Preference, Belief, and Similarity

Preference, Belief, and Similarity
Selected Writings

by Amos Tversky
edited by Eldar Shafir

A Bradford Book
The MIT Press
Cambridge, Massachusetts
London, England

This book was set in Times New Roman on 3B2 by Asco Typesetters, Hong Kong and was printed and bound in the United States of America.

Library of Congress Cataloging-in-Publication Data

Tversky, Amos.
  Preference, belief, and similarity : selected writings / by Amos Tversky ; edited by Eldar Shafir.
    p.   cm.
  "A Bradford book."
  Includes bibliographical references and index.
  ISBN 978-0-262-20144-5 (hc. : alk. paper) — ISBN 978-0-262-70093-1 (pb. : alk. paper)
  1. Cognitive psychology. 2. Decision making. 3. Judgment. 4. Tversky, Amos. I. Shafir, Eldar.
II. Title.
BF201 .T78 2003
153—dc21   2002032164

Contents

Introduction and Biography

Amos Tversky was a towering figure in the field of cognitive psychology and in the decision sciences. His research had enormous influence; he created new areas of study and helped transform related disciplines. His work was innovative, exciting, aesthetic, and ingenious. This book brings together forty of Tversky's original articles, which he and the editor chose together during the last months of Tversky's life. Because it includes only a fragment of Tversky's published work, this book cannot provide a full sense of his remarkable achievements. Instead, this collection of favorites is intended to capture the essence of Tversky's phenomenal mind for those who did not have the fortune to know him, and will provide a cherished memento to those whose lives he enriched.

Tversky was born on March 16, 1937, in Haifa, Israel. His father was a veterinarian, and his mother was a social worker and later a member of the first Israeli Parliament. He received his Bachelor of Arts degree, majoring in philosophy and psychology, from Hebrew University in Jerusalem in 1961, and his Doctor of Philosophy degree in psychology from the University of Michigan in 1965. Tversky taught at Hebrew University (1966–1978) and at Stanford University (1978–1996), where he was the inaugural Davis-Brack Professor of Behavioral Sciences and Principal Investigator at the Stanford Center on Conflict and Negotiation. After 1992 he also held an appointment as Senior Visiting Professor of Economics and Psychology and Permanent Fellow of the Sackler Institute of Advanced Studies at Tel Aviv University.

Tversky wrote his dissertation, which won the University of Michigan's Marquis Award, under the supervision of Clyde Coombs. His early work in mathematical psychology focused on the study of individual choice behavior and the analysis of psychological measurement. Almost from the beginning, Tversky's work explored the surprising implications of simple and intuitively compelling psychological assumptions for theories that, until then, seemed self-evident. In one oft-cited early work (chapter 19), Tversky showed how a series of pair-wise choices could yield intransitive patterns of preference. To do this, he created a set of options such that the difference on an important dimension was negligible between adjacent alternatives, but proved to be consequential once it accumulated across a number of such comparisons, yielding a reversal of preference between the first and the last. This was of theoretical significance since the transitivity of preferences is one of the fundamental axioms of utility theory. At the same time, it provided a revealing glimpse into the psychological processes involved in choices of that kind.

In his now-famous model of similarity (chapter 1), Tversky made a number of simple psychological assumptions: items are mentally represented as collections of features, with the similarity between them an increasing function of the features that they have in common, and a decreasing function of their distinct features. In addition, feature weights are assumed to depend on the nature of the task so that, for example, common features matter more in judgments of similarity, whereas distinctive features receive more attention in judgments of dissimilarity. Among other things, this simple theory was able to explain asymmetries in similarity judgments (A may be more similar to B than B is to A), and the fact that item A may be perceived as quite similar to item B and item B quite similar to item C, but items A and C may nevertheless be perceived as highly dissimilar (chapter 3). In many ways, these early papers foreshadowed the immensely elegant work to come. They were predicated on the technical mastery of relevant normative theories, and explored simple and compelling psychological principles until their unexpected theoretical implications became apparent, and often striking.

Tversky's long and extraordinarily influential collaboration with Daniel Kahneman began in 1969 and spanned the fields of judgment and decision making. (For a sense of the impact, consider the fact that the two papers most representative of their collaboration, chapters 8 and 22 in this book, register 3035 and 2810 citations, respectively, in the Social Science Citation Index in the two decades spanning 1981–2001.) Having recognized that intuitive predictions and judgments of probability do not follow the principles of statistics or the laws of probability, Kahneman and Tversky embarked on the study of biases as a method for investigating judgmental heuristics. The beauty of the work was most apparent in the interplay of psychological intuition with normative theory, accompanied by memorable demonstrations.

The research showed that people's judgments often violate basic normative principles. At the same time, it showed that they exhibit sensitivity to these principles' normative appeal. The coexistence of fallible intuitions and an underlying appreciation for normative judgment yields a subtle picture of probabilistic reasoning. An important theme in Tversky's work is a rejection of the claim that people are not smart enough or sophisticated enough to grasp the relevant normative considerations. Rather, Tversky attributes the recurrent and systematic errors that he finds to people's reliance on intuitive judgment and heuristic processes in situations where the applicability of normative criteria is not immediately apparent. This approach runs through much of Tversky's work. The experimental demonstrations are noteworthy not simply because they contradict a popular and highly influential normative theory; rather, they are memorable precisely because people who exhibit these errors typically find the demonstrations highly compelling, yet surprisingly inconsistent with their own assumptions about how they make decisions.

Psychological common sense formed the basis for some of Tversky's most profound and original insights. A fundamental assumption underlying normative theories is the extensionality principle: options that are extensionally equivalent are assigned the same value, and extensionally equivalent events are assigned the same probability. These theories, in other words, are about options and events in the world: alternative descriptions of the same thing are still about the same thing, and hence similarly evaluated. Tversky's analyses, on the other hand, focus on the mental representations of the relevant constructs. The extensionality principle is deemed descriptively invalid because alternative descriptions of the same options or events often produce systematically different judgments and preferences. The way a decision problem is described—for example, in terms of gains or losses—can trigger conflicting risk attitudes and thus lead to discrepant preferences with respect to the same final outcomes (chapter 24); similarly, alternative descriptions of the same event bring to mind different instances and thus can yield discrepant likelihood judgments (chapter 14). Preferences as well as judgments appear to be constructed, not merely revealed, in the elicitation process, and their construction depends on the framing of the problem, the method of elicitation, and the valuations and attitudes that these trigger.

Behavior, Tversky's research made clear, is the outcome of normative ideals that people endorse upon reflection, combined with psychological tendencies and processes that intrude upon and shape behavior, independently of any deliberative intent. Tversky had a unique ability to master the technicalities of the normative requirements and to intuit, and then experimentally demonstrate, the vagaries and consequences of the psychological processes that impinged on them. He was an intellectual giant whose work has an exceptionally broad appeal; his research is known to economists, philosophers, statisticians, political scientists, sociologists, and legal theorists, among others. He published more than 120 papers and co-wrote or co-edited 10 books. (A complete bibliography is printed at the back of this book.) Tversky's main research interests spanned a large variety of topics, some of which are better represented in this book than others, and can be roughly divided into three general areas: similarity, judgment, and preference. The articles in this collected volume are divided into corresponding sections and appear in chronological order within each section.

Many of Tversky's papers are both seminal and definitive. Reading a Tversky paper offers the pleasure of watching a craftsman at work: he provides a clear map of a domain that had previously seemed confusing, and then offers a new set of tools and ideas for thinking about the problem. Tversky's writings have had remarkable longevity: the research he did early in his career has remained at the center of attention for several decades, and the work he was doing toward the end of his life will affect theory and research for a long time to come. Special issues of *The Quarterly Journal of Economics* (1997), the *Journal of Risk and Uncertainty* (1998), and *Cognitive Psychology* (1999) have been dedicated to Tversky's memory, and various obituaries and articles about Tversky have appeared in places ranging from *The Wall Street Journal* (1996) and *The New York Times* (1996), to the *Journal of Medical Decision Making* (1996), *American Psychologist* (1998), *Thinking & Reasoning* (1997), and *The MIT Encyclopedia of Cognitive Science* (1999), to name a few.

Tversky won many awards for his diverse accomplishments. As a young officer in a paratroops regiment, he earned Israel's highest honor for bravery in 1956 for rescuing a soldier. He won the Distinguished Scientific Contribution Award of the American Psychological Association in 1982, a MacArthur Prize in 1984, and the Warren Medal of the Society of Experimental Psychologists in 1995. He was elected to the American Academy of Arts and Sciences in 1980, to the Econometric Society in 1993, and to the National Academy of Sciences as a foreign member in 1985. He received honorary doctorates from the University of Goteborg, the State University of New York at Buffalo, the University of Chicago, and Yale University.

Tversky managed to combine discipline and joy in the conduct of his life in a manner that conveyed a great sense of freedom and autonomy. His habit of working through the night helped protect him from interruptions and gave him the time to engage at leisure in his research activities, as well as in other interests, including a lifelong love of Hebrew literature, a fascination with modern physics, and an expert interest in professional basketball. He was tactful but firm in rejecting commitments that would distract him: "For those who like that sort of thing," Amos would say with his characteristic smile as he declined various engagements, "that's the sort of thing they like." To his friends and collaborators, Amos was a delight. He found great joy in sharing ideas and experiences with people close to him, and his joy was contagious. Many friends became research collaborators, and many collaborators became close friends. He would spend countless hours developing an idea, delighting in it, refining it. "Let's get this right," he would say—and his ability to do so was unequaled.

Amos Tversky continued his research and teaching until his illness made that impossible, just a few weeks before his death. He died of metastatic melanoma on June 2, 1996, at his home in Stanford, California. He was in the midst of an enormously productive time, with over fifteen papers and several edited volumes in press. Tversky is survived by his wife, Barbara, who was a fellow student at the University of Michigan and then a fellow professor of psychology at Stanford University, and by his three children, Oren, Tal, and Dona. This book is dedicated to them.

Eldar Shafir

Postscript

In October 2002 The Royal Swedish Academy of Sciences awarded the Nobel Memorial Prize in Economic Sciences to Daniel Kahneman, "for having integrated insights from psychological research into economic science, especially concerning human judgment and decision-making under uncertainty." The work Kahneman had done together with Amos Tversky, the Nobel citation explained, formulated alternative theories that better account for observed behavior. The Royal Swedish Academy of Sciences does not award prizes posthumously, but took the unusual step of acknowledging Tversky in the citation. "Certainly, we would have gotten this together," Kahneman said on the day of the announcement. Less than two months later, Amos Tversky posthumously won the prestigious 2003 Grawemeyer Award together with Kahneman. The committee of the Grawemeyer Award, which recognizes powerful ideas in the arts and sciences, noted, "It is difficult to identify a more influential idea than that of Kahneman and Tversky in the human sciences." Reacting to the award, Kahneman said, "My joy is mixed with the sadness of not being able to share the experience with Amos Tversky, with whom the work was done." It is with a similar mixture of joy and sadness that we turn to Amos's beautiful work.

Sources

1. Tversky, A. (1977). Features of similarity. *Psychological Review*, 84, 327–352. Copyright © 1977 by the American Psychological Association. Reprinted with permission.

2. Sattath, S., and Tversky, A. (1977). Additive similarity trees. *Psychometrika*, 42, 319–345.

3. Tversky, A., and Gati, I. (1978). Studies of similarity. In E. Rosch and B. Lloyd (Eds.), *Cognition and Categorization*, (79–98), Hillsdale, N.J.: Erlbaum.

4. Gati, I., and Tversky, A. (1984). Weighting common and distinctive features in perceptual and conceptual judgments, *Cognitive Psychology*, 16, 341–370.

5. Tversky, A., and Hutchinson, J. W. (1986). Nearest neighbor analysis of psychological spaces. *Psychological Review*, 93, 3–22. Copyright © 1986 by the American Psychological Association. Reprinted with permission.

6. Sattath, S., and Tversky, A. (1987). On the relation between common and distinctive feature models. *Psychological Review*, 94, 16–22. Copyright © 1987 by the American Psychological Association. Reprinted with permission.

7. Tversky, A., and Kahneman, D. (1971). Belief in the law of small numbers. *Psychological Bulletin*, 76, 105–110.

8. Tversky, A., and Kahneman, D. (1974). Judgment under uncertainty: Heuristics and biases. *Science*, 185, 1124–1131. Reprinted with permission from Science. Copyright 1974 American Association for the Advancement of Science.

9. Tversky, A., and Kahneman, D. (1983). Extensional vs. intuitive reasoning: The conjunction fallacy in probability judgment. *Psychological Review*, 91, 293–315. Copyright © 1983 by the American Psychological Association. Reprinted with permission.

10. Tversky, A., and Gilovich, T. (1989). The cold facts about the "hot hand" in basketball. *Chance*, 2(1), 16–21. Reprinted with permission from CHANCE. Copyright 1989 by the American Statistical Association. All rights reserved.

11. Tversky, A., and Gilovich, T. (1989). The hot hand: Statistical reality or cognitive illusion? *Chance*, 2(4), 31–34. Reprinted with permission from CHANCE. Copyright 1989 by the American Statistical Association. All rights reserved.

12. Griffin, D., and Tversky, A. (1992). The weighing of evidence and the determinants of confidence. *Cognitive Psychology*, 24, 411–435.

13. Liberman, V., and Tversky, A. (1993). On the evaluation of probability judgments: Calibration, resolution and monotonicity. *Psychological Bulletin*, 114, 162–173.

14. Tversky, A., and Koehler, D. J. (1994). Support theory: A nonextensional representation of subjective probability. *Psychological Review*, 101, 547–567. Copyright © 1994 by the American Psychological Association. Reprinted with permission.

15. Redelmeier, D. A., and Tversky, A. (1996). On the belief that arthritis pain is related to the weather. *Proc. Natl. Acad. Sci.*, 93, 2895–2896. Copyright 1996 National Academy of Sciences, U.S.A.

16. Rottenstreich, Y., and Tversky, A. (1997). Unpacking, repacking, and anchoring: Advances in support theory. *Psychological Review*, 104(2), 406–415. Copyright © 1997 by the American Psychological Association. Reprinted with permission.

17. Tversky, A. (1964). On the optimal number of alternatives at a choice point. *Journal of Mathematical Psychology*, 2, 386–391.

18. Tversky, A., and Russo, E. J. (1969). Substitutability and similarity in binary choices. *Journal of Mathematical Psychology*, 6, 1–12.

19. Tversky, A. (1969). The intransitivity of preferences. *Psychological Review*, 76, 31–48. Copyright © 1969 by the American Psychological Association. Reprinted with permission.

20. Tversky, A. (1972). Elimination by aspects: A theory of choice. *Psychological Review*, 79, 281–299. Copyright © 1972 by the American Psychological Association. Reprinted with permission.

21. Tversky, A., and Sattath, S. (1979). Preference trees. *Psychological Review*, 86, 542–573. Copyright © 1979 by the American Psychological Association. Reprinted with permission.

22. Kahneman, D., and Tversky, A. (1979). Prospect theory: An analysis of decision under risk. *Econometrica*, 47, 263–291. Copyright The Econometric Society.

23. McNeil, B., Pauker, S., Sox, H. Jr., and Tversky, A. (1982). On the elicitation of preferences for alternative therapies. *New England Journal of Medicine*, 306, 1259–1262. Copyright © 1982 Massachusetts Medical Society. All rights reserved.

24. Tversky, A., and Kahneman, D. (1986). Rational choice and the framing of decisions. *The Journal of Business*, 59, Part 2, S251–S278.

25. Quattrone, G. A., and Tversky, A. (1988). Contrasting rational and psychological analyses of political choice. *American Political Science Review*, 82(3), 719–736.

26. Heath, F., and Tversky, A. (1991). Preference and belief: Ambiguity and competence in choice under uncertainty. *Journal of Risk and Uncertainty*, 4(1), 5–28. Reprinted with kind permission from Kluwer Academic Publishers.

27. Tversky, A., and Kahneman, D. (1992). Advances in prospect theory: Cumulative representation of uncertainty. *Journal of Risk and Uncertainty*, 5, 297–323. Reprinted with kind permission from Kluwer Academic Publishers.

28. Shafir, E., and Tversky, A. (1992). Thinking through uncertainty: Nonconsequential reasoning and choice. *Cognitive Psychology*, 24(4), 449–474.

29. Kahneman, D., and Tversky, A. (1995). Conflict resolution: A cognitive perspective. In K. Arrow, R. Mnookin, L. Ross, A. Tversky, and R. Wilson (Eds.), Barriers to the Negotiated Resolution of Conflict, (49–67). New York: Norton.

30. Tversky, A., and Fox, C. R. (1995). Weighing risk and uncertainty. *Psychological Review*, 102(2), 269–283. Copyright © 1995 by the American Psychological Association. Reprinted with permission.

31. Fox, C. R., and Tversky, A. (1995). Ambiguity aversion and comparative ignorance. *Quarterly Journal of Economics*, 110, 585–603. © 1995 by the President and Fellows of Harvard College and the Massachusetts Institute of Technology.

32. Fox, C. R., and Tversky, A. (1998). A belief-based account of decision under uncertainty. *Management Science*, 44(7), 879–895.

33. Quattrone, G. A., and Tversky, A. (1986). Self-deception and the voter's illusion. In Jon Elster (Ed.), *The Multiple Self*, (35–58), New York: Cambridge University Press. Reprinted with permission of Cambridge University Press.

34. Tversky, A., Sattath, S., and Slovic, P. (1988). Contingent weighting in judgment and choice. *Psychological Review*, 95(3), 371–384. Copyright © 1988 by the American Psychological Association. Reprinted with permission.

35. Tversky, A., and Thaler, R. (1990). Anomalies: Preference reversals. *Journal of Economic Perspectives*, 4(2), 201–211.

36. Redelmeier, D. A., and Tversky, A. (1990). Discrepancy between medical decisions for individual patients and for groups. *New England Journal of Medicine*, 322, 1162–1164. Copyright © 1990 Massachusetts Medical Society. All rights reserved.

37. Tversky, A., and Kahneman, D. (1991). Loss aversion in riskless choice: A reference-dependent model. *Quarterly Journal of Economics*, 107(4), 1039–1061. © 1991 by the President and Fellows of Harvard College and the Massachusetts Institute of Technology.

38. Tversky, A., and Griffin, D. (1991). Endowment and contrast in judgments of well-being. In F. Strack, M. Argyle, and N. Schwartz (Eds.), *Subjective Well-being: An Interdisciplinary Perspective* (101–118). Elmsford, NY: Pergamon Press.

39. Shafir, E., Simonson, I., and Tversky, A. (1993). Reason-based choice. *Cognition*, 49, 11–36. Reprinted from Cognition with permission from Elsevier Science. Copyright 1993.

40. Kelman, M., Rottenstreich, Y., and Tversky, A. (1996). Context-dependence in legal decision making. *The Journal of Legal Studies*, 25, 287–318. Reprinted with permission of the University of Chicago.

SIMILARITY

Editor's Introductory Remarks

Early in his career as a mathematical psychologist Tversky developed a deep interest in the formalization and conceptualization of similarity. The notion of similarity is ubiquitous in psychological theorizing, where it plays a fundamental role in theories of learning, memory, knowledge, perception, and judgment, among others. When Tversky began his work in this area, geometric models dominated the theoretical analysis of similarity relations; in these models each object is represented by a point is some multidimensional coordinate space, and the metric distances between points reflect the similarities between the respective objects.

Tversky found it more intuitive to represent stimuli in terms of their many qualitative features rather than a few quantitative dimensions. In this contrast model of similarity (chapter 1), Tversky challenges the assumptions that underlie the geometric approach to similarity and develops an alternative approach based on feature matching. He began with simple psychological assumptions couched in an aesthetic formal treatment, and was able to predict surprising facts about the perception of similarity and to provide a compelling reinterpretation of previously known facts.

According to the contrast model, items are represented as collections of features. The perceived similarity between items is an increasing function of the features that they have in common, and a decreasing function of the features on which they differ. In addition, each set of common and distinctive features is weighted differentially, depending on the context, the order of comparison, and the particular task at hand. For example, common features are weighted relatively more in judgments of similarity, whereas distinctive features receive more attention in judgments of dissimilarity. Among other things, the theory is able to explain asymmetries in similarity judgments (A can be more similar to B than B is to A), the non-complementary nature of similarity and dissimilarity judgments (A and B may be both more similar to one another and more different from one another than are C and D), and triangle inequality (item A may be perceived as quite similar to item B and item B quite similar to item C, but items A and C may nevertheless be perceived as highly dissimilar) (Tversky & Gati 1982). These patterns of similarity judgments, which Tversky and his colleagues compellingly documented, are inconsistent with geometric representations (where, for example, the distance from A to B needs to be the same as that between B and A, etc.). The logic and implications of the contrast model are further summarized and given a less technical presentation by Tversky and Itamar Gati in chapter 3.

In a further investigation of how best to represent similarity relations (chapter 2), Shmuel Sattath and Tversky consider the representation of similarity data in the form of additive trees, and compare it to alternative representational schemes, particularly spatial representations that are limited in some of the ways suggested above.

In the additive tree model, objects are represented by the external nodes of a tree, and the dissimilarity between objects is the length of the path joining them. As it turns out, the effect of common features can be better captured by trees than by spatial representations. In fact, an additive tree can be interpreted as a feature tree, with each object viewed as a set of features, and each arc representing the set of features shared by all objects that follow from that arc. (An additive tree is a special case of the contrast model in which symmetry and the triangle inequality hold, and the feature space allows a tree structure.)

Further exploring the adequacy of the geometric models, chapter 5 applies a "nearest neighbor" analysis to similarity data. The technical analysis essentially shows that geometric models are severely restricted in the number of objects that they can allow to share the same nearest (for example, most similar) neighbor. Using one hundred different data sets, Tversky and Hutchinson show that while perceptual data often satisfy the bounds imposed by geometric representations, the conceptual data sets typically do not. In particular, in many semantic fields a focal element (such as the superordinate category) is the nearest neighbor of most of the category instances. Tversky shows that such a popular nearest neighbor, while inconsistent with a geometric representation, can be captured by an additive tree in which the category name (for example, *fruit*) is the nearest neighbor of all its instances.

Tversky and his coauthors conclude that some similarity data are better described by a tree, whereas other data may be better captured by a spatial configuration. Emotions or sound, for example, may be characterized by a few dimensions that differ in intensity, and may thus be natural candidates for a dimensional representation. Other items, however, have a hierarchical classification involving various qualitative attributes, and may thus be better captured by tree representations.

A formal procedure based on the contrast model is developed in chapter 4 in order to assess the relative weight of common to distinctive features. By adding the same component (for example, cloud) to two stimuli (for example, landscapes) or to one of the stimuli only, Gati and Tversky are able to assess the impact of that component as a common or as a distinctive feature. Among other things, they find that in verbal stimuli common features loom larger than distinctive features (as if the differences between stimuli are acknowledged and one focuses on the search for common features), whereas in pictorial stimuli distinctive features loom larger than common features (consistent with the notion that commonalities are treated as background and the search is for distinctive features.)

The theoretical relationship between common- and distinctive-feature models is explored in chapter 6, where Sattath and Tversky show that common-feature models and distinctive-feature models can produce different orderings of dissimilarity between objects. They further show that the choice of a model and the specification of a feature structure are not always determined by the dissimilarity data and, in particular, that the relative weights of common and distinctive features observed in chapter 4 can depend on the feature structure induced by the addition of dimensions. Chapter 6 concludes with general commentary regarding the observation that the form of measurement models often is not dictated by the data. This touches on the massive project on the foundations of measurement that Tversky co-authored (Krantz, Luce, Suppes, and Tversky, 1971; Suppes, Krantz, Luce, and Tversky, 1989; Luce, Krantz, Suppes, and Tversky, 1990), but which is not otherwise represented in this collection.

1 Features of Similarity

Amos Tversky

Similarity plays a fundamental role in theories of knowledge and behavior. It serves as an organizing principle by which individuals classify objects, form concepts, and make generalizations. Indeed, the concept of similarity is ubiquitous in psychological theory. It underlies the accounts of stimulus and response generalization in learning, it is employed to explain errors in memory and pattern recognition, and it is central to the analysis of connotative meaning.

Similarity or dissimilarity data appear in different forms: ratings of pairs, sorting of objects, communality between associations, errors of substitution, and correlation between occurrences. Analyses of these data attempt to explain the observed similarity relations and to capture the underlying structure of the objects under study.

The theoretical analysis of similarity relations has been dominated by geometric models. These models represent objects as points in some coordinate space such that the observed dissimilarities between objects correspond to the metric distances between the respective points. Practically all analyses of proximity data have been metric in nature, although some (e.g., hierarchical clustering) yield tree-like structures rather than dimensionally organized spaces. However, most theoretical and empirical analyses of similarity assume that objects can be adequately represented as points in some coordinate space and that dissimilarity behaves like a metric distance function. Both dimensional and metric assumptions are open to question.

It has been argued by many authors that dimensional representations are appropriate for certain stimuli (e.g., colors, tones) but not for others. It seems more appropriate to represent faces, countries, or personalities in terms of many qualitative features than in terms of a few quantitative dimensions. The assessment of similarity between such stimuli, therefore, may be better described as a comparison of features rather than as the computation of metric distance between points.

A metric distance function, δ, is a scale that assigns to every pair of points a nonnegative number, called their distance, in accord with the following three axioms:

Minimality: $\delta(a, b) \geq \delta(a, a) = 0.$

Symmetry: $\delta(a, b) = \delta(b, a).$

The triangle inequality: $\delta(a, b) + \delta(b, c) \geq \delta(a, c).$

To evaluate the adequacy of the geometric approach, let us examine the validity of the metric axioms when δ is regarded as a measure of dissimilarity. The minimality axiom implies that the similarity between an object and itself is the same for all objects. This assumption, however, does not hold for some similarity measures. For example, the probability of judging two identical stimuli as "same" rather that "different" is not constant for all stimuli. Moreover, in recognition experiments the off-diagonal entries often exceed the diagonal entries; that is, an object is identified as another object more frequently than it is identified as itself. If identification probability is interpreted as a measure of similarity, then these observations violate minimality and are, therefore, incompatible with the distance model.

Similarity has been viewed by both philosophers and psychologists as a prime example of a symmetric relation. Indeed, the assumption of symmetry underlies essentially all theoretical treatments of similarity. Contrary to this tradition, the present paper provides empirical evidence for asymmetric similarities and argues that similarity should not be treated as a symmetric relation.

Similarity judgments can be regarded as extensions of similarity statements, that is, statements of the form "a is like b." Such a statement is directional; it has a subject, a, and a referent, b, and it is not equivalent in general to the converse similarity statement "b is like a." In fact, the choice of subject and referent depends, at least in part, on the relative salience of the objects. We tend to select the more salient stimulus, or the prototype, as a referent, and the less salient stimulus, or the variant, as a subject. We say "the portrait resembles the person" rather than "the person resembles the portrait." We say "the son resembles the father" rather than "the father resembles the son." We say "an ellipse is like a circle," not "a circle is like an ellipse," and we say "North Korea is like Red China" rather than "Red China is like North Korea."

As will be demonstrated later, this asymmetry in the *choice* of similarity statements is associated with asymmetry in *judgments* of similarity. Thus, the judged similarity of North Korea to Red China exceeds the judged similarity of Red China to North Korea. Likewise, an ellipse is more similar to a circle than a circle is to an ellipse. Apparently, the direction of asymmetry is determined by the relative salience of the stimuli; the variant is more similar to the prototype than vice versa.

The directionality and asymmetry of similarity relations are particularly noticeable in similies and metaphors. We say "Turks fight like tigers" and not "tigers fight like Turks." Since the tiger is renowned for its fighting spirit, it is used as the referent rather than the subject of the simile. The poet writes "my love is as deep as the ocean," not "the ocean is as deep as my love," because the ocean epitomizes depth. Sometimes both directions are used but they carry different meanings. "A man is like a tree" implies that man has roots; "a tree is like a man" implies that the tree has a life history. "Life is like a play" says that people play roles. "A play is like life" says that a play can capture the essential elements of human life. The relations between the interpretation of metaphors and the assessment of similarity are briefly discussed in the final section.

The triangle inequality differs from minimality and symmetry in that it cannot be formulated in ordinal terms. It asserts that one distance must be smaller than the sum of two others, and hence it cannot be readily refuted with ordinal or even interval data. However, the triangle inequality implies that if a is quite similar to b, and b is quite similar to c, then a and c cannot be very dissimilar from each other. Thus, it sets a lower limit to the similarity between a and c in terms of the similarities between a and b and between b and c. The following example (based on William James) casts some doubts on the psychological validity of this assumption. Consider the similarity between countries: Jamaica is similar to Cuba (because of geographical proximity); Cuba is similar to Russia (because of their political affinity); but Jamaica and Russia are not similar at all.

This example shows that similarity, as one might expect, is not transitive. In addition, it suggests that the perceived distance of Jamaica to Russia exceeds the perceived distance of Jamaica to Cuba, plus that of Cuba to Russia—contrary to the triangle inequality. Although such examples do not necessarily refute the triangle inequality, they indicate that it should not be accepted as a cornerstone of similarity models.

It should be noted that the metric axioms, by themselves, are very weak. They are satisfied, for example, by letting $\delta(a, b) = 0$ if $a = b$, and $\delta(a, b) = 1$ if $a \neq b$. To specify the distance function, additional assumptions are made (e.g., intradimensional subtractivity and interdimensional additivity) relating the dimensional structure of the objects to their metric distances. For an axiomatic analysis and a critical discussion of these assumptions, see Beals, Krantz, and Tversky (1968), Krantz and Tversky (1975), and Tversky and Krantz (1970).

In conclusion, it appears that despite many fruitful applications (see e.g., Carroll & Wish, 1974; Shepard, 1974), the geometric approach to the analysis of similarity faces several difficulties. The applicability of the dimensional assumption is limited, and the metric axioms are questionable. Specifically, minimality is somewhat problematic, symmetry is apparently false, and the triangle inequality is hardly compelling.

The next section develops an alternative theoretical approach to similarity, based on feature matching, which is neither dimensional nor metric in nature. In subsequent sections this approach is used to uncover, analyze, and explain several empirical phenomena, such as the role of common and distinctive features, the relations between judgrnents of similarity and difference, the presence of asymmetric similarities, and the effects of context on similarity. Extensions and implications of the present development are discussed in the final section.

Feature Matching

Let $\Delta = \{a, b, c, \ldots\}$ be the domain of objects (or stimuli) under study. Assume that each object in Δ is represented by a set of features or attributes, and let A, B, C denote the sets of features associated with the objects a, b, c, respectively. The features may correspond to components such as eyes or mouth; they may represent concrete properties such as size or color; and they may reflect abstract attributes such as quality or complexity. The characterization of stimuli as feature sets has been employed in the analysis of many cognitive processes such as speech perception (Jakobson, Fant, & Halle, 1961), pattern recognition (Neisser, 1967), perceptual learning (Gibson, 1969), preferential choice (Tversky, 1972), and semantic judgment (Smith, Shoben, & Rips, 1974).

Two preliminary comments regarding feature representations are in order. First, it is important to note that our total data base concerning a particular object (e.g., a person, a country, or a piece of furniture) is generally rich in content and complex in form. It includes appearance, function, relation to other objects, and any other property of the object that can be deduced from our general knowledge of the world. When faced with a particular task (e.g., identification or similarity assessment) we extract and compile from our data base a limited list of relevant features on the basis of which we perform the required task. Thus, the representation of an object as a collection of features is viewed as a product of a prior process of extraction and compilation.

Second, the term *feature* usually denotes the value of a binary variable (e.g., voiced vs. voiceless consonants) or the value of a nominal variable (e.g., eye color). Feature representations, however, are not restricted to binary or nominal variables; they are also applicable to ordinal or cardinal variables (i.e., dimensions). A series of tones that differ only in loudness, for example, could be represented as a sequence of nested sets where the feature set associated with each tone is included in the feature sets associated with louder tones. Such a representation is isomorphic to a directional unidimensional structure. A nondirectional unidimensional structure (e.g., a series of tones that differ only in pitch) could be represented by a chain of overlapping sets. The set-theoretical representation of qualitative and quantitative dimensions has been investigated by Restle (1959).

Let $s(a, b)$ be a measure of the similarity of a to b defined for all distinct a, b in Δ. The scale s is treated as an ordinal measure of similarity. That is, $s(a, b) > s(c, d)$ means that a is more similar to b than c is to d. The present theory is based on the following assumptions.

1. MATCHING:

$$s(a, b) = F(A \cap B, A - B, B - A).$$

The similarity of a to b is expressed as a function F of three arguments: $A \cap B$, the features that are common to both a and b; $A - B$, the features that belong to a but not to b; $B - A$, the features that belong to b but not to a. A schematic illustration of these components is presented in figure 1.1.

2. MONOTONICITY:

$$s(a, b) \geq s(a, c)$$

whenever

$$A \cap B \supset A \cap C, \quad A - B \subset A - C,$$

and

$$B - A \subset C - A.$$

Moreover, the inequality is strict whenever either inclusion is proper.

That is, similarity increases with addition of common features and/or deletion of distinctive features (i.e., features that belong to one object but not to the other). The monotonicity axiom can be readily illustrated with block letters if we identify their features with the component (straight) lines. Under this assumption, E should be more similar to F than to I because E and F have more common features than E and I. Furthermore, I should be more similar to F than to E because I and F have fewer distinctive features than I and E.

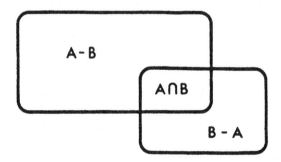

Figure 1.1
A graphical illustration of the relation between two feature sets.

Any function F satisfying assumptions 1 and 2 is called a *matching function*. It measures the degree to which two objects—viewed as sets of features—match each other. In the present theory, the assessment of similarity is described as a feature-matching process. It is formulated, therefore, in terms of the set-theoretical notion of a matching function rather than in terms of the geometric concept of distance.

In order to determine the functional form of the matching function, additional assumptions about the similarity ordering are introduced. The major assumption of the theory (independence) is presented next; the remaining assumptions and the proof of the representation theorem are presented in the appendix. Readers who are less interested in formal theory can skim or skip the following paragraphs up to the discussion of the representation theorem.

Let Φ denote the set of all features associated with the objects of Δ, and let $X, Y, Z, \ldots$ etc. denote collections of features (i.e., subsets of Φ). The expression $F(X, Y, Z)$ is defined whenever there exists a, b in Δ such that $A \cap B = X$, $A - B = Y$, and $B - A = Z$, whence $s(a, b) = F(A \cap B, A - B, B - A) = F(X, Y, Z)$. Next, define $V \simeq W$ if one or more of the following hold for some X, Y, Z: $F(V, Y, Z) = F(W, Y, Z)$, $F(X, V, Z) = F(X, W, Z)$, $F(X, Y, V) = F(X, Y, W)$.

The pairs (a, b) and (c, d) are said to *agree* on one, two, or three components, respectively, whenever one, two, or three of the following hold: $(A \cap B) \simeq (C \cap D)$, $(A - B) \simeq (C - D)$, $(B - A) \simeq (D - C)$.

3. INDEPENDENCE Suppose the pairs (a, b) and (c, d), as well as the pairs (a', b') and (c', d'), agree on the same two components, while the pairs (a, b) and (a', b'), as well as the pairs (c, d) and (c', d'), agree on the remaining (third) component. Then

$$s(a, b) \geq s(a', b') \quad \text{iff} \quad s(c, d) \geq s(c', d').$$

To illustrate the force of the independence axiom consider the stimuli presented in figure 1.2, where

$A \cap B = C \cap D = \text{round profile} = X$,

$A' \cap B' = C' \cap D' = \text{sharp profile} = X'$,

$A - B = C - D = \text{smiling mouth} = Y$,

$A' - B' = C' - D' = \text{frowning mouth} = Y'$,

$B - A = B' - A' = \text{straight eyebrow} = Z$,

$D - C = D' - C' = \text{curved eyebrow} = Z'$.

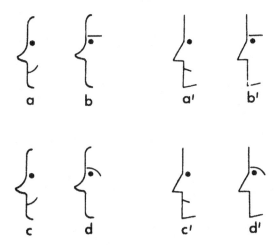

Figure 1.2
An illustration of independence.

By independence, therefore,

$$s(a, b) = F(A \cap B, A - B, B - A)$$

$$= F(X, Y, Z) \geq F(X', Y', Z)$$

$$= F(A' \cap B', A' - B', B' - A')$$

$$= s(a', b')$$

if and only if

$$s(c, d) = F(C \cap D, C - D, D - C)$$

$$= F(X, Y, Z') \geq F(X', Y', Z')$$

$$= F(C' \cap D', C' - D', D' - C')$$

$$= s(c', d').$$

Thus, the ordering of the joint effect of any two components (e.g., X, Y vs. X', Y') is independent of the fixed level of the third factor (e.g., Z or Z').

It should be emphasized that any test of the axioms presupposes an interpretation of the features. The independence axiom, for example, may hold in one interpretation and fail in another. Experimental tests of the axioms, therefore, test jointly the adequacy of the interpretation of the features and the empirical validity of the assumptions. Furthermore, the above examples should not be taken to mean that stimuli (e.g., block letters, schematic faces) can be properly characterized in terms of their components. To achieve an adequate feature representation of visual forms, more global properties (e.g., symmetry, connectedness) should also be introduced. For an interesting discussion of this problem, in the best tradition of Gestalt psychology, see Goldmeier (1972; originally published in 1936).

In addition to matching (1), monotonicity (2), and independence (3), we also assume solvability (4), and invariance (5). Solvability requires that the feature space under study be sufficiently rich that certain (similarity) equations can be solved. Invariance ensures that the equivalence of intervals is preserved across factors. A rigorous formulation of these assumptions is given in the Appendix, along with a proof of the following result.

Representation Theorem Suppose assumptions 1, 2, 3, 4, and 5 hold. Then there exist a similarity scale S and a nonnegative scale f such that for all a, b, c, d in Δ,

(i) $S(a, b) \geq S(c, d)$ iff $s(a, b) \geq s(c, d)$;

(ii) $S(a, b) = \theta f(A \cap B) - \alpha f(A - B) - \beta f(B - A)$, for some $\theta, \alpha, \beta \geq 0$;

(iii) f and S are interval scales.

The theorem shows that under assumptions 1–5, there exists an interval similarity scale S that preserves the observed similarity order and expresses similarity as a linear combination, or a contrast, of the measures of the common and the distinctive features. Hence, the representation is called the *contrast model*. In parts of the following development we also assume that f satisfies feature additivity. That is, $f(X \cup Y) = f(X) + f(Y)$ whenever X and Y are disjoint, and all three terms are defined.[1]

Note that the contrast model does not define a single similarity scale, but rather a family of scales characterized by different values of the parameters θ, α, and β. For example, if $\theta = 1$ and α and β vanish, then $S(a, b) = f(A \cap B)$; that is, the similarity between objects is the measure of their common features. If, on the other hand, $\alpha = \beta = 1$ and θ vanishes then $-S(a, b) = f(A - B) + f(B - A)$; that is, the dissimilarity between objects is the measure of the symmetric difference between the respective feature sets. Restle (1961) has proposed these forms as models of similarity and psychological distance, respectively. Note that in the former model ($\theta = 1$, $\alpha = \beta = 0$), similarity between objects is determined only by their common features, whereas in the latter model ($\theta = 0$, $\alpha = \beta = 1$), it is determined by their distinctive features only. The contrast model expresses similarity between objects as a weighted difference of the measures of their common and distinctive features, thereby allowing for a variety of similarity relations over the same domain.

The major constructs of the present theory are the contrast rule for the assessment of similarity, and the scale f, which reflects the salience or prominence of the various features. Thus, f measures the contribution of any particular (common or distinctive) feature to the similarity between objects. The scale value f(A) associated with stimulus a is regarded, therefore, as a measure of the overall salience of that stimulus. The factors that contribute to the salience of a stimulus include intensity, frequency, familiarity, good form, and informational content. The manner in which the scale f and the parameters (θ, α, β) depend on the context and the task are discussed in the following sections.

Let us recapitulate what is assumed and what is proven in the representation theorem. We begin with a set of objects, described as collections of features, and a similarity ordering which is assumed to satisfy the axioms of the present theory. From these assumptions, we derive a measure f on the feature space and prove that the similarity ordering of object pairs coincides with the ordering of their contrasts, defined as linear combinations of the respective common and distinctive features. Thus, the measure f and the contrast model are derived from qualitative axioms regarding the similarity of objects.

The nature of this result may be illuminated by an analogy to the classical theory of decision under risk (von Neumann & Morgenstern, 1947). In that theory, one starts with a set of prospects, characterized as probability distributions over some consequence space, and a preference order that is assumed to satisfy the axioms of the theory. From these assumptions one derives a utility scale on the consequence space and proves that the preference order between prospects coincides with the order of their expected utilities. Thus, the utility scale and the expectation principle are derived from qualitative assumptions about preferences. The present theory of similarity differs from the expected-utility model in that the characterization of objects as feature sets is perhaps more problematic than the characterization of uncertain options as probability distributions. Furthermore, the axioms of utility theory are proposed as (normative) principles of rational behavior, whereas the axioms of the present theory are intended to be descriptive rather than prescriptive.

The contrast model is perhaps the simplest form of a matching function, yet it is not the only form worthy of investigation. Another matching function of interest is the *ratio model*,

$$S(a, b) = \frac{f(A \cap B)}{f(A \cap B) + \alpha f(A - B) + \beta f(B - A)}, \quad \alpha, \beta \geq 0,$$

where similarity is normalized so that S lies between 0 and 1. The ratio model generalizes several set-theoretical models of similarity proposed in the literature. If $\alpha = \beta = 1$, $S(a, b)$ reduces to $f(A \cap B)/f(A \cup B)$ (see Gregson, 1975, and Sjöberg, 1972). If $\alpha = \beta = \frac{1}{2}$, $S(a, b)$ equals $2f(A \cap B)/(f(A) + f(B))$ (see Eisler & Ekman, 1959). If $\alpha = 1$ and $\beta = 0$, $S(a, b)$ reduces to $f(A \cap B)/f(A)$ (see Bush & Mosteller, 1951). The present framework, therefore, encompasses a wide variety of similarity models that differ in the form of the matching function F and in the weights assigned to its arguments.

In order to apply and test the present theory in any particular domain, some assumptions about the respective feature structure must be made. If the features associated with each object are explicitly specified, we can test the axioms of the theory directly and scale the features according to the contrast model. This approach, however, is generally limited to stimuli (e.g., schematic faces, letters, strings of symbols) that are constructed from a fixed feature set. If the features associated with the objects under study cannot be readily specified, as is often the case with natural stimuli, we can still test several predictions of the contrast model which involve only general qualitative assumptions about the feature structure of the objects. Both approaches were employed in a series of experiments conducted by Itamar Gati and the present author. The following three sections review and discuss our main findings, focusing primarily on the test of qualitative predictions. A more detailed description of the stimuli and the data are presented in Tversky and Gati (in press).

Asymmetry and Focus

According to the present analysis, similarity is not necessarily a symmetric relation. Indeed, it follows readily (from either the contrast or the ratio model) that

$$s(a, b) = s(b, a) \quad \text{iff} \quad \alpha f(A - B) + \beta f(B - A) = \alpha f(B - A) + \beta f(A - B)$$

$$\text{iff} \quad (\alpha - \beta)f(A - B) = (\alpha - \beta)f(B - A).$$

Hence, $s(a, b) = s(b, a)$ if either $\alpha = \beta$, or $f(A - B) = f(B - A)$, which implies $f(A) = f(B)$, provided feature additivity holds. Thus, symmetry holds whenever the objects are equal in measure ($f(A) = f(B)$) or the task is nondirectional ($\alpha = \beta$). To interpret the latter condition, compare the following two forms:

(i) Assess the degree to which a and b are similar to each other.

(ii) Assess the degree to which a is similar to b.

In (i), the task is formulated in a nondirectional fashion; hence it is expected that $\alpha = \beta$ and $s(a, b) = s(b, a)$. In (ii), on the other hand, the task is directional, and hence α and β may differ and symmetry need not hold.

If $s(a, b)$ is interpreted as the degree to which a is similar to b, then a is the subject of the comparison and b is the referent. In such a task, one naturally focuses on the subject of the comparison. Hence, the features of the subject are weighted more heavily than the features of the referent (i.e., $\alpha > \beta$). Consequently, similarity is reduced more by the distinctive features of the subject than by the distinctive features of the referent. It follows readily that whenever $\alpha > \beta$,

$$s(a, b) > s(b, a) \quad \text{iff} \quad f(B) > f(A).$$

Thus, the focusing hypothesis (i.e., $\alpha > \beta$) implies that the direction of asymmetry is determined by the relative salience of the stimuli so that the less salient stimulus is more similar to the salient stimulus than vice versa. In particular, the variant is more similar to the prototype than the prototype is to the variant, because the prototype is generally more salient than the variant.

Similarity of Countries

Twenty-one pairs of countries served as stimuli. The pairs were constructed so that one element was more prominent than the other (e.g., Red China–North Vietnam, USA–Mexico, Belgium–Luxemburg). To verify this relation, we asked a group of 69 subjects[2] to select in each pair the country they regarded as more prominent. The proportion of subjects that agreed with the a priori ordering exceeded $\frac{2}{3}$ for all pairs except one. A second group of 69 subjects was asked to choose which of two phrases they preferred to use: "country a is similar to country b," or "country b is similar to country a." In all 21 cases, most of the subjects chose the phrase in which the less prominent country served as the subject and the more prominent country as the referent. For example, 66 subjects selected the phrase "North Korea is similar to Red China" and only 3 selected the phrase "Red China is similar to North Korea." These results demonstrate the presence of marked asymmetries in the choice of similarity statements, whose direction coincides with the relative prominence of the stimuli.

To test for asymmetry in direct judgments of similarity, we presented two groups of 77 subjects each with the same list of 21 pairs of countries and asked subjects to rate their similarity on a 20-point scale. The only difference between the two groups was the order of the countries within each pair. For example, one group was asked to assess "the degree to which the USSR is similar to Poland," whereas the second group was asked to assess "the degree to which Poland is similar to the USSR." The lists were constructed so that the more prominent country appeared about an equal number of times in the first and second positions.

For any pair (p, q) of stimuli, let p denote the more prominent element, and let q denote the less prominent element. The average $s(q, p)$ was significantly higher than the average $s(p, q)$ across all subjects and pairs: t test for correlated samples yielded $t(20) = 2.92$, $p < .01$. To obtain a statistical test based on individual data, we computed for each subject a directional asymmetry score defined as the average similarity for comparisons with a prominent referent; that is, $s(q, p)$, minus the average similarity for comparisons with a prominent subject, $s(p, q)$. The average difference was significantly positive: $t(153) = 2.99$, $p < .01$.

The above study was repeated using judgments of difference instead of judgments of similarity. Two groups of 23 subjects each participated in this study. They received the same list of 21 pairs except that one group was asked to judge the degree to which country a differed from country b, denoted $d(a, b)$, whereas the second group was asked to judge the degree to which country b was different from country a, denoted $d(b, a)$. If judgments of difference follow the contrast model, and $\alpha > \beta$, then we expect the prominent stimulus p to differ from the less prominent stimulus q more than q differs from p; that is, $d(p, q) > d(q, p)$. This hypothesis was tested using the same set of 21 pairs of countries and the prominence ordering established earlier. The average $d(p, q)$, across all subjects and pairs, was significantly higher than the average $d(q, p)$: t test for correlated samples yielded $t(20) = 2.72$, $p < .01$. Furthermore, the average asymmetry score, computed as above for each subject, was significantly positive, $t(45) = 2.24$, $p < .05$.

Similarity of Figures

A major determinant of the salience of geometric figures is goodness of form. Thus, a "good figure" is likely to be more salient than a "bad figure," although the latter is generally more complex. However, when two figures are roughly equivalent with respect to goodness of form, the more complex figure is likely to be more salient. To investigate these hypotheses and to test the asymmetry prediction, two sets of eight pairs of geometric figures were constructed. In the first set, one figure in each pair (denoted p) had better form than the other (denoted q). In the second set, the two figures in each pair were roughly matched in goodness of form, but one figure (denoted p) was richer or more complex than the other (denoted q). Examples of pairs of figures from each set are presented in figure 1.3.

A group of 69 subjects was presented with the entire list of 16 pairs of figures, where the two elements of each pair were displayed side by side. For each pair, the subjects were asked to indicate which of the following two statements they preferred

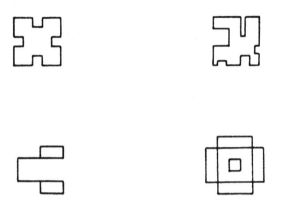

Figure 1.3
Examples of pairs of figures used to test the prediction of asymmetry. The top two figures are examples of a pair (from the first set) that differs in goodness of form. The bottom two are examples of a pair (from the second set) that differs in complexity.

to use: "The left figure is similar to the right figure," or "The right figure is similar to the left figure." The positions of the stimuli were randomized so that p and q appeared an equal number of times on the left and on the right. The results showed that in each one of the pairs, most of the subjects selected the form "q is similar to p." Thus, the more salient stimulus was generally chosen as the referent rather than the subject of similarity statements.

To test for asymmetry in judgments of similarity, we presented two groups of 67 subjects each with the same 16 pairs of figures and asked the subjects to rate (on a 20-point scale) the degree to which the figure on the left was similar to the figure on the right. The two groups received identical booklets, except that the left and right positions of the figures in each pair were reversed. The results showed that the average $s(q, p)$ across all subjects and pairs was significantly higher than the average $s(p, q)$. A t test for correlated samples yielded $t(15) = 2.94$, $p < .01$. Furthermore, in both sets the average asymmetry scores, computed as above for each subject, were significantly positive: In the first set $t(131) = 2.96$, $p < .01$, and in the second set $t(131) = 2.79$, $p < .01$.

Similarity of Letters
A common measure of similarity between stimuli is the probability of confusing them in a recognition or an identification task: The more similar the stimuli, the more likely they are to be confused. While confusion probabilities are often asymmetric (i.e., the probability of confusing a with b is different from the probability of con-

fusing b with a), this effect is typically attributed to a response bias. To eliminate this interpretation of asymmetry, one could employ an experimental task where the subject merely indicates whether the two stimuli presented to him (sequentially or simultaneously) are identical or not. This procedure was employed by Yoav Cohen and the present author in a study of confusion among block letters.

The following eight block letters served as stimuli: ⌐, ⊏, ⊓, ☐, ⊨, ⨌, ⨆, ⨄. All pairs of letters were displayed on a cathode-ray tube, side by side, on a noisy background. The letters were presented sequentially, each for approximately 1 msec. The right letter always followed the left letter with an interval of 630 msec in between. After each presentation the subject pressed one of two keys to indicate whether the two letters were identical or not.

A total of 32 subjects participated in the experiment. Each subject was tested individually. On each trial, one letter (known in advance) served as the standard. For one half of the subjects the standard stimulus always appeared on the left, and for the other half of the subjects the standard always appeared on the right. Each one of the eight letters served as a standard. The trials were blocked into groups of 10 pairs in which the standard was paired once with each of the other letters and three times with itself. Since each letter served as a standard in one block, the entire design consisted of eight blocks of 10 trials each. Every subject was presented with three replications of the entire design (i.e., 240 trials). The order of the blocks in each design and the order of the letters within each block were randomized.

According to the present analysis, people compare the variable stimulus, which serves the role of the subject, to the standard (i.e., the referent). The choice of standard, therefore, determines the directionality of the comparison. A natural partial ordering of the letters with respect to prominence is induced by the relation of inclusion among letters. Thus, one letter is assumed to have a larger measure than another if the former includes the latter. For example, $\sqsubseteq$ includes $\vDash$ and $\sqsubset$ but not $\square$. For all 19 pairs in which one letter includes the other, let p denote the more prominent letter and q denote the less prominent letter. Furthermore, let $s(a, b)$ denote the percentage of times that the subject judged the variable stimulus a to be the same as the standard b.

It follows from the contrast model, with $\alpha > \beta$, that the proportion of "same" responses should be larger when the variable is included in the standard than when the standard is included in the variable, that is, $s(q, p) > s(p, q)$. This prediction was borne out by the data. The average $s(q, p)$ across all subjects and trials was 17.1%, whereas the average $s(p, q)$ across all subjects and trials was 12.4%. To obtain a statistical test, we computed for each subject the difference between $s(q, p)$ and $s(p, q)$ across all trials. The difference was significantly positive, $t(31) = 4.41$, $p < .001$.

These results demonstrate that the prediction of directional asymmetry derived from the contrast model applies to confusion data and not merely to rated similarity.

Similarity of Signals

Rothkopf (1957) presented 598 subjects with all ordered pairs of the 36 Morse Code signals and asked them to indicate whether the two signals in each pair were the same or not. The pairs were presented in a randomized order without a fixed standard. Each subject judged about one fourth of all pairs.

Let $s(a, b)$ denote the percentage of "same" responses to the ordered pair (a, b), i.e., the percentage of subjects that judged the first signal a to be the same as the second signal b. Note that a and b refer here to the first and second signal, and not to the variable and the standard as in the previous section. Obviously, Morse Code signals are partially ordered according to temporal length. For any pair of signals that differ in temporal length, let p and q denote, respectively, the longer and shorter element of the pair.

From the total of 555 comparisons between signals of different length, reported in Rothkopf (1957), $s(q, p)$ exceeds $s(p, q)$ in 336 cases, $s(p, q)$ exceeds $s(q, p)$ in 181 cases, and $s(q, p)$ equals $s(p, q)$ in 38 cases, $p < .001$, by sign test. The average difference between $s(q, p)$ and $s(p, q)$ across all pairs is 3.3%, which is also highly significant. A t test for correlated samples yields $t(554) = 9.17$, $p < .001$.

The asymmetry effect is enhanced when we consider only those comparisons in which one signal is a proper subsequence of the other. (For example, $\cdot\cdot$ is a subsequence of $\cdot\cdot\text{-}$ as well as of $\cdot\text{-}\cdot$). From a total of 195 comparisons of this type, $s(q, p)$ exceeds $s(p, q)$ in 128 cases, $s(p, q)$ exceeds $s(q, p)$ in 55 cases, and $s(q, p)$ equals $s(p, q)$ in 12 cases, $p < .001$ by sign test. The average difference between $s(q, p)$ and $s(p, q)$ in this case is 4.7%, $t(194) = 7.58$, $p < .001$.

A later study following the same experimental paradigm with somewhat different signals was conducted by Wish (1967). His signals consisted of three tones separated by two silent intervals, where each component (i.e., a tone or a silence) was either short or long. Subjects were presented with all pairs of 32 signals generated in this fashion and judged whether the two members of each pair were the same or not.

The above analysis is readily applicable to Wish's (1967) data. From a total of 386 comparisons between signals of different length, $s(q, p)$ exceeds $s(p, q)$ in 241 cases, $s(p, q)$ exceeds $s(q, p)$ in 117 cases, and $s(q, p)$ equals $s(p, q)$ in 28 cases. These data are clearly asymmetric, $p < .001$ by sign test. The average difference between $s(q, p)$ and $s(p, q)$ is 5.9%, which is also highly significant, $t(385) = 9.23$, $p < .001$.

In the studies of Rothkopf and Wish there is no a priori way to determine the directionality of the comparison, or equivalently to identify the subject and the referent. However, if we accept the focusing hypothesis ($\alpha > \beta$) and the assumption that longer signals are more prominent than shorter ones, then the direction of the observed asymmetry indicates that the first signal serves as the subject that is compared with the second signal that serves the role of the referent. Hence, the directionality of the comparison is determined, according to the present analysis, from the prominence ordering of the stimuli and the observed direction of asymmetry.

Rosch's Data

Rosch (1973, 1975) has articulated and supported the view that perceptual and semantic categories are naturally formed and defined in terms of focal points, or prototypes. Because of the special role of prototypes in the formation of categories, she hypothesized that (i) in sentence frames involving hedges such as "a is essentially b," focal stimuli (i.e., prototypes) appear in the second position; and (ii) the perceived distance from the prototype to the variant is greater than the perceived distance from the variant to the prototype. To test these hypotheses, Rosch (1975) used three stimulus domains: color, line orientation, and number. Prototypical colors were focal (e.g., pure red), while the variants were either non-focal (e.g., off-red) or less saturated. Vertical, horizontal, and diagonal lines served as prototypes for line orientation, and lines of other angles served as variants. Multiples of 10 (e.g., 10, 50, 100) were taken as prototypical numbers, and other numbers (e.g., 11, 52, 103) were treated as variants.

Hypothesis (i) was strongly confirmed in all three domains. When presented with sentence frames such as "____ is virtually ____," subjects generally placed the prototype in the second blank and the variant in the first. For instance, subjects preferred the sentence "103 is virtually 100" to the sentence "100 is virtually 103." To test hypothesis (ii), one stimulus (the standard) was placed at the origin of a semicircular board, and the subject was instructed to place the second (variable) stimulus on the board so as "to represent his feeling of the distance between that stimulus and the one fixed at the origin." As hypothesized, the measured distance between stimuli was significantly smaller when the prototype, rather than the variant, was fixed at the origin, in each of the three domains.

If focal stimuli are more salient than non-focal stimuli, then Rosch's findings support the present analysis. The hedging sentences (e.g., "a is roughly b") can be regarded as a particular type of similarity statements. Indeed, the hedges data are in perfect agreement with the choice of similarity statements. Furthermore, the observed asymmetry in distance placement follows from the present analysis of asymmetry and the natural assumptions that the standard and the variable serve, respectively, as referent and subject in the distance-placement task. Thus, the placement of b at distance t from a is interpreted as saying that the (perceived) distance from b to a equals t.

Rosch (1975) attributed the observed asymmetry to the special role of distinct prototypes (e.g., a perfect square or a pure red) in the processing of information. In the present theory, on the other hand, asymmetry is explained by the relative salience of the stimuli. Consequently, it implies asymmetry for pairs that do not include the prototype (e.g., two levels of distortion of the same form). If the concept of prototypicality, however, is interpreted in a relative sense (i.e., a is more prototypical than b) rather than in an absolute sense, then the two interpretations of asymmetry practically coincide.

Discussion

The conjunction of the contrast model and the focusing hypothesis implies the presence of asymmetric similarities. This prediction was confirmed in several experiments of perceptual and conceptual similarity using both judgmental methods (e.g., rating) and behavioral methods (e.g., choice).

The asymmetries discussed in the previous section were observed in *comparative* tasks in which the subject compares two given stimuli to determine their similarity. Asymmetries were also observed in *production* tasks in which the subject is given a single stimulus and asked to produce the most similar response. Studies of pattern recognition, stimulus identification, and word association are all examples of production tasks. A common pattern observed in such studies is that the more salient object occurs more often as a response to the less salient object than vice versa. For example, "tiger" is a more likely associate to "leopard" than "leopard" is to "tiger." Similarly, Garner (1974) instructed subjects to select from a given set of dot patterns one that is similar—but not identical—to a given pattern. His results show that "good" patterns are usually chosen as responses to "bad" patterns and not conversely.

This asymmetry in production tasks has commonly been attributed to the differential availability of responses. Thus, "tiger" is a more likely associate to "leopard" than vice versa, because "tiger" is more common and hence a more available response than "leopard." This account is probably more applicable to situations where the subject must actually produce the response (as in word association or pattern recognition) than to situations where the subject merely selects a response from some specified set (as in Garner's task).

Without questioning the importance of response availability, the present theory suggests another reason for the asymmetry observed in production tasks. Consider the following translation of a production task to a question-and-answer scheme.

Question: What is a like? Answer: a is like b. If this interpretation is valid and the given object a serves as a subject rather than as a referent, then the observed asymmetry of production follows from the present theoretical analysis, since $s(a, b) > s(b, a)$ whenever $f(B) > f(A)$.

In summary, it appears that proximity data from both comparative and production tasks reveal significant and systematic asymmetries whose direction is determined by the relative salience of the stimuli. Nevertheless, the symmetry assumption should not be rejected altogether. It seems to hold in many contexts, and it serves as a useful approximation in many others. It cannot be accepted, however, as a universal principle of psychological similarity.

Common and Distinctive Features

In the present theory, the similarity of objects is expressed as a linear combination, or a contrast, of the measures of their common and distinctive features. This section investigates the relative impact of these components and their effect on the relation between the assessments of similarity and difference. The discussion concerns only symmetric tasks, where $\alpha = \beta$, and hence $s(a, b) = s(b, a)$.

Elicitation of Features

The first study employs the contrast model to predict the similarity between objects from features that were produced by the subjects. The following 12 vehicles served as stimuli: bus, car, truck, motorcycle, train, airplane, bicycle, boat, elevator, cart, raft, sled. One group of 48 subjects rated the similarity between all 66 pairs of vehicles on a scale from 1 (no similarity) to 20 (maximal similarity). Following Rosch and Mervis (1975), we instructed a second group of 40 subjects to list the characteristic features of each one of the vehicles. Subjects were given 70 sec to list the features that characterized each vehicle. Different orders of presentation were used for different subjects.

The number of features per vehicle ranged from 71 for airplane to 21 for sled. Altogether, 324 features were listed by the subjects, of which 224 were unique and 100 were shared by two or more vehicles. For every pair of vehicles we counted the number of features that were attributed to both (by at least one subject), and the number of features that were attributed to one vehicle but not to the other. The frequency of subjects that listed each common or distinctive feature was computed.

In order to predict the similarity between vehicles from the listed features, the measures of their common and distinctive features must be defined. The simplest measure is obtained by counting the number of common and distinctive features produced by the subjects. The product-moment correlation between the (average) similarity of objects and the number of their common features was .68. The correlation between the similarity of objects and the number of their distinctive features was −.36. The multiple correlation between similarity and the numbers of common and distinctive features (i.e., the correlation between similarity and the contrast model) was .72.

The counting measure assigns equal weight to all features regardless of their frequency of mention. To take this factor into account, let X_a denote the proportion of subjects who attributed feature X to object a, and let N_X denote the number of objects that share feature X. For any a, b, define the measure of their common features by $f(A \cap B) = \sum X_a X_b / N_X$, where the summation is over all X in A $\cap$ B, and the measure of their distinctive features by

$$f(A - B) + f(B - A) = \sum Y_a + \sum Z_b$$

where the summations range over all $Y \in A - B$ and $Z \in B - A$, that is, the distinctive features of a and b, respectively. The correlation between similarity and the above measure of the common features was .84; the correlation between similarity and the above measure of the distinctive features was −.64. The multiple correlation between similarity and the measures of the common and the distinctive features was .87.

Note that the above methods for defining the measure f were based solely on the elicited features and did not utilize the similarity data at all. Under these conditions, a perfect correlation between the two should not be expected because the weights associated with the features are not optimal for the prediction of similarity. A given feature may be frequently mentioned because it is easily labeled or recalled, although it does not have a great impact on similarity, and vice versa. Indeed, when the features were scaled using the additive tree procedure (Sattath & Tversky, in press) in which the measure of the features is derived from the similarities between the objects, the correlation between the data and the model reached .94.

The results of this study indicate that (i) it is possible to elicit from subjects detailed features of semantic stimuli such as vehicles (see Rosch & Mervis, 1975); (ii) the listed features can be used to predict similarity according to the contrast model with a reasonable degree of success; and (iii) the prediction of similarity is improved when frequency of mention and not merely the number of features is taken into account.

Similarity versus Difference

It has been generally assumed that judgments of similarity and difference are complementary; that is, judged difference is a linear function of judged similarity with a slope of −1. This hypothesis has been confirmed in several studies. For example, Hosman and Kuennapas (1972) obtained independent judgments of similarity and difference for all pairs of lowercase letters on a scale from 0 to 100. The product–moment correlation between the judgments was −.98, and the slope of the regression line was −.91. We also collected judgments of similarity and difference for 21 pairs of countries using a 20-point rating scale. The sum of the two judgments for each pair was quite close to 20 in all cases. The product–moment correlation between the ratings was again −.98. This inverse relation between similarity and difference, however, does not always hold.

Naturally, an increase in the measure of the common features increases similarity and decreases difference, whereas an increase in the measure of the distinctive features decreases similarity and increases difference. However, the relative weight assigned to the common and the distinctive features may differ in the two tasks. In the assessment of similarity between objects the subject may attend more to their common features, whereas in the assessment of difference between objects the subject may attend more to their distinctive features. Thus, the relative weight of the common features will be greater in the former task than in the latter task.

Let $d(a, b)$ denote the perceived difference between a and b. Suppose d satisfies the axioms of the present theory with the reverse inequality in the monotonicity axiom, that is, $d(a, b) \leq d(a, c)$ whenever $A \cap B \supset A \cap C$, $A - B \subset A - C$, and $B - A \subset C - A$. Furthermore, suppose s also satisfies the present theory and assume (for simplicity) that both d and s are symmetric. According to the representation theorem, therefore, there exist a nonnegative scale f and nonnegative constants θ and λ such that for all a, b, c, e,

$$s(a, b) > s(c, e) \quad \text{iff} \quad \theta f(A \cap B) - f(A - B) - f(B - A)$$
$$> \theta f(C \cap E) - f(C - E) - f(E - C),$$

and

$$d(a, b) > d(c, e) \quad \text{iff} \quad f(A - B) + f(B - A) - \lambda f(A \cap B)$$
$$> f(C - E) + f(E - C) - \lambda f(C \cap E).$$

The weights associated with the distinctive features can be set equal to 1 in the symmetric case with no loss of generality. Hence, θ and λ reflect the *relative* weight of the common features in the assessment of similarity and difference, respectively.

Note that if θ is very large then the similarity ordering is essentially determined by the common features. On the other hand, if λ is very small, then the difference ordering is determined primarily by the distinctive features. Consequently, both $s(a, b) > s(c, e)$ and $d(a, b) > d(c, e)$ may be obtained whenever

$$f(A \cap B) > f(C \cap E)$$

and

$$f(A - B) + f(B - A) > f(C - E) + f(E - C).$$

That is, if the common features are weighed more heavily in judgments of similarity than in judgments of difference, then a pair of objects with many common and many distinctive features may be perceived as both more similar and more different than another pair of objects with fewer common and fewer distinctive features.

To test this hypothesis, 20 sets of four countries were constructed on the basis of a pilot test. Each set included two pairs of countries: a prominent pair and a nonprominent pair. The prominent pairs consisted of countries that were well known to our subjects (e.g., USA–USSR, Red China–Japan). The nonprominent pairs consisted of countries that were known to the subjects, but not as well as the prominent ones (e.g., Tunis–Morocco, Paraguay–Ecuador). All subjects were presented with the same 20 sets. One group of 30 subjects selected between the two pairs in each set the pair of countries that were more *similar*. Another group of 30 subjects selected between the two pairs in each set the pair of countries that were more *different*.

Let Π_s and Π_d denote, respectively, the percentage of choices where the prominent pair of countries was selected as more similar or as more different. If similarity and difference are complementary (i.e., $\theta = \lambda$), then $\Pi_s + \Pi_d$ should equal 100 for all pairs. On the other hand, if $\theta > \lambda$, then $\Pi_s + \Pi_d$ should exceed 100. The average value of $\Pi_s + \Pi_d$, across all sets, was 113.5, which is significantly greater than 100, $t(59) = 3.27$, $p < .01$.

Moreover, on the average, the prominent pairs were selected more frequently than the nonprominent pairs in both the similarity and the difference tasks. For example, 67% of the subjects in the similarity group selected West Germany and East Germany as more similar to each other than Ceylon and Nepal, while 70% of the subjects in the difference group selected West Germany and East Germany as more different from each other than Ceylon and Nepal. These data demonstrate how the relative weight of the common and the distinctive features varies with the task and support the hypothesis that people attend more to the common features in judgments of similarity than in judgments of difference.

Similarity in Context

Like other judgments, similarity depends on context and frame of reference. Some-times the relevant frame of reference is specified explicitly, as in the questions, "How similar are English and French with respect to sound?" "What is the similarity of a pear and an apple with respect to taste?" In general, however, the relevant feature space is not specified explicitly but rather inferred from the general context.

When subjects are asked to assess the similarity between the USA and the USSR, for instance, they usually assume that the relevant context is the set of countries and that the relevant frame of reference includes all political, geographical, and cultural features. The relative weights assigned to these features, of course, may differ for different people. With natural, integral stimuli such as countries, people, colors, and sounds, there is relatively little ambiguity regarding the relevant feature space. How-ever, with artificial, separable stimuli, such as figures varying in color and shape, or lines varying in length and orientation, subjects sometimes experience difficulty in evaluating overall similarity and occasionally tend to evaluate similarity with respect to one factor or the other (Shepard, 1964) or change the relative weights of attributes with a change in context (Torgerson, 1965).

In the present theory, changes in context or frame of reference correspond to changes in the measure of the feature space. When asked to assess the political simi-larity between countries, for example, the subject presumably attends to the political aspects of the countries and ignores, or assigns a weight of zero to, all other features. In addition to such restrictions of the feature space induced by explicit or implicit instructions, the salience of features and hence the similarity of objects are also influenced by the effective context (i.e., the set of objects under consideration). To understand this process, let us examine the factors that determine the salience of a feature and its contribution to the similarity of objects.

The Diagnosticity Principle

The salience (or the measure) of a feature is determined by two types of factors: intensive and diagnostic. The former refers to factors that increase intensity or signal-to-noise ratio, such as the brightness of a light, the loudness of a tone, the saturation of a color, the size of a letter, the frequency of an item, the clarity of a picture, or the vividness of an image. The diagnostic factors refer to the classificatory significance of features, that is, the importance or prevalence of the classifications that are based on these features. Unlike the intensive factors, the diagnostic factors are highly sensitive to the particular object set under study. For example, the feature "real" has no diagnostic value in the set of actual animals since it is shared by all actual animals and hence cannot be used to classify them. This feature, however, acquires considerable diagnostic value if the object set is extended to include legendary animals, such as a centaur, a mermaid, or a phoenix.

When faced with a set of objects, people often sort them into clusters to reduce information load and facilitate further processing. Clusters are typically selected so as to maximize the similarity of objects within a cluster and the dissimilarity of objects from different clusters. Hence, the addition and/or deletion of objects can alter the clustering of the remaining objects. A change of clusters, in turn, is expected to increase the diagnostic value of features on which the new clusters are based, and therefore, the similarity of objects that share these features. This relation between similarity and grouping—called the diagnosticity hypothesis—is best explained in terms of a concrete example. Consider the two sets of four schematic faces (displayed in figure 1.4), which differ in only one of their elements (p and q).

The four faces of each set were displayed in a row and presented to a different group of 25 subjects who were instructed to partition them into two pairs. The most frequent partition of set 1 was c and p (smiling faces) versus a and b (nonsmiling faces). The most common partition of set 2 was b and q (frowning faces) versus a and c (nonfrowning faces). Thus, the replacement of p by q changed the grouping of a: In set 1 a was paired with b, while in set 2 a was paired with c.

According to the above analysis, smiling has a greater diagnostic value in set 1 than in set 2, whereas frowning has a greater diagnostic value in set 2 than in set 1. By the diagnosticity hypothesis, therefore, similarity should follow the grouping. That is, the similarity of a (which has a neutral expression) to b (which is frowning) should be greater in set 1, where they are grouped together, than in set 2, where they are grouped separately. Likewise, the similarity of a to c (which is smiling) should be greater in set 2, where they are grouped together, than in set 1, where they are not.

To test this prediction, two different groups of 50 subjects were presented with sets 1 and 2 (in the form displayed in figure 1.4) and asked to select one of the three faces below (called the choice set) that was most similar to the face on the top (called the target). The percentage of subjects who selected each of the three elements of the choice set is presented below the face. The results confirmed the diagnosticity hypothesis: b was chosen more frequently in set 1 than in set 2, whereas c was chosen more frequently in set 2 than in set 1. Both differences are statistically significant, $p < .01$. Moreover, the replacement of p by q actually reversed the similarity ordering: In set 1, b is more similar to a than c, whereas in set 2, c is more similar to a than b.

A more extensive test of the diagnosticity hypothesis was conducted using semantic rather than visual stimuli. The experimental design was essentially the same,

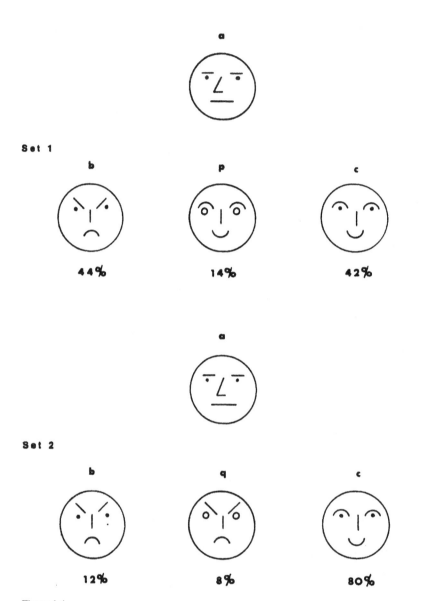

Figure 1.4
Two sets of schematic faces used to test the diagnosticity hypothesis. The percentage of subjects who selected each face (as most similar to the target) is presented below the face.

```
┌─────────────────────────────────────────────────────┐
│                      a                               │
│                   Austria                            │
│   Set 1                                              │
│           b            p            c                │
│         Sweden      Poland       Hungary             │
│          49%          15%          36%               │
│                                                      │
│                                                      │
│                      a                               │
│                   Austria                            │
│   Set 2                                              │
│           b            q            c                │
│         Sweden      Norway       Hungary             │
│          14%          26%          60%               │
└─────────────────────────────────────────────────────┘
```

Figure 1.5
Two sets of countries used to test the diagnosticity hypothesis. The percentage of subjects who selected each country (as most similar to Austria) is presented below the country.

except that countries served as stimuli instead of faces. Twenty pairs of matched sets of four countries of the form $\{a, b, c, p\}$ and $\{a, b, c, q\}$ were constructed. An example of two matched sets is presented in figure 1.5.

Note that the two matched sets (1 and 2) differ only by one element (p and q). The sets were constructed so that a (in this case Austria) is likely to be grouped with b (e.g., Sweden) in set 1, and with c (e.g., Hungary) in set 2. To validate this assumption, we presented two groups of 25 subjects with all sets of four countries and asked them to partition each quadruple into two pairs. Each group received one of the two matched quadruples, which were displayed in a row in random order. The results confirmed our prior hypothesis regarding the grouping of countries. In every case but one, the replacement of p by q changed the pairing of the target country in the predicted direction, $p < .01$ by sign test. For example, Austria was paired with Sweden by 60% of the subjects in set 1, and it was paired with Hungary by 96% of the subjects in set 2.

To test the diagnosticity hypothesis, we presented two groups of 35 subjects with 20 sets of four countries in the format displayed in figure 1.5. These subjects were asked to select, for each quadruple, the country in the choice set that was most similar to the target country. Each group received exactly one quadruple from each pair. If the similarity of b to a, say, is independent of the choice set, then the proportion of subjects who chose b rather than c as most similar to a should be the same regardless of whether the third element in the choice set is p or q. For example, the proportion of subjects who select Sweden rather than Hungary as most similar to Austria should be independent of whether the odd element in the choice set is Norway or Poland.

In contrast, the diagnosticity hypothesis implies that the change in grouping, induced by the substitution of the odd element, will change the similarities in a predictable manner. Recall that in set 1 Poland was paired with Hungary, and Austria with Sweden, while in set 2 Norway was paired with Sweden, and Austria with Hungary. Hence, the proportion of subjects who select Sweden rather than Hungary (as most similar to Austria) should be higher in set 1 than in set 2. This prediction is strongly supported by the data in figure 1.5, which show that Sweden was selected more frequently than Hungary in set 1, while Hungary was selected more frequently than Sweden in set 2.

Let b(p) denote the percentage of subjects who chose country b as most similar to a when the odd element in the choice set is p, and so on. As in the above examples, the notation is chosen so that b is generally grouped with q, and c is generally grouped with p. The differences $b(p) - b(q)$ and $c(q) - c(p)$, therefore, reflect the effects of the odd elements, p and q, on the similarity of b and c to the target a. In the absence of context effects, both differences should equal 0, while under the diagnosticity hypothesis both differences should be positive. In figure 1.5, for example, $b(p) - b(q) = 49 - 14 = 35$, and $c(q) - c(p) = 60 - 36 = 24$. The average difference, across all pairs of quadruples, equals 9%, which is significantly positive, $t(19) = 3.65$, $p < .01$.

Several variations of the experiment did not alter the nature of the results. The diagnosticity hypothesis was also confirmed when (i) each choice set contained four elements, rather than three, (ii) the subjects were instructed to rank the elements of each choice set according to their similarity to the target, rather than to select the most similar element, and (iii) the target consisted of two elements, and the subjects were instructed to select one element of the choice set that was most similar to the two target elements. For further details, see Tversky and Gati (in press).

The Extension Effect

Recall that the diagnosticity of features is determined by the classifications that are based on them. Features that are shared by all the objects under consideration cannot be used to classify these objects and are, therefore, devoid of diagnostic value. When the context is extended by the enlargement of the object set, some features that had been shared by all objects in the original context may not be shared by all objects in the broader context. These features then acquire diagnostic value and increase the similarity of the objects that share them. Thus, the similarity of a pair of objects in the original context will usually be smaller than their similarity in the extended context.

Essentially the same account was proposed and supported by Sjöberg[3] in studies of similarity between animals, and between musical instruments. For example, Sjöberg showed that the similarities between string instruments (banjo, violin, harp, electric guitar) were increased when a wind instrument (clarinet) was added to this set. Since the string instruments are more similar to each other than to the clarinet, however, the above result may be attributed, in part at least, to subjects' tendency to standardize the response scale, that is, to produce the same average similarity for any set of comparisons.

This effect can be eliminated by the use of a somewhat different design, employed in the following study. Subjects were presented with pairs of countries having a common border and assessed their similarity on a 20-point scale. Four sets of eight pairs were constructed. Set 1 contained eight pairs of European countries (e.g., Italy–Switzerland). Set 2 contained eight pairs of American countries (e.g., Brazil–Uruguay). Set 3 contained four pairs from set 1 and four pairs from set 2, while set 4 contained the remaining pairs from sets 1 and 2. Each one of the four sets was presented to a different group of 30–36 subjects.

According to the diagnosticity hypothesis, the features "European" and "American" have no diagnostic value in sets 1 and 2, although they both have a diagnostic value in sets 3 and 4. Consequently, the overall average similarity in the heterogeneous sets (3 and 4) is expected to be higher than the overall average similarity in the homogeneous sets (1 and 2). This prediction was confirmed by the data, $t(15) = 2.11$, $p < .05$.

In the present study all similarity assessments involve only homogeneous pairs (i.e., pairs of countries from the same continent sharing a common border). Unlike Sjöberg's[3] study, which extended the context by introducing nonhomogeneous pairs, our experiment extended the context by constructing heterogeneous sets composed of homogeneous pairs. Hence, the increase of similarity with the enlargement of context, observed in the present study, cannot be explained by subjects' tendency to equate the average similarity for any set of assessments.

The Two Faces of Similarity
According to the present analysis, the salience of features has two components: intensity and diagnosticity. The intensity of a feature is determined by perceptual and cognitive factors that are relatively stable across contexts. The diagnostic value of a feature is determined by the prevalence of the classifications that are based on it, which change with the context. The effects of context on similarity, therefore, are treated as changes in the diagnostic value of features induced by the respective changes in the grouping of the objects.

This account was supported by the experimental finding that changes in grouping (produced by the replacement or addition of objects) lead to corresponding changes in the similarity of the objects. These results shed light on the dynamic interplay between similarity and classification. It is generally assumed that classifications are determined by similarities among the objects. The preceding discussion supports the converse hypothesis: that the similarity of objects is modified by the manner in which they are classified. Thus, similarity has two faces: causal and derivative. It serves as a basis for the classification of objects, but it is also influenced by the adopted classification. The diagnosticity principle which underlies this process may provide a key to the analysis of the effects of context on similarity.

Discussion

In this section we relate the present development to the representation of objects in terms of clusters and trees, discuss the concepts of prototypicality and family resemblance, and comment on the relation between similarity and metaphor.

Features, Clusters, and Trees

There is a well-known correspondence between features or properties of objects and the classes to which the objects belong. A red flower, for example, can be characterized as having the feature "red," or as being a member of the class of red objects. In this manner we associate with every feature in Φ the class of objects in Δ which possesses that feature. This correspondence between features and classes provides a direct link between the present theory and the clustering approach to the representation of proximity data.

In the contrast model, the similarity between objects is expressed as a function of their common and distinctive features. Relations among overlapping sets are often represented in a Venn diagram (see figure 1.1). However, this representation becomes cumbersome when the number of objects exceeds four or five. To obtain useful graphic representations of the contrast model; two alternative simplifications are entertained.

First, suppose the objects under study are all equal in prominence, that is, $f(A) = f(B)$ for all a, b in Δ. Although this assumption is not strictly valid in general, it may serve as a reasonable approximation in certain contexts. Assuming feature additivity and symmetry, we obtain

$$S(a, b) = \theta f(A \cap B) - f(A - B) - f(B - A)$$

$$= \theta f(A \cap B) + 2f(A \cap B) - f(A - B) - f(B - A) - 2f(A \cap B)$$

$$= (\theta + 2)f(A \cap B) - f(A) - f(B)$$

$$= \lambda f(A \cap B) + \mu,$$

since $f(A) = f(B)$ for all a, b in Δ. Under the present assumptions, therefore, similarity between objects is a linear function of the measure of their common features.

Since f is an additive measure, $f(A \cap B)$ is expressible as the sum of the measures of all the features that belong to both a and b. For each subset Λ of Δ, let $\Phi(\Lambda)$ denote the set of features that are shared by all objects in Λ, and are not shared by any object that does not belong to Λ. Hence,

$$S(a, b) = \lambda f(A \cap B) + \mu$$
$$= \lambda\left(\sum f(X)\right) + \mu \quad X \in A \cap B$$
$$= \lambda\left(\sum f(\Phi(\Lambda))\right) + \mu \quad \Lambda \supset \{a, b\}.$$

Since the summation ranges over all subsets of Δ that include both a and b, the similarity between objects can be expressed as the sum of the weights associated with all the sets that include both objects.

This form is essentially identical to the additive clustering model proposed by Shepard and Arabie[4]. These investigators have developed a computer program, ADCLUS, which selects a relatively small collection of subsets and assigns weight to each subset so as to maximize the proportion of (similarity) variance accounted for by the model. Shepard and Arabie[4] applied ADCLUS to several studies including Shepard, Kilpatric, and Cunningham's (1975) on judgments of similarity between the integers 0 through 9 with respect to their abstract numerical character. A solution with 19 subsets accounted for 95% of the variance. The nine major subsets (with the largest weights) are displayed in table 1.1 along with a suggested interpretation. Note that all the major subsets are readily interpretable, and they are overlapping rather than hierarchical.

Table 1.1
ADCLUS Analysis of the Similarities among the Integers 0 through 9 (from Shepard & Arabie[4])

Rank	Weight	Elements of subset	Interpretation of subset
1st	.305	2 4 8	powers of two
2nd	.288	6 7 8 9	large numbers
3rd	.279	3 6 9	multiples of three
4th	.202	0 1 2	very small numbers
5th	.202	1 3 5 7 9	odd numbers
6th	.175	1 2 3	small nonzero numbers
7th	.163	5 6 7	middle numbers (largish)
8th	.160	0 1	additive and multiplicative identities
9th	.146	0 1 2 3 4	smallish numbers

The above model expresses similarity in terms of common features only. Alternatively, similarity may be expressed exclusively in terms of distinctive features. It has been shown by Sattath[5] that for any symmetric contrast model with an additive measure f, there exists a measure g defined on the same feature space such that

$$S(a, b) = \theta f(A \cap B) - f(A - B) - f(B - A)$$

$$= \lambda - g(A - B) - g(B - A) \quad \text{for some } \lambda > 0.$$

This result allows a simple representation of dissimilarity whenever the feature space Φ is a tree (i.e., whenever any three objects in Δ can be labeled so that $A \cap B = A \cap C \subset B \cap C$). Figure 1.6 presents an example of a feature tree, constructed by Sattath and Tversky (in press) from judged similarities between lowercase letters, obtained by Kuennapas and Janson (1969). The major branches are labeled to facilitate the interpretation of the tree.

Each (horizontal) arc in the graph represents the set of features shared by all the objects (i.e., letters) that follow from that arc, and the arc length corresponds to the measure of that set. The features of an object are the features of all the arcs which lead to that object, and its measure is its (horizontal) distance to the root. The tree distance between objects a and b is the (horizontal) length of the path joining them, that is, $f(A - B) + f(B - A)$. Hence, if the contrast model holds, $\alpha = \beta$, and Φ is a tree, then dissimilarity (i.e., $-S$) is expressible as tree distance.

A feature tree can also be interpreted as a hierarchical clustering scheme where each arc length represents the weight of the cluster consisting of all the objects that follow from that arc. Note that the tree in figure 1.6 differs from the common hierarchical clustering tree in that the branches differ in length. Sattath and Tversky (in press) describe a computer program, ADDTREE, for the construction of additive feature trees from similarity data and discuss its relation to other scaling methods.

It follows readily from the above discussion that if we assume both that the feature set Φ is a tree, and that $f(A) = f(B)$ for all a, b in Δ, then the contrast model reduces to the well-known hierarchical clustering scheme. Hence, the additive clustering model (Shepard & Arabie)[4], the additive similarity tree (Sattath & Tversky, in press), and the hierarchical clustering scheme (Johnson, 1967) are all special cases of the contrast model. These scaling models can thus be used to discover the common and distinctive features of the objects under study. The present development, in turn, provides theoretical foundations for the analysis of set-theoretical methods for the representation of proximities.

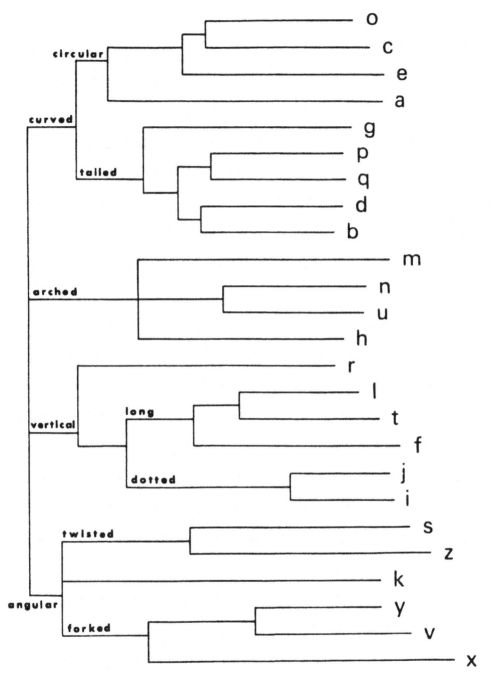

Figure 1.6
The representation of letter similarity as an additive (feature) tree. From Sattath and Tversky (in press).

Similarity, Prototypicality, and Family Resemblance

Similarity is a relation of proximity that holds between two objects. There exist other proximity relations such as prototypicality and representativeness that hold between an object and a class. Intuitively, an object is prototypical if it exemplifies the category to which it belongs. Note that the prototype is not necessarily the most typical or frequent member of its class. Recent research has demonstrated the importance of prototypicality or representativeness in perceptual learning (Posner & Keele, 1968; Reed, 1972), inductive inference (Kahneman & Tversky, 1973), semantic memory (Smith, Rips, & Shoben, 1974), and the formation of categories (Rosch & Mervis, 1975). The following discussion analyzes the relations of prototypicality and family resemblance in terms of the present theory of similarity.

Let $P(a, \Lambda)$ denote the (degree of) prototypicality of object a with respect to class Λ, with cardinality n, defined by

$$P(a, \Lambda) = p_n \left(\lambda \sum f(A \cap B) - \sum (f(A - B) + f(B - A)) \right),$$

where the summations are over all b in Λ. Thus, $P(a, \Lambda)$ is defined as a linear combination (i.e., a contrast) of the measures of the features of a that are shared with the elements of Λ and the features of a that are not shared with the elements of Λ. An element a of Λ is a *prototype* if it maximizes $P(a, \Lambda)$. Note that a class may have more than one prototype.

The factor p_n reflects the effect of category size on prototypicality, and the constant λ determines the relative weights of the common and the distinctive features. If $p_n = 1/n$, $\lambda = 0$, and $\alpha = \beta = 1$, then $P(a, \Lambda) = 1/n \sum S(a, b)$ (i.e., the prototypicality of a with respect to Λ equals the average similarity of a to all members of Λ). However, in line with the focusing hypotheses discussed earlier, it appears likely that the common features are weighted more heavily in judgments of prototypicality than in judgments of similarity.

Some evidence concerning the validity of the proposed measure was reported by Rosch and Mervis (1975). They selected 20 objects from each one of six categories (furniture, vehicle, fruit, weapon, vegetable, clothing) and instructed subjects to list the attributes associated with each one of the objects. The prototypicality of an object was defined by the number of attributes or features it shared with each member of the category. Hence, the prototypicality of a with respect to Λ was defined by $\sum N(a, b)$, where $N(a, b)$ denotes the number of attributes shared by a and b, and the summation ranges over all b in Λ. Clearly, the measure of prototypicality employed by Rosch and Mervis (1975) is a special case of the proposed measure, where λ is large and $f(A \cap B) = N(a, b)$.

These investigators also obtained direct measures of prototypicality by instructing subjects to rate each object on a 7-point scale according to the extent to which it fits the "idea or image of the meaning of the category." The rank correlations between these ratings and the above measure were quite high in all categories: furniture, .88; vehicle, .92; weapon, .94; fruit, .85; vegetable, .84; clothing, .91. The rated prototypicality of an object in a category, therefore, is predictable by the number of features it shares with other members of that category.

In contrast to the view that natural categories are definable by a conjunction of critical features, Wittgenstein (1953) argued that several natural categories (e.g., a game) do not have any attribute that is shared by all their members, and by them alone. Wittgenstein proposed that natural categories and concepts are commonly characterized and understood in terms of family resemblance, that is, a network of similarity relations that link the various members of the class. The importance of family resemblance in the formation and processing of categories has been effectively underscored by the work of Rosch and her collaborators (Rosch, 1973; Rosch & Mervis, 1975; Rosch, Mervis, Gray, Johnson, & Boyes-Braem, 1976). This research demonstrated that both natural and artificial categories are commonly perceived and organized in terms of prototypes, or focal elements, and some measure of proximity from the prototypes. Furthermore, it lent substantial support to the claim that people structure their world in terms of basic semantic categories that represent an optimal level of abstraction. Chair, for example, is a basic category; furniture is too general and kitchen chair is too specific. Similarly, car is a basic category; vehicle is too general and sedan is too specific. Rosch argued that the basic categories are selected so as to maximize family resemblance—defined in terms of cue validity.

The present development suggests the following measure for family resemblance, or category resemblance. Let Λ be some subset of Δ with cardinality n. The category resemblance of Λ denoted $R(\Lambda)$ is defined by

$$R(\Lambda) = r_n\left(\lambda \sum f(A \cap B) - \sum (f(A - B) + f(B - A))\right),$$

the summations being over all a, b in Λ. Hence, category resemblance is a linear combination of the measures of the common and the distinctive features of all pairs of objects in that category. The factor r_n reflects the effect of category size on category resemblance, and the constant λ determines the *relative* weight of the common and the distinctive features. If $\lambda = 0$, $\alpha = \beta = 1$, and $r_n = 2/n(n-1)$, then

$$R(\Lambda) = \frac{\sum S(a, b)}{\binom{n}{2}},$$

the summation being over all a, b in Λ; that is, category resemblance equals average similarity between all members of Λ. Although the proposed measure of family resemblance differs from Rosch's, it nevertheless captures her basic notion that family resemblance is highest for those categories which "have the most attributes common to members of the category and the least attributes shared with members of other categories" (Rosch et al., 1976, p. 435).

The maximization of category resemblance could be used to explain the formation of categories. Thus, the set Λ rather than Γ is selected as a natural category whenever $R(\Lambda) > R(\Gamma)$. Equivalently, an object a is added to a category Λ whenever $R(\{\Lambda \cup a\}) > R(\Lambda)$. The fact that the preferred (basic) categories are neither the most inclusive nor the most specific imposes certain constraints on r_n.

If $r_n = 2/n(n-1)$ then $R(\Lambda)$ equals the average similarity between all members of Λ. This index leads to the selection of minimal categories because average similarity can generally be increased by deleting elements. The average similarity between sedans, for example, is surely greater than the average similarity between cars; nevertheless, car rather than sedan serves as a basic category. If $r_n = 1$ then $R(\Lambda)$ equals the sum of the similarities between all members of Λ. This index leads to the selection of maximal categories because the addition of objects increases total similarity, provided S is nonnegative.

In order to explain the formation of intermediate-level categories, therefore, category resemblance must be a compromise between an average and a sum. That is, r_n must be a decreasing function of n that exceeds $2/n(n-1)$. In this case, $R(\Lambda)$ increases with category size whenever average similarity is held constant, and vice versa. Thus, a considerable increase in the extension of a category could outweigh a small reduction in average similarity.

Although the concepts of similarity, prototypicality, and family resemblance are intimately connected, they have not been previously related in a formal explicit manner. The present development offers explications of similarity, prototypicality, and family resemblance within a unified framework, in which they are viewed as contrasts, or linear combinations, of the measures of the appropriate sets of common and distinctive features.

Similes and Metaphors

Similes and metaphors are essential ingredients of creative verbal expression. Perhaps the most interesting property of metaphoric expressions is that despite their novelty and nonliteral nature, they are usually understandable and often informative. For example, the statement that Mr. X resembles a bulldozer is readily understood as saying that Mr. X is a gross, powerful person who overcomes all obstacles in getting a job done. An adequate analysis of connotative meaning should account for man's ability to interpret metaphors without specific prior learning. Since the message conveyed by such expressions is often pointed and specific, they cannot be explained in terms of a few generalized dimensions of connotative meaning, such as evaluation or potency (Osgood, 1962). It appears that people interpret similes by scanning the feature space and selecting the features of the referent that are applicable to the subject (e.g., by selecting features of the bulldozer that are applicable to the person). The nature of this process is left to be explained.

There is a close tie between the assessment of similarity and the interpretation of metaphors. In judgments of similarity one assumes a particular feature space, or a frame of reference, and assesses the quality of the match between the subject and the referent. In the interpretation of similes, one assumes a resemblance between the subject and the referent and searches for an interpretation of the space that would maximize the quality of the match. The same pair of objects, therefore, can be viewed as similar or different depending on the choice of a frame of reference.

One characteristic of good metaphors is the contrast between the prior, literal interpretation, and the posterior, metaphoric interpretation. Metaphors that are too transparent are uninteresting; obscure metaphors are uninterpretable. A good metaphor is like a good detective story. The solution should not be apparent in advance to maintain the reader's interest, yet it should seem plausible after the fact to maintain coherence of the story. Consider the simile "An essay is like a fish." At first, the statement is puzzling. An essay is not expected to be fishy, slippery, or wet. The puzzle is resolved when we recall that (like a fish) an essay has a head and a body, and it occasionally ends with a flip of the tail.

Notes

This paper benefited from fruitful discussions with Y. Cohen, I. Gati, D. Kahneman, L. Sjöberg, and S. Sattath.

1. To derive feature additivity from qualitative assumptions, we must assume the axioms of an extensive structure and the compatibility of the extensive and the conjoint scales; see Krantz et al. (1971, Section 10.7).

2. The subjects in all our experiments were Israeli college students, ages 18–28. The material was presented in booklets and administered in a group setting.

3. Sjöberg, L. A cognitive theory of similarity. *Göteborg Psychological Reports* (No. 10), 1972.

4. Shepard, R. N., & Arabie, P. Additive cluster analysis of similarity data. *Proceedings of the U.S.–Japan Seminar on Theory, Methods, and Applications of Multidimensional Scaling and Related Techniques.* San Diego, August 1975.

5. Sattath, S. *An equivalence theorem.* Unpublished note, Hebrew University, 1976.

References

Beals, R., Krantz, D. H., & Tversky, A. Foundations of multidimensional scaling. *Psychological Review*, 1968, *75*, 127–142.

Bush, R. R., & Mosteller, F. A model for stimulus generalization and discrimination. *Psychological Review*, 1951, *58*, 413–423.

Carroll, J. D., & Wish, M. Multidimensional perceptual models and measurement methods. In E. C. Carterette & M. P. Friedman (Eds.), *Handbook of perception*. New York: Academic Press, 1974.

Eisler, H., & Ekman, G. A mechanism of subjective similarity. *Acta Psychologica*, 1959, *16*, 1–10.

Garner, W. R. *The processing of information and structure*. New York: Halsted Press, 1974.

Gibson, E. *Principles of perceptual learning and development*. New York: Appleton-Century-Crofts, 1969.

Goldmeier, E. Similarity in visually perceived forms. *Psychological Issues*, 1972, *8*, 1–136.

Gregson, R. A. M. *Psychometrics of similarity*. New York: Academic Press, 1975.

Hosman, J., & Kuennapas, T. *On the relation between similarity and dissimilarity estimates* (Report No. 354). University of Stockholm, Psychological Laboratories, 1972.

Jakobson, R., Fant, G. G. M., & Halle, M. *Preliminaries to speech analysis: The distinctive features and their correlates*. Cambridge, Mass.: MIT Press, 1961.

Johnson, S. C. Hierarchical clustering schemes. *Psychometrika*, 1967, *32*, 241–254.

Kahneman, D., & Tversky, A. On the psychology of prediction. *Psychological Review*, 1973, *80*, 237–251.

Krantz, D. H., Luce, R. D., Suppes, P., & Tversky, A. *Foundations of measurement* (Vol. 1). New York: Academic Press, 1971.

Krantz, D. H., & Tversky, A. Similarity of rectangles: An analysis of subjective dimensions. *Journal of Mathematical Psychology*, 1975, *12*, 4–34.

Kuennapas, T., & Janson, A. J. Multidimensional similarity of letters. *Perceptual and Motor Skills*, 1969, *28*, 3–12.

Neisser, U. *Cognitive psychology*. New York: Appleton-Century-Crofts, 1967.

Osgood, C. E. Studies on the generality of affective meaning systems. *American Psychologist*, 1962, *17*, 10–28.

Posner, M. I., & Keele, S. W. On the genesis of abstract ideas. *Journal of Experimental Psychology*, 1968, *77*, 353–363.

Reed, S. K. Pattern recognition and categorization. *Cognitive Psychology*, 1972, *3*, 382–407.

Restle, F. A metric and an ordering on sets. *Psychometrika*, 1959, *24*, 207–220.

Restle, F. *Psychology of judgment and choice*. New York: Wiley, 1961.

Rosch, E. On the internal structure of perceptual and semantic categories. In T. E. Moore (Ed.), *Cognitive development and the acquisition of language*. New York: Academic Press, 1973.

Rosch, E. Cognitive reference points. *Cognitive Psychology*, 1975, *7*, 532–547.

Rosch, E., & Mervis, C. B. Family resemblances: Studies in the internal structure of categories. *Cognitive Psychology*, 1975, *7*, 573–603.

Rosch, E., Mervis, C. B., Gray, W., Johnson, D., & Boyes-Braem, P. Basic objects in natural categories. *Cognitive Psychology*, 1976, *8*, 382–439.

Rothkopf, E. Z. A measure of stimulus similarity and errors in some paired-associate learning tasks. *Journal of Experimental Psychology*, 1957, *53*, 94–101.

Sattath, S., & Tversky, A. Additive similarity trees. *Psychometrika*, in press.

Shepard, R. N. Attention and the metric structure of the stimulus space. *Journal of Mathematical Psychology*, 1964, *1*, 54–87.

Shepard, R. N. Representation of structure in similarity data: Problems and prospects. *Psychometrika*, 1974, *39*, 373–421.

Shepard, R. N., Kilpatric, D. W., & Cunningham, J. P. The internal representation of numbers. *Cognitive Psychology*, 1975, *7*, 82–138.

Smith, E. E., Rips, L. J., & Shoben, E. J. Semantic memory and psychological semantics. In G. H. Bower (Ed.), *The psychology of learning and motivation* (Vol. 8). New York: Academic Press, 1974.

Smith, E. E., Shoben, E. J., & Rips, L. J. Structure and process in semantic memory: A featural model for semantic decisions. *Psychological Review*, 1974, *81*, 214–241.

Torgerson, W. S. Multidimensional scaling of similarity. *Psychometrika*, 1965, *30*, 379–393.

Tversky, A. Elimination by aspects: A theory of choice. *Psychological Review*, 1972, *79*, 281–299.

Tversky, A., & Gati, I. Studies of similarity. In E. Rosch & B. Lloyd (Eds.), *On the nature and principle of formation of categories*. Hillsdale, N.J.: Erlbaum, in press.

Tversky, A., & Krantz, D. H. The dimensional representation and the metric structure of similarity data. *Journal of Mathematical Psychology*, 1970, *7*, 572–597.

von Neumann, J., & Morgenstern, O. *Theory of games and economic behavior*. Princeton, N.J.: Princeton University Press, 1947.

Wish, M. A model for the perception of Morse Code-like signals. *Human Factors*, 1967, *9*, 529–540.

Wittgenstein, L. *Philosophical investigations*. New York: Macmillan, 1953.

Appendix: An Axiomatic Theory of Similarity

Let $\Delta = \{a, b, c, \ldots\}$ be a collection of objects characterized as sets of features, and let A, B, C, denote the sets of features associated with a, b, c, respectively. Let $s(a, b)$ be an ordinal measure of the similarity of a to b, defined for all distinct a, b in Δ. The present theory is based on the following five axioms. Since the first three axioms are discussed in the paper, they are merely restated here; the remaining axioms are briefly discussed.

1. MATCHING: $s(a, b) = F(A \cap B, A - B, B - A)$ where F is some real-valued function in three arguments.

2. MONOTONICITY: $s(a, b) \geq s(a, c)$ whenever $A \cap B \supset A \cap C$, $A - B \subset A - C$, and $B - A \subset C - A$. Moreover, if either inclusion is proper then the inequality is strict.

Let Φ be the set of all features associated with the objects of Δ, and let X, Y, Z, etc. denote subsets of Φ. The expression $F(X, Y, Z)$ is defined whenever there exist a, b in Δ such that $A \cap B = X$, $A - B = Y$, and $B - A = Z$, whence $s(a, b) = F(X, Y, Z)$. Define $V \simeq W$ if one or more of the following hold for some X, Y, Z: $F(V, Y, Z) = F(W, Y, Z)$, $F(X, V, Z) = F(X, W, Z)$, $F(X, Y, V) = F(X, Y, W)$. The pairs (a, b) and (c, d) *agree* on one, two, or three components, respectively, whenever one, two, or three of the following hold: $(A \cap B) \simeq (C \cap D)$, $(A - B) \simeq (C - D)$, $(B - A) \simeq (D - C)$.

3. INDEPENDENCE: Suppose the pairs (a, b) and (c, d), as well as the pairs (a', b') and (c', d'), agree on the same two components, while the pairs (a, b) and (a', b'), as well as the pairs (c, d) and (c', d'), agree on the remaining (third) component. Then

$$s(a, b) \geq s(a', b') \quad \text{iff} \quad s(c, d) \geq s(c', d').$$

4. SOLVABILITY:

(i) For all pairs (a, b), (c, d), (e, f), of objects in Δ there exists a pair (p, q) which agrees with them, respectively, on the first, second, and third component, that is, $P \cap Q \simeq A \cap B$, $P - Q \simeq C - D$, and $Q - P \simeq F - E$.

(ii) Suppose $s(a, b) > t > s(c, d)$. Then there exist e, f with $s(e, f) = t$, such that if (a, b) and (c, d) agree on one or two components, then (e, f) agrees with them on these components.

(iii) There exist pairs (a, b) and (c, d) of objects in Δ that do not agree on any component.

Unlike the other axioms, solvability does not impose constraints on the similarity order; it merely asserts that the structure under study is sufficiently rich so that certain equations can be solved. The first part of axiom 4 is analogous to the existence of a factorial structure. The second part of the axiom implies that the range of s is a real interval: There exist objects in Δ whose similarity matches any real value that is bounded by two similarities. The third part of axiom 4 ensures that all arguments of F are essential.

Let Φ_1, Φ_2, and Φ_3 be the sets of features that appear, respectively, as first, second, or third arguments of F. (Note that $\Phi_2 = \Phi_3$.) Suppose X and X' belong to Φ_1, while Y and Y' belong to Φ_2. Define $(X, X')_1 \simeq (Y, Y')_2$ whenever the two intervals are matched, that is, whenever there exist pairs (a, b) and (a', b') of equally similar objects in Δ which agree on the third factor. Thus, $(X, X')_1 \simeq (Y, Y')_2$ whenever

$$s(a, b) = F(X, Y, Z) = F(X', Y', Z) = s(a', b').$$

This definition is readily extended to any other pair of factors. Next, define $(V, V')_i \simeq (W, W')_i$, $i = 1, 2, 3$ whenever $(V, V')_i \simeq (X, X')_j \simeq (W, W')_i$, for some $(X, X')_j$, $j \neq i$. Thus, two intervals on the same factor are equivalent if both match the same interval on another factor. The following invariance axiom asserts that if two intervals are equivalent on one factor, they are also equivalent on another factor.

5. INVARIANCE: Suppose V, V', W, W' belong to both Φ_i and Φ_j, $i, j = 1, 2, 3$. Then

$$(V, V')_i \simeq (W, W')_i \quad \text{iff} \quad (V, V')_j \simeq (W, W')_j.$$

REPRESENTATION THEOREM

Suppose axioms 1–5 hold. Then there exist a similarity scale S and a nonnegative scale f such that for all a, b, c, d in Δ

(i) $S(a, b) \geq S(c, d)$ iff $s(a, b) \geq s(c, d)$,

(ii) $S(a, b) = \theta f(A \cap B) - \alpha f(A - B) - \beta f(B - A)$, for some $\theta, \alpha, \beta \geq 0$.

(iii) f and S are interval scales.

While a self-contained proof of the representation theorem is quite long, the theorem can be readily reduced to previous results.

Recall that Φ_i is the set of features that appear as the ith argument of F, and let $\Psi_i = \Phi_i / \simeq$, $i = 1, 2, 3$. Thus, Ψ_i is the set of equivalence classes of Φ_i with respect to $\simeq$. It follows from axioms 1 and 3 that each Ψ_i is well defined, and it follows from axiom 4 that $\Psi = \Psi_1 \times \Psi_2 \times \Psi_3$ is equivalent to the domain of F. We wish to show that Ψ, ordered by F, is a three-component, additive conjoint structure, in the sense of Krantz, Luce, Suppes, and Tversky (1971, Section 6.11.1).

This result, however, follows from the analysis of decomposable similarity structures, developed by Tversky and Krantz (1970). In particular, the proof of part (c) of theorem 1 in that paper implies that, under axioms 1, 3, and 4, there exist nonnegative functions f_i defined on Ψ_i, $i = 1, 2, 3$, so that for all a, b, c, d in Δ

$$s(a, b) \geq s(c, d)   \text{iff}   S(a, b) \geq S(c, d)$$

where

$$S(a, b) = f_1(A \cap B) + f_2(A - B) + f_3(B - A),$$

and f_1, f_2, f_3 are interval scales with a common unit.

According to axiom 5, the equivalence of intervals is preserved across factors. That is, for all V, V', W, W' in $\Phi_i \cap \Phi_j$, $i, j = 1, 2, 3$,

$$f_i(V) - f_i(V') = f_i(W) - f_i(W')   \text{iff}   f_j(V) - f_j(V') = f_j(W) - f_j(W').$$

Hence by part (i) of theorem 6.15 of Krantz et al. (1971), there exist a scale f and constants θ_i such that $f_i(X) = \theta_i f(X)$, $i = 1, 2, 3$. Finally, by axiom 2, S increases in f_1 and decreases in f_2 and f_3. Hence, it is expressible as

$$S(a, b) = \theta f(A \cap B) - \alpha f(A - B) - \beta f(B - A),$$

for some nonnegative constants θ, α, β.

2 Additive Similarity Trees

Shmuel Sattath and Amos Tversky

The two goals of research on the representation of proximity data are the development of theories for explaining similarity relations and the construction of scaling procedures for describing and displaying similarities between objects. Indeed, most representations of proximity data can be regarded either as similarity theories or as scaling procedures. These representations can be divided into two classes: spatial models and network models. The spatial models—called multidimensional scaling—represent each object as a point in a coordinate space so that the metric distances between the points reflect the observed proximities between the objects. Network models represent each object as a node in a connected graph, typically a tree, so that the relations between the nodes in the graph reflect the observed proximity relations among the objects.

This chapter investigates tree representations of similarity data. We begin with a critical discussion of the familiar hierarchical clustering scheme [Johnson, 1967], and present a more general representation, called the additive tree. A computer program (ADDTREE) for the construction of additive trees from proximity data is described and illustrated using several sets of data. Finally, the additive tree is compared with multidimensional scaling from both empirical and theoretical standpoints.

Consider the proximity matrix presented in table 2.1, taken from a study by Henley [1969]. The entries of the table are average ratings of dissimilarity between the respective animals on a scale from 0 (maximal similarity) to 10 (maximal dissimilarity). Such data have commonly been analyzed using the hierarchical clustering scheme (HCS) that yields a hierarchy of nested clusters. The application of this scaling procedure to table 2.1 is displayed in figure 2.1.

The construction of the tree proceeds as follows. The two objects which are closest to each other (e.g., donkey and cow) are combined first, and are now treated as a single element, or cluster. The distance between this new element, z, and any other element, y, is defined as the minimum (or the average) of the distances between y and the members of z. This operation is repeated until a single cluster that includes all objects is obtained. In such a representation the objects appear as the external nodes of the tree, and the distance between objects is the height of their meeting point, or equivalently, the length of the path joining them.

This model imposes severe constraints on the data. It implies that given two disjoint clusters, all intra-cluster distances are smaller than all inter-cluster distances, and that all the inter-cluster distances are equal. This property is called the ultrametric inequality, and the representation is denoted an ultrametric tree. The ultrametric

Table 2.1
Dissimilarities between Animals

	Donkey	Cow	Pig
Camel	5.0	5.6	7.2
Donkey		4.6	5.7
Cow			4.9

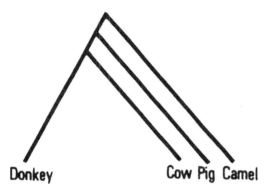

Figure 2.1
The representation of table 2.1 as an HCS.

inequality, however, is often violated by data, see, e.g., Holman [note 1]. To illustrate, note that according to figure 2.1, camel should be equally similar to donkey, cow and pig, contrary to the data of table 2.1.

The limitations of the ultrametric tree have led several psychologists, e.g., Carroll and Chang [1973], Carroll [1976], Cunningham [note 2, note 3], to explore a more general structure, called an additive tree. This structure appears under different names including: weighted tree, free tree, path-length tree, and unrooted tree, and its formal properties were studied extensively, see, e.g., Buneman [1971, pp. 387–395; 1974], Dobson [1974], Hakimi and Yau [1964], Patrinos and Hakimi [1972], Turner and Kautz [1970, sections III–4 and III–6]. The representation of table 2.1 as an additive tree is given in figure 2.2. As in the ultrametric tree, the external nodes correspond to objects and the distance between objects is the length of the path joining them. A formal definition of an additive tree is presented in the next section.

It is instructive to compare the two representations of table 2.1 displayed in figures 2.1 and 2.2. First, note that the clustering is different in the two figures. In the ultra-

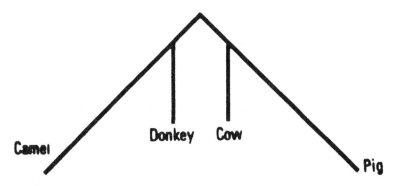

Figure 2.2
The representation of table 2.1 as an additive tree, in rooted form.

metric tree (figure 2.1), cow and donkey form a single cluster that is subsequently joined by pig and camel. In the additive tree (figure 2.2), camel with donkey form one cluster, and cow with pig form another cluster. Second, in the additive tree, unlike the ultrametric tree, intra-cluster distances may exceed inter-cluster distances. For example, in figure 2.2 cow and donkey belong to different clusters although they are the two closest animals. Third, in an additive tree, an object outside a cluster is no longer equidistant from all objects inside the cluster. For example, both cow and pig are closer to donkey than to camel.

The differences between the two models stem from the fact than in the ultrametric tree (but not in an additive tree) the external nodes are all equally distant from the root. The greater flexibility of the additive tree permits a more faithful representation of data. Spearman's rank correlation, for example, between the dissimilarities of table 2.1 and the tree distances is 1.00 for the additive tree and 0.64 for the ultrametric tree.

Note that the distances in an additive tree do not depend on the choice of root. For example, the tree of figure 2.2 can be displayed in unrooted form, as shown in figure 2.3. Nevertheless, it is generally more convenient to display similarity trees in a rooted form.

Analysis of Trees

In this section we define ultrametric and additive trees, characterize the conditions under which proximity data can be represented by these models, and describe the structure of the clusters associated with them.

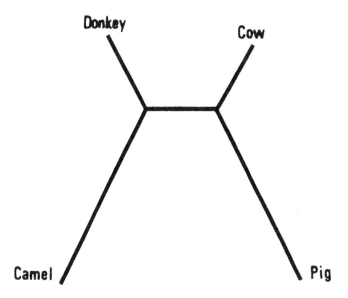

Figure 2.3
The representation of table 2.1 as an additive tree, in unrooted form.

Representation of Dissimilarity

A *tree* is a (finite) connected graph without cycles. Hence, any two nodes in a tree are connected by exactly one path. An *additive tree* is a tree with a metric in which the distance between nodes is the length of the path (i.e., the sum of the arc-lengths) that joins them. An additive tree with a distinguished node (named the root) which is equidistant from all external nodes is called an *ultrametric tree*. Such trees are normally represented with the root on top, (as in figure 2.1) so that the distance between external nodes is expressible as the height of the lowest (internal) node that lies above them.

A *dissimilarity measure* d on a finite set of objects $S = \{x, y, z, \ldots\}$ is a non-negative function on $S \times S$ such that $d(x, y) = d(y, x)$, and $d(x, y) = 0$ iff $x = y$. A tree (ultrametric or additive) *represents* a dissimilarity measure on S iff the external nodes of the tree can be associated with the objects of S so that the tree distances between external nodes coincide with the dissimilarities between the respective objects.

If a dissimilarity measure d on S is represented by an ultrametric tree, then the relation among any three objects in S has the form depicted in figure 2.4. It follows, therefore, that for all x, y, z in S

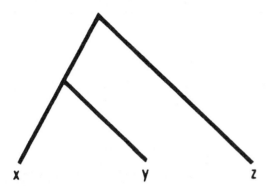

Figure 2.4
The relations among three objects in an ultrametric tree.

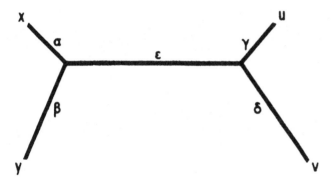

Figure 2.5
The relations among four objects in an additive tree.

$d(x, y) \leq \max\{d(x, z), d(y, z)\}$.

This property, called the *ultrametric inequality*, is both necessary and sufficient for the representation of a dissimilarity measure by an ultrametric tree [Johnson, 1967; Jardine & Sibson, 1971]. As noted in the previous section, however, the ultrametric inequality is very restrictive. It implies that for any three objects in S, two of the dissimilarities are equal and the third does not exceed them. Thus the dissimilarities among any three objects must form either an equilateral triangle or an isosceles triangle with a narrow base.

An analogous analysis can be applied to additive trees. If a dissimilarity measure d on S is represented by an additive tree, then the relations among any four objects in S has the form depicted in figure 2.5, with non-negative $\alpha, \beta, \gamma, \delta, \varepsilon$. It follows, therefore, that in this case

$$d(x, y) + d(u, v) = \alpha + \beta + \gamma + \delta$$

$$\leq \alpha + \beta + \gamma + \delta + 2\varepsilon$$

$$= d(x, u) + d(y, v)$$

$$= d(x, v) + d(y, u).$$

Hence, any four objects can be labeled so as to satisfy the above inequality.

Consequently, in an additive tree,

$$d(x, y) + d(u, v) \leq \max\{d(x, u) + d(y, v), d(x, v) + d(y, u)\}$$

for all x, y, u, v in S (not necessarily distinct).

It is easy to verify that this condition, called the *additive inequality* (or the four-points condition), follows from the ultrametric inequality and implies the triangle inequality. It turns out that the additive inequality is both necessary and sufficient for the representation of a dissimilarity measure by an additive tree. For a proof of this assertion, see, e.g., Buneman [1971, pp. 387–395; 1974], Dobson [1974]. To illustrate the fact that the additive inequality is less restrictive than the ultrametric inequality, note that the distances between any four points on a line satisfy the former but not the latter.

The ultrametric and the additive trees differ in the number of parameters employed in the representation. In an ultrametric tree all $\binom{n}{2}$ inter-point distances are determined by at most $n - 1$ parameters where n is the number of elements in the object set S. In an additive tree, the distances are determined by at most $2n - 3$ parameters.

Trees and Clusters

A dissimilarity measure, d, can be used to define different notions of clustering, see, e.g., Sokal and Sneath [1973]. Two types of clusters—tight and loose—are now introduced and their relations to ultrametric and additive trees are discussed.

A nonempty subset A of S is a *tight cluster* if

$$\max_{x, y \in A} d(x, y) < \min_{\substack{x \in A \\ z \in S - A}} d(x, z).$$

That is, A is a tight cluster whenever the dissimilarity between any two objects in A is smaller than the dissimilarity between any object in A and any object outside A, i.e., in $S - A$. It follows readily that a subset A of an ultrametric tree is a tight cluster iff there is an arc such that A is the set of all objects that lie below that arc. In figure 2.1, for example, {donkey, cow} and {donkey, cow, pig} are tight clusters whereas {cow, pig} and {cow, pig, camel} are not.

A subset A of S is a *loose cluster* if for any x, y in A and u, v in $S - A$

$$d(x, y) + d(u, v) < \min\{d(x, u) + d(y, v), d(x, v) + d(y, u)\}.$$

In figure 2.5, for example, the binary loose clusters are $\{x, y\}$ and $\{u, v\}$. Let A, B denote disjoint nonempty loose clusters; let $D(A), D(B)$ denote the average intra-cluster dissimilarities of A and B, respectively; and let $D(A, B)$ denote the average inter-cluster dissimilarity between A and B. It can be shown that $1/2(D(A) + D(B)) < D(A, B)$. That is, the mean of the average dissimilarity within loose clusters is smaller than the average dissimilarity between loose clusters.

The deletion of an arc divides a tree into two subtrees, thereby partitioning S into two nonempty subsets. It follows readily that, in an additive tree, both subsets are loose clusters, and all loose clusters can be obtained in this fashion. Thus, an additive tree induces a family of loose clusters whereas an ultrametric tree defines a family of tight clusters. In table 2.1, for example, the cluster {Donkey, Cow} is tight but not loose, whereas the clusters {Donkey, Camel} and {Cow, Pig} are loose but not tight, see figures 2.1 and 2.2. Scaling methods for the construction of similarity trees are generally based on clustering: HCS is based on tight clusters, whereas the following procedure for the construction of additive trees is based on loose clusters.

Computational Procedure

This section describes a computer algorithm, ADDTREE, for the construction of additive similarity trees. Its input is a symmetric matrix of similarities or dissimilarities, and its output is an additive tree.

If the additive inequality is satisfied without error, then the unique additive tree that represents the data can be constructed without difficulty. In fact, any proof of the sufficiency of the additive inequality provides an algorithm for the errorless case. The problem, therefore, is the development of an efficient algorithm that constructs an additive tree from fallible data.

This problem has two components: (i) construction, which consists of finding the most appropriate tree-structure, (ii) estimation, which consists of finding the best estimates of arc-lengths. In the present algorithm the construction of the tree proceeds in stages by clustering objects so as to maximize the number of sets satisfying the additive inequality. The estimation of arc lengths is based on the least square criterion. The two components of the program are now described in turn.

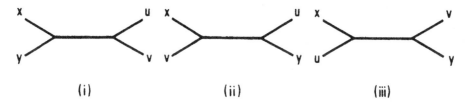

Figure 2.6
The three possible configurations of four objects in an additive tree.

Construction

In an additive tree, any four distinct objects, x, y, u, v, appear in one of the configurations of figure 2.6. The patterns of distances which correspond to the configurations of figure 2.6 are:

(i) $d(x, y) + d(u, v) < d(x, u) + d(y, v) = d(x, v) + d(y, u)$

(ii) $d(x, v) + d(y, u) < d(x, u) + d(y, v) = d(x, y) + d(u, v)$

(iii) $d(x, u) + d(y, v) < d(x, y) + d(u, v) = d(x, v) + d(y, u).$

Our task is to select the most appropriate configuration on the basis of an observed dissimilarity measure δ. It is easy to see that any four objects can be relabeled so that

$$\delta(x, y) + \delta(u, v) \leq \delta(x, u) + \delta(y, v) \leq \delta(x, v) + \delta(y, u).$$

It is evident, in this case, that configuration (i) represents these dissimilarities better than (ii) or (iii). Hence, we obtain the following rule for choosing the best configuration for any set of four elements: label the objects so as to satisfy the above inequality, and select configuration (i). The objects x and y (as well as u and v) are then called *neighbors*. The construction of the tree proceeds by grouping elements on the basis of the neighbors relation. The major steps of the construction are sketched below.

For each pair x, y, ADDTREE examines all objects u, v and counts the number of quadruples in which x and y are neighbors. The pair x, y with the highest score is selected, and its members are combined to form a new element z which replaces x and y in the subsequent analysis. The dissimilarity between z and any other element u is set equal to $(\delta(u, x) + \delta(u, y))/2$. The pair with the next highest score is selected next. If its elements have not been previously selected, they are combined as above, and the scanning of pairs is continued until all elements have been selected. Ties are treated here in a natural manner.

This grouping process is first applied to the object set S yielding a collection of elements which consists of the newly formed elements together with the original elements that were not combined in this process. The grouping process is then applied repeatedly to the outcome of the previous phase until the number of remaining elements is three. Finally, these elements are combined to form the last element, which is treated as the root of the tree.

It is possible to show that if only one pair of elements are combined in each phase, then perfect subtrees in the data appear as subtrees in the representation. In particular, any additive tree is reproduced by the above procedure.

The construction procedure described above uses sums of dissimilarities to define neighbors and to compute distances to the new (constructed) elements. Strictly speaking, this procedure is applicable to cardinal data, i.e., data measured on interval or ratio scales. For ordinal data, a modified version of the algorithm has been developed. In this version, the neighbors relation is introduced as follows. Suppose δ is an ordinal dissimilarity scale, and

$$\delta(x, y) < \delta(x, u), \quad \delta(x, y) < \delta(x, v),$$

$$\delta(u, v) < \delta(y, v), \quad \delta(u, v) < \delta(y, w).$$

Then we conclude that x and y (as well as u and v) are *neighbors*. (If the inequalities on the left [right] alone hold, then x and y [as well as u and v] are called *semi-neighbors*, and are counted as half neighbors.)

If x and y are neighbors in the ordinal sense, they are also neighbors in the cardinal sense, but the converse is not true. In the cardinal case, every four objects can be partitioned into two pairs of neighbors; in the ordinal case, this property does not always hold since the defining inequality may fail for all permutations of the objects. To define the distances to the new elements in the ordinal version of the algorithm, some ordinal index of average dissimilarity, e.g., mean rank or median, can be used.

Estimation

Although the construction of the tree is independent of the estimation of arc lengths, the two processes are performed in parallel. The parameters of the tree are estimated, employing a least-square criterion. That is, the program minimizes

$$\sum_{x, y \in S} (d(x, y) - \delta(x, y))^2,$$

where d is the distance function of the tree. Since an additive tree with n objects has $m \le 2n - 3$ parameters (arcs), one obtains the equation $CX = \delta$ where δ is the vector of dissimilarities, X is the vector of (unknown) arc lengths, and C is an $\binom{n}{2} \times m$

matrix where

$$c_{ij} = \begin{cases} 1 & \text{if the } i\text{-th tree-distance includes the } j\text{-th arc} \\ 0 & \text{otherwise} \end{cases}$$

The least-square solution of $CX = \delta$ is $X = (C^T C)^{-1} C^T \delta$, provided $C^T C$ is positive definite. In general, this requires inverting an $m \times m$ matrix which is costly for moderate m and prohibitive for large m. However, an exact solution that requires no matrix inversion and greatly simplifies the estimation process can be obtained by exploiting the following property of additive trees. Consider an arc and remove its endpoints; this divides the tree into a set of disjoint subtrees. The least-square estimate of the length of that arc is a function of (i) the average distances between the subtrees and (ii) the number of objects in each subtree. The proof of this proposition, and the description of that function are long and tedious and are therefore omitted. It can also be shown that all negative estimates (which reflect error) should be set equal to zero.

The present program constructs a rooted additive tree. The graphical representation of a rooted tree is unique up to permutations of its subtrees. To select an informative graphical representation, the program permutes the objects so as to maximize the correspondence of the similarity between objects and the ordering of their positions in the display—subject to the constraint imposed by the structure of the tree. Under the same constraint, the program can also permute the objects so as to maximize the ordinal correlation (γ) with any prespecified ordering.

Comparison of Algorithms

Several related methods have recently been proposed. Carroll [1976] discussed two extensions of HCS. One concerns an ultrametric tree in which internal as well as external nodes represent objects [Carroll & Chang, 1973]. Another concerns the representation of a dissimilarity matrix as the sum of two or more ultrametric trees [Carroll & Pruzansky, note 4]. The first effective procedure for constructing an additive tree for fallible similarity data was presented by Cunningham [note 2, note 3]. His program, like ADDTREE, first determines the tree structure, and then obtains least-square estimates of arc-lengths. However, there are two problems with Cunningham's program. First, in the presence of noise, it tends to produce degenerate trees with few internal nodes. This problem becomes particularly severe when the number of objects is moderate or large. To illustrate, consider the additive tree presented in figure 2.8, and suppose that, for some reason or another (e.g., errors of measurement), monkey was rated as extremely similar to squirrel. In Cunningham's program, this single datum produces a drastic change in the structure of the tree: It eliminates the arcs labeled "rodents" and "apes," and combines all rodents and apes into a single cluster. In ADDTREE, on the other hand, this datum produces only a minor change. Second, Cunningham's estimation procedure requires the inversion of a $\binom{n}{4} \times \binom{n}{4}$ matrix, which restricts the applicability of the program to relatively small data sets, say under 15 objects.

ADDTREE overcomes the first problem by using a "majority" rule rather than a "veto" rule to determine the tree structure, and it overcomes the second problem by using a more efficient method of estimation. The core memory required for ADDTREE is of the order of n^2, hence it can be applied to sets of 100 objects, say, without any difficulty. Furthermore, ADDTREE is only slightly more costly than HCS, and less costly than a multidimensional scaling program in two dimensions.

Applications

This section presents applications of ADDTREE to several sets of similarity data and compares them with the results of multidimensional scaling and HCS.

Three sets of proximity data are analyzed. To each data set we apply the cardinal version of ADDTREE, the average method of HCS [Johnson, 1967], and smallest space analysis [Guttman, 1968; Lingoes, 1970] in 2 and 3 dimensions-denoted SSA/2D and SSA/3D, respectively. (The use of the ordinal version of ADDTREE, and the min method of HCS did not change the results substantially.) For each representation we report two measures of correspondence between the solution and the original data: the product-moment correlation r, and Kruskal's ordinal measure of stress defined as

$$\left[\frac{\sum_x \sum_y (d(x, y) - \hat{d}(x, y))^2}{\sum_x \sum_y d(x, y)^2} \right]^{1/2}$$

where d is the distance in the respective representation, and $\hat{d}$ is an appropriate order-preserving transformation of the original dissimilarities [Kruskal, 1964].

Since ADDTREE and HCS yielded similar tree structures in all three data sets, only the results of the former are presented along with the two-dimensional (Euclidean) configurations obtained by SSA/2D. The two-dimensional solution was chosen for comparison because (i) it is the most common and most interpretable spatial representation, and (ii) the number of parameters of a two-dimensional solution is the same as the number of parameters in an additive tree.

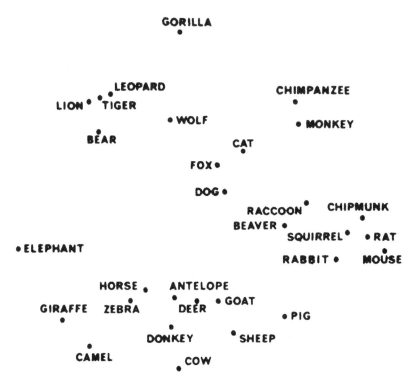

Figure 2.7
Representation of animal similarity (Henley, 1969) by SSA/2D.

Similarity of Animals

Henley [1969] obtained average dissimilarity ratings between animals from a homogeneous group of 18 subjects. Each subject rated the dissimilarity between all pairs of 30 animals on a scale from 0 to 10.

The result of SSA/2D is presented in figure 2.7. The horizontal dimension is readily interpreted as size, with elephant and mouse at the two extremes, and the vertical dimension may be thought of as ferocity [Henley, 1969], although the correspondence is far from perfect.

The result of ADDTREE is presented in figure 2.8 in parallel form. In this form all branches are parallel, and the distance between two nodes is the sum of the *horizontal* arcs on the path joining them. Clearly, every (rooted) tree can be displayed in parallel form which we use because of its convenience.

In an additive tree the root is not determined by the distances, and any point on the tree can serve as a root. Nevertheless, different roots induce different hierarchies

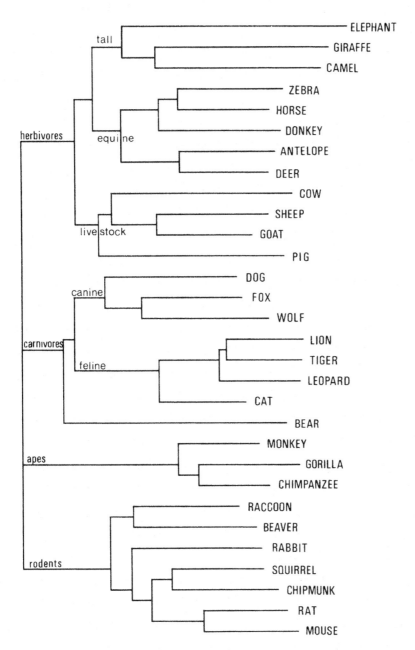

Figure 2.8
Representation of animal similarity (Henley, 1969) by ADDTREE.

Table 2.2
Correspondence Indices (Animals)

	ADDTREE	HCS	SSA/2D	SSA/3D
Stress	.07	.10	.17	.11
r	.91	.84	.86	.93

of partitions or clusters. ADDTREE provides a root that tends to minimize the variance of the distances to the external nodes. Other criteria for the selection of a root could readily be incorporated. The choice of a root for an additive tree is analogous to the choice of a coordinate system in (euclidean) multidimensional scaling. Both choices do not alter the distances, yet they usually affect the interpretation of the configuration.

In figure 2.8 the 30 animals are first partitioned into four major clusters: herbivores, carnivores, apes, and rodents. The major clusters in the figure are labeled to facilitate the interpretation. Each of these clusters is further partitioned into finer clusters. For example, the carnivores are partitioned into three clusters: felines (including cat, leopard, tiger, and lion), canines (including dog, fox, and wolf), and bear.

Recall that in a rooted tree, each arc defines a cluster which consists of all the objects that follow from it. Thus, each arc can be interpreted as the features shared by all objects in that cluster and by them alone. The length of the arc can thus be viewed as the weight of the respective features, or as a measure of the distinctiveness of the respective cluster. For example, the apes in figure 2.8 form a highly distinctive cluster because the arc labeled "apes" is very long. The interpretation of additive trees as feature trees is discussed in the last section.

The obtained (vertical) order of the animals in figure 2.8 from top to bottom roughly corresponds to the dimension of size, with elephant and mouse at the two endpoints. The (horizontal) distance of an animal from the root reflects its average distance from other animals. For example, cat is closer to the root than tiger, and indeed cat is more similar, on the average, to other animals than tiger. Note that this property of the data cannot be represented in an ultrametric tree in which all objects are equidistant from the root.

The correspondence indices for animal similarity are given in table 2.2.

Similarity of Letters

The second data set consists of similarity judgments between all lower-case Swedish letters obtained by Kuennapas and Janson [1969]. They reported average similarity

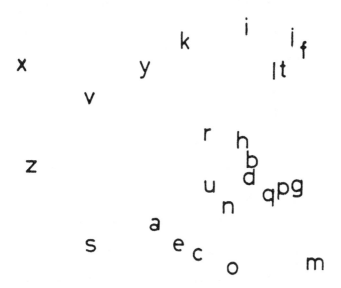

Figure 2.9
Representation of letter similarity (Kuennapas an Janson, 1969) by SSA/2D.

ratings for 57 subjects using a 0–100 scale. The modified letters $å, ö, ä$ are omitted from the present analysis. The result of SSA/2D is displayed in figure 2.9. The typeset in the figure is essentially identical to that used in the experiment. The vertical dimension in figure 2.9 might be interpreted as round-vs.-straight. No interpretable second dimension, however, emerges from the configuration.

The result of ADDTREE is presented in figure 2.10 which reveals a distinct set of interpretable clusters. The obtained clusters exhibit excellent correspondence with the factors derived by Kuennapas and Janson [1969] via a principle-component analysis. These investigators obtained six major factors which essentially coincide with the clustering induced by the additive tree. The factors together with their high-loading letters are as follows:

Factor I: roundness (o, c, e)

Factor II: roundness attached to veritical linearity (p, q, b, g, d)

Factor III: parallel vertical linearity (n, m, h, u)

Factor IV: zigzaggedness (s, z)

Factor V: angularity open upward (v, y, x)

Factor VI: vertical linearity (t, f, l, r, j, i)

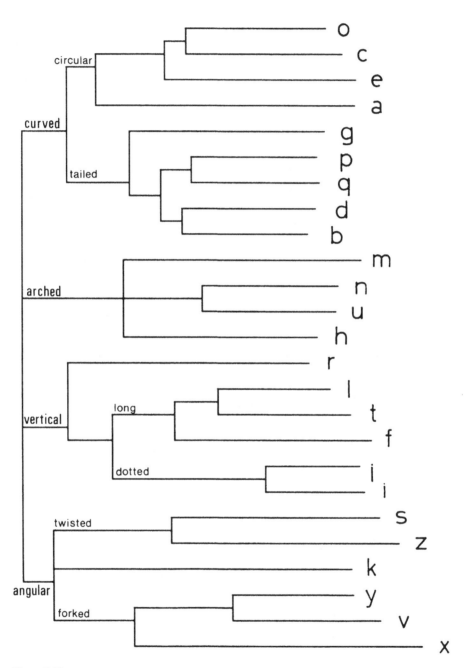

Figure 2.10
Representation of letter similarity (Kuennapas and Janson, 1969) by ADDTREE.

Table 2.3
Correspondence Indices (Letters)

	ADDTREE	HCS	SSA/2D	SSA/3D
Stress	.08	.11	.24	.16
r	.87	.82	.76	.84

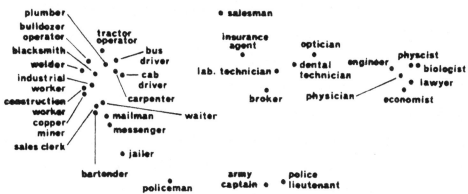

Figure 2.11
Representation of similarity between occupations (Kraus, 1976) by SSA/2D.

The vertical ordering of the letters in figure 2.10 is interpretable as roundness vs. angularity. It was obtained by the standard permutation procedure with the additional constraint that *o* and *x* are the end-points.

The correspondence indices for letter similarity are presented in table 2.3.

Similarity of Occupations

Kraus [note 5] instructed 154 Israeli subjects to classify 90 occupations into disjoint classes. The proximity between occupations was defined as the number of subjects who placed them in the same class. A representative subset of 35 occupations was selected for analysis.

The result of SSA/2D is displayed in figure 2.11. The configuration could be interpreted in terms of two dimensions: white collar vs. blue collar, and autonomy vs. subordination. The result of ADDTREE is presented in figure 2.12 which yields a

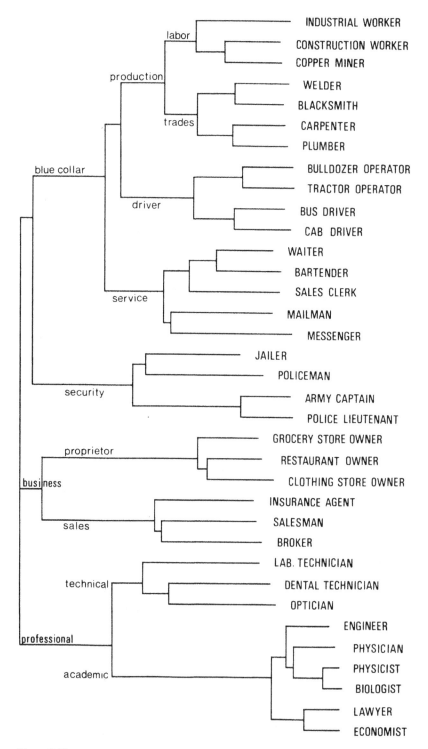

Figure 2.12
Representation of similarity between occupations (Kraus, 1976) by ADDTREE.

Table 2.4
Correspondence Indices (Occupations)

	ADDTREE	HCS	SSA/2D	SSA/3D
Stress	.06	.06	.15	.09
r	.96	.94	.86	.91

coherent classification of occupations. Note that while some of the obtained clusters (e.g., blue collar, academicians) also emerge from figure 2.11, others (e.g., security, business) do not. The vertical ordering of occupations produced by the program corresponds to collar color, with academic white collar at one end and manual blue collar at the other.

The correspondence indices for occupations are presented in table 2.4.

In the remainder of this section we comment on the robustness of tree structures and discuss the appropriateness of tree vs. spatial representations.

Robustness

The stability of the representations obtained by ADDTREE was examined using artificial data. Several additive trees (consisting of 16, 24, and 32 objects) were selected. Random error was added to the resulting distances according to the following rule: to each distance d we added a random number selected from a uniform distribution over $[-d/3, +d/3]$. Thus, the expected error of measurement for each distance is 1/6 of its length. Several sets of such data were analyzed by ADDTREE. The correlations between the solutions and the data were around .80. Nevertheless, the original tree-structures were recovered with very few errors indicating that tree structures are fairly robust. A noteworthy feature of ADDTREE is that as the noise level increases, the internal arcs become shorter. Thus, when the signal-to-noise ratio is low, the major clusters are likely to be less distinctive.

In all three data sets analyzed above, the ordinal and the cardinal versions of ADDTREE produce practically the same tree-structures. This observation suggests that the tree-structure is essentially determined by the ordinal properties of the data. To investigate this question, we have performed order-preserving transformations on several sets of real and artificial data, and applied ADDTREE to them. The selected transformations were the following: ranking, and $d \rightarrow d^\theta$, $\theta = 1/4, 1/3, 1/2, 1, 2, 3, 4$. The obtained tree-structures for the different transformations were highly similar. There was a tendency, however, for the high-power transformations to produce non-centered subtrees such as figure 2.1.

Tree vs. Spatial Representations

The applications of ADDTREE described above yielded interpretable tree structures. Furthermore, the tree distances reproduced the observed measures of similarity, or dissimilarity, to a reasonably high degree of approximation. The application
of HCS to the same data yielded similar tree structures, but the reproduction of the
observed proximities was, naturally, less satisfactory in all three data sets.

The comparison of ADDTREE with SSA indicates that the former provided a
better account of the data than the latter, as measured by the product-moment correlation and by the stress coefficient. The fact that ADDTREE achieved lower stress
in all data sets is particularly significant because SSA/3D has more free parameters,
and it is designed to minimize stress while ADDTREE is not. Furthermore, while the
clusters induced by the trees were readily interpretable, the dimensions that emerged
from the spatial representations were not always readily interpretable. Moreover, the
major dimension of the spatial solutions (e.g., size of animals, and prestige of occupations) also emerged as the vertical ordering in the corresponding trees.

These results indicate that some similarity data are better described by a tree than
by a spatial configuration. Naturally, there are other data for which dimensional
models are more suitable, see, e.g., Fillenbaum and Rapoport [1971], and Shepard
[1974]. The appropriateness of tree vs. spatial representation depends on the nature
of the task and the structure of the stimuli. Some object sets have a natural product
structure, e.g., emotions may be described in terms of intensity and pleasantness;
sound may be characterized in terms of intensity and frequency. Such object sets are
natural candidates for dimensional representations. Other objects sets have a hierarchical structure that may result, for instance, from an evolutionary process in which
all objects have an initial common structure and later develop additional distinctive
features. Alternatively, a hierarchal structure may result from people's tendency to
classify objects into mutually exclusive categories. The prevalence of hierarchical
classifications can be attributed to the added complexity involved in the introduction
of cross classifications with overlapping clusters. Structures generated by an evolutionary process or classification scheme are likely candidates for tree representations.

It is interesting to note that tree and spatial models are opposing in the sense that
very simple configurations of one model are incompatible with the other model. For
example, a square grid in the plane cannot be adequately described by an additive
tree. On the other hand, an additive tree with a single internal node cannot be adequately represented by a non-trivial spatial model [Holman, 1972]. These observations suggest that the two models may be appropriate for different data and may
capture different aspects of the same data.

Discussion

Feature Trees

As was noted earlier, a rooted additive tree can be interpreted as a feature tree. In this interpretation, each object is viewed as a set of features. Furthermore, each arc represents the set of features shared by all the objects that follow from that arc, and the arc length corresponds to the measure of that set. Hence, the features of an object are the features of all arcs which lead to that object, and its measure is its distance from the root. The tree-distance d between any two objects, therefore, corresponds to their set-distance, i.e., the measure of the symmetric difference between the respective feature sets:

$$d(x, y) = f(X - Y) + f(Y - X)$$

where X, Y are the feature sets associated with the objects x, y, respectively, and f is the measure of the feature space.

A more general model of similarity, based on feature matching, was developed in Tversky [1977]. In this theory, the dissimilarity between x and y is monotonically related to

$$d(x, y) = \alpha f(X - Y) + \beta f(Y - X) - \theta f(X \cap Y) \quad \alpha, \beta, \theta \geq 0,$$

where X, Y, and f are defined as above. According to this form (called the contrast model) the dissimilarity between objects is expressed as a linear combination of the measures of their common and distinctive features. Thus, an additive tree is a special case of the contrast model in which symmetry and the triangle inequality hold, and the feature space has a tree structure.

Decomposition of Trees

There are three types of additive trees that have a particularly simple structure: ultrametric, singular, and linear. In an ultrametric tree all objects are equidistant from the root. A *singular* tree is an additive tree with a single internal node. A *linear* tree, or a line, is an additive tree in which all objects lie on a line (see figure 2.13). Recall that an additive tree is ultrametric iff it satisfies the ultrametric inequality. An additive tree is singular iff for each object x in S there exists a length $\bar{x}$ such that $d(x, y) = \bar{x} + \bar{y}$. An additive tree is a line iff the triangle equality $d(x, y) + d(y, z) = d(x, z)$ holds for any three elements in S. Note that all three types of trees have no more than n parameters.

Throughout this section let T, T_1, T_2, etc. be additive trees defined on the same set of objects. T_1 is said to be *simpler* than T_2 iff the graph of T_1 (i.e., the structure

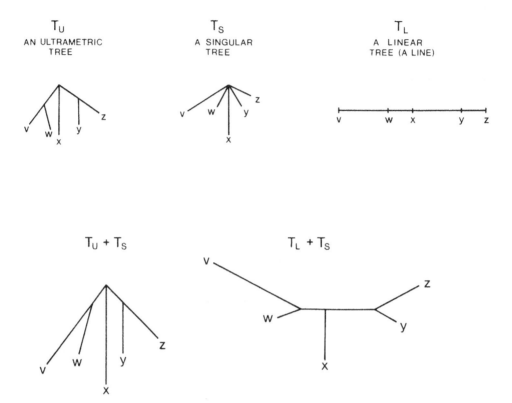

Figure 2.13
An illustration of different types of additive trees.

without the metric) is obtained from the graph of T_2 by cancelling one or more internal arcs and joining their endpoints. Hence, a singular tree is simpler than any other tree defined on the same object set. If T_1 and T_2 are both simpler than some T_3, then T_1 and T_2 are said to be *compatible*. (Note that compatibility is not transitive.) Let d_1 and d_2 denote, respectively, the distance functions of T_1 and T_2. It is not difficult to prove that the distance function $d = d_1 + d_2$ can be represented by an additive tree iff T_1 and T_2 are compatible. (Sufficiency follows from the fact that the sum of two trees with the same graph is a tree with the same graph. The proof of necessity relies on the fact that for any two incompatible trees there exists a quadruple on which they are incompatible.)

This result indicates that data which are not representable by a single additive tree may nevertheless be represented as the sum of incompatible additive trees. Such representations are discussed by Carroll and Pruzansky [note 3].

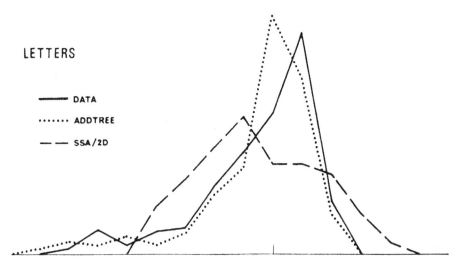

LETTERS

——— DATA

······· ADDTREE

— — SSA/2D

Figure 2.14
Distributions of dissimilarities and distances between letters.

Another implication of the above result is that tree-structures are preserved by the addition of singular trees. In particular, the sum of an ultrametric tree T_U and a singular tree T_S is an additive tree T with the same graph as T_U (see Figure 2.13). This leads to the converse question: can an additive tree T be expressed as $T_U + T_S$? An interesting observation (attributed to J. S. Farris) is that the distance function d of an additive tree T can be expressed as $d(x, y) = d_U(x, y) + \bar{x} + \bar{y}$, where d_U is the distance function of an ultrametric tree, and $\bar{x}, \bar{y}$ are real numbers (not necessarily positive). If all these numbers are non-negative then d is decomposable into an ultrametric and a singular tree, i.e., $d = d_U + d_S$. It is readily verified that T is expressible as $T_U + T_S$ iff there is a point on T whose distance to any internal node does not exceed its distance to any external node. Another structure of interest is obtained by the addition of a singular tree T_S and a line T_L (see figure 2.13). It can be shown that an additive tree T is expressible as $T_S + T_L$ iff no more than two internal arcs meet at any node.

Distribution of Distances
Figure 2.14 presents the distribution of dissimilarities between letters [from Kuennapas & Janson, 1969] along with the corresponding distributions of distances derived via ADDTREE, and via SSA/2D. The distributions of derived distances were standardized so as to have the same mean and variance as the distribution of the observed dissimilarities.

Note that the distribution of dissimilarities and the distribution of distances in the additive tree are skewed to the left, whereas the distribution of distances from the two-dimensional representation is skewed to the right. This pattern occurs in all three data sets, and reflects a general phenomenon.

In an additive tree, there are generally many large distances and few small distances. This follows from the observation that in most rooted trees, there are fewer pairs of objects that belong to the same cluster than pairs of objects that belong to different clusters. In contrast, a convex Euclidean configuration yields many small distances and fewer large distances. Indeed, under fairly natural conditions, the two models can be sharply distinguished by the skewness of their distance distribution.

The skewness of a distribution can be defined in terms of different criteria, e.g., the relation between the mean and the median, or the third central moment of the distribution. We employ here another notion of skewness that is based on the relation between the mean and the midpoint. A distribution is skewed to the left, according to the mean-midpoint criterion, iff the mean μ exceeds the midpoint $\lambda = 1/2 \max_{x,y} d(x, y)$. The distribution is skewed to the right, according to the mean-midpoint criterion, iff $\mu < \lambda$. From a practical standpoint, the mean-midpoint criterion has two drawbacks. First, it requires ratio scale data. Second, it is sensitive to error since it depends on the maximal distance. As demonstrated below, however, this criterion is useful for the investigation of distributions of distances.

A rooted additive tree (with n objects) is *centered* iff no subtree contains more than $n/2 + n(\bmod 2)$ objects. (Note that this bound is $n/2$ when n is even, and $(n + 1)/2$ when n is odd.) In an additive tree, one can always select a root such that the resulting rooted tree is centered. For example, the tree in figure 2.2 is centered around its root, whereas the tree in figure 2.1 is not. We can now state the following.

SKEWNESS THEOREM

I. Consider an additive tree T that is expressible as a sum of an ultrametric tree T_U and a singular tree T_S such that (i) T_U is centered around its natural root, and (ii) in T_S the longest arc is no longer than twice the shortest arc. Then the distribution of distances satisfies $\mu > \lambda$.

II. In a bounded convex subset of the Euclidean plane with the uniform measure, the distribution of distances satisfies $\mu < \lambda$.

Part I of the theorem shows that in an additive tree the distribution of distances is skewed to the left (according to the mean-midpoint criterion) whenever the distances between the centered root and the external nodes do not vary "too much." This property is satisfied, for example, by the trees in figures 2.8 and 2.10, and by T_U, T_S, and $T_U + T_S$ in figure 2.13. Part II of the theorem shows that in the Euclidean plane the distribution of distances is skewed to the right, in the above sense, whenever the set of points "has no holes." The proof of the Skewness Theorem is given in the appendix.

The theorem provides a sharp separation of these two families of representations in terms of the skewness of their distance distribution. This result does not hold for additive trees and Euclidean representations in general. In particular, it can be shown that the distribution of distances between all points on the circumference of a circle (which is a Euclidean representation, albeit nonconvex) is skewed to the left. This fact may explain the presence of "holes" in some configurations obtained through multidimensional scaling [see Cunningham, note 3, figure 1.1]. It can also be shown that the distribution of distances between all points on a line (which is a limiting case of an additive tree which cannot be expressed as $T_U + T_S$) is skewed to the right. Nevertheless, the available computational and theoretical evidence indicates that the distribution of distances in an additive tree is generally skewed to the left, whereas in a Euclidean representation it is generally skewed to the right. This observation suggests the intriguing possibility of evaluating the appropriateness of these representations on the basis of distributional properties of observed dissimilarities.

Appendix
Proof of the Skewness Theorem

Part I
Consider an additive tree $T = T_U + T_S$ with n external nodes. Hence,

$$\mu = \frac{\sum d(x, y)}{\binom{n}{2}} = \frac{\sum d_U(x, y)}{\binom{n}{2}} + \frac{\sum d_S(x, y)}{\binom{n}{2}} = \mu_U + \mu_S$$

and

$$\lambda = \tfrac{1}{2} \max d(x, y) \geq \lambda_U + l_S$$

where $\lambda_U = 1/2 \max d_U(x, y)$ is the distance between the root and the external nodes in the ultrametric tree, and l_S is the length of the longest arc in the singular tree. To show that T satisfies $\mu > \lambda$, it suffices to establish the inequalities: $\mu_U > \lambda_U$ and $\mu_S > l_S$ for its ultrametric and singular components. The inequality $\mu_S > l_S$ follows at once from the assumption that, in the singular tree, the shortest arc is not less than half the longest arc. To prove $\mu_U > \lambda_U$, suppose the ultrametric tree has k subtrees, with $n_1, n_2, \ldots n_k$ objects, that originate directly from the root. Since the tree is centered $n_i \leq n/2 + n \pmod 2$ where $n = \sum_i n_i$. Clearly $\mu_U = \sum_{x,y} d_U(x, y)/n(n-1)$. We show that $\sum_{x,y} d_U(x, y) > n(n-1)\lambda_U$.

Let P be the set of all pairs of objects that are connected through the root. Hence,

$$\sum_{(x,y)} d_U(x, y) \geq \sum_{(x,y) \in P} d_U(x, y) = 2\lambda_U \sum_{i=1}^{k} n_i(n - n_i)$$

where the equality follows from the fact that $d_U(x, y) = 2\lambda_U$ for all (x, y) in P. Therefore, it suffices to show that $2 \sum_i n_i(n - n_i) > n(n-1)$, or equivalently that $n^2 + n > 2 \sum_i n_i^2$. It can be shown that, subject to the constraint $n_i \leq n/2 + n \pmod 2$, the sum $\sum_i n_i^2$ is maximal when $k = 2$. In this case, it is easy to verify that $n^2 + n > 2(n_1^2 + n_2^2)$ since $n_1, n_2 = n/2 \pm n \pmod 2$.

Part II

Croften's Second Theorem on convex sets [see Kendall & Moran, 1963, pp. 64–66] is used to establish part II of the Skewness Theorem.

Let S be a bounded convex set in the plane, hence

$$\mu = \frac{\iiiint_S ((x_1 - x_2)^2 + (y_1 - y_2)^2)^{1/2} \, dx_1 \, dy_1 \, dx_2 \, dy_2}{\iiiint_S dx_1 \, dy_1 \, dx_2 \, dy_2}$$

We replace the coordinates (x_1, y_1, x_2, y_2) by $(p, \theta, \rho_1, \rho_2)$ where p and θ are the polar coordinates of the line joining (x_1, y_1) and (x_2, y_2), and ρ_1, ρ_2 are the distances from the respective points to the projection of the origin on that line. Thus,

$$x_1 = \rho_1 \sin \theta + p \cos \theta, \quad y_1 = -\rho_1 \cos \theta + p \sin \theta,$$

$$x_2 = \rho_2 \sin \theta + p \cos \theta, \quad y_2 = -\rho_2 \cos \theta + p \sin \theta.$$

Since the Jacobian of this transformation is $\rho_2 - \rho_1$,

$$\mu = \frac{\iiiint |\rho_1 - \rho_2|^2 \, d\rho_1 \, d\rho_2 \, dp \, d\theta}{\iiiint |\rho_1 - \rho_2| \, d\rho_1 \, d\rho_2 \, dp \, d\theta}.$$

To prove that $\mu < \lambda$ we show that for every p and θ

$$\lambda \geq \frac{\iint |\rho_1 - \rho_2|^2 \, d\rho_1 \, d\rho_2}{\iint |\rho_1 - \rho_2|^2 \, d\rho_1 \, d\rho_2}.$$

Given some p and θ, let L be the length of the cord in S whose polar coordinates are p, θ. Hence,

$$\int_a^b dp_1 \int |p_1 - p_2|^n \, dp_2 = \int_a^b dp_1 \left(\int_a^{p_1} (p_1 - p_2)^n \, dp_2 + \int_{p_1}^b (p_2 - p_1)^n \, dp_2 \right)$$

$$= \int_a^b dp_1 \left(-\frac{(p_1 - p_2)^{n+1}}{n+1} \bigg|_a^{p_1} + \frac{(p_2 - p_1)^{n+1}}{n+1} \bigg|_{p_1}^b \right)$$

$$= \int_a^b \frac{(p_1 - a)^{n+1} + (b - p_1)^{n+1}}{n+1} \, dp_1$$

$$= \frac{1}{(n+1)(n+2)} ((p_1 - a)^{n+2} - (b - p_1)^{n+2}) \big|_a^b$$

$$= \frac{(b - a)^{n+2} + (b - a)^{n+2}}{(n+1)(n+2)}$$

$$= \frac{2L^{n+2}}{(n+1)(n+2)}$$

where a and b are the distances from the endpoints of the chord to the projection of the origin on that chord, whence $L = b - a$. Consequently,

$$\frac{\int\int |p_1 - p_2|^2 \, dp_1 \, dp_2}{\int\int |p_1 - p_2| \, dp_1 \, dp_2} = \frac{L}{2} \leq \lambda$$

since λ is half the supremal chord-length. Moreover, $L/2 < \lambda$ for a set of chords with positive measure, hence $\mu < \lambda$.

Notes

We thank Nancy Henley and Vered Kraus for providing us with data, and Jan deLeeuw for calling our attention to relevant literature. The work of the first author was supported in part by the Psychology Unit of the Israel Defense Forces.

1. Holman, E. W. *A test of the hierarchical clustering model for dissimilarity data.* Unpublished manuscript, University of California at Los Angeles, 1975.

2. Cunningham, J. P. *Finding an optimal tree realization of a proximity matrix.* Paper presented at the mathematical psychology meeting, Ann Arbor, August, 1974.

3. Cunningham, J. P. *Discrete representations of psychological distance and their applications in visual memory.* Unpublished doctoral dissertation. University of California at San Diego, 1976.

4. Carroll, J. D., & Pruzansky, S. *Fitting of hierarchical tree structure (HTS) models, mixture of HTS models, and hybrid models, via mathematical programming and alternating least squares,* paper presented at

the US–Japan Seminar on Theory, Methods, and Applications of Multidimensional Scaling and related techniques, San Diego, August, 1975.

5. Kraus, personal communication, 1976.

References

Buneman, P. The recovery of trees from measures of dissimilarity. In F. R. Hodson, D. G. Kendall, & P. Tautu (Eds.), *Mathematics in the Archaeological and Historical Sciences*. Edinburgh: Edinburgh University Press, 1971.

Buneman, P. A note on the metric properties of trees. *Journal of Combinatorial Theory*, 1974, *17*(B), 48–50.

Carroll, J. D. Spatial, non-spatial and hybrid models for scaling. *Psychometrika*, 1976, *41*, 439–463.

Carroll, J. D., & Chang, J. J. A method for fitting a class of hierarchical tree structure models to dissimilarities data and its application to some "body parts" data of Miller's. *Proceedings, 81st Annual Convention, American Psychological Association*, 1973, *8*, 1097–1098.

Dobson, J. Unrooted trees for numerical taxonomy. *Journal of Applied Probability*, 1974, *11*, 32–42.

Fillenbaum, S., & Rapoport, A. *Structures in the subjective lexicon*. New York: Academic Press, 1971.

Guttman, L. A general nonmetric technique for finding the smallest coordinate space for a configuration of points. *Psychometrika*, 1968, *33*, 469–506.

Hakimi, S. L., & Yau, S. S. Distance matrix of a graph and its realizability. *Quarterly of Applied Mathematics*, 1964, *22*, 305–317.

Henley, N. M. A psychological study of the semantics of animal terms. *Journal of Verbal Learning and Verbal Behavior*, 1969, *8*, 176–184.

Holman, E. W. The relation between hierarchical and Euclidean models for psychological distances. *Psychometrika*, 1972, *37*, 417–423.

Jardine, N., & Sibson, R. *Mathematical taxonomy*. New York: Wiley, 1971.

Johnson, S. C. Hierarchical clustering schemes. *Psychometrika*, 1967, *32*, 241–254.

Kendall, M. G., & Moran, M. A. *Geometrical Probability*. New York: Hafner Publishing Company, 1963.

Kruskal, J. B. Multidimensional scaling by optimizing goodness of fit to a nonmetric hypothesis. *Psychometrika*, 1964, *29*, 1–27.

Kuennapas, T., & Janson, A. J. Multidimensional similarity of letters. *Perceptual and Motor Skills*, 1969, *28*, 3–12.

Lingoes, J. C. An IBM 360/67 program for Guttman–Lingoes smallest space analysis-PI. *Behavioral Science*, 1970, *15*, 536–540.

Patrinos, A. N., & Hakimi, S. L. The distance matrix of a graph and its tree realization. *Quarterly of Applied Mathematics*, 1972, *30*, 255–269.

Shepard, R. N. Representation of structure in similarity data: Problems and prospects. *Psychometrika*, 1974, *39*, 373–421.

Sneath, P. H. A., & Sokal, R. R. *Numerical taxonomy: the principles and practice of numerical classification*. San Francisco: W. H. Freeman, 1973.

Turner, J., & Kautz, W. H. A survey of progress in graph theory in the Soviet Union. *Siam Review*, 1970, *12*, 1–68. (Supplement)

Tversky, A. Features of similarity. *Psychological Review*, 1977, *84*, 327–352.

3 Studies of Similarity

Amos Tversky and Itamar Gati

Any event in the history of the organism is, in a sense, unique. Consequently, recognition, learning, and judgment presuppose an ability to categorize stimuli and classify situations by similarity. As Quine (1969) puts it: "There is nothing more basic to thought and language than our sense of similarity; our sorting of things into kinds" [p. 116]. Indeed, the notion of similarity—that appears under such different names as proximity, resemblance, communality, representativeness, and psychological distance—is fundamental to theories of perception, learning, and judgment. This chapter outlines a new theoretical analysis of similarity and investigates some of its empirical consequences.

The theoretical analysis of similarity relations has been dominated by geometric models. Such models represent each object as a point in some coordinate space so that the metric distances between the points reflect the observed similarities between the respective objects. In general, the space is assumed to be Euclidean, and the purpose of the analysis is to embed the objects in a space of minimum dimensionality on the basis of the observed similarities, see Shepard (1974).

In a recent paper (Tversky, 1977), the first author challenged the dimensional-metric assumptions that underlie the geometric approach to similarity and developed an alternative feature-theoretical approach to the analysis of similarity relations. In this approach, each object a is characterized by a set of features, denoted A, and the observed similarity of a to b, denoted $s(a,b)$, is expressed as a function of their common and distinctive features (see figure 3.1). That is, the observed similarity $s(a,b)$ is expressed as a function of three arguments: $A \cap B$, the features shared by a and b; $A - B$, the features of a that are not shared by b; $B - A$, the features of b that are not shared by a. Thus the similarity between objects is expressed as a feature-matching function (i.e., a function that measures the degree to which two sets of features match each other) rather than as the metric distance between points in a coordinate space.

The theory is based on a set of qualitative assumptions about the observed similarity ordering. They yield an interval similarity scale S, which preserves the observed similarity order [i.e., $S(a,b) > S(c,d)$ iff $s(a,b) > s(c,d)$], and a scale f, defined on the relevant feature space such that

$$S(a,b) = \theta f(A \cap B) - \alpha f(A - B) - \beta f(B - A) \quad \text{where } \theta, \alpha, \beta \geq 0. \tag{1}$$

According to this form, called the *contrast model*, the similarity of a to b is described as a linear combination (or a contrast) of the measures of their common

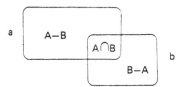

Figure 3.1
A graphical illustration of the relation between two feature sets.

and distinctive features. Naturally, similarity increases with the measure of the common features and decreases with the measure of the distinctive features.

The contrast model does not define a unique index of similarity but rather a family of similarity indices defined by the values of the parameters θ, α, and β. For example, if $\theta = 1$, and $\alpha = \beta = 0$, then $S(a, b) = f(A \cap B)$; that is, similarity equals the measure of the common features. On the other hand, if $\theta = 0$, and $\alpha = \beta = 1$, then $-S(a, b) = f(A - B) + f(B - A)$; that is, the dissimilarity of a to b equals the measure of the symmetric difference of the respective feature sets, see Restle (1961). Note that in the former case ($\theta = 1$, $\alpha = \beta = 0$), the similarity between objects is determined only by their common features, whereas in the latter case ($\theta = 0$, $\alpha = \beta = 1$), it is determined by their distinctive features only. The contrast model expresses similarity between objects as the weighted difference of the measures of their common and distinctive features, thereby allowing for a variety of similarity relations over the same set of objects.

The contrast model is formulated in terms of the parameters (θ, α, β) that characterize the task, and the scale f, which reflects the salience or prominence of the various features. Thus f measures the contribution of any particular (common or distinctive) feature to the similarity between objects. The scale value $f(A)$ associated with stimulus a is regarded, therefore, as a measure of the overall salience of that stimulus. The factors that contribute to the salience of a stimulus include: intensity, frequency, familiarity, good form, and informational content. The manner in which the scale f and the parameters (θ, α, β) depend on the context and the task are discussed in the following sections.

This chapter employs the contrast model to analyze the following three problems: the relation between judgments of similarity and difference; the nature of asymmetric similarities; and the effects of context on similarity. All three problems concern changes in similarity induced, respectively, by the formulation of the *task* (as judgment of similarity or as judgment of difference), the *direction* of comparison, and the effective *context* (i.e., the set of objects under consideration).

To account for the effects of these manipulations within the present theoretical framework, we introduce several hypotheses that relate focus of attention to the experimental task. In particular, it is assumed that people attend more to common features in judgments of similarity than in judgments of difference, that people attend more to the subject than to the referent of the comparison, and that people attend primarily to features that have classificatory significance.

These hypotheses are formulated in terms of the contrast model and are tested in several experimental studies of similarity. For a more comprehensive treatment of the contrast model and a review of relevant data (including the present studies), see Tversky (1977).

Similarity versus Difference

What is the relation between judgments of similarity and judgements of difference? Some authors emphasized that the two judgments are conceptually independent; others have treated them as perfectly correlated. The data appear to support the latter view. For example, Hosman and Kuennapas (1972) obtained independent judgments of similarity and difference for all pairs of lower-case letters on a scale from 0 to 100. The product-moment correlation between the judgments was $-.98$, and the slope of the regression line was $-.91$. We also collected judgments of similarity and difference for 21 pairs of countries using a 20-point rating scale. The product moment correlation between the ratings was again $-.98$. The near-perfect negative correlation between similarity and difference, however, does not always hold.

In applying the contrast model to judgments of similarity and of difference, it is reasonable to assume that enlarging the measure of the common features increases similarity and decreases difference, whereas enlarging the measure of the distinctive features decreases similarity and increases difference. More formally, let $s(a,b)$ and $d(a,b)$ denote ordinal measures of similarity and difference, respectively. Thus $s(a,b)$ is expected to increase with $f(A \cap B)$ and to decrease with $f(A - B)$ and with $f(B - A)$, whereas $d(a,b)$ is expected to decrease with $f(A \cap B)$ and to increase with $f(A - B)$ and with $f(B - A)$.

The relative weight assigned to the common and the distinctive features may differ in the two judgments because of a change in focus. In the assessment of similarity between stimuli, the subject may attend more to their common features, whereas in the assessment of difference between stimuli, the subject may attend more to their distinctive features. Stated differently, the instruction to consider similarity may lead the subject to focus primarily on the features that contribute to the similarity of the stimuli, whereas the instruction to consider difference may lead the subject to focus primarily on the features that contribute to the difference between the stimuli. Consequently, the relative weight of the common features is expected to be greater in the assessment of similarity than in the assessment of difference.

To investigate the consequences of this focusing hypothesis, suppose that both similarity and difference measures satisfy the contrast model with opposite signs but with different weights. Furthermore, suppose for simplicity that both measures are symmetric. Hence, under the contrast model, there exist non-negative constants θ and λ such that

$$s(a,b) > s(c,e) \quad \text{iff} \quad \theta f(A \cap B) - f(A - B) - f(B - A)$$
$$> \theta f(C \cap E) - f(C - E) - f(E - C), \tag{2}$$

and

$$d(a,b) > d(c,e) \quad \text{iff} \quad f(A - B) + f(B - A) - \lambda f(A \cap B)$$
$$> f(C - E) + F(E - C) - \lambda f(C \cap E) \tag{3}$$

The weights associated with the distinctive features can be set equal to 1 in the symmetric case with no loss of generality. Hence, θ and λ reflect the *relative* weight of the common features in the assessment of similarity and difference, respectively.

Note that if θ is very large, then the similarity ordering is essentially determined by the common features. On the other hand, if λ is very small, then the difference ordering is determined primarily by the distinctive features. Consequently, both $s(a,b) > s(c,e)$ and $d(a,b) > d(c,e)$ may be obtained whenever

$$f(A \cap B) > f(C \cap E) \quad \text{and} \quad f(A - B) + f(B - A) > f(C - E) + f(E - C). \tag{4}$$

That is, if the common features are weighed more heavily in judgments of similarity than in judgments of difference, then a pair of objects with many common and many distinctive features may be perceived as both more similar and more different than another pair of objects with fewer common and fewer distinctive features.

Study 1: Similarity versus Difference
All subjects that took part in the experiments reported in this chapter were undergraduate students majoring in the social sciences from the Hebrew University in Jerusalem and the Ben-Gurion University in Beer-Sheba. They participated in the studies as part of the requirements for a psychology course. The material was presented in booklets and administered in the classroom. The instructions were printed

Table 3.1
Percentage of Subjects That Selected the Prominent Pair in the Similarity Group (Π_s) and in the Difference Group (Π_d)

Prominent Pairs	Nonprominent Pairs	Π_s	Π_d	$\Pi_s + \Pi_d$
1 W. Germany–E. Germany	Ceylon–Nepal	66.7	70.0	136.7
2 Lebanon–Jordan	Upper Volta–Tanzania	69.0	43.3	112.3
3 Canada–U.S.A.	Bulgaria–Albania	80.0	16.7	96.7
4 Belgium–Holland	Peru–Costa Rica	78.6	21.4	100.0
5 Switzerland–Denmark	Pakistan–Mongolia	55.2	28.6	83.8
6 Syria–Iraq	Liberia–Kenya	63.3	28.6	91.9
7 U.S.S.R.–U.S.A.	Paraguay–Ecuador	20.0	100.0	120.0
8 Sweden–Norway	Thailand–Burma	69.0	40.7	109.7
9 Turkey–Greece	Bolivia–Honduras	51.7	86.7	138.4
10 Austria–Switzerland	Zaire–Madagascar	79.3	24.1	103.4
11 Italy–France	Bahrain–Yemen	44.8	70.0	114.8
12 China–Japan	Guatemala–Costa Rica	40.0	93.1	133.1
13 S. Korea–N. Korea	Nigeria–Zaire	63.3	60.0	123.3
14 Uganda–Libya	Paraguay–Ecuador	23.3	65.5	88.8
15 Australia–S. Africa	Iceland–New Zealand	57.1	60.0	117.1
16 Poland–Czechoslovakia	Colombia–Honduras	82.8	37.0	119.8
17 Portugal–Spain	Tunis–Morocco	55.2	73.3	128.5
18 Vatican–Luxembourg	Andorra–San Marino	50.0	85.7	135.7
19 England–Ireland	Pakistan–Mongolia	80.0	58.6	138.6
20 Norway–Denmark	Indonesia–Philippines	51.7	25.0	76.7
Average		59.1	54.4	113.5

in the booklet and also read aloud by the experimenter. The different forms of each booklet were assigned randomly to different subjects.

Twenty sets of four countries were constructed. Each set included two pairs of countries: a prominent pair and a nonprominent pair. The prominent pairs consisted of countries that were well known to the subjects (e.g., U.S.A.–U.S.S.R.). The non-prominent pairs consisted of countries that were known to our subjects but not as well as the prominent pairs (e.g., Paraguay–Ecuador). This assumption was verified in a pilot study in which 50 subjects were presented with all 20 quadruples of countries and asked to indicate which of the two pairs include countries that are more prominent, or better known. For each quadruple, over 85% of the subjects ordered the pairs in accord with our a priori ordering. All 20 sets of countries are displayed in table 3.1.

Two groups of 30 subjects each participated in the main study. All subjects were presented with the same 20 sets in the same order. The pairs within each set were arranged so that the prominent pairs appeared an equal number of times on the left and on the right. One group of subjects—the similarity group—selected between the two pairs of each set the pair of countries that are more similar. The second group of subjects—the difference group—selected between the two pairs in each set the pair of countries that are more different.

Let Π_s and Π_d denote, respectively, the percentage of subjects who selected the prominent pair in the similarity task and in the difference task. (Throughout this chapter, percentages were computed relative to the number of subjects who responded to each problem, which was occasionally smaller than the total number of subjects.) These values are presented in table 3.1 for all sets. If similarity and difference are complementary (i.e., $\theta = \lambda$), then the sum $\Pi_s + \Pi_d$ should equal 100 for all pairs. On the other hand, if $\theta > \lambda$, then this sum should exceed 100. The average value of $\Pi_s + \Pi_d$ across all subjects and sets is 113.5, which is significantly greater than 100 ($t = 3.27, df = 59, p < .01$). Moreover, table 3.1 shows that, on the average, the prominent pairs were selected more frequently than the nonprominent pairs both under similarity instructions (59.1%) and under difference instructions (54.4%), contrary to complementarity. These results demonstrate that the relative weight of the common and the distinctive features vary with the nature of the task and support the focusing hypothesis that people attend more to the common features in judgments of similarity than in judgments of difference.

Directionality and Asymmetry

Symmetry has been regarded as an essential property of similarity relations. This view underlies the geometric approach to the analysis of similarity, in which dissimilarity between objects is represented as a metric distance function. Although many types of proximity data, such as word associations or confusion probabilities, are often nonsymmetric, these asymmetries have been attributed to response biases. In this section, we demonstrate the presence of systematic asymmetries in direct judgments of similarity and argue that similarity should not be viewed as a symmetric relation. The observed asymmetries are explained in the contrast model by the relative salience of the stimuli and the directionality of the comparison.

Similarity judgments can be regarded as extensions of similarity statements (i.e., statements of the form "a is like b"). Such a statement is directional; it has a subject, a, and a referent, b, and it is not equivalent in general to the converse similarity statement "b is like a." In fact, the choice of a subject and a referent depends, in part at least, on the relative salience of the objects. We tend to select the more salient stimulus, or the prototype, as a referent and the less salient stimulus, or the variant, as a subject. Thus we say "the portrait resembles the person" rather than "the person resembles the portrait." We say "the son resembles the father" rather than "the father resembles the son," and we say "North Korea is like Red China" rather than "Red China is like North Korea."

As is demonstrated later, this asymmetry in the *choice* of similarity statements is associated with asymmetry in *judgments* of similarity. Thus the judged similarity of North Korea to Red China exceeds the judged similarity of Red China to North Korea. In general, the direction of asymmetry is determined by the relative salience of the stimuli: The variant is more similar to the prototype than vice versa.

If $s(a, b)$ is interpreted as the degree to which a is similar to b, then a is the subject of the comparison and b is the referent. In such a task, one naturally focuses on the subject of the comparison. Hence, the features of the subject are weighted more heavily than the features of the referent (i.e., $\alpha > \beta$). Thus similarity is reduced more by the distinctive features of the subject than by the distinctive features of the referent. For example, a toy train is quite similar to a real train, because most features of the toy train are included in the real train. On the other hand, a real train is not as similar to a toy train, because many of the features of a real train are not included in the toy train.

It follows readily from the contrast model, with $\alpha > \beta$, that

$$s(a, b) > s(b, a) \quad \text{iff} \quad \theta f(A \cap B) - \alpha f(A - B) - \beta f(B - A)$$

$$> \theta f(A \cap B) - \alpha f(B - A) - \beta f(A - B) \tag{5}$$

$$\text{iff} \quad f(B - A) > f(A - B).$$

Thus $s(a, b) > s(b, a)$ whenever the distinctive features of b are more salient than the distinctive features of a, or whenever b is more prominent than a. Hence, the conjunction of the contrast model and the focusing hypothesis ($\alpha > \beta$) implies that the direction of asymmetry is determined by the relative salience of the stimuli so that the less salient stimulus is more similar to the salient stimulus than vice versa.

In the contrast model, $s(a, b) = s(b, a)$ if either $f(A - B) = f(B - A)$ or $\alpha = \beta$. That is, symmetry holds whenever the objects are equally salient, or whenever the comparison is nondirectional. To interpret the latter condition, compare the following two forms:

1. Assess the degree to which a and b are similar to each other.

2. Assess the degree to which a is similar to b.

In (1), the task is formulated in a nondirectional fashion, and there is no reason to emphasize one argument more than the other. Hence, it is expected that $\alpha = \beta$ and

$s(a,b) = s(b,a)$. In (2), on the other hand, the task is directional, and hence the subject is likely to be the focus of attention rather than the referent. In this case, asymmetry is expected, provided the two stimuli are not equally salient. The directionality of the task and the differential salience of the stimuli, therefore, are necessary and sufficient for asymmetry.

In the following two studies, the directional asymmetry prediction, derived from the contrast model, is tested using semantic (i.e., countries) and perceptual (i.e., figures) stimuli. Both studies employ essentially the same design. Pairs of stimuli that differ in salience are used to test for the presence of asymmetry in the choice of similarity statements and in direct assessments of similarity.

Study 2: Similarity of Countries

In order to test the asymmetry prediction, we constructed 21 pairs of countries so that one element of the pair is considerably more prominent than the other (e.g., U.S.A.–Mexico, Belgium–Luxembourg). To validate this assumption, we presented all pairs to a group of 68 subjects and asked them to indicate in each pair the country they regard as more prominent. In all cases except one, more than two-thirds of the subjects agreed with our initial judgment. All 21 pairs of countries are displayed in table 3.2, where the more prominent element of each pair is denoted by p and the less prominent by q.

Next, we tested the hypothesis that the more prominent element is generally chosen as the referent rather than as the subject of similarity statements. A group of 69 subjects was asked to choose which of the following two phrases they prefer to use: "p is similar to q," or "q is similar to p." The percentage of subjects that selected the latter form, in accord with our hypothesis, is displayed in table 3.2 under the label Π. It is evident from the table that in all cases the great majority of subjects selected the form in which the more prominent country serves as a referent.

To test the hypothesis that $s(q,p) > s(p,q)$, we instructed two groups of 77 subjects each to assess the similarity of each pair on a scale from 1 (no similarity) to 20 (maximal similarity). The two groups were presented with the same list of 21 pairs, and the only difference between the two groups was the order of the countries within each pair. For example, one group was asked to assess "the degree to which Red China is similar to North Korea," whereas the second group was asked to assess "the degree to which North Korea is similar to Red China." The lists were balanced so that the more prominent countries appeared about an equal number of times in the first and second position. The average ratings for each ordered pair, denoted $s(p,q)$ and $s(q,p)$ are displayed in table 3.2. The average $s(q,p)$ was significantly higher than the average $s(p,q)$ across all subjects and pairs. A t-test for correlated samples

Table 3.2
Average Similarities and Differences for 21 Pairs of Countries

p	q	Π	s(p, q)	s(q, p)	d(p, q)	d(q, p)
1 U.S.A.	Mexico	91.1	6.46	7.65	11.78	10.58
2 U.S.S.R.	Poland	98.6	15.12	15.18	6.37	7.30
3 China	Albania	94.1	8.69	9.16	14.56	12.16
4 U.S.A.	Israel	95.6	9.70	10.65	13.78	12.53
5 Japan	Philippines	94.2	12.37	11.95	7.74	5.50
6 U.S.A.	Canada	97.1	16.96	17.33	4.40	3.82
7 U.S.S.R.	Israel	91.1	3.41	3.69	18.41	17.25
8 England	Ireland	97.1	13.32	13.49	7.50	5.04
9 W. Germany	Austria	87.0	15.60	15.20	6.95	6.67
10 U.S.S.R.	France	82.4	5.21	5.03	15.70	15.00
11 Belgium	Luxembourg	95.6	15.54	16.14	4.80	3.93
12 U.S.A.	U.S.S.R.	65.7	5.84	6.20	16.65	16.11
13 China	N. Korea	95.6	13.13	14.22	8.20	7.48
14 India	Ceylon	97.1	13.91	13.88	5.51	7.32
15 U.S.A.	France	86.8	10.42	11.09	10.58	10.15
16 U.S.S.R.	Cuba	91.1	11.46	12.32	11.50	10.50
17 England	Jordan	98.5	4.97	6.52	15.81	14.95
18 France	Israel	86.8	7.48	7.34	12.20	11.88
19 U.S.A.	W. Germany	94.1	11.30	10.70	10.25	11.96
20 U.S.S.R.	Syria	98.5	6.61	8.51	12.92	11.60
21 France	Algeria	95.6	7.86	7.94	10.58	10.15

yielded $t = 2.92$, $df = 20$, and $p < .01$. To obtain a statistical test based on individual data, we computed for each subject a directional asymmetry score, defined as the average similarity for comparisons with a prominent referent [i.e., $s(q, p)$ minus the average similarity for comparison with a prominent subject, i.e., $s(p, q)$]. The average difference (.42) was significantly positive: $t = 2.99$, $df = 153$, $p < .01$.

The foregoing study was repeated with judgments of difference instead of judgments of similarity. Two groups of 23 subjects each received the same list of 21 pairs, and the only difference between the groups, again, was the order of the countries within each pair. For example, one group was asked to assess "the degree to which the U.S.S.R. is different from Poland," whereas the second group was asked to assess "the degree to which Poland is different from the U.S.S.R." All subjects were asked to rate the difference on a scale from 1 (minimal difference) to 20 (maximal difference).

If judgments of difference follow the contrast model (with opposite signs) and the focusing hypothesis ($\alpha > \beta$) holds, then the prominent stimulus p is expected to differ from the less prominent stimulus q more than q differs from p [i.e., $d(p, q) > d(q, p)$]. The average judgments of difference for all ordered pairs are displayed in table 3.2.

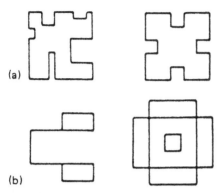

Figure 3.2
Examples of pairs of figures used to test the prediction of asymmetry. (a) Example of a pair of figures (from set 1) that differ in goodness of form. (b) Example of a pair of figures (from set 2) that differ in complexity.

The average $d(p, q)$ across all subjects and pairs was significantly higher than the average $d(q, p)$. A t-test for correlated samples yielded $t = 2.72$, $df = 20$, $p < .01$. Furthermore, the average difference between $d(p, q)$ and $d(q, p)$, computed as previously for each subject (.63), was significantly positive: $t = 2.24$, $df = 45$, $p < .05$. Hence, the predicted asymmetry was confirmed in direct judgments of both similarity and difference.

Study 3: Similarity of Figures
Two sets of eight pairs of geometric figures served as stimuli in the present study. In the first set, one figure in each pair, denoted p, had better form than the other, denoted q. In the second set, the two figures in each pair were roughly equivalent with respect to goodness of form, but one figure, denoted p, was richer or more complex than the other, denoted q. Examples of pairs of figures from each set are presented in figure 3.2.

We hypothesized that both goodness of form and complexity contribute to the salience of geometric figures. Moreover, we expected a "good figure" to be more salient than a "bad figure," although the latter is generally more complex. For pairs of figures that do not vary much with respect to goodness of form, however, the more complex figure is expected to be more salient.

A group of 69 subjects received the entire list of 16 pairs of figures. The two elements of each pair were displayed side by side. For each pair, the subjects were asked to choose which of the following two statements they preferred to use: "the left figure is similar to the right figure," or "the right figure is similar to the left figure." The positions of the figures were randomized so that p and q appeared an equal number of times on the left and on the right. The proportion of subjects that selected the form "q is similar to p" exceeded 2/3 in all pairs except one. Evidently, the more salient figure (defined as previously) was generally chosen as the referent rather than as the standard.

To test for asymmetry in judgments of similarity, we presented two groups of 66 subjects each with the same 16 pairs of figures and asked the subjects to rate (on a 20-point scale) the degree to which the figure on the left is similar to the figure on the right. The two groups received identical booklets, except that the left and right positions of the figures in each pair were reversed. The data shows that the average $s(q, p)$ across all subjects and pairs was significantly higher than the average $s(p, q)$. A t-test for correlated samples yielded $t = 2.94$, $df = 15$, $p < .01$. Furthermore, in both sets the average difference between $s(q, p)$ and $s(p, q)$ computed as previously for each individual subject (.56) were significantly positive. In set 1, $t = 2.96$, $df = 131$, $p < .01$, and in set 2, $t = 2.79$, $df = 131$, $p < .01$.

The preceding two studies revealed the presence of systematic and significant asymmetries in judgments of similarity between countries and geometric figures. The results support the theoretical analysis based on the contrast model and the focusing hypothesis, according to which the features of the subject are weighted more heavily than the features of the referent. Essentially the same results were obtained by Rosch (1975) using a somewhat different design. In her studies, one stimulus (the standard) was placed at the origin of a semicircular board, and the subject was instructed to place the second (variable) stimulus on the board so as "to represent his feeling of the distance between that stimulus and the one fixed at the origin." Rosch used three stimulus domains: color, line orientation, and number. In each domain, she paired prominent, or focal, stimuli with nonfocal stimuli. For example, a pure red was paired with an off-red, a vertical line was paired with a diagonal line, and a round number (e.g., 100) was paired with a nonround number (e.g., 103).

In all three domains, Rosch found that the measured distance between stimuli was smaller when the more prominent stimulus was fixed at the origin. That is, the similarity of the variant to the prototype was greater than the similarity of the prototype to the variant. Rosch also showed that when presented with sentence frames containing hedges such as "____ is virtually ____," subjects generally placed the prototype in the second blank and the variant in the first. For example, subjects preferred the sentence "103 is virtually 100" to the sentence "100 is virtually 103."

In contrast to direct judgments of similarity, which have traditionally been viewed as symmetric, other measures of similarity such as confusion probability or association were known to be asymmetric. The observed asymmetries, however, were commonly attributed to a response bias. Without denying the important role of response biases, asymmetries in identification tasks occur even in situations to which a response bias interpretation does not apply (e.g., in studies where the subject indicates whether two presented stimuli are identical or not). Several experiments employing this paradigm obtained asymmetric confusion probabilities of the type predicted by the present analysis. For a discussion of these data and their implications, see Tversky (1977).

Context Effects

The preceding two sections deal with the effects of the formulation of the task (as judgment of similarity or of difference) and of the direction of comparison (induced by the choice of subject and referent) on similarity. These manipulations were related to the parameters (θ, α, β) of the contrast model through the focusing hypothesis. The present section extends this hypothesis to describe the manner in which the measure of the feature space f varies with a change in context.

The scale f is generally not invariant with respect to changes in context or frame of reference. That is, the salience of features may vary widely depending on implicit or explicit instructions and on the object set under consideration. East Germany and West Germany, for example, may be viewed as highly similar from a geographical or cultural viewpoint and as quite dissimilar from a political viewpoint. Moreover, the two Germanys are likely to be viewed as more similar to each other in a context that includes many Asian and African countries than in a context that includes only European countries.

How does the salience of features vary with changes in the set of objects under consideration? We propose that the salience of features is determined, in part at least, by their diagnosticity (i.e., classificatory significance). A feature may acquire diagnostic value (and hence become more salient) in a particular context if it serves as a basis for classification in that particular context. The relations between similarity and diagnosticity are investigated in several studies that show how the similarity between a given pair of countries is varied by changing the context in which they are embedded.

Study 4: The Extension of Context
According to the preceding discussion, the diagnosticity of features is determined by the prevalence of the classifications that are based on them. Hence, features that are

Table 3.3
Average Similarities of Countries in Homogeneous (s_1) and Heterogeneous (s_2) Contexts

	Countries	$s_0(a,b)$	$s_e(a,b)$
American countries	Panama–Costa Rica	12.30	13.29
	Argentina–Chile	13.17	14.36
	Canada–U.S.A.	16.10	15.86
	Paraguay–Bolivia	13.48	14.43
	Mexico–Guatemala	11.36	12.81
	Venezuela–Colombia	12.06	13.06
	Brazil–Uruguay	13.03	14.64
	Peru–Ecuador	13.52	14.61
European countries	England–Ireland	13.88	13.37
	Spain–Portugal	15.44	14.45
	Bulgaria–Greece	11.44	11.00
	Sweden–Norway	17.09	15.03
	France–W. Germany	10.88	11.81
	Yugoslavia–Austria	8.47	9.86
	Italy–Switzerland	10.03	11.14
	Belgium–Holland	15.39	17.06

shared by all the objects under study are devoid of diagnostic value, because they cannot be used to classify these objects. However, when the context is extended by enlarging the object set, some features that had been shared by all objects in the original context may not be shared by all objects in the broader context. These features then acquire diagnostic value and increase the similarity of the objects that share them. Thus the similarity of a pair of objects in the original context is usually smaller than their similarity in the extended context.

To test this hypothesis, we constructed a list of pairs of countries with a common border and asked subjects to assess their similarity on a 20-point scale. Four sets of eight pairs were constructed. Set 1 contained eight pairs of American countries, set 2 contained eight pairs of European countries, set 3 contained four pairs from set 1 and four pairs from set 2, and set 4 contained the remaining pairs from sets 1 and 2. Each one of the four sets was presented to a different group of 30–36 subjects. The entire list of 16 pairs is displayed in table 3.3.

Recall that the features "American" and "European" have no diagnostic value in sets 1 and 2, although they both have diagnostic value in sets 3 and 4. Consequently, the overall average similarity in the heterogeneous sets (3 and 4) is expected to be higher than the overall average similarity in the homogeneous sets (1 and 2). The average similarity for each pair of countries obtained in the homogeneous and the heterogeneous contexts, denoted s_0 and s_e, respectively, are presented in table 3.3.

In the absence of context effects, the similarity for any pair of countries should be independent of the list in which it was presented. In contrast, the average difference between s_e and s_o (.57) is significantly positive: $t = 2.11$, $df = 15$, $p < .05$.

Similar results were obtained in an earlier study by Sjöberg (1972) who showed that the similarities between string instruments (banjo, violin, harp, electric guitar) were increased when a wind instrument (clarinet) was added to this set. Hence, Sjöberg found that the similarity in the homogeneous pairs (i.e., pairs of string instruments) was increased when heterogeneous pairs (i.e., a string instrument and a wind instrument) were introduced into the list. Because the similarities in the homogeneous pairs, however, are greater than the similarities in the heterogeneous pairs, the above finding may be attributed, in part at least, to the common tendency of subjects to standardize the response scale (i.e., to produce the same average similarity for any set of comparisons).

Recall that in the present study all similarity assessments involve only homogeneous pairs (i.e., pairs of countries from the same continent sharing a common border). Unlike Sjöberg's (1972) study that extended the context by introducing heterogeneous pairs, our experiment extended the context by constructing heterogeneous lists composed of homogeneous pairs. Hence, the increase of similarity with the enlargement of context, observed in the present study, cannot be explained by the tendency to standardize the response scale.

Study 5: Similarity and Clustering

When faced with a set of stimuli, people often organize them in clusters to reduce information load and facilitate further processing. Clusters are typically selected in order to maximize the similarity of objects within the cluster and the dissimilarity of objects from different clusters. Clearly, the addition and/or deletion of objects can alter the clustering of the remaining objects. We hypothesize that changes in clustering (induced by the replacement of objects) increase the diagnostic value of the features on which the new clusters are based and consequently the similarity of objects that share these features. Hence, we expect that changes in context which affect the clustering of objects will affect their similarity in the same manner.

The procedure employed to test this hypothesis (called the *diagnosticity hypothesis*) is best explained in terms of a concrete example, taken from the present study. Consider the two sets of four countries displayed in figure 3.3, which differ only in one of their elements (*p* or *q*).

The sets were constructed so that the natural clusterings of the countries are: *p* and *c* vs. *a* and *b* in set 1; and *b* and *q* vs. *c* and *a* in set 2. Indeed, these were the modal classifications of subjects who were asked to partition each quadruple into two

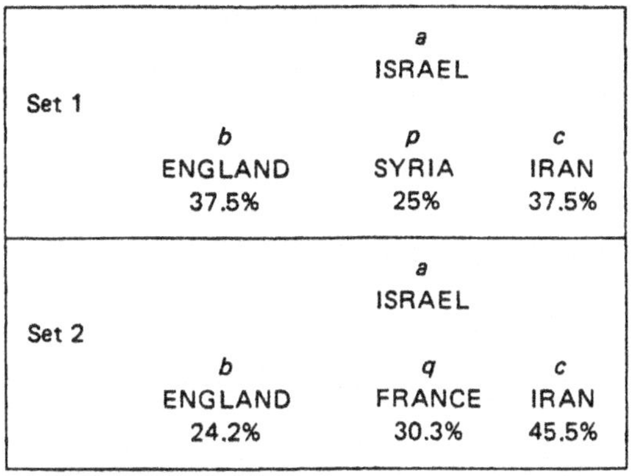

Figure 3.3
An example of two matched sets of countries used to test the diagnosticity hypothesis. The percentage of
subjects that ranked each country below (as most similar to the target) is presented under the country.

pairs. In set 1, 72% of the subjects partitioned the set into Moslem countries (Syria
and Iran) vs. non-Moslem countries (England and Israel); whereas in set 2, 84%
of the subjects partitioned the set into European countries (England and France) vs.
Middle-Eastern countries (Iran and Israel). Hence, the replacement of p by q
changed the pairing of a: In set 1, a was paired with b; whereas in set 2, a was paired
with c. The diagnosticity hypothesis implies that the change in clustering, induced by
the substitution of the odd element (p or q), should produce a corresponding change
in similarity. That is, the similarity of England to Israel should be greater in set 1,
where it is natural to group them together, than in set 2 where it is not. Likewise, the
similarity of Iran to Israel should be greater in set 2, where they tend to be grouped
together, than in set 1 where they are not.

To investigate the relation between clustering and similarity, we constructed 20
pairs of sets of four countries of the form (a, b, c, p) and (a, b, c, q), whose elements
are listed in table 3.4. Two groups of 25 subjects each were presented with 20 sets
of four countries and asked to partition each quadruple into two pairs. Each group
received one of the two matched quadruples, displayed in a row in random order.

Let $a_p(b, c)$ denote the percentage of subjects that paired a with b rather than with
c when the odd element was p, etc. the difference $D(p, q) = a_p(b, c) - a_q(b, c)$,
therefore, measures the effect of replacing q by p on the tendency to classify a with b
rather than with c. The values of $D(p, q)$ for each one of the pairs is presented in the
last column of table 3.4. The results show that, in all cases, the replacement of q by p
changed the pairing of a in the expected direction; the average difference is 61.4%.

Table 3.4
Classification and Similarity Data for the Test of the Diagnosticity Hypothesis

	a	b	c	q	p	$b(p) - b(q)$	$c(q) - c(p)$	$D(p,q)$
1	U.S.S.R.	Poland	China	Hungary	India	6.1	24.2	66.7
2	England	Iceland	Belgium	Madagascar	Switzerland	10.4	-7.5	68.8
3	Bulgaria	Czechoslovakia	Yugoslavia	Poland	Greece	13.7	19.2	56.6
4	U.S.A.	Brazil	Japan	Argentina	China	11.2	30.2	78.3
5	Cyprus	Greece	Crete	Turkey	Malta	9.1	-6.1	63.2
6	Sweden	Finland	Holland	Iceland	Switzerland	6.5	6.9	44.1
7	Israel	England	Iran	France	Syria	13.3	8.0	87.5
8	Austria	Sweden	Hungary	Norway	Poland	3.0	15.2	60.0
9	Iran	Turkey	Kuwait	Pakistan	Iraq	-6.1	0.0	58.9
10	Japan	China	W. Germany	N. Korea	U.S.A.	24.2	6.1	66.9
11	Uganda	Libya	Zaire	Algeria	Angola	23.0	-1.0	48.8
12	England	France	Australia	Italy	New Zealand	36.4	15.2	73.3
13	Venezuela	Colombia	Iran	Brazil	Kuwait	0.3	31.5	60.7
14	Yugoslavia	Hungary	Greece	Poland	Turkey	9.1	9.1	76.8
15	Libya	Algeria	Syria	Tunis	Jordan	3.0	24.2	73.2
16	China	U.S.S.R.	India	U.S.A.	Indonesia	30.3	-3.0	42.2
17	France	W. Germany	Italy	England	Spain	-12.1	30.3	74.6
18	Cuba	Haiti	N. Korea	Jamaica	Albania	-9.1	0.0	35.9
19	Luxembourg	Belgium	Monaco	Holland	San Marino	30.3	6.1	52.2
20	Yugoslavia	Czechoslovakia	Austria	Poland	France	3.0	24.2	39.6

Next, we presented two groups of 33 subjects each with 20 sets of four countries in the format displayed in figure 3.3. The subjects were asked to rank, in each quadruple, the three countries below (called the *choice set*) in terms of their similarity to the country on the top (called the *target*). Each group received exactly one quadruple from each pair. If the similarity of b to a, say, is independent of the choice set, then the proportion of subjects who ranked b rather than c as most similar to a should be independent of whether the third element in the choice set is p or q. For example, the proportion of subjects who ranked England rather than Iran as most similar to Israel should be the same whether the third element in the choice set is Syria or France. In contrast, the diagnosticity hypothesis predicts that the replacement of Syria (which is grouped with Iran) by France (which is grouped with England) will affect the ranking of similarity so that the proportion of subjects that ranked England rather than Iran as most similar to Israel is greater in set 1 than in set 2.

Let $b(p)$ denote the percentage of subjects who ranked country b as most similar to a when the odd element in the choice set is p, etc. Recall that b is generally grouped with q, and c is generally grouped with p. The differences $b(p) - b(q)$ and $c(q) - c(p)$, therefore, measure the effects of the odd elements, p and q, on the similarity of b and c to the target a. The value of these differences for all pairs of quadruples are presented in table 3.4. In the absence of context effects, the differences should equal 0, while under the diagnosticity hypothesis, the differences should be positive. In figure 3.3, for example, $b(p) - b(q) = 37.5 - 24.2 = 13.3$, and $c(q) - c(p) = 45.5 - 37.5 = 8$. The average difference across all pairs of quadruples was 11%, which is significantly positive: $t = 6.37$, $df = 19$, $p < .01$.

An additional test of the diagnosticity hypothesis was conducted using a slightly different design. As in the previous study, we constructed pairs of sets that differ in one element only (p or q). Furthermore, the sets were constructed so that b is likely to be grouped with q, and c is likely to be grouped with p. Two groups of 29 subjects were presented with all sets of five countries in the format displayed in figure 3.4. These subjects were asked to select, for each set, the country in the choice set below that is most similar to the two target countries above. Each group received exactly one set of five countries from each pair. Thus the present study differs from the previous one in that: (1) the target consists of a pair of countries (a_1 and a_2) rather than of a single country; and (2) the subjects were instructed to select an element of the choice set that is most similar to the target rather than to rank all elements of the choice set.

The analysis follows the previous study. Specifically, let $b(p)$ denote the proportion of subjects who selected country b as most similar to the two target countries

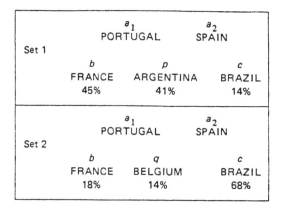

Figure 3.4
Two sets of countries used to test the diagnosticity hypothesis. The percentage of subjects who selected each country (as most similar to the two target countries) is presented below the country.

when the odd element in the choice set was p, etc. Hence, under the diagnosticity hypothesis, the differences $b(p) - b(q)$ and $c(q) - c(p)$ should both be positive, whereas under the assumption of context independence, both differences should equal 0. The values of these differences for all 12 pairs of sets are displayed in table 3.5. The average difference across all pairs equals 10.9%, which is significantly positive: $t = 3.46$, $df = 11$, $p < .01$.

In figure 3.4, for example, France was selected, as most similar to Portugal and Spain, more frequently in set 1 (where the natural grouping is: Brazil and Argentina vs. Portugal, Spain, and France) than in set 2 (where the natural grouping is: Belgium and France vs. Portugal, Spain, and Brazil). Likewise, Brazil was selected, as most similar to Portugal and Spain, more frequently in set 2 than in set 1. Moreover, in this particular example, the replacement of p by q actually reversed the proximity order. In set 1, France was selected more frequently than Brazil; in set 2, Brazil was chosen more frequently than France.

There is considerable evidence that the grouping of objects is determined by the similarities among them. The preceding studies provide evidence for the *converse* (diagnosticity) hypothesis that the similarity of objects is modified by the manner in which they are grouped. Hence, similarity serves as a basis for the classification of objects, but it is also influenced by the adopted classification. The diagnosticity principle that underlies the latter process may provide a key to the understanding of the effects of context on similarity.

Table 3.5
Similarity Data for the Test of the Diagnosticity Hypothesis

	a_1	a_2	b	c	p	q	$b(p) - b(q)$	$c(q) - c(p)$
1	China	U.S.S.R.	Poland	U.S.A.	England	Hungary	18.8	1.6
2	Portugal	Spain	France	Brazil	Argentina	Belgium	27.0	54.1
3	New Zealand	Australia	Japan	Canada	U.S.A.	Philippines	27.2	-12.4
4	Libya	Algeria	Syria	Uganda	Angola	Jordan	13.8	10.3
5	Australia	New Zealand	S. Africa	England	Ireland	Rhodesia	-0.1	13.8
6	Cyprus	Malta	Sicily	Crete	Greece	Italy	0.0	3.4
7	India	China	U.S.S.R.	Japan	Philippines	U.S.A.	-6.6	14.8
8	S. Africa	Rhodesia	Ethiopia	New Zealand	Canada	Zaire	33.4	5.9
9	Iraq	Syria	Lebanon	Libya	Algeria	Cyprus	9.6	20.3
10	U.S.A.	Canada	Mexico	England	Australia	Panama	6.0	13.8
11	Holland	Belgium	Denmark	France	Italy	Sweden	5.4	-8.3
12	Australia	England	Cyprus	U.S.A.	U.S.S.R.	Greece	5.4	5.1

Discussion

The investigations reported in this chapter were based on the contrast model according to which the similarity between objects is expressed as a linear combination of the
measures of their common and distinctive features. The results provide support for the
general hypothesis that the parameters of the contrast model are sensitive to manipulations that make the subject focus on certain features rather than on others. Consequently, similarities are not invariant with respect to the marking of the attribute
(similarity vs. difference), the directionality of the comparison [$s(a, b)$ vs. $s(b, a)$], and
the context (i.e., the set of objects under consideration). In accord with the focusing
hypothesis, study 1 shows that the relative weight attached to the common features is
greater in judgments of similarity than in judgments of difference (i.e., $\theta > \lambda$). Studies
2 and 3 show that people attach greater weight to the subject of a comparison than to
its referent (i.e., $\alpha > \beta$). Studies 4 and 5 show that the salience of features is determined, in part, by their diagnosticity (i.e., by their classificatory significance).

What are the implications of the present findings to the analysis and representation
of similarity relations? First, they indicate that there is no unitary concept of similarity that is applicable to all different experimental procedures used to elicit proximity data. Rather, it appears that there is a wide variety of similarity relations
(defined on the same domain) that differ in the weights attached to the various arguments of the feature-matching function. Experimental manipulations that call attention to the common features, for example, are likely to increase the weight assigned
to these features. Likewise, experimental manipulations (e.g., the introduction of a
standard) that emphasize the directionality of the comparison are likely to produce
asymmetry. Finally, changes in the natural clustering of the objects under study are
likely to highlight those features on which the clusters are based.

Although the violations of complementarity, symmetry, and context independence
are statistically significant and experimentally reliable in the sense that they were
observed with different stimuli under different experimental conditions, the effects are
relatively small. Consequently, complementarity, symmetry, or context independence
may provide good first approximations to similarity data. Scaling models that are
based on these assumptions, therefore, should not be rejected off-hand. A Euclidean
map may provide a very useful and parsimonious description of complex data, even
though its underlying assumptions (e.g., symmetry, or the triangle inequality) may be
incorrect. At the same time, one should not treat such a representation, useful as it
might be, as an adequate psychological theory of similarity. An analogy to the measurement of physical distance illustrates the point. The knowledge that the earth is
round does not prevent surveyors from using plane geometry to calculate small distances on the surface of the earth. The fact that such measurements often provide

excellent approximations to the data, however, should not be taken as evidence for the flat-earth model.

Finally, two major objections have been raised against the usage of the concept of similarity [see e.g., Goodman (1972)]. First, it has been argued that similarity is relative and variable: Objects can be viewed as either similar or different depending on the context and frame of reference. Second, similarity often does not account for our inductive practice but rather is inferred from it; hence, the concept of similarity lacks explanatory power.

Although both objections have some merit, they do not render the concept of similarity empirically uninteresting or theoretically useless. The present studies, like those of Shepard (1964) and Torgerson (1965), show that similarity is indeed relative and variable, but it varies in a lawful manner. A comprehensive theory, therefore, should describe not only how similarity is assessed in a given situation but also how it varies with a change of context. The theoretical development, outlined in this chapter, provides a framework for the analysis of this process.

As for the explanatory function of similarity, it should be noted that similarity plays a dual role in theories of knowledge and behavior: It is employed as an independent variable to explain inductive practices such as concept formation, classification, and generalization; but it is also used as a dependent variable to be explained in terms of other factors. Indeed, similarity is as much a summary of past experience as a guide for future behavior. We expect similar things to behave in the same way, but we also view things as similar because they behave in the same way. Hence, similarities are constantly updated by experience to reflect our ever-changing picture of the world.

References

Goodman, N. Seven strictures on similarity. In N. Goodman, *Problems and projects.* New York: Bobbs-Merril, 1972.

Hosman, J., and Kuennapas, T. On the relation between similarity and dissimilarity estimates. Report No. 354, Psychological Laboratories, The University of Stockholm, 1972.

Quine, W. V. Natural kinds. In W. V. Quine, *Ontological relativity and other essays.* New York: Columbia University Press, 1969.

Restle, F. *Psychology of judgment and choice.* New York: Wiley, 1961.

Rosch, E. Cognitive reference points. *Cognitive Psychology*, 1975, *7*, 532–547.

Shepard, R. N. Attention and the metric structure of the stimulus space. *Journal of Mathematical Psychology*, 1964, *1*, 54–87.

Shepard, R. N. Representation of structure in similarity data: Problems and prospects. *Psychometrika*, 1974, *39*, 373–421.

Sjöberg, L. A cognitive theory of similarity. *Goteborg Psychological Reports*, 1972, *2*(No. 10).

Torgerson, W. S. Multidimensional scaling of similarity. *Psychometrika*, 1965, *30*, 379–393.

Tversky, A. Features of similarity. *Psychological Review*, 1977, *84*, 327–352.

4 Weighting Common and Distinctive Features in Perceptual and Conceptual Judgments

Itamar Gati and Amos Tversky

The proximity between objects or concepts is reflected in a variety of responses including judgments of similarity and difference, errors of identification, speed of recognition. generalization gradient, and free classification. Although the proximity orders induced by these tasks are highly correlated in general, the observed data also reflect the nature of the process by which they are generated. For example, we observed that the digits 6 and 9 are judged as more similar than 6 and 8 although the latter pair is more frequently confused in a recognition task (Keren & Baggen, 1981). Evidently, the fact that 6 and 9 are related by a rotation has a greater impact on rated similarity than on confusability, which is more sensitive to the number of non-matching line segments.

The proximity between objects can be described in terms of their common and their distinctive features, whose relative weight varies with the nature of the task. Distinctive features play a dominant role in tasks that require discrimination. The detection of a distinctive feature establishes a difference between stimuli, regardless of the number of common features. On the other hand, common features appear to play a central role in classification, association, and figurative speech. A common feature can be used to classify objects or to associate ideas, irrespective of the number of distinctive features. Thus, one common feature can serve as a basis for metaphor, whereas one distinctive feature is sufficient to determine nonidentity. In other tasks, such as judgments of similarity and dissimilarity, both common and distinctive features appear to play significant roles.

The present research employs the contrast model (Tversky, 1977) to assess the relative weight of common to distinctive features. In the first part of the article we review the theoretical model, describe the estimation method, and discuss a validation procedure. In the second part of the article we analyze judgment of similarity and dissimilarity of a variety of conceptual and perceptual stimuli.

The contrast model expresses the similarity of objects in terms of their common and distinctive features. In this model, each stimulus i is represented as a set of measurable features, denoted $\mathbf{i}$, and the similarity of i and j is a function of three arguments: $\mathbf{i} \cap \mathbf{j}$, the feature shared by i and j; $\mathbf{i} - \mathbf{j}$, the features of i that do not belong to j; $\mathbf{j} - \mathbf{i}$, the features of j that do not belong to i. The contrast model is based on a set of ordinal assumptions that lead to the construction of (nonnegative) scales g and f defined on the relevant collections of common and distinctive features such that $s(i, j)$, the observed similarity of i and j, is monotonically related to

$$S(i, j) = g(\mathbf{i} \cap \mathbf{j}) - \alpha f(\mathbf{i} - \mathbf{j}) - \beta f(\mathbf{j} - \mathbf{i}), \quad \alpha, \beta > 0. \qquad (1)$$

This model describes the similarity of i and j as a linear combination, or a contrast, of the measures of their common and distinctive features.[1] This form generalizes the original model in which $g(x) = \theta f(x)$, $\theta > 0$. The contrast model represents a family of similarity relations that differ in the degree of asymmetry (α/β) and the weight of the common relative to the distinctive features. The present analysis is confined to the symmetric case where $\alpha = \beta = 1$. Note that the contrast model expresses S as an additive function of g and f, but it does not require that either g or f be additive in their arguments. Evidence presented later in the article indicates that both g and f are subadditive in the sense that $g(xy) < g(x) + g(y)$ where xy denotes the combination or the union of x and y.

Estimation

We distinguish between additive attributes defined by the presence or absence of a particular feature (e.g., mustache), and substitutive attributes (e.g., eye color) defined by the presence of exactly one element from a given set. Some necessary conditions for the characterization of additive attributes are discussed later (see also Gati & Tversky, 1982). Let bpx, bq, bqy, etc., denote stimuli with a common background b, substitutive components p and q, and additive components x and y. That is, each stimulus in the domain includes the same background b, one and only one of the substitutive components, p or q, and any combination of the additive components: x, y, both, or neither. To assess the effect of an additive component x as a common feature, denoted $C(x)$, we add x to both bp and bq and compare the similarity between bpx and bqx to the similarity between bp and bq. The difference between these similarities can be taken as an estimate of $C(x)$. Formally, define

$$
\begin{aligned}
C(x) &= S(bpx, bqx) - S(bp, bq) \\
&= [g(bx) - f(p) - f(q)] - [g(b) - f(p) - f(q)] \quad \text{by (1)} \\
&= g(bx) - g(b) \\
&= g(x)
\end{aligned}
\tag{2}
$$

provided $g(bx) = g(b) + g(x)$. Since the background b is shared by all stimuli in the domain the above equation may hold even when g is not additive in general. Previous research (Gati & Tversky, 1982; Tversky & Gati, 1982) suggests that rated similarity is roughly linear in the derived scale, hence the observed scale s can be used as an approximation of the derived scale S.

To assess the effect of an additive component x as a distinctive feature, denoted $D(x)$, we add x to one stimulus (bp) but not to the other (bpy) and compare the similarity between bp and bpy to the similarity between bpx and bpy. The difference between these similarities can be taken as an estimate of $D(x)$. Formally, define

$$D(x) = S(bp, bpy) - S(bpx, bpy)$$
$$= [g(bp) - f(y)] - [g(bp) - f(x) - f(y)] \quad \text{by (1)} \tag{3}$$
$$= f(x).$$

(We could have estimated $D(x)$ by $s(p, q) - s(px, q)$ but this difference yields $f(px) - f(p)$, which is likely to underestimate $f(x)$ because of subadditivity.)

The impact of x as a common feature relative to its impact as a distinctive feature is defined as

$$W(x) = C(x)/[C(x) + D(x)]$$
$$= g(x)/[g(x) + f(x)], \quad \text{by (2) and (3).} \tag{4}$$

The value of $W(x)$ ranges from 0 (when $C(x) = 0$) to 1 (when $D(x) = 0$), and $W(x) = \frac{1}{2}$ when $C(x) = D(x)$, reflecting the relative weight of common to distinctive features. Unlike $C(x)$ and $D(x)$ that are likely to vary widely depending on the salience of x, $W(x)$ is likely to be more stable across different components and alternative response scales. Note that $C(x)$, $D(x)$, and $W(x)$ are all well defined in terms of the similarity scale S, regardless of the validity of the contrast model and/or the proposed componential analysis. These assumptions are needed, however, to justify the interpretation of $C(x)$ and $D(x)$, respectively, as $g(x)$ and $f(x)$. The componential analysis and the estimation process are illustrated below in terms of a few selected experimental examples.

Figure 4.1 presents two pairs of landscapes (p, q) and (px, qx). Note that p and q are substitutive while x is additive. To simplify the notation we supress the background b that is shared by all stimuli under discussion. Note that the lower pictures are obtained by adding a cloud (x) to the upper pictures. Hence the differences between their similarities provides an estimate of the contribution of a cloud as a common feature.

The similarities between these pictures were rated by the subjects on a scale from 1 (very low similarity) to 20 (very high similarity). Using average similarity we obtained

$$C(x) = s(px, qx) - s(p, q)$$
$$= 5.4 - 4.1 = 1.3.$$

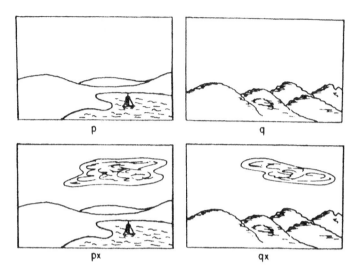

Figure 4.1
Landscapes used to estimate C (p, hills and lake; q, mountain range; x, cloud).

Figure 4.2 presents two other pairs of landscapes (p, py) and (px, py) where the second pair is obtained by adding a cloud (x) to only one element (p) of the first pair. Hence, the difference between the similarities of the two pairs provides an estimate of the contribution of a cloud as a distinctive feature. In our data

$$D(x) = s(p, py) - s(px, py)$$

$$= 15.0 - 11.3 = 3.7.$$

$W(x)$ can now be obtained from $C(x)$ and $D(x)$ by $W(x) = 1.3/(1.3 + 3.7) = .26$. Thus, the addition of the cloud to only one picture reduced their similarity by an amount that is almost three times as large as the increase in similarity obtained by adding it to both pictures. As we shall see later, this is a typical result for pictorial stimuli.

Note that the clouds in the two bottom pictures in figure 4.1 are not identical. Hence, the value of $C(x)$ should be interpreted as the effect of adding *a cloud* to both pictures, not as the effect of adding the *same cloud* to both pictures. Naturally, C, and hence W, will be higher when the critical components are identical than when they are not.

The same estimation procedure can also be applied to verbal stimuli. We illustrate the procedure in a study of similarity of professional and social stereotypes in Israel.

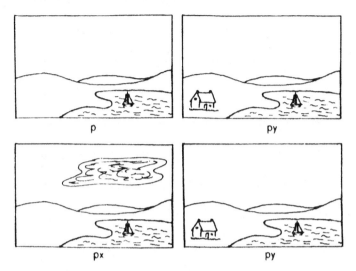

Figure 4.2
Landscapes used to estimate D (p, hills and lake; x, cloud; y, house).

The common background b corresponds to an adult male. The substitutive attributes were a dentist (p) and an accountant (q); the additive attributes were a naturalist (x) and a member of the nationalist party (y). To assess the impact of "naturalist" as a common component, we compared the similarity between "an accountant" and "a dentist," $s(p,q)$, to the similarity between "an accountant who is a naturalist" and a "dentist who is a naturalist," $s(px, qx)$. Using the average rated similarity between descriptions, we obtained

$$C(x) = s(px, qx) - s(p, q)$$

$$= 13.5 - 6.3 = 7.2.$$

To assess the impact of "naturalist" as a distinctive component, we compared the similarity between "an accountant" and "an accountant who is a member of the nationalist party," $s(p, py)$, to the similarity between "an accountant who is a naturalist" and "an accountant who is a member of the nationalist party," $s(px, py)$. In this case,

$$D(x) = s(p, py) - s(px, py)$$

$$= 14.9 - 13.2 = 1.7,$$

and

$$W(x) = 7.2/(7.2 + 1.7) = .81.$$

The addition of the attribute "naturalist" to both descriptions has a much greater impact on similarity than the addition of the same attribute to one description only. The difference in W between pictorial and verbal stimuli is the central topic of this article. Note that the similarities between the basic pairs $s(p, q)$ and $s(p, py)$, to which we added common or distinctive components, respectively, were roughly the same for the pictorial and the verbal stimuli. Hence the difference in W cannot be attributed to variations in baseline similarity.

Independence of Components

The interpretation of $C(x)$ and $D(x)$ in terms of the contribution of x as a common and as a distinctive component, respectively, assumes independence among the relevant components. In the present section we analyze this assumption, discuss the conditions under which it is likely to hold or fail and exhibit four formal properties that are used to detect dependence among components and to validate the proposed estimation procedure. Note that the present concept of independence among features, employed in (2) and (3), does not imply the stronger requirement of additivity.

We use the term "feature" to describe any property, characteristic, or aspect of a stimulus that is relevant to the task under study. The features used to characterize a picture may include physically distinct parts, called components, such as a cloud or a house, as well as abstract global attributes such as symmetry or attractiveness. The same object can be characterized in terms of different sets of features that correspond to different descriptions or different levels of analysis. A face can be described, for example, by its eyes, nose, and mouth and these features may be further analyzed into more basic constituents. In order to simplify the estimation process, we have attempted to construct stimuli with independent components. To verify the independence of components, we examine the following testable conditions:

Positivity of C: $s(px, qx) > s(p, q),$ $\hspace{3cm}$ (5)

that is, the addition of x to both p and q increases similarity.

Positivity of D: $s(p, py) > s(px, py),$ $\hspace{2.8cm}$ (6)

that is, the addition of x to p but not to py decreases similarity. The positivity conditions are satisfied in the preceding examples of landscape drawings and person descriptions, but they do not always hold. For example, ⌐ and ⊓ are judged as more similar than ⊏ and ▢, although the latter pair is obtained from the former by adding the lower horizontal line to both stimuli. Hence, the addition of a common component decreases rather than increases similarity contrary to the positivity of C. This addition, however, results in closing one of the figures, thereby introducing a global distinctive feature (open vs closed). This example shows that the proximity of letters cannot be expressed in terms of their local components (i.e., line segments); they require global features as well (see, e.g., Keren & Baggen, 1981). The positivity of D is also violated in this context: ⊓ is less similar to ⌐ then to ⊏ although the latter contains an additional distinctive component. Conceptual comparisons can violate (6) as well. For example, an accountant who climbs mountains (py) is more similar to an accountant who plays basketball (px) than to an accountant (p) without a specified hobby because the two hobbies (x and y) have features in common. Hence, the addition of a distinctive component (basketball player) increases rather than decreases similarity.

Formally, the hobbies x and y can be expressed as $x = zx'$ and $y = zy'$, where z denotes the features shared by the two hobbies, and x' and y' denote their unique features. Thus, x and y are essentially substitutive rather than additive. Consequently,

$$S(p, py) = g(p) - f(zy')$$

$$S(px, py) = g(pz) - f(y') - f(x').$$

Hence, $D(x) = s(p, py) - s(px, py) < 0$ if the impact of the unique part of x, $f(x')$, is much smaller than the impact of the part shared by x and y, $g(z)$.

These examples, which yield negative estimates of C and D do not invalidate the feature-theoretical approach although they complicate its applications; they show that the experimental operation of adding a component to a pair of stimuli or to one stimulus only may confound common and distinctive features. In particular, the addition of a common component (e.g., a line segment) to a pair of stimuli may also introduce distinctive features and the addition of a distinctive component (e.g., a hobby) may also introduce common features.

In order to validate the interpretation of C and D, we designed stimuli with physically separable components, and we tested the independence of the critical components in each study. More specifically, we tested the positivity of C and of D, (5) and (6), as well as two other ordinal conditions, (7) and (8), that detect interactions among the relevant components.

Exchangeability: $s(px, q) = s(p, qx)$. (7)

In the present studies, the substitutive components were constructed to be about equally salient so that $f(p) = f(q)$. This hypothesis is readily verified by the observation that $s(px, p)$ equals $s(qx, q)$ to a good first approximation. In this case, $s(px, q)$ should equal $s(p, qx)$, that is, exchanging the position of the additive component should not affect similarity. Feature exchangeability (7) fails when a global feature is overlooked. For example, let p and q denote $\sqcap$ and $\sqcap$ and let x denote the lower horizontal line. It is evident that the similarity of $\sqsubset$ and $\sqcap$, $s(px, q)$, exceeds the similarity of $\sqcap$ and $\square$, $s(p, qx)$, contrary to (7), because the distinction between open and closed figures was not taken into account. Exchangeability also fails when the added component, x, has more features in common, say, with p than with q. A naturalist, for example, shares more features with a biologist than with an accountant. Consequently, the similarity between a biologist and an accountant–naturalist is greater than the similarity between an accountant and a biologist–naturalist.

Feature exchangeability, on the other hand, was supported in the comparisons of landscapes and of professionals described in the previous section. Adding the cloud (x) to the mountain (p) or the lake (q) did not have a significant effect on rated similarity. The addition of the attribute "naturalist" (x) to an accountant (p) or a dentist (q) also confirmed feature exchangeability. Because (7) was violated when "dentist" was replaced by "biologist" we can estimate the impact of "naturalist" for the pair "accountant–dentist" but not for the pair "accountant–biologist."

The final test of independence concerns the following inequality

Balance: $s(p, pxy) \geq s(px, py)$.   (8)

According to the proposed analysis $s(p, pxy) = g(p) - f(xy)$, whereas $s(px, py) = g(p) - f(x) - f(y)$. Because f is generally subadditive, or at most additive ($f(xy) \leq f(x) + f(y)$), the above inequality is expected to hold. Indeed, (8) was satisfied in the examples of landscapes and professionals. On the other hand, (8) is violated if the balanced stimuli (px and py) with the same "number" of additive components are more similar than the unbalanced stimuli (p and pxy) that vary in the "number" of additive components. For example, consider trips to several European countries, with a 1-week stay in each. The similarity between a trip to England and France and a trip to England and Italy is greater than the similarity between a trip to England, France, and Italy and a trip to England only. Because the former trips are of equal duration while the latter are not, the unbalanced trips have more distinctive features that reduce their similarity.

The preceding discussion exhibits the major qualitative conditions under which the addition of a physically distinct component to one or to two stimuli can be interpreted as the addition of a distinctive or a common feature, respectively. In the next part of the article we verify these conditions for several domains in order to validate the assessment of *W*.

Experiments

In order to compare the weights of common and of distinctive features in conceptual and perceptual comparisons, it is important to estimate *W* for many different stimuli. In the conceptual domain, we investigated verbal descriptions of people in terms of personality traits, political affinities, hobbies, and professions. We also studied other compound verbal stimuli (meals, farms, symptoms, trips) that can be characterized in terms of separable additive components. In the perceptual domain we investigated schematic faces and landscape drawings. We also studied verbal descriptions of pictorial stimuli.

Method

SUBJECTS   In all studies the subjects were undergraduate students from the Hebrew University between 20 and 30 years old. Approximately equal numbers of males and females took part in the studies.

PROCEDURE   The data were gathered in group sessions, lasting 8 to 15 min. The stimuli were presented in booklets, each page including six pairs of verbal stimuli or two pairs of pictorial stimuli. The ordering of the pairs was randomized with the constraint that identical stimuli did not appear in consecutive pairs. The positions of the stimuli (left–right for pictorial stimuli or top–bottom for verbal stimuli) were counterbalanced and the ordering of pages randomized. The first page of each booklet included the instructions, followed by three to six practice trials to familiarize the subject with the stimuli and the task. Subjects were instructed to assess the similarity between each pair of stimuli on a 20-point scale, where 1 denotes low similarity and 20 denotes very high similarity.

Person Descriptions (Studies 1–3)

In studies 1–3 the stimuli were verbal descriptions of people composed of one substitutive and two additive components (study 1) or three additive components (studies 2 and 3).

Study 1—Professional Stereotypes

STIMULI   Schematic descriptions of people characterized by one substitutive attribute: profession (*p* or *q*) and two additive attributes: hobby (*x*) and political affiliation (*y*) (see table 4.1).

Table 4.1
Stimuli for Study 1—Professionals

	Set			
Attribute	1	2	3	4
Profession				
p	Engineer	Cab driver	High school teacher	Dentist
q	Lawyer	Barber	Tax collector	Accountant
Hobby				
x	Soccer	Chess	Cooking	Naturalist
Political affiliation				
y	Gush Emunim (religious nationalist)	Moked (new left)	Mapam (Socialist)	Herut (nationalist)

DESIGN   Four sets of attributes were employed as shown in table 4.1 and for each set eight descriptions were constructed according to a factorial design with three binary attributes. Thus, each description consisted of one of the two professions, with or without a hobby or political affiliation. A complete design yields 28 pair comparisons for each set. To avoid excessive repetitions, four different booklets were prepared by selecting seven pairs from each set so that each subject was presented with all 28 types of comparisons. The four booklets were randomly distributed among 154 subjects.

RESULTS   The top part of table 4.2 presents the average estimates of $C(x)$ and $D(x)$ for all additive components in all four sets from study 1. Recall that

$$C(x) = s(px, qx) - s(p, q) \quad \text{and}$$

$$D(x) = s(p, py) - s(px, py).$$

Table 4.2 presents estimates of $C(x)$ and of $D(x)$ for all similarity comparisons in which x was added, respectively, to both stimuli or to one stimulus only. We have investigated the independence of all additive components by testing conditions (5) through (8) in the aggregate data. Values of $C(x)$ and of $D(x)$ whose 95% confidence interval includes zero, are marked by $+$. Estimates of $W(x) = C(x)/[C(x) + D(x)]$ are presented only for those additive components which yield positive estimates of C and of D, satisfy balance (8), and do not produce significant violation of exchangeability (7).

All estimates of C and of D were nonnegative and 12 out of 16 were significantly greater than zero by a t test ($p < .05$). Balance was confirmed for all components.

Table 4.2
Estimates of the Relative Weights of Common to Distinctive Features in Judgments of Similarity between Person Descriptions

Study	Stimuli	N		Component	C		D	W
1	Professionals	154		Politics				
	$R_1 = .97$			Relígous nationalist	5.13		2.17	.70
	$R_2 = .97$			New left	5.85		0.44+	.93
	$R_3 = .98$			Socialist	4.36		1.41	.76
	$R_4 = .95$			Nationalist	5.00		0.54+	.90
				Hobby				
				Soccer playing	3.23		0.63+	—
				Chess	4.28		1.75	.71
				Cooking	4.14		0.97+	—
				Naturalist	5.60		1.61	.78
2	Students (set A)	48		Politics				
	$R = .95$		x_1	Religious nationalist	5.00		3.08	.62
			x_2	Socialist	4.56	>	1.73	.72
				Hobbies				
			y_1	Soccer fan	5.40	>	1.44	.79
			y_2	Naturalist	5.90	>	0.27+	—
				Personality				
			z_1	Arrogant	6.10	>	2.88	.68
			z_2	Anxious	4.98	>	2.04	.71
	Students (set B)	46		Politics				
	$R = .95$		x_1	New left	4.04	>	1.41	—
			x_2	Liberal center	3.13		1.26	.71
				Hobby				
			y_1	Soccer fan	4.33	>	0.37+	.92
			y_2	Amateur photographer	3.07	>	0.63+	.83
				Personality				
			z_1	Arrogant	7.28	>	1.33+	.85
			z_2	Outgoing	5.89	>	1.15+	.84
3	Matches	66	x_1	Twice divorced	2.96	>	1.76	.63
	$R = .97$		x_2	Outgoing	2.11	>	0.96+	.69

Note: + Values of C and D that are not statistically different from zero by a *t* test ($p < .05$); —, missing estimates due to failure of independence; >, statistically significant difference between C and D by a *t* test ($p < .05$).

No estimates of W are given for two hobbies where exchangeability was violated. In all eight cases, $C(x)$ was greater than $D(x)$. However, the present design does not yield within-subject estimates of C and D, hence in this study we do not test the significance of the difference between them separately for each component. To obtain an estimate of W within the data of each subject, we have pooled the four different sets of study 1, and computed the average C and D across all additive components for which independence was not rejected in the aggregate data. The median W, within the data of each subject, was .80 and for 77% of the subjects W exceeded $\frac{1}{2}$.

The multiple correlations between the judgments and the best linear combination of the components are given in the left-hand side of table 4.2. The multiple correlations R_1, R_2, R_3, R_4, which refer to the corresponding sets defined in table 4.1, exceed .95 in all cases. Note that, like the preceding analysis, the linear regression model assumes the independence of the critical components and a linear relation between s and S. However, it also requires the additivity of both g and f that is not assumed in the contrast model. The multiple correlation coefficient is reported in the corresponding table for each of the following studies.

Study 2—Students

STIMULI   Stimuli were verbal descriptions of Israeli students with three types of additive attributes: political affiliation, hobbies, and personality traits. Two different attributes of each type were used (see table 4.2, study 2, set A).

DESIGN   For each additive component x_i, $i = 1, 2$, we presented subjects with four pairs of stimuli required to estimate C and D. In the present design, which includes only additive components,

$$C(x_i) = s(x_i y_j, x_i z_j) - s(y_j, z_j) \quad \text{and}$$

$$D(x_i) = s(y_j, y_j z_j) - s(x_i y_j, y_j z_j).$$

Exchangeability was tested by comparing the pairs $s(x_i y_j, z_j)$ and $s(y_j, x_i z_j)$. In addition, each subject also assessed $s(y_j, x_i y_j z_j)$ and $s(x_i y_j, x_i y_j z_j)$. Thus, for each additive component x_i, we constructed 8 pairs of descriptions for a total of 48 pairs. The design was counterbalanced so that half of the subjects evaluated the pairs with $i = j$, and the other half evaluated the pairs with $i \neq j$.

The entire study was replicated using a different set of political affiliations, hobbies, and personality traits (see table 4.2, study 2, set B). Two groups, of 48 and 46 subjects, assessed the similarity between the descriptions from set A and set B, respectively.

RESULTS   The two sets were analyzed separately. For each component x_i, we computed $C(x_i)$ and $D(x_i)$ after pooling the results across the two bases (y_1z_1 and y_2z_2). The values of C and D for each component are displayed in table 4.2.

As in study 1 all estimates of C and of D were nonnegative, and 19 out of 24 estimates were significantly positive. Balance was confirmed for all components. Exchangeability was violated for "naturalist" and for "new left"; hence no estimates of W are given for these components. In all cases, $C(x)$ was greater than $D(x)$ and the difference was statistically significant for 10 out of 12 cases by a t test ($p < .05$). To obtain an estimate of W within the data of each subject, we computed the average C and D across all additive components that satisfy independence. The median W was .71 for set A and .86 for set B, and 73 and 87% of the subjects in sets A and B, respectively, yielded $W > \frac{1}{2}$.

Study 3—Matches

STIMULI   The stimuli were descriptions of people modeled after marriage advertisements in Israeli newpapers. All marriage applicants were male with a college degree, described by various combinations of the attributes:"religious" (y_1), "wealthy" (z_1), "has a doctorate degree" (y_2), and "interested in music"(z_2). The two critical additive attributes were "twice divorced" (x_1) and "outgoing" (x_2).

DESIGN   As in the previous study, 8 pairs were constructed for each critical attribute, hence, the subjects ($N = 66$) assessed the similarity of 16 pairs of descriptions.

RESULTS   Similarity judgments were pooled across bases separately for each critical component: the values of C, D, and W are displayed in table 4.2. For both components exchangeability and balance were confirmed, C and D were positive, and $C(x)$ was greater than $D(x)$. The median W was 57 and for 56% of the subjects exceeded $\frac{1}{2}$.

Compound Verbal Stimuli (Studies 4–7)

In the preceding studies W was greater than $\frac{1}{2}$ for all tested additive components. It could be argued that there might be some ambiguity regarding the interpretation of missing components in person description. For instance, the absence of a political affiliation from a description of a person may be interpreted either as a lack of interest in politics or as missing information that may be filled by a guess, regarding the likely political affiliation of the person in question. The following studies employ other compound verbal stimuli, meals, farms, symptoms, and trips, in which this ambiguity does not arise. For example, a "trip to England and France" does not suggest a visit to an additional country.

Table 4.3
Stimuli for Study 4—Meals

Attribute	Set			
	1	2	3	4
Entree				
p	Steak & French fries	Grilled chicken & rice	Kabab, rice, & beans	Sausages & sauerkraut
q	Veal cutlet & vegetables	Tongue & baked potatoes	Stuffed pepper with meat & rice	Meatballs & macaroni
First course				
x	Mushroom omelet	Onion soup	Tahini & hummus	Deviled egg
Dessert				
y	Chocolate mousse	Almond torte	Baklava	Apricots

Study 4—Meals

STIMULI   The stimuli were descriptions of meals characterized by one substitutive attribute: the entrée (p or q) and two additive attributes: first course (x) and dessert (y, see table 4.3).

DESIGN   All eight possible descriptions were constructed following a factorial design with three binary attributes. Each meal was described by one of the two entrées, with or without a first course and/or dessert. Four sets of eight meals were constructed, as shown in table 4.3. To avoid excessive repetition entailed by a complete pair comparison design, we followed the four-group design employed in study 1. The four booklets were randomly distributed among 100 subjects.

RESULTS   The data were analyzed as in study 1. The values of C, D, and W are displayed in table 4.4. All estimates of C and D were nonnegative, and 14 out of 16 were significantly greater than zero. Exchangeability (7) and balance (8) were confirmed for all attributes, $C(x)$ was greater than $D(x)$ for seven out of eight components. The present design does not yield within-subject estimates of C and D, hence we do not test the significance of the difference between them separately for each component. Table 4.4 also presents the multiple correlations between the judgments and the linear regression model for the four sets of study 4 as well as for studies 5–7. W was computed within the data of each subject as in study 1. The median W was .56, and 54% of the subjects W exceeded $\frac{1}{2}$.

Table 4.4
Estimates of the Relative Weights of Common to Distinctive Features in Judgments of Similarity between Verbal Descriptions of Compound Objects: Meals, Farms, Trips, and Symptoms

Study	Stimuli	N		Component		C		D	W
4	Meals			First course					
	$R_1 = .96$	100		Mushroom omelette		5.08		3.78	.57
	$R_2 = .97$			Onion soup		3.91		1.90	.67
	$R_3 = .97$			Hummus & Tahini		4.87		1.06+	.82
	$R_4 = .98$			Deviled egg		3.52		2.98	.54
				Dessert					
				Chocolate mousse		4.48		3.62	.55
				Almond torte		4.05		3.44	.54
				Baklava		3.14		1.10+	.74
				Apricots		3.01		3.04	.50
5	Farms								
	$R = .96$	79	x_1	Beehive		4.52	>	2.08	.68
			x_2	Fish		3.99		3.04	.57
			x_3	Cows		5.02	>	3.14	.62
			x_4	Chickens		4.49	>	2.34	.66
6	Symptoms								
	$R_A = .95$	90	x_1	Nausea	m-	6.12	>	0.84+	.88
			x_2	Mild headache		3.64	>	−0.54+	—
	$R_B = .96$	87	x_3	Rash		5.74	>	2.12	.73
			x_4	Diarrhea		5.32	>	1.74	—
7	Trips								
	$R = .93$	87	x_1	France		4.56	>	0.44+	.91
			x_2	Ireland		3.66	>	1.63	.69
			x_3	England		3.57		3.23	.53
			x_4	Denmark		4.82	>	2.25	.68

Note: + Values of C and D that are not statistically different from zero by a t test ($p < .05$); —, missing estimates due to failure of independence; >, statistically significant difference between C and D by a t test ($p < .05$).

Study 5—Farms

STIMULI Stimuli were descriptions of farms characterized by 1, 2, or 3 additive components: vegetables (y_1), peanuts (z_1), wheat (y_2), cotton (z_2), beehive (x_1), fish (x_2), vineyard (y_3), apples (z_3), strawberries (y_4), flowers (z_4), cows (x_3), and chickens (x_4).

DESIGN For each critical component x_i, $i = 1, \ldots, 4$, we presented subjects with the following four pairs of stimuli required to estimate C and D:

$$C(x_i) = s(x_i y_j, x_i z_j) - s(y_j, z_j) \quad \text{and}$$

$$D(x_i) = s(y_j, y_j z_j) - s(x_i y_j, y_j z_j).$$

Exchangeability was tested by comparing the pairs $s(x_i y_j, z_j)$ and $s(y_j, x_i z_j)$. In addition, each subject also assessed $s(y_j, x_i y_j z_j)$ and $s(x_i y_j, x_i y_j z_j)$. Thus, for each additive component x_i, 8 pairs of descriptions were constructed for a total of 32 pairs. The design was counterbalanced so that about half of the subjects ($N = 39$) compared the pairs with $i = j$; the other half ($N = 40$) compared the pairs obtained by interchanging x_1 with x_2, and x_3 with x_4.

RESULTS   The data analysis followed that of study 2. The values of C, D, and W are displayed in table 4.4. All estimates of C and D were significantly positive. Exchangeability (7) and balance (8) were confirmed for all attributes. $C(x)$ was significantly greater than $D(x)$ for three components. The median W, within the data of each subject, was .72, and for 66% of the subjects W exceeded $\frac{1}{2}$.

Study 6—Symptoms

STIMULI   Stimuli were two sets of medical symptoms. Set A included cough (y_1), rapid pulse (z_1), side pains (y_2), general weakness (z_2), nausea and vomiting (x_1), mild headache (x_2). Set B included fever (y_3), side pains (z_3), headache (y_4), cold sweat (z_4), rash (x_3), diarrhea (x_4).

DESIGN   The study 3 design was used; $N = 90$ in set A and $N = 87$ in set B.

RESULTS   The data of each set were analyzed separately; the results are displayed in table 4.4. Balance was confirmed for all components. No estimates of W for "mild headache" and for "diarrhea" are presented since D was not positive for the former, and exchangeability (7) was violated for the latter. For the two other symptoms all conditions of independence were satisfied. $C(x)$ was significantly greater than $D(x)$ for all four critical components. The median W, within the data of each subject, was .78 in set A and .66 in set B, and 70 and 69% of the subjects in sets A and B, respectively, yielded $W > \frac{1}{2}$.

Study 7—Trips

STIMULI   Stimuli were descriptions of trips consisting of visits to one, two, or three European countries; the duration of each trip was 17 days. The components were Switzerland (y_1), Italy (z_1), Austria (y_2), Romania (z_2), France (x_1), Ireland (x_2), Spain (y_3), Greece (z_3), Sweden (y_4), Belgium (z_4), England (x_3), Denmark (x_4).

DESIGN   The study 5 design was used: $N = 87$.

RESULTS   The data were analyzed as in study 5, and the results are displayed in table 4.4. All estimates of C and D were positive and only one was not statistically signifi-

Figure 4.3
Faces.

cant. Exchangeability (7) and balance (8) were confirmed for all attributes. $C(x)$ was significantly greater than $D(x)$ for three components. The median W, within the data of each subject, was .68, and for 68% of the subjects W exceeded $\frac{1}{2}$.

Discussion of Studies 1–7
The data from studies 1–7 are generally compatible with the contrast model and the proposed componential analysis: judged similarity increased with the addition of a common feature and decreased with the addition of a distinctive feature. Furthermore, with few exceptions, the additive components under discussion satisfied the conditions of independence, that is, they yielded positive C and D, and they confirmed exchangeability and balance. The multiple regression analysis provided further support for the independence of the components and for the linearity of the response scale. The major finding of the preceding studies is that $C(x) > D(x)$, or W exceeded $\frac{1}{2}$, for all tested components except one. In the next set of studies, we estimate W from similarity judgments between pictorial stimuli and explore the effect of stimulus modality on the relative weight of common to distinctive features.

Pictorial Stimuli (Studies 8–11)

Study 8—Faces

STIMULI   Stimuli were schematic faces with 1, 2, or 3 additive components: beard (x), glasses (y), hat (z). The eight stimuli are displayed in figure 4.3.

Table 4.5
Estimates of the Relative Weight of Common to Distinctive Features in Judgments of Similarity between Pictorial Stimuli: Faces, Profiles, Figures, Landscapes, and Sea Scenes

Study	Stimuli	N	Component	C		D	W
8	Faces						
	$R = .97$	60	Beard	1.88	<	3.68	.34
			Glasses	0.08+	<	3.52	.02
			Hat	0.28+	<	2.83	.09
9	Profiles						
	$R = .98$	97	Mouth	2.15	<	3.87	.36
			Eyebrow	1.50	<	4.09	.27
10	Landscapes A						
	$R = .99$	85	Cloud	2.28	<	3.71	.38
			Tree	2.32	<	4.24	.35
	Landscapes B						
	$R = .99$	77	Cloud	1.30	<	3.70	.26
			House	1.23	<	4.26	.22
11	Sea scenes						
	$R = .84$	34	Island	1.94	<	3.59'	.35'
			Boat	1.26+	<	3.85'	.25'

Note: + Values of C and D that are not statistically different from zero by a t test ($p < .05$); >, statistically significant difference between C and D by a t test ($p < .05$); ', estimates based on D' rather than on D.

DESIGN   For each additive component x, the subject assessed the similarity of the following five pairs: (y, z), (yx, z), (xy, xz), (y, yz), (xyz, xy). All subjects ($N = 60$) evaluated 5×3 pairs.

RESULTS   In the present design, which includes three additive components, the following comparisons were used:

$$C(x) = s(xy, xz) - s(y, z)$$

$$D(x) = s(y, yz) - s(xy, yz).$$

Exchangeability was tested by comparing $s(xy, z)$ and $s(y, xz)$. Balance was tested by comparing $D'(x)$ defined as $s(y, z) - s(y, xz)$ with $D(x)$. As in (8), because f is generally subadditive, we expect $D(x) > D'(x)$. Thus, $D(x) < D'(x)$ indicates a violation of balance.

The results are displayed in table 4.5. All six estimates of C and of D were positive and four of them were statistically significant. Exchangeability and balance were confirmed for all attributes. $D(x)$ was significantly greater than $C(x)$ for all compo-

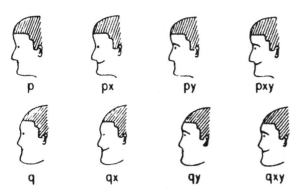

Figure 4.4
Profiles.

nents. The median within-subject W was .06, and for 78% of the subjects W was less than $\frac{1}{2}$.

Study 9—Profiles

STIMULI   Stimuli were eight schematic profiles following a factorial design with three binary attributes: profile type (p or q), mouth (x), eyebrow (y). Each stimulus was characterized by one of the two profiles and by the presence or absence of a mouth and/or an eyebrow. The set of all eight profiles is presented in figure 4.4.

DESIGN   All 28 possible pairs of profiles were presented to 97 subjects.

RESULTS   The data were analyzed as in study 1 and the results are displayed in table 4.5. All estimates of C and D were significantly positive and exchangeability and balance were also confirmed. As in the previous study, $D(x)$ was significantly greater than $C(x)$ for both attributes. The median within-subject W was .35, and for 72% of the subjects W was less than $\frac{1}{2}$.

Study 10—Landscapes

STIMULI   Stimuli were two sets of landscapes drawings. Set A is displayed in figure 4.5 and set B in figure 4.1. In each set the background was substitutive: hills (p) or mountains (q). The additive components in set A were a cloud (x) and a tree (y). The additive components in set B were a cloud (x) and a house (y).

DESIGN   Twelve pairs of stimuli were constructed for each set of stimuli: (p, q), (xp, xq), (yp, yq), (xyp, xyq), (xp, yp), (p, yp), (p, xyp), (p, xp), (px, q), (p, qx),

Figure 4.5
Landscapes (set A).

(py, q), (p, qy). Eighty-five subjects rated the similarity between pairs of set A and seventy-seven subjects rated the similarity between the pairs of set B.

RESULTS   The data were analyzed separately in each set. Table 4.5 presents the values of $C(x)$, $D(x)$, $C(y)$, and $D(y)$, all of which were significantly positive. Exchangeability and balance were also confirmed. $D(x)$ was significantly greater than $C(x)$ for both attributes in each set. Note that in set A the same cloud was added to both pictures, whereas in set B different clouds were used. The results reflect this difference: while $D(x)$ was almost the same for both sets, $C(x)$ was substantially higher in set A where the clouds were identical than in set B where they were not. The median within-subject W was .42 for set A and .36 for set B, and 59 and 71% of the subjects, respectively, yielded $W < \frac{1}{2}$.

Study 11—Sea Scenes

STIMULI   Stimuli were drawings of sea scenes characterized by one substitutive attribute: calm sea (p) or stormy sea (q), and two additive attributes: island (x) and/or boat (y). Figure 4.6 displays two stimuli: qx and py.

DESIGN   The design was identical to that of study 10, $N = 34$.

RESULTS   The data were analyzed as in study 10. Tests of independence showed that exchangeability was confirmed, but balance was violated. Specifically, $s(px, py)$ was greater than $s(p, pxy)$, presumably because the addition of an island (x) to p but not to py introduces a common (a large object in the sea) as well as a distinctive feature. As a consequence, the values of $D(x)$ were not always positive. Hence the following procedure was used to estimate $f(x)$:

$$D'(x) = S(p, py) - S(p, pxy)$$
$$= g(p) - f(y) - [g(p) - f(xy)]$$
$$= f(xy) - f(y).$$

This procedure provides a proper estimate of $f(x)$ whenever f is approximately additive. The subadditivity of f, however, makes $D'(x)$ an underestimate of $f(x)$, whereas the violation of balance implied by $s(p, pxy) < s(px, py)$ makes $D'(x)$ an overestimate of $f(x)$. The obtained values of D' and $W' = C/(C + D')$ should be interpreted in light of these considerations. The values of C, D', and W' are displayed in table 4.5. The values of C and D' were all positive, three were significantly positive, and $D'(x)$ was significantly greater than $C(x)$ for both components. The median within-subject W' was .35, and for 69% of the subjects W' was less than $\frac{1}{2}$.

Discussion of Studies 8–11

The data from studies 8–11 were generally compatible with the proposed analysis and the conditions of independence were satisfied by most additive components, as in studies 1–7. The major difference between the two sets of studies is that the values of W were below $\frac{1}{2}$ for the pictorial stimuli and above $\frac{1}{2}$ for the verbal stimuli. To test whether this difference is attributable to modality or to content we constructed verbal analogs for two of the pictorial stimuli (faces and sea scenes) and compared W across modality for matched stimuli.

Verbal Analogs of Pictorial Stimuli (Studies 12–15)

Study 12—Verbal Description of Faces

STIMULI Stimuli were verbal descriptions of schematic faces with three additive components: beard, glasses, hat, designed to match the faces of figure 4.3.

DESIGN Design was the same as in study 8, $N = 46$.

PROCEDURE The subjects were instructed to assess the similarity between pairs of verbal descriptions. They were asked to assume that in addition to the additive features, each schematic face is characterized by a circle with two dots for eyes, a line for a mouth, a nose, ears, and hair. The subject then evaluated the similarity between, say, "A face with a beard and glasses" (xy) and "A face with glasses and a hat" (xz).

RESULTS The estimates of C, D, and W for each component are displayed in table 4.6. For all components $C(x)$ was significantly positive, but $D(x)$ was not. Exchange-

Table 4.6
Estimates of the Relative Weights of Common to Distinctive Features in Judgments of Similarity between
Verbal Descriptions of Pictorial Stimuli: Schematic Faces and Sea Scenes

Study	Stimuli	N	Component	C		D	W
12	Faces						
	$R = .98$	46	Beard	3.44	>	0.48+	.88
			Glasses	2.41	>	−0.02+	—
			Hat	2.94	>	0.46+	.86
13	Faces (imagery)						
	$R = .92$	39	Beard	6.08	>	1.45	.81
			Glasses	5.76	>	1.74	.77
			Hat	4.63	>	1.66	.74
14	Sea scenes						
	$R = .97$	44	Island	1.75		0.95+′	.65′
			Boat	1.89		0.77+′	.71′
15	Sea scenes (imagery)						
	$R = .72$	42	Island	1.55		1.55′	.50′
			Boat	1.88		2.79′	.40′

Note: + Values of C and D that are not statistically different from zero by a t test ($p < .05$); —, missing estimates due to failure of independence; >, statistically significant difference between C and D by a t test ($p < .05$); ′, estimates based on D' rather than on D.

ability and balance were confirmed in all cases. As in the conceptual rather than the perceptual comparisons, the values of $C(x)$ were significantly greater than $D(x)$ for all three components. Since D (glasses) was not positive, W was not computed for this component. The median within-subject W was .80, and for 70% of the subjects W exceeded $\frac{1}{2}$.

Study 13—Imagery of Faces

PROCEDURE   Study 13 was identical to study 12 in all respects except that the subjects ($N = 39$) first rated the similarity between the drawings of the schematic faces (figure 4.3) following the procedure described in study 8. Immediately afterward they rated the similarity between the verbal descriptions of these faces following the procedure described in study 12. These subjects, then, were able to imagine the pictures of the faces while evaluating their verbal descriptions.

RESULTS   The data were analyzed as in study 12 and the values of C, D, and W are displayed in table 4.6. All estimates of C and D were significantly positive. Exchangeability and balance were also confirmed. As in study 12, $C(x)$ was significantly greater than $D(x)$ for all three components. The median within-subject W was .80, and for 74% of the subjects W exceeded $\frac{1}{2}$.

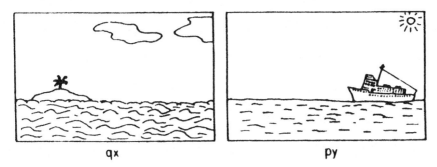

Figure 4.6
Sea scenes.

Study 14—Verbal Descriptions of Sea Scenes

STIMULI   Stimuli were verbal descriptions of sea scenes designed to match the pictures of study 11, see figure 4.6.

DESIGN   Design was the same as in study 11, $N = 44$. Subjects were instructed to rate the similarity between verbal descriptions of "sea scenes of the type that appear in children's books."

RESULTS   The data were analyzed as in study 11, and the values of C, D, and W are displayed in table 4.6. Exchangeability was confirmed, but, as in study 11, balance was violated for both island and boat precisely in the same manner. Consequently, D' was used instead of D. All estimates of C and D' were positive, the estimates of C significantly, but the differences between C and D' were not statistically significant. The median within-subject $W' = C/(C + D')$ was .57, and for 49% of the subjects W' exceeded $\frac{1}{2}$.

Study 15—Imagery of Sea Scenes

PROCEDURE   Study 15 was identical to study 14 in all respects except that the subjects ($N = 42$) were first presented with the pictures shown in figure 4.6 that portrays a boat on a calm sea, and an island in a stormy sea. The subjects had 2 min to look at the drawings. They were then given a booklet containing the verbal descriptions of the sea scenes used in study 14, with the following instructions:

In this questionnaire you will be presented with verbal descriptions of sea scenes of the type you have seen. Your task is to imagine each of the described scenes as concretely as possible according to the examples you just saw, and to judge the similarity between them.

Table 4.7
Comparison of the Weights of Common and Distinctive Features in Different Modalities

Stimuli	Component	Modality			t
		Verbal $C - D$	Imagery $C - D$	Pictorial $C - D$	
Faces	Beard	2.96	4.63	−1.80	3.72**
	Glasses	2.43	4.02	−3.43	4.31**
	Hat	2.48	2.97	−2.55	4.96**
Sea scenes	Island	0.80	0.00	−1.65	1.70*
	Boat	1.11	−0.90	−2.59	2.54**

* $p < .05$.
** $p < .01$.

Each verbal description was preceded by the phrase "Imagine ____" e.g., "Imagine a boat on a calm sea," "Imagine an island in a stormy sea."

RESULTS   The data were analyzed as in studies 11 and 14. Exchangeability was confirmed, but balance was violated as in studies 11 and 14. The values of C, D', and W' for each component are displayed in table 4.6. All estimates of C and D' were significantly positive but the differences between C and D' were not statistically significant. The median within-subject W' was .57, and for 48 percent of the subjects W' exceeded $\frac{1}{2}$.

Discussion of Studies 12–15
The results of studies 12 and 14 yielded $W > \frac{1}{2}$, indicating that verbal descriptions of faces and sea scenes were evaluated like other verbal stimuli, not like their pictorial counterparts. This result supports the hypothesis that the observed differences in W are due, in part at least, to modality and that they cannot be explained by the content of the stimuli. The studies of imagery (studies 13 and 15) yielded values of W that are only slightly lower than the corresponding estimates for the verbal stimuli (see table 4.6).

   To examine the difference between the verbal and the pictorial conditions we computed $C(x) - D(x)$ for each subject, separately for each component. These values are presented in table 4.7 along with the t statistic used to test the difference between the verbal and the pictorial stimuli. Table 4.7 shows that in all five comparisons $C - D$ was significantly higher in the verbal than in the pictorial condition.

Individual Differences
Although the present study did not focus on individual differences, we obtained individual estimates of W for a group of 88 subjects who rated the similarity of (a)

schematic faces (figure 4.3), (b) verbal descriptions of these faces (study 12), and (c) descriptions of students (study 2, set A). The product–moment correlations, across subjects, were $r_{ab} = .20$, $r_{ac} = .15$, $r_{bc} = .14$.

Judgments of Dissimilarity

We have replicated three of the conceptual studies and two of the perceptual studies using rating of dissimilarity instead of rating of similarity. The results are summarized in table 4.8. As in the previous studies, the verbal stimuli yielded $C > D$ for most components (11 out of 14), whereas the pictorial stimuli yielded $C < D$ in all five cases. The estimates of W within the data of each subject revealed the same pattern.

A comparison of similarity and dissimilarity judgments shows that $C - D$ was greater in the former than in the latter task in 12 out of 13 conceptual comparisons ($t(12) = 5.35, p < .01$) and in 3 out of 5 perceptual comparisons (n.s.).

Subadditivity of C and D

The design of the present studies allows a direct test of the subadditivity of g and f, namely, that the contribution of a common (distinctive) feature decreases with the presence of additional common (distinctive) features. To test this hypothesis, define

$$C'(x) = S(pxy, qxy) - S(py, qy)$$
$$= [g(xy) - f(p) - f(q)] - [g(y) - f(p) - f(q)]$$
$$= g(xy) - g(y),$$

and

$$D'(x) = S(p, py) - S(p, pxy)$$
$$= [g(p) - f(y)] - [g(p) - f(xy)]$$
$$= f(xy) - f(y).$$

Hence, $C'(x)$ and $D'(x)$, respectively, provide estimates of the contribution of x as a second (in addition to y) common or distinctive feature. If g and f are subadditive, then $C(x) > C'(x)$ and $D(x) > D'(x)$. In the verbal stimuli, $C(x)$ exceeded $C'(x)$ in all 42 components, with a mean difference of 2.99, $t(41) = 19.79$, $p < .01$; $D(x)$ exceeded $D'(x)$ in 29 out of 42 components, with a mean difference of 0.60, $t(41) = 3.55$, $p < .01$. In the pictorial stimuli $C(x)$ exceeded $C'(x)$ in 6 out of 9 components, with a mean difference of 0.54, $t(8) = 1.71$, n.s.; $D(x)$ exceeded $D'(x)$ in 7 out of 9 comparisons, with a mean difference of 1.04, $t(8) = 2.96$, $p < .01$. Study

Table 4.8
Estimates of the Relative Weights of Common to Distinctive Features in Judgments of Dissimilarity

Stimuli	N		Component	C		D	W
Verbal							
Students							
(Study 2, set A)	45		Politics				
$R = .93$		x_1	Religious nationalist	2.89		4.51	0.39
		x_2	Socialist	2.40		0.82+	0.75
			Hobbies				
		y_1	Soccer Fan	3.71	>	−0.31+	(1.00)
		y_2	Naturalist	3.29		1.93	—
			Personality				
		z_1	Anxious	2.31		1.26	0.65
		z_2	Nervous	4.24		2.53	0.63
Farms							
(Study 5)	50	x_1	Beehive	4.86		3.16	0.61
$R = .96$		x_2	Fish	3.22		3.70	0.47
		x_3	Cows	3.66		4.16	0.47
		x_4	Chickens	3.86		3.50	0.52
Trips							
(Study 7)	44	x_1	France	4.09	>	1.36	0.75
$R = .90$		x_2	Ireland	2.61		1.64	0.61
		x_3	England	3.09		2.80	0.53
		x_4	Denmark	3.07		1.89	0.62
Pictorial							
Faces							
(Study 8)	46		Beard	0.52+	<	3.65	0.12
$R = .96$			Glasses	0.76+	<	3.80	0.17
			Hat	0.00+	<	3.30	0.00
Landscapes							
(Study 11, set B)	21		Clouds	0.71+	<	3.57	0.17
$R = .99$			House	0.62+	<	2.71	0.19

Note: + Values of C and D that are not statistically different from zero by a t test ($p < .05$); —, missing estimates due to failure of independence; >, statistically significant difference between C and D by a t test ($p < .05$).

11, where D' was used instead of D, was excluded from this analysis. As expected, the subadditivity of C was more pronounced in the conceptual domain, whereas the subadditivity of D was more pronounced in the perceptual domain.

Discussion

In the first part of this chapter we developed a method for estimating the relative weight W of common to distinctive features for independent components of separable stimuli. In the second part of the chapter we applied this method to several conceptual and perceptual domains. The results may be summarized as follows: (a) the independence assumption was satisfied by many, though not all, components; (b) in verbal stimuli, common features were generally weighted more heavily than distinctive features; (c) in pictorial stimuli, distinctive features were generally weighted more heavily than common features; (d) in verbal descriptions of pictorial stimuli, as in verbal stimuli, common features were weighted more heavily than distinctive features; (e) similarity judgments yielded higher estimates of W than dissimilarity judgments, particularly for verbal stimuli; (f) the impact of any common (distinctive) feature decreases with the addition of other common (distinctive) features. An overview of the results is presented in figure 4.7, which displays the estimates of W of all components for both judgments.

These findings suggest the presence of two different modes of comparison of objects that focus either on their common or on their distinctive features. In the first mode, the differences between the stimuli are acknowledged and one searches for common features. In the second mode, the commonalities between the objects are treated as background and one searches for distinctive features. The near-perfect separation between the verbal and the pictorial stimuli, summarized in figure 4.7, suggests that conceptual comparisons follow the first mode that focuses on common features while perceptual comparisons follow the second mode that focuses on distinctive features.

This hypothesis is compatible with previous findings. Keren and Baggen (1981) investigated recognition errors among rectangular digits, and reanalyzed confusion among capital letters (obtained by Gilmore, Hersh, Caramazza, & Griffin, 1979). Using a linear model, where the presence or absence of features were represented by dummy variables, they found that distinctive features were weighted more than twice as much as common features for both digits and letters. An unpublished study by Yoav Cohen of confusion among computer-generated letters (described in Tversky, 1977) found little or no effect of common features and a large effect of distinctive

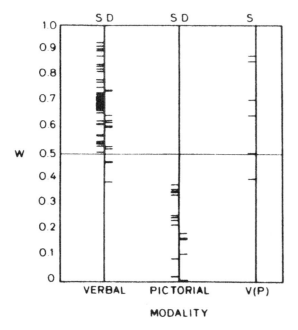

Figure 4.7
Distribution of W in verbal and pictorial comparisons. V(P) refers to verbal descriptions of pictorial stimuli
(S—Similarity, D—Dissimilarity).

features. A different pattern of results emerged from studies of similarity and typicality in semantic categories. Rosch and Mervis (1975) found that the judged typicality of an instance (e.g., robin) of a category (e.g., bird) is highly correlated with the total number of elicited features that a robin shares with other birds. A different study based on elicited features (reported in Tversky, 1977) found that the similarity between vehicles was better predicted by their common than by their distinctive features.

The finding of greater W for verbal than for pictorial stimuli is intriguing but the exact locus of the effect is not entirely clear. Several factors, including the design, the task, the display, the interpretation and the modality of the stimuli, may all contribute to the observed results. We shall discuss these factors in turn from least to most pertinent for the modality hypothesis.

Baseline Similarity
The relative impact of any common or distinctive feature depends on baseline similarity. If the comparison stimuli are highly similar, one is likely to focus primarily on

their distinctive features; if the comparison stimuli are dissimilar, one is likely to focus primarily on their common features. This shift of focus is attributable to the subadditivity of g and f that was demonstrated in the previous section. The question arises, then, whether the difference in W between verbal and pictorial stimuli can be explained by the difference in baseline similarity.

This hypothesis was tested in the matched studies (8 vs 13 and 11 vs 15) in which the subjects evaluated verbal stimuli (faces and sea scenes) after seeing their pictorial counterparts. The analysis of schematic faces revealed that the average similarity of the pair (p, q), to which we added a common feature, was much higher for the pictures (10.6) than for their verbal descriptions (4.9), and the average similarity for the pair (p, py), to which we added a distinctive feature, was also higher for the pictures (14.7) than for their verbal descriptions (12.1). Thus, the rated similarity between the verbal descriptions was substantially lower than that between the pictures, even though the verbal stimuli were evaluated after the pictures. Consequently, the difference in W for schematic faces may be explained by variation in baseline similarity. However, the analysis of sea scenes did not support this conclusion. Despite a marked difference in W between the verbal and the pictorial stimuli, the analysis showed no systematic difference in baseline similarity. The average similarity $s(p, q)$ was 9.9 and 9.2, respectively, for the pictorial and the verbal stimuli; the corresponding values of $s(p, py)$ were 11.4 and 11.8.

There is further evidence that the variation in W cannot be attributed to the variations in baseline similarity. A comparison of person descriptions (studies 1 and 2) with the landscapes (study 11, sets A and B), for example, shows a marked difference in W despite a rough match in baseline similarities. The average similarity, $s(p, q)$, was actually lower for landscapes (4.9) than for persons (6.2), and the average similarities $s(p, py)$ were 14.4 and 14.1, respectively. Furthermore, we obtained similar values of W for faces and landscapes although the baseline similarities for landscapes were substantially higher. We conclude that the basic difference between verbal and pictorial stimuli cannot be explained by baseline similarity alone.

Task Effect

We have proposed that judgments of similarity focus on common features whereas judgments of dissimilarity focus on distinctive features. This hypothesis was confirmed for both verbal and pictorial stimuli (see figure 4.7 and Tversky & Gati, 1978, 1982). If the change of focus from common to distinctive features can be produced by explicit instructions (i.e., to rate similarity or dissimilarity), perhaps it can also be produced by an implicit suggestion induced by the task that is normally performed in the two modalities. Specifically, it could be argued that verbal stimuli are usually categorized (e.g., Linda is an active feminist), a task that depends primarily on common features. On the other hand, pictorial stimuli often call for a discrimination (e.g., looking for a friend in a crowd), a task that depends primarily on distinctive features. If similarity judgments reflect the weighting associated with the task that is typically applied to the stimuli in question, then the difference in W may be attributed to the predominance of categorization in the conceptual domain and to the prevalence of discrimination in the perceptual domain. This hypothesis implies that the difference between the two modalities should be considerably smaller in tasks (e.g., recall or generalization) that are less open to subjective interpretation than judgments of similarity and dissimilarity.

Processing Considerations

The verbal stimuli employed in the present studies differ from the pictorial ones in structure as well as in form: they were presented as lists of separable objects or adjectives and not as integrated units like faces or scenes. This difference in structure could affect the manner in which the stimuli are processed and evaluated. In particular, the verbal components are more likely to be processed serially and evaluated in a discrete fashion, whereas the pictorial components are more likely to be processed in parallel and evaluated in a more "holistic" fashion. As a consequence, common components may be more noticeable in the verbal realm—where they retain their separate identity—than in the perceptual realm—where they tend to fade into the general common background. This hypothesis, suggested to us by Lennart Sjöberg, can be tested by varying the representation of the stimuli. In particular, one may construct pictorial stimuli (e.g., mechanical drawings) that induce a more discrete and serial processing. Conversely, one may construct "holistic" verbal stimuli by embedding the critical components in an appropriately devised story, or by using words that express a combination of features (e.g., bachelor, as an unmarried male).

Interpretation

A major difference between verbal and pictorial representations is that words designate objects while pictures depict them. A verbal code is merely a conventional symbol for the object it designates. In contrast, a picture shares many features with the object it describes. There is a sense in which pictorial stimuli are "all there" while the comprehension of verbal stimuli requires retrieval or construction, which demands additional mental effort. It is possible, then, that both the presence and the absence of features are treated differently in a depictive system than in a designative system. This hypothesis suggests that different interpretations of the same picture could affect W. For example, the same visual display is expected to yield higher W when it is interpreted as a symbolic code than when it is interpreted only as a pattern of dots.

Figure 4.8
Faces.

Modality

Finally, it is conceivable that the difference between pictorial and verbal stimuli observed in the present studies is due, in part at least, to an inherent difference between pictures and words. In particular, studies of divided visual field (see, e.g., Beaumont, 1982) suggest that "the right hemisphere is better specialized for difference detection, while the left hemisphere is better specialized for sameness detection" (Egath & Epstein, 1972, p. 218). The observed difference in W may reflect the correspondence between cerebral hemisphere and stimulus modality.

Whatever the cause of the difference in W between verbal and pictorial stimuli, variations in W within each modality are also worth exploring. Consider, for example, the schematic faces displayed in figure 4.8, which were included in study 8. It follows from (1) that the top face (bx) will be classified with the enriched face ($bxyz$) of W is sufficiently large, and that it will be classified with the basic face (b) if W is small. Variations in W could reflect differences in knowledge and outlook: children may produce higher values than adults, and novices may produce higher values than more knowledgeable respondents.

The assessments of C, D, and W are based on the contrast model (Tversky, 1977). Initially we applied this model to the analysis of asymmetric proximities, of the discrepancy between similarity and dissimilarity judgments, and of the role of diagnosticity and the effect of context (Tversky & Gati, 1978). These analyses were based on qualitative properties and they did not require a complete specification of the relevant feature space. Further analyses of qualitative and quantitative attributes (Gati & Tversky, 1982; Tversky & Gati, 1982) incorporated additional assumptions regarding the separability of attributes and the representation of qualitative and quantitative dimensions, respectively, as chains and nestings. The present chapter extends previous applications of the contrast model in two directions. First, we employed a more general form of the model in which the measures of the common and the distinctive features (g and f) are no longer proportional. Second, we investigated a particular class of separable stimuli with independent components. Although the separability of the stimuli and the independence of components do not always hold, we were able to identify a variety of stimuli in which these assumptions were satisfied, to a reasonable degree of approximation. In these cases it was possible to estimate g and f for several critical components and to compare the obtained valued of W across domains, tasks, and modalities. The contrast model, in conjunction with the proposed componential analysis, provides a method for analyzing the role of common and of distinctive features, which may illuminate the nature of conceptual and perceptual comparisons.

Notes

This research was supported by a grant from the United States–Israel Binational Science Foundation (BSF). Jerusalem, Israel. The preparation of this report was facilitated by the Goldie Rotman Center for Cognitive Science in Education of the Hebrew University. We thank Efrat Neter for her assistance throughout the study.

1. Equation (1) is derived from the original theory by deleting the invariance axiom (Tversky, 1977, p. 351).

References

Beaumont, J. G. (1982). *Divided visual field studies of cerebral organization*. London: Academic Press.

Egath, H., & Epstein, J. (1972). Differential specialization of the cerebral hemispheres for the perception of sameness and difference. *Perception and Psychophysics*, 12, 218–220.

Gati, I., & Tversky, A. (1982). Representations of qualitative and quantitative dimensions. *Journal of Experimental Psychology: Human Perception and Performance*, 8, 325–340.

Gilmore, G. C., Hersh, H., Caramazza, A., & Griffin, J. (1979). Multidimensional letter recognition derived from recognition errors. *Perception & Psychophysics*, 25, 425–431.

Keren, G., & Baggen, S. (1981). Recognition models of alphanumeric characters. *Perception & Psychophysics*, 29, 234–246.

Rosch, E., & Mervis, C. B. (1975). Family resemblances: Studies in the internal structure of categories. *Cognitive Psychology*, 7, 573–605.

Tversky, A. (1977). Features of similarity. *Psychological Review*, 84, 327–352.

Tversky, A., & Gati, I. (1978). Studies of similarity. In E. Rosch & B. Lloyd (Eds.), *Cognition and categorization*. Hillsdale, NJ: Erlbaum.

Tversky, A., & Cati, I. (1982). Similarity, separability and the triangle inequality. *Psychological Review*, 89, 123–154.

5 Nearest Neighbor Analysis of Psychological Spaces

Amos Tversky and J. Wesley Hutchinson

Proximity data are commonly used to infer the structure of the entities under study and to embed them in an appropriate geometric or classificatory structure. The geometric approach represents objects as points in a continuous multidimensional space so that the order of the distances between the points reflects the proximities between the respective objects (see Coombs, 1964; Guttman, 1971; Shepard, 1962a, 1962b, 1974, 1980). Alternatively, objects can be described in terms of their common and distinctive features (Tversky, 1977) and represented by discrete clusters (see, e.g., Carroll, 1976; Johnson, 1967; Sattath & Tversky, 1977; Shepard & Arabie, 1979; Sokal, 1974).

The geometric and the classificatory approaches to the representation of proximity data are often compatible, but some data appear to favor one type of representation over another. Multidimensional scaling seems particularly appropriate for perceptual stimuli, such as colors and sounds, that vary along a small number of continuous dimensions, and Shepard (1984) made a compelling argument for the spatial nature of certain mental representations. On the other hand, clustering representations seem particularly appropriate for conceptual stimuli, such as people or countries, that appear to be characterized by a large number of discrete features.

Several criteria can be used for assessing which structure, if any, is appropriate for a given data set, including interpretability, goodness of fit, tests of critical axioms, and analyses of diagnostic statistics. The interpretability of a scaling solution is perhaps the most important consideration, but it is not entirely satisfactory because it is both subjective and vague. Furthermore, it is somewhat problematic to evaluate a (scaling) procedure designed to discover new patterns by the degree to which its results are compatible with prior knowledge. Most formal assessments of the adequacy of scaling models are based on some overall measure of goodness of fit, such as stress or proportion of variance explained by a linear or monotone representation of the data. These indices are often useful and informative, but they have several limitations. Because fit improves by adding more parameters, the stress of a multidimensional scaling solution decreases with additional dimensions, and the fit of a clustering model improves with the inclusion of additional clusters. Psychological theories rarely specify in advance the number of free parameters; hence, it is often difficult to compare and evaluate goodness of fit. Furthermore, global measures of correspondence are often insensitive to relatively small but highly significant deviations. The flat earth model, for example, provides a good fit to the distances between cities in California, although the deviations from the model could be detected by properly designed tests.

It is desirable, therefore, to devise testable procedures that are sufficiently powerful to detect meaningful departures from the model and that are not too sensitive to the dimensionality of the parameter space. Indeed, the metric axioms (e.g., symmetry, the triangle inequality) and the dimensional assumptions (e.g., interdimensional additivity and intradimensional subtractivity) underlying multidimensional scaling have been analyzed and tested by several investigators (e.g., Beals, Krantz, & Tversky, 1968; Gati & Tversky, 1982; Krantz & Tversky, 1975; Tversky & Gati, 1982; Tversky & Krantz, 1969, 1970; Wender, 1971; Wiener-Ehrlich, 1978). However, the testing of axioms or other necessary properties of spatial models often requires prior identification of the dimensions and construction of special configurations that are sometimes difficult to achieve, particularly for natural stimuli.

Besides the evaluation of overall goodness of fit and the test of metric and dimensional axioms, one may investigate statistical properties of the observed and the recovered proximities that can help diagnose the nature of the data and shed light on the adequacy of the representation. The present chapter investigates diagnostic properties based on nearest neighbor data. In the next section we introduce two ordinal properties of proximity data, *centrality* and *reciprocity*; discuss their implications; and illustrate their diagnostic significance. The theoretical values of these statistics are compared with the values observed in 100 proximity matrices reported in the literature. The results and their implications are discussed in the final section.

Centrality and Reciprocity

Given a symmetric measure d of dissimilarity, or distance, an object i is the nearest neighbor of j if $d(j, i) < d(j, k)$ for all k, provided i, j, and k are distinct. The relation "i is the nearest neighbor of j" arises in many contexts. For example, i may be rated as most similar to j, i can be the most common associate of j in a word association task, j may be confused with i more often than with any other letters in a recognition task, or i may be selected as j's best friend in a sociometric rating. Nearest neighbor data are often available even when a complete ordering of all interpoint distances cannot be obtained, either because the object set is too large or because quarternary comparisons (e.g., i likes j more than k likes l) are difficult to make.

For simplicity, we assume that the proximity order has no ties, or that ties are broken at random, so that every object has exactly one nearest neighbor. Note that the symmetry of d does not imply the symmetry of the nearest neighbor relation. If i is the nearest neighbor of j, j need not be the nearest neighbor of i. Let $S = \{0, 1, \ldots, n\}$ be the set of objects or entities under study, and let N_i, $0 \le i \le n$, be the number of elements in S whose nearest neighbor is i. The value of N_i reflects the centrality or the "popularity" of i with respect to S: $N_i = 0$ if there is no element in S whose nearest neighbor is i, and $N_i = n$ if i is the nearest neighbor of all other elements. Because every object has exactly one nearest neighbor, $N_0 + \cdots + N_n = n + 1$, and their average is always 1. That is,

$$\frac{1}{n+1}\sum_{i=0}^{n} N_i = 1.$$

To measure the centrality of the entire set S, we use the second sample moment

$$C = \frac{1}{n+1}\sum_{i=0}^{n} N_i^2,$$

which equals the sample variance plus 1 (Tversky, Rinott, & Newman, 1983). The centrality index C ranges from 1 when each point is the nearest neighbor of exactly one point to $(n^2 + 1)/(n + 1)$ when there exists one point that is everyone's nearest neighbor. More generally, C is high when S includes a few elements with high N and many elements with zero N, and C is low when the elements of S do not vary much in popularity.

The following example from unpublished data by Mervis, Rips, Rosch, Shoben, and Smith (1975), cited in Rosch and Mervis (1975), illustrates the computation of the centrality statistic and demonstrates the diagnostic significance of nearest neighbor data. Table 5.1 presents the average ratings of relatedness between fruits on a scale from 0 (*unrelated*) to 4 (*highly related*). The column entry that is the nearest neighbor of each row entry is indexed, and the values of N_i, $0 \leq i \leq 20$, appear in the bottom line. Table 5.1 shows that the category name *fruit* is the nearest neighbor of all but two instances: *lemon*, which is closer to *orange*, and *date*, which is closer to *olive*. Thus, $C = (18^2 + 2^2 + 1^2)/21 = 15.67$, which is not far from the maximal attainable value of $(20^2 + 1)/21 = 19.10$.

Note that many conceptual domains have a hierarchical structure (Rosch, 1978) involving a superordinate (e.g., *fruit*), its instances (e.g., *orange*, *apple*), and their subordinates (e.g., *Jaffa orange*, *Delicious apple*). To construct an adequate representation of people's conception of such a domain, the proximity among concepts at different levels of the hierarchy has to be assessed. Direct judgments of similarity are not well suited for this purpose because it is unnatural to rate the similarity of an instance (e.g., *grape*) to a category (e.g., *fruit*). However, there are other types of data (e.g., ratings of relatedness, free associations, substitution errors) that can serve as a basis for scaling objects together with their higher order categories.

Table 5.1
Mean Ratings of Relatedness between 20 Common Fruits and the Superordinate (Fruit) on a 5-Point Scale (Mervis et al., 1975)

Fruit	0	1	2	3	4	5	6	7	8	9	10	11	12	13	14	15	16	17	18	19	20
0. Fruit		3.12[a]	3.04	2.97	2.96	3.09	2.98	3.08	3.04	2.92	3.03	2.97	2.90	2.84	2.93	2.76	2.73	2.38	2.06	1.71	2.75
1. Orange	3.12[a]		2.20	1.69	2.20	1.97	2.13	1.69	1.53	1.57	2.69	1.77	1.54	1.45	1.76	1.56	1.56	1.33	1.43	1.05	2.80
2. Apple	3.04[a]	2.20		1.75	2.23	2.33	2.07	2.04	1.73	1.62	1.55	1.54	1.37	1.33	1.51	1.91	1.31	1.14	1.55	1.19	1.56
3. Banana	2.97[a]	1.69	1.75		1.74	1.93	1.63	1.32	1.46	1.59	1.36	1.54	1.45	1.37	1.26	1.21	1.36	1.29	1.07	0.98	1.53
4. Peach	2.96[a]	2.20	2.23	1.74		2.40	2.74	2.26	1.58	1.84	1.64	1.44	1.60	1.39	1.65	1.55	1.46	1.32	1.41	1.09	1.48
5. Pear	3.09[a]	1.97	2.33	1.93	2.40		2.15	2.06	1.58	1.75	1.63	1.44	1.35	1.69	1.51	1.21	1.26	1.24	1.24	0.96	1.59
6. Apricot	2.98[a]	2.13	2.07	1.63	2.74	2.15		2.29	1.77	1.80	1.55	1.42	1.55	1.41	1.51	1.52	1.80	1.12	1.24	1.23	1.53
7. Plum	3.08[a]	1.69	2.04	1.32	2.26	2.06	2.29		2.35	1.74	1.34	1.37	1.95	1.34	1.50	1.68	2.10	1.36	1.50	1.46	1.35
8. Grapes	3.04[a]	1.53	1.73	1.46	1.58	1.58	1.77	2.35		2.07	1.57	1.29	2.35	1.51	1.35	1.70	2.04	1.03	1.18	1.48	1.31
9. Strawberry	2.92[a]	1.57	1.62	1.59	1.84	1.75	1.80	1.74	2.07		1.38	1.58	2.73	1.50	1.27	1.45	1.68	1.12	1.53	1.22	1.37
10. Grapefruit	3.03[a]	2.69	1.55	1.36	1.64	1.77	1.55	1.34	1.57	1.38		2.10	1.40	1.83	2.15	1.61	1.24	1.44	1.13	0.89	2.46
11. Pineapple	2.97[a]	1.77	1.54	1.54	1.44	1.63	1.42	1.55	1.57	1.58	2.10		1.29	1.50	1.78	1.46	1.31	1.73	0.97	0.90	1.72
12. Blueberry	2.90[a]	1.54	1.37	1.45	1.60	1.44	1.55	1.95	2.35	2.73	1.40	1.29		1.00	1.27	1.52	1.47	1.12	1.02	1.30	1.30
13. Watermelon	2.84[a]	1.45	1.33	1.37	1.39	1.35	1.41	1.34	1.51	1.50	1.83	1.50	1.27		2.75	1.60	1.13	1.07	1.26	0.86	1.20
14. Honeydew	2.93[a]	1.76	1.51	1.26	1.65	1.69	1.51	1.50	1.35	1.27	2.15	1.78	1.52	2.75		1.46	1.19	1.41	1.06	0.87	1.46
15. Pomegranate	2.76[a]	1.56	1.91	1.21	1.55	1.51	1.52	1.68	1.70	1.45	1.61	1.46	1.52	1.60	1.46		1.54	1.60	1.29	1.11	1.37
16. Date	2.73[a]	1.33	1.31	1.36	1.46	1.21	1.80	2.10	2.04	1.68	1.24	1.31	1.47	1.13	1.19	1.54		1.60	1.02	1.87	1.23
17. Coconut	2.38[a]	1.34	1.14	1.29	1.32	1.26	1.13	1.36	1.03	1.12	1.44	1.73	1.12	1.07	1.41	1.60	1.60		1.11	0.97	1.26
18. Tomato	2.06[a]	1.43	1.55	1.07	1.41	1.24	1.24	1.50	1.18	1.53	1.13	0.97	1.02	1.26	1.06	1.29	1.02	1.11		1.08	0.93
19. Olive	1.71	1.05	1.19	0.98	1.09	0.96	1.23	1.46	1.48	1.22	0.89	0.90	1.30	0.86	0.87	1.11	1.87[a]	0.97	1.08		1.25
20. Lemon	2.75	2.80[a]	1.56	1.53	1.48	1.59	1.53	1.35	1.31	1.37	2.46	1.72	1.30	1.20	1.46	1.37	1.23	1.26	0.93	1.25	
N_i	18	2	0	0	0	0	0	0	0	0	0	0	0	0	0	0	1	0	0	0	0

Note: On the 5-point scale, $0 = unrelated$ and $4 = highly\ related.$
[a] The column entry that is the nearest neighbor of the row entry.

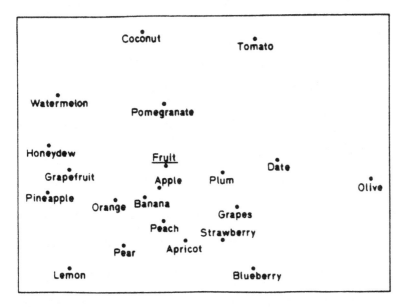

Figure 5.1
Two-dimensional Euclidean solution (KYST) for judgments of relatedness between fruits (table 5.1).

Figure 5.1 displays the two-dimensional scaling solution for the fruit data, obtained by KYST (Kruskal, Young, & Seery, 1973). In this representation the objects are described as points in the plane, and the proximity between the objects is expressed by their (Euclidean) distance. The spatial solution of figure 5.1 places the category name *fruit* in the center of the configuration, but it is the nearest neighbor of only 2 points (rather than 18), and the centrality of the solution is only 1.76 as compared with 15.67 in the original data! Although the two-dimensional solution appears reasonable in that similar fruits are placed near each other, it fails to capture the centrality of these data because the Euclidean model severely restricts the number of points that can share the same nearest neighbor.

In one dimension, a point cannot be the nearest neighbor of more than 2 points. In two dimensions, it is easy to see that in a regular hexagon the distance between the vertices and the center is equal to the distances between adjacent vertices. Consequently, disallowing ties, the maximal number of points with a common nearest neighbor is 5, corresponding to the center and the five vertices of a regular, or a nearly regular, pentagon. It can be shown that the maximal number of points in three dimensions that share the same nearest neighbor is 11. Bounds for high-dimensional spaces are discussed by Odlyzko and Sloane (1979).

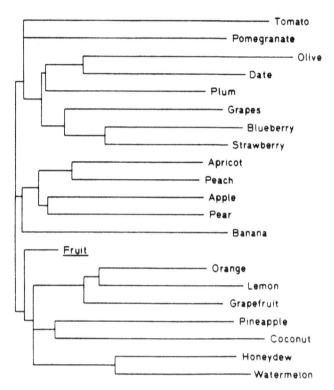

Figure 5.2
Additive tree solution (ADDTREE) for judgments of relatedness between fruits (table 5.1).

Figure 5.2 displays the additive tree (ADDTREE: Sattath & Tversky, 1977) representation of the fruit data. In this solution, the objects appear as the terminal nodes of the tree, and the distance between objects is given by their horizontal path length. (The vertical lines are drawn for graphical convenience.) An additive tree, unlike a two-dimensional map, can accommodate high centrality. Indeed, the category *fruit* in figure 5.2 is the nearest neighbor of all its instances. This tree accounts for 82% and 87%, respectively, of the linearly explained and the monotonically explained variance in the data, compared with 47% and 76% for the two-dimensional solution. (Note that, unlike additive trees, ultrametric trees are not able to accommodate high centrality because all objects must be equidistant from the root of the tree.) Other representations of high centrality data, which combine Euclidean and hierarchical components, are discussed in the last section.

The centrality statistic C that is based on the distribution of N_i, $0 \le i \le n$, measures the degree to which elements of S share a nearest neighbor. Another property of nearest neighbor data, called reciprocity, is measured by a different statistic (Schwarz & Tversky, 1980). Recall that each element i of S generates a rank order of all other elements of S by their proximity to i. Let R_i be the rank of i in the proximity order of its nearest neighbor. For example, if each member of a class ranks all others in terms of closeness of friendship, then R_i is i's position in the ranking of her best friend. Thus, $R_i = 1$ if i is the best friend of her best friend, and $R_i = n$ if i is the worst friend of her best friend. The reciprocity of the entire set is defined by the sample mean

$$R = \frac{1}{n+1} \sum_{i=0}^{n} R_i.$$

R is minimal when the nearest neighbor relation is symmetric, so that every object is the nearest neighbor of its nearest neighbor and $R = 1$. R is maximal when one element of S is the nearest neighbor of all others, so that $R = (1 + 1 + 2 + \cdots + n)/(n+1) = n/2 + 1/(n+1)$. Note that high R implies low reciprocity and vice versa.

To illustrate the calculation of R, we present in table 5.2 the conditional proximity order induced by the fruit data of table 5.1. That is, each row of table 5.2 includes the rank order of all 20 column elements according to their proximity to the given row element. Recall that j is the nearest neighbor of i if column j receives the rank 1 in row i. In this case, R_i is given by the rank of column i in row j. These values are marked by superscripts in table 5.2, and the distribution of R_i appears in the bottom line. The reciprocity statistic, then, is

$$R = \frac{1}{21} \sum_{i=0}^{20} R_i = \frac{181}{21} = 8.62.$$

As with centrality, the degree of reciprocity in the ADDTREE solution ($R = 9.38$) is comparable to that of the data, whereas the KYST solution yields a considerably lower value ($R = 2.81$) than the data.

Examples and Constraints

To appreciate the diagnostic significance of R and its relation to C, consider the patterns of proximity generated by the graphs in figures 5.3, 5.4, and 5.5, where the

Table 5.2
Conditional Proximity Order of Fruits Induced by the Mean Ratings Given in Table 5.1

Fruit	0	1	2	3	4	5	6	7	8	9	10	11	12	13	14	15	16	17	18	19	20
0. Fruit	1[a]	1[a]	4[a]	8[a]	10[a]	2[a]	7[a]	3[a]	5[a]	13[a]	6[a]	9[a]	12[a]	14[a]	11[a]	15[a]	17[a]	18[a]	19[a]	20	16
1. Orange	1		4	10	5	7	6	11	14	12	3	8	13	15	9	16	19	18	17	20	2[a]
2. Apple	1	4		8	3	2	5	6	9	10	12	14	16	17	15	7	18	19	13	20	11
3. Banana	1	5	8		4	2	6	15	10	7	13	8	12	11	17	18	14	16	19	20	9
4. Peach	1	6	3	4		3	2	4	12	7	13	16	11	18	9	13	15	19	17	20	14
5. Pear	1	6	5	7	3		4	5	13	9	8	11	18	16	10	14	20	17	18	20	12
6. Apricot	1	5	6	10	2	4		3	8	7	11	16	17	15	12	14	5	20	18	19	13
7. Plum	1	10	7	20	4	6	3		2	9	18	15	8	17	12	11	5	16	13	14	17
8. Grapes	1	12	9	15	10	10	6	2		4	11	18	3	13	16	8	5	20	19	14	17
9. Strawberry	1	12	11	10	7	6	5	7	4		16	11	2	14	18	15	8	20	13	19	3
10. Grapefruit	2	2	13	16	8	7	12	17	10	15		5	14	6	4	9	13	5	19	20	3
11. Pineapple	1	4	9	10	5	11	6	15	17	8	2		18	11	3	12	16	5	19	20	6
12. Blueberry	1	7	13	11	10	12	4	4	3	2	12	16		20	17	8	9	18	19	14	15
13. Watermelon	1	8	14	17	9	6	13	13	5	6	3	7	19	20	2	4	17	18	15	20	16
14. Honeydew	1	5	8	7	6	6	10	10	14	15	3	4	16	2	15	11	18	13	19	20	12
15. Pomegranate	1	8	2	9	4	13	11	4	3	16	5	14	12	6	15		10	7	18	20	17
16. Date	1	12	13	11	10	17	14	7	3	6	15	2	9	19	18	8		7	20	4[a]	16
17. Coconut	1	8	10	10	9	11	7	4	19	15	5	19	16	18	6	3	4		17	20	12
18. Tomato	1	5	15	15	6	9	10	4	11	3	12	17	17	8	16	7	18	13		14	20
19. Olive	2	13	14	14	11	16	7	4	3	8	18	17	5	20	19	10	1	15	12		6
20. Lemon	2	1	7	7	9	5	8	13	14	11	3	4	15	19	10	12	18	16	20	17	
R_i	1	4	8	10	2	7	3	5	13	16	9	12	14	11	15	17	18	19	4	4	2

[a] The rank of each column entry in the proximity order of its nearest neighbor.

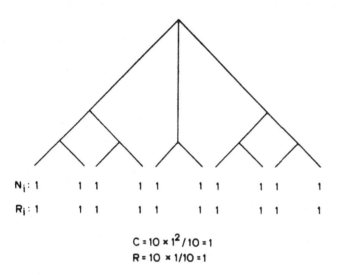

N_i: 1   1 1   1 1   1 1   1 1   1

R_i: 1   1 1   1 1   1 1   1 1   1

$$C = 10 \times 1^2 / 10 = 1$$
$$R = 10 \times 1/10 = 1$$

Figure 5.3
A binary tree.

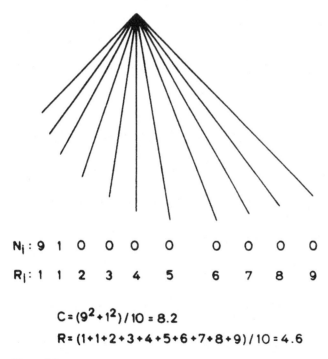

N_i: 9 1 0   0   0   0   0   0   0   0

R_i: 1 1 2   3   4   5   6   7   8   9

$$C = (9^2 + 1^2)/10 = 8.2$$
$$R = (1+1+2+3+4+5+6+7+8+9)/10 = 4.6$$

Figure 5.4
A singular tree.

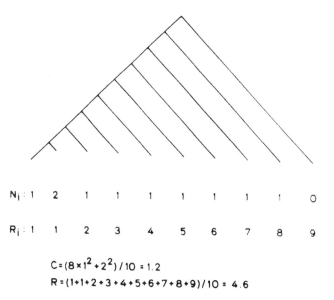

N_i : 1   2   1   1   1   1   1   1   1   0

R_i : 1   1   2   3   4   5   6   7   8   9

$$C = (8 \times 1^2 + 2^2)/10 = 1.2$$
$$R = (1+1+2+3+4+5+6+7+8+9)/10 = 4.6$$

Figure 5.5
A nested tree.

distance between points is given by the length of the path that joins them. The distributions of N_i and of R_i are also included in the figures along with the values of C and R. Recall that R is the mean of the distribution of R_i whereas C is the second moment of the distribution of N_i.

Figure 5.3 presents a binary tree where the nearest neighbor relation is completely symmetric; hence, both C and R are minimal and equal to 1. Figure 5.4 presents a singular tree, also called a *star* or a *fan*. In this structure the shortest branch is always the nearest neighbor of all other branches; hence, both C and R achieve their maximal values. Figure 5.5 presents a nested tree, or a *brush*, where the nearest neighbor of each point lies on the shorter adjacent branch; hence, C is very low because only the longest branch is not a nearest neighbor of some point. On the other hand, R is maximal because each point is closer to all the points that lie on shorter branches than to any point that lies on a longer branch. Another example of such structure is the sequence $\{\frac{1}{2}, \frac{1}{4}, \frac{1}{8}, \ldots\}$, where each number is closest to the next number in the sequence and closer to all smaller numbers than to any larger number. This produces minimal C and maximal R. In a sociometric context, figure 5.3 corresponds to a group that is organized in pairs (e.g., married couples), figure 5.4 corresponds to a group with a focal element (e.g., a leader), and figure 5.5 corresponds to a certain type of hierarchical organization (e.g., military ranks) in which each position is closer to all of its subordinates than to any of its superiors.

These examples illustrate three patterns of proximity that yield low C and low R (figure 5.3), high C and high R (figure 5.4), and low C with high R (figure 5.5). The statistics R and C, therefore, are not redundant: both are required to distinguish the brush from the fan and from the binary tree. However, it is not possible to achieve high C and low R because they are constrained by the inequality $C \leq 2R - 1$.

To derive this inequality suppose i is the nearest neighbor of k elements so that $N_i = k$, $0 \leq k \leq n$. Because the R_is associated with these elements are their ranking from i, the set of k ranks must include a value $\geq k$, a value $\geq k - 1$, and so forth. Hence, each N_i contributes at least $N_i + (N_i - 1) + \cdots + 1 = (N_i + 1)N_i/2$ to the sum $R_0 + \cdots + R_n = (n + 1)R$. Consequently,

$$(n + 1)R \geq \frac{1}{2}\sum_{i=0}^{n}(N_i + 1)N_i,$$

$$2R \geq \frac{1}{n+1}\left(\sum_{i=0}^{n}N_i{}^2 + \sum_{i=0}^{n}N_i\right) = C + 1,$$

and $C \leq 2R - 1$.

This relation, called the CR inequality, restricts the feasible values of these statistics to the region above the solid line in figure 5.6 that displays the CR plane in logarithmic coordinates. The figure also presents the values of R and C from the previous examples. Because both C and R are greater than or equal to 1, the origin is set at $(1, 1)$. As seen in the figure, high C requires high R, low R requires low C, but low C is compatible with high R. Recall that the maximal values of C and R, respectively, are $(n^2 + 1)/(n + 1)$ and $n/2 + 1/(n + 1)$, which approach $n - 1$ and $n/2$ as n becomes large. These maximal values approximate the boundary implied by the CR inequality.

Geometry and Statistics

In the preceding discussion we introduced two statistics based on nearest neighbor data and investigated their properties. We also demonstrated the diagnostic potential of nearest neighbor data by showing that high centrality values cannot be achieved in low-dimensional representations because the dimensionality of the solution space sets an upper bound on the number of points that can share the same nearest neighbor. High values of C therefore may be used to rule out two- or three-dimensional representations, but they are less useful for higher dimensions because the bound

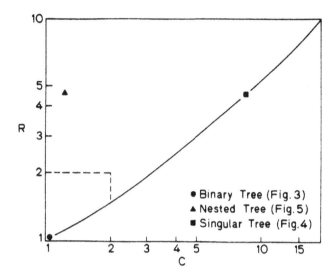

Figure 5.6
The C and R values (on logarithmic coordinates) for the trees shown in figures 5.3, 5.4, and 5.5. (The boundary implied by the CR inequality is shown by the solid curve. The broken lines denote the upper bound imposed by the geometric sampling model.)

increases rapidly with the dimensionality of the space. Furthermore, the theoretical bound is usually too high for scaling applications. For example, a value of $N_i = 18$, observed in table 5.1, can be achieved in a four-dimensional space. However, the four-dimensional KYST solution of these data yielded a maximal N_i of only 4. It is desirable, therefore, to obtain a more restrictive bound that is also applicable to high-dimensional solutions.

Recent mathematical developments (Newman & Rinott, in press; Newman, Rinott, & Tversky, 1983; Schwarz & Tversky, 1980; Tversky, Rinott, & Newman, 1983) obtained much stricter upper bounds on C and on R by assuming that S is a sample of independent and identically distributed points from some continuous distribution in a d-dimensional Euclidean space. In this case, the asymptotic values of C and of R cannot exceed 2, regardless of the dimensionality of the space and the form of the underlying distribution of points. (We will refer to the combined assumptions of statistical sampling and spatial representation as the geometric sampling model, or more simply, the GS model.)

It is easy to show that the probability that a point, selected at random from some continuous univariate distribution, is the nearest neighbor of k points is $\frac{1}{4}$ for $k = 0$, $\frac{1}{2}$ for $k = 1$, $\frac{1}{4}$ for $k = 2$, and 0 for $k > 2$. (These results are exact for a uniform distribution and approximate for other continuous univariate distributions.) In the one-dimensional case, therefore, $C = \left(\frac{1}{4} \times 0\right) + \left(\frac{1}{2} \times 1\right) + \left(\frac{1}{4} \times 4\right) = 1.5$. Simulations (Maloney, 1983; Roberts, 1969) suggest that the corresponding values in two and three dimensions are 1.63 and 1.73, respectively. And Newman et al. (1983) showed that C approaches 2 as the number of dimensions increases without bound. Thus, the limiting value of C, as the number of points becomes very large, ranges from 1.5, in the one-dimensional case, to 2, when the number of dimensions tends to infinity. Simulations (Maloney, 1983) show that the asymptotic results provide good approximations even for moderately small samples (e.g., 36) drawn from a wide range of continuous multivariate distributions. The results do not hold, however, when the number of dimensions is very large in relation to the number of points. For a review of the major theorems, see Tversky et al. (1983); the derivation of the limiting distribution of N_i, under several statistical models, is given in Newman and Rinott (in press) and in Newman et al. (1983).

Theoretical and computational analyses show that the upper bound of the GS model is fairly robust with respect to random error, or noisy data. First, Newman et al. (1983) proved that C does not exceed 2 when the distances between objects are randomly ordered. Second, Maloney's (1983) simulation showed that the addition of normal random error to the measured distance between points has a relatively small effect on centrality, although it increases the dimensionality of the space. Maloney also showed that for a uniform distribution of n points in the n-dimensional unit cube, for example, the observed centrality values exceed 2 but do not reach 3. This finding illustrates the general theoretical point that the upper bound of the GS model need not hold when the number of dimensions is very large in relation to the number of points (see Tversky et al. 1983). It also shows that extreme values of C (like those observed in the fruit data of table 5.1) cannot be produced by independent and identically distributed points even when the number of dimensions equals the number of data points.

The analysis of reciprocity (Schwarz & Tversky, 1980) led to similar results. The asymptotic value of R ranges from 1.5 in the unidimensional case to 2 when the dimensionality tends to infinity or when distances are randomly ordered. The probability that one is the nearest neighbor of one's nearest neighbor is $1/R$, which ranges from $\frac{2}{3}$ to $\frac{1}{2}$. Again, simulations show that the results provide good approximations for relatively small samples. Thus, the GS model imposes severe bounds on the centrality and the reciprocity of data.

The plausibility of the GS model depends on the nature of the study. Some investigators have actually used an explicit sampling procedure to select Munsell color clips (Indow & Aoki, 1983), to generate shapes (Attneave, 1957), or to construct dot patterns (Posner & Keele, 1968). In most cases, however, stimuli have been constructed following a factorial design, selected according to some rule (e.g., the most common elements of a class), or chosen informally without an explicit rationale. The relevance of the GS bounds in these cases is discussed in the next section.

Applications

In this section we analyze nearest neighbor data from 100 proximity matrices, covering a wide range of stimuli and dependent measures. The analysis demonstrates the diagnostic function of C and of R and sheds light on the conditions that give rise to high values of these statistics.

Our data base encompasses a variety of perceptual and conceptual domains. The perceptual studies include visual stimuli (e.g., colors, letters, and various figures and shapes); auditory stimuli (e.g., tones, musical scale notes, and consonant phonemes); and a few gustatory and olfactory stimuli. The conceptual studies include many different verbal stimuli, such as animals, occupations, countries, and environmental risks. Some studies used a representative collection of the elements of a natural category including their superordinate (e.g., *apple*, *orange*, and *fruit*). These sets were entered into the data base twice, with and without the category name. In assembling the data base, we were guided by a desire to span the range of possible types of data. Therefore, as a sample of published proximity matrices, our collection is probably biased toward data that yield extremely high or extremely low values of C and R. The data base also includes more than one dependent measure (e.g., similarity ratings, confusion probabilities, associations) for the following stimulus domains: colors, letters, emotions, fruit, weapons, animals, environmental risks, birds, occupations, and body parts. A description of the data base is presented in the appendix.

Data Analysis
Multidimensional scaling (MDS) solutions in two and in three dimensions were constructed for all data sets using the KYST procedure (Kruskal et al., 1973). The analysis is confined to these solutions because higher dimensional ordinal solutions are not very common in the literature. To avoid inferior solutions due to local minima, we used 10 different starting configurations for each set of data. Nine runs were started from random configurations, and one was started from a metric (i.e., interval) MDS configuration. If a solution showed clear signs of degeneracy (see Shepard, 1974), the interval solution was obtained. The final scaling results, then, are based on more than 2,000 separate KYST solutions.

Table 5.3 presents, for each data set, the values of C and R computed from the scaling solutions and the values obtained from the observed data. The table also reports a measure of fit (stress formula 1) that was minimized by the scaling procedure. Table 5.4 summarizes the results for each class of stimuli, and figure 5.7 plots the C and R values for all data sets in logarithmic coordinates.

It is evident that for more than one half of the data sets, the values of C and R exceed the asymptotic value of 2 implied by the GS model. Simulations suggest that the standard deviation of C and R for samples of 20 points from three-dimensional Euclidean spaces, under several distributions, is about 0.25 (Maloney, 1983; Schwarz & Tversky, 1980). Hence, observed values that exceed 3 cannot be attributed to sampling errors. Nevertheless, 23% of the data sets yielded values of C greater than 3 and 33% yielded values of R greater than 3. In fact, the obtained values of C and R fell within the GS bounds (1.5–2.0) for only 37% and 25% of the data, respectively.

To facilitate the interpretation of the results, we organize the perceptual and the conceptual stimuli in several groups. Perceptual stimuli are divided into colors, letters, other visual stimuli, auditory stimuli, and gustatory/olfactory stimuli (see tables 5.3 and 5.4). This classification reflects differences in sense modality with further subdivision of visual stimuli according to complexity. The conceptual stimuli are divided into four classes: categorical ratings, attribute-based categories, categorical associations, and assorted semantic stimuli. The categorical ratings data came from two unpublished studies (Mervis et al., 1975; Smith & Tversky, 1981). In the study by Mervis et al., subjects rated, on a 5-point scale, the degree of relatedness between instances of seven natural categories that included the category name. The instances were chosen to span the range from the most typical to fairly atypical instances of the category. In the study by Smith and Tversky, subjects rated the degree of relatedness between instances of four categories that included either the immediate superordinate (e.g., *rose*, *tulip*, and *flower*) or a distant superordinate (e.g., *rose*, *tulip*, and *plant*). Thus, for each category there are two sets of independent judgments differing only in the level of the superordinates. This study also included four sets of attribute-based categories, that is, sets of objects that shared a single attribute and little else. The attribute name, which is essentially the common denominator of the instances (e.g., *apple*, *blood*, and *red*), was also included in the set.

The categorical associations data were obtained from the association norms derived by Marshall and Cofer (1970), who chose exemplars that spanned the range of production frequencies reported by Cohen, Bousefield, and Whitmarsh (1957). Eleven of these categories were selected for analysis. The proximity of word i to word j was defined by the sum of the relative frequency of producing i as an associate to j and the relative frequency of producing j as an associate to i, where the production

Table 5.3
Nearest Neighbor Statistics for 100 Sets of Proximity Data and Their Associated Two-Dimensional (2-D) and Three-Dimensional (3-D) KYST Solutions

Data description	N	max N_i			C			R			Stress	
		Data	3-D	2-D	Data	3-D	2-D	Data	3-D	2-D	3-D	2-D
Perceptual												
Colors												
1. Lights	14	2	2	2	1.43	1.43	1.29	1.43	1.50	1.50	.013	.023
2. Chips	10	2	2	2	1.60	1.60	1.40	1.50	1.40	1.20	.010	.062
3. Chips	20	2	3	3	1.60	1.70	1.90	1.50	1.85	1.60	.104	.171
4. Chips	21	2	2	2	1.29	1.48	1.48	1.14	1.38	1.33	.049	.075
5. Chips	24	3	2	2	1.50	1.42	1.50	1.46	1.33	1.54	.034	.088
6. Chips	21	3	4	3	1.86	2.05	1.95	1.48	1.62	1.71	.053	.086
7. Chips	9	2	2	3	1.44	1.44	2.11	1.33	1.33	1.67	.016	.043
Letters												
8. Lowercase	25	4	3	3	1.88	1.72	2.12	1.68	1.72	1.88	.141	.214
9. Lowercase	25	4	2	2	1.80	1.64	1.56	1.56	1.48	1.64	.144	.213
10. Uppercase	9	2	2	2	1.67	1.67	1.67	1.78	1.67	1.44	.015	.091
11. Uppercase	9	2	2	2	1.67	1.67	1.44	1.44	1.44	1.44	.029	.087
12. Uppercase	26	3	3	2	1.69	1.78	1.46	1.73	1.92	1.38	.129	.212
13. Uppercase	26	3	2	3	1.62	1.46	1.93	1.73	1.50	1.58	.185	.267
Other visual												
14. Visual illusions	45	4	4	3	2.16	2.07	1.71	3.58	3.33	2.64	.113	.152
15. Polygons	16	2	2	2	1.25	1.63	1.88	1.38	1.56	1.69	.081	.165
16. Plants	16	2	2	2	1.63	1.38	1.50	1.38	1.25	1.38	.118	.176
17. Dot figures	16	2	2	3	1.25	1.62	1.62	1.19	1.44	1.44	.094	.176
18. Walls figures	16	2	2	4	1.38	1.38	2.12	1.50	1.38	1.56	.096	.175
19. Circles	9	2	2	2	1.44	1.22	1.44	1.56	1.33	1.56	.009	.046
20. Response positions	9	2	2	2	1.44	1.44	1.67	2.56	2.33	2.22	.003	.015
21. Arabic numerals	10	2	2	2	1.80	1.60	1.40	1.80	1.40	1.20	.060	.115

Auditory

22. Sine wave	12	2	2	1.67	1.83	1.83	1.58	1.50	1.58	.069	.115
23. Square waves	12	2	2	1.33	1.33	1.50	1.83	1.83	2.25	.035	.058
24. Musical tones	13	3	3	2.39	1.62	1.46	3.62	1.77	1.46	.107	.165
25. Consonant phonemes	16	2	3	1.50	1.75	1.63	1.44	1.56	2.38	.066	.139
26. Morse code	36	2	2	1.28	1.56	1.28	1.25	1.64	1.36	.131	.194
27. Vowels	12	3	3	2.17	1.83	1.83	1.67	1.50	1.42	.035	.091

Gustatory and olfactory

28. Wines	15	3	3	2.07	1.93	1.80	2.87	2.47	2.13	.134	.213
29. Wines	15	3	3	4.60	2.33	1.67	4.27	2.80	2.73	.138	.202
30. Amino acids	20	4	3	2.60	1.90	2.10	4.60	3.45	4.25	.117	.179
31. Odors	21	3	2	1.57	1.57	1.38	1.71	1.76	1.76	.156	.217

Conceptual

Assorted semantic

32. Animals	30	3	3	1.87	1.60	1.80	2.27	1.90	1.90	.096	.131
33. Emotions	15	3	2	1.80	1.67	1.40	1.93	1.87	1.80	.010	.035
34. Emotions	30	3	3	2.00	1.87	1.73	1.83	1.73	1.77	.073	.132
35. Linguistic forms	8	1	1	1.00	1.00	1.00	1.00	1.00	1.00	.010	.031
36. Journals	8	3	2	2.00	1.50	2.25	1.75	1.38	1.75	.121	.206
37. Societal risks	30	4	3	1.86	1.53	1.60	2.93	2.17	1.63	.055	.108
38. Societal risks	30	4	3	1.93	1.53	1.67	2.30	1.97	1.83	.046	.080
39. Societal risks	30	3	4	1.86	1.93	1.80	2.83	2.27	2.00	.049	.089
40. Birds	15	2	2	2.33	1.53	1.67	2.27	1.87	1.67	.063	.134
41. Students	16	2	1	1.13	1.13	1.00	1.13	1.19	1.00	.077	.135
42. Animals	30	3	3	1.73	1.60	1.80	2.07	1.57	2.00	.091	.152
43. Varied objects	36	2	2	1.56	1.57	1.50	1.28	1.36	1.50	.089	.157
44. Attribute words	30	4	3	1.93	1.67	1.80	2.10	2.00	1.87	.082	.132
45. Occupations	35	3	3	1.63	1.57	1.51	1.37	1.60	1.66	.068	.134
46. Body parts	20	3	3	1.70	1.90	1.70	2.00	1.85	1.80	.046	.124
47. Countries	17	2	3	1.58	1.71	1.47	1.29	1.47	1.47	.098	.186
48. Countries	17	4	2	2.18	1.59	1.59	1.76	1.35	1.29	.106	.200
49. Numbers	10	2	2	1.60	1.40	1.20	2.00	1.30	1.30	.077	.139
50. Countries	12	4	2	2.33	1.83	1.67	1.83	1.67	1.33	.107	.188
51. Maniocs	25	7	3	3.88	1.72	1.64	7.64	6.00	4.64	.131	.185
52. Maniocs	22	4	3	2.46	1.73	1.54	6.73	6.09	4.82	.121	.176

Table 5.3 (continued)

Data description	N	max N_i Data	3-D	2-D	C Data	3-D	2-D	R Data	3-D	2-D	Stress 3-D	2-D
Categorical ratings 1 (with superordinate)												
53. Fruits	21	18	2	3	15.67	1.76	1.76	8.62	2.81	2.10	.146	.210
54. Furniture	21	10	3	3	5.38	1.95	1.95	5.00	2.81	2.14	.114	.193
55. Sports	21	8	2	3	4.33	1.48	1.86	3.43	1.43	1.62	.126	.186
56. Tools	21	12	2	3	7.38	1.57	1.76	5.86	2.10	1.86	.156	.226
57. Vegetables	21	14	3	3	9.86	1.95	1.95	6.57	2.33	2.14	.130	.188
58. Vehicles	21	7	4	2	3.10	2.05	1.48	3.86	2.00	2.24	.120	.183
59. Weapons	21	14	4	2	9.76	2.05	1.57	6.48	2.57	2.33	.111	.169
Categorical ratings 1 (without superordinate)												
60. Fruits	20	2	3	3	1.50	2.30	1.70	2.75	3.05	2.25	.125	.188
61. Furniture	20	3	3	3	2.40	2.00	1.60	3.05	2.45	2.15	.105	.195
62. Sports	20	3	2	3	1.90	1.20	1.80	1.80	1.10	1.60	.110	.171
63. Tools	20	3	2	3	1.80	1.60	1.70	2.15	2.20	1.90	.141	.212
64. Vegetables	20	4	2	3	2.71	1.60	1.70	2.70	2.25	2.20	.109	.166
65. Vehicles	20	3	3	2	1.70	1.70	1.60	2.30	1.90	2.20	.103	.164
66. Weapons	20	4	2	2	2.10	1.90	1.80	2.90	2.70	2.50	.091	.145
Categorical ratings 2 (with superordinate)												
67. Flowers	7	3	3	2	1.86	1.86	1.57	1.71	1.71	1.57	.009	.045
68. Trees	7	4	2	2	2.71	1.86	1.86	2.14	1.71	2.14	.032	.101
69. Birds	7	6	3	3	5.29	1.86	1.84	3.14	2.14	2.43	.024	.098
70. Fish	7	6	4	2	5.29	3.00	1.86	3.14	2.14	1.43	.010	.056
Categorical ratings 2 (with distant superordinate)												
71. Flowers	7	2	2	2	1.29	1.29	1.57	1.43	1.14	1.43	.009	.006
72. Trees	7	2	2	3	1.57	1.57	1.86	1.71	1.86	2.29	.001	.023
73. Birds	7	4	5	3	2.71	3.86	1.86	2.71	3.14	2.14	.008	.008
74. Fish	7	2	2	2	1.57	1.86	1.57	2.00	2.00	2.29	.009	.009

Categorical associations (with superordinate)

75. Birds	18	17	3	4	16.11	1.89	2.22	8.56	1.83	2.00	.031	.090
76. Body parts	17	4	3	4	2.41	2.18	2.65	2.47	2.06	2.53	.046	.096
77. Clothes	17	3	3	3	1.94	1.82	1.82	1.71	2.18	1.88	.067	.114
78. Drinks	16	12	3	3	9.38	2.50	1.88	6.13	3.06	1.88	.088	.142
79. Earth formations	19	4	3	2	2.37	1.53	1.63	2.47	1.47	1.58	.235	.333
80. Fruits	17	12	3	3	8.76	1.82	2.06	5.47	2.29	2.65	.047	.118
81. House parts	17	11	3	2	7.59	2.06	1.82	5.47	2.24	2.06	.049	.093
82. Musical instruments	18	11	4	2	7.22	2.78	1.67	4.94	2.78	1.83	.063	.108
83. Professions	17	6	2	3	4.18	1.35	1.94	5.88	1.24	1.65	.245	.345
84. Weapons	17	4	2	2	2.65	1.47	1.59	3.53	2.29	1.71	.037	.084
85. Weather	17	8	4	3	4.88	2.18	2.06	4.53	3.12	2.41	.066	.112

Categorical associations (without superordinate)

86. Birds	17	4	2	2	2.65	1.35	1.56	4.41	1.35	1.47	.250	.349
87. Body parts	16	4	2	2	2.63	1.63	1.50	3.00	1.63	1.44	.229	.326
88. Clothes	16	4	3	3	2.12	1.88	1.88	1.69	2.13	1.81	.047	.097
89. Drinks	15	4	3	3	2.07	2.80	1.93	2.07	2.33	2.20	.049	.103
90. Earth formations	18	4	3	2	2.22	1.67	1.33	2.44	1.44	1.50	.236	.334
91. Fruit	16	3	2	3	1.75	1.38	1.88	2.25	1.31	1.69	.229	.330
92. House parts	16	2	2	2	1.75	1.38	1.38	3.38	1.31	1.31	.240	.339
93. Musical instruments	17	2	2	3	1.24	1.47	1.71	1.71	1.59	1.59	.018	.058
94. Professions	16	5	3	2	2.75	1.88	1.50	4.06	1.50	1.44	.243	.345
95. Weapons	16	4	2	2	2.25	1.25	1.38	2.94	1.13	1.38	.224	.325
96. Weather	16	5	4	2	3.75	3.00	1.75	3.81	3.25	2.06	.037	.090

Attribute-based categories

97. Red	7	6	4	3	5.29	3.57	2.14	3.14	2.43	2.00	.008	.059
98. Circle	7	6	6	2	5.29	5.29	1.57	3.14	3.14	1.57	.013	.093
99. Smell	7	6	4	3	5.29	3.00	2.14	3.14	2.29	2.00	.023	.084
100. Sound	7	6	3	3	5.29	2.71	2.43	3.14	2.43	2.86	.010	.093

Table 5.4
Means and Standard Deviations for C and R for Each Stimulus Group

Stimulus group	N	C		R		C/R	
		M	SD	M	SD	M	SD
Perceptual							
Colors	7	1.53	0.18	1.41	0.13	1.09	0.08
Letters	6	1.72	0.10	1.65	0.13	1.05	0.11
Other visual	8	1.54	0.31	1.89	0.81	0.89	0.21
Auditory	6	1.72	0.46	1.90	0.87	0.97	0.24
Gustatory/olfactory	4	2.71	1.33	3.36	1.33	0.82	0.24
All perceptual	31	1.76	0.62	1.92	0.90	0.97	0.19
Conceptual							
Assorted semantic	21	1.92	0.57	2.40	1.67	0.93	0.25
Categorical ratings 1 (with superordinate)	7	7.93	4.28	5.69	1.78	1.32	0.33
Categorical ratings 1 (without superordinate)	7	2.02	0.42	2.52	0.45	0.81	0.17
Categorical ratings 2 (with superordinate)	4	3.79	1.77	2.53	0.72	1.43	0.30
Categorical ratings 2 (with distant superordinate)	4	1.78	0.63	1.96	0.55	0.90	0.09
Categorical associations (with superordinate)	11	6.14	4.28	4.65	2.00	1.22	0.37
Categorical associations (without superordinate)	11	2.29	0.66	2.89	0.94	0.83	0.21
Attribute-based categories	4	5.29	0.00	3.14	0.00	1.68	0.00
All conceptual	69	3.57	3.06	3.21	1.80	1.06	0.35

frequencies were divided by the total number of responses to each stimulus word. The proximity for the category name was estimated from the norms of Cohen et al. (1957). All of the remaining studies involving conceptual stimuli are classified as assorted semantic stimuli. These include both simple concepts (e.g., occupations, numbers) as well as compound concepts (e.g., sentences, descriptions of people).

Figure 5.7 and table 5.4 show that some of the stimulus groups occupy fairly specific regions in the CR plane. All colors and letters and most of the other visual and auditory data yielded C and R values that are less than 2, as implied by the GS model. In contrast, 20 of the 26 sets of data that included the superordinate yielded values of C and R that are both greater than 3. These observations suggest that high C and R values occur primarily in categorical rating and categorical associations, when the category name is included in the set. Furthermore, high C values are found primarily when the category name is a basic-level object (e.g., *fruit, bird, fish*) rather

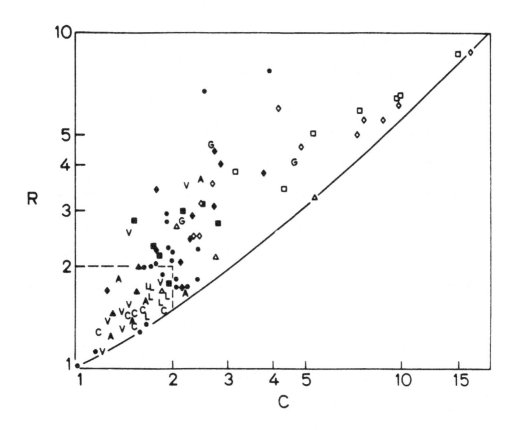

C Colors
L Letters
V Other Visual
A Auditory
G Gustatory or Olfactory
• Miscellaneous Semantic
□ Categorical Ratings I (with superordinate)
■ Categorical Ratings I (without superordinate)
△ Categorical Ratings II (with superordinate)
▲ Categorical Ratings II (with distant superordinate)
◇ Categorical Associations (with superordinate)
♦ Categorical Associations (without superordinate)
▽ Attribute Based Categories

Figure 5.7
The C and R values (on logarithmic coordinates) for 100 data sets. (The CR inequality is shown by a solid curve, and the geometric sampling bound is denoted by a broken line.)

than a superordinate-level object (e.g., *vehicle, clothing, animal*); see Rosch (1978) and Rosch, Mervis, Gray, Johnson, and Boyes-Braem (1976). When the category name was excluded from the analysis, the values of C and R were substantially reduced, although 12 of 22 data sets still exceeded the upper limit of the GS model. For example, when the superordinate *weather* was eliminated from the categorical association data, the most typical weather conditions (*rain* and *storm*) became the foci, yielding C and R values of 3.75 and 3.81, respectively. There were also cases in which a typical instance of a category was the nearest neighbor of more instances than the category name itself. For example, in the categorical association data, *doctor* was the nearest neighbor of six professions, whereas the category name (*profession*) was the nearest neighbor of only five professions.

A few data sets did not reach the lower bound imposed by the GS model. In particular, all seven factorial designs yielded C that was less than 1.5 and in six of seven cases, the value of R was also below 1.5.

The dramatic violations of the GS bound, however, need not invalidate the spatial model. A value of R or C that is substantially greater than 2 indicates that either the geometric model is inappropriate or the statistical assumption is inadequate. To test these possibilities, the nearest neighbor statistics (C and R) of the data can be compared with those derived from the scaling solution. If the values match, there is good reason to believe that the data were generated by a spatial model that does not satisfy the statistical assumption. However, if the values of C and R computed from the data are much greater than 2 while the values derived from the solution are less than 2, the spatial solution is called into question.

The data summarized in tables 5.3 and 5.4 reveal marked discrepancies between the data and their solutions. The three-dimensional solutions, for instance, yield C and R that exceed 3 for only 6% and 10% of the data sets, respectively. The relations between the C and R values of the data and the values computed from the three-dimensional solutions are presented in figures 5.8 and 5.9. For comparison we also present the corresponding plots for ADDTREE (Sattath & Tversky, 1977) for a subset of 35 data sets. The correlations between observed and predicted values in figures 5.8 and 5.9 indicate that the trees tend to reflect the centrality ($r^2 = .64$) and the reciprocity ($r^2 = .80$) of the data. In contrast, the spatial solutions do not match either the centrality ($r^2 = .10$) or the reciprocity ($r^2 = .37$) of the data and yield low values of C and R, as implied by the statistical assumption. The MDS solutions are slightly more responsive to R than to C, but large values of both indices are grossly underestimated by the spatial representations.

The finding that trees represent nearest neighbor data better than low-dimensional spatial models does not imply that tree models are generally superior to spatial rep-

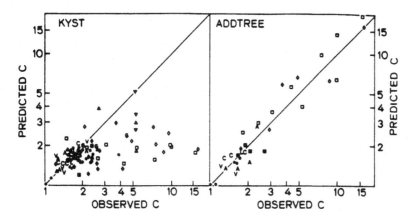

Figure 5.8
Values of *C* computed from 100 three-dimensional KYST solutions and a subset of 35 ADDTREE solutions (predicted *C*) plotted against the values of *C* computed from the corresponding data (observed *C*).

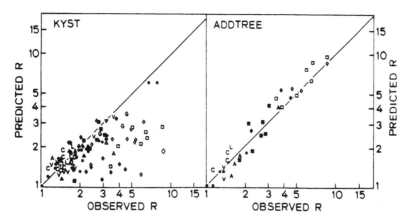

Figure 5.9
Values of *R* computed from 100 three-dimensional KYST solutions and a subset of 35 ADDTREE solutions (predicted *R*) plotted against the values of *R* computed from the corresponding data (observed *R*).

resentations. Other patterns, such as product structures, are better represented by multidimensional scaling or overlapping clusters than by simple trees. Because trees can accommodate any achievable level of C and R (see figures 5.3–5.5), and because no natural analog to the GS model is readily available for trees, C and R are more useful diagnostics for low-dimensional spatial models than for trees. Other indices that can be used to compare trees and spatial models are discussed by Pruzansky, Tversky, and Carroll (1982). The present article focuses on spatial solutions, not on trees; the comparison between them is introduced here merely to demonstrate the diagnostic significance of C and R. An empirical comparison of trees and spatial solutions of various data is reported in Fillenbaum and Rapoport (1971).

A descriptive analysis of the data base revealed that similarity ratings and word associations produced, on the average, higher C and R than same–different judgments or identification errors. However, these response measures were confounded with the distinction between perceptual and conceptual data. Neither the number of objects in the set nor the fit of the (three-dimensional) solution correlated significantly with either C or R.

Finally, the great majority of visual and auditory stimulus sets had values of C and R that were less than 2, and most factorial designs had values of C and R that were less than 1.5. Extremely high values of C and R were invariably the result of a single focal element that was the nearest neighbor of most other elements. Moderately high values of C and R, however, also arise from other patterns involving multiple foci and outliers.

Foci and Outliers

A set has multiple foci if it contains two or more elements that are the nearest neighbors of more than one element. We distinguish between two types of multiple foci: local and global. Let S_i be the set of elements in S whose nearest neighbor is i. (Thus, N_i is the number of elements in S_i.) A focal element i is said to be local if it is closer to all elements of S_i than to any other member of S. That is, $d(i, a) < d(i, b)$ for all $a \in S_i$ and $b \in S - S_i$. Two or more focal elements are called global foci if they function together as a single focal element. Specifically, i and j are a pair of global foci if they are each other's nearest neighbors and if they induce an identical (or nearly identical) proximity order on the other elements. Suppose $a \in S_i$ and $b \in S_j$, $a \neq j$ and $b \neq i$. If i and j are local foci, then $d(i, a) < d(i, b)$ and $d(j, a) > d(j, b)$. On the other hand, if i and j are a pair of global foci, then $d(i, a) \leq d(i, b)$ if $d(j, a) \leq d(j, b)$. Thus, local foci suggest distinct clusters, whereas global foci suggest a single cluster.

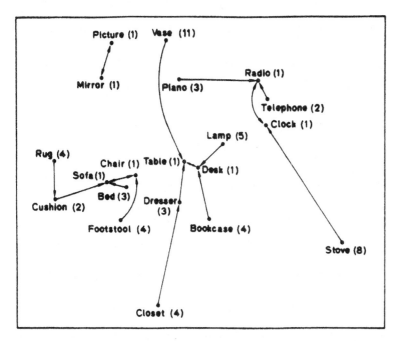

Figure 5.10
Nearest neighbor relations, represented by arrows, superimposed on a two-dimensional KYST solution of proximity ratings between instances of furniture (Mervis et al., 1975; Data Set 61). (The R value of each instance is given in parentheses.)

Figure 5.10 illustrates both local and global foci in categorical ratings of proximity between instances of furniture (Mervis et al. 1975; data set 61). The nearest neighbor of each instance is denoted by an arrow that is superimposed on the two-dimensional KYST solution of these data. The reciprocity of each instance (i.e., its rank from its nearest neighbor) is given in parentheses. Figure 5.10 reveals four foci that are the nearest neighbor of three elements each. These include two local foci, *sofa* and *radio*, and a pair of global foci, *table* and *desk*.

The R values show that *sofa* is closest to *chair*, *cushion*, and *bed*, whereas *radio* is closest to *clock*, *telephone*, and *piano*. These are exactly the instances that selected *sofa* and *radio*, respectively, as their nearest neighbor. It follows readily that for a local focal element i, $R_a \leq N_i$ for any a $\in S_i$. That is, the R value of an element cannot exceed the nearest neighbor count of the relevant local focus. In contrast, *table* and *desk* behave like global foci: They are each other's nearest neighbor, and they induce a similar (though not identical) proximity order on the remaining instances.

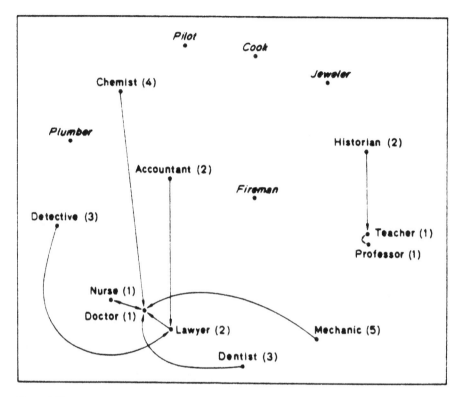

Figure 5.11
Nearest neighbor relations, represented by arrows, superimposed on a two-dimensional KYST solution of association between professions (Marshall & Cofer, 1970; Data Set 94). (The R value of each instance is given in parentheses. Outliers are italicized.)

Multiple foci produce intermediate C and R whose values increase with the size of the cluster. Holding the distribution of N_i (and hence the value of C) constant, R is generally greater for global than for local foci. Another characteristic that affects R but not C is the presence of outliers. A collection of elements are called *outliers* if they are furthest away from all other elements. Thus, k is an outlier if $d(i, k) > d(i, j)$ for all i and for any nonoutlier j. Figure 11 illustrates a collection of outliers in the categorical associations between professions derived from word association norms (Marshall & Cofer, 1970; data set 94).

Figure 5.11 reveals two local foci (*teacher, doctor*) and five outliers (*plumber, pilot, cook, jeweler, fireman*) printed in italics. These outliers were not elicited as an association to any of the other professions, nor did they produce any other profession as

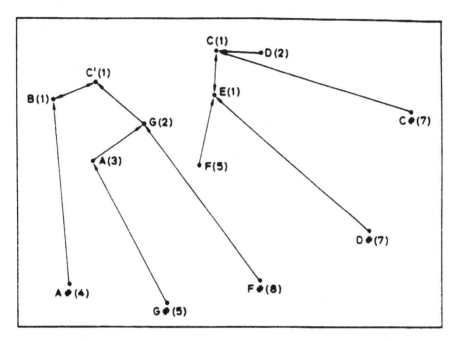

Figure 5.12
Nearest neighbor relations, represented by arrows, superimposed on a two-dimensional KYST solution of judgments of dissimilarity between musical notes (Krumhansl, 1979; Data Set 24). (The R value of each instance is given in parentheses.)

an association. Consequently, no arrows for these elements are drawn; they are all maximally distant from all other elements, including each other. For the purpose of computing R, the outliers were ranked last and the ties among them were broken at random.

Note that the arrows, which depict the nearest neighbor relation in the data, are not always compatible with the multidimensional scaling solution. For example, in the categorical association data, *doctor* is the nearest neighbor of *chemist* and *mechanic*. In the spatial solution of figure 5.11, however, *chemist* is closer to *plumber* and to *accountant*, whereas *mechanic* is closer to *dentist* and to *lawyer*.

A different pattern of foci and outliers arising from judgments of musical tones (Krumhansl, 1979; data set 24) is presented in figure 5.12. The stimuli were the 13 notes of the chromatic scale, and the judgments were made in the context of the C major scale. The nearest neighbor graph approximates two sets of global foci, (C, E) and (B, C', G), and a collection of five outliers, (A♯, G♯, F♯, D♯, C♯). In the data, the scale notes are closer to each other than to the nonscale notes (i.e., the five sharps). In addition, each nonscale note is closer to some scale note than to any other nonscale note. This property of the data, which is clearly seen in the nearest neighbor graph, is not satisfied by the two-dimensional solution in which all nonscale notes have other nonscale notes as their nearest neighbors.

The presence of outliers increases R but has little or no impact on C because an outlier is not the nearest neighbor of any point. Indeed, the data of figures 5.11 and 5.12 yield low C/R ratios of .66 and .68, respectively, as compared with an overall mean ratio of about 1 (see table 5.4). In contrast, a single focal element tends to produce a high C/R ratio, as well as high C and R. Indeed, $C/R > 1$ in 81% of the cases where the category name is included in the set, but $C/R > 1$ in only 35% of the remaining conceptual data. Thus, a high C/R suggests a single focus, whereas a low C/R suggests outliers.

Discussion

Our theoretical analysis of nearest neighbor relations has two thrusts: diagnostic and descriptive. We have demonstrated the diagnostic significance of nearest neighbor statistics for geometric representations, and we have suggested that centrality and reciprocity could be used to identify and describe certain patterns of proximity data.

Nearest neighbor statistics may serve three diagnostic functions. First, the dimensionality of a spatial representation sets an absolute upper bound on the number of points that can share the same nearest neighbor. A nearest neighbor count that exceeds 5 or 11 could be used to rule out, respectively, a two- ro a three-dimensional representation. Indeed, the fruit data (table 5.1) and some of the other conceptual data described in table 5.3 produce centrality values that cannot be accommodated in a low-dimensional space.

Second, a much stricter bound on C and R is implied by the GS model that appends to the geometric assumptions of multidimensional scaling the statistical assumption that the points under study represent a sample from some continuous multivariate distribution. In this model both C and R are less than 2, regardless of the dimensionality of the solution space. If the statistical assumption is accepted, at least as first approximation, the adequacy of a multidimensional scaling representation can be assessed by testing whether C or R fall in the permissible range. The plausibility of the statistical assumption depends both on the nature of the stimuli and the manner in which they are selected. Because the centrality of multidimensional scaling solutions is similar to that implied by the GS model, the observed high values of C cannot be attributed to the sampling assumption alone; it casts some doubt on the geometric assumption.

Third, aside from the geometric and the statistical assumptions, one can examine whether the nearest neighbor statistics of the data match the values computed from their multidimensional scaling solutions. The finding that, for much of the conceptual data, the former are considerably greater than the latter points to some limitation of the spatial solutions and suggests alternative representations. On the other hand, the finding that much of the perceptual data are consistent with the GS bound supports the geometric interpretation of these data.

Other diagnostic statistics for testing spatial solutions (and trees) are based on the distribution of the interpoint distances. For example, Sattath and Tversky (1977) showed that the distribution of interpoint distances arising from a convex configuration of points in the plane exhibits positive skewness whereas the distribution of interpoint distances induced by ultrametric and by many additive trees tends to exhibit negative skewness (see Pruzansky et al., 1982). These authors also showed in a simulation study that the proportion of elongated triangles (i.e., triples of point with two large distances and one small distance) tends to be greater for points generated by an additive tree than for points sampled from the Euclidean plane. A combination of skewness and elongation effectively distinguished data sets that were better described by a plane from those that were better fit by a tree. Unlike the present analysis that is purely ordinal, however, skewness and elongation assume an interval scale measure of distance or proximity, and they are not invariant under monotone transformations.

Diagnostic statistics in general and nearest neighbor indices in particular could help choose among alternative representations, although this choice is commonly based on nonstatistical criteria such as interpretability and simplicity of display. The finding of high C and R in the conceptual domain suggests that these data may be better represented by clustering models (e.g., Carroll, 1976; Corter & Tversky, 1985; Cunningham, 1978; Johnson, 1967; Sattath & Tversky, 1977; Shepard & Arabie, 1979) than by low-dimensional spatial models. Indeed, Pruzansky et al. (1982) observed in a sample of 20 studies that conceptual data were better fit by an additive tree than by a two-dimensional space whereas the perceptual data exhibited the opposite pattern. This observation may be due to the hierarchical character of much conceptual data, as suggested by the present analysis. Alternatively, conceptual data may generally have more dimensions than perceptual data, and some high-dimensional configurations are better approximated by a tree than by a two- or a three-dimensional solution. The relative advantage of trees may also stem from the fact that they can represent the effect of common features better than spatial solutions. Indeed, studies of similarity judgments showed that the weight of common features (relative to distinctive features) is greater in conceptual than in perceptual stimuli (Gati & Tversky, 1984).

High centrality data can also be fit by hybrid models combining both hierarchical and spatial components (see, e.g., Carroll, 1976; Krumhansl, 1978, 1983; Winsberg & Carroll, 1984). For example, dissimilarity can be expressed by $D(x, y) + d(x) + d(y)$, where $D(x, y)$ is the distance between x and y in a common Euclidean space and $d(x)$ and $d(y)$ are the distances from x and y to that common space. Note that $d(x) + d(y)$ is the distance between x and y in a singular tree having no internal structure (see figure 5.4). This model, therefore, can be interpreted as a sum of a spatial (Euclidean) distance and a (singular) tree distance. Because a singular tree produces maximal C and R, the hybrid model can accommodate a wide range of nearest neighbor data.

To illustrate this model we applied the Marquardt (1963) method of nonlinear least-squares regression to the fruit data presented in table 5.1. This procedure yielded a two-dimensional Euclidean solution, similar to figure 5.1, and a function, d, that associates a positive additive constant with each of the instances. The solution fits the data considerably better ($r^2 = .91$) than does the three-dimensional Euclidean solution ($r^2 = .54$) with the same number of parameters. As expected, the additive constant associated with the superordinate was much smaller than the constants associated with the instances. Normalizing the scale so that $\max[D(x, y)] = D(olive, grapefruit) = 1$ yields $d(fruit) = .11$, compared with $d(orange) = .27$ for the most typical fruit and $d(coconut) = .67$ for a rather atypical fruit. As a consequence, the hybrid model—like the additive tree of figure 5.2—produces maximal values of C and R.

The above hybrid model is formally equivalent to the symmetric form of the spatial density model of Krumhansl (1978). The results of the previous analysis, however, are inconsistent with the spatial density account in which the dissimilarity between points increases with the local densities of the spatial regions in which they are located. According to this theory, the constants associated with *fruit* and *orange*, which lie in a relatively dense region of the space, should be greater than those associated with *tomato* or *coconut*, which lie in sparser regions of the space (see figure 5.1). The findings that the latter values are more than twice as large as the former indicates that the additive constants of the hybrid model reflect nontypicality or unique attributes rather than local density (see also Krumhansl 1983).

From a descriptive standpoint, nearest neighbor analysis offers new methods for investigating proximity data in the spirit of exploratory data analysis. The patterns of centrality and reciprocity observed in the data may reveal empirical regularities and illuminate interesting phenomena. For example, in the original analyses of the categorical rating data, the superordinate was located in the center of a two-dimensional configuration (see, e.g., Smith & Medin, 1981). This result was interpreted as indirect confirmation of the usefulness of the Euclidean model, which recognized the central role of the superordinate. The present analysis highlights the special role of the superordinate but shows that its high degree of centrality is inconsistent with a low-dimensional spatial representation. The analysis of the categorical data also reveals that nearest neighbor relations follow the direction of increased typicality. In the data of Mervis et al. (1975), where all instances are ordered by typicality, the less typical instance is the nearest neighbor of the more typical instance in 53 of 74 cases for which the nearest neighbor relation is not symmetric (data sets 60–66, excluding the category name). Finally, the study of local and global foci and of outliers may facilitate the analysis of the structure of natural categories (cf. Medin & Smith, 1984; Smith & Medin, 1981). It is hoped that the conceptual and computational tools afforded by nearest neighbor analysis will enrich the description, the analysis, and the interpretation of proximity data.

Note

This work has greatly benefited from discussions with Larry Maloney, Yosef Rinott, Gideon Schwarz, and Ed Smith.

References

Arabie, P., & Rips, L. J. (1972). [Similarity between animals]. Unpublished data.

Attneave, F. (1957). Transfer of experience with a class schema to identification learning of patterns and shapes. *Journal of Experimental Psychology, 54,* 81–88.

Beals, R., Krantz, D. H., & Tversky, A. (1968). The foundations of multidimensional scaling. *Psychological Review, 75,* 127–142.

Berglund, B., Berglund, V., Engen, T., & Ekman, G. (1972). Multidimensional analysis of twenty-one odors. *Reports of the Psychological Laboratories, University of Stockholm* (Report No. 345). Stockholm, Sweden: University of Stockholm.

Block, J. (1957). Studies in the phenomenology of emotions. *Journal of Abnormal and Social Psychology, 54,* 358–363.

Boster, X. (1980). *How the expectations prove the rule: An analysis of informant disagreement in aguaruna manioc identification.* Unpublished doctoral dissertation, University of California, Berkeley.

Bricker, P. D., & Pruzansky, S. A. (1970). *A comparison of sorting and pair-wise similarity judgment techniques for scaling auditory stimuli.* Unpublished paper, Bell Laboratories, Murray Hill, NJ.

Carroll, J. D. (1976). Spatial, non-spatial, and hybrid models for scaling. *Psychometrika, 41,* 439–463.

Carroll, J. D., & Chang, J. J. (1973). A method for fitting a class of hierarchical tree structure models to dissimilarities data and its application to some "body parts" data of Miller's. *Proceedings of the 81st Annual Convention of the American Psychological Association, 8,* 1097–1098.

Carroll, J. D., & Wish, M. (1974). Multidimensional perceptual models and measurement methods. In E. C. Carterette & M. P. Friedman (Eds.), *Handbook of perception* (Vol. 2, pp. 391–447). New York: Academic Press.

Clark, H. H., & Card, S. K. (1969). Role of semantics in remembering comparative sentences. *Journal of Experimental Psychology, 82,* 545–553.

Cohen, B. H., Bousefield, W. A., & Whitmarsh, G. A. (1957, August). *Cultural norms for verbal items in 43 categories* (University of Connecticut Tech. Rep. No. 22). Storrs: University of Connecticut.

Coombs, C. H. (1964). *A theory of data.* New York: Wiley.

Corter, J., & Tversky, A. (1985). *Extended similarity trees.* Unpublished manuscript, Stanford University.

Cunningham, J. P. (1978). Free trees and bidirectional trees as representations of psychological distance. *Journal of Mathematical Psychology, 17,* 165–188.

Ekman, G. (1954). Dimensions of color vision. *Journal of Psychology, 38,* 467–474.

Fillenbaum, S., & Rapoport, A. (1971). *Structures in the subjective lexicon: An experimental approach to the study of semantic fields.* New York: Academic Press.

Fischhoff, B., Slovic, P., Lichtenstein, S., Read, S., & Combs, B. (1978). How safe is safe enough? A psychometric study of attitudes towards technological risks and benefits. *Policy Sciences, 9,* 127–152.

Fish, R. S. (1981). *Color: Studies of its perceptual, memory and linguistic representation.* Unpublished doctoral dissertation, Stanford University.

Frijda, N. H., & Philipszoon, E. (1963). Dimensions of recognition of expression. *Journal of Abnormal and Social Psychology, 66,* 45–51.

Furnas, G. W. (1980). *Objects and their features: The metric representation of two-class data.* Unpublished doctoral dissertation, Stanford University.

Gati, I. (1978). *Aspects of psychological similarity.* Unpublished doctoral dissertation, Hebrew University of Jerusalem.

Gati, I., & Tversky, A. (1982). Representations of qualitative and quantitative dimensions. *Journal of Experimental Psychology: Human Perception and Performance, 8,* 325–340.

Gati, I., & Tversky, A. (1984). Weighting common and distinctive features in perceptual and conceptual judgments. *Cognitive Psychology, 16,* 341–370.

Gregson, R. A. M. (1976). A comparative evaluation of seven similarity models. *British Journal of Mathematical and Statistical Psychology, 29,* 139–156.

Guttman, L. (1971). Measurement as structural theory. *Psychometrika, 36,* 465–506.

Henley, N. M. (1969). A psychological study of the semantics of animal terms. *Journal of Verbal Learning and Behavior, 8,* 176–184.

Hosman, J., & Künnapas, T. (1972). On the relation between similarity and dissimilarity estimates. *Reports from the Psychological Laboratory, University of Stockholm* (Report No. 354, pp. 1–8). Stockholm, Sweden: University of Stockholm.

Hutchinson, J. W., & Lockhead, G. R. (1975). Categorization of semantically related words. *Bulletin of the Psychonomic Society, 6,* 427.

Indow, T., & Aoki, N. (1983). Multidimensional mapping of 178 Munsell colors. *Color Research and Application, 8,* 145–152.

Indow, T., & Kanazawa, K. (1960). Multidimensional mapping of Munsell colors varying in hue, chroma, and value. *Journal of Experimental Psychology, 59,* 330–336.

Indow, T., & Uchizono, T. (1960). Multidimensional mapping of Munsell colors varying in hue and chroma. *Journal of Experimental Psychology, 59,* 321–329.

Jenkins, J. J. (1970). The 1952 Minnesota word association norms. In L. Postman & G. Keppel (Eds.), *Norms of free association.* New York: Academic Press.

Johnson, S. C. (1967). Hierarchical clustering schemes. *Psychometrika, 32,* 241–254.

Krantz, D. H., & Tversky, A. (1975). Similarity of rectangles: An analysis of subjective dimensions. *Journal of Mathematical Psychology, 12,* 4–34.

Kraus, V. (1976). *The structure of occupations in Israel.* Unpublished doctoral dissertation, Hebrew University of Jerusalem.

Krumhansl, C. L. (1978). Concerning the applicability of geometric models to similarity data: The interrelationship between similarity and spatial density. *Psychological Review, 85,* 445–463.

Krumhansl, C. L. (1979). The psychological representation of musical pitch in a tonal context. *Cognitive Psychology, 11,* 346–374.

Krumhansl, C. L. (1983, August). *Set-theoretic and spatial models of similarity: Some considerations in application.* Paper presented at the meeting of the Society for Mathematical Psychology, Boulder, CO.

Kruskal, J. B., Young, F. W., & Seery, J. B. (1973). *How to use KYST, a very flexible program to do multidimensional scaling and unfolding.* Unpublished paper. Bell Laboratories, Murray Hill, NJ.

Künnapas, T. (1966). Visual perception of capital letters: Multidimensional ratio scaling and multidimensional similarity. *Scandinavian Journal of Psychology, 7,* 188–196.

Künnapas, T. (1967). Visual memory of capital letters: Multidimensional ratio scaling and multidimensional similarity. *Perceptual and Motor Skills, 25,* 345–350.

Künnapas, T., & Janson, A. J. (1969). Multidimensional similarity of letters. *Perceptual and Motor Skills, 28,* 3–12.

Maloney, L. T. (1983). Nearest neighbor analysis of point processes: Simulations and evaluations. *Journal of Mathematical Psychology, 27,* 235–250.

Marquardt, D. W. (1963). An algorithm for least-squares estimation of nonlinear parameters. *Journal of the Society of Industrial and Applied Mathematics, 11,* 431–441.

Marshall, G. R., & Cofer, C. N. (1970). Single-word free-association norms for 328 responses from the Connecticut cultural norms for verbal items in categories. In L. Postman & G. Keppel (Eds.), *Norms of free association* (pp. 320–360). New York: Academic Press.

Medin, D. L., & Smith, E. E. (1984). Concepts and concept formation. *Annual Review of Psychology, 35,* 113–138.

Mervis, C. B., Rips, L., Rosch, E., Shoben, E. J., & Smith, E. E. (1975). [Relatedness of concepts]. Unpublished data.

Miller, G. A., & Nicely, P. E. (1955). An analysis of perceptual confusions among some English consonants. *Journal of the Acoustical Society of America, 27,* 338–352.

Newman, C. M., & Rinott, Y. (in press). Nearest neighbors and Voronoi volumes in high dimensional point processes with various distance functions. *Advances in Applied Probability.*

Newman, C. M., Rinott, Y., & Tversky, A. (1983). Nearest neighbors and Voronoi regions in certain point processes. *Advances in Applied Probability, 15,* 726–751.

Odlyzko, A. M., & Sloane, J. A. (1979). New bounds on the number of unit spheres that can touch a unit sphere in *n* dimensions. *Journal of Combinatorial Theory, 26,* 210–214.

Podgorny, P., & Garner, W. R. (1979). Reaction time as a measure of inter- and intrasubjective similarity: Letters of the alphabet. *Perception and Psychophysics, 26,* 37–52.

Posner, M. I., & Keele, S. W. (1968). On the genesis of abstract ideas. *Journal of Experimental Psychology, 77,* 353–363.

Pruzansky, S., Tversky, A., & Carroll, J. D. (1982). Spatial versus tree representations of proximity data. *Psychometrika, 47,* 3–24.

Roberts, F. D. K. (1969). Nearest neighbors in a Poisson ensemble. *Biometrika, 56,* 401–406.

Robinson, J. P., & Hefner, R. (1967). Multidimensional differences in public and academic perceptions of nations. *Journal of Personality and Social Psychology, 7,* 251–259.

Rosch, E. (1978). Principles of categorization. In E. Rosch & B. B. Floyd (Eds.), *Cognition and categorization*. Hillsdale, NJ: Erlbaum.

Rosch, E., & Mervis, C. B. (1975). Family resemblances: Studies in the internal structure of categories. *Cognitive Psychology, 7*, 573–605.

Rosch, E., Mervis, C. B., Gray, W., Johnson, D., & Boyes-Braem, P. (1976). Basic objects in natural categories. *Cognitive Psychology, 3*, 382–439.

Rothkopf, E. Z. (1957). A measure of stimulus similarity and errors in some paired-associate learning tasks. *Journal of Experimental Psychology, 53*, 94–101.

Sattath, S., & Tversky, A. (1977). Additive similarity trees. *Psychometrika, 42*, 319–345.

Schwarz, G., & Tversky, A. (1980). On the reciprocity of proximity relations. *Journal of Mathematical Psychology, 22*, 157–175.

Shepard, R. N. (1958). Stimulus and response generalization: Tests of a model relating generalization to distance in psychological space. *Journal of Experimental Psychology, 55*, 509–523.

Shepard, R. N. (1962a). The analysis of proximities: Multidimensional scaling with an unknown distance function. Part I. *Psychometrika, 27*, 125–140.

Shepard, R. N. (1962b). The analysis of proximities: Multidimensional scaling with an unknown distance function. Part II. *Psychometrika, 27*, 219–246.

Shepard, R. N. (1974). Representation of structure in similarity data: Problems and prospects. *Psychometrika, 39*, 373–421.

Shepard, R. N. (1980). Multidimensional scaling, tree-fitting, and clustering. *Science, 210*, 390–398.

Shepard, R. N. (1984). Ecological constraints on internal representation: Resonant kinematics of perceiving, imagining, thinking, and dreaming. *Psychological Review, 91*, 417–447.

Shepard, R. N., & Arabie, P. (1979). Additive clustering: Representation of similarities as combinations of discrete overlapping properties. *Psychological Review, 86*, 87–123.

Shepard, R. N., Kilpatric, D. W., & Cunningham, J. P. (1975). The internal representation of numbers. *Cognitive Psychology, 7*, 82–138.

Smith, E. E., & Medin, D. L. (1981). *Categories and concepts*. Cambridge, MA: Harvard University Press.

Smith, E. E., & Tversky, A. (1981). [The centrality effect]. Unpublished data.

Sokal, R. R. (1974). Classification: Purposes, principles, progress, prospects. *Science, 185*, 1115–1123.

Starr, C. (1969). Social benefit versus technological risk. *Science, 165*, 1232–1238.

Stringer, P. (1967). Cluster analysis of non-verbal judgments of facial expressions. *British Journal of Mathematical and Statistical Psychology, 20*, 71–79.

Terbeek, D. A. (1977). A cross-language multidimensional scaling study of vowel perception. *UCLA Working Papers in Phonetics*, (Report No. 37).

Tversky, A. (1977). Features of similarity. *Psychological Review, 84*, 327–352.

Tversky, A., & Gati, I. (1982). Similarity, separability, and the triangle inequality. *Psychological Review, 89*, 123–154.

Tversky, A., & Krantz, D. H. (1969). Similarity of schematic faces: A test of interdimensional additivity. *Perception and Psychophysics, 5*, 124–128.

Tversky, A., & Krantz, D. H. (1970). The dimensional representation and the metric structure of similarity data. *Journal of Mathematical Psychology, 7*, 572–596.

Tversky, A., Rinott, Y., & Newman, C. M. (1983). Nearest neighbor analysis of point processes: Applications to multidimensional scaling. *Journal of Mathematical Psychology, 27*, 235–250.

Wender, K. (1971). A test of the independence of dimensions in multidimensional scaling. *Perception & Psychophysics, 10*, 30–32.

Wiener-Ehrlich, W. K. (1978). Dimensional and metric structures in multidimensional scaling. *Perception & Psychophysics, 24*, 399–414.

Winsberg, S., & Carroll, J. D. (1984, June). *A nonmetric method for a multidimensional scaling model postulating common and specific dimensions.* Paper presented at the meeting of the Psychometric Society, Santa Barbara, CA.

Winton, W., Ough, C. S., & Singleton, V. L. (1975). Relative distinctiveness of varietal wines estimated by the ability of trained panelists to name the grape variety correctly. *American Journal of Enological Viticulture, 26*, 5–11.

Wish, M. (1970). Comparisons among multidimensional structures of nations based on different measures of subjective similarity. In L. von Bertalanffy & A. Rapoport (Eds.), *General systems* (Vol. 15, pp. 55–65). Ann Arbor, MI: Society for General Systems Research.

Yoshida, M., & Saito, S. (1969). Multidimensional scaling of the taste of amino acids. *Japanese Psychological Research, 11*, 149–166.

Appendix

This appendix describes each of the studies included in the data base. The descriptions are organized and numbered as in table 5.3. For each data set the following information is provided: (a) the source of the data, (b) the number and type of stimuli used in the study, (c) the design for construction of the stimulus set, (d) the method of measuring proximity, and (e) miscellaneous comments. When selection was not specified by the investigator, the design is labeled *natural selection* in (c).

Perceptual Data

Colors

1. (a) Ekman (1954); (b) 14 spectral (i.e., single wavelength) lights; (c) spanned the visible range at equal intervals; (d) ratings of similarity; (e) the stimuli represent the so-called color circle.

2. (a) Fish (1981); (b) 10 Color-Aid Silkscreen color sheets and their corresponding color names; (c) color circle plus black and white; (d) dissimilarity ratings; (e) stimuli were restricted to those colors for which common English names existed; the data were symmetrized by averaging.

3. (a) Furnas (1980); (b) 20 Color-Aid Silkscreen color sheets; (c) natural selection; (d) dissimilarity ratings.

4. (a) Indow and Uchizono (1960); (b) 21 Munsell color chips; (c) varied in hue and chroma over a wide range; (d) spatial distance was used to indicate dissimilarity; (e) the data were symmetrized by averaging.

5. (a) Indow and Kanazawa (1960); (b) 24 Munsell color chips; (c) varied in hue, value, and chroma over a wide range; (d) spatial distance was used to indicate dissimilarity; (e) the data were symmetrized by averaging.

6. (a) Indow and Uchizono (1960); (b) 21 Munsell color chips; (c) varied in hue and chroma over a wide range; (d) spatial distance was used to indicate dissimilarity; (e) the data were symmetrized by averaging.

7. (a) Shepard (1958); (b) nine Munsell color chips; (c) partial factorial spanning five levels of value and chroma for shades of red; (d) average confusion probabilities across responses in a stimulus identification task.

Letters

8. (a) Hosman and Künnapas (1972); (b) 25 lowercase Swedish letters; (c) natural selection; (d) dissimilarity ratings.

9. (a) Künnapas and Janson (1969); (b) 25 lowercase Swedish letters; (c) natural selection; (d) similarity ratings; (e) data were symmetrized by averaging.

10. (a) Künnapas (1966); (b) nine uppercase Swedish letters; (c) natural selection; (d) ratings of visual similarity; (e) visual presentation; the data were symmetrized by averaging.

11. (a) Künnapas (1967); (b) nine uppercase Swedish letters; (c) natural selection; (d) ratings of visual similarity; (e) auditory presentation; the data were symmetrized by averaging.

12. (a) Podgorny and Garner (1979); (b) 26 uppercase English letters; (c) complete alphabet; (d) dissimilarity ratings; (e) data were symmetrized by averaging.

13. (a) Podgorny and Garner (1979); (b) 26 uppercase English letters; (c) complete alphabet; (d) discriminative reaction times; (e) data were symmetrized by averaging.

Other Visual

14. (a) Coren (personal communication, February, 1980); (b) 45 visual illusions; (c) natural selection; (d) correlations across subjects of the magnitudes of the illusions.

15. (a) Gati (1978); (b) 16 polygons; (c) 4×4 factorial design that varied shape and size; (d) dissimilarity ratings.

16. (a) Gati and Tversky (1982); (b) 16 plants; (c) 4×4 factorial design that varied the shape of the pot and the elongation of the leaves; (d) dissimilarity ratings; (e) from table 1 in the source reference.

17. (a) Gregson (1976); (b) 16 dot figures; (c) 4×4 factorial design that varied the horizontal and vertical distances between two dots; (d) similarity ratings.

18. (a) Gregson (1976); (b) 16 figures consisting of pairs of brick wall patterns; (c) 4×4 factorial design that varied the heights of the left and right walls in the figure; (d) similarity ratings.

19. (a) Shepard (1958); (b) nine circles; (c) varied in diameter only; (d) average confusion probabilities across responses in a stimulus identification task.

20. (a) Shepard (1958); (b) nine letters and numbers; (c) natural selection; (d) average confusion probabilities between responses across stimulus–response mappings; (e) responses consisted of placing an electric probe into one of nine holes, which were arranged in a line inside a rectangular slot.

21. (a) Shepard, Kilpatric, and Cunningham (1975); (b) 10 single-digit Arabic numerals (i.e., 0–9); (c) complete set; (d) dissimilarity ratings; (e) stimuli were judged as Arabic numerals (cf. data set 49).

Auditory

22. (a) Bricker and Pruzansky (1970); (b) 12 sine wave tones; (c) 4×3 factorial design that varied modulation frequency (4 levels) and modulation percentage (3 levels); (d) dissimilarity ratings.

23. (a) Bricker and Pruzansky (1970); (b) 12 square wave tones; (c) 4×3 factorial design that varied modulation frequency (4 levels) and modulation percentage (3 levels); (d) dissimilarity ratings.

24. (a) Krumhansl (1979); (b) 13 musical tones; (c) complete set; the notes of the chromatic scale for one octave; (d) similarity ratings; (e) one of three musical contexts (i.e., an ascending C major scale, a descending C major scale, and the C major chord) was played prior to each stimulus pair, the data were averaged across contexts and symmetrized by averaging across presentation order.

25. (a) Miller and Nicely (1955); (b) consonant phonemes; (c) complete set; (d) probability of confusion in a stimulus–response identification task; (e) stimuli were presented with varying levels of noise; symmetrized data are taken from Carroll and Wish (1974).

26. (a) Rothkopf (1975); (b) 36 Morse code signals: 26 letters and 10 digits; (c) complete set; (d) probability of confusion in a same–different task; (e) symmetrized by averaging.

27. (a) Terbeek (1977); (b) 12 vowel sounds; (c) varied in four linguistic features; (d) triadic comparisons.

Gustatory and Olfactory

28. (a) Winton, Ough, and Singleton (1975); (b) 15 varieties of California white wines vinted in 1972; (c) availability from University of California, Davis, Experimental Winery; (d) confusion probabilities in a free identification task; (e) expert judges were used, and they were unaware of the composition of the stimulus set; therefore, the response set was limited only by their knowledge of the varieties of white wines.

29. (a) Winton, Ough, and Singleton (1975); (b) 15 varieties of California white wines vinted in 1973; (c) availability from University of California, Davis, Experimental Winery; (d) confusion probabilities in a free identification task; (e) same as data set 28.

30. (a) Yoshida and Saito (1969); (b) 20 taste stimuli composed of 16 amino acids; three concentrations of monosodium glutamate and sodium chloride as reference points; (c) natural selection; (d) dissimilarity ratings.

31. (a) Berglund, Berglund, Engen, and Ekman (1972); (b) 21 odors derived from various chemical compounds; (c) natural selection; (d) similarity ratings.

Conceptual Stimuli

Assorted Semantic

32. (a) Arabie and Rips (1972); (b) 30 animal names; (c) natural selection; (d) similarity ratings; (e) replication of Henley (1969; data set 42) using similarity ratings instead of dissimilarity.

33. (a) Block (1957); (b) 15 emotion words; (c) natural selection; (d) correlations across 20 semantic differential connative dimensions; (e) female sample.

34. (a) Stringer (1967); (b) 30 facial expressions of emotions; (c) taken from Frijda and Philipszoon (1963); (d) frequency of not being associated in a free sorting task; (e) the study also found general agreement among subjects regarding spontaneous verbal labels for the emotion portayed by each facial expression.

35. (a) Clark and Card (1969); (b) eight linguistic forms; (c) $2 \times 2 \times 2$ factorial design varying comparative/equative verb phrases, positive/negative, and marked/unmarked adjectives across sentences; (d) confusions between the forms in a cued recall task; (e) from Table 1 in the source reference; symmetrized by averaging.

36. (a) Coombs (1964); (b) 10 psychological journals; (c) natural selection; (d) frequency of citations between the journals; (e) data were converted to conditional probabilities and symmetrized by averaging.

37. (a) Fischhoff, Slovic, Lichtenstein, Read, and Combs (1978); (b) 30 societal risks; (c) natural selection, included the eight items used by Starr (1969); (d) correlations between risks across average ratings for nine risk factors; (e) nonexpert sample.

38. (a) Fischhoff et al. (1978); (b) 30 societal risks; (c) natural selection; included the eight items used by Starr (1969); (d) nine-dimensional Euclidean distances between risks based on average ratings for nine risk factors; (e) nonexpert sample.

39. (a) Fischhoff et al. (1978); (b) 30 societal risks; (c) natural selection; included the eight items used by Starr (1969); (d) nine-dimensional Euclidean distances between risks based on average ratings for nine risk factors; (e) expert sample.

40. (a) Furnas (1980); (b) 15 bird names; (c) chosen to span the Rosch (1978) typicality norms; (d) dissimilarity ratings.

41. (a) Gati (1978; cited in Tversky & Gati, 1982); (b) 16 descriptions of students; (c) 4 × 4 design that varied major field of study and political affiliation; (d) dissimilarity ratings.

42. (a) Henley (1969); (b) 30 animal names; (c) natural selection; (d) dissimilarity ratings; (e) replicated by Arabie and Rips (1972; data set 32) using similarity ratings.

43. (a) Hutchinson and Lockhead (1975); (b) 36 words for various objects; (c) 6 words were selected from each of six categories such that each set of 6 could be naturally subdivided into two sets of 3; (d) dissimilarity ratings; (e) subcategories were chosen to conform to a cross classification based on common versus rare objects.

44. (a) Jenkins (1970); (b) 30 attribute words; (c) all attribute words contained in the Kent–Rosanoff word association test; (d) word associations, specifically the conditional probability that a particular response was given as an associate to a particular stimulus word (computed as a proportion of all responses); (e) contains many pairs of opposites.

45. (a) Kraus (1976); (b) 35 occupations; (c) natural selection; (d) similarity ratings.

46. (a) Miller (as reported by Carroll & Chang, 1973); (b) 20 names of body parts; (c) natural selection; (d) frequency of co-occurrence in a sorting task; (e) given in table 1 of the source reference.

47. (a) Robinson and Hefner (1967); (b) 17 names of countries; (c) chosen to span most geographic regions, and high similarity pairs were avoided; (d) the percentage of times that each country was chosen as 1 of the 3 most similar to the reference country; (e) public sample; 9 reference countries per subject.

48. (a) Robinson and Hefner (1967); (b) 17 names of countries; (c) chosen to span most geographic regions, and high similarity pairs were avoided; (d) the percentage

of times that each country was chosen as 1 of the 3 most similar to the reference country; (e) academic sample; 17 reference countries per subject.

49. (a) Shepard et al. (1975); (b) 10 single-digit Arabic numerals (i.e., 0–9); (c) complete set; (d) dissimilarity ratings; (e) stimuli were judged as abstract concepts (cf. data set 21).

50. (a) Wish (1970); (b) 12 names of countries; (c) based on Robinson and Hefner (1967); (d) similarity ratings; (e) pilot data for the referenced study.

51. (a) Boster (1980); (b) a set of (hard to name) maniocs, which are a type of edible root; (c) natural selection; (d) percentage agreement between 25 native informants regarding the names of the maniocs; (e) although the stimuli were maniocs in this experiment, the items for which proximity was measured in this anthropological study were the informants.

52. (a) Boster (1980); (b) a set of (easily named) maniocs, which are a type of edible root; (c) natural selection; (d) percentage agreement between 21 native informants regarding the names of the maniocs; (e) although the stimuli were maniocs in this experiment, the items for which proximity was measured in this anthropological study were the informants.

Categorical Ratings 1 (With Superordinate)

53–59. (a) Mervis et al. (1975); (b) 20 names of exemplars and the name of the category for each of the seven categories: fruit (53), furniture (54), sports (55), tools (56), vegetables (57), vehicles (58), and weapons (59); (c) stimuli for each category were chosen to span a large range of prototypicality as measured in a previous study; (d) relatedness judgments; (e) these data are identical to those for data sets 60 through 66 except that they include observations for the proximity between exemplars and the category names for each category.

Categorical Ratings 1 (Without Superordinate)

60–66. (a) Mervis et al. (1975); (b) 20 names of exemplars and the name of the category for each of the seven categories: fruit (60), furniture (61), sports (62), tools (63), vegetables (64), vehicles (65), and weapons (66); (c) stimuli for each category were chosen to span a large range of prototypicality as measured in a previous study; (d) relatedness judgments; (e) these data are identical to those for data sets 53 through 59 except that they do not include observations for the proximity between exemplars and the category names for each category.

Categorical Ratings 2 (With Superordinate)

67–70. (a) Smith and Tversky (1981); (b) six names of exemplars and the category name for the four categories: flowers (67), trees (68), birds (69), and fish (70); (c) natural selection; (d) relatedness judgments; (e) the exemplars are the same as for data sets 71 through 74; however, the data were based on independent judgments by different subjects.

Categorical Ratings 2 (With Distant Superordinate)

71–74. (a) Smith and Tversky (1981); (b) six names of exemplars and the name of a distant superordinate (i.e., plant or animal) for the four categories: flowers (71), trees (72), birds (73), and fish (74); (c) natural selection; (d) relatedness judgments; (e) the exemplars are the same as for data sets 66 through 70; however, the data were based on independent judgments by different subjects.

Categorical Associations (With Superordinate)

75–85. (a) Marshall and Cofer (1970); (b) between 15 and 18 (see table 5.3) exemplars and the category name for each of the categories: birds (75), body parts (76), clothes (77), drinks (78), earth formations (79), fruit (80), house parts (81), musical instruments (82), professions (83), weapons (84), and weather (85); (c) exemplars were selected to span the production frequencies reported by Cohen et al. (1957); (d) the conditional probability that a particular exemplar or the category name was given as an associate to an exemplar (computed as a proportion of all responses) was based on the Marshall and Cofer norms; the likelihood that a particular exemplar was given as a response to the category name (computed as a proportion of all responses) was based on the Cohen et al. norms; (e) the data were symmetrized by averaging.

Categorical Associations (Without Superordinate)

86–96. (a) Marshall and Cofer (1970); (b) between 15 and 18 (see table 5.3) exemplars for each of the categories: birds (86), body parts (87), clothes (88), drinks (89), earth formations (90), fruit (91), house parts (92), musical instruments (93), professions (94), weapons (95), and weather (96); (c) exemplars were selected to span the production frequencies reported by Cohen et al. (1957); (d) the conditional probability that a particular exemplar was given as an associate to an exemplar (computed as a proportion of all responses) was based solely on the Marshall and Cofer norms;

(e) the data were symmetrized by averaging and are identical to data sets 75 through 85, except that the proximities between the category name and the exemplars have been excluded.

Attribute-Based Categories

97–100. (a) Smith and Tversky (1981); (b) each data set contained an attribute word and six objects that possessed the attribute; the attributes were red (97), circle (98), smell (99), and sound (100); (c) stimuli chosen to have little in common other than the named attribute; (d) relatedness judgments.

6 On the Relation between Common and Distinctive Feature Models

Shmuel Sattath and Amos Tversky

The classification of objects (e.g., countries, events, animals, books) plays an important role in the organization of knowledge. Objects can be classified on the basis of features they share; they can also be classified on the basis of their distinctive features. There is a well-known correspondence between predicates (or features) and classes (or clusters). For example, the predicate "two legged" can be viewed as a feature that describes some animals; it can also be seen as a class consisting of all animals that have two legs. The relation between a feature and the corresponding cluster is essentially that between the *intension* (i.e., the meaning) of a concept and its *extension* (i.e., the set of objects to which it applies). The clusters or features used to classify objects can be specified in advance or else derived from some measure of similarity or dissimilarity between the objects via a suitable model. Conversely, a clustering model can be used to predict the observed dissimilarity between the objects. The present chapter investigates the relationship between the classificatory structure of objects and the dissimilarity between them.

Consider a set of objects s, a set of features S, and a mapping that associates each object b in s with a set of features B in S. We assume that both s and S are finite, and we use lowercase letters $a, b, \ldots$ to denote objects in s and uppercase letters to denote features or sets of features. The feature structure associated with s is described by a matrix $M = (m_{ij})$, where $m_{ij} = 1$ if Feature i belongs to Object j and $m_{ij} = 0$ otherwise.

Let $d(a, b)$ be a symmetric and positive $[d(a, b) = d(b, a) > 0]$ index of dissimilarity between a and b. We assume $a \neq b$ and exclude self-dissimilarity. Perhaps the simplest rule that relates the dissimilarity of objects to their feature structure is the *common features* (CF) model. In this model,

$$d(a, b) = K - g(A \cap B)$$

$$= K - \sum_{X \in A \cap B} g(X) \tag{1}$$

where K is a positive constant and g is an additive measure defined on the subsets of S. That is, g is a real-valued non-negative function satisfying $g(X \cup Y) = g(X) + g(Y)$ whenever X and Y are disjoint. To simplify the notation we write $g(X)$ for $g(\{X\})$, and so on.

The CF model offers a natural representation of the proximity between objects: The smaller the measure of their common features the greater the dissimilarity

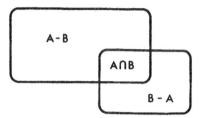

Figure 6.1
A graphic representation of the measures of the common and the distinctive features of a pair of objects.

between the objects (see figure 6.1). This model arises in many contexts: It serves as a basis for several hierarchical clustering procedures (e.g., Hartigan, 1975), and it underlies the additive clustering model of Shepard and Arabie (1979). It has also been used to assess the commonality and the prototypicality of concepts (see Rosch & Mervis, 1975; Smith & Medin, 1981).

An alternative conception of dissimilarity is expressed by the *distinctive features* (DF) model. In this model,

$$d(a,b) = f(A - B) + f(B - A)$$
$$= \sum_{X \in A\Delta B} f(X)$$

(2)

where $A - B$ is the set of features of a that do not belong to b, $A\Delta B = (A - B) \cup (B - A)$, and f is an additive measure defined on the subsets of S. This model, also called the *symmetric difference* metric, was introduced to psychology by Restle (1961). It encompasses the Hamming distance as well as the city-block metric (Shepard, 1980). It also underlies several scaling methods (e.g., Corter & Tversky, 1986; Eisler & Roskam, 1977).

We investigate in this article the relations among the CF model, the DF model, and the feature matrix M. We assume that any feature included in the matrix has a positive weight (i.e., measure); features with zero weight are excluded because they do not affect the dissimilarity of objects. Hence, M defines the *support* of the measure, that is, the set of elements for which it is nonzero.

Consider first the special case in which all objects have a unit weight. That is,

$$f(A) = \sum_{X \in A} f(X) = 1$$

for all a in s. In this case, the measure of the distinctive features of any pair of objects is a linear function of the measure of their common features. Specifically,

$$d(a, b) = f(A - B) + f(B - A)$$

$$= f(A) + f(B) - 2f(A \cap B)$$

$$= 2 - 2f(A \cap B)$$

$$= K - g(A \cap B),$$

where $K = 2$ and $g = 2f$. Hence the two models are indistinguishable if all objects are weighted equally, as in the ultrametric tree (Jardine & Sibson, 1971; Johnson, 1967), in which all objects are equidistant from the root. Indeed, this representation can be interpreted either as a CF model or as a DF model.

Given a feature matrix M, however, the two models are not compatible in general. This is most easily seen in a nested structure. To illustrate, consider the (identi-kit) faces presented in figure 6.2, where each face consists of a basic frame Z (including eyes, nose, and mouth) plus one, two, or three additive components: beard (Y), glasses (X), and moustache (W). In the present discussion, we identify the features of the faces with their distinct physical components.

According to the CF model, then,

$$d(ZY, ZX) = K - g(Z) = d(ZY, ZXW),$$

but

$$d(ZY, ZX) = K - g(Z) > K - g(Z) - g(W)$$

$$= d(ZYW, ZXW).$$

In the DF model, on the other hand,

$$d(ZY, ZX) = f(Y) + f(X) < f(Y) + f(X) + f(W)$$

$$= d(ZY, ZXW),$$

but

$$d(ZY, ZX) = f(Y) + f(X) = d(ZYW, ZXW).$$

The two models, therefore, induce different dissimilarity orders[1] on the faces in figure 6.2; hence they are empirically distinguishable, given a feature matrix M. Nevertheless, we show below that if the data satisfy one model, relative to some feature matrix M, then the other model will also be satisfied, relative to a different

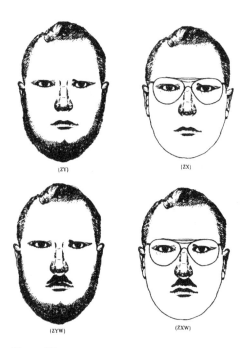

Figure 6.2
Identi-kit faces with a common frame (Z) and 3 additive features: beard (Y), glasses (X), and moustache (W).

feature matrix M'. The two representations are generally different, but they have the same number of free parameters.

Theorem: Let d be a dissimilarity index on s^2, and suppose there is an additive measure g on S and a constant $K > g(B)$, for all b in s, such that

(i) $d(a,b) = K - g(A \cap B)$.

Then there is an additive measure f on S such that

(ii) $d(a,b) = f(A \Delta B) = f(A - B) + f(B - A)$.

Conversely, if there is an additive measure f satisfying (ii) then there exists an additive measure g and a constant K such that (i) holds. Thus, d satisfies the common features model if and only if it satisfies the distinctive features model, up to an additive constant.

To prove this theorem, we define f in terms of g and vice versa and show that the models reduce to each other. The actual proof is given in propositions 1 and 2 of the

Table 6.1
A Feature Matrix for the Faces of Figure 6.2

| | Objects | | | |
| | a | b | c | d |
Features	(ZY)	(ZX)	(ZYW)	(ZXW)
Z	1	1	1	1
Y	1	0	1	0
X	0	1	0	1
W	0	0	1	1

mathematical appendix. Here we describe the transformations relating f and g and illustrate the equivalence of the models.

For any b in s, let $\hat{B} \notin B$ denote a *complementary* feature of b, that is, a feature shared by all objects in s except b. With no loss of generality we can assume that each object has a single complementary feature.

To show how the CF model reduces to the DF model, assume (i) and define f on S as follows:

$$f(X) = \begin{cases} [K + g(\hat{B}) - g(B)]/2 & \text{if } X = \hat{B} \text{ for some } b \in s \\ g(X)/2 & \text{otherwise.} \end{cases} \tag{3}$$

Note that in the CF model $\hat{B}$ enters into all the dissimilarities that do not involve b, whereas in the DF model $\hat{B}$ enters into all the dissimilarities that involve b and into them only. The translation of one model into another is made by changing the relative weights assigned to these features. The above definition sets $f = g/2$ and adds to the measure of each complementary feature a linear function of the overall measure of the respective object.

To obtain the CF model from the DF model assume (ii) and define g on S by

$$g(X) = \begin{cases} 2f(\hat{B}) + f(B) & \text{if } X = \hat{B} \text{ for some } b \in s \\ 2f(X) & \text{otherwise.} \end{cases} \tag{4}$$

Thus, $g = 2f$ for all elements of S except the complementary features, whose values are further augmented by the overall measures of the respective objects.

We next illustrate these transformations and the equivalence of the two models using the dissimilarities between the faces in figure 6.2. The feature matrix associated with these objects is presented in table 6.1. Each column in the matrix represents an object in s, and each row corresponds to a feature in S. Table 6.2 presents above the diagonal the dissimilarities between the objects according to the CF model and below

Table 6.2
Dissimilarities between the Faces of Figure 6.2 Computed According to the CF Model (above Diagonal)
and the DF Model (below Diagonal)

	Objects			
	a	b	c	d
Objects	(ZY)	(ZX)	(ZYW)	(ZXW)
a	—	$K - g(Z)$	$K - g(Z) - g(Y)$	$K - g(Z)$
b	$f(X) + f(Y)$	—	$K - g(Z)$	$K - g(Z) - g(X)$
c	$f(W)$	$f(X) + f(Y) + f(W)$	—	$K - g(Z) - g(W)$
d	$f(X) + f(Y) + f(W)$	$f(W)$	$f(X) + f(Y)$	—

Table 6.3
An Extended Feature Matrix for the Faces of Figure 6.2

	Objects					
	a	b	c	d		
Features	(ZY)	(ZX)	(ZYW)	(ZXW)	f'	g'
Z	1	1	1	1	$g(Z)/2$	$2f(Z)$
Y	1	0	1	0	$g(Y)/2$	$2f(Y)$
X	0	1	0	1	$g(X)/2$	$2f(X)$
W	0	0	1	1	$g(W)/2$	$2f(W)$
$\hat{A}$	0	1	1	1	$[K - g(Z) - g(Y)]/2$	$f(Z) + f(Y)$
$\hat{B}$	1	0	1	1	$[K - g(Z) - g(X)]/2$	$f(Z) + f(X)$
$\hat{C}$	1	1	0	1	$[K - g(Z) - g(Y) - g(W)]/2$	$f(Z) + f(Y) + f(W)$
$\hat{D}$	1	1	1	0	$[K - g(Z) - g(X) - g(W)]/2$	$f(Z) + f(X) + f(W)$

the diagonal the dissimilarities according to the DF model, using the feature matrix of table 6.1. Table 6.2 shows that the two models are incompatible. In the CF model $d(a,b) = d(b,c) = d(a,d) > d(a,c), d(b,d), d(c,d)$. In the DF model, on the other hand, $d(a,b) = d(c,d)$, $d(a,c) = d(b,d)$, $d(a,d) = d(b,c)$, and $d(a,d) > d(a,b)$, $d(a,c)$. The CF model and the DF model, therefore, do not agree when restricted to the feature matrix of table 6.1. However, the two models become equivalent if we extend the feature matrix (see table 6.3) by including the complementary features. The new measures f' (derived from g via equation 3) and g' (derived from f via equation 4) are presented in the last two columns of the table.

To illustrate the equivalence theorem let us examine first how the CF dissimilarities, presented above the diagonal in table 6.2, can be represented by the DF model. To do so we turn to the extended feature matrix (table 6.3) and compute the dissimilarities according to the DF model using the derived measure f'. For example,

$$d(a,b) = f'(Y) + f'(X) + f'(\hat{A}) + f'(\hat{B})$$
$$= [g(Y) + g(X) + K - g(Z) - g(Y) + K - g(Z) - g(X)]/2$$
$$= K - g(Z).$$

It is easy to verify that these DF dissimilarities coincide with the original CF dissimilarities. To represent the original DF dissimilarities, presented below the diagonal in table 6.2, by the CF model we turn again to the extended feature matrix (table 6.3) add apply the CF model using the derived measure g'. Letting

$$K = \sum_{a \in s} f(A)$$
$$= 2[2f(Z) + f(Y) + f(X) + f(W)]$$

yields, for example,

$$d(a,b) = K - g'(Z) - g'(\hat{C}) - g'(\hat{D})$$
$$= K - [2f(Z) + f(Z) + f(Y) + f(W) + f(Z) + f(X) + f(W)]$$
$$= f(Y) + f(X).$$

Again, it is easy to verify that these CF dissimilarities coincide with the original DF dissimilarities as required. It appears that the extension of the matrix introduces four additional parameters corresponding to the weights of the complementary features. These parameters, however, are not independent. For example, $g'(Z) + g'(Y) = 2g'(\hat{A})$. Because the new measures are defined in terms of the old ones, the original and the extended solutions have the same number of free parameters.

To summarize, consider an object set s with a feature matrix M and an extended feature matrix M'. The preceding discussion establishes the following conclusions: First, given a feature matrix M the DF and the CF models do not always coincide. Moreover, in the example of figure 6.2 with the "natural" feature matrix of table 6.2, the two models yield different dissimilarity orders. Second, any set of DF dissimilarities in M can be represented as CF dissimilarities in the extended feature matrix M' and vice versa. Thus, one model can be "translated" into the other provided the original feature matrix (i.e., the support of the measure) can be extended to include the complementary features. Third, because M' is generally different than M, the two representations yield different clusters or features. Nevertheless, the two solutions have the same number of free parameters (i.e., degrees of freedom) because f' is defined by g and g' is defined by f (see table 6.3). The two representations, therefore, have the same dimensionality even though they do not have the same support.

These results show that unless the feature structure is constrained in advance, the CF model and the DF model cannot be compared on the basis of goodness-of-fit because they fit the data equally well. As a consequence, the models cannot be distinguished on the basis of the observed dissimilarity alone. On the other hand, the scaling solutions derived from the two models are not identical and one may be preferable to the other. In particular, a solution that includes complementary features may be harder to interpret than a solution that does not. Besides simplicity and interpretability, the choice between the representations can be based on additional empirical considerations. For example, we may prefer a solution that is consistent with the results of a free classification of the objects under study. The choice of a feature structure may also benefit from the ingenious experimental analysis of Triesman and Souther (1985).

The formal equivalence of the CF and the DF models is a special case of a more general result regarding the contrast model (Tversky, 1977) in which the dissimilarity of objects is expressed as a function of the measures of their common and their distinctive features. In the symmetric additive version of this model

$$d(a,b) = tf(A\Delta B) + (t-1)g(A \cap B), \quad 0 \le t \le 1. \tag{5}$$

This form reduces to the CF model (up to an additive constant) when $t = 0$, and it reduces to the DF model when $t = 1$. If g and f are additive measures (they need not be additive in general) and the underlying feature matrix includes the complementary features, then the parameter t is not identifiable. That is, if there are additive measures g and f and a constant $0 \le t \le 1$ such that equation 5 holds, then for any $0 \le t' \le 1$ there are additive measures f' and g' such that

$$d(a,b) = t'f'(A\Delta B) + (t'-1)g'(A \cap B)$$

up to an additive constant (see proposition 3 in the mathematical appendix). Note that the previous theorem corresponds to the case where $t = 0$ and $t' = 1$ or vice versa.

This result shows that in the additive version of the contrast model the parameter t (reflecting the weight of the distinctive relative to the common features) can be meaningfully assessed only for feature structures that do not include the complementary features. Indeed, Gati and Tversky (1984) constructed such structures by adding a separable component either to one or to two stimuli. Using equation 5, these authors estimated t for a dozen different domains and found higher values of t for perceptual than for conceptual stimuli. The present analysis shows that these conclusions depend on the feature structure induced by the addition of physical components.

The preceding discussion demonstrated the nonuniqueness of the parameter t in an extended feature matrix. We next discuss the nonuniqueness of the feature matrix associated with the distinctive features model. Recall that in this model

$$d(a,b) = f(A\Delta B) = f(A - B) + f(B - A) = \sum_i f_i e_i(a,b)$$

where f_i is the weight of the i-th feature, and

$$e_i(a,b) = \begin{cases} 1 & \text{if } m_{ia} \neq m_{ib} \\ 0 & \text{if } m_{ia} = m_{ib} \end{cases}$$

Thus, e_i is nonzero only for the features of $A\Delta B$, that is, features that belong to one of the objects but not to the other. It follows readily from the DF model that interchanging all zeros and ones in the i-th row of the feature matrix leaves e_i and hence $d(a,b)$ unchanged. Furthermore, it is redundant to add a new feature that is the mirror image of an old one because interchanging all 0's and 1's in the row corresponding to the old feature renders the two features identical. A DF solution, therefore, does not represent a unique feature matrix but rather a family of feature matrices—called a *classification structure*—whose members are related to each other by interchanging all 0's and 1's in one or more rows of the matrix and deleting redundant features. A classification structure determines which objects are classified together according to each feature, but it does not distinguish between the presence and absence of that feature. The relation between a feature matrix and the classification structure to which it belongs mirrors the relation between an additive and a substitutive feature (Tversky & Gati, 1982). The former is defined in terms of presence or absence, whereas the latter merely distinguishes between the two levels of each attribute. (Nonbinary attributes can always be reduced to binary ones using dummy variables.)

Because the DF model does not distinguish among feature matrices that belong to the same classification structure, the interpretation of this model in terms of a particular feature matrix (e.g., tables 6.1 and 6.3) cannot be based on observed dissimilarities. The following example taken from an unpublished study of dissimilarity between countries illustrates this point. The average ratings of dissimilarity between countries were analyzed using the ADDTREE program for fitting an additive tree (Sattath & Tversky, 1977). Figure 6.3 presents the subtree obtained for five selected countries.

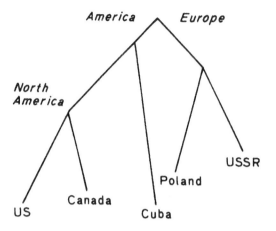

Figure 6.3
A tree representation of the dissimilarity between five countries.

In an additive tree the dissimilarity between objects (e.g., countries) is given by the length of the path that joins the respective endpoints. The feature matrix that corresponds to the tree of figure 6.3 is given in table 6.4. Each arc of the tree can be interpreted as a feature, or a set of features, that belong to all objects that follow from this arc. Thus, the first five features in table 6.4 correspond to the unique features of each of the five countries. The sixth and seventh features correspond to the features shared, respectively, by USSR and Poland (labeled European) and by U.S. and Canada (labeled North American). Finally, the eighth feature is shared by the three American countries (Cuba, U.S., and Canada).

Inspection of table 6.4 reveals that feature 8 is redundant because it is the mirror image of feature 6. Hence, we can delete feature 8 and replace it by another redundant feature that is the mirror image of feature 7. Because the new feature is shared by Cuba, Poland, and USSR, it is labeled Communist. Figure 6.4 displays a tree representation in which the new feature replaces feature 8. Note that in figure 6.3, Cuba joins the American countries, whereas in figure 6.4 it joins the Communist countries. Although the two figures yield different clustering, the dissimilarities between the countries are identical because the two respective feature matrices belong to the same classification structure, represented by the unrooted tree of figure 6.5. This tree generates the same dissimilarities as the rooted trees of figures 6.3 and 6.4, but it does not yield a hierarchical clustering of the objects. The choice of a root for an additive tree (e.g., figure 6.5) corresponds to the choice of a particular feature matrix (e.g., table 6.4) from the respective classification structure. The rooting of the

Table 6.4
A Labeled Feature Matrix for the Tree Representation of Judged Dissimilarity between Countries

	Countries				
Feature	U.S.	Canada	Cuba	Poland	USSR
1. U.S.	1	0	0	0	0
2. Canada	0	1	0	0	0
3. Cuba	0	0	1	0	0
4. Poland	0	0	0	1	0
5. USSR	0	0	0	0	1
6. Europe	0	0	0	1	1
7. North America	1	1	0	0	0
8. America	1	1	1	0	0
(Communist	0	0	1	1	1)

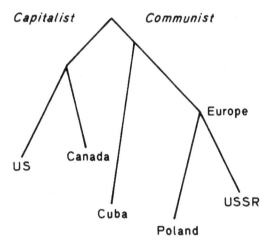

Figure 6.4
A tree representation of the dissimilarity between five countries.

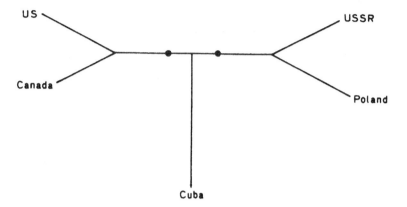

Figure 6.5
An unrooted tree representation of the dissimilarity between five countries. (The points used as roots in figures 6.3 and 6.4, respectively, correspond to the right and left dots in this figure.)

tree is analogous to the selection of a coordinate system for a configuration of points obtained by (Euclidean) multidimensional scaling. Both constructions are introduced to enhance the interpretation of the data, but they are not implied by the observed dissimilarities.

Discussion

This chapter shows that a data set that can be represented by the common features (CF) model can also be represented by the distinctive features (DF) model and vice versa, although the two representations involve different features. Furthermore, the DF model does not distinguish between feature matrices that belong to the same classification structure. It could be argued that the lack of uniqueness implied by these results exposes a basic limitation of linear feature models that are not sufficiently constrained to determine the form of the model (CF or DF), which must be chosen on the basis of other considerations.

In reply we argue that similar problems of indeterminacy arise in other measurement systems as well, including the physical measurement of weight and distance. The classical theory for the measurement of extensive attributes (e.g., mass, length, time) has three primitive notions: a set of objects, a process of comparing the objects with respect to the attribute in question, and an operation of concatenation of objects. For example, in the measurement of mass the objects are compared by placing them on the two sides of a pan balance and the concatenation of objects is performed by putting them on the same side of the balance. In the measurement of length the objects may be viewed as rigid rods that are concatenated by combining their endpoints. The theory assumes that the comparison process yields a transitive ordering of the objects with respect to the attribute in question, and that if c is heavier (longer) than b then the concatenation of c and a is heavier (longer) than the concatenation of b and a. These axioms, in conjunction with others of a more technical nature, lead to the construction of an additive scale of mass, m, satisfying $m(a * b) = m(a) + m(b)$ where $*$ denotes the concatenation operation.

Assuming additivity, m is a ratio scale: It is unique except for the unit of measurement. Contrary to common belief, however, the additive representation itself is not determined by the data. The observations (as well as the axioms) are also compatible, for example, with a multiplicative representation in which $m(a * b) = m(a)m(b)$, or with a Pythagorian representation in which $m(a * b) = [m(a)^2 + m(b)^2]^{1/2}$; (see Krantz, Luce, Suppes and Tversky, 1971, section 3.9). Although the additive form appears simpler and more natural, it is not dictated by the observations, and we cannot test which form is correct. If an additive representation exists, so does the multiplicative and the Pythagorian, as well as many others. It may come as a surprise to many readers that the form of our measurement models—of dissimilarity as well as of mass and distance—is not determined by the data. Indeed, the careful separation of the empirical and the conventional aspects of numerical models is perhaps the major contribution of measurement theory to both the physical and the social sciences.

Note

1. Indeed, the observation that both inequalities may hold has led to the development of the contrast model (Tversky, 1977), discussed later in this chapter, in which dissimilarity depends on both common or distinctive features.

References

Corter, J., & Tversky, A. (1986). Extended similarity trees. *Psychometrika, 51*, 429–451.

Eisler, H., & Roskam, E. (1977). Multidimensional similarity: An experimental and theoretical comparison of vector, distance, and set theoretical models. I. Models and internal consistency of data. *Acta Psychologica, 41*, 1–46.

Gati, I., & Tversky, A. (1984). Weighting common and distinctive features in perceptual and conceptual judgments. *Cognitive Psychology, 16*, 341–370.

Hartigan, J. A. (1975). *Clustering algorithms.* New York: Wiley.

Jardine, N., & Sibson, R. (1971). *Mathematical taxonomy.* London: Wiley.

Johnson, S. C. (1967). Hierarchical clustering schemes. *Psychometrika, 32*, 241–254.

Krantz, D. H., Luce, R. D., Suppes, P., & Tversky, A. (1971). *Foundations of measurement* (Vol. 1). New York: Academic Press.

Restle, F. (1961). *Psychology of judgment and choice*. New York: Wiley.

Rosch, E., & Mervis, C. B. (1975). Family resemblance: Studies in the internal structure of categories. *Cognitive Psychology*, 7, 573–603.

Sattath, S., & Tversky, A. (1977). Additive similarity trees. *Psychometrika, 42*, 319–345.

Smith, E. E., & Medin, D. L. (1981). *Categories and concepts*. Cambridge, MA: Harvard University Press.

Shepard, R. N. (1980). Multidimensional scaling, tree-fitting, and clustering. *Science, 210*, 390–398.

Shepard, R. N., & Arabie, P. (1979). Additive clustering: Representation of similarities as combinations of discrete overlapping properties. *Psychological Review, 30*, 87–123.

Triesman, A., & Souther, J. (1985). Search asymmetry: A diagnostic for preattentive processing of separable features. *Journal of Experimental Psychology: General, 114*, 285–310.

Tversky, A. (1977). Features of similarity. *Psychological Review, 84*, 327–352.

Tversky, A., & Gati, I. (1982). Separability, similarity and the triangle inequality, *Psychological Review, 89*, 123–154.

Mathematical Appendix

PROPOSITION 1   Suppose there is an additive measure g on S and constant $K > g(B)$, for all b in s, such that

(i) $d(a, b) = K - g(A \cap B)$.

Then there is an additive measure f on S such that

(ii) $d(a, b) = f(A \Delta B)$.

Proof   Define

$$f(X) = \begin{cases} [K + g(\hat{B}) - g(B)]/2 & \text{if } X = \hat{B} \text{ for some } b \in s, \\ g(X)/2 & \text{otherwise.} \end{cases}$$

We show that for any a, b in s, $f(A \Delta B) = K - g(A \cap B)$.

$$
\begin{aligned}
f(A \Delta B) &= f(A - B) + f(B - A) \\
&= f(\hat{B}) + f((A - B) - \hat{B}) + f(\hat{A}) + f((B - A) - \hat{A}) \\
&= [K - g(B) + g(\hat{B}) + g((A - B) - \hat{B})]/2 \\
&\quad + [K - g(A) + g(\hat{A}) + g((B - A) - \hat{A})]/2 \\
&= K + [-g(B) + g(A - B) - g(A) + g(B - A)]/2 \\
&= K + [-2g(A \cap B)]/2 \\
&= K - g(A \cap B).
\end{aligned}
$$

PROPOSITION 2   Suppose there is an additive measure f on S such that

(i) $d(a, b) = f(A \Delta B)$.

Then there exists an additive measure g and a constant K such that

(ii) $d(a, b) = K - g(A \cap B)$.

Proof   Define

$$g(X) = \begin{cases} 2f(\hat{B}) + f(B) & \text{if } X = \hat{B} \text{ for some } b \in s, \\ 2f(X) & \text{otherwise.} \end{cases}$$

Let

$$K = \sum_{a \in s} f(A), \quad L = \sum_{a \in s} f(\hat{A}), \quad M = \sum_{a \in s} g(\hat{A}) = 2L + K,$$

and let $\hat{S} = \{\hat{B} : b \in s\}$. Hence,

$$K - g(A \cap B) = K - \left[g(A \cap B - \hat{S}) + \sum_{X \in A \cap B \cap \hat{S}} g(X) \right]$$

$$= K - \left[g(A \cap B - \hat{S}) + \sum_{X \in \acute{S}} g(X) - g(\hat{A}) - g(\hat{B}) \right]$$

$$= K - g(A \cap B - \hat{S}) - M + g(\hat{A}) + g(\hat{B})$$

$$= K - M + 2f(\hat{A}) + f(A) + 2f(\hat{B}) + f(B) - 2f(A \cap B - \hat{S})$$

$$= K - M + f(A) + f(B) + 2(f(\hat{A}) + f(\hat{B}))$$

$$\quad - 2\left(f(A \cap B) - \sum_{X \in A \cap B \cap \hat{S}} f(X) \right)$$

$$= K - M + f(A) + f(B) + 2(f(\hat{A}) + f(\hat{B})) - 2f(A \cap B)$$

$$\quad + 2\left(\sum_{X \in \hat{S}} f(X) - f(\hat{A}) - f(\hat{B}) \right)$$

$$= K - M + f(A \Delta B) + 2L$$

$$= f(A \Delta B).$$

PROPOSITION 3 Suppose there are additive measures g and f on S and a constant $0 \leq t \leq 1$ such that

$$d(a,b) = tf(A\Delta B) + (t-1)g(A \cap B).$$

Then for any $0 \leq t' \leq 1$ there are additive measures g', f' and a constant K such that

$$d(a,b) = t'f'(A\Delta B) + (t'-1)g'(A\Delta B) + K.$$

Proof By Proposition 1 there is a measure f'' so that

$$d(a,b) = tf(A\Delta B) + (t-1)f''(A\Delta B) + M.$$

Define $f' = f + f''$, hence

$$d(a,b) = f'(A\Delta B) + M.$$

By Proposition 2 there is a constant L and a measure g' so that

$$f'(A\Delta B) = g'(A \cap B) + L$$

thus

$$(t-1)f'(A\Delta B) = (t-1)g'(A \cap B) + (1-t)L$$

and

$$d(a,b) = t'f'(A\Delta B) + (t'-1)f'(A\Delta B) + M$$
$$= t'f'(A\Delta B) + (t'-1)g'(A \cap B) + K,$$

where

$$K = M + (t'-1)L.$$

JUDGMENT

Editor's Introductory Remarks

Research on human judgment changed dramatically and definitively after Tversky's enormously influential work. Research in the late fifties and early sixties first introduced Bayesian notions to the empirical study of human judgment, and surmised that people are reasonably good intuitive statisticians. Tversky's collaboration with Daniel Kahneman on the "heuristics and biases" program began in this milieu. Their first paper, on the belief in the law of small numbers (chapter 7), suggests that naïve respondents as well as trained scientists have strong but misguided intuitions about random sampling. In particular, Tversky and Kahneman suggest that people expect (1) randomly drawn samples to be highly representative of the population from which they are drawn, (2) sampling to be a self-correcting process and, consequently, (3) the variability of samples to be less than is typically observed. These expectations were shown to lead to systematic misperception of chance events, which Tversky later applied to the analyses of widely held yet misguided beliefs—"the hot hand in basketball," studied in collaboration with Tom Gilovich (chapters 10 and 11), and the belief that arthritis pain is related to the weather, investigated with Don Redelmeier (chapter 15).

Cognitive and perceptual biases that operate regardless of motivational factors formed the core of the remarkably creative and highly influential "heuristics and biases" program. Having recognized that intuitive predictions and judgments of probability do not follow the principles of statistics or the laws of probability, Tversky and Kahneman embarked on the study of biases as a method for investigating judgmental heuristics. In an article in *Science* (chapter 8), they documented three heuristics—representativeness, availability, and anchoring and adjustment—that people employ in assessing probabilities and in predicting values. In settings where the relevance of simple probabilistic rules was made transparent, people often were shown to reveal appropriate statistical intuitions. In richer contexts, however, they often rely on heuristics that do not obey simple formal considerations and can thus lead to fallacious judgments. According to the representativeness heuristic, for example, the likelihood that item A belongs to class B is judged by the degree to which A resembles B. Prior probabilities and sample sizes, both of which are highly relevant to likelihood, have no impact on how representative an item appears and are thus neglected. This can lead to memorable errors such as the "conjunction fallacy," wherein a conjunction, because it appears more representative, is judged more probable than one of its conjuncts (chapter 9).

The conjunction fallacy and other judgmental errors violate the most fundamental axioms of probability. Interestingly, however, even if a person's judgment is coherent, it may nonetheless be misguided. Normative judgment requires that the person be not only coherent but also "well calibrated." Consider a set of propositions, each of which a person judges to be true with a probability of .70. If the person is right about seventy percent of these, then the person is said to be well calibrated. If she is right about less than or more than seventy percent, then she is said to be over-confident or underconfident, respectively. Calibration, furthermore, does not ensure informativeness, as illustrated, for example, by a judge who predicts the sex of each newborn with a probability of .50, and is thus well calibrated, yet entirely unable to discriminate. Tversky published insightful analyses of these issues, particularly as they shed light on judgmental strategies and underlying human abilities. In one instance (chapter 13), Varda Liberman and Tversky draw subtle distinctions among different characteristics of judgments of probability and among different manifes-tations of overconfidence. The notion that people focus on the strength of the evi-dence (for example, the warmth of a letter of reference) with insufficient regard for its weight (for example, how well the writer knows the candidate) is used by Dale Grif-fin & Tversky (chapter 12) to explain various systematic biases in probabilistic judg-ment including the failure to appreciate regression phenomena, the tendency to show overconfidence (when the evidence is remarkable but its weight is low), and occa-sional underconfidence (when the evidence is unremarkable but its weight is high).

A fundamental assumption underlying normative theories is the extensionality principle: options that are extensionally equivalent are assigned the same value, and extensionally equivalent events are assigned the same probability. These theories, in other words, are about options and events in the world, whereas Tversky's analyses focus on how the relevant constructs are mentally represented. The extensionality principle is deemed descriptively invalid because alternative descriptions of the same event can yield different representations and thus produce systematically different judgments. In his final years, Tversky returned to the study of judgment and col-laborated with Derek Koehler on a theory, called support theory, that formally dis-tinguishes between events in the world and the manner in which they are mentally represented (chapter 14). In support theory, probabilities are attached not to events, as in standard normative models, but rather to descriptions of events, called hypoth-eses. Probability judgments, according to the theory, are based on the support (that is, strength of evidence) of the focal hypothesis relative to that of alternative, or residual, hypotheses. The theory distinguishes between explicit and implicit dis-junctions. *Explicit disjunctions* are hypotheses that list their individual components (for example, "a car crash due to road construction, or due to driver fatigue, or due to break failure"), whereas *implicit disjunctions* ("a car crash") do not. According to the theory, unpacking a description of an event into disjoint components (that is, from an implicit to an explicit disjunction) generally increases its support and, hence, its perceived likelihood. Unpacking can increase support by bringing to mind neglected possibilities or by increasing the impact of unpacked components. As a result, different descriptions of the same event can give rise to different judgments. In light of findings that emerged subsequent to the original publication, Tversky and Yuval Rottenstreich developed a generalization of support theory (chapter 16.) In Tversky's inimitable style, support theory makes sense of a variety of fascinating observations in the context of a highly general and aesthetic theoretical structure. As before, these chapters show the interplay of psychological intuition with normative theory, accompanied by memorable demonstrations.

7 Belief in the Law of Small Numbers

Amos Tversky and Daniel Kahneman

"Suppose you have run an experiment on 20 subjects, and have obtained a significant result which confirms your theory ($z = 2.23$, $p < .05$, two-tailed). You now have cause to run an additional group of 10 subjects. What do you think the probability is that the results will be significant, by a one-tailed test, separately for this group?"

If you feel that the probability is somewhere around .85, you may be pleased to know that you belong to a majority group. Indeed, that was the median answer of two small groups who were kind enough to respond to a questionnaire distributed at meetings of the Mathematical Psychology Group and of the American Psychological Association.

On the other hand, if you feel that the probability is around .48, you belong to a minority. Only 9 of our 84 respondents gave answers between .40 and .60. However, .48 happens to be a much more reasonable estimate than .85.[1]

Apparently, most psychologists have an exaggerated belief in the likelihood of successfully replicating an obtained finding. The sources of such beliefs, and their consequences for the conduct of scientific inquiry, are what this chapter is about. Our thesis is that people have strong intuitions about random sampling; that these intuitions are wrong in fundamental respects; that these intuitions are shared by naive subjects and by trained scientists; and that they are applied with unfortunate consequences in the course of scientific inquiry.

We submit that people view a sample randomly drawn from a population as highly representative, that is, similar to the population in all essential characteristics. Consequently, they expect any two samples drawn from a particular population to be more similar to one another and to the population than sampling theory predicts, at least for small samples.

The tendency to regard a sample as a representation is manifest in a wide variety of situations. When subjects are instructed to generate a random sequence of hypothetical tosses of a fair coin, for example, they produce sequences where the proportion of heads in any short segment stays far closer to .50 than the laws of chance would predict (Tune 1964). Thus, each segment of the response sequence is highly representative of the "fairness" of the coin. Similar effects are observed when subjects successively predict events in a randomly generated series, as in probability learning experiments (Estes, 1964) or in other sequential games of chance. Subjects act as if *every* segment of the random sequence must reflect the true proportion: if the sequence has strayed from the population proportion, a corrective bias in the other direction is expected. This has been called the gambler's fallacy.

The heart of the gambler's fallacy is a misconception of the fairness of the laws of chance. The gambler feels that the fairness of the coin entitles him to expect that any deviation in one direction will soon be cancelled by a corresponding deviation in the other. Even the fairest of coins, however, given the limitations of its memory and moral sense, cannot be as fair as the gambler expects it to be. This fallacy is not unique to gamblers. Consider the following example:

The mean IQ of the population of eighth graders in a city is *known* to be 100. You have selected a random sample of 50 children for a study of educational achievements. The first child tested has an IQ of 150. What do you expect the mean IQ to be for the whole sample?

The correct answer is 101. A surprisingly large number of people believe that the expected IQ for the sample is still 100. This expectation can be justified only by the belief that a random process is self-correcting. Idioms such as "errors cancel each other out" reflect the image of an active self-correcting process. Some familiar processes in nature obey such laws: a deviation from a stable equilibrium produces a force that restores the equilibrium. The laws of chance, in contrast, do not work that way: deviations are not canceled as sampling proceeds, they are merely diluted.

Thus far, we have attempted to describe two related intuitions about chance. We proposed a representation hypothesis according to which people believe samples to be very similar to one another and to the population from which they are drawn. We also suggested that people believe sampling to be a self-correcting process. The two beliefs lead to the same consequences. Both generate expectations about characteristics of samples, and the variability of these expectations is less than the true variability, at least for small samples.

The law of large numbers guarantees that very large samples will indeed be highly representative of the population from which they are drawn. If, in addition, a self-corrective tendency is at work, then small samples should also be highly representative and similar to one another. People's intuitions about random sampling appear to satisfy the law of small numbers, which asserts that the law of large numbers applies to small numbers as well.

Consider a hypothetical scientist who lives by the law of small numbers. How would his belief affect his scientific work? Assume our scientist studies phenomena whose magnitude is small relative to uncontrolled variability, that is, the signal-to-noise ratio in the messages he receives from nature is low. Our scientist could be a meteorologist, a pharmacologist, or perhaps a psychologist.

If he believes in the law of small numbers, the scientist will have exaggerated confidence in the validity of conclusions based on small samples. To illustrate, suppose he is engaged in studying which of two toys infants will prefer to play with. Of the first five infants studied, four have shown a preference for the same toy. Many a psychologist will feel some confidence at this point, that the null hypothesis of no preference is false. Fortunately, such a conviction is not a sufficient condition for journal publication, although it may do for a book. By a quick computation, our psychologist will discover that the probability of a result as extreme as the one obtained is as high as $\frac{3}{8}$ under the null hypothesis.

To be sure, the application of statistical hypothesis testing to scientific inference is beset with serious difficulties. Nevertheless, the computation of significance levels (or likelihood ratios, as a Bayesian might prefer) forces the scientist to evaluate the obtained effect in terms of a *valid* estimate of sampling variance rather than in terms of his subjective biased estimate. Statistical tests, therefore, protect the scientific community against overly hasty rejections of the null hypothesis (i.e., type I error) by policing its many members who would rather live by the law of small numbers. On the other hand, there are no comparable safeguards against the risk of failing to confirm a valid research hypothesis (i.e., type II error).

Imagine a psychologist who studies the correlation between need for achievement and grades. When deciding on sample size, he may reason as follows: "What correlation do I expect? $r = .35$. What N do I need to make the result significant? (Looks at table.) $N = 33$. Fine, that's my sample." The only flaw in this reasoning is that our psychologist has forgotten about sampling variation, possibly because he believes that any sample must be highly representative of its population. However, if his guess about the correlation in the population is correct, the correlation in the sample is about as likely to lie below or above .35. Hence, the likelihood of obtaining a significant result (i.e., the power of the test) for $N = 33$ is about .50.

In a detailed investigation of statistical power, J. Cohen (1962, 1969) has provided plausible definitions of large, medium, and small effects and an extensive set of computational aids to the estimation of power for a variety of statistical tests. In the normal test for a difference between two means, for example, a difference of $.25\sigma$ is small, a difference of $.50\sigma$ is medium, and a difference of 1σ is large, according to the proposed definitions. The mean IQ difference between clerical and semiskilled workers is a medium effect. In an ingenious study of research practice, J. Cohen (1962) reviewed all the statistical analyses published in one volume of the *Journal of Abnormal and Social Psychology*, and computed the likelihood of detecting each of the three sizes of effect. The average power was .18 for the detection of small effects, .48 for medium effects, and .83 for large effects. If psychologists typically expect medium effects and select sample size as in the above example, the power of their studies should indeed be about .50.

Cohen's analysis shows that the statistical power of many psychological studies is ridiculously low. This is a self-defeating practice: it makes for frustrated scientists and inefficient research. The investigator who tests a valid hypothesis but fails to obtain significant results cannot help but regard nature as untrustworthy or even hostile. Furthermore, as Overall (1969) has shown, the prevalence of studies deficient in statistical power is not only wasteful but actually pernicious: it results in a large proportion of invalid rejections of the null hypothesis among published results.

Because considerations of statistical power are of particular importance in the design of replication studies, we probed attitudes concerning replication in our questionnaire.

Suppose one of your doctoral students has completed a difficult and time-consuming experiment on 40 animals. He has scored and analyzed a large number of variables. His results are generally inconclusive, but one before-after comparison yields a highly significant $t = 2.70$, which is surprising and could be of major theoretical significance.

Considering the importance of the result, its surprisal value, and the number of analyses that your student has performed, would you recommend that he replicate the study before publishing? If you recommend replication, how many animals would you urge him to run?

Among the psychologists to whom we put these questions there was overwhelming sentiment favoring replication: it was recommended by 66 out of 75 respondents, probably because they suspected that the single significant result was due to chance. The median recommendation was for the doctoral student to run 20 subjects in a replication study. It is instructive to consider the likely consequences of this advice. If the mean and the variance in the second sample are actually identical to those in the first sample, then the resulting value of t will be 1.88. Following the reasoning of note 1, the student's chance of obtaining a significant result in the replication is only slightly above one-half (for $p = .05$, one-tail test). Since we had anticipated that a replication sample of 20 would appear reasonable to our respondents, we added the following question:

Assume that your unhappy student has in fact repeated the initial study with 20 additional animals, and has obtained an insignificant result in the same direction, $t = 1.24$. What would you recommend now? Check one: [the numbers in parentheses refer to the number of respondents who checked each answer]

(a) He should pool the results and publish his conclusion as fact. (0)

(b) He should report the results as a tentative finding. (26)

(c) He should run another group of [median 20] animals. (21)

(d) He should try to find an explanation for the difference between the two groups. (30)

Note that regardless of one's confidence in the original finding, its credibility is surely enhanced by the replication. Not only is the experimental effect in the same direction in the two samples but the magnitude of the effect in the replication is fully two-thirds of that in the original study. In view of the sample size (20), which our respondents recommended, the replication was about as successful as one is entitled to expect. The distribution of responses, however, reflects continued skepticism concerning the student's finding following the recommended replication. This unhappy state of affairs is a typical consequence of insufficient statistical power.

In contrast to Responses b and c, which can be justified on some grounds, the most popular response, Response d, is indefensible. We doubt that the same answer would have been obtained if the respondents had realized that the difference between the two studies does not even approach significance. (If the variances of the two samples are equal, t for the difference is .53.) In the absence of a statistical test, our respondents followed the representation hypothesis: as the difference between the two samples was larger than they expected, they viewed it as worthy of explanation. However, the attempt to "find an explanation for the difference between the two groups" is in all probability an exercise in explaining noise.

Altogether our respondents evaluated the replication rather harshly. This follows from the representation hypothesis: if we expect all samples to be very similar to one another, then almost all replications of a valid hypothesis should be statistically significant. The harshness of the criterion for successful replication is manifest in the responses to the following question:

An investigator has reported a result that you consider implausible. He ran 15 subjects, and reported a significant value, $t = 2.46$. Another investigator has attempted to duplicate his procedure, and he obtained a nonsignificant value of t with the same number of subjects. The direction was the same in both sets of data.

You are reviewing the literature. What is the highest value of t in the second set of data that you would describe as a failure to replicate?

The majority of our respondents regarded $t = 1.70$ as a failure to replicate. If the data of two such studies ($t = 2.46$ and $t = 1.70$) are pooled, the value of t for the combined data is about 3.00 (assuming equal variances). Thus, we are faced with a paradoxical state of affairs, in which the same data that would increase our confidence in the finding when viewed as part of the original study, shake our confidence when viewed as an independent study. This double standard is particularly disturbing since, for many reasons, replications are usually considered as independent studies, and hypotheses are often evaluated by listing confirming and disconfirming reports.

Contrary to a widespread belief, a case can be made that a replication sample should often be larger than the original. The decision to replicate a once obtained finding often expresses a great fondness for that finding and a desire to see it accepted by a skeptical community. Since that community unreasonably demands that the replication be independently significant, or at least that it approach significance, one must run a large sample. To illustrate, if the unfortunate doctoral student whose thesis was discussed earlier assumes the validity of his initial result ($t = 2.70$, $N = 40$), and if he is willing to accept a risk of only .10 of obtaining a t lower than 1.70, he should run approximately 50 animals in his replication study. With a somewhat weaker initial result ($t = 2.20$, $N = 40$), the size of the replication sample required for the same power rises to about 75.

That the effects discussed thus far are not limited to hypotheses about means and variances is demonstrated by the responses to the following question:

You have run a correlational study, scoring 20 variables on 100 subjects. Twenty-seven of the 190 correlation coefficients are significant at the .05 level; and 9 of these are significant beyond the .01 level. The mean absolute level of the significant correlations is .31, and the pattern of results is very reasonable on theoretical grounds. How many of the 27 significant correlations would you expect to be significant again, in an exact replication of the study, with $N = 40$?

With $N = 40$, a correlation of about .31 is required for significance at the .05 level. This is the mean of the significant correlations in the original study. Thus, only about half of the originally significant correlations (i.e., 13 or 14) would remain significant with $N = 40$. In addition, of course, the correlations in the replication are bound to differ from those in the original study. Hence, by regression effects, the initially significant coefficients are most likely to be reduced. Thus, 8 to 10 repeated significant correlations from the original 27 is probably a generous estimate of what one is entitled to expect. The median estimate of our respondents is 18. This is more than the number of repeated significant correlations that will be found if the correlations are recomputed for 40 subjects randomly selected from the original 100! Apparently, people expect more than a mere duplication of the original statistics in the replication sample; they expect a duplication of the significance of results, with little regard for sample size. This expectation requires a ludicrous extension of the representation hypothesis; even the law of small numbers is incapable of generating such a result.

The expectation that patterns of results are replicable almost in their entirety provides the rationale for a common, though much deplored practice. The investigator who computes all correlations between three indexes of anxiety and three indexes of dependency will often report and interpret with great confidence the single significant correlation obtained. His confidence in the shaky finding stems from his belief that the obtained correlation matrix is highly representative and readily replicable.

In review, we have seen that the believer in the law of small numbers practices science as follows:

1. He gambles his research hypotheses on small samples without realizing that the odds against him are unreasonably high. He overestimates power.

2. He has undue confidence in early trends (e.g., the data of the first few subjects) and in the stability of observed patterns (e.g., the number and identity of significant results). He overestimates significance.

3. In evaluating replications, his or others', he has unreasonably high expectations about the replicability of significant results. He underestimates the breadth of confidence intervals.

4. He rarely attributes a deviation of results from expectations to sampling variability, because he finds a causal "explanation" for any discrepancy. Thus, he has little opportunity to recognize sampling variation in action. His belief in the law of small numbers, therefore, will forever remain intact.

Our questionnaire elicited considerable evidence for the prevalence of the belief in the law of small numbers.[2] Our typical respondent is a believer, regardless of the group to which he belongs. There were practically no differences between the median responses of audiences at a mathematical psychology meeting and at a general session of the American Psychological Association convention, although we make no claims for the representativeness of either sample. Apparently, acquaintance with formal logic and with probability theory does not extinguish erroneous intuitions. What, then, can be done? Can the belief in the law of small numbers be abolished or at least controlled?

Research experience is unlikely to help much, because sampling variation is all too easily "explained." Corrective experiences are those that provide neither motive nor opportunity for spurious explanation. Thus, a student in a statistics course may draw repeated samples of given size from a population, and learn the effect of sample size on sampling variability from personal observation. We are far from certain, however, that expectations can be corrected in this manner, since related biases, such as the gambler's fallacy, survive considerable contradictory evidence.

Even if the bias cannot be unlearned, students can learn to recognize its existence and take the necessary precautions. Since the teaching of statistics is not short on admonitions, a warning about biased statistical intuitions may not be out of place. The obvious precaution is computation. The believer in the law of small numbers has incorrect intuitions about significance level, power, and confidence intervals. Significance levels are usually computed and reported, but power and confidence limits are not. Perhaps they should be.

Explicit computation of power, relative to some reasonable hypothesis, for instance, J. Cohen's (1962, 1969) small, large, and medium effects, should surely be carried out before any study is done. Such computations will often lead to the realization that there is simply no point in running the study unless, for example, sample size is multiplied by four. We refuse to believe that a serious investigator will knowingly accept a .50 risk of failing to confirm a valid research hypothesis. In addition, computations of power are essential to the interpretation of negative results, that is, failures to reject the null hypothesis. Because readers' intuitive estimates of power are likely to be wrong, the publication of computed values does not appear to be a waste of either readers' time or journal space.

In the early psychological literature, the convention prevailed of reporting, for example, a sample mean as $M \pm PE$, where PE is the probable error (i.e., the 50% confidence interval around the mean). This convention was later abandoned in favor of the hypothesis-testing formulation. A confidence interval, however, provides a useful index of sampling variability, and it is precisely this variability that we tend to underestimate. The emphasis on significance levels tends to obscure a fundamental distinction between the size of an effect and its statistical significance. Regardless of sample size, the size of an effect in one study is a reasonable estimate of the size of the effect in replication. In contrast, the estimated significance level in a replication depends critically on sample size. Unrealistic expectations concerning the replicability of significance levels may be corrected if the distinction between size and significance is clarified, and if the computed size of observed effects is routinely reported. From this point of view, at least, the acceptance of the hypothesis-testing model has not been an unmixed blessing for psychology.

The true believer in the law of small numbers commits his multitude of sins against the logic of statistical inference in good faith. The representation hypothesis describes a cognitive or perceptual bias, which operates regardless of motivational factors. Thus, while the hasty rejection of the null hypothesis is gratifying, the rejection of a cherished hypothesis is aggravating, yet the true believer is subject to both. His intuitive expectations are governed by a consistent misperception of the world rather than by opportunistic wishful thinking. Given some editorial prodding, he may be willing to regard his statistical intuitions with proper suspicion and replace impression formation by computation whenever possible.

Notes

1. The required estimate can be interpreted in several ways. One possible approach is to follow common research practice, where a value obtained in one study is taken to define a plausible alternative to the null

hypothesis. The probability requested in the question can then be interpreted as the power of the second test (i.e., the probability of obtaining a significant result in the second sample) against the alternative hypothesis defined by the result of the first sample. In the special case of a test of a mean with known variance, one would compute the power of the test against the hypothesis that the population mean equals the mean of the first sample. Since the size of the second sample is half that of the first, the computed probability of obtaining $z \geq 1.645$ is only .473. A theoretically more justifiable approach is to interpret the requested probability within a Bayesian framework and compute it relative to some appropriately selected prior distribution. Assuming a uniform prior, the desired posterior probability is .478. Clearly, if the prior distribution favors the null hypothesis, as is often the case, the posterior probability will be even smaller.

2. W. Edwards (1968, 25) has argued that people fail to extract sufficient information or certainty from probabilistic data; he called this failure conservatism. Our respondents can hardly be described as conservative. Rather, in accord with the representation hypothesis, they tend to extract more certainty from the data than the data, in fact, contain.

References

Cohen, J. The statistical power of abnormal-social psychological research. *Journal of Abnormal and Social Psychology*, 1962, 65, 145–153.

Cohen, J. *Statistical power analysis in the behavioral sciences.* New York: Academic Press, 1969.

Edwards, W. Conservatism in human information processing. In B. Kleinmuntz (Ed.), *Formal representation of human judgment.* New York: Wiley, 1968.

Estes, W. K. Probability learning. In A. W. Melton (Ed.), *Categories of human learning.* New York: Academic Press, 1964.

Overall, J. E. Classical statistical hypothesis testing within the context of Bayesian theory. *Psychological Bulletin*, 1969, 71, 285–292.

Tune, G. S. Response preferences: A review of some relevant literature. *Psychological Bulletin*, 1964, 61, 286–302.

8 Judgment under Uncertainty: Heuristics and Biases

Amos Tversky and Daniel Kahneman

Many decisions are based on beliefs concerning the likelihood of uncertain events such as the outcome of an election, the guilt of a defendant, or the future value of the dollar. These beliefs are usually expressed in statements such as "I think that ...," "chances are ...," "It is unlikely that ...," etc. Occasionally, beliefs concerning uncertain events are expressed in numerical form as odds or subjective probabilities. What determines such beliefs? How do people assess the probability of an uncertain event or the value of an uncertain quantity? The theme of the present paper is that people rely on a limited number of heuristic principles which reduce the complex tasks of assessing probabilities and predicting values to simpler judgmental operations. In general, these heuristics are quite useful, but sometimes they lead to severe and systematic errors.

The subjective assessment of probability resembles the subjective assessment of physical quantities such as distance or size. These judgments are all based on data of limited validity, which are processed according to heuristic rules. For example, the apparent distance of an object is determined in part by its clarity. The more sharply the object is seen, the closer it appears to be. This rule has some validity, because in any given scene the more distant objects are seen less sharply than nearer objects. However, the reliance on this rule leads to systematic errors in the estimation of distance. Specifically, distances are often overestimated when visibility is poor because the contours of objects are blurred. On the other hand, distances are often underestimated when visibility is good because the objects are sharply seen. Thus, the reliance on blur as a cue leads to characteristic biases in the judgment of distance. Systematic errors which are associated with heuristic rules are also common in the intuitive judgment of probability. The following sections describe three heuristics that are employed to assess probabilities and to predict values. Biases to which these heuristics lead are enumerated and the applied and theoretical implications of these observations are discussed.

Representativeness

Many of the probabilistic questions with which people are concerned belong to one of the following types: What is the probability that object *A* belongs to class *B*? What is the probability that event *A* originates from process *B*? What is the probability that process *A* will generate event *B*? In answering such questions people typically rely on the representativeness heuristic, in which probabilities are evaluated by the degree to which A is representative of B, i.e., by the degree of similarity between them. For example, when A is highly representative of B, the probability that A originates from B is judged to be high. On the other hand, if A is not similar to B, the probability that A originates from B is judged to be low.

For an illustration of judgment by representativeness, consider an individual who has been described by a former neighbor as follows: "Steve is very shy and withdrawn, invariably helpful, but with little interest in people, or in the world of reality. A meek and tidy soul, he has a need for order and structure, and a passion for detail." How do people assess the probability that Steve is engaged in each of several occupations (e.g., farmer, salesman, airline pilot, librarian, physician)? How do people order these occupations from most to least likely? In the representativeness heuristic, the probability that Steve is a librarian, for example, is assessed by the degree to which he is representative or similar to the stereotype of a librarian. Indeed, research with problems of this type has shown that people order the occupations by probability and by similarity in exactly the same way.[1] As will be shown below, this approach to the judgment of probability leads to serious errors because similarity, or representativeness, is not influenced by several factors which should affect judgments of probability.

Insensitivity to Prior Probability of Outcomes

One of the factors that have no effect on representativeness but should have a major effect on probability is the prior probability, or base-rate frequency, of the outcomes. In the case of Steve, for example, the fact that there are many more farmers than librarians in the population should enter into any reasonable estimate of the probability that Steve is a librarian rather than a farmer. Considerations of base-rate frequency, however, do not affect the similarity of Steve to the stereotypes of librarians and farmers. If people evaluate probability by representativeness, therefore, prior probabilities will be neglected. This hypothesis was tested in an experiment where prior probabilities were explicitly manipulated.[1] Subjects were shown brief personality descriptions of several individuals, allegedly sampled at random from a group of 100 professionals—engineers and lawyers. The subjects were asked to assess, for each description, the probability that it belonged to an engineer rather than to a lawyer. In one experimental condition, subjects were told that the group from which the descriptions had been drawn consisted of 70 engineers and 30 lawyers. In another condition, subjects were told that the group consisted of 30 engineers and 70 lawyers. The odds that any particular description belongs to an engineer rather than to a lawyer should be higher in the first condition, where there is a majority of engineers, than in the second condition, where there is a majority of lawyers. Specifically, it can be shown by applying Bayes' rule that the ratio of these odds should be $(.7/.3)^2 = 5.44$ for each description. In a sharp violation of Bayes' rule, the subjects in the two conditions produced essentially the same probability judgments. Apparently, subjects evaluated the likelihood that a particular description belonged to an engineer rather than to a lawyer by the degree to which this description was representative of the two stereotypes, with little or no regard for the prior probabilities of the categories.

The subjects correctly utilized prior probabilities when they had no other information. In the absence of a personality sketch they judged the probability that an unknown individual is an engineer to be .7 and .3 respectively, in the two base-rate conditions. However, prior probabilities were effectively ignored when a description was introduced, even when this description was totally uninformative. The responses to the following description illustrate this phenomenon:

Dick is a 30-year old man. He is married with no children. A man of high ability and high motivation, he promises to be quite successful in his field. He is well liked by his colleagues.

This description was intended to convey no information relevant to the question of whether Dick is an engineer or a lawyer. Consequently, the probability that Dick is an engineer should equal the proportion of engineers in the group, as if no description had been given. The subjects, however, judged the probability of Dick being an engineer to be .5 regardless of whether the stated proportion of engineers in the group was .7 or .3. Evidently, people respond differently when given no evidence and when given worthless evidence. When no specific evidence is given—prior probabilities are properly utilized; when worthless evidence is given—prior probabilities are ignored.[1]

Insensitivity to Sample Size

To evaluate the probability of obtaining a particular result in a sample drawn from a specified population, people typically apply the representativeness heuristic. That is, they assess the likelihood of a sample result (e.g., that the average height in a random sample of ten men will be 6'0") by the similarity of this result to the corresponding parameter (i.e., to the average height in the population of men). The similarity of a sample statistic to a population parameter does not depend on the size of the sample. Consequently, if probabilities are assessed by representativeness, then the judged probability of a sample statistic will be essentially independent of sample size. Indeed, when subjects assessed the distributions of average height for samples of various sizes, they produced identical distributions. For example, the probability of obtaining an average height greater than 6'0" was assigned the same value for samples of 1000, 100, and 10 men.[2] Moreover, subjects failed to appreciate the role of sample size even when it was emphasized in the formulation of the problem. Consider the following question:

A certain town is served by two hospitals. In the larger hospital about 45 babies are born each day, and in the smaller hospital about 15 babies are born each day. As you know, about 50% of all babies are boys. The exact percentage of baby boys, however, varies from day to day. Sometimes it may be higher than 50%, sometimes lower.

For a period of one year, each hospital recorded the days on which more than 60% of the babies born were boys. Which hospital do you think recorded more such days?

- The larger hospital (21)
- The smaller hospital (21)
- About the same (i.e., within 5% of each other) (53).

The values in parentheses are the number of undergraduate students who chose each answer.

Most subjects judged the probability of obtaining more than 60% boys to be the same in the small and in the large hospital, presumably because these events are described by the same statistic and are therefore equally representative of the general population. In contrast, sampling theory entails that the expected number of days on which more than 60% of the babies are boys is much greater in the small hospital than in the large one, because a large sample is less likely to stray from 50%. This fundamental notion of statistics is evidently not part of people's repertoire of intuitions.

A similar insensitivity to sample size has been reported in judgments of posterior probability, i.e., of the probability that a sample has been drawn from one population rather than from another. Consider the following example:

Imagine an urn filled with balls, of which $\frac{2}{3}$ are of one color and $\frac{1}{3}$ of another. One individual has drawn 5 balls from the urn, and found that 4 were red and 1 was white. Another individual has drawn 20 balls and found that 12 were red and 8 were white. Which of the two individuals should feel more confident that the urn contains $\frac{2}{3}$ red balls and $\frac{1}{3}$ white balls, rather than the opposite? What odds should each individual give?

In this problem, the correct posterior odds are 8 to 1 for the 4:1 sample and 16 to 1 for the 12:8 sample, assuming equal prior probabilities. However, most people feel that the first sample provides much stronger evidence for the hypothesis that the urn is predominantly red, because the proportion of red balls is larger in the first than in the second sample. Here again, intuitive judgments are dominated by the sample proportion and are essentially unaffected by the size of the sample, which plays a crucial role in the determination of the actual posterior odds.[2] In addition, intuitive estimates of posterior odds are far less extreme than the correct values. The under-estimation of the impact of evidence has been observed repeatedly in problems of this type.[3,4] It has been labeled "conservatism."

Misconceptions of Chance

People expect that a sequence of events generated by a random process will represent the essential characteristics of that process even when the sequence is short. In considering tosses of a coin, for example, people regard the sequence HTHTTH to be more likely than the sequence HHHTTT, which does not appear random, and also more likely than the sequence HHHHTH, which does not represent the fairness of the coin.[2] Thus, people expect that the essential characteristics of the process will be represented, not only globally in the entire sequence, but also locally in each of its parts. A locally representative sequence, however, deviates systematically from chance expectation: it contains too many alternations and too few runs. Another consequence of the belief in local representativeness is the well-known gambler's fallacy. After observing a long run of *red* on the roulette wheel, for example, most people erroneously believe that *black* is now due, presumably because the occurrence of *black* will result in a more representative sequence than the occurrence of an additional *red*. Chance is commonly viewed as a self-correcting process where a deviation in one direction induces a deviation in the opposite direction to restore the equilibrium. In fact, deviations are not "corrected" as a chance process unfolds, they are merely diluted.

Misconceptions of chance are not limited to naive subjects. A study of the statistical intuitions of experienced research psychologists[5] revealed a lingering belief in what may be called the "law of small numbers" according to which even small samples are highly representative of the populations from which they are drawn. The responses of these investigators reflected the expectation that a valid hypothesis about a population will be represented by a statistically significant result in a sample—with little regard for its size. As a consequence, the researchers put too much faith in the results of small samples, and grossly overestimated the replicability of such results. In the actual conduct of research, this bias leads to the selection of samples of inadequate size and to over-interpretation of findings.

Insensitivity to Predictability

People are sometimes called upon to make numerical predictions, e.g., of the future value of a stock, the demand for a commodity, or the outcome of a football game. Such predictions are often made by representativeness. For example, suppose one is given a description of a company, and is asked to predict its future profit. If the description of the company is very favorable, a very high profit will appear most representative of that description; if the description is mediocre, a mediocre performance will appear most representative, etc. Now, the degree of favorableness of the description is unaffected by the reliability of that description or by the degree to which it permits accurate prediction. Hence, if people predict solely in terms of the favorableness of the description, their predictions will be insensitive to the reliability of the evidence and to the expected accuracy of the prediction.

This mode of judgment violates the normative statistical theory where the extremeness and the range of predictions are controlled by considerations of predictability. When predictability is nil, the same prediction should be made in all cases. For example, if the descriptions of companies provide no information relevant to profit, then the same value (e.g., average profit) should be predicted for all companies. If predictability is perfect, of course, the values predicted will match the actual values, and hence the range of predictions will equal the range of outcomes. In general, the higher the predictability, the wider the range of predicted values.

Several studies of numerical prediction have demonstrated that intuitive predictions violate this rule, and that subjects show little or no regard for considerations of predictability.[1] In one of these studies, subjects were presented with several paragraphs, each describing the performance of a student-teacher during a particular practice lesson. Some subjects were asked to *evaluate* the quality of the lesson described in the paragraph in percentile scores, relative to a specified population. Other subjects were asked to *predict*, also in percentile scores, the standing of each student-teacher five years after the practice lesson. The judgments made under the two conditions were identical. That is, the prediction of a remote criterion (success of a teacher after five years) was identical to the evaluation of the information on which the prediction was based (the quality of the practice lesson). The students who made these predictions were undoubtedly aware of the limited predictability of teaching competence on the basis of a single trial lesson five years earlier. Nevertheless, their predictions were as extreme as their evaluations.

The Illusion of Validity

As we have seen, people often predict by selecting the outcome (e.g., an occupation) that is most representative of the input (e.g., the description of a person). The confidence they have in their prediction depends primarily on the degree of representativeness (i.e., on the quality of the match between the selected outcome and the input) with little or no regard for the factors that limit predictive accuracy. Thus, people express great confidence in the prediction that a person is a librarian when given a description of his personality which matches the stereotype of librarians, even if the description is scanty, unreliable or outdated. The unwarranted confidence which is produced by a good fit between the predicted outcome and the input information may be called the illusion of validity. This illusion persists even when the judge is aware of the factors that limit the accuracy of his predictions. It is a common observation that psychologists who conduct selection interviews often experience considerable confidence in their predictions, even when they know of the vast literature that shows selection interviews to be highly fallible. The continued reliance on the clinical interview for selection, despite repeated demonstrations of its inadequacy, amply attests to the strength of this effect.

The internal consistency of a pattern of inputs, e.g., a profile of test scores, is a major determinant of one's confidence in predictions based on these inputs. Thus, people express more confidence in predicting the final grade-point average of a student whose first-year record consists entirely of *B*'s, than in predicting the grade-point average of a student whose first-year record includes many *A*'s and *C*'s. Highly consistent patterns are most often observed when the input variables are highly redundant or correlated. Hence, people tend to have great confidence in predictions based on redundant input variables. However, an elementary result in the statistics of correlation asserts that, given input variables of stated validity, a prediction based on several such inputs can achieve higher accuracy when they are independent of each other than when they are redundant or correlated. Thus, redundancy among inputs decreases accuracy even as it increases confidence, and people are often confident in predictions that are quite likely to be off the mark.[1]

Misconceptions of Regression

Suppose a large group of children have been examined on two equivalent versions of an aptitude test. If one selects ten children from among those who did best on one of the two versions, he will find their performance on the second version to be somewhat disappointing, on the average. Conversely, if one selects ten children from among those who did worst on one version, they will be found, on the average, to do somewhat better on the other version. More generally, consider two variables X and Y which have the same distribution. If one selects individuals whose average score deviates from the mean of X by k units then, by and large, their average deviation from the mean of Y will be less than k. These observations illustrate a general phenomenon known as regression toward the mean, which was first documented by Galton over one hundred years ago.

In the normal course of life, we encounter many instances of regression toward the mean, e.g., in the comparison of the height of fathers and sons, of the intelligence of husbands and wives, or of the performance of individuals on consecutive examinations. Nevertheless, people do not develop correct intuitions about this phenomenon. First, they do not expect regression in many contexts where it is bound to occur. Second, when they recognize the occurrence of regression, they often invent spurious causal explanations for it.[1] We suggest that the phenomenon of regression remains elusive because it is incompatible with the belief that the predicted outcome should be maximally representative of the input, and hence that the value of the outcome variable should be as extreme as the value of the input variable.

The failure to recognize the import of regression can have pernicious consequences as illustrated by the following observation.[1] In a discussion of flight training, experienced instructors noted that praise for an exceptionally smooth landing is typically followed by a poorer landing on the next try, while harsh criticism after a rough landing is usually followed by an improvement on the next try. The instructors concluded that verbal rewards are detrimental to learning while verbal punishments are beneficial—contrary to accepted psychological doctrine. This conclusion is unwarranted because of the presence of regression toward the mean. As in other cases of repeated examination, an improvement will usually follow a poor performance and a deterioration will usually follow an outstanding performance—even if the instructor does not respond to the trainee's achievement on the first attempt. Because the instructors had praised their trainees after good landings and admonished then after poor ones, they reached the erroneous and potentially harmful conclusion that punishment is more effective than reward.

Thus, the failure to understand the effect of regression leads one to overestimate the effectiveness of punishment and to underestimate the effectiveness of reward. In social interaction as well as in intentional training, rewards are typically administered when performance is good and punishments are typically administered when performance is poor. By regression alone, therefore, behavior is most likely to improve after punishment and most likely to deteriorate after reward. Consequently, the human condition is such that, by chance alone, one is most often rewarded for punishing others and most often punished for rewarding them. People are generally not aware of this contingency. In fact, the elusive role of regression in determining the apparent consequences of reward and punishment seems to have escaped the notice of students of this area.

Availability

There are situations in which people assess the frequency of a class or the probability of an event by the ease with which instances or occurrences can be brought to mind. For example, one may assess the risk of heart attack among middle aged people by recalling such occurrences among one's acquaintances. Similarly, one may evaluate the probability that a given business venture will fail by imagining various difficulties which it could encounter. This judgmental heuristic is called availability. Availability is a useful clue for assessing frequency or probability because, in general, instances of large classes are recalled better and faster than instances of less frequent classes. However, availability is also affected by other factors besides frequency and probability. Consequently, the reliance on availability leads to predictable biases, some of which are illustrated below.

Biases Due to the Retrievability of Instances

When the frequency of a class is judged by the availability of its instances, a class whose instances are easily retrieved will appear more numerous than a class of equal frequency whose instances are less retrievable. In an elementary demonstration of this effect, subjects heard a list of well-known personalities of both sexes and were subsequently asked to judge whether the list contained more names of men than of women. Different lists were presented to different groups of subjects. In some of the lists the men were relatively more famous than the women, and in others the women were relatively more famous than the men. In each of the lists, the subjects erroneously judged the class consisting of the more famous personalities to be the more numerous.[6]

In addition to familiarity, there are other factors (e.g., salience) which affect the retrievability of instances. For example, the impact of seeing a house burning, on the subjective probability of such accidents is probably greater than the impact of reading about a fire in the local paper. Furthermore, recent occurrences are likely to be relatively more available than earlier occurrences. It is a common experience that the subjective probability of traffic accidents rises temporarily when one sees a car overturned by the side of the road.

Biases Due to the Effectiveness of a Search Set

Suppose one samples a word (of three letters or more) at random from an English text. Is it more likely that the word starts with r or that r is its third letter? People approach this problem by recalling words that begin with r (e.g., road) and words that have r in the third position (e.g., car) and assess relative frequency by the ease with which words of the two types come to mind. Because it is much easier to search for words by their first than by their third letter, most people judge words that begin with a given consonant to be more numerous than words in which the same consonant appears in the third position. They do so even for consonants (e.g., r or k) that are actually more frequent in the third position than in the first.[6]

Different tasks elicit different search sets. For example, suppose you are asked to rate the frequency with which abstract words (e.g., thought, love) and concrete words (e.g., door, water) appear in written English. A natural way to answer this question is to search for contexts in which the word could appear. It seems easier to think of contexts in which an abstract concept is mentioned (e.g., "love" in love stories) than to think of contexts in which a concrete word (e.g., "door") is mentioned. If the frequency of words is judged by the availability of the contexts in which they appear, abstract words will be judged as relatively more numerous than concrete words. This bias has been observed in a recent study[7] which showed that the judged frequency of occurrence of abstract words was much higher than that of concrete words of the same objective frequency. Abstract words were also judged to appear in a much greater variety of contexts than concrete words.

Biases of Imaginability

Sometimes, one has to assess the frequency of a class whose instances are not stored in memory but can be generated according to a given rule. In such situations, one typically generates several instances, and evaluates frequency or probability by the ease with the relevant instances can be constructed. However, the ease of constructing instances does not always reflect their actual frequency, and this mode of evaluation is prone to biases. To illustrate, consider a group of 10 people who form committees of k members, $2 \leq k \leq 8$. How many different committees of k members can be formed? The correct answer to this problem is given by the binomial coefficient $\binom{10}{k}$ which reaches a maximum of 252 for $k = 5$. Clearly, the number of committees of k members equals the number of committees of $(10 - k)$ members because any committee of k members defines a unique group of $(10 - k)$ non-members.

One way to answer this question without computation is to mentally construct committees of k members, and to evaluate their number by the ease with which they come to mind. Committees of few members, say 2, are more available that committees of many members, say 8. The simplest scheme for the construction of committees is a partition of the group into disjoint sets. One readily sees that it is easy to construct five disjoint committees of 2 members, while it is impossible to generate even two disjoint committees of 8 members. Consequently, if frequency is assessed by imaginability, or by availability for construction, the small committees will appear more numerous than larger committees, in contrast to the correct symmetric bell-shaped function. Indeed, when naive subjects were asked to estimate the number of distinct committees of various sizes, their estimates were a decreasing monotonic function of committee size.[6] For example, the median estimate of the number of committees of 2 members was 70, while the estimate for committees of 8 members was 20 (the correct answer is 45 in both cases).

Imaginability plays an important role in the evaluation of probabilities in real-life situations. The risk involved in an adventurous expedition, for example, is evaluated by imagining contingencies with which the expedition is not equipped to cope. If many such difficulties are vividly portrayed, the expedition can be made to appear exceedingly dangerous, although the ease with which disasters are imagined need not reflect their actual likelihood. Conversely, the risk involved in an undertaking may be grossly underestimated if some possible dangers are either difficult to conceive, or simply do not come to mind.

Illusory Correlation

Chapman and Chapman[8] have described an interesting bias in the judgment of the frequency with which two events co-occur. They presented naive judges with information concerning several hypothetical mental patients. The data for each patient consisted of a clinical diagnosis and a drawing of a person made by the patient. Later the judges estimated the frequency with which each diagnosis (e.g., paranoia or suspiciousness) had been accompanied by various features of the drawing (e.g., peculiar eyes). The subjects markedly overestimated the frequency of co-occurrence of natural associates, such as suspiciousness and peculiar eyes. This effect was labeled illusory correlation. In their erroneous judgments of the data to which they had been exposed, naive subjects "rediscovered" much of the common but unfounded clinical lore concerning the interpretation of the draw-a-person test. The illusory correlation effect was extremely resistant to contradictory data. It persisted even when the correlation between symptom and diagnosis was actually negative, and it prevented the judges from detecting relationships that were in fact present.

Availability provides a natural account for the illusory-correlation effect. The judgment of how frequently two events co-occur could be based on the strength of the associative bond between them. When the association is strong, one is likely to conclude that the events have been frequently paired. Consequently, strong associates will be judged to have occurred frequently together. According to this view, the illusory correlation between suspiciousness and peculiar drawing of the eyes, for example, is due to the fact that suspiciousness is more readily associated with the eyes than with any other part of the body.

Life-long experience has taught us that, in general, instances of large classes are recalled better and faster than instances of less frequent classes; that likely occurrences are easier to imagine than unlikely ones; and that the associative connections between events are strengthened when the events frequently co-occur. As a consequence, man has at his disposal a procedure (i.e., the availability heuristic) for estimating the numerosity of a class, the likelihood of an event or the frequency of co-ocurrences, by the ease with which the relevant mental operations of retrieval, construction, or association can be performed. However, as the preceding examples have demonstrated, this valuable estimation procedure is subject to systematic errors.

Adjustment and Anchoring

In many situations, people make estimates by starting from an initial value which is adjusted to yield the final answer. The initial value, or starting point, may be suggested by the formulation of the problem, or else it may be the result of a partial computation. Whatever the source of the initial value, adjustments are typically insufficient.[4] That is, different starting prints yield different estimates, which are biased towards the initial values. We call this phenomenon anchoring.

Insufficient Adjustment

In a demonstration of the anchoring effect, subjects were asked to estimate various quantities, stated in percentages (e.g., the percentage of African countries in the U.N.). For each question a starting value between 0 and 100 was determined by spinning a wheel of fortune in the subjects' presence. The subjects were instructed to indicate whether the given (arbitrary) starting value was too high or too low, and then to reach their estimate by moving upward or downward from that value. Different groups were given different starting values for each problem. These arbitrary values had a marked effect on the estimates. For example, the median estimates of the percentage of African countries in the U.N. were 25% and 45%, respectively, for groups which received 10% and 65% as starting points. Payoffs for accuracy did not reduce the anchoring effect.

Anchoring occurs not only when the starting point is given to the subject but also when the subject bases his estimate on the result of some incomplete computation. A study of intuitive numerical estimation illustrates this effect. Two groups of high-school students estimated, within 5 seconds, a numerical expression that was written on the blackboard. One group estimated the product $8 \times 7 \times 6 \times 5 \times 4 \times 3 \times 2 \times 1$, while another group estimated the product $1 \times 2 \times 3 \times 4 \times 5 \times 6 \times 7 \times 8$. To rapidly answer such questions people may perform a few steps of computation and estimate the product by extrapolation or adjustment. Because adjustments are typically insufficient, this procedure should lead to underestimation. Furthermore, because the result of the first few steps of multiplication (performed from left to right) is higher in the descending sequence than in the ascending sequence, the former expression should be judged larger than the latter. Both predictions were confirmed. The median estimate for the ascending sequence was 512, while the median estimate for the descending sequence was 2,250. The correct answer is 40,320.

Biases in the Evaluation of Conjunctive and Disjunctive Events

In a recent study,[9] subjects were given the opportunity to bet on one of two events. Three types of events were used; (i) simple events, e.g., drawing a red marble from a bag containing 50% red marbles and 50% white marbles; (ii) conjunctive events, e.g., drawing a red marble 7 times in succession, with replacement, from a bag containing 90% red marbles and 10% white marbles; (iii) disjunctive events, e.g., drawing a red marble at least once in 7 successive tries, with replacement, from a bag containing 10% red marbles and 90% white marbles. In this problem, a significant majority of subjects preferred to bet on the conjunctive event (the probability of which is .48) rather than on the simple event, the probability of which is .50. Subjects also preferred to bet on the simple event rather than on the disjunctive events which has a probability of .52. Thus, most subjects bet on the less likely event in both comparisons. This pattern of choices illustrates a general finding. Studies of choice among gambles and of judgments of probability indicate that people tend to overestimate the probability of conjunctive events[10] and to underestimate the probability of disjunctive events. These biases are readily explained as effects of anchoring. The stated probability of the elementary event (e.g., of success at any one stage) provides a natural starting point for the estimation of the probabilities of both conjunctive and disjunctive events. Since adjustment from the starting point is typically insufficient, the final estimates remain too close to the probabilities of the elementary events in both cases. Note that the overall probability of a conjunctive event is lower than the probability of each elementary event, whereas the overall probability of a disjunctive event is higher than the probability of each elementary event. As a consequence of anchoring, the overall probability will be overestimated in conjunctive problems and underestimated in disjunctive problems.

Biases in the evaluation of compound events are particularly significant in the context of planning. The successful completion of an undertaking (e.g., the development of a new product) typically has a conjunctive character: for the undertaking to succeed each of a series of events must occur. Even when each of these events is very likely, the overall probability of success can be quite low if the number of events is large. The general tendency to overestimate the probability of conjunctive events leads to unwarranted optimism in the evaluation of the likelihood that a plan will succeed, or that a project will be completed on time. Conversely, disjunctive structures are typically encountered in the evaluation of risks. A complex system (e.g., a nuclear reactor or a human body) will malfunction if any of its essential components fails. Even when the likelihood of failure in each component is slight, the probability of an overall failure can be high if many components are involved. Because of anchoring, people will tend to underestimate the probabilities of failure in complex systems. Thus, the direction of the anchoring bias can sometimes be inferred from the structure of the event. The chain-like structure of conjunctions leads to over-estimation, the funnel-like structure of disjunctions leads to underestimation.

Anchoring in the Assessment of Subjective Probability Distributions

For many purposes (e.g., the calculation of posterior probabilities, decision-theoretical analyses) a person is required to express his beliefs about a quantity (e.g., the value of the Dow-Jones on a particular day) in the form of a probability distri-bution. Such a distribution is usually constructed by asking the person to select values of the quantity that correspond to specified percentiles of his subjective prob-ability distribution. For example, the judge may be asked to select a number X_{90} such that his subjective probability that this number will be higher than the value of the Dow-Jones is .90. That is, he should select X_{90} so that he is just willing to accept 9 to 1 odds that the Dow-Jones will not exceed X_{90}. A subjective probability distribution for the value of the Dow-Jones can be constructed from several such judgments cor-responding to different percentiles (e.g., X_{10}, X_{25}, X_{75}, X_{99}, etc.).

By collecting subjective probability distributions for many different quantities, it is possible to test the judge for proper calibration. A judge is properly (or externally) calibrated in a set of problems if exactly $\Pi\%$ of the true values of the assessed quan-tities fall below his stated values of X_Π. For example, the true values should fall below X_{01} for 1% of the quantities and above X_{99} for 1% of the quantities. Thus, the true values should fall in the confidence interval between X_{01} and X_{99} on 98% of the problems.

Several investigators (see notes 11, 12, 13) have obtained probability distributions for many quantities from a large number of judges. These distributions indicated large and systematic departures from proper calibration. In most studies, the actual values of the assessed quantities are either smaller than X_{01} or greater than X_{99} for about 30% of the problems. That is, the subjects state overly narrow confidence intervals which reflect more certainty than is justified by their knowledge about the assessed quantities. This bias is common to naive and to sophisticated subjects, and it is not eliminated by introducing proper scoring rules which provide incentives for external calibration. This effect is attributable, in part at least, to anchoring. To select X_{90} for the value of the Dow-Jones, for example, it is natural to begin by thinking about one's best estimate of the Dow-Jones and to adjust this value upward. If this adjustment—like most others—is insufficient, then X_{90} will not be sufficiently extreme. A similar anchoring effect will occur in the selection of X_{10} which is pre-sumably obtained by adjusting one's best estimate downwards. Consequently, the confidence interval between X_{10} and X_{90} will be too narrow, and the assessed probability distribution will be too tight. In support of this interpretation it can be shown that subjective probabilities are systematically altered by a procedure in which one's best estimate does not serve as an anchor.

Subjective probability distributions for a given quantity (the Dow-Jones average) can be obtained in two different ways: (i) by asking the subject to select values of the Dow-Jones that correspond to specified percentiles of his probability distribution and (ii) by asking the subject to assess the probabilities that the true value of the Dow-Jones will exceed some specified values. The two procedures are formally equivalent and should yield identical distributions. However, they suggest different modes of adjustment from different anchors. In procedure (i), the natural starting point is one's best estimate of the quantity. In procedure (ii), on the other hand, the subject may be anchored on the value stated in the question. Alternatively, he may be anchored on even odds, or 50-50 chances, which is a natural starting point in the estimation of likelihood. In either case, procedure (ii) should yield less extreme odds than procedure (i).

To contrast the two procedures, a set of 24 quantities (such as the air distance from New Delhi to Peking) was presented to a group of subjects who assessed either X_{10} or X_{90} for each problem. Another group of subjects received the median judgment of the first group for each of the 24 quantities. They were asked to assess the odds that each of the given values exceeded the true value of the relevant quantity. In the absence of any bias, the second group should retrieve the odds specified to the first group, that is, 9:1. However, if even odds or the stated value serve as anchors, the odds of the second group should be less extreme, that is, closer to 1:1. Indeed, the median odds stated by this group, across all problems, were 3:1. When the judgments of the two groups were tested for external calibration, it was found that subjects in the first group were too extreme, while subjects in the second group were too conservative.

Discussion

This chapter has been concerned with cognitive biases which stem from the reliance on judgmental heuristics. These biases are not attributable to motivational effects such as wishful thinking or the distortion of judgments by payoffs and penalties. Indeed, several of the severe errors of judgment reported earlier were observed despite the fact that subjects were encouraged to be accurate and were rewarded for the correct answers.[2,6]

The reliance on heuristics and the prevalence of biases are not restricted to laymen. Experienced researchers are also prone to the same biases—when they think intuitively. For example, the tendency to predict the outcome that best represents the data, with insufficient regard for prior probability, has been observed in the intuitive judgments of individuals who had extensive training in statistics.[1,5] Although the statistically sophisticated avoid elementary errors (e.g., the gambler's fallacy), their intuitive judgments are liable to similar fallacies in more intricate and less transparent problems.

It is not surprising that useful heuristics such as representativeness and availability are retained, even though they occasionally lead to errors in prediction or estimation. What is perhaps surprising is the failure of people to infer from life-long experience such fundamental statistical rules as regression toward the mean, or the effect of sample size on sampling variability. Although everyone is exposed in the normal course of life to numerous examples from which these rules could have been induced, very few people discover the principles of sampling and regression on their own. Statistical principles are not learned from everyday experience because the relevant instances are not coded appropriately. For example, we do not discover that successive lines in a text differ more in average word length than do successive pages, because we simply do not attend to the average word length of individual lines or pages. Thus, we do not learn the relation between sample size and sampling variability, although the data for such learning is present in abundance whenever we read.

The lack of an appropriate code also explains why people usually do not detect the biases in their judgments of probability. A person could conceivably learn whether his judgments are externally calibrated by keeping a tally of the proportion of events that actually occur among those to which he assigns the same probability. However, it is not natural to group events by their judged probability. In the absense of such grouping it is impossible for an individual to discover, for example, that only 50% of the predictions to which he has assigned a probability of .9 or higher actually came true.

The empirical analysis of cognitive biases has implications for the theoretical and applied role of judged probabilities. Modern decision theory[14,15] regards subjective probability as the quantified opinion of an idealized person. Specifically, the subjective probability of a given event is defined by the set of bets about this event which such a person is willing to accept. An internally consistent, or coherent, subjective probability measure can be derived for an individual if his choices among bets satisfy certain principles (i.e., the axioms of the theory). The derived probability is subjective in the sense that different individuals are allowed to have different probabilities for the same event. The major contribution of this approach is that it provides a rigorous subjective interpretation of probability which is applicable to unique events and is embedded in a general theory of rational decision.

It should perhaps be noted that while subjective probabilities can sometimes be inferred from preferences among bets, they are normally not formed in this fashion. A person bets on Team *A* rather than on Team *B* because he believes that Team *A* is more likely to win; he does not infer this belief from his betting preferences. Thus, in reality, subjective probabilities determine preferences among bets and are not derived from them as in the axiomatic theory of rational decision.[14]

The inherently subjective nature of probability has led many students to the belief that coherence, or internal consistency, is the only valid criterion by which judged probabilities should be evaluated. From the standpoint of the formal theory of subjective probability, any set of internally consistent probability judgments is as good as any other. This criterion is not entirely satisfactory because an internally consistent set of subjective probabilities can be incompatible with other beliefs held by the individual. Consider a person whose subjective probabilities for all possible outcomes of a coin-tossing game reflect the gambler's fallacy. That is, his estimate of the probability of *tails* on any toss increases with the number of consecutive *heads* that preceded that toss. The judgments of such a person could be internally consistent and therefore acceptable as adequate subjective probabilities according to the criterion of the formal theory. These probabilities, however, are incompatible with the generally-held belief that a coin has no memory and is therefore incapable of generating sequential dependencies. For judged probabilities to be considered adequate, or rational, internal consistency is not enough. The judgments must be compatible with the entire web of beliefs held by the individual. Unfortunately, there can be no simple formal procedure for assessing the compatibility of a set of probability judgments with the judge's total system of beliefs. The rational judge will nevertheless strive for compatibility, even though internal consistency is more easily achieved and assessed. In particular, he will attempt to make his probability judgments compatible with his knowledge about (i) the subject-matter; (ii) the laws of probability; (iii) his own judgmental heuristics and biases.

References and Notes

This article was published with minor modifications, in *Science* 185 (1974), 1124–1131, 27 September 1974. Copyright 1974 by the American Association for the Advancement of Science whose permission to reproduce it here is gratefully acknowledged.

This research was supported by the Advanced Research Projects Agency of the Department of Defense and was monitored by ONR under Contract No. N00014-73-C-0438 to Oregon Research Institute. Additional support was provided by the Research and Development Authority of the Hebrew University.

1. Kahneman, D. and Tversky, A., 'On the Psychology of Prediction', *Psychological Review* 80 (1973), 237–251.

2. Kahneman, D. and Tversky, A., 'Subjective Probability: A Judgment of Representativeness', *Cognitive Psychology* 3 (1972), 430–454.

3. Edwards, W., 'Conservatism in Human Information Processing', in B. Kleinmuntz (ed.), *Formal Representation of Human Judgment*, Wiley, New York, 1968, pp. 17–52.

4. Slovic, P. and Lichtenstein, S., 'Comparison of Bayesian and Regression Approaches to the Study of Information Processing in Judgment', *Organizational Behavior and Human Performance* 6 (1971), 649–744.

5. Tversky, A. and Kahneman, D., 'The Belief in the Law of Small Numbers', *Psychological Bulletin* 76 (1971), 105–110.

6. Tversky, A. and Kahneman, D., 'Availability: A Heuristic for Judging Frequency and Probability', *Cognitive Psychology* 5 (1973), 207–232.

7. Galbraith, R. C. and Underwood, B. J., 'Perceived Frequency of Concrete and Abstract Words', *Memory & Cognition* 1 (1973), 56–60.

8. Chapman, L. J. and Chapman, J. P., 'Genesis of Popular but Erroneous Psychodiagnostic Observations', *Journal of Abnormal Psychology* 73 (1967), 193–204.
   Chapman, L. J. and Chapman, J. P., 'Illusory Correlation as an Obstacle to the Use of Valid Psychodiagnostic Signs', *Journal of Abnormal Psychology* 74 (1969), 271–280.

9. Bar-Hillel, M., 'Compounding Subjective Probabilities', *Organizational Behavior and Human Performance* 9 (1973), 396–406.

10. Cohen, J., Chesnick, E. I., and Haran, D., 'A Confirmation of the Inertial-ψ Effect in Sequential Choice and Decision', *British Journal of Psychology* 63 (1972), 41–46.

11. Alpert, M. and Raiffa, H., 'A Report on the Training of Probability Assessors', Unpublished manuscript, Harvard University, 1969.

12. C. Staël von Holstein, 'Two Techniques for Assessment of Subjective Probability Distributions—An Experimental Study', *Acta Psychologica* 35 (1971), 478–494.

13. Winkler, R. L., 'The Assessment of Prior Distributions in Bayesian Analysis', *Journal of the American Statistical Association* 62 (1967), 776–800.

14. Savage, L. J., *The Foundations of Statistics*, Wiley, New York, 1954.

15. de Finetti, B., 'Probability: Interpretation', in D. L. Sills (ed.), *International Encyclopedia of the Social Sciences* 13 (1968), 496–504.

9 Extensional versus Intuitive Reasoning: The Conjunction Fallacy in Probability Judgment

Amos Tversky and Daniel Kahneman

Uncertainty is an unavoidable aspect of the human condition. Many significant choices must be based on beliefs about the likelihood of such uncertain events as the guilt of a defendant, the result of an election, the future value of the dollar, the outcome of a medical operation, or the response of a friend. Because we normally do not have adequate formal models for computing the probabilities of such events, intuitive judgment is often the only practical method for assessing uncertainty.

The question of how lay people and experts evaluate the probabilities of uncertain events has attracted considerable research interest in the last decade (see, e.g., Einhorn & Hogarth, 1981; Kahneman, Slovic, & Tversky, 1982; Nisbett & Ross, 1980). Much of this research has compared intuitive inferences and probability judgments to the rules of statistics and the laws of probability. The student of judgment uses the probability calculus as a standard of comparison much as a student of perception might compare the perceived sizes of objects to their physical sizes. Unlike the correct size of objects, however, the "correct" probability of events is not easily defined. Because individuals who have different knowledge or who hold different beliefs must be allowed to assign different probabilities to the same event, no single value can be correct for all people. Furthermore, a correct probability cannot always be determined even for a single person. Outside the domain of random sampling, probability theory does not determine the probabilities of uncertain events—it merely imposes constraints on the relations among them. For example, if A is more probable than B, then the complement of A must be less probable than the complement of B.

The laws of probability derive from extensional considerations. A probability measure is defined on a family of events and each event is construed as a set of possibilities, such as the three ways of getting a 10 on a throw of a pair of dice. The probability of an event equals the sum of the probabilities of its disjoint outcomes. Probability theory has traditionally been used to analyze repetitive chance processes, but the theory has also been applied to essentially unique events where probability is not reducibe to the relative frequency of "favorable" outcomes. The probability that the man who sits next to you on the plane is unmarried equals the probability that he is a bachelor plus the probability that he is either divorced or widowed. Additivity applies even when probability does not have a frequentistic interpretation and when the elementary events are not equiprobable.

The simplest and most fundamental qualitative law of probability is the extension rule: If the extension of A includes the extension of B (i.e., $A \supset B$) then $P(A) \geq P(B)$. Because the set of possibilities associated with a conjunction A&B is included in the set of possibilities associated with B, the same principle can also be expressed by the conjunction rule $P(A\&B) \leq P(B)$: A conjunction cannot be more probable than one of its constituents. This rule holds regardless of whether A and B are independent and is valid for any probability assignment on the same sample space. Furthermore, it applies not only to the standard probability calculus but also to nonstandard models such as upper and lower probability (Dempster, 1967; Suppes, 1975), belief function (Shafer, 1976), Baconian probability (Cohen, 1977), rational belief (Kyburg, in press), and possibility theory (Zadeh, 1978).

In contrast to formal theories of belief, intuitive judgments of probability are generally not extensional. People do not normally analyze daily events into exhaustive lists of possibilities or evaluate compound probabilities by aggregating elementary ones. Instead, they commonly use a limited number of heuristics, such as representativeness and availability (Kahneman et al. 1982). Our conception of judgmental heuristics is based on *natural assessments* that are routinely carried out as part of the perception of events and the comprehension of messages. Such natural assessments include computations of similarity and representativeness, attributions of causality, and evaluations of the availability of associations and exemplars. These assessments, we propose, are performed even in the absence of a specific task set, although their results are used to meet task demands as they arise. For example, the mere mention of "horror movies" activates instances of horror movies and evokes an assessment of their availability. Similarly, the statement that Woody Allen's aunt had hoped that he would be a dentist elicits a comparison of the character to the stereotype and an assessment of representativeness. It is presumably the mismatch between Woody Allen's personality and our stereotype of a dentist that makes the thought mildly amusing. Although these assessments are not tied to the estimation of frequency or probability, they are likely to play a dominant role when such judgments are required. The availability of horror movies may be used to answer the question, "What proportion of the movies produced last year were horror movies?," and representativeness may control the judgment that a particular boy is more likely to be an actor than a dentist.

The term *judgmental heuristic* refers to a strategy—whether deliberate or not—that relies on a natural assessment to produce an estimation or a prediction. One of the manifestations of a heuristic is the relative neglect of other considerations. For example, the resemblance of a child to various professional stereotypes may be given too much weight in predicting future vocational choice, at the expense of other pertinent data such as the base-rate frequencies of occupations. Hence, the use of judgmental heuristics gives rise to predictable biases. Natural assessments can affect judgments in other ways, for which the term *heuristic* is less apt. First, people sometimes misinterpret their task and fail to distinguish the required judgment from the natural assessment that the problem evokes. Second, the natural assessment may act as an anchor to which the required judgment is assimiliated, even when the judge does not intend to use the one to estimate the other.

Previous discussions of errors of judgment have focused on deliberate strategies and on misinterpretations of tasks. The present treatment calls special attention to the processes of anchoring and assimiliation, which are often neither deliberate nor conscious. An example from perception may be instructive: If two objects in a picture of a three-dimensional scene have the same picture size, the one that appears more distant is not only seen as "really" larger but also as larger in the picture. The natural computation of real size evidently influences the (less natural) judgment of picture size, although observers are unlikely to confuse the two values or to use the former to estimate the latter.

The natural assessments of representativeness and availability do not conform to the extensional logic of probability theory. In particular, a conjunction can be more representative than one of its constituents, and instances of a specific category can be easier to retrieve than instances of a more inclusive category. The following demonstration illustrates the point. When they were given 60 sec to list seven-letter words of a specified form, students at the University of British Columbia (UBC) produced many more words of the form _ _ _ _ing than of the form _ _ _ _ _n_, although the latter class includes the former. The average numbers of words produced in the two conditions were 6.4 and 2.9, respectively, $t(44) = 4.70$, $p < .01$. In this test of availability, the increased efficacy of memory search suffices to offset the reduced extension of the target class.

Our treatment of the availability heuristic (Tversky & Kahneman, 1973) suggests that the differential availability of *ing* words and of _n_ words should be reflected in judgments of frequency. The following questions test this prediction.

In four pages of a novel (about 2,000 words), how many words would you expect to find that have the form _ _ _ _ing (seven-letter words that end with "ing")? Indicate your best estimate by circling one of the values below:

0   1–2   3–4   5–7   8–10   11–15   16+.

A second version of the question requested estimates for words of the form _ _ _ _ _ n_. The median estimates were 13.4 for *ing* words ($n = 52$), and 4.7 for _n_ words ($n = 53$, $p < .01$, by median test), contrary to the extension rule. Similar results were obtained for the comparison of words of the form _ _ _ _ _ly with words of the form _ _ _ _ _l_; the median estimates were 8.8 and 4.4, respectively.

This example illustrates the structure of the studies reported in this article. We constructed problems in which a reduction of extension was associated with an increase in availability or representativeness, and we tested the conjunction rule in judgments of frequency or probability. In the next section we discuss the representativeness heuristic and contrast it with the conjunction rule in the context of person perception. The third section describes conjunction fallacies in medical prognoses, sports forecasting, and choice among bets. In the fourth section we investigate probability judgments for conjunctions of causes and effects and describe conjunction errors in scenarios of future events. Manipulations that enable respondents to resist the conjunction fallacy are explored in the fifth section, and the implications of the results are discussed in the last section.

Representative Conjunctions

Modern research on categorization of objects and events (Mervis & Rosch, 1981; Rosch, 1978; Smith & Medin, 1981) has shown that information is commonly stored and processed in relation to mental models, such as prototypes and schemata. It is therefore natural and economical for the probability of an event to be evaluated by the degree to which that event is representative of an appropriate mental model (Kahneman & Tversky, 1972, 1973; Tversky & Kahneman, 1971, 1982). Because many of the results reported here are attributed to this heuristic, we first briefly analyze the concept of representativeness and illustrate its role in probability judgment.

Representativeness is an assessment of the degree of correspondence between a sample and a population, an instance and a category, an act and an actor or, more generally, between an outcome and a model. The model may refer to a person, a coin, or the world economy, and the respective outcomes could be marital status, a sequence of heads and tails, or the current price of gold. Representativeness can be investigated empirically by asking people, for example, which of two sequences of heads and tails is more representative of a fair coin or which of two professions is more representative of a given personality. This relation differs from other notions of proximity in that it is distinctly directional. It is natural to describe a sample as more or less representative of its parent population or a species (e.g., robin, penguin) as more or less representative of a superordinate category (e.g., bird). It is awkward to describe a population as representative of a sample or a category as representative of an instance.

When the model and the outcomes are described in the same terms, representativeness is reducible to similarity. Because a sample and a population, for example, can be described by the same attributes (e.g., central tendency and variability), the sample appears representative if its salient statistics match the corresponding parameters of the population. In the same manner, a person seems representative of a social group if his or her personality resembles the stereotypical member of that group. Representativeness, however, is not always reducible to similarity; it can also reflect causal and correlational beliefs (see, e.g., Chapman & Chapman, 1967; Jennings, Amabile, & Ross, 1982; Nisbett & Ross, 1980). A particular act (e.g., suicide) is representative of a person because we attribute to the actor a disposition to commit the act, not because the act resembles the person. Thus, an outcome is representative of a model if the salient features match or if the model has a propensity to produce the outcome.

Representativeness tends to covary with frequency: Common instances and frequent events are generally more representative than unusual instances and rare events. The representative summer day is warm and sunny, the representative American family has two children, and the representative height of an adult male is about 5 feet 10 inches. However, there are notable circumstances where representativeness is at variance with both actual and perceived frequency. First, a highly specific outcome can be representative but infrequent. Consider a numerical variable, such as weight, that has a unimodal frequency distribution in a given population. A narrow interval near the mode of the distribution is generally more representative of the population than a wider interval near the tail. For example, 68% of a group of Stanford University undergraduates ($N = 105$) stated that it is more representative for a female Stanford student "to weigh between 124 and 125 pounds" than "to weigh more than 135 pounds." On the other hand, 78% of a different group ($N = 102$) stated that among female Stanford students there are more "women who weigh more than 135 pounds" than "women who weigh between 124 and 125 pounds." Thus, the narrow modal interval (124–125 pounds) was judged to be more representative but less frequent than the broad tail interval (above 135 pounds).

Second, an attribute is representative of a class if it is very diagnostic, that is, if the relative frequency of this attribute is much higher in that class than in a relevant reference class. For example, 65% of the subjects ($N = 105$) stated that it is more representative for a Hollywood actress "to be divorced more than 4 times" than "to vote Democratic." Multiple divorce is diagnostic of Hollywood actresses because it is part of the stereotype that the incidence of divorce is higher among Hollywood actresses than among other women. However, 83% of a different group ($N = 102$) stated that, among Hollywood actresses, there are more "women who vote Democratic" than "women who are divorced more than 4 times." Thus, the more diagnostic attribute was judged to be more representative but less frequent than an attribute (voting Democratic) of lower diagnosticity. Third, an unrepresentative instance of a category can be fairly representative of a superordinate category. For example, chicken is a worse exemplar of a bird than of an animal, and rice is an unrepresentative vegetable, although it is a representative food.

The preceding observations indicate that representativeness is nonextensional: It is not determined by frequency, and it is not bound by class inclusion. Consequently, the test of the conjunction rule in probability judgments offers the sharpest contrast between the extensional logic of probability theory and the psychological principles of representativeness. Our first set of studies of the conjunction rule were conducted in 1974, using occupation and political affiliation as target attributes to be predicted singly or in conjunction from brief personality sketches (see Tversky & Kahneman, 1982, for a brief summary). The studies described in the present section replicate and extend our earlier work. We used the following personality sketches of two fictitious individuals, Bill and Linda, followed by a set of occupations and avocations associated with each of them.

Bill is 34 years old. He is intelligent, but unimaginative, compulsive, and generally lifeless. In school, he was strong in mathematics but weak in social studies and humanities.

Bill is a physician who plays poker for a hobby.

Bill is an architect.

Bill is an accountant. (A)

Bill plays jazz for a hobby. (J)

Bill surfs for a hobby.

Bill is a reporter.

Bill is an accountant who plays jazz for a hobby. (A&J)

Bill climbs mountains for a hobby.

Linda is 31 years old, single, outspoken, and very bright. She majored in philosophy. As a student, she was deeply concerned with issues of discrimination and social justice, and also participated in anti-nuclear demonstrations.

Linda is a teacher in elementary school.

Linda works in a bookstore and takes Yoga classes.

Linda is active in the feminist movement. (F)

Linda is a psychiatric social worker.

Linda is a member of the League of Women Voters.

Linda is a bank teller. (T)

Linda is an insurance salesperson.

Linda is a bank teller and is active in the feminist movement. (T&F)

As the reader has probably guessed, the description of Bill was constructed to be representative of an accountant (A) and unrepresentative of a person who plays jazz for a hobby (J). The description of Linda was constructed to be representative of an active feminist (F) and unrepresentative of a bank teller (T). We also expected the ratings of representativeness to be higher for the classes defined by a conjunction of attributes (A&J for Bill, T&F for Linda) than for the less representative constituent of each conjunction (J and T, respectively).

A group of 88 undergraduates at UBC ranked the eight statements associated with each description by "the degree to which Bill (Linda) resembles the typical member of that class." The results confirmed our expectations. The percentages of respondents who displayed the predicted order (A > A&J > J for Bill; F > T&F > T for Linda) were 87% and 85%, respectively. This finding is neither surprising nor objectionable. If, like similarity and prototypicality, representativeness depends on both common and distinctive features (Tversky, 1977), it should be enhanced by the addition of shared features. Adding eyebrows to a schematic face makes it more similar to another schematic face with eyebrows (Gati & Tversky, 1982). Analogously, the addition of feminism to the profession of bank teller improves the match of Linda's current activities to her personality. More surprising and less acceptable is the finding that the great majority of subjects also rank the conjunctions (A&J and T&F) as more *probable* than their less representative constituents (J and T). The following sections describe and analyze this phenomenon.

Indirect and Subtle Tests
Experimental tests of the conjunction rule can be divided into three types: *indirect* tests, *direct-subtle* tests and *direct-transparent* tests. In the indirect tests, one group of subjects evaluates the probability of the conjunction, and another group of subjects evaluates the probability of its constituents. No subject is required to compare a conjunction (e.g., "Linda is a bank teller and a feminist") to its constituents. In the direct-subtle tests, subjects compare the conjunction to its less representative constituent, but the inclusion relation between the events is not emphasized. In the direct-transparent tests, the subjects evaluate or compare the probabilities of the conjunction and its constituent in a format that highlights the relation between them.

The three experimental procedures investigate different hypotheses. The indirect procedure tests whether probability judgments conform to the conjunction rule; the direct-subtle procedure tests whether people will take advantage of an opportunity to compare the critical events; the direct-transparent procedure tests whether people will obey the conjunction rule when they are compelled to compare the critical events. This sequence of tests also describes the course of our investigation, which

Table 9.1
Tests of the Conjunction Rule in Likelihood Rankings

Subjects	Problem	Direct test				Indirect test		
		V	R(A&B)	R(B)	N	R(A&B)	R(B)	Total N
Naive	Bill	92	2.5	4.5	94	2.3	4.5	88
	Linda	89	3.3	4.4	88	3.3	4.4	86
Informed	Bill	86	2.6	4.5	56	2.4	4.2	56
	Linda	90	3.0	4.3	53	2.9	3.9	55
Sophisticated	Bill	83	2.6	4.7	32	2.5	4.6	32
	Linda	85	3.2	4.3	32	3.1	4.3	32

Note: V = percentage of violations of the conjunction rule; R(A&B) and R(B) = mean rank assigned to A&B and to B, respectively; N = number of subjects in the direct test; Total N = total number of subjects in the indirect test, who were about equally divided between the two groups.

began with the observation of violations of the conjunction rule in indirect tests and proceeded—to our increasing surprise—to the finding of stubborn failures of that rule in several direct-transparent tests.

Three groups of respondents took part in the main study. The statistically *naive* group consisted of undergraduate students at Stanford University and UBC who had no background in probability or statistics. The *informed* group consisted of first-year graduate students in psychology and in education and of medical students at Stanford who were all familiar with the basic concepts of probability after one or more courses in statistics. The *sophisticated* group consisted of doctoral students in the decision science program of the Stanford Business School who had taken several advanced courses in probability, statistics, and decision theory.

Subjects in the main study received one problem (either Bill or Linda) first in the format of a direct test. They were asked to rank all eight statements associated with that problem (including the conjunction, its separate constituents, and five filler items) according to their probability, using 1 for the most probable and 8 for the least probable. The subjects then received the remaining problem in the format of an indirect test in which the list of alternatives included either the conjunction or its separate constituents. The same five filler items were used in both the direct and the indirect versions of each problem.

Table 9.1 presents the average ranks (R) of the conjunction R(A&B) and of its less representative constituents R(B), relative to the set of five filler items. The percentage of violations of the conjunction rule in the direct test is denoted by V. The results can be summarized as follows: (a) the conjunction is ranked higher than its less likely constituents in all 12 comparisons, (b) there is no consistent difference between the ranks of the alternatives in the direct and indirect tests, (c) the overall incidence of violations of the conjunction rule in direct tests is 88%, which virtually coincides with the incidence of the corresponding pattern in judgments of representativeness, and (d) there is no effect of statistical sophistication in either indirect or direct tests.

The violation of the conjunction rule in a direct comparison of B to A&B is called the *conjunction fallacy*. Violations inferred from between-subjects comparisons are called *conjunction errors*. Perhaps the most surprising aspect of table 9.1 is the lack of any difference between indirect and direct tests. We had expected the conjunction to be judged more probable than the less likely of its constituents in an indirect test, in accord with the pattern observed in judgments of representativeness. However, we also expected that even naive respondents would notice the repetition of some attributes, alone and in conjunction with others, and that they would then apply the conjunction rule and rank the conjunction below its constituents. This expectation was violated, not only by statistically naive undergraduates but even by highly sophisticated respondents. In both direct and indirect tests, the subjects apparently ranked the outcomes by the degree to which Bill (or Linda) matched the respective stereotypes. The correlation between the mean ranks of probability and representativeness was .96 for Bill and .98 for Linda. Does the conjunction rule hold when the relation of inclusion is made highly transparent? The studies described in the next section abandon all subtlety in an effort to compel the subjects to detect and appreciate the inclusion relation between the target events.

Transparent Tests

This section describes a series of increasingly desperate manipulations designed to induce subjects to obey the conjunction rule. We first presented the description of Linda to a group of 142 undergraduates at UBC and asked them to check which of two alternatives was more probable:

Linda is a bank teller. (T)
Linda is a bank teller and is active in the feminist movement. (T&F)

The order of alternatives was inverted for one half of the subjects, but this manipulation had no effect. Overall, 85% of respondents indicated that T&F was more probable than T, in a flagrant violation of the conjunction rule.

Surprised by the finding, we searched for alternative interpretations of the subjects' responses. Perhaps the subjects found the question too trivial to be taken literally and consequently interpreted the inclusive statement T as T&not-F; that is, "Linda is a bank teller and is *not* a feminist." In such a reading, of course, the observed judgments would not violate the conjunction rule. To test this interpretation, we asked a new group of subjects ($N = 119$) to assess the probability of T and of T&F on a

9-point scale ranging from 1 (extremely unlikely) to 9 (extremely likely). Because it is sensible to rate probabilities even when one of the events includes the other, there was no reason for respondents to interpret T as T&not-F. The pattern of responses obtained with the new version was the same as before. The mean ratings of probability were 3.5 for T and 5.6 for T&F, and 82% of subjects assigned a higher rating to T&F than they did to T.

Although subjects do not spontaneously apply the conjunction rule, perhaps they can recognize its validity. We presented another group of UBC undergraduates with the description of Linda followed by the two statements, T and T&F, and asked them to indicate which of the following two arguments they found more convincing.

Argument 1. Linda is more likely to be a bank teller than she is to be a feminist bank teller, because every feminist bank teller is a bank teller, but some women bank tellers are not feminists, and Linda could be one of them.

Argument 2. Linda is more likely to be a feminist bank teller than she is likely to be a bank teller, because she resembles an active feminist more than she resembles a bank teller.

The majority of subjects (65%, $n = 58$) chose the invalid resemblance argument (argument 2) over the valid extensional argument (argument 1). Thus, a deliberate attempt to induce a reflective attitude did not eliminate the appeal of the representativeness heuristic.

We made a further effort to clarify the inclusive nature of the event T by representing it as a disjunction. (Note that the conjunction rule can also be expressed as a disjunction rule $P(\text{A or B}) \geq P(\text{B})$). The description of Linda was used again, with a 9-point rating scale for judgments of probability, but the statement T was replaced by

Linda is a bank teller whether or not she is active in the feminist movement. (T*)

This formulation emphasizes the inclusion of T&F in T. Despite the transparent relation between the statements, the mean ratings of likelihood were 5.1 for T&F and 3.8 for T* ($p < .01$, by t test). Furthermore, 57% of the subjects ($n = 75$) committed the conjunction fallacy by rating T&F higher than T*, and only 16% gave a lower rating to T&F than to T*.

The violations of the conjunction rule in direct comparisons of T&F to T* are remarkable because the extension of "Linda is a bank teller whether or not she is active in the feminist movement" clearly includes the extension of "Linda is a bank teller and is active in the feminist movement." Many subjects evidently failed to draw extensional inferences from the phrase "whether or not," which may have been taken to indicate a weak disposition. This interpretation was supported by a between-subjects comparison, in which different subjects evaluated T, T*, and T&F on a 9-point scale after evaluating the common filler statement, "Linda is a psychiatric social worker." The average ratings were 3.3 for T, 3.9 for T*, and 4.5 for T&F, with each mean significantly different from both others. The statements T and T* are of course extensionally equivalent, but they are assigned different probabilities. Because feminism fits Linda, the mere mention of this attribute makes T* more likely than T, and a definite commitment to it makes the probability of T&F even higher!

Modest success in loosening the grip of the conjunction fallacy was achieved by asking subjects to choose whether to bet on T or on T&F. The subjects were given Linda's description, with the following instruction:

If you could win $10 by betting on an event, which of the following would you choose to bet on? (Check one)

The percentage of violations of the conjunction rule in this task was "only" 56% ($n = 60$), much too high for comfort but substantially lower than the typical value for comparisons of the two events in terms of probability. We conjecture that the betting context draws attention to the conditions in which one bet pays off whereas the other does not, allowing some subjects to discover that a bet on T dominates a bet on T&F.

The respondents in the studies described in this section were statistically naive undergraduates at UBC. Does statistical education eradicate the fallacy? To answer this question, 64 graduate students of social sciences at the University of California, Berkeley and at Stanford University, all with credit for several statistics courses, were given the rating-scale version of the direct test of the conjunction rule for the Linda problem. For the first time in this series of studies, the mean rating for T&F (3.5) was lower than the rating assigned to T (3.8), and only 36% of respondents committed the fallacy. Thus, statistical sophistication produced a majority who conformed to the conjunction rule in a transparent test, although the incidence of violations was fairly high even in this group of intelligent and sophisticated respondents.

Elsewhere (Kahneman & Tversky, 1982a), we distinguished between positive and negative accounts of judgments and preferences that violate normative rules. A positive account focuses on the factors that produce a particular response; a negative account seeks to explain why the correct response was not made. The positive analysis of the Bill and Linda problems invokes the representativeness heuristic. The stubborn persistence of the conjunction fallacy in highly transparent problems, however, lends special interest to the characteristic question of a negative analysis: Why do intelligent and reasonably well-educated people fail to recognize the applicability of the conjunction rule in transparent problems? Postexperimental interviews and class discussions with many subjects shed some light on this question. Naive as well as sophisticated subjects generally noticed the nesting of the target events in the direct-transparent test, but the naive, unlike the sophisticated, did not appreciate its significance for probability assessment. On the other hand, most naive subjects did not attempt to defend their responses. As one subject said after acknowledging the validity of the conjunction rule, "I thought you only asked for my opinion."

The inverviews and the results of the direct transparent tests indicate that naive subjects do not spontaneously treat the conjunction rule as decisive. Their attitude is reminiscent of children's responses in a Piagetian experiment. The child in the pre-conservation stage is not altogether blind to arguments based on conservation of volume and typically expects quantity to be conserved (Bruner 1966). What the child fails to see is that the conservation argument is decisive and should overrule the perceptual impression that the tall container holds more water than the short one. Similarly, naive subjects generally endorse the conjunction rule in the abstract, but their application of this rule to the Linda problem is blocked by the compelling impression that T&F is more representative of her than T is. In this context, the adult subjects reason as if they had not reached the stage of formal operations. A full understanding of a principle of physics, logic, or statistics requires knowledge of the conditions under which it prevails over conflicting arguments, such as the height of the liquid in a container or the representativeness of an outcome. The recognition of the decisive nature of rules distinguishes different developmental stages in studies of conservation; it also distinguishes different levels of statistical sophistication in the present series of studies.

More Representative Conjunctions

The preceding studies revealed massive violations of the conjunction rule in the domain of person perception and social stereotypes. Does the conjunction rule fare better in other areas of judgment? Does it hold when the uncertainty regarding the target events is attributed to chance rather than to partial ignorance? Does expertise in the relevant subject matter protect against the conjunction fallacy? Do financial incentives help respondents see the light? The following studies were designed to answer these questions.

Medical Judgment

In this study we asked practicing physicians to make intuitive predictions on the basis of clinical evidence.[1] We chose to study medical judgment because physicians possess expert knowledge and because intuitive judgments often play an important role in medical decision making. Two groups of physicians took part in the study. The first group consisted of 37 internists from the greater Boston area who were taking a postgraduate course at Harvard University. The second group consisted of 66 internists with admitting privileges in the New England Medical Center. They were given problems of the following type:

A 55-year-old woman had pulmonary embolism documented angiographically 10 days after a cholecystectomy.

Please rank order the following in terms of the probability that they will be among the conditions experienced by the patient (use 1 for the most likely and 6 for the least likely). Naturally, the patient could experience more than one of these conditions.

dyspnea and hemiparesis (A&B)   syncope and tachycardia

calf pain   hemiparesis (B)

pleuritic chest pain   hemoptysis

The symptoms listed for each problem included one, denoted B, which was judged by our consulting physicians to be nonrepresentative of the patient's condition, and the conjunction of B with another highly representative symptom denoted A. In the above example of pulmonary embolism (blood clots in the lung), dyspnea (shortness of breath) is a typical symptom, whereas hemiparesis (partial paralysis) is very atypical. Each participant first received three (or two) problems in the indirect format, where the list included either B or the conjunction A&B, but not both, followed by two (or three) problems in the direct format illustrated above. The design was balanced so that each problem appeared about an equal number of times in each format. An independent group of 32 physicians from Stanford University were asked to rank each list of symptoms "by the degree to which they are representative of the clinical condition of the patient."

The design was essentially the same as in the Bill and Linda study. The results of the two experiments were also very similar. The correlation between mean ratings by probability and by representativeness exceeded .95 in all five problems. For every one of the five problems, the conjunction of an unlikely symptom with a likely one was judged more probable than the less likely constituent. The ranking of symptoms was the same in direct and indirect tests: The overall mean ranks of A&B and of B, respectively, were 2.7 and 4.6 in the direct tests and 2.8 and 4.3 in the indirect tests. The incidence of violations of the conjunction rule in direct tests ranged from 73% to 100%, with an average of 91%. Evidently, substantive expertise does not displace representativeness and does not prevent conjunction errors.

Can the results be interpreted without imputing to these experts a consistent violation of the conjunction rule? The instructions used in the present study were espe-

cially designed to eliminate the interpretation of symptom B as an exhaustive description of the relevant facts, which would imply the absence of symptom A. Participants were instructed to rank symptoms in terms of the probability "that they will
be among the conditions experienced by the patient." They were also reminded that
"the patient could experience more than one of these conditions." To test the effect
of these instructions, the following question was included at the end of the questionnaire:

In assessing the probability that the patient described has a particular symptom X, did you
assume that (check one)

X is the *only* symptom experienced by the patient?

X is *among* the symptoms experienced by the patient?

Sixty of the 62 physicians who were asked this question checked the second
answer, rejecting an interpretation of events that could have justified an apparent
violation of the conjunction rule.

An additional group of 24 physicians, mostly residents at Stanford Hospital, participated in a group discussion in which they were confronted with their conjunction
fallacies in the same questionnaire. The respondents did not defend their answers,
although some references were made to "the nature of clinical experience." Most
participants appeared surprised and dismayed to have made an elementary error of
reasoning. Because the conjunction fallacy is easy to expose, people who committed
it are left with the feeling that they should have known better.

Predicting Wimbledon

The uncertainty encountered in the previous studies regarding the prognosis of a
patient or the occupation of a person is normally attributed to incomplete knowledge
rather than to the operation of a chance process. Recent studies of inductive reasoning about daily events, conducted by Nisbett, Krantz, Jepson, and Kunda (1983),
indicated that statistical principles (e.g., the law of large numbers) are commonly
applied in domains such as sports and gambling, which include a random element.
The next two studies test the conjunction rule in predictions of the outcomes of a
sports event and of a game of chance, where the random aspect of the process is
particularly salient.

A group of 93 subjects, recruited through an advertisement in the University of
Oregon newspaper, were presented with the following problem in October 1980:

Suppose Bjorn Borg reaches the Wimbledon finals in 1981. Please rank order the following
outcomes from most to least likely.

A. Borg will win the match (1.7)

B. Borg will lose the first set (2.7)

C. Borg will lose the first set but win the match (2.2)

D. Borg will win the first set but lose the match (3.5)

The average rank of each outcome (1 = most probable, 2 = second most probable, etc.) is given in parentheses. The outcomes were chosen to represent different levels of strength for the player, Borg, with A indicating the highest strength; C, a rather lower level because it indicates a weakness in the first set; B, lower still because it only mentions this weakness; and D, lowest of all.

After winning his fifth Wimbledon title in 1980, Borg seemed extremely strong. Consequently, we hypothesized that Outcome C would be judged more probable than Outcome B, contrary to the conjunction rule, because C represents a better performance for Borg than does B. The mean rankings indicate that this hypothesis was confirmed; 72% of the respondents assigned a higher rank to C than to B, violating the conjunction rule in a direct test.

Is it possible that the subjects interpreted the target events in a nonextensional manner that could justify or explain the observed ranking? It is well-known that connectives (e.g., *and, or, if*) are often used in ordinary language in ways that depart from their logical definitions. Perhaps the respondents interpreted the conjunction (A and B) as a disjunction (A or B), an implication, (A implies B), or a conditional statement (A if B). Alternatively, the event B could be interpreted in the presence of the conjunction as B and not-A. To investigate these possibilities, we presented to another group of 56 naive subjects at Stanford University the hypothetical results of the relevant tennis match, coded as sequences of wins and losses. For example, the sequence LWWLW denotes a five-set match in which Borg lost (L) the first and the third sets but won (W) the other sets and the match. For each sequence the subjects were asked to examine the four target events of the original Borg problem and to indicate, by marking + or −, whether the given sequence was consistent or inconsistent with each of the events.

With very few exceptions, all of the subjects marked the sequences according to the standard (extensional) interpretation of the target events. A sequence was judged consistent with the conjunction "Borg will lose the first set but win the match" when both constituents were satisfied (e.g., LWWLW) but not when either one or both constituents failed. Evidently, these subjects did not interpret the conjunction as an implication, a conditional statement, or a disjunction. Furthermore, both LWWLW and LWLWL were judged consistent with the inclusive event "Borg will lose the first set," contrary to the hypothesis that the inclusive event B is understood in the context of the other events as "Borg will lose the first set and the match." The classification of sequences therefore indicated little or no ambiguity regarding the extension of the target events. In particular, all sequences that were classified as instances of B&A were also classified as instances of B, but some sequences that were classified as instances of B were judged inconsistent with B&A, in accord with the standard interpretation in which the conjunction rule should be satisfied.

Another possible interpretation of the conjunction error maintains that instead of assessing the probability $P(B/E)$ of hypothesis B (e.g., that Linda is a bank teller) in light of evidence E (Linda's personality), subjects assess the inverse probability $P(E/B)$ of the evidence given to the hypothesis in question. Because $P(E/A\&B)$ may well exceed $P(E/B)$, the subjects' responses could be justified under this interpretation. Whatever plausibility this account may have in the case of Linda, it is surely inapplicable to the present study where it makes no sense to assess the conditional probability that Borg will reach the finals given the outcome of the final match.

Risky Choice

If the conjunction fallacy cannot be justified by a reinterpretation of the target events, can it be rationalized by a nonstandard conception of probability? On this hypothesis, representativeness is treated as a legitimate nonextensional interpretation of probability rather than as a fallible heuristic. The conjunction fallacy, then, may be viewed as a misunderstanding regarding the meaning of the word *probability*. To investigate this hypothesis we tested the conjunction rule in the following decision problem, which provides an incentive to choose the most probable event, although the word *probability* is not mentioned.

Consider a regular six-sided die with four green faces and two red faces. The die will be rolled 20 times and the sequence of greens (G) and reds (R) will be recorded. You are asked to select one sequence, from a set of three, and you will win $25 if the sequence you chose appears on successive rolls of the die. Please check the sequence of greens and reds on which you prefer to bet.

1. RGRRR

2. GRGRRR

3. GRRRRR

Note that sequence 1 can be obtained from sequence 2 by deleting the first G. By the conjunction rule, therefore, sequence 1 must be more probable than sequence 2. Note also that all three sequences are rather unrepresentative of the die because they contain more Rs than Gs. However, sequence 2 appears to be an improvement over sequence 1 because it contains a higher proportion of the more likely color. A group of 50 respondents were asked to rank the events by the degree to which they are representative of the die; 88% ranked sequence 2 highest and sequence 3 lowest. Thus, sequence 2 is favored by representativeness, although it is dominated by sequence 1.

A total of 260 students at UBC and Stanford University were given the choice version of the problem. There were no significant differences between the populations, and their results were pooled. The subjects were run in groups of 30 to 50 in a classroom setting. About one half of the subjects ($N = 125$) actually played the gamble with real payoffs. The choice was hypothetical for the other subjects. The percentages of subjects who chose the dominated option of sequence 2 were 65% with real payoffs and 62% in the hypothetical format. Only 2% of the subjects in both groups chose sequence 3.

To facilitate the discovery of the relation between the two critical sequences, we presented a new group of 59 subjects with a (hypothetical) choice problem in which sequence 2 was replaced by RGRRRG. This new sequence was preferred over sequence 1, RGRRR, by 63% of the respondents, although the first five elements of the two sequences were identical. These results suggest that subjects coded each sequence in terms of the proportion of Gs and Rs and ranked the sequences by the discrepancy between the proportions in the two sequences (1/5 and 1/3) and the expected value of 2/3.

It is apparent from these results that conjunction errors are not restricted to misunderstandings of the word *probability*. Our subjects followed the representativeness heuristic even when the word was not mentioned and even in choices involving substantial payoffs. The results further show that the conjunction fallacy is not restricted to esoteric interpretations of the connective *and*, because that connective was also absent from the problem. The present test of the conjunction rule was direct, in the sense defined earlier, because the subjects were required to compare two events, one of which included the other. However, informal interviews with some of the respondents suggest that the test was subtle: The relation of inclusion between sequences 1 and 2 was apparently noted by only a few of the subjects. Evidently, people are not attuned to the detection of nesting among events, even when these relations are clearly displayed.

Suppose that the relation of dominance between sequences 1 and 2 is called to the subjects' attention. Do they immediately appreciate its force and treat it as a decisive argument for sequence 1? The original choice problem (without sequence 3) was presented to a new group of 88 subjects at Stanford University. These subjects, however, were not asked to select the sequence on which they preferred to bet but only to indicate which of the following two arguments, if any, they found correct.

Argument 1: The first sequence (RGRRR) is more probable than the second (GRGRRR) because the second sequence is the same as the first with an additional G at the beginning. Hence, every time the second sequence occurs, the first sequence must also occur. Consequently, you can win on the first and lose on the second, but you can never win on the second and lose on the first.

Argument 2: The second sequence (GRGRRR) is more probable than the first (RGRRR) because the proportions of R and G in the second sequence are closer than those of the first sequence to the expected proportions of R and G for a die with four green and two red faces.

Most of the subjects (76%) chose the valid extensional argument over an argument that formulates the intuition of representativeness. Recall that a similar argument in the case of Linda was much less effective in combating the conjunction fallacy. The success of the present manipulation can be attributed to the combination of a chance setup and a gambling task, which promotes extensional reasoning by emphasizing the conditions under which the bets will pay off.

Fallacies and Misunderstandings

We have described violations of the conjunction rule in direct tests as a fallacy. The term *fallacy* is used here as a psychological hypothesis, not as an evaluative epithet. A judgment is appropriately labeled a fallacy when most of the people who make it are disposed, after suitable explanation, to accept the following propositions: (a) They made a nontrivial error, which they would probably have repeated in similar problems, (b) the error was conceptual, not merely verbal or technical, and (c) they *should* have known the correct answer or a procedure to find it. Alternatively, the same judgment could be described as a failure of communication if the subject misunderstands the question or if the experimenter misinterprets the answer. Subjects who have erred because of a misunderstanding are likely to reject the propositions listed above and to claim (as students often do after an examination) that they knew the correct answer all along, and that their error, if any, was verbal or technical rather than conceptual.

A psychological analysis should apply interpretive charity and should avoid treating genuine misunderstandings as if they were fallacies. It should also avoid the temptation to rationalize any error of judgment by ad hoc interpretations that the respondents themselves would not endorse. The dividing line between fallacies and misunderstandings, however, is not always clear. In one of our earlier studies, for example, most respondents stated that a particular description is more likely to belong to a physical education teacher than to a teacher. Strictly speaking, the latter category includes the former, but it could be argued that *teacher* was understood in this problem in a sense that excludes physical education teacher, much as *animal* is

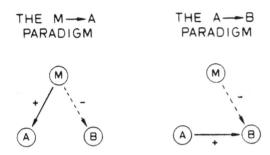

THE M—►A   THE A—►B
PARADIGM   PARADIGM

Figure 9.1
Schematic representation of two experimental paradigms used to test the conjunction rule. (Solid and broken arrows denote strong positive and negative association, respectively, between the model M, the basic target B, and the added target A.)

often used in a sense that excludes insects. Hence, it was unclear whether the apparent violation of the extension rule in this problem should be described as a fallacy or as a misunderstanding. A special effort was made in the present studies to avoid ambiguity by defining the critical event as an intersection of well-defined classes, such as bank tellers and feminists. The comments of the respondents in postexperimental discussions supported the conclusion that the observed violations of the conjunction rule in direct tests are genuine fallacies, not just misunderstandings.

Causal Conjunctions

The problems discussed in previous sections included three elements: a causal model M (Linda's personality); a basic target event B, which is unrepresentative of M (she is a bank teller); and an added event A, which is highly representative of the model M (she is a feminist). In these problems, the model M is positively associated with A and is negatively associated with B. This structure, called the M → A paradigm, is depicted on the left-hand side of figure 9.1. We found that when the sketch of Linda's personality was omitted and she was identified merely as a "31-year-old woman," almost all respondents obeyed the conjunction rule and ranked the conjunction (bank teller and active feminist) as less probable than its constituents. The conjunction error in the original problem is therefore attributable to the relation between M and A, not to the relation between A and B.

The conjunction fallacy was common in the Linda problem despite the fact that the stereotypes of bank teller and feminist are mildly incompatible. When the constituents of a conjunction are highly incompatible, the incidence of conjunction errors is greatly reduced. For example, the conjunction "Bill is bored by music and plays jazz for a hobby" was judged as less probable (and less representative) than its constituents, although "bored by music" was perceived as a probable (and representative) attribute of Bill. Quite reasonably, the incompatibility of the two attributes reduced the judged probability of their conjunction.

The effect of compatibility on the evaluation of conjunctions is not limited to near contradictions. For instance, it is more representative (as well as more probable) for a student to be in the upper half of the class in both mathematics and physics or to be in the lower half of the class in both fields than to be in the upper half in one field and in the lower half in the other. Such observations imply that the judged probability (or representativeness) of a conjunction cannot be computed as a function (e.g., product, sum, minimum, weighted average) of the scale values of its constituents. This conclusion excludes a large class of formal models that ignore the relation between the constituents of a conjunction. The viability of such models of conjunctive concepts has generated a spirited debate (Jones, 1982; Osherson & Smith, 1981, 1982; Zadeh, 1982; Lakoff, reference note 1).

The preceding discussion suggests a new formal structure, called the A → B paradigm, which is depicted on the right-hand side of figure 9.1. Conjunction errors occur in the A → B paradigm because of the direct connection between A and B, although the added event, A, is not particularly representative of the model, M. In this section of the article we investigate problems in which the added event, A, provides a plausible cause or motive for the occurrence of B. Our hypothesis is that the strength of the causal link, which has been shown in previous work to bias judgments of conditional probability (Tversky & Kahneman, 1980), will also bias judgments of the probability of conjunctions (see Beyth-Marom, reference note 2). Just as the thought of a personality and a social stereotype naturally evokes an assessment of their similarity, the thought of an effect and a possible cause evokes an assessment of causal impact (Ajzen, 1977). The natural assessment of propensity is expected to bias the evaluation of probability.

To illustrate this bias in the A → B paradigm consider the following problem, which was presented to 115 undergraduates at Stanford University and UBC:

A health survey was conducted in a representative sample of adult males in British Columbia of all ages and occupations.
    Mr. F. was included in the sample. He was selected by chance from the list of participants.
    Which of the following statements is more probable? (check one)

Mr. F. has had one or more heart attacks.

Mr. F. has had one or more heart attacks and he is over 55 years old.

This seemingly transparent problem elicited a substantial proportion (58%) of conjunction errors among statistically naive respondents. To test the hypothesis that these errors are produced by the causal (or correlational) link between advanced age and heart attacks, rather than by a weighted average of the component probabilities, we removed this link by uncoupling the target events without changing their marginal probabilities.

A health survey was conducted in a representative sample of adult males in British Columbia of all ages and occupations.
    Mr. F. and Mr. G. were both included in the sample. They were unrelated and were selected by chance from the list of participants.
    Which of the following statements is more probable? (check one)

Mr. F. has had one or more heart attacks.
Mr. F. has had one or more heart attacks and Mr. G. is over 55 years old.

Assigning the critical attributes to two independent individuals eliminates in effect the A → B connection by making the events (conditionally) independent. Accordingly, the incidence of conjunction errors dropped to 29% ($N = 90$).

The A → B paradigm can give rise to dual conjunction errors where A&B is perceived as more probable than each of its constituents, as illustrated in the next problem.

Peter is a junior in college who is training to run the mile in a regional meet. In his best race, earlier this season, Peter ran the mile in 4:06 min. Please rank the following outcomes from most to least probable.

Peter will run the mile under 4:06 min.
Peter will run the mile under 4 min.
Peter will run the second half-mile under 1:55 min.
Peter will run the second half-mile under 1:55 min. and will complete the mile under 4 min.
Peter will run the first half-mile under 2:05 min.

The critical event (a sub-1:55 minute second half *and* a sub-4 minute mile) is clearly defined as a conjunction and not as a conditional. Nevertheless, 76% of a group of undergraduate students from Stanford University ($N = 96$) ranked it above one of its constituents, and 48% of the subjects ranked it above both constituents. The natural assessment of the relation between the constituents apparently contaminated the evaluation of their conjunction. In contrast, no one violated the extension rule by ranking the second outcome (a sub-4 minute mile) above the first (a sub-4:06 minute mile). The preceding results indicate that the judged probability of a conjunction cannot be explained by an averaging model because in such a model P(A&B) lies between P(A) and P(B). An averaging process, however, may be responsible for some conjunction errors, particularly when the constituent probabilities are given in a numerical form.

Motives and Crimes

A conjunction error in a motive–action schema is illustrated by the following problem—one of several of the same general type administered to a group of 171 students at UBC:

John P. is a meek man, 42 years old, married with two children. His neighbors describe him as mild-mannered, but somewhat secretive. He owns an import–export company based in New York City, and he travels frequently to Europe and the Far East. Mr. P. was convicted once for smuggling precious stones and metals (including uranium) and received a suspended sentence of 6 months in jail and a large fine.

Mr. P. is currently under police investigation.

Please rank the following statements by the probability that they will be among the conclusions of the investigation. Remember that other possibilities exist and that more than one statement may be true. Use 1 for the most probable statement, 2 for the second, etc.

Mr. P. is a child molester.

Mr. P. is involved in espionage and the sale of secret documents.

Mr. P. is a drug addict.

Mr. P. killed one of his employees.

One half of the subjects ($n = 86$) ranked the events above. Other subjects ($n = 85$) ranked a modified list of possibilities in which the last event was replaced by

Mr. P. killed one of his employees to prevent him from talking to the police.

Although the addition of a possible motive clearly reduces the extension of the event (Mr. P. might have killed his employee for other reasons, such as revenge or self-defense), we hypothesized that the mention of a plausible but nonobvious motive would increase the perceived likelihood of the event. The data confirmed this expectation. The mean rank of the conjunction was 2.90, whereas the mean rank of the inclusive statement was 3.17 ($p < .05$, by t test). Furthermore, 50% of the respondents ranked the conjunction as more likely than the event that Mr. P. was a drug addict, but only 23% ranked the more inclusive target event as more likely than drug addiction. We have found in other problems of the same type that the mention of a cause or motive tends to increase the judged probability of an action when the suggested motive (a) offers a reasonable explanation of the target event, (b) appears fairly likely on its own, (c) is nonobvious, in the sense that it does not immediately come to mind when the outcome is mentioned.

We have observed conjunction errors in other judgments involving criminal acts in both the A → B and the M → A paradigms. For example, the hypothesis that a policeman described as violence prone was involved in the heroin trade was ranked less likely (relative to a standard comparison set) than a conjunction of allegations— that he is involved in the heroin trade and that he recently assaulted a suspect. In that example, the assault was not causally linked to the involvement in drugs, but it made the combined allegation more representative of the suspect's disposition. The implications of the psychology of judgment to the evaluation of legal evidence deserve careful study because the outcomes of many trials depend on the ability of a judge or a jury to make intuitive judgments on the basis of partial and fallible data (see Rubinstein, 1979; Saks & Kidd, 1981).

Forecasts and Scenarios

The construction and evaluation of scenarios of future events are not only a favorite pastime of reporters, analysts, and news watchers. Scenarios are often used in the context of planning, and their plausibility influences significant decisions. Scenarios for the past are also important in many contexts, including criminal law and the writing of history. It is of interest, then, to evaluate whether the forecasting or reconstruction of real-life events is subject to conjunction errors. Our analysis suggests that a scenario that includes a possible cause and an outcome could appear more probable than the outcome on its own. We tested this hypothesis in two populations: statistically naive students and professional forecasters.

A sample of 245 UBC undergraduates were requested in April 1982 to evaluate the probability of occurrence of several events in 1983. A 9-point scale was used, defined by the following categories: less than .01%, .1%, .5%, 1%, 2%, 5%, 10%, 25%, and 50% or more. Each problem was presented to different subjects in two versions: one that included only the basic outcome and another that included a more detailed scenario leading to the same outcome. For example, one half of the subjects evaluated the probability of

a massive flood somewhere in North America in 1983, in which more than 1000 people drown.

The other half of the subjects evaluated the probability of

an earthquake in California sometime in 1983, causing a flood in which more than 1000 people drown.

The estimates of the conjunction (earthquake and flood) were significantly higher than the estimates of the flood ($p < .01$, by a Mann-Whitney test). The respective geometric means were 3.1% and 2.2%. Thus, a reminder that a devastating flood could be caused by the anticipated California earthquake made the conjunction of an earthquake and a flood appear more probable than a flood. The same pattern was observed in other problems.

The subjects in the second part of the study were 115 participants in the Second International Congress on Forecasting held in Istanbul, Turkey, in July 1982. Most of the subjects were professional analysts, employed by industry, universities, or research institutes. They were professionally involved in forecasting and planning, and many had used scenarios in their work. The research design and the response scales were the same as before. One group of forecasters evaluated the probability of

a complete suspension of diplomatic relations between the USA and the Soviet Union, sometime in 1983.

The other respondents evaluated the probability of the same outcome embedded in the following scenario:

a Russian invasion of Poland, and a complete suspension of diplomatic relations between the USA and the Soviet Union, sometime in 1983.

Although *suspension* is necessarily more probable than *invasion and suspension*, a Russian invasion of Poland offered a plausible scenario leading to the breakdown of diplomatic relations between the superpowers. As expected, the estimates of probability were low for both problems but significantly higher for the conjunction *invasion and suspension* than for *suspension* ($p < .01$, by a Mann–Whitney test). The geometric means of estimates were .47% and .14%, respectively. A similar effect was observed in the comparison of the following outcomes:

a 30% drop in the consumption of oil in the US in 1983.
a dramatic increase in oil prices and a 30% drop in the consumption of oil in the US in 1983.

The geometric means of the estimated probability of the first and the second outcomes, respectively, were .22% and .36%. We speculate that the effect is smaller in this problem (although still statistically significant) because the basic target event (a large drop in oil consumption) makes the added event (a dramatic increase in oil prices) highly available, even when the latter is not mentioned.

Conjunctions involving hypothetical causes are particularly prone to error because it is more natural to assess the probability of the effect given the cause than the joint probability of the effect and the cause. We do not suggest that subjects deliberately adopt this interpretation; rather we propose that the higher conditional estimate serves as an anchor that makes the conjunction appear more probable.

Attempts to forecast events such as a major nuclear accident in the United States or an Islamic revolution in Saudi Arabia typically involve the construction and evaluation of scenarios. Similarly, a plausible story of how the victim might have been killed by someone other than the defendant may convince a jury of the existence of reasonable doubt. Scenarios can usefully serve to stimulate the imagination, to establish the feasibility of outcomes, or to set bounds on judged probabilities (Kirkwood & Pollock, 1982; Zentner, 1982). However, the use of scenarios as a prime instrument for the assessment of probabilities can be highly misleading. First, this procedure favors a conjunctive outcome produced by a sequence of likely steps (e.g., the successful execution of a plan) over an equally probable disjunctive outcome (e.g., the failure of a careful plan), which can occur in many unlikely ways (Bar-Hillel, 1973; Tversky & Kahneman, 1973). Second, the use of scenarios to assess probability is especially vulnerable to conjunction errors. A detailed scenario consisting of causally linked and representative events may appear more probable than a subset of these events (Slovic, Fischhoff, & Lichtenstein, 1976). This effect contributes to the appeal of scenarios and to the illusory insight that they often provide. The attorney who fills in guesses regarding unknown facts, such as motive or mode of operation, may strengthen a case by improving its coherence, although such additions can only lower probability. Similarly, a political analyst can improve scenarios by adding plausible causes and representative consequences. As Pooh-Bah in the *Mikado* explains, such additions provide "corroborative details intended to give artistic verisimilitude to an otherwise bald and unconvincing narrative."

Extensional Cues

The numerous conjunction errors reported in this article illustrate people's affinity for nonextensional reasoning. It is nonetheless obvious that people can understand and apply the extension rule. What cues elicit extensional considerations and what factors promote conformity to the conjunction rule? In this section we focus on a single estimation problem and report several manipulations that induce extensional reasoning and reduce the incidence of the conjunction fallacy. The participants in the studies described in this section were statistically naive students at UBC. Mean estimates are given in parentheses.

A health survey was conducted in a sample of adult males in British Columbia, of all ages and occupations.

Please give your best estimate of the following values:

What percentage of the men surveyed have had one or more heart attacks? (18%)

What percentage of the men surveyed both are over 55 years old and have had one or more heart attacks? (30%)

This version of the health-survey problem produced a substantial number of conjunction errors among statistically naive respondents: 65% of the respondents ($N = 147$) assigned a strictly higher estimate to the second question than to the first.[2] Reversing the order of the constituents did not significantly affect the results.

The observed violations of the conjunction rule in estimates of relative frequency are attributed to the A → B paradigm. We propose that the probability of the conjunction is biased toward the natural assessment of the strength of the causal or statistical link between age and heart attacks. Although the statement of the question appears unambiguous, we considered the hypothesis that the respondents who committed the fallacy had actually interpreted the second question as a request to assess a conditional probability. A new group of UBC undergraduates received the same problem, with the second question amended as follows:

Among the men surveyed who are over 55 years old, what percentage have had one or more heart attacks?

The mean estimate was 59% ($N = 55$). This value is significantly higher than the mean of the estimates of the conjunction (45%) given by those subjects who had committed the fallacy in the original problem. Subjects who violate the conjunction rule therefore do not simply substitute the conditional $P(B/A)$ for the conjunction $P(A\&B)$.

A seemingly inconsequential change in the problem helps many respondents avoid the conjunction fallacy. A new group of subjects ($N = 159$) were given the original questions but were also asked to assess the "percentage of the men surveyed who are over 55 years old" prior to assessing the conjunction. This manipulation reduced the incidence of conjunction error from 65% to 31%. It appears that many subjects were appropriately cued by the requirement to assess the relative frequency of both classes before assessing the relative frequency of their intersection.

The following formulation also facilitates extensional reasoning:

A health survey was conducted in a sample of 100 adult males in British Columbia, of all ages and occupations.

Please give your best estimate of the following values:

How many of the 100 participants have had one or more heart attacks?

How many of the 100 participants both are over 55 years old and have had one or more heart attacks?

The incidence of the conjunction fallacy was only 25% in this version ($N = 117$). Evidently, an explicit reference to the number of individual cases encourages subjects to set up a representation of the problems in which class inclusion is readily perceived and appreciated. We have replicated this effect in several other problems of the same general type. The rate of errors was further reduced to a record 11% for a group ($N = 360$) who also estimated the number of participants over 55 years of age prior to the estimation of the conjunctive category. The present findings agree with the results of Beyth-Marom (reference note 2), who observed higher estimates for conjunctions in judgments of probability than in assessments of frequency.

The results of this section show that nonextensional reasoning sometimes prevails even in simple estimates of relative frequency in which the extension of the target event and the meaning of the scale are completely unambiguous. On the other hand, we found that the replacement of percentages by frequencies and the request to assess both constituent categories markedly reduced the incidence of the conjunction fallacy. It appears that extensional considerations are readily brought to mind by seemingly inconsequential cues. A contrast worthy of note exists between the effectiveness of extensional cues in the health-survey problem and the relative inefficacy of the methods used to combat the conjunction fallacy in the Linda problem (argument, betting, "whether or not"). The force of the conjunction rule is more readily appreciated when the conjunctions are defined by the intersection of concrete classes than by a combination of properties. Although classes and properties are equivalent from a logical standpoint, they give rise to different mental representations in which different relations and rules are transparent. The formal equivalence of properties to classes is apparently not programmed into the lay mind.

Discussion

In the course of this project we studied the extension rule in a variety of domains; we tested more than 3,000 subjects on dozens of problems, and we examined numerous variations of these problems. The results reported in this article constitute a representative though not exhaustive summary of this work.

The data revealed widespread violations of the extension rule by naive and sophisticated subjects in both indirect and direct tests. These results were interpreted within the framework of judgmental heuristics. We proposed that a judgment of probability or frequency is commonly biased toward the natural assessment that the problem evokes. Thus, the request to estimate the frequency of a class elicits a search for exemplars, the task of predicting vocational choice from a personality sketch evokes a comparison of features, and a question about the co-occurrence of events induces an assessment of their causal connection. These assessments are not constrained by the extension rule. Although an arbitrary reduction in the extension of an event typically reduces its availability, representativeness, or causal coherence, there are numerous occasions in which these assessments are higher for the restricted than for the inclusive event. Natural assessments can bias probability judgment in three ways: The respondents (a) may use a natural assessment deliberately as a strategy of estimation, (b) may be primed or anchored by it, or (c) may fail to appreciate the difference between the natural and the required assessments.

Logic versus Intuition

The conjunction error demonstrates with exceptional clarity the contrast between the extensional logic that underlies most formal conceptions of probability and the natural assessments that govern many judgments and beliefs. However, probability judgments are not always dominated by nonextensional heuristics. Rudiments of probability theory have become part of the culture, and even statistically naive adults can enumerate possibilities and calculate odds in simple games of chance (Edwards, 1975). Furthermore, some real-life contexts encourage the decomposition of events. The chances of a team to reach the playoffs, for example, may be evaluated as follows: "Our team will make it if we beat team B, which we should be able to do since we have a better defense, or if team B loses to both C and D, which is unlikely since neither one has a strong offense." In this example, the target event (reaching the playoffs) is decomposed into more elementary possibilities that are evaluated in an intuitive manner.

Judgments of probability vary in the degree to which they follow a decompositional or a holistic approach and in the degree to which the assessment and the aggregation of probabilities are analytic or intuitive (see, e.g., Hammond & Brehmer, 1973). At one extreme there are questions (e.g., What are the chances of beating a given hand in poker?) that can be answered by calculating the relative frequency of "favorable" outcomes. Such an analysis possesses all the features associated with an extensional approach: It is decompositional, frequentistic, and algorithmic. At the other extreme, there are questions (e.g., What is the probability that the witness is telling the truth?) that are normally evaluated in a holistic, singular, and intuitive manner (Kahneman & Tversky, 1982b). Decomposition and calculation provide some protection against conjunction errors and other biases, but the intuitive element cannot be entirely eliminated from probability judgments outside the domain of random sampling.

A direct test of the conjunction rule pits an intuitive impression against a basic law of probability. The outcome of the conflict is determined by the nature of the evidence, the formulation of the question, the transparency of the event structure, the appeal of the heuristic, and the sophistication of the respondents. Whether people obey the conjunction rule in any particular direct test depends on the balance of these factors. For example, we found it difficult to induce naive subjects to apply the conjunction rule in the Linda problem, but minor variations in the health-survey question had a marked effect on conjunction errors. This conclusion is consistent with the results of Nisbett et al. (1983), who showed that lay people can apply certain statistical principles (e.g., the law of large numbers) to everyday problems and that the accessibility of these principles varied with the content of the problem and increased significantly with the sophistication of the respondents. We found, however, that sophisticated and naive respondents answered the Linda problem similarly in indirect tests and only parted company in the most transparent versions of the problem. These observations suggest that statistical sophistication did not alter intuitions of representativeness, although it enabled the respondents to recognize in direct tests the decisive force of the extension rule.

Judgment problems in real life do not usually present themselves in the format of a within-subjects design or of a direct test of the laws of probability. Consequently, subjects' performance in a between-subjects test may offer a more realistic view of everyday reasoning. In the indirect test it is very difficult even for a sophisticated judge to ensure that an event has no subset that would appear more probable than it does and no superset that would appear less probable. The satisfaction of the extension rule could be ensured, without direct comparisons of A&B to B, if all events in the relevant ensemble were expressed as disjoint unions of elementary possibilities. In many practical contexts, however, such analysis is not feasible. The physician, judge, political analyst, or entrepreneur typically focuses on a critical target event and is rarely prompted to discover potential violations of the extension rule.

Studies of reasoning and problem solving have shown that people often fail to understand or apply an abstract logical principle even when they can use it properly in concrete familiar contexts. Johnson-Laird and Wason (1977), for example, showed that people who err in the verification of *if then* statements in an abstract format often succeed when the problem evokes a familiar schema. The present results exhibit the opposite pattern: People generally accept the conjunction rule in its abstract form (B is more probable than A&B) but defy it in concrete examples, such as the Linda and Bill problems, where the rule conflicts with an intuitive impression.

The violations of the conjunction rule were not only prevalent in our research, they were also sizable. For example, subjects' estimates of the frequency of seven-letter words ending with *ing* were three times as high as their estimates of the frequency of seven letter words ending with $\_n\_$. A correction by a factor of three is the smallest change that would eliminate the inconsistency between the two estimates. However, the subjects surely know that there are many $\_n\_$ words that are not *ing* words (e.g., *present, content*). If they believe, for example, that only one half of the $\_n\_$ words end with *ing*, then a 6:1 adjustment would be required to make the entire system coherent. The ordinal nature of most of our experiments did not permit an estimate of the adjustment factor required for coherence. Nevertheless, the size of the effect was often considerable. In the rating-scale version of the Linda problem, for example, there was little overlap between the distributions of ratings for T&F and for T. Our problems, of course, were constructed to elicit conjunction errors, and they do not provide an unbiased estimate of the prevalence of these errors. Note, however, that the conjunction error is only a symptom of a more general phenomenon: People tend to overestimate the probabilities of representative (or available) events and/or underestimate the probabilities of less representative events. The violation of the conjunction rule demonstrates this tendency even when the "true" probabilities are unknown or unknowable. The basic phenomenon may be considerably more common than the extreme symptom by which it was illustrated.

Previous studies of the subjective probability of conjunctions (e.g., Bar-Hillel, 1973; Cohen & Hansel, 1957; Goldsmith, 1978; Wyer, 1976; Beyth-Marom, reference note 2) focused primarily on testing the multiplicative rule $P(A\&B) = P(B)P(A/B)$. This rule is strictly stronger than the conjunction rule; it also requires cardinal rather than ordinal assessments of probability. The results showed that people generally overestimate the probability of conjunctions in the sense that $P(A\&B) > P(B)P(A/B)$. Some investigators, notably Wyer and Beyth-Marom, also reported data that are inconsistent with the conjunction rule.

Conversing under Uncertainty

The representativeness heuristic generally favors outcomes that make good stories or good hypotheses. The conjunction *feminist bank teller* is a better hypothesis about Linda than *bank teller*, and the scenario of a Russian invasion of Poland followed by a diplomatic crisis makes a better story than simply *diplomatic crisis*. The notion of a good story can be illuminated by extending the Gricean concept of cooperativeness (Grice, 1975) to conversations under uncertainty. The standard analysis of conversation rules assumes that the speaker knows the truth. The maxim of quality enjoins him or her to say only the truth. The maxim of quantity enjoins the speaker to say all of it, subject to the maxim of relevance, which restricts the message to what the listener needs to know. What rules of cooperativeness apply to an uncertain speaker, that is, one who is uncertain of the truth? Such a speaker can guarantee absolute quality only for tautological statements (e.g., "Inflation will continue so long as prices rise"), which are unlikely to earn high marks as contributions to the conversation. A useful contribution must convey the speaker's relevant beliefs even if they are not certain. The rules of cooperativeness for an uncertain speaker must therefore allow for a trade-off of quality and quantity in the evaluation of messages. The expected value of a message can be defined by its information value if it is true, weighted by the probability that it is true. An uncertain speaker may wish to follow the maxim of value: Select the message that has the highest expected value.

The expected value of a message can sometimes be improved by increasing its content, although its probability is thereby reduced. The statement "Inflation will be in the range of 6% to 9% by the end of the year" may be a more valuable forecast than "Inflation will be in the range of 3% to 12%," although the latter is more likely to be confirmed. A good forecast is a compromise between a point estimate, which is sure to be wrong, and a 99.9% credible interval, which is often too broad. The selection of hypotheses in science is subject to the same trade-off: A hypothesis must risk refutation to be valuable, but its value declines if refutation is nearly certain. Good hypotheses balance informativeness against probable truth (Good, 1971). A similar compromise obtains in the structure of natural categories. The basic level category *dog* is much more informative than the more inclusive category *animal* and only slightly less informative than the narrower category *beagle*. Basic level categories have a privileged position in language and thought, presumably because they offer an optimal combination of scope and content (Rosch, 1978). Categorization under uncertainty is a case in point. A moving object dimly seen in the dark may be appropriately labeled *dog*, where the subordinate *beagle* would be rash and the superordinate *animal* far too conservative.

Consider the task of ranking possible answers to the question, "What do you think Linda is up to these days?" The maxim of value could justify a preference for T&F over T in this task, because the added attribute *feminist* considerably enriches the description of Linda's current activities, at an acceptable cost in probable truth. Thus, the analysis of conversation under uncertainty identifies a pertinent question that is legitimately answered by ranking the conjunction above its constituent. We do not believe, however, that the maxim of value provides a fully satisfactory account of the conjunction fallacy. First, it is unlikely that our respondents interpret the request to rank statements by their probability as a request to rank them by their expected (informational) value. Second, conjunction fallacies have been observed in numerical estimates and in choices of bets, to which the conversational analysis simply does not apply. Nevertheless, the preference for statements of high expected (informational) value could hinder the appreciation of the extension rule. As we suggested in the discussion of the interaction of picture size and real size, the answer to a question can be biased by the availability of an answer to a cognate question—even when the respondent is well aware of the distinction between them.

The same analysis applies to other conceptual neighbors of probability. The concept of surprise is a case in point. Although surprise is closely tied to expectations, it does not follow the laws of probability (Kahneman & Tversky, 1982b). For example, the message that a tennis champion lost the first set of a match is more surprising than the message that she lost the first set but won the match, and a sequence of four consecutive heads in a coin toss is more surprising than four heads followed by two tails. It would be patently absurd, however, to bet on the less surprising event in each of these pairs. Our discussions with subjects provided no indication that they interpreted the instruction to judge probability as an instruction to evaluate surprise. Furthermore, the surprise interpretation does not apply to the conjunction fallacy observed in judgments of frequency. We conclude that surprise and informational value do not properly explain the conjunction fallacy, although they may well contribute to the ease with which it is induced and to the difficulty of eliminating it.

Cognitive Illusions

Our studies of inductive reasoning have focused on systematic errors because they are diagnostic of the heuristics that generally govern judgment and inference. In the words of Helmholtz (1881/1903), "It is just those cases that are not in accordance with reality which are particularly instructive for discovering the laws of the processes by which normal perception originates." The focus on bias and illusion is a research strategy that exploits human error, although it neither assumes nor entails that people are perceptually or cognitively inept. Helmholtz's position implies that perception is not usefully analyzed into a normal process that produces accurate percepts and a distorting process that produces errors and illusions. In cognition, as in perception, the same mechanisms produce both valid and invalid judgments. Indeed, the evidence does not seem to support a "truth plus error" model, which assumes a coherent system of beliefs that is perturbed by various sources of distortion and error. Hence, we do not share Dennis Lindley's optimistic opinion that "inside every incoherent person there is a coherent one trying to get out," (Lindley, reference note 3) and we suspect that incoherence is more than skin deep (Tversky & Kahneman, 1981).

It is instructive to compare a structure of beliefs about a domain, (e.g., the political future of Central America) to the perception of a scene (e.g., the view of Yosemite Valley from Glacier Point). We have argued that intuitive judgments of all relevant marginal, conjunctive, and conditional probabilities are not likely to be coherent, that is, to satisfy the constraints of probability theory. Similarly, estimates of distances and angles in the scene are unlikely to satisfy the laws of geometry. For example, there may be pairs of political events for which $P(A)$ is judged greater than $P(B)$ but $P(A/B)$ is judged less than $P(B/A)$—see Tversky and Kahneman (1980). Analogously, the scene may contain a triangle ABC for which the A angle appears greater than the B angle, although the BC distance appears to be smaller than the AC distance.

The violations of the qualitative laws of geometry and probability in judgments of distance and likelihood have significant implications for the interpretation and use of these judgments. Incoherence sharply restricts the inferences that can be drawn from subjective estimates. The judged ordering of the sides of a triangle cannot be inferred from the judged ordering of its angles, and the ordering of marginal probabilities cannot be deduced from the ordering of the respective conditionals. The results of the present study show that it is even unsafe to assume that $P(B)$ is bounded by $P(A\&B)$. Furthermore, a system of judgments that does not obey the conjunction rule cannot be expected to obey more complicated principles that presuppose this rule, such as Bayesian updating, external calibration, and the maximization of expected utility. The presence of bias and incoherence does not diminish the normative force of these principles, but it reduces their usefulness as descriptions of behavior and hinders their prescriptive applications. Indeed, the elicitation of unbiased judgments and the reconciliation of incoherent assessments pose serious problems that presently have no satisfactory solution (Lindley, Tversky & Brown, 1979; Shafer & Tversky, reference note 4).

The issue of coherence has loomed larger in the study of preference and belief than in the study of perception. Judgments of distance and angle can readily be compared to objective reality and can be replaced by objective measurements when accuracy matters. In contrast, objective measurements of probability are often unavailable, and most significant choices under risk require an intuitive evaluation of probability. In the absence of an objective criterion of validity, the normative theory of judgment under uncertainty has treated the coherence of belief as the touchstone of human rationality. Coherence has also been assumed in many descriptive analyses in psychology, economics, and other social sciences. This assumption is attractive because the strong normative appeal of the laws of probability makes violations appear implausible. Our studies of the conjunction rule show that normatively inspired theories that assume coherence are descriptively inadequate, whereas psychological analyses that ignore the appeal of normative rules are, at best, incomplete. A comprehensive account of human judgment must reflect the tension between compelling logical rules and seductive nonextensional intuitions.

Notes

This research was supported by Grant NR 179-058 from the U.S. Office of Naval Research. We are grateful to friends and colleagues, too numerous to list by name, for their useful comments and suggestions on an earlier draft of this article.
1. We are grateful to Barbara J. McNeil, Harvard Medical School, Stephen G. Pauker, Tufts University School of Medicine, and Edward Baer, Stanford Medical School, for their help in the construction of the clinical problems and in the collection of the data.

2. The incidence of the conjunction fallacy was considerably lower (28%) for a group of advanced undergraduates at Stanford University ($N = 62$) who had completed one or more courses in statistics.

Reference Notes

1. Lakoff, G. *Categories and cognitive models* (Cognitive Science Report No. 2). Berkeley: University of California, 1982.

2. Beyth-Marom, R. *The subjective probability of conjunctions* (Decision Research Report No. 81–12). Eugene, Oregon: Decision Research, 1981.

3. Lindley, Dennis, Personal communication, 1980.

4. Shafer, G., & Tversky, A. *Weighing evidence: The design and comparisons of probability thought experiments*. Unpublished manuscript, Stanford University, 1983.

References

Ajzen, I. Intuitive theories of events and the effects of base-rate information on prediction. *Journal of Personality and Social Psychology*, 1977, *35*, 303–314.

Bar-Hillel, M. On the subjective probability of compound events. *Organizational Behavior and Human Performance*, 1973, *9*, 396–406.

Bruner, J. S. On the conservation of liquids. In J. S. Bruner, R. R. Olver, & P. M. Greenfield, et al. (Eds.), *Studies in cognitive growth*. New York: Wiley, 1966.

Chapman, L. J., & Chapman, J. P. Genesis of popular but erroneous psychodiagnostic observations. *Journal of Abnormal Psychology*, 1967, *73*, 193–204.

Cohen, J., & Hansel, C. M. The nature of decision in gambling: Equivalence of single and compound subjective probabilities. *Acta Psychologica*, 1957, *13*, 357–370.

Cohen, L. J. *The probable and the provable*. Oxford, England: Clarendon Press, 1977.

Dempster, A. P. Upper and lower probabilities induced by a multivalued mapping. *Annals of Mathematical Statistics*, 1967, *38*, 325–339.

Edwards, W. Comment. *Journal of the American Statistical Association*, 1975, *70*, 291–293.

Einhorn, H. J., & Hogarth, R. M. Behavioral decision theory: Processes of judgment and choice. *Annual Review of Psychology*, 1981, *32*, 53–88.

Gati, I., & Tversky, A. Representations of qualitative and quantitative dimensions. *Journal of Experimental Psychology: Human Perception and Performance*, 1982, *8*, 325–340.

Goldsmith, R. W. Assessing probabilities of compound events in a judicial context. *Scandinavian Journal of Psychology*, 1978, *19*, 103–110.

Good, I. J. The probabilistic explication of information, evidence, surprise, causality, explanation, and utility. In V. P. Godambe & D. A. Sprott (Eds.), *Foundations of statistical inference: Proceedings on the foundations of statistical inference*. Toronto, Ontario, Canada: Holt, Rinehart & Winston, 1971.

Grice, H. P. Logic and conversation. In G. Harman & D. Davidson (Eds.), *The logic of grammar*. Encino, Calif.: Dickinson, 1975.

Hammond, K. R., & Brehmer, B. Quasi-rationality and distrust: Implications for international conflict. In L. Rappoport & D. A. Summers (Eds.), *Human judgment and social interaction*. New York: Holt, Rinehart & Winston, 1973.

Helmholtz, H. von. *Popular lectures on scientific subjects* (E. Atkinson, trans.). New York: Green, 1903. (Originally published, 1881.)

Jennings, D., Amabile, T., & Ross, L. Informal covariation assessment. In D. Kahneman, P. Slovic, & A. Tversky (Eds.), *Judgment under uncertainty: Heuristics and biases*. New York: Cambridge University Press, 1982.

Johnson-Laird, P. N., & Wason, P. C. A theoretical analysis of insight into a reasoning task. In P. N. Johnson-Laird & P. C. Wason (Eds.), *Thinking*. Cambridge, England: Cambridge University Press, 1977.

Jones, G. V. Stacks not fuzzy sets: An ordinal basis for prototype theory of concepts. *Cognition*, 1982, *12*, 281–290.

Kahneman, D., Slovic, P., & Tversky, A. (Eds.) *Judgment under uncertainty: Heuristics and biases*. New York: Cambridge University Press, 1982.

Kahneman, D., & Tversky, A. Subjective probability: A judgment of representativeness. *Cognitive Psychology*, 1972, *3*, 430–454.

Kahneman, D., & Tversky, A. On the psychology of prediction. *Psychological Review*, 1973, *80*, 237–251.

Kahneman, D., & Tversky, A. On the study of statistical intuitions. *Cognition*, 1982, *11*, 123–141. (a)

Kahneman, D., & Tversky, A. Variants of uncertainty. *Cognition*, 1982, *11*, 143–157. (b)

Kirkwood, C. W., & Pollock, S. M. Multiple attribute scenarios, bounded probabilities, and threats of nuclear theft. *Futures*, 1982, *14*, 545–553.

Kyburg, H. E. Rational belief. *The Behavioral and Brain Sciences*, in press.

Lindley, D. V., Tversky, A., & Brown, R. V. On the reconciliation of probability assessments. *Journal of the Royal Statistical Society*, 1979, *142*, 146–180.

Mervis, C. B., & Rosch, E. Categorization of natural objects. *Annual Review of Psychology*, 1981, *32*, 89–115.

Nisbett, R. E., Krantz, D. H., Jepson, C., & Kunda, Z. The use of statistical heuristics in everyday inductive reasoning. *Psychological Review*, 1983, *90*, 339–363.

Nisbett, R., & Ross, L. *Human inference: Strategies and shortcomings of social judgment*. Englewood Cliffs, N.J.: Prentice-Hall, 1980.

Osherson, D. N., & Smith, E. E. On the adequacy of prototype theory as a theory of concepts. *Cognition*, 1981, *9*, 35–38.

Osherson, D. N., & Smith, E. E. Gradedness and conceptual combination. *Cognition*, 1982, *12*, 299–318.

Rosch, E. Principles of categorization. In E. Rosch & B. B. Lloyd (Eds.), *Cognition and categorization*. Hillsdale, N.J.: Erlbaum, 1978.

Rubinstein, A. False probabilistic arguments vs. faulty intuition. *Israel Law Review*, 1979, *14*, 247–254.

Saks, M. J., & Kidd, R. F. Human information processing and adjudication: Trials by heuristics. *Law & Society Review*, 1981, *15*, 123–160.

Shafer, G. *A mathematical theory of evidence*. Princeton, N.J.: Princeton University Press, 1976.

Slovic, P., Fischhoff, B., & Lichtenstein, S. Cognitive processes and societal risk taking. In J. S. Carroll & J. W. Payne (Eds.), *Cognition and social behavior*. Potomac, Md.: Erlbaum, 1976.

Smith, E. E., & Medin, D. L. *Categories and concepts*. Cambridge, Mass.: Harvard University Press, 1981.

Suppes, P. Approximate probability and expectation of gambles. *Erkenntnis*, 1975, *9*, 153–161.

Tversky, A. Features of similarity. *Psychological Review*, 1977, *84*, 327–352.

Tversky, A., & Kahneman, D. Belief in the law of small numbers. *Psychological Bulletin*, 1971, *76*, 105–110.

Tversky, A., & Kahneman, D. Availability: A heuristic for judging frequency and probability. *Cognitive Psychology*, 1973, *5*, 207–232.

Tversky, A., & Kahneman, D. Causal schemas in judgments under uncertainty. In M. Fishbein (Ed.), *Progress in social psychology*. Hillsdale, N.J.: Erlbaum, 1980.

Tversky, A., & Kahneman, D. The framing of decisions and the psychology of choice. *Science*, 1981, *211*, 453–458.

Tversky, A., & Kahneman, D. Judgments of and by representativeness. In D. Kahneman, P. Slovic, & A. Tversky (Eds.), *Judgment under uncertainty: Heuristics and biases*. New York: Cambridge University Press, 1982.

Wyer, R. S., Jr. An investigation of the relations among probability estimates. *Organizational Behavior and Human Performance*, 1976, *15*, 1–18.

Zadeh, L. A. Fuzzy sets as a basis for a theory of possibility. *Fuzzy Sets and Systems*, 1978, *1*, 3–28.

Zadeh, L. A. A note on prototype theory and fuzzy sets. *Cognition*, 1982, *12*, 291–297.

Zentner, R. D. Scenarios, past, present and future. *Long Range Planning*, 1982, *15*, 12–20.

10 The Cold Facts about the "Hot Hand" in Basketball

Amos Tversky and Thomas Gilovich

You're in a world all your own. It's hard to describe. But the basket seems to be so wide. No matter what you do, you know the ball is going to go in.
—Purvis Short, of the NBA's Golden State Warriors

This statement describes a phenomenon known to everyone who plays or watches the game of basketball, a phenomenon known as the "hot hand." The term refers to the putative tendency for success (and failure) in basketball to be self-promoting or self-sustaining. After making a couple of shots, players are thought to become relaxed, to feel confident, and to "get in a groove" such that subsequent success becomes more likely. The belief in the hot hand, then, is really one version of a wider conviction that "success breeds success" and "failure breeds failure" in many walks of life. In certain domains it surely does—particularly those in which a person's reputation can play a decisive role. However, there are other areas, such as most gambling games, in which the belief can be just as strongly held, but where the phenomenon clearly does not exist.

What about the game of basketball? Does success in this sport tend to be self-promoting? Do players occasionally get a "hot hand"?

Misconceptions of Chance Processes

One reason for questioning the widespread belief in the hot hand comes from research indicating that people's intuitive conceptions of randomness do not conform to the laws of chance. People commonly believe that the essential characteristics of a chance process are represented not only globally in a large sample, but also locally in each of its parts. For example, people expect even short sequences of heads and tails to reflect the fairness of a coin and to contain roughly 50% heads and 50% tails. Such a locally representative sequence, however, contains too many alternations and not enough long runs.

This misconception produces two systematic errors. First, it leads many people to believe that the probability of heads is greater after a long sequence of tails than after a long sequence of heads; this is the notorious gamblers' fallacy. Second, it leads people to question the randomness of sequences that contain the expected number of runs because even the occurrence of, say, four heads in a row—which is quite likely in even relatively small samples—makes the sequence appear non-representative. Random sequences just do not look random.

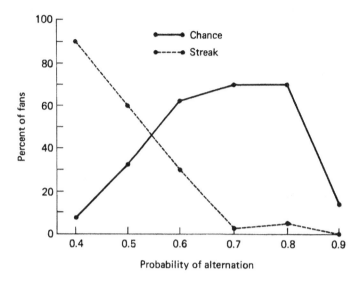

Figure 10.1
Percentage of basketball fans classifying sequences of hits and misses as examples of streak shooting or chance shooting, as a function of the probability of alternation within the sequences.

Perhaps, then, the belief in the hot hand is merely one manifestation of this fundamental misconception of the laws of chance. Maybe the streaks of consecutive hits that lead players and fans to believe in the hot hand do not exceed, in length or frequency, those expected in any random sequence.

To examine this possibility, we first asked a group of 100 knowledgeable basketball fans to classify sequences of 21 hits and misses (supposedly taken from a basketball player's performance record) as *streak shooting, chance shooting*, or *alternating shooting*. Chance shooting was defined as runs of hits and misses that are just like those generated by coin tossing. Streak shooting and alternating shooting were defined as runs of hits and misses that are longer or shorter, respectively, than those observed in coin tossing. All sequences contained 11 hits and 10 misses, but differed in the probability of alternation, $p(a)$, or the probability that the outcome of a given shot would be different from the outcome of the previous shot. In a random (i.e., independent) sequence, $p(a) = .5$; streak shooting and alternating shooting arise when $p(a)$ is less than or greater than .5, respectively. Each respondent evaluated six sequences, with $p(a)$ ranging from .4 to .9. Two (mirror image) sequences were used for each level of $p(a)$ and presented to different respondents.

The percentage of respondents who classified each sequence as "streak shooting" or "chance shooting" is presented in figure 10.1 as a function of $p(a)$. (The percentage of "alternating shooting" is the complement of these values.) As expected, people perceive streak shooting where it does not exist. The sequence of $p(a) = .5$, representing a perfectly random sequence, was classified as streak shooting by 65% of the respondents. Moreover, the perception of chance shooting was strongly biased against long runs: The sequences selected as the best examples of chance shooting were those with probabilities of alternation of .7 and .8 instead of .5.

It is clear, then, that a common misconception about the laws of chance can distort people's observations of the game of basketball: Basketball fans "detect" evidence of the hot hand in perfectly random sequences. But is this the main determinant of the widespread conviction that basketball players shoot in streaks? The answer to this question requires an analysis of shooting statistics in real basketball games.

Cold Facts from the NBA

Although the precise meaning of terms like "the hot hand" and "streak shooting" is unclear, their common use implies a shooting record that departs from coin tossing in two essential respects (see box 10.1). First, the frequency of streaks (i.e., moderate or long runs of successive hits) must exceed what is expected by a chance process with a constant hit rate. Second, the probability of a hit should be greater following a hit than following a miss, yielding a positive serial correlation between the outcomes of successive shots.

To examine whether these patterns accurately describe the performance of players in the NBA, the field-goal records of individual players were obtained for 48 home games of the Philadelphia 76ers during the 1980–1981 season. Table 10.1 presents, for the nine major players of the 76ers, the probability of a hit conditioned on 1, 2, and 3 hits and misses. The overall hit rate for each player, and the number of shots he took, are presented in column 5. A comparison of columns 4 and 6 indicates that for eight of the nine players the probability of a hit is actually higher following a miss (mean = .54) than following a hit (mean = .51), contrary to the stated beliefs of both players and fans. Column 9 presents the (serial) correlations between the outcomes of successive shots. These correlations are not significantly different than zero except for one player (Dawkins) whose correlation is negative. Comparisons of the other matching columns (7 vs. 3, and 8 vs. 2) provide further evidence against streak shooting. Additional analyses show that the probability of a hit (mean = .57) following a "cold" period (0 or 1 hits in the last 4 shots) is higher than the probability of a hit (mean = .50) following a "hot" period (3 or 4 hits in the last 4 shots). Finally, a series of Wald-Wolfowitz runs tests revealed that the observed number of

---

What People Mean by the "Hot Hand" and "Streak Shooting"

Although all that people mean by streak shooting and the hot hand can be rather complex, there is a strong consensus among those close to the game about the core features of non-stationarity and serial dependence. To document this consensus, we interviewed a sample of 100 avid basketball fans from Cornell and Stanford. A summary of their responses are given below. We asked similar questions of the players whose data we analyzed—members of the Philadelphia 76ers—and their responses matched those we report here.

Does a player have a better chance of making a shot after having just made his last two or three shots than he does after having just missed his last two or three shots?

Yes   91%
No   9%

When shooting free throws, does a player have a better chance of making his second shot after making his first shot than after missing his first shot?

Yes   68%
No   32%

Is it important to pass the ball to someone who has just made several (2, 3, or 4) shots in a row?

Yes   84%
No   16%

Consider a hypothetical player who shoots 50% from the field.

What is your estimate of his field goal percentage for those shots that he takes after having just made a shot?

Mean = 61%

What is your estimate of his field goal percentage for those shots that he takes after having just missed a shot?

Mean = 42%

---

runs in the players' shooting records does not depart from chance expectation except for one player (Dawkins) whose data, again, run counter to the streak-shooting hypothesis. Parallel analyses of data from two other teams, the New Jersey Nets and the New York Knicks, yielded similar results.

Although streak shooting entails a positive dependence between the outcomes of successive shots, it could be argued that both the runs test and the test for a positive correlation are not sufficiently powerful to detect occasional "hot" stretches embedded in longer stretches of normal performance. To obtain a more sensitive test of stationarity (suggested by David Freedman) we partitioned the entire record of

Table 10.1
Probability of Making a Shot Conditioned on the Outcome of Previous Shots for Nine Members of the Philadelphia 76ers; Hits Are Denoted H, Misses Are M

Player	$P(H/3M)$	$P(H/2M)$	$P(H/1M)$	$P(H)$	$P(H/1H)$	$P(H/2H)$	$P(H/3H)$	Serial correlation r
Clint Richardson	.50	.47	.56	.50 (248)	.49	.50	.48	−.020
Julius Erving	.52	.51	.51	.52 (884)	.53	.52	.48	.016
Lionel Hollins	.50	.49	.46	.46 (419)	.46	.46	.32	−.004
Maurice Cheeks	.77	.60	.60	.56 (339)	.55	.54	.59	−.038
Caldwell Jones	.50	.48	.47	.47 (272)	.45	.43	.27	−.016
Andrew Toney	.52	.53	.51	.46 (451)	.43	.40	.34	−.083
Bobby Jones	.61	.58	.58	.54 (433)	.53	.47	.53	−.049
Steve Mix	.70	.56	.52	.52 (351)	.51	.48	.36	−.015
Darryl Dawkins	.88	.73	.71	.62 (403)	.57	.58	.51	−.142*
Weighted mean	.56	.53	.54	.52	.51	.50	.46	−.039

Note: The number of shots taken by each player is given in parentheses in column 5.
* $p < .01$.

each player into non-overlapping series of four consecutive shots. We then counted the number of series in which the player's performance was high (3 or 4 hits), moderate (2 hits) or low (0 or 1 hits). If a player is occasionally "hot," his record must include more high-performance series than expected by chance. The numbers of high, moderate, and low series for each of the nine Philadelphia 76ers were compared to the expected values, assuming independent shots with a constant hit rate (taken from column 5 of table 10.1). For example, the expected percentages of high-, moderate-, and low-performance series for a player with a hit rate of .50 are 31.25%, 37.5%, and 31.25%, respectively. The results provided no evidence for non-stationarity or streak shooting as none of the nine chi-squares approached statistical significance. The analysis was repeated four times (starting the partition into quadruples at the first, second, third, and fourth shot of each player), but the results were the same. Combining the four analyses, the overall observed percentages of high, medium, and low series are 33.5%, 39.4%, and 27.1%, respectively, whereas the expected percentages are 34.4%, 36.8%, and 28.8%. The aggregate data yield slightly fewer high and low series than expected by independence, which is the exact opposite of the pattern implied by the presence of hot and cold streaks.

At this point, the lack of evidence for streak shooting could be attributed to the contaminating effects of shot selection and defensive strategy. Streak shooting may exist, the argument goes, but it may be masked by a hot player's tendency to take more difficult shots and to receive more attention from the defensive team. Indeed, the best shooters on the team (e.g., Andrew Toney) do not have the highest hit rate, presumably because they take more difficult shots. This argument however, does not explain why players and fans erroneously believe that the probability of a hit is greater following a hit than following a miss, nor can it account for the tendency of knowledgeable observers to classify random sequences as instances of streak shooting. Nevertheless, it is instructive to examine the performance of players when the difficulty of the shot and the defensive pressure are held constant. Free-throw records provide such data. Free throws are shot, usually in pairs, from the same location and without defensive pressure. If players shoot in streaks, their shooting percentage on the second free throws should be higher after having made their first shot than after having missed their first shot. Table 10.2 presents the probability of hitting the second free throw conditioned on the outcome of the first free throw for nine Boston Celtics players during the 1980–1981 and the 1981–1982 seasons.

These data provide no evidence that the outcome of the second shot depends on the outcome of the first. The correlation is negative for five players and positive for the remaining four, and in no case does it approach statistical significance.

Table 10.2
Probability of Hitting a Second Free Throw (H_2) Conditioned on the Outcome of the First Free Throw (H_1 or M_1) for Nine Members of the Boston Celtics

Player	$P(H_2/M_1)$	$P(H_2/H_1)$	Serial correlation r
Larry Bird	.91 (53)	.88 (285)	−.032
Cedric Maxwell	.76 (128)	.81 (302)	.061
Robert Parish	.72 (105)	.77 (213)	.056
Nate Archibald	.82 (76)	.83 (245)	.014
Chris Ford	.77 (22)	.71 (51)	−.069
Kevin McHale	.59 (49)	.73 (128)	.130
M. L. Carr	.81 (26)	.68 (57)	−.128
Rick Robey	.61 (80)	.59 (91)	−.019
Gerald Henderson	.78 (37)	.76 (101)	−.022

Note: The number of shots on which each probability is based is given in parentheses.

The Cold Facts from Controlled Experiments

To test the hot hand hypothesis, under controlled conditions, we recruited 14 members of the men's varsity team and 12 members of the women's varsity team at Cornell University to participate in a shooting experiment. For each player, we determined a distance from which his or her shooting percentage was roughly 50%, and we drew two 15-foot arcs at this distance from which the player took 100 shots, 50 from each arc. When shooting baskets, the players were required to move along the arc so that consecutive shots were never taken from exactly the same spot.

The analysis of the Cornell data parallels that of the 76ers. The overall probability of a hit following a hit was .47, and the probability of a hit following a miss was .48. The serial correlation was positive for 12 players and negative for 14 (mean $r = .02$). With the exception of one player ($r = .37$) who produced a significant positive correlation (and we might expect one significant result out of 26 just by chance), both the serial correlations and the distribution of runs indicated that the outcomes of successive shots are statistically independent.

We also asked the Cornell players to predict their hits and misses by betting on the outcome of each upcoming shot. Before every shot, each player chose whether to bet *high*, in which case he or she would win 5 cents for a hit and lose 4 cents for a miss, or to bet *low*, in which case he or she would win 2 cents for a hit and lose 1 cent for a miss. The players were advised to bet high when they felt confident in their shooting ability and to bet low when they did not. We also obtained betting data from another player who observed the shooter and decided, independently, whether to bet high or low on each trial. The players' payoffs included the amount of money won or lost on the bets made as shooters and as observers.

The players were generally unsuccessful in predicting their performance. The average correlation between the shooters' bets and their performance was .02, and the highest positive correlation was .22. The observers were also unsuccessful in predicting the shooter's performance (mean $r = .04$). However, the bets made by both shooters and observers *were* correlated with the outcome of the shooters' previous shot (mean $r = .40$ for the shooters and .42 for the observers). Evidently, both shooters and observers relied on the outcome of the previous shot in making their predictions, in accord with the hot-hand hypothesis. Because the correlation between successive shots was negligible (again, mean $r = .02$), this betting strategy was not superior to chance, although it did produce moderate agreement between the bets of the shooters and the observers (mean $r = .22$).

The Hot Hand as Cognitive Illusion

To summarize what we have found, we think it may be helpful to clarify what we have *not* found. Most importantly, our research does not indicate that basketball shooting is a purely chance process, like coin tossing. Obviously, it requires a great deal of talent and skill. What we have found is that, contrary to common belief, a player's chances of hitting are largely independent of the outcome of his or her previous shots. Naturally, every now and then, a player may make, say, nine of ten shots, and one may wish to claim—after the fact—that he was hot. Such use, however, is misleading if the length and frequency of such streaks do not exceed chance expectation.

Our research likewise does not imply that the number of points that a player scores in different games or in different periods within a game is roughly the same. The data merely indicate that the probability of making a given shot (i.e., a player's shooting *percentage*) is unaffected by the player's prior performance. However, players' willingness to shoot may well be affected by the outcomes of previous shots. As a result, a player may score more points in one period than in another not because he shoots better, but simply because he shoots more often. The absence of streak shooting does not rule out the possibility that other aspects of a player's performance, such as defense, rebounding, shots attempted, or points scored, could be subject to hot and cold periods. Furthermore, the present analysis of basketball data does not say whether baseball or tennis players, for example, go through hot and cold periods. Our research does not tell us anything general about sports, but it does suggest a generalization about people, namely that they tend to "detect" patterns even where none exist, and to overestimate the degree of clustering in sports events, as in other sequential data. We attribute the discrepancy between the observed basketball sta-tistics and the intuitions of highly interested and informed observers to a general misconception of the laws of chance that induces the expectation that random sequences will be far more balanced than they generally are, and creates the illusion that there are patterns or streaks in independent sequences.

This account explains both the formation and maintenance of the belief in the hot hand. If independent sequences are perceived as streak shooting, no amount of exposure to such sequences will convince the player, the coach, or the fan that the sequences are actually independent. In fact, the more basketball one watches, the more one encounters what appears to be streak shooting. This misconception of chance has direct consequences for the conduct of the game. Passing the ball to the hot player, who is guarded closely by the opposing team, may be a non-optimal strategy if other players who do not appear hot have a better chance of scoring. Like other cognitive illusions, the belief in the hot hand could be costly.

Additional Reading

Gilovich, T., Vallone, R., and Tversky, A. (1985). "The hot hand in basketball: On the misperception of random sequences." *Cognitive Psychology*, 17, 295–314.

Kahneman, D., Slovic, P., and Tversky, A. (1982). "Judgment under uncertainty: Heuristics and biases." New York: Cambridge University Press.

Tversky, A. and Kahneman, D. (1971). "Belief in the law of small numbers." *Psychological Bulletin*, 76, 105–110.

Tversky, A. and kahneman, D. (1974). "Judgment under uncertainty: Heuristics and biases." *Science*, 185, 1124–1131.

Wagenaar, W. A. (1972). "Generation of random sequences by human subjects: A critical survey of liter-ature." *Psychological Bulletin*, 77, 65–72.

11 The "Hot Hand": Statistical Reality or Cognitive Illusion?

Amos Tversky and Thomas Gilovich

Myths die hard. Misconceptions of chance are no exception. Despite the knowledge that coins have no memory, people believe that a sequence of heads is more likely to be followed by a tail than by another head. Many observers of basketball believe that the probability of hitting a shot is higher following a hit than following a miss, and this conviction is at the heart of the belief in the "hot hand" or "streak shooting." Our previous analyses showed that experienced observers and players share this belief although it is not supported by the facts. We found no evidence for a positive serial correlation in either pro-basketball data or a controlled shooting experiment, and the frequency of streaks of various lengths was not significantly different from that expected by chance.

Larkey, Smith, and Kadane (LSK) challenged our conclusion. Like many other believers in streak shooting, they felt that we must have missed something and proceeded to search for the elusive hot hand. To this end, LSK collected a new data set consisting of 39 National Basketball Association (NBA) games from the 1987–1988 season and analyzed the records of 18 outstanding players. LSK first computed the probability of a hit given a hit or a miss on the player's previous shot. The results, which essentially replicate our findings, provide no evidence for the hot hand: Half the players exhibited a positive serial correlation, the other half exhibited a negative serial correlation, and the overall average was essentially zero.

Statistical versus Psychological Questions

LSK dismiss these results because the analysis extends beyond "cognitively manageable chunks of shooting opportunities" on which the belief in the hot hand is based. Their argument confounds the statistical question of whether the hot hand exists with the psychological question of why people believe in the hot hand—whether it exists or not. We shall address the two questions separately, starting with the statistical facts.

LSK argue, in effect, that the hot hand is a local (short-lived) phenomenon that operates only when a player takes successive shots within a short time span. By computing, as we did, a player's serial correlation for all successive shots, regardless of temporal proximity, we may have diluted and masked any sign of the hot hand. The simplest test of this hypothesis is to compute the serial correlation for successive shots that are in close temporal proximity. LSK did not perform this test but they were kind enough to share their data. Using their records, we computed for each

Table 11.1
Shooting Statistics for the 18 Players Studied by LSK

Player	(1) r_1	(2) r	(3) AT	(4) PS	(5) $P(T/H)$	(6) $P(T/M)$
Jordan	.05	.03	40.4	28.3	.30	.31
Bird	.12	.14	39.0	25.1	.33	.23
McHale	−.02	−.07	37.3	12.0	.22	.21
Parish	−.04	.11	31.2	9.9	.15	.15
D. Johnson	−.07	−.11	34.7	11.2	.16	.23
Ainge	.14	.01	37.3	17.6	.13	.14
D. Wilkins	−.09	−.09	36.0	27.6	.40*	.26
E. Johnson	−.18	−.05	36.6	14.1	.20	.30
A-Jabbar	−.18	.02	28.8	12.8	.19	.21
Worthy	.07	.03	35.4	16.4	.24	.26
Scott	.00	.04	37.6	19.0	.19	.16
Aguirre	−.04	−.08	33.9	22.6	.35*	.14
Dantley	.06	.01	31.1	12.0	.34*	.13
Laimbeer	−.04	−.08	35.3	13.3	.22*	.11
Dumars	−.08	−.04	33.3	13.6	.27	.19
Thomas	−.04	.00	36.1	19.9	.29	.24
V. Johnson	.02	.04	23.6	13.6	.45*	.20
Rodman	−.02	−.06	26.2	10.1	.07	.14
Mean	−.02	−.01	34.1	16.6	.25	.20

Notes:
(1) Serial correlation (r_1) between the outcome of successive shots separated by at most one shot of another player on the same team.
(2) Serial correlation (r) between the outcome of all successive shots, taken from LSK.
(3) Average playing time (AT) in minutes for the 1987/1988 season.
(4) Percent of the team's shots (PS) taken by each player during the 1987/1988 season.
(5) Probability of taking the team's next shot if the player hit the previous shot, $P(T/H)$.
(6) Probability of taking the team's next shot if the player missed the previous shot, $P(T/M)$.
*Statistical significance ($p < .05$) of the difference between $P(T/H)$ and $P(T/M)$.

player the serial correlation r_1 for all pairs of successive shots that are separated by at most one shot by another player on the same team. This condition restricts the analysis to cases in which the time span between shots is generally less than a minute and a half. The results, presented in the first column of table 11.1, do not support the locality hypothesis. The serial correlations are negative for 11 players, positive for 6 players, and the overall mean is −.02. None of the correlations are statistically significant. The comparison of the local serial correlation r_1, with the regular serial correlation r, presented in the second column of table 11.1, shows that the hot-hand hypothesis does not fair better in the local analysis described above than in the original global analysis. (Restricting the local analysis to shots that are separated by at most 3, 2, or 0 shots by another teammate yielded similar results.)

On Testing the Locality Hypothesis

It is not clear why LSK did not submit the locality hypothesis to a straightforward test. Instead, they computed a rather unusual statistic that appears to produce an extreme result for one of the 18 players, Vinnie "the Microwave" Johnson, who has a reputation as a streak shooter. On the strength of this observation, LSK argue that the judgments of our respondents stand somewhat vindicated, and conclude that "it's OK to believe in the hot hand." We believe that this conclusion is unwarranted for several reasons.

As our survey shows, it is widely believed that the hot hand applies to most players. On average, a player's chances of hitting a shot were judged to be nearly 20% higher following a hit than following a miss. There is hardly a basketball game broadcast on the radio or TV without repeated references to one player or another suddenly getting hot. Because LSK's entire argument is based on the performance of a single player, we could rest our case right there. Although it is not evident in a casual reading of LSK, the case for Vinnie Johnson is based on a single observation: a run of 7 consecutive hits within a 20-shot sequence. This incident enters repeatedly into the LSK statistics, as a single run of 7, as 2 runs of 6, as 3 runs of 5, etc. If we discard this episode, the case for the Microwave goes up in smoke: All the "traumatic" statistics vanish (the 7/7 and 6/6 entries in table 6, and the 7/8 and 6/7 entries in table 7), and the remaining values are substantially reduced. It is hard to see how the widespread belief in the hot hand or the erroneous estimates of our respondents can be justified by the performance of Vinnie Johnson during a single Pistons-Lakers game. But let us ignore these doubts for the moment and examine what might be special about Vinnie's record.

LSK argue that Vinnie Johnson's shooting accomplishments set him apart from other great shooters such as Larry Bird and Michael Jordan. How did LSK reach this conclusion? They did it with a model. LSK constructed a statistical model of basketball which assumes that a player's probability of taking the next shot in the game (γ) and his probability of hitting any given shot (P) are constant throughout all games. The claim that Vinnie's performance is much less probable than that of other great players is based solely on the contention that Vinnie's seven-hit streak is unlikely under the LSK model. As we shall show, this model is inappropriate, hence its failure to accommodate Vinnie's record provides no evidence for streak shooting.

LSK estimated γ by the proportion of shots taken by each player throughout all games. For example, Vinnie took about 13% of the Pistons' shots, who took about 50% of the shots in all the games they played, so Vinnie's γ is $.13 \times .5 = .065$. Under this interpretation of γ, however, the LSK model is patently false because the probability that a player will take the next shot must be higher when he is on the court than when he is sitting on the bench. Because Vinnie plays on average about two quarters per game, his actual shooting rate must be approximately twice as high as that estimated by LSK, who did not take playing time into account. Thus, he is much more likely to hit several shots in a row within a 20-shot sequence than computed by LSK. Furthermore, the bias produced by this method is more severe for a player like Vinnie Johnson who averages less than 24 minutes per game than for a player like Michael Jordan who plays on average more than 40 minutes per game. Columns 3 and 4 of table 11.1 present the average playing time (AT) and the percentage of a team's shots (PS) taken by each player, for the 1987–1988 season. Note that Vinnie has the lowest average playing time among the 18 players investigated by LSK.

The trouble with the analysis of LSK goes beyond the inadequacy of the estimation procedure. As suggested in our original article, a player who believes in the hot hand may be more likely to take a shot following a recent hit than following a recent miss. Indeed, a great majority of the players and fans who answered our questionnaires endorsed the proposition that "it is important to pass the ball to someone who has just made several shots in a row." Columns 5 and 6 of table 11.1 present, for each player, the probability of his taking the team's next shot given that he has hit or missed his team's previous shot, denoted $P(T/H)$ and $P(T/M)$, respectively. The results show that the probability that Vinnie will take the Pistons' next shot is .45 if he has hit the Pistons' previous shot, and it is only .20 if he has missed the Pistons' previous shot. This difference, which is statistically significant, is the highest among the 18 players studied by LSK. Four other players also produced significant differences. In contrast, the probability that the NBA scoring leader, Michael Jordan, will take his team's next shot is practically the same (.30 and .31) regardless of whether he hits or misses the previous shot.

Comparing columns 5 and 6 with columns 1 and 2 indicates that Vinnie is distinguished from other players by his greater willingness to take a shot following a previous hit, not by his chances of making a shot following a previous hit. The overall correlation between the outcome of successive shots by Vinnie is .04; and the (local) correlation between successive shots that are separated by at most one shot by a teammate is only .02. The tendency to shoot more after a hit than a miss might add to the belief that Vinnie is a streak shooter, but it provides no evidence for the validity of this belief because a higher probability of shooting does not imply a higher probability of hitting.

The hot-hand and streak shooting concern the probability (P) that a player will *hit* the next shot given his previous hits and misses, not the probability (γ) that a player will *take* the next shot. LSK constructed a model in which both P and γ do not depend on previous hits and misses, observed that this model seems inappropriate for Vinnie Johnson, and concluded that he must be a streak shooter. This reasoning is fallacious because, as we have shown, the failure of the model is caused by variations in γ, not in P. It is ironic that LSK have committed the very error that they have falsely accused us of committing, namely reaching unjustified conclusions on the basis of an unrealistic model. Contrary to their claim, we did not assume that basketball is a binomial process. Such an assumption is not needed in order to compare people's intuitive estimates of $P(H/H)$ and $P(H/M)$ with the actual relative frequencies. It is regrettable that, in their eagerness to vindicate the belief in the hot hand, LSK have misrepresented our position.

A final note. We looked at the videotape and did not find Vinnie's seven-hit streak. LSK have mistakenly coded a sequence of four hits, one miss, and two hits (in the fifth Piston-Laker playoff game) as a seven-hit streak. When this error is corrected, Vinnie Johnson no longer stands out in their analysis. Recall that the entire case of LSK rests on Vinnie's alleged seven-hit streak and the assumption of a constant shooting rate (γ). A closer examination of the data shows that this assumption is false, and that Vinnie's streak did not happen. Should we believe in the hot hand?

Editor's Introductory Remarks to Chapter 11

Like chapter 10, this article by Tversky and Gilovich concerns the phenomenon known as "the hot hand" in basketball. The two articles are among Tversky's most celebrated instances of debunking the layperson's intuitions. Soon after the preceding article appeared, it triggered a critical response from Larkey, Smith, and Kadane (LSK), which the next chapter addresses. What follows here is a brief synopsis of LSK's article. (The interested reader can refer back to the original piece and to Gilovich, Vallone, and Tversky 1985, which presents further analyses in greater detail.)

In their article, "It's Okay to believe in the hot hand," Larkey, Smith, and Kadane (1989) propose "a different conception of how observers' beliefs in streak shooting are based on NBA player shooting performances." They find that the data Tversky and Gilovich analyze, in the form of isolated individual-player shooting sequences, "are in a very different form than the data usually available to observers qua believers in streak shooting." The latter data, they explain, come in the form of "individual players' shooting efforts in the very complicated context of an actual game," and, among other things, are a function of "how that player's shooting activities interact with the activities of other players." For example, LSK propose that two players both with five consecutive field goal successes will be perceived very differently if one's consecutive successes are interspersed throughout the game, whereas the other's occur in a row, without teammates scoring any points in between. For their revised analyses, LSK devise a statistical model of players' shooting behavior in the context of a game. They find that Vinnie Johnson—a player with the reputation for being "the most lethal streak shooter in basketball"—"is different than other players in the data in terms of noticeable, memorable field goal shooting accomplishments," and reckon that "Johnson's reputation as a streak shooter is apparently well deserved." "Basketball fans and coaches who once believed in the hot hand and streak shooting and who have been worried about the adequacy of their cognitive apparatus since the publication of Tversky and Gilovich's original work," conclude LSK, "can relax and once again enjoy watching the game."

Reference

Larkey, P., Smith, R., and Kadane, J. B. (1989). "It's Okay to Believe in the Hot Hand," *Chance*, pp. 22–30.

12 The Weighing of Evidence and the Determinants of Confidence

Dale Griffin and Amos Tversky

The weighing of evidence and the formation of belief are basic elements of human thought. The question of how to evaluate evidence and assess confidence has been addressed from a normative perspective by philosophers and statisticians; it has also been investigated experimentally by psychologists and decision researchers. One of the major findings that has emerged from this research is that people are often more confident in their judgments than is warranted by the facts. Overconfidence is not limited to lay judgment or laboratory experiments. The well-publicized observation that more than two-thirds of small businesses fail within 4 years (Dun & Bradstreet, 1967) suggests that many entrepreneurs overestimate their probability of success (Cooper, Woo, & Dunkelberg, 1988). With some notable exceptions, such as weather forecasters (Murphy & Winkler, 1977) who receive immediate frequentistic feedback and produce realistic forecasts of precipitation, overconfidence has been observed in judgments of physicians (Lusted, 1977), clinical psychologists (Oskamp, 1965), lawyers (Wagenaar & Keren, 1986), negotiators (Neale & Bazerman, 1990), engineers (Kidd, 1970), and security analysts (Staël von Holstein, 1972). As one critic described expert prediction, "often wrong but rarely in doubt."

Overconfidence is common but not universal. Studies of calibration have found that with very easy items, overconfidence is eliminated, and underconfidence is often observed (Lichtenstein, Fischhoff, & Phillips, 1982). Furthermore, studies of sequential updating have shown that posterior probability estimates commonly exhibit conservatism or underconfidence (Edwards, 1968). In the present paper, we investigate the weighting of evidence and propose an account that explains the pattern of overconfidence and underconfidence observed in the literature.[1]

The Determinants of Confidence

The assessment of confidence or degree of belief in a given hypothesis typically requires the integration of different kinds of evidence. In many problems, it is possible to distinguish between the strength, or extremeness, of the evidence and its weight, or predictive validity. When we evaluate a letter of recommendation for a graduate student written by a former teacher, we may wish to consider two separate aspects of the evidence: (i) how positive or warm is the letter? and (ii) how credible or knowledgeable is the writer? The first question refers to the strength or extremeness of the evidence, whereas the second question refers to its weight or credence. Similarly, suppose we wish to evaluate the evidence for the hypothesis that a coin is biased in favor of heads rather than in favor of tails. In this case, the proportion of heads in a sample reflects the strength of evidence for the hypothesis in question, and the size of the sample reflects the credence of these data. The distinction between the strength of evidence and its weight is closely related to the distinction between the size of an effect (e.g., a difference between two means) and its reliability (e.g., the standard error of the difference). Although it is not always possible to decompose the impact of evidence into the separate contributions of strength and weight, there are many contexts in which they can be varied independently. A strong or a weak recommendation may come from a reliable or unreliable source, and the same proportion of heads can be observed in a small or large sample.

Statistical theory and the calculus of chance prescribe rules for combining strength and weight. For example, probability theory specifies how sample proportion and sample size combine to determine posterior probability. The extensive experimental literature on judgment under uncertainty indicates that people do not combine strength and weight in accord with the rules of probability and statistics. Rather, intuitive judgments are overly influenced by the degree to which the available evidence is representative of the hypothesis in question (Dawes, 1988; Kahneman, Slovic, & Tversky, 1982; Nisbett & Ross, 1980). If people were to rely on representativeness alone, their judgments (e.g., that a person being interviewed will be a successful manager) would depend only on the strength of their impression (e.g., the degree to which the individual in question "looks like" a successful manager) with no regard for other factors that control predictive validity. In many situations, however, it appears that people do not neglect these factors altogether. Instead, we propose, people focus on the strength of the evidence—as they perceive it—and then make some adjustment in response to its weight.

In evaluating a letter of recommendation, we suggest, people first attend to the warmth of the recommendation and then make allowance for the writer's limited knowledge. Similarly, when judging whether a coin is biased in favor of heads or in favor of tails, people focus on the proportion of heads in the sample and then adjust their judgment according to the number of tosses. Because such an adjustment is generally insufficient (Slovic & Lichtenstein, 1971; Tversky & Kahneman, 1974), the strength of the evidence tends to dominate its weight in comparison to an appropriate statistical model. Furthermore, the tendency to focus on the strength of the evidence leads people to underutilize other variables that control predictive validity, such as base rate and discriminability. This treatment combines judgment by representativeness, which is based entirely on the strength of an impression, with an anchoring and adjustment process that takes the weight of the evidence into account, albeit insufficiently. The role of anchoring in impression formation has been addressed by Quattrone (1982).

This hypothesis implies a distinctive pattern of overconfidence and underconfidence. If people are highly sensitive to variations in the extremeness of evidence and not sufficiently sensitive to variations in its credence or predictive validity, then judgments will be overconfident when strength is high and weight is low, and they will be underconfident when weight is high and strength is low. As is shown below, this hypothesis serves to organize and summarize much experimental evidence on judgment under uncertainty.

Consider the prediction of success in graduate school on the basis of a letter of recommendation. If people focus primarily on the warmth of the recommendation with insufficient regard for the credibility of the writer, or the correlation between the predictor and the criterion, they will be overconfident when they encounter a glowing letter based on casual contact, and they will be underconfident when they encounter a moderately positive letter from a highly knowledgeable source. Similarly, if people's judgments regarding the bias of a coin are determined primarily by the proportion of heads and tails in the sample with insufficient regard for sample size, then they will be overconfident when they observe an extreme proportion in a small sample, and underconfident when they observe a moderate proportion in a large sample.

In this article, we test the hypothesis that overconfidence occurs when strength is high and weight is low, and underconfidence occurs when weight is high and strength is low. The first three experiments are concerned with the evaluation of statistical hypotheses, where strength of evidence is defined by sample proportion. In the second part of the paper, we extend this hypothesis to more complex evidential problems and investigate its implications for judgments of confidence.

Evaluating Statistical Hypotheses

Study 1: Sample Size
We first investigate the relative impact of sample proportion (strength) and sample size (weight) in an experimental task involving the assessment of posterior probability. We presented 35 students with the following instructions:

Imagine that you are spinning a coin, and recording how often the coin lands heads and how often the coin lands tails. Unlike tossing, which (on average) yields an equal number of heads and tails, spinning a coin leads to a bias favoring one side or the other because of slight imperfections on the rim of the coin (and an uneven distribution of mass). Now imagine that you know that this bias is 3/5. It tends to land on one side 3 out of 5 times. But you do not know if this bias is in favor of heads or in favor of tails.

Subjects were then given various samples of evidence differing in sample size (from 3 to 33) and in the number of heads (from 2 to 19). All samples contained a majority of

Table 12.1
Stimuli and Responses for Study 1

Number of heads (h)	Number of tails (t)	Sample size (n)	Posterior probability $P(H \mid D)$	Median confidence (in %)
2	1	3	.60	63.0
3	0	3	.77	85.0
3	2	5	.60	60.0
4	1	5	.77	80.0
5	0	5	.88	92.5
5	4	9	.60	55.0
6	3	9	.77	66.9
7	2	9	.88	77.0
9	8	17	.60	54.5
10	7	17	.77	59.5
11	6	17	.88	64.5
19	14	33	.88	60.0

heads, and subjects were asked to estimate the probability (from .5 to 1) that the bias favored heads (H) rather than tails (T). Subjects received all 12 combinations of sample proportion and sample size shown in table 12.1. They were offered a prize of \$20 for the person whose judgments most closely matched the correct values.

Table 12.1 also presents, for each sample of data (D), the posterior probability for hypothesis H (a 3:2 bias in favor of heads) computed according to Bayes' Rule. Assuming equal prior probabilities, Bayes' Rule yields

$$\log\left(\frac{P(H \mid D)}{P(T \mid D)}\right) = n\left(\frac{h - t}{n}\right) \log\left(\frac{.6}{.4}\right),$$

where h and t are the number of heads and tails, respectively, and $n = h + t$ denotes sample size. The first term on the right-hand side, n, represents the weight of evidence. The second term, the difference between the proportion of heads and tails in the sample, represents the strength of the evidence for H against T. The third term, which is held constant in this study, is the discriminability of the two hypotheses, corresponding to d' in signal detection theory. Plotting equal-support lines for strength and weight in logarithmic coordinates yields a family of parallel straight lines with a slope of -1, as illustrated by the dotted lines in figure 12.1. (To facilitate interpretation, the strength dimension is defined as h/n which is linearly related to $(h - t)/n$.) Each line connects all data sets that provide the same support for hypothesis H. For example, a sample of size 9 with 6 heads and 3 tails, and a sample of size 17 with 10 heads and 7 tails, yields the same posterior probability (.77) for H

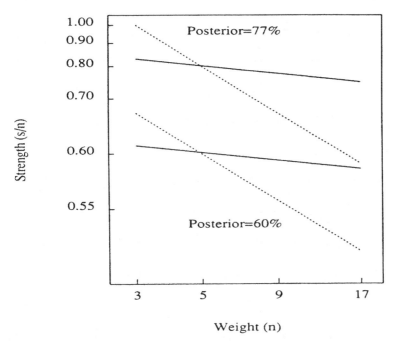

Figure 12.1
Equal support lines for strength and sample size.

over T. Thus the point (9, 6/9) and the point (17, 10/17) both lie on the upper line. Similarly, the lower line connects the data sets that yield a posterior probability of .60 in favor of H (see table 12.1).

To compare the observed judgments with Bayes' Rule, we first transformed each probability judgment into log odds and then, for each subject as well as the median data, regressed the logarithm of these values against the logarithms of strength, $(h - t)/n$, and of weight, n, separately for each subject. The regressions fit the data quite well: multiple R was .95 for the median data and .82 for the median subject. According to Bayes' Rule, the regression weights for strength and weight in this metric are equal (see figure 12.1). In contrast, the regression coefficient for strength was larger than the regression coefficient for weight for 30 out of 35 subjects ($p < .001$ by sign test). Across subjects, the median ratio of these coefficients was 2.2 to 1 in favor of strength.[2] For the median data, the observed regression weight for strength (.81) was almost 3 times larger than that for weight (.31).

The equal-support lines obtained from the regression analysis are plotted in figure 12.1 as solid lines. The comparison of the two sets of lines highly reveal

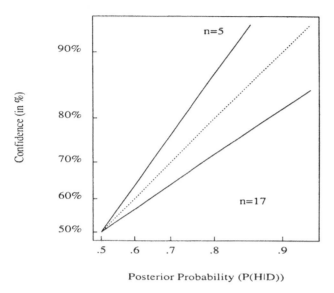

Figure 12.2
Sample size and confidence.

two noteworthy observations. First, the intuitive lines are much shallower than the Bayesian lines, indicating that the strength of evidence dominates its weight. Second, for a given level of support (e.g., 60% or 77%), the Bayesian and the intuitive lines cross, indicating overconfidence where strength is high and weight is low, and underconfidence where strength is low and weight is high. As is seen later, the crossing point is determined primarily by the discriminability of the competing hypotheses (d').

Figure 12.2 plots the median confidence for a given sample of evidence as a function of the (Bayesian) posterior probability for two separate sample sizes. The best-fitting lines were calculated using the log odds metric. If the subjects were Bayesian, the solid lines would coincide with the dotted line. Instead, intuitive judgments based on the small sample ($n = 5$) were overconfident, whereas the judgments based on the larger sample ($n = 17$) were underconfident.

The results described in table 12.1 are in general agreement with previous results that document the non-normative nature of intuitive judgment (for reviews see, e.g., Kahneman, Slovic, & Tversky, 1982; von Winterfeldt & Edwards, 1986). Moreover, they help reconcile apparently inconsistent findings. Edwards and his colleagues (e.g., Edwards, 1968), who used a sequential updating paradigm, argued that people are conservative in the sense that they do not extract enough information from sample data. On the other hand, Tversky & Kahneman (1971), who investigated the role of sample size in researchers' confidence in the replicability of their results, concluded that people (even those trained in statistics) make radical inferences on the basis of small samples. Figures 12.1 and 12.2 suggest how the dominance of sample proportion over sample size could produce both findings. In some updating experiments conducted by Edwards, subjects were exposed to large samples of data typically of moderate strength. This is the context in which we expect underconfidence or conservatism. The situations studied by Tversky & Kahneman, on the other hand, involve moderately strong effects based on fairly small samples. This is the context in which overconfidence is likely to prevail. Both conservatism and overconfidence, therefore, can be generated by a common bias in the weighting of evidence, namely the dominance of strength over weight.

As was noted earlier, the tendency to focus on the strength of the evidence leads people to neglect or underweight other variables, such as the prior probability of the hypothesis in question or the discriminability of the competing hypotheses. These effects are demonstrated in the following two studies. All three studies reported in this section employ a within-subject design, in which both the strength of the evidence and the mitigating variable (e.g., sample size) are varied within subjects. This procedure may underestimate the dominance of strength because people tend to respond to whatever variable is manipulated within a study whether or not it is normative to do so (Fischhoff & Bar-Hillel, 1984). Indeed, the neglect of sample size and base-rate information has been most pronounced in between-subject comparisons (Kahneman & Tversky, 1972).

Study 2: Base Rate
Considerable research has demonstrated that people tend to neglect background data (e.g., base rates) in the presence of specific evidence (Kahneman, Slovic, & Tversky, 1982; Bar-Hillel, 1983). This neglect can lead either to underconfidence or overconfidence, as is shown below. We asked 40 students to imagine that they had three different foreign coins, each with a known bias of $3:2$. As in study 1, subjects did not know if the bias of each coin was in favor of heads (H) or in favor of tails (T). The subjects' prior probabilities of the two hypotheses (H and T) were varied. For one-half of the subjects, the probability of H was .50 for one type of coin, .67 for a second type of coin, and .90 for a third type of coin. For the other half of the subjects, the prior probabilities of H were .50, .33, and .10. Subjects were presented with samples of size 10, which included from 5 to 9 heads. They were then asked to give their confidence (in %) that the coin under consideration was biased in favor of heads. Again, a $20 prize was offered for the person whose judgments most closely

Table 12.2
Stimuli and Responses for Study 2

Number of heads (out of 10)	Prior probability (Base rate)	Posterior probability $P(H \mid D)$	Median confidence (in %)
5	9:1	.90	60.0
6	9:1	.95	70.0
7	9:1	.98	85.0
8	9:1	.99	92.5
9	9:1	.996	98.5
5	2:1	.67	55.0
6	2:1	.82	65.0
7	2:1	.91	71.0
8	2:1	.96	82.5
9	2:1	.98	90.0
5	1:1	.50	50.0
6	1:1	.69	60.0
7	1:1	.84	70.0
8	1:1	.92	80.0
9	1:1	.96	90.0
5	1:2	.33	33.0
6	1:2	.53	50.0
7	1:2	.72	57.0
8	1:2	.85	77.0
9	1:2	.93	90.0
5	1:9	.10	22.5
6	1:9	.20	45.0
7	1:9	.36	60.0
8	1:9	.55	80.0
9	1:9	.74	85.0

matched the correct values. Table 12.2 summarizes the sample data, the posterior probability for each sample, and subjects' median confidence judgments. It is clear that our subjects overweighted strength of evidence and under-weighted the prior probability.

Figure 12.3 plots median judgments of confidence as a function of (Bayesian) posterior probability for high (.90) and low (.10) prior probabilities of H. The figure also displays the best-fitting lines for each condition. It is evident from the figure that subjects were overconfident in the low base rate condition and underconfident in the high base rate condition.

These results are consistent with Grether's (1980, 1990) studies on the role of the representativeness heuristic in judgments of posterior probability. Unlike the present study, where both prior probabilities and data were presented in numerical form,

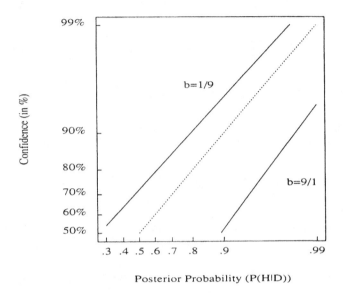

Figure 12.3
Base rate and confidence.

Grether's procedure involved random sampling of numbered balls from a bingo cage. He found that subjects overweighted the likelihood ratio relative to prior probability, as implied by representativeness, and that monetary incentives reduced but did not eliminate base rate neglect. Grether's results, like those found by Camerer (1990) in his extensive study of market trading, contradict the claim of Gigerenzer, Hell, and Blank (1988) that explicit random sampling eliminates base rate neglect. Evidence that explicit random sampling alone does not reduce base rate neglect is presented in Griffin (1991).

Our analysis implies that people are prone to overconfidence when the base rate is low and to underconfidence when the base rate is high. Dunning, Griffin, Milojkovic, and Ross (1990) observed this pattern in a study of social prediction. In their study, each subject interviewed a target person before making predictions about the target's preferences and behavior (e.g., "If this person were offered a free subscription, which magazine would he choose: *Playboy* or *New York Review of Books*?"). The authors presented each subject with the empirically derived estimates of the base rate frequency of the responses in question (e.g., that 68% of prior respondents preferred *Playboy*). To investigate the effect of empirical base rates, Dunning et al. analyzed separately the predictions that agreed with the base rate (i.e., "high" base rate predictions) and the predictions that went against the base rate (i.e., "low" base rate predictions). Overconfidence was much more pronounced when base rates were low (confidence = 72%, accuracy = 49%) than when base rates were high (confidence = 79%, accuracy = 75%). Moreover, for items with base rates that exceeded 75%, subjects' predictions were actually underconfident. This is exactly the pattern implied by the hypothesis that subjects evaluate the probability that a given person would prefer *Playboy* over the *New York Review of Books* on the basis of their impression of that person with little or no regard for the empirical base rate, that is, the relative popularity of the two magazines in the target population.

Study 3: Discriminability

When we consider the question of which of two hypotheses is true, confidence should depend on the degree to which the data fit one hypothesis better than the other. However, people seem to focus on the strength of evidence for a given hypothesis and neglect how well the same evidence fits an alternate hypothesis. The Barnum effect is a case in point. It is easy to construct a personality sketch that will impress many people as a fairly accurate description of their own characteristics because they evaluate the description by the degree to which it fits their personality with little or no concern for whether it fits others just as well (Forer, 1949). To explore this effect in a chance setup, we presented 50 students with evidence about two types of foreign coins. Within each type of coin, the strength of evidence (sample proportion) varied from 7/12 heads to 10/12 heads. The two types of coins differed in their characteristic biases. Subjects were instructed:

Imagine that you are spinning a foreign coin called a *quinta*. Suppose that half of the quintas (the "X" type) have a .6 bias towards heads (that is, heads comes up on 60% of the spins for X-quintas) and half of the quintas (the "Y" type) have a .75 bias toward tails (that is, tails comes up on 75% of the spins for Y-quintas). Your job is to determine if this is an X-quinta or a Y-quinta.

They then received the samples of evidence displayed in table 12.3. After they gave their confidence that each sample came from an X-quinta or a Y-quinta, subjects were asked to make the same judgments for A-libnars (which have a .6 bias toward heads) and B-libnars (which have a .5 chance of heads). The order of presentation of coins was counterbalanced.

Table 12.3 summarizes the sample data, the posterior probability for each sample, and subjects' median confidence judgments. The comparison of the confidence judgments to the Bayesian posterior probabilities indicates that our subjects focused primarily on the degree to which the data fit the favored hypothesis with insufficient regard for how well they fit the alternate hypothesis (Fischhoff & Beyth-Marom,

Table 12.3
Stimuli and Responses for Study 3

Number of heads (out of 12)	Separation of hypotheses (d')	Posterior probability $P(H \mid D)$	Median confidence (in %)
7	.6 vs .5	.54	55.0
8	.6 vs .5	.64	66.0
9	.6 vs .5	.72	75.0
10	.6 vs .5	.80	85.0
7	.6 vs .25	.95	65.0
8	.6 vs .25	.99	70.0
9	.6 vs .25	.998	80.0
10	.6 vs .25	.999	90.0

1983). Figure 12.4 plots subjects' median confidence judgments against the Bayesian posterior probability both for low discriminability and high discriminability comparisons. When the discriminability between the hypotheses was low (when the coin's bias was either .6 or .5) subjects were slightly overconfident, when the discriminability between the hypotheses was high (when the bias was either .6 or .25) subjects were grossly underconfident.

In the early experimental literature on judgments of posterior probability, most studies (e.g., Peterson, Schneider, & Miller, 1965) examined symmetric hypotheses that were highly discriminable (e.g., 3:2 versus 2:3) and found consistent underconfidence. In accord with our hypothesis, however, studies which included pairs of hypotheses of low discriminability found overconfidence. For example, Peterson and Miller (1965) found overconfidence in posterior probability judgments when the respective ratios were 3:2 and 3:4, and Phillips and Edwards (1966) found overconfidence when the ratios were 11:9 and 9:11.

Confidence in Knowledge

The preceding section shows that people are more sensitive to the strength of evidence than to its weight. Consequently, people are overconfident when strength is high and weight is low, and underconfident when strength is low and weight is high. This conclusion, we propose, applies not only to judgments about chance processes such as coin spinning, but also to judgments about uncertain events such as who will win an upcoming election, or whether a given book will make the best-seller list. When people assess the probability of such events they evaluate, we suggest, their

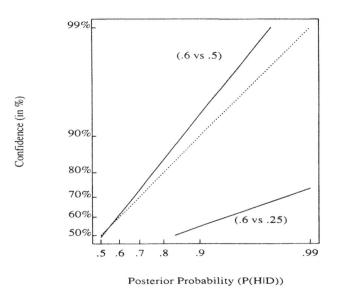

Figure 12.4
Discriminability and confidence.

impression of the candidate or the book. These impressions may be based on a casual observation or on extensive knowledge of the preferences of voters and readers. In an analogy to a chance setup, the extremeness of an impression may be compared to sample proportion, and the credence of an impression may correspond to the size of the sample, or to the discriminability of the competing hypotheses. If people focus on the strength of the impression with insufficient appreciation of its weight, then the pattern of overconfidence and underconfidence observed in the evaluation of chance processes should also be present in evaluations of non-statistical evidence.

In this section, we extend this hypothesis to complex evidential problems where strength and weight cannot be readily defined. We first compare the prediction of self and of others. Next, we show how the present account gives rise to the "difficulty effect." Finally, we explore the determinants of confidence in general-knowledge questions, and relate the confidence-frequency discrepancy to the illusion of validity.

Study 4: Self versus Other

In this study, we ask people to predict their own behavior, about which they presumably know a great deal, and the behavior of others, about which they know less. If people base their confidence primarily on the strength of their impression with insufficient regard for its weight, we expect more overconfidence in the prediction of others than in the prediction of self.

Fourteen pairs of same-sex students, who did not know each other, were asked to predict each other's behavior in a task involving risk. They were first given 5 min to interview each other, and then they sat at individual computer terminals where they predicted their own and their partner's behavior in a Prisoner's Dilemma–type game called "The Corporate Jungle." On each trial, participants had the option of "merging" their company with their partner's company (i.e., cooperating), or "taking over" their partner's company (i.e., competing). If one partner tried to merge and the other tried to take over, the cooperative merger took a steep loss and the corporate raider made a substantial gain. However, if both partners tried a takeover on the same trial, they both suffered a loss. There were 20 payoff matrices, some designed to encourage cooperation and some designed to encourage competition.

Subjects were asked to predict their own behavior for 10 of the payoff matrices and the behavior of the person they had interviewed for the other 10. The order of the two tasks was counterbalanced, and each payoff matrix appeared an equal number of times in each task. In addition to predicting cooperation or competition for each matrix, subjects indicated their confidence in each prediction (on a scale from 50% to 100%). Shortly after the completion of the prediction task, subjects played 20 trials against their opponents, without feedback, and received payment according to the outcomes of the 20 trials.

The analysis is based on 25 subjects who completed the entire task. Overall, subjects were almost equally confident in their self predictions ($M = 84\%$) and in their predictions of others ($M = 83\%$), but they were considerably more accurate in predicting their own behavior ($M = 81\%$) than in predicting the behavior of others ($M = 68\%$). Thus, people exhibited considerable overconfidence in predictions of others, but were relatively well-calibrated in predicting themselves (see figure 12.5).

In some circumstances, where the strength of evidence is not extreme, the prediction of one's own behavior may be underconfident. In the case of a job choice, for example, underconfidence may arise if a person has good reasons for taking job A and good reasons for taking job B, but fails to appreciate that even a small advantage for job A over B would generally lead to the choice of A. If confidence in the choice of A over B reflects the balance of arguments for the two positions (Koriat, Lichtenstein, & Fischhoff, 1980), then a balance of 2 to 1 would produce confidence of about 2/3, although the probability of choosing A over B is likely to be higher. Over the past few years, we have discreetly approached colleagues faced with a choice between job offers, and asked them to estimate the probability that they will

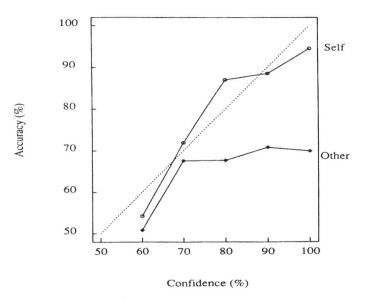

Figure 12.5
Predicting self and other.

choose one job over another. The average confidence in the predicted choice was a modest 66%, but only 1 of the 24 respondents chose the opinion to which he or she initially assigned a lower probability, yielding an overall accuracy rate of 96%. It is noteworthy that there are situations in which people exhibit overconfidence even in predicting their own behavior (Vallone, Griffin, Lin, & Ross, 1990). The key variable, therefore, is not the target of prediction (self versus other) but rather the relation between the strength and the weight of the available evidence.

The tendency to be confident about the prediction of the behavior of others, but not of one's own behavior, has intriguing implications for the analysis of decision making. Decision analysts commonly distinguish between decision variables that are controlled by the decision maker and state variables that are not under his or her control. The analysis proceeds by determining the values of decision variables (i.e., decide what you want) and assigning probabilities to state variables (e.g., the behavior of others). Some decision analysts have noted that their clients often wish to follow an opposite course: determine or predict (with certainty) the behavior of others and assign probabilities to their own choices. After all, the behavior of others should be predictable from their traits, needs, and interests, whereas our own behavior is highly flexible and contingent on changing circumstances (Jones & Nisbett, 1972).

The Effect of Difficulty

The preceding analysis suggests that people assess their confidence in one of two competing hypotheses on the basis of their balance of arguments for and against this hypothesis, with insufficient regard for the quality of the data. This mode of judgment gives rise to overconfidence when people form a strong impression on the basis of limited knowledge and to underconfidence when people form a moderate impression on the basis of extensive data.

The application of this analysis to general knowledge questions is complicated by the fact that strength and weight cannot be experimentally controlled as in studies 1–3. However, in an analogy to a chance setup, let us suppose that the balance of arguments for a given knowledge problem can be represented by the proportion of red and white balls in a sample. The difficulty of the problem can be represented by the discriminability of the two hypotheses, that is, the difference between the probability of obtaining a red ball under each of the two competing hypotheses. Naturally, the greater the difference, the easier the task, that is, the higher the posterior probability of the more likely hypothesis on the basis of any given sample. Suppose confidence is given by the balance of arguments, that is, the proportion of red balls in the sample. What is the pattern of results predicted by this model?

Figure 12.6 displays the predicted results (for a sample of size 10) for three pairs of hypotheses that define three levels of task difficulty: an "easy" task where the probability of getting red balls under the competing hypotheses are respectively .50 and .40; a "difficult" task, where the probabilities are .50 and .45; and an "impossible" task, where the probability of drawing a red ball is .5 under both hypotheses. We have chosen nonsymmetric hypotheses for our example to allow for an initial bias that is often observed in calibration data.

It is instructive to compare the predictions of this model to the results of Lichtenstein & Fischhoff (1977) who investigated the effect of task difficulty (see figure 12.7). Their "easy" items (accuracy = 85%) produced underconfidence through much of the confidence range, their "difficult" items (accuracy = 61%) produced overconfidence through most of the confidence range, and their "impossible" task (discriminating European from American handwriting, accuracy = 51%) showed dramatic overconfidence throughout the entire range.

A comparison of figures 12.6 and 12.7 reveals that our simple chance model reproduces the pattern of results observed by Lichtenstein & Fischhoff (1977): slight underconfidence for very easy items, consistent overconfidence for difficult items, and dramatic overconfidence for "impossible" items. This pattern follows from the assumption that judged confidence is controlled by the balance of arguments for the competing hypotheses. The present account, therefore, can explain the observed relation between task difficulty and overconfidence (see Ferrell & McGoey, 1980).

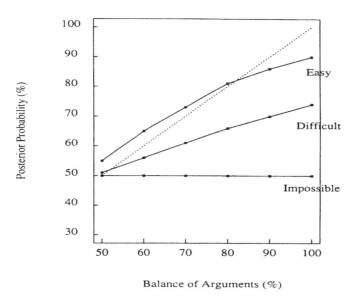

Figure 12.6
Predicted calibration for item difficulty.

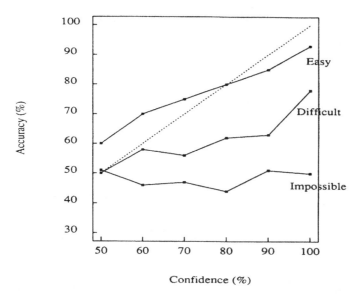

Figure 12.7
Calibration plots for item difficulty.

The difficulty effect is one of the most consistent findings in the calibration literature (Lichtenstein & Fischhoff, 1977; Lichtenstein, Fischhoff, & Phillips, 1982; Yates, 1990). It is observed not only in general knowledge questions, but also in clinical diagnoses (Oskamp, 1962), predictions of future events (contrast Fischhoff & MacGregor, 1982, versus Wright & Wisudha, 1982), and letter identification (Keren, 1988). Moreover, the difficulty effect may contribute to other findings that have been interpreted in different ways. For example, Keren (1987) showed that world-class bridge players were well-calibrated, whereas amateur players were overconfident. Keren interpreted this finding as an optimism bias on the part of the amateur players. In addition, however, the professionals were significantly more accurate than the amateurs in predicting the outcome of bridge hands and the difference in difficulty could have contributed to the difference in overconfidence.

The difficulty effect can also explain the main finding of a study by Gigerenzer, Hoffrage, & Kleinbolting (1991). In this study, subjects in one group were presented with pairs of cities and asked to choose the city with the larger population and indicate their confidence in each answer. The items were randomly selected from a list of all large West German cities. Subjects in a second group were presented with general knowledge questions (e.g., Was the zipper invented before or after 1920?) and instructed to choose the correct answer and assess their confidence in that answer. Judgments about the population of cities were fairly well calibrated, but responses to the general knowledge questions exhibited overconfidence. However, the two tasks were not equally difficult: average accuracy was 72% for the city judgments and only 53% for the general knowledge questions. Hence, the presence of overconfidence in the latter but not in the former could be entirely due to the difficulty effect, documented by Lichtenstein & Fischhoff (1977). Indeed, when Gigerenzer et al. (1991) selected a set of city questions that were matched in difficulty to the general knowledge questions, the two domains yielded the same degree of overconfidence. The authors did not acknowledge the fact that their study confounded item generation (representative versus selective) with task difficulty (easy versus hard). Instead, they interpret their data as confirmation for their theory that overconfidence in individual judgments is a consequence of item selection and that it disappears when items are randomly sampled from some natural environment. This prediction is tested in the following study.

Study 5: The Illusion of Validity

In this experiment, subjects compared pairs of American states on several attributes reported in the *1990 World Almanac*. To ensure representative sampling, we randomly selected 30 pairs of American states from the set of all possible pairs of states.

Subjects were presented with pairs of states (e.g., Alabama, Oregon) and asked to choose the state that was higher on a particular attribute and to assess the probability that their answer was correct. According to Gigerenzer et al. (1991), there should be no overconfidence in these judgments because the states were randomly selected from a natural reference class. In contrast, our account suggests that the degree of overconfidence depends on the relation between the strength and weight of the evidence. More specifically, overconfidence will be most pronounced when the weight of evidence is low and the strength of evidence is high. This is likely to arise in domains in which people can readily form a strong impression even though these impressions have low predictive validity. For example, an interviewer can form a strong impression of the quality of the mind of a prospective graduate student even though these impressions do not predict the candidate's performance (Dawes, 1979).

The use of natural stimuli precludes the direct manipulation of strength and weight. Instead, we used three attributes that vary in terms of the strength of impression that subjects are likely to form and the amount of knowledge they are likely to have. The three attributes were the number of people in each state (population), the high-school graduation rate in each state (education), and the difference in voting rates between the last two presidential elections in each state (voting). We hypothesized that the three attributes would yield different patterns of confidence and accuracy. First, we expected people to be more knowledgeable about population than about either education or voting. Second, we expected greater confidence in the prediction of education than in the prediction of voting because people's images or stereotypes of the various states are more closely tied to the former than the latter. For example, people are likely to view one state as more "educated" than another if it has more famous universities or if it is associated with more cultural events. Because the correlations between these cues and high-school graduation rates are very low, however, we expected greater overconfidence for education than for population or voting. Thus, we expected high accuracy and high confidence for population, low accuracy and low confidence for voting, and low accuracy and higher confidence for education.

To test these hypotheses, 298 subjects each evaluated half (15) of the pairs of states on one of the attributes. After subjects had indicated their confidence for each of the 15 questions, they were asked to estimate how many of the 15 questions they had answered correctly. They were reminded that by chance alone the expected number of correct answers was 7.5.

Table 12.4 presents mean judgments of confidence, accuracy, and estimated frequency of correct answers for each of the three attributes. Judgments of confidence exhibited significant overconfidence ($p < .01$) for all three attributes, contradicting

Table 12.4
Confidence and Accuracy for Study 6

	Population $N = 93$	Voting $N = 77$	Education $N = 118$
Confidence	74.7	59.7	65.6
Accuracy	68.2	51.2	49.8
Conf-Acc	6.5	8.5	15.8
Frequency	51.3	36.1	41.2

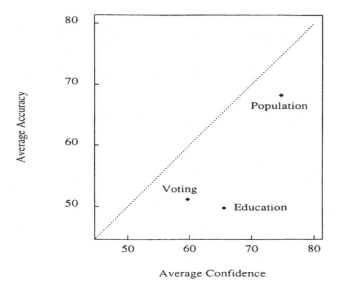

Figure 12.8
Confidence and accuracy for three attributes.

the claim that "If the set of general-knowledge tasks is randomly sampled from a natural environment, we expect overconfidence to be zero" (Gigerenzer et al., 1991, p. 512). Evidently there is a great deal more to overconfidence than the biased selection of items.

The observed pattern of confidence and accuracy is consistent with our hypothesis, as can be seen in figure 12.8. This figure plots average accuracy against average confidence, across all subjects and items, for each of the three attributes. For population, people exhibited considerable accuracy and moderate overconfidence. For voting, accuracy was at chance level, but overconfidence was again moderate. For education, too, accuracy was at chance level, but overconfidence was massive.

The present results indicate that overconfidence cannot be fully explained by the effect of difficulty. Population and voting produced comparable levels of overconfidence (6.5 versus 8.5, $t < 1$, ns) despite a large difference in accuracy (68.2 versus 51.2, $p < .001$). On the other hand, there is much greater overconfidence in judgments about education than about voting (15.8 versus 8.5, $p < .01$) even though their level of accuracy was nearly identical (49.8 versus 51.2, $t < 1$, ns).

This analysis may shed light on the relation between overconfidence and expertise. When predictability is reasonably high, experts are generally better calibrated than lay people. Studies of race oddsmakers (Griffith, 1949; Hausch, Ziemba, & Rubinstein, 1981; McGlothlin, 1956) and expert bridge players (Keren, 1987) are consistent with this conclusion. When predictability is very low, however, experts may be more prone to overconfidence than novices. If the future state of a mental patient, the Russian economy, or the stock market cannot be predicted from present data, then experts who have rich models of the system in question are more likely to exhibit overconfidence than lay people who have a very limited understanding of these systems. Studies of clinical psychologists (e.g., Oskamp, 1965) and stock market analysts (e.g., Yates, 1990) are consistent with this hypothesis.

Frequency versus Confidence
We now turn to the relation between people's confidence in the validity of their individual answers and their estimates of the overall hit rate. A sportscaster, for example, can be asked to assess his confidence in the prediction of each game as well as the number of games he expects to predict correctly. According to the present account, these judgments are not expected to coincide because they are based on different evidence. A judgment of confidence in a particular case, we propose, depends primarily on the balance of arguments for and against a specific hypothesis, e.g., the relative strength of two opposing teams. Estimated frequency of correct prediction, on the other hand, is likely to be based on a general evaluation of the difficulty of the task, the knowledge of the judge, or past experience with similar problems. Thus, the overconfidence observed in average judgments of confidence need not apply to global judgments of expected accuracy. Indeed, table 12.4 shows that estimated frequencies were substantially below the actual frequencies of correct prediction. In fact, the latter estimates were below chance for two of the three attributes.[3] Similar results have been observed by other investigators (e.g., Gigerenzer et al., 1991; May, 1986; Sniezek & Switzer, 1989). Evidently, people can maintain a high degree of confidence in the validity of specific answers even when they know that their overall hit rate is not very high.[4] This phenomenon has been called the "illusion of validity" (Kahneman & Tversky, 1973): people often make

confident predictions about individual cases on the basis of fallible data (e.g., personal interviews or projective tests) even when they know that these data have low predictive validity (Dawes, Faust, & Meehl, 1989).

The discrepancy between estimates of frequency and judgments of confidence is an interesting finding but it does not undermine the significance of overconfidence in individual items. The latter phenomenon is important because people's decisions are commonly based on their confidence in their assessment of individual events, not on their estimates of their overall hit rate. For example, an extensive survey of new business owners (Cooper, Woo, & Dunkelberg, 1988) revealed that entrepreneurs were, on average, highly optimistic (i.e., overconfident) about the success of their specific new ventures even when they were reasonably realistic about the general rule of failure for ventures of that kind. We suggest that decisions to undertake new ventures are based primarily on beliefs about individual events, rather than about overall base rates. The tendency to prefer an individual or "inside" view rather than a statistical or "outside" view represents one of the major departures of intuitive judgment from normative theory (Kahneman & Lovallo, 1991; Kahneman & Tversky, 1982).

Finally, note that people's performance on the frequency task leaves much to be desired. The degree of underestimation in judgments of frequency was comparable, on average, to the degree of overconfidence in individual judgments of probability (see table 12.4). Furthermore, the correlation across subjects between estimated and actual frequency was negligible for all three attributes (+.10 for population, −.10 for voting, and +.15 for education). These observations do not support the view that people estimate their hit rate correctly, and that the confidence–frequency discrepancy is merely a manifestation of their inability to evaluate the probability of unique events. Research on overconfidence has been criticized by some authors on the grounds that it applies a frequentistic criterion (the rate of correct prediction) to a nonfrequentistic or subjective concept of probability. This objection, however, overlooks the fact that a Bayesian expects to be calibrated (Dawid, 1982), hence the theory of subjective probability permits the comparison of confidence and accuracy.

Concluding Remarks

The preceding study demonstrated that the overconfidence observed in calibration experiments is not an artifact of item selection or a byproduct of test difficulty. Furthermore, overconfidence is not limited to the prediction of discrete events; it has consistently been observed in the assessment of uncertain quantities (Alpert & Raiffa, 1982).

The significance of overconfidence to the conduct of human affairs can hardly be overstated. Although overconfidence is not universal, it is prevalent, often massive, and difficult to eliminate (Fischhoff, 1982). This phenomenon is significant not only because it demonstrates the discrepancy between intuitive judgments and the laws of chance, but primarily because confidence controls action (Heath & Tversky, 1991). It has been argued (see e.g., Taylor & Brown, 1988) that overconfidence—like optimism—is adaptive because it makes people feel good and moves them to do things that they would not have done otherwise. These benefits, however, may be purchased at a high price. Overconfidence in the diagnosis of a patient, the outcome of a trial, or the projected interest rate could lead to inappropriate medical treatment, bad legal advice, and regrettable financial investments. It can be argued that people's willingness to engage in military, legal, and other costly battles would be reduced if they had a more realistic assessment of their chances of success. We doubt that the benefits of overconfidence outweigh its costs.

Notes

This work was supported by a NSERC research grant to the first author and by Grant 89-0064 from the Air Force Office of Scientific Research to the second author. The paper has benefited from discussions with Robyn Dawes, Baruch Fischhoff, and Daniel Kahneman.

1. A person is said to exhibit overconfidence if she overestimates the probability of her favored hypothesis. The appropriate probability estimate may be determined empirically (e.g., by a person's hit rate) or derived from an appropriate model.

2. To explore the effect of the correlation between strength and weight, we replicated our experiment with another set of stimuli that were selected to have a smaller correlation between the two independent variables ($r = -.27$ as compared to $r = -.64$). The results for this set of stimuli were remarkably similar to those reported in the text, i.e., the regression weights for the median data yielded a ratio of nearly 2 to 1 in favor of strength.

3. One possible explanation for this puzzling observation is that subjects reported the number of items they knew with certainty, without correction for guessing.

4. This is the statistical version of the paradoxical statement "I believe in all of my beliefs, but I believe that some of my beliefs are false."

References

Alpert, M., & Raiffa, H. (1982). A progress report on the training of probability assessors. In D. Kahneman, P. Slovic, & A. Tversky (Eds.), *Judgment under uncertainty: Heuristics and biases* (pp. 294–305). Cambridge: Cambridge University Press.

Bar-Hillel, M. (1983). The base rate fallacy controversy. In R. W. Scholz (Ed.), *Decision making under uncertainty* (pp. 39–61). Amsterdam: North-Holland.

Camerer, C. (1990). Do markets correct biases in probability judgment? Evidence from market experiments. In L. Green & J. H. Kagel (Eds.), *Advances in behavioral economics*, Vol. 2 (pp. 126–172).

Cooper, A. C., Woo, Carolyn, Y., & Dunkelberg, W. C. (1988). Entrepreneurs' perceived chances for success. *Journal of Business Venturing*, 3, 97–108.

Dawes, R. M. (1979). The robust beauty of improper linear models in decision making. *American Psychologist*, 34, 571–582.

Dawes, R. M. (1988). *Rational choice in an uncertain world*. New York: Harcourt Brace Jovanovich.

Dawes, R. M., Faust, D., & Meehl, P. E. (1989). Clinical versus actuarial judgment. *Science*, 243, 1668–1674.

Dawid, A. P. (1982). The well-calibrated Bayesian. *Journal of the American Statistical Association*, 77, 605–613.

Dun & Bradstreet. (1967). *Patterns of success in managing a business*. New York: Dun and Bradstreet.

Dunning, D., Griffin, D. W., Milojkovic, J., & Ross, L. (1990). The overconfidence effect in social prediction. *Journal of Personality and Social Psychology*, 58, 568–581.

Edwards, W. (1968). Conservatism in human information processing. In B. Kleinmuntz (Ed.), *Formal representation of human judgment* (pp. 17–52). New York: Wiley.

Ferrell, W. R., & McGoey, P. J. (1980). A model of calibration for subjective probabilities. *Organizational Behavior and Human Performance*, 26, 32–53.

Fischhoff, B. (1982). Debiasing. In D. Kahneman, P. Slovic, & A. Tversky (Eds.), *Judgment under uncertainty: Heuristics and biases* (pp. 422–444). New York: Cambridge.

Fischhoff, B., & Bar-Hillel, M. (1984). Focusing techniques: A shortcut to improving probability judgments? *Organizational Behavior and Human Performance*, 34, 175–194.

Fischhoff, B., & Beyth-Marom, R. (1983). Hypothesis evaluation from a Bayesian perspective. *Psychological Review*, 90, 239–260.

Fischhoff, B., & MacGregor, D. (1982). Subjective confidence in forecasts. *Journal of Forecasting*, 1, 155–172.

Forer, B. (1949). The fallacy of personal validation: A classroom demonstration of gullibility. *Journal of Abnormal and Social Psychology*, 44, 118–123.

Gigerenzer, G., Hell, W., & Blank, H. (1988). Presentation and content: The use of base rates as a continuous variable. *Journal of Experimental Psychology: Human Perception and Performance*, 14, 513–525.

Gigerenzer, G., Hoffrage, U., & Kleinbolting, H. (1991). Probabilistic mental models: A Brunswikian theory of confidence. *Psychological Review*, 98, 506–528.

Grether, D. M. (1980). Bayes' rule as a descriptive model: The representativeness heuristic. *The Quarterly Journal of Economics*, 95, 537–557.

Grether, D. M. (1990). *Testing Bayes' rule and the representativeness heuristic: Some experimental evidence* (Social Science Working Paper 724). Pasadena, CA: Division of the Humanities and Social Sciences, California Institute of Technology.

Griffin, D. W. (1991). *On the use and neglect of base rates*. Unpublished manuscript, Department of Psychology, University of Waterloo.

Griffith, R. M. (1949). Odds adjustments by American horse-race bettors. *American Journal of Psychology*, 62, 290–294.

Hausch, D. B., Ziemba, W. T., & Rubinstein, M. (1981). Efficiency of the market for racetrack betting. *Management Science*, 27, 1435–1452.

Heath, F., & Tversky, A. (1991). Preference and belief: Ambiguity and competence in choice under uncertainty. *Journal of Risk and Uncertainty*, 4, 5–28.

Jones, E. E., & Nisbett, R. E. (1972). *The actor and the observer: Divergent perceptions of the causes of behavior*. Morristown, NJ: General Learning Press.

Kahneman, D., & Lovallo, D. (1991). Bold forecasting and timid decisions: A cognitive perspective on risk taking. In R. Rumelt, P. Schendel, & D. Teece (Eds.), *Fundamental issues in strategy*. Cambridge: Harvard University Press, forthcoming.

Kahneman, D., Slovic, P., & Tversky, A. (1982). *Judgment under uncertainty: Heuristics and biases*. Cambridge: Cambridge University Press.

Kahneman, D., & Tversky, A. (1972). Subjective probability: A judgment of representativeness. *Cognitive Psychology*, 3, 430–454.

Kahneman, D., & Tversky, A. (1973). On the psychology of prediction. *Psychological Review*, 80, 237–251.

Kahneman, D., & Tversky, A. (1982). Intuitive prediction: Biases and corrective procedures. In D. Kahneman, P. Slovic, & A. Tversky (Eds.), *Judgment under uncertainty: Heuristics and biases* (pp. 414–421). Cambridge: Cambridge University Press.

Keren, G. (1987). Facing uncertainty in the game of bridge: A calibration study. *Organizational Behavior and Human Decision Processes*, 39, 98–114.

Keren, G. (1988). On the ability of monitoring non-veridical perceptions and uncertain knowledge: Some calibration studies. *Acta Psychologica*, 67, 95–119.

Kidd, J. B. (1970). The utilization of subjective probabilities in production planning. *Acta Psychologica*, 34, 338–347.

Koriat, A., Lichtenstein, S., & Fischhoff, B. (1980). Reasons for confidence. *Journal of Experimental Psychology: Human Learning and Memory*, 6, 107–118.

Lichtenstein, S., & Fischhoff, B. (1977). Do those who know more also know more about how much they know? The calibration of probability judgments. *Organizational Behavior and Human Performance*, 20, 159–183.

Lichtenstein, S., Fischhoff, B., & Phillips, L. D. (1982). Calibration of probabilities: The state of the art to 1980. In D. Kahneman, P. Slovic, & A. Tversky (Eds.), *Judgment under uncertainty: Heuristics and biases* (pp. 306–334). Cambridge: Cambridge University Press.

Lusted, L. B. (1977). *A study of the efficacy of diagnostic radiologic procedures: Final report on diagnostic efficacy*. Chicago: Efficacy Study Committee of the American College of Radiology.

McGlothlin, W. H. (1956). Stability of choices among uncertain alternatives. *American Journal of Psychology*, 69, 604–615.

May, R. S. (1986). Inferences, subjective probability and frequency of correct answers: A cognitive approach to the overconfidence phenomenon. In B. Brehmer, H Jungermann, P. Lourens, & G. Sevo'n (Eds.), *New directions in research on decision making* (pp. 175–189). Amsterdam: North-Holland.

Murphy, A. H., & Winkler, R. L. (1977). Can weather forecasters formulate reliable probability forecasts of precipitation and temperature? *National Weather Digest*, 2, 2–9.

Neale, M. A., & Bazerman, M. H. (1990). *Cognition and rationality in negotiation*. New York: The Free Press, forthcoming.

Nisbett, R. E., & Ross, L. (1980). *Human inference: Strategies and shortcomings of human judgment*. Englewood Cliffs, NJ: Prentice-Hall.

Oskamp, S. (1962). The relationship of clinical experience and training methods to several criteria of clinical prediction. *Psychological Monographs*, 76 (28, Whole, No. 547).

Oskamp, S. (1965). Overconfidence in case-study judgments. *The Journal of Consulting Psychology*, 29, 261–265.

Peterson, C. R., & Miller, A. J. (1965). Sensitivity of subjective probability revision. *Journal of Experimental Psychology*, 70, 117–121.

Peterson, C. R., Schneider, R. J., & Miller, A. J. (1965). Sample size and the revision of subjective probabilities. *Journal of Experimental Psychology*, 69, 522–527.

Phillips, L. D., & Edwards, W. (1966). Conservatism in a simple probability inference task. *Journal of Experimental Psychology*, 72, 346–354.

Quattrone, G. A. (1982). Overattribution and unit formation: When behavior engulfs the person. *Journal of Personality and Social Psychology*, 42, 593–607.

Slovic, P., & Lichtenstein, S. (1971). Comparison of Bayesian and regression approaches to the study of information processing in judgment. *Organizational Behavior and Human Performance*, 6, 649–744.

Sniezek, J. A., & Switzer, F. S. (1989). *The over-underconfidence paradox: High Pi's but poor unlucky me.* Paper presented at the Judgment and Decision Making Society annual meeting in Atlanta, Georgia.

Staël von Holstein, C.-A. S. (1972). Probabilistic forecasting: An experiment related to the stock market. *Organizational Behavior and Human Performance*, 8, 139–158.

Taylor, S. E., & Brown, J. D. (1988). Illusion and well-being: A social psychological perspective on mental health. *Psychological Bulletin*, 103, 193–210.

Tversky, A., & Kahneman, D. (1971). The belief in the law of small numbers. *Psychological Bulletin*, 76, 105–110.

Tversky, A., & Kahneman, D. (1974). Judgment under uncertainty: Heuristics and biases. *Science*, 185, 1124–1131.

Vallone, R. P., Griffin, D. W., Lin, S., & Ross, L. (1990). The overconfident prediction of future actions and outcomes by self and others. *Journal of Personality and Social Psychology*, 58, 582–592.

von Winterfeldt, D., & Edwards, W. (1986). *Decision analysis and behavioral research.* New York: Cambridge University Press.

Wagenaar, W. A., & Keren, G. (1986). Does the expert know? The reliability of predictions and confidence ratings of experts. In E. Hollnagel, G. Maneini, & D. Woods (Eds.), *Intelligent decision support in process environments* (pp. 87–107.) Berlin: Springer.

Wright, G., & Wisudha, A. (1982). Distribution of probability assessments for almanac and future event questions. *Scandinavian Journal of Psychology*, 23, 219–224.

Yates, J. F. (1990). *Judgment and Decision Making.* Englewood Cliffs, NJ: Prentice–Hall.

13 On the Evaluation of Probability Judgments: Calibration, Resolution, and Monotonicity

Varda Liberman and Amos Tversky

Much research on judgment under uncertainty has focused on the comparison of probability judgments with the corresponding relative frequency of occurrence. In a typical study, judges are presented with a series of prediction or knowledge problems and asked to assess the probability of the events in question. Judgments of probability or confidence are used both in research (Lichtenstein, Fischhoff, & Phillips, 1982; Wallsten & Budescu, 1983) and in practice. For example, weather forecasters often report the probability of rain (Murphy & Daan, 1985), and economists are sometimes called upon to estimate the chances of recession (Zarnowitz & Lambros, 1987).

The two main criteria used to evaluate such judgments are calibration and resolution. A judge is said to be calibrated if his or her probability judgments match the corresponding relative frequency of occurrence. More specifically, consider all events to which the judge assigns a probability p; the judge is calibrated if the proportion of events in that class that actually occur equals p. Calibration is a desirable property, especially for communication, but it does not ensure informativeness. A judge can be properly calibrated and entirely noninformative if, for example, he or she predicts the sex of each newborn with probability 1/2. An ideal judge should also be able to resolve uncertainty, namely, to discriminate between events that do and do not occur. In particular, such a judge assigns a probability 1 to all the events that occur and a probability 0 to all the events that do not. In practice, of course, people are neither calibrated nor do they exhibit perfect resolution. To evaluate probability judgments, therefore, researchers investigate the observed departures from calibration and resolution.

In the present article, we discuss some conceptual problems regarding the evaluation of probability judgments. In the first section, we distinguish between two representations of probability judgments: the designated form, which is based on a particular coding of the outcomes, and the inclusive form, which takes into account all events and their complements. The two forms yield the same overall measure of performance, but they give rise to different measures of calibration and resolution. We illustrate the differences between the indices derived from the designated and the inclusive representations and show that the same judgments can yield different values of the designated indices depending on the designation chosen by the analyst. In the second section, we distinguish between two types of overconfidence, specific and generic, and show that they are logically independent of calibration. *Specific* overconfidence refers to the overestimation of the probability of a specific designated hypothesis (e.g., rain). *Generic* overconfidence refers to the overestimation of the probability of the hypothesis that the judge considers most likely. In the third section, we treat probability judgments as an ordinal scale, discuss alternative measures of monotonicity, and propose an ordinal index of performance. In the final section, we apply this measure to several studies of probability judgment and compare it with the standard measures of calibration and resolution. The relevant mathematical results are reviewed in the appendix.

Calibration and Resolution

Consider a binary assessment task. Throughout this section, we assume that on each trial, the judge assigns a probability p_i to the event E_i and a probability $1 - p_i$ to its complement.[1] The results of a series of probability judgments are often summarized by a calibration plot that describes the observed rate of occurrence as a function of stated probability. There are two forms of calibration plots. In the *designated form*, a target event is preselected for each problem, independently of the judge's response, and the data are displayed in terms of the probabilities assigned to these events, disregarding their complements. In contrast, the *inclusive form* incorporates, for each problem, the probabilities assigned to the two complementary events. The designated form is commonly used when all the judgments refer to a common hypothesis (e.g., rain vs. no rain, victory for the home team vs. victory for the visiting team), and the inclusive form is typically used in general-knowledge problems for which there is no common hypothesis. The form, however, is not dictated by the hypotheses under consideration. The inclusive form can be used in the presence of a common hypothesis, and the designated form can be employed in its absence, using an arbitrary selection of target events.

By complementarity, the calibration plot for the inclusive form in the binary case satisfies the following symmetry: If the point (q, f_q) is included in the plot, then the point $(1 - q, 1 - f_q)$ is also included in the plot (i.e., $f_{1-q} = 1 - f_q$). Therefore, authors normally display the *reduced form*, which plots the observed rate of occurrence only for probability judgments that exceed one half; the rest follows from complementarity. Note that the reduced form includes one event from each complementary pair but the target event in this case depends on the assessor's judgment; it cannot be specified in advance as required by the designated form. The reduced plot, therefore, should not be confused with the designated plot; it is merely a parsimonious representation of the inclusive plot. To distinguish between the designated and the inclusive forms, we use P to denote the set of judgments of the designated events and Q to denote the set of all judgments. Thus, Q includes each judgment in P as well as its complement.

We wish to emphasize that the inclusive and the designated forms are alternative representations of probability judgments, not alternative methods of elicitation. In some experiments, subjects are asked to assess the probability of a specific event (e.g., rain, recession), whereas in other studies, subjects first select the hypothesis they consider most likely and then assess its probability. Alternatively, the subject may be asked to divide a chance wheel into two sectors so as to match the probabilities of two complementary events. This procedure, used by decision analysts, requires the subject to consider simultaneously the event and its complement, thereby avoiding the need to specify a target event. Although the experimental procedure could influence people's judgments, these data can be represented in either the designated or the inclusive form, irrespective of the method of elicitation.

The most common measure of overall performance is the quadratic loss function proposed by Brier (1950) in the context of weather forecasting. Let x_i be an indicator that equals 1 if event E_i occurs and 0 otherwise. Brier's loss function or probability score $S(P)$ is given by

$$\frac{1}{n}\sum_{i=1}^{n}(p_i - x_i)^2,$$

where n denotes the number of elements in P. Because $(p_i - x_i)^2 = [(1 - p_i) - (1 - x_i)]^2$, we obtain the same value of S whether it is computed using the designated or the inclusive form, that is, $S(P) = S(Q)$.

This index provides a measure of overall performance in which lower values indicate better performance. Unlike the linear loss function, which encourages strategic responses, the quadratic rule is incentive compatible; to minimize the expected score, the judge should report his or her "true" probability (Winkler, 1986). Furthermore, the quadratic score can be decomposed into several interpretable components (Murphy, 1973; Sanders, 1963; Yates, 1982). Murphy (1972) considered two decompositions, one based on the designated form and one based on the inclusive form.[2] In the designated decomposition, see the appendix, part A,

$$S = f(1 - f) - \frac{1}{n}\sum_{p \in P}N_p(f_p - f)^2 + \frac{1}{n}\sum_{p \in P}N_p(p - f_p)^2$$

$$= V - R' + C',$$

(1)

where N_p is the number of times the judged probability of the designated event equals p, f_p is the relative frequency of occurrence in that class, and f is the overall relative frequency of the designated event.

The third term on the right-hand side (C') measures the discrepancy between the observed hit rate (f_p) and the identity line, the second term (R') measures the variability of the hit rate around the overall base rate (f), and the first term (V) is the variance of the outcome variable. Note that V does not depend on the judgments. (We use primes to denote characteristics of the designated judgments.) The indices C' and R' are commonly interpreted as measures of calibration and resolution, respectively (see e.g., Lichtenstein et al., 1982; Murphy & Winkler, 1992; Yaniv, Yates, & Smith, 1991). Note that good performance is represented by low values of C' and high values of R'.

Two features of this decomposition are worth noting. First, all the components of Equation 1 remain unchanged if the designated outcome (e.g., rain) and its complement (e.g., no rain) are interchanged throughout. Thus, V, R', and C' do not depend on the labeling of the designation, although they depend on the designation itself. Second, it follows from the standard decomposition of the total variance that $V - R'$ is the variance of the (designated) outcome variable that cannot be explained by the judgments.

Murphy (1972) also considered another decomposition of S that is based on the inclusive form. In this decomposition, which incorporates the judged probabilities of all events and their complements,

$$S = .25 - \frac{1}{2n}\sum_{q \in Q} N_q(f_q - .5)^2 + \frac{1}{2n}\sum_{q \in Q} N_q(q - f_q)^2$$

$$= .25 - R + C,$$

(2)

where N_q is the number of times the judge assigns a probability q to either the designated event or to its complement and f_q refers to the relative frequency of occurrence in that class. Thus, for every $q \in Q$, $N_q = N_p + N_{1-p}$, and f_q is a weighted average of f_p and $1 - f_{1-p}$.

The major difference between the two decompositions is that equation 1 incorporates only the judgments of the designated events, whereas equation 2 includes their complements as well. Hence, Q has $2n$ elements. The inclusion of the complements changes the outcome variable: In the designated case, it has mean f and variance $f(1 - f)$, whereas in the inclusive case, it has mean .50 and variance .25. Thus, the first term (.25) on the right-hand side of equation 2 is the variance of the (inclusive) outcome variable, the second term (R) measures the variability of the calibration plot around the overall mean (.50), and the third term (C) reflects overall calibration. Here, $.25 - R$ is the variance of the outcome variable that cannot be explained by the judgments.

Table 13.1
An Example of Multiple Designation

Game	Visitors	Winner	$P(V, H)$	$P(A, B)$
1	A	B	.25 (0)	.25 (0)
2	B	B	.75 (1)	.25 (0)
3	A	B	.25 (0)	.25 (0)
4	B	A	.75 (0)	.25 (1)
5	A	B	.75 (0)	.75 (0)
6	B	A	.25 (0)	.75 (1)
7	A	A	.75 (1)	.75 (1)
8	B	A	.25 (0)	.75 (1)
Mean			.50 (.25)	.50 (.50)
C'			.0625	0

Note: $P(V, H)$ = probability of visiting team beating home team, $P(A, B)$ = probability of As beating Bs, C' = correspondence between hit rate and judged probability.

Both the designated indices (C' and R') and the inclusive indices (C and R) are widely used in the literature, but the conceptual differences between them are not properly appreciated. We next discuss the interpretation of these measures, starting with calibration. It is evident from the comparison of the inclusive index C and the designated index C' that the former measures calibration at large, whereas the latter measures calibration relative to a specific designated hypothesis. That is, C measures the degree to which the judge's scale is calibrated. Thus, $C = 0$ iff the hit rate among all the events to which the judge assigns a probability p is equal to p. In contrast, C' measures the correspondence between hit rate and judged probability only for the designated events. A judge can be properly calibrated at large (i.e., $C = 0$) and exhibit a bias with respect to a particular designation, yielding $C' > 0$. Moreover, different designations produce different values of C', as illustrated in the example described in table 13.1.

Consider a sportscaster who assesses the probabilities of the outcomes of 8 basketball games between two teams, the As and the Bs. Half of the games are played on the As' home court, and the other half are played on the Bs' home court. The visiting team and the winner of each game in the series are given in the second and third columns of table 13.1. Note that the As and the Bs each won 50% of their games (4 out of 8) and that the visiting team won 25% of the games (2 out of 8).

The probabilities assigned by the sportscaster can be analyzed in terms of two different designations: (a) the visiting team versus the home team and (b) the As versus the Bs. The fourth column of table 13.1 contains the sportscaster's probability judgments for the proposition "the visiting team beats the home team," denoted

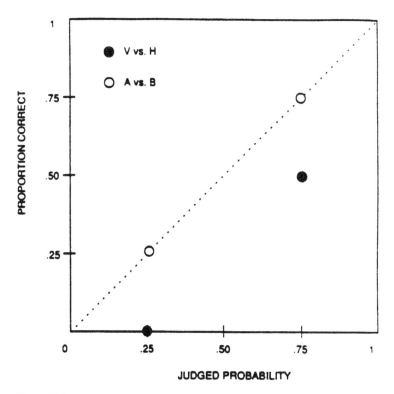

Figure 13.1
Calibration graph for the two designations of the data from table 13.1 (V = visiting team, H = home team, A = A team, B = B team).

$P(V, H)$. The fifth column of table 13.1 contains the sportscaster's probability judgments for the proposition "the As beat the Bs," denoted $P(A, B)$. In this example, the assessor uses only two values, .25 and .75; this feature simplifies the analysis but it is not essential. The table also indicates, beside each judgment, whether the event in question occurred (1) or did not occur (0).

Inspection of column 4 reveals that the sportscaster is not properly calibrated with respect to the (V, H) designation: Average judged probability for victory by the visiting team equals .50, whereas the corresponding hit rate is only .25, yielding $C' = .0625$. Analysis of the same set of judgments in terms of the As versus the Bs (see column 5) reveals perfect calibration (i.e., $C' = 0$). Figure 13.1 contains the calibration plot for the data of table 13.1. The black circles show that the judge is overconfident in predicting victory for the visiting team, thereby underestimating the home court advantage. On the other hand, the open circles indicate that the judge has no bias in favor of either team. Hence, the same set of judgments yields different values of C' depending on the choice of designation.

The problem of multiple designation has escaped attention, we believe, because investigators normally describe the data in terms of one preferred designation (e.g., victory for the home team) and report C' (and R') in terms of this designation. In many situations, of course, there is a natural designation, but it is often difficult to justify the exclusion of all others. Even in the classical problem of forecasting the probability of rain, one can think of other meaningful designations, such as, "Will tomorrow's weather be different from today's?"

It might be tempting to deal with the problem of multiple designations by defining the assessor's task in terms of a preferred designation. This approach, however, does not solve the problem because we have no way of knowing how the judge actually thinks about the events in question. In the example above, the sportscaster may be asked to assess the probability of victory by the visiting team, yet he or she may think in terms of a victory by the As, or in terms of both designations and perhaps some others. This does not imply that C' is meaningless or noninformative. It only indicates that C' should be interpreted as a measure of bias with respect to a particular designation, not as a measure of calibration at large.

The value of the inclusive index, of course, does not depend on the designation. In this example, $C = 0$, as in the (A, B) designation of column 5 in table 13.1. In general, the value of C is equal to the minimal value of C'. This follows from the fact that $C \leq C'$ (see part B of the appendix) and the observation that there always exists a designation for which $C' = C$.

The problem of multiple designations applies with equal force to the interpretation of the resolution index R'. Recall that the inclusive index R measures the variability of the calibration plot around .5, whereas the designated index R' measures the variability around the base rate of the designated event (see equation 1). Because alternative designations induce different outcome variables, with different base rates, the same set of judgments can yield markedly different values of R', as illustrated below. Note that R can be either smaller or larger than R'.

Consider a political analyst who predicts the outcomes of gubernatorial elections in 10 different states, in which 5 of the incumbents are Republicans and 5 are Democrats. Suppose that the analyst predicts, with probability 1, that the challenger will beat the incumbent in all 10 races, and suppose further that these predictions are confirmed. There are two natural designations in this case. The results of the election can be coded in terms of victory for the challenger or for the incumbent. Alternatively, they can be coded in terms of a victory for a Republican or for a Democrat.

The two designations induce different outcome variables. In the former, the outcome variable has a mean of 1 and no variance, because all of the races were won by the challengers. In the latter, the outcome variable has a mean .50 and variance .25, because the races were evenly split between Republicans and Democrats. As a consequence, the analyst obtains the *maximal* value of R', namely .25, in the Republican versus Democrat designation, and the *minimal* value of R', namely 0, in the challenger versus incumbent designation. The value of R', therefore, depends critically on the choice of designation.

The designated index R' measures the assessor's ability to improve the prediction of the designated outcome variable beyond the base rate of that variable; it does not measure the assessor's general ability to distinguish between events that do and do not occur. As shown above, a perfect judge, who predicts all outcomes without error, can obtain $R' = 0$. In contrast, the inclusive measure R always assigns the maximal value (.25) to an assessor who predicts without error.

The inclusive and the designated measures of resolution may be used to describe and summarize the observed judgments; also they can be used to evaluate the performance of the assessor and its usefulness for others. One might argue that R' is preferable to R because a judge who achieves perfect resolution when the base rate of the outcome variable is 1 (or 0) is less informative and less useful than a judge who achieves perfect resolution when the base rate of the outcome variable is .5 (see Yaniv et al., 1991 for a discussion of this issue). Although this is often the case, the evaluation problem is more complicated. First, as the preceding example shows, different designations give rise to different base rates. Should we use, for example, the base rate for Republicans versus Democrats, which equals .5, or the base rate for the challenger versus the incumbent, which equals 1? In the absence of a unique designation, it is not clear what is the relevant base rate. But suppose, for the sake of argument, that there is a unique designation. If we evaluate the judge's performance relative to the base rate of this designation (using R'), then a judge who predicts the base rate in each case receives $R' = 0$ and is therefore treated as totally uninformative. This evaluation may be reasonable if the base rate of the outcome variable is generally known, but not otherwise.

Consider, for example, a physician who assesses for each patient the probability of success of a particular medical treatment. Suppose the physician assigns a probability .9 for each of the patients and that the treatment is indeed successful in 90% of the cases. How shall we evaluate this performance? If the rate of success for this treatment is generally known, the physician is clearly uninformative. However, if the medical treatment in question is new and its rate of success is unknown, the physician's assessments may be highly informative. Hence, the informativeness and the usefulness of a set of judgments depend on the prior knowledge of the user, which may or may not coincide with the base rate of the outcome variable. Because the prior knowledge of the user is not part of the formal definition of the problem, none of the available indices provide a fully satisfactory measure of the usefulness of the assessor.

We conclude this section with a brief discussion of the reasons for using the designated and the inclusive analyses. To begin with, there are many situations in which only the inclusive analysis can be applied, because there is no common hypothesis or a nonarbitrary designation. Examples of such tasks include multiple-choice tests of general knowledge or the diagnosis of patients in an emergency room where the set of relevant diagnoses varies from case to case. Recall that the inclusive indices depend only on the assessor's judgment and the actual state of the world, whereas the designated indices also depend on the designation chosen by the analyst. To justify this choice and the use of the designated indices, the investigator should have a good reason (a) for selecting a particular designation (e.g., Republicans vs. Democrats rather than incumbents vs. challengers), and (b) for focusing on the prediction of a particular outcome (e.g., a victory by a Democrat) separately from the prediction of its complement.

The designated analysis has been sometimes recommended on the ground that the judge was asked to assess the probability of a particular outcome (e.g., the probability that a manuscript would be accepted, not the probability that it would be rejected). This argument, however, is not very compelling because the manner in which the judge thinks about the event in question is not dictated by the wording of the question. (How about the probability that the manuscript will not be rejected?) There is a better rationale for the designated analysis, namely, an interest in the presence or absence of a bias regarding a specific hypothesis. Such a bias can be observed in the designated plot but not in the inclusive plot. Indeed, the former is more popular than the latter, especially in the binary case, in which the inclusive plot can be constructed from the designated plot but not vice versa. This relation no longer holds in the nonbinary case, in which the judge assesses the probabilities of three of more outcomes. In this case, the inclusive plot incorporates some data that are excluded from the designated plot.

In summary, the inclusive analysis is appropriate when we are interested in the assessor's use of the probability scale, irrespective of the particular outcome. The designated analysis, on the other hand, is relevant when we are interested in the prediction of a specific outcome. (An investigator, of course, may choose to focus on any outcome, e.g., rain on the weekend, even when most judgments of rain do not involve this outcome.) The preceding discussion indicates that both the designated and the inclusive indices can be useful for describing and evaluating probability judgments. Furthermore, the appreciation of their differences could facilitate the selection of indices and their interpretation.

Calibration and Confidence

One of the major findings that has emerged from the study of intuitive judgment is the prevalence of overconfidence. Overconfidence is manifested in different forms, such as nonregressive predictions (Kahneman, Slovic, & Tversky, 1982) and the overestimation of the accuracy of clinical judgments (Dawes, Faust, & Meehl, 1989). Within the calibration paradigm, we distinguish between two manifestations of overconfidence, which we call *specific* and *generic*.[3] A person is said to exhibit *specific overconfidence* (or bias, Yates, 1990) if he or she overestimates the probability of a specific hypothesis or a designated outcome. (Note that specific overconfidence in a given hypothesis entails specific underconfidence in the complementary hypothesis.) A person is said to exhibit *generic overconfidence* if he or she overestimates the probability of the hypothesis that he or she considers most likely. The two concepts of overconfidence are distinct. A person may exhibit specific overconfidence either with or without generic overconfidence. An assessor who overestimates the probability that the visiting team will win a basketball game may or may not overestimate the probability of the outcome that he or she considers more likely. The two phenomena can have different causes. Inadequate appreciation of the home court advantage, for example, is likely to produce specific, not generic, overconfidence.

Specific overconfidence implies $C' > 0$ for the relevant designation, whereas generic overconfidence implies $C > 0$ in the binary case. Thus, generic overconfidence is represented by probability judgments that are more extreme (i.e., closer to 0 or 1) than the corresponding hit rates. Generic overconfidence, however, is no longer equivalent to extremeness when the number of outcomes is greater than two, because in that case, the highest judged probability can be less than one half. In Oskamp's (1965) well-known study, for example, clinical psychologists chose one out of five outcomes describing a real patient and assessed their confidence in their prediction. By the end of the session, average confidence was about 45%, whereas average hit rate was only .25. These data exhibited massive generic overconfidence, but the judgments were less extreme (i.e., closer to .50) than the corresponding hit rate.

It is tempting to try to reconcile extremeness and generic overconfidence in the n outcome case by defining extremeness relative to $1/n$. Indeed, confidence of .45 is more extreme than a hit rate of .25 relative to a chance baseline of .20. Unfortunately, this approach does not work in general. Consider an assessor who assigns probabilities $(.4, .3, .3)$ to three outcomes whose respective rates of occurrence are $(.2, .2, .6)$. These judgments exhibit generic overconfidence: The assessor overestimates the probability of the outcome he or she considers most likely. The judgments, however, are less extreme (i.e., closer to $1/3$) than the actual relative frequencies. Furthermore, in the nonbinary case, there is no compelling ordering of all probability vectors with respect to extremeness; alternative metrics yield different orders. Moreover, in the nonbinary case, generic overconfidence may coexist with $C = 0$.

The preceding discussion shows that except for the binary case, calibration and overconfidence are logically distinct. Both noncalibration and overconfidence (or underconfidence) represent biased assessments. However, C describes a global bias, aggregated over all assignments; specific overconfidence (or C') describes a bias in the assessment of a specific hypothesis; and generic overconfidence reflects a bias in the assessment of one's favored hypothesis. It is important to distinguish among these effects because they could have different theoretical and practical implications.

Ordinal Analysis

The use of calibration and resolution for evaluating human judgment has been criticized on the ground that assessments of probability may not be readily translatable into relative frequencies. Although many experiments provide explicit frequentistic instructions, it could be argued that the person who says that she is "90% sure" does not necessarily expect to be correct 90% of the time. According to this view, being "90% sure" is an expression of high confidence that should not be given a frequentistic interpretation. Whatever the merit of this objection, it may be instructive to treat and evaluate probability judgments as an ordinal scale.

Suppose a judge classifies each of n uncertain events into one of k ordered categories. The categories may be defined verbally (e.g., very likely, likely, rather unlikely) or they may correspond to numerical judgments of probability. The results can be described by a $2 \times k$ matrix in which the columns correspond to the k judgment categories, and the rows indicate whether the event occurred, see figure 13.2. The cell entries n_{1i} and n_{0i} denote the number of events assigned by the judge to category i, $1 \leq i \leq k$, that did and did not occur, respectively. For example, consider a judge who rates each of n candidates on a 5-point scale in terms of their chances of passing a given test. Suppose we do not attach a probability to each level and treat them instead as an ordinal scale. How shall we evaluate the performance of the judge? Because calibration refers to the numerical correspondence between the response scale and the respective rate of occurrence, it does not have an ordinal analogue. Accuracy or resolution, on the other hand, can be evaluated ordinally by comparing

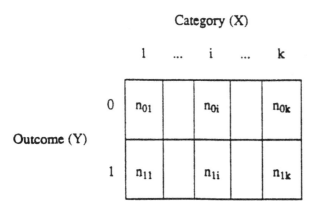

Category (X)

Figure 13.2
An Outcome × Judgment matrix.

the proportion of pairs of candidates that are ordered correctly to the proportion of pairs of candidates that are ordered incorrectly.

We interpret each pair of judgments (i.e., assigning one event to category i and another to category j) as an indirect comparison (i.e., that one event is more likely than the other, or that they are perceived as equiprobable). Given n events, there are $N = n(n-1)/2$ comparisons that can be partitioned into the following five types: the number of valid distinctions

$$v = \sum_{i<j} n_{0i}n_{1j},$$

the number of wrong distinctions

$$w = \sum_{i>j} n_{0i}n_{1j},$$

the number of comparisons that are tied on X only

$$x = \sum_{i} n_{0i}n_{1i},$$

the number of comparisons that are tied on Y only

$$y = \sum_{i<j} (n_{0i}n_{0j} + n_{1i}n_{1j}),$$

and the number of comparisons that are tied on both X and Y

$$z = \sum_{i,j} n_{ij}(n_{ij} - 1)/2.$$

Clearly, $N = v + w + x + y + z$.

There is an extensive literature on ordinal measures of association. We seek a measure that is appropriate for the present problem. Following the seminal work of Goodman and Kruskal (1954, 1959), we define a generalized ordinal measure of association by

$$G = \frac{v - w}{v + w + \delta_1 x + \delta_2 y + \delta_3 z}, \quad \delta_i = 0, 1, \text{ for } i = 1, 2, 3. \tag{3}$$

Thus, G is the difference between the number of concordant and discordant pairs divided by the total number of "relevant" pairs (Wilson, 1974). Equation 3 defines a family of indices that differ only in the type of ties that are included in the set of relevant pairs.[4] Note that ties are unavoidable because the number of events generally exceed the number of categories.

The best-known member of this family of indices is Goodman and Kruskal's $\gamma = (v - w)/(v + w)$, obtained by setting $\delta_1 = \delta_2 = \delta_3 = 0$. This measure is widely used, but it is not well suited for our purposes because it ignores all ties. Consequently, a judge could obtain a perfect score by producing a small number of correct judgments and a large number of ties. To illustrate the problem, consider the hypothetical example displayed in figure 13.3a, in which a judge evaluated 20 events using three categories: low, medium, and high probability. In this case, $v = 10 + 9 = 19$ and $w = 0$; hence $\gamma = 1$. Using γ to evaluate performance, therefore, would encourage the judge to make a few "safe" judgments and tie all others (e.g., by using the middle category as in figure 13.3a.

An alternative measure, $(v - w)/(v + w + x + y)$, obtained by setting $\delta_1 = \delta_2 = 1$ and $\delta_3 = 0$, was proposed by Wilson (1974). This index takes into account all comparisons that are tied either on X or on Y, but not on both. Unlike γ, this measure penalizes the assessor for discrimination failures, but the penalty is too sweeping. As illustrated in figure 13.3b, an assessor can achieve perfect ordinal resolution (i.e., a complete separation of the events that did and did not occur), yet the value of Wilson's index is only 2/3 rather than 1.

The preceding examples suggest the desired refinement. Note that contingency tables for probability judgments are generally asymmetric: The outcome variable has only two values (0 and 1), whereas the judgment scale normally includes more than

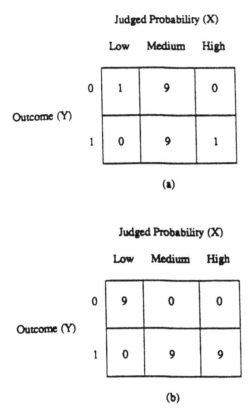

Figure 13.3
Hypothetical Outcome × Judgment matrix.

two values. Therefore, the assessor is bound to assign events with a common fate to different categories, but he or she may be able to distinguish occurrences from non-occurrences without error. Hence, one may wish to penalize the assessor for assigning events with a different fate to the same category (i.e., ties on X) but not for assigning events with a common fate to different categories (i.e., ties on Y).

To formalize this argument, we define the following notion. An Outcome × Judgment matrix is *separable* if $w = x = 0$. In other words, a matrix is separable if there exists a category j so that any event that is rated above j occurs and any event that is rated at or below j does not occur. An ordinal measure of association is said to satisfy the separability criterion whenever it assigns the maximal value to a matrix if and only if the matrix is separable. It follows readily that among the generalized measures of association defined by equation 3, there is only one index, obtained by setting $\delta_1 = 1$, $\delta_2 = \delta_3 = 0$, that satisfies the separability criterion. This measure, denoted M for *monotonicity*, is given by

$$M = \frac{v - w}{v + w + x}.$$ (4)

This formula was first introduced by Somers (1962) in a different context. He sought an asymmetric measure to distinguish between the contributions of the dependent and the independent variable. The above measure was further discussed by Freeman (1986), Kim (1971), and Wilson (1974), who concluded that it is the measure of choice for testing the hypothesis that Y is a (weakly) monotonic function of X. Indeed, applying M to figure 13.3a yields a fairly low score, $19/(19 + 81) = .19$, unlike the perfect score assigned by γ; and applying M to the separable matrix of figure 13.3b yields a perfect score, in contrast to the intermediate value (2/3) of Wilson's index. Thus, M provides an adequate index of performance that can be interpreted as an ordinal measure of the judge's ability to distinguish between events that do and do not occur. It vanishes iff $v = w$, and it equals 1 iff $w = x = 0$. Other ordinal indices for confidence judgments are discussed by Nelson (1984). To the best of our knowledge, however, no other measure of ordinal association discussed in the literature satisfies the separability criterion.

Applications

In this section, we compare the monotonicity index M with the standard measures of performance and illustrate the difference between the designated and the inclusive indices in three sets of data reported in the literature.[5]

Comparing Verbal and Numerical Judgments
There is considerable interest in the relation between verbal and numerical judgments of belief (see, e.g., Mosteller & Youtz, 1990, and the following commentary). To investigate this question, Wallsten, Budescu, and Zwick (in press) conducted an extensive study in which each subject ($N = 21$) evaluated the probability of some 300 propositions (e.g., "The Monroe Doctrine was proclaimed before the Republican party was founded") and of their complements. The data satisfied the assumption of complementarity used in the calculation of the inclusive indices. In addition to the numerical assessments, the respondents also evaluated all propositions and their complements, using a set of ordered verbal expressions (e.g., improbable, doubtful,

likely) selected separately by each subject. To compare the quality of the two modes of judgment, the authors devised scaling procedures that converted the verbal expressions to numerical estimates and computed the designated measures of calibration and resolution for the numerical judgments and for the scaled verbal expressions. Because subjects evaluated each proposition and its complement and because the estimates were roughly additive, there were essentially no differences between the designated and the inclusive indices in this case.

One advantage of the ordinal analysis discussed above is that it can be used to compare verbal and numerical judgments without converting the former into the latter. Accordingly, we applied the monotonicity measure to both the verbal and numerical judgments of each subject. The mean value of M was .489 in the numerical data and .456 in the verbal data, $t(21) = 2.03$, $p < .06$. The mean value of R' was .056 in the numerical data and .050 in the scaled verbal data, $t(21) = 2.4$, $p < .05$. Both measures, therefore, indicated better performance in the numerical than in the verbal mode. The product–moment correlation, across subjects, between M and R' was .975 in the numerical data and .978 in the verbal data. (The negative correlations between M and S were almost as high, but those between M and C' were substantially lower.) These results support the interpretation of M as an ordinal measure of resolution, which can be used to evaluate verbal expressions of belief without converting them to numbers.

Recession Forecast

The next data set was taken from a survey of professional economic forecasters conducted by the National Bureau for Economic Research and the American Statistical Association (Zarnowitz, 1985; Zarnowitz & Lambros, 1987). Each member of the panel was asked, among other things, to assess the probability of a recession, defined as a decline in the real gross national product from the last quarter. The survey was conducted at the beginning of the second month of each quarter (i.e., four times per year), and each participant was asked to provide five probability assessments; one for the current quarter (Q0) and one for each of the following four quarters, denoted Q1 through Q4. The present analysis is based on the work of Braun and Yaniv (1992), who selected a subsample of 40 forecasters for whom a substantial number of predictions were available.

Figures 13.4 and 13.5 contain, respectively, the designated and the inclusive calibration plots for the prediction of recession in the current quarter, pooled across all 40 forecasters. The number of observations is given for each point. The designated plot (figure 13.4) indicates the presence of specific overconfidence, or bias, favoring

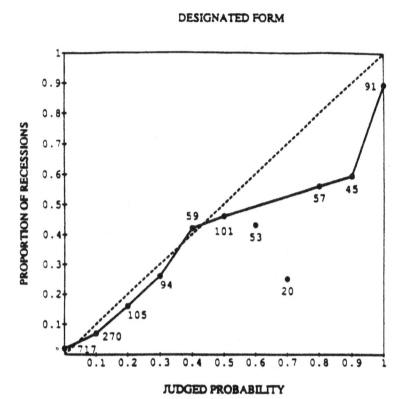

Figure 13.4
Designated calibration plot for the forecast of recession. (The solid line connects adjacent nondecreasing points.)

recession. Overall, mean confidence in the prediction of recession was 24%, whereas the overall rate of recession was only 19%. The inclusive plot (figure 13.5) reveals a modest departure from calibration, indicating generic overconfidence. Overall mean confidence in the forecaster's favored hypothesis was 91%, compared with a hit rate of 81%. Recall that specific overconfidence in the prediction of recession can be associated with generic overconfidence, generic underconfidence, or neither.

Conclusions based on aggregate plots (e.g., figures 13.4 and 13.5) should be validated in the data of individual respondents, because aggregation over subjects can alter the picture. The pooled data can be perfectly calibrated, for example, if the probability of recession is overestimated by some subjects and underestimated by others. The following discussion is based on the analysis of individual data.

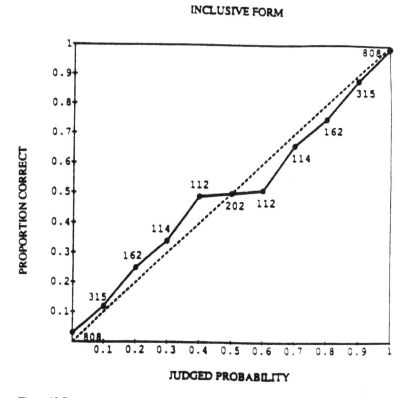

Figure 13.5
Inclusive calibration plot of the forecast of recession. (The solid line connects adjacent nondecreasing points.)

For each of the 40 forecasters, we computed, separately for each quarter, C' and R' using the designated form (equation 1) and C and R using the inclusive form (equation 2). We also computed the Brier score S and the monotonicity index M (equation 3) separately for each subject. The means of these measures are presented in figures 13.6, 13.7, and 13.8 for each of the five quarters. The vertical lines denote ± 1 standard error.

Figure 13.6 displays the mean values of C and C'. It shows that C is significantly smaller than C', and that both C and C' are relatively insensitive to the prediction horizon, with the possible exception of Q4. Figure 13.7 displays the mean values of R and R'. As expected, both measures of resolution are higher for short-term than for long-term predictions. In addition, R is substantially greater than R'. Recall that $C' \geq C$ (see the appendix, part B), but there is no necessary relation between R

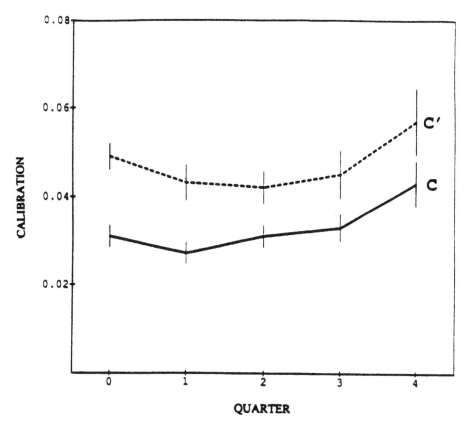

Figure 13.6
Calibration measures (C and C') for forecasts of recession.

and R'. However, R is bounded by .25, whereas R' is bounded by the variance of the designated outcome variable V, which equals $(.19)(.81) = .15$. This fact may help explain the observed difference between R and R'. Taken together, figures 13.6 and 13.7 show that the inclusive measures are more flattering than the designated measures.

Figure 13.8 contains the mean values of the ordinal measure M and the cardinal measure S. To facilitate the comparison of the two indices, we "matched" their ranges by plotting the linear transform $S^* = 1 - 4S$ instead of S. Note that S^*, like M, equals 1 if the judge is perfect, and S^* equals 0 if the judge makes the same forecast (i.e., .5) in each case. As expected, both M and S^* decrease as the prediction horizon increases. Indeed, the forecasts for the current quarter (Q0) are reasonably

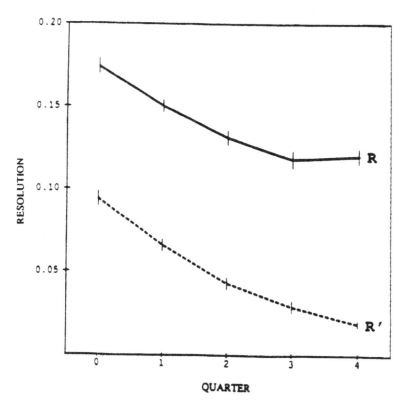

Figure 13.7
Resolution measures (R and R') for forecasts of recession.

accurate ($M = .74$, $S^* = .57$), but the forecasts for the last quarter (Q4) are no better than chance ($M = -.06$, $S^* = .31$). To interpret the value of S^*, note that forecasting the base rate of recession (.19) in every case yields $S = .81(.19)^2 + .19(.81)^2 = .154$, which gives an S^* of .384. In terms of the Brier score, therefore, the economists' forecasts for the last two quarters are inferior, on average, to a flat base rate; for discussion, see Braun and Yaniv (1992).

Figure 13.8 also shows that the slope of M is steeper than the slope of S^*. Perhaps more important, M is more sensitive than S^* in the sense that it yields greater separation (i.e., smaller overlap) between the distributions of performance measures for successive quarters. As a consequence, it provides a more powerful statistical test for differences in performance. For example, the hypothesis that the quality of forecasts

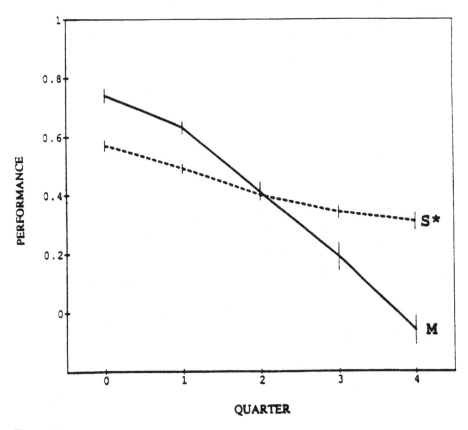

Figure 13.8
Performance measures (M and S^*) for forecasts of recession.

is the same for the last two quarters can be soundly rejected for M but not for S^*. The respective t statistics are 5.2 and 1.2

To explore further the relations between the indices we computed, separately for each forecaster in each quarter, the product–moment correlation between the ordinal measure M and the standard measures S, R, and C. The average correlation, across all subjects and periods, between M and S is $-.64$, between M and R is $.51$, and between M and C is $-.36$. Thus, M correlates quite highly with the Brier score S, slightly lower with the resolution measure R, and still lower with the calibration measure C. The average correlation between C and R is only $-.17$. Taken together with the observation that C does not vary greatly across quarters, whereas R, S^*, and

M decrease from Q0 to Q4, it appears that the degree of calibration is relatively insensitive to the accuracy of prediction.

Categorical Prediction

Fischhoff, MacGregor, and Lichtenstein (1983) introduced a novel elicitation procedure that requires sorting events prior to their evaluation. Subjects were presented with 50 general-knowledge questions. Each question had two alternative answers, one correct and one incorrect. In the first phase, subjects went through all 50 items and chose, in each case, the answer they thought was correct. After the selection phase, subjects were instructed to sort the items into a fixed number of piles and assign to each pile a number (between .5 and 1) that expresses the probability that the chosen answer for each item in the pile is correct. Four different groups of 50, 42, 38, and 32 subjects sorted the same 50 items into three, four, five, or six piles, respectively.

For each subject, we computed the values of S, C, R, and M. Because the pattern of results was essentially independent of the number of piles, we pooled the individual estimates across the four conditions.[6] The average value of S was .255, yielding an S^* of $-.020$, which provides no new evidence of knowledge because an S^* of 0 can be achieved by assigning a probability of one half to all items. In contrast, the ordinal analysis yields an average M of .287, which shows that the subjects performed considerably better than chance. Indeed, M was positive for 90% of the subjects ($p < .001$ by sign test), but S^* was positive for only 46% of the subjects. Hence, the hypothesis of total ignorance could be rejected for M but not for S. In other words, M provided a more sensitive measure of performance in the sense that it detected knowledge that was not detected by the Brier score. This situation occurred because $S^* = 0$ (or, equivalently, $S = .25$) either when the judge is totally ignorant and assigns probability .5 to all items or when the judge possesses some knowledge but is heavily penalized by the quadratic scoring rule. Therefore, an S^* of 0 does not have an unequivocal interpretation: It may represent either total ignorance and proper calibration or a combination of partial knowledge and poor calibration. This problem does not arise with respect to the ordinal index because $M = 0$ iff the judge produces an equal number of valid and invalid distinctions (i.e., $v = w$).

The pattern of correlations between the indices is similar to that observed in the predictions of recession, but the actual correlations are considerably higher. The average correlation, across all subjects and conditions, between M and S is $-.88$, between M and R is .82, and between M and C is $-.68$. The average correlation between R and C is only $-.40$. These results reinforce the previous conclusion that calibration is only weakly related to accuracy.

To interpret the correlations between the measures, recall that S as well as C and C' depend on the actual numerical values assessed by the judge, M depends on their order only, whereas R and R' depend merely on the equivalence classes formed by the judge, irrespective of their labels. Changing the judged probability of each event from p to $1 - p$, for example, has no effect on R and R', although it has a profound effect on all other measures. Note that M, like R, reflects the assessor's ability to distinguish among likely and less likely events, independent of the use of the probability scale. Hence, M is conceptually closer to R than to C. However, nonmonotonicity in the calibration plot ($q > r$ but $f_q < f_r$) affects the Brier score (S) through C, not through R. Consequently, we expected (a) a moderate correlation between M and C, (b) a substantial correlation between M and R, and (c) an even higher correlation between M and S because S incorporates both C and R. The correlations observed in the previous studies confirmed these expectations.

Summary and Conclusions

We discussed in this chapter three distinctions that pertain to the analysis and the evaluation of probability judgments: inclusive versus designated representations, generic versus specific overconfidence, and ordinal versus cardinal measures of performance. We argued that the inclusive and the designated indices measure different characteristics of probability judgments. Specifically, the inclusive indices C and R measure calibration and resolution at large, whereas the designated indices C' and R' measure, respectively, the bias associated with a particular designation and the improvement—beyond the base rate—in the prediction of a designated outcome variable. Both the inclusive and the designated indices could convey useful information, but the latter—unlike the former—are contingent on the coding of the outcomes.

We also distinguished calibration from two types of overconfidence: specific overconfidence, namely, overestimating the probability of a specific hypothesis, and generic confidence, namely, overestimating the probability of the hypothesis that is considered most likely. In the binary case, specific overconfidence implies $C' > 0$, whereas generic overconfidence implies $C > 0$. Finally, we proposed an ordinal measure of performance based on the separability criterion that can be used in addition to, or instead of, the standard measures. Applications of the ordinal analysis to several data sets suggest that the proposed index of monotonicity provides a reasonably sensitive and informative measure of performance. We conclude that the evaluation of probability judgments involves subtle conceptual problems and that the analysis of these data may benefit from the use of alternative representations and the comparison of different measures.

Notes

Varda Liberman, Open University of Israel, Tel Aviv, Israel; Amos Tversky, Department of Psychology, Stanford University.

This article has benefited from the comments of Alan Murphy, Ilan Yaniv, Frank Yates, Tom Wallsten, and Bob Winkler. The work was supported by Air Force Office of Scientific Research Grant 89-0064 and by National Science Foundation Grant SES-9109535, to Amos Tversky.

1. If a judge insists on assigning, say, probability .4 to an event and probability .3 to its complement, there is little point in assessing the calibration of these data; however, they could be treated ordinally.

2. He used the terms *scalar* and *vector representations* to describe what we call *inclusive* and *designated forms*, respectively.

3. Underconfidence is defined similarly.

4. Note that the extensions of Kendall's τ to tied observations are not consistent with the formulation above and, as a result, do not have a probabilistic interpretation.

5. We are grateful to Braun and Yaniv, to Fischhoff, MacGregor, and Lichtenstein, and to Wallsten, Budescu, and Zwick for providing us with their primary unpublished data.

6. Fischhoff, MacGregor, and Lichtenstein (1983) found no significant differences in overconfidence among the four groups.

References

Braun, P., & Yaniv, I. (1992). A case study of expert judgment: Economists' probabilities versus base-rate model forecasts. *Journal of Behavioral Decision Research, 5*, 217–231.

Brier, G. W. (1950). Verification of forecasts expressed in terms of probability. *Monthly Weather Review*, 1–3.

Dawes, R. M., Faust, D., & Meehl, P. E. (1989). Clinical versus actuarial judgment. *Science, 243*, 1668–1674.

Fischhoff, B., MacGregor, D., & Lichtenstein, S. (1983). *Categorical confidence* (Tech. Rep. No. 81-10). Eugene, OR: Decision Research Corporation.

Freeman, L. C. (1986). Order-based statistics and monotonicity: A family of ordinal measures of association. *Journal of Mathematical Sociology, 12*(1), 49–69.

Goodman, L. A., & Kruskal, W. H. (1954). Measures of association for cross-classifications. *Journal of the American Statistical Association, 49*, 733–764.

Goodman, L. A., & Kruskal, W. H. (1959). Measures of association for cross-classifications: II. Further discussion and references. *Journal of the American Statistical Association, 54*, 123–163.

Kahneman, D., Slovic, P., & Tversky, A. (1982). *Judgment under uncertainty: Heuristics and biases.* Cambridge, England: Cambridge University Press.

Kim, J. O. (1971). Predictive measures of ordinal association. *American Journal of Sociology, 76*, 891–907.

Lichtenstein, S., Fischhoff, B., & Phillips, L. (1982). Calibration of probabilities: The state of the art to 1980. In D. Kahneman, P. Slovic, & A. Tversky (Eds.), *Judgment under uncertainty: Heuristics and biases.* New York: Cambridge University Press.

Mosteller, F., & Youtz, C. (1990). Quantifying probabilistic expressions. *Statistical Science, 6*, 2–34.

Murphy, A. H. (1972). Scalar and vector partitions of the probability score: Part I. Two-state situation. *Journal of Applied Meteorology, 11*, 273–282.

Murphy, A. H. (1973). A new vector partition of the probability score. *Journal of Applied Meteorology, 12*, 595–600.

Murphy, A. H., & Daan, H. (1985). Forecast evaluation. In A. H. Murphy & R. W. Katz (Eds.), *Probability, statistics, and decision making in the atmospheric sciences* (pp. 379–437). Boulder, CO: Westview Press.

Murphy, A. H., & Winkler, R. L. (1992). Diagnostic verification of probability forecasts. *International Journal of Forecasting, 7*, 435–455.

Nelson, T. O. (1984). A comparison of current measures of accuracy of feeling-of-knowing predictions. *Psychological Bulletin, 95*, 109–133.

Oskamp, S. (1965). Overconfidence in case-study judgments. *Journal of Consulting Psychology, 29*, 261–265.

Sanders, F. (1963). On subjective probability forecasting. *Journal of Applied Meteorology, 1*, 191–201.

Somers, R. H. (1962). A new asymmetric measure of association for ordinal variables. *American Sociological Review, 27*, 799–811.

Wallsten, T. S., & Budescu, D. V. (1983). Encoding subjective probabilities: A psychological and psychometric review. *Management Science, 29*, 151–173.

Wallsten, T. S., Budescu, D. V., & Zwick, R. (in press). Comparing the calibration and coherence of numerical and verbal probability judgments. *Management Science.*

Wilson, T. P. (1974). Measures of association for bivariate ordinal hypotheses. In H. M. Blalock (Ed.), *Measurement in the social sciences* (pp. 327–341). Chicago: Aldine.

Winkler, R. L. (1986). On "good probability appraisers." In P. Goel & A. Zellner (Eds.), *Bayesian inference and decision techniques* (pp. 265–278). Amsterdam: North-Holland.

Yaniv, I., Yates, J. F., & Smith, J. E. K. (1991). Measures of discrimination skill in probabilistic judgment. *Psychological Bulletin, 110*, 611–617.

Yates, J. F. (1982). External correspondence: Decompositions of the mean probability score. *Organizational Behavior and Human Performance, 30*, 132–156.

Yates, J. F. (1990). *Judgment and decision making.* Englewood Cliffs, NJ: Prentice-Hall.

Zarnowitz, V. (1985). Rational expectations and macroeconomic forecasts. *Journal of Business and Economic Statistics, 3*, 293–311.

Zarnowitz, V., & Lambros, L. A. (1987). Consensus and uncertainty in economic prediction. *Journal of Political Economy, 95*, 591–621.

Appendix

This appendix is included to make the present treatment self-contained. The basic results can be found in Murphy (1972, 1973); they are restated here in terms of the present notation.

Part A
We first establish the decomposition:

$$S = \frac{1}{n}\sum_p N_p(p - f_p)^2 + f(1 - f) - \frac{1}{n}\sum_p N_p(f_p - f)^2 = C' + V - R'.$$

Recall that the score S is defined by

$$S = \frac{1}{n}\sum_{i=1}^{n}(p_i - \chi_i)^2,$$

where p_i is the judged probability of the event E_i and x_i equals 1 if E_i occurs and 0 otherwise.

Let N_p = the number of times the judged probability of the designated event equals p, f_p = the relative frequency of occurrence in that class, $I(p) = \{i : p_i = p\}$, f = the overall frequency of the designated event. Then

$$S = \frac{1}{n}\sum_{p}\sum_{I(p)}(p - \chi_i)^2.$$

Because

$$\sum_{I(p)}\chi_i = \sum_{I(p)}\chi_i^2 = f_p N_p,$$

$$\sum_{I(p)}(p - \chi_i)^2 = N_p p^2 - 2p f_p N_p + f_p N_p$$
$$= N_p(p^2 - 2p f_p + f_p^2) + N_p(f_p - f_p^2)$$
$$= N_p(p - f_p)^2 + N_p f_p(1 - f_p).$$

Thus,

$$S = \frac{1}{n}\sum_{p}\sum_{I(p)}(p - \chi_i)^2$$

$$= \frac{1}{n}\sum_{p}N_p(p - f_p)^2 + \frac{1}{n}\sum_{p}N_p f_p(1 - f_p)$$

$$= \frac{1}{n}\sum_{p}N_p(p - f_p)^2 + \frac{1}{n}\sum_{p}N_p f_p - \frac{1}{n}\sum_{p}N_p f_p^2.$$

Note that

$$\frac{1}{n}\sum_{p}N_p f_p = f$$

and

$$\frac{1}{n}\sum_p N_p f_p^2 = \frac{1}{n}\sum_p N_p (f_p - f)^2 + f^2.$$

Hence,

$$S = \frac{1}{n}\sum_p N_p (p - f_p)^2 + f - \frac{1}{n}\sum_p N_p (f_p - f)^2 - f^2$$

$$= \frac{1}{n}\sum_p N_p (p - f_p)^2 + f(1 - f) - \frac{1}{n}\sum_p N_p (f_p - f)^2$$

$$= C' + V - R'.$$

Part B

We next show that $C \le C'$ where

$$C' = \frac{1}{n}\sum_p N_p (p - f_q)^2$$

and

$$C' = \frac{1}{2n}\sum_q N_q (q - f_q)^2 = \frac{1}{2n}\sum_p (N_p + N_{1-p})(p - f_q)^2$$

where

$$f_q = \frac{N_p f_p + N_{1-p}(1 - f_{1-p})}{N_p + N_{1-p}}$$

But,

$$\frac{1}{n}\sum_p N_p (p - f_p)^2 = \frac{1}{2n}\sum_p 2N_p (p - f_p)^2$$

$$= \frac{1}{2n}\sum_p [N_p (p - f_p)^2 + N_{1-p}(1 - p - f_{1-p})^2],$$

so we have to prove that

$$(N_p + N_{1-p})(p - f_q)^2 \le N_p (p - f_p)^2 + N_{1-p}(1 - p - f_{1-p})^2$$

or

$$(N_p + N_{1-p})f_q^2 \le N_p f_p^2 + N_{1-p}(1 - f_{1-p})^2.$$

Using the fact that

$$f_q = \frac{N_p f_p + N_{1-p}(1 - f_{1-p})}{N_p + N_{1-p}},$$

it suffices to show that

$$[N_p f_p + N_{1-p}(1 - f_{1-p})]^2 \le (N_p + N_{1-p})[N_p f_p^2 + N_{1-p}(1 - f_{1-p})]^2$$

or

$$2f_p(1 - f_{1-p}) \le f_p^2 + (1 - f_{1-p})^2,$$

which is clearly true.

14 Support Theory: A Nonextensional Representation of Subjective Probability

Amos Tversky and Derek J. Koehler

Both laypeople and experts are often called upon to evaluate the probability of uncertain events such as the outcome of a trial, the result of a medical operation, the success of a business venture, or the winner of a football game. Such assessments play an important role in deciding, respectively, whether to go to court, undergo surgery, invest in the venture, or bet on the home team. Uncertainty is usually expressed in verbal terms (e.g., unlikely or probable), but numerical estimates are also common. Weather forecasters, for example, often report the probability of rain (Murphy, 1985), and economists are sometimes required to estimate the chances of recession (Zarnowitz, 1985). The theoretical and practical significance of subjective probability has inspired psychologists, philosophers, and statisticians to investigate this notion from both descriptive and prescriptive standpoints.

Indeed, the question of whether degree of belief can, or should be, represented by the calculus of chance has been the focus of a long and lively debate. In contrast to the Bayesian school, which represents degree of belief by an additive probability measure, there are many skeptics who question the possibility and the wisdom of quantifying subjective uncertainty and are reluctant to apply the laws of chance to the analysis of belief. Besides the Bayesians and the skeptics, there is a growing literature on what might be called revisionist models of subjective probability. These include the Dempster–Shafer theory of belief (Dempster, 1967; Shafer, 1976), Zadeh's (1978) possibility theory, and the various types of upper and lower probabilities (e.g., see Suppes, 1974; Walley, 1991). Recent developments have been reviewed by Dubois and Prade (1988), Gilboa and Schmeidler (in press), and Mongin (in press). Like the Bayesians, the revisionists endorse the quantification of belief, using either direct judgments or preferences between bets, but they find the calculus of chance too restrictive for this purpose. Consequently, they replace the additive measure, used in the classical theory, with a nonadditive set function satisfying weaker requirements.

A fundamental assumption that underlies both the Bayesian and the revisionist models of belief is the extensionality principle: Events with the same extension are assigned the same probability. However, the extensionality assumption is descriptively invalid because alternative descriptions of the same event often produce systematically different judgments. The following three examples illustrate this phenomenon and motivate the development of a descriptive theory of belief that is free from the extensionality assumption.

1. Fischhoff, Slovic, and Lichtenstein (1978) asked car mechanics, as well as laypeople, to assess the probabilities of different causes of a car's failure to start. They

found that the mean probability assigned to the residual hypothesis—"The cause of failure is something other than the battery, the fuel system, or the engine"—increased from .22 to .44 when the hypothesis was broken up into more specific causes (e.g., the starting system, the ignition system). Although the car mechanics, who had an average of 15 years of experience, were surely aware of these possibilities, they discounted hypotheses that were not explicilty mentioned.

2. Tversky and Kahneman (1983) constructed many problems in which both probability and frequency judgments were not consistent with set inclusion. For example, one group of subjects was asked to estimate the number of seven-letter words in four pages of a novel that end with *ing*. A second group was asked to estimate the number of seven-letter words that end with $\_n\_$. The median estimate for the first question (13.4) was nearly three times higher than that for the second (4.7), presumably because it is easier to think of seven-letter words ending with *ing* than to think of seven-letter words with *n* in the sixth position. It appears that most people who evaluated the second category were not aware of the fact that it includes the first.

3. Violations of extensionality are not confined to probability judgments; they are also observed in the evaluation of uncertain prospects. For example, Johnson, Hershey, Meszaros, and Kunreuther (1993) found that subjects who were offered (hypothetical) health insurance that covers hospitalization for any disease or accident were willing to pay a higher premium than subjects who were offered health insurance that covers hospitalization for any reason. Evidently, the explicit mention of disease and accident increases the perceived chances of hospitalization and, hence, the attractiveness of insurance.

These observations, like many others described later in this article, are inconsistent with the extensionality principle. We distinguish two sources of nonextensionality. First, extensionality may fail because of memory limitation. As illustrated in example 2, a judge cannot be expected to recall all of the instances of a category, even when he or she can recognize them without error. An explicit description could remind people of relevant cases that might otherwise slip their minds. Second, extensionality may fail because different descriptions of the same event may call attention to different aspects of the outcome and thereby affect their relative salience. Such effects can influence probability judgments even when they do not bring to mind new instances or new evidence.

The common failures of extensionality, we suggest, represent an essential feature of human judgment, not a collection of isolated examples. They indicate that probability judgments are attached not to events but to descriptions of events. In this article, we present a theory in which the judged probability of an event depends on the explicitness of its description. This treatment, called *support theory*, focuses on direct judgments of probability, but it is also applicable to decision under uncertainty. The basic theory is introduced and characterized in the next section. The experimental evidence is reviewed in the subsequent section. In the final section, we extend the theory to ordinal judgments, discuss upper and lower indicators of belief, and address descriptive and prescriptive implications of the present development.

Support Theory

Let T be a finite set including at least two elements, interpreted as states of the world. We assume that exactly one state obtains but it is generally not known to the judge. Subsets of T are called *events*. We distinguish between events and descriptions of events, called *hypotheses*. Let H be a set of hypotheses that describe the events in T. Thus, we assume that each hypothesis $A \in H$ corresponds to a unique event $A' \subset T$. This is a many-to-one mapping because different hypotheses, say A and B, may have the same extension (i.e., $A' = B'$). For example, suppose one rolls a pair of dice. The hypotheses "The sum is 3" and "The product is 2" are different descriptions of the same event; namely, one die shows 1 and the other shows 2. We assume that H is finite and that it includes at least one hypothesis for each event. The following relations on H are induced by the corresponding relations on T. A is *elementary* if $A' \in T$. A is *null* if $A' = \varnothing$. A and B are *exclusive* if $A' \cap B' = \varnothing$. If A and B are in H, and they are exclusive, then their explicit disjunction, denoted $A \vee B$, is also in H. Thus, H is closed under exclusive disjunction. We assume that $\vee$ is associative and commutative and that $(A \vee B)' = A' \cup B'$.

A key feature of the present formulation is the distinction between explicit and implicit disjunctions. A is an *implicit disjunction*, or simply an implicit hypothesis, if it is neither elementary nor null, and it is not an explicit disjunction (i.e., there are no exclusive nonnull B, C in H such that $A = B \vee C$). For example, suppose A is "Ann majors in a natural science," B is "Ann majors in a biological science," and C is "Ann majors in a physical science." The explicit disjunction, $B \vee C$ ("Ann majors in either a biological or a physical science"), has the same extension as A (i.e., $A' = (B \vee C)' = B' \cup C'$), but A is an implicit hypothesis because it is not an explicit disjunction. Note that the explicit disjunction $B \vee C$ is defined for any exclusive $B, C \in H$, whereas a coextensional implicit disjunction may not exist because some events cannot be naturally described without listing their components.

An *evaluation frame* (A, B) consists of a pair of exclusive hypotheses: The first element A is the *focal* hypothesis that the judge evaluates, and the second element B

is the *alternative* hypothesis. To simplify matters, we assume that when A and B are exclusive, the judge perceives them as such, but we do not assume that the judge can list all of the constituents of an implicit disjunction. In terms of the above example, we assume that the judge knows, for instance, that genetics is a biological science, that astronomy is a physical science, and that the biological and the physical sciences are exclusive. However, we do not assume that the judge can list all of the biological or the physical sciences. Thus, we assume recognition of inclusion but not perfect recall.

We interpret a person's probability judgment as a mapping P from an evaluation frame to the unit interval. To simplify matters we assume that $P(A, B)$ equals zero if and only if A is null and that it equals one if and only if B is null; we assume that A and B are not both null. Thus, $P(A, B)$ is the judged probability that A rather than B holds, assuming that one and only one of them is valid. Obviously, A and B may each represent an explicit or an implicit disjunction. The extensional counterpart of $P(A, B)$ in the standard theory is the conditional probability $P(A' \mid A' \cup B')$. The present treatment is nonextensional because it assumes that probability judgment depends on the descriptions A and B, not just on the events A' and B'. We wish to emphasize that the present theory applies to the hypotheses entertained by the judge, which do not always coincide with the given verbal descriptions. A judge presented with an implicit disjunction may, nevertheless, think about it as an explicit disjunction, and vice versa.

Support theory assumes that there is a ratio scale s (interpreted as degree of support) that assigns to each hypothesis in H a nonnegative real number such that, for any pair of exclusive hypotheses $A, B \in$ H,

$$P(A, B) = \frac{s(A)}{s(A) + s(B)}. \tag{1}$$

If B and C are exclusive, A is implicit, and $A' = (B \vee C)'$, then

$$s(A) \leq s(B \vee C) = s(B) + s(C). \tag{2}$$

Equation 1 provides a representation of subjective probability in terms of the support of the focal and the alternative hypotheses. Equation 2 states that the support of an implicit disjunction A is less than or equal to that of a coextensional explicit disjunction $B \vee C$ that equals the sum of the support of its components. Thus, support is additive for explicit disjunctions and subadditive for implicit ones.

The subadditivity assumption, we suggest, represents a basic principle of human judgment. When people assess their degree of belief in an implicit disjunction, they do not normally unpack the hypothesis into its exclusive components and add their support, as required by extensionality. Instead, they tend to form a global impression that is based primarily on the most representative or available cases. Because this mode of judgment is selective rather than exhaustive, unpacking tends to increase support. In other words, we propose that the support of a summary representation of an implicit hypothesis is generally less than the sum of the support of its exclusive components. Both memory and attention may contribute to this effect. Unpacking a category (e.g., death from an unnatural cause) into its components (e.g., homicide, fatal car accidents, drowning) might remind people of possibilities that would not have been considered otherwise. Moreover, the explicit mention of an outcome tends to enhance its salience and hence its support. Although this assumption may fail in some circumstances, the overwhelming evidence for subadditivity, described in the next section, indicates that these failures represent the exception rather than the rule.

The support associated with a given hypothesis is interpreted as a measure of the strength of evidence in favor of this hypothesis that is available to the judge. The support may be based on objective data (e.g., the frequency of homicide in the relevant population) or on a subjective impression mediated by judgmental heuristics, such as representativeness, availability, or anchoring and adjustment (Kahneman, Slovic, & Tversky, 1982). For example, the hypothesis "Bill is an accountant" may be evaluated by the degree to which Bill's personality matches the stereotype of an accountant, and the prediction "An oil spill along the eastern coast before the end of next year" may be assessed by the ease with which similar accidents come to mind. Support may also reflect reasons or arguments recruited by the judge in favor of the hypothesis in question (e.g., if the defendant were guilty, he would not have reported the crime). Because judgments based on impressions and reasons are often nonextensional, the support function is nonmonotonic with respect to set inclusion. Thus, $s(B)$ may exceed $s(A)$ even though $A' \supset B'$. Note, however, that $s(B)$ cannot exceed $s(B \vee C)$. For example, if the support of a category is determined by the availability of its instances, then the support of the hypothesis that a randomly selected word ends with *ing* can exceed the support of the hypothesis that the word ends with $\_n\_$. Once the inclusion relation between the categories is made transparent, the $\_n\_$ hypothesis is replaced by "*ing* or any other $\_n\_$," whose support exceeds that of the *ing* hypothesis.

The present theory provides an interpretation of subjective probability in terms of relative support. This interpretation suggests that, in some cases, probability judgment may be predicted from independent assessments of support. This possibility is explored later. The following discussion shows that, under the present theory, support can be derived from probability judgments, much as utility is derived from preferences between options.

Consequences

Support theory has been formulated in terms of the support function s, which is not directly observable. We next characterize the theory in terms of the observed index P. We first exhibit four consequences of the theory and then show that they imply equations 1 and 2. An immediate consequence of the theory is *binary complementarity*:

$$P(A, B) + P(B, A) = 1. \tag{3}$$

A second consequence is *proportionality*:

$$\frac{P(A, B)}{P(B, A)} = \frac{P(A, B \vee C)}{P(B, A \vee C)}, \tag{4}$$

provided that A, B, and C are mutually exclusive and B is not null. Thus, the "odds" for A against B are independent of the additional hypothesis C.

To formulate the next condition, it is convenient to introduce the probability ratio $R(A, B) = P(A, B)/P(B, A)$, which is the odds for A against B. Equation 1 implies the following *product rule*:

$$R(A, B)R(C, D) = R(A, D)R(C, B), \tag{5}$$

provided that A, B, C, and D are not null and the four pairs of hypotheses in Equation 5 are pairwise exclusive. Thus, the product of the odds for A against B and for C against D equals the product of the odds for A against D and for C against B. To see the necessity of the product rule, note that, according to equation 1, both sides of equation 5 equal $s(A)s(C)/s(B)s(D)$. Essentially the same condition has been used in the theory of preference trees (Tversky & Sattath, 1979).

Equations 1 and 2 together imply the *unpacking principle*. Suppose B, C, and D are mutually exclusive, A is implicit, and $A' = (B \vee C)'$. Then

$$P(A, D) \leq P(B \vee C, D) = P(B, C \vee D) + P(C, B \vee D). \tag{6}$$

The properties of s entail the corresponding properties of P: Judged probability is additive for explicit disjunctions and subadditive for implicit disjunctions. In other words, unpacking an implicit disjunction may increase, but not decrease, its judged probability. Unlike equations 3–5, which hold in the standard theory of probability, the unpacking principle (equation 6) generalizes the classical model. Note that this assumption is at variance with lower probability models, including Shafer's (1976), which assume extensionality and superadditivity (i.e., $P(A' \cup B') \geq P(A') + P(B')$ if $A' \cap B' = \varnothing$).

There are two conflicting intuitions that yield nonadditive probability. The first intuition, captured by support theory, suggests that unpacking an implicit disjunction enhances the salience of its components and consequently increases support. The second intuition, captured by Shafer's (1976) theory, among others, suggests that—in the face of partial ignorance—the judge holds some measure of belief "in reserve" and does not distribute it among all elementary hypotheses, as required by the Bayesian model. Although Shafer's theory is based on a logical rather than a psychological analysis of belief, it has also been interpreted by several authors as a descriptive model. Thus, it provides a natural alternative to be compared with the present theory.

Whereas proportionality (equation 4) and the product rule (equation 5) have not been systematically tested before, a number of investigators have observed binary complementarity (equation 3) and some aspects of the unpacking principle (equation 6). These data, as well as several new studies, are reviewed in the next section. The following theorem shows that the above conditions are not only necessary but also sufficient for support theory. The proof is given in the appendix.

THEOREM 1   Suppose $P(A, B)$ is defined for all exclusive $A, B \in H$ and that it vanishes if and only if A is null. Equations 3–6 hold if and only if there exists a nonnegative ratio scale s on H that satisfies equations 1 and 2.

The theorem shows that if probability judgments satisfy the required conditions, it is possible to scale the support or strength of evidence associated with each hypothesis without assuming that hypotheses with the same extension have equal support. An ordinal generalization of the theory, in which P is treated as an ordinal rather than cardinal scale, is presented in the final section. In the remainder of this section, we introduce a representation of subadditivity and a treatment of conditioning.

Subadditivity

We extend the theory by providing a more detailed representation of subadditivity. Let A be an implicit hypothesis with the same extension as the explicit disjunction of the elementary hypotheses $A_1, \ldots, A_n$; that is, $A' = (A_1 \vee \cdots \vee A_n)'$. Assume that any two elementary hypotheses, B and C, with the same extension have the same support; that is, $B', C' \in T$ and $B' = C'$ implies $s(B) = s(C)$. It follows that, under this assumption we can write

$$s(A) = w_{1A}s(A_1) + \cdots + w_{nA}s(A_n), \quad 0 \leq w_{iA} \leq 1, \ i = 1, \ldots, n. \tag{7}$$

In this representation, the support of each elementary hypothesis is "discounted" by its respective weight, which reflects the degree to which the judge attends to the hypothesis in question. If $w_{iA} = 1$ for all i, then $s(A)$ is the sum of the support of its elementary hypotheses, as in an explicit disjunction. On the other hand, $w_{jA} = 0$ for some j indicates that A_j is effectively ignored. Finally, if the weights add to one, then $s(A)$ is a weighted average of the $s(A_i)$, $1 \leq i \leq n$. We hasten to add that equation 7 should not be interpreted as a process of deliberate discounting in which the judge assesses the support of an implicit disjunction by discounting the assessed support of the corresponding explicit disjunction. Instead, the weights are meant to represent the result of an assessment process in which the judge evaluates A without explicitly unpacking it into its elementary components. It should also be kept in mind that elementary hypotheses are defined relative to a given sample space. Such hypotheses may be broken down further by refining the level of description.

Note that whereas the support function is unique, except for a unit of measurement, the "local" weights w_{iA} are not uniquely determined by the observed probability judgments. These data, however, determine the "global" weights w_A defined by

$$s(A) = w_A[s(A_1) + \cdots + s(A_n)], \quad 0 \leq w_A \leq 1. \tag{8}$$

The global weight w_A, which is the ratio of the support of the corresponding implicit (A) and explicit ($A_1 \vee \cdots \vee A_n$) disjunctions, provides a convenient measure of the degree of subadditivity induced by A. The degree of subadditivity, we propose, is influenced by several factors, one of which is the interpretation of the probability scale. Specifically, subadditivity is expected to be more pronounced when probability is interpreted as a propensity of an individual case than when it is equated with, or estimated by, relative frequency. Kahneman and Tversky (1979, 1982) referred to these modes of judgment as singular and distributional, respectively, and argued that the latter is usually more accurate than the former[1] (see also Reeves & Lockhart, 1993). Although many events of interest cannot be interpreted in frequentistic terms, there are questions that can be framed in either a distributional or a singular mode. For example, people may be asked to assess the probability that an individual, selected at random from the general population, will die as a result of an accident. Alternatively, people may be asked to assess the percentage (or relative frequency) of the population that will die as a result of an accident. We propose that the implicit disjunction "accident" is more readily unpacked into its components (e.g., car accidents, plane crashes, fire, drowning, poisoning) when the judge considers the entire population rather than a single person. The various causes of death are all represented in the population's mortality statistics but not in the death of a single person. More generally, we propose that the tendency to unpack an implicit disjunction is stronger in the distributional than in the singular mode. Hence, a frequentistic formulation is expected to produce less discounting (i.e., higher ws) than a formulation that refers to an individual case.

Conditioning

Recall that $P(A, B)$ is interpreted as the conditional probability of A, given A or B. To obtain a general treatment of conditioning, we enrich the hypothesis set H by assuming that if A and B are distinct elements of H, then their conjunction, denoted AB, is also in H. Naturally, we assume that conjunction is associative and commutative and that $(AB)' = A' \cap B'$. We also assume distributivity, that is, $A(B \vee C) = AB \vee AC$. Let $P(A, B \mid D)$ be the judged probability that A rather than B holds, given some data D. In general, new evidence (i.e., a different state of information) gives rise to a new support function s_D that describes the revision of s in light of D. In the special case in which the data can be described as an element of H, which merely restricts the hypotheses under consideration, we can represent conditional probability by

$$P(A, B \mid D) = \frac{s(AD)}{s(AD) + s(BD)}, \tag{9}$$

provided that A and B are exclusive but $A \vee B$ and D are not.

Several comments on this form are in order. First, note that if s is additive, then equation 9 reduces to the standard definition of conditional probability. If s is subadditive, as we have assumed throughout, then judged probability depends not only on the description of the focal and the alternative hypotheses but also on the description of the evidence D. Suppose $D' = (D_1 \vee D_2)'$, D_1 and D_2 are exclusive, and D is implicit. Then

$$P(A, B \mid D_1 \vee D_2) = \frac{s(AD_1 \vee AD_2)}{s(AD_1 \vee AD_2) + s(BD_1 \vee BD_2)}.$$

But because $s(AD) \leq s(AD_1 \vee AD_2)$ and $s(BD) \leq s(BD_1 \vee BD_2)$ by subadditivity, the unpacking of D may favor one hypothesis over another. For example, the judged probability that a woman earns a very high salary given that she is a university professor is likely to increase when "university" is unpacked into "law school, business school, medical school, or any other school" because of the explicit mention of high-paying positions. Thus, equation 9 extends the application of subadditivity to the representation of evidence. As we show later, it also allows us to compare the impact of different bodies of evidence, provided they can be described as elements of H.

Consider a collection of $n \geq 3$ mutually exclusive and exhaustive (nonnull) hypotheses, $A_1 \ldots A_n$, and let $\bar{A}_i$ denote the negation of A_i that corresponds to an implicit disjunction of the remaining hypotheses. Consider two items of evidence, $B, C \in H$, and suppose that each A_i is more compatible with B than with C in the sense that $s(BA_i) \geq s(CA_i)$, $1 \leq i \leq n$. We propose that B induces more subadditivity than C so that $s(B\bar{A}_i)$ is discounted more heavily than $s(C\bar{A}_i)$ (i.e., $w_{B\bar{A}_i} \leq w_{C\bar{A}_i}$; see equation 7). This assumption, called *enhancement*, suggests that the assessments of $P(A_i, \bar{A}_i \mid B)$ will be generally higher than those of $P(A_i, \bar{A}_i \mid C)$. More specifically, we propose that the sum of the probabilities of $A_i \ldots A_n$, each evaluated by different judges,[2] is no smaller under B than under C. That is,

$$\sum_{i=1}^{n} P(A_i, \bar{A}_i \mid B) \geq \sum_{i=1}^{n} P(A_i, \bar{A}_i \mid C). \tag{10}$$

Subadditivity implies that both sums are greater than or equal to one. The preceding inequality states that the sum is increased by evidence that is more compatible with the hypotheses under study. It is noteworthy that enhancement suggests that people are inappropriately responsive to the prior probability of the data, whereas base-rate neglect indicates that people are not sufficiently responsive to the prior probability of the hypotheses. The following schematic example illustrates an implication of enhancement and compares it with other models.

Suppose that a murder was committed by one (and only one) of several suspects. In the absence of any specific evidence, assume that all suspects are considered about equally likely to have committed the crime. Suppose further that a preliminary investigation has uncovered a body of evidence (e.g., motives and opportunities) that implicates each of the suspects to roughly the same degree. According to the Bayesian model, the probabilities of all of the suspects remain unchanged because the new evidence is nondiagnostic. In Shafer's theory of belief functions, the judged probability that the murder was committed by one suspect rather than by another generally increases with the amount of evidence; thus, it should be higher after the investigation than before. Enhancement yields a different pattern: The binary probabilities (i.e., of one suspect against another) are expected to be approximately one half, both before and after the investigation, as in the Bayesian model. However, the probability that the murder was committed by a particular suspect (rather than by any of the others) is expected to increase with the amount of evidence. Experimental tests of enhancement are described in the next section.

Data

In this section, we discuss the experimental evidence for support theory. We show that the interpretation of judged probability in terms of a normalized subadditive support function provides a unified account of several phenomena reported in the literature; it also yields new predictions that have not been tested heretofore. This section consists of four parts. In the first part, we investigate the effect of unpacking and examine factors that influence the degree of subadditivity. In the second, we relate probability judgments to direct ratings of evidence strength. In the third, we investigate the enhancement effect and compare alternative models of belief. In the final part, we discuss the conjunction effect, hypothesis generation, and decision under uncertainty.

Studies of Unpacking

Recall that the unpacking principle (equation 6) consists of two parts: additivity for explicit disjunctions and subadditivity for implicit disjunctions, which jointly entail nonextensionality. (Binary complementarity [equation 3] is a special case of additivity.) Because each part alone is subject to alternative interpretations, it is important to test additivity and subadditivity simultaneously. For this reason, we first describe several new studies that have tested both parts of the unpacking principle within the same experiment, and then we review previous research that provided the impetus for the present theory.

Study 1: Causes of Death   Our first study followed the seminal work of Fischhoff et al. (1978) on fault trees, using a task similar to that studied by Russo and Kolzow (1992). We asked Stanford undergraduates ($N = 120$) to assess the likelihood of various possible causes of death. The subjects were informed that each year approximately 2 million people in the United States (nearly 1% of the population) die from different causes, and they were asked to estimate the probability of death from a variety of causes. Half of the subjects considered a single person who had recently died and assessed the probability that he or she had died from each in a list of specified causes. They were asked to assume that the person in question had been randomly selected from the set of people who had died the previous year. The other half, given a frequency judgment task, assessed the percentage of the 2 million deaths in the previous year attributable to each cause. In each group, half of the subjects were promised that the 5 most accurate subjects would receive $20 each.

Each subject evaluated one of two different lists of causes, constructed such that he or she evaluated either an implicit hypothesis (e.g., death resulting from natural causes) or a coextensional explicit disjunction (e.g., death resulting from heart disease, cancer, or some other natural cause), but not both. The full set of causes considered is listed in table 14.1. Causes of death were divided into natural and unnatural types. Each type had three components, one of which was further divided into seven subcomponents. To avoid very small probabilities, we conditioned these seven subcomponents on the corresponding type of death (i.e., natural or unnatural). To provide subjects with some anchors, we informed them that the probability or

Table 14.1
Mean Probability and Frequency Estimates for Causes of Death in Study 1, Comparing Evaluations of Explicit Disjunctions with Coextensional Implicit Disjunctions

	Mean estimate (%)		
Hypothesis	Probability	Frequency	Actual %
Three-component			
P(heart disease)	22	18	34.1
P(cancer)	18	20	23.1
P(other natural cause)	33	29	35.2
$\sum$(natural cause)	73	67	92.4
P(natural cause)	58	56	
$\sum/P$	1.26	1.20	
P(accident)	32	30	4.4
P(homicide)	10	11	1.1
P(other unnatural cause)	11	12	2.1
$\sum$(unnatural cause)	53	53	7.6
P(unnatural cause)	32	39	
$\sum/P$	1.66	1.36	
Seven-component			
P(respiratory cancer | natural)	12	11	7.1
P(digestive cancer | natural)	8	7	5.9
P(genitourinary cancer | natural)	5	3	2.7
P(breast cancer | natural)	13	9	2.2
P(urinary cancer | natural)	7	3	1.0
P(leukemia | natural)	8	6	1.0
P(other cancer | natural)	17	10	5.1
$\sum$(cancer | natural)	70	49	25.0
P(cancer | natural)	32	24	
$\sum/P$	2.19	2.04	
P(auto accident | unnatural)	33	33	30.3
P(firearm accident | unnatural)	7	12	1.3
P(accidental fall | unnatural)	6	4	7.9
P(death in fire | unnatural)	4	5	2.6
P(drowning | unnatural)	5	4	2.6
P(accidental poisoning | unnatural)	4	3	3.9
P(other accident | unnatural)	24	17	9.2
$\sum$(accident | unnatural)	83	78	57.9
P(accident | unnatural)	45	48	
$\sum/P$	1.84	1.62	

Note: Actual percentages were taken from the 1990 *U.S. Statistical Abstract.* $\sum$ = sum of mean estimates.

frequency of death resulting from respiratory illness is about 7.5% and the probability or frequency of death resulting from suicide is about 1.5%.

Table 14.1 shows that, for both probability and frequency judgments, the mean estimate of an implicit disjunction (e.g., death from a natural cause) is smaller than the sum of the mean estimates of its components (heart disease, cancer, or other natural causes), denoted $\sum$ (natural causes). Specifically, the former equals 58%, whereas the latter equals $22\% + 18\% + 33\% = 73\%$. All eight comparisons in table 14.1 are statistically significant ($p < .05$) by Mann–Whitney U test. (We used a nonparametric test because of the unequal variances involved when comparing a single measured variable with a sum of measured variables.)

Throughout this article, we use the ratio of the probabilities assigned to coextensional explicit and implicit hypotheses as a measure of subadditivity. The ratio in the preceding example is 1.26. This index, called the *unpacking factor*, can be computed directly from probability judgments, unlike w, which is defined in terms of the support function. Subadditivity is indicated by an unpacking factor greater than 1 and a value of w less than 1. It is noteworthy that subadditivity, by itself, does not imply that explicit hypotheses are overestimated or that implicit hypotheses are underestimated relative to an appropriate objective criterion. It merely indicates that the former are judged as more probable than the latter.

In this study, the mean unpacking factors were 1.37 for the three-component hypotheses and 1.92 for the seven-component hypotheses, indicating that the degree of subadditivity increased with the number of components in the explicit disjunction. An analysis of medians rather than means revealed a similar pattern, with somewhat smaller differences between packed and unpacked versions. Comparison of probability and frequency tasks showed, as expected, that subjects gave higher and thus more subadditive estimates when judging probabilities than when judging frequencies, $F(12, 101) = 2.03$, $p < .05$. The average unpacking factors were 1.74 for probability and 1.56 for frequency.

The judgments generally overestimated the actual values, obtained from the 1990 *U.S. Statistical Abstract*. The only clear exception was heart disease, which had an actual probability of 34% but received a mean judgment of 20%. Because subjects produced higher judgments of probability than of frequency, the former exhibited greater overestimation of the actual values, but the correlation between the estimated and actual values (computed separately for each subject) revealed no difference between the two tasks. Monetary incentives did not improve the accuracy of people's judgments.

The following design provides a more stringent test of support theory and compares it with alternative models of belief. Suppose $A_1, A_2,$ and B are mutually exclusive and exhaustive; $A' = (A_1 \vee A_2)'$; A is implicit; and $\bar{A}$ is the negation of A. Consider the following observable values:

$\alpha = P(A, B)$;

$\beta = P(A_1 \vee A_2, B)$;

$\gamma_1 = P(A_1, A_2 \vee B)$, $\gamma_2 = P(A_2, A_1 \vee B)$, $\gamma = \gamma_1 + \gamma_2$;   and

$\delta_1 = P(A_1, \bar{A}_1)$, $\delta_2 = (A_2, \bar{A}_2)$, $\delta = \delta_1 + \delta_2$.

Different models of belief imply different orderings of these values:

support theory, $\alpha \leq \beta = \gamma \leq \delta$;

Bayesian model, $\alpha = \beta = \gamma = \delta$;

belief function, $\alpha = \beta \geq \gamma = \delta$;   and

regressive model, $\alpha = \beta \leq \gamma = \delta$.

Support theory predicts $\alpha \leq \beta$ and $\gamma \leq \delta$ due to the unpacking of the focal and residual hypotheses, respectively; it also predicts $\beta = \gamma$ due to the additivity of explicit disjunctions. The Bayesian model implies $\alpha = \beta$ and $\gamma = \delta$, by extensionality, and $\beta = \gamma$, by additivity. Shafer's theory of belief functions also assumes extensionality, but it predicts $\beta \geq \gamma$ because of superadditivity. The above data, as well as numerous studies reviewed later, demonstrate that $\alpha < \delta$, which is consistent with support theory but inconsistent with both the Bayesian model and Shafer's theory.

The observation that $\alpha < \delta$ could also be explained by a *regressive model* that assumes that probability judgments satisfy extensionality but are biased toward .5 (e.g., see Erev, Wallsten, & Budescu, 1994). For example, the judge might start with a "prior" probability of .5 that is not revised sufficiently in light of the evidence. Random error could also produce regressive estimates. If each individual judgment is biased toward .5, then β, which consists of a single judgment, would be less than γ, which is the sum of two judgments. On the other hand, this model predicts no difference between α and β, each of which consists of a single judgment, or between γ and δ, each of which consists of two. Thus, support theory and the regressive model make different predictions about the source of the difference between α and δ. Support theory predicts subadditivity for implicit disjunctions (i.e., $\alpha \leq \beta$ and $\gamma \leq \delta$) and additivity for explicit disjunctions (i.e., $\beta = \gamma$), whereas the regressive model assumes extensionality (i.e., $\alpha = \beta$ and $\gamma = \delta$) and subadditivity for explicit disjunctions (i.e., $\beta \leq \gamma$).

Table 14.2
Mean and Median Probability Estimates for Various Causes of Death

Probability judgments	Mean	Median
$\beta = P(\text{accident or homicide, OUC})$	64	70
$\gamma_1 = P(\text{accident, homicide or OUC})$	53	60
$\gamma_2 = P(\text{homicide, accident or OUC})$	16	10
$\gamma = \gamma_1 + \gamma_2$	69	70
$\delta_1 = P(\text{accident, OUC})$	56	65
$\delta_2 = P(\text{homicide, OUC})$	24	18
$\delta = \delta_1 + \delta_2$	80	83

Note: OUC = other unnatural causes.

To contrast these predictions, we asked different groups (of 25 to 30 subjects each) to assess the probability of various unnatural causes of death. All subjects were told that a person had been randomly selected from the set of people who had died the previous year from an unnatural cause. The hypotheses under study and the corresponding probability judgments are summarized in table 14.2. The first row, for example, presents the judged probability β that death was caused by an accident or a homicide rather than by some other unnatural cause. In accord with support theory, $\delta = \delta_1 + \delta_2$ was significantly greater than $\gamma = \gamma_1 + \gamma_2$, $p < .05$ (by Mann–Whitney U test), but γ was not significantly greater than β, contrary to the prediction of the regressive model. Nevertheless, we do not rule out the possibility that regression toward .5 could yield $\beta < \gamma$, which would contribute to the discrepancy between α and δ. A generalization of support theory that accommodates such a pattern is considered in the final section.

Study 2: Suggestibility and Subadditivity Before turning to additional demonstrations of unpacking, we discuss some methodological questions regarding the elicitation of probability judgments. It could be argued that asking a subject to evaluate a specific hypothesis conveys a subtle (or not so subtle) suggestion that the hypothesis is quite probable. Subjects, therefore, might treat the fact that the hypothesis has been brought to their attention as information about its probability. To address this objection, we devised a task in which the assigned hypotheses carried no information so that any observed subadditivity could not be attributed to experimental suggestion.

Stanford undergraduates ($N = 196$) estimated the percentage of U.S. married couples with a given number of children. Subjects were asked to write down the last digit of their telephone numbers and then to evaluate the percentage of couples having exactly that many children. They were promised that the 3 most accurate respondents would be awarded $10 each. As predicted, the total percentage attributed to the numbers 0 through 9 (when added across different groups of subjects) greatly exceeded 1. The total of the means assigned by each group was 1.99, and the total of the medians was 1.80. Thus, subadditivity was very much in evidence, even when the selection of focal hypothesis was hardly informative. Subjects overestimated the percentage of couples in all categories, except for childless couples, and the discrepancy between the estimated and the actual percentages was greatest for the modal couple with 2 children. Furthermore, the sum of the probabilities for 0, 1, 2, and 3 children, each of which exceeded .25, was 1.45. The observed subadditivity, therefore, cannot be explained merely by a tendency to overestimate very small probabilities.

Other subjects ($N = 139$) were asked to estimate the percentage of U.S. married couples with "less than 3," "3 or more," "less than 5," or "5 or more" children. Each subject considered exactly one of the four hypotheses. The estimates added to 97.5% for the first pair of hypotheses and to 96.3% for the second pair. In sharp contrast to the subadditivity observed earlier, the estimates for complementary pairs of events were roughly additive, as implied by support theory. The finding of binary complementarity is of special interest because it excludes an alternative explanation of subadditivity according to which the evaluation of evidence is biased in favor of the focal hypothesis.

Subadditivity in Expert Judgments   Is subadditivity confined to novices, or does it also hold for experts? Redelmeier, Koehler, Liberman, and Tversky (1993) explored this question in the context of medical judgments. They presented physicians at Stanford University ($N = 59$) with a detailed scenario concerning a woman who reported to the emergency room with abdominal pain. Half of the respondents were asked to assign probabilities to two specified diagnoses (gastroenteritis and ectopic pregnancy) and a residual category (none of the above); the other half assigned probabilities to five specified diagnoses (including the two presented in the other condition) and a residual category (none of the above). Subjects were instructed to give probabilities that summed to one because the possibilities under consideration were mutually exclusive and exhaustive. If the physicians' judgments conform to the classical theory, then the probability assigned to the residual category in the two-diagnosis condition should equal the sum of the probabilities assigned to its unpacked components in the five-diagnosis condition. Consistent with the predictions of support theory, however, the judged probability of the residual in the two-diagnosis condition (mean = .50) was significantly lower than that of the unpacked components in the five-diagnosis condition (mean $= .69$). $p < .005$ (Mann–Whitney U test).

In a second study, physicians from Tel Aviv University ($N = 52$) were asked to consider several medical scenarios consisting of a one-paragraph statement including the patient's age, gender, medical history, presenting symptoms, and the results of any tests that had been conducted. One scenario, for example, concerned a 67-year-old man who arrived in the emergency room suffering a heart attack that had begun several hours earlier. Each physician was asked to assess the probability of one of the following four hypotheses: patient dies during this hospital admission (A); patient is discharged alive but dies within 1 year (B); patient lives more than 1 but less than 10 years (C); or patient lives more than 10 years (D). Throughout this article, we refer to these as *elementary judgments* because they pit an elementary hypothesis against its complement, which is an implicit disjunction of all of the remaining elementary hypotheses. After assessing one of these four hypotheses, all respondents assessed $P(A, B)$, $P(B, C)$, and $P(C, D)$ or the complementary set. We refer to these as *binary judgments* because they involve a comparison of two elementary hypotheses.

As predicted, the elementary judgments were substantially subadditive. The means of the four groups in the preceding example were 14% for A, 26% for B, 55% for C, and 69% for D, all of which overestimated the actual values reported in the medical literature. In problems like this, when individual components of a partition are evaluated against the residual, the denominator of the unpacking factor is taken to be 1; thus, the unpacking factor is simply the total probability assigned to the components (summed over different groups of subjects). In this example, the unpacking factor was 1.64. In sharp contrast, the binary judgments (produced by two different groups of physicians) exhibited near-perfect additivity, with a mean total of 100.5% assigned to complementary pairs.

Further evidence for subadditivity in expert judgment has been provided by Fox, Rogers, and Tversky (1994), who investigated 32 professional options traders at the Pacific Stock Exchange. These traders made probability judgments regarding the closing price of Microsoft stock on a given future date (e.g., that it will be less than $88 per share). Microsoft stock is traded at the Pacific Stock Exchange, and the traders are commonly concerned with the prediction of its future value. Nevertheless, their judgments exhibited the predicted pattern of subadditivity and binary complementarity. The average unpacking factor for a fourfold partition was 1.47, and the average sum of complementary binary events was 0.98. Subadditivity in expert judgments has been documented in other domains by Fischhoff et al. (1978), who studied auto mechanics, and by Dube-Rioux and Russo (1988), who studied restaurant managers.

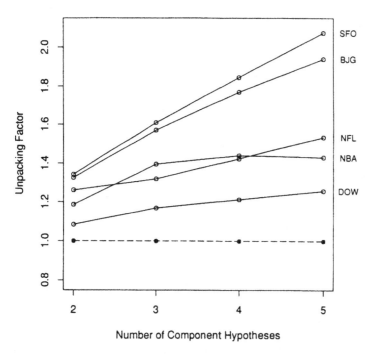

Figure 14.1
Unpacking factors from Tversky and Fox's (1994) data. SFO = San Francisco temperature; BJG = Beijing temperature; NFL = 1991 National Football League Super Bowl; NBA = National Basketball Association playoff; DOW = weekly change in Dow–Jones index.

Review of Previous Research   We next review other studies that have provided tests of support theory. Tversky and Fox (1994) asked subjects to assign probabilities to various intervals in which an uncertain quantity might fall, such as the margin of victory in the upcoming Super Bowl or the change in the Dow–Jones Industrial Average over the next week. When a given event (e.g., "Buffalo beats Washington") was unpacked into individually evaluated components (e.g., "Buffalo beats Washington by less than 7 points" and "Buffalo beats Washington by at least 7 points"), subjects' judgments were substantially subadditive. Figure 14.1 plots the unpacking factor obtained in this study as a function of the number of component hypotheses in the explicit disjunction. Judgments for five different types of event are shown: future San Francisco temperature (SFO), future Beijing temperature (BJG), the outcome of the Super Bowl of the National Football League (NFL), the outcome of a playoff game of the National Basketball Association (NBA), and weekly change in the Dow–Jones index (DOW). Recall that an unpacking factor greater than 1 (i.e., fall-

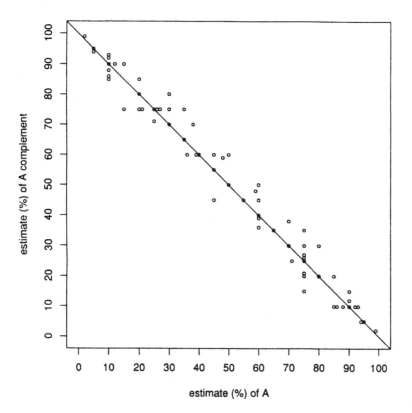

Figure 14.2
A test of binary complementarity based on Tversky and Fox (1994).

ing above the dashed line in the plot) indicates subadditivity. The results displayed in figure 14.1 reveal consistent subadditivity for all sources that increases with the number of components in the explicit disjunction.

Figure 14.2 plots the median probabilities assigned to complementary hypotheses. (Each hypothesis is represented twice in the plot, once as the focal hypothesis and once as the complement.) As predicted by support theory, judgments of intervals representing complementary pairs of hypotheses were essentially additive, with no apparent tendency toward either subadditivity or superadditivity.

Further evidence for binary complementarity comes from an extensive study conducted by Wallsten, Budescu, and Zwick (1992),[3] who presented subjects with 300 propositions concerning world history and geography (e.g., "The Monroe Doctrine was proclaimed before the Republican Party was founded") and asked them to esti-

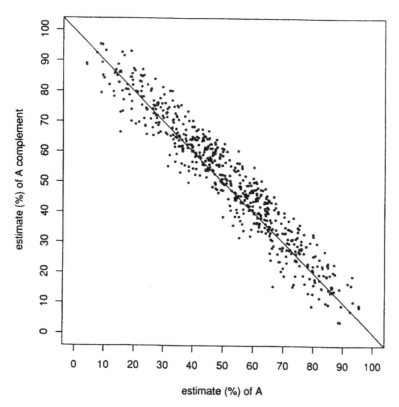

Figure 14.3
A test of binary complementarity based on Wallsten, Budescu, and Zwick (1992).

mate the probability that each was true. True and false (complementary) versions of each proposition were presented on different days. Figure 14.3 plots the mean probabilities assigned to each of the propositions in both their true and false versions using the format of figure 14.2. Again, the judgments are additive (mean = 1.02) through the entire range.

We next present a brief summary of the major findings and list both current and previous studies supporting each conclusion.

SUBADDITIVITY   Unpacking an implicit hypothesis into its component hypotheses increases its total judged probability, yielding subadditive judgments. Tables 14.3 and 14.4 list studies that provide tests of the unpacking condition. For each experiment, the probability assigned to the implicit hypothesis and the total probability

Table 14.3
Results of Experiments Using Qualitative Hypotheses: Average Probability Assigned to Coextensional Implicit and Explicit Disjunctions and the Unpacking Factor Measuring the Degree of Subadditivity

Study and topic	n	Explicit P	Implicit P	Unpacking factor
Fischhoff, Slovic, & Lichtenstein (1978)				
Car failure, Experiment 1	4	0.54	.18	3.00
Car failure, Experiment 5	2	0.27	.20	1.35
Car failure, Experiment 6 (experts)	4	0.44	.22	2.00
Mehle, Gettys, Manning, Baca, & Fisher (1981): college majors	6	0.27	.18	1.50
Russo & Kolzow (1992)				
Causes of death	4	0.55	.45	1.22
Car failure	4	0.55	.27	2.04
Koehler & Tversky (1993)				
College majors	4	1.54	1.00[a]	1.54
College majors	5	2.51	1.00[a]	2.51
Study 1: causes of death	3	0.61	.46	1.33
	7	0.70	.37	1.86
Study 4: crime stories	4	1.71	1.00[a]	1.71
Study 5: college majors	4	1.76	1.00[a]	1.76

Note: The number of components in the explicit disjunction is denoted by n. Numbered studies with no citation refer to the present article.

[a] Because the components partition the space, it is assumed that a probability of 1.00 would have been assigned to the implicit disjunction.

assigned to its components in the explicit disjunction are listed along with the resulting unpacking factor. All of the listed studies used an experimental design in which the implicit disjunction and the components of the explicit disjunction were evaluated independently, either by separate groups of subjects or by the same subjects but with a substantial number of intervening judgments. The probabilities are listed as a function of the number of components in the explicit disjunction and are collapsed over all other independent variables. Table 14.3 lists studies in which subjects evaluated the probability of qualitative hypotheses (e.g., the probability that Bill W. majors in psychology); table 14.4 lists studies in which subjects evaluated quantitative hypotheses (e.g., the probability that a randomly selected adult man is between 6 ft and 6 ft 2 in. tall).

The tables show that the observed unpacking factors are, without exception, greater than one, indicating consistent subadditivity. The fact that subadditivity is observed both for qualitative and for quantitative hypotheses is instructive. Subadditivity in assessments of qualitative hypotheses can be explained, in part at least, by the failure to consider one or more component hypotheses when the event in

Table 14.4
Results of Experiments Using Quantitative Hypotheses: Average Probability Assigned to Coextensional Implicit and Explicit Disjunctions and the Unpacking Factor Measuring the Degree of Subadditivity

Study and topic	n	Explicit P	Implicit P	Unpacking factor
Teigen (1974b)				
Experiment 1: binomial	2	0.66	.38	1.73
outcomes	3	0.84	.38	2.21
	5	1.62	1.00[a]	1.62
	9	2.25	1.00[a]	2.25
Teigen (1974b)				
Experiment 2: heights of	2	0.58	.36	1.61
students	4	1.99	.76	2.62
	5	2.31	.75	3.07
	6	2.55	1.00[a]	2.55
Teigen (1974a)				
Experiment 2: binomial	11	4.25	1.00[a]	4.25
outcomes				
Olson (1976)				
Experiment 1: gender	2	0.13	.10	1.30
distribution	3	0.36	.21	1.71
	5	0.68	.40	1.70
	9	0.97	.38	2.55
Peterson and Pitz (1988)				
Experiment 3: baseball	3	1.58	1.00[a]	1.58
victories				
Tversky and Fox (1994):	2	0.77	.62	1.27
uncertain quantities	3	1.02	.72	1.46
	4	1.21	.79	1.58
	5	1.40	.84	1.27
Study 2: number of children	10	1.99	1.00[a]	1.99

Note: The number of components in the explicit disjunction is denoted by n. Numbered Study with no citation refers to the peresent article.
[a] Because the components partition the space, it is assumed that a probability of 1.00 would have been assigned to the implicit disjunction.

Table 14.5
Results of Experiments Testing Binary Complementarity: Average Total Probability Assigned to Complementary Pairs of Hypotheses, Between-Subjects Standard Deviations, and the Number of Subjects in the Experiment

Study and topic	Mean total P	SD	N
Wallsten, Budescu, & Zwick (1992): general knowledge	1.02	0.06	23
Tversky & Fox (1994)			
NBA playoff	1.00	0.07	27
Super Bowl	1.02	0.07	40
Dow-Jones	1.00	0.10	40
San Francisco temperature	1.02	0.13	72
Beijing temperature	0.99	0.14	45
Koehler & Tversky (1993): college majors[a]	1.00		170
Study 2: number of children[a]	0.97		139
Study 4: crime stories[a]	1.03		60
Study 5: college majors[a]	1.05		115

Note: Numbered studies with no citation refer to the present article. NBA = National Basketball Association.
[a] A given subject evaluated either the event or its complement, but not both.

question is described in an implicit form. The subadditivity observed in judgments of quantitative hypotheses, however, cannot be explained as a retrieval failure. For example, Teigen (1974b, experiment 2) found that the judged proportion of college students whose heights fell in a given interval increased when that interval was broken into several smaller intervals that were assessed separately. Subjects evaluating the implicit disjunction (i.e., the large interval), we suggest, did not overlook the fact that the interval included several smaller intervals; rather, the unpacking manipulation enhanced the salience of these intervals and, hence, their judged probability. Subadditivity, therefore, is observed even in the absence of memory limitations.

NUMBER OF COMPONENTS   The degree of subadditivity increases with the number of components in the explicit disjunction. This follows readily from support theory: Unpacking an implicit hypothesis into exclusive components increases its total judged probability, and additional unpacking of each component should further increase the total probability assigned to the initial hypothesis. Tables 14.3 and 14.4 show, as expected, that the unpacking factor generally increases with the number of components (see also figure 14.1).

BINARY COMPLEMENTARITY   The judged probabilities of complementary pairs of hypotheses add to one. Table 14.5 lists studies that have tested this prediction. We considered only studies in which the hypothesis and its complement were evaluated independently, either by different subjects or by the same subjects but with a substantial number of intervening judgments. (We provide the standard deviations for the experiments that used the latter design.) Table 14.5 shows that such judgments generally add to one. Binary complementarity indicates that people evaluate a given hypothesis relative to its complement. Moreover, it rules out alternative interpretations of subadditivity in terms of a suggestion effect or a confirmation bias. These accounts imply a bias in favor of the focal hypothesis yielding $P(A, B) + P(B, A) > 1$, contrary to the experimental evidence. Alternatively, one might be tempted to attribute the subadditivity observed in probability judgments to subjects' lack of knowledge of the additivity principle of probability theory. This explanation, however, fails to account for the observed subadditivity in frequency judgments (in which additivity is obvious) and for the finding of binary complementarity (in which additivity is consistently satisfied).

The combination of binary complementarity and subadditive elementary judgments, implied by support theory, is inconsistent with both Bayesian and revisionist models. The Bayesian model implies that the unpacking factor should equal one because the unpacked and packed hypotheses have the same extension. Shafer's theory of belief functions and other models of lower probability require an unpacking factor of less than one, because they assume that the subjective probability (or belief) of the union of disjoint events is generally greater than the sum of the probabilities of its exclusive constituents. Furthermore, the data cannot be explained by the dual of the belief function (called the plausibility function) or, more generally, by an upper probability (e.g., see Dempster, 1967) because this model requires that the sum of the assessments of complementary events exceed unity, contrary to the evidence. Indeed, if $P(A, B) + P(B, A) = 1$ (see table 14.5), then both upper and lower probability reduce to the standard additive model. The experimental findings, of course, do not invalidate the use of upper and lower probability, or belief functions, as formal systems for representing uncertainty. However, the evidence reviewed in this section indicates that these models are inconsistent with the principles that govern intuitive probability judgments.

PROBABILITY VERSUS FREQUENCY   Of the studies discussed earlier and listed in tables 14.3 and 14.4, some (e.g., Fischhoff et al., 1978) used frequency judgments and others (e.g., Teigen, 1974a, 1974b) used probability judgments. The comparison of the two tasks, summarized in table 14.6, confirms the predicted pattern: Subadditivity holds for both probability and frequency judgments, and the former are more subadditive than the latter.

Table 14.6
Results of Experiments Comparing Probability and Frequency Judgments: Unpacking Factor Computed from Mean Probability Assigned to Coextensional Explicit and Implicit Disjunctions

Study and topic	n	Unpacking factor	
		Probability	Frequency
Teigen (1974b)			
Experiment 1: binomial outcomes	2	1.73	1.26
	5	2.21	1.09
	9	2.25	1.24
Teigen (1974b)			
Experiment 2: heights of students	6	2.55	1.68
Koehler & Tversky (1993): college majors	4	1.72	1.37
Study 1: causes of death	3	1.44	1.28
	7	2.00	1.84

Note: The number of components in the explicit disjunction is denoted by n. Numbered studies with no citation refer to the present article.

Scaling Support

In the formal theory developed in the preceding section, the support function is derived from probability judgments. Is it possible to reverse the process and predict probability judgments from direct assessments of evidence strength? Let $\hat{s}(A)$ be the rating of the strength of evidence for hypothesis A. What is the relation between such ratings and the support estimated from probability judgments? Perhaps the most natural assumption is that the two scales are monotonically related; that is, $\hat{s}(A) \geq \hat{s}(B)$ if and only if (iff) $s(A) \geq s(B)$. This assumption implies, for example, that $P(A, B) \geq \frac{1}{2}$ iff $\hat{s}(A) \geq \hat{s}(B)$, but it does not determine the functional form relating $\hat{s}$ and s. To further specify the relation between the scales, it may be reasonable to assume, in addition, that support ratios are also monotonically related. That is, $\hat{s}(A)/\hat{s}(B) \geq \hat{s}(C)/\hat{s}(D)$ iff $s(A)/s(B) \geq s(C)/s(D)$.

It can be shown that if the two monotonicity conditions are satisfied, and both scales are defined, say, on the unit interval, then there exists a constant $k > 0$ such that the support function derived from probability judgments and the support function assessed directly are related by a power transformation of the form $s = \hat{s}^k$. This gives rise to the *power model*

$$R(A, B) = P(A, B)/P(B, A) = [\hat{s}(A)/\hat{s}(B)]^k,$$

yielding

$$\log R(A, B) = k \log[\hat{s}(A)/\hat{s}(B)].$$

We next use this model to predict judged probability from independent assessments of evidence strength obtained in two studies.

Study 3: Basketball Games   Subjects ($N = 88$) were NBA fans who subscribe to a computer news group. We posted a questionnaire to this news group and asked readers to complete and return it by electronic mail within 1 week. In the questionnaire, subjects assessed the probability that the home team would win in each of 20 upcoming games. These 20 outcomes constituted all possible matches among five teams (Phoenix, Portland, Los Angeles Lakers, Golden State, and Sacramento) from the Pacific Division of the NBA, constructed such that, for each pair of teams, two games were evaluated (one for each possible game location). Use of this "expert" population yielded highly reliable judgments, as shown, among other things, by the fact that the median value of the correlation between an individual subject's ratings and the set of mean judgments was .93.

After making their probability judgments, subjects rated the strength of each of the five teams. The participants were instructed:

First, choose the team you believe is the strongest of the five, and set that team's strength to 100. Assign the remaining teams ratings in proportion to the strength of the strongest team. For example, if you believe that a given team is half as strong as the strongest team (the team you gave a 100), give that team a strength rating of 50.

We interpreted these ratings as a direct assessment of support.

Because the strength ratings did not take into account the home court effect, we collapsed the probability judgments across the two possible locations of the match. The slope of the regression line predicting $\log R(A, B)$ from $\log[\hat{s}(A)/\hat{s}(B)]$ provided an estimate of k for each subject. The median estimate of k was 1.8, and the mean was 2.2; the median R^2 for this analysis was .87. For the aggregate data, k was 1.9 and the resulting R^2 was .97. The scatterplot in figure 14.4 exhibits excellent correspondence between mean prediction based on team strength and mean judged probability. This result suggests that the power model can be used to predict judged probability from assessments of strength that make no reference to chance or uncertainty. It also reinforces the psychological interpretation of s as a measure of evidence strength.

Study 4: Crime Stories   This study was designed to investigate the relation between judged probability and assessed support in a very different context and to explore the enhancement effect, described in the next subsection. To this end, we adapted a task introduced by Teigen (1983) and Robinson and Hastie (1985) and presented subjects with two criminal cases. The first was an embezzlement at a computer-parts manu-

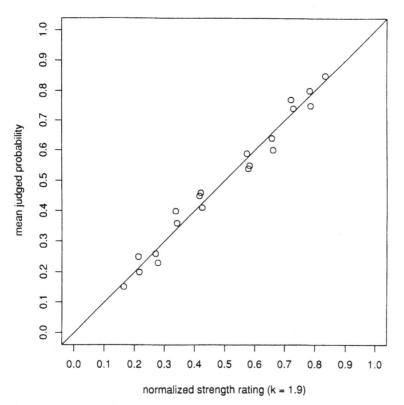

Figure 14.4
Judged probability for basketball games as a function of normalized strength ratings.

facturing company involving four suspects (a manager, a buyer, an accountant, and a seller). The second case was a murder that also involved four suspects (an activist, an artist, a scientist, and a writer). In both cases, subjects were informed that exactly one suspect was guilty. In the low-information condition, the four suspects in each case were introduced with a short description of their role and possible motive. In the high-information condition, the motive of each suspect was strengthened. In a manner resembling the typical mystery novel, we constructed each case so that all the suspects seemed generally more suspicious as more evidence was revealed.

Subjects evaluated the suspects after reading the low-information material and again after reading the high-information material. Some subjects ($N = 60$) judged the probability that a given suspect was guilty. Each of these subjects made two elementary judgments (that a particular suspect was guilty) and three binary judgments (that suspect A rather than suspect B was guilty) in each case. Other subjects ($N = 55$) rated the suspiciousness of a given suspect, which we took as a direct assessment of support. These subjects rated two suspects per case by providing a number between 0 (indicating that the suspect was "not at all suspicious") and 100 (indicating that the suspect was "maximally suspicious") in proportion to the suspiciousness of the suspect.

As in the previous study, we assumed binary complementarity and estimated k by a logarithmic regression of $R(A, B)$ against the suspiciousness ratio. For these data, k was estimated to be .84, and R^2 was .65. Rated suspiciousness, therefore, provides a reasonable predictor of the judged probability of guilt. However, the relation between judged probability and assessed support was stronger in the basketball study than in the crime study. Furthermore, the estimate of k was much smaller in the latter than in the former. In the basketball study, a team that was rated twice as strong as another was judged more than twice as likely to win; in the crime stories, however, a character who was twice as suspicious as another was judged less than twice as likely to be guilty. This difference may be due to the fact that the judgments of team strength were based on more solid data than the ratings of suspiciousness.

In the preceding two studies, we asked subjects to assess the overall support for each hypothesis on the basis of all the available evidence. A different approach to the assessment of evidence was taken by Briggs and Krantz (1992; see also Krantz, Ray, & Briggs, 1990). These authors demonstrated that, under certain conditions, subjects can assess the degree to which an isolated item of evidence supports each of the hypotheses under consideration. They also proposed several rules for the combination of independent items of evidence, but they did not relate assessed support to judged probability.

The Enhancement Effect

Recall that assessed support is noncompensatory in the sense that evidence that increases the support of one hypothesis does not necessarily decrease the support of competing hypotheses. In fact, it is possible for new evidence to increase the support of all elementary hypotheses. We have proposed that such evidence will enhance subadditivity. In this section, we describe several tests of enhancement and compare support theory with the Bayesian model and with Shafer's theory.

We start with an example discussed earlier, in which one of several suspects has committed a murder. To simplify matters, assume that there are four suspects who, in the absence of specific evidence (low information), are considered equally likely to be guilty. Suppose further evidence is then introduced (high information) that implicates each of the suspects to roughly the same degree, so that they remain equally probable. Let L and H denote, respectively, the evidence available under low- and high-information conditions. Let $\bar{A}$ denote the negation of A, that is, "Suspect A is not guilty." According to the Bayesian model, then, $P(A, B \mid H) = P(A, B \mid L) = \frac{1}{2}$, $P(A, \bar{A} \mid H) = P(A, \bar{A} \mid L) = \frac{1}{4}$, and so forth.

In contrast, Shafer's (1976) belief-function approach requires that the probabilities assigned to each of the suspects add to less than one and suggests that the total will be higher in the presence of direct evidence (i.e., in the high-information condition) than in its absence. As a consequence, $\frac{1}{2} \geq P(A, B \mid H) \geq P(A, B \mid L)$, $\frac{1}{4} \geq P(A, \bar{A} \mid H) \geq P(A, \bar{A} \mid L)$, and so forth. In other words, both the binary and the elementary judgments are expected to increase as more evidence is encountered. In the limit, when no belief is held in reserve, the binary judgments approach one half and the elementary judgments approach one fourth.

The enhancement assumption yields a different pattern, namely $P(A, B \mid H) = P(A, B \mid L) = \frac{1}{2}$, $P(A, \bar{A} \mid H) \geq P(A, \bar{A} \mid L) \geq \frac{1}{4}$, and so forth. As in the Bayesian model, the binary judgments are one half; in contrast to that model, however, the elementary judgments are expected to exceed one fourth and to be greater under high- than under low-information conditions. Although both support theory and the belief-function approach yield greater elementary judgments under high- than under low-information conditions, support theory predicts that they will exceed one fourth in both conditions, whereas Shafer's theory requires that these probabilities be less than or equal to one fourth.

The assumption of equally probable suspects is not essential for the analysis. Suppose that initially the suspects are not equally probable, but the new evidence does not change the binary probabilities. Here, too, the Bayesian model requires additive judgments that do not differ between low- and high-information conditions; the belief-function approach requires superadditive judgments that become less superadditive as more information is encountered; and the enhancement assumption predicts subadditive judgments that become more subadditive with the addition of (compatible) evidence.

Evaluating Suspects

With these predictions in mind, we turn to the crime stories of study 4. Table 14.7 displays the mean suspiciousness ratings and elementary probability judgments of each suspect in the two cases under low- and high-information conditions. The table shows that, in all cases, the sums of both probability judgments and suspiciousness ratings exceed one. Evidently, subadditivity holds not only in probability judgment

Table 14.7
Mean Suspiciousness Rating and Judged Probability of Each Suspect under Low- and High-Information Conditions

Case and suspect	Suspiciousness		Probability	
	Low information	High information	Low information	High information
Case 1: embezzlement				
Accountant	41	53	40	45
Buyer	50	58	42	48
Manager	47	51	48	59
Seller	32	48	37	42
Total	170	210	167	194
Case 2: murder				
Activist	32	57	39	57
Artist	27	23	37	30
Scientist	24	43	34	40
Writer	38	60	33	54
Total	122	184	143	181

but also in ratings of evidence strength or degree of belief (e.g., that a given subject is guilty). Further examination of the suspiciousness ratings shows that all but one of the suspects increased in suspiciousness as more information was provided. In accord with our prediction, the judged probability of each of these suspects also increased with the added information, indicating enhanced subadditivity (see equation 10). The one exception was the artist in the murder case, who was given an alibi in the high-information condition and, as one would expect, subsequently decreased both in suspiciousness and in probability. Overall, both the suspiciousness ratings and the probability judgments were significantly greater under high- than under low-information conditions ($p < .001$ for both cases by t test).

From a normative standpoint, the support (i.e., suspiciousness) of all the suspects could increase with new information, but an increase in the probability of one suspect should be compensated for by a decrease in the probability of the others. The observation that new evidence can increase the judged probability of all suspects was made earlier by Robinson and Hastie (1985; Van Wallendael & Hastie, 1990). Their method differed from ours in that each subject assessed the probability of all suspects, but this method too produced substantial subadditivity, with a typical unpacking factor of about two. These authors rejected the Bayesian model as a descriptive account and proposed Shafer's theory as one viable alternative. As was noted earlier, however, the observed subadditivity is inconsistent with Shafer's theory, as well as the Bayesian model, but it is consistent with the present account.

In the crime stories, the added evidence was generally compatible with all of the hypotheses under consideration. Peterson and Pitz (1988, experiment 3), however, observed a similar effect with mixed evidence, which favored some hypotheses but not others. Their subjects were asked to assess the probability that the number of games won by a baseball team in a season fell in a given interval on the basis of one, two, or three cues (team batting average, earned run average, and total home runs during that season). Unbeknownst to subjects, they were asked, over a large number of problems, to assign probabilities to all three components in a partition (e.g., less than 80 wins, between 80 and 88 wins, and more than 88 wins). As the number of cues increased, subjects assigned a greater probability, on average, to all three intervals in the partition, thus exhibiting enhanced subadditivity. The unpacking factors for these data were 1.26, 1.61, and 1.86 for one, two, and three cues, respectively. These results attest to the robustness of the enhancement effect, which is observed even when the added evidence favors some, but not all, of the hypotheses under study.

Study 5: College Majors   In this study, we tested enhancement by replacing evidence rather than by adding evidence as in the previous study. Following Mehle, Gettys, Manning, Baca, and Fisher (1981), we asked subjects ($N = 115$) to assess the probability that a social science student at an unspecified midwestern university majored in a given field. Subjects were told that, in this university, each social science student has one and only one of the following four majors: economics, political science, psychology, and sociology.

Subjects estimated the probability that a given student had a specified major on the basis of one of four courses the student was said to have taken in his or her second year. Two of the courses (statistics and Western civilization) were courses typically taken by social science majors; the other two (French literature and physics) were courses not typically taken by social science majors. This was confirmed by an independent group of subjects ($N = 36$) who evaluated the probability that a social science major would take each one of the four courses. Enhancement suggests that the typical courses will yield more subadditivity than the less typical courses because they give greater support to each of the four majors.

Each subject made both elementary and binary judgments. As in all previous studies, the elementary judgments exhibited substantial subadditivity (mean unpacking factor $= 1.76$), whereas the binary judgments were essentially additive (mean unpacking factor $= 1.05$). In the preceding analyses, we have used the unpacking factor as an overall measure of subadditivity associated with a set of mutually exclusive hypotheses. The present experiment also allowed us to estimate w (see equation 8), which provides a more refined measure of subadditivity because it is

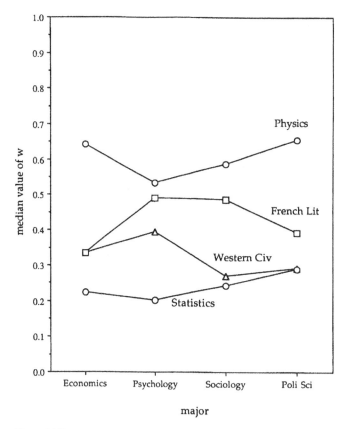

Figure 14.5
Median value of w for predictions of college majors, plotted separately for each course. Lit = literature;
Civ = civilization; Poli Sci = political science.

estimated separately for each of the implicit hypotheses under study. For each
course, we first estimated the support of each major from the binary judgments and
then estimated w for each major from the elementary judgments using the equation

$$P(A, \bar{A}) = \frac{s(A)}{s(A) + w_{\bar{A}}[s(B) + s(C) + s(D)]},$$

where A, B, C, and D denote the four majors.

This analysis was conducted separately for each subject. The average value of w
across courses and majors was .46, indicating that a major received less than half of
its explicit support when it was included implicitly in the residual. Figure 14.5 shows

the median value of w (over subjects) for each major, plotted separately for each of the four courses. In accord with enhancement, the figure shows that the typical courses, statistics and Western civilization, induced more subadditivity (i.e., lower w) than the less typical courses, physics and French literature. However, for any given course, w was roughly constant across majors. Indeed, a two-way analysis of variance yielded a highly significant effect of course, $F(3, 112) = 31.4$, $p < .001$, but no significant effect of major, $F(3, 112) < 1$.

Implications

To this point, we have focused on the direct consequences of support theory. We conclude this section by discussing the conjunction effect, hypothesis generation, and decision under uncertainty from the perspective of support theory.

The Conjunction Effect Considerable research has documented the conjunction effect, in which a conjunction AB is judged more probable than one of its constituents A. The effect is strongest when an event that initially seems unlikely (e.g., a massive flood in North America in which more than 1,000 people drown) is supplemented by a plausible cause or qualification (e.g., an earthquake in California causing a flood in which more than 1,000 people drown), yielding a conjunction that is perceived as more probable than the initially implausible event of which it is a proper subset (Tversky & Kahneman, 1983). Support theory suggests that the implicit hypothesis A is not unpacked into the coextensional disjunction $AB \vee A\bar{B}$ of which the conjunction is one component. As a result, evidence supporting AB is not taken to support A. In the flood problem, for instance, the possibility of a flood caused by an earthquake may not come readily to mind; thus, unless it is mentioned explicitly, it does not contribute any support to the (implicit) flood hypothesis. Support theory implies that the conjunction effect would be eliminated in these problems if the implicit disjunction were unpacked before its evaluation (e.g., if subjects were reminded that a flood might be caused by excessive rainfall or by structural damage to a reservoir caused by an earthquake, an engineering error, sabotage, etc.).

The greater tendency to unpack either the focal or the residual hypothesis in a frequentistic formulation may help explain the finding that conjunction effects are attenuated, though not eliminated, when subjects estimate frequency rather than probability. For example, the proportion of subjects who judged the conjunction "X is over 55 years old and has had at least one heart attack" as more probable than the constituent event "X has had at least one heart attack" was significantly greater in a probabilistic formulation than in a frequentistic formulation (Tversky & Kahneman, 1983).

It might be instructive to distinguish two different unpacking operations. In *conjunctive unpacking*, an (implicit) hypothesis (e.g., nurse) is broken down into exclusive conjunctions (e.g., male nurse and female nurse). Most, but not all, initial demonstrations of the conjunction effect were based on conjunctive unpacking. In *categorical unpacking*, a superordinate category (e.g., unnatural death) is broken down into its "natural" components (e.g., car accident, drowning, and homicide). Most of the demonstrations reported in this article are based on categorical unpacking. A conjunction effect using categorical unpacking has been described by Bar-Hillel and Neter (1993), who found numerous cases in which a statement (e.g., "Daniela's major is literature") was ranked as more probable than a more inclusive implicit disjunction (e.g., "Daniela's major is in humanities"). These results held both for subjects' direct estimates of probabilities and for their willingness to bet on the relevant events.

Hypothesis Generation   All of the studies reviewed thus far asked subjects to assess the probability of hypotheses presented to them for judgment. There are many situations, however, in which a judge must generate hypotheses as well as assess their likelihood. In the current treatment, the generation of alternative hypotheses entails some unpacking of the residual hypothesis and, thus, is expected to increase its support relative to the focal hypothesis. In the absence of explicit instructions to generate alternative hypotheses, people are less likely to unpack the residual hypothesis and thus will tend to overestimate specified hypotheses relative to those left unspecified.

This implication has been confirmed by Gettys and his colleagues (Gettys, Mehle, & Fisher, 1986; Mehle et al., 1981), who have found that, in comparison with veridical values, people generally tend to overestimate the probability of specified hypotheses presented to them for evaluation. Indeed, overconfidence that one's judgment is correct (e.g., Lichtenstein, Fischhoff, & Phillips, 1982) may sometimes arise because the focal hypothesis is specified, whereas its alternatives often are not. Mehle et al. (1981) used two manipulations to encourage unpacking of the residual hypothesis: One group of subjects was provided with exemplar members of the residual, and another was asked to generate its own examples. Both manipulations improved performance by decreasing the probability assigned to specified alternatives and increasing that assigned to the residual. These results suggest that the effects of hypothesis generation are due to the additional hypotheses it brings to mind, because simply providing hypotheses to the subject has the same effect. Using a similar manipulation, Dube-Rioux and Russo (1988) found that generation of alternative hypotheses increased the judged probability of the residual relative to that of specified categories and attenuated the effect of omitting a category. Examination of the number of instances generated by the subjects showed that, when enough instances were produced, the effect of category omission was eliminated altogether.

Now consider a task in which subjects are asked to generate a hypothesis (e.g., to guess which film will win the best picture Oscar at the next Academy Awards ceremony) before assessing its probability. Asking subjects to generate the most likely hypothesis might actually lead them to consider several candidates in the process of settling on the one they prefer. This process amounts to a partial unpacking of the residual hypothesis, which should decrease the judged probability of the focal hypothesis. Consistent with this prediction, a recent study (Koehler, 1994) found that subjects asked to generate their own hypotheses assigned them a lower probability of being true than did other subjects presented with the same hypotheses for evaluation. The interpretation of these results—that hypothesis generation makes alternative hypotheses more salient—was tested by two further manipulations. First, providing a closed set of specified alternatives eliminated the difference between the generation and evaluation conditions. In these circumstances, the residual should be represented in the same way in both conditions. Second, inserting a distracter task between hypothesis generation and probability assessment was sufficient to reduce the salience of alternatives brought to mind by the generation task, increasing the judged probability of the focal hypothesis.

Decision Under Uncertainty   This article has focused primarily on numerical judgments of probability. In decision theory, however, subjective probabilities are generally inferred from preferences between uncertain prospects rather than assessed directly. It is natural to inquire, then, whether unpacking affects people's decisions as well as their numerical judgments. There is considerable evidence that it does. For example, Johnson et al. (1993) observed that subjects were willing to pay more for flight insurance that explicitly listed certain events covered by the policy (e.g., death resulting from an act of terrorism or mechanical failure) than for a more inclusive policy that did not list specific events (e.g., death from any cause).

Unpacking can affect decisions in two ways. First, as has been shown, unpacking tends to increase the judged probability of an uncertain event. Second, unpacking can increase an event's impact on the decision, even when its probability is known. For example, Tversky and Kahneman (1986) asked subjects to choose between two lotteries that paid different amounts depending on the color of a marble drawn from a box. (As an inducement to consider the options with care, subjects were informed that one tenth of the participants, selected at random, would actually play the gambles they chose.) Two different versions of the problem were used, which differed only in the description of the outcomes. The fully unpacked version 1 was as follows:

Box A:	90% white	6% red	1% green	1% blue	2% yellow
	$0	win $45	win $30	lose $15	lose $15

Box B:	90% white	6% red	1% green	1% blue	2% yellow
	$0	win $45	win $45	lose $10	lose $15

It is not difficult to see that box B dominates box A; indeed, all subjects chose box B in this version. Version 2 combined the two outcomes resulting in a loss of $15 in box A (i.e., blue and yellow) and the two outcomes resulting in a gain of $45 in box B (i.e., red and green):

Box A:	90% white	6% red		1% green	3% yellow/blue
	$0	win $45		win $30	lose $15

Box B:	90% white	7% red/green	1% blue	2% yellow
	$0	win $45	lose $10	lose $15

In accord with subadditivity, the combination of events yielding the same outcome makes box A more attractive because it packs two losses into one and makes box B less attractive because it packs two gains into one. Indeed, 58% of subjects chose box A in version 2, even though it was dominated by box B. Starmer and Sugden (1993) further investigated the effect of unpacking events with known probabilities (which they called an event-splitting effect) and found that a prospect generally becomes more attractive when an event that yields a positive outcome is unpacked into two components. Such results demonstrate that unpacking affects decisions even when the probabilities are explicitly stated.

The role of unpacking in choice was further illustrated by Redelmeier et al. (in press). Graduating medical students at the University of Toronto ($N = 149$) were presented with a medical scenario concerning a middle-aged man suffering acute shortness of breath. Half of the respondents were given a packed description that noted that "obviously, many diagnoses are possible ... including pneumonia." The other half were given an unpacked description that mentioned other potential diagnoses (pulmonary embolus, heart failure, asthma, and lung cancer) in addition to pneumonia. The respondents were asked whether or not they would prescribe antibiotics in such a case, a treatment that is effective against pneumonia but not against the other potential diagnoses mentioned in the unpacked version. The unpacking manipulation was expected to reduce the perceived probability of pneumonia and, hence, the respondents' inclination to prescribe antibiotics. Indeed, a significant majority (64%) of respondents given the unpacked description chose not to prescribe antibiotics, whereas respondents given the packed description were almost evenly divided between prescribing (47%) and not prescribing them. Singling out pneumonia increased the tendency to select a treatment that is effective for pneumonia, even though the presenting symptoms were clearly consistent with a number of well-known alternative diagnoses. Evidently, unpacking can affect decisions, not only probability assessments.

Although unpacking plays an important role in probability judgment, the cognitive mechanism underlying this effect is considerably more general. Thus, one would expect unpacking effects even in tasks that do not involve uncertain events. For example, van der Pligt, Eiser, and Spears (1987, experiment 1) asked subjects to assess the current and ideal distribution of five power sources (nuclear, coal, oil, hydro, solar/wind/wave) and found that a given power source was assigned a higher estimate when it was evaluated on its own than when its four alternatives were unpacked (see also Fiedler & Armbruster, 1994; Pelham, Sumarta, & Myaskovsky, 1994). Such results indicate that the effects of unpacking reflect a general characteristic of human judgment.

Extensions

We have presented a nonextensional theory of belief in which judged probability is given by the relative support, or strength of evidence, of the respective focal and alternative hypotheses. In this theory, support is additive for explicit disjunctions of exclusive hypotheses and subadditive for implicit disjunctions. The empirical evidence confirms the major predictions of support theory: (a) Probability judgments increase by unpacking the focal hypothesis and decrease by unpacking the alternative hypothesis; (b) subjective probabilities are complementary in the binary case and subadditive in the general case; and (c) subadditivity is more pronounced for probability than for frequency judgments, and it is enhanced by compatible evidence. Support theory also provides a method for predicting judged probability from independent assessments of evidence strength. Thus, it accounts for a wide range of empirical findings in terms of a single explanatory construct.

In this section, we explore some extensions and implications of support theory. First, we consider an ordinal version of the theory and introduce a simple parametric representation. Second, we address the problem of vagueness, or imprecision, by characterizing upper and lower probability judgments in terms of upper and lower support. Finally, we discuss the implications of the present findings for the design of elicitation procedures for decision analysis and knowledge engineering.

Ordinal Analysis

Throughout the chapter, we have treated probability judgment as a quantitative measure of degree of belief. This measure is commonly interpreted in terms of a reference chance process. For example, assigning a probability of two thirds to the hypothesis that a candidate will be elected to office is taken to mean that the judge considers this hypothesis as likely as drawing a red ball from an urn in which two thirds of the balls are red. Probability judgment, therefore, can be viewed as an outcome of a thought experiment in which the judge matches degree of belief to a standard chance process (see Shafer & Tversky, 1985). This interpretation, of course, does not ensure either coherence or calibration.

Although probability judgments appear to convey quantitative information, it might be instructive to analyze these judgments as an ordinal rather than a cardinal scale. This interpretation gives rise to an ordinal generalization of support theory. Suppose there is a nonnegative scale s defined on H and a strictly increasing function F such that, for all A, B in H,

$$P(A, B) = F\left(\frac{s(A)}{s(A) + s(B)}\right),\tag{11}$$

where $s(C) \leq s(A \vee B) = s(A) + s(B)$ whenever A and B are exclusive, C is implicit, and $C' = (A \vee B)'$.

An axiomatization of the ordinal model lies beyond the scope of the present article. It is noteworthy, however, that to obtain an essentially unique support function in this case, we have to make additional assumptions, such as the following *solvability condition* (Debreu, 1958): If $P(A, B) \geq z \geq P(A, D)$, then there exists $C \in H$ such that $P(A, C) = z$. This idealization may be acceptable in the presence of a random device, such as a chance wheel with sectors that can be adjusted continuously. The following theorem shows that, assuming the ordinal model and the solvability condition, binary complementarity and the product rule yield a particularly simple parametric form that coincides with the model used in the preceding section to relate assessed and derived support. The proof is given in the appendix.

THEOREM 2   Assume the ordinal model (equation 11) and the solvability condition. Binary complementarity (equation 3) and the product rule (equation 5) hold if and only if there exists a constant $k \geq 0$ such that

$$P(A, B) = \frac{s(A)^k}{s(A)^k + s(B)^k}.\tag{12}$$

This representation, called the power model, reduces to the basic model if $k = 1$. In this model, judged probability may be more or less extreme than the respective

Probability (%):	0	5	10	15	20	25	30	35	40	45	50	55	60	65	70	75	80	85	90	95	100
Clearly too high																		×	×	×	×
Slightly too high																×	×				
ABOUT RIGHT															×						
Slightly too low										×	×	×	×	×							
Clearly too low	×	×	×	×	×	×	×	×	×												

Figure 14.6
Example of the staircase method used to elicit upper and lower probabilities.

relative support depending on whether k is greater or less than one. Recall that the experimental data, reviewed in the preceding section, provide strong evidence for the inequality $\alpha < \delta$. That is, $P(A, B) \leq P(A_1, B) + P(A_2, B)$ whenever A_1, A_2, and B are mutually exclusive; A is implicit; and $A' = (A_1 \vee A_2)'$. We also found evidence (see table 14.2) for the equality $\beta = \gamma$, that is, $P(A_1 \vee A_2, B) = P(A_1, A_2 \vee B) + P(A_2, A_1 \vee B)$, but this property has not been extensively tested. Departures from additivity induced, for example, by regression toward .5 could be represented by a power model with $k < 1$, which implies $\alpha < \beta < \gamma < \delta$. Note that, for explicit disjunctions of exclusive hypotheses, the basic model (equations 1 and 2), the ordinal model (equation 11), and the power model (equation 12) all assume additive support, but only the basic model entails additive probability.

Upper and Lower Indicators
Probability judgments are often vague and imprecise. To interpret and make proper use of such judgments, therefore, one needs to know something about their range of uncertainty. Indeed, much of the work on nonstandard probability has been concerned with formal models that provide upper and lower indicators of degree of belief. The elicitation and interpretation of such indicators, however, present both theoretical and practical problems. If people have a hard time assessing a single definite value for the probability of an event, they are likely to have an even harder time assessing two definite values for its upper and lower probabilities or generating a second-order probability distribution. Judges may be able to provide some indication regarding the vagueness of their assessments, but such judgments, we suggest, are better interpreted in qualitative, not quantitative, terms.

To this end, we have devised an elicitation procedure in which upper and lower probability judgments are defined verbally rather than numerically. This procedure, called the *staircase method*, is illustrated in figure 14.6. The judge is presented with an uncertain event (e.g., an eastern team rather than a western team will win the next NBA title) and is asked to check one of the five categories for each probability value. The lowest value that is not "clearly too low" (.45) and the highest value that is not "clearly too high" (.80), denoted P_* and P^*, respectively, may be taken as the lower and upper indicators. Naturally, alternative procedures involving a different number of categories, different wording, and different ranges could yield different indicators. (We assume that the labeling of the categories is symmetric around the middle category.) The staircase method can be viewed as a qualitative analog of a second-order probability distribution or of a fuzzy membership function.

We model P_* and P^* in terms of lower and upper support functions, denoted s_* and s^*, respectively. We interpret these scales as low and high estimates of s and assume that, for any A, $s_*(A) \leq s(A) \leq s^*(A)$. Furthermore, we assume that P_* and P^* can be expressed as follows:

$$P_*(A, B) = \frac{s_*(A)}{s_*(A) + s^*(B)}$$

and

$$P^*(A, B) = \frac{s^*(A)}{s^*(A) + s_*(B)}.$$

According to this model, the upper and lower indicators are generated by a slanted reading of the evidence; $P^*(A, B)$ can be interpreted as a probability judgment that is biased in favor of A and against B, whereas $P_*(A, B)$ is biased against A and in favor of B. The magnitude of the bias reflects the vagueness associated with the basic judgment, as well as the characteristics of the elicitation procedure. Within a given procedure, however, we can interpret the interval (P_*, P^*) as a comparative index of imprecision. Thus, we may conclude that one judgment is less vague than another if the interval associated with the first assessment is included in the interval associated with the second assessment. Because the high and low estimates are unlikely to be more precise or more reliable than the judge's best estimate, we regard P_* and P^* as supplements, not substitutes, for P.

To test the proposed representation against the standard theory of upper and lower probability (e.g., see Dempster, 1967; Good, 1962); we investigated people's predictions of the outcomes of the NFL playoffs for 1992–1993. The study was run the week before the two championship games in which Buffalo was to play Miami for the title of the American Football Conference (AFC), and Dallas was to play San Francisco for the title of the National Football Conference (NFC). The winners of these games would play each other two weeks later in the Super Bowl. The subjects were 135 Stanford students who volunteered to participate in a study of football prediction in exchange for a single California Lottery ticket. Half of the subjects assessed the probabilities that the winner of the Super Bowl would be Buffalo, Miami, an NFC team. The other half of the subjects assessed the probabilities that the winner of the Super Bowl would be Dallas, San Francisco, an AFC team. All subjects assessed probabilities for the two championship games. The focal and the alternative hypotheses for these games were counterbalanced. Thus, each subject made five probability assessments using the staircase method illustrated in figure 14.6.

Subjects' best estimates exhibited the pattern of subadditivity and binary complementarity observed in previous studies. The average probabilities of each of the four teams winning the Super Bowl added to 1.71; the unpacking factor was 1.92 for the AFC teams and 1.48 for the NFC teams. In contrast, the sum of the average probability of an event and its complement was 1.03. Turning to the analysis of the upper and the lower assessments, note that the present model implies $P_*(A, B) + P^*(B, A) = 1$, in accord with the standard theory of upper and lower probability. The data show that this condition holds to a very close degree of approximation, with an average sum of 1.02.

The present model, however, does not generally agree with the standard theory of upper and lower probability. To illustrate the discrepancy, suppose A and B are mutually exclusive and $C' = (A \vee B)'$. The standard theory requires that $P_*(A, \bar{A}) + P_*(B, \bar{B}) \leq P_*(C, \bar{C})$, whereas the present account suggests the opposite inequality when C is implicit. The data clearly violate the standard theory: The average lower probabilities of winning the Super Bowl were .21 for Miami and .21 for Buffalo but only .24 for their implicit disjunction (i.e., an AFC team). Similarly, the average lower probabilities of winning the Super Bowl were .25 for Dallas and .41 for San Francisco but only .45 for an NFC team. These data are consistent with the present model, assuming the subadditivity of s_*, but not with the standard theory of lower probability.

Prescriptive Implications

Models of subjective probability or degree of belief serve two functions: descriptive and prescriptive. The literature on nonstandard probability models is primarily prescriptive. These models are offered as formal languages for the evaluation of evidence and the representation of belief. In contrast, support theory attempts to describe the manner in which people make probability judgments, not to prescribe how people should make these judgments. For example, the proposition that judged probability increases by unpacking the focal hypothesis and decreases by unpacking the alternative hypothesis represents a general descriptive principle that is not endorsed by normative theories, additive or nonadditive.

Despite its descriptive nature, support theory has prescriptive implications. It could aid the design of elicitation procedures and the reconciliation of inconsistent assessments (Lindley, Tversky, & Brown, 1979). This role may be illuminated by a perceptual analogy. Suppose a surveyor has to construct a map of a park on the basis of judgments of distance between landmarks made by a fallible observer. A knowledge of the likely biases of the observer could help the surveyor construct a better map. Because observers generally underestimate distances involving hidden areas, for example, the surveyor may discard these assessments and compute the respective distances from other assessments using the laws of plane geometry. Alternatively, the surveyor may wish to reduce the bias by applying a suitable correction factor to the estimates involving hidden areas. The same logic applies to the elicitation of probability. The evidence shows that people tend to underestimate the probability of an implicit disjunction, especially the negation of an elementary hypothesis. This bias may be reduced by asking the judge to contrast hypotheses of comparable level of specificity instead of assessing the probability of a specific hypothesis against its complement.

The major conclusion of the present research is that subjective probability, or degree of belief, is nonextensional and hence nonmeasurable in the sense that alternative partitions of the space can yield different judgments. Like the measured length of a coastline, which increases as a map becomes more detailed, the perceived likelihood of an event increases as its description becomes more specific. This does not imply that judged probability is of no value, but it indicates that this concept is more fragile than suggested by existing formal theories. The failures of extensionality demonstrated in this article highlight what is perhaps the fundamental problem of probability assessment, namely the need to consider unavailable possibilities. The problem is especially severe in tasks that require the generation of new hypotheses or the construction of novel scenarios. The extensionality principle, we argue, is normatively unassailable but practically unachievable because the judge cannot be expected to fully unpack any implicit disjunction. People can be encouraged to unpack a category into its components, but they cannot be expected to think of all relevant conjunctive unpackings or to generate all relevant future scenarios. In this respect, the assessment of an additive probability distribution may be an impossible task. The judge could, of course, ensure the additivity of any given set of judgments, but this does not ensure that additivity will be preserved by further refinement.

The evidence reported here and elsewhere indicates that both qualitative and quantitative assessments of uncertainty are not carried out in a logically coherent fashion, and one might be tempted to conclude that they should not be carried out at all. However, this is not a viable option because, in general, there are no alternative procedures for assessing uncertainty. Unlike the measurement of distance, in which fallible human judgment can be replaced by proper physical measurement, there are no objective procedures for assessing the probability of events such as the guilt of a defendant, the success of a business venture, or the outbreak of war. Intuitive judgments of uncertainty, therefore, are bound to play an essential role in people's deliberations and decisions. The question of how to improve their quality through the design of effective elicitation methods and corrective procedures poses a major challenge to theorists and practitioners alike.

Notes

This research has been supported by Grant SES-9109535 from the National Science Foundation to Amos Tversky and by a National Defense Science and Engineering fellowship to Derek J. Koehler.

We are grateful to Maya Bar-Hillel, Todd Davies, Craig Fox, Daniel Kahneman, David Krantz, Glenn Shafer, Eldar Shafir, and Peter Wakker for many helpful comments and discussions.

1. Gigerenzer (1991) has further argued that the biases observed in probability judgments of unique events disappear in judgments of frequency, but the data reviewed here and elsewhere are inconsistent with this claim.

2. Enhancement, like subadditivity, may not hold when a person evaluates these probabilities at the same time because this task introduces additional constraints.

3. We thank the authors for making their data available to us.

References

Aczel, J. (1966). *Lectures on functional equations and their applications.* San Diego, CA: Academic Press.

Bar-Hillel, M., & Neter, E. (1993). How alike is it versus how likely is it: A disjunction fallacy in stereotype judgments. *Journal of Personality and Social Psychology, 65,* 1119–1131.

Briggs, L. K., & Krantz, D. H. (1992). Judging the strength of designated evidence. *Journal of Behavioral Decision Making, 5,* 77–106.

Debreu, G. (1958). Stochastic choice and cardinal utility. *Econometrica, 26,* 440–444.

Dempster, A. P. (1967). Upper and lower probabilities induced by a multivalued mapping. *Annals of Mathematical Statistics, 38,* 325–339.

Dube-Rioux, L., & Russo, J. E. (1988). An availability bias in professional judgment. *Journal of Behavioral Decision Making, 1,* 223–237.

Dubois, D., & Prade, H. (1988). Modelling uncertainty and inductive inference: A survey of recent non-additive probability systems. *Acta Psychologica, 68,* 53–78.

Erev, I., Wallsten, T. S., & Budescu, D. V. (1994). Simultaneous over- and underconfidence: The role of error in judgment processes. *Psychological Review, 101,* 519–527.

Fiedler, K., & Armbruster, T. (1994). Two halfs may be more than one whole. *Journal of Personality and Social Psychology, 66,* 633–645.

Fischhoff, B., Slovic, P., & Lichtenstein, S. (1978). Fault trees: Sensitivity of estimated failure probabilities to problem representation. *Journal of Experimental Psychology: Human Perception and Performance, 4*, 330–344.

Fox, C. R., Rogers, B., & Tversky, A. (1994). *Decision weights for options traders.* Unpublished manuscript, Stanford University, Stanford, CA.

Gettys, C. F., Mehle, T., & Fisher, S. (1986). Plausibility assessments in hypothesis generation. *Organizational Behavior and Human Decision Processes, 37*, 14–33.

Gigerenzer, G. (1991). How to make cognitive illusions disappear: Beyond "heuristics and biases." In W. Stroche & M. Hewstone (Eds.), *European review of social psychology* (Vol. 2, pp. 83–115). New York: Wiley.

Gilboa, I., & Schmeidler, D. (in press). Additive representations of non additive measures and the Choquet integral. *Annals of Operation Research.*

Good, I. J. (1962). Subjective probability as the measure of a nonmeasurable set. In E. Nagel, P. Suppes, & A. Tarski (Eds.), *Logic, methodology, and philosophy of sciences* (pp. 319–329). Stanford, CA: Stanford University Press.

Johnson, E. J., Hershey, J., Meszaros, J., & Kunreuther, H. (1993). Framing, probability distortions, and insurance decisions. *Journal of Risk and Uncertainty, 7*, 35–51.

Kahneman, D., Slovic, P., & Tversky, A. (Eds.). (1982). *Judgment under uncertainty: Heuristics and biases.* Cambridge, England: Cambridge University Press.

Kahneman, D., & Tversky, A. (1979). Intuitive prediction: Biases and corrective procedures. *TIMS Studies in Management Science, 12*, 313–327.

Kahneman, D., & Tversky, A. (1982). Variants of uncertainty. *Cognition, 11*, 143–157.

Koehler, D. J. (1994). Hypothesis generation and confidence in judgment. *Journal of Experimental Psychology: Learning, Memory, and Cognition, 20*, 461–469.

Koehler, D. J., & Tversky, A. (1993). *The enhancement effect in probability judgment.* Unpublished manuscript, Stanford University, Stanford, CA.

Krantz, D. H., Ray, B., & Briggs, L. K. (1990). *Foundations of the theory of evidence: The role of schemata.* Unpublished manuscript, Columbia University, New York.

Lichtenstein, S., Fischhoff, B., & Phillips, L. (1982). Calibration of probabilities: The state of the art to 1980. In D. Kahneman, P. Slovic, & A. Tversky (Eds.), *Judgment under uncertainty: Heuristics and biases,* (pp. 306–334). Cambridge, England: Cambridge University Press.

Lindley, D. V., Tversky, A., & Brown, R. V. (1979). On the reconciliation of probability assessments. *Journal of the Royal Statistical Society, 142*, 146–180.

Mehle, T., Gettys, C. F., Manning, C., Baca, S., & Fisher, S. (1981). The availability explanation of excessive plausibility assessment. *Acta Psychologica, 49*, 127–140.

Mongin, P. (in press). Some connections between epistemic logic and the theory of nonadditive probability. In P. W. Humphreys (Ed.), *Patrick Suppes: Scientific philosopher.* Dordrecht, Netherlands: Kluwer.

Murphy, A. H. (1985). Probabilistic weather forecasting. In A. H. Murphy & R. W. Katz (Eds.), *Probability, statistics, and decision making in the atmospheric sciences* (pp. 337–377). Boulder, CO: Westview Press.

Olson, C. L. (1976). Some apparent violations of the representativeness heuristic in human judgment. *Journal of Experimental Psychology: Human Perception and Performance, 2*, 599–608.

Pelham, B. W., Sumarta, T. T., & Myaskovsky, L. (1994). The easy path from many to much: The numerosity heuristic. *Cognitive Psychology, 26*, 103–133.

Peterson, D. K., & Pitz, G. F. (1988). Confidence, uncertainty, and the use of information. *Journal of Experimental Psychology: Learning, Memory, and Cognition, 14*, 85–92.

Redelmeier, D., Koehler, D. J., Liberman, V., & Tversky, A. (in press). Probability judgment in medicine: Discounting unspecified alternatives. *Medical Decision Making.*

Reeves, T., & Lockhart, R. S. (1993). Distributional vs. singular approaches to probability and errors in probabilistic reasoning. *Journal of Experimental Psychology: General, 122,* 207–226.

Robinson, L. B., & Hastie, R. (1985). Revision of beliefs when a hypothesis is eliminated from consideration. *Journal of Experimental Psychology: Human Perception and Performance, 4,* 443–456.

Russo, J. E., & Kolzow, K. J. (1992). *Where is the fault in fault trees?* Unpublished manuscript, Cornell University, Ithaca, N.Y.

Shafer, G. (1976). *A mathematical theory of evidence.* Princeton, N.J.: Princeton University Press.

Shafer, G., & Tversky, A. (1985). Languages and designs for probability judgment. *Cognitive Science, 9,* 309–339.

Starmer, C., & Sugden, R. (1993). Testing for juxtaposition and event-splitting effects. *Journal of Risk and Uncertainty, 6,* 235–254.

Statistical abstract of the United States. (1990). Washington, DC: U.S. Dept. of Commerce, Bureau of the Census.

Suppes, P. (1974). The measurement of belief. *Journal of the Royal Statistical Society, B, 36,* 160–191.

Teigen, K. H. (1974a). Overestimation of subjective probabilities. *Scandinavian Journal of Psychology, 15,* 56–62.

Teigen, K. H. (1974b). Subjective sampling distributions and the additivity of estimates. *Scandinavian Journal of Psychology, 15,* 50–55.

Teigen, K. H. (1983). Studies in subjective probability III: The unimportance of alternatives. *Scandinavian Journal of Psychology, 24,* 97–105.

Tversky, A., & Fox, C. (1994). *Weighing risk and uncertainty.* Unpublished manuscript, Stanford University, Stanford, CA.

Tversky, A., & Kahneman, D. (1983). Extensional vs. intuitive reasoning: The conjunction fallacy in probability judgment. *Psychological Review, 91,* 293–315.

Tversky, A., & Kahneman, D. (1986). Rational choice and the framing of decisions, Part 2. *Journal of Business, 59,* 251–278.

Tversky, A., & Sattath, S. (1979). Preference trees. *Psychological Review, 86,* 542–573.

van der Pligt, J., Eiser, J. R., & Spears, R. (1987). Comparative judgments and preferences: The influence of the number of response alternatives. *British Journal of Social Psychology, 26,* 269–280.

Van Wallendael, L. R., & Hastie, R. (1990). Tracing the footsteps of Sherlock Holmes: Cognitive representations of hypothesis testing. *Memory & Cognition, 18,* 240–250.

Walley, P. (1991). *Statistical reasoning with imprecise probabilities.* London: Chapman & Hall.

Wallsten, T. S., Budescu, D. V., & Zwick, R. (1992). Comparing the calibration and coherence of numerical and verbal probability judgments. *Management Science, 39,* 176–190.

Zadeh, L. A. (1978). Fuzzy sets as a basis for a theory of possibility. *Fuzzy Sets & Systems, 1,* 3–28.

Zarnowitz, V. (1985). Rational expectations and macroeconomic forecasts. *Journal of Business and Economic Statistics, 3,* 293–311.

Appendix

THEOREM 1: Suppose $P(A, B)$ is defined for all disjoint $A, B \in H$, and it vanishes if and only if (iff) $A' = \varnothing$. Equations 3–6 (see text) hold iff there exists a nonnegative ratio scale s on H that satisfies equations 1 and 2.

Proof: Necessity is immediate. To establish sufficiency, we define s as follows. Let $E = \{A \in H : A' \in T\}$ be the set of elementary hypotheses. Select some $D \in E$ and set $s(D) = 1$. For any other elementary hypothesis $C \in E$, such that $C' \neq D'$, define $s(C) = P(C, D)/P(D, C)$. Given any hypothesis $A \in H$ such that $A' \neq T, \varnothing$, select some $C \in E$ such that $A' \cap C' = \varnothing$ and define $s(A)$ through

$$\frac{s(A)}{s(C)} = \frac{P(A, C)}{P(C, A)};$$

that is,

$$s(A) = \frac{P(A, C)P(C, D)}{P(C, A)P(D, C)}.$$

To demonstrate that $s(A)$ is uniquely defined, suppose $B \in E$ and $A' \cap B' = \varnothing$. We want to show that

$$\frac{P(A, C)P(C, D)}{P(C, A)P(D, C)} = \frac{P(A, B)P(B, D)}{P(B, A)P(D, B)}.$$

By proportionality (equation 4), the left-hand ratio equals

$$\frac{P(A, C \vee B)P(C, D \vee B)}{P(C, A \vee B)P(D, C \vee B)}$$

and the right-hand ratio equals

$$\frac{P(A, B \vee C)P(B, D \vee C)}{P(B, A \vee C)P(D, B \vee C)}.$$

Canceling common terms, it is easy to see that the two ratios are equal iff

$$\frac{P(C, D \vee B)}{P(B, D \vee C)} = \frac{P(C, A \vee B)}{P(B, A \vee C)},$$

which holds because both ratios equal $P(C, B)/P(B, C)$, again by proportionality.

   To complete the definition of s, let $s(A) = 0$ whenever $A' = \varnothing$. For $A' = T$, we distinguish two cases. If A is explicit, that is, $A = B \vee C$ for some exclusive $B, C \in H$, set $s(A) = s(B) + s(C)$. If A is implicit, let $s(A)$ be the minimum value of s over all explicit descriptions of T.

   To establish the desired representation, we first show that for any exclusive $A, B \in H$, such that $A', B' \neq T, \varnothing$, $s(A)/s(B) = P(A, B)/P(B, A)$. Recall that T includes at least two elements. Two cases must be considered.

First, suppose $A' \cup B' \neq T$; hence, there exists an elementary hypothesis C such that $A' \cap C' = B' \cap C' = \emptyset$. In this case,

$$\frac{s(A)}{s(B)} = \frac{P(A,C)/P(C,A)}{P(B,C)/P(C,B)} = \frac{P(A,C \vee B)/P(C,A \vee B)}{P(B,C \vee A)/P(C,B \vee A)} = \frac{P(A,B)}{P(B,A)}$$

by repeated application of proportionality.

Second, suppose $A' \cup B' = T$. In this case, there is no $C' \in T$ that is not included in either A' or B', so the preceding argument cannot be applied. To show that $s(A)/s(B) = P(A,B)/P(B,A)$, suppose $C, D \in E$ and $A' \cap C' = B' \cap D' = \emptyset$. Hence,

$$\frac{s(A)}{s(B)} = \frac{s(A)s(C)s(D)}{s(C)s(D)s(B)}$$

$$= \frac{P(A,C)P(C,D)P(D,B)}{P(C,A)P(D,C)P(B,D)}$$

$$= R(A,C)R(C,D)R(D,B)$$

$$= R(A,B) \quad \text{(by the product rule [Equation 5])}$$

$$= P(A,B)/P(B,A) \quad \text{(as required)}.$$

For any pair of exclusive hypotheses, therefore, we obtain $P(A,B)/P(B,A) = s(A)/s(B)$, and $P(A,B) + P(B,A) = 1$, by binary complementarity. Consequently, $P(A,B) = s(A)/[s(A) + s(B)]$ and s is unique up to a choice of unit, which is determined by the value of $s(D)$.

To establish the properties of s, recall that unpacking (equation 6) yields $P(D,C) \leq P(A \vee B, C) = P(A, B \vee C) + P(B, A \vee C)$ whenever $D' = A' \cup B'$, A and B are exclusive, and D is implicit. The inequality on the left-hand side implies that

$$\frac{s(D)}{s(D) + s(C)} \leq \frac{s(A \vee B)}{s(A \vee B) + s(C)};$$

hence, $s(D) \leq s(A \vee B)$. The equality on the right-hand side implies that

$$\frac{s(A \vee B)}{s(A \vee B) + s(C)} = \frac{s(A)}{s(A) + s(B \vee C)} + \frac{s(B)}{s(B) + s(A \vee C)}.$$

To demonstrate that the additivity of P implies the additivity of s, suppose A, B, and C are nonnull and mutually exclusive. (If $A' \cup B' = T$, the result is immediate.)

Hence, by proportionality,

$$\frac{s(A)}{s(B)} = \frac{P(A, B)}{P(B, A)} = \frac{P(A, B \vee C)}{P(B, A \vee C)} = \frac{s(A)/[s(A) + s(B \vee C)]}{s(B)/[s(B) + s(A \vee C)]}.$$

Consequently, $s(A) + s(B \vee C) = s(B) + s(A \vee C) = s(C) + s(A \vee B)$. Substituting these relations in the equation implied by the additivity of P yields $s(A \vee B) = s(A) + s(B)$, which completes the proof of theorem 1.

THEOREM 2:   Assume the ordinal model (equation 11) and the solvability condition. Binary complementarity (equation 3) and the product rule (equation 5) hold iff there exists a constant $k \geq 0$ such that

$$P(A, B) = \frac{s(A)^k}{s(A)^k + s(B)^k}.$$

Proof: It is easy to verify that equations 3 and 5 are implied by the power model (equation 12). To derive this representation, assume that the ordinal model and the solvability condition are satisfied. Then there exists a nonnegative scale s, defined on H, and a strictly increasing function F from the unit interval into itself such that for all $A, B \in$ H,

$$P(A, B) = F\left[\frac{s(A)}{s(A) + s(B)}\right].$$

By binary complementarity, $P(A, B) = 1 - P(B, A)$; hence, $F(z) = 1 - F(1 - z)$, $0 \leq z \leq 1$. Define the function G by

$$R(A, B) = \frac{P(A, B)}{P(B, A)} = \frac{F\{s(A)/[s(A) + s(B)]\}}{F\{s(B)/[s(B) + s(A)]\}} = G[s(A)/s(B)], \quad B' \neq \varnothing.$$

Applying the product rule, with $s(C) = s(D)$, yields $G[s(A)/s(B)] = G[s(A)/s(C)]G[s(C)/s(B)]$; hence, $G(xy) = G(x)G(y)$, $x, y \geq 0$. This is a form of the Cauchy equation, whose solution is $G(x) = x^k$ (see Aczel, 1966). Consequently, $R(A, B) = s(A)^k/s(B)^k$ and, by binary complementarity,

$$P(A, B) = \frac{s(A)^k}{s(A)^k + s(B)^k}, \quad k \geq 0 \text{ (as required).}$$

15 On the Belief That Arthritis Pain Is Related to the Weather

Donald A. Redelmeier and Amos Tversky

For thousands of years people have believed that arthritis pain is influenced by the weather. Hippocrates around 400 B.C. discussed the effects of winds and rains on chronic diseases in his book *Air, Water, and Places* (1). In the nineteenth century, several authors suggested that variations in barometric pressure, in particular, were partially responsible for variations in the intensity of arthritis pain (2–4). To the current day, such beliefs are common among patients, physicians, and interested observers throughout the world (5–14). Furthermore, these beliefs have led to recommendations that patients move to milder climates or spend time in a climate-controlled chamber to lessen joint pain (15–17).

The research literature, however, has not established a clear association between arthritis pain and the weather. No study using objective measures of inflammation has found positive results (18, 19), and studies using subjective measures of pain have been conflicting. Some find that an increase in barometric pressure tends to increase pain (20), others find that it tends to decrease pain (21), and others find no association (22, 23). Some investigators argue that only a simultaneous change in pressure and humidity influences arthritis pain (24), but others find no such pattern (25). Several studies report that weather effects are immediate (20), whereas others suggest a lag of several days (26). Due to the lack of clear evidence, medical textbooks—which once devoted chapters to the relation of weather and rheumatic disease—now devote less than a page to the topic (27, 28).

The contrast between the strong belief that arthritis pain is related to the weather and the weak evidence found in the research literature is puzzling. How do people acquire and maintain the belief? Research on judgment under uncertainty indicates that both laypeople and experts sometimes detect patterns where none exist. In particular, people often perceive positive serial correlations in random sequences of coin tosses (29), stockmarket prices (30), or basketball shots (31). We hypothesize that a similar bias occurs in the evaluation of correlations between pairs of time series, and that it contributes to the belief that arthritis pain is related to the weather. We explored this hypothesis by testing (*i*) whether arthritis patients' perceptions are consistent with their data and (*ii*) whether people perceive associations between uncorrelated time series.

We obtained data from rheumatoid arthritis patients ($n = 18$) on pain (assessed by the patient), joint tenderness (evaluated by the physician), and functional status (based on a standard index) measured twice a month for 15 months (32). We also obtained local weather reports on barometric pressure, temperature, and humidity

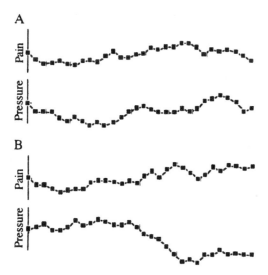

Figure 15.1
Random walk sequences. The upper sequence in each pair represents daily arthritis pain for 30 consecutive observations; the lower sequence represents daily barometric pressure during the same period. For both *A* and *B*, the correlation between changes in pain and changes in pressure is 0.00.

for the corresponding time period. Finally, we interviewed patients about their beliefs concerning their arthritis pain. All patients but one believed that their pain was related to the weather, and all but two believed the effects were strong, occurred within a day, and were related to barometric pressure, temperature, or humidity.

We computed the correlations between pain and the specific weather component and lag mentioned by each patient. The mean of these correlations was 0.016 and none was significant at $P < 0.05$. We also computed the correlation between pain and barometric pressure for each patient, using nine different time lags ranging from 2 days forward to 2 days backward in 12-hr increments. The mean of these correlations was 0.003, and only 6% were significant at $P < 0.05$. Similar results were obtained in analyses using the two other measures of arthritis and the two other measures of the weather. Furthermore, we found no consistent pattern among the few statistically significant correlations.

We next presented college students ($n = 97$) with pairs of sequences displayed graphically. The top sequence was said to represent a patient's daily arthritis pain over 1 month, and the bottom sequence was said to represent daily barometric pressure during the same month (figure 15.1). Each sequence was generated as a normal random walk and all participants evaluated six pairs of sequences: a positively correlated pair ($r = +0.50$), a negatively correlated pair ($r = -0.50$), and four uncorrelated pairs. Participants were asked to classify each pair of sequences as (*i*) positively related, (*ii*) negatively related, or (*iii*) unrelated. Positively related sequences were defined as follows: "An increase in barometric pressure is more likely to be accompanied by an increase in arthritis pain rather than a decrease on that day (and a decrease in barometric pressure is more likely to be accompanied by a decrease rather than an increase in arthritis pain on that day)." Negatively related sequences and unrelated sequences were defined similarly.

We found that the positively correlated pair and the negatively correlated pair were correctly classified by 89% and 93% of respondents, respectively. However, some uncorrelated pairs were consistently classified as related. For example, the two uncorrelated sequences in figure 15.1A were judged as positively related by 87%, as negatively related by 2%, and as unrelated by 11% of participants. The two uncorrelated sequences in figure 15.1B were judged as positively related by 3%, as negatively related by 79%, and as unrelated by 18% of participants. The remaining two pairs of uncorrelated sequences were correctly classified by 59% and 64% of participants. Evidently, the intuitive notion of association differs from the statistical concept of association.

Our results indicate that people tend to perceive an association between uncorrelated time series. We attribute this phenomenon to selective matching, the tendency to focus on salient coincidences, thereby capitalizing on chance and neglecting contrary evidence (33–35). For arthritis, selective matching leads people to look for changes in the weather when they experience increased pain, and pay little attention to the weather when their pain is stable. For graphs, selective matching leads people to focus on segments where the two sequences seem to move together (in the same or opposite direction), with insufficient regard to other aspects of the data. In both cases, a single day of severe pain and extreme weather might sustain a lifetime of belief in a relation between them. The cognitive processes involved in evaluating graphs are different from those involved in evaluating past experiences, yet all intuitive judgments of covariation are vulnerable to selective matching.

Several psychological factors could contribute to the belief that arthritis pain is related to the weather, in addition to general plausibility and traditional popularity. The desire to have an explanation for a worsening of pain may encourage patients to search for confirming evidence and neglect contrary instances (36). This search is facilitated by the availability of multiple components and time lags for linking changes in arthritis to changes in the weather (37). Selective memory may further enhance the belief that arthritis pain is related to the weather if coincidences are more memorable than mismatches (38). Selective matching, therefore, can be enhanced by both motivational and memory effects; our study of graphs, however, suggests that it can operate even in the absence of these effects.

Selective matching can help explain both the prevalent belief that arthritis pain is related to the weather and the failure of medical research to find consistent correlations. Our study, of course, does not imply that arthritis pain and the weather are unrelated for all patients. Furthermore, it is possible that daily measurements over many years of our patients would show a stronger correlation than observed in our data, at least for some patients. However, it is doubtful that sporadic correlations could justify the widespread and strongly held beliefs about arthritis and the weather. The observation that the beliefs are just as prevalent in San Diego (where the weather is mild and stable) as in Boston (where the weather is severe and volatile) casts further doubt on a purely physiological explanation (39). People's beliefs about arthritis pain and the weather may tell more about the workings of the mind than of the body.

References

1. Adams, F. (1991) *The Genuine Works of Hippocrates* (Williams & Wilkins, Baltimore).

2. Webster, J. (1859) *Lancet* i, 588–589.

3. Mitchel, S. W. (1877) *Am. J. Med. Sci.* 73, 305–329.

4. Everett, J. T. (1879) *Med. J. Exam.* 38, 253–260.

5. Abdulpatakhov, D. D. (1969) *Vopr. Revm.* 9, 72–76.

6. Nava, P., & Seda, H. (1964) *Bras. Med.* 78, 71–74.

7. Pilger, A. (1970) *Med. Klin. Munich* 65, 1363–1365.

8. Hollander, J. L. (1963) *Arch. Environ. Health* 6, 527–536.

9. Guedj, D., & Weinberger, A. (1990) *Ann. Rheum. Dis.* 49, 158–159.

10. Lawrence, J. S. (1977) *Rheumatism in Population* (Heinemann Med. Books, London), pp. 505–517.

11. Rose, M. B. (1974) *Physiotherapy* 60, 306–309.

12. Rasker, J. J., Peters, H. J. G., & Boon, K. L. (1986) *Scand. J. Rheumatol.* 15, 27–36.

13. Laborde, J. M., Dando, W. A., & Powers, M. J. (1986) *Soc. Sci. Med.* 23, 549–554.

14. Shutty, M. S., Cundiff, G., & DeGood, D. E. (1992) *Pain* 49, 199–204.

15. Hill, D. F., & Holbrook, W. P. (1942) *Clinics* 1, 577–581.

16. Balfour, W. (1916) *Observations with Cases Illustrative of a New, Simple, and Expeditious Mode of Curing Rheumatism and Sprains* (Muirhead, Edinburgh).

17. Edstrom, G., Lundin, G., & Wramner, T. (1948) *Ann. Rheum. Dis.* 7, 76–92.

18. Latman, N. S. (1981) *J. Rheumatol.* 8, 725–729.

19. Latman, N. S. (1980) *N. Engl. J. Med.* 303, 1178.

20. Rentschler, E. B., Vanzant, F. R., & Rowntree, L. G. (1929) *J. Am. Med. Assoc.* 92, 1995–2000.

21. Guedj, D. (1990) *Ann. Rheum. Dis.* 49, 158–159.

22. Dordick, I. (1958) *Weather* 13, 359–364.

23. Patberg, W. R., Nienhuis, R. L. F., & Veringa, F. (1985) *J. Rheumatol.* 12, 711–715.

24. Hollander, J. L., & Yeostros, S. J. (1963) *Bull. Am. Meteorol. Soc.* 44, 489–494.

25. Sibley, J. T. (1985) *J. Rheumatol.* 12, 707–710.

26. Patberg, W. R. (1989) *Arthritis Rheum.* 32, 1672–1629.

27. Hollander, J. L., ed. (1960) *Arthritis and Allied Conditions* (Lea & Febiger, Philadelphia), 6th ed., pp. 577–581.

28. McCarty, D. J., ed. (1989) *Arthritis and Allied Conditions* (Lea & Febiger, Philadelphia), 11th ed., p. 25.

29. Bar-Hillel, M., & Wagenaar, W. (1991) *Adv. Appl. Math.* 12, 428–454.

30. Malkiel, B. G. (1990) *A Random Walk Down Wall Street* (Norton, New York).

31. Gilovich, T., Vallone, R., & Tversky, A. (1985) *Cognit. Psychol.* 17, 295–314.

32. Ward, M. M. (1993) *J. Rheumatol.* 21, 17–21.

33. Kahneman, D., Slovic, P., & Tversky, A., eds. (1982) *Judgment Under Uncertainty: Heuristics and Biases* (Cambridge Univ. Press, New York).

34. Nisbett, R., & Ross, L. (1980) *Human Inference: Strategies and Shortcomings of Social Judgment* (Prentice–Hall, London), pp. 90–112.

35. Gilovich, T. (1991) *How We Know What Isn't So: The Fallibility of Human Reasoning in Everyday Life* (The Free Press, New York).

36. Chapman, L. J., & Chapman, J. P. (1969) *J. Abnorm. Psychol.* 74, 271–280.

37. Abelson, R. P. (1995) *Statistics as Principled Argument* (Lawrence Erlbaum, Hillsdale, N.J.), pp. 7–8.

38. Tversky, A., & Kahneman, D. (1973) *Cognit. Psychol.* 5, 207–232.

39. Jamison, R. N., Anderson, K. O., & Slater, M. A. (1995) *Pain* 61, 309–315.

16 Unpacking, Repacking, and Anchoring: Advances in Support Theory

Yuval Rottenstreich and Amos Tversky

The study of intuitive probability judgment has shown that people often do not follow the extensional logic of probability theory (see, e.g., Kahneman, Slovic, & Tversky, 1982). In particular, alternative descriptions of the same event can give rise to different probability judgments, and a specific event (e.g., that 1,000 people will die in an earthquake) may appear more likely than a more inclusive event (e.g., that 1,000 people will die in a natural disaster). To accommodate such findings, Tversky and Koehler (1994) have developed a nonextensional theory of belief in which subjective probability is not attached to events, as in other models, but to descriptions of events, called *hypotheses*. According to this account, called *support theory*, each hypothesis A has a support value, $s(A)$, corresponding to the strength of the evidence for this hypothesis. The judged probability, $P(A, B)$, that hypothesis A rather than B holds, assuming that one and only one of them obtains, is given by

$$P(A, B) = \frac{s(A)}{s(A) + s(B)}.$$

Thus, judged probability is interpreted in terms of the support of the focal hypothesis A relative to the alternative hypothesis B. The key assumption of support theory is that unpacking a description of an event (e.g., a plane crash, C) into disjoint components (e.g., an accidental plane crash, C_a, caused by human error or mechanical failure, or a nonaccidental plane crash, C_n, caused by terrorism or sabotage) generally increases its support. Thus, the support of the explicit disjunction $C_a \vee C_n$ is equal to or greater than the support of the implicit disjunction C that does not mention any cause. That is, $s(C) \le s(C_a \vee C_n)$. The rationale for this assumption is twofold. First, unpacking an implicit hypothesis may remind people of possibilities they might have overlooked. Second, the explicit mention of a possibility tends to increase its salience and hence its perceived support.

Support theory provides a unified framework for the analysis and the interpretation of a wide range of findings. It predicts that the judged probability of an event increases by unpacking the focal hypothesis and decreases by unpacking the alternative hypothesis. For instance, the judged probability that a given person will die a natural rather than an unnatural death increases by listing various causes of natural death (e.g., heart attack, stroke, cancer) and decreases by listing various causes of unnatural death (e.g., car accident, homicide, fire). Furthermore, support theory implies that the judged probability of a hypothesis plus the judged probability of its complement, evaluated by different groups of participants, adds up to one. For finer partitions, however, the sum of the judged probabilities of a set of mutually exclusive and exhaustive hypotheses generally is greater than one. These predictions have been confirmed in numerous studies; earlier experiments are reviewed by Tversky and Koehler (1994), some later experiments are discussed by Fox and Tversky (in press).

This article presents a significant generalization of support theory that allows subadditivity for explicit disjunctions. To illustrate this extension, consider the possibilities that the winner of the next presidential election in the United States will be a Democrat (*Dem*), a Republican (*Rep*), or an Independent (*Ind*). The original version of support theory assumes that support is additive for explicit disjunctions, with the result that $s(Rep \vee Ind) = s(Rep) + s(Ind)$, and consequently, judged probability (P) is also additive for explicit disjunctions as in the standard theory of probability. As is shown next, however, several observations suggest that support is subadditive for explicit disjunctions such that $s(Rep \vee Ind) \leq s(Rep) + s(Ind)$, and hence

$$P(Rep \vee Ind, Dem) \leq P(Rep, Dem \vee Ind) + P(Ind, Rep \vee Dem).$$

That is, the judged probability that the winner of the upcoming election will be a Republican or an Independent rather than a Democrat is less than or equal to the judged probability that the winner will be a Republican rather than a Democrat or an Independent plus the judged probability that the winner will be an Independent rather than a Republican or a Democrat. More generally, we assume that if A and B are mutually exclusive hypotheses, and (A_1, A_2) is recognized as a partition of A, then $s(A) \leq s(A_1 \vee A_2) \leq s(A_1) + s(A_2)$. This assumption regarding the support function s imposes the following constraints on the observed measure P. In particular, the left inequality implies a testable condition, called *implicit subadditivity*,

$$P(A, B) = \frac{s(A)}{s(A) + s(B)}$$

$$\leq \frac{s(A_1 \vee A_2)}{s(A_1 \vee A_2) + s(B)} \quad \text{because } s(A) \leq s(A_1 \vee A_2)$$

$$= P(A_1 \vee A_2, B).$$

And the right inequality implies a second testable condition, called *explicit subadditivity*,

$$P(A_1 \vee A_2, B) = \frac{s(A_1 \vee A_2)}{s(A_1 \vee A_2) + s(B)}$$

$$\leq \frac{s(A_1) + s(A_2)}{s(A_1) + s(A_2) + s(B)} \quad \text{because } s(A_1 \vee A_2) \leq s(A_1) + s(A_2)$$

$$\leq \frac{s(A_1)}{s(A_1) + s(B \vee A_2)} + \frac{s(A_2)}{s(A_2) + s(B \vee A_1)} \quad \text{by the same logic}$$

$$= P(A_1, B \vee A_2) + P(A_2, B \vee A_1).$$

Note that probability theory requires additivity throughout, whereas the theory of belief functions (Shafer, 1976) assumes superadditivity. Thus, support theory and Shafer's theory depart from the probability calculus in opposite directions. The contrast between the two theories is discussed in the last section.

Before addressing the cognitive processes that give rise to explicit subadditivity, we discuss three issues regarding the interpretation of support theory. First, we wish to emphasize that the predictions of the theory, notably binary complementarity, that is, $P(A, B) + P(B, A) = 1$, concern hypotheses not events. This distinction is particularly important in tasks where the alternative to the focal hypothesis is not explicitly stated. Consider, for example, the outcome of a race between an incumbent and a challenger, and let *In* denote the hypothesis that the incumbent will win the race and *Ch* denote the hypothesis that the challenger will win the race. Support theory implies that the judged probability of *In* plus the judged probability of not-*In* (i.e., the incumbent will not win the race) equals one, but the theory is not committed to the prediction that the judged probability of *In* plus the judged probability of *Ch* will equal one. In this simple example it is immediately obvious that *Ch* is the same as not-*In*, hence additivity is likely to hold, assuming it is clear that there are no other candidates and that ties are excluded. However, when the hypotheses under discussion are more complicated and the setting is less familiar, additivity need not hold (see Gonzales & Bonini, 1995; Macchi, Osherson, & Legrenzi, 1995).

Second, the unpacking inequality $s(A) \leq s(A_1 \vee A_2)$ is assumed to hold only when the judge knows, or believes, that $A_1 \vee A_2$ has the same extension as A. Thus, the theory predicts that the judged probability that a patient has meningitis (M), for example, is less than or equal to the judged probability that the patient has either viral meningitis or nonviral meningitis because their disjunction is clearly coextensional with M. However, the theory does not require that the judged probability of meningitis will be less than or equal to the judged probability of either viral meningitis (M_v) or bacterial meningitis (M_b), unless the judge happens to know that $M_v \vee M_b$ is coextensional with M. Note that a judge presented with the explicit disjunction $M_v \vee M_b$ may recognize that it has the same extension as the implicit disjunction M even though, presented with M alone, the judge may not be able to unpack it into M_v and M_b. Thus, the theory permits recognition without recall.

Third, the present theory expresses an observed probability judgment, $P(A, B)$, in terms of the underlying support, $s(A)$ and $s(B)$, of the individual hypotheses.

Although it is possible, in some cases, to predict judged probability from independent assessments of support (see Tversky & Koehler, 1994), the present theory treats support as a psychological construct derived from probability judgment. A formal statement of the theory is presented in the Appendix. It provides necessary and sufficient conditions for the representation of probability judgments in terms of subadditive support; it also provides a simple method for constructing an essentially unique support function from observed judgments of probability.

Let us turn now from the interpretation of support theory to the main topic of this article, namely the psychological processes that can produce explicit subadditivity. More specifically, we investigate two such mechanisms, repacking and anchoring, that are discussed in turn.

As noted in the original version of the theory, a judge presented with an explicit disjunction may, nevertheless, think about it as an implicit disjunction, and vice versa. Consider, for example, the probability that a particular student majors in industrial, mechanical, or electrical engineering. A judge presented with such an explicit disjunction may repack the various disciplines and evaluate the implicit disjunction *engineering*. Because unpacking increases support, repacking reduces support giving rise to explicit subadditivity. Furthermore, we expect more explicit subadditivity for disjunctions of similar components than for disjunctions of dissimilar components because similar components are more easily repacked.

A second source of explicit subadditivity is the use of anchoring and adjustment. Instead of assessing independently the support of each component of an explicit disjunction and then adding the separate assessments, the judge may assess one of the components (perhaps the larger or the more familiar) and then adjust this value upward to accommodate the other components. Because such adjustments are generally insufficient (Poulton, 1994; Slovic & Lichtenstein, 1968; Tversky & Kahneman, 1974), the use of this heuristic is likely to produce explicit subadditivity. An individual who is asked to assess the combined population of the United States and Canada, for example, may anchor on the U.S. population and then adjust it upward, without making an explicit assessment of the population of Canada. If frequency, probability, or support are evaluated in this manner, we expect subadditivity for explicit disjunctions, even if their components are not repacked.

The effects of repacking and anchoring are explored in the following studies. Studies 1 and 2 test both implicit and explicit subadditivity in intuitive judgments of probability. Studies 3 and 4 investigate explicit subadditivity in judgments of frequency.

Study 1: Implicit and Explicit Subadditivity

This study employs two problems that have the same formal structure. Let A_1, A_2, and B denote three mutually exclusive and exhaustive hypotheses, and let A be an implicit disjunction of A_1 and A_2. In each problem, different groups of participants evaluated the implicit disjunction $P(A, B)$, the explicit disjunction $P(A_1 \vee A_2, B)$, the component, $P(A_1, A_2 \vee B)$, and the component $P(A_2, A_1 \vee B)$.

A total of 178 Stanford students participated in the study to fulfill course requirements. They were divided into four groups of roughly equal size. Every group evaluated both problems, each in a different condition. The two problems were embedded in a packet that included several other questionnaires, unrelated to the present study. Participants received the packet in class, completed it in their free time, and returned it anonymously 1 week later.

The first problem concerns the outcome of the next presidential election in the United States. Participants in the implicit group evaluated "the probability that the winner of the next presidential election will not be a Democrat." Participants in the explicit group evaluated the probability that "the winner of the next presidential election will be a Republican or an Independent rather than a Democrat." Participants in the two remaining groups evaluated either "the probability that the winner of the next presidential election will be a Republican rather than a Democrat or an Independent" or "the probability that the winner of the next presidential election will be an Independent rather than a Democrat or a Republican."

The second problem concerns the outcome of a criminal trial. All participants read the following scenario:

Susan L. has accused her boss, Frank G., of unwelcome sexual advances and the promise of promotion in exchange for sexual favors. Frank G. denies any wrongdoing. The case has been brought before a jury consisting of seven men and five women. There were no eyewitnesses, but Susan's boyfriend has testified that she told him about the incidents in question. The jury is now deliberating.

Participants in the implicit group evaluated "the probability that this trial will not result in a guilty verdict." Participants in the explicit group evaluated "the probability of either a not guilty verdict or a hung jury rather than a guilty verdict." Participants in the two remaining groups evaluated either "the probability of a not guilty verdict rather than a guilty verdict or a hung jury" or "the probability of a hung jury rather than a not guilty verdict or a guilty verdict."

Table 16.1 presents median probability judgments for each of the two problems. Although support theory does not require strict inequalities for implicit and explicit

Table 16.1
Median Probability Judgments Used to Test Implicit and Explicit Subadditivity in Study 1

Probability judgments	Problem 1: presidential election	Problem 2: criminal trial
$\alpha = P(A, B)$	60	50
$\beta = P(A_1 \lor A_2, B)$	60	60
$\gamma = P(A_1, A_2 \lor B)$	59	58
$\delta = P(A_2, A_1 \lor B)$	5	40

Note: In Problem 1, A_1 = Republican, A_2 = Independent, A = not Democrat, and B = Democrat. In Problem 2, A_1 = not guilty, A_2 = hung jury, A = result other than guilty, and B = guilty.

subadditivity, the statistical tests reported in this article test the strict version of these inequalities against the null hypothesis of equality. In particular, we used the Mann–Whitney statistic to test the hypothesis that the judged probability of the implicit disjunction, $P(A, B)$, is strictly smaller than the judged probability of the explicit disjunction, $P(A_1 \lor A_2, B)$. This analysis provides some evidence for implicit subadditivity in Problem 2 ($p < .05$, one-sided) but not in problem 1. We used the same statistic to test the hypothesis that the judged probability of the explicit disjunction, $P(A_1 \lor A_2, B)$, is strictly smaller than the sum of the judged probabilities of the single components, $P(A_1, A_2 \lor B) + P(A_2, A_1 \lor B)$. Because the latter were assessed by different groups of participants, we generated 100 "synthetic" distributions of such sums by pairing at random participants from the two groups. The median of the Mann–Whitney statistics across these distributions was significant in both Problem 1 (median $p < .05$) and Problem 2 (median $p < .0001$). Thus, strict explicit subadditivity was confirmed for both problems, and strict implicit subadditivity was observed in the trial problem but not in the election problem. The latter observation is not too surprising because here the implicit disjunction, non-Democrat, is naturally unpacked into the explicit disjunction, Republican or Independent.

Study 2: Causal Versus Temporal Unpacking

If implicit and explicit subadditivity are generated by different mechanisms, as suggested above, their relative contributions should vary depending on the nature of the partition. Some partitions are expected to induce primarily implicit subadditivity, whereas others are expected to produce primarily explicit subadditivity. The following study explores these effects and estimates their relative contributions.

Participants in the study were 165 Stanford students attending an introductory economics class. They answered, in a classroom setting, a few questions concerning the probability of various causes of death. Participants were informed that

Each year in the United States, approximately 2 million people (or 1% of the population) die from a variety of causes. In this questionnaire you will be asked to estimate the probability that a randomly selected death is due to one cause rather than another. Obviously, you are not expected to know the exact figures, but everyone has some idea about the prevalence of various causes of death. To give you a feel for the numbers involved, note that 1.5% of deaths each year are attributable to suicide.

This study consists of two cases. In case 1 the focal hypothesis, homicide (H) is unpacked according to the causal agent: homicide by an acquaintance (H_a) and homicide by a stranger (H_s). In case 2 the same focal hypothesis, H is unpacked according to the time of occurrence: daytime homicide (H_d) and nighttime homicide (H_n). The alternative hypothesis in all judgments is accidental death (X).

In this study, unlike the previous one, the focal and the alternative hypotheses are not exhaustive; the cause of death may be other than homicide or accident. Thus, participants here are asked to evaluate the conditional probability of the focal against the alternative hypothesis, assuming that one and only one of them holds. It is essential, of course, that participants understand and respect this assumption. Because the alternative hypothesis (X) in this design is held constant, probability theory requires additivity of odds, not of conditional probability. In particular, it implies $R(H_a \vee H_s, X) = R(H_a, X) + R(H_s, X)$, where $R(A, B)$ denotes the probability ratio $P(A, B)/P(B, A)$, provided $P(B, A) \neq 0$.

We conjectured that the causal partition is more likely to bring to mind additional possibilities than the temporal partition. Homicide by an acquaintance suggests domestic violence or a partners' quarrel, whereas homicide by a stranger suggests armed robbery or drive-by shooting. In contrast, daytime homicide and nighttime homicide are less likely to bring to mind disparate acts and hence are more readily repacked as an implicit disjunction. Consequently, we expect more implicit subadditivity in case 1, due to enhanced availability, and more explicit subadditivity in case 2, due to repacking of the explicit disjunction.

The study was designed as follows. In case 1, the participants were randomly divided into three groups. One group ($N = 55$) evaluated the probability of the implicit disjunction that a randomly selected death is a homicide rather than an accidental death, $P(H, X)$. A second group ($N = 54$) evaluated the probability of the explicit disjunction that a randomly selected death is a homicide committed by an acquaintance or a homicide committed by a stranger rather than an accidental death, $P(H_a \vee H_s, X)$. A third group ($N = 56$) evaluated the probability of the two individual components, $P(H_a, X)$ and $P(H_s, X)$.

Case 2 was presented to the same participants a few weeks later. The design and the procedures were the same, except for the use of the temporal partition instead of

Table 16.2
Median Probability Judgments (P) and Estimated Supports (s) and Weights (w) for the Two Partitions in Study 2

	Homicide unpacked	
	Case 1 (causal agent):	Case 2 (by time):
Hypothesis	acquaintance vs. stranger	day vs. night
Implicit	$P(H, X) = .20$	$P(H, X) = .20$
Explicit	$P(H_a \vee H_s, X) = .25$	$P(H_d \vee H_n, X) = .20$
	$P(H_a, X) = .15$	$P(H_d, X) = .10$
	$P(H_s, X) = .15$	$P(H_n, X) = .21$
Implicit	$s(H) = .25$	$s(H) = .25$
Explicit	$s(H_a \vee H_s) = .33$	$s(H_d \vee H_n) = .25$
	$s(H_a) + s(H_s) = .18 + .18 = .36$	$s(H_d) + s(H_n) = .11 + .29 = .40$
Implicit (I)	$w_{III} = .25/.33 = .76$	$w_{III} = .25/.25 = 1.00$
Explicit (E)	$w_{HE} = .33/.36 = .92$	$w_{HE} = .25/.40 = .63$
Global	$w_H = .25/.36 = .69$	$w_H = .25/.40 = .63$

Note: H denotes homicide, X denotes accidental death, and H_a, H_s, H_d, H_n denote, respectively, homicide by an acquaintance, by a stranger, during daytime, and during nighttime.

the causal partition. As above, the participants were randomly divided into three groups. One group ($N = 53$) evaluated the implicit disjunction $P(H, X)$; a second group ($N = 53$) evaluated the explicit disjunction $P(H_a \vee H_n, X)$; and a third group ($N = 56$) evaluated the two individual components, $P(H_d, X)$ and $P(H_n, X)$. The median estimates for both cases are presented in the upper part of table 16.2.

The lower part of table 16.2 presents the supports and the weights derived from the median judgments, as will be shown later. Note that according to support theory, the odds $P(A, B)/[1 - P(A, B)]$ equal $s(A)/s(B)$. Letting $s(X) = 1$, the support of each focal hypothesis in this study equals the odds of this hypothesis against the alternative X. For example,

$$s(H) = \frac{s(H)}{s(X)} = \frac{P(H, X)}{1 - P(H, X)} = \frac{.20}{.80} = .25.$$

Other support values were obtained similarly.

Support theory offers simple measures of implicit and explicit subadditivity. Let $(A_1, \ldots, A_n)$ be a partition of the implicit hypothesis A. The ratio

$$w_A = \frac{s(A)}{s(A_1) + \cdots + s(A_n)}$$

provides a global measure of the degree of subadditivity induced by the above partition. Note that $w_A = 1$ if probability judgments are additive, and $w_A < 1$ if they exhibit either implicit or explicit subadditivity. Thus, lower w implies greater sub-additivity. To assess the separate contributions of implicit and explicit subadditivity, define

$$w_{AI} = \frac{s(A)}{s(A_1 \vee \cdots \vee A_n)}$$

$$w_{AE} = \frac{s(A_1 \vee \cdots \vee A_n)}{s(A_1) + \cdots + s(A_n)}$$

so that $w_A = w_{AI}w_{AE}$. Hence, the global measure of subadditivity, w_A, is decomposed into its implicit (w_{AI}) and explicit (w_{AE}) components that can be estimated from the data.

Applying the preceding analysis to the data of table 16.2 reveals more implicit subadditivity in case 1 ($w_{HI} = .76$) than in case 2 ($w_{HI} = 1.00$), and more explicit subadditivity in case 2 ($w_{HI} = .62$) than in case 1 ($w_{HE} = .92$). Strict implicit sub-additivity was tested by comparing the supports of the implicit and explicit dis-junctions in each case, that is, $s(H)$ versus $s(H_a \vee H_s)$ and $s(H)$ versus $s(H_d \vee H_n)$, using the Mann–Whitney statistic. Strict explicit subadditivity was tested by com-paring the sum of the supports of the component hypotheses, within the data of a participant, to the support of the corresponding explicit disjunction, that is $s(H_a) + s(H_s)$ versus $s(H_a \vee H_s)$ and $s(H_d) + s(H_n)$ versus $s(H_d \vee H_n)$. The analysis yielded significant strict implicit subadditivity in case 1 ($p < .01$) but not in case 2, and significant strict explicit subadditivity in case 2 ($p < .005$), but not in case 1. These findings support our conjecture that the causal partition induces more implicit subadditivity, whereas the temporal partition induces more explicit subadditivity.

Study 3: Similar Versus Dissimilar Components

Although support theory has been conceived as a model of probability judgment, it can be readily applied to assessments of percentage or relative frequency (Tversky & Koehler, 1994). Moreover, judgments of absolute frequency can serve as support for certain hypotheses. For example, the probability that it will snow in Chicago next November may be based on an estimate of the frequency of snowy and nonsnowy Novembers in the last decade. It is instructive, therefore, to test whether assessed frequency satisfies implicit and explicit subadditivity. One might expect that judg-ments of absolute frequency are less vulnerable to these biases because the additivity of frequency is simpler and more intuitive than the additivity of probability.

The study of frequency judgment also provides an opportunity for testing another potential source of explicit subadditivity, namely a regressive bias towards the midpoint of the scale (e.g., .5), reflecting either response bias or random error (see, e.g., Erev, Wallsten, & Budescu, 1994). This account implies explicit subadditivity when the two components are below the midpoint and explicit superadditivity when the two components are above the midpoint. Because the probability scale is bounded by one, the above prediction cannot be tested using judgments of probability or relative frequency, but it can be readily tested in judgments of absolute frequency.

The participants, 152 Stanford students, were asked to estimate the number of fellow undergraduates majoring in particular fields. They were recruited through ads placed in *The Stanford Daily* and were paid for their participation. Participants were run in groups of 8–12 members. In addition to the judgments of frequency, students participated in several unrelated two-person games. Participants were given the following instructions:

Consider all Stanford students who have declared *one* major. We would like you to estimate the number of students majoring in particular fields. Obviously, you are not expected to know the exact figures. We are interested in your impressions regarding the popularity of different majors.

For your information, 120 students major in History. Using this number as a standard of comparison, please give your best estimates of the following. The three most accurate respondents will receive a prize of $20.

Twenty-four majors, listed in table 16.3, were divided into three sets of 8. From each set of 8 majors, we constructed four pairs of similar majors (e.g., mathematics and computer science), and four pairs of dissimilar majors (e.g., mathematics and Italian). Participants were randomly divided into three groups. The participants in each group evaluated each of the 8 individual majors from one set (e.g., "The number of students majoring in mathematics"), the four similar pairs of majors from another set (e.g., "The total number of students majoring either in political science or international relations"), and the four dissimilar pairs from a third set (e.g., "The total number of students majoring either in chemistry or English"). Thus, each participant encountered each major exactly once.

Explicit subadditivity implies that the estimated number of students in a given pair of majors is less than or equal to the sum of the estimates of the individual majors. If this phenomenon is driven, at least in part, by participants' tendency to repack the individual components, then we should expect greater subadditivity for similar than for dissimilar pairs because it is easier and more natural to pack related majors (e.g., mathematics and computer science) than unrelated majors (e.g., mathematics and

Table 16.3
Median Frequency Estimates and the Actual Number of Students in Each Major (Study 3)

Major	Median estimate	Actual number
Biology	250	265
Chemistry	100	51
Chemical engineering	70	56
Civil engineering	95	64
Communication	65	66
Comparative literature	40	6
Computer science	100	104
Electrical engineering	100	102
Earth systems	50	66
Economics	200	261
English	120	200
French	25	7
Geology	36	3
Industrial engineering	70	64
International relations	100	96
Italian	20	1
Mathematics	50	9
Mechanical engineering	100	97
Petroleum engineering	30	1
Philosophy	50	18
Political science	150	135
Public policy	80	72
Sociology	80	35
Symbolic systems	30	44

Italian). Finally, if participants estimate the total number of students who major in one of two fields by anchoring on the larger major and making an insufficient upward adjustment, then we expect the judgments to be more sensitive to the larger than to the smaller component of each pair.

Table 16.3 presents median estimates for each of the 24 majors, along with the official numbers. The correlation between the estimated and correct values is .93, and the average absolute deviation of prediction is 24, indicating that our respondents had a reasonably good idea of the relative popularity of the various majors at their university.

Tables 16.4 and 16.5 present, separately for similar and dissimilar pairs, the median frequency estimates for the pairs, denoted F_{AB}, the median sums of frequency estimates of the individual majors, computed within the data of each participant and denoted $F_A + F_B$, and the ratio of these values. The results provide strong evidence

Table 16.4
Median Frequency Estimates for Each Similar Pair (F_{AB}), Median Sum of Estimated Components $(F_A + F_B)$, and Their Ratio (Study 3)

Similar pair	Median estimate (F_{AB})	Median sum $(F_A + F_B)$	$\left(\dfrac{F_{AB}}{F_A + F_B}\right)$
Chemical engineering and petroleum engineering	50	110	.45
Geology and earth systems	50	110	.45
Mechanical engineering and civil engineering	100	200	.50
Biology and chemistry	200	360	.56
Philosophy and symbolic systems	50	90	.56
Political science and international relations	150	260	.58
English and comparative literature	105	160	.66
Economics and public policy	190	275	.69
Math and computer science	130	173	.75
Communication and sociology	115	150	.77
French and Italian	40	50	.80
Electrical engineering and industrial engineering	180	160	1.13
Median			.62

Table 16.5
Median Frequency Estimates for Each Dissimilar Pair (F_{AB}), Median Sum of Estimated Components $(F_A + F_B)$, and Their Ratio (Study 3)

Dissimilar pair	Median estimate (F_{AB})	Median sum $(F_A + F_B)$	$\left(\dfrac{F_{AB}}{F_A + F_B}\right)$
Industrial engineering and political science	145	238	.61
Philosophy and earth systems	70	114	.61
Chemistry and English	150	230	.65
Chemical engineering and public policy	80	120	.67
Mechanical engineering and sociology	150	220	.68
Computer science and French	100	135	.74
Electrical engineering and international relations	150	195	.77
Geology and symbolic systems	50	65	.77
Communication and civil engineering	120	155	.77
Economics and petroleum engineering	200	250	.80
Biology and comparative literature	220	270	.81
Mathematics and Italian	58	70	.83
Median			.76

for subadditivity: The estimate of the pair is less than the sum of the individual estimates in 23 of 24 cases, and the mean value of $F_{AB}/(F_A + F_B)$ across all pairs is only .69. This effect cannot be explained by a regression towards a central value (e.g., 120, which was given as a standard of comparison) because subadditivity is very much in evidence for both large and small pairs of majors. Recall that a symmetric error model predicts subadditivity for pairs of small majors and superadditivity for pairs of large majors, contrary to the data in tables 16.4 and 16.5.

In accord with repacking, the similar pairs tend to be more subadditive than the dissimilar pairs: The values of $F_{AB}/(F_A + F_B)$ are generally lower in table 16.4 than in table 16.5 ($p < .05$ by a one-sided Mann–Whitney test). However, the presence of strict explicit subadditivity in both cases suggests an anchoring and adjustment process.

To test this account we compared, separately for similar and dissimilar pairs, the median estimate of each pair, F_{AB}, with the higher of the two medians of estimates for individual majors forming the pair, denoted F_H. For similar pairs, the mean value of F_H was 108, whereas the mean value of F_{AB} was 113, ($t = .22$, ns). For dissimilar pairs, the mean value of F_H was 111, whereas the mean value of F_{AB} was 124 ($t = .56$, ns). Thus, the estimates for the pairs (overall mean $= 119$) are much closer to the higher of the two majors (overall mean $= 109$) than to the sum of the individual estimates (overall mean $= 165$). These data are consistent with the notion that participants estimated the pairs by focusing on the larger component.

Study 4: Anchoring and Adjustment

If instead of evaluating each major separately and then adding these individual estimates, participants evaluate pairs of majors by adjusting one of the estimates, then participants who had already evaluated one of the majors are likely to use this estimate as an anchor. In this case, the frequency estimate of a pair is higher when the participants had estimated beforehand the higher rather than the lower component of that pair. To test this prediction we selected 12 pairs of majors and identified each of their components as high or low according to the median estimates in table 16.3. The participants ($N = 81$) were recruited and run as in the preceding study. They were divided randomly into three groups. All participants evaluated all 12 pairs. Prior to this task, however, each group evaluated a different set of 8 single majors. The single majors were selected so that for each pair of majors one group evaluated beforehand the high or more popular major, a second group evaluated the low or less popular major, and a third group did not evaluate either of the individual components prior to the evaluation of the pair. The order of presentation of both individual majors and pairs of majors was randomized.

If people focus on their prior estimate, we expect participants who first evaluated the high component of a pair to give higher estimates than participants who first evaluated the low component of that pair. And if, in the absence of a prior estimate, people tend to choose the larger of the two majors as an anchor because it is closer to the required estimate, we expect participants who made no prior estimate for a given pair to be closer to those who evaluated the high component than to those who evaluated the low component.

The results confirmed both predictions. The mean estimate for a pair of majors in the high condition was 251 students, whereas the mean estimate for a pair of majors in the low condition was 202 students ($t = 3.50$, $p < .001$). The mean estimate in the neutral condition was 237, significantly higher than the median estimate in the low condition ($t = 1.96$, $p = .05$) but not significantly lower than the mean estimate in the high condition ($t = .70$, ns).

Summary and Discussion

The present extension of support theory distinguishes between implicit subadditivity, induced by unpacking, and explicit subadditivity, resulting from the difference between the assessment of an explicit disjunction and separate assessments of its disjoint components. We have proposed that the former is caused by enhanced availability, whereas the latter is produced, in part at least, by repacking or anchoring. Consequently, different partitions are likely to give rise to different patterns of subadditivity. Study 1 established strict implicit and explicit subadditivity in judgments of unconditional probability. Study 2 showed that a causal partition produced more implicit subadditivity, whereas a temporal partition produced more explicit subadditivity, in judgments of conditional probability. Study 3 demonstrated greater explicit subadditivity for similar than for dissimilar components in judgments of frequency. Study 4 suggested that people follow an anchoring and adjustment heuristic that focuses on the larger, or the more familiar, component and increases the assessment of that component slightly to accommodate the larger extension.

The use of an anchoring and adjustment heuristic in this context is somewhat surprising because it seems easy to estimate the components separately and then add the estimates. Evidently, people are reluctant to add uncertain quantities. If they do not know the population of Spain and also do not know the population of Portugal, they are reluctant to estimate each of these numbers separately and add their guesses.

Instead, they apparently form an overall impression of the combined population of the two states that is determined primarily by the larger of the two. Taken together, the present results imply that an adequate model of probability or frequency judgment should be able to accommodate both implicit and explicit subadditivity. The current version of support theory provides such a model.

We conclude with a discussion of the relation between support theory and Shafer's (1976) theory of belief functions. Although the theory of belief functions is based on logical rather than psychological considerations, it has been interpreted by several authors as a descriptive model of belief. In this theory, as in many other models, the belief in the disjunction of disjoint events is greater than or equal to the sum of the beliefs in each of the components. Thus, support theory and the theory of belief functions depart from the Bayesian model in opposite directions: Support theory predicts subadditivity, whereas the theory of belief functions assumes superadditivity. Using the notation of table 16.1, probability theory requires $\alpha = \beta = \gamma + \delta$, Shafer's theory assumes $\alpha = \beta \geq \gamma + \delta$, and support theory implies $\alpha \leq \beta \leq \gamma + \delta$.

The experimental literature provides strong evidence that judged probability of both lay people and experts is subadditive rather than superadditive (see, e.g., Tversky & Koehler, 1994; Fox & Tversky, in press). For example, options traders who evaluated a set of four mutually exclusive and exhaustive hypotheses regarding the closing price of Microsoft stock did not hold any belief in reserve, as required by the theory of belief functions. On the contrary, the sum of the probabilities assigned to these hypotheses was substantially greater than 1,[1] and options traders were actually willing to bet on these values (Fox, Rogers, & Tversky, 1996). Although we do not wish to claim that superadditivity cannot arise in certain circumstances, the experimental evidence suggests that such instances represent the exception rather than the rule.

What then is the psychological basis for the superadditivity assumption that underlies post-Bayesian models of degree of belief? The answer to this question goes back to Keynes's (1921) distinction between the balance of evidence in favor of a given proposition and the weight (or strength) of evidence for this proposition. Keynes has argued that the standard notion of probability can represent the balance of evidence but not the weight of evidence because a probability of one half, for example, may result either from strong evidence for and strong evidence against the proposition in question or from weak evidence for and weak evidence against that proposition. Following Keynes, we suggest that superadditivity often holds for judgments of evidence strength, that is, of the degree to which a designated body of evidence supports a particular hypothesis (see Briggs & Krantz, 1992), but it does not hold for probability judgments that reflect the global balance of evidence.

The contrast between these notions is most pronounced in situations where there is good evidence for some general hypothesis but there is no specific evidence for any of its components. Suppose, for example, that there is very strong evidence that a particular person was murdered, but there is no evidence regarding the identity of the killer. Let H, H_a, and H_s denote, respectively, homicide, homicide by an acquaintance, and homicide by a stranger. If people can make sensible assessments of the degree to which the evidence confirms each of these hypotheses (say on a scale from 0 to 1), we expect these assessments to be close to 1 for H, and close to 0 for H_a and for H_s, in accord with Shafer's (1976) model. On the other hand, the judged probabilities of H_a and H_s are expected to be substantially greater than 0, and their sum may even exceed the judged probability of H. Judgments of strength of evidence, we suggest, reflect the degree to which a specific body of evidence confirms a particular hypothesis, whereas judgments of probability express the relative support for the competing hypotheses based on the judge's general knowledge and prior belief. The two types of judgments, therefore, are expected to follow different rules. Indeed, Krantz (1991) has argued that Shafer's model is more suitable for judgments of evidence strength than for judgments of probability.

Because there is very little data on judgments of evidence strength, we can only speculate about the rules they follow. It appears that in the absence of specific evidence, as in the homicide example earlier, such judgments are likely to be superadditive. However, judgments of evidence strength are unlikely to be superadditive in general. To illustrate, consider a body of evidence, for example, a fragment of Linda's diary expressing moral objection to sexist language. Such evidence, we suggest, can provide stronger support for the hypothesis that Linda is a feminist bank teller than for the more inclusive hypothesis that Linda is a bank teller. This pattern, of course, is not only subadditive; it is actually nonmonotonic. Similarly, a postcard with an Alpine scene appears to provide stronger evidence for the hypothesis that it came from Switzerland than for the hypothesis that it came from Europe (see e.g., Bar-Hillel & Neter, 1993). In these cases the evidence matches the narrower hypothesis better than it matches the broader hypothesis, hence an assessment based on matching (or representativeness) can give rise to nonmonotonicity in judgment of evidence strength, as well as in judgment of probability (Tversky & Kahneman, 1983).

To summarize, the experimental evidence described here and elsewhere indicates that probability judgments, which are based on the balance of evidence, are generally subadditive. The preceding discussion, however, suggests that judgments of the strength of a designated body of evidence may exhibit a different pattern. Such judgments are likely to be superadditive when there is little evidence for each of the component hypotheses, and they are likely to be subadditive (or even nonmonotonic) when the evidence strongly favors one of the components. Whether or not these conjectures are valid, we suggest that the discussion of alternative representations of belief can be illuminated by the distinction between probability judgments based on the balance of evidence and judgments of the strength of a specific body of evidence.

Notes

This work was supported by National Science Foundation Grant SBR-9408684 and by National Institutes of Health Grant MH-53046.

We are indebted to Daniel Kahneman for suggesting the use of anchoring as a source of explicit subadditivity and to Peter Wakker for insightful comments on the formal theory. We also thank Derek Koehler, David Krantz, and Sivan Rottenstreich for helpful discussions.

1. On the other hand, the prevalence of additivity for binary partitions, called binary complementarity, excludes the dual of the belief function, called the plausibility function. It follows readily that under binary complementarity all models of upper and lower probability reduce to the standard additive model.

References

Bar-Hillel, M., & Neter, E. (1993). How alike is it versus how likely it is: A disjunction fallacy in probability judgments. *Journal of Personality and Social Psychology, 65,* 1119–1131.

Briggs, L., & Krantz, D. (1992). Judging the strength of designated evidence. *Journal of Behavioral Decision Making, 5,* 77–106.

Erev, I., Wallsten, T. S., & Budescu, D. V. (1994). Simultaneous over- and underconfidence: The role of error in judgment processes. *Psychological Review, 101,* 519–527.

Fox, C. R., Rogers, B. A., & Tversky, A. (1996). Options traders exhibit subadditive decision weights. *Journal of Risk and Uncertainty, 13,* 5–19.

Fox, C. R., & Tversky, A. (in press). A belief-based account of decision under uncertainty. In D. Kahneman & A. Tversky (Eds.), *Choices, values, and frames.* Cambridge, England: Cambridge University Press.

Gonzales, M., & Bonini, N. (1995). *Probability judgments in two-outcome situations: What induces a defect in complementarity?* Unpublished manuscript, Centre de Recherche en Psychologie Cognitive, University de Provence, Aix-en-Provence, France.

Kahneman, D., Slovic, P., & Tversky, A. (1982). *Judgment under uncertainty: Heuristics and biases.* Cambridge, England: Cambridge University Press.

Keynes, J. M. (1921). *A treatise on probability.* London: Macmillan.

Krantz, D. H. (1991). From indices to mappings: The representational approach to measurement. In D. R. Brown & E. K. Smith (Eds.), *Frontiers of mathematical psychology: Essays in honor of Clyde Coombs* (pp. 1–52). New York: Springer-Verlag.

Macchi, L., Osherson, D., & Legrenzi, P. (1995, November). *Superadditivity with complementary pairs of hypotheses.* Paper presented at the annual meeting of the Society for Judgment and Decision Making, Los Angeles.

Poulton, E. C. (1994). *Behavioral decision theory: A new approach.* Cambridge, England: Cambridge University Press.

Shafer, G. (1976). *A mathematical theory of evidence.* Princeton, NJ: Princeton University Press.

Slovic, P., & Lichtenstein, S. (1968). Relative importance of probabilities and payoffs in risk taking. *Journal of Experimental Psychology Monographs, 78*(3, Pt. 2).

Tversky, A., & Kahneman, D. (1974). Judgment under uncertainty: Heuristics and biases. *Science, 185*, 1124–1131.

Tversky, A., & Kahneman, D. (1983). Extensional vs. intuitive reasoning: The conjunction fallacy in probability judgment. *Psychological Review, 91*, 293–315.

Tversky, A., & Koehler, D. J. (1994). Support theory: A nonextensional representation of subjective probability. *Psychological Review, 101*, 547–567.

Appendix

Support Theory

This section presents a self-contained, formal statement of support theory and provides necessary and sufficient conditions for the present model in terms of judged probability. This analysis extends the treatment of Tversky and Koehler (1994, theorem 1) by introducing explicit subadditivity and by restricting the assumption of implicit subadditivity.

Let T be a finite set including at least two elements, interpreted as states of the world. We assume that exactly one state obtains but it is generally not known to the judge. Subsets of T are called *events*. We distinguish between events and description of events, called *hypotheses*. We use H to denote the set of hypotheses that describe the events in T and prime ($'$) to denote the mapping that associates hypotheses with events. Thus, we assume that each hypothesis $A \in$ H corresponds to a unique event $A' \in$ T. Different hypotheses may describe the same event. For example, consider rolling a pair of dice. The hypotheses "the sum is 3" and "the product is 2" describe the same event: One die shows 1, and the other shows 2. We assume that H is finite and that it includes at least one hypothesis for each event. A is elementary if $A' \in$ T. A is null if $A' = \varnothing$. A and B are exclusive if $A' \cap B' = \varnothing$. If A and B are in H, and they are exclusive and nonnull, then their explicit disjunction, denoted $A \vee B$, is also in H. We assume that $\vee$ is associative and commutative and that $(A \vee B)' = A' \cup B'$.

Support theory distinguishes between explicit and implicit disjunctions. Formally, A is an implicit disjunction, or simply an implicit hypothesis, if it is neither elementary nor null, and it is not an explicit disjunction (i.e., there are no exclusive nonnull B, C in H such that $A = B \vee C$). For example, the explicit disjunction, "Homicide by an acquaintance or by a stranger," has the same extension as "Homicide," but the latter is an implicit hypothesis because it is not an explicit disjunction.

An evaluation frame (A, B) consists of a pair of exclusive hypotheses: The first element, A, is the focal hypothesis that the judge evaluates, and the second element,

B, is the alternative hypothesis. We interpret a person's probability judgment as a mapping P from an evaluation frame to the unit interval. To simplify matters, we assume that $P(A, B)$ equals zero if and only if A is null and equals one if and only if B is null. Thus, $P(A, B)$ is the judged probability that A rather than B holds, assuming that one and only one of them obtains. Obviously, A and B may each represent an explicit or an implicit disjunction. The extensional counterpart of $P(A, B)$ in probability theory is the conditional probability $P(A' \mid A' \cup B')$. Support theory is nonextensional because it assumes that probability judgment depends on the descriptions A and B, not on the events A' and B'.

As in the original version of the theory, we assume *binary complementarity:*

$$P(A, B) + P(B, A) = 1, \qquad\qquad \text{(Condition 1)}$$

which follows readily from the equation relating judged probability and support. To formulate the next two assumptions, we introduce the probability ratio $R(A, B) = P(A, B)/P(B, A)$, which is the odds for A against B, assuming B is nonnull. The use of odds is merely a notational device, not a change in the response scale. Our second assumption is the *product rule:*

$$R(A, B)R(B, D) = R(A, C)R(C, D) \quad \text{and}$$
$$\qquad\qquad \text{(Condition 2)}$$
$$R(A, B)R(B, D) = R(A, D),$$

where each equation holds whenever the arguments of R in that equation are exclusive. Note that according to support theory, $R(A, B) = s(A)/s(B)$. Hence the product rule follows from this form by cancellation. This assumption is slightly stronger than the product rule used in the original version of the theory.[A1]

Our third assumption, called the *odds inequality*, replaces the unpacking condition of the original theory. Suppose A_1, A_2, and B are mutually exclusive, A is implicit, and $A_1 \vee A_2$ is recognized as a partition of A. That is, $(A_1 \vee A_2)' = A'$, and the judge recognizes that $A_1 \vee A_2$ has the same extension as A. Then

$$R(A, B) \le R(A_1 \vee A_2, B) \le R(A_1, B) + R(A_2, B). \qquad \text{(Condition 3)}$$

Note that under the classical probability axioms both inequalities reduce to equalities. The recognition requirement, which restricts the assumption of implicit subadditivity, was not explicitly stated in the original version of the theory, although it was assumed in its applications.

The following theorem shows that conditions 1, 2, and 3 are both necessary and sufficient for the extended version of support theory.

THEOREM: Suppose $P(A, B)$ is defined for all exclusive $A, B \in H$ and that it vanishes if and only if A is null. Conditions 1, 2, and 3 hold if and only if there exists a non-negative ratio scale s on H such that for any pair of exclusive hypotheses A, B

$$P(A, B) = \frac{s(A)}{s(A) + s(B)}. \qquad \text{(Condition 4)}$$

Furthermore, if A_1 and A_2 are exclusive, A is implicit, and $(A_1 \vee A_2)$ is recognized as a partition of A then

$$s(A) \leq s(A_1 \vee A_2) \leq s(A_1) + s(A_2). \qquad \text{(Condition 5)}$$

Proof: Necessity is straightforward. To prove sufficiency we assume Conditions 1, 2, and 3 and construct the support function s. Let $E = \{A \in H \mid A' \in T\}$ be the set of elementary hypotheses. Select some $D \in E$ and set $s(D) = 1$. For any other elementary hypothesis $C \in E$ such that $C' \neq D'$, set $s(C) = R(C, D)$. Given any $A \in H$ such that $A' \neq T, \varnothing$, select some $C \in E$ such that $A' \cap C' = \varnothing$ and either $C = D$ or $C' \neq D'$. Set $s(A) = R(A, D)$ if $C = D$ and $s(A) = R(A, C)R(C, D)$ otherwise. It is easy to verify that the product rule (Condition 2), $R(A, B)R(B, D) = R(A, C)R(C, D)$ and $R(A, B)R(B, D) = R(A, D)$, ensures that $s(A)$ is independent of the choice of C. Apply the second equation when A and D are exclusive, and the first equation when they are not. To complete the construction of s, set $s(A) = 0$ when $A' = \varnothing$. When $A' = T$, set $s(A) = \min \sum s(B_n)$, where the minimum is taken over all explicit disjunctions $B = B_1 \vee \cdots \vee B_n$ such that $B' = T$.

To establish the representation for $P(A, B)$, suppose $A' \cap D' = \varnothing$. Thus, $s(A) = R(A, D)$. Furthermore, there exists $C \in E$ such that $s(B) = R(B, C)R(C, D)$. By the product rule, therefore, $s(B) = R(B, A)R(A, D)$, and $s(A)/s(B) = R(A, B)$. Applying binary complementarity (Condition 1), yields $P(A, B) = s(A)/[s(A) + s(B)]$ for all disjoint $A, B \in H$, where s is unique up to a choice of unit determined by the value of $s(D)$.

Finally, implicit subadditivity, $s(A) \leq s(A_1 \vee A_2)$, and explicit subadditivity, $s(A_1 \vee A_2) \leq s(A_1) + s(A_2)$, (see Condition 5), follow respectively from the left hand and the right hand of the odds inequality (Condition 3), $R(A, B) \leq R(A_1 \vee A_2, B) \leq R(A_1, B) + R(A_2, B)$, provided $A' \neq T$. Otherwise, these inequalities follow from the definition of $s(A)$ for $A' = T$.

Appendix Note

A1. The first part of condition 2 is equivalent to the product rule used in the original theory; the second part of condition 2 is implied by but does not imply the proportionality assumption of the original theory.

PREFERENCE

Editor's Introductory Remarks

Amos Tversky studied individual choice behavior throughout his career. His early work focused on probabilistic models of choice, that is, models that assume a random process in which the same choice is not always made even under seemingly identical conditions. Most theoretical work on probabilistic preferences was based on the notion of independence among alternatives. In an early study by Tversky and J. Russo (chapter 18), the assumptions of independence and substitutability were shown to be equivalent, all capturing the fundamental principle that pair-wise choice probabilities could be expressed as a function of an underlying scale value, such that if two alternatives are equivalent in one context, they are substitutable for each other in any context. While this principle dominated the theoretical work in the field, Tversky focused on findings showing that choice probabilities were affected not only by the scale values of alternatives but also by comparability issues that could not be captured by any model that assigns values in a context-independent manner. In particular, similarity altered discrimination between stimuli and, because similarity could be varied without changing the stimuli's scale values, independence was violated.

Considerations of discrimination and context already appeared in Tversky's first published paper (chapter 17), in which he investigated the number of alternatives at a choice point that, under certain theoretical assumptions, would optimize discriminability. Related considerations later proved central to his insightful analysis of the intransitivity of preferences (chapter 19). There, he relied on the psychology of just-noticeable differences to predict violations of transitivity, one of the most basic axioms of the normative theory of choice. That article raised a number of issues that proved pivotal in Tversky's later work. It addressed the tension between observed violations of transitivity on the one hand, and subjects' strong endorsement of transitivity and their reluctance to admit to its violation on the other. It also addressed the difficulty of reaching clear conclusions concerning the rational status of such violations in the absence of a compelling analysis of the mechanisms and costs involved. Simplification in the choice process, Tversky suggested, may prove extremely useful, even if occasionally it fails to yield the optimal choice. When difficulty and precision are taken into account, a component-wise evaluation may prove superior to independent evaluation despite the fact that the latter necessarily maintains transitivity whereas the former does not. Of main interest to Tversky was not only the systematic violation of normative principles but what these violations revealed about the psychological mechanisms governing choice.

Continued interest in processes that violate independence led to Tversky's elimination-by-aspects model (chapter 20), a theory of choice based on a covert sequential-elimination process, which was able to account for observed dependencies among options. A considerably more parsimonious version of the model, in which choice alternatives are represented in a treelike graph, was later developed in collaboration with Shmuel Sattath (chapter 21). According to these models, the probability of selecting an option depends not only on its overall value, but also on its relations to the other options available. In particular, "irrelevant alternatives" can influence choice probabilities because the introduction of an alternative "hurts" similar alternatives more than dissimilar ones. Unlike their classical counterparts, these models allow for the effects of different agendas on choice probabilities.

The empirical study of decision making was motivated largely by earlier work in economics. A notable development was the publication of von Neumann and Morgenstern's normative treatment of expected utility (1947), which, along with ensuing modifications, showed that a few compelling axioms, when satisfied, imply that a person's choices can be thought of as favoring the alternative with the highest subjective expected utility. In the seventies, Tversky worked with Daniel Kahneman on a descriptive theory of risky choice, known as prospect theory (chapter 22.) Prospect theory incorporates a number of fundamental psychological principles of choice that differ in important ways from those envisioned by the normative account. The theory predicts decision patterns that dozens of studies have confirmed empirically, and which contrast directly with the fundamental assumptions of expected utility theory. Mathematically elegant and psychologically insightful, prospect theory has had a major influence in the social sciences. (The original publication in 1979 appears to be the most cited paper ever published in the prestigious journal *Econometrica*.) Whereas the original formulation of the theory was technically limited to choice between risky monetary gambles involving at most two nonzero outcomes, a new version of the model was later developed that applied to uncertain as well as to risky prospects with any number of outcomes (chapter 27).

Among other things, prospect theory posits a value function with three important properties: (1) it is defined on gains and losses rather than total wealth, which captures the fact that individuals normally treat outcomes as departures from some reference point, rather than in terms of final assets; (2) it is steeper for losses than for gains: thus, a loss of $X is more aversive than a gain of $X is attractive, yielding what is referred to as "loss aversion"; and (3) it is concave for gains and convex for losses, which yields risk aversion in the domain of gains and risk seeking in the domain of losses (except for very low probabilities, where these patterns reverse).

The above properties may seem compelling and unobjectionable; yet, they lead to normatively problematic consequences. Because people are risk averse or risk seeking depending on whether they face apparent gains or losses, decision situations can arise in which alternative descriptions of the same decision problem give rise to different choices. This is known as a *framing effect* and is in violation of the principle of invariance, which requires that logically equivalent representations of a decision problem, as well as logically equivalent methods of elicitation, yield the same preferences (chapter 24).

Prospect theory also makes a number of psychological assumptions about the impact of probabilities. According to the theory, the value of each outcome is multiplied by a decision weight, which transforms the relevant probability into its impact on the decision-maker. Decision weights represent a distortion that captures the impact of events on the valuation of prospects, not merely the perceived likelihood of those events. In particular, a nonlinear transformation of the probability scale is assumed, which overweights low probabilities and underweights moderate and high probabilities. Tversky and Craig Fox (chapter 30) extend this nonlinear transformation from risk (where the probabilities associated with outcomes are assumed to be known) to uncertainty (where the probabilities are not known). An event is found to have greater impact when it turns possibility into certainty (the certainty effect), or impossibility into possibility, than when it merely adjusts the likelihood of a possibility. Also, people appear to be less sensitive to uncertainty than to risk, which is consistent with a two-stage process in which the decision maker first assesses the probability of an uncertain event, then transforms this value via the weighting function. One of Tversky's last major theoretical contributions was a cohesive account of decision under uncertainty (chapter 32) that incorporates judgments of probability assumed to satisfy support theory with decisions under risk, assumed to satisfy prospect theory.

Tversky conducted several studies documenting the occurrence of framing effects, certainty effects, and other biases in real-life decisions involving lay people as well as experts. In a medical study in collaboration with McNeil, Pauker, and Sox (chapter 23), a large number of outpatients, physicians, and graduate students were presented with alternative therapies for lung cancer, and their choices were shown to be influenced by presumably immaterial variations in the nature of the presentation. In a study involving choices between political candidates and public referendum issues, George Quattrone and Tversky (chapter 25) document framing effects, loss aversion, and other patterns that are predicted by prospect theory but inconsistent with fundamental normative assumptions. In a similar vein, Kahneman and Tversky (chapter 29) explore the implications for conflict resolution of several cognitive phenomena that have emerged from the study of decision making, including loss aversion, optimistic overconfidence, and the certainty effect. They suggest that such biases can hinder negotiation and the successful resolution of conflict.

As a result of observations in the earlier work, Tversky became particularly interested in the relationship between uncertainty and preference. In an investigation of the relationship between probability judgments and preferences between bets, Chip Heath and Tversky (chapter 26) propose the competence hypothesis, according to which people prefer to bet on beliefs in situations in which they feel competent or knowledgeable, but prefer to bet on chance when they feel incompetent or ignorant. Interestingly, this pattern is inconsistent with the familiar "ambiguity aversion," which predicts a general preference for betting on chance over beliefs whose probability is ambiguous. Along related lines, Fox and Tversky (chapter 31) present the comparative ignorance hypothesis: aversion to ambiguity, which emerges only in comparative settings, is produced by a comparison with less ambiguous events or with more knowledgeable individuals.

The foregoing findings call into question the fundamental notion of inferring beliefs from preferences. Most conceptions of decision making under uncertainty—both normative and descriptive—are consequentialist in the sense that decisions are presumed to be determined by an assessment of the potential consequences and their perceived likelihood. However, Shafir and Tversky (chapter 28) document situations in which people reason and make choices in a non-consequentialist manner. For example, people who eventually make the same choice regardless of how the uncertainty is resolved are seen to make a different choice while the situation is still uncertain, contrary to consequentialism. Quattrone and Tversky (chapter 33) manipulate the diagnostic and causal effectiveness of actions, and thereby illustrate another violation of consequentialism. They show that people are prone to select actions that are diagnostic of auspicious outcomes even when the actions clearly do not facilitate the outcome. Among other things, they document "diagnostic voting," where the belief that one's actions are diagnostic of the actions of relevant others appears to increase the reported willingness to vote, despite the fact that this action is unlikely to affect the final outcome in any way.

Foremost in Tversky's research is the realization that preferences tend to be shaped by psychological processes that act independently of normative considerations that the person might endorse upon reflection. Such processes underlie the study of contingent preferences, where purportedly immaterial variations in description, context, or procedure alter respondents' relative weighting of attributes and, consequently, their preferences. In the prototypical example, people choose one bet over another but then price the second bet above the first, a phenomenon known as "preference reversal." Tversky and Richard Thaler (chapter 35) suggest that the major cause of preference reversals is a differential weighting of probability and payoffs in choice versus pricing. In particular, experimental evidence indicates that an attribute of an option is given more weight when it is compatible with the response format than when it is not. Because the price that the subject assigns to a bet is expressed in dollars, the payoffs of the bet, also expressed in dollars, are weighted more heavily in pricing than in choice. This causes the bet with the higher payoff to be evaluated more favorably in pricing than in choice and can give rise to preference reversals.

Tversky, Shmuel Sattath, and Paul Slovic (chapter 34) contrast choice with another procedure called "matching" in which the decision maker adjusts one option to match another. They show that the more prominent dimension tends to loom larger in choice than in matching or in pricing tasks. They then discuss models in which the trade-off between attributes is contingent on the nature of the response, and raise conceptual as well as practical questions concerning the nature, the meaning, and the assessment of preference.

Redelmeier and Tversky explore contingent preferences in medical contexts (chapter 36) and suggest that looking at a problem from different perspectives can change the relative weight assigned to attributes and thus lead to different choices. They show that practicing physicians give more weight to a patient's personal concerns when they consider the patient as an individual, and more weight to criteria of effectiveness and cost when they consider the patient as part of a group. As a result, these physicians make different decisions when evaluating an individual patient than when considering a group of comparable patients (a discrepancy also found in the judgments of lay people).

The influence of different reference states plays a major role in the treatment of loss aversion in riskless choice (chapter 37). Loss aversion, it is suggested, accounts for the large disparity often observed between the minimum people are willing to accept to give up an item and the maximum they would be willing to pay to acquire it. This has far-reaching consequences for economic choices and for the willingness to depart from the status quo. Tversky and Kahneman propose a reference-dependent theory which posits a preference relation indexed to specific reference states as a way to capture the relevant patterns.

Other violations of context-independence are revealed in studies involving legal decision-making (chapter 40), where Kelman, Rottenstreich, and Tversky focus on two phenomena: compromise and contrast. Compromise refers to the finding that the same option is evaluated more favorably when it is intermediate rather than extreme in the offered set, and contrast refers to the fact that an option is evaluated more favorably in the presence of similar options that are inferior to it.

Related contextual effects are highlighted in Tversky and Dale Griffin's application to judgments of well being (chapter 38). The hedonic impact of an event, they suggest, reflects a balance of its endowment and contrast effects. The endowment effect of an event represents its direct contribution to one's satisfaction. Good news and positive experiences make people happier; bad news and hard times diminish their well being. Events also have an indirect contrast effect on the evaluation of subsequent events. A positive experience makes people happy, but it also renders similar experiences less exciting. A negative experience makes people unhappy, but it helps them to appreciate subsequent experiences that are less bad. Interesting implications are drawn for the notion of Pareto optimality, which is fundamental to welfare economics, since—to the extent that contrast plays a significant role—policies that ignore contrast effects can technically improve everybody's lot while still creating widespread unhappiness.

When faced with the need to choose, decision makers often seek and construct reasons in order to resolve the conflict and justify their choice. Different frames, contexts, and elicitation procedures highlight different aspects of the options and bring forth different reasons and considerations that influence decision. In chapter 39, Shafir and Tversky consider the role of reasons in the making of decisions. An analysis based on reasons, they suggest, can accommodate framing and elicitation effects and can incorporate the comparative influences and considerations of perspective, conflict, and context that typically remain outside the purview of value maximization.

Tversky's collection of articles concerning the study and nature of preferences (of which the present volume represents only a small subset) is truly remarkable. All the more so, reading Tversky's work makes one wish he had the opportunity to go even further.

Probabilistic Models of Choice

17 On the Optimal Number of Alternatives at a Choice Point

Amos Tversky

Consider any test task or questionnaire which can be represented as a sequence of choice points at each of which one out of a set of alternatives is chosen. Multiple-choice tests, mazes or personality check lists are examples. Given a fixed total number of alternatives for the whole test, we wish to find the optimal number of choice points and the optimal number of alternatives at each choice point.

Let k be the total number of alternatives, and let x_i denote the number of alternatives at the ith choice point. Thus:

$$\sum_{i=1}^{r} x_i = k \tag{1}$$

where r is the number of choice points.

Three criteria for optimality which one may attempt to maximize will be considered.

(a) Discrimination capacity: the number n of possible distinct response patterns of a given test

$$n = \prod_{i=1}^{r} x_i \tag{2}$$

For example, consider a multiple-choice diagnostic test or an attitude questionnaire based on Likert-type items. Let every sequence of responses be regarded as a different "personality type" or "attitude profile." Thus, by maximizing n, we maximize the number of distinct types or profiles among which the test enables us to discriminate.

(b) Power: defined as 1 minus the probability of attaining perfect performance by chance alone. Assuming equal probability of guessing for all alternatives:

$$\text{Power} = 1 - \left(\prod_{i=1}^{r} x_i \right)^{-1} \tag{3}$$

Clearly, we are interested in constructing tests with maximal power.

(c) Uncertainty associated with the set $[A]$ of all possible response patterns to a given task.

$$H[A] = -\sum_{i=1}^{n} p_i \log_2 p_i = \log_2 \prod_{i=1}^{r} x_i \tag{4}$$

Since the three criteria proposed are strictly monotonically related to each other, maximizing (2) maximizes (3) and (4) as well. If the same number of alternatives is used at each choice point, i.e., $x_i = x_j$, for any i and j then

$$n = \prod_{i=1}^{r} x_i = x^r \tag{5}$$

and since $x \cdot r = k$

$$n = x^{k/x}.$$

Let us denote by $f_k(x)$ the discrimination function $x^{k/x}$ of such a test. $f_k(x)$ can be maximized by setting $(d/dx)f_k(x) = 0$.

$$\frac{d}{dx} f_k(x) = \frac{d}{dx}(x^{k/x}) = \frac{d}{dx}(e^{\ln x^{k/x}})$$

$$= e^{\ln x^{k/x}} \frac{d}{dx}(\ln x^{k/x}) = x^{k/x}\left(\frac{k}{x^2} - \ln x \frac{k}{x^2}\right) \tag{6}$$

$$= x^{k/x} \frac{k}{x^2}(1 - \ln x)$$

Since both x and k are positive $(d/dx)f_k(x) = 0$ and only if

$$1 - \ln x = 0, \quad \ln x = 1, \quad \text{or} \quad x = e.$$

Thus $f(x)$ has a unique maximum at $x = e = 2.718$.

A family of discrimination functions for some different values of k is given in figure 17.1. Note that though the value of $f_k(x)$ depends rather heavily on k, the location of its maximum is completely independent of k.

(Note, incidentally, that the well-known function $f(p_i) = -p_i \log_2 p_i$, is a logarithmic transformation of the discrimination function $f_k(x)$ where $k = 1$. The above result may be used to solve for its maximum.

Let $\log_2 y = -p_i \log_2 p_i$ and let $x = 1/p_i$. Hence:

$$y = \left(\frac{1}{p_i}\right)^{p_i} = x^{1/x} = f_1(x) \tag{7}$$

By (6), $f_1(x)$ is maximum at $x = e$. Indeed $-p_i \log_2 p_i$ is maximum at $p_i = 1/e = 0.368$.)

Since x stands for the number of alternatives, we want to find the integer which is closest to the maximum point. Since $f_k(x)$ is single-peaked it should be either 2 or 3.

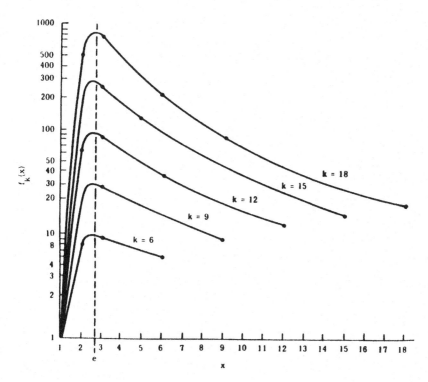

Figure 17.1
A family of discrimination function $f_k(x)$ for some different values of k. The dots on the curves denote the points at which both x and k/x are integers.

To show that 3 gives the desired solution we have to show that $f_k(3) > f_k(2)$ for any $k > 0$, i.e., $3^{k/3} > 2^{k/2}$. Raising both sides of the above equation to the $6/k$ power yields the desired result.

Hence the use of three alternatives at each choice point will maximize discrimination capacity, power, and uncertainty of the test.

The final result for the case in which both x and k/r are integers is given by the following theorem.

THEOREM Consider any sequence of positive integers $x_1, x_2 \cdots x_r$ such that $\sum_{i=1}^{r} x_i = k$. A sequence for which $\prod_{i=1}^{r} x_i$ is maximum will include a maximal number of 3's without including any 1.

That is, the best solution will include either (i) $k/3$ choice points with 3 alternatives each, or (ii) $(k - 4)/3$ choice points with 3 alternatives each and a single choice point with 4 alternatives, or (iii) $(k-2)/3$ choice points with 3 alternatives each and a single choice point with 2 alternatives, depending on whether the remainder of k when divided by 3 is zero, one, or two, i.e., whether $k \bmod(3)$ equals 0, 1, or 2.

The proof of the theorem is as follows: For every sequence of positive integers, denoted by S, with a fixed sum, k, which is not in any one of the forms (i), (ii), or (iii) it is possible to construct another sequence denoted by S' with the following properties:

(1) $\sum S' = \sum S = k$.

(2) $\prod S' > \prod S$.

(3) S' is in one of the forms (i), (ii), or (iii).

The construction of such a sequence is done by successive replacements of elements in the original sequence which do not change its sum. Let S be any sequence of positive integers. If it contains 1, delete the 1 by adding it to some other element. The new sequence obtained will have a greater product since

$$x + 1 > x \cdot 1 \quad \text{for any} \quad x \geq 1. \tag{8}$$

If the sequence contains 2's or 3's, leave them unchanged. If the sequence contains 4, replace it by a pair of 2's, leaving both the sum and the product unchanged.

Next, any even x can be expressed as $2t$ for some positive integer t. Hence replace any even $x > 4$ by its corresponding t-tuple of 2's. The product of the new sequence will exceed that of the old one since

$$2^t > 2t \quad \text{for any} \quad t > 2. \tag{9}$$

Similarly, any odd $x > 3$ can be expressed as $2t + 3$ for some positive integer t. Thus we may replace any odd $x > 3$ by a single 3 and its corresponding t-tuple of 2's. This replacement will increase the product of the sequence because

$$2^t \cdot 3 > 2t + 3. \tag{10}$$

Repeated application of these replacements will yield a sequence consisting of 2's and 3's only.

Finally, replace any triple of 2's by a pair of 3's, thus increasing the product since

$$3^2 > 2^3. \tag{11}$$

The final sequence thus obtained will be in one and only one of the desired forms (i), (ii), or (iii). The maximality of $\prod S'$ for this sequence follows from the inequalities (8) through (11).

The form of the desired sequence S' is unique except for order and except in case (ii) in which either a single 4 or a pair of 2's may be used.

Alternatively, the above theorem may be stated as follows: Consider all sequences of positive integers $x_1, x_2, \ldots, x_r$ with a fixed product k, i.e., $\prod_{i=1}^{r} x_i = k$. The sequence for which $\sum_{i=1}^{r} x_i$ is minimum will include a maximal number of 3's without including any 1.

Discussion

The criteria proposed will be maximized by constructing tasks whose alternatives are of the form given by the above theorem. Certainly, additional criteria may be considered in deciding upon the number of alternatives to be used. There are, however, instances in which the above result may be directly applicable.

Whenever the amount of time spent on the test is proportional to its total number of alternatives, the use of three alternatives at each choice point will maximize the amount of information obtained per time unit. This seems to be true of multiple-choice tests consisting of questions like: "which of the following passages best describes X's position?" in which the amount of time spent on the question is negligible compared to the time spent on choosing among the alternatives. The result is applicable, however, even in instances in which the proportionality assumption does not hold. All that is needed is that the relative gain in information will exceed the relative loss in time.

An estimate of the relative gain (or loss) of information, power, and discriminability as a function of some different values of x for a given k can be obtained from the graph of $f_k(x)$ in figure 17.1. Whenever additional criteria are explicitly introduced, the above estimate may be taken into account in constructing an optimally-designed task.

There exists some empirical evidence (Pressey, 1962), based on the study of auto-instructional items, which indicates that three-alternative test items are indeed optimal. Since neither time nor the total number of alternatives was controlled, the results are only suggestive.

Finally, the above result may shed some light on the study of information coding and processing. In a paper entitled "Information transmission with elementary auditory displays," Sumby, Chambliss, and Pollack (1958) have used a set of auditory signals as an alphabet. They employed four stimulus variables, with two, three, and five alternatives per variable. In summarizing the results Garner (1962) says: "Their results showed that three alternatives per variable gave the best performance, agreeing with the suggestion in the Pollack and Ficks (1954) results that three levels per dimension are better than two. Certainly, at this stage it seems that the maximum information transmission will be obtained with humans when no more than three alternatives are used with a single variable, but with many variables involved," (pp. 122–123). In other words, the data show that perceptual discrimination, measured by the amount of information transmitted, was maximized when each one of the dimensions has three levels.

One may hypothesize that the discriminability of the stimuli, or the memory load associated with them, is directly related to the total number of levels summed over dimensions. The fact that amplitude, for example, is a relevant dimension does not contribute to the S's memory load; rather, it is the number of levels of amplitude which hinders discrimination. The total number of levels, however, was shown to be minimal whenever three-level factors are employed. If the above hypothesis is true, it follows that the use of three-level factors will minimize confusion and decrease memory load. This problem seems worthy of experimental investigation. Taken together with Garner's conclusions concerning human capacities to process multi-dimensional information, these results suggest that the use of three levels per dimension may be the most efficient way to code and process information.

Notes

This research was supported by the Air Force Office of Scientific Research under contract AF-AFOSR-196-63, and by Public Health Service Research grant MH-04236.

I wish to thank J. Give'on for his helpful suggestions and Dr. R. M. Dawes for calling my attention to the relationships between the finding of Pollack and Ficks and the result reported here.

References

Garner, W. R. *Uncertainty and structure as psychological concepts.* New York: Wiley, 1962.

Pollack, I., and Ficks, L. Information of elementary multidimensional auditory displays. *J. acoust. Soc. Amer.*, 1954, 26, 155–158.

Pressey, S. L. Basic unresolved teaching-machine problems, *Theory and Practice*, 1962, 1, No. 1.

Sumby, W. H., Chambliss, D., and Pollack, I. Information transmission with elementary auditory displays. *J. acoust. Soc. Amer.*, 1958, 30, 423–429.

18 Substitutability and Similarity in Binary Choices

Amos Tversky and J. Edward Russo

Most probabilistic theories of choice behavior are based on a fundamental principle that has appeared in several different forms. The assumptions of simple scalability, strong stochastic transitivity, substitutability, and independence are different versions of the same basic principle. In the first part of the paper, these four assumptions are shown to be logically equivalent. In the second part, this principle is contrasted with an alternative hypothesis in an experimental study involving judgments of relative size.

To introduce the various conditions, let S be a set of alternatives or stimuli, denoted $x, y, \ldots$, and let $P(x, y)$ be the probability that x is chosen over y. More specifically, we assume that $P(x, y) + P(y, x) = 1$ and that $P(x, x) = \frac{1}{2}$, for all x, y in S. Furthermore, it is assumed that all choice probabilities are neither 0 nor 1, that is, all preferences or discriminations are imperfect. These probabilities are usually estimated by the relative frequencies observed in binary choice experiments.

A set of binary choice probabilities satisfies *simple scalability* if there are real-valued functions F and u such that for all x, y in S

$$P(x, y) = F[u(x), u(y)], \tag{1}$$

where F is strictly increasing in its first argument and strictly decreasing in the second. This property, introduced by Krantz (1964), states that the effect of each stimulus, x, can be summarized by a single scale value, $u(x)$. Two alternatives are thus equivalent if, and only if, they have the same scale value. (Krantz's original formulation is slightly weaker as F must only be one-to-one in each argument. The two formulations, however, are equivalent if F is continuous in both arguments.)

Equation 1 is probably the most general formulation of independence between alternatives. The more elaborate choice models, such as Thurstone's (1927, case V) and Luce's (1959), require the stronger assumption that

$$P(x, y) = F[u(x) - u(y)].$$

The difference between the two assumptions is that in the former F is a function in two variables, $u(x)$ and $u(y)$, whereas in the latter it is a function of their difference. A detailed analysis of the relationships among the various probabilistic choice models can be found in Luce and Suppes (1965).

Despite its generality, simple scalability has several testable consequences. In particular, it implies that if $P(x, y)$ and $P(y, z)$ exceed one half then $P(x, z)$ exceeds both of them. This property, called *strong stochastic transitivity* (SST), is a probabilistic version of transitivity. Stated formally,

$$P(x, y) \geq \tfrac{1}{2} \quad \text{and} \quad P(y, z) \geq \tfrac{1}{2} \quad \text{imply} \quad P(x, z) \geq \max[P(x, y), P(y, z)], \tag{2}$$

where strict inequality in both hypotheses entails strict inequality in the conclusion. (The present formulation of SST is slightly stronger than the usual one, as the requirement of strict inequality is typically omitted.)

To derive (2) from (1), suppose $P(x, y) \geq \tfrac{1}{2} = P(y, y)$, hence $F[u(x), u(y)] \geq F[u(y), u(y)]$ and $u(x) \geq u(y)$ since F is increasing in its first argument. Consequently, $F[u(x), u(z)] \geq F[u(y), u(z)]$ or, $P(x, z) \geq P(y, z)$. Similarly, $P(y, z) \geq \tfrac{1}{2} = P(z, z)$ implies $u(y) \geq u(z)$ and $P(x, z) \geq P(x, y)$, since F is decreasing in its second argument. Finally, it is easy to verify that strict inequality in both hypotheses yields strict inequality in the conclusion, which completes the proof.

Strong stochastic transitivity, in turn, implies the following *substitutability* condition for all x, y, z in S.

$$P(x, z) \geq P(y, z) \quad \text{if and only if} \quad P(x, y) \geq \tfrac{1}{2}. \tag{3}$$

This property may also be stated as a conjunction of two implications: (i) $P(x, z) > P(y, z)$ implies $P(x, y) > \tfrac{1}{2}$, and (ii) $P(x, z) = P(y, z)$ implies $P(x, y) = \tfrac{1}{2}$. The equivalence of the two forms is readily established.

To derive (3), assume (i) is false; hence $P(x, z) > P(y, z)$ but $P(y, x) \geq \tfrac{1}{2}$. There are two cases to be considered, $P(x, z) \geq \tfrac{1}{2}$ and $\tfrac{1}{2} > P(x, z)$. First, suppose $P(x, z) \geq \tfrac{1}{2}$; hence by SST $P(y, z) \geq P(x, z)$, contrary to our hypothesis. Second, suppose $\tfrac{1}{2} > P(x, z)$; hence by hypothesis $\tfrac{1}{2} > P(y, z)$ or $P(z, y) > \tfrac{1}{2}$, but since $P(y, x) \geq \tfrac{1}{2}$ it follows from SST that $P(z, x) \geq P(z, y)$, contrary to our hypothesis that $P(x, z) > P(y, z)$.

Next, assume (ii) is false; hence $P(x, z) = P(y, z)$ but $P(x, y) \neq \tfrac{1}{2}$, say $P(x, y) > \tfrac{1}{2}$. There are three cases to be considered, $P(x, z) > \tfrac{1}{2}$, $\tfrac{1}{2} > P(x, z)$, and $P(x, z) = \tfrac{1}{2}$. First, suppose $P(x, z) = P(y, z) > \tfrac{1}{2}$; hence by SST, $P(x, z) > P(y, z)$, a contradiction. Second, suppose $\tfrac{1}{2} > P(x, z)$ or $P(z, x) > \tfrac{1}{2}$; hence by SST $P(z, y) > P(z, x)$ or $P(x, z) > P(y, z)$, a contradiction. Finally, suppose $P(x, z) = \tfrac{1}{2} = P(z, y)$; hence by SST $P(x, y) = \tfrac{1}{2}$ as required. This completes the derivation of the substitutability condition. Essentially the same result was obtained by Block and Marschak (1960, theorem 4.1).

A set of binary choice probabilities satisfies the *independence* condition if for any x, y, z, w in S,

$$P(x, z) \geq P(y, z) \quad \text{if and only if} \quad P(x, w) \geq P(y, w). \tag{4}$$

Thus, if two stimuli (x, y) are ordered according to their choice probabilities relative to some fixed standard then, under equation 4, the ordering is independent of the particular standard. Essentially the same property plays an important role in the theory of conjoint measurement (see Tversky 1967). To derive independence from substitutability, suppose $P(x, z) \geq P(y, z)$; hence by applying (3) twice, $P(x, y) \geq \frac{1}{2}$ and $P(x, w) \geq P(y, w)$ as required.

The independence condition, in turn, implies simple scalability. To demonstrate, choose a fixed element z and define a real-valued function u on S by $u(x) = P(x, z)$. Next, define another real-valued function F by the equation $F[u(x), u(y)] = P(x, y)$. To show that F is well defined, suppose $u(x) = u(x')$ and $u(y) = u(y')$. Then $P(x, z) = P(x', z)$ so $P(x, y) = P(x', y)$ by (4). Also, $P(y, z) = P(y', z)$, so $P(y, x') = P(y', x')$ by (4). Hence, $P(x, y) = P(x', y')$, i.e., $F[u(x), u(y)] = F[u(x'), u(y')]$. Reversing these steps shows that F is one-to-one in each component. Finally, to show that F is strictly increasing in the first argument, suppose $u(x') > u(x)$; hence, by construction together with independence, $P(x', y) > P(x, y)$ and $F[u(x'), u(y)] > F[u(x), u(y)]$ as required. An analogous argument applied to the second component shows that F is strictly decreasing in the second component, which completes the derivation of simple scalability. Essentially the same result was established by Krantz (1964, theorem 4).

Using transitivity of implications, the previous discussion is summarized by the following result.

THEOREM   The following conditions are equivalent:

(i)   simple scalability,

(ii)   strong stochastic transitivity,

(iii)   substitutability, and

(iv)   independence.

All four properties, therefore, capture the same principle that pairwise choice probabilities can be expressed as a monotone function of some underlying scale values in such a way that if two alternatives are equivalent in one context, they are substitutable for each other in any context.

Although this principle has dominated much of the theoretical work in the field, research exists indicating that choice probabilities are affected by comparability factors which cannot be accounted for by any model based on simple scalability. In particular, Coombs (1958) presented subjects with gray color patches varying in brightness and asked them to select that patch closest to their ideal image of gray. As predicted by Coombs' unfolding theory, SST was violated for some specified triples of stimuli that lay on both sides of the subject's ideal point. More recently, Krantz (1967) has demonstrated serious violations of simple scalability in judgments of similarity between pairs of monochromatic colors. Krantz showed that the probability of choosing one pair of stimuli as more similar than another pair is affected by comparability factors between the pairs, over and above the similarity between the elements of each pair. These results indicate that choice probabilities reflect not only the scale values of the alternatives, but also the degree of difficulty of the comparison. Consequently, substitutability is violated as alternatives may be substitutable in some contexts but not in others.

The similarity between stimuli has long been considered a determinant of the degree of comparability between them. In fact, it has been hypothesized that for a fixed difference between the psychological scale values, the more similar the stimuli, the easier the comparison or the discrimination between them.

The present study investigated the simple scalability principle and the above similarity hypothesis in judgments of relative size. Geometric figures, varying in size and shape independently, were used as stimuli. The subjects were asked to judge which of two figures presented to them had a bigger area. Each stimulus was paired with each of two standards that were maximally dissimilar from each other with respect to shape. If simple scalability holds, then the orders of the choice probabilities obtained under the two standards should coincide. This is precisely the independence condition of equation 4. If, on the other hand, shape similarity facilitates judgments of relative size, then the independence condition must be violated by some specified pairs of stimuli. The two opposing predictions are contrasted in the following experiment.

Method

Stimuli

The stimuli consisted of two sets of geometric figures: rectangles and lenses, where a lens was a figure formed by the intersection of two circles of equal radii. Each set contained 20 variable stimuli varying in size and shape, and two standard stimuli of the same size but with different shapes. The 20 stimuli in each set formed a factorial design with four size levels and five shape levels. The size levels were determined by the ratio of the stimulus area to the area of the standards. The ratios of .91, .94, 1.06, and 1.09 were used in both sets. The shape levels were determined by the ratio of width to length in the rectangle set and by the ratio of the minor axis to the major

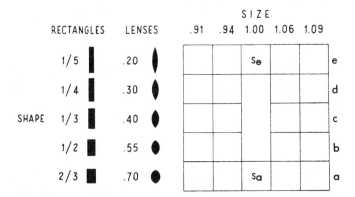

Figure 18.1
An illustration of the stimulus sets.

axis in the lens set. The ratios used in the rectangles were 2/3, 1/2, 1/3, 1/4, and 1/5, while the ratios used in the lenses were .70, .55, .40, .30, and .20. The shape levels of both sets were denoted by the letters a through e. In both sets the standards had the two extreme shape levels. One standard (s_a) was closest to a square (or a circle), while the other standard (s_e) had the most elongated shape. A schematic illustration of the stimulus sets including sets of rectangles and lenses with the same area and all five different shape levels is presented in figure 18.1.

Subjects
One hundred and sixty-eight inmates of the Detroit House of Correction participated in the experiment. Seven subjects were deleted because they failed to perform the task according to instructions. Of the remaining subjects, 78 were presented with rectangles and 83 were presented with lenses.

Procedure
Each standard was paired with all 20 variable stimuli from the same set, yielding a total of 40 pair comparisons between rectangles and 40 pair comparisons between lenses. The subjects were asked to judge which member of a pair had the larger area. The stimuli were projected on a screen for a period of about 10 sec, under normal viewing conditions. The experimental session consisted of a practice period and three replications of a complete stimulus set (40 pair comparisons). The presentation order was randomized. The session, including the practice period, lasted about 2 hr, and the subjects were run in groups of approximately 45 each. In order to motivate the

subjects, payments were given on the basis of the proportion of correct responses. Payments consisted of packs of cigarettes, which are used as currency in the prison; the average subject received about three packs.

Results

The data consist of a set of 5×4 matrices in which the rows correspond to the shape levels, the columns correspond to the size levels, and the cell entries are the relative frequencies of choosing the variable stimulus over the standard. Since each standard was compared with all variable stimuli, two such data matrices were obtained for each subject. The first test of the independence principle was based on the comparisons where the variable stimulus had one of the two extreme shape levels. Hence, only the bottom and the top rows of each data matrix were utilized in this analysis. These rows correspond to the stimuli with the least and the most elongated shapes, designated by a and e, respectively.

Let x_{ai} and x_{ei}, $i = 1, \ldots, 4$, denote stimuli of the two extreme shapes (a and e) and the same size (i). If the independence principle is valid, then for any size level, i,

$$P(x_{ai}, s_a) \geq P(x_{ei}, s_a) \quad \text{if and only if} \quad P(x_{ai}, s_e) \geq P(x_{ei}, s_e). \tag{5}$$

That is, the order of the choice probabilities is independent of the standard. If, however, the similarity hypothesis is valid and shape similarity facilitates the judgments, then the more similar the stimuli with respect to shape, the easier the size discrimination between them. Consequently, the comparison between x_{ai} and s_a is easier than that between x_{ei} and s_a, since s_a and x_{ai} have the same shape. Similarly, the comparison between x_{ei} and s_e is easier than that between x_{ai} and s_e since s_e and x_{ei} have the same shape. If both variable stimuli in equation 5 were of the same subjective area and if both standards were of the same subjective area, then the similarity hypothesis would imply that

$$P(x_{ai}, s_a) \geq P(x_{ei}, s_a) \quad \text{if and only if} \quad P(x_{ei}, s_e) \geq P(x_{ai}, s_e). \tag{6}$$

That is, opposite orders should be obtained under the two standards, in direct contradiction to the earlier prediction. Since in the present design, however, the stimuli in the pairs (s_a, s_e) and (x_{ai}, x_{ei}) are of equal objective rather than subjective area, equation 6 is not a necessary consequence of the similarity hypothesis. Nevertheless, one would expect equation 6 to be satisfied for some pairs of stimuli if the similarity hypothesis is true.

Table 18.1
The Frequency Distributions of the Individuals' M Values

M	Rectangles	Lenses	Total
$+1$	12	16	28
$+\frac{1}{3}$	3	4	7
0	9	11	20
$-\frac{1}{3}$	3	2	5
-1	36	32	68

To compare the predictions of (5) and (6), the following measure (M) of the degree of correspondence between the orders obtained under the two standards was devised. To each size level ($i = 1, 2, 3, 4$), $+1$ was assigned if equation 5 was satisfied, and -1 was assigned if equation 6 was satisfied. The cases in which a tie occurred in at least one of the two orders do not provide an adequate basis for comparing the orders and were, therefore, discounted from the analysis. The value of M for a given individual is simply the sum of the $+1$'s and -1's (over the four size levels) normalized by the number of untied comparisons. Thus, M ranges from $+1$ to -1, where $+1$ is predicted by equation 5, -1 is predicted by equation 6, and 0 is expected on the basis of random choice. The value of M is essentially an average Kendall's tau where tau is based on two stimuli only.

The distributions of the M values are presented in table 18.1. The obtained distributions were positively skewed in both stimulus sets. The average M values were $-.38$ for rectangles and $-.24$ for lenses, both of which were significantly ($p < .05$) negative according to the significance test for Kendall's tau.

The overall relative frequencies of choosing the variable stimuli over the standards, totaled for all subjects, are given in table 18.2. The group data provide strong support for the similarity hypothesis and strong evidence against the independence principle, which is violated in all cases. In every column of table 18.2, the cell entries are ordered oppositely under the two standards in complete agreement with equation 6.

The only implication of the similarity hypothesis that is independent of perceived area values is that violations of independence should be due to shape similarity. That is, if the discrimination between s_a and x is better than that between s_a and y whereas the discrimination between s_e and x is worse than that between s_e and y, then s_a should be more similar to x than to y, and s_e should be more similar to y than to x. Letting $Q(x, y)$ denote the proportion of correct area judgments between x and y, it is readily seen that any strict violation of independence is expressible in the form

Table 18.2
The Overall Frequency of Choosing the Variable Stimulus as Larger than the Standard

Standard	Shape	Size level			
		1	2	3	4
Rectangles					
s_a	e	93	106	154	180
	a	23	41	205	208
s_e	e	16	26	198	210
	a	58	73	117	125
Lenses					
s_a	e	129	153	202	203
	a	40	48	222	232
s_e	e	37	49	211	215
	a	44	56	100	102

Table 18.3
The Proportions of Pairs of Stimuli which Violate the Independence Principle and Are Compatible with the Similarity Hypothesis

	Rectangles	Lenses	Total
Set I	80/83	62/72	142/155
Set II	41/60	28/42	69/102
Total	121/143	90/114	211/257

$$Q(x, s_a) > Q(y, s_a) \quad \text{and} \quad Q(y, s_e) > Q(x, s_e) \tag{7}$$

To test the similarity hypothesis, two sets of pairs of variable stimuli, where the elements in each pair have the same area, were employed in this analysis. Set I contains all such pairs where one element has shape a and the other element has shape e, while set II contains all such pairs where one element has shape b and the other element has shape d. In accord with the natural partial order of shape similarity between stimuli, all pairs from sets I and II were classified as follows: a pair of variable stimuli (x, y) satisfying (7) is compatible with the similarity hypothesis if and only if x is less elongated than y. That is, if either (x, y) belongs to set I and x has shape a while y has shape e, or if (x, y) belongs to set II and x has shape b while y has shape d. The proportions of pairs of rectangles and lenses, from sets I and II, which satisfy (7) and are compatible with the similarity hypothesis are given in table 18.3. If all violations of independence were due to indiscriminability or random error, then only one half of the violations should be compatible with the similarity hypothesis. However, all the entries of table 18.3 are significantly greater than one half. (The proportion of

Table 18.4
The Frequency Distribution of the Individuals' Tau-Values

Tau	Rectangles	Lenses	Total
+0.76– + 1.00	1	0	1
+0.51– + 0.75	5	5	10
+0.26– + 0.50	7	5	12
+0.01– + 0.25	9	11	20
0	8	8	16
−0.01– − 0.25	15	6	21
−0.26– − 0.50	17	17	34
−0.51– − 0.75	11	17	28
−0.76– − 1.00	5	14	19

pairs of lenses from set II is significant at the .05 level, whereas all other proportions are significant at the .01 level.) The results show that most violations of independence are attributable to similarity, and that this effect is stronger in set I that in set II where the similarity differences are less extreme. The results of set II show that the similarity hypothesis is supported even when the variable stimuli do not have the same shape as the standards.

The final analysis was also based on the frequencies of correct area judgments. From the original 5×4 frequency matrices of each subject, a 5×1 column vector was computed whose entries were the number of correct choices for each shape level, summed over areas. Two such vectors were obtained for each subject, one under each standard, and the rank order correlation (Kendall's tau) between the two vectors was computed. The independence principle predicts a perfect positive correlation between the two vectors. A zero correlation is expected under the assumption of random choice, and a perfect negative correlation is expected under the similarity hypothesis provided stimuli with equal objective area are equal in subjective area. Since the stimuli were not equated in subjective area, however, one would expect a negative but not a perfect correlation. The distributions of the tau values from each stimulus set are presented in table 18.4. The obtained distributions were positively skewed, as 102 subjects had negative values as compared with 43 subjects with positive values. The average tau was −.15 for the rectangles and −.26 for the lenses, both of which were significantly negative ($p < .01$) according to a test for the significance of Kandall's tau.

The relative frequencies (totaled over subjects) of correct choices for each shape level under the two standards are shown in figure 18.2 for the rectangles and figure 18.3 for the lenses.

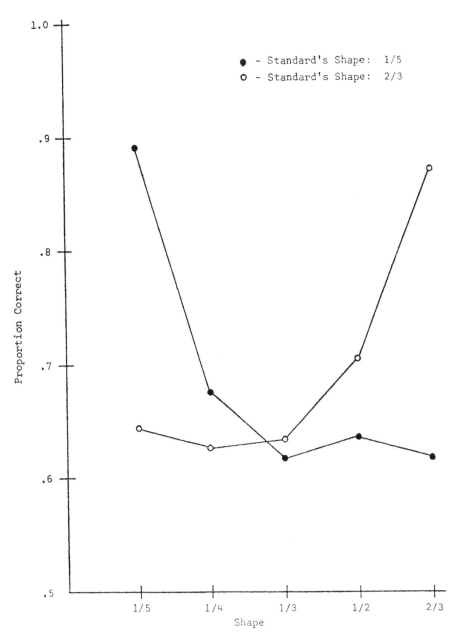

Figure 18.2
Proportion of correct choice between rectangles ($N = 936$) summed over subjects and area values.

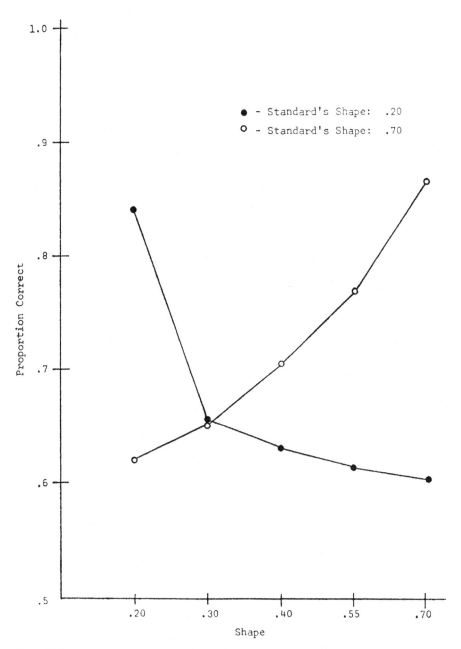

Figure 18.3
Proportion of correct choices between lenses ($N = 996$) summed over subjects and area values.

The orderings of these values, under the two standards, appear inversely related to each other and monotonically related to similarity, in accordance with the similarity hypothesis and in contradiction to the independence principle.

Discussion

Two incompatible principles of choice were compared in the present study. The data provide evidence against the independence principle and for the similarity hypothesis. It was found that the similarity between stimuli facilitates the discrimination between them. But since the similarity between two stimuli can be varied without changing their scale values, simple scalability, and hence independence, must be violated.

Although these findings hold for both types of stimuli (rectangles and lenses), their applicability to other stimuli and to different types of judgments are left to be explored. If, as available data indicate, simple scalability is violated in many contexts, then both theoretical and applied research on choice behavior should be fundamentally reevaluated.

Is this the end of simple scalability? Not necessarily. It should be recalled that in the present study, the stimuli were paired so as to maximize the similarity effect. Simple scalability may still hold for more homogeneous sets of pair comparisons. Moreover, all violations of simple scalability have been obtained in studies of pair comparisons. This, however, is not the only empirical procedure for estimating binary choice probabilities. Alternatively, a single-stimulus method may be employed to obtain replicated magnitude estimates for each stimulus. The $P(x, y)$ may then be defined as the probability that a value assigned to x exceeds a value assigned to y. In this method each stimulus is presented alone so that comparability factors cannot operate. Simple scalability may very well be satisfied by choice probabilities estimated in this fashion.

Finally, to the extent that the similarity hypothesis is applicable to the decisions of consumers or voters, it suggests the intriguing possibility of influencing choice probabilities between products or candidates by manipulating the similarity between them.

Notes

This work was supported in part by Public Health Service Grant MH-04236 and by National Science Foundation Grant GM-6782 to the University of Michigan.

We thank David H. Krantz and H. William Morrison for their many helpful suggestions and criticism based on an earlier version of this paper.

References

Block, H. D., and Marschak, J. Random orderings and stochastic theories of responses. *In* I. Olkin, S. Ghurye, W. Hoeffding, W. Madow, and H. Mann (Eds.), *Contributions to probability and statistics.* Stanford: Stanford Univer. Press, 1960.

Coombs, C. H. On the use of inconsistency of preferences in psychological measurement. *Journal of Experimental Psychology,* 1958, 55, 1–7.

Krantz, D. H. The scaling of small and large color differences. Unpublished doctoral dissertation, University of Pennsylvania, 1964.

Krantz, D. H. Rational distance functions for multidimensional scaling. *Journal of Mathematical Psychology,* 1967, 4, 226–245.

Luce, R. D. *Individual choice behavior: A theoretical analysis.* New York: Wiley, 1959.

Luce, R. D., and Suppes, P. Preference, utility, and subjective probability. *In* R. D. Luce, R. R. Bush, and E. Galanter (Eds.), *Handbook of mathematical psychology,* vol. 3. New York: Wiley, 1965, pp. 249–410.

Thurstone, L. L. A law of comparative judgment. *Psychological Review,* 1927, 34, 273–286.

Tversky, A. Additivity, utility, and subjective probability. *Journal of Mathematical Psychology,* 1967, 4, 175–201.

19 Intransitivity of Preferences

Amos Tversky

Whenever we choose which car to buy, which job to take, or which bet to play we exhibit preference among alternatives. The alternatives are usually multidimensional in that they vary along several attributes or dimensions that are relevant to the choice. In searching for the laws that govern such preferences, several decision principles have been proposed and investigated. The simplest and probably the most basic principle of choice is the transitivity condition.

A preference-or-indifference relation, denoted $\gtrsim$, is transitive if for all x, y, and z

$$x \gtrsim y \quad \text{and} \quad y \gtrsim z \quad \text{imply} \quad x \gtrsim z. \tag{1}$$

Transitivity is of central importance to both psychology and economics. It is the cornerstone of normative and descriptive decision theories (Edwards, 1954, 1961; Luce & Suppes, 1965; Samuelson, 1953), and it underlies measurement models of sensation and value (Luce & Galanter, 1963; Suppes & Zinnes, 1963). The essential role of the transitivity assumption in measurement theories stems from the fact that it is a necessary condition for the existence of an ordinal (utility) scale, u, such that for all x and y,

$$u(x) \geq u(y) \quad \text{if and only if} \quad x \gtrsim y. \tag{2}$$

Transitivity is also a sufficient condition for the existence of such a scale, provided the number of alternatives is finite, or countable.

Individuals, however, are not perfectly consistent in their choices. When faced with repeated choices between x and y, people often choose x in some instances and y in others. Furthermore, such inconsistencies are observed even in the absence of systematic changes in the decision maker's taste which might be due to learning or sequential effects. It seems, therefore, that the observed inconsistencies reflect inherent variability or momentary fluctuation in the evaluative process. This consideration suggests that preference should be defined in a probabilistic fashion. To do so, let $P(x, y)$ be the probability of choosing x in a choice between x and y, where $P(x, y) + P(y, x) = 1$. Preference can now be defined by

$$x \gtrsim y \quad \text{if and only if} \quad P(x, y) \geq \tfrac{1}{2}. \tag{3}$$

The inconsistency of the choices is thus incorporated into the preference relation as x is said to be preferred to y only when it is chosen over y more than half the time. Restating the transitivity axiom in terms of this definition yields

$$P(x, y) \geq \tfrac{1}{2} \quad \text{and} \quad P(y, z) \geq \tfrac{1}{2} \quad \text{imply} \quad P(x, z) \geq \tfrac{1}{2}. \tag{4}$$

This condition, called weak stochastic transitivity, or WST, is the most general probabilistic version of transitivity. Violations of this property cannot be attributable to inconsistency alone.

Despite the almost universal acceptance of the transitivity axiom, in either algebraic or probabilistic form, one can think of several choice situations where it may be violated. Consider, for example, a situation in which three alternatives, x, y, and z, vary along two dimensions, I and II, and where their values on these dimensions are given by the following payoff matrix.

		Dimensions	
		I	II
	x	2ε	6ε
Alternatives	y	3ε	4ε
	z	4ε	2ε

The alternatives may be job applicants varying in intelligence (I) and experience (II), where the entries are the candidates' scores on the corresponding scales or dimensions. Suppose the subject (S) uses the following decision rule in choosing between each pair of alternatives: if the difference between the alternatives on dimension I is (strictly) greater than ε, choose the alternative that has the higher value on dimension I. If the difference between the alternatives on dimension I is less than or equal to ε, choose the alternative that has the higher value on dimension II. It is easy to see that this seemingly reasonable decision rule yields intransitive preferences when applied to the above matrix. Since the differences between x and y and between y and z on the first dimension are not greater than ε, the choice is made on the basis of the second dimension and hence x is chosen over y and y is chosen over z. But since the difference between x and z on the first dimension is greater than ε, z is chosen over x yielding an intransitive chain of preferences.

Formally, such a structure may be characterized as a lexicographic semiorder, abbreviated LS, where a semiorder (Luce, 1956) or a just noticeable difference structure is imposed on a lexicographic ordering. As an illustration, let us restate this rule in terms of the selection of applicants. An employer, regarding intelligence as far more important than experience, may choose the brighter of any pair of candidates. Cognizant that intelligence scores are not perfectly reliable, the employer may decide to regard one candidate as brighter than another one only if the difference between their IQ scores exceeds 3 points, for example. If the difference between the applicants is less than 3 points, the employer considers the applicants equally bright and chooses the more experienced candidate. Essentially the same example was discussed by Davidson, McKinsey, and Suppes (1955). Such a decision rule is particularly appealing whenever the relevant dimension is noisy as a consequence of imperfect discrimination or unreliability of available information. Where this decision rule is actually employed by indiduals, WST must be rejected.

Other theoretical considerations proposed by Savage (1951), May (1954), Quandt (1956), and Morrison (1962) suggest that WST may be violated under certain conditions. No conclusive violations of WST, however, have been demonstrated in studies of preferences although Morrison (1962) provided some evidence for predictable intransitivities in judgments of relative numerosity, and Shepard (1964) produced a striking circularity in judgments of relative pitch. Several preference experiments have tested WST, for example, Edwards (1953), May (1954), Papandreou, Sauerlander, Bownlee, Hurwicz, and Franklin (1957), Davis (1958), Davidson and Marschak (1959), Chipman (1960), and Griswold and Luce (1962). All these studies failed to detect any significant violation of WST.

The present paper attempts to explore the conditions under which transitivity holds or fails to hold. First, the LS described above is utilized to construct alternatives which yield stochastically intransitive data. The conditions under which WST is violated are studied within the framework of a general additive difference choice model and their implications for the psychology of choice are discussed.

Experiments

General Considerations
The purpose of the following studies was to create experimental situations in which individuals would reveal consistent patterns of intransitive choices. The experiments are not addressed to the question of whether human preferences are, in general, transitive; but rather to the question of whether reliable intransitivities can be produced, and under what conditions. The construction of the alternatives was based on the LS described in the introduction. The application of the LS to a specific experimental situation, however, raises serious identification problems.

In the first place, the LS may be satisfied by some, but not all, individuals. One must identify, therefore, the Ss that satisfy the model. This, however, is not an easy task since even if the LS is satisfied by all people, they may differ in the manner in which the alternatives are perceived or processed. Different individuals can characterize the same alternatives in terms of different sets of attributes. For example, one employer may evaluate job applicants in terms of their intelligence and experience whereas another employer may evaluate them in terms of their competence and

Table 19.1
The Gambles Employed in Experiment I

Gamble	Probability of winning	Payoff (in $)	Expected value (in $)
a	7/24	5.00	1.46
b	8/24	4.75	1.58
c	9/24	4.50	1.69
d	10/24	4.25	1.77
e	11/24	4.00	1.83

sociability. Similarly, one S may conceptualize (two-outcome) gambles in terms of odds and stakes, while another may view them in terms of their expectation, variance, and skewness. Since the predictions of the model are based on the dimensional structure of the alternatives, this structure has to be specified separately for each S. In order to induce Ss to use the same dimensional framework, alternatives that are defined and displayed in terms of a given dimensional representation have been employed.

Then, even if all individuals satisfy the LS relative to the same dimensions, they may still vary in their preference threshold as well as in the relative importance that they attribute to the dimensions. A difference between an IQ of 123 and an IQ of 127, for instance, may appear significant to some people and negligible to others.

These considerations suggest treating each S as a separate experiment and constructing the alternatives according to the dimensions and the spacing he uses. Alternatively, one may select, for a critical test, those Ss who satisfy a specified criterion relative to a given representation. (It should be noted that the preselection of Ss or alternatives, on the basis of an independent criterion, is irrelevant to the question of whether WST is consistently violated for any given S.) Both methods are employed in the following studies. The first study investigates choice between gambles while the second one is concerned with the selection of college applicants.

Experiment I
The present study investigates preferences between simple gambles. All gambles were of the form (x, p, o) where one receives a payoff of $\$x$ if a chance event p occurs, and nothing if p does not occur. The chance events were generated by spinning a spinner on a disc divided into a black and a white sector. The probability of winning corresponded to the relative size of the black sector. The gambles employed in the study are described in table 19.1.

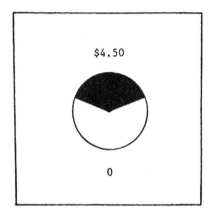

Figure 19.1
An illustration of a gamble card.

Each gamble was displayed on a card showing the payoff and a disc with the corresponding black and white sectors. An illustration of a gamble card is given in figure 19.1. Note that, unlike the outcomes, the probabilities were not displayed in a numerical form. Consequently, no exact calculation of expected values was possible. The gambles were constructed so that the expected value increased with probability and decreased with payoff.

Since the present design renders the evaluation of payoff differences easier than that of probability differences, it was hypothesized that at least some Ss would ignore small probability differences, and choose between adjacent gambles on the basis of the payoffs. (Gambles are called adjacent if they are a step apart along the probability or the value scale.) Since expected value, however, is negatively correlated with payoff, it was further hypothesized that for gambles lying far apart in the chain, Ss would choose according to expected value, or the probability of winning. Such a pattern of preference must violate transitivity somewhere along the chain (from *a* to *e*).

In order to identify Ss who might exhibit this preference pattern, 18 Harvard undergraduates were invited to a preliminary session. The Ss were run individually. On each trial the experimenter presented S with a pair of gamble cards and asked him which of the gambles he would rather play. No indifference judgment was allowed. The Ss were told that a single trial would be selected at the end of the session and that they would be able to play the gamble they had chosen on that trial. They were also told that the outcome of this gamble would be their only payoff.

To minimize the memory of earlier choices in order to allow independent replications within one session a set of five "irrelevant" gambles was constructed. These gambles were of the same general form (x, p, o) but they differed from the critical gambles in probabilities and payoffs.

In the preliminary session, all Ss were presented with all pairs of adjacent gambles $(a, b; b, c; c, d; d, e)$ as well as with the single pair of extreme gambles (a, e). In addition, all 10 pair comparisons of the "irrelevant" gambles were presented. Each of the 15 pairs was replicated 3 times. The order of presentation was randomized within each of the three blocks.

The following criterion was used to identify the potentially intransitive Ss. On the majority of the adjacent pairs (i.e., three out of the four) S had to prefer the alternative with the higher payoff, while on the extreme pair, he had to prefer the one with the higher expected value (i.e., choose e over a). A gamble was said to be preferred over another one if it was chosen on at least two out of the three replications of that pair. Eight out of the 18 Ss satisfied the above criterion and were invited to participate in the main experiment.

The experiment consisted of five test sessions, one session every week. In each session, all 10 pair comparisons of the test gambles along with all 10 pair comparisons of the "irrelevant" gambles were presented. Each of the 20 pairs was replicated four times in each session. The position of the gambles (right-left) and the order of the pairs were randomized within each block of 20 pairs. The Ss were run individually under the same procedure as in the preliminary session. Each of the test sessions lasted approximately $\frac{3}{4}$ of an hour. The choice probabilities of all eight Ss between the five gambles are shown in table 19.2. Violations of WST are marked by superscript x and violations of the LS are marked by superscript y.

The data indicate that although two Ss (7 and 8) seemed to satisfy WST, it was violated by the rest of the Ss. Furthermore, all violations were in the expected direction, and almost all of them were in the predicted locations. That is, people chose between adjacent gambles according to the payoff and between the more extreme gambles according to probability, or expected value. This result is extremely unlikely under the hypothesis that the intransitivities are due to random choices. Had this been the case, one should have expected the violations to be uniformly distributed with an equal number of violations in each of the two directions.

To further test the statistical significance of the results, likelihood ratio tests of both WST and the LS were conducted for each S. This test compares a restrictive model (or hypothesis) denoted M_1 (such as WST or the LS) where the parameter space is constrained, with a nonrestrictive model, denoted M_0, which is based on an unconstrained parameter space. The test statistic is the ratio of the maximum value

Table 19.2
Proportion of Times that the Row Gamble Was Chosen over the Column Gamble by Each of the Eight Subjects

| Subject | Gamble | Gamble | | | | |
		a	b	c	d	e
1	a	—	.75	.70	.45[x]	.15[x]
	b		—	.85	.65	.40[x]
	c			—	.80	.60
	d				—	.85
	e					—
2	a	—	.40[y]	.65	.50	.25[x]
	b		—	.70	.40[xy]	.35[x]
	c			—	.75	.55
	d				—	.75
	e					—
3	a	—	.75	.70	.60	.25[x]
	b		—	.80	.65	.40[x]
	c			—	.95	.80
	d				—	1.00
	e					—
4	a	—	.50	.45	.20	.05
	b		—	.65[x]	.35	.10
	c			—	.70[x]	.40
	d				—	.85[x]
	e					—
5	a	—	.75	.65	.35[x]	.60[y]
	b		—	.80	.55	.30[x]
	c			—	.65	.65
	d				—	.70
	e					—
6	a	—	1.00	.90	.65	.20[x]
	b		—	.80	.75	.55
	c			—	.90	.65
	d				—	.75
	e					—
7	a	—	.45[y]	.65	.60	.60[y]
	b		—	.60	.40[xy]	.65
	c			—	.50	.75
	d				—	.70
	e					—
8	a	—	.60	.70	.75	.85[y]
	b		—	.65	.75	.85
	c			—	.60	.80
	d				—	.40[y]
	e					—

[x] Violations of WST.
[y] Violations of the LS.

Table 19.3
Likelihood Ratio Test for all Subjects under WST and the LS

Subject	$Q(WST, M_0)$	df	$p <$	$Q(LS, M_0)$	df	$p <$	$Q(WST, LS)$
1	11.82	3	.01	.00	0	—	11.82
2	7.84	3	.05	.00	0	—	7.84
3	6.02	2	.05	.00	0	—	6.02
4	15.94	3	.01	.00	0	—	15.94
5	5.18	2	.10	.40	1	.75	4.78
6	7.36	1	.01	.00	0	—	7.36
7	.40	1	.75	1.80	3	.50	−1.20
8	.00	0	—	11.62	2	.01	−11.62

Note: $Q(M_1, M_0) = -2 \ln \frac{L^*(M_1)}{L^*(M_0)}$.

of the likelihood function of the sample under the restrictive model, denoted $L^*(M_1)$, to the maximum value of the likelihood function of the sample under the nonrestrictive model, denoted $L^*(M_0)$. For a large sample size, the quantity

$$Q(M_1, M_0) = -2 \ln \frac{L^*(M_1)}{L^*(M_0)}$$

has a chi-square distribution with a number of degrees of freedom that equals the number of constrained parameters. Using this distribution, one can test the null hypothesis that the data were generated by the restrictive model. For further details, see Mood (1950).

In the present study, $L^*(M_0)$ is simply the product of the binomial probabilities, while $L^*(M_1)$ is obtained from it by substituting a value of one-half in the above product for those choice probabilities that were incompatible with the particular restrictive model. The tested version of the LS was that in the (four) pairs of adjacent gambles, preferences are according to payoff while in the most extreme pair of gambles, preferences are according to expected value. The obtained chi-square values with the associated degrees of freedom and significance levels are displayed in table 19.3.

The table shows that WST is rejected at the .05 level for five Ss, while the LS is rejected for one S only. It is important to note that the test for rejecting WST is very conservative in that it depends only on the magnitude of the violations and ignores their (predicted) location and direction.

The last column of table 19.3 reports the Q values corresponding to the ratio of the maximum likelihoods of WST and the LS. Since both models are of the restrictive

Table 19.4
Gamble Sets I, II, and III

Set	Probability	Payoff	Expected value
I	7/24	5.00	1.46
	8/24	4.75	1.58
	9/24	4.50	1.69
	10/24	4.25	1.77
	11/24	4.00	1.83
II	8/24	5.00	1.67
	10/24	4.75	1.98
	12/24	4.50	2.25
	14/24	4.25	2.48
	16/24	4.00	2.67
III	7/24	3.70	1.08
	8/24	3.60	1.20
	9/24	3.50	1.31
	10/24	3.40	1.42
	11/24	3.30	1.51

type and the two chi-squares are not independent the distribution of this statistic is not known. Nevertheless, its values are substantially positive for six out of the eight Ss, suggesting that the LS accounts for the data better than WST.

In a postexperimental interview, S_4 described his behavior as follows: "There is a small difference between Gambles a and b or b and c etc., so I would pick the one with the higher payoff. However, there is a big difference between Gambles a and e or b and e etc., so I would pick the one with the higher probability." This is, in fact, a good description of his actual choices. When asked whether this type of behavior might lead to intransitivities, he replied, "I do not think so, but I am not sure." The Ss did not remember for sure whether any of the pairs were replicated during the experiment, although they were sure that most gambles appeared in more than one pair in any one of the sessions. When the transitivity assumption was explained to the Ss, they reacted by saying that although they did not pay special attention to it, they were almost certain that their preferences were transitive.

The degree of intransitivity obtained in an experiment depends critically on the spacing of the alternatives and the selection of the display. To study the effects of changes in the payoff or the probability structure, three sets of gambles portrayed in table 19.4 were compared.

Note that set I is the one used in the main experiment. Set II was obtained from it by increasing the probability differences between adjacent gambles, and set III by decreasing the payoff differences between them. All sets were constructed so that the expected value increased with the probability of winning and decreased with the payoff.

To compare the three sets, 36 Harvard undergraduates (who did not participate in the earlier sessions) were invited for a single session. Each S was presented with five pairs of gambles from each one of the three sets. These included the four pairs of adjacent gambles and the single pair of extreme gambles from each set. Each of the 15 pairs was replicated three times, in a randomized presentation order. The Ss were run individually under the procedure employed in the earlier sessions. Furthermore, the same criterion for circularity was investigated. That is, S had to choose between most (three out of four) adjacent gambles according to payoff and between the extreme gamble according to probability. The results showed that, out of the 36 Ss, 13 satisfied the criterion in set I, 6 satisfied the criterion in set II and 8 satisfied the criterion in set III. These findings indicate that the probability and the payoff differences used in set I yield more intransitivities than those used in sets II and III.

Experiment II

The second experimental task is the selection of college applicants. Thirty-six undergraduates were presented with pairs of hypothetical applicants and were asked to choose the one that they would rather accept. Each applicant was described by a profile portraying his percentile ranks on three evaluative dimensions, labeled I, E, and S. The Ss were told that dimension I reflects intellectual ability, dimension E reflects emotional stability, and dimension S reflects social facility. An illustrative profile is shown in figure 19.2.

The Ss were further told that the profiles were constructed by a selection committee on the basis of high school grades, intelligence and personality tests, letters of recommendation, and a personal interview. Using this information, all applicants were ranked with respect to the three dimensions and the three corresponding percentile ranks constitute the applicant's profile. The Ss were then told that

The college selection committee is interested in learning student opinion concerning the type of applicants that should be admitted to the school. Therefore, you are asked to select which you would admit from each of several pairs of applicants. Naturally, intellectual ability would be the most important factor in your decision, but the other factors are of some value, too. Also, you should bear in mind that the scores are based on the committee's ranking and so they may not be perfectly reliable.

The study consisted of two parts: a preliminary session and a test session. The profiles used in the preliminary session are given in table 19.5.

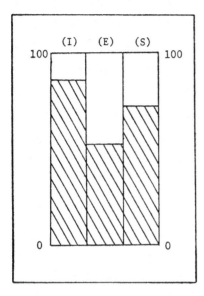

Figure 19.2
An illustrative applicant's profile.

Table 19.5
The 10 Profiles Used in the Preliminary Session of Experiment II

Applicant	Dimensions		
	I	E	S
a	63	96	95
b	66	90	85
c	69	84	75
d	72	78	65
e	75	72	55
f	78	66	45
g	81	60	35
h	84	54	25
i	87	48	15
j	90	42	5

Note: I = intellectual ability, E = emotional stability, S = social facility.

The profiles were constructed such that there was a perfect negative correlation between the scores on dimension I and the scores on dimensions E and S. The (absolute) difference between a pair of profiles on dimension I is referred to as their I difference. A choice between profiles is said to be compatible with (or according to) dimension I whenever the profile with the higher score on that dimension is selected, and it is said to be incompatible with dimension I whenever the profile with the lower score on that dimension is selected.

Since dimension I is the most important to the present task, and since the graphical display hinders the evaluation of small I difference it was hypothesized that the LS would be satisfied by some of the Ss. For small I differences these Ss would choose according to dimensions E and S, but for large I differences they would choose according to dimension I. The purpose of the preliminary session was to identify Ss who behaved in that fashion and to collect preference data that could be employed in constructing new sets of profiles to be used in the test session.

The Ss were run individually. On each trial the experimenter presented S with a pair of profiles and asked him to make a choice. Indifference judgment was not allowed. The Ss were presented with all 45 pair comparisons of the 10 profiles in the same randomized order.

The criterion for participation in the test session was that at least six out of nine choices between the adjacent profiles $(a, b; b, c; c, d; d, e; e, f; f, g; g, h; h, i; i, j)$ were according to dimensions E and S and at least seven out of the 10 choices between the extreme profiles $(a, j; a, i; a, h; a, g; b, j; b, i; b, h; c, j; c, i; d, j)$ were according to dimension I. Fifteen out of the 36 Ss satisfied this criterion and were invited to the test session.[1]

Using the data obtained in the preliminary session, the following procedure was employed to construct a special set of five profiles for each S. Let $n(\delta)$ denote the number of choices (made by a given S in the preliminary session) between profiles whose I difference was at most δ and that were incompatible with dimension I. Similarly, let $m(\delta)$ denote the number of choices between profiles whose I difference was at least δ and that were compatible with Dimension I. Note that $\delta = 3, 6, 9, \ldots, 27$ and that, by the selection criterion employed, $n(3) \geq 6$ and $m(18) \geq 7$ for all the selected Ss. The values of $n(\delta)$ and $m(\delta)$ were computed for each S and the value of δ' for which $n(\delta) + m(\delta)$ is maximized was obtained.

To illustrate the procedure, the choices made by S_8 in the preliminary session, along with the values of $n(\delta)$, $m(\delta)$, and $n(\delta) + m(\delta)$ are shown in table 19.6. A value of 1 in an entry indicates that the profile in that row was selected over the profile in that column. A value of 0 indicates the opposite.

Table 19.6
Choices Made by S_8 in the Preliminary Session and the Resulting Values of $n(\delta)$, $m(\delta)$, and $n(\delta) + m(\delta)$

Profile	a	b	c	d	e	f	g	h	i	j	δ	$n(\delta)$	$m(\delta)$	$n(\delta) + m(\delta)$
a		1	1	0	0	0	1	0	0	0	27	23	1	24
b			1	1	1	0	0	0	1	0	24	23	3	26
c				1	0	1	1	0	0	0	21	23	5	28
d					1	1	0	1	1	0	18	22	8	30
e						0	1	1	0	1	15	21	11	32
f							1	1	1	0	12	19	15	34
g								1	0	0	9	17	18	35
h									0	1	6	13	20	33
i										1	3	7	22	29
j														

Note: The preference of a row profile over a column profile is denoted by a 1, and the reverse preference is denoted by 0.

Note that the diagonals of table 19.6 represent pairs of profiles that have equal I differences, and that these differences increase with the distance from the main (lowest) diagonal. Thus, pairs of adjacent profiles are on the lowest diagonal while pairs of extreme profiles are on the higher diagonals. Inspection of table 19.6 reveals that most choices on the three lower diagonals were incompatible with dimension I, while most choices on the six upper diagonals were compatible with dimension I. The value of δ which maximizes $n(\delta) + m(\delta)$ is 9, which is taken as an estimate of the preference threshold ε. (It should be noted that ε was originally defined as a subjective rather than objective difference. Consequently, it need not be independent of the location of the scores, and different estimates of δ' may be obtained for different parts of the scale. In the present study, however, only a single estimate of ε was obtained for each S.)

On the basis of these estimates, Ss were divided into four groups, and a special set of profiles was constructed for each group. The new sets were constructed so that the intermediate I differences equaled the estimated threshold, ε, for each S. More specifically, the I differences in the four pairs of adjacent profiles $(a, b; b, c; c, d; d, e)$ were smaller than ε, the I differences in the three pairs of extreme profiles $(a, e; a, d; b, e)$ were larger than ε, and the I differences in the three pairs of intermediate profiles $(a, c; b, d; c, e)$ equaled ε. The four sets of profiles, constructed for the test session, are shown in table 19.7. Note that in each of the sets of table 19.7 there is a perfect negative correlation between dimension I and dimensions E and S, and that the profiles are equally spaced. The four sets differ from each other in the location and the spacing of the profiles. The differences between adjacent profiles on dimensions I, E, and

Table 19.7
Four Sets of Profiles Constructed for Experiment II

Set	Profiles	Dimensions		
		I	E	S
I	a	69	84	75
	b	72	78	65
	c	75	72	55
	d	78	66	45
	e	81	60	35
II	a	66	90	85
	b	72	80	70
	c	78	70	55
	d	84	60	40
	e	90	50	25
III	a	54	90	95
	b	63	78	75
	c	72	66	55
	d	81	54	35
	e	90	42	15
IV	a	42	96	96
	b	54	80	73
	c	66	64	50
	d	78	48	27
	e	90	32	4

Note: I = intellectual ability, E = emotional stability, S = social facility.

S respectively are 3, 6, and 10 in set I; 6, 10, and 15 in set II; 9, 12, and 20 in set III; 12, 16, and 23 in set IV. Under the hypothesized model this construction was designed to yield preference patterns where choices between the four adjacent profiles are incompatible with dimension I, whereas choices between the three extreme profiles are compatible with dimension I.

The test session took place approximately 2 weeks after the preliminary session. The Ss were reminded of the instructions and the nature of the task. They were run individually, and each one was presented with all 10 pair comparisons of the five new profiles along with all 10 pair comparisons of five "irrelevant" profiles introduced to minimize recall of the earlier decisions. Each of the 20 pairs was replicated three times during the session. The order of presentation was identical for all Ss and it was randomized within each block of 20 pairs. The choice frequencies of all 10 critical pairs of profiles are shown in table 19.8 for each S. Since only three replications of each pair comparison were obtained, the likelihood ratio test could not be properly

Table 19.8
Frequencies of Selecting the First Element of Each Pair over the Second, Totaled over the Three Replications

Subject	Set	Pair a,b	b,c	c,d	d,e	a,c	b,d	c,e	a,d	b,e	a,e	π	WST(π)	LS(π)
1	I	3	3	2	1	2	1	2	1	0	0	.4	.213	.316
2	I	2	1	2	3	2	1	2	0	0	0	.2	.196	.292
3	I	3	2	3	2	1	2	3	0	0	0	.4	.262	.303
4	II	3	3	2	3	1	0	0	0	0	0	.3	.125	.241
5	II	0	0	0	0	0	0	0	0	0	0	.0	.000	.300
6	II	3	2	3	1	2	1	2	2	0	1	.3	.171	.285
7	II	3	3	3	1	2	1	1	0	0	0	.2	.197	.295
8	II	3	3	3	1	2	1	1	0	0	0	.3	.125	.242
9	II	3	2	3	3	1	2	3	2	1	0	.4	.237	.281
10	III	3	3	2	3	2	2	2	1	0	0	.5	.324	.391
11	III	3	3	3	3	2	3	3	1	2	1	.4	.238	.366
12	III	2	1	2	3	2	1	2	0	0	0	.2	.196	.292
13	III	3	2	2	3	2	1	0	1	1	0	.3	.228	.275
14	IV	2	2	3	3	1	0	2	1	1	0	.3	.228	.275
15	IV	3	2	3	3	2	2	2	2	0	0	.4	.238	.372
Total												.307	.199	.302

Note: The values of π denote the observed proportions of intransitive triples, whereas the values of LS(π) and WST(π) denote the expected proportions under the two models, respectively.

applied to these data. Instead, the maximum likelihood estimates of the choice probabilities, under both WST and the LS, were obtained for each S. The observed proportion of triples violating WST, denoted π, was then compared with the expected proportions, based on the maximum likelihood estimates under WST and the LS, denoted WST(π) and LS(π) respectively. Table 19.8 shows that the observed values of π exceed the maximum likelihood estimates of π under WST for all but one S ($p < .01$ by a sign test). Furthermore, the LS predicted the observed proportions better than WST for 11 out of 15 Ss. Finally, the overall proportion of intransitive triples (.307) is significantly higher ($p < .01$) than the value expected under WST (.199), but it is not significantly different from the value expected under the LS (.302), according to a chi-square test. Hence, WST is rejected because both the overall proportion of intransitive triples and the π values of a significant majority of Ss exceed their expected value under WST.

The Ss were interviewed at the end of the test session. None of the Ss realized that his preferences were intransitive. Moreover, a few Ss denied this possibility emphatically and asked to see the experimenter's record. When faced with his own intransitivities one S said "I must have made a mistake somewhere." When the LS was explained to that S, however, he commented, "It is a reasonable way to make choices. In fact, I have probably made some decisions that way." The relation between the model and its logical consequences was obviously not apparent to our S.

Theory

The empirical studies showed that, under appropriate experimental conditions, the behavior of some people is intransitive. Moreover, the intransitivities are systematic, consistent, and predictable. What type of choice theory is needed to explain intransitive preferences between multidimensional alternatives?

The lexicographic semiorder that was employed in the construction of the alternatives for the experiments is one such model. It is not, however, the only model that can account for the results. Furthermore, despite its intuitive appeal, it is based on a noncompensatory principle that is likely to be too restrictive in many contexts. In this section, two choice theories are introduced and their relationships to the transitivity principle are studied.

Let $A = A_1 \times \cdots \times A_n$ be a set of multidimensional alternatives with elements of the form $x = (x_1, \ldots, x_n)$, $y = (y_1, \ldots, y_n)$, where x_i $(i = 1, \ldots, n)$ is the value of alternative x on dimension i. Note that the components of x may be nominal scale values rather than real numbers. A theory of choice between such alternatives is essentially a decision rule which determines when x is preferred to y, or when $p(x, y) > \frac{1}{2}$. A more elaborate theory may also provide an explicit formula for $P(x, y)$.

In examining the process of choice between multidimensional alternatives, two different methods of evaluation have been considered (Morrison, 1962). The first is based on independent evaluations. According to this method, one evaluates the two alternatives, x and y, separately, and assigns scale values, $u(x)$ and $u(y)$, to each of them. Alternative x is, then, preferred to alternative y if and only if $u(x) > u(y)$. The scale value assigned to an alternative is a measure of its utility, or subjective value, which is assumed to depend on the subjective values of its components. More specifically, there are scales $u_1, \ldots, u_n$ defined on $A_1, \ldots, A_n$ respectively such that $u_i(x_i)$ is the subjective value of the ith component of alternative x. It is further assumed that the overall utility of an alternative is expressable as a specified function of the scale values of its components. Among the various possible functional relations, the additive combination rule has been most thoroughly investigated. According to the additive (conjoint measurement) model, the subjective value of an alternative is simply the sum of the subjective value of its components.

Stated formally, a preference structure satisfies the *additive model* if there exist real-valued functions $u, u_1, \ldots, u_n$ such that

$$x \gtrsim y \quad \text{if and only if} \quad u(x) = \sum_{i=1}^{n} u_i(x_i) \geq \sum_{i=1}^{n} u_i(y_i) = u(y). \tag{5}$$

Axiomatic analyses of this model, which are based on ordinal assumptions, have been provided by Debreu (1960), Luce and Tukey (1964), Krantz (1964), and Luce (1966) under solvability conditions. Necessary and sufficient conditions for additivity have been discussed by Adams and Fagot (1959), Scott (1964), and Tversky (1967b). For some of the empirical applications of the model, see Shepard (1964) and Tversky (1967a). Note that the commonly applied multiple-regression model is a special case of the additive model where all the subjective scales are linear.

The second method of evaluation is based on comparisons of component-wise differences between the alternatives. According to this method one considers quantities of the form $\delta_i = u_i(x_i) - u_i(y_i)$ which correspond to the difference between the subjective values of x and y on the ith dimension. To each such quantity, one applies a difference function, ϕ_i, which determines the contribution of the particular subjective difference to the overall evaluation of the alternatives. The quantity $\phi_i(\delta_i)$ can be viewed, therefore, as the "advantage" or the "disadvantage" (depending on whether δ_i is positive or negative) of x over y with respect to dimension i. With this interpretation in mind, it is natural to require that $\phi_i(-\delta) = -\phi_i(\delta)$. The obtained values of $\phi_i(\delta_i)$ are, then, summed over all dimensions, and x is preferred over y whenever the resulting sum is positive.

Stated formally, a preference structure satisfies the *additive difference model* if there exist real-valued functions $u_1, \ldots, u_n$ and increasing continuous functions $\phi_1, \ldots, \phi_n$ defined on some real intervals such that

$$x \gtrsim y \quad \text{if and only if} \quad \sum_{i=1}^{n} \phi_i[u_i(x_i) - u_i(y_i)] \geq 0 \tag{6}$$

where $\quad \phi_i(-\delta) = -\phi_i(\delta) \quad$ for all i.

An axiomatic analysis of the additive difference model will be presented elsewhere. Essentially the same model was proposed by Morrison (1962). A set of ordinal axioms yielding a (symmetric) additive difference model of similarity (rather than preference) judgments has been given by Beals, Krantz, and Tversky (1968).

A comparison of the additive model (equation 5) with the additive difference model (equation 6) from a psychological viewpoint reveals that they suggest different ways of processing and evaluating the alternatives. A schematic illustration of the difference is given below.

$$x = (x_1, \ldots, x_i, \ldots, x_n) \rightarrow \sum_{i=1}^{n} u_i(x_i)$$

$$y = (y_1, \ldots, y_i, \ldots, y_n) \rightarrow \sum_{i=1}^{n} u_i(y_i)$$

$$\downarrow$$

$$\sum_{i=1}^{n} \phi_i[u_i(x_i) - u_i(y_i)]$$

In the simple additive model, the alternatives are first processed "horizontally," by adding the scale values of the components, and the resulting sums are then compared to determine the choice. In the additive difference model, on the other hand, the alternatives are first processed "vertically," by making intradimensional evaluations, and the results of these vertical comparisons are then added to determine the choice. Although the two models suggest different processing strategies, the additive model is formally a special case of the additive difference model where all the difference functions are linear. To verify this fact, suppose $\phi_i(\delta_i) = t_i\delta_i$ for some positive t_i and for all i. Consequently,

$$\sum_{i=1}^{n} \phi_i[u_i(x_i) - u_i(y_i)] = \sum_{i=1}^{n} t_i u_i(x_i) - \sum_{i=1}^{n} t_i u_i(y_i).$$

Thus, if we let $v_i(x_i) = t_i u_i(x_i)$ for all i, then equation 6 can be written as $x \gtrsim y$ if and only if

$$\sum_{i=1}^{n} v_i(x_i) \geq \sum_{i=1}^{n} v_i(y_i)$$

which is the additive model of equation 5.

Hence, if the difference functions are linear the two models (but not necessarily the processing strategies) coincide. The vertical processing strategy is, thus, compatible with the additive model if and only if the difference functions are linear.

The proposed processing strategies, as well as the models associated with them, are certainly affected by the way in which the information is displayed. More specifically, the additive model is more likely to be used when the alternatives are displayed sequentially (i.e., one at a time), while the additive difference model is more likely to be used when the dimensions are displayed sequentially. Two different types of political campaigns serve as a case in point. In one type of campaign, each candidate appears separately and presents his views on all the relevant issues. In the second type the various issues are raised separately and each candidate presents his view on that particular issue. It is argued that the "horizontal" evaluation method, or the simple additive model, is more likely to be used in the former situation, while the "vertical" evaluation method, or the additive difference model, is more likely to be used in the latter situation.

Although different evaluation methods may be used in different situations, there are several general considerations which favor the additive difference model. In the first place, it is considerably more general, and can accommodate a wider variety of preference structures. The LS, for example, is a limiting case of this model where one (or more) of the difference functions approaches a step function where $\phi(\delta) = 0$ whenever $\delta \leq \varepsilon$. Second, intradimensional comparison may simplify the evaluation task. If one alternative is slightly better than another one on all relevant dimensions, it will be immediately apparent in a component-wise comparison and the choice will indeed be easy. If the alternatives, however, are evaluated independently this dominance relation between the alternatives may be obscured, which would certainly complicate the choice process. But even if no such dominance relation exists, it may still be easier to use approximation methods when the evaluation is based on component-wise comparisons. One common approximation procedure is based on "canceling out" differences that are equal, or nearly equal, thus reducing the number of dimensions that have to be considered. In deciding which of two houses to buy, for example, one may feel that the differences in style and location cancel each other out and the choice problem reduces to one of deciding whether it is worth spending $x more for a larger house. It is considerably more difficult to employ this procedure when the two alternatives are evaluated independently.

Finally, intradimensional evaluations are simpler and more natural than inter-dimensional ones simply because the compared quantities are expressed in terms of the same units. It is a great deal simpler to evaluate the difference in intelligence between two candidates than to evaluate the combined effect of intelligence and emotional stability. In choosing between two n-dimensional alternatives, one makes $2n$ interdimensional evaluations when the alternatives are evaluated independently according to the additive model, but only n interdimensional evaluations along with n intradimensional evaluations according to the additive difference model.

Now that the two models have been defined and compared, their relationships to the transitivity principle are investigated. It can be readily seen that the simple additive model satisfies the transitivity principle, for the assumptions that x is preferred to y, and y is preferred to z imply that $u(x) > u(y)$ and $u(y) > u(z)$. Hence, $u(x) > u(z)$, which implies that x must be preferred to z. Note that the argument does not depend on the additivity assumption. Transitivity must, therefore, be satisfied by any model where a scale value is assigned to each alternative and the preferences are compatible with equations 2 or 3.

Under what conditions does the additive difference model satisfy the transitivity principle? The answer to this question is given by the following result, which depends on the dimensionality of the alternatives.[2]

THEOREM: If the additive difference model (equation 6) is satisfied then the following assertions hold whenever the difference functions are defined.

1. For $n \geq 3$, transitivity holds if and only if all difference functions are linear. That is, $\phi_i(\delta) = t_i\delta$ for some positive t_i and for all i.
2. For $n = 2$, transitivity holds if and only if $\phi_1(\delta) = \phi_2(t\delta)$ for some positive t.
3. For $n = 1$, transitivity is always satisfied.

The proof is given in the appendix. The theorem shows that the transitivity assumption imposes extremely strong constraints on the form of the difference functions. In the two-dimensional case, the difference functions applied to the two dimensions must be identical except for a change of unit of their domain. If the alternatives have three or more dimensions, then transitivity is both necessary and sufficient for the linearity of all the difference functions. Recall that under the linearity assumption, the additive difference model reduces to the simple additive model, which has already been shown to satisfy transitivity. The above theorem asserts, however, that this is the only case in which the transitivity assumption is compatible with the additive difference model. Put differently, if the additive difference model is satisfied and if even one difference function is nonlinear, as is likely to be the case in some situations, then transitivity must be violated somewhere in the system. The experimental identification of these intransitivities in the absence of knowledge of the form of the difference functions might be very difficult indeed. The LS employed in the design of the experimental research is based on one extreme form of nonlinearity where one of the difference functions is, or can be approximated by, a step function. The above theorem suggests a new explanation of the intransitivity phenomenon, in terms of the form of the difference functions, which may render it more plausible than it seemed before.

Most of the choice mechanisms that have been purported to yield intransitivities (including the LS) are based on the notion of shifting attention, or switching dimensions, from one choice to another. Consequently, they assume that some relevant information describing the alternatives is ignored or discarded on particular choices. In contrast to this notion, intransitivities can occur in the additive difference model in a fully compensatory system where all the information is utilized in the evaluation process.

Both the additive model and the additive difference model can be extended in a natural way. To do so, let F be an increasing function and suppose that all choice probabilities are neither 0 and 1. The (extended) additive model is said to be satisfied whenever equation 5 holds and

$$P(x, y) = F\left[\sum_{i=1}^{n} u_i(x_i) - \sum_{i=1}^{n} u_i(y_i)\right]. \tag{7}$$

Similarly, the (extended) additive difference model is said to be satisfied whenever equation 6 holds and

$$P(x, y) = F\left(\sum_{i=1}^{n} \phi_i[u_i(x_i) - u_i(y_i)]\right). \tag{8}$$

Both models are closely related to the Fechnerian or the strong utility model (see Luce & Suppes, 1965). This model asserts that there exists a function u and a distribution function F such that

$$P(x, y) = F[u(x) - u(y)]. \tag{9}$$

Note that equation 7 is a special case of equation 9, where the utilities are additive, while equation 8 is an additive generalization of equation 9 to the multidimensional case. The two most developed probabilistic models of Thurstone (1927, case V) and Luce (1959) can be obtained from the Fechnerian model by letting F be the normal or the logistic distribution function respectively.

It can be easily shown that equation 9 and, hence, equation 7 satisfy not only WST, but also a stronger probabilistic version of transitivity called strong stochastic transitivity, or SST. According to this condition, if $P(x, y) \geq \frac{1}{2}$ and $P(y, z) \geq \frac{1}{2}$ then both $P(x, z) \geq P(x, y)$ and $P(x, z) \geq P(y, z)$.

Clearly, SST implies WST but not conversely. However, if equation 8 is valid with $n \geq 3$, and if WST is satisfied, then according to the above theorem, equation 8 reduces to equation 7 which satisfies SST as well. Thus, we obtain the somewhat surprising result that, under the extended additive difference model, with $n \geq 3$, WST and SST are equivalent.

Discussion

In the introduction, a choice model (the LS) yielding intransitive preferences was described. This model was employed in the design of two studies which showed that, under specified experimental conditions, consistent intransitivities can be obtained. The theoretical conditions under which intransitivities occur were studied within the framework of a general additive difference model. The results suggest that in the absence of a model that guides the construction of the alternatives, one is unlikely to detect consistent violations of WST. The absence of an appropriate model combined with the lack of sufficiently powerful statistical tests may account for the failure to reject WST in previous investigations.

Most previous tests of WST have been based on comparison between the observed proportion of intransitive triples, π, and the expected proportion under WST. As Morrison (1963) pointed out, however, this approach leads to difficulties arising from the fact that in a complete pair comparison design only a limited proportion of triples can, in principle, be intransitive. Specifically, the expected value of π for an S who is diabolically (or maximally) intransitive is $\dfrac{k+1}{4(k-2)}$ where k is the number of alternatives. As k increases, this expression approaches one-fourth, which is the expected value of π under the hypothesis of random choice (i.e., $P(x, y) = \frac{1}{2}$ for all x, y). Morrison argued, therefore, that unless the intransitive triples can be identified in advance, it is practically impossible (with a large number of alternatives) to distinguish between the diabolically intransitive S and the random S on the basis of the observed value of π. These considerations suggest that a more powerful test of WST can be obtained by using many replications of a few well-chosen alternatives rather than by using a few replications of many alternatives. The latter approach, however, has been employed in most studies of preference.

What are the implications of the present results for the analysis of choice behavior?

Casual observations, as well as the comments made by Ss, suggest that the LS (or some other nonlinear version of the additive difference model) is employed in some realworld decisions, and that the resulting intransitivities can also be observed outside the laboratory. Consider, for example, a person who is about to purchase a compact car of a given make. His initial tendency is to buy the simplest model for $2089. Nevertheless, when the saleman presents the optional accessories, he first decides to add power steering, which brings the price to $2167, feeling that the price difference is relatively negligible. Then, following the same reasoning, he is willing to add $47 for a good car radio, and then an additional $64 for power brakes. By repeating this process several times, our consumer ends up with a $2593 car, equipped with all the available accessories. At this point, however, he may prefer the simplest car over the fancy one, realizing that he is not willing to spend $504 for all the added features, although each one of them alone seemed worth purchasing.

When interviewed after the experiment, the vast majority of Ss said that people are and should be transitive. Some Ss found it very difficult to believe that they had exhibited consistent intransitivities. If intransitivities of the type predicted by the additive difference model, however, are manifest in choice behavior why were Ss so confident that their choices are transitive?

In the first place, transitivity is viewed, by college undergraduates at least, as a logical principle whose violation represents an error of judgment or reasoning. Consequently, people are not likely to admit the existence of consistent intransitivities. Second, in the absence of replications, one can always attribute intransitivities to a change in taste that took place between choices. The circular preferences of the car buyer, for example, may be explained by the hypothesis that, during the choice process, the consumer changed his mind with regard to the value of the added accessories. If this hypothesis is misapplied, the presence of genuine intransitivities is obscured. Finally, most decisions are made in a sequential fashion. Thus, having chosen y over x and then z over y, one is typically committed to z and may not even compare it with x, which has already been eliminated. Furthermore, in many choice situations the eliminated alternative is no longer available so there is no way of finding out whether our preferences are transitive or not. These considerations suggest that in actual decisions, as well as in laboratory experiments, people are likely to overlook their own intransitivities.

Transitivity, however, is one of the basic and the most compelling principles of rational behavior. For if one violates transitivity, it is a well-known conclusion that he is acting, in effect, as a "money-pump." Suppose an individual prefers y to x, z to y, and x to z. It is reasonable to assume that he is willing to pay a sum of money to replace x by y. Similarly, he should be willing to pay some amount of money to replace y by z and still a third amount to replace z by x. Thus, he ends up with the alternative he started with but with less money. In the context of the selection of applicants, intransitivity implies that, if a single candidate is to be selected in a series of pair comparisons, then the chosen candidate is a function of the order in which the pairs are presented. Regardless of whether this is the case or not, it is certainly an undesirable property of a decision rule.

As has already been mentioned, the normative character of the transitivity assumption was recognized by Ss. In fact, some evidence (MacCrimmon, 1965) indicates that when people are faced with their own intransitivities they tend to modify their choices according to the transitivity principle. Be this as it may, the fact remains that, under the appropriate experimental conditions, some people are intransitive and these intransitivities cannot be attributed to momentary fluctuations or random variability.

Is this behavior necessarily irrational? We tend to doubt it. It seems impossible to reach any definite conclusion concerning human rationality in the absence of a detailed analysis of the sensitivity of the criterion and the cost involved in evaluating the alternatives. When the difficulty (or the cost) of the evaluations and the consistency (or the error) of the judgments are taken into account, a model based on component-wise evaluation, for example, may prove superior to a model based on independent evaluation despite the fact that the former is not necessarily transitive while the latter is. When faced with complex multidimensional alternatives, such as job offers, gambles, or candidates, it is extremely difficult to utilize properly all the available information. Instead, it is contended that people employ various approximation methods that enable them to process the relevant information in making a decision. The particular approximation scheme depends on the nature of the alternatives as well as on the ways in which they are presented or displayed. The lexicographic semiorder is one such an approximation. In general, these simplification procedures might be extremely useful in that they can approximate one's "true preference" very well. Like any approximation, they are based on the assumption that the approximated quantity is independent of the approximation method. That is, in using such methods in making decisions we implicitly assume that the world is not designed to take advantage of our approximation methods. The present experiments, however, were designed with exactly that goal in mind. They attempted to produce intransitivity by capitalizing on a particular approximation method. This approximation may be very good in general, despite the fact that it yields intransitive choices in some specially constructed situations. The main interest in the present results lies not so much in the fact that transitivity can be violated but rather in what these violations reveal about the choice mechanism and the approximation method that govern preference between multidimensional alternatives.

Notes

This work was supported in part by United States Public Health Service Grant MH-04236 and by National Science Foundation Grant GM-6782 to the University of Michigan and in part by Carnegie Corporation of New York B-3233 to Harvard University, Center for Cognitive Studies.

The author wishes to thank H. William Morrison for his helpful comments and David H. Krantz for his valuable assistance, including the suggestion of the likelihood ratio test.

1. In some pilot studies in which Ss were run in a group and only two dimensional profiles were used the proportion of Ss satisfying the above criterion was considerably lower.

2. In referring to the dimensionality of the alternatives, denoted n, only nontrivial dimensions having more than one value are considered. The fact that transitivity holds whenever $n = 2$ and $\phi_1 = \phi_2$ has been recognized by Morrison (1962, p. 19).

References

Adams, E., & Fagot, R. A model of riskless choice. *Behavioral Science*, 1959, 4, 1–10.

Beals, R., Krantz, D. H., & Tversky, A. The foundations of multidimensional scaling. *Psychological Review*, 1968, 75, 127–142.

Chipman, J. S. Stochastic choice and subjective probability. In D. Willner (Ed.), *Decisions, values and groups*, vol. I. Oxford: Pergamon Press, 1960.

Debreu, G. Topological methods in cardinal utility theory. In K. J. Arrow, S. Karlin, & P. Suppes (Eds.), *Mathematical methods in the social sciences.* Stanford: Stanford University Press, 1960.

Davidson, D., & Marshak, J. Experimental tests of stochastic decision theories. In C. W. Churchman & P. Ratoosh (Eds.), *Measurement: Definitions and theories.* New York: Wiley, 1959.

Davidson, D., McKinsey, J. C. C., & Suppes, P. Outlines of a formal theory of value. *Philosophy of Science*, 1955, 22, 140–160.

Davis, J. M. The transitivity of preferences. *Behavioral Science*, 1958, 3, 26–33.

Edwards, W. Probability-preferences in gambling. *American Journal of Psychology*, 1953, 59, 290–294.

Edwards, W. The theory of decision making. *Psychological Bulletin*, 1954, 51, 380–416.

Edwards, W. Behavioral decision theory. *Annual Review of Psychology*, 1961, 12, 473–498.

Griswold, B. J., & Luce, R. D. Choice among uncertain outcomes: A test of a decomposition and two assumptions of transitivity. *American Journal of Psychology*, 1962, 75, 35–44.

Krantz, D. H. Conjoint measurement: The Luce-Tukey axiomatization and some extensions. *Journal of Mathematical Psychology*, 1964, 1, 248–277.

Luce, R. D. Semiorders and a theory of utility discrimination. *Econometrica*, 1956, 24, 178–191.

Luce, R. D. *Individual choice behavior.* New York: Wiley, 1959.

Luce, R. D. Two extensions of conjoint measurement. *Journal of Mathematical Psychology*, 1966, 3, 348–370.

Luce, R. D., & Galanter, E. Psychophysical scaling. In R. D. Luce, R. R. Bush, & E. Galanter (Eds.), *Handbook of mathematical psychology*, vol. I. New York: Wiley, 1963.

Luce, R. D., & Suppes, P. Preference, utility, and subjective probability. In R. D. Luce, R. R. Bush, & E. Galanter (Eds.), *Handbook of mathematical psychology*, vol. III. New York: Wiley, 1965.

Luce, R. D., & Tukey, J. W. Simultaneous conjoint measurement: A new type of fundamental measurement. *Journal of Mathematical Psychology*, 1964, 1, 1–27.

MacCrimmon, K. R. An experimental study of the decision making behavior of business executives. Unpublished doctoral dissertation, University of California, Los Angeles, 1965.

May, K. O. Intransitivity, utility, and the aggregation of preference patterns. *Econometrica*, 1954, 22, 1–13.

Mood, A. *Introduction to the theory of statistics.* New York: McGraw-Hill, 1950.

Morrison, H. W. Intransitivity of paired comparison choices. Unpublished doctoral dissertation, University of Michigan, 1962.

Morrison, H. W. Testable conditions for triads of paired comparison choices. *Psychometrika*, 1963, 28, 369–390.

Papandreou, A. G., Sauerlander, O. H., Brownlee, O. H., Hurwicz, L., & Franklin, W. A test of a stochastic theory of choice. *University of California Publications in Economics*, 1957, 16, 1–18.

Quandt, R. E. Probabilistic theory of consumer behavior. *Quarterly Journal of Economics*, 1956, 70, 507–536.

Samuelson, P. A. *Foundations of economic analysis.* Cambridge: Harvard University Press, 1953.

Savage, L. J. The theory of statistical decision. *Journal of the Americal Statistical Association*, 1951, 46, 55–57.

Scott, D. Measurement models and linear inequalities. *Journal of Mathematical Psychology*, 1964, 1, 233–248.

Shepard, R. N. On subjectively optimum selection among multiattribute alternatives. In M. W. Shelly & G. L. Bryan (Eds.), *Human judgments and optimality.* New York: Wiley, 1964.

Suppes, P., & Zinnes, J. L. Basic measurement theory. In R. D. Luce, R. R. Bush, & E. Galanter (Eds.), *Handbook of mathematical psychology*, vol. I. New York: Wiley, 1963.

Thurstone, L. L. A law of comparative judgment. *Psychological Review*, 1927, 34, 273–286.

Tversky, A. Additivity, utility and subjective probability. *Journal of Mathematical Psychology*, 1967, 4, 175–202. (a)

Tversky, A. A general theory of polynominal con joint measurement. *Journal of Mathematical Psychology*, 1967, 4, 1–20. (b)

Appendix

THEOREM   If the additive difference model (equation 6) is satisfied, then the following assertions hold whenever the difference functions are defined.

1. For $n \geq 3$, transitivity holds if and only if all difference functions are linear. That is, $\phi_i(\delta) = t_i \delta$ for some real t_i and for all i.

2. For $n = 2$, transitivity holds if and only if $\phi_1(\delta) = \phi_2(t\delta)$ for some real t.

3. For $n = 1$, transitivity is always satisfied.

Proof   By WST, $P(x, y) = \frac{1}{2}$ and $P(y, z) = \frac{1}{2}$ imply $P(x, z) = \frac{1}{2}$. Hence, according to the additive difference model there exist functions $u_1, \ldots, u_n$ and increasing continuous functions $\phi_1, \ldots, \phi_n$ defined on some real intervals of the form $(-\delta_i, \delta_i)$ such that

$$\sum_{i=1}^{n} \phi_i[u_i(x_i) - u_i(y_i)] = 0$$

and

$$\sum_{i=1}^{n} \phi_i[u_i(y_i) - u_i(z_i)] = 0$$

imply

$$\sum_{i=1}^{n} \phi_i[u_i(x_i) - u_i(z_i)] = 0,$$

where $\phi_i(-\delta) = -\phi_i(\delta)$. Letting

$$\alpha_i = u_i(x_i) - u_i(y_i) \quad \text{and} \quad \beta_i = u_i(y_i) - u_i(z_i)$$

yields

$$(^*) \quad \sum_{i=1}^{n} \phi_i(\alpha_i) = 0 \quad \text{and} \quad \sum_{i=1}^{n} \phi_i(\beta_i) = 0$$

imply

$$\sum_{i=1}^{n} \phi_i(\alpha_i + \beta_i) = 0.$$

First, suppose $n = 1$, hence $(^*)$ reduces to:

$$\phi(\alpha) = 0, \quad \phi(\beta) = 0 \quad \text{imply} \quad \phi(\alpha + \beta) = 0.$$

But since ϕ is increasing, and $\phi(0) = -\phi(0) = 0$, $\alpha = \beta = 0 = \alpha + \beta$, and hence the above equation is always satisfied.

Next, suppose $n = 2$, hence, by $(^*)$, $\phi_1(\alpha_1) + \phi_2(\alpha_2) = 0$ and $\phi_1(\beta_1) + \phi_2(\beta_2) = 0$ imply $\phi_1(\alpha_1 + \beta_1) + \phi_2(\alpha_2 + \beta_2) = 0$. Since $\phi_i(-\delta) = -\phi_i(\delta)$, the above relation can be rewritten as $\phi_1(\alpha_1) = \phi_2(-\alpha_2)$ and $\phi_1(\beta_1) = \phi_2(-\beta_2)$ imply $\phi_1(\alpha_1 + \beta_1) = \phi_2(-\alpha_2 - \beta_2)$. Consequently, by letting $\alpha_1 = \beta_1$ and $\alpha_2 = \beta_2$, and repeating the argument n times, we obtain $\phi_1(\alpha) = \phi_2(\beta)$ implies $\phi_1(n\alpha) = \phi_2(n\beta)$ for any positive integer n for which both $\phi_1(n\alpha)$ and $\phi_2(n\beta)$ are defined.

Since all difference functions are continuously increasing and since they all vanish at zero, one can select positive a, b such that $\phi_1(a), \phi_2(b)$ are defined and such that $\phi_1(a) = \phi_2(b)$. Hence, for any positive integers m, n for which $\phi_1\left(\dfrac{m}{n}a\right)$ and $\phi_2\left(\dfrac{m}{n}b\right)$ are defined, $\phi_1\left(\dfrac{a}{n}\right)$ and $\phi_2\left(\dfrac{b}{n}\right)$ are also defined. Furthermore, $\phi_1\left(\dfrac{a}{n}\right) = \phi_2\left(\dfrac{b}{n}\right)$, for otherwise a strict inequality must hold. Suppose $\phi_1\left(\dfrac{a}{n}\right) < \phi_2\left(\dfrac{b}{n}\right)$, hence there exists c such that $\phi_1\left(\dfrac{a}{n}\right) = \phi_2(c) < \phi_2\left(\dfrac{b}{n}\right)$. Consequently, $c < \dfrac{b}{n}$, or $nc < b$, and $\phi_2(nc)$ is defined. Hence, $\phi_2(nc) = \phi_1(a) = \phi_2(b)$ and $nc = b$, a contradiction. By the symmetry of the situation, a similar contradiction is obtained if $\phi_2\left(\dfrac{a}{n}\right) > \phi_2\left(\dfrac{b}{n}\right)$.

Therefore, $\phi_1(a) = \phi_2(b)$ implies $\phi_1\left(\dfrac{a}{n}\right) = \phi_2\left(\dfrac{b}{n}\right)$ for all n.

Next, let $t = \dfrac{b}{a}$ and suppose that both $\phi_1(c)$ and $\phi_2(tc)$ are defined. Thus, for any $\delta \geq 0$, there exist m, n such that $c - \delta \leq \dfrac{m}{n}a \leq c$, and hence $\dfrac{b}{a}(c - \delta) \leq \dfrac{b}{a}\dfrac{m}{n}a \leq \dfrac{b}{a}c$. Consequently, $\phi_1(c - \delta) \leq \phi_1\left(\dfrac{m}{n}a\right) \leq \phi_1(c)$ and $\phi_2\left[\dfrac{b}{a}(c - \delta)\right] \leq \phi_2\left(\dfrac{m}{n}b\right) \leq \phi_2\left(\dfrac{b}{a}c\right)$. As δ approaches 0, however, $\phi_1(c - \delta) = \phi_1(c)$ and $\phi_2\left[\dfrac{b}{a}(c - \delta)\right] = \phi_2\left(\dfrac{b}{a}c\right)$, and since $\phi_1\left(\dfrac{m}{n}a\right) = \phi_2\left(\dfrac{m}{n}b\right)$, by hypothesis, $\phi_1(c) = \phi_2(tc)$ as required. Conversely, if $\phi_1(c) = \phi_2(tc)$ it follows readily that equation $(^*)$ is satisfied which completes the proof of this case.

Finally, suppose $n \geq 3$. Since we can let all but three differences be zero, we consider the case where $n = 3$. Hence,

$$\phi_1(\alpha_1) + \phi_2(\alpha_2) + \phi_3(\alpha_3) = 0$$

and

$$\phi_1(\beta_1) + \phi_2(\beta_2) + \phi_3(\beta_3) = 0$$

imply $\phi_1(\alpha_1 + \beta_1) + \phi_2(\alpha_2 + \beta_2) + \phi_3(\alpha_3 + \beta_3) = 0$. By the earlier result, however, $\phi_i(\delta) = \phi_j(t_j\delta)$ for $i, j = 1, 2, 3$. Hence, the above implication is expressible as

$$\phi(\alpha) + \phi(\beta) = \phi(\delta) \quad \text{and} \quad \phi(\alpha') + \phi(\beta') = \phi(\delta')$$

imply

$\phi(\alpha + \alpha') + \phi(\beta + \beta') = \phi(\delta + \delta')$.

Define ψ such that $\phi(\alpha) + \phi(\beta) = \phi[\psi(\alpha, \beta)]$ for all α, β. Hence,

$$\phi(\alpha + \alpha') + \phi(\beta + \beta') = \phi[\psi(\alpha + \alpha', \beta + \beta')]$$
$$= \phi(\delta + \delta')$$
$$= \phi[\psi(\alpha, \beta) + \psi(\alpha', \beta')].$$

Hence, $\psi(\alpha, \beta) + \psi(\alpha', \beta') = \psi(\alpha + \alpha', \beta + \beta')$ and ψ is linear in α, β. Therefore, $\phi(\alpha) + \psi(\beta) = \phi(p\alpha + q\beta)$ for some real p, q. If we let $\beta = 0$, we get $\phi(\alpha) = \phi(p\alpha)$ hence $p = 1$. Similarly, if we let $\alpha = 0$, we get $\phi(\beta) = \phi(q\beta)$ hence $q = 1$. Consequently, $\phi(\alpha) + \phi(\beta) = \phi(\alpha + \beta)$ and ϕ if linear as required. The converse for any $n \geq 3$ is immediate which completes the proof of this theorem.

20 Elimination by Aspects: A Theory of Choice

Amos Tversky

When faced with a choice among several alternatives, people often experience uncertainty and exhibit inconsistency. That is, people are often not sure which alternative they should select, nor do they always make the same choice under seemingly identical conditions. In order to account for the observed inconsistency and the reported uncertainty, choice behavior has been viewed as a probabilistic process.

Probabilistic theories of preference differ with respect to the nature of the mechanism that is assumed to govern choice. Some theories (e.g., Thurstone, 1927, 1959) attribute a random element to the determination of subjective value, while others (e.g., Luce, 1959) attribute a random element to the decision rule. Most theoretical work on probabilistic preferences has been based on the notion of independence among alternatives. This notion, however, is incompatible with some observed patterns of preferences which exhibit systematic dependencies among alternatives.

This chapter develops a probabilistic theory of choice, based on a covert elimination process, which accounts for observed dependencies among alternatives. The first section analyzes the independence assumption; the second section formulates a theory of choice and discusses its consequences; some experimental tests of the theory are reported in the third section; and its psychological implications are explored in the fourth and final section.

We begin by introducing some notation. Let $T = \{x, y, z, \ldots\}$ be a finite set, interpreted as the total set of alternatives under consideration. We use $A, B, C, \ldots$, to denote specific nonempty subsets of T, and $A_i, B_j, C_k, \ldots$, to denote variables ranging over nonempty subsets of T. Thus, $\{A_i \mid A_i \supseteq B\}$ is the set of all subsets of T which includes B. The number of elements in A is denoted by a. Proper and nonproper set inclusion are denoted, respectively, by $\supset$ and $\supseteq$. The empty set is denoted by ϕ. The probability of choosing an alternative x from an offered set $A \subseteq T$ is denoted $P(x, A)$. Naturally, we assume $P(x, A) \geq 0$, $\sum_{x \in A} P(x, A) = 1$ for any A, and $P(x, A) = 0$ for any $x \notin A$. For brevity, we write $P(x; y)$ for $P(x, \{x, y\})$, $P(x; y, z)$ for $P(x, \{x, y, z\})$, etc. A realvalued, nonnegative function in one argument is called a *scale*. Choice probability is typically estimated by relative frequency in repeated choices. It should be kept in mind, however, that other empirical interpretations of choice probability, such as confidence judgments (which are applicable to unique choice situations), might also be adopted.

Perhaps the most general formulation of the notion of independence from irrelevant alternatives is the assumption that the alternatives can be scaled so that each choice probability is expressible as a monotone function of the scale values of the

respective alternatives. This assumption, called *simple scalability*, was first investigated by Krantz (1964, appendix A). Formally, simple scalability holds if and only
if there exists a scale u defined on the alternatives of T and functions F_n in n arguments, $2 \leq n \leq t$, such that for any $A = \{x, \dots, z\} \subseteq T$,

$$P(x, A) = F_a[u(x), \dots, u(z)], \tag{1}$$

where each F_a is strictly increasing in the first argument and strictly decreasing in the
remaining $a - 1$ arguments provided $P(x, A) \neq 0, 1$. This assumption underlies most
theoretical work in the field. The theory of Luce (1959), for example, is a special case
of this assumption where

$$P(x, A) = F_a[u(x), \dots, u(z)]$$

$$= \frac{u(x)}{\sum\limits_{y \in A} u(y)}. \tag{2}$$

Despite its generality, simple scalability (equation 1) has strong testable consequences. In particular, it implies that for all $x, y \in A$,

$$P(x; y) \geq 1/2 \quad \text{iff} \quad P(x, A) \geq P(y, A), \quad \text{provided} \quad P(y, A) \neq 0. \tag{3}$$

Equation 3 asserts that the ordering of x and y, by choice probability, is independent of the offered set.[1] Thus, if x is preferred to y in one context (e.g., $P(x; y) \geq
1/2$), then x is preferred to y in any context. Furthermore, if $P(x; y) = 1/2$ then
$P(x, A) = P(y, A)$ for any A which contains both x and y. Thus, if an individual is
indifferent between x and y, then he should choose them with equal probability from
any set which contains them.

This assumption, however, is not valid in general, as suggested by several counterexamples and demonstrated in many experiments (see Becker, DeGroot, & Marschak, 1963b; Chipman, 1960; Coombs, 1958; Krantz, 1967; Tversky & Russo,
1969). To motivate the present development, let us examine the arguments against
simple scalability starting with an example proposed by Debreu (1960).

Suppose you are offered a choice among the following three records: a suite by
Debussy, denoted D, and two different recordings of the same Beethoven symphony,
denoted B_1 and B_2. Assume that the two Beethoven recordings are of equal quality,
and that you are undecided between adding a Debussy or a Beethoven to your
record collection. Hence, $P(B_1; B_2) = P(D; B_1) = P(D; B_2) = 1/2$. It follows readily
from equation 3 that $P(D; B_1, B_2) = 1/3$. This conclusion, however, is unacceptable on intuitive grounds because the basic conflict between Debussy and Beethoven

is not likely to be affected by the addition of another Beethoven recording. Instead, it is suggested that in choosing among the three records, B_1 and B_2 are treated as one alternative to be compared with D. Consequently, one would expect that $P(D; B_1, B_2)$ will be close to one-half, while $P(B_1; B_2, D) = P(B_2; B_1, D)$ will be close to one-fourth, contrary to simple scalability (equation 1). Empirical support for Debreu's hypothesis was presented by Becker et al. (1963b) in a study of choice among gambles. Although Debreu's example was offered as a criticism of Luce's model (equation 2), it applies to any model based on simple scalability.

Previous efforts to resolve this problem (e.g., Estes, 1960) attempted to redefine the alternatives so that B_1 and B_2 are no longer viewed as different alternatives. Although this idea has some appeal, it does not provide a satisfactory account of our problem. First, B_1 and B_2 are not only physically distinct, but they can also be perfectly discriminable. Hence, there is no independent basis for treating them as indistinguishable. Second, the process of redefining choice alternatives itself requires an adequate theoretical analysis. Finally, data show that the principle of independence from irrelevant alternatives is violated in a manner that cannot be readily accounted for by grouping choice alternatives. More specifically, it appears that the addition of an alternative to an offered set "hurts" alternatives that are similar to the added alternative more than those that are dissimilar to it. Such an effect (of which Debreu's example is a special case) requires a more drastic revision of the principles underlying our models of choice.

The following example provides another illustration of the inadequacy of simple scalability. Suppose each of two travel agencies, denoted 1 and 2, offers tours of Europe (E) and of the Far East (F). Let $T = \{E_1, F_1, E_2, F_2\}$ where letters denote the destination of the tours, and the subscripts denote the respective agencies. Let us assume, for simplicity, that the decision maker is equally attracted by Europe and by the Far East, and that he has no reason to prefer one travel agency over the other. Consequently, all binary choice probabilities equal one-half, and the probability of choosing each tour from the total set equals one-fourth. It follows from equation 3, in this case, that all trinary probabilities must equal one-third. However, an examination of the problem suggests that in fact none of the trinary probabilities equals one-third; instead, some of them equal one-half while the others equal one-fourth.

Consider, for example, the set $\{E_1, F_1, F_2\}$. Since the distinction between the agencies is treated as irrelevant, the problem reduces to the choice between a tour of Europe and a tour of the Far East. If the latter is chosen, then either one of the agencies can be selected. Consequently, $P(E_1; F_1, F_2) = 1/2$, and $P(F_1; F_2, E_1) = P(F_2; F_1, E_1) = 1/4$. An identical argument applies to all other triples. Besides violating simple scalability, this example demonstrates that the same set of binary (or quarternary) probabilities can give rise to different trinary probabilities and hence the latter cannot be determined by the former. Put differently, this example shows that the probabilities of choosing alternatives from a given set, A, cannot be computed, in general, from the probabilities of choosing these alternatives from the subsets and the supersets of A. This observation imposes a high lower bound on the complexity of any adequate theory of choice.

A minor modification of an example due to L. J. Savage (see Luce & Suppes, 1965, pp. 334–335), which is based on binary comparisons only, illustrates yet another difficulty encountered by simple scalability. Imagine an individual who has to choose between a trip to Paris and a trip to Rome. Suppose he is indifferent between the two trips so that $P(\text{Paris}; \text{Rome}) = 1/2$. When the individual is offered a new alternative which consists of the trip to Paris plus a \$1 bonus, denoted Paris+, he will undoubtedly prefer it over the original trip to Paris with certainty so that $P(\text{Paris}+; \text{Paris}) = 1$. It follows from equation 3, then, that $P(\text{Paris}+; \text{Rome}) = 1$, which is counterintuitive. For if our individual cannot decide between Paris and Rome, it is unlikely that a relatively small bonus would resolve the conflict completely and change the choice probability from 1/2 to 1. Rather, we expect $P(\text{Paris}+; \text{Rome})$ to be closer to 1/2 than to 1. Experimental data (e.g., Tversky & Russo, 1969) support this intuition. Choice probabilities, therefore, reflect not only the utilities of the alternatives in question, but also the difficulty of comparing them. Thus, an extreme choice probability (i.e., close to 0 or 1) can result from either a large discrepancy in value or from an easy comparison, as in the case of the added bonus. The comparability of the alternatives, however, cannot be captured by their scale values, and hence simple scalability must be rejected. The above examples demonstrate that the substitution of one alternative for another, which is equivalent to it in some contexts, does not necessarily preserve choice probability in any context. The substitution affects the comparability among the alternatives, which in turn influences choice probability.

An alternative approach to the development of probabilistic theories of choice treats the utility of each alternative as a random variable rather than a constant. Specifically, it is assumed that there exists a random vector $\mathbf{U} = (\mathbf{U}_x, \ldots, \mathbf{U}_z)$ on $T = \{x, \ldots, z\}$ (i.e., for any $y \in T$, $\mathbf{U}_y$ is a random variable) such that

$$P(x, A) = P(\mathbf{U}_x \geq \mathbf{U}_y \text{ for all } y \in A). \qquad [4]$$

Models of this type are called random utility models. The only random utility models which have been seriously investigated assume that the random variables are independent. However, an extension of the last example (see Luce & Raiffa, 1957, p. 375) is shown to violate any independent random utility model. To demonstrate, consider the trips to Paris and Rome with and without the added bonus.

The expected binary choice probabilities in this case are $P(\text{Paris}+; \text{Paris}) = 1$, $P(\text{Rome}+; \text{Rome}) = 1$ but $P(\text{Paris}+; \text{Rome}) < 1$ and $P(\text{Rome}+; \text{Paris}) < 1$.

Assuming an independent random utility model, the first two equations above imply that there is no overlap between the distributions representing Paris and Paris+, nor is there an overlap between the distributions representing Rome and Rome+. The last two inequalities above imply that there must be some overlap between the distributions representing Rome and Paris+, as well as between the distributions representing Paris and Rome+. It is easy to verify that these conclusions are mutually inconsistent, and hence the above choice probabilities are incompatible with any independent random utility model. The representation of choice alternatives by independent random variables, therefore, appears too restrictive in general since, like simple scalability, it is incompatible with some eminently reasonable patterns of preference. In discussing the difficulties encountered by probabilistic theories of choice, Luce and Suppes (1965) wrote:

It appears that such criticisms, although usually directed toward specific models, are really much more sweeping objections to all our current preference theories. They suggest that we cannot hope to be completely successful in dealing with preferences until we include some mathematical structure over the set of outcomes that are simply substitutable for one another and those that are special cases of others. Such functional and logical relations among the outcomes seem to have a sharp control over the preference probabilities, and they cannot long be ignored [p. 337].

Theory

The present development describes choice as a covert sequential elimination process. Suppose that each alternative consists of a set of aspects of characteristics,[2] and that at every stage of the process, an aspect is selected (from those included in the available alternatives) with probability that is proportional to its weight. The selection of an aspect eliminates all the alternatives that do not include the selected aspect, and the process continues until a single alternative remains. If a selected aspect is included in all the available alternatives, no alternative is eliminated and a new aspect is selected. Consequently, aspects that are common to all the alternatives under consideration do not affect choice probabilities. Since the present theory describes choice as an elimination process governed by successive selection of aspects, it is called the elimination-by-aspects (EBA) model.

In contemplating the purchase of a new car, for example, the first aspect selected may be automatic transmission: this will eliminate all cars that do not have this feature. Given the remaining alternatives, another aspect, say a $3000 price limit, is selected and all cars whose price exceeds this limit are excluded. The process continues until all cars but one are eliminated. This decision rule is closely related to the lexicographic model (see Coombs, 1964; Fishburn, 1968), where an ordering of the relevant attributes is specified a priori. One chooses, then, the alternative that is best relative to the first attribute; if some alternatives are equivalent with respect to the first attribute, one chooses from them the alternative that is best relative to the second attribute, and so on. The present model differs from the lexicographic model in that here no fixed prior ordering of aspects (or attributes) is assumed, and the choice process is inherently probabilistic.

More formally, consider a mapping that associates with each $x \in T$ a nonempty set $x' = \{\alpha, \beta, \ldots\}$ of elements which are interpreted as the aspects of x. An alternative x is said to include an aspect α whenever $\alpha \in x'$. The aspects could represent values along some fixed quantitative or qualitative dimensions (e.g., price, quality, comfort), or they could be arbitrary features of the alternatives that do not fit into any simple dimensional structure. The characterization of alternatives in terms of aspects is not necessarily unique. Furthermore, we generally do not know what aspects are considered by an individual in any particular choice problem. Nevertheless, as is demonstrated later, this knowledge is not required in order to apply the present model, and its descriptive validity can be determined independently of any particular characterization of the alternatives.

To clarify the formalization of the model, let us first examine a simple example. Consider a three-alternative set $T = \{x, y, z\}$, where the collections of aspects associated with the respective alternatives are

$$x' = \{\alpha_1, \alpha_2, \theta_1, \theta_2, \rho_1, \rho_2, \omega\},$$

$$y' = \{\beta_1, \beta_2, \theta_1, \theta_2, \sigma_1, \sigma_2, \omega\},$$

and

$$z' = \{\gamma_1, \gamma_2, \rho_1, \rho_2, \sigma_1, \sigma_2, \omega\}.$$

A graphical representation of the structure of the alternatives and their aspects is presented in figure 20.1. It is readily seen that α_i, β_i, and γ_i ($i = 1, 2$) are, respectively, the unique aspects of x, y, and z; that θ_i, σ_i, and ρ_i are, respectively, the aspects shared by x and y, by y and z, and by x and z; and that ω is shared by all three alternatives. Since the selection of ω does not eliminate any alternative, it can be discarded from further considerations. Let u be a scale which assigns to each aspect a positive number representing its utility or value, and let K be the sum of the scale values of all the aspects under consideration, that is, $K = \sum_\alpha u(\alpha)$ where the sum-

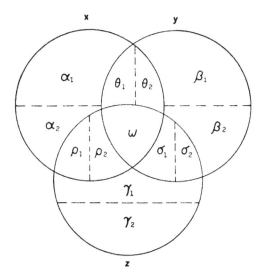

Figure 20.1
A graphical representation of aspects in the three-alternative case.

mation ranges over all the aspects except ω. Using these notations we now compute $P(x, T)$.

Note first that x can be chosen directly from T if either α_1 or α_2 is selected in the first stage (in which case both y and z are eliminated). This occurs with probability $[u(\alpha_1) + u(\alpha_2)]/K$. Alternatively, x can be chosen via $\{x, y\}$ if either θ_1 or θ_2 is selected in the first stage (in which case z is eliminated), and then x is chosen over y. This occurs with probability $[u(\theta_1) + u(\theta_2)] \times P(x; y)/K$. Finally, x can be chosen via $\{x, z\}$ if either ρ_1 or ρ_2 is selected in the first stage (in which case y is eliminated), and then x is chosen over z. This occurs with probability $[u(\rho_1) + u(\rho_2)]P(x; z)/K$. Since the above paths leading to the choice of x from T are all disjoint,

$$P(x, T) = (1/K)(u(\alpha_1) + u(\alpha_2) + [u(\theta_1) + u(\theta_2)]P(x; y) + [u(\rho_1) + u(\rho_2)]P(x; z)) \quad [5]$$

where

$$P(x; y) = \frac{u(\alpha_1) + u(\alpha_2) + u(\rho_1) + u(\rho_2)}{u(\alpha_1) + u(\alpha_2) + u(\rho_1) + u(\rho_2) + u(\beta_1) + u(\beta_2) + u(\sigma_1) + u(\sigma_2)}, \text{ etc.}$$

More generally, let T be any finite set of alternatives. For any $A \subseteq T$ let $A' = \{\alpha \mid \alpha \in x' \text{ for some } x \in A\}$, and $A^0 = \{\alpha \mid \alpha \in x' \text{ for all } x \in A\}$. Thus, A' is the set of aspects that belongs to at least one alternative in A, and A^0 is the set of aspects that belongs to all the alternatives in A. In particular, T' is the set of all aspects under consideration, while T^0 is the set of aspects shared by all the alternatives under study. Given any aspect $\alpha \in T'$, let A_α denote those alternatives of A which include α, that is, $A_\alpha = \{x \mid x \in A \ \& \ \alpha \in x'\}$.

The elimination-by-aspects model asserts that there exists a positive scale u defined on the aspects (or more specifically on $T' - T^0$) such that for all $x \in A \subseteq T$

$$P(x, A) = \frac{\sum\limits_{\alpha \in x' - A^0} u(\alpha)P(x, A_\alpha)}{\sum\limits_{\beta \in A' - A^0} u(\beta)} \qquad [6]$$

provided the denominator does not vanish. Note that the summations in the numerator and the denominator of equation 6 range, respectively, over all aspects of x and A except those that are shared by all elements of A. Hence, the denominator of equation 6 vanishes only if all elements of A share the same aspects, in which case it is assumed that $P(x, A) = 1/a$.

Equation 6 is a recursive formula. It expresses the probability of choosing x from A as a weighted sum of the probabilities of choosing x from the various subsets of A (i.e., A_α for $\alpha \in x'$), where the weights (i.e., $u(\alpha)/\sum u(\beta)$) correspond to the probabilities of selecting the respective aspects of x.

Consider a special case of the elimination-by-aspects model where all pairs of alternatives share the same aspects, that is, $x' \cap y' = z' \cap w'$ for all $x, y, z, w \in T$. Since aspects that are common to all the alternatives of T do not affect the choice process, the alternatives can be treated as (pairwise) disjoint, that is, $x' \cap y' = \phi$ for all $x, y \in T$. In this case, equation 6 reduces to

$$P(x, A) = \frac{\sum\limits_{\alpha \in x'} u(\alpha)}{\sum\limits_{\beta \in A'} u(\beta)}$$

since $\alpha \in x'$ implies $A_\alpha = \{x\}$, and $P(x, \{x\}) = 1$. Letting

$$u(x) = \sum\limits_{\alpha \in x'} u(\alpha)$$

yields

$$P(x, A) = \frac{u(x)}{\sum\limits_{y \in A} u(y)}.$$

Hence, in the present theory, Luce's model (equation 2) holds whenever the alternatives can be regarded as composed of disjoint aspects.

Next, examine another special case of the model where only binary choice probabilities are considered. In this case, we obtain

$$P(x; y) = \frac{\sum\limits_{\alpha \in x' - y'} u(\alpha)}{\sum\limits_{\alpha \in x' - y'} u(\alpha) + \sum\limits_{\beta \in y' - x'} u(\beta)}$$

$$= \frac{u(x' - y')}{u(x' - y') + u(y' - x')},$$ [7]

where $x' - y' = \{\alpha \mid \alpha \in x' \ \& \ \alpha \notin y'\}$ is the set of aspects that belongs to x but not to y; $y' - x' = \{\beta \mid \beta \in y' \ \& \ \beta \notin x'\}$ is the set of aspects that belongs to y but not to x; and $u(x' - y') = \sum_{\alpha \in x' - y'} u(\alpha)$. Equation 7 coincides with Restle's (1961) model. The EBA model, therefore, generalizes the choice models of Luce and of Restle.

The elimination-by-aspects model has been formulated above in terms of a scale u defined over the set of relevant aspects. It appears that the application of the model presupposes prior characterization of the alternatives in terms of their aspects. However, it turns out that this is not necessary because the EBA model can be formulated purely in terms of the alternatives, or more specifically, in terms of the subsets of T.

To illustrate the basic idea, consider the example presented in figure 20.1. There we assume that $\alpha_i, \beta_i, \ldots$ $(i = 1, 2)$ are all distinct aspects. According to the elimination-by-aspects model, however, there is no need to distinguish between aspects that lead to the same outcome. For example, the selection of either α_1 or α_2 eliminates both y and z; the selection of either θ_1 or θ_2 eliminates z; and the selection of either ρ_1 or ρ_2 eliminates y. From the standpoint of the elimination-by-aspects model, therefore, there is no need to differentiate between α_1 and α_2, between θ_1 and θ_2, or between ρ_1 and ρ_2. Thus we can group all the aspects that belong to x alone, all the aspects that belong to x and y but not to z, etc. Let $\{\bar{x}\}$ denote the aspects that belong to x alone (i.e., α_1 and α_2), $\{\overline{x, y}\}$ the aspects that belong only to x and y (i.e., θ_1 and θ_2), $\{\overline{x, z}\}$ the aspects that belong only to x and z (i.e., ρ_1 and ρ_2), etc.[3] The representation of the grouped aspects in the three-alternative case is displayed in figure 20.2.

The scale value of a collection of aspects is defined as the sum of the scale value of its members, that is, $U(\bar{x}) = u(\alpha_1) + u(\alpha_2)$, $U(\overline{x, y}) = u(\theta_1) + u(\theta_2)$, etc. For simplicity of notation we write $U(\bar{x})$ for $U(\{\bar{x}\})$, $U(\overline{x, y})$ for $U(\{\overline{x, y}\})$, etc. Thus, equation 5 is expressible as

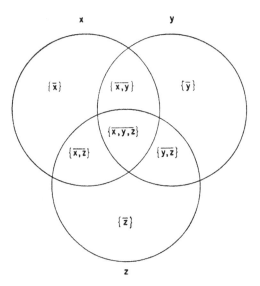

Figure 20.2
A graphical representation of the grouped aspects in the three-alternative case.

$$P(x, T) = \frac{U(\bar{x}) + U(\overline{x,y})P(x; y) + U(\overline{x,z})P(x; z)}{U(\bar{x}) + U(\bar{y}) + U(\bar{z}) + U(\overline{x,y}) + U(\overline{x,z}) + U(\overline{y,z})} \qquad [8]$$

where

$$P(x; y) = \frac{U(\bar{x}) + U(\overline{x,z})}{U(\bar{x}) + U(\bar{y}) + U(\overline{x,z}) + U(\overline{y,z})}, \quad \text{etc.}$$

The essential difference between equations 5 and 8 lies in the domain of the scales: in equation 5, u is defined over individual aspects, whereas in equation 8 U is defined over collections of aspects which are associated, respectively, with the subsets of T. The method by which equation 5 is translated into equation 8 can be applied in general.

Each proper subset A of T is associated with the set $\bar{A}$ of all aspects that are included in *all* the alternatives of A and are not included in *any* of the alternatives that do not belong to A. That is, $\bar{A} = \{\alpha \in T' \mid \alpha \in x' \text{ for all } x \in A \ \& \ \alpha \notin y' \text{ for any } y \notin A\}$. The scale U is defined by $U(\bar{A}) = \sum_{\alpha \in \bar{A}} u(\alpha)$. It is shown in the appendix that the elimination-by-aspects model, defined in equation 6, holds if and only if there exists a scale U defined on $\{\bar{A}_i \mid A_i \subset T\}$ such that for all $x \in A \subseteq T$

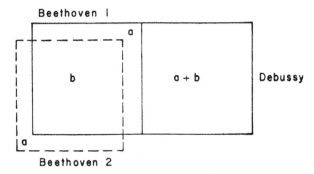

Figure 20.3

$$P(x, A) = \frac{\sum_{B_i \not\supseteq A} U(\bar{B}_i) P(x, A \cap B_i)}{\sum_{A_j \in \mathscr{A}} U(\bar{A}_j)} \tag{9}$$

where $\mathscr{A} = \{A_j \mid A_j \cap A \neq A, \phi\}$, provided the denominator does not vanish. (According to the present theory, the denominator can vanish only if $P(x, A) = 1/a$.) The significance of this result lies in showing how the elimination-by-aspects model can be formulated in terms of the subsets of T without reference to specific aspects. Note that for $A \subset T$, $U(\bar{A})$ is *not* a measure of the value of the alternatives of A; rather it is a measure of all the evaluative aspects that are shared by all the alternatives of A and by them only. Thus, $U(\bar{A})$ can be viewed as a measure of the unique advantage of the alternatives of A. The reader is invited to verify that in the three-alternative case, equation 9 reduces to equation 8.

Before discussing the consequences of the EBA model, let us examine how it resolves the counterexamples described in the previous section. First, consider Debreu's record selection problem where $T = \{D, B_1, B_2\}$. Naturally, the two Beethoven recordings have much more in common with each other than either of them has with the Debussy record. Assume, for simplicity, that any aspect shared by D and one of the B records is also shared by the other B record, hence D can be treated as (aspectwise) disjoint of both B_1 and B_2. Suppose $U(\bar{B}_1) = U(\bar{B}_2) = a$, $U(\overline{B_1, B_2}) = b$, and $U(\bar{D}) = a + b$. A graphical illustration of this representation is shown in figure 20.3.

It follows readily, under these assumptions, that all the binary choice probabilities are equal, since

$$P(B_1; B_2) = \frac{a}{2a} = \frac{1}{2} = \frac{a+b}{2(a+b)}$$

$$= P(D; B_1) = P(D; B_2),$$

yet the trinary choice probabilities are unequal, since

$$P(D; B_1, B_2) = \frac{a+b}{3a+2b} > \frac{a+b(a/2a)}{3a+2b}$$

$$= P(B_1; B_2, D) = P(B_2; B_1, D).$$

In fact, as a (or a/b) approaches 0, the left-hand side approaches $1/2$ while the right-hand side approaches $1/4$. Hence, according to the elimination-by-aspects model, all three records can be pairwise equivalent, and yet the probability of choosing D from the entire set can be as high as $1/2$ whenever B_1 and B_2 include the same aspects.

Second, consider Savage's problem of choosing between trips, and let $T = \{P, R, P+, R+\}$, where P and R denote, respectively, trips to Paris and Rome, while $+$ denotes a small monetary bonus. Here it is natural to suppose that Paris+ includes Paris (in the sense that all aspects of the latter trip are included in the former). On the other hand, Paris+ does not include Rome because each of these trips has some aspects that are not shared by the other. Similarly, Rome+ includes Rome but not Paris. The relations among the four alternatives are illustrated in figure 20.4.

Letting $U(\overline{P+}) = U(\overline{R+}) = a$, and $U(\overline{P, P+}) = U(\overline{R, R+}) = b$, yields

$$P(P; R) = \frac{b}{2b} = \frac{1}{2} = \frac{a+b}{2(a+b)} = P(P+; R+),$$

$$P(P+; P) = P(R+; R) = \frac{a}{a} = 1, \quad \text{and}$$

$$P(P+; R) = P(R+; P) = \frac{a+b}{a+2b},$$

which can take any value between $1/2$ and 1, depending on the relative weight of the bonus. Thus, the above pattern of binary choice probabilities, which violates simple scalability (equation 1) and any independent random utility model (equation 4), arises naturally in the present model. Essentially the same solution to this problem (which involves only binary probabilities) has been proposed by Restle (1961).

The reader is invited to show how the elimination-by-aspects model can accommodate the example described earlier of choice among tours of Europe or the Far East with each of two travel agencies.

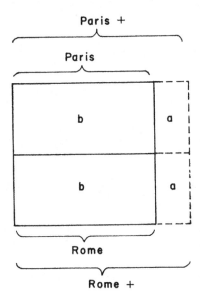

Figure 20.4
A graphical illustration of the analysis of the choice between trips.

Consequences

In the following discussion we assume that the elimination-by-aspects model is valid, and list some of its testable consequences. The derivations of these properties are presented in Tversky (1972).

Regularity: For all $x \in A \subseteq B$, $P(x, A) \geq P(x, B)$.   [10]

Regularity asserts that the probability of choosing an alternative from a given set cannot be increased by enlarging the offered set. This is probably the weakest form of noninteraction among alternatives. Although regularity seems innocuous, it is worth noting that the replacement of $\geq$ by $>$ in equation 10 violates the expected preference pattern in the record selection problem.

The following consequence of the elimination-by-aspects model involves binary probabilities only. Since it generalizes the algebraic notion of transitivity, it is called *moderate stochastic transitivity*.

Moderate stochastic transitivity: $P(x; y) \geq 1/2$ and $P(y; z) \geq 1/2$ imply

$$P(x; z) \geq \min[P(x; y), P(y; z)].$$ [11]

If we replace min by max in the conclusion of equation 11, we obtain a stronger condition called *strong stochastic transitivity*. This latter property (which is not a consequence of the present model) is essentially equivalent to simple scalability in the binary case. If we replace the conclusion of equation 11 by $P(x; z) \geq 1/2$, we obtain a weaker condition called *weak stochastic transitivity*, which is a consequence of the existence of an ordinal utility scale satisfying $u(x) \geq u(y)$ iff $P(x; y) \geq 1/2$.

The next consequence of the EBA model has not been investigated previously to the best of my knowledge. It relates binary and trinary choice probabilities by a property called the *multiplicative inequality*.

Multiplicative inequality: $P(x; y, z) \geq P(x; y)P(x; z)$.   [12]

The multiplicative inequality asserts that the probability of choosing x from $\{x, y, z\}$ is at least as large as the probability of choosing x from both $\{x, y\}$ and $\{x, z\}$ in two independent choices. It is conjectured that the elimination-by-aspects model implies a much stronger form of the multiplicative inequality, namely, $P(x, A \cup B) \geq P(x, A)P(x, B)$ for all $A, B \subseteq T$.

Equations 10 and 12 can be combined to yield

$$\min[P(x; y), P(x; z)] \geq P(x; y, z) \geq P(x; y)P(x; z).$$ [13]

Thus, trinary choice probabilities are bounded from above by regularity, and from below by the multiplicative inequality. A geometric representation of equation 13 which displays the admissible range of $P(x; y, z)$ given the values of $P(x; y)$ and $P(x; z)$ is given in figure 20.5. It shows that the trinary probability must lie between the lower and upper surfaces generated, respectively, by the multiplicative inequality (equation 12) and regularity (equation 10).

The significance of the above consequences stems from the fact that they provide measurement-free tests of the elimination-by-aspects model, that is, tests which do not require estimation of parameters.

For a given set of alternatives T, the elimination-by-aspects model has $2^t - 3$ free parameters, or U values (the number of proper nonempty subsets of T minus an arbitrary unit of measurement), while the number of independent data points of the form $P(x, A)$, $x \in A \subseteq T$, is

$$\sum_{n=2}^{t} (n-1) \binom{t}{n} = (t-2)2^{t-1} + 1.$$

Hence, there are always at least as many data points as parameters in the present model; the former exceeds the latter whenever $t > 3$. In general, therefore, the scale

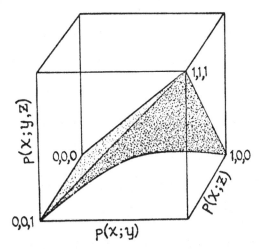

Figure 20.5
A geometric representation of the admissible values (shaded region) of the trinary probability $P(x; y, z)$ given the binary probabilities $P(x; y)$ and $P(x; z)$, under equation 13.

values are uniquely determined by the choice probabilities except in some particular situations, for example, when $P(x, A) = 1/a$ for all $x \in A \subseteq T$.

Even in the case where $t = 3$, in which the number of parameters (five) equals the number of data points, the choice probabilities are severely constrained. The volume of the subspace generated by the present model is less than $1/2\%$ of the volume of the entire parameter space which is a five-dimensional unit hypercube. The probability that a point sampled at random, from a uniform distribution over the parameter space, satisfies the present model, therefore, is less than .005 in this case.

Additional consequences and further developments of the elimination-by-aspects model are presented in Tversky (1972). They include a generalization of the present model, an extension to ranking, and a proof that the EBA model is a random utility model, though not an independent one.

Tests

In contrast to the many theoretical studies of probabilistic models of preference (see, e.g., Becker et al., 1963a; Luce & Suppes, 1965; Marschak, 1960; Morrison, 1963), there have been relatively few empirical studies in which these models were tested. Moreover, much of the available data are limited to binary choices, and most studies report and analyze only group data (see, e.g., Rumelhart & Greeno, 1971).

Unfortunately, group data usually do not permit adequate testing of theories of individual choice behavior because, in general, the compatibility of such data with the theory is neither a necessary nor a sufficient condition for its validity. (For an instructive illustration of this point, see Luce, 1959, p. 8.) The scarcity of appropriate data in an area of considerable theoretical interest is undoubtedly due to the difficulties involved in obtaining adequate estimates of choice probabilities for an individual subject, particularly outside the domain of psychophysics.

Two consequences of the present model were tested in previous studies. In an experiment involving choice among gambles, Becker et al. (1963b) showed that although simple scalability (equation 1) is systematically violated, the regularity condition (equation 10) is generally satisfied. Similarly, although strong stochastic transitivity was violated in several studies (e.g., Coombs, 1958; Krantz, 1967; Tversky & Russo, 1969), moderate stochastic transitivity was usually supported. (For some specified conditions under which moderate stochastic transitivity, as well as weak stochastic transitivity, is violated, see Tversky, 1969.) The fact that simple scalability and strong stochastic transitivity are often violated while regularity and moderate stochastic transitivity are typically satisfied provides some support, albeit nonspecific, for the present theory. The following experimental work was designed to obtain a more direct test of the EBA model.

Method

To test the model, three different tasks were selected. The stimuli in Task A were random dot patterns, in a square frame, varying in size (of square) and density (of dots). Subjects were presented with pairs and triples of frames and instructed to choose, in each case, the frame which contained the largest number of dots. The stimuli in Task B were profiles of college applicants with different intelligence (I) and motivation (M) scores. The scores were expressed in percentiles (relative to the population of college applicants), and displayed as bar graphs. Subjects were presented with pairs and triples of such profiles and asked to select, in each case, the applicant they considered the most promising. The stimuli in Task C were two-outcome gambles of the form (p, x), in which one wins \$$x$ with probability p and nothing otherwise. Each gamble was displayed as a pie diagram, where the probabilities of winning and not winning were represented, respectively, by the black and white sectors of the pie. Subjects were presented with pairs and triples of gambles and were asked to choose the gamble they would prefer to play. (At the end of the study, each subject actually played for money five of the gambles chosen by him in the course of the study. The gambles were played by spinning an arrow on a wheel of fortune and the subjects won the indicated amont if the arrow landed on the black sector of the wheel.) Examples of the three types of stimuli are shown in figure 20.6.

A dot pattern   **A gamble**   **A score profile**

Figure 20.6
Typical stimulus slides from each of the three tasks.

The same eight subjects participated in all three tasks. They were students in a Jerusalem high school, ages 16–18. Subjects were run in a single group. The stimuli were projected on slides and each subject indicated his choices by checking an appropriate box on his response sheet. The study consisted of 12 one-hour sessions, three times a week, for four weeks. The first two sessions were practice sessions in which the problems and the procedure were introduced and the subjects familiarized themselves with the stimuli of the task.

Each experimental session included all three tasks, and the ordering of the tasks was randomized across sessions. Within each task, subjects were presented with various pairs and triples formed from a basic set of $4 \times 4 = 16$ two-dimensional stimuli. One set of three stimuli of each type was isolated and replicated more than other sets. The entire triple was replicated 30 times (three per session) while each of the pairs within this triple was replicated 20 times (two per session). The following discussion is concerned with the analysis of these triples. Each triple was constructed so that no alternative dominates another one with respect to both dimensions, and so that two of the elements, called x and y, are very similar to each other, while the third element, z, is relatively dissimilar to each of them.[4]

The subjects were paid a flat fee for the completion of all the sessions. In addition, each subject received a bonus proportional to the number of correct numerosity judgments made by him, and was allowed to play, for money, five gambles selected randomly from those chosen by him during the study.

Results
The analysis of the results begins by testing the constant-ratio rule which is essentially equivalent to Luce's (1959) model. According to this rule,

$$\frac{P(x; y)}{P(y; x)} = \frac{P(x, A)}{P(y, A)} \quad x, y \in A, \tag{14}$$

provided the denominators do not vanish. The constant-ratio rule is a strong version of the principle of independence from irrelevant alternatives. It requires that the ratio of $P(x, A)$ and $P(y, A)$ (not merely their order as required by simple scalability) be independent of the offered set A.

Let $T = \{x, y, z\}$, and define

$$P_y(x; z) = \frac{P(x, T)}{P(x, T) + P(z, T)},$$

$$P_x(y; z) = \frac{P(y, T)}{P(y, T) + P(z, T)}.$$

Hence, by the constant-ratio rule,

$$P(x; z) = P_y(x; z) \quad \text{and}$$

$$P(y; z) = P_x(y; z). \tag{15}$$

Put differently, the binary probability $P(x; z)$ should equal $P_y(x; z)$, computed from the trinary probabilities, since under equation 14 the presence of y is "irrelevant" to the choice between x and z.

In the present study, the alternatives were designed so that x and y are much more similar to each other than either of them is to z. Hence, the similarity hypothesis that is incorporated into the elimination-by-aspects model predicts that the addition of alternative y to the set $\{x, z\}$ will reduce $P(x, T)$ proportionally more than $P(z, T)$. That is, the similar alternative, x, will lose relatively more than the dissimilar alternative, z, by the addition of y. Likewise, y is expected to lose relatively more than z by the introduction of x. Contrary to the constant-ratio rule, therefore, the similarity hypothesis implies

$$P(x; z) > P_y(x; z) \quad \text{and}$$

$$P(y; z) > P_x(y; z). \tag{16}$$

To test the constant-ratio rule, the observed (binary) relative frequencies $\hat{P}(x, z)$ and $\hat{P}(y, z)$ were compared, respectively, with $\hat{P}_y(x; z)$ and $\hat{P}_x(y; z)$ computed from the trinary relative frequencies, separately for each one of the subjects. The observed and the computed values for all subjects are shown in table 20.1 for each of the three tasks.

It seems that the constant-ratio model (equation 14) holds in the psychophysical task (A), and that it fails in the two preference tasks (B and C) in the manner predicted by the similarity hypothesis (equation 16). Out of 16 individual comparisons

Table 20.1
Observed and Predicted Proportions (under the Constant-Ratio Model) for Each Task

Subject	Task A (dots)				Task B (applicants)				Task C (gambles)			
	$\hat{P}(x;z)$	$\hat{P}_y(x;z)$	$\hat{P}(y;z)$	$\hat{P}_x(y;z)$	$\hat{P}(x;z)$	$\hat{P}_y(x;z)$	$\hat{P}(y;z)$	$\hat{P}_x(y;z)$	$\hat{P}(x;z)$	$\hat{P}_y(x;z)$	$\hat{P}(y;z)$	$\hat{P}_x(y;z)$
1	.50	.43	.45	.43	.65	.44	.30	.26	.35	.12	.50	.46
2	.60	.27	.35	.33	.55	.37	.75	.58	.60	.53	.70	.68
3	.25	.38	.40	.41	.55	.38	.60	.41	.25	.26	.50	.29
4	.70	.75	.30	.67	.40	.46	.40	.32	.60	.43	.70	.35
5	.65	.52	.35	.39	.65	.45	.55	.40	.20	.16	.50	.41
6	.40	.39	.45	.52	.35	.20	.40	.38	.65	.54	.60	.44
7	.15	.26	.45	.44	.75	.77	.35	.40	.55	.42	.65	.50
8	.15	.14	.45	.57	.55	.52	.40	.29	.55	.35	.70	.43
Overall proportion	.425	.405	.400	.466	.556	.463	.469	.388	.469	.354	.606	.466
p		ns		ns		$<.05$		$<.10$		$<.01$		$<.01$

in each task (two per subject), equation 16 was satisfied in 13 and 15 cases, respectively, in Tasks B and C ($p < .05$ in each case[5]), and only in 7 cases in Task A. Essentially the same result was found in additional analyses.

The relatively small number of observations does not permit an adequate test of individual comparisons. Hence, the observed and the computed choice frequencies were pooled over subjects. The results of a chi-square test of equation 15 against equation 16, based on these data, are shown in the last row of table 20.1 for each comparison in each of the tasks. The same pattern emerges from the analysis of the pooled data: the observed proportions are significantly higher than the computed ones in tasks B and C, but not in task A.

Since the constant-ratio model is not acceptable, in general, the simplest version of the elimination-by-aspects model, which is compatible with the similarity hypothesis, was selected next. Recall that the test stimuli were designed so that x and y are very similar to each other while z is relatively dissimilar to either of them (see footnote 4). Thus, we assume that neither x nor y share with z any aspect that they do not share with each other. Consequently, aside from the aspects shared by all three stimuli, z can be regarded as (aspectwise) disjoint from both x and y. That is, we assume that, to a reasonable degree of approximation, $U(\overline{x,z}) = U(\overline{y,z}) = 0$. This assumption reduces the number of free parameters (from five to three) at the cost of some loss in generality.

Let $U(\bar{x}) = a$, $U(\bar{y}) = b$, $U(\bar{z}) = c$, and $U(\overline{x,y}) = d$ (see Figure 7). Under this special case of the model, there exist nonnegative a, b, c, and d such that

$$P(x; y) = \frac{a}{a+b}, \quad P(y; z) = \frac{b+d}{b+d+c}, \quad P(x; z) = \frac{a+d}{a+d+c},$$

$$P(x; y, z) = \frac{a + d\frac{a}{a+b}}{a+b+c+d}, \quad \text{and} \quad P(z; x, y) = \frac{c}{a+b+c+d}.$$

[17]

For three alternatives, there are five independent data points (three binary and two trinary). In the absence of any restrictions on the parameters, the likelihood function of the data is maximized by using the observed relative frequencies as estimates of the parameters, in which case the dimensionality of the parameter space, denoted $d(\Omega)$, equals five. In the above version (equation 17) of the elimination-by-aspects model, we can set c, say, arbitrarily, whence the observed proportions are all expressible in terms of three parameters (a, b, and d), and the dimensionality of the restricted parameter space, denoted $d(\omega)$, equals three. Let λ be the likelihood ratio $L(\omega)/L(\Omega)$, where L denotes the maximum value of the likelihood function under

Table 20.2
Values of the Test Statistic and the Estimated Values of d for Each Subject in Each of the Tasks

Subject	Task A (dots)		Task B (applicants)		Task C (gambles)	
	χ^2	d	χ^2	d	χ^2	d
1	.133	.29	2.179	.14	.040	.46
2	3.025	.89	1.634	.92	.001	.58
3	.849	0	.159	1.18	2.022	.14
4	5.551*	0	6.864*	.51	1.053	1.56
5	.951	0	.428	1.23	.887	0
6	.401	0	.405	.42	.157	1.18
7	3.740	0	.083	0	.304	1.00
8	4.112	0	.038	.37	1.241	1.44

Note: $df = 2$.
* $p = .1$.

the respective model. If equation 17 holds, then the statistic $-2 \ln \lambda$ has an approximate chi-square distribution with $d(\Omega) - d(\omega) = 2$ degrees of freedom.

Chandler's (1969) STEPIT program was employed to obtain maximum likelihood estimates of the parameters under equation 17 with $c = 1$. The values of the test statistics are reported in table 20.2, along with the estimates of d, for each subject in all tasks.

Table 20.2 exhibits a very good correspondence between the observed proportions and the tested version (equation 17) of the EBA model: only 2 out of 24 tests permit rejecting the model at the conservative .1 level. It should perhaps be noted that a correspondence between observed choice probabilities and the elimination-by-aspects model does not necessarily imply that the subjects are actually following a strategy of elimination by aspects. They might, in fact, employ a different strategy that is well approximated by the elimination-by-aspects model. The study of the actual strategies employed by subjects in choice experiments may perhaps be advanced by investigating choice probabilities in conjunction with other data such as reaction time, eye movements, or verbal protocols.

The relation between the predictions of the constant-ratio model (equation 15) and the similarity hypothesis (equation 16) can be further investigated using the obtained estimates of the parameter d, reported in table 20.2. It is easy to verify that the constant-ratio model is compatible with equation 17 if and only if $d = 0$, while the similarity hypothesis implies $d > 0$. Hence, if the former holds, the estimates of d should be close to 0, whereas if the latter holds, the estimates should be substantially positive. (The magnitude of d should be interpreted in the light of the facts that all

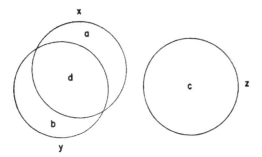

Figure 20.7
A graphical illustration of the tested version of the EBA model (equation 17).

parameters are nonnegative and $c = 1$, see equation 17 and figure 20.7.) Inspection of table 20.2 reveals that the majority of the d estimates in task A are zero, while the majority of the d estimates in tasks B and C are substantially positive. This agrees with the results of previous analyses (summarized in table 20.1) according to which the constant-ratio model is satisfied in task A, but not in tasks B and C.

Taken together, the experimental findings suggest the hypothesis that the constant-ratio model is valid for choice among *unitary* alternatives (e.g., dots, colors, sounds) that are usually evaluated as wholes, but not for *composite* alternatives (e.g., gambles, applicants) that tend to be evaluated in terms of their attributes or components. This hypothesis is closely related to a suggestion made by Luce (1959):

If we call a decision that is not subdivided into simpler decisions an elementary choice, then possibly we can hope to find Axiom 1 [Luce's choice axiom] directly confirmed for elementary choices but probably not for more complex ones [p. 133].

Research on multidimensional scaling based on similarity, or proximity, data (e.g., Shepard, 1964a; Torgerson, 1965) has also shown that judgments of unitary and composite stimuli (sometimes referred to as analyzable and unanalyzable) are governed by different rules. Much additional research, however, is required in order to assess the validity and the generality of the proposed hypothesis.

Finally, the distinction between unitary and composite stimuli is logically independent of whether the inconsistency reflected in choice probabilities is attributable to imperfect discrimination or to a conflict among incompatible criteria. (For a discussion of this last distinction, see Block & Marschak, 1960.) Although choice experiments in psychophysics typically involve imperfect discrimination with unitary stimuli while preference experiments are usually concerned with conflict among composite alternatives, the other two combinations also exist.

Discussion

Strategic Implications

A major feature of the elimination-by-aspects model is that the probability of selecting an alternative depends not only on its overall value, but also on its relations to the other available alternatives. This gives rise to study of strategic factors in the design and the presentation of choice alternatives. Specifically, the present model provides a method for investigating questions concerning optimal design or location of alternatives in order to maximize (or minimize) choice probability under specified constraints. The following examples are intended to illustrate the scope and the nature of such a study.

First, consider a problem of binary comparisons. Suppose y and z are given, and we search for x such that $P(x; y)$ is maximized under the constraints that z has no aspects in common with any other alternative, and that $P(y; z)$ and $P(x; z)$ are fixed. By the former constraint, z can be viewed as a standard of comparison. Hence, the latter constraint can be interpreted as meaning that the overall values of y and of x (evaluated relative to z) are held fixed. Thus, only the position of x relative to y can be varied to maximize $P(x; y)$. Under these conditions, the present model implies that if $P(x; z) > P(y; z)$, x' should include as much of y' as possible. If, on the other hand, $P(x; z) < P(y; z)$, x' should include as little of y' as possible. The degree of overlap between x' and y' can be regarded as an index of the difficulty of comparing them. If x' includes y', the comparison is trivial, and $P(x; y)$ is maximal. If x' and y' are disjoint, the comparison is much more difficult, and $P(x; y)$ is less extreme.

In the light of this interpretation, the above result asserts that it is in the best interest of the favored alternative to make the comparison as easy as possible, while it is in the best interest of the nonfavored alternative to make the comparison as difficult as possible. This certainly makes sense: any increase in the difficulty of comparing the alternatives adds "error" to the judgment process and makes $P(x; y)$ closer to $1/2$. According to this logic, drastically different policies are prescribed depending on whether x is the favored or the nonfavored alternative. Advertising campaigns based on slogans such as "All aspirins are the same—why pay more?" and "This car is completely different from any other car in its class," illustrate, respectively, the policies recommended to the favored and the nonfavored alternatives. Note that these policies could be employed in the design of products as well as in their advertisements.

Second, let $T = \{x, y, \ldots, z\}$ and suppose that all pairwise choice probabilities are fixed and that we wish to select a set $A \subseteq T$ which includes both x and y so that the ratio $P(x, A)/P(y, A)$ is maximized. According to the elimination-by-aspects model, the above ratio is maximized when A consists of alternatives (which are not dominated by y) that "cover" as much of y as possible without "covering" much of x. If x and y are products in some market A, for example, then the present model predicts that the relative advantage of x over y is maximized when the other available products are as similar to y and dissimilar to x as possible. The example of choice among records discussed in the introduction and the similarity effect demonstrated in table 20.1 illustrate the point. Note that this maximization problem cannot be investigated in Luce's model (equation 2), for example, since by the constant-ratio rule $P(x, A)/P(y, A) = P(x; y)/P(y; x)$, $x, y \in A$, and hence is independent of A. According to the EBA model, in contrast, the above ratio can, in principle, be arbitrarily large, provided $P(x; y) \neq 0$.

Thus, if the present theory is valid, one can take advantage of the so-called "irrelevant alternatives" to influence choice probabilities. This result is based on the idea that the introduction of an additional alternative "hurts" similar alternatives more than dissimilar ones. This is a familiar notion in the context of group choice. The present development suggests that it is an important determinant of individual choice behavior as well. In practice, problems such as the design of a product or a political campaign involve many specific constraints concerning the nature of the product or the candidate. To the extent that these constraints can be translated into the present framework, the elimination-by-aspects model can be used (or abused) to determine the optimal design, or location, of choice alternatives.

Psychological Interpretation

The EBA model accounts for choice in terms of a covert elimination process based on sequential selection of aspects. Any such sequence of aspects can be regarded as a particular state of mind which leads to a unique choice. In light of this interpretation, the choice mechanism at any given moment in time is entirely deterministic; the probabilities merely reflect the fact that at different moments in time different states of mind (leading to different choices) may prevail. According to the present theory, choice probability is an increasing function of the values of the relevant aspects. Indeed, the elimination-by-aspects model is compensatory in nature despite the fact that at any given instant in time, the choice is assumed to follow a conjunctive (or a lexicographic) strategy. Thus, the present model is compensatory "globally" with respect to choice probability but not "locally" with regard to any particular state of mind.

In the proposed model, aspects are interpreted as desirable features; the selection of any particular aspect leads to elimination of all alternatives that do not contain the selected aspect. Following the present development, one can formulate a dual model where aspects are interpreted as disadvantages, or regrets, associated with the alternatives. According to such a model, the selection of a particular aspect leads to the elimination of all alternatives that contain the selected aspect. This model is also based on the notion of elimination by aspects, except that here an alternative is chosen if and only if none of its aspects is selected, whereas in the model developed in this paper an alternative is selected if and only if it includes all the selected aspects. The former model may be more appropriate when the defining features of the alternatives are naturally viewed as undesirable. In choosing among various insurance policies, for example, it may be more natural to apply the strategy of elimination by aspects to the various risks and premiums, treated as disadvantages or regrets, than to interpret them as relative advantages with respect to some reference points.[6]

Although the present model has been introduced and discussed in terms of aspects, we have shown that it requires no specific assumptions concerning the structure of these aspects. In the course of the investigation, however, assumptions concerning the structure and/or the relative weights of aspects were sometimes introduced. In discussing the Paris–Rome problem, for example, we assumed that Paris+ (i.e., a trip to Paris plus an added bonus) includes Paris in the sense that all aspects of the latter are included in the former. Similarly, in analyzing Debreu's example, we assumed that the two recordings B_1 and B_2 of the Beethoven symphony are very similar to each other, whereas the suite by Debussy is relatively dissimilar to either of them. Essentially the same assumption was employed in the analysis of the experimental data. In all these instances, specific assumptions about the structure or the relative weights of aspects were added to the model on the basis of some prior analysis of the alternatives. The addition of such assumptions strengthens the predictions of the model and tightens its empirical interpretation. These assumptions, however, must be carefully examined because the inadequacy of an added assumption can erroneously be interpreted as a failure of model.

To illustrate this point, consider the following example of choice between articles of clothing. Let J denote a jacket, S a pair of matching slacks, and C a coat. Suppose that the coat is more valuable than the jacket, so $P(C; J) > 1/2$. But since the slacks and the jacket are well matched, $P(JS; CS) > 1/2$, where JS and CS denote the options consisting of the combined respective articles. Both JS and CS share the same article, S; hence one might be tempted to interpret S as a collection of aspects shared by the two alternatives. According to the elimination-by-aspects model, such aspects could be deleted without affecting the choice process. Consequently, under the proposed interpretation of S, $P(JS; CS) = P(J; C)$ contrary to the assumptions.

Further reflection, however, reveals that the interpretation of S as a collection of aspects common to both options is inappropriate. The fact that the jacket and the slacks form an attractive outfit implies that this alternative has some gestaltlike properties, or that the option JS includes some aspects that are not included in either J or S alone. Hence, the fact that the option JS includes both J and S as components does not, by itself, justify the conclusion that the aspects of JS can be partitioned into those associated with J and S alone.

Rational Choice and the Logic of Elimination by Aspects
The following television commercial serves to introduce the problem. "There are more than two dozen companies in the San Francisco area which offer training in computer programming." The announcer puts some two dozen eggs and one walnut on the table to represent the alternatives, and continues: "Let us examine the facts. How many of these schools have on-line computer facilities for training?" The announcer removes several eggs. "How many of these schools have placement services that would help find you a job?" The announcer removes some more eggs. "How many of these schools are approved for veterans' benefits?" This continues until the walnut alone remains. The announcer cracks the nutshell, which reveals the name of the company and concludes: "This is all you need to know in a nutshell."

This commercial illustrates the logic of elimination by aspects; it also suggests that this logic has some normative appeal as a method of choosing among many complex alternatives. The appeal of this logic stems primarily from the fact that it is easy to state, defend, and apply. In choosing among many complex alternatives such as new cars or job offers, one typically faces an overwhelming amount of relevant information. Optimal policies for choosing among such alternatives usually require involved computations based on the weights assigned to the various relevant factors, or on the compensation rates associated with the critical variables. Since man's intuitive computational facilities are quite limited (Shepard, 1964b; Slovic & Lichtenstein, 1971), the above method is difficult to apply.

Moreover, it seems that people are reluctant to accept the principle that (even very important) decisions should depend on computations based on subjective estimates of likelihoods or values in which the decision maker himself has only limited confidence. When faced with an important decision, people appear to search for an analysis of the situation and a compelling principle of choice which will resolve the decision problem by offering a clear-cut choice without relying on estimation of relative weights, or on numerical computations. (Altogether people seem to have more confidence in the rationality of their decisions than in the validity of their intuitive estimates, and the fact that the former depends on the latter is often met with a mixture of resistance and unhappiness.)

The strategy of elimination by aspects (illustrated by the above commercial) provides an example of such a principle: It is relatively easy to apply, it involves no numerical computations, and it is easy to explain and justify in terms of a priority ordering defined on the aspects. Inasmuch as people look for a decision rule that not only looks sensible, but which also seems easy to defend to oneself as well as to others, the principle of elimination by aspects appears attractive. Its uncritical application, however, may lead to very poor decisions. For virtually any available alternative, no matter how inadequate it might be, one can devise a sequence of selected aspects or, equivalently, describe a particular state of mind that leads to the choice of that alternative.

Indeed, the purpose of advertisement is to induce a state of mind in the decision maker which will result in the purchase of the advertised product. This is typically accomplished by increasing the salience and the availability of the desired state of mind. Being influenced by such factors, people are often lured into adopting a state of mind which, upon further reflection, appears atypical or inadequate. Shepard (1964b) tells of a person who is induced to purchase the *Encyclopedia Britannica* by imagining how he would read it in his free time and impress his friends with his newly acquired knowledge. Only after failing to consult the *Encyclopedia Britannica* for a long period of time does the person realize how inappropriate the state of mind was that had led him to purchase those many dusty volumes.

From a normative standpoint, the major flaw in the principle of elimination by aspects lies in its failure to ensure that the alternatives retained are, in fact, superior to those which are eliminated.

In the problem addressed by the above commercial, for instance, the existence of placement services that would help the trainee to find a job is certainly a desirable aspect of the advertised program. Its use as a criterion for elimination, however, may lead to the rejection of programs whose overall quality exceeds that of the advertised one despite the fact that they do not offer placement services.

In general, therefore, the strategy of elimination by aspects cannot be defended as a rational procedure of choice. On the other hand, there may be many contexts in which it provides a good approximation to much more complicated compensatory models and could thus serve as a useful simplification procedure. The conditions under which the approximation is adequate, and the manner in which this principle could be utilized to facilitate and improve decision making, are subjects for future investigations.

Notes

The research was supported, in part, by National Science Foundation Grant GB-6782. Much of the work reported in this paper was accomplished while the author was a Fellow at the Center for Advanced Study in the Behavioral Sciences, Stanford, California, during 1970–1971.

I wish to thank the Center for the generous hospitality. I am grateful to David H. Krantz for many invaluable discussions throughout the years, to Maya Bar-Hillel for her assistance in both theoretical and experimental phases of the investigation, and to Edward N. Pugh for his help in the analysis of the data. I have also benefited from discussions with Clyde H. Coombs, Robyn M. Dawes, R. Duncan Luce, Jacob Marschak, J. E. Russo, and Paul Slovic.

1. Simple scalability is, in fact, equivalent (see Tversky, 1972) to the following *order independence* assumption. For $x, y \in A - B$, and $z \in B$, $P(x, A) \geq P(y, A)$ iff $P(z, B \cup \{x\}) \leq P(z, B \cup \{y\})$ provided the terms on the two sides of either inequality are not both 0 or 1.

2. The representation of choice alternatives as collections of measurable aspects was developed by Restle (1961) who formulated a binary choice model based on this representation. As will be shown later, the present theory reduces to Restle's in the two-alternative case. A related representation of choice alternatives was developed by Lancaster (1966) who assumed that economic goods possess, or give rise to, multiple characteristics (or aspects) in fixed proportion, and that these characteristics determine the consumer's choice. Lancaster's theory, however, is nonprobabilistic.

3. In this paper, the superbar is used exclusively to denote collections of aspects. It should not be confused with a common use of this symbol to denote set complement.

4. The following stimuli were employed in the study. Task A: $x = (13 \times 13, 4/5)$, $y = (14 \times 14, 3/4)$, and $z = (28 \times 28, 1/5)$ where the first component of each stimulus is the size of the underlying matrix used to generate the pattern, and the second component is the proportion of cells of the matrix that contain dots. Task B: $x = (78, 25)$, $y = (75, 35)$, and $z = (60, 90)$ where the first and second components of each pair denote, respectively, intelligence and motivation scores of the applicants. Task C: $x = (1/5, 4.00)$, $y = (1/4, 3.50)$, and $z = (2/3, 1.00)$, where the first and second component of each pair are, respectively, the probability of winning and the amount to be won in each of the gambles in Israeli pounds.

5. This significance level should be interpreted with caution because of the potential dependency between the observations of each subject.

6. George Miller remarked that people seem to be better at finding what is wrong with an alternative than what is good about it. This certainly is true of some people, who might then find the "negative" version of the model less objectionable or more compatible with their way of thinking.

References

Becker, G. M., DeGroot, M. H., & Marschak, J. Stochastic models of choice behavior. *Behavioral Science*, 1963, 8, 41–55. (a)

Becker, G. M., DeGroot, M. H., & Marschak, J. Probabilities of choices among very similar objects. *Behavioral Science*, 1963, 8, 306–311. (b)

Block, H. D., & Marschak, J. Random orderings and stochastic theories of responses. In I. Olkin, S. Ghurye, W. Hoeffding, W. Madow, & H. Mann (Eds.), *Contributions to probability and statistics.* Stanford: Stanford University Press, 1960.

Chandler, J. P. STEPIT—Finds local minima of a smooth function of several parameters. *Behavioral Science*, 1969, 14, 81–82.

Chipman, J. S. Stochastic choice and subjective probability. In D. Willner (Ed.), *Decisions, values, and groups*, vol. 1. New York: Pergamon Press, 1960.

Coombs, C. H. On the use of inconsistency of preferences in psychological measurement. *Journal of Experimental Psychology*, 1958, 55, 1–7.

Coombs, C. H. *A theory of data*. New York: Wiley, 1964.

Debreu, G. Review of R. D. Luce, Individual choice behavior: A theoretical analysis. *American Economic Review*, 1960, 50, 186–188.

Estes, W. K. A random-walk model for choice behavior. In K. J. Arrow, S. Karlin, & P. Suppes (Eds.), *Mathematical methods in the social sciences, 1959*. Stanford: Stanford University Press, 1960.

Fishburn, P. C. Utility theory. *Management Science*, 1968, 13, 435–453.

Krantz, D. H. *The scaling of small and large color differences*. (Doctoral dissertation, University of Pennsylvania) Ann Arbor, Mich.: University Microfilms, 1964. No. 65–5777.

Krantz, D. H. Rational distance function for multidimensional scaling. *Journal of Mathematical Psychology*, 1967, 4, 226–245.

Lancaster, K. J. A new approach to consumer theory. *Journal of Political Economy*, 1966, 74, 132–157.

Luce, R. D. *Individual choice behavior: A thoretical analysis*. New York: Wiley, 1959.

Luce, R. D., & Raiffa, H. *Games and decisions*. New York: Wiley, 1957.

Luce, R. D., & Suppes, P. Preference, utility, and subjective probability. In R. D. Luce, R. R. Bush, & E. Galanter (Eds.), *Handbook of mathematical psychology, III*. New York: Wiley, 1965.

Marschak, J. Binary-choice constraints and random utility indicators. In K. J. Arrow, S. Karlin, & P. Suppes (Eds.), *Mathematical methods in the social sciences, 1959*. Stanford: Stanford University Press, 1960.

Morrison, H. W. Testable conditions for triads of paired comparison choices. *Psychometrika*, 1963, 28, 369–390.

Restle, F. *Psychology of judgment and choice*. New York: Wiley, 1961.

Rumelhart, D. L., & Greeno, J. G. Similarity between stimuli: An experimental test of the Luce and Restle choice models. *Journal of Mathematical Psychology*, 1971, 8, 370–381.

Shepard, R. N. Attention and the metric structure of the stimulus space. *Journal of Mathematical Psychology*, 1964, 1, 54–87. (a)

Shepard, R. N. On the subjectively optimum selection among multiattribute alternatives. In M. W. Shelly & G. L. Bryan (Eds.), *Human judgments and optimality*. New York: Wiley, 1964. (b)

Slovic, P., & Lichtenstein, S. C. comparison of Bayesian and regression approaches to the study of information processing in judgment. *Organizational Behavior and Human Performance*, 1971, 6, 649–744.

Thurstone, L. L. A law of comparative judgment. *Psychological Review*, 1927, 34, 273–286.

Thurstone, L. L. *The measurement of values*. Chicago: University of Chicago Press, 1959.

Torgerson, W. S. Multidimensional scaling of similarity. *Psychometrika*, 1965, 30, 379–393.

Tversky, A. Intransitivity of preferences. *Psychological Review*, 1969, 76, 31–48.

Tversky, A. Choice by elimination. *Journal of Mathematical Psychology*, 1972, in press.

Tversky, A., & Russo, J. E. Similarity and substitutability in binary choices. *Journal of Mathematical Psychology*, 1969, 6, 1–12.

Appendix

This appendix estalishes the equivalence of the two formulations (equations 6 and 9) of the elimination-by-aspects model. Let T be a finite set of alternatives. For each $x \in T$, let x' denote the set of aspects associated with x. For any $A \subseteq T$, define $A' = \{\alpha \mid \alpha \in x' \text{ for some } x \in A\}$, $A^0 = \{\alpha \mid \alpha \in x' \text{ for all } x \in A\}$, and $\bar{A} = \{\alpha \mid \alpha \in x'$

for all $x \in A$ & $\alpha \notin y$ for any $y \notin A$}. We wish to show that there exists a positive scale u on $T' - T^0$ satisfying equation 6 if and only if there exists a scale U on $\{\bar{A}_i \,|\, A_i \subset T\}$ satisfying equation 9.

It follows at once from the above definitions that $\{\bar{A}_i \,|\, A_i \subset T\}$ forms a partition of $T' - T^0$, since any $\alpha \in T' - T^0$ belongs to exactly one $\bar{A}_i$. Suppose equation 6 holds. For any $A \subset T$, define $U(\bar{A}) = \sum_{\alpha \in \bar{A}} u(\alpha)$. By the positivity of u, U is nonnegative and $U(\bar{A}) = 0$ iff $\bar{A} = \phi$. Note that if $\alpha, \beta \in \bar{B}$ then for all $A \subset T$, $A_\alpha = A_\beta = A \cap B$. Furthermore, since $\{\bar{B}_i \,|\, x \in B_i\}$ forms a partition of x', the numerator in equation 6 can be expressed as

$$\sum_{\alpha \in x' - A^0} P(x, A_\alpha) u(\alpha) = \sum_{x \in B_i \not\supseteq A} \; \sum_{\alpha \in \bar{B}_i} P(x, A_\alpha) u(\alpha)$$

$$= \sum_{x \in B_i \not\supseteq A} P(x, A \cap B_i) \sum_{\alpha \in \bar{B}_i} u(\alpha)$$

$$= \sum_{B_i \not\supseteq A} P(x, A \cap B_i) U(\bar{B}_i).$$

(The condition $x \in B_i$ under the summation sign is deleted because for any $x \notin B_i$, $P(x, A \cap B_i) = 0$. Similarly, since $\{\beta \,|\, \beta \in A' - A^0\} = \{\beta \,|\, \beta \in \bar{A}_j$ for some A_j such that $A_j \not\supseteq A$ and $A_j \cap A \neq \phi\}$, the denominator in equation 6 can be expressed as

$$\sum_{\beta \in A' - A^0} u(\beta) = \sum_{A_j \in \mathscr{A}} U(\bar{A}_j)$$

where

$$\mathscr{A} = \{A_j \,|\, A_j \cap A \neq A, \phi\}.$$

Thus, equation 6 reduces to equation 9, since

$$\frac{\displaystyle\sum_{\alpha \in x' - A^0} u(\alpha) P(x, A_\alpha)}{\displaystyle\sum_{\beta \in A' - A^0} u(\beta)} = \frac{\displaystyle\sum_{B_i \not\supseteq A} U(\bar{B}_i) P(x, A \cap B_i)}{\displaystyle\sum_{A_j \in \mathscr{A}} U(\bar{A}_j)}$$

Conversely, suppose equation 9 holds. That is, there exists a scale U such that $P(x, A)$ is given by the right-hand side of the above equation. For any $x \in T$, let $x' = \{A_i \subset T \,|\, x \in A_i\}$, and $u = U$, hence equation 9 reduces to equation 6. Finally, if either of the above denominators vanishes, so does the other.

21 Preference Trees

Amos Tversky and Shmuel Sattath

The analysis of choice behavior has concerned many students of social science. Choices among political candidates, market products, investment plans, transportation modes, and professional careers have been investigated by economists, political scientists, and psychologists using a variety of empirical and theoretical methods. An examination of the empirical literature indicates that choice behavior is often inconsistent, hierarchical, and context dependent.

Inconsistency refers to the observation that people sometimes make different choices under seemingly identical conditions. Although inconsistency can be explained as the result of learning, satiation, or change in taste, it tends to persist even when the effects of these factors are controlled or minimized. Furthermore, even in an essentially unique choice situation that cannot be replicated, people often experience doubt regarding their decisions and feel that in a different state of mind, they might have made a different choice. The observed inconsistency and the experienced uncertainty associated with choice behavior have led several investigators to conceptualize choice as a probabilistic process and to use the concept of choice probability as a basis for the measurement of strength of preference (Luce, 1959; Marschak, 1960; Thurstone, 1927).

Choice among many alternatives appears to follow a hierarchical elimination process. When faced with many alternatives (e.g., job offers, houses, cars), people appear to eliminate various subsets of alternatives sequentially according to some hierarchical structure, rather than scanning all the options in an exhaustive manner. This strategy is particularly appealing when the number of alternatives is large and an exhaustive evaluation is either not feasible or costly in time and effort. Indeed, these considerations have led several theorists (notably Simon, 1957) to modify the classical criterion of maximization and to view the choice process as a search for an acceptable alternative that satisfies certain criteria. Such a search is naturally executed by a sequential elimination procedure.

Choice behavior appears to be context dependent. That is, the strength of preference of one alternative over another depends on the context of the other available alternatives. Furthermore, choice probability depends not only on the values of the alternatives but also on their similarity or comparability (see, e.g., Tversky, 1972b). An analysis of the structural relations among the alternatives, therefore, is an essential element of any theory that purports to explain the effects of similarity and context on choice.

This article develops a probabilistic, context-dependent choice model—called *preference tree*—based on a hierarchical elimination process. The first part illustrates the tree model and investigates its formal properties and their psychological significance. In the second part, the model is applied to several sets of choice data that are represented as preference trees. The problem of constrained choice is investigated in the third section, and the implications of the tree model are discussed in the last section.

Theory

To motivate and develop the theory of preference trees, we discuss, first, the more general model of elimination by aspects (EBA). According to this model (Tversky, 1972a, 1972b), each alternative is viewed as a collection of measurable aspects, and choice is described as a covert process of eliminations. At each stage in the process, one selects an aspect (from those included in the available alternatives) with probability that is proportional to its measure. The selection of an aspect eliminates all alternatives that do not include this aspect, and the process continues until a single alternative remains. Consider, for example, the choice of a restaurant for dinner. The first aspect selected may be seafood; this eliminates all restaurants that do not serve acceptable seafood. From the remaining alternatives another aspect, say a price level, is selected, and all alternatives that do not meet this criterion are eliminated. The process continues until one restaurant—which includes all the selected aspects—remains.

To characterize this process in formal terms, some notation is introduced. Let $T = \{x, y, z, \ldots\}$ be the total finite set of alternatives under study, and let A, B, C denote nonempty subsets of T. Let $P(x, A)$ be the probability of choosing alternative x from an offered set A. Naturally,

$$\sum_{x \in A} P(x, A) = 1$$

for all $A \subset T$, and $P(x, A) = 0$ for $x \notin A$. For simplicity, we write $P(x, y)$ for $P(x, \{x, y\})$. Choice probabilities are typically estimated from relative frequency of selecting x on repeated choices from A. Next, consider a mapping that associates each x in T with a finite nonempty set $x' = \{\alpha, \beta, \ldots\}$ of elements that are interpreted as the aspects of x. An alternative x is said to include an aspect α whenever α is an element of x'. The present theory represents choice alternatives as collections of aspects that denote all valued attributes of the options including quantitative attributes (e.g., price, quality) and nominal attributes (e.g., automatic transmission on a

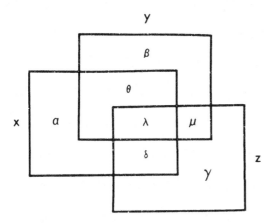

Figure 21.1
Schematic representation of three alternatives, x, y, and z, with their associated feature sets denoted α, β, and so on.

car, fried rice on a menu). The present analysis, however, does not require prior identification of the aspects associated with each alternative.

For any subset A of T, let A' be the set of aspects that belong to at least one alternative in A; that is, $A' = \{\alpha \mid \alpha \in x' \text{ for some } x \in A\}$. In particular, T' is the family of all aspects under consideration. For any α in T', let $A_\alpha = \{x \in A \mid \alpha \in x'\}$ denote the set of all alternatives of A that include α. Note that A' is a set of aspects, and A_α is a set of alternatives. Using these constructs, the EBA model can now be defined as follows.

A family of choice probabilities $P(x, A)$, $x \in A \subset T$, satisfies EBA if there exists a nonnegative scale u defined on T' such that for all $x \in A \subset T$

$$P(x, A) = \frac{\sum\limits_{\alpha \in x'} u(\alpha) P(x, A_\alpha)}{\sum\limits_{\beta \in A'} u(\beta)}. \tag{1}$$

This recursive formula, which defines the EBA model, expresses the probability of choosing x from A as a weighted sum of the probabilities $P(x, A_\alpha)$ of choosing x from proper subsets of A. It is easy to show that aspects common to all alternatives under consideration do not affect choice probability and will, therefore, be discarded.

To illustrate the model, consider the case of three alternatives where $A = \{x, y, z\}$, and let $x' = \{\alpha, \theta, \delta, \lambda\}$, $y' = \{\beta, \theta, \mu, \lambda\}$, and $z' = \{\gamma, \delta, \mu, \lambda\}$ (see figure 21.1). Thus,

$A_\alpha = \{x\}$, $A_\theta = \{x, y\}$, $A_\delta = \{x, z\}$, $A_\lambda = \{x, y, z\}$, and so on. Discarding λ, which is shared by all alternatives, and normalizing the scale u such that $u(\alpha) + u(\beta) + u(\gamma) + u(\delta) + u(\theta) + u(\mu) = 1$ yields

$$P(x, A) = u(\alpha)P(x, A_\alpha) + u(\theta)P(x, A_\theta) + u(\delta)P(x, A_\delta)$$

$$= u(\alpha) + u(\theta)P(x, y) + u(\delta)P(x, z),$$

where

$$P(x, y) = \frac{u(\alpha) + u(\delta)}{u(\alpha) + u(\delta) + u(\beta) + u(\mu)} = \frac{u(x' - y')}{u(x' - y') + u(y' - x')}.$$

This equation for binary choice probabilities coincides with Restle's (1961) model. According to the EBA model, x can be chosen from A (a) if α is selected first, (b) if θ is selected first and then either α or δ are selected later, and (c) if δ is selected first and then either α or θ are selected later. The probability of choosing x from A, therefore, is the sum of the probabilities associated with these outcomes.

Since there may be many aspects that are unique to x or common to x and y only, α, θ, and so on should be interpreted as collections of aspects. However, for the purposes of the present treatment, it is possible to combine all aspects that are unique to x and treat them as a single aspect. Formally, for any nonempty proper subset A of T let $\bar{A} = \{\alpha \mid \alpha \in x'$ for all $x \in A$ and $\alpha \notin y'$ for any $y \in T - A\}$. Thus, $\bar{A}$ is the set of aspects shared by all alternatives of A that are not shared by any alternative in $T - A$, and $\{\bar{A} \mid A \neq T, \varnothing\}$ is a partition of the set of all aspects into $2^n - 2$ aspect sets. To avoid additional notation we use α, β, and others, to denote these aspect sets and suppress the distinction between individual aspects and collections of aspects.

If all pairs of distinct alternatives in T are disjoint aspectwise, that is, $x' \cap y'$ is null, then $P(x, A_\alpha) = 1$ for any α in x', hence equation 1 reduces to

$$P(x, A) = \frac{\sum_{\alpha \in x'} u(\alpha)}{\sum_{\beta \in A'} u(\beta)} = \frac{u(x)}{\sum_{y \in A} u(y)},$$

where

$$u(x) = \sum_{\alpha \in x'} u(\alpha). \tag{2}$$

This is the choice model developed by Luce (1959, 1977). When all choice probabilities are nonzero, Luce's model is equivalent to the assumption that the ratio

$P(x, A)/(P(y, A)$ is a constant that depends on x and y but not on the offered set A. Hence, it is called the constant-ratio model (CRM). This model is simple and parsimonious; it expresses all probabilities of choice among n alternatives in terms of n scale values. (Since the unit of measurement is arbitrary, the number of independent parameters to be estimated is one less the number of scale values.) The CRM, however, fails to account for the effects of similarity between alternatives on choice probability, as shown by several authors (e.g., Debreu, 1960; Luce & Suppes, 1965; Restle, 1961; Rumelhart & Greeno, 1971; Tversky, 1972b). The relevant experimental studies were reviewed by Luce (1977).

In contrast, EBA provides a natural explanation of the similarity effect. Furthermore, it has several testable consequences that impose considerable constraints on observed choice probabilities and permit a measurement-free test of a model. The EBA model, however, does not restrict the structure of the aspects in any way, and hence it yields a large number of scale values $(2^n - 2)$, limiting its use as a scaling model. In particular, EBA cannot be estimated from binary choice probabilities, since the number of parameters exceeds the number of data points. The question arises, then, whether EBA can be significantly simplified by imposing some structure on the set of aspects. Stated differently, can we formulate an adequate theory of choice that is less restrictive than CRM and more parsimonious than EBA? We can view CRM as the set-theoretical analogue of a unidimensional representation and EBA as the counterpart of a high dimensional representation. What, then, is the analogue of low dimensionality in a set-theoretical representation?

In this article we investigate the representation of choice alternatives as a treelike graph. A graph is a collection of points, called nodes, some of which are linked directly by lines called edges or links. A sequence of adjacent links with no cycles is called a path. A (rooted) tree is a graph (containing a distinguished node called the root) in which any two nodes are joined by a unique path. For ease of reference, we place the root at the top of the tree and the terminal nodes at the bottom, as in figure 21.2. To interpret a rooted tree as a family of aspect sets, we associate each terminal node of the tree with a single alternative in T and each link of the tree with the set of aspects that are shared by all the alternatives that include (or follow from) that link and are not shared by any of the alternatives that do not include that link. Naturally, the length of each link in the tree represents the measure of the respective set of aspects. Hence, the set of all aspects that belong to a given alternative is represented by the path from the root of the tree to the terminal node associated with the alternative, and the length of the path represents the overall measure of the alternative.

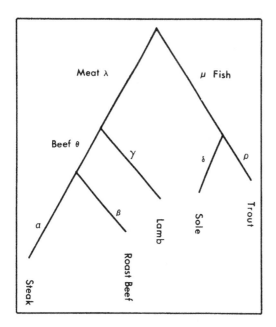

Figure 21.2
Tree representation of the choice among entrees.

An illustrative example of a tree representation of a menu is presented in figure 21.2. The set of alternatives consists of five entrees (steak, roast beef, lamb, sole, and trout) that appear as the terminal nodes of the tree. Thus, the link labelled λ represents the aspects shared by all meat entrees but not fish, θ represents the aspects shared by steak and roast beef but not lamb or fish, and γ represents the unique aspects of lamb. The names of the alternatives are displayed vertically and the suggested labels of the clusters (defined by the links) are displayed horizontally.

A tree representation imposes constraints on the family $T^* = \{x' \mid x \in T\}$ of aspect sets associated with a given set of alternatives. In particular, a tree defines a hierarchical structure on the alternatives in T induced by associating each link α of the tree with the set $T_\alpha = \{x \in T \mid \alpha \in x'\}$ of all alternatives that include or follow from that link. In figure 21.2, for example, $T_\mu = \{$sole, trout$\}$ and $T_\alpha = \{$steak$\}$. It is easy to verify that for any two links α, β in a tree, either $T_\alpha \supset T_\beta$, $T_\beta \supset T_\alpha$, or $T_\alpha \cap T_\beta$ is empty. The constraints implied by the tree greatly restrict the structure under consideration and drastically reduce the number of parameters from $2^n - 2$ (the number of proper nonempty subsets of T) to $2n - 2$ that correspond to the maximal number of links in a tree with n terminal nodes. To appreciate the nature of the constraints, note that the paths that connect any three terminal nodes with the root either all meet at the same node or two paths join at one node and the third path joins them at a higher node, that is, one that is closer to the root. In figure 21.2, for example, steak and roast beef join first, and then lamb joins them later.

This property of trees implies the following inclusion rule: For all x, y, z in T, either $x' \cap y' \supset x' \cap z'$ or $x' \cap z' \supset x' \cap y'$. That is, one out of any two binary intersections of three alternatives includes the other. Equivalently, any subset of T with three elements contains one alternative, say z, such that $z' \cap x' = z' \cap y'$, which in turn is included in $x' \cap y'$. We denote this relation by $(x, y)z$, with or without a comma. Thus, the tree in figure 21.2 is described as ((steak, roast beef) lamb) (sole, trout). The upper portion of figure 21.3 illustrates the inclusion rule by a Venn diagram, and the lower portion of figure 21.3 displays the corresponding tree. A comparison of figure 21.1 and the upper portion of figure 21.3 reveals that under the inclusion rule, two out of the three binary intersections coincide with the triple intersection $(x' \cap z' = y' \cap z' = x' \cap y' \cap z')$, hence the number of parameters or aspect sets reduces in this case from six to four, excluding λ, which represents the aspects shared by all three alternatives. The following elementary result, proved in appendix A, shows that the inclusion rule is not only necessary but also sufficient for representation by a tree.

STRUCTURE THEOREM.   A family $\{x' \mid x \in T\}$ of aspect sets is representable by a tree iff either $x' \cap y' \supset x' \cap z'$ or $x' \cap z' \supset x' \cap y'$ for all x, y, z in T.

When the family $\{x' \mid x \in T\}$ of aspect sets satisfies the inclusion rule, the process of elimination by aspects reduces to elimination by tree (EBT). That is, one selects a link from the tree (with probability that is proportional to its length) and then eliminates all alternatives that do not include the selected link. The same process is then applied to the selected branch until one alternative remains. In figure 21.3, for example, $P(x, \{x, y, z\}) = u(\alpha) + u(\theta)u(\alpha)/[u(\alpha) + u(\beta)]$ and $P(z, \{x, y, z\}) = u(\gamma)$, assuming the measure u is normalized so that $u(\alpha) + u(\beta) + u(\gamma) + u(\theta) = 1$. Elimination by tree, then, is simply the application of elimination by aspects to a tree structure. Note that CRM corresponds to a degenerate tree or a bush with only one internal node—the root.

Hierarchical Elimination

The representation of choice alternatives as a tree suggests an alternative decision model in which the tree is viewed as a hierarchy of choice points.[1] This theory, called

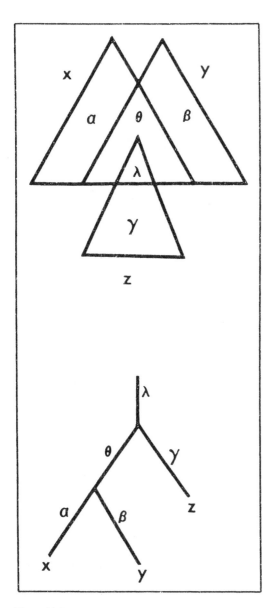

Figure 21.3
An illustration of the inclusion rule $x' \cap y' \supset x' \cap z'$ as a Venn-diagram (above) and as a tree (below).

the *hierarchical elimination model* (HEM), can be described as follows. One begins at the top of the tree and selects first among the major branches or the links that follow directly from the root. One then proceeds to the next choice point at the bottom of the selected link, and the process is repeated until the chosen branch contains a single alternative. The probability of choosing an alternative x from an offered set A is the product of the probabilities of selecting the branches containing x at each stage of the process, and the probability of selecting a branch is proportional to its overall weight. For example, the probability of choosing trout from the choice set presented in figure 21.2 equals the probability of selecting fish over meat multiplied by the probability of choosing trout over sole. Thus, each node in the tree is treated as a choice point, and one proceeds in order from the top to the bottom of the hierarchy.

To define the HEM in a more formal manner, let A_α denote the set of alternatives in A that include the link α, that is, $A_\alpha = \{x \in A \mid \alpha \in x'\}$. Define $\alpha \mid \beta$ if β follows directly from α, that is, $A_\alpha \supset A_\beta$, and $A_\gamma \supset A_\beta$ implies $A_\gamma \supset A_\alpha$. Let $u(\alpha)$ denote the length of α, and let $m(\alpha)$ be the measure or total length of all links that follow from α, including α. In figure 21.3, for example, $0 \mid \alpha$, $0 \mid \beta$, and $m(0) = u(\alpha) + u(\beta) + u(0)$. If T^* is a tree and $A \subset T$, $A^* = \{x' \mid x \in A\}$ is also a tree that is referred to as a subtree of T. Naturally, the relation $\mid$ and the measure u on T^* induce corresponding relations and measures on A^*. Finally, for $B \subset A$, let $P(B, A)$ denote the probability that the alternative selected from A is also an element of B, that is,

$$P(B, A) = \sum_{x \in B} P(x, A).$$

A family of choice probabilities, $P(x, A)$, $x \in A \subset T$, is said to satisfy HEM if there exists a tree T^* with a measure u such that the following three conditions hold:

(a) If $\gamma \mid \beta$ and $\beta \mid \alpha$ then $P(A_\alpha, A_\gamma) = P(A_\alpha, A_\beta) P(A_\beta, A_\gamma)$;

(b) if $\gamma \mid \beta$ and $\gamma \mid \alpha$ then $\dfrac{P(A_\alpha, A_\gamma)}{P(A_\beta, A_\gamma)} = \dfrac{m(\alpha)}{m(\beta)}$, provided $P(A_\beta, A_\gamma) \neq 0$.   (3)

(c) The above conditions also hold for any subtree A^* of T^*, with the induced structure on A^*.

The first condition implies that the probability of selecting x from T is the product of the probabilities of selecting the branches that contain x at each junction. This condition is readily testable, since it is formulated directly in terms of choice probability with no reference to the scale u. The second condition states that the probabilities of selecting one branch rather than another at a given junction are proportional to the weights of the respective branches—defined as the total length of all their links. If we view each junction as a pan balance and the weight of each subtree as mass, then b can be interpreted as a weighing process where the probability of choice among subtrees is proportional to their masses. The third condition ensures that a and b apply not only to the entire tree but also to any subtree obtained by deleting alternatives from T. To avoid complications we assume that any two alternatives have some distinctive aspect with a nonzero measure, however small.

The notion of hierarchical elimination and the idea of elimination by tree represent different comceptions of the choice process that assume a tree structure. EBT describes $P(x, A)$ as a weighted sum of the probabilities $P(x, A_\alpha)$ of selecting x from the various subsets of A. In HEM, on the other hand, $P(x, A)$ is expressed as a product of the probabilities $P(A_\alpha, A_\beta)$, $\beta \mid \alpha$ of selecting a subtree containing x at each level in the hierarchy. Compare, for example, the two formulas for the probability of choosing steak from the set of entrees T displayed in figure 21.2. To simplify the notation, we suppress the scale u and write α for $u(\alpha)$, and so on. Furthermore, the scale is normalized so that $\alpha + \beta + \gamma + \delta + \rho + \theta + \lambda + \mu = 1$. According to EBT, then

$$P(\text{Steak}, T) = \alpha + \theta\left(\frac{\alpha}{\alpha + \beta}\right) + \lambda\left[\left(\frac{\alpha}{\alpha + \beta + \gamma + \theta}\right) + \left(\frac{\theta}{\alpha + \beta + \gamma + \theta}\right) \times \left(\frac{\alpha}{\alpha + \beta}\right)\right],$$

whereas according to HEM,

$$P(\text{Steak}, T) = (\alpha + \beta + \gamma + \theta + \lambda) \times \left(\frac{\alpha + \beta + \theta}{\alpha + \beta + \gamma + \theta}\right) \times \left(\frac{\alpha}{\alpha + \beta}\right).$$

The difference in form reflects a difference in processing strategy. EBT assumes free access; that is, each aspect can be selected (as a basis for elimination) at any stage of the process. On the other hand, HEM assumes sequential access; that is, aspects are considered in a fixed hierarchical fashion. The constrast between models based on random and on sequential access can also be found in theoretical analyses of memory and pattern recognition.

It would appear that EBT is applicable to decisions, such as the selection of a restaurant or the choice of a movie, for which there is no fixed sequence of choice points, whereas HEM seems appropriate for decisions that induce a natural hierarchy of choice points. A student who has to decide what to do after graduation, for example, is more likely to consider the alternatives in a hierarchical manner. That is, first decide whether to go to graduate school, travel, or take a job, and only then evaluate in detail the relevant alternatives, e.g., graduate schools, travel plans, or job opportunities. The preceding discussion suggests that EBT and HEM capture different decision strategies that might be followed in different situations. However, the following theorem establishes a rather surprising result that despite the difference in mathematical form and psychological interpretation, the two models are actually equivalent.

EQUIVALENCE THEOREM.   EBT and HEM are equivalent; that is, any set of choice probabilities satisfies one model iff it satisfies the other.

The proof of the equivalence theorem is given in appendix B. It shows that, given a tree T^* with a measure u, EBT and HEM yield identical choice probabilities, and hence it is impossible to discriminate between these strategies on the basis of these data alone. It might be possible, however, that other data such as verbal protocols, reaction time, or eye movements can be used to distinguish between the two strategies. To avoid confusion, we shall use the term *preference tree* or *pretree* to denote the choice probabilities generated by EBT or by HEM, irrespective of the particular strategy.

An immediate corollary of the equivalence of EBT and HEM is that any alternating strategy consisting of a mixture of EBT is also equivalent to them. For example, a person may choose a restaurant according to EBT and select an entree according to HEM, or vice versa. It is a remarkable fact that all the various strategies obtained by alternating EBT and HEM yield identical choice probabilities. Thus, pretree provides a versatile representation of choice that is compatible with both random-access and sequential-access strategies.

Consequences

We turn now to discuss general properties and testable consequences of the tree model, starting with the similarity effect. There are two distinct ways in which the similarity between alternatives affects choice probability. First, similarity, or the presence of common aspects, creates statistical dependence among alternatives. If x has more in common with y than with z, for example, then the addition of x to the set $\{z, y\}$ tends to hurt the similar alternative y more than the less similar one z. In the extreme case in which x is almost identical to y, the addition of x will divide the probability of choosing y by two and leave the probability of choosing z unchanged. Second, similarity facilitates comparison. If x is more similar to y than to z and $P(y, z) = \frac{1}{2}$, then $P(x, z)$ will be less extreme than $P(x, y)$, that is, closer to $\frac{1}{2}$. Thus, the more similar pair generally yields a more extreme choice probability because similarity facilitates the comparison between the alternatives.

To illustrate the effects of similarity, consider a hypothetical example of choice among transportation modes. Suppose the available alternatives include two airlines, a_1 and a_2, and two trains, t_1 and t_2. Suppose further that there is no reason to prefer one airline over the other, but train t_2 has a very slight but clear advantage over t_1, since it makes one less stop along the way. Because the train is more comfortable but the plane is faster, suppose one is undecided whether to fly or take a train. Hence,

$$P(a_1, a_2) = \tfrac{1}{2}, \quad P(t_2, t_1) = 1,$$

and

$$P(a_1, t_1) = P(a_2, t_1) = \tfrac{1}{2}.$$

Let $P(x, xyz)$ denote $P(x, \{x, y, z\})$. It follows at once from CRM that $P(t_1, t_1 a_1 a_2) = \tfrac{1}{3}$. Introspection suggests, however, that the selection from $\{t_1, a_1, a_2\}$ is likely to be viewed as a choice between a train and a plane, so a_1 and a_2 are treated as one alternative that is compared with t_1. Consequently, $P(t_1, t_1 a_1 a_2)$ will be close to $\tfrac{1}{2}$, and the two other trinary choice probabilities will be close to $\tfrac{1}{4}$. The commonality between a_1 and a_2, therefore, produces a statistical dependence that increases the relative advantage of the odd alternative t_1.

Furthermore, CRM implies that if two alternatives are equivalent in one context, then they are substitutable in any context. That is, it should be possible to substitute one for the other without changing choice probability. Since $P(a_1, t_1) = \tfrac{1}{2}$ and $P(t_2, t_1) = 1$, we obtain by substitution $P(t_2, a_1) = 1$. This result, however, seems implausible because the slight, albeit definite, advantage of t_2 over t_1 is not likely to eliminate all conflict in the choice between t_2 and a_1. $P(t_2, a_1)$, therefore, is expected to be significantly smaller than 1, contrary to CRM. (Further discussions of this problem, originally presented by Debreu, 1960, can be found in Luce and Suppes, 1965, pp. 334–335; and Tversky, 1972b, pp. 282–284.)

Figure 21.4 represents the above example as a preference tree. It is easy to verify that according to the tree model with $\alpha = \beta$ and $\theta + \alpha = \delta$, $P(a_1, a_2) = P(t_1, a_1) = P(t_1, a_2) = \tfrac{1}{2}$, $P(t_2, t_1) = 1$, but $P(t_2, a_2) = (\gamma + \delta)/(\gamma + 2\delta)$, which approaches $\tfrac{1}{2}$ as γ approaches 0. Furthermore, $P(t_1, t_1 a_1 a_2) = \delta/(2\delta + \alpha)$, which approaches $\tfrac{1}{2}$ as α approaches 0. Hence the tree model provides a simple and parsimonious account of the similarity effects that are incompatible with CRM.

The effects of similarity on choice probability can also be explained by a Thurstonian or a random utility model such as the additive-random-aspect model (Tversky, 1972a). In this development each aspect α is represented by a random variable $\mathbf{V}_\alpha$, each x in T is represented by the random variable $\mathbf{V}_x = \sum_{\alpha \in x'} \mathbf{V}_\alpha$ and, following the random utility model, $P(x, A) = P(\mathbf{V}_x > \mathbf{V}_y \text{ for all } y \in A)$. This model, like EBA,

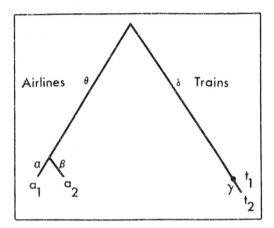

Figure 21.4
A preference tree for the choice among modes of transportation.

accounts for the observed dependence among the alternatives in terms of their common aspects, which produce positive correlations among the respective random variables. An additive-random-aspect model differs from the present development in that the aspects are represented by random variables rather than by constants and choice is described as a comparison of sums of random variables rather than as a sequential elimination process. Nevertheless, it was shown (Tversky, 1972a) that EBA, and hence pretree, is also expressible as a random utility model, though not necessarily an additive one. A random utility analogue of the tree model, developed by McFadden (reference note 1), is discussed later.

The following testable properties were derived from EBA (see Sattath & Tversky, 1976; Tversky, 1972a, 1972b). Since EBT is a special case of EBA, these properties apply to the tree model as well.

Moderate stochastic transitivity   If $P(x,y) \geq \frac{1}{2}$ and $P(y,z) \geq \frac{1}{2}$, then $P(x,z) \geq \min(P(x,y), P(y,z))$. This is a probabilistic form of the transitivity assumption. Note that the tree model does not entail the stronger property in which *min* is replaced by *max*.

Regularity $P(x,A) \geq P(x,A \cup B)$. The probability of selecting x from a given offered set cannot be increased by enlarging that set.

The multiplicative inequality $P(x, A \cap B) \geq P(x,A)P(x,B)$. The probability of selecting x from $A \cap B$ is at least as large as the probability of choosing x from both A and B in two independent choices.

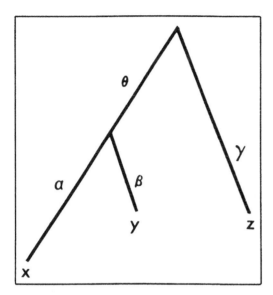

Figure 21.5
A preference tree for three alternatives, x, y, and z.

The properties discussed so far follow from the general EBA model. We turn now to some new properties of binary choice probabilities that characterize the tree model. To simplify the exposition, we introduce the probability ratio $R(x, y) = P(x,y)/P(y,x)$ and restrict the discussion to the case in which $P(x,y) \neq 0$ so that $R(x, y)$ is always well defined. The results can be readily extended to deal with choice probabilities that equal 0 or 1. Consider, first, the case of three alternatives, and note that any subtree of three elements has the form portrayed in figure 21.5 except for the permutation of the alternatives and the possibility of vanishing links. We use the parentheses notation to describe the structure of the tree; for example, the tree in figure 21.5 is described by $(xy)z$ and the tree in figure 21.4 by $(a_1 a_2)(t_1 t_2)$.

Using the notation of figure 21.5, it follows at once that $R(x, y) = \alpha/\beta$ is more extreme (i.e., further from 1) than $R(x, z)/R(y, z) = (\alpha + \theta)/(\beta + \theta)$. Hence any three elements that form a subtree $(xy)z$ satisfy the following trinary condition.

If $R(x, y) \geq 1$, then

$$R(x, y) \geq \frac{R(x, z)}{R(y, z)} \geq 1, \tag{4}$$

where a strict inequality in the hypothesis implies strict inequalities in the conclusion and an equality in the hypothesis implies equalities in the conclusion.

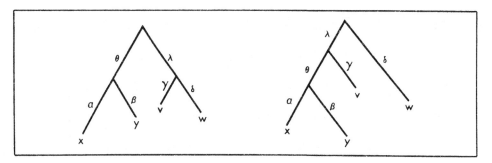

Figure 21.6
Preference trees for four alternatives, x, y, v, and w.

The trinary condition (equation 4) reflects the similarity hypothesis in that the commonality between alternatives enhances their discriminability. This is seen most clearly in the case where $\theta > 0$, $\alpha > \beta$, and $\beta + \theta = \gamma$, that is, $R(x, y) > 1$ and $R(y, z) = 1$. (See figure 21.5.) According to the trinary condition, $R(x, y) = \alpha/\beta > (\alpha + \theta)/(\beta + \theta) = R(x, z)$. Although y and z are pairwise equivalent, $P(x, y)$ exceeds $P(x, z)$ because x shares more aspects with y than with z. Note that when θ vanishes, $R(x, y) = R(x, z)/R(y, z)$, as required by CRM. In this case, where $(xy)z$, $(xz)y$, and $(zy)x$ all hold, we omit the parentheses altogether and write xyz.

Next, let us consider sets of four alternatives. It is easy to verify that up to permutations of alternatives, any subtree of four elements has one of the two forms displayed in figure 21.6, including degenerate forms with one or more vanishing links. It follows readily that in the tree $(xy)(vw)$, portrayed in the left portion of figure 21.6,

$$\frac{R(x,v)}{R(y,v)} = \frac{(\alpha+\theta)/(\gamma+\lambda)}{(\beta+\theta)/(\gamma+\lambda)} = \frac{(\alpha+\theta)/(\delta+\lambda)}{(\beta+\theta)/(\delta+\lambda)} = \frac{R(x,w)}{R(y,w)}. \tag{5}$$

If we interpret $R(x, v)/R(y, v)$ as an indirect measure of preference for x over y, measured relative to a standard v, then the above quarternary condition asserts that this measure is the same for different standards (v and w) provided that the pairs (x, y) and (v, w) belong to distinct clusters.

If the relation among the four alternatives under consideration has the form depicted at the right portion of figure 21.6, that is $((xy)v)w$ then the following quarternary condition holds.

$$\frac{R(x,v) - R(y,v)}{R(x,w) - R(y,w)} = \frac{(\alpha-\beta)/\gamma}{(\alpha-\beta)/\delta} = \frac{(\alpha+\theta-\gamma)/\gamma}{(\alpha+\theta-\gamma)/\delta} = \frac{R(x,v) - R(v,v)}{R(x,w) - R(v,w)}. \tag{6}$$

Note that under CRM the quarternary conditions hold for any four alternatives.

At this point, the reader may suspect that the consideration of more elaborate tree structures involving larger sets of alternatives will yield additional independent consequences. However, the following theorem shows that the trinary and the quarternary conditions are not only necessary but are also sufficient to ensure the representation of *binary* choice probabilities as a preference tree.

REPRESENTATION THEOREM.   A set of nonzero binary choice probabilities satisfies the tree model with a given structure iff the trinary (equation 4) and the quarternary (equations 5 and 6) conditions are satisfied relative to that structure.

The theorem shows that if equations 4, 5, and 6 are satisfied relative to some tree structure, then there exists a ratio scale u defined on that structure such that

$$P(x, y) = \frac{u(x' - y')}{u(x' - y') + u(y' - x')}$$

and

$$R(x, y) = \frac{u(x' - y')}{u(y' - x')}.$$

Recall that $u(x' - y')$ is the measure of the aspects of x that are not included in y or the length of the path from the terminal node associated with x to the meeting point of the paths from x and y to the root.

The proof of the representation theorem is presented in appendix C. This result shows, in effect, how to construct a preference tree from binary choice probabilities whenever the necessary conditions hold. The trinary and quarternary conditions are readily testable, given any specified tree structure. Moreover, they can be used to determine which structure, if any, is compatible with the data. Recall that at least one permutation of every triple must satisfy equation 4 and at least one permutation of every quadruple must satisfy equation 5 or equation 6. Hence, by finding the appropriate permutations of all triples and quadruples, any tree structure that is compatible with the data will emerge. It can be verified that the scale values (i.e., the lengths of the links associated with a particular tree structure) are uniquely determined up to an arbitrary unit of measurement whenever binary choice probabilities are not one half. The tree structure, however, is not always unique. That is, a given set of binary choice probabilities could be compatible with more than one tree structure. An example of this kind is presented in appendix D, along with a proof of the proposition that the tree structure is uniquely determined by the set of binary and trinary choice probabilities.

Furthermore, if both binary and trinary choice probabilities are available, they must satisfy the following conditions. Suppose the tree model holds with $(xy)z$ (see figure 21.5), then

$$\frac{P(x,z)}{P(z,x)} = \frac{\alpha + 0}{\gamma} \geq \frac{\alpha + 0\alpha/(\alpha + \beta)}{\gamma} = \frac{P(x,xyz)}{P(z,xyz)} \tag{7}$$

and

$$\frac{P(x,y)}{P(y,x)} = \frac{\alpha}{\beta} = \frac{\alpha + 0\alpha/(\alpha + \beta)}{\beta + 0\beta/(\alpha + \beta)} = \frac{P(x,xyz)}{P(y,xyz)}, \tag{8}$$

provided all choice probabilities are nonzero. Thus, according to the tree model with $(xy)z$, the constant-ratio rule (equation 8) holds for the adjacent pair (x,y), but not for the split pair (x,z). Note that this rule is violated by equation 7 in the direction implied by the similarity hypothesis for $(xy)z$. Since y is closer to x than to z in that structure (in the sense that $y' \cap x' \supset y' \cap z'$), the addition of y to the set $\{x,z\}$ reduces the probability of choosing x proportionally more than the probability of choosing z. On the other hand, since z is equally distant from x and from y (in the sense that $x' \cap z' = y' \cap z'$), the addition of z to the set $\{x,y\}$ reduces the probabilities of choosing x and y by the same factor.

Aggregate Probabilities

So far, we have modeled the process by which an individual chooses among alternatives. Because of the difficulties in obtaining independent repeated choices from the same individual, most available data consist of the proportions of individuals who selected the various alternatives, referred to as group data or aggregate probabilities. It should be emphasized that these data do not pertain to group decision making, they merely characterize the aggregate preferences of different individuals.

It is well-known that most probabilistic models for individual choice (including CRM and EBA) are not preserved by aggregation. That is, group probabilities could violate the model even though each individual satisfies it, and vice versa. Consider, for instance, the case of three individuals, 1, 2, 3, and three alternatives, x, y, z. Suppose the observed choice probabilities $P(x,y)$, $P(y,z)$, and $P(z,x)$ are, respectively, .75, .75, and .15 for individual 1; .15, .75, and .75 for individual 2; and .75, .15, and .75 for individual 3. The individual choice probabilities all satisfy EBA, but the expected aggregate probabilities .55, .55, and .55, respectively, violate EBA. Hence, the validity of EBA as a model for individual choice is neither necessary nor sufficient for its validity as an aggregate model. Nevertheless, we contend that similar principles govern both types of choice data and propose a new interpretation of EBA as an aggregate model.

Suppose each individual chooses in accordance with the following sequential elimination rule. Given an offered set A, select some (nonempty) subset of A, say B, and eliminate all the alternatives that do not belong to B. Repeat the process until the selected subset consists of a single alternative. Let $Q_A(B)$ be the proportion of subjects who first select B when presented with the offered set A, that is, the proportion of subjects who eliminate all elements of $A - B$ in the first stage. Naturally,

$$\sum_{B_i \subset A} Q_A(B_i) = 1,$$

and $Q_A(A) = 1$ iff A consists of a single alternative. Note that $Q_A(B)$ is an elimination probability, not a choice probability. The two constructs are related via the following equation.

$$P(x, A) = \sum_{B_i \subset A} Q_A(B_i) P(x, B_i). \tag{9}$$

Thus, the proportion of subjects who choose x from A is obtained by summing, over all proper subsets B_i of A, the proportion of individuals who first select B_i multiplied by the proportion of subjects who choose x from the selected subset. This general elimination model, by itself, does not restrict the observed choice probabilities because we can always set $Q_A(B) = P(x, A)$, if $B = \{x\}$, and $Q_A(B) = 0$ otherwise. Nevertheless, it provides a method for characterizing probabilistic choice models in terms of the constraints they impose on the elimination probabilities.

A family of elimination probabilities, $Q_A(B)$, $B \subset A \subset T$, satisfies proportionality iff for all A, B, C, B_i, C_j in T,

$$\frac{Q_A(B)}{Q_A(C)} = \frac{\sum Q_T(B_i)}{\sum Q_T(C_j)}, \tag{10}$$

where the summations range, respectively, over all subsets B_i, C_j of T such that $B_i \cap A = B$ and $C_j \cap A = C$. It is assumed that the denominators are either both positive or both zero. This condition implies that for any $A \subset T$, the values of Q_A are computable from the values of Q_T. More specifically, the percentage of subjects who first select B when presented with the offered set A is proportional to the percentage of subjects presented with the total set T who first select any subset B_i that includes, in addition to B, only elements that do not belong to A.

To illustrate the proportionality condition, consider the choice among entrees. Let $T = \{r, s, t\}$ and $A = \{r, t\}$, where r, s, and t denote, respectively, roast beef, steak, and trout. According to proportionality, therefore,

$$\frac{Q_A(r)}{Q_A(t)} = \frac{Q_T(r) + Q_T(r, s)}{Q_T(t) + Q_T(t, s)}.$$

Note that in the binary case, where $A = \{r, t\}$, $Q_A(r) = P(r, A) = P(r, t)$.

The rationale behind the proportionality condition is the assumption that upon restricting the offered set from T to A, all individuals who first selected $B \cup C$ from T, $C \subset T - A$, will now select B from A, since the alternatives of C are no longer available. For example, those who first selected $\{r, s\}$ from T will select roast beef when restricted to A because now steak is not on the menu. The following theorem shows that the (aggregate) process described above is compatible with EBA.

AGGREGATION THEOREM.   A set of aggregate choice probabilities on T is compatible with EBA iff there exist elimination probabilities on T that satisfy equations 9 and 10.

The proof of this theorem is readily reduced to earlier results. (See the appendix in Tversky, 1972b, and theorem 2 in Tversky, 1972a.) They show that if equation 9 and equation 10 hold, then

$$P(x, A) = \frac{\sum Q(B_i) P(x, A \cap B_i)}{\sum Q(B_i)},$$

where $Q(B_i) = Q_T(B_i)$ and the summations range over all $B_i \subset T$ such that $B_i \cap A$ is nonempty. This form, in turn, is shown to be equivalent to EBA. Hence, the aggregation theorem provides a new interpretation of EBA as a model for group data.

It is instructive to compare the above version of the EBA model to the original version defined in equation 1. First, note that the scale $Q(B)$ is not a measure of the overall value of the alternatives of B. Rather, it reflects the degree to which they form a good cluster, as evinced by the proportion of subjects who first selected B when presented with T. The counterpart of $Q(B)$ in the original version of the EBA model is $u(\bar{B})$, the measure of the aspects that belong to *all* alternatives of B and do not belong to *any* alternative in $T - B$.

The individual version of the EBA model assumes that at any point in time, one has a fixed ordering of the relevant aspect sets, which, in turn, induces a (lexicographic) ordering of the available alternatives. However, at a different point in time, one may be in a different state of mind that yields different ordering of aspects and alternatives. Indeed, the stochastic component was introduced into the model to accommodate such momentary fluctuations. The new aggregate version of EBA assumes that each individual has a fixed ordering of the relevant aspect sets, and the stochastic component of the model is associated with differences between individuals rather than with changes within an individual. Hence, the former version explains choice probabilities in terms of an intraindividual distribution of states of mind, whereas the latter version explains the data in terms of an interindividual distribution of tastes.

The EBA model may provide a useful model of aggregate data because the same principles that give rise to EBA as a model of individual choice appear to apply to group data. As a case in point, let us reexamine the similarity effect using the transportation problem discussed earlier. Suppose the group is divided equally between the train t_1 and the plane a_1 and is also equally divided between the two airlines a_1 and a_2. Hence,

$$P(t_1, a_1) = P(a_1, a_2) = \tfrac{1}{2}.$$

We propose that the proportion of individuals who choose the train t_1 from the offered set $\{t_1, a_1, a_2\}$ lies between $\tfrac{1}{2}$ and $\tfrac{1}{3}$ because the addition of a_2 to $\{t_1, a_1\}$ is likely to affect those who chose a_1 more than those who chose t_1. More generally, the addition of a new alternative or product (e.g., a low-tar cigarette or a liberal candidate) hurts similar alternatives (e.g., other low-tar cigarettes and other liberal candidates) more than less similar alternatives.

Furthermore, as in the case of individual choice, the similarity between options appears to enhance the discrimination between them. Suppose that each individual prefers train t_2 over train t_1, since it is slightly faster. Suppose further that the group is equally divided between a_1 and t_1, so $P(a_1, t_1) = \tfrac{1}{2}$. Contrary to CRM, which implies $P(t_2, a_1) = 1$, we predict that $P(t_2, a_1)$ is likely to be between $\tfrac{1}{2}$ and 1 because many of those who prefer a_1 over t_1 are not likely to switch from a plane to a train because of the slight, albeit clear, advantage of the faster train. Since the same correlational pattern emerges from both individual and group data, the EBA model may be applicable to both, although the assumptions and the parameters of the model have different interpretations in the two cases.

Consider, for example, the assumption that the alternative set $T = \{a_1, a_2, t_1\}$ in the transportation problem has a tree structure $(a_1 a_2)t_1$. In the individual version, the tree assumption implies that any aspect shared by the train and any one of the airlines is also shared by the other airline. In the aggregate case, the tree assumption entails that both $Q_T(a_1, t_1)$ and $Q_T(a_2, t_1)$ vanish; that is, nobody eliminates from T

one airline only. Hence, if all individuals share the same tree structure but not necessarily the same preferences, the aggregate data will generally exhibit the same qualitative structure. The actual measure derived from aggregate data, however, does not relate to the measures derived from individual data in any simple manner.

Applications

In this section we apply the tree model to several sets of individual and aggregate choice probabilities reported in the literature, construct tree representations for these data, and test pretree against CRM. As was demonstrated in the previous section, the trinary and the quarternary conditions provide necessary and sufficient conditions for the representation of binary choice probabilities as a preference tree. For error-free data, therefore, these conditions can readily be applied to find a tree structure that is compatible with the data. Since data are fallible, however, the construction of the most appropriate tree structure, the estimation of link lengths, and the evaluation of the adequacy of the tree model pose nontrivial computational and statistical problems.

In this article we do not develop a comprehensive solution to the construction, estimation, and evaluation problems. Instead, we rely on independent judgments (e.g., similarity data) for the construction of the tree and employ standard iterative maximization methods to estimate its parameters. To evaluate goodness of fit, we test the tree model, assuming the hypothesized tree structure, against the binary version of Luce's CRM.

It has been shown by Luce (1959) that the binary CRM, according to which $P(x, y) = v(x)/(v(x) + v(y))$, is essentially equivalent to the following product rule:

$$P(x, y)P(y, z)P(z, x) = P(x, z)P(z, y)P(y, x),$$

that is,

$$R(x, y)R(y, z)R(z, x) = 1. \tag{11}$$

Thus, any two intransitive cycles through the same set of alternatives are equiprobable. On the other hand, the trinary condition (equation 4) yields

$$\text{If } P(x, y) > \tfrac{1}{2} \text{ and } (xy)z, \quad \text{then} \quad R(x, y)R(y, z)R(z, x) > 1, \tag{12}$$

or

$$P(x, y)P(y, z)P(z, x) > P(x, z)P(z, y)P(y, x).$$

Any hypothesized tree structure, therefore, can be examined to test whether the product rule is violated in the predicted direction.

The analysis of the data proceeds as follows. We start with a given set of individual or collective pair comparison data along with a hypothesized tree structure, derived from a priori considerations or inferred from other data. Maximum likelihood estimates for both CRM and pretree are obtained using Chandler's (1969) iterative program (STEPIT), and the two models are compared via a likelihood ratio test. In addition, we perform an estimate-free comparison of the two models by contrasting the product rule (equation 11) and the trinary inequality (equation 12).

Choice between Celebrities

Rumelhart and Greeno (1971) investigated the effects of similarity on choice probability and compared the choice models of Luce (1959) and Restle (1961). The stimuli were nine celebrities including three politicians (L. B. Johnson, Harold Wilson, Charles De-Gaulle), three athletes (Johnny Unitas, Carl Yastrzemski, A. J. Foyt), and three movie stars (Brigitte Bardot, Elizabeth Taylor, Sophia Loren). The subjects ($N = 234$) were presented with all 36 pairs of names and were instructed to choose for each pair "the person with whom they would rather spend an hour discussing a topic of their choosing" (p. 372).

On the basis of a chi-square test for goodness of fit applied to the aggregate choice probabilities, Rumelhart and Greeno (1971) were able to reject Luce's model, $\chi^2(28) = 78.2$, $p < .001$, but not a particular version of Restle's model, $\chi^2(19) = 21.9$, $p > .25$. Recall that Restle's model coincides with the binary form of the EBA model.

The list of celebrities used in this study naturally suggests the following tree structure with three branches corresponding to the three different occupations represented in the list: (LBJ, HW, CDG) (JU, CY, AJF) (BB, ET, SL). The estimates of the parameters of the tree,[2] displayed in figure 21.7, are identical to those obtained by Edgell, Geisler, and Zinnes (1973), who corrected the procedure used by Rumelhart and Greeno (1971) and proposed a simplification of the model that amounts to the above tree structure. The tree model appears to fit the data well, $\chi^2(25) = 30.0$, $p > .20$, although it has only three more parameters than Luce's model.

Since pretree includes CRM, the likelihood ratio test can be used to test and compare them. The test is based on the fact that if model 1 is valid and includes model 2, then under the standard assumptions, $-2\ ln(L_1/L_2)$ has a chi-square distribution with $d_1 - d_2$ degree of freedom, where L_1 and L_2 denote the likelihood functions of model 1 and model 2 and d_1 and d_2 denote the respective numbers of parameters. If the inclusive model is saturated, that is, imposes no constraints, then the above test is

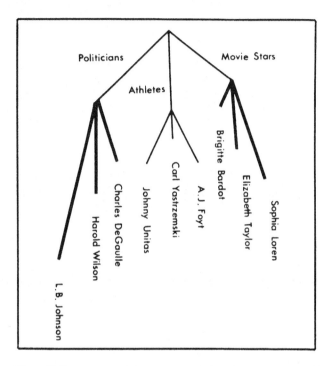

Figure 21.7
Preference tree for choice among celebrities.

equivalent to the common chi-square test for goodness of fit. When the likelihood ratio test is applied to the present data, CRM is rejected in favor of pretree, $\chi^2(3) = 48.2$, $p < .001$. The average absolute deviation between predicted and observed probabilities is .036 for CRM and .023 for pretree.

It should be noted (see Falmagne, reference note 2) that the test statistics for pretree do not have an exact chi-square distribution because the parameter space associated with the model is constrained not only by the equations implied by the quarternary conditions but also by the trinary inequality. The result, however, is a stricter test of pretree, since the inequalities imposed on the solution can only reduce goodness of fit.

Since the product rule (equation 11) and the trinary inequality (equation 12) are the key binary properties that give rise, respectively, to CRM and pretree, it is instructive to compare them directly. Using the tree structure presented in figure 21.7, the trinary inequality applies in $9 \times 6 = 54$ triples, and it is satisfied in 89% of the cases. Because the various triples are not independent, no simple statistical test is readily available. To obtain some indication about the size of the effect, we computed the value of $R(xyz) = R(x, y)R(y, z)R(z, x)$ for all triples satisfying $(xy)z$ and $R(x, y) > 1$. The median of these values equals 1.40, and the interquartile range is 1.13–1.68. Recall that under CRM the trinary inequality is expected to hold in 50% of the cases and the median $R(xyz)$ should equal one. The summary statistics for all the studies in this section are presented in table 21.1.

Political Choice

The next three data sets were obtained from Lennart Sjöberg, who collected both similarity and preference data for several sets of stimuli and showed a positive correlation between interstimulus distances (derived from multi-dimensional scaling) and the standard deviation of utility differences (derived from a Thurstonian model). Sjöberg (1977) and Sjöberg and Capozza (1975) conducted parallel studies of preferences for Swedish and Italian political parties. In these experiments 215 Swedish students and 195 Italian students were presented with all pairs of the seven leading Swedish and Italian parties, respectively. The subjects first rated the similarity between all 21 pairs of parties on a scale from 1 to 9 and then indicated for each pair which party they preferred. In addition, the subjects were presented with all 35 triples of parties and were asked to choose one party from each triple.

The average similarities between the parties were first used to construct an additive similarity tree according to the ADDTREE method developed by Sattath and Tversky (1977). In this construction, which generalizes the familiar hierarchical clustering scheme, the stimuli are represented as terminal nodes in a tree so that the dissimilarity between stimuli corresponds to the length of the path that joins them. For illustration, we present in figure 21.8 the ADDTREE solution for the similarities between the Swedish parties. The product-moment correlation between rated similarities and path length is $-.96$. Assuming the tree structure derived from ADDTREE, Chandler's (1969) STEPIT program was employed to search for maximum likelihood estimates of the parameters of pretree, using the observed choice probabilities. The obtained preference tree for the Swedish data is presented in figure 21.9, and the preference tree for the Italian data is presented in figure 21.10.

Several comments about the relations between similarity and preference trees are in order. First, the rules for computing dissimilarity and preference from a given tree are different. The dissimilarity between x and y is represented by the length of the path (i.e., the sum of the links) that connects x and y, and the degree of preference $R(x, y)$ is represented by the ratio of the respective paths. Second, the numerical estimates of the links in the two representations tend to differ systematically. In gen-

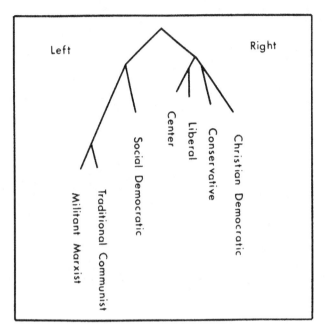

Figure 21.8
Additive tree (ADDTREE) representation of the similarities between Swedish political parties.

eral, the distances between the root and the terminal nodes vary much more in a preference tree (due to the presence of extreme choice probabilities) than in a similarity tree. Furthermore, some links that appear in the similarity tree sometimes vanish in the estimation of pretree (as can be seen by comparing figures 21.8 and 21.9), indicating the presence of aspects that affect judged similarity but not choice probability. Third, the root in a similarity tree is essentially arbitrary, since the distance between nodes is unaffected by the choice of root. The probability of choice in pretree, however, is highly sensitive to the choice of a root. Consequently, several alternative roots were tried and the best-fitting structure was selected in each case.

Tests of goodness of fit indicate that pretree provides an excellent account of the Swedish data, $\chi^2(11) = 5.8$, $p > .5$, with an average absolute deviation of .012, compared with $\chi^2(15) = 49.1$, $p < .001$, with an average absolute deviation of .038 for CRM. Pretree also provides a reasonable account of the Italian data, $\chi^2(11) = 19.5$, $p > .05$, with an average absolute deviation of .023, compared with $\chi^2(15) = 67.6$, $p < .001$, with an average absolute deviation of .042 for CRM. The applications of the likelihood ratio test indicate that pretree fits these data signifi-

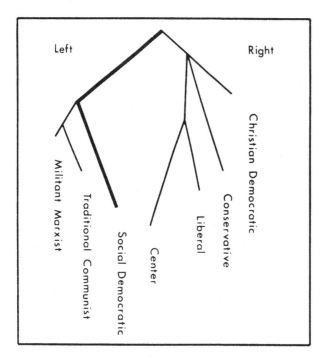

Figure 21.9
Preference tree for choice among Swedish political parties.

cantly better than CRM; the test statistics are $\chi^2(4) = 43.3$, $p < .001$, for the Swedish data and $\chi^2(4) = 48.1$, $p < .001$, for the Italian data. Furthermore, for the Swedish data, the trinary inequality is satisfied in 96% of the cases ($N = 23$), the median $R(xyz)$ equals 1.73, and the interquartile range is 1.38–2.27. For the Italian data, the trinary inequality is satisfied in 78% of the cases ($N = 18$), the median $R(xyz)$ equals 1.74, and the interquartile range is .93–2.78.

The availability of both binary and trinary probabilities in the political studies permitted an additional test of pretree. Recall from equation 7 that the tree model implies

$$\frac{P(x,z)}{P(z,x)} > \frac{P(x,xyz)}{P(z,xyz)}, \quad \text{provided } (xy)z,$$

whereas CRM implies that the two ratios are equal. For the Swedish data, the above inequality is satisfied in 87% of the cases ($N = 46$), the median $P(x,z)P(z,xyz)/$

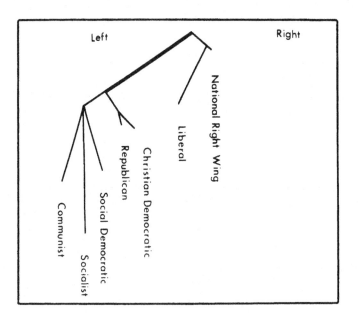

Figure 21.10
Preference tree for choice among Italian political parties.

$P(z, x)P(x, xyz)$ equals 1.28, and the interquartile range is 1.12–1.64. For the Italian data, the inequality is satisfied in 81% of the cases ($N = 36$), the median of the above product ratio equals 1.19, and the interquartile range is .86–2.28. Note that under CRM

$$P(x, z)P(z, xyz)/P(z, x)P(x, xyz) = u(x)u(z)/u(z)u(x) = 1.$$

Choice between Academic Disciplines

In a third study conducted by Sjöberg (1977), the alternatives consisted of the following 12 academic disciplines that comprise the social science program at the University of Göteborg in Göteborg, Sweden: psychology, education, sociology, anthropology, geography, political science, law, economic history, economics, business administration, statistics, and computer science. A group of 85 students from that university first rated the similarity between all pairs of disciplines on a 9-point scale and then indicated for each of the 66 pairs the discipline they preferred.

As in the two preceding analyses, the tree structure was obtained via ADDTREE, and STEPIT was employed to search for maximum likelihood estimates of the parameters.

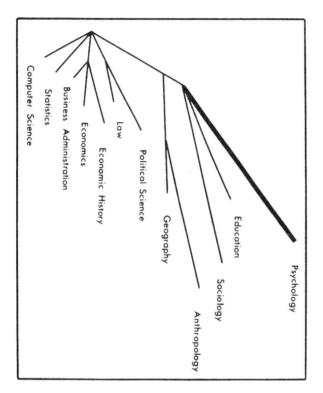

Figure 21.11
Preference tree for choice among social sciences.

The resulting preference tree for the choice between the 12 social sciences is presented in figure 21.11.

A chi-square test for goodness of fit yields $\chi^2(50) = 45.5$, $p > .25$, for pretree, compared with $\chi^2(55) = 69.1$, $p > .05$, for CRM, and the likelihood ratio test rejects CRM in favor of pretree, $\chi^2(5) = 23.6$, $p < .001$. The average absolute deviation between predicted and observed probabilities is .025 for pretree and .035 for CRM. Finally, the trinary inequality is satisfied in 84% of the cases ($N = 86$), the median $R(xyz)$ equals 1.52, and the interquartile range is 1.21–1.86.

Choice between Shades of Gray

In a classic study of unfolding theory, Coombs (1958) used as stimuli 12 patches of gray that varied in brightness. The subjects were presented with all possible sets of 4 stimuli and were asked to rank them from the most to the least representative gray.

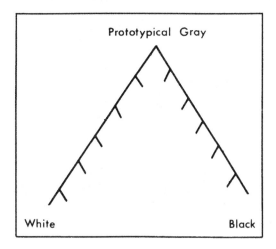

Figure 21.12
A schematic preference tree for the choice between shades of gray.

Binary choice probabilities were estimated for each subject by the proportion of rank orders in which one stimulus was ranked above the other. The data provided strong support for Coomb's probabilistic unfolding model, in which the stimuli are represented as random variables and the derived choice probabilities reflect momentary fluctuations in one's perceptions of the stimuli as well as in one's notion of the ideal gray.

To represent Coombs' data as a tree, consider a line representing variation in brightness (with white and black at the two endpoints) that is folded in the middle at a point corresponding to the prototypical gray. The stimuli can now be represented as small branches stemming from this folded line (see figure 21.12). Because of the large number of zeros and ones in these data, we did not attempt to estimate the tree. Instead, we inferred from the data the characteristic folding point of each subject and used the induced tree structure to compare, separately for each subject, the trinary inequality against the product rule, letting $P(x, y)$ denote the probability that x is judged to be farther than y from the prototypical gray. Triples involving zero probability were excluded from the analysis. The results for each one of the four subjects, presented in the bottom part of table 21.1, show that the product rule (equation 11) is violated in the manner implied by the trinary inequality (equation 12).

Table 21.1 summarizes the analyses of the studies discussed in this section. The left-hand part of the table describes the statistics for the trinary inequality, where N is the number of tested triples, π is the percentage of triples that confirm the trinary

Table 21.1
Summary Statistics for the Comparison of the Constant-Ratio Model (CRM) and Pretree

Study	Trinary inequality statistics					CRM			Pretree			Difference	
	N	π	R	R_1	R_3	d	χ^2	df	d	χ^2	df	χ^2	df
Rumelhart & Greeno (1971)													
Celebrities	54	89	1.40	1.13	1.68	0.36	78.2**	28	.023	30.0	25	48.2**	3
Sjöberg (1977)													
Swedish parties	23	96	1.73	1.38	2.27	.038	49.1**	15	.012	5.8	11	43.3**	4
Sjöberg & Capozza (1975)													
Italian parties	18	78	1.74	.93	2.78	.042	67.6**	15	.023	19.5	11	48.1**	4
Sjöberg (1977)													
Social sciences	86	84	1.52	1.21	1.86	.035	69.1	55	.025	45.5	50	23.6**	5
Coombs (1958)													
Shades of gray													
Subject 1	99	83	2.06	1	4								
Subject 2	139	76	5.08	1	9								
Subject 3	127	70	1.45	.58	3.52								
Subject 4	184	94	6.66	2.84	100								

Note: $\pi = \%$ triples confirming the trinary inequality. R is median value of $R(xyz) = R(x,y)R(y,z) \cdot R(z,x)$. $R_1 =$ First quartile of distribution of $R(xyz)$. $R_3 =$ third quartile of distribution of $R(xyz)$. $d =$ average absolute deviation between observed and predicted choice probabilities. * $p < .05$. ** $p < .001$.

inequality, R is the median value of $R(xyz) = R(x,y)R(y,z)R(z,x)$, and R_1 and R_3 are the first and third quartiles of the distribution of $R(xyz)$. The right-hand part of table 21.1 describes the measures of goodness of fit for both CRM and pretree, where d is the average absolute deviation between observed and predicted choice probabilities.

Tree Representation of Choice Data

The examination of the trinary inequality provides an estimate-free comparison of CRM and pretree. The results described in table 21.1 show that in all data sets, CRM is violated in the direction implied by the similarity hypothesis and the assumed tree structure. The statistical tests for the correspondence between models and data indicate that pretree offers an adequate account of the data that is significantly better than the account offered by CRM. Apparently, the introduction of a few additional parameters that correspond to aspects shared by some of the alternatives results in a substantial improvement in goodness of fit. Furthermore, pretree yields interpretable hierarchical representations of the alternatives under study along with the measures of the relevant aspect sets.

The preceding analyses relied on similarity data or on a priori considerations to construct the tree structure and used choice probabilities to test the model and to estimate the tree. This procedure avoids the difficulty involved in using the same data for constructing the tree and for testing its validity. It is also attractive because similarity data are easily obtained and they are typically more stable and less variable than preferences. An examination of Sjöberg's data, for example, shows that subjects who reveal markedly different preferences tend, nevertheless, to exhibit considerable agreement in judgments of similarity. The only drawback of this procedure is that it fails to produce the best tree whenever the similarities and the preferences follow different structures. The development of an effective algorithm for constructing a tree from fallible preferences and the development of appropriate estimation and testing procedures remain open problems for future research.

The correspondence between the observed and the predicted choice probabilities indicates that the tree structures inferred from judgments of similarity generally agree with the structures implied by the observed choice probabilities. This result supports the notion of correspondence between similarity and preference structures originated by Coombs (1964) and underscores the potential use of similarity scaling techniques in the analysis of choice behavior. Other analyses of the relations between the representations of similarity and of preference, based on multidimensional scaling, are reported by Carroll (1972), Nygren and Jones (1977), Sjöberg (1977), and Stefflre (1972).

Constrained Choice and the Effect of Agenda

The preceding development, like other models of choice, deals with the selection of a single element from some offered set. The present section investigates choice that is constrained by a partition imposed on the offered set. For example, the choice of an alternative from the set $\{x, y, v, w\}$ can be constrained by the requirement to choose first between $\{x, y\}$ and $\{v, w\}$ and then to choose a single element from the selected pair. Constraints of this type are common; they could be imposed by others, induced by circumstances, or adopted for convenience.

For example, the decision regarding a new appointment is sometimes introduced as an initial decision between a senior and a junior appointment, followed by a later choice among the respective junior or senior candidates. Deadlines and other time limits provide another source of constraint. Suppose the alternatives of $A \subset T$, for example, are no longer available after April 1. Prior to this date, therefore, one has to decide whether to choose an element of A or to select an element from $T - A$, in which case the choice of a particular element can be delayed. The selection of an agenda and the grouping of options for voting (which have long been recognized as influential procedures) are familiar examples of external constraints.

There are many situations, however, in which a person constrains his choice to reduce cost or effort. Consider, for example, a consumer who intends to purchase one item from a set $\{x, y, v, w\}$ of four competing products. Suppose there are two stores in town that are quite distant from each other; one store carries only x and y, and the other carries only v and w. Under such circumstances, the consumer is likely to select first a store and then a product, because he has to decide which store to enter but he does not have to choose a product before entering the store. Similarly, people typically select a restaurant first and an entree later—even when they are thoroughly familiar with the available menus. Thus, the need to make some decisions (e.g., of a restaurant) at an early stage and the common tendency to delay decisions (e.g., of an entree) to a later stage constrain the sequence of choices leading to the selected alternative.

The effect of an agenda on group decision making has been investigated by an economist, Charles R. Plott, and a lawyer, Michael E. Levine, from Caltech. Levine and Plott (1977) conducted an ingenious study of a flying club, to which they belong, whose members had to decide on the size and composition of the club's aircraft fleet. There were a few hundred competing alternatives, and the group was to meet once and decide by a majority vote. Levine and Plott constructed an agenda designed to maximize the chances of selecting the alternative they preferred. The group followed this agenda, and indeed chose the option favored by the authors. A second study demonstrated the impact of agenda under controlled laboratory conditions. Plott and Levine (1978) developed a model of individual voting behavior and used it to construct an agenda for each alternative, designed to enhance the selection of that alternative. The results indicate that although the specific model was not fully supported, the imposed agenda had a substantial effect on group choice.

A Theoretical Analysis

An agenda or a constraint imposed on an offered set induces a hierarchical structure or a tree on that set. Suppose, for example, that $\{B, C, D\}$ is a partition of A; hence, under the constraint $[[B][C]][D]$, the choice of an alternative from A proceeds by first choosing between D and $B \cup C$ and then choosing between B and C, if D is eliminated in the first stage. It is essential to distinguish here between the intrinsic tree structure (defined in terms of the relations among the aspects that characterize the alternatives) and the imposed structure that characterizes the external constraints. The choice among $\{x, y, v, w\}$, for example, whose aspects form the tree $(xy)(vw)$, may be constrained by the requirement to choose first between $\{x, w\}$ and $\{y, v\}$. To avoid confusion we use parentheses, for example, $(xy)v$, to characterize the intrinsic tree, and brackets, for example, $[xy]z$, to denote the imposed constraints.

Let $P(x, [A][B])$, $x \in A$, $A \cap B = \phi$ denote the probability of selecting x from $A \cup B$, subject to the constraint of choosing first between A and B. The present treatment is based on the following assumption.

$$P(x, [A][B]) = P(x, A)P(A, A \cup B)$$

$$= P(x, A) \sum_{y \in A} P(y, A \cup B). \tag{13}$$

That is, the probability of choosing x under $[A][B]$ is decomposable into two independent choices: The choice of x from A and the choice of A from $[A][B]$. Furthermore, the latter choice is reduced to the selection of any element of A from the offered set $A \cup B$. Hence for $A = \{x, y\}$ and $B = \{v, w\}$, $P(x, [xy][vw]) = P(x, y)(P(x, xyvw) + P(y, xyvw))$. Equation 13 does not assume any choice model, it merely expresses the probability of a constrained choice in terms of the probabilities of nonconstrained choices.

A choice model is called invariant if the probability of choice is unaffected by constraints imposed on offered sets. Thus, invariance implies that $P(x, [A][B]) = P(x, A \cup B)$ for all $x \in A \cup B$. It is easy to see that CRM is invariant. In fact, the invariance condition is equivalent to Luce's (1959) choice axiom, which asserts that $P(x, A) = P(x, B)P(B, A)$ whenever $B \subset A$ and $P(x, A) > 0$. Consequently, Luce's model is the only invariant theory of choice; all other models violate invariance in one form or another.

Two hierarchical structures or trees defined on the same set of alternatives are called compatible iff there exists a third tree, defined on the same alternatives, that is a refinement of both. Refinement is used here in a nonstrict sense so that every tree is a refinement of itself. Thus, $((xy)z)(uvw)$ is compatible with $(xyz)((uv)w)$ because both are coarsenings of $((xy)z)((uv)w)$. On the other hand, $(xy)z$ and $(xz)y$ are incompatible, since there is no tree that is a refinement of both. Note that the (degenerate) tree structure implied by CRM is compatible with any tree. The relation between the instrinsic preference tree and the imposed agenda is described in the following theorem.

COMPATIBILITY THEOREM.   If equation 13 holds and pretree is valid, then a set of choice probabilities is unaffected by constraints iff the constraints are compatible with the structure of the tree.

A proof of the theorem is given in appendix E. The following discussion explores the simplest example of the effect of agenda. Suppose that $T = \{x, y, z\}$, pretree holds and the intrinsic tree is $(xy)z$. Let α, β, and γ denote the measures of the unique aspects of x, y, and z, respectively, and let θ denote the measure of the aspects shared by x and y. (See figure 21.5.) Setting $\alpha + \beta + \gamma + \theta = 1$, yields

$$P(x, xyz) = \alpha + \theta\alpha/(\alpha + \beta), \quad P(y, xyz) = \beta + \theta\beta/(\alpha + \beta), \quad P(z, xyz) = \gamma.$$

There are three nontrivial constraints in this case. The first, $[xy]z$, coincides with the tree structure, hence it does not influence choice probability. The other two partitions, $[xz]y$ and $[yz]x$, are symmetric with respect to x and y, hence we investigate only the former. By equation 13 we have $P(y, [xz]y) = P(y, xyz)$. More generally, an imposed partition, for example, $[xz]y$, does not change the probability of selecting the isolated alternative, for example, y. The imposed constraint, however, can have a substantial effect on the probability of selecting other alternatives, for example, x and z. Since

$$P(x, [xz]y) = P(x, z)(P(x, xyz) + P(z, xyz)),$$

then

$$P(x, [xz]y) > P(x, xyz)$$

iff

$$P(z, xyz)P(x, z) > P(x, xyz)P(z, x).$$

In the tree model, with $(xy)z$, this inequality is always satisfied (see equation 7) because

$$\frac{P(x, z)}{P(z, x)} = \frac{\alpha + \theta}{\gamma} > \frac{\alpha + \theta\alpha/(\alpha + \beta)}{\gamma} = \frac{P(x, xyz)}{P(z, xyz)},$$

hence, $P(x, [xz]y) > P(x, xyz)$. Imposing the partition $[xz]y$, therefore, on the tree $(xy)z$ is beneficial to x, immaterial for y, and harmful to z.

To interpret this result, recall that x and y share more aspects with each other than with z. In the absence of external constraints, z benefits directly from the competition between x and y, as demonstrated by the above inequality that shows that x loses proportionally more than z by the addition of y to the set $\{x, z\}$. The constraint $[xz]y$ reduces, in effect, the direct competition between x and y and enhances x at the expense of z.

A numerical example illustrates this effect. Suppose $\alpha = .0001$, $\beta = .0999$, $\theta = .4$, and $\gamma = .5$. In a free choice, therefore, $P(z, xyz) = .5$, $P(y, xyz) = .4995$, and

$P(x, xyz) = .0005$ because x is practically dominated by y. Under the constraint $[xz]y$, however, the probabilities of choosing z, y, and x, respectively, are .2761, .4995, and .2244. Thus, the imposed partition increases the probability of choosing x from .0005 to .2244. This occurs because x fares well against z, but performs badly against y. In a regular choice, where x is compared directly to y, its chances are negligible. Under the partition $[xz]y$, however, these chances improve greatly because there is an even chance to eliminate y in the first stage and a close to even chance to eliminate z in the second stage.

The above treatment of constrained choice should be viewed as a first approximation because its assumptions probably do not always hold. First, the alternatives in question may not form a tree. Second, the independence condition (embodied in equation 13) may fail in many situations. Finally, the probability of selecting A over B may not equal $\sum_{x \in A} P(x, A \cup B)$—particularly when A and B have a different number of elements that could induce a bias to choose the larger or the smaller set. Nevertheless, the proposed model appears to provide a promising method for the analysis of constrained choice.

Constrained Choices among Prospects and Applicants

This experiment investigates the effect of agenda on individual choice and tests the implications of the preceding analysis. Two parallel studies are reported using hypothetical prospects (study 1) and college applicants (study 2) as choice alternatives. Each prospect was described as having $p\%$ chance to win $\$a$ and $(100 - p)\%$ chance to win nothing, denoted $(\$a, p\%)$. Each applicant was characterized by a high school grade point average (GPA) and an average score on the Scholastic Aptitude Test (SAT). The subjects were reminded that the SAT has a maximum of 800, with an average of about 500, and that GPA is computed by letting A = 4, B = 3, and so on.

One hundred students from Stanford University, Stanford, California, participated in each of the two studies. Every subject was presented individually with 10 triples of alternatives, each displayed on a separate card. Each triple was divided into a *pair* of alternatives and an *odd* alternative, and the subject was instructed to decide first whether he or she preferred the odd alternative or one of the members of the pair. If the odd alternative was selected, the elements of the triple were not considered again. If the pair was selected, the subject was given an opportunity to choose between its members after the presentation of all 10 triples. The delay was designed to reduce the dependence between the trinary and the binary choices.

The subjects in study 1 were asked to imagine that they were actually faced with the choice between the displayed prospects and to indicate the decision they would have made in each case. The subjects in study 2 were asked to select from each triple the applicant that they preferred. Subjects were reminded that their task was to express their preferences rather than to predict which applicant was most likely to be admitted to college. The participants in both studies were asked to consider each choice carefully and to treat each triple as a separate choice problem.

The alternatives in each triple, denoted x, y, z, were constructed so that (a) x and y are very similar, (b) z is not very similar to either x or y, and (c) the advantage of y over x on one dimension appears greater than the advantage of x over y on the other dimension so that y is preferable to x. In study 1, z is a sure prospect, whereas x and y are risky prospects with similar probabilities and outcomes and with y superior to x in expected value. For example, $x = (\$40, 75\%)$, $y = (\$50, 70\%)$, and $z = \$25$ for sure, denoted $(\$25)$. In study 2, x and y are applicants with relatively high GPA and moderate SAT, and z is an applicant with a relatively low GPA and fairly high SAT. For example, $x = (3.5, 562)$, $y = (3.4, 596)$, and $z = (2.5, 725)$. The results of a pilot study indicated that .1 on the GPA scale is roughly equivalent to 20 SAT points. According to this criterion for overall quality, applicant y is "better" than x in all cases. All triples of prospects and applicants are displayed in tables 21.2 and 21.3.

The present experiment was designed to compare choice under $[xy]z$ with choice under $[xz]y$. Hence, for each triple, half of the subjects had to choose first between the pair (x, y) and z, and the remaining half had to choose first between the pair (x, z) and y. Each subject made five choices under $[xy]z$ and five choices under $[xz]y$. The order of triples and constraints, as well as the positions of the option cards (i.e., left, center, right) were all counterbalanced.

Because alternatives x and y have much more in common with each other than with z, the tree structure that best approximates the triples is $(xy)z$. Hence, the constraint $[xy]z$ is compatible with the natural structure of the alternatives, whereas the constraint $[xz]y$ is not. The preceding analysis implies that the latter should enhance the choice of x, hinder the choice of z, and have no substantial effect on the choice of y. Stated formally,

$$d(x) = P(x, [xz]y) - P(x, [xy]z) > 0,$$

$$d(y) = P(y, [xz]y) - P(y, [xy]z) = 0,$$

and

$$d(z) = P(z, [xz]y) - P(z, [xy]z) < 0.$$

Obviously, in the absence of any effect due to the imposed constraints, $d(x) = d(y) = d(z) = 0$. The proportions of subjects who chose x and y in each triple under

Table 21.2
Probabilities of Choice among Prospects under Two Different Constraints: Study 1

Triple	Alternatives			Constraints				Effects		
				[xy]z		[xz]y				
	x ($\$$, %)	y ($\$$, %)	z ($\$$)	$P(x, [xy]z)$	$P(z, [xy]z)$	$P(x, [xz]y)$	$P(z, [xz]y)$	$d(x)$	$d(y)$	$d(z)$
1	(40, 75)	(50, 70)	(25)	.08	.22	.18	.20	.10	−.08	−.02
2	(80, 15)	(75, 20)	(10)	.12	.40	.24	.32	.12	−.04	−.08
3	(65, 90)	(75, 85)	(55)	.12	.42	.20	.46	.08	−.12	.04
4	(120, 5)	(85, 10)	(5)	.08	.54	.18	.38	.10	.06	−.16
5	(75, 30)	(100, 25)	(20)	.04	.54	.20	.48	.16	−.10	−.06
6	(125, 35)	(120, 40)	(35)	.04	.44	.18	.32	.14	−.02	−.12
7	(30, 65)	(40, 60)	(15)	.18	.36	.30	.40	.12	−.16	.04
8	(35, 95)	(45, 90)	(30)	.06	.40	.16	.28	.10	.02	−.12
9	(50, 85)	(60, 80)	(40)	.04	.48	.22	.30	.18	.00	−.18
10	(65, 25)	(95, 20)	(15)	.02	.42	.24	.28	.22	−.08	−.14
M				.078	.422	.210	.342	.132	−.052	−.080

Note: $\$$ = amount to be won. % = chances to win. $d(x) = P(x, [xz]y) - P(x, [xy]z)$, $d(y) = P(y, [xy]z) - P(y, [xz]y)$, $d(z) = P(z, [xz]y) - P(z, [xy]z)$. Numbers in parentheses indicate choice alternatives.

Table 21.3
Probabilities of Choice among Applicants under Two Different Constraints: Study 2

Triple	Alternatives (GPA. SAT)			Constraints				Effects		
				[xy]z		[xz]y				
	x	y	z	$P(x, [xy]z)$	$P(z, [xy]z)$	$P(x, [xz]y)$	$P(z, [xz]y)$	$d(x)$	$d(y)$	$d(z)$
1	(3.3, 654)	(3.2, 692)	(2.2, 773)	.16	.40	.30	.32	.14	−.06	−.08
2	(3.6, 592)	(3.5, 625)	(2.6, 785)	.18	.38	.28	.26	.10	.02	−.12
3	(3.5, 579)	(3.7, 571)	(2.5, 701)	.00	.48	.18	.40	.18	−.10	−.08
4	(3.1, 602)	(3.0, 641)	(2.1, 730)	.14	.36	.22	.26	.08	.02	−.10
5	(2.9, 521)	(3.1, 515)	(2.3, 703)	.04	.50	.20	.34	.16	.00	−.16
6	(2.8, 666)	(2.9, 661)	(2.0, 732)	.06	.40	.26	.24	.20	−.04	−.16
7	(3.8, 587)	(3.7, 629)	(2.6, 744)	.14	.38	.28	.30	.14	−.06	−.08
8	(3.4, 600)	(3.6, 590)	(2.4, 755)	.06	.40	.24	.30	.18	−.08	−.10
9	(3.7, 718)	(3.9, 712)	(3.1, 798)	.00	.40	.20	.22	.20	−.02	−.18
10	(3.5, 562)	(3.4, 596)	(2.5, 725)	.20	.28	.26	.30	.06	−.08	.02
M				.098	.398	.242	.294	.144	−.040	−.104

Note: GPA = grade point average. SAT = Scholastic Aptitude Test. $d(x) = P(x, [xz]y) − P(x, [xy]z)$, $d(y) = P(y, [xy]z) − P(y, [xz]y)$, $d(z) = P(z, [xz]y) − P(z, [xy]z)$.
Numbers in parentheses indicate choice alternatives.

the two constraints are presented in tables 21.2 and 21.3 along with the values of $d(x)$, $d(y)$, and $d(z)$ defined above.

The results reported in tables 21.2 and 21.3 tend to confirm the predicted pattern of choices. In both studies the values of $d(x)$ are all positive, and the values of $d(z)$ are negative with a few small exceptions. Furthermore, in both study 1 and study 2, the means of $d(x)$ are significantly positive, yielding $t(9) = 9.2$ and $t(9) = 8.6$, respectively, $p < .001$, whereas the means of $d(z)$ are significantly negative, yielding $t(9) = -3.0$, $p < .05$, in study 1, and $t(9) = -5.5$, $p < .001$, in study 2. The means of $d(y)$ were also negative, yielding $t(9) = -2.3$ and $t(9) = -2.8$, respectively, $.01 < p < .05$. Hence, the shift from the natural constraint $[xy]z$ to the constraint $[xz]y$ increases the chances of x and decreases the chances of z and, to a lesser extent, of y. The latter effect, which departs from the predicted pattern, may reflect a response bias against the odd alternative.

The pattern of results described above seems to exclude two alternative simple models that produce an agenda effect. Suppose choices are made at random so that one chooses between the odd and the paired alternatives with equal probability. As a consequence,

$$d(x) = P(x, [xz]y) - P(x, [xy]z) = \tfrac{1}{2} \times \tfrac{1}{2} - \tfrac{1}{2} \times \tfrac{1}{2} = 0,$$

$$d(y) = P(y, [xz]y) - P(y, [xy]z) = \tfrac{1}{2} - \tfrac{1}{2} \times \tfrac{1}{2} = \tfrac{1}{4} > 0,$$

and

$$d(z) = P(z, [xz]y) - P(z, [xy]z) = \tfrac{1}{2} \times \tfrac{1}{2} - \tfrac{1}{2} = -\tfrac{1}{4} < 0,$$

which are incompatible with the experimental findings.

The random choice model gives a distinct advantage to the odd alternative, hence its failure suggests a different model, according to which the odd alternative suffers a setback perhaps because people prefer to delay the choice and avoid commitment. This hypothesis, however, implies $d(x) = 0$, $d(y) < 0$ and $d(z) > 0$—again contrary to the data.

Since all triples have the same structure, it is possible to pool all x choices, y choices, and z choices across triples and test our hypotheses within the data of each subject. Let $P_i(x, [xz]y)$ denote the proportion of triples in which subject i made an x choice under the constraint $[xz]y$, and so forth. Let $d_i(x) = P_i(x, [xz]y) - P_i(x, [xy]z)$, $d_i(z) = P(z, [xz]y) - P_i(z, [xy]z)$, and let $D_i = d_i(x) - d_i(z)$. Thus, D_i measures the advantage of x over z due to the shift from $[xy]z$ to $[xz]y$. Recall that in the absence of an agenda effect, $d_i(x) = d_i(z) = D_i = 0$, whereas under the proposed model, $d_i(x) > 0 > d_i(z)$, hence, D_i has a positive expectation. The means of the D_i distributions are .21 in study 1 and .25 in study 2, which are significantly positive, yielding $t(99) = 4.2$ and $t(99) = 5.8$, respectively, $p < .001$ in both cases. In study 1, 60% of the D_is are positive and 22% negative; in study 2, 62% are positive and 18% negative. Hence, the predicted pattern of choices is also confirmed in a within-subjects comparison in which choices are pooled over trials rather than over subjects.

In summary, the data show that imposed constraints have a significant impact on choice behavior and confirm the major predictions of the proposed model of constrained choice. The present results about individual choice, which are based on the correlational pattern among the alternatives, should be distinguished from the results of Plott and Levine (1978), who demonstrated the effect of agenda on the outcome of group decision based on majority vote. An agenda often introduces strategic considerations that could affect the outcome of a voting process even if it does not change the ordering of the options for any single individual, much as group decision can be intransitive even when its members are all transitive. Although different effects seem to contribute to the failure of invariance in individual and in collective choice, they are probably both present, for example, in many forms of committee decision making. The influence of procedural constraints on either individual or social choice emerges as a subject of great theoretical and practical significance. For if the choice of a new staff member, for example, depends on whether the initial decision concerns the nature of the appointment (e.g., junior vs. senior) or the field (e.g., perception vs. social), then the order in which decisions are made becomes an important component of the choice process that cannot be treated merely as a procedural matter.

The present model of individual choice under constraints may serve three related functions. First, it could be used to predict the manner in which choices among political candidates, market products, or public policies are affected by the introduction or the change of agendas. Second, the model may be used to construct an agenda to maximize the probability of a desired outcome. Experienced politicians and seasoned marketeers are undoubtedly aware of the effects of grouping and separating options. A formal model may nevertheless prove useful, particularly in complex decisions for which the number of alternatives is large and computational demands exceed cognitive limitations. Third, the model can be employed by a group or a committee as a framework for the discussion and comparison of different agendas. Although an optimal or a fair agenda may not exist, the analysis might help clarify the issues and facilitate the choice. If all members of the group, for example, perceive the available options in terms of the same tree structure, even though they have different weights and preferences, then the use of an agenda that is compatible with that structure is recommended because it ensures invariance. The applications of the present development for the construction, selection, and evaluation of agendas remain to be developed.

Discussion

Individual choice behavior is variable, complex, and context dependent, and the attempts to model it are at best incomplete. Even the most basic axioms of preference are consistently violated under certain circumstances. (See, e.g., Kahneman & Tversky, 1979; Lichtenstein & Slovic 1971; Tversky, 1969.) The present treatment does not attempt to develop a comprehensive theory of choice, but analyzes in detail a particular strategy that appears to govern several decision processes. There are undoubtedly decision processes that are not compatible with pretree. Some of them could perhaps be explained by EBA, but others may require different theoretical treatments. The selection of a choice model, however, generally involves a balance between generality or scope on the one hand and simplicity or predictive power on the other. Pretree may be regarded as an intermediate model that is much less restrictive than CRM, since it is compatible with the similarity hypothesis; yet it is much more parsimonious than the general EBA model, since it has at most $2n - 2$ rather than $2^n - 2$ parameters.

Furthermore, the tree model may provide a useful approximation to a more complex structure in the same way that a two-dimensional solution often provides a useful representation of a higher dimensional structure. Consider, for example, a person who is about to take a 1-week trip to a single European country and is offered a choice between France (F) and Italy (I) and between a luxury tour (L) and an economy tour (E). Naturally, the luxury tour is much more comfortable, but it is also considerably more expensive than the economy tour. It is easy to see that the four available alternatives, F_L, F_E, I_L, I_E, do not satisfy the inclusion rule because for any triple, each alternative shares different aspects with the other two. Hence, the EBA model cannot be reduced to a tree in this case, although it can be approximated by a tree—provided one of the attributes looms much larger than the others.

Suppose the decision maker is concerned about the site of the trip (Italy vs. France), but is not overly concerned about comfort or price. In this case, the weights associated with the tour type (luxury vs. economy) would be small in comparison with the weights associated with the sites. Hence, the observed choice probabilities may be approximated fairly well by the tree $(F_L F_E) (I_L I_E)$. On the other hand, if the decision maker is much more concerned about the type of tour than about its site, his choice probabilities will be better described by the tree $(F_L I_L) (F_E I_E)$. The quality of either approximation depends on the degree to which one attribute dominates the other, and it can be assessed directly by examining the trinary and the quarternary conditions. An extension of the tree model that deals with factorial structures will be described elsewhere.

Hierarchical or treelike models of choice have been recently employed by students of economics and market research who investigate questions such as the share of the market to be captured by a new product or the probability that a consumer will switch from one brand to another. Luce's (1959) model provides the simplest answers to such questions, but as we have already seen, it is too restrictive. Perhaps the simplest way of extending CRM is to assume that the offered set of alternatives can be partitioned into classes so that the model holds within each homogeneous class, even though it does not hold for heterogeneous sets.

This assumption underlies the analysis of brand switching developed by the Hendry Corporation and described by Kalwani and Morrison (1977). According to the Hendry model, the probability that a consumer will purchase a new brand, given that he switched from his old one, is proportional to the market share of the new brand, provided the two brands belong to the same class of the partition. The application of this model, therefore, requires prior identification of an appropriate partition or tree structure, which is presumably constructed on the basis of informed intuition. The similarity-based scaling procedure employed in this article and the test of the necessary trinary and quarternary conditions could perhaps be used to construct and validate the partition to which the analysis of brand switching is applied.

The partition of the alternatives into homogeneous classes satisfying CRM was also used by McFadden (1976; McFadden, reference note 1) in his theoretical and empirical analyses of probabilistic choice. As an economist, McFadden was primarily interested in aggregate demand for alternatives (e.g., different modes of transportation) as a function of measured attributes of the alternatives and the decision makers (e.g., cost, travel time, income). The Thurstonian, or random utility, model provides a natural framework for such an analysis that assumes, in accord with classical economic theory, that each individual maximizes his utility function defined over the relevant set of alternatives; the random component reflects the sampling of individuals with different utility functions.

McFadden (reference note 1) began with the multinomial logit (MNL) model in which

$$P(x, A) = \exp \sum_i x_i \theta_i \Big/ \sum_{y \in A} \exp \sum_i y_i \theta_i,$$

where $x_1, \ldots, x_n$ are specified attributes of x and $\theta_1, \ldots, \theta_n$ are parameters estimated from the data. This is clearly a special case of Luce's model (equation 2), where $\log u(x)$ is a linear function in the parameters $\theta_1, \ldots, \theta_n$. It is expressible as a random utility model by assuming an extreme value distribution $F(t) = \exp[-\exp - (at + b)]$, $a > 0$. (See, e.g., Luce, 1977; Yellott, 1977.)

The MNL has been applied to several economic problems, notably transportation planning (McFadden, 1976), but the failure of context independence led McFadden (reference note 1) to develop a more general family of choice models, called *generalized extreme value models*, that are compatible with the similarity hypothesis. One model from this family, called the *nested logit model*, assumes a tree structure in which the probabilities of choice at each level of the tree conform to the MNL model (see McFadden, reference note 1). Although the nested logit model does not coincide with pretree, the two models are sufficiently close that the former may be regarded as a random utility counterpart of the latter.

Psychological models of individual choice fall into three overlapping classes: decomposition models, probabilistic models, and process models. Decomposition models express the overall value of each alternative as a function of the scale values associated with its components. This class includes all variations of expected utility theory as well as the various adding and averaging models. Probabilistic models relate choice data to an underlying value structure through a probabilistic process. The models of Thurstone and Luce are prominent examples. Process models attempt to capture the mental operations that are performed in the course of a decision. This approach, pioneered by Simon, has led to the development of computer models designed to simulate the decision-making process. Pretree, like the more general EBA, belongs to all three classes. It is a decomposition model that expresses the overall value of an alternative as an additive combination of the values of its aspects. Unlike most decomposition models, however, the relation between the observed choice and the underlying value structure is probabilistic, and the formal theory is interpretable as a process model of choice behavior that is based on successive eliminations following a tree structure.

This article exhibits three correspondence relations (a) the equivalence of elimination by tree and the hierarchical elimination model, (b) the compatibility of aggregate choice and the individual EBA model, and (c) the correspondence between preference and similarity trees. The three results, however, have different theoretical and empirical status. The equivalence of EBT and HEM is a mathematical fact that permits the application of the tree model to both random and hierarchical decision processes. The second result offers a new interpretation of EBA as an aggregate choice model, thereby providing a rationale for applying EBA to aggregate data. Finally, the compatibility of similarity and preference trees is an empirical observation that suggests that the two processes are related through a common underlying structure.

Notes

This work was supported by the Office of Naval Research under Contract N00014-79-C-0077 to Stanford University.

    This article has benefited from discussions with R. M. Dawes, J. C. Falmagne, W. Hutchinson, D. H. Krantz, D. Kahneman, and D. McFadden. We are particularly grateful to L. Sjöberg for making his data available to us and to I. Gati and P. Smith for their help in the analysis of the data.

1. The present notion of a preference tree should be distinguished from the concept of a decision tree commonly used in the analysis of decisions under uncertainty.

2. To obtain compact figures, we use a heavy line (see figure 21.7) to indicate double length and an extra heavy line (see figure 21.11) to indicate tenfold length.

Reference Notes

1. McFadden, D. *Econometric models for probabilistic choices* (Cowles Foundation Discussion Paper). Unpublished manuscript, Yale University, 1978.

2. Falmagne, J. C. *Probabilistic theories of measurement*. Paper presented at the Soviet-American Seminar on Decision Models, Tbilisi, Soviet Union, April 1979.

References

Carroll, J. D. Individual differences and multidimensional scaling. In R. N. Shepard, A. K. Romney, & S. B. Nerlove (Eds.), *Multidimensional scaling: Theory and applications in the behavioral sciences* (vol. 1). New York: Seminar Press, 1972.

Chandler, J. P. STEPIT—Finds local minima of a smooth function of several parameters. *Behavioral Science*, 1969, *14*, 81–82.

Coombs, C. H. On the use of inconsistency of preferences in psychological measurement. *Journal of Experimental Psychology*, 1958, *55*, 1–7.

Coombs, C. H. *A theory of data*. New York: Wiley, 1964.

Debreu, G. Review of R. D. Luce, Individual choice behavior: A theoretical analysis. *American Economic Review*, 1960, *50*, 186–188.

Edgell, S. E., Geisler, W. S., III, & Zinnes, J. L. A note on a paper by Rumelhart and Greeno. *Journal of Mathematical Psychology*, 1973, *10*, 86–90.

Kahneman, D., & Tversky, A. Prospect theory: An analysis of decision under risk. *Econometrica*, 1979, *47*, 263–291.

Kalwani, M. V., & Morrison, D. G. A parsimonious description of the Hendry system. *Management Science*, 1977, *23*, 467–477.

Levine, M. E., & Plott, C. R. Agenda influence and its implications. *Virginia Law Review*, 1977, *63*, 561–604.

Lichtenstein, S., & Slovic, P. Reversal of preference between bids and choices in gambling decisions. *Journal of Experimental Psychology*, 1971, *89*, 46–55.

Luce, R. D. *Individual choice behavior: A theoretical analysis*. New York: Wiley, 1959.

Luce, R. D. The choice axiom after twenty years. *Journal of Mathematical Psychology*, 1977, *15*, 215–233.

Luce, R. D., & Suppes, P. Preference, utility, and subjective probability. In R. D. Luce, R. R. Bush, & E. Galanter (Eds.), *Handbook of mathematical psychology* (vol. 3). New York: Wiley, 1965.

Marschak, J. Binary-choice constraints and random utility indicators. In K. J. Arrow, S. Karlin, & P. Suppes (Eds.), *Mathematical methods in the social sciences*. Stanford, Calif.: Stanford University Press, 1960.

McFadden, D. Quantal choice analysis. A survey. *Annals of Economic and Social Measurement*, 1976, *5*, 363–390.

Nygren, T. E., & Jones, L. E. Individual differences in perception and preferences for political candidates. *Journal of Experimental Social Psychology*, 1977, *13*, 182–197.

Plott, C. R., & Levine, M. E. A model of agenda influence on committee decision. *American Economic Review*, 1978, *68*, 146–160.

Restle, F. *Psychology of judgment and choice*. New York: Wiley, 1961.

Rumelhart, D. L., & Greeno, J. G. Similarity between stimuli: An experimental test of the Luce and Restle choice models. *Journal of Mathematical Psychology*, 1971, *8*, 370–381.

Sattath, S., & Tversky, A. Unite and conquer: A multiplicative inequality for choice probabilities. *Econometrica*, 1976, *44*, 79–89.

Sattath, S., & Tversky, A. Additive similarity trees. *Psychometrika*, 1977, *42*, 319–345.

Simon, H. A. *Models of man*. New York: Wiley, 1957.

Sjöberg, L. Choice frequency and similarity. *Scandinavian Journal of Psychology*, 1977, *18*, 103–115.

Sjöberg, L., & Capozza, D. Preference and cognitive structure of Italian political parties. *Italian Journal of Psychology*, 1975, *2*, 391–402.

Stefflre, V. Some applications of multidimensional scaling to social science problems. In A. K. Romney, R. N. Shepard, & S. B. Nerlove (Eds.), *Multidimensional scaling: Theory and applications in the behavioral sciences* (vol. 2). New York: Seminar Press, 1972.

Thurstone, L. L. A law of comparative judgment. *Psychological Review*, 1927, *34*, 273–286.

Tversky, A. Intransitivity of preferences. *Psychological Review*, 1969, *76*, 31–48.

Tversky, A. Choice by elimination. *Journal of Mathematical Psychology*, 1972, *9*, 341–367. (a)

Tversky, A. Elimination by aspects: A theory of choice. *Psychological Review*, 1972, *79*, 281–299. (b)

Yellott, J. I., Jr. The relationship between Luce's choice axiom, Thurstone's theory of comparative judgment, and the double exponential distribution. *Journal of Mathematical Psychology*, 1977, *15*, 109–144.

Appendix A
Proof of the Structure Theorem

To show that a tree representation of $T^* = \{x' \mid x \in T\}$ implies the inclusion rule, let $t(x)$ denote the path from the root of the tree to the terminal node associated with x.

For any x, y, z in T, there are four possible tree structures, and they all satisfy the inclusion rule as shown below. (a) If $t(x)$ and $t(y)$ meet below $t(z)$, then $x' \cap y' \supset x' \cap z'$. (b) If $t(x)$ and $t(z)$ meet below $t(y)$, then $x' \cap z' \supset x' \cap y'$. (c) If $t(y)$ and $t(z)$ meet below $t(x)$, then $x' \cap y' = x' \cap z'$. (d) If $t(x)$, $t(y)$, and $t(z)$ all meet at the same node, then $x' \cap y' = x' \cap z'$.

To establish the sufficiency of the inclusion rule, let $T_\alpha = \{x \in T \mid \alpha \in x'\}$, and let $S(T)$ be the set of all T_α for any α in T'. To prove that $T^* = \{x' \mid x \in T\}$ is a tree, it suffices to show that $S(T)$ is a hierarchical clustering. That is, for any α, β in T', either $T_\alpha \supset T_\beta$, $T_\beta \supset T_\alpha$, or $T_\alpha \cap T_\beta$ is empty. Suppose $S(T)$ is not a hierarchical clustering. Then there exist some distinct aspects α, β in T' and some x, y, z in T such that $x \in T_\alpha \cap T_\beta$, $y \in T_\alpha - T_\beta$, and $z \in T_\beta - T_\alpha$. Hence, α is included in $x' \cap y'$, β is included in $x' \cap z'$, but α is not included in z' and β is not included in y'. Consequently, $x' \cap y'$ neither includes nor is included in $x' \cap z'$, and the inclusion rule is violated, as required.

Appendix B
Proof of the Equivalence Theorem

(i) EBT implies HEM.

If EBT holds for T, then it must also hold for any $A \subset T$ with the induced tree structure. Hence, it suffices to demonstrate the first two parts of equation 3.

(a) If $\gamma \mid \beta$ and $\beta \mid \alpha$, then $P(A_\alpha, A_\gamma) = P(A_\alpha, A_\beta)P(A_\beta, A_\gamma)$.

(b) If $\gamma \mid \beta$ and $\gamma \mid \alpha$, then $\dfrac{P(A_\alpha, A_\gamma)}{P(A_\beta, A_\gamma)} = \dfrac{m(\alpha)}{m(\beta)}$, provided $m(\beta) \neq 0$.

We begin with the following auxiliary result. If $\beta \mid \alpha$, then

$$P(x, A_\beta) = P(x, A_\alpha)\frac{m(\alpha)}{m(\beta) - u(\beta)}.$$

Let $\alpha_1, \ldots, \alpha_n$ be a sequence of links leading from x to α. That is, $A_{\alpha_1} = \{x\}$, $\alpha_{i+1} \mid \alpha_i$, $i = 1, \ldots, n-1$, and $\alpha_n = \alpha$. Assuming EBT and $\beta \mid \alpha$,

$$P(x, A_\beta) = \frac{u(\alpha_n)}{m(\beta) - u(\beta)}P(x, A_{\alpha_n}) + \frac{u(\alpha_{n-1})}{m(\beta) - u(\beta)}P(x, A_{\alpha_{n-1}}) + \cdots$$

$$+ \frac{u(\alpha_1)}{m(\beta) - u(\beta)}P(x, A_{\alpha_1})$$

$$= \frac{u(\alpha_n)}{m(\beta) - u(\beta)} P(x, A_{\alpha_n}) + \frac{m(\alpha_n) - u(\alpha_n)}{m(\beta) - u(\beta)} \left(\frac{u(\alpha_{n-1})}{m(\alpha_n) - u(\alpha_n)} P(x, A_{\alpha_{n-1}}) + \cdots \right.$$

$$\left. + \frac{u(\alpha_1)}{m(\alpha_n) - u(\alpha_n)} P(x, A_{\alpha_1}) \right)$$

$$= \frac{u(\alpha_n)}{m(\beta) - u(\beta)} P(x, A_{\alpha_n}) + \frac{m(\alpha_n) - u(\alpha_n)}{m(\beta) - u(\beta)} P(x, A_{\alpha_n})$$

$$= \frac{m(\alpha)}{m(\beta) - u(\beta)} P(x, A_\alpha)$$

as required. To prove b we assume that $\gamma \,|\, \beta$ and $\gamma \,|\, \alpha$, hence

$$\frac{P(A_\alpha, A_\gamma)}{P(A_\beta, A_\gamma)} = \frac{\sum\limits_{x \in A_\alpha} P(x, A_\gamma)}{\sum\limits_{x \in A_\beta} P(x, A_\gamma)}$$

$$= \frac{\sum\limits_{x \in A_\alpha} P(x, A_\alpha) \dfrac{m(\alpha)}{m(\gamma) - u(\gamma)}}{\sum\limits_{x \in A_\beta} P(x, A_\beta) \dfrac{m(\beta)}{m(\gamma) - u(\gamma)}}$$

$$= \frac{m(\alpha)}{m(\beta)},$$

since $\sum_{x \in A_\alpha} P(x, A_\alpha) = \sum_{x \in A_\beta} P(x, A_\beta) = 1$.

To prove a, suppose $\gamma \,|\, \beta$ and $\beta \,|\, \alpha$. By our auxiliary result

$$P(A_\beta, A_\gamma) = \sum_{x \in A_\beta} P(x, A_\gamma) = m(\beta)/(m(\gamma) - u(\gamma)),$$

and

$$P(A_\alpha, A_\gamma) = \sum_{x \in A_\alpha} P(x, A_\gamma)$$

$$= \sum_{x \in A_\alpha} P(x, A_\beta) \frac{m(\beta)}{m(\gamma) - u(\gamma)}$$

$$= P(A_\alpha, A_\beta) \frac{m(\beta)}{m(\gamma) - u(\gamma)}$$

$$= P(A_\alpha, A_\beta) P(A_\beta, A_\gamma).$$

(ii) HEM implies EBT.

We have to show that for any $A \subset T$, $P(x, A)$ satisfies equation 1. The proof is by induction on the cardinality of A. Let $\alpha_1, \ldots, \alpha_n$ be the sequence of segments leading from x to the root of A. That is, $\{x\} = A_{\alpha_1}$, $\alpha_{i+1} \mid \alpha_i$, $i = 1, \ldots, n-1$, and $A_{\alpha_n} = A$. If $\gamma \mid \beta$, $x \in A_\beta$, and equation 3 holds, then

$$P(x, A_\gamma) = \frac{m(\beta)}{m(\gamma) - u(\gamma)} P(x, A_\beta).$$

Thus, using the inductive hypothesis, we obtain

$$P(x, A_{\alpha_n}) = \frac{m(\alpha_{n-1})}{m(\alpha_n) - u(\alpha_n)} P(x, A_{\alpha_{n-1}})$$

$$= \frac{u(\alpha_{n-1})}{m(\alpha_n) - u(\alpha_n)} P(x, A_{\alpha_{n-1}}) + \frac{m(\alpha_{n-1}) - u(\alpha_{n-1})}{m(\alpha_n) - u(\alpha_n)} P(x, A_{\alpha_{n-1}})$$

$$= \frac{u(\alpha_{n-1})}{m(\alpha_n) - u(\alpha_n)} P(x, A_{\alpha_{n-1}}) + \frac{m(\alpha_{n-1}) - u(\alpha_{n-1})}{m(\alpha_n) - u(\alpha_n)} \left[\frac{\sum_{i=1}^{n-2} u(\alpha_i) P(x, A_{\alpha_i})}{m(\alpha_{n-1}) - u(\alpha_{n-1})} \right]$$

$$= \frac{\sum_{i=1}^{n-1} u(\alpha_i) P(x, A_{\alpha_i})}{m(\alpha_n) - u(\alpha_n)},$$

which is the recursive expression for $P(x, A)$.

Appendix C
Proof of the Representation Theorem

The proof is divided into a series of lemmas. Let P_T denote the set of binary choice probabilities defined for all pairs of elements in T.

LEMMA 1. If $T = \{x, y, z\}$, then P_T satisfies pretree with $(xy)z$ iff the trinary inequality (equation 4) is satisfied in this form.

Proof. Necessity is obvious. To prove sufficiency, we use the notation of figure 21.5, where $R(x, y) \geq 1$. Set $\alpha = 1$, $\beta = R(y, x)$, and select $\theta \geq 0$ so that $[R(x, z) - R(y, z)]\theta = R(y, z) - R(y, x)R(x, z)$, and let $\gamma = R(z, x)(1 + \theta)$. Note that when $R(x, y) > 1$, θ is uniquely defined and positive, and when $R(x, y) = 1$, θ can be chosen arbitrarily.

Let $\overline{\mathbf{P}}_T$ be the set of binary probabilities obtained by using the above expressions for α, β, γ, and θ in the defining equations of the model. It can be verified, after some algebra, that $\overline{\mathbf{P}}_T = P_T$ as required.

Before we go further, note that if P_T satisfies pretree with $(xy)z$ and $R(x, y) > 1$, then $\beta/\alpha = R(y, x)$. Furthermore,

$$\frac{\dfrac{\theta}{\alpha}+1}{\dfrac{\theta}{\alpha}+\dfrac{\beta}{\alpha}} = \frac{\theta+\alpha}{\theta+\beta} = \frac{R(x,z)}{R(y,z)} \quad \text{implies} \quad \frac{\theta}{\alpha} = \frac{R(y,z)-R(y,x)R(x,z)}{R(x,z)-R(y,z)},$$

and

$$\frac{1+\dfrac{\theta}{\alpha}}{\dfrac{\gamma}{\alpha}} = \frac{\alpha+\theta}{\gamma} = R(x,z) \quad \text{implies} \quad \frac{\gamma}{\alpha} = R(z,x)\left(1+\frac{R(y,z)-R(y,x)R(x,z)}{R(x,z)-R(y,z)}\right)$$

$$= \frac{1-R(y,x)}{R(x,z)-R(y,z)}.$$

Hence, the lengths of all links are determined up to multiplication by a positive constant. Furthermore, the present model readily entails the following property.

LEMMA 2.   Suppose A and $B = \{x, y, v\}$ are sets of objects such that $y, v \in A$ and $x \notin A$, and suppose that both P_A and P_B satisfy pretree. (It is assumed that $P(v, y)$ is the same in both structures.) Then the measures on A' and B' can be selected so that $u(v' - y')$ as well as $u(y' - v')$ are the same in both measures.

LEMMA 3.   Suppose $A = \{x, y, v\}$ and $B = \{y, v, w\}$ satisfy pretree, with representing measures u_A and u_B, in the forms $(xy)v$ and $(yv)w$, respectively. If $C = A \cup B = \{x, y, v, w\}$ satisfies the appropriate quarternary condition with $(xy)(vw)$ or with $((xy)v)w$, then there exists a representing measure u on C' that extends both u_A and u_B. Naturally, we assume that u_A and u_B were selected according to Lemma 2.

Proof.   Consider the form $(xy)(vw)$ (see the left portion of figure 21.6). By lemma 2, $u_A(\beta + \theta) = u_B(\beta + \theta)$ and $u_A(\lambda + \gamma) = u_B(\lambda + \gamma)$. Hence, u_A and u_B can be used to define a measure u on C'. To show that u is a representing measure on C' we have to show that $R(x, w) = u(\theta + \alpha)/u(\lambda + \delta)$. Since C satisfies pretree, it follows from equation 5 that

$$R(x, w) = R(y, w)R(x, v)R(v, y)$$

$$= \frac{u(\beta + \theta)u(\alpha + \theta)u(\lambda + \gamma)}{u(\lambda + \delta)u(\lambda + \gamma)u(\beta + \theta)}$$

$$= \frac{u(\theta + \alpha)}{u(\lambda + \delta)}.$$

Next, consider the form $((xy)v)w$ (see the right portion of figure 21.6). Here, we have to show that $R(x, w) = u(\alpha + \theta + \lambda)/u(\delta)$. Applying equation 6, it follows that

$$R(x, w) = \frac{(1 - R(x, v))R(y, w) + R(v, w)(R(x, v) - R(y, v))}{1 - R(y, v)}$$

$$= \frac{\left(1 - \dfrac{u(\alpha + \theta)}{u(\gamma)}\right)\dfrac{u(\beta + \theta + \lambda)}{u(\delta)} + \dfrac{u(\gamma + \lambda)}{u(\delta)}\left(\dfrac{u(\alpha + \theta)}{u(\gamma)} - \dfrac{u(\beta + \theta)}{u(\gamma)}\right)}{1 - \dfrac{u(\beta + \theta)}{u(\gamma)}}$$

$$= \frac{u(\alpha + \theta + \lambda)}{u(\delta)},$$

as required.

LEMMA 4. P_T satisfies pretree with a specified structure iff for every $S \subset T$ with four elements or less, P_S satisfies pretree relative to the same structure.

Proof.   Necessity is immediate. Sufficiency is proved by induction on the cardinality of T, denoted n. Suppose $n > 4$, and assume that the lemma holds for any cardinality smaller than n.

Suppose $(xy)v$ holds for any v in T. Let $A = T - \{x\}$ and $B = \{x, y, v\}$. By the induction hypothesis, both P_A and P_B satisfy pretree with the appropriate structure. By lemma 2 we can assume, with no loss of generality, that the measures of y and v in A' coincide with their measures in B'. Since any aspect in T' appears either in A' or in B' and since the aspects that appear in both trees have the same measure, we can define the measure of any aspect in T' by its measure in A' or in B'. Letting $\bar{P}$ denote the calculated binary probability function, we show that $\bar{P}_T = P_T$.

Since $\bar{P}_A = P_A$ and $\bar{P}_B = P_B$, it remains to be shown that $\bar{P}(x, w) = P(x, w)$ for any $w \in T - B$.

Let $C = \{x, y, v, w\}$, which satisfies pretree, by assumption, with either $(xy)(vw)$ or $((xy)v)w$. Since $C = B \cup \{y, v, w\}$, lemma 3 implies that the representing measure on C' coincides with the restriction to C' of the defined measure on T'. Hence, $\bar{P}(x, w) = P(x, w)$ as required.

In conclusion, lemma 3 together with lemma 1 shows that the trinary and the quarternary conditions are necessary and sufficient for the representation of quadruples. Lemma 4 shows that if pretree is satisfied by all quadruples, then it is satisfied by the entire object set. This completes the proof of the representation theorem.

Appendix D
Uniqueness Considerations

It follows readily from the representation theorem that given a tree structure, the measure u is unique up to multiplication by a positive constant whenever none of the binary choice probabilities equals $\frac{1}{2}$. We show that the tree structure is uniquely determined by the binary and the trinary choice probabilities, but not by the binary data alone.

To show that binary choice probabilities do not always determine a unique tree structure, consider two different trees $(xy)z$ and $(yz)x$, and let α, β, γ denote, respectively, the unique aspects of x, y, z. Let θ denote the aspects shared by x and y, and let λ denote the aspects shared by y and z. Let u and v be the measures associated with $(xy)z$ and $(yz)x$, respectively, and suppose that

$$u(\alpha) = 2, \quad u(\beta) = 1, \quad u(\gamma) = 1, \quad \text{and} \quad u(\theta) = 2;$$

$$v(\alpha) = 8, \quad v(\beta) = 3, \quad v(\gamma) = 1, \quad \text{and} \quad v(\lambda) = 1.$$

By the assumed tree structures, $u(\lambda) = v(\theta) = 0$. It is easy to verify that the two trees yield identical binary choice probabilities: $P(x, y) = \frac{2}{3}$, $P(y, z) = \frac{3}{4}$, $P(x, z) = \frac{4}{5}$. We next show that the tree structure is uniquely determined by the binary *and* the trinary choice probabilities, provided all binary probabilities are nonzero. Consider a tree $(xy)z$ with a measure u, and aspects α, β, γ, θ defined as above. Assume $u(\alpha)$, $u(\beta)$, $u(\gamma)$, and $u(\theta)$ are nonzero. It follows from $(xy)z$ that

$$\frac{P(x, y)}{P(y, x)} = \frac{u(\alpha)}{u(\beta)} = \frac{u(\alpha) + u(\theta)u(\alpha)/(u(\alpha) + u(\beta))}{u(\beta) + u(\theta)u(\beta)/(u(\alpha) + u(\beta))} = \frac{P(x, xyz)}{P(y, xyz)}.$$

Suppose the data were compatible with another tree structure, say $(yz)x$ with no loss of generality. By the same argument

$$\frac{P(y, z)}{P(z, y)} = \frac{P(y, xyz)}{P(z, xyz)},$$

and

$$\frac{u(\beta) + u(\theta)}{u(\gamma)} = \frac{u(\beta) + u(\theta)u(\beta)/(u(\alpha) + u(\beta))}{u(\gamma)},$$

hence $u(\alpha)$ or $u(\theta)$ vanishes, a contradiction. Given binary and trinary probabilities, therefore, the structure of any triple and, hence, of the entire tree is uniquely determined.

Appendix E
Proof of the Compatibility Theorem

It follows readily from HEM (see equation 3) that

$$P(x, A) = P(x, A_1)P(A_1, A_2) \ldots P(A_{n-1}, A_n)$$

for some sequence $A_1, \ldots, A_n$, such that $A_n = A$ and $A_i \subset A_{i+1}$, $i = 1, \ldots, n - 1$. We show first that the sequence can be chosen so that $a_i = i + 1$, $1 \leq i \leq n$, where a_i is the cardinality of A_i. This condition is obviously satisfied in a binary tree in which each node joins, at most, two links. Suppose then that the tree contains three links that meet at the same node, for example, $\delta \mid \gamma$, $\delta \mid \beta$, and $\delta \mid \alpha$. Hence, by part b of equation 3,

$$P(A_\alpha, A_\delta) = \frac{m(\alpha)}{m(\alpha) + m(\beta) + m(\gamma)} = \frac{m(\alpha)}{m(\alpha) + m(\beta)} \times \frac{m(\alpha) + m(\beta)}{m(\alpha) + m(\beta) + m(\gamma)}$$

$$= P(A_\alpha, A_\alpha \cup A_\beta)P(A_\alpha \cup A_\beta, A_\delta),$$

and the result is readily extended to nodes with k links. Under pretree, therefore, $P(x, A)$ is expressible as a product where each factor $P(A_i, A_{i+1})$ is a probability of choosing between two branches.

Under equation 13, the probability of selecting x from A under a specified agenda equals $P(x, B_1)P(B_1, B_2) \ldots P(B_m, A)$, for some $B_1 \subset B_2 \cdots \subset B_m \subset A$. By compatibility, there exists a tree and hence a binary tree that refines both the agenda and the intrinsic tree structure. By the above argument, $P(x, A)$ is expressible as a product $P(x, A_1)P(A_1, A_2) \ldots P(A_{n-1}, A_n)$, where $a_i = i + 1$, $1 \leq i \leq n$, corresponding to a binary tree that refines both structures. Thus, each B_j, $j = 1, \ldots, m$, appears among the $A_{i'}$s $i = 1, \ldots, n$. Suppose $B_j = A_i$ and $B_{j+1} = A_{i+t}$, hence

$$P(B_j, B_{j+1}) = P(A_i, A_{i+t}) = \prod_{k=i}^{i+t-1} P(A_k, A_{k+1}),$$

and

$$P(x, A) = P(x, A_1)P(A_1, A_2)\dots P(A_{n-1}, A_n) = P(x, B_1)P(B_1, B_2)\dots P(B_m, A).$$

Hence, choice probability is unaffected by an agenda that is compatible with the intrinsic structure of a preference tree.

If the agenda is not compatible with the intrinsic tree, there exists some x, y, z in T such that both $(xy)z$ and $[xz]y$ hold. It is easy to verify (see the discussion in the text) that $P(x, xyz) \neq P(x, [xz]y)$ in this case, which establishes the necessity of the compatability condition.

Choice under Risk and Uncertainty

22 Prospect Theory: An Analysis of Decision under Risk

Daniel Kahneman and Amos Tversky

Introduction

Expected utility theory has dominated the analysis of decision making under risk. It has been generally accepted as a normative model of rational choice [24], and widely applied as a descriptive model of economic behavior, e.g. [15, 4]. Thus, it is assumed that all reasonable people would wish to obey the axioms of the theory [47, 36], and that most people actually do, most of the time.

The present chapter describes several classes of choice problems in which preferences systematically violate the axioms of expected utility theory. In the light of these observations we argue that utility theory, as it is commonly interpreted and applied, is not an adequate descriptive model and we propose an alternative account of choice under risk.

Critique

Decision making under risk can be viewed as a choice between prospects or gambles. A prospect $(x_1, p_1; \ldots; x_n, p_n)$ is a contract that yields outcome x_i with probability p_i, where $p_1 + p_2 + \cdots + p_n = 1$. To simplify notation, we omit null outcomes and use (x, p) to denote the prospect $(x, p; 0, 1 - p)$ that yields x with probability p and 0 with probability $1 - p$. The (riskless) prospect that yields x with certainty is denoted by (x). The present discussion is restricted to prospects with so-called objective or standard probabilities.

The application of expected utility theory to choices between prospects is based on the following three tenets.

(i) Expectation: $U(x_1, p_1; \ldots; x_n, p_n) = p_1 u(x_1) + \cdots + p_n u(x_n)$.

That is, the overall utility of a prospect, denoted by U, is the expected utility of its outcomes.

(ii) Asset Integration: $(x_1, p_1; \ldots; x_n, p_n)$ is acceptable at asset position w iff $U(w + x_1, p_1; \ldots; w + x_n, p_n) > u(w)$.

That is, a prospect is acceptable if the utility resulting from integrating the prospect with one's assets exceeds the utility of those assets alone. Thus, the domain of the utility function is final states (which include one's asset position) rather than gains or losses.

Although the domain of the utility function is not limited to any particular class of consequences, most applications of the theory have been concerned with monetary outcomes. Furthermore, most economic applications introduce the following additional assumption.

(iii) Risk Aversion: u is concave $(u'' < 0)$.

A person is risk averse if he prefers the certain prospect (x) to any risky prospect with expected value x. In expected utility theory, risk aversion is equivalent to the concavity of the utility function. The prevalence of risk aversion is perhaps the best known generalization regarding risky choices. It led the early decision theorists of the eighteenth century to propose that utility is a concave function of money, and this idea has been retained in modern treatments (Pratt [33], Arrow [4]).

In the following sections we demonstrate several phenomena which violate these tenets of expected utility theory. The demonstrations are based on the responses of students and university faculty to hypothetical choice problems. The respondents were presented with problems of the type illustrated below.

Which of the following would you prefer?

A: 50% chance to win 1,000,   B: 450 for sure.
    50% chance to win nothing;

The outcomes refer to Israeli currency. To appreciate the significance of the amounts involved, note that the median net monthly income for a family is about 3,000 Israeli pounds. The respondents were asked to imagine that they were actually faced with the choice described in the problem, and to indicate the decision they would have made in such a case. The responses were anonymous, and the instructions specified that there was no "correct" answer to such problems, and that the aim of the study was to find out how people choose among risky prospects. The problems were presented in questionnaire form, with at most a dozen problems per booklet. Several forms of each questionnaire were constructed so that subjects were exposed to the problems in different orders. In addition, two versions of each problem were used in which the left-right position of the prospects was reversed.

The problems described in this paper are selected illustrations of a series of effects. Every effect has been observed in several problems with different outcomes and probabilities. Some of the problems have also been presented to groups of students and faculty at the University of Stockholm and at the University of Michigan. The pattern of results was essentially identical to the results obtained from Israeli subjects.

The reliance on hypothetical choices raises obvious questions regarding the validity of the method and the generalizability of the results. We are keenly aware of these problems. However, all other methods that have been used to test utility theory also suffer from severe drawbacks. Real choices can be investigated either in the field, by naturalistic or statistical observations of economic behavior, or in the laboratory. Field studies can only provide for rather crude tests of qualitative predictions, because probabilities and utilities cannot be adequately measured in such contexts. Laboratory experiments have been designed to obtain precise measures of utility and probability from actual choices, but these experimental studies typically involve contrived gambles for small stakes, and a large number of repetitions of very similar problems. These features of laboratory gambling complicate the interpretation of the results and restrict their generality.

By default, the method of hypothetical choices emerges as the simplest procedure by which a large number of theoretical questions can be investigated. The use of the method relies on the assumption that people often know how they would behave in actual situations of choice, and on the further assumption that the subjects have no special reason to disguise their true preferences. If people are reasonably accurate in predicting their choices, the presence of common and systematic violations of expected utility theory in hypothetical problems provides presumptive evidence against that theory.

Certainty, Probability, and Possibility

In expected utility theory, the utilities of outcomes are weighted by their probabilities. The present section describes a series of choice problems in which people's preferences systematically violate this principle. We first show that people overweight outcomes that are considered certain, relative to outcomes which are merely probable—a phenomenon which we label the *certainty effect*.

The best known counter-example to expected utility theory which exploits the certainty effect was introduced by the French economist Maurice Allais in 1953 [2]. Allais' example has been discussed from both normative and descriptive standpoints by many authors [28, 38]. The following pair of choice problems is a variation of Allais' example, which differs from the original in that it refers to moderate rather than to extremely large gains. The number of respondents who answered each problem is denoted by N, and the percentage who choose each option is given in brackets.

Problem 1: Choose between

A:	2,500 with probability	.33,	B: 2,400 with certainty.
	2,400 with probability	.66,	
	0 with probability	.01;	

$N = 72$ [18]   [82]*

Problem 2: Choose between

    C: 2,500 with probability .33,   D: 2,400 with probability .34,
         0 with probability   .67;   0 with probability   .66.
$N = 72$ [83]*   [17]

The data show that 82 per cent of the subjects chose B in problem 1, and 83 per cent of the subjects chose C in problem 2. Each of these preferences is significant at the .01 level, as denoted by the asterisk. Moreover, the analysis of individual patterns of choice indicates that a majority of respondents (61 per cent) made the modal choice in both problems. This pattern of preferences violates expected utility theory in the manner originally described by Allais. According to that theory, with $u(0) = 0$, the first preference implies

$$u(2,400) > .33u(2,500) + .66u(2,400) \qquad \text{or} \qquad .34u(2,400) > .33u(2,500)$$

while the second preference implies the reverse inequality. Note that problem 2 is obtained from problem 1 by eliminating a .66 chance of winning 2400 from both prospects under consideration. Evidently, this change produces a greater reduction in desirability when it alters the character of the prospect from a sure gain to a probable one, than when both the original and the reduced prospects are uncertain.

A simpler demonstration of the same phenomenon, involving only two-outcome gambles is given below. This example is also based on Allais [2].

Problem 3:

    A: (4,000, .80),   or   B: (3,000).
$N = 95$ [20]   [80]*

Problem 4:

    C: (4,000, .20),   or   D: (3,000, .25).
$N = 95$ [65]*   [35]

In this pair of problems as well as in all other problem-pairs in this section, over half the respondents violated expected utility theory. To show that the modal pattern of preferences in problems 3 and 4 is not compatible with the theory, set $u(0) = 0$, and recall that the choice of B implies $u(3,000)/u(4,000) > 4/5$, whereas the choice of C implies the reverse inequality. Note that the prospect $C = (4,000, .20)$ can be expressed as $(A, .25)$, while the prospect $D = (3,000, .25)$ can be rewritten as $(B, .25)$. The substitution axiom of utility theory asserts that if B is preferred to A, then any (probability) mixture (B, p) must be preferred to the mixture (A, p). Our subjects did not obey this axiom. Apparently, reducing the probability of winning from 1.0 to .25 has a greater effect than the reduction from .8 to .2. The following pair of choice problems illustrates the certainty effect with non-monetary outcomes.

Problem 5:

	A:	50% chance to win a three-week tour of England, France, and Italy;	B:	A one-week tour of England, with certainty.
$N = 72$	[22]		[78]*	

Problem 6:

	C:	5% chance to win a three-week tour of England, France, and Italy;	D:	10% chance to win a one-week tour of England.
$N = 72$	[67]*		[33]	

The certainty effect is not the only type of violation of the substitution axiom. Another situation in which this axiom fails is illustrated by the following problems.

Problem 7:

	A:	(6,000, .45),	B:	(3,000, .90).
$N = 66$	[14]		[86]*	

Problem 8:

	C:	(6,000, .001),	D:	(3,000, .002).
$N = 66$	[73]*		[27]	

Note that in problem 7 the probabilities of winning are substantial (.90 and .45), and most people choose the prospect where winning is more probable. In problem 8, there is a *possibility* of winning, although the probabilities of winning are minuscule (.002 and .001) in both prospects. In this situation where winning is possible but not probable, most people choose the prospect that offers the larger gain. Similar results have been reported by MacCrimmon and Larsson [28].

The above problems illustrate common attitudes toward risk or chance that cannot be captured by the expected utility model. The results suggest the following empirical generalization concerning the manner in which the substitution axiom is violated. If (y, pq) is equivalent to (x, p), then (y, pqr) is preferred to (x, pr), $0 < p, q, r < 1$.

Table 22.1
Preferences between Positive and Negative Prospects

Positive prospects				Negative prospects			
Problem 3: $N = 95$	(4,000, .80) [20]	<	(3,000). [80]*	Problem 3′: $N = 95$	(−4,000, .80) [92]*	>	(−3,000). [8]
Problem 4: $N = 95$	(4,000, .20) [65]*	>	(3,000, .25). [35]	Problem 4′: $N = 95$	(−4,000, .20) [42]	<	(−3,000, .25). [58]
Problem 7: $N = 66$	(3,000, .90) [86]*	>	(6,000, .45). [14]	Problem 7′: $N = 66$	(−3,000, .90) [8]	<	(−6,000, .45). [92]*
Problem 8: $N = 66$	(3,000, .002) [27]	<	(6,000, .001). [73]*	Problem 8′: $N = 66$	(−3,000, .002) [70]*	>	(−6,000, .001). [30]

This property is incorporated into an alternative theory, developed in the second part of the chapter.

The Reflection Effect

The previous section discussed preferences between positive prospects, i.e., prospects that involve no losses. What happens when the signs of the outcomes are reversed so that gains are replaced by losses? The left-hand column of table 22.1 displays four of the choice problems that were discussed in the previous section, and the right-hand column displays choice problems in which the signs of the outcomes are reversed. We use −x to denote the loss of x, and > to denote the prevalent preference, i,e., the choice made by the majority of subjects.

In each of the four problems in table 22.1 the preference between negative prospects is the mirror image of the preference between positive prospects. Thus, the reflection of prospects around 0 reverses the preference order. We label this pattern the *reflection effect*.

Let us turn now to the implications of these data. First, note that the reflection effect implies that risk aversion in the positive domain is accompanied by risk seeking in the negative domain. In problem 3′, for example, the majority of subjects were willing to accept a risk of .80 to lose 4,000, in preference to a sure loss of 3,000, although the gamble has a lower expected value. The occurrence of risk seeking in choices between negative prospects was noted early by Markowitz [29]. Williams [48] reported data where a translation of outcomes produces a dramatic shift from risk aversion to risk seeking. For example, his subjects were indifferent between (100, .65; −100, .35) and (0), indicating risk aversion. They were also indifferent between (−200, .80) and (−100), indicating risk seeking. A recent review by Fishburn and Kochenberger [14] documents the prevalence of risk seeking in choices between negative prospects.

Second, recall that the preferences between the positive prospects in table 22.1 are inconsistent with expected utility theory. The preferences between the corresponding negative prospects also violate the expectation principle in the same manner. For example, problems 3' and 4', like problems 3 and 4, demonstrate that outcomes which are obtained with certainty are overweighted relative to uncertain outcomes. In the positive domain, the certainty effect contributes to a risk averse preference for a sure gain over a larger gain that is merely probable. In the negative domain, the same effect leads to a risk seeking preference for a loss that is merely probable over a smaller loss that is certain. The same psychological principle—the overweighting of certainty—favors risk aversion in the domain of gains and risk seeking in the domain of losses.

Third, the reflection effect eliminates aversion for uncertainty or variability as an explanation of the certainty effect. Consider, for example, the prevalent preferences for (3,000) over (4,000, .80) and for (4,000, .20) over (3,000, .25). To resolve this apparent inconsistency one could invoke the assumption that people prefer prospects that have high expected value and small variance (see, e.g., Allais [2]; Markowitz [30]; Tobin [41]). Since (3,000) has no variance while (4,000, .80) has large variance, the former prospect could be chosen despite its lower expected value. When the prospects are reduced, however, the difference in variance between (3,000, .25) and (4,000, .20) may be insufficient to overcome the difference in expected value. Because (−3,000) has both higher expected value and lower variance than (−4,000, .80), this account entails that the sure loss should be preferred, contrary to the data. Thus, our data are incompatible with the notion that certainty is generally desirable. Rather, it appears that certainty increases the aversiveness of losses as well as the desirability of gains.

Probabilistic Insurance
The prevalence of the purchase of insurance against both large and small losses has been regarded by many as strong evidence for the concavity of the utility function for money. Why otherwise would people spend so much money to purchase insurance policies at a price that exceeds the expected actuarial cost? However, an examination of the relative attractiveness of various forms of insurance does not support the notion that the utility function for money is concave everywhere. For example, people often prefer insurance programs that offer limited coverage with low or zero deductible over comparable policies that offer higher maximal coverage with higher

deductibles—contrary to risk aversion (see, e.g., Fuchs [16]). Another type of insurance problem in which people's responses are inconsistent with the concavity hypothesis may be called probabilistic insurance. To illustrate this concept, consider the following problem, which was presented to 95 Stanford University students.

Problem 9: Suppose you consider the possibility of insuring some property against damage, e.g., fire or theft. After examining the risks and the premium you find that you have no clear preference between the options of purchasing insurance or leaving the property uninsured.

It is then called to your attention that the insurance company offers a new program called *probabilistic insurance*. In this program you pay half of the regular premium. In case of damage, there is a 50 per cent chance that you pay the other half of the premium and the insurance company covers all the losses; and there is a 50 per cent chance that you get back your insurance payment and suffer all the losses. For example, if an accident occurs on an odd day of the month, you pay the other half of the regular premium and your losses are covered; but if the accident occurs on an even day of the month, your insurance payment is refunded and your losses are not covered.

Recall that the premium for full coverage is such that you find this insurance barely worth its cost.

Under these circumstances, would you purchase probabilistic insurance:

	Yes,	No.
$N = 95$	[20]	[80]*

Although problem 9 may appear contrived, it is worth noting that probabilistic insurance represents many forms of protective action where one pays a certain cost to reduce the probability of an undesirable event—without eliminating it altogether. The installation of a burglar alarm, the replacement of old tires, and the decision to stop smoking can all be viewed as probabilistic insurance.

The responses to problem 9 and to several other variants of the same question indicate that probabilistic insurance is generally unattractive. Apparently, reducing the probability of a loss from p to $p/2$ is less valuable than reducing the probability of that loss from $p/2$ to 0.

In contrast to these data, expected utility theory (with a concave u) implies that probabilistic insurance is superior to regular insurance. That is, if at asset position w one is just willing to pay a premium y to insure against a probability p of losing x, then one should definitely be willing to pay a smaller premium ry to reduce the probability of losing x from p to $(1 - r)p$, $0 < r < 1$. Formally, if one is indifferent between $(w - x, p; w, 1 - p)$ and $(w - y)$, then one should prefer probabilistic insurance $(w - x, (1 - r)p; w - y, rp; w - ry, 1 - p)$ over regular insurance $(w - y)$.

To prove this proposition, we show that

$$pu(w - x) + (1 - p)u(w) = u(w - y)$$

implies

$$(1 - r)pu(w - x) + rpu(w - y) + (1 - p)u(w - ry) > u(w - y).$$

Without loss of generality, we can set $u(w - x) = 0$ and $u(w) = 1$. Hence, $u(w - y) = 1 - p$, and we wish to show that

$$rp(1 - p) + (1 - p)u(w - ry) > 1 - p \qquad \text{or} \qquad u(w - ry) > 1 - rp$$

which holds if and only if u is concave.

This is a rather puzzling consequence of the risk aversion hypothesis of utility theory, because probabilistic insurance appears intuitively riskier than regular insurance, which entirely eliminates the element of risk. Evidently, the intuitive notion of risk is not adequately captured by the assumed concavity of the utility function for wealth.

The aversion for probabilistic insurance is particularly intriguing because all insurance is, in a sense, probabilistic. The most avid buyer of insurance remains vulnerable to many financial and other risks which his policies do not cover. There appears to be a significant difference between probabilistic insurance and what may be called contingent insurance, which provides the certainty of coverage for a specified type of risk. Compare, for example, probabilistic insurance against all forms of loss or damage to the contents of your home and contingent insurance that eliminates all risk of loss from theft, say, but does not cover other risks, e.g., fire. We conjecture that contingent insurance will be generally more attractive than probabilistic insurance when the probabilities of unprotected loss are equated. Thus, two prospects that are equivalent in probabilities and outcomes could have different values depending on their formulation. Several demonstrations of this general phenomenon are described in the next section.

The Isolation Effect

In order to simplify the choice between alternatives, people often disregard components that the alternatives share, and focus on the components that distinguish them (Tversky [44]). This approach to choice problems may produce inconsistent preferences, because a pair of prospects can be decomposed into common and distinctive components in more than one way, and different decompositions sometimes lead to different preferences. We refer to this phenomenon as the *isolation effect*.

Problem 10: Consider the following two-stage game. In the first stage, there is a probability of .75 to end the game without winning anything, and a probability of .25 to move into the second stage. If you reach the second stage you have a choice between

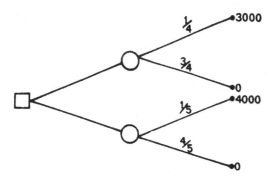

Figure 22.1
The representation of problem 4 as a decision tree (standard formulation).

(4,000, .80)   and   (3,000).

Your choice must be made before the game starts, i.e., before the outcome of the first stage is known.

Note that in this game, one has a choice between .25 × .80 = .20 chance to win 4,000, and a .25 × 1.0 = .25 chance to win 3,000. Thus, in terms of final outcomes and probabilities one faces a choice between (4,000, .20) and (3,000, .25), as in problem 4 above. However, the dominant preferences are different in the two problems. Of 141 subjects who answered problem 10, 78 per cent chose the latter prospect, contrary to the modal preference in problem 4. Evidently, people ignored the first stage of the game, whose outcomes are shared by both prospects, and considered problem 10 as a choice between (3,000) and (4,000, .80), as in problem 3 above.

The standard and the sequential formulations of problem 4 are represented as decision trees in figures 22.1 and 22.2, respectively. Following the usual convention, squares denote decision nodes and circles denote chance nodes. The essential difference between the two representations is in the location of the decision node. In the standard form (figure 22.1), the decision maker faces a choice between two risky prospects, whereas in the sequential form (figure 22.2) he faces a choice between a risky and a riskless prospect. This is accomplished by introducing a dependency between the prospects without changing either probabilities or outcomes. Specifically, the event "not winning 3,000" is included in the event "not winning 4,000" in the sequential formulation, while the two events are independent in the standard formulation. Thus, the outcome of winning 3,000 has a certainty advantage in the sequential formulation, which it does not have in the standard formulation.

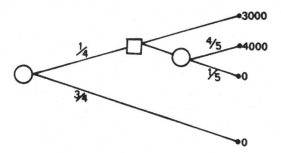

Figure 22.2
The representation of problem 10 as a decision tree (sequential formulation).

The reversal of preferences due to the dependency among events is particularly significant because it violates the basic supposition of a decision-theoretical analysis, that choices between prospects are determined solely by the probabilities of final states.

It is easy to think of decision problems that are most naturally represented in one of the forms above rather than in the other. For example, the choice between two different risky ventures is likely to be viewed in the standard form. On the other hand, the following problem is most likely to be represented in the sequential form. One may invest money in a venture with some probability of losing one's capital if the venture fails, and with a choice between a fixed agreed return and a percentage of earnings if it succeeds. The isolation effect implies that the contingent certainty of the fixed return enhances the attractiveness of this option, relative to a risky venture with the same probabilities and outcomes.

The preceding problem illustrated how preferences may be altered by different representations of probabilities. We now show how choices may be altered by varying the representation of outcomes.

Consider the following problems, which were presented to two different groups of subjects.

Problem 11: In addition to whatever you own, you have been given 1,000. You are now asked to choose between

    A: (1,000, .50),   and   B: (500).

$N = 70$ [16]   [84]*

Problem 12: In addition to whatever you own, you have been given 2,000. You are now asked to choose between

C: (−1,000, .50),   and   D: (−500).
N = 68 [69*]   [31]

The majority of subjects chose B in the first problem and C in the second. These preferences conform to the reflection effect observed in table 22.1, which exhibits risk aversion for positive prospects and risk seeking for negative ones. Note, however, that when viewed in terms of final states, the two choice problems are identical. Specifically,

A = (2,000, .50; 1,000, .50) = C,   and   B = (1,500) = D.

In fact, problem 12 is obtained from problem 11 by adding 1,000 to the initial bonus, and subtracting 1,000 from all outcomes. Evidently, the subjects did not integrate the bonus with the prospects. The bonus did not enter into the comparison of prospects because it was common to both options in each problem.

The pattern of results observed in problems 11 and 12 is clearly inconsistent with utility theory. In that theory, for example, the same utility is assigned to a wealth of $100,000, regardless of whether it was reached from a prior wealth of $95,000 or $105,000. Consequently, the choice between a total wealth of $100,000 and even chances to own $95,000 or $105,000 should be independent of whether one currently owns the smaller or the larger of these two amounts. With the added assumption of risk aversion, the theory entails that the certainty of owning $100,000 should always be preferred to the gamble. However, the responses to problem 12 and to several of the previous questions suggest that this pattern will be obtained if the individual owns the smaller amount, but not if he owns the larger amount.

The apparent neglect of a bonus that was common to both options in problems 11 and 12 implies that the carriers of value or utility are changes of wealth, rather than final asset positions that include current wealth. This conclusion is the cornerstone of an alternative theory of risky choice, which is described in the following sections.

Theory

The preceding discussion reviewed several empirical effects which appear to invalidate expected utility theory as a descriptive model. The remainder of the chapter presents an alternative account of individual decision making under risk, called prospect theory. The theory is developed for simple prospects with monetary outcomes and stated probabilities, but it can be extended to more involved choices. Prospect theory distinguishes two phases in the choice process: an early phase of editing and a subsequent phase of evaluation. The editing phase consists of a preliminary analysis of the offered prospects, which often yields a simpler representation of these prospects. In the second phase, the edited prospects are evaluated and the prospect of highest value is chosen. We next outline the editing phase, and develop a formal model of the evaluation phase.

The function of the editing phase is to organize and reformulate the options so as to simplify subsequent evaluation and choice. Editing consists of the application of several operations that transform the outcomes and probabilities associated with the offered prospects. The major operations of the editing phase are described below.

Coding. The evidence discussed in the previous section shows that people normally perceive outcomes as gains and losses, rather than as final states of wealth or welfare. Gains and losses, of course, are defined relative to some neutral reference point. The reference point usually corresponds to the current asset position, in which case gains and losses coincide with the actual amounts that are received or paid. However, the location of the reference point, and the consequent coding of outcomes as gains or losses, can be affected by the formulation of the offered prospects, and by the expectations of the decision maker.

Combination. Prospects can sometimes be simplified by combining the probabilities associated with identical outcomes. For example, the prospect $(200, .25; 200, .25)$ will be reduced to $(200, .50)$, and evaluated in this form.

Segregation. Some prospects contain a riskless component that is segregated from the risky component in the editing phase. For example, the prospect $(300, .80; 200, .20)$ is naturally decomposed into a sure gain of 200 and the risky prospect $(100, .80)$. Similarly, the prospect $(-400, .40; -100, .60)$ is readily seen to consist of a sure loss of 100 and of the prospect $(-300, .40)$.

The preceding operations are applied to each prospect separately. The following operation is applied to a set of two or more prospects.

Cancellation. The essence of the isolation effects described earlier is the discarding of components that are shared by the offered prospects. Thus, our respondents apparently ignored the first stage of the sequential game presented in problem 10, because this stage was common to both options, and they evaluated the prospects with respect to the results of the second stage (see figure 22.2). Similarly, they neglected the common bonus that was added to the prospects in problems 11 and 12. Another type of cancellation involves the discarding of common constituents, i.e., outcome-probability pairs. For example, the choice between $(200, .20; 100, .50; -50, .30)$ and $(200, .20; 150, .50; -100, .30)$ can be reduced by cancellation to a choice between $(100, .50; -50, .30)$ and $(150, .50; -100, .30)$.

Two additional operations that should be mentioned are simplification and the detection of dominance. The first refers to the simplification of prospects by rounding probabilities or outcomes. For example, the prospect $(101, .49)$ is likely to be recoded as an even chance to win 100. A particularly important form of simplification involves the discarding of extremely unlikely outcomes. The second operation involves the scanning of offered prospects to detect dominated alternatives, which are rejected without further evaluation.

Because the editing operations facilitate the task of decision, it is assumed that they are performed whenever possible. However, some editing operations either permit or prevent the application of others. For example, $(500, .20; 101, .49)$ will appear to dominate $(500, .15; 99, .51)$ if the second constituents of both prospects are simplified to $(100, .50)$. The final edited prospects could, therefore, depend on the sequence of editing operations, which is likely to vary with the structure of the offered set and with the format of the display. A detailed study of this problem is beyond the scope of the present treatment. In this paper we discuss choice problems where it is reasonable to assume either that the original formulation of the prospects leaves no room for further editing, or that the edited prospects can be specified without ambiguity.

Many anomalies of preference result from the editing of prospects. For example, the inconsistencies associated with the isolation effect result from the cancellation of common components. Some intransitivities of choice are explained by a simplification that eliminates small differences between prospects (see Tversky [43]). More generally, the preference order between prospects need not be invariant across contexts, because the same offered prospect could be edited in different ways depending on the context in which it appears.

Following the editing phase, the decision maker is assumed to evaluate each of the edited prospects, and to choose the prospect of highest value. The overall value of an edited prospect, denoted V, is expressed in terms of two scales, π and v.

The first scale, π, associates with each probability p a decision weight $\pi(p)$, which reflects the impact of p on the over-all value of the prospect. However, π is not a probability measure, and it will be shown later that $\pi(p) + \pi(1 - p)$ is typically less than unity. The second scale, v, assigns to each outcome x a number $v(x)$, which reflects the subjective value of that outcome. Recall that outcomes are defined relative to a reference point, which serves as the zero point of the value scale. Hence, v measures the value of deviations from that reference point, i.e., gains and losses.

The present formulation is concerned with simple prospects of the form $(x, p; y, q)$, which have at most two non-zero outcomes. In such a prospect, one receives x with probability p, y with probability q, and nothing with probability $1 - p - q$, where $p + q \leq 1$. An offered prospect is strictly positive if its outcomes are all positive, i.e., if $x, y > 0$ and $p + q = 1$; it is strictly negative if its outcomes are all negative. A prospect is regular if it is neither strictly positive nor strictly negative.

The basic equation of the theory describes the manner in which π and v are combined to determine the over-all value of regular prospects.

If $(x, p; y, q)$ is a regular prospect (i.e., either $p + q < 1$, or $x \geq 0 \geq y$, or $x \leq 0 \leq y$), then

$$V(x, p; y, q) = \pi(p)v(x) + \pi(q)v(y) \tag{1}$$

where $v(0) = 0$, $\pi(0) = 0$, and $\pi(1) = 1$. As in utility theory, V is defined on prospects, while v is defined on outcomes. The two scales coincide for sure prospects, where $V(x, 1.0) = V(x) = v(x)$.

Equation (1) generalizes expected utility theory by relaxing the expectation principle. An axiomatic analysis of this representation is sketched in the appendix, which describes conditions that ensure the existence of a unique π and a ratio-scale v satisfying equation (1).

The evaluation of strictly positive and strictly negative prospects follows a different rule. In the editing phase such prospects are segregated into two components: (i) the riskless component, i.e., the minimum gain or loss which is certain to be obtained or paid; (ii) the risky component, i.e., the additional gain or loss which is actually at stake. The evaluation of such prospects is described in the next equation.

If $p + q = 1$ and either $x > y > 0$ or $x < y < 0$, then

$$V(x, p; y, q) = v(y) + \pi(p)[v(x) - v(y)]. \tag{2}$$

That is, the value of a strictly positive or strictly negative prospect equals the value of the riskless component plus the value-difference between the outcomes, multiplied by the weight associated with the more extreme outcome. For example, $V(400, .25;$ $100, .75) = v(100) + \pi(.25)[v(400) - v(100)]$. The essential feature of equation (2) is that a decision weight is applied to the value-difference $v(x) - v(y)$, which represents the risky component of the prospect, but not to $v(y)$, which represents the riskless component. Note that the right-hand side of equation (2) equals $\pi(p)v(x) +$ $[1 - \pi(p)]v(y)$. Hence, equation (2) reduces to equation (1) if $\pi(p) + \pi(1 - p) = 1$. As will be shown later, this condition is not generally satisfied.

Many elements of the evaluation model have appeared in previous attempts to modify expected utility theory. Markowitz [29] was the first to propose that utility be defined on gains and losses rather than on final asset positions, an assumption which has been implicitly accepted in most experimental measurements of utility (see, e.g., [7, 32]). Markowitz also noted the presence of risk seeking in preferences among positive as well as among negative prospects, and he proposed a utility function which has convex and concave regions in both the positive and the negative domains. His treatment, however, retains the expectation principle; hence it cannot account for the many violations of this principle; see, e.g., table 22.1.

The replacement of probabilities by more general weights was proposed by Edwards [9], and this model was investigated in several empirical studies (e.g., [3, 42]). Similar models were developed by Fellner [12], who introduced the concept of decision weight to explain aversion for ambiguity, and by van Dam [46] who attempted to scale decision weights. For other critical analyses of expected utility theory and alternative choice models, see Allais [2], Coombs [6], Fishburn [13], and Hansson [22].

The equations of prospect theory retain the general bilinear form that underlies expected utility theory. However, in order to accomodate the effects described in the first part of the paper, we are compelled to assume that values are attached to changes rather than to final states, and that decision weights do not coincide with stated probabilities. These departures from expected utility theory must lead to normatively unacceptable consequences, such as inconsistencies, intransitivities, and violations of dominance. Such anomalies of preference are normally corrected by the decision maker when he realizes that his preferences are inconsistent, intransitive, or inadmissible. In many situations, however, the decision maker does not have the opportunity to discover that his preferences could violate decision rules that he wishes to obey. In these circumstances the anomalies implied by prospect theory are expected to occur.

The Value Function

An essential feature of the present theory is that the carriers of value are changes in wealth or welfare, rather than final states. This assumption is compatible with basic principles of perception and judgment. Our perceptual apparatus is attuned to the evaluation of changes or differences rather than to the evaluation of absolute magnitudes. When we respond to attributes such as brightness, loudness, or temperature, the past and present context of experience defines an adaptation level, or reference point, and stimuli are perceived in relation to this reference point [23]. Thus, an object at a given temperature may be experienced as hot or cold to the touch depending on the temperature to which one has adapted. The same principle applies to non-sensory attributes such as health, prestige, and wealth. The same level of wealth, for example, may imply abject poverty for one person and great riches for another—depending on their current assets.

The emphasis on changes as the carriers of value should not be taken to imply that the value of a particular change is independent of initial position. Strictly speaking, value should be treated as a function in two arguments: the asset position that serves as reference point, and the magnitude of the change (positive or negative) from that reference point. An individual's attitude to money, say, could be described by a book, where each page presents the value function for changes at a particular asset position. Clearly, the value functions described on different pages are not identical: they are likely to become more linear with increases in assets. However, the preference order of prospects is not greatly altered by small or even moderate variations in asset position. The certainty equivalent of the prospect (1,000, .50), for example, lies between 300 and 400 for most people, in a wide range of asset positions. Consequently, the representation of value as a function in one argument generally provides a satisfactory approximation.

Many sensory and perceptual dimensions share the property that the psychological response is a concave function of the magnitude of physical change. For example, it is easier to discriminate between a change of 3° and a change of 6° in room temperature, than it is to discriminate between a change of 13° and a change of 16°. We propose that this principle applies in particular to the evaluation of monetary changes. Thus, the difference in value between a gain of 100 and a gain of 200 appears to be greater than the difference between a gain of 1,100 and a gain of 1,200. Similarly, the difference between a loss of 100 and a loss of 200 appears greater than the difference between a loss of 1,100 and a loss of 1,200, unless the larger loss is intolerable. Thus, we hypothesize that the value function for changes of wealth is normally concave above the reference point ($v''(x) < 0$, for $x > 0$) and often convex below it ($v''(x) > 0$, for $x < 0$). That is, the marginal value of both gains and losses generally decreases with their magnitude. Some support for this hypothesis has been reported by Galanter and Pliner [17], who scaled the perceived magnitude of monetary and non-monetary gains and losses.

The above hypothesis regarding the shape of the value function was based on responses to gains and losses in a riskless context. We propose that the value function which is derived from risky choices shares the same characteristics, as illustrated in the following problems.

Problem 13:

| (6,000, .25), | or | (4,000, .25; 2,000, .25). |
| $N = 68$ [18] | | [82]* |

Problem 13':

$$(-6,000, .25), \quad \text{or} \quad (-4,000, .25; -2,000, .25).$$
$$N = 64 \quad [70]^* \quad\quad\quad\quad\quad [30]$$

Applying equation 1 to the modal preference in these problems yields

$$\pi(.25)v(6,000) < \pi(.25)[v(4,000) + v(2,000)] \quad \text{and}$$

$$\pi(.25)v(-6,000) > \pi(.25)[v(-4,000) + v(-2,000)].$$

Hence, $v(6,000) < v(4,000) + v(2,000)$ and $v(-6,000) > v(-4,000) + v(-2,000)$. These preferences are in accord with the hypothesis that the value function is concave for gains and convex for losses.

Any discussion of the utility function for money must leave room for the effect of special circumstances on preferences. For example, the utility function of an individual who needs $60,000 to purchase a house may reveal an exceptionally steep rise near the critical value. Similarly, an individual's aversion to losses may increase sharply near the loss that would compel him to sell his house and move to a less desirable neighborhood. Hence, the derived value (utility) function of an individual does not always reflect "pure" attitudes to money, since it could be affected by additional consequences associated with specific amounts. Such perturbations can readily produce convex regions in the value function for gains and concave regions in the value function for losses. The latter case may be more common since large losses often necessitate changes in life style.

A salient characteristic of attitudes to changes in welfare is that losses loom larger than gains. The aggravation that one experiences in losing a sum of money appears to be greater than the pleasure associated with gaining the same amount [17]. Indeed, most people find symmetric bets of the form $(x, .50; -x, .50)$ distinctly unattractive. Moreover, the aversiveness of symmetric fair bets generally increases with the size of the stake. That is, if $x > y \geq 0$, then $(y, .50; -y, .50)$ is preferred to $(x, .50; -x, .50)$. According to equation (1), therefore,

$$v(y) + v(-y) > v(x) + v(-x) \quad \text{and} \quad v(-y) - v(-x) > v(x) - v(y).$$

Setting $y = 0$ yields $v(x) < -v(-x)$, and letting y approach x yields $v'(x) < v'(-x)$, provided v', the derivative of v, exists. Thus, the value function for losses is steeper than the value function for gains.

In summary, we have proposed that the value function is (i) defined on deviations from the reference point; (ii) generally concave for gains and commonly convex for losses; (iii) steeper for losses than for gains. A value function which satisfies these

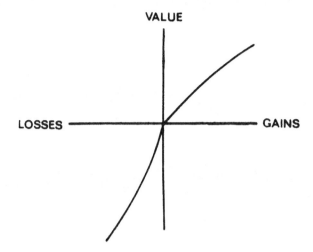

Figure 22.3
A hypothetical value function.

properties is displayed in figure 22.3. Note that the proposed S-shaped value function is steepest at the reference point, in marked contrast to the utility function postulated by Markowitz [29] which is relatively shallow in that region.

Although the present theory can be applied to derive the value function from preferences between prospects, the actual scaling is considerably more complicated than in utility theory, because of the introduction of decision weights. For example, decision weights could produce risk aversion and risk seeking even with a linear value function. Nevertheless, it is of interest that the main properties ascribed to the value function have been observed in a detailed analysis of von Neumann–Morgenstern utility functions for changes of wealth (Fishburn and Kochenberger [14]). The functions had been obtained from thirty decision makers in various fields of business, in five independent studies [5, 18, 19, 21, 40]. Most utility functions for gains were concave, most functions for losses were convex, and only three individuals exhibited risk aversion for both gains and losses. With a single exception, utility functions were considerably steeper for losses than for gains.

The Weighting Function

In prospect theory, the value of each outcome is multiplied by a decision weight. Decision weights are inferred from choices between prospects much as subjective probabilities are inferred from preferences in the Ramsey–Savage approach. However, decision weights are not probabilities: they do not obey the probability axioms and they should not be interpreted as measures of degree or belief.

Consider a gamble in which one can win 1,000 or nothing, depending on the toss of a fair coin. For any reasonable person, the probability of winning is .50 in this situation. This can be verified in a variety of ways, e.g., by showing that the subject is indifferent between betting on heads or tails, or by his verbal report that he considers the two events equiprobable. As will be shown below, however, the decision weight $\pi(.50)$ which is derived from choices is likely to be smaller than .50. Decision weights measure the impact of events on the desirability of prospects, and not merely the perceived likelihood of these events. The two scales coincide (i.e., $\pi(p) = p$) if the expectation principle holds, but not otherwise.

The choice problems discussed in the present paper were formulated in terms of explicit numerical probabilities, and our analysis assumes that the respondents adopted the stated values of p. Furthermore, since the events were identified only by their stated probabilities, it is possible in this context to express decision weights as a function of stated probability. In general, however, the decision weight attached to an event could be influenced by other factors, e.g., ambiguity [10, 11].

We turn now to discuss the salient properties of the weighting function π, which relates decision weights to stated probabilities. Naturally, π is an increasing function of p, with $\pi(0) = 0$ and $\pi(1) = 1$. That is, outcomes contingent on an impossible event are ignored, and the scale is normalized so that $\pi(p)$ is the ratio of the weight associated with the probability p to the weight associated with the certain event.

We first discuss some properties of the weighting function for small probabilities. The preferences in problems 8 and 8' suggest that for small values of p, π is a subadditive function of p, i.e., $\pi(rp) > r\pi(p)$ for $0 < r < 1$. Recall that in problem 8, (6,000, .001) is preferred to (3,000, .002). Hence

$$\frac{\pi(.001)}{\pi(.002)} > \frac{v(3,000)}{v(6,000)} > \frac{1}{2} \quad \text{by the concavity of } v.$$

The reflected preferences in problem 8' yield the same conclusion. The pattern of preferences in problems 7 and 7', however, suggests that subadditivity need not hold for large values of p.

Furthermore, we propose that very low probabilities are generally overweighted, that is, $\pi(p) > p$ for small p. Consider the following choice problems.

Problem 14:

$$(5,000, .001), \quad \text{or} \quad (5).$$
$N = 72 \quad [72]^* \qquad\qquad\qquad [28]$

Problem 14′:

$$(-5,000, .001), \quad \text{or} \quad (-5).$$
$$N = 72 \quad [17] \qquad\qquad\qquad [83]^*$$

Note that in problem 14, people prefer what is in effect a lottery ticket over the expected value of that ticket. In problem 14′, on the other hand, they prefer a small loss, which can be viewed as the payment of an insurance premium, over a small probability of a large loss. Similar observations have been reported by Markowitz [29]. In the present theory, the preference for the lottery in problem 14 implies $\pi(.001)v(5,000) > v(5)$, hence $\pi(.001) > v(5)/v(5,000) > .001$, assuming the value function for gains is concave. The readiness to pay for insurance in problem 14′ implies the same conclusion, assuming the value function for losses is convex.

It is important to distinguish overweighting, which refers to a property of decision weights, from the overestimation that is commonly found in the assessment of the probability of rare events. Note that the issue of overestimation does not arise in the present context, where the subject is assumed to adopt the stated value of p. In many real-life situations, overestimation and overweighting may both operate to increase the impact of rare events.

Although $\pi(p) > p$ for low probabilities, there is evidence to suggest that, for all $0 < p < 1$, $\pi(p) + \pi(1 - p) < 1$. We label this property subcertainty. It is readily seen that the typical preferences in any version of Allias' example (see, e.g., problems 1 and 2) imply subcertainty for the relevant value of p. Applying equation (1) to the prevalent preferences in problems 1 and 2 yields, respectively,

$$v(2,400) > \pi(.66)v(2,400) + \pi(.33)v(2,500),$$

i.e.,

$$[1 - \pi(.66]v(2,400) > \pi(.33)v(2,500)$$

and

$$\pi(.33)v(2,500) > \pi(.34)v(2,400);$$

hence,

$$1 - \pi(.66) > \pi(.34), \quad \text{or} \quad \pi(.66) + \pi(.34) < 1.$$

Applying the same analysis to Allais' original example yields $\pi(.89) + \pi(.11) < 1$, and some data reported by MacCrimmon and Larsson [28] imply subcertainty for additional values of p.

The slope of π in the interval $(0, 1)$ can be viewed as a measure of the sensitivity of preferences to changes in probability. Subcertainty entails that π is regressive with respect to p, i.e., that preferences are generally less sensitive to variations of probability than the expectation principle would dictate. Thus, subcertainty captures an essential element of people's attitudes to uncertain events, namely that the sum of the weights associated with complementary events is typically less than the weight associated with the certain event.

Recall that the violations of the substitution axiom discussed earlier in this paper conform to the following rule: If (x, p) is equivalent to (y, pq) then (x, pr) is not preferred to (y, pqr), $0 < p, q, r \leq 1$. By equation (1),

$$\pi(p)v(x) = \pi(pq)v(y) \quad \text{implies} \quad \pi(pr)v(x) \leq \pi(pqr)v(y);$$

hence,

$$\frac{\pi(pq)}{\pi(p)} \leq \frac{\pi(pqr)}{\pi(pr)}.$$

Thus, for a fixed ratio of probabilities, the ratio of the corresponding decision weights is closer to unity when the probabilities are low than when they are high. This property of π, called subproportionality, imposes considerable constraints on the shape of π: it holds if and only if $\log \pi$ is a convex function of $\log p$.

It is of interest to note that subproportionality together with the overweighting of small probabilities imply that π is subadditive over that range. Formally, it can be shown that if $\pi(p) > p$ and subproportionality holds, then $\pi(rp) > r\pi(p)$, $0 < r < 1$, provided π is monotone and continuous over $(0, 1)$.

Figure 22.4 presents a hypothetical weighting function which satisfies overweighting and subadditivity for small values of p, as well as subcertainty and subproportionality. These properties entail that π is relatively shallow in the open interval and changes abruptly near the end-points where $\pi(0) = 0$ and $\pi(1) = 1$. The sharp drops or apparent discontinuities of π at the endpoints are consistent with the notion that there is a limit to how small a decision weight can be attached to an event, if it is given any weight at all. A similar quantum of doubt could impose an upper limit on any decision weight that is less than unity. This quantal effect may reflect the categorical distinction between certainty and uncertainty. On the other hand, the simplification of prospects in the editing phase can lead the individual to discard events of extremely low probability and to treat events of extremely high probability as if they were certain. Because people are limited in their ability to comprehend and evaluate extreme probabilities, highly unlikely events are either ignored or overweighted, and

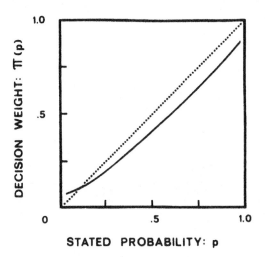

Figure 22.4
A hypothetical weighting function.

the difference between high probability and certainty is either neglected or exaggerated. Consequently, π is not well-behaved near the end-points.

The following example, due to Zeckhauser, illustrates the hypothesized nonlinearity of π. Suppose you are compelled to play Russian roulette, but are given the opportunity to purchase the removal of one bullet from the loaded gun. Would you pay as much to reduce the number of bullets from four to three as you would to reduce the number of bullets from one to zero? Most people feel that they would be willing to pay much more for a reduction of the probability of death from 1/6 to zero than for a reduction from 4/6 to 3/6. Economic considerations would lead one to pay more in the latter case, where the value of money is presumably reduced by the considerable probability that one will not live to enjoy it.

An obvious objection to the assumption that $\pi(p) \neq p$ involves comparisons between prospects of the form $(x, p; x, q)$ and $(x, p'; x, q')$, where $p + q = p' + q' < 1$. Since any individual will surely be indifferent between the two prospects, it could be argued that this observation entails $\pi(p) + \pi(q) = \pi(p') + \pi(q')$, which in turn implies that π is the identity function. This argument is invalid in the present theory, which assumes that the probabilities of identical outcomes are combined in the editing of prospects. A more serious objection to the nonlinearity of π involves potential violations of dominance. Suppose $x > y > 0$, $p > p'$, and $p + q = p' + q' < 1$; hence, $(x, p; y, q)$ dominates $(x, p'; y, q')$. If preference obeys dominance, then

$$\pi(p)v(x) + \pi(q)v(y) > \pi(p')v(x) + \pi(q')v(y),$$

or

$$\frac{\pi(p) - \pi(p')}{\pi(q') - \pi(q)} > \frac{v(y)}{v(x)}.$$

Hence, as y approaches x, $\pi(p) - \pi(p')$ approaches $\pi(q') - \pi(q)$. Since $p - p' = q' - q$, π must be essentially linear, or else dominance must be violated.

Direct violations of dominance are prevented, in the present theory, by the assumption that dominated alternatives are detected and eliminated prior to the evaluation of prospects. However, the theory permits indirect violations of dominance, e.g., triples of prospects so that A is preferred to B, B is preferred to C, and C dominates A. For an example, see Raiffa [34, p. 75].

Finally, it should be noted that the present treatment concerns the simplest decision task in which a person chooses between two available prospects. We have not treated in detail the more complicated production task (e.g., bidding) where the decision maker generates an alternative that is equal in value to a given prospect. The asymmetry between the two options in this situation could introduce systematic biases. Indeed, Lichtenstein and Slovic [27] have constructed pairs of prospects A and B, such that people generally prefer A over B, but bid more for B than for A. This phenomenon has been confirmed in several studies, with both hypothetical and real gambles, e.g., Grether and Plott [20]. Thus, it cannot be generally assumed that the preference order of prospects can be recovered by a bidding procedure.

Because prospect theory has been proposed as a model of choice, the inconsistency of bids and choices implies that the measurement of values and decision weights should be based on choices between specified prospects rather than on bids or other production tasks. This restriction makes the assessment of v and π more difficult because production tasks are more convenient for scaling than pair comparisons.

Discussion

In the final section we show how prospect theory accounts for observed attitudes toward risk, discuss alternative representations of choice problems induced by shifts of reference point, and sketch several extensions of the present treatment.

Risk Attitudes

The dominant pattern of preferences observed in Allais' example (problems 1 and 2) follows from the present theory iff

$$\frac{\pi(.33)}{\pi(.34)} > \frac{v(2{,}400)}{v(2{,}500)} > \frac{\pi(.33)}{1 - \pi(.66)}.$$

Hence, the violation of the independence axiom is attributed in this case to sub-certainty, and more specifically to the inequality $\pi(.34) < 1 - \pi(.66)$. This analysis shows that an Allais-type violation will occur whenever the v-ratio of the two non-zero outcomes is bounded by the corresponding π-ratios.

Problems 3 through 8 share the same structure, hence it suffices to consider one pair, say problems 7 and 8. The observed choices in these problems are implied by the theory iff

$$\frac{\pi(.001)}{\pi(.002)} > \frac{v(3{,}000)}{v(6{,}000)} > \frac{\pi(.45)}{\pi(.90)}.$$

The violation of the substitution axiom is attributed in this case to the sub-proportionality of π. Expected utility theory is violated in the above manner, there-fore, whenever the v-ratio of the two outcomes is bounded by the respective π-ratios. The same analysis applies to other violations of the substitution axiom, both in the positive and in the negative domain.

We next prove that the preference for regular insurance over probabilistic insur-ance, observed in Problem 9, follows from prospect theory—provided the probability of loss is overweighted. That is, if $(-x, p)$ is indifferent to $(-y)$, then $(-y)$ is preferred to $(-x, p/2; -y, p/2; -y/2, 1 - p)$. For simplicity, we define for $x \geq 0$, $f(x) = -v(-x)$. Since the value function for losses is convex, f is a concave function of x. Applying prospect theory, with the natural extension of equation 2, we wish to show that

$$\pi(p)f(x) = f(y) \quad \text{implies}$$

$$f(y) \leq f(y/2) + \pi(p/2)[f(y) - f(y/2)] + \pi(p/2)[f(x) - f(y/2)]$$
$$= \pi(p/2)f(x) + \pi(p/2)f(y) + [1 - 2\pi(p/2)]f(y/2).$$

Substituting for $f(x)$ and using the concavity of f, it suffices to show that

$$f(y) \leq \frac{\pi(p/2)}{\pi(p)}f(y) + \pi(p/2)f(y) + f(y)/2 - \pi(p/2)f(y)$$

or

$$\pi(p)/2 \leq \pi(p/2), \quad \text{which follows from the subadditivity of } \pi.$$

According to the present theory, attitudes toward risk are determined jointly by v and π, and not solely by the utility function. It is therefore instructive to examine the conditions under which risk aversion or risk seeking are expected to occur. Consider the choice between the gamble (x, p) and its expected value (px). If $x > 0$, risk seeking is implied whenever $\pi(p) > v(px)/v(x)$, which is greater than p if the value function for gains is concave. Hence, overweighting $(\pi(p) > p)$ is necessary but not sufficient for risk seeking in the domain of gains. Precisely the same condition is necessary but not sufficient for risk aversion when $x < 0$. This analysis restricts risk seeking in the domain of gains and risk aversion in the domain of losses to small probabilities, where overweighting is expected to hold. Indeed these are the typical conditions under which lottery tickets and insurance policies are sold. In prospect theory, the overweighting of small probabilities favors both gambling and insurance, while the S-shaped value function tends to inhibit both behaviors.

Although prospect theory predicts both insurance and gambling for small probabilities, we feel that the present analysis falls far short of a fully adequate account of these complex phenomena. Indeed, there is evidence from both experimental studies [37], survey research [26], and observations of economic behavior, e.g., service and medical insurance, that the purchase of insurance often extends to the medium range of probabilities, and that small probabilities of disaster are sometimes entirely ignored. Furthermore, the evidence suggests that minor changes in the formulation of the decision problem can have marked effects on the attractiveness of insurance [37]. A comprehensive theory of insurance behavior should consider, in addition to pure attitudes toward uncertainty and money, such factors as the value of security, social norms of prudence, the aversiveness of a large number of small payments spread over time, information and misinformation regarding probabilities and outcomes, and many others. Some effects of these variables could be described within the present framework, e.g., as changes of reference point, transformations of the value function, or manipulations of probabilities or decision weights. Other effects may require the introduction of variables or concepts which have not been considered in this treatment.

Shifts of Reference

So far in this paper, gains and losses were defined by the amounts of money that are obtained or paid when a prospect is played, and the reference point was taken to be the status quo, or one's current assets. Although this is probably true for most choice problems, there are situations in which gains and losses are coded relative to an expectation or aspiration level that differs from the status quo. For example, an unexpected tax withdrawal from a monthly pay check is experienced as a loss, not as a reduced gain. Similarly, an entrepreneur who is weathering a slump with greater success than his competitors may interpret a small loss as a gain, relative to the larger loss he had reason to expect.

The reference point in the preceding examples corresponded to an asset position that one had expected to attain. A discrepancy between the reference point and the current asset position may also arise because of recent changes in wealth to which one has not yet adapted [29]. Imagine a person who is involved in a business venture, has already lost 2,000 and is now facing a choice between a sure gain of 1,000 and an even chance to win 2,000 or nothing. If he has not yet adapted to his losses, he is likely to code the problem as a choice between $(-2,000, .50)$ and $(-1,000)$ rather than as a choice between $(2,000, .50)$ and $(1,000)$. As we have seen, the former representation induces more adventurous choices than the latter.

A change of reference point alters the preference order for prospects. In particular, the present theory implies that a negative translation of a choice problem, such as arises from incomplete adaptation to recent losses, increases risk seeking in some situations. Specifically, if a risky prospect $(x, p; -y, 1 - p)$ is just acceptable, then $(x - z, p; -y - z, 1 - p)$ is preferred over $(-z)$ for $x, y, z > 0$, with $x > z$.

To prove this proposition, note that

$$V(x, p; y, 1 - p) = 0 \quad \text{iff} \quad \pi(p)v(x) = -\pi(1 - p)v(-y).$$

Furthermore,

$$
\begin{aligned}
V(x &- z, p; -y - z, 1 - p) \\
&= \pi(p)v(x - z) + \pi(1 - p)v(-y - z) \\
&> \pi(p)v(x) - \pi(p)v(z) + \pi(1 - p)v(-y) \\
&\quad + \pi(1 - p)v(-z) \quad \text{by the properties of } v, \\
&= -\pi(1 - p)v(-y) - \pi(p)v(z) + \pi(1 - p)v(-y) \\
&\quad + \pi(1 - p)v(-z) \quad \text{by substitution,} \\
&= -\pi(p)v(z) + \pi(1 - p)v(-z) \\
&> v(-z)[\pi(p) + \pi(1 - p)] \quad \text{since } v(-z) < -v(z), \\
&> v(-z) \quad \text{by subcertainty.}
\end{aligned}
$$

This analysis suggests that a person who has not made peace with his losses is likely to accept gambles that would be unacceptable to him otherwise. The well known observation [31] that the tendency to bet on long shots increases in the course of the betting day provides some support for the hypothesis that a failure to adapt to losses or to attain an expected gain induces risk seeking. For another example, consider an individual who expects to purchase insurance, perhaps because he has owned it in the past or because his friends do. This individual may code the decision to pay a premium y to protect against a loss x as a choice between $(-x + y, p; y, 1 - p)$ and (0) rather than as a choice between $(-x, p)$ and $(-y)$. The preceding argument entails that insurance is likely to be more attractive in the former representation than in the latter.

Another important case of a shift of reference point arises when a person formulates his decision problem in terms of final assets, as advocated in decision analysis, rather than in terms of gains and losses, as people usually do. In this case, the reference point is set to zero on the scale of wealth and the value function is likely to be concave everywhere [39]. According to the present analysis, this formulation essentially eliminates risk seeking, except for gambling with low probabilities. The explicit formulation of decision problems in terms of final assets is perhaps the most effective procedure for eliminating risk seeking in the domain of losses.

Many economic decisions involve transactions in which one pays money in exchange for a desirable prospect. Current decision theories analyze such problems as comparisons between the status quo and an alternative state which includes the acquired prospect minus its cost. For example, the decision whether to pay 10 for the gamble $(1,000, .01)$ is treated as a choice between $(990, .01; -10, .99)$ and (0). In this analysis, readiness to purchase the positive prospect is equated to willingness to accept the corresponding mixed prospect.

The prevalent failure to integrate riskless and risky prospects, dramatized in the isolation effect, suggests that people are unlikely to perform the operation of subtracting the cost from the outcomes in deciding whether to buy a gamble. Instead, we suggest that people usually evaluate the gamble and its cost separately, and decide to purchase the gamble if the combined value is positive. Thus, the gamble $(1,000, .01)$ will be purchased for a price of 10 if $\pi(.01)v(1,000) + v(-10) > 0$.

If this hypothesis is correct, the decision to pay 10 for $(1,000, .01)$, for example, is no longer equivalent to the decision to accept the gamble $(990, .01; -10, .99)$. Furthermore, prospect theory implies that if one is indifferent between $(x(1 - p), p; -px, 1 - p)$ and (0) then one will not pay px to purchase the prospect (x, p). Thus, people are expected to exhibit more risk seeking in deciding whether to accept a fair gamble than in deciding whether to purchase a gamble for a fair price. The location of the reference point, and the manner in which choice problems are coded and edited emerge as critical factors in the analysis of decisions.

Extensions

In order to encompass a wider range of decision problems, prospect theory should be extended in several directions. Some generalizations are immediate; others require further development. The extension of equations (1) and (2) to prospects with any number of outcomes is straightforward. When the number of outcomes is large, however, additional editing operations may be invoked to simplify evaluation. The manner in which complex options, e.g., compound prospects, are reduced to simpler ones is yet to be investigated.

Although the present chapter has been concerned mainly with monetary outcomes, the theory is readily applicable to choices involving other attributes, e.g., quality of life or the number of lives that could be lost or saved as a consequence of a policy decision. The main properties of the proposed value function for money should apply to other attributes as well. In particular, we expect outcomes to be coded as gains or losses relative to a neutral reference point, and losses to loom larger than gains.

The theory can also be extended to the typical situation of choice, where the probabilities of outcomes are not explicitly given. In such situations, decision weights must be attached to particular events rather than to stated probabilities, but they are expected to exhibit the essential properties that were ascribed to the weighting function. For example, if A and B are complementary events and neither is certain, $\pi(A) + \pi(B)$ should be less than unity—a natural analogue to subcertainty.

The decision weight associated with an event will depend primarily on the perceived likelihood of that event, which could be subject to major biases [45]. In addition, decision weights may be affected by other considerations, such as ambiguity or vagueness. Indeed, the work of Ellsberg [10] and Fellner [12] implies that vagueness reduces decision weights. Consequently, subcertainty should be more pronounced for vague than for clear probabilities.

The present analysis of preference between risky options has developed two themes. The first theme concerns editing operations that determine how prospects are perceived. The second theme involves the judgmental principles that govern the evaluation of gains and losses and the weighting of uncertain outcomes. Although both themes should be developed further, they appear to provide a useful framework for the descriptive analysis of choice under risk.

Appendix

In this appendix we sketch an axiomatic analysis of prospect theory. Since a complete self-contained treatment is long and tedious, we merely outline the essential steps and exhibit the key ordinal properties needed to establish the bilinear representation of equation (1). Similar methods could be extended to axiomatize equation (2).

Consider the set of all regular prospects of the form $(x, p; y, q)$ with $p + q < 1$. The extension to regular prospects with $p + q = 1$ is straightforward. Let $\gtrsim$ denote the relation of preference between prospects that is assumed to be connected, symmetric and transitive, and let $\simeq$ denote the associated relation of indifference. Naturally, $(x, p; y, q) \simeq (y, q; x, p)$. We also assume, as is implicit in our notation, that $(x, p; 0, q) \simeq (x, p; 0, r)$, and $(x, p; y, 0) \simeq (x, p; z, 0)$. That is, the null outcome and the impossible event have the property of a multiplicative zero.

Note that the desired representation (equation (1)) is additive in the probability-outcome pairs. Hence, the theory of additive conjoint measurement can be applied to obtain a scale V which preserves the preference order, and interval scales f and g in two arguments such that

$$V(x, p; y, q) = f(x, p) + g(y, q).$$

The key axioms used to derive this representation are:

Independence: $(x, p; y, q) \gtrsim (x, p; y'q')$ iff $(x', p'; y, q) \gtrsim (x', p'; y', q')$.

Cancellation: If $(x, p; y'q') \gtrsim (x', p'; y, q)$ and $(x', p'; y'', q'') \gtrsim (x'', p''; y', q')$, then $(x, p; y'', q'') \gtrsim (x'', p''; y, q)$.

Solvability: If $(x, p; y, q) \gtrsim (z, r) \gtrsim (x, p; y'q')$ for some outcome z and probability r, then there exist y'', q'' such that

$$(x, p; y''q'') \simeq (z, r).$$

It has been shown that these conditions are sufficient to construct the desired additive representation, provided the preference order is Archimedean [8, 25]. Furthermore, since $(x, p; y, q) \simeq (y, q; x, p)$, $f(x, p) + g(y, q) = f(y, q) + g(x, p)$, and letting $q = 0$ yields $f = g$.

Next, consider the set of all prospects of the form (x, p) with a single non-zero outcome. In this case, the bilinear model reduces to $V(x, p) = \pi(p)v(x)$. This is the multiplicative model, investigated in [35] and [25]. To construct the multiplicative representation we assume that the ordering of the probability-outcome pairs satisfies independence, cancellation, solvability, and the Archimedean axiom. In addition, we assume sign dependence [25] to ensure the proper multiplication of signs. It should be noted that the solvability axiom used in [35] and [25] must be weakened because the probability factor permits only bounded solvability.

Combining the additive and the multiplicative representations yields

$$V(x, p; y, q) = f[\pi(p)v(x)] + f[\pi(q)v(y)].$$

Finally, we impose a new distributivity axiom:

$$(x, p; y, p) \simeq (z, p) \quad \text{iff} \quad (x, q; y, q) \simeq (z, q).$$

Applying this axiom to the above representation, we obtain

$$f[\pi(p)v(x)] + f[\pi(p)v(y)] = f[\pi(p)v(z)]$$

implies

$$f[\pi(q)v(x)] + f[\pi(q)v(y)] = f[\pi(q)v(z)].$$

Assuming, with no loss of generality, that $\pi(q) < \pi(p)$, and letting $\alpha = \pi(p)v(x)$, $\beta = \pi(p)v(y)$, $\gamma = \pi(p)v(z)$, and $\theta = \pi(q)/\pi(p)$, yields $f(\alpha) + f(\beta) = f(\gamma)$ implies $f(\theta\alpha) + f(\theta\beta) = f(\theta\gamma)$ for all $0 < \theta < 1$.

Because f is strictly monotonic we can set $\gamma = f^{-1}[f(\alpha) + f(\beta)]$. Hence, $\theta\gamma = \theta f^{-1}[f(\alpha) + f(\beta)] = f^{-1}[f(\theta\alpha) + f(\theta\beta)]$.

The solution to this functional equation is $f(\alpha) = k\alpha^c$ [1]. Hence, $V(x, p; y, q) = k[\pi(p)v(x)]^c + k[\pi(q)v(y)]^c$, for some $k, c > 0$. The desired bilinear form is obtained by redefining the scales π, v, and V so as to absorb the constants k and c.

Notes

This work was supported in part by grants from the Harry F. Guggenheim Foundation and from the Advanced Research Projects Agency of the Department of Defense and was monitored by Office of Naval Research under Contract N00014-78-C-0100 (ARPA Order No. 3469) under Subcontract 78-072-0722 from Decisions and Designs, Inc. to Perceptronics, Inc. We also thank the Center for Advanced Study in the Behavioral Sciences at Stanford for its support.
    We are indebted to David H. Krantz for his help in the formulation of the appendix.

References

[1] Aczél, J. *Lectures on Functional Equations and Their Applications.* New York: Academic Press, 1966.

[2] Allais, M. "Le Comportement de l'Homme Rationnel devant le Risque, Critique des Postulats et Axiomes de l'Ecole Americaine," *Econometrica,* 21 (1953), 503–546.

[3] Anderson, N. H., and J. C. Shanteau. "Information Integration in Risky Decision Making," *Journal of Experimental Psychology,* 84 (1970), 441–451.

[4] Arrow, K. J. *Essays in the Theory of Risk-Bearing.* Chicago: Markham, 1971.

[5] Barnes, J. D., and J. E. Reinmuth. "Comparing Imputed and Actual Utility Functions in a Competitive Bidding Setting," *Decision Sciences,* 7 (1976), 801–812.

[6] Coombs, C. H. "Portfolio Theory and the Measurement of Risk," in *Human Judgment and Decision Processes*, ed. by M. F. Kaplan and S. Schwartz. New York: Academic Press, 1975, pp. 63–85.

[7] Davidson, D., P. Suppes, and S. Siegel. *Decision-Making: An Experimental Approach*. Stanford: Stanford University Press, 1957.

[8] Debreu, G. "Topological Methods in Cardinal Utility Theory," *Mathematical Methods in the Social Sciences*, ed. by K. J. Arrow, S. Karlin, and P. Suppes. Stanford: Stanford University Press, 1960, pp. 16–26.

[9] Edwards, W. "Subjective Probabilities Inferred from Decisions," *Psychological Review*, 69 (1962), 109–135.

[10] Ellsberg, D. "Risk, Ambiguity and the Savage Axioms," *Quarterly Journal of Economics*, 75 (1961), 643–669.

[11] Fellner, W. "Distortion of Subjective Probabilities as a Reaction to Uncertainty," *Quarterly Journal of Economics*, 75 (1961), 670–690.

[12] ———. *Probability and Profit—A Study of Economic Behavior Along Bayesian Lines*. Homewood, Illinois: Richard D. Irwin, 1965.

[13] Fishburn, P. C. "Mean-Risk Analysis with Risk Associated with Below-Target Returns," *American Economic Review*, 67 (1977), 116–126.

[14] Fishburn, P. C., and G. A. Kochenberger. "Two-Piece von Neumann-Morgenstern Utility Functions," forthcoming.

[15] Friedman, M., and L. J. Savage. "The Utility Analysis of Choices Involving Risks," *Journal of Political Economy*, 56 (1948), 279–304.

[16] Fuchs, V. R. "From Bismark to Woodcock: The 'Irrational' Pursuit of National Health Insurance," *Journal of Law and Economics*, 19 (1976), 347–359.

[17] Galanter, E., and P. Pliner. "Cross-Modality Matching of Money against Other Continua," in *Sensation and Measurement*, ed. by H. R. Moskowitz et al. Dordrecht, Holland: Reidel, 1974, pp. 65–76.

[18] Grayson, C. J. *Decisions under Uncertainty: Drilling Decisions by Oil and Gas Operators*. Cambridge, Massachusetts: Graduate School of Business, Harvard University, 1960.

[19] Green, P. E. "Risk Attitudes and Chemical Investment Decisions," *Chemical Engineering Progress*, 59 (1963), 35–40.

[20] Grether, D. M., and C. R. Plott. "Economic Theory of Choice and the Preference Reversal Phenomenon," *American Economic Review*, forthcoming.

[21] Halter, A. N., and G. W. Dean. *Decisions under Uncertainty*. Cincinnati: South Western Publishing Co., 1971.

[22] Hansson, B. "The Appropriateness of the Expected Utility Model," *Erkenntnis*, 9 (1975), 175–194.

[23] Helson, H. *Adaptation-Level Theory*. New York: Harper, 1964.

[24] Keeney, R. L., and H. Raiffa. *Decisions with Multiple Objectives: Preferences and Value Tradeoffs*. New York: Wiley, 1976.

[25] Krantz, D. H., D. R. Luce, P. Suppes, and A. Tversky. *Foundations of Measurement*. New York: Academic Press, 1971.

[26] Kunreuther, H., R. Ginsberg, L. Miller, P. Sagi, P. Slovic, B. Borkan, and N. Katz. *Disaster Insurance Protection: Public Policy Lessons*. New York: Wiley, 1978.

[27] Lichtenstein, S., and P. Slovic. "Reversal of Preference Between Bids and Choices in Gambling Decisions," *Journal of Experimental Psychology*, 89 (1971), 46–55.

[28] MacCrimmon, K. R., and S. Larsson. "Utility Theory: Axioms versus Paradoxes," in *Expected Utility Hypothesis and the Allais Paradox*, ed. by M. Allais and O. Hagen, forthcoming in *Theory and Decision*.

[29] Markowitz, H. "The Utility of Wealth," *Journal of Political Economy*, 60 (1952), 151–158.

[30] ———. *Portfolio Selection*. New York: Wiley, 1959.

[31] McGlothlin, W. H. "Stability of Choices among Uncertain Alternatives," *American Journal of Psychology*, 69 (1956), 604–615.

[32] Mosteller, F., and P. Nogee. "An Experimental Measurement of Utility," *Journal of Political Economy*, 59 (1951), 371–404.

[33] Pratt, J. W. "Risk Aversion in the Small and in the Large," *Econometrica*, 32 (1964), 122–136.

[34] Raiffa, H. *Decision Analysis: Introductory Lectures on Choices Under Uncertainty*. Reading, Massachusetts: Addison-Wesley, 1968.

[35] Roskies, R. "A Measurement Axiomatization for an Essentially Multiplicative Representation of Two Factors," *Journal of Mathematical Psychology*, 2 (1965), 266–276.

[36] Savage, L. J. *The Foundations of Statistics*. New York: Wiley, 1954.

[37] Slovic, P., B. Fischhoff, S. Lichtenstein, B. Corrigan, and B. Coombs. "Preference for Insuring against Probable Small Losses: Insurance Implications," *Journal of Risk and Insurance*, 44 (1977), 237–258.

[38] Slovic, P., and A. Tversky. "Who Accepts Savage's Axiom?," *Behavioral Science*, 19 (1974), 368–373.

[39] Spetzler, C. S. "The Development of Corporate Risk Policy for Capital Investment Decisions," *IEEE Transactions on Systems Science and Cybernetics*, SSC-4 (1968), 279–300.

[40] Swalm, R. O. "Utility Theory—Insights into Risk Taking," *Harvard Business Review*, 44 (1966), 123–136.

[41] Tobin, J. "Liquidity Preferences as Behavior Towards Risk," *Review of Economic Studies*, 26 (1958), 65–86.

[42] Tversky, A. "Additivity, Utility, and Subjective Probability," *Journal of Mathematical Psychology*, 4 (1967), 175–201.

[43] ———. "Intransitivity of Preferences," *Psychological Review*, 76 (1969), 31–48.

[44] ———. "Elimination by Aspects: A Theory of Choice," *Psychological Review*, 79 (1972), 281–299.

[45] Tversky, A., and D. Kahneman. "Judgment under Uncertainty: Heuristics and Biases," *Science*, 185 (1974), 1124–1131.

[46] van Dam, C. "Another Look at Inconsistency in Financial Decision-Making," presented at the Seminar on Recent Research in Finance and Monetary Economics, Cergy-Pontoise, March, 1975.

[47] von Neumann, J., and O. Morgenstern. *Theory of Games and Economic Behavior*, Princeton: Princeton University Press, 1944.

[48] Williams, A. C. "Attitudes toward Speculative Risks as an Indicator of Attitudes toward Pure Risks," *Journal of Risk and Insurance*, 33 (1966), 577–586.

23 On the Elicitation of Preferences for Alternative Therapies

Barbara J. McNeil, Stephen G. Pauker, Harold C. Sox, Jr., and Amos Tversky

There is a growing appreciation in the general public and the medical profession of the need to incorporate patients' preferences into medical decision making. To achieve this goal, the physican must provide the patient with data about the possible outcomes of the available therapies, and the patient must be able to comprehend and use these data. In this chapter we investigate how people use statistical information regarding the possible outcomes of alternative therapies. We have focused on a particular medical problem (operable lung cancer) and asked the participants to choose between surgery and radiation therapy on the basis of simple descriptions of their possible consequences. Four variables were investigated: the input data presented to the subjects (life expectancy or cumulative probability), the characterization or framing of the outcomes (in terms of mortality or in terms of survival), the identification of the treatments (surgery or radiation therapy vs. unidentified treatments labeled "A" and "B"), and the population of respondents (physicians, patients, and graduate students).

Methods

The Clinical Problem
Lung cancer was selected for study because it offers a clear-cut choice between two alternative therapies—irradiation and surgery—that yield different patterns of survival probabilities. A previous study of this problem, using a formal decision-analytic approach,[1,2] found that an appreciable number of patients preferred radiation therapy to surgery despite the lower long-term survival associated with radiation therapy,[3] presumably because it does not involve the risk of perioperative death.

As in the previous study on lung cancer, we used data reported by Mountain and his colleagues on the results of surgery[4,5] and data reported by Hilton[6] on the results of radiation therapy for operable lung cancer. These reports and others indicate that for 60-year-old patients treated with surgery the average operative mortality rate is 10 per cent, and the average five-year survival rate is about 34 per cent. The survival rates at one, two, three, and four years are 68, 51, 40, and 35 per cent, respectively. For radiation therapy there is essentially no treatment mortality, and the five-year survival rate is 22 per cent; survival rates at one, two, three, and four years are 77, 44, 28, and 23 per cent, respectively. Other data from the National Cancer Institute on the excess risk of death from lung cancer and on age-specific annual mortality rates were used to adjust the survival data to other age groups.[7] The comparison of the two treatments shows that surgery offers better long-term prospects at the cost of a greater immediate risk.

Input Data

Two types of data were used. The first type, called cumulative-probability data, included the probability of survival (or death) immediately after the treatment, one year after the treatment, and five years after the treatment. The one-year point was chosen because it represents the short-term range in which survival after radiation therapy is higher than survival after surgery; the five-year point was chosen because it is commonly used in medicine to evaluate and compare alternative treatments. The second type, called life-expectancy data, included the probability of survival (or death) immediately after the treatment and the life expectancy associated with each treatment—that is, the average number of years lived after the treatment.

The survival curve describing the results after surgery has a longer tail (i.e., it is more skewed to the right) than the survival curve for radiation therapy. Thus, the proportion of patients who will survive more than 10 years, for example, is greater for surgery than for radiation therapy. Consequently, the use of life expectancy, which is affected by the long tail, is expected to make surgery appear more attractive than it would with the use of one-year and five-year survival rates, which are not affected by the long tail.

Identification of Treatment

For about half the respondents, the input data were identified as resulting from surgery or radiation therapy; for the remaining respondents, the treatments were not identified and the alternatives were labeled "A" and "B." The input data describing the results of A were identical to the results of surgery, and the data describing the results of B were identical to those of radiation therapy. This variation was introduced to assess the extent to which choices are determined by prior conceptions (or misconceptions) about surgery and radiation therapy.

Framing of Outcome

The cumulative probabilities presented to about half the subjects referred to survival after a particular time—e.g., to a 68 per cent chance of living for more than one year. The cumulative probabilities presented to the rest of the subjects referred to mortality—e.g., to a 32 per cent chance of dying by the end of one year. Recent work by cognitive psychologists on the framing of decision problems indicates that the characterization of outcomes in terms of the probability of survival rather than the probability of death can have a substantial effect on people's preferences.[8,9]

More specifically, this work suggested that the impact of perioperative mortality on the comparison between the two treatments would be greater when it was framed as a difference between mortality rates of 0 per cent and 10 per cent, than when it was framed as a difference between survival rates of 100 per cent and 90 per cent. Because the risk of perioperative death is the major disadvantage of surgery relative to radiation therapy, we hypothesized that surgery would be selected more frequently when the problem was described in terms of the probability of living than when it was described in terms of the probability of dying.

Subject Population

Three groups of respondents were investigated: patients, physicians, and students. None of the subjects were known to have lung cancer. The patients were 238 men with chronic medical problems who were being treated as outpatients by internists at the Palo Alto Veterans Administration Medical Center. Their ages ranged from 40 to 80 years, with an average age of 58 years, which is similar to the age distribution of patients with lung cancer. The physicians were 424 radiologists whose ages ranged from 28 to 67 years, with an average age of 43 years; these subjects were taking postgraduate courses at the Harvard Medical School and the Brigham and Women's Hospital. Since physicians normally have an essential role in the choice of therapy, their own preferences are of considerable interest. The third group consisted of 491 graduate students from Stanford Business School, who had completed several courses in statistics and decision theory. Their average age was 29 years. They were included in the study so that we could examine the effects of age and analytic training.

We expected the students, who were younger than both the patients and the physicians, to choose surgery more often than the other two groups. We also expected the physicians and the students, who had more formal training than the patients, to be less affected by the variation in framing.

Procedure

Each subject was assigned to one of four conditions defined by the combinations of label (identified or unidentified) and frame (living or dying). The number of subjects in each group is shown in table 23.1. All subjects received both cumulative-probability data and life-expectancy data, in that order. All subjects received the input data appropriate for their age group. Subjects who received the input data in an identified format and with outcome presented as the probability of dying were given the following instructions.

Table 23.1
Numbers of Subjects Given Data in Various Ways

Population	Outcome Presented as Probability of Dying		Outcome Presented as Probability of Living	
	Treatment Identified	Treatment Unidentified	Treatment Identified	Treatment Unidentified
Patients	60	60	59	59
Physicians	80	135	87	122
Students	196	64	101	130

Surgery for lung cancer involves an operation on the lungs. Most patients are in the hospital for two or three weeks and have some pain around their incisions; they spend a month or so recuperating at home. After that, they generally feel fine.

Radiation therapy for lung cancer involves the use of radiation to kill the tumor and requires coming to the hospital about four times a week for six weeks. Each treatment takes a few minutes and during the treatment, patients lie on a table as if they were having an x-ray. During the course of the treatment, some patients develop nausea and vomiting, but by the end of the six weeks they also generally feel fine.

Thus, after the initial six or so weeks, patients treated with either surgery or radiation therapy feel about the same.

Next, the subjects were presented with the following cumulative probability data, which were also displayed in a table.

Of 100 people having surgery, *10* will die during treatment, *32* will have died by one year, and *66* will have died by five years. Of 100 people having radiation therapy, none will die during treatment, *23* will die by one year, and *78* will die by five years.
   Which treatment would you prefer?

After the subjects made a choice, they were told that the above data summarized the experience of many hospitals and that they would now be asked to consider new information pertaining to a specific hospital and to make a new choice on the basis of these data.

At this single hospital, 10 per cent of the patients who have surgery die during the perioperative period. The patients who survive treatment have a life expectancy (e.g., average number of remaining years) of *6.8* years. The life expectancy of all patients who undergo surgery (including those who die in the postoperative period) is *6.1* years. With radiation therapy, nobody dies during treatment, and the life expectancy of the patients who undergo radiation therapy is *4.7* years.
   Which treatment would you prefer?

Table 23.2
Percentages of Subjects Choosing Radiation Therapy over Surgery

| | Outcome and Treatment Variables | | | | |
| | Dying | | Living | | |
Type of Data	identified treatment	unidentified treatment	identified treatment	unidentified treatment	Overall
(No. of subjects)	(336)	(259)	(247)	(311)	(1153)
Cumulative probability*					
Patients	40	68	22	31	40
Physicians	50	62	16	51	47
Students	43	53	17	27	35
Overall	44	61	18	37	40
Life expectancy[†]					
Patients	35	50	19	27	28
Physicians	28	39	9	41	31
Students	21	41	9	24	22
Overall	25	42	11	31	27

* Immediately after treatment and at one and five years thereafter.
[†] Probability of surviving or dying from immediate treatment plus life expectancy thereafter. The dichotomy between probability of dying and probability of living in this group applies only to the data concerning the immediate treatment period.

The subjects who received the data in an unidentified format were presented with different background information:

Both treatment A and treatment B are medications which are administered to the patient hospitalized for cancer. Both are given intravenously and neither one has significant side effects. Treatments A and B are considered equal except in their survival rates.

The input data concerning cumulative probability and life expectancy were the same as those for the identified treatments except that surgery and radiation therapy were replaced by "A" and "B," respectively. For the subjects who received the input data expressed in terms of the probability of survival, the probability of dying was replaced throughout by the probability of living. The patients were interviewed individually. The physicians and the students responded to a written questionnaire.

Results

The percentages of respondents who chose radiation therapy rather than surgery are shown in table 23.2 for each of the experimental conditions. The results for the

cumulative-probability condition and for the life-expectancy condition were sub-
mitted to two separate 3-by-2-by-2 analyses of variance after an arcsin transformation.[10] The effects of all four independent variables were significant ($P < 0.001$).
Moreover, table 23.2 reveals a highly regular pattern: with one minor exception there
are no "cross-over" interactions among the major dependent variables—input data,
identification of treatment, and the outcome frame. For example, all entries under
"cumulative probability" exceed the corresponding entries under "life expectancy."
We shall summarize the main effects in turn.

Input Data

As expected, subjects who had received life-expectancy data chose radiation therapy
less frequently overall (27 per cent) than did subjects who had received cumulative-
probability data (40 per cent). An examination of individual choices revealed that 59
per cent of the subjects chose surgery under both types of data and 26 per cent chose
radiation therapy under both types. Hence, 85 per cent of the respondents made
the same choice under both conditions. Fourteen per cent of the respondents chose
radiation therapy in the cumulative-probability condition and surgery in the life-
expectancy condition; only 1 per cent made the opposite choices.

Identification of Treatment

Overall, radiation therapy was chosen 42 per cent of the time when it was not identified and only 26 per cent of the time when it was identified. Evidently, identification
of the two treatments favors surgery over radiation therapy.

Framing of Outcome

As predicted, surgery was relatively less attractive in the mortality frame (probability
of dying) than in the survival frame (probability of living). On the average, radiation
therapy was preferred to surgery 42 per cent of the time in the mortality frame and
25 per cent of the time in the survival frame.

Subject Population

Radiation therapy was least popular among the students (28 per cent of all responses), somewhat more popular among the patients (34 per cent), and most popular among the physicians (39 per cent). The general pattern of preferences, however,
was very similar in all three groups despite large differences in age, income, and
lifestyle.

Discussion

We presented a large number of outpatients, physicians, and graduate students with information describing the possible outcomes of two alternative therapies for lung cancer. The respondents appeared to comprehend and use these data. An interview with the patients after the experiment indicated that they understood the data and were able to recall important items of information. However, the choices of both naive subjects (patients) and sophisticated subjects (physicians) were influenced by several variations in the nature of the data and the form in which they were presented.

The finding that data on life expectancy favored surgery where as data on cumulative probability favored radiation therapy is not surprising in view of the fact that the survival distribution for surgery is much more skewed than the survival distribution for radiation therapy. However, this result illustrates the difficulty of selecting appropriate summary data; seemingly reasonable statistics (e.g., the mean or the median of a distribution) are likely to bias the decision maker in favor of one therapy or another.

The finding that radiation therapy was less attractive when the treatments were identified indicates that people relied more on preexisting beliefs regarding the treatments than on the statistical data presented to them. We do not know, however, whether these beliefs were based on valid evidence or reflected a widely shared bias against radiation therapy. In the former case, the input data should be expanded to include additional information that was presumably used by the subjects in the identified format only. In the latter case, subjects should be informed before the elicitation process in an attempt to reduce their biases.

Perhaps our most notable finding is the effect on people's choices of presenting the data in terms of survival or death. Surgery appeared to be much more attractive when the outcomes were framed in terms of the probability of survival rather than in terms of the probability of death. We attribute this result to the fact that the risk of perioperative death looms larger when it is presented in terms of mortality than when it is presented in terms of survival. Unlike the preceding effects, which can be justified or at least rationalized, this effect of using different terminology to describe outcome represents a cognitive illusion. The effect observed in this study is large (25 per cent vs. 42 per cent) and consistent: It holds for both cumulative-probability and life-expectancy data, for both identified and unidentified treatments, and for all three populations of subjects. Much to our surprise, the effect was not generally smaller for the physicians (who had considerable experience in evaluating medical data) or for the graduate students (who had received statistical training) than for the patients (who had neither).

One might be tempted to conclude from this study that there is no point in devising methods for the explicit elicitation of patients' preferences, since they are so susceptible to the way the data are presented, and to implicit suggestions and other biases. However, it should be noted that the preferences expressed by the physicians, which are likely to play an important part in the advice they give to patients, were subject to the same biases. In addition, there is little reason to believe that more informal procedures in which the treatments are described in general terms without quantitative statistical data are less susceptible to the effects of different methods of presentation.

Variations in types of data presentation can be used to assess the sensitivity of preferences with respect to the available alternatives. If a patient prefers surgery over radiation therapy, for example, whether the data are presented as cumulative probabilities or as life expectancy and whether the probabilities are presented in terms of mortality or in terms of survival, the preference may be assumed to be reasonably certain. If, on the other hand, a change of presentation leads to a reversal of preference, then additional data, discussions, or analyses are probably needed. We suggest that an awareness of the effects of presentation among physicians and patients could help reduce bias and improve the quality of medical decision making.

Notes

Supported in part by the Henry J. Kaiser Family Foundation. Dr. Pauker is a recipient of a research Career Development Award (K04-GM-00349).
    We are indebted to our volunteers for the generous gift of their time for this study.

References

1. Raiffa H. Decision analysis: introductory lectures on choices under uncertainty. Reading, Mass.: Addison-Wesley, 1968.

2. Keeney RL, and Raiffa H. Decision with multiple objectives: preferences and value tradeoffs. New York: John Wiley, 1976.

3. McNeil BJ, Weichselbaum R, and Pauker SG. Fallacy of the five-year survival in lung cancer. N Engl J Med. 1978; 299:1397–401.

4. Mountain CT. The relationship of prognosis to morphology and the anatomic extent of disease: studies of a new clinical staging system. In: Israel L, and Chahinian AP, eds. Lung cancer: natural history, prognosis, and therapy. New York: Academic Press, 1976:107–40.

5. Mountain CF, Carr DT, and Anderson WAD. A system for clinical staging of lung cancer. Am J Roentgenol Radium Ther Nucl Med. 1974; 120:130–8.

6. Hilton G. Present position relating to cancer of the lung: results with radio-therapy alone. Thorax. 1960; 15:17–8.

7. Axtell LM, Cutler SJ, and Myers MH, eds. End results in cancer (report no. 4). Bethesda, Md.: National Cancer Institute, 1972. (DHEW publication no. (NIH) 73-272).

8. Kahneman D, and Tversky A. Prospect theory: an analysis of decision under risk. Econometrica. 1979; 47:263–91.

9. Tversky A, and Kahneman D. The framing of decisions and the psychology of choice. Science. 1981; 211:453–8.

10. Snedecor GW, and Cochran WG. Statistical methods. 6th ed. Ames, Iowa: Iowa State University Press, 1967.

24 Rational Choice and the Framing of Decisions

Amos Tversky and Daniel Kahneman

The modern theory of decision making under risk emerged from a logical analysis of games of chance rather than from a psychological analysis of risk and value. The theory was conceived as a normative model of an idealized decision maker, not as a description of the behavior of real people. In Schumpeter's words, it "has a much better claim to being called a logic of choice than a psychology of value" (1954, p. 1058).

The use of a normative analysis to predict and explain actual behavior is defended by several arguments. First, people are generally thought to be effective in pursuing their goals, particularly when they have incentives and opportunities to learn from experience. It seems reasonable, then, to describe choice as a maximization process. Second, competition favors rational individuals and organizations. Optimal decisions increase the chances of survival in a competitive environment, and a minority of rational individuals can sometimes impose rationality on the whole market. Third, the intuitive appeal of the axioms of rational choice makes it plausible that the theory derived from these axioms should provide an acceptable account of choice behavior.

The thesis of the present chapter is that, in spite of these a priori arguments, the logic of choice does not provide an adequate foundation for a descriptive theory of decision making. We argue that the deviations of actual behavior from the normative model are too widespread to be ignored, too systematic to be dismissed as random error, and too fundamental to be accommodated by relaxing the normative system. We first sketch an analysis of the foundations of the theory of rational choice and then show that the most basic rules of the theory are commonly violated by decision makers. We conclude from these findings that the normative and the descriptive analyses cannot be reconciled. A descriptive model of choice is presented, which accounts for preferences that are anomalous in the normative theory.

A Hierarchy of Normative Rules

The major achievement of the modern theory of decision under risk is the derivation of the expected utility rule from simple principles of rational choice that make no reference to long-run considerations (von Neumann and Morgenstern 1944). The axiomatic analysis of the foundations of expected utility theory reveals four substantive assumptions—cancellation, transitivity, dominance, and invariance— besides the more technical assumptions of comparability and continuity. The substantive assumptions can be ordered by their normative appeal, from the cancellation condition, which has been challenged by many theorists, to invariance, which has been accepted by all. We briefly discuss these assumptions.

Cancellation. The key qualitative property that gives rise to expected utility theory is the "cancellation" or elimination of any state of the world that yields the same outcome regardless of one's choice. This notion has been captured by different formal properties, such as the substitution axiom of von Neumann and Morgenstern (1944), the extended sure-thing principle of Savage (1954), and the independence condition of Luce and Krantz (1971). Thus, if A is preferred to B, then the prospect of winning A if it rains tomorrow (and nothing otherwise) should be preferred to the prospect of winning B if it rains tomorrow because the two prospects yield the same outcome (nothing) if there is no rain tomorrow. Cancellation is necessary to represent preference between prospects as the maximization of expected utility. The main argument for cancellation is that only one state will actually be realized, which makes it reasonable to evaluate the outcomes of options separately for each state. The choice between options should therefore depend only on states in which they yield different outcomes.

Transitivity. A basic assumption in models of both risky and riskless choice is the transitivity of preference. This assumption is necessary and essentially sufficient for the representation of preference by an ordinal utility scale u such that A is preferred to B whenever $u(A) > u(B)$. Thus transitivity is satisfied if it is possible to assign to each option a value that does not depend on the other available options. Transitivity is likely to hold when the options are evaluated separately but not when the consequences of an option depend on the alternative to which it is compared, as implied, for example, by considerations of regret. A common argument for transitivity is that cyclic preferences can support a "money pump," in which the intransitive person is induced to pay for a series of exchanges that returns to the initial option.

Dominance. This is perhaps the most obvious principle of rational choice: if one option is better than another in one state and at least as good in all other states, the dominant option should be chosen. A slightly stronger condition—called stochastic dominance—asserts that, for unidimensional risky prospects, A is preferred to B if the cumulative distribution of A is to the right of the cumulative distribution of B. Dominance is both simpler and more compelling than cancellation and transitivity, and it serves as the cornerstone of the normative theory of choice.

Invariance. An essential condition for a theory of choice that claims normative status is the principle of invariance: different representations of the same choice problem should yield the same preference. That is, the preference between options should be independent of their description. Two characterizations that the decision maker, on reflection, would view as alternative descriptions of the same problem should lead to the same choice—even without the benefit of such reflection. This principle of invariance (or extensionality [Arrow 1982]), is so basic that it is tacitly assumed in the characterization of options rather than explicitly stated as a testable axiom. For example, decision models that describe the objects of choice as random variables all assume that alternative representations of the same random variables should be treated alike. Invariance captures the normative intuition that variations of form that do not affect the actual outcomes should not affect the choice. A related concept, called consequentialism, has been discussed by Hammond (1985).

The four principles underlying expected utility theory can be ordered by their normative appeal. Invariance and dominance seem essential, transitivity could be questioned, and cancellation has been rejected by many authors. Indeed, the ingenious counterexamples of Allais (1953) and Ellsberg (1961) led several theorists to abandon cancellation and the expectation principle in favor of more general representations. Most of these models assume transitivity, dominance, and invariance (e.g., Hansson 1975; Allais 1979; Hagen 1979; Machina 1982; Quiggin 1982; Weber 1982; Chew 1983; Fishburn 1983; Schmeidler 1984; Segal 1984; Yaari 1984; Luce and Narens 1985). Other developments abandon transitivity but maintain invariance and dominance (e.g., Bell 1982; Fishburn 1982, 1984; Loomes and Sugden 1982). These theorists responded to observed violations of cancellation and transitivity by weakening the normative theory in order to retain its status as a descriptive model. However, this strategy cannot be extended to the failures of dominance and invariance that we shall document. Because invariance and dominance are normatively essential and descriptively invalid, a theory of rational decision cannot provide an adequate description of choice behavior.

We next illustrate failures of invariance and dominance and then review a descriptive analysis that traces these failures to the joint effects of the rules that govern the framing of prospects, the evaluation of outcomes, and the weighting of probabilities. Several phenomena of choice that support the present account are described.

Failures of Invariance

In this section we consider two illustrative examples in which the condition of invariance is violated and discuss some of the factors that produce these violations.

The first example comes from a study of preferences between medical treatments (McNeil et al. 1982). Respondents were given statistical information about the outcomes of two treatments of lung cancer. The same statistics were presented to some respondents in terms of mortality rates and to others in terms of survival rates. The respondents then indicated their preferred treatment. The information was presented as follows.[1]

Problem 1 (Survival frame)

Surgery: Of 100 people having surgery 90 live through the post-operative period, 68 are alive at the end of the first year and 34 are alive at the end of five years.

Radiation Therapy: Of 100 people having radiation therapy all live through the treatment, 77 are alive at the end of one year and 22 are alive at the end of five years.

Problem 1 (Mortality frame)

Surgery: Of 100 people having surgery 10 die during surgery or the post-operative period, 32 die by the end of the first year and 66 die by the end of five years.

Radiation Therapy: Of 100 people having radiation therapy, none die during treatment, 23 die by the end of one year and 78 die by the end of five years.

The inconsequential difference in formulation produced a marked effect. The overall percentage of respondents who favored radiation therapy rose from 18% in the survival frame ($N = 247$) to 44% in the mortality frame ($N = 336$). The advantage of radiation therapy over surgery evidently looms larger when stated as a reduction of the risk of immediate death from 10% to 0% rather than as an increase from 90% to 100% in the rate of survival. The framing effect was not smaller for experienced physicians or for statistically sophisticated business students than for a group of clinic patients.

Our next example concerns decisions between conjunctions of risky prospects with monetary outcomes. Each respondent made two choices, one between favorable prospects and one between unfavorable prospects (Tversky and Kahneman 1981, p. 454). It was assumed that the two selected prospects would be played independently.

Problem 2 ($N = 150$). Imagine that you face the following pair of concurrent decisions. First examine both decisions, then indicate the options you prefer.

Decision (i) Choose between:
A. a sure gain of $240 [84%]
B. 25% chance to gain $1000 and 75% chance to gain nothing [16%]

Decision (ii) Choose between:
C. a sure loss of $750 [13%]
D. 75% chance to lose $1000 and 25% chance to lose nothing [87%]

The total number of respondents in denoted by N, and the percentage who chose each option is indicated in brackets. (Unless otherwise specified, the data were obtained from undergraduate students at Stanford University and at the University of British Columbia.) The majority choice in decision i is risk averse, while the majority choice in decision ii is risk seeking. This is a common pattern: choices involving gains are usually risk averse, and choices involving losses are often risk seeking—except when the probability of winning or losing is small (Fishburn and Kochenberger 1979; Kahneman and Tversky 1979; Hershey and Schoemaker 1980).

Because the subjects considered the two decisions simultaneously, they expressed, in effect, a preference for the portfolio A and D over the portfolio B and C. However, the preferred portfolio is actually dominated by the rejected one! The combined options are as follows.

A & D: 25% chance to win $240 and 75% chance to lose $760.
B & C: 25% chance to win $250 and 75% chance to lose $750.

When the options are presented in this aggregated form, the dominant option is invariably chosen. In the format of problem 2, however, 73% of respondents chose the dominated combination A and D, and only 3% chose B and C. The contrast between the two formats illustrates a violation of invariance. The findings also support the general point that failures of invariance are likely to produce violations of stochastic dominance and vice versa.

The respondents evidently evaluated decisions i and ii separately in problem 2, where they exhibited the standard pattern of risk aversion in gains and risk seeking in losses. People who are given these problems are very surprised to learn that the combination of two preferences that they considered quite reasonable led them to select a dominated option. The same pattern of results was also observed in a scaled-down version of problem 2, with real monetary payoff (see Tversky and Kahneman 1981, p. 458).

As illustrated by the preceding examples, variations in the framing of decision problems produce systematic violations of invariance and dominance that cannot be defended on normative grounds. It is instructive to examine two mechanisms that could ensure the invariance of preferences: canonical representations and the use of expected actuarial value.

Invariance would hold if all formulations of the same prospect were transformed to a standard canonical representation (e.g., a cumulative probability distribution of the same random variable) because the various versions would then all be evaluated in the same manner. In problem 2, for example, invariance and dominance would both be preserved if the outcomes of the two decisions were aggregated prior to evaluation. Similarly, the same choice would be made in both versions of the medical problem if the outcomes were coded in terms of one dominant frame (e.g., rate of survival). The observed failures of invariance indicate that people do not spontaneously aggregate concurrent prospects or transform all outcomes into a common frame.

The failure to construct a canonical representation in decision problems contrasts with other cognitive tasks in which such representations are generated automatically and effortlessly. In particular, our visual experience consists largely of canonical representations: objects do not appear to change in size, shape, brightness, or color when we move around them or when illumination varies. A white circle seen from a sharp angle in dim light appears circular and white, not ellipsoid and grey. Canonical representations are also generated in the process of language comprehension, where listeners quickly recode much of what they hear into an abstract propositional form that no longer discriminates, for example, between the active and the passive voice and often does not distinguish what was actually said from what was implied or presupposed (Clark and Clark 1977). Unfortunately, the mental machinery that transforms percepts and sentences into standard forms does not automatically apply to the process of choice.

Invariance could be satisfied even in the absence of a canonical representation if the evaluation of prospects were separately linear, or nearly linear, in probability and monetary value. If people ordered risky prospects by their actuarial values, invariance and dominance would always hold. In particular, there would be no difference between the mortality and the survival versions of the medical problem. Because the evaluation of outcomes and probabilities is generally non-linear, and because people do not spontaneously construct canonical representations of decisions, invariance commonly fails. Normative models of choice, which assume invariance, therefore cannot provide an adequate descriptive account of choice behavior. In the next section we present a descriptive account of risky choice, called prospect theory, and explore its consequences. Failures of invariance are explained by framing effects that control the representation of options, in conjunction with the nonlinearities of value and belief.

Framing and Evaluation of Outcomes

Prospect theory distinguishes two phases in the choice process: a phase of framing and editing, followed by a phase of evaluation (Kahneman and Tversky 1979). The first phase consists of a preliminary analysis of the decision problem, which frames the effective acts, contingencies, and outcomes. Framing is controlled by the manner in which the choice problem is presented as well as by norms, habits, and expectancies of the decision maker. Additional operations that are performed prior to evaluation include cancellation of common components and the elimination of options that are seen to be dominated by others. In the second phase, the framed prospects are evaluated, and the prospect of highest value is selected. The theory distinguishes two ways of choosing between prospects: by detecting that one dominates another or by comparing their values.

For simplicity, we confine the discussion to simple gambles with numerical probabilities and monetary outcomes. Let $(x, p; y, q)$ denote a prospect that yields x with probability p and y with probability q and that preserves the status quo with probability $(1 - p - q)$. According to prospect theory, there are values $v(\cdot)$, defined on gains and losses, and decision weights $\pi(\cdot)$, defined on stated probabilities, such that the overall value of the prospect equals $\pi(p)v(x) + \pi(q)v(y)$. A slight modification is required if all outcomes of a prospect have the same sign.[2]

The Value Function

Following Markowitz (1952), outcomes are expressed in prospect theory as positive or negative deviations (gains or losses) from a neutral reference outcome, which is assigned a value of zero. Unlike Markowitz, however, we propose that the value function is commonly S shaped, concave above the reference point, and convex below it, as illustrated in figure 24.1. Thus the difference in subjective value between a gain of $100 and a gain of $200 is greater than the subjective difference between a gain of $1,100 and a gain of $1,200. The same relation between value differences holds for the corresponding losses. The proposed function expresses the property that the effect of a marginal change decreases with the distance from the reference point in either direction. These hypotheses regarding the typical shape of the value function may not apply to ruinous losses or to circumstances in which particular amounts assume special significance.

A significant property of the value function, called *loss aversion*, is that the response to losses is more extreme than the response to gains. The common reluctance to accept a fair bet on the toss of a coin suggests that the displeasure of losing a sum of money exceeds the pleasure of winning the same amount. Thus the proposed value function is (i) defined on gains and losses, (ii) generally concave for gains and convex for losses, and (iii) steeper for losses than for gains. These properties of the value function have been supported in many studies of risky choice involving monetary outcomes (Fishburn and Kochenberger 1979; Kahneman and Tversky 1979; Hershey and Schoemaker 1980; Payne, Laughhunn, and Crum 1980) and human lives (Tver-

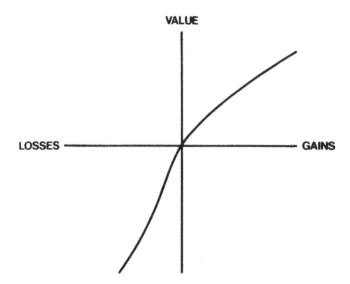

Figure 24.1
A typical value function.

sky 1977; Eraker and Sox 1981; Tversky and Kahneman 1981; Fischhoff 1983). Loss aversion may also contribute to the observed discrepancies between the amount of money people are willing to pay for a good and the compensation they demand to give it up (Bishop and Heberlein 1979; Knetsch and Sinden 1984). This effect is implied by the value function if the good is valued as a gain in the former context and as a loss in the latter.

Framing Outcomes
The framing of outcomes and the contrast between traditional theory and the present analysis are illustrated in the following problems.

Problem 3 ($N = 126$): Assume yourself richer by $300 than you are today. You have to choose between

a sure gain of $100 [72%]

50% chance to gain $200 and 50% chance to gain nothing [28%]

Problem 4 ($N = 128$): Assume yourself richer by $500 than you are today. You have to choose between

a sure loss of $100 [36%]

50% chance to lose nothing and 50% chance to lose $200 [64%]

As implied by the value function, the majority choice is risk averse in problem 3 and risk seeking in problem 4, although the two problems are essentially identical. In both cases one faces a choice between $400 for sure and an even chance of $500 or $300. Problem 4 is obtained from problem 3 by increasing the initial endowment by $200 and subtracting this amount from both options. This variation has a substantial effect on preferences. Additional questions showed that variations of $200 in initial wealth have little or no effect on choices. Evidently, preferences are quite insensitive to small changes of wealth but highly sensitive to corresponding changes in reference point. These observations show that the effective carriers of values are gains and losses, or changes in wealth, rather than states of wealth as implied by the rational model.

The common pattern of preferences observed in problems 3 and 4 is of special interest because it violates not only expected utility theory but practically all other normatively based models of choice. In particular, these data are inconsistent with the model of regret advanced by Bell (1982) and by Loomes and Sugden (1982) and axiomatized by Fishburn (1982). This follows from the fact that problems 3 and 4 yield identical outcomes and an identical regret structure. Furthermore, regret theory cannot accommodate the combination of risk aversion in problem 3 and risk seeking in problem 4—even without the corresponding changes in endowment that make the problems extensionally equivalent.

Shifts of reference can be induced by different decompositions of outcomes into risky and riskless components, as in the above problems. The reference point can also be shifted by a mere labeling of outcomes, as illustrated in the following problems (Tversky and Kahneman 1981, p. 453).

Problem 5 ($N = 152$): Imagine that the U.S. is preparing for the outbreak of an unusual Asian disease, which is expected to kill 600 people. Two alternative programs to combat the disease have been proposed. Assume that the exact scientific estimates of the consequences of the programs are as follows:

If Program A is adopted, 200 people will be saved. [72%]

If Program B is adopted, there is 1/3 probability that 600 people will be saved, and 2/3 probability that no people will be saved. [28%]

In problem 5 the outcomes are stated in positive terms (lives saved), and the majority choice is accordingly risk averse. The prospect of certainly saving 200 lives is more attractive than a risky prospect of equal expected value. A second group of respondents was given the same cover story with the following descriptions of the alternative programs.

Problem 6 ($N = 155$):

If Program C is adopted 400 people will die. [22%]

If Program D is adopted there is 1/3 probability that nobody will die, and 2/3 probability that 600 people will die. [78%]

In problem 6 the outcomes are stated in negative terms (lives lost), and the majority choice is accordingly risk seeking. The certain death of 400 people is less acceptable than a two-thirds chance that 600 people will die. Problems 5 and 6, however, are essentially identical. They differ only in that the former is framed in terms of the number of lives saved (relative to an expected loss of 600 lives if no action is taken), whereas the latter is framed in terms of the number of lives lost.

On several occasions we presented both versions to the same respondents and discussed with them the inconsistent preferences evoked by the two frames. Many respondents expressed a wish to remain risk averse in the "lives saved" version and risk seeking in the "lives lost" version, although they also expressed a wish for their answers to be consistent. In the persistence of their appeal, framing effects resemble visual illusions more than computational errors.

Discounts and Surcharges

Perhaps the most distinctive intellectual contribution of economic analysis is the systematic consideration of alternative opportunities. A basic principle of economic thinking is that opportunity costs and out-of-pocket costs should be treated alike. Preferences should depend only on relevant differences between options, not on how these differences are labeled. This principle runs counter to the psychological tendencies that make preferences susceptible to superficial variations in form. In particular, a difference that favors outcome A over outcome B can sometimes be framed either as an advantage of A or as a disadvantage of B by suggesting either B or A as the neutral reference point. Because of loss aversion, the difference will loom larger when A is neutral and B-A is evaluated as a loss than when B is neutral and A-B is evaluated as a gain. The significance of such variations of framing has been noted in several contexts.

Thaler (1980) drew attention to the effect of labeling a difference between two prices as a surcharge or a discount. It is easier to forgo a discount than to accept a surcharge because the same price difference is valued as a gain in the former case and as a loss in the latter. Indeed, the credit card lobby is said to insist that any price difference between cash and card purchases should be labeled a cash discount rather than a credit surcharge. A similar idea could be invoked to explain why the price response to slack demand often takes the form of discounts or special concessions

(Stigler and Kindahl 1970). Customers may be expected to show less resistance to the eventual cancellation of such temporary arrangements than to outright price increases. Judgments of fairness exhibit the same pattern (Kahneman, Knetsch, and Thaler, in this issue).

Schelling (1981) has described a striking framing effect in a context of tax policy. He points out that the tax table can be constructed by using as a default case either the childless family (as is in fact done) or, say, the modal two-child family. The tax difference between a childless family and a two-child family is naturally framed as an exemption (for the two-child family) in the first frame and as a tax premium (on the childless family) in the second frame. This seemingly innocuous difference has a large effect on judgments of the desired relation between income, family size, and tax. Schelling reported that his students rejected the idea of granting the rich a larger exemption than the poor in the first frame but favored a larger tax premium on the childless rich than on the childless poor in the second frame. Because the exemption and the premium are alternative labels for the same tax differences in the two cases, the judgments violate invariance. Framing the consequences of a public policy in positive or in negative terms can greatly alter its appeal.

The notion of a money illusion is sometimes applied to workers' willingness to accept, in periods of high inflation, increases in nominal wages that do not protect their real income—although they would strenuously resist equivalent wage cuts in the absence of inflation. The essence of the illusion is that, whereas a cut in the nominal wage is always recognized as a loss, a nominal increase that does not pre-serve real income may be treated as a gain. Another manifestation of the money illusion was observed in a study of the perceived fairness of economic actions (Kahneman, Knetsch, and Thaler, in press). Respondents in a telephone interview evaluated the fairness of the action described in the following vignette, which was presented in two versions that differed only in the bracketed clauses.

A company is making a small profit. It is located in a community experiencing a recession with substantial unemployment [but no inflation/and inflation of 12%]. The company decides to [decrease wages and salaries 7%/increase salaries only 5%] this year.

Although the loss of real income is very similar in the two versions, the proportion of respondents who judged the action of the company "unfair" or "very unfair" was 62% for a nominal reduction but only 22% for a nominal increase.

Bazerman (1983) has documented framing effects in experimental studies of bargaining. He compared the performance of experimental subjects when the outcomes of bargaining were formulated as gains or as losses. Subjects who bargained over the allocation of losses more often failed to reach agreement and more often failed to discover a Pareto-optimal solution. Bazerman attributed these observations to the general propensity toward risk seeking in the domain of losses, which may increase the willingness of both participants to risk the negative consequences of a deadlock.

Loss aversion presents an obstacle to bargaining whenever the participants evaluate their own concessions as losses and the concessions obtained from the other party as gains. In negotiating over missiles, for example, the subjective loss of security associated with dismantling a missile may loom larger than the increment of security produced by a similar action on the adversary's part. If the two parties both assign a two-to-one ratio to the values of the concessions they make and of those they obtain, the resulting four-to-one gap may be difficult to bridge. Agreement will be much easier to achieve by negotiators who trade in "bargaining chips" that are valued equally, regardless of whose hand they are in. In this mode of trading, which may be common in routine purchases, loss aversion tends to disappear (Kahneman and Tversky 1984).

The Framing and Weighting of Chance Events

In expected-utility theory, the utility of each possible outcome is weighted by its probability. In prospect theory, the value of an uncertain outcome is multiplied by a decision weight $\pi(p)$, which is a monotonic function of p but is not a probability. The weighting function π has the following properties. First, impossible events are discarded, that is, $\pi(0) = 0$, and the scale is normalized so that $\pi(1) = 1$, but the function is not well behaved near the end points (Kahneman and Tversky 1979). Second, for low probabilities, $\pi(p) > p$, but $\pi(p) + \pi(1 - p) \leq 1$ (subcertainty). Thus low probabilities are overweighted, moderate and high probabilities are underweighted, and the latter effect is more pronounced than the former. Third, $\pi(pr)/\pi(p) < \pi(pqr)/\pi(pq)$ for all $0 < p, q, r \leq 1$ (subproportionality). That is, for any fixed probability ratio r, the ratio of decision weights is closer to unity when the probabilities are low than when they are high, for example, $\pi(.1)/\pi(.2) > \pi(.4)/\pi(.8)$. A hypothetical weighting function that satisfies these properties is shown in figure 24.2. Its consequences are discussed in the next section.[3]

Nontransparent Dominance
The major characteristic of the weighting function is the overweighting of probability differences involving certainty and impossibility, for example, $\pi(1.0) - \pi(.9)$ or $\pi(.1) - \pi(0)$, relative to comparable differences in the middle of the scale, for example, $\pi(.3) - \pi(.2)$. In particular, for small p, π is generally subadditive, for example,

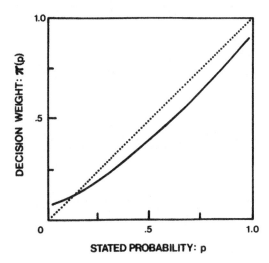

Figure 24.2
A typical weighting function.

$\pi(.01) + \pi(.06) > \pi(.07)$. This property can lead to violations of dominance, as illustrated in the following pair of problems.

Problem 7 ($N = 88$). Consider the following two lotteries, described by the percentage of marbles of different colors in each box and the amount of money you win or lose depending on the color of a randomly drawn marble. Which lottery do you prefer?

Option A

90% white	6% red	1% green	1% blue	2% yellow
$0	win $45	win $30	lose $15	lose $15

Option B

90% white	6% red	1% green	1% blue	2% yellow
$0	win $45	win $45	lose $10	lose $15

It is easy to see that option B dominates option A: for every color the outcome of B is at least as desirable as the outcome of A. Indeed, all respondents chose B over A. This observation is hardly surprising because the relation of dominance is highly transparent, so the dominated prospect is rejected without further processing. The next problem is effectively identical to problem 7, except that colors yielding identical outcomes (red and green in B and yellow and blue in A) are combined. We have proposed that this operation is commonly performed by the decision maker if no dominated prospect is detected.

Problem 8 ($N = 124$). Which lottery do you prefer?

Option C

90% white	6% red	1% green	3% yellow
$0	win $45	win $30	lose $15

Option D

90% white	7% red	1% green	2% yellow
$0	win $45	lose $10	lose $15

The formulation of problem 8 simplifies the options but masks the relation of dominance. Furthermore, it enhances the attractiveness of C, which has two positive outcomes and one negative, relative to D, which has two negative outcomes and one positive. As an inducement to consider the options carefully, participants were informed that one-tenth of them, selected at random, would actually play the gambles they chose. Although this announcement aroused much excitement, 58% of the participants chose the dominated alternative C. In answer to another question the majority of respondents also assigned a higher cash equivalent to C than to D. These results support the following propositions. (i) Two formulations of the same problem elicit different preferences, in violation of invariance. (ii) The dominance rule is obeyed when its application is transparent. (iii) Dominance is masked by a frame in which the inferior option yields a more favorable outcome in an identified state of the world (e.g., drawing a green marble). (iv) The discrepant preferences are consistent with the subadditivity of decision weights. The role of transparency may be illuminated by a perceptual example. Figure 24.3 presents the well-known Müller-Lyer illusion: the top line appears longer than the bottom line, although it is in fact shorter. In figure 24.4, the same patterns are embedded in a rectangular frame, which makes it apparent that the protruding bottom line is longer than the top one. This judgment has the nature of an inference, in contrast to the perceptual impression that mediates judgment in figure 24.3. Similarly, the finer partition introduced in problem 7 makes it possible to conclude that option D is superior to C, without assessing their values. Whether the relation of dominance is detected depends on framing as well as on the sophistication and experience of the decision maker. The dominance relation in problems 8 and 1 could be transparent to a sophisticated decision maker, although it was not transparent to most of our respondents.

Certainty and Pseudocertainty

The overweighting of outcomes that are obtained with certainty relative to outcomes that are merely probable gives rise to violations of the expectation rule, as first noted by Allais (1953). The next series of problems (Tversky and Kahneman 1981,

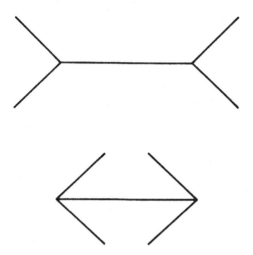

Figure 24.3
The Müller-Lyer illusion.

p. 455) illustrates the phenomenon discovered by Allais and its relation to the weighting of probabilities and to the framing of chance events. Chance events were realized by drawing a single marble from a bag containing a specified number of favorable and unfavorable marbles. To encourage thoughtful answers, one-tenth of the participants, selected at random, were given an opportunity to play the gambles they chose. The same respondents answered problems 9–11, in that order.

Problem 9 ($N = 77$). Which of the following options do you prefer?

A. a sure gain of $30 [78%]
B. 80% chance to win $45 and 20% chance to win nothing [22%]

Problem 10 ($N = 81$). Which of the following options do you prefer?

C. 25% chance to win $30 and 75% chance to win nothing [42%]
D. 20% chance to win $45 and 80% chance to win nothing [58%]

Note that problem 10 is obtained from problem 9 by reducing the probabilities of winning by a factor of four. In expected utility theory a preference for A over B in problem 9 implies a preference for C over D in problem 10. Contrary to this prediction, the majority preference switched from the lower prize ($30) to the higher one ($45) when the probabilities of winning were substantially reduced. We called this phenomenon the *certainty effect* because the reduction of the probability of winning from certainty to .25 has a greater effect than the corresponding reduction from .8 to .2. In prospect theory, the modal choice in problem 9 implies $v(45)\pi(.80) < v(30)\pi(1.0)$, whereas the modal choice in problem 10 implies $v(45)\pi(.20) > v(30)\pi(.25)$. The observed violation of expected utility theory, then, is implied by the curvature of π (see figure 24.2) if

$$\frac{\pi(.20)}{\pi(.25)} > \frac{v(30)}{v(45)} > \frac{\pi(.80)}{\pi(1.0)}.$$

Allais's problem has attracted the attention of numerous theorists, who attempted to provide a normative rationale for the certainty effect by relaxing the cancellation rule (see, e.g., Allais 1979; Fishburn 1982, 1983; Machina 1982; Quiggin 1982; Chew 1983). The following problem illustrates a related phenomenon, called the *pseudocertainty effect*, that cannot be accommodated by relaxing cancellation because it also involves a violation of invariance.

Problem 11 ($N = 85$): Consider the following two stage game. In the first stage, there is a 75% chance to end the game without winning anything, and a 25% chance to move into the second stage. If you reach the second stage you have a choice between:

E. a sure win of $30 [74%]

F. 80% chance to win $45 and 20% chance to win nothing [26%]

Your choice must be made before the outcome of the first stage is known.

Because there is one chance in four to move into the second stage, prospect E offers a .25 probability of winning $30, and prospect F offers a $.25 \times .80 = .20$ probability of winning $45. Problem 11 is therefore identical to problem 10 in terms of probabilities and outcomes. However, the preferences in the two problems differ: most subjects made a risk-averse choice in problem 11 but not in problem 10. We call this phenomenon the pseudocertainty effect because an outcome that is actually uncertain is weighted as if it were certain. The framing of problem 11 as a two-stage game encourages respondents to apply cancellation: the event of failing to reach the second stage is discarded prior to evaluation because it yields the same outcomes in both options. In this framing problems 11 and 9 are evaluated alike.

Although problems 10 and 11 are identical in terms of final outcomes and their probabilities, problem 11 has a greater potential for inducing regret. Consider a decision maker who chooses F in problem 11, reaches the second stage, but fails to win the prize. This individual knows that the choice of E would have yielded a gain of $30. In problem 10, on the other hand, an individual who chooses D and fails to win cannot know with certainty what the outcome of the other choice would have been. This difference could suggest an alternative interpretation of the pseudo-certainty effect in terms of regret (e.g., Loomes and Sugden 1982). However, the certainty and the pseudocertainty effects were found to be equally strong in a modi-fied version of problems 9–11 in which opportunities for regret were equated across problems. This finding does not imply that considerations of regret play no role in decisions. (For examples, see Kahneman and Tversky [1982, p. 710].) It merely indi-cates that Allais's example and the pseudocertainty effect are primarily controlled by the nonlinearity of decision weights and the framing of contingencies rather than by the anticipation of regret.[4]

The certainty and pseudocertainty effects are not restricted to monetary outcomes. The following problem illustrates these phenomena in a medical context. The respondents were 72 physicians attending a meeting of the California Medical Asso-ciation. Essentially the same pattern of responses was obtained from a larger group ($N = 180$) of college students.

Problem 12 ($N = 72$). In the treatment of tumors there is sometimes a choice between two types of therapies: (i) a radical treatment such as extensive surgery, which involves some risk of imminent death, (ii) a moderate treatment, such as limited surgery or radiation therapy. Each of the following problems describes the possible outcome of two alternative treatments, for three different cases. In considering each case, suppose the patient is a 40-year-old male. Assume that without treatment death is imminent (within a month) and that only one of the treatments can be applied. Please indicate the treatment you would prefer in each case.

Case 1

Treatment A: 20% chance of imminent death and 80% chance of normal life, with an expected longevity of 30 years. [35%]

Treatment B: certainty of a normal life, with an expected longevity of 18 years. [65%]

Case 2

Treatment C: 80% chance of imminent death and 20% chance of normal life, with an expected longevity of 30 years. [68%]

Treatment D: 75% chance of imminent death and 25% chance of normal life, with an expected longevity of 18 years. [32%]

Case 3

Consider a new case where there is a 25% chance that the tumor is treatable and a 75% chance that it is not. If the tumor is not treatable, death is imminent. If the tumor is treatable, the outcomes of the treatment are as follows:

Treatment E: 20% chance of imminent death and 80% chance of normal life, with an expected longevity of 30 years. [32%]

Treatment F: certainty of normal life, with an expected longevity of 18 years. [68%]

The three cases of this problem correspond, respectively, to problems 9–11, and the same pattern of preferences is observed. In case 1, most respondents make a risk-averse choice in favor of certain survival with reduced longevity. In case 2, the moderate treatment no longer ensures survival, and most respondents choose the treatment that offers the higher expected longevity. In particular, 64% of the physicians who chose B in case 1 selected C in case 2. This is another example of Allais's certainty effect.

The comparison of cases 2 and 3 provides another illustration of pseudocertainty. The cases are identical in terms of the relevant outcomes and their probabilities, but the preferences differ. In particular, 56% of the physicians who chose C in case 2 selected F in case 3. The conditional framing induces people to disregard the event of the tumor not being treatable because the two treatments are equally ineffective in this case. In this frame, treatment F enjoys the advantage of pseudocertainty. It appears to ensure survival, but the assurance is conditional on the treatability of the tumor. In fact, there is only a .25 chance of surviving a month if this option is chosen.

The conjunction of certainty and pseudocertainty effects has significant implications for the relation between normative and descriptive theories of choice. Our results indicate that cancellation is actually obeyed in choices—in those problems that make its application transparent. Specifically, we find that people make the same choices in problems 11 and 9 and in cases 3 and 1 of problem 12. Evidently, people "cancel" an event that yields the same outcomes for all options, in two-stage or nested structures. Note that in these examples cancellation is satisfied in problems that are formally equivalent to those in which it is violated. The empirical validity of cancellation therefore depends on the framing of the problems.

The present concept of framing originated from the analysis of Allais's problems by Savage (1954, pp. 101–4) and Raiffa (1968, pp. 80–86), who reframed these examples in an attempt to make the application of cancellation more compelling. Savage and Raiffa were right: naive respondents indeed obey the cancellation axiom when its application is sufficiently transparent.[5] However, the contrasting preferences in different versions of the same choice (problems 10 and 11 and cases 2 and 3 of problem 12) indicate that people do not follow the same axiom when its application is not transparent. Instead, they apply (non-linear) decision weights to the probabilities as stated. The status of cancellation is therefore similar to that of dominance: both rules are intuitively compelling as abstract principles of choice, consistently obeyed in transparent problems and frequently violated in nontransparent ones. Attempts to rationalize the preferences in Allais's example by discarding the cancellation axiom face a major difficulty: they do not distinguish transparent formulations in which cancellation is obeyed from nontransparent ones in which it is violated.

Discussion

In the preceding sections we challenged the descriptive validity of the major tenets of expected utility theory and outlined an alternative account of risky choice. In this section we discuss alternative theories and argue against the reconciliation of normative and descriptive analyses. Some objections of economists to our analysis and conclusions are addressed.

Descriptive and Normative Considerations

Many alternative models of risky choice, designed to explain the observed violations of expected utility theory, have been developed in the last decade. These models divide into the following four classes. (i) Nonlinear functionals (e.g., Allais 1953, 1979; Machina 1982) are obtained by eliminating the cancellation condition altogether. These models do not have axiomatizations leading to a (cardinal) measurement of utility, but they impose various restrictions (i.e., differentiability) on the utility functional. (ii) The expectations quotient model (axiomatized by Chew and MacCrimmon 1979; Weber 1982; Chew 1983; Fishburn 1983) replaces cancellation by a weaker substitution axiom and represents the value of a prospect by the ratio of two linear functionals. (iii) Bilinear models with nonadditive probabilities (e.g., Kahneman and Tversky 1979; Quiggin 1982; Schmeidler 1984; Segal 1984; Yaari 1984; Luce and Narens 1985) assume various restricted versions of cancellation (or substitution) and construct a bilinear representation in which the utilities of outcomes are weighted by a nonadditive probability measure or by some nonlinear transform of the probability scale. (iv) Nontransitive models represent preferences by a bivariate utility function. Fishburn (1982, 1984) axiomatized such models, while Bell (1982) and Loomes and Sugden (1982) interpreted them in terms of expected regret. For further theoretical developments, see Fishburn (1985).

The relation between models and data is summarized in table 24.1. The stub column lists the four major tenets of expected utility theory. Column 1 lists the major empirical violations of these tenets and cites a few representative references. Column 2 lists the subset of models discussed above that are consistent with the observed violations.

The conclusions of table 24.1 may be summarized as follows. First, all the above models (as well as some others) are consistent with the violations of cancellation

Table 24.1
Summary of Empirical Violations and Explanatory Models

Tenet	Empirical violation	Explanatory model
Cancellation	Certainty effect (Allais 1953, 1979; Kahneman and Tversky 1979) (problems 9–10, and 12 [cases 1 and 2])	All models
Transitivity	Lexicographic semiorder (Tversky 1969) Preference reversals (Slovic and Lichtenstein 1983)	Bivariate models
Dominance	Contrasting risk attitudes (problem 2) Subadditive decision weights (problem 8)	Prospect theory
Invariance	Framing effects (problems 1, 3–4, 5–6, 7–8, 10–11, and 12)	Prospect theory

produced by the certainty effect.[6] Therefore, Allais's "paradox" cannot be used to compare or evaluate competing nonexpectation models. Second, bivariate (nontransitive) models are needed to explain observed intransitivities. Third, only prospect theory can accommodate the observed violations of (stochastic) dominance and invariance. Although some models (e.g., Loomes and Sugden 1982; Luce and Narens 1985) permit some limited failures of invariance, they do not account for the range of framing effects described in this article.

Because framing effects and the associated failures of invariance are ubiquitous, no adequate descriptive theory can ignore these phenomena. On the other hand, because invariance (or extensionality) is normatively indispensable, no adequate prescriptive theory should permit its violation. Consequently, the dream of constructing a theory that is acceptable both descriptively and normatively appears unrealizable (see also Tversky and Kahneman 1983).

Prospect theory differs from the other models mentioned above in being unabashedly descriptive and in making no normative claims. It is designed to explain preferences, whether or not they can be rationalized. Machina (1982, p. 292) claimed that prospect theory is "unacceptable as a descriptive model of behavior toward risk" because it implies violations of stochastic dominance. But since the violations of dominance predicted by the theory have actually been observed (see problems 2 and 8), Machina's objection appears invalid.

Perhaps the major finding of the present article is that the axioms of rational choice are generally satisfied in transparent situations and often violated in nontransparent ones. For example, when the relation of stochastic dominance is transparent (as in the aggregated version of problem 2 and in problem 7), practically everyone selects the dominant prospect. However, when these problems are framed so that the relation of dominance is no longer transparent (as in the segregated version of problem 2 and in problem 8), most respondents violate dominance, as predicted. These results contradict all theories that imply stochastic dominance as well as others (e.g., Machina 1982) that predict the same choices in transparent and non-transparent contexts. The same conclusion applies to cancellation, as shown in the discussion of pseudocertainty. It appears that both cancellation and dominance have normative appeal, although neither one is descriptively valid.

The present results and analysis—particularly the role of transparency and the significance of framing—are consistent with the conception of bounded rationality originally presented by Herbert Simon (see, e.g., Simon 1955, 1978; March 1978; Nelson and Winter 1982). Indeed, prospect theory is an attempt to articulate some of the principles of perception and judgment that limit the rationality of choice.

The introduction of psychological considerations (e.g., framing) both enriches and complicates the analysis of choice. Because the framing of decisions depends on the language of presentation, on the context of choice, and on the nature of the display, our treatment of the process is necessarily informal and incomplete. We have identified several common rules of framing, and we have demonstrated their effects on choice, but we have not provided a formal theory of framing. Furthermore, the present analysis does not account for all the observed failures of transitivity and invariance. Although some intransitivities (e.g., Tversky 1969) can be explained by discarding small differences in the framing phase, and others (e.g., Raiffa 1968, p. 75) arise from the combination of transparent and nontransparent comparisons, there are examples of cyclic preferences and context effects (see, e.g., Slovic, Fischhoff, and Lichtenstein 1982; Slovic and Lichtenstein 1983) that require additional explanatory mechanisms (e.g., multiple reference points and variable weights). An adequate account of choice cannot ignore these effects of framing and context, even if they are normatively distasteful and mathematically intractable.

Bolstering Assumptions

The assumption of rationality has a favored position in economics. It is accorded all the methodological privileges of a self-evident truth, a reasonable idealization, a tautology, and a null hypothesis. Each of these interpretations either puts the hypothesis of rational action beyond question or places the burden of proof squarely on any alternative analysis of belief and choice. The advantage of the rational model is compounded because no other theory of judgment and decision can ever match it in scope, power, and simplicity.

Furthermore, the assumption of rationality is protected by a formidable set of defenses in the form of bolstering assumptions that restrict the significance of any observed violation of the model. In particular, it is commonly assumed that substantial violations of the standard model are (i) restricted to insignificant choice problems, (ii) quickly eliminated by learning, or (iii) irrelevant to economics because of the corrective function of market forces. Indeed, incentives sometimes improve the quality of decisions, experienced decision makers often do better than novices, and the forces of arbitrage and competition can nullify some effects of error and illusion. Whether these factors ensure rational choices in any particular situation is an empirical issue, to be settled by observation, not by supposition.

It has frequently been claimed (see, e.g., Smith 1985) that the observed failures of rational models are attributable to the cost of thinking and will thus be eliminated by proper incentives. Experimental findings provide little support for this view. Studies reported in the economic and psychological literature have shown that errors that are prevalent in responses to hypothetical questions persist even in the presence of significant monetary payoffs. In particular, elementary blunders of probabilistic reasoning (Grether 1980; Tversky and Kahneman 1983), major inconsistencies of choice (Grether and Plott 1979; Slovic and Lichtenstein 1983), and violations of stochastic dominance in nontransparent problems (see problem 2 above) are hardly reduced by incentives. The evidence that high stakes do not always improve decisions is not restricted to laboratory studies. Significant errors of judgment and choice can be documented in real world decisions that involve high stakes and serious deliberation. The high rate of failures of small businesses, for example, is not easily reconciled with the assumptions of rational expectations and risk aversion.

Incentives do not operate by magic: they work by focusing attention and by prolonging deliberation. Consequently, they are more likely to prevent errors that arise from insufficient attention and effort than errors that arise from misperception or faulty intuition. The example of visual illusion is instructive. There is no obvious mechanism by which the mere introduction of incentives (without the added opportunity to make measurements) would reduce the illusion observed in figure 24.3, and the illusion vanishes—even in the absence of incentives—when the display is altered in figure 24.4. The corrective power of incentives depends on the nature of the particular error and cannot be taken for granted.

The assumption of the rationality of decision making is often defended by the argument that people will learn to make correct decisions and sometimes by the evolutionary argument that irrational decision makers will be driven out by rational ones. There is no doubt that learning and selection do take place and tend to improve efficiency. As in the case of incentives, however, no magic is involved. Effective learning takes place only under certain conditions: it requires accurate and immediate feedback about the relation between the situational conditions and the appropriate response. The necessary feedback is often lacking for the decisions made by managers, entrepreneurs, and politicians because (i) outcomes are commonly

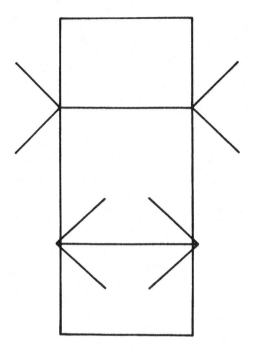

Figure 24.4
A transparent version of the Müller-Lyer illusion.

delayed and not easily attributable to a particular action; (ii) variability in the environment degrades the reliability of the feedback, especially where outcomes of low probability are involved; (iii) there is often no information about what the outcome would have been if another decision had been taken; and (iv) most important decisions are unique and therefore provide little opportunity for learning (see Einhorn and Hogarth 1978). The conditions for organizational learning are hardly better. Learning surely occurs, for both individuals and organizations, but any claim that a particular error will be eliminated by experience must be supported by demonstrating that the conditions for effective learning are satisfied.

Finally, it is sometimes argued that failures of rationality in individual decision making are inconsequential because of the corrective effects of the market (Knez, Smith, and Williams 1985). Economic agents are often protected from their own irrational predilections by the forces of competition and by the action of arbitrageurs, but there are situations in which this mechanism fails. Hausch, Ziemba, and Rubenstein (1981) have documented an instructive example: the market for win bets at the racetrack is efficient, but the market for bets on place and show is not. Bettors commonly underestimate the probability that the favorite will end up in second or third place, and this effect is sufficiently large to sustain a contrarian betting strategy with a positive expected value. This inefficiency is found in spite of the high incentives, of the unquestioned level of dedication and expertise among participants in racetrack markets, and of obvious opportunities for learning and for arbitrage.

Situations in which errors that are common to many individuals are unlikely to be corrected by the market have been analyzed by Haltiwanger and Waldman (1985) and by Russell and Thaler (1985). Furthermore, Akerlof and Yellen (1985) have presented their near-rationality theory, in which some prevalent errors in responding to economic changes (e.g., inertia or money illusion) will (i) have little effect on the individual (thereby eliminating the possibility of learning), (ii) provide no opportunity for arbitrage, and yet (iii) have large economic effects. The claim that the market can be trusted to correct the effect of individual irrationalities cannot be made without supporting evidence, and the burden of specifying a plausible corrective mechanism should rest on those who make this claim.

The main theme of this article has been that the normative and the descriptive analyses of choice should be viewed as separate enterprises. This conclusion suggests a research agenda. To retain the rational model in its customary descriptive role, the relevant bolstering assumptions must be validated. Where these assumptions fail, it is instructive to trace the implications of the descriptive analysis (e.g., the effects of loss aversion, pseudocertainty, or the money illusion) for public policy, strategic decision making, and macroeconomic phenomena (see Arrow 1982; Akerlof and Yellen 1985).

Notes

This work was supported by contract N00014-84-K-0615 from the Office of Naval Research to Stanford University. The present article reviews our work on decision making under risk from a new perspective, discussed primarily in the first and last sections. Most of the empirical demonstrations have been reported in earlier publications. Problems 3, 4, 7, 8, and 12 are published here for the first time.

1. All problems are presented in the text exactly as they were presented to the participants in the experiments.

2. If $p + q = 1$ and either $x > y > 0$ or $x < y < 0$, the value of a prospect is given by $v(y) + \pi(p)[v(x) - v(y)]$, so that decision weights are not applied to sure outcomes.

3. The extension of the present analysis to prospects with many (nonzero) outcomes involves two additional steps. First, we assume that continuous (or multivalued) distributions are approximated, in the framing phase, by discrete distributions with a relatively small number of outcomes. For example, a uniform distribution on the interval $(0, 90)$ may be represented by the discrete prospect $(0, .1; 10, .1; \ldots; 90, .1)$. Second, in the multiple-outcome case the weighting function, $\pi_p(p_i)$, must depend on the probability vector p, not only on the component p_i, $i = 1, \ldots, n$. For example, Quiggin (1982) uses the function

$\pi_p(p_i) = \pi(p_i)/[\pi(p_1) + \cdots + \pi(p_n)]$. As in the two-outcome case, the weighting function is assumed to satisfy subcertainty, $\pi_p(p_1) + \cdots + \pi_p(p_n) \leq 1$, and subproportionality.

4. In the modified version—problems 9'–11'—the probabilities of winning were generated by drawing a number from a bag containing 100 sequentially numbered tickets. In problem 10', the event associated with winning \$45 (drawing a number between one and 20) was included in the event associated with winning \$30 (drawing a number between one and 25). The sequential setup of problem 11 was replaced by the simultaneous play of two chance devices: the roll of a die (whose outcome determines whether the game is on) and the drawing of a numbered ticket from a bag. The possibility of regret now exists in all three problems, and problem 10' and 11' no longer differ in this respect because a decision maker would always know the outcomes of alternative choices. Consequently, regret theory cannot explain either the certainty effect (9' vs. 10') or the pseudocertainty effect (10' vs. 11') observed in the modified problems.

5. It is noteworthy that the conditional framing used in problems 11 and 12 (case 3) is much more effective in eliminating the common responses to Allais's paradox than the partition framing introduced by Savage (see, e.g., Slovic and Tversky 1974). This is probably due to the fact that the conditional framing makes it clear that the critical options are identical—after eliminating the state whose outcome does not depend on one's choice (i.e., reaching the second stage in problem 11, an untreatable tumor in problem 12, case 3).

6. Because the present article focuses on prospects with known probabilities, we do not discuss the important violations of cancellation due to ambiguity (Ellsberg 1961).

References

Akerlof, G. A., and Yellen, J. 1985. Can small deviations from rationality make significant differences to economic equilibria? *American Economic Review* 75:708–20.

Allais, M. 1953. Le comportement de l'homme rationnel devant le risque: Critique des postulats et axiomes de l'Ecole Américaine. *Econometrica* 21:503–46.

Allais, M. 1979. The foundations of a positive theory of choice involving risk and a criticism of the postulates and axioms of the American School. In M. Allais and O. Hagen (eds.), *Expected Utility Hypotheses and the Allais Paradox*. Dordrecht: Reidel.

Arrow, K. J. 1982. Risk perception in psychology and economics. *Economic Inquiry* 20:1–9.

Bazerman, M. H. 1983. Negotiator judgment. *American Behavioral Scientist* 27:211–28.

Bell, D. E. 1982. Regret in decision making under uncertainty. *Operations Research* 30:961–81.

Bishop, R. C., and Heberlein, T. A. 1979. Measuring values of extra-market goods: Are indirect measures biased? *American Journal of Agricultural Economics* 61:926–30.

Chew, S. H. 1983. A generalization of the quasilinear mean with applications to the measurement of income inequality and decision theory resolving the Allais paradox. *Econometrica* 51:1065–92.

Chew, S. H., and MacCrimmon, K. 1979. Alpha utility theory, lottery composition, and the Allais paradox. Working Paper no. 686. Vancouver: University of British Columbia.

Clark, H. H., and Clark, E. V. 1977. *Psychology and Language.* New York: Harcourt Brace Jovanovich.

Einhorn, H. J., and Hogarth, R. M. 1978. Confidence in judgment: Persistence of the illusion of validity. *Psychological Review* 85:395–416.

Ellsberg, D. 1961. Risk, ambiguity, and the Savage axioms. *Quarterly Journal of Economics* 75:643–69.

Eraker, S. E., and Sox, H. C. 1981. Assessment of patients' preferences for therapeutic outcomes. *Medical Decision Making* 1:29–39.

Fischhoff, B. 1983. Predicting frames. *Journal of Experimental Psychology: Learning, Memory and Cognition* 9:103–16.

Fishburn, P. C. 1982. Nontransitive measurable utility. *Journal of Mathematical Psychology* 26:31–67.

Fishburn, P. C. 1983. Transitive measurable utility. *Journal of Economic Theory* 31:293–317.

Fishburn, P. C. 1984. SSB utility theory and decision making under uncertainty. *Mathematical Social Sciences* 8:253–85.

Fishburn, P. C. 1985. Uncertainty aversion and separated effects in decision making under uncertainty. Working paper. Murray Hill, N.J.: AT&T Bell Labs.

Fishburn, P. C., and Kochenberger, G. A. 1979. Two-piece von Neumann–Morgenstern utility functions. *Decision Sciences* 10:503–18.

Grether, D. M. 1980. Bayes rule as a descriptive model: The representativeness heuristic. *Quarterly Journal of Economics* 95:537–57.

Grether, D. M., and Plott, C. R. 1979. Economic theory of choice and the preference reversal phenomenon. *American Economic Review* 69:623–38.

Hagen, O. 1979. Towards a positive theory of preferences under risk. In M. Allais and O. Hagen (eds.), *Expected Utility Hypotheses and the Allais Paradox*. Dordrecht: Reidel.

Haltiwanger, J., and Waldman, M. 1985. Rational expectations and the limits of rationality: An analysis of heterogeneity. *American Economic Review* 75:326–40.

Hammond, P. 1985. Consequential behavior in decision trees and expected utility. Institute for Mathematical Studies in the Social Sciences Working Paper no. 112. Stanford, Calif.: Stanford University.

Hansson, B. 1975. The appropriateness of the expected utility model. *Erkenntnis* 9:175–93.

Hausch, D. B.; Ziemba, W. T.; and Rubenstein, M. E. 1981. Efficiency of the market for racetrack betting. *Management Science* 27:1435–52.

Hershey, J. C., and Schoemaker, P. J. H. 1980. Risk taking and problem context in the domain of losses: An expected utility analysis. *Journal of Risk and Insurance* 47:111–32.

Kahneman, D.; Knetsch, J. L.; and Thaler, R. H. In this issue. Fairness and the assumptions of economics.

Kahneman, D.; Knetsch, J. L.; and Thaler, R. In press. Perceptions of fairness: Entitlements in the market. *American Economic Review*.

Kahneman, D., and Tversky, A. 1979. Prospect theory: An analysis of decision under risk. *Econometrica* 47:263–91.

Kahneman, D., and Tversky, A. 1982. The psychology of preferences. *Scientific American* 246:160–73.

Kahneman, D., and Tversky, A. 1984. Choices, values, and frames. *American Psychologist* 39:341–50.

Knetsch, J. L., and Sinden, J. A. 1984. Willingness to pay and compensation demanded: Experimental evidence of an unexpected disparity in measures of value. *Quarterly Journal of Economics* 99:507–21.

Knez, P.; Smith, V. L.; and Williams, A. W. 1985. Individual rationality, market rationality and value estimation. *American Economic Review: Papers and Proceedings* 75:397–402.

Loomes, G., and Sugden, R. 1982. Regret theory: An alternative theory of rational choice under uncertainty. *Economic Journal* 92:805–24.

Luce, R. D., and Krantz, D. H. 1971. Conditional expected utility. *Econometrica* 39:253–71.

Luce, R. D., and Narens, L. 1985. Classification of concatenation measurement structures according to scale type. *Journal of Mathematical Psychology* 29:1–72.

Machina, M. J. 1982. "Expected utility" analysis without the independence axiom. *Econometrica* 50:277–323.

McNeil, B. J.; Pauker, S. G.; Sox, H. C., Jr.; and Tversky, A. 1982. On the elicitation of preferences for alternative therapies. *New England Journal of Medicine* 306:1259–62.

March, J. G. 1978. Bounded rationality, ambiguity, and the engineering of choice. *Bell Journal of Economics* 9:587–608.

Markowitz, H. 1952. The utility of wealth. *Journal of Political Economy* 60:151–58.

Nelson, R. R., and Winter, S. G. 1982. *An Evolutionary Theory of Economic Change*. Cambridge, Mass.: Harvard University Press.

Payne, J. W.; Laughhunn, D. J.; and Crum, R. 1980. Translation of gambles and aspiration level effects in risky choice behavior. *Management Science* 26:1039–60.

Quiggin, J. 1982. A theory of anticipated utility. *Journal of Economic Behavior and Organization* 3:323–43.

Raiffa, H. 1968. *Decision Analysis: Introductory Lectures on Choices under Uncertainty*. Reading, Mass.: Addison-Wesley.

Russell, T., and Thaler, R. 1985. The relevance of quasi-rationality in competitive markets. *American Economic Review* 75:1071–82.

Savage, L. J. 1954. *The Foundations of Statistics*. New York: Wiley.

Schelling, T. C. 1981. Economic reasoning and the ethics of policy. *Public Interest* 63:37–61.

Schmeidler, D. 1984. Subjective probability and expected utility without additivity. Preprint Series no. 84. Minneapolis: University of Minnesota, Institute for Mathematics and Its Applications.

Schumpeter, J. A. 1954. *History of Economic Analysis*. New York: Oxford University Press.

Segal, U. 1984. Nonlinear decision weights with the independence axiom. Working Paper in Economics no. 353. Los Angeles: University of California, Los Angeles.

Simon, H. A. 1955. A behavioral model of rational choice. *Quarterly Journal of Economics* 69:99–118.

Simon, H. A. 1978. Rationality as process and as product of thought. *American Economic Review: Papers and Proceedings* 68:1–16.

Slovic, P.; Fischhoff, B.; and Lichtenstein, S. 1982. Response mode, framing, and information processing effects in risk assessment. In R. M. Hogarth (ed.), *New Directions for Methodology of Social and Behavioral Science: Question Framing and Response Consistency*. San Francisco: Jossey-Bass.

Slovic, P., and Lichtenstein, S. 1983. Preference reversals: A broader perspective. *American Economic Review* 73:596–605.

Slovic, P., and Tversky, A. 1974. Who accepts Savage's axiom? *Behavioral Science* 19:368–73.

Smith, V. L. 1985. Experimental economics: Reply. *American Economic Review* 75:265–72.

Stigler, G. J., and Kindahl, J. K. 1970. *The Behavior of Industrial Prices*. New York: National Bureau of Economic Research.

Thaler, R. H. 1980. Towards a positive theory of consumer choice. *Journal of Economic Behavior and Organization* 1:39–60.

Tversky, A. 1969. Intransitivity of preferences. *Psychological Review* 76:105–10.

Tversky, A. 1977. On the elicitation of preferences: Descriptive and prescriptive considerations. In D. E. Bell, R. L. Keeney, and H. Raiffa (eds.), *Conflicting Objectives in Decisions*. New York: Wiley.

Tversky, A., and Kahneman, D. 1981. The framing of decisions and the psychology of choice. *Science* 211:453–58.

Tversky, A., and Kahneman, D. 1983. Extensional versus intuitive reasoning: The conjunction fallacy in probability judgment. *Psychological Review* 90:293–315.

von Neumann, J., and Morgenstern, O. 1944. *Theory of Games and Economic Behavior*. Princeton, N.J.: Princeton University Press.

Weber, R. J. 1982. The Allais paradox, Dutch auctions, and alpha-utility theory. Working paper. Evanston, Ill.: Northwestern University.

Yaari, M. E. 1984. Risk aversion without decreasing marginal utility. Report Series in Theoretical Economics. London: London School of Economics.

25 Contrasting Rational and Psychological Analyses of Political Choice

George A. Quattrone and Amos Tversky

The assumption of individual rationality plays a central role in the social sciences, especially in economics and political science. Indeed, it is commonly assumed that most if not all economic and political agents obey the maxims of consistency and coherence leading to the maximization of utility. This notion has been captured by several models that constitute the rational theory of choice including the expected utility model for decision making under risk, the riskless theory of choice among commodity bundles, and the Bayesian theory for the updating of belief. These models employ different assumptions about the nature of the options and the information available to the decision maker, but they all adopt the principles of coherence and invariance that underlie the prevailing notion of rationality.

The rational theory of choice has been used to prescribe action as well as to describe the behavior of consumers, entrepreneurs, voters, and politicians. The use of the rational theory as a descriptive model has been defended on the grounds that people are generally effective in pursuing their goals, that the axioms underlying the theory are intuitively compelling, and that evolution and competition favor rational individuals over less rational ones. The objections to the rationality assumption were primarily psychological. The human animal, it has been argued, is often controlled by emotions and desires that do not fit the model of calculating rationality. More recent objections to the maximization doctrine have been cognitive rather than motivational. Following the seminal work of Herbert Simon (1955, 1978) and the emergence of cognitive psychology, it has become evident that human rationality is bounded by limitations on memory and computational capabilities. Furthermore, the experimental analysis of inference and choice has revealed that the cognitive machinery underlying human judgment and decision making is often inconsistent with the maxims of rationality. These observations have led to the development of a descriptive analysis of judgment and choice that departs from the rational theory in many significant respects (see, e.g., Abelson and Levi 1985; Dawes 1988; Kahneman, Slovic, and Tversky 1982; Tversky and Kahneman 1986).

We contrast the rational theory of choice with a descriptive psychological analysis, using a series of questions involving political candidates and public referenda. These problems are used to illustrate the differences between rational and descriptive theories of choice and to test their predictions. Some of the questions probed our respondents' views about familiar political issues, such as the Equal Rights Amendment and the prevalence of crime in black neighborhoods compared to white neighborhoods. In other cases involving the test of general hypotheses, such as risk aversion, we introduced hypothetical problems in order to achieve experimental control and eliminate the influence of irrelevant factors. The use of hypothetical problems raises obvious questions regarding the generality and the applicability of the finding. Nevertheless, we believe that the use of carefully worded questions can address key issues regarding people's values and beliefs so long as respondents take the questions seriously and have no particular reason to disguise or misrepresent their true preferences. Under these conditions hypothetical questions can be used to compare alternative theories of political choice that cannot be readily tested using available survey and voting data. Our results, of course, do not provide definitive conclusions about political decision making, but they may shed light on the formation of political judgment and stimulate new hypotheses that can be tested in national election surveys in the years to come.

We focus on expected utility theory, which is the major normative theory of decision making under risk (von Neumann and Morgenstern 1947; Raiffa 1968; Savage 1954). This model is contrasted with prospect theory, a descriptive analysis developed by Kahneman and Tversky (1979, 1984). The first section deals with the role of the reference point and its impact on the choice between political candidates. In the second section we test the assumption of invariance and contrast it with a psychophysical analysis of numerical scales. The third section deals with the perception and the weighting of chance events, and the role of uncertainty in choice. The fourth section addresses the classical issue of the rationality of voting. It contrasts, again, a rational analysis based on the probability of casting a decisive vote with a less rational analysis that incorporates an element of self-deception. The implications of the present analysis are discussed in the fifth and final section.

Reference Effects, Risk Attitudes, and Loss Aversion

The standard utility function, derived from the expected utility model, has two essential characteristics. First, it is defined on wealth, or final asset position. Thus, a person with wealth W accepts an even chance to win $1,000 or lose $500 if the difference between the utility of $W + \$1,000$ and the utility of W (the upside) exceeds the difference between the utility of W and the utility of $W - \$500$ (the downside). Second, the utility function is concave; that is, the subjective value of an additional dollar diminishes with the total amount of money one has. The first assumption (asset integration) is necessitated by basic considerations of coherence. The second assumption (concavity) was introduced by Bernoulli (1954) to accommodate the

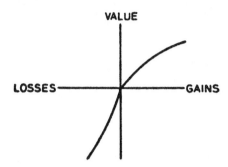

Figure 25.1
A hypothetical value function.

common observations of risk aversion, and it has played an essential role in economics. A person is risk-averse if he or she prefers a sure outcome over a risky prospect that has an equal or greater expected value. For example, most people prefer $100 for sure over an even chance to win $200 or nothing. Risk aversion is implied by the concavity of the utility scale because the utility of $2x$ is less than twice the utility of x.

Although risk aversion is quite common, particularly for prospects with positive outcomes, risk seeking is also prevalent, particularly for prospects with negative outcomes. For example, most people find a sure loss of $100 more aversive than an even chance to lose $200 or nothing. To explain the combination of risk aversion and risk seeking, prospect theory replaces the traditional concave utility function for wealth by an S-shaped function for changes of wealth. In this theory, therefore, the carriers of values are positive or negative changes (i.e., gains and losses) defined relative to a neutral reference point. Furthermore, the value function is assumed to be concave above the reference point and convex below it, giving rise to risk aversion in the domain of gains and risk seeking in the domain of losses. As in the classical theory, it is assumed that the difference between $100 and $200 is subjectively larger than the (numerically equivalent) difference between $1,100 and $1,200. Unlike the classical theory, however, it is assumed that the difference between a loss of $100 and a loss of $200 is subjectively larger than the numerically equivalent difference between a loss of $1,100 and a loss of $1,200. Thus, the value function of prospect theory is steepest at the origin and it gets shallower as one moves away from the reference point in either direction. An important property of the value function— called loss aversion—is that the downside is considerably steeper than the upside;

that is, losses loom larger than the corresponding gains. A typical value function with these characteristics is given in figure 25.1.

Attitudes towards Risk

Expected utility theory and prospect theory yield different predictions. The classical theory predicts risk aversion independent of the reference point, whereas prospect theory predicts risk aversion in the domain of gains and risk seeking in the domain of losses (except for small probabilities). Furthermore, prospect theory implies that shifts in the reference point induced by the framing of the problem will have predictable effects on people's risk preferences. These phenomena are illustrated in the following four problems, each involving a choice between alternative political prospects.

The respondents to these and other problems reported in this article were under-graduates at Stanford University or at the University of California at Berkeley. The problems were presented in a questionnaire in a classroom setting. Each problem involved a simple choice between two candidates or positions on a public referen-dum. The respondents were asked to imagine actually facing the choice described, and they wee assured that the responses were anonymous and that there were no correct or incorrect answers. The number of respondents in this and all subsequent problems is denoted by N, and the percentage who chose each outcome is given in parentheses.

Problem 1 ($N = 89$)

Suppose there is a continent consisting of five nations, Alpha, Beta, Gamma, Delta, and Epsilon. The nations all have very similar systems of government and economics, are members of a continental common market, and are therefore expected to produce very similar standards of living and rates of inflation. Imagine you are a citizen of Alpha, which is about to hold its presidential election. The two presidential candidates, Brown and Green, differ from each other primarily in the policies they are known to favor and are sure to implement. These poli-cies were studied by Alpha's two leading economists, who are of equal expertise and are impartial as to the result of the election. After studying the policies advocated by Brown and Green and the policies currently being pursued by the other four nations, each economist made a forecast. The forecast consisted of three predictions about the expected standard of living index (SLI). The SLI measures the goods and services consumed (directly or indirectly) by the average citizen yearly. It is expressed in dollars per capita so that the higher the SLI the higher the level of economic prosperity. The three projections concerned

1. the average SLI to be expected among the nations Beta, Gamma, Delta, and Epsilon

2. the SLI to be expected by following Brown's policy

3. the SLI to be expected by following Green's policy

The forecasts made by each economist are summarized in the following table:

Projected SLI in Dollars per Capita

	Other four nations	Brown's policy	Green's policy
Economist 1	$43,000	$65,000	$51,000
Economist 2	$45,000	$43,000	$53,000

Suppose that as a citizen of Alpha, you were asked to cast your vote for Brown or Green. On the basis of the information provided, whom would you vote for? [Brown, 28%; Green, 72%]

A second group of respondents received the same cover story as in problem 1, but the economists' forecasts about the other four nations were altered. The forecasts made about the candidates remained the same.

Problem 2 (N = 96)

Projected SLI in Dollars per Capita

	Other four nations	Brown's policy	Green's policy
Economist 1	$63,000	$65,000	$51,000
Economist 2	$65,000	$43,000	$53,000

Suppose that as a citizen of Alpha, you were asked to cast your vote for Brown or Green. On the basis of the information provided, whom would you vote for? [Brown, 50%; Green, 50%]

Comparing the responses to problems 1 and 2 shows that the choice between Brown and Green was influenced by the projected SLI in other countries. This effect can be explained in terms of the value function of prospect theory. Because the two economists were said to be impartial and of equal expertise, we assume that respondents gave equal weight to their projections. Hence, the actuarial expected value of Brown's policy ($54,000) is about the same as that of Green's policy ($52,000). However, Brown is riskier than Green in the sense that the outcomes projected for Brown have greater spread than those projected for Green. Therefore, Brown would profit from risk seeking and Green from risk aversion. According to prospect theory, an individual's attitude towards risk depends on whether the outcomes are perceived as gains or losses, relative to the reference point.

In problems 1 and 2 it seems reasonable to adopt the average SLI projected for the other nations as a point of reference, because all five nations were said to have comparable standards of living. The reference point then will be about $44,000 in problem 1 and $64,000 in problem 2. Outcomes projected for Brown and Green would, therefore, be treated as gains in the first problem and as losses in the second. As a consequence, the value function entails more risk aversion in problem 1 than in problem 2. In fact, significantly more respondents opted for the relatively risk-free Green in problem 1 (72%) than in problem 2 (50%) ($p < .005$ by chi-square). Another factor that may have contributed to the finding is a tendency for people to discount the highly discrepant projection for the risky candidate, Brown (i.e., the one made by economist 1 in problem 1 and by economist 2 in problem2). Although this consideration may have played a role in the present case, the same shift in attitudes towards risk have been observed in many other problems in which this account does not apply (Tversky and Kahneman 1986).

To address whether the predictions based on the value function apply to other attributes besides money, we included in the same questionnaire one of two problems in which the rate of inflation was the outcome of the choice.

Problem 3 ($N = 76$)

Now imagine that several years have passed and that there is another presidential contest between two new candidates, Frank and Carl. The same two economists studied the candidates' preferred policies and made a projection. This time, however, the forecast concerned the projected rate of inflation. The forecasts made by each economist are summarized in the following table:

Projected Rate of Inflation (%)

	Other four nations	Frank's policy	Carl's policy
Economist 1	24	16	4
Economist 2	26	14	26

Suppose that as a citizen of Alpha, you were asked to cast your vote for Frank or Carl. On the basis of the information provided, whom would you vote for? [Frank, 74%; Carl, 26%]

A second group of respondents received the same cover story as in problem 3, but the economists' forecasts about the other four nations were altered. The forecasts made about the candidates remained the same.

Problem 4 ($N = 75$)

Projected Rate of Inflation (%)

	Other four nations	Frank's policy	Carl's policy
Economist 1	4	16	4
Economist 2	6	14	26

Suppose that as a citizen of Alpha, you were asked to cast your vote for Frank or Carl. On the basis of the information provided, whom would you vote for? [Frank, 52%; Carl, 48%]

The analysis of problems 3 and 4 closely follows that of problems 1 and 2. The expected rate of inflation was 15% for both candidates. However, this value was below the expected continental rate of 25% in problem 3 and above the expected continental rate of 5% in problem 4. Because high inflation is undesirable, values below reference are likely to be viewed as gains, whereas values above reference are likely to be viewed as losses. Assuming that the continental rate of inflation was taken as a point of reference, the results confirmed the prediction of prospect theory that the more risky candidate (Carl) would obtain more votes in problem 4 (48%) than in problem 3 (26%) ($p < .01$ by chi-square).

Together, the responses to problems 1–4 confirm the prediction of prospect theory that people are risk-averse in the domain of gains and risk-seeking in the domain of losses, where gains and losses were defined relative to the outcomes projected for other countries. These results may shed light on the so-called incumbency-oriented voting hypothesis. Numerous investigators have shown that the evaluation of an incumbent party is responsive to fluctuations in the national economy. In general, incumbent presidents and congressional candidates of the same party benefit at the polls from improving economic conditions whereas they suffer from deteriorating conditions (Kramer 1971). These results can be understood, in part, as a consequence of the divergent attitudes towards risks for outcomes involving gains and losses. Following Shepsle (1972), we maintain that incumbents are usually regarded by voters as less risky than the challengers, who are often unknowns and whose policies could drastically alter the current trends, for better or for worse. If people are risk-averse for gains and risk-seeking for losses, the less risky incumbent should fare better when conditions are good than when they are bad. This analysis assumes that the reelection of the incumbent is perceived by voters as a continuation of the current trends, which is attractive when times are good. In contrast, the election of the challenger offers a political gamble that is worth taking when "four more years" of the incumbent is viewed as an unsatisfactory state.

It is important to distinguish this analysis of incumbency-oriented voting from the more common explanation that "when times are bad you throw the rascals out." In the latter account, voters are thought to regard a credible challenger as having to be better than the incumbent, who "got us into this mess to begin with." The present account, in contrast, is based on the notion that the challenger is *riskier* than the incumbent, not necessarily better overall. In problems 2 and 4, the risky candidates profit from hard times even though their expected value was no better than that of the relatively riskless candidates. Obviously, however, a challenger whose expected value is substantially below the incumbent's is unlikely to be elected even in the presence of substantial risk seeking.

In light of this discussion, it is interesting to share an unsolicited response given by one of our participants, who received problem 4 in the winter of 1981. This respondent penciled in *Carter* over Frank, the less risky candidate, and *Reagan* over Carl, the riskier candidate. Recall that in this problem the outcomes were less desirable than the reference point. Evidently, our respondent—who voted for Carl—believed that the erstwhile incumbent Carter would have guaranteed the continuation of unacceptable economic conditions, while the erstwhile challenger Reagan, with his risky "new" theories, might have made matters twice as bad as they were or might have been able to restore conditions to a satisfactory level. Because economic and global conditions were widely regarded as unacceptable in 1980, the convexity of the value function for losses may have contributed to the election of a risky presidential prospect, namely Reagan.

Loss Aversion

A significant feature of the value function is that losses loom larger than gains. For example, the displeasure associated with losing a sum of money is generally greater than the pleasure associated with winning the same amount. This property, called *loss aversion*, is depicted in figure 25.1 by the steeper slope for outcomes below the reference point than for those above.

An important consequence of loss aversion is a preference for the status quo over alternatives with the same expected value. For example, most people are reluctant to accept a bet that offers equal odds of winning and losing x number of dollars. This reluctance is consistent with loss aversion, which implies that the pain associated with the loss would exceed the pleasure associated with the gain, or $v(x) < -v(-x)$. This observation, however, is also consistent with the concavity of the utility function, which implies that the status quo (i.e., the prospect yielding one's current level of wealth with certainty) is preferred to any risky prospect with the same expected value. These accounts can be discriminated from each other because in utility theory the greater impact of losses than of gains is tied to the presence of risk. In the present analysis, however, loss aversion also applies to riskless choice. Consider the following example: Let $x = (x_i, x_u)$ and $y = (y_i, y_u)$ denote two economic policies that produce inflation rates of x_i and y_i and unemployment rates of x_u and y_u. Suppose $x_i > y_i$ but $x_u < y_u$; that is, y produces a lower rate of inflation than x but at the price of a higher rate of unemployment. If people evaluate such policies as positive or negative changes relative to a neutral multiattribute reference point and if the (multiattribute) value function exhibits loss aversion, people will exhibit a reluctance to trade; that is, if at position x (the status quo) people are indifferent between x and y, then at position y they would not be willing to switch to x (Kahneman and Tversky 1984). We test this prediction in the following pair of problems.

Problem 5 (N = 91)

Imagine there were a presidential contest between two candidates, Frank and Carl. Frank wishes to keep the level of inflation and unemployment at its current level. The rate of inflation is currently at 42%, and the rate of unemployment is currently at 15%. Carl proposes a policy that would decrease the rate of inflation by 19% while increasing the rate of unemployment by 7%. Suppose that as a citizen of Alpha, you were asked to cast your vote for either Frank or Carl. Please indicate your vote. [Frank, 65%; Carl, 35%]

Problem 6 (N = 89)

Imagine there were a presidential contest between two candidates, Frank and Carl. Carl wishes to keep the rate of inflation and unemployment at its current level. The rate of inflation is currently at 23%, and the rate of unemployment is currently at 22%. Frank proposes a policy that would increase the rate of inflation by 19% while decreasing the rate of unemployment by 7%. suppose that as a citizen of Alpha you wee asked to cast your vote for either Frank or Carl. Please indicate your vote. [Frank, 39%; Carl, 61%]

It is easy to see that problems 5 and 6 offer the same choice between Frank's policy (42%, 15%) and Carl's policy (23%, 22%). The problems differ only in the location of the status quo, which coincides with Frank's policy in problem 5 and with Carl's policy in problem 6. As implied by the notion of multiattribute loss aversion, the majority choice in both problems favored the status quo ($p < .001$ by chi-square). The reluctance to trade is in this instance incompatible with standard utility theory, in which the preference between two policies should not depend on whether one or the other is designated as the status quo. In terms of a two-dimensional value function, defined on changes in inflation and unemployment, the present results imply that both $v(19, -7)$ and $v(-19, 7)$ are less than $v(0, 0) = 0$.

We have seen that the combination of risk aversion for gains and risk seeking for losses is consistent with incumbency-oriented voting: incumbents profit from good times, and challengers from bad times. We wish to point out that loss aversion is consistent with another widely accepted generalization, namely that the incumbent enjoys a distinct advantage over the challenger. This effect is frequently attributed to such advantages of holding office as that of obtaining free publicity while doing one's job and being perceived by voters as more experienced and effective at raising funds (Kiewiet 1982). To these considerations, the present analysis of choice adds the consequences of the value function. Because it is natural to take the incumbent's policy as the status quo—the reference point to which the challenger's policy is compared—and because losses loom larger than gains, it follows that the incumbent enjoys a distinct advantage. As we argued earlier, the introduction of risk or uncertainty also tends to favor the incumbent under conditions that enhance risk aversion; that is, when the general conditions are good or even acceptable, voters are likely to play it safe and opt for the relatively riskless incumbent. Only when conditions become unacceptable will the risky challenger capture an edge. Hence, the properties of the value function are consistent with the generally observed incumbency effects, as well as with the exceptions that are found during hard times.

Loss aversion may play an important role in bargaining and negotiation. The process of making compromises and concessions may be hindered by loss aversion, because each party may view its own concessions as losses that loom larger than the gains achieved by the concessions of the adversary (Bazerman 1983; Tversky and Kahneman 1986). In negotiating over missiles, for example, each superpower may sense a greater loss in security from the dismantling of its own missiles than it senses a gain in security from a comparable reduction made by the other side. This difficulty is further compounded by the fact, noted by several writers (e.g., Lebow and Stein 1987; Ross 1986), that the very willingness of one side to make a particular concession (e.g., eliminate missiles from a particular location) immediately reduces the perceived value of this concession.

An interesting example of the role of the reference point in the formation of public opinion was brought to our attention by the actor Alan Alda. The objective of the Equal Rights Amendment (ERA) can be framed in two essentially equivalent ways. On the one hand, the ERA can be presented as an attempt to eliminate discrimination against women. In this formulation, attention is drawn to the argument that equal rights for women are not currently guaranteed by the constitution, a negative state that the ERA is designed to undo. On the other hand, the ERA can be framed as legislation designed to improve women's status in society. This frame emphasizes what is to be gained from the amendment, namely, better status and equal rights for women. If losses loom larger than gains, then support for the ERA should be greater among those who are exposed to the frame that emphasizes the elimination of discrimination than the improvement of women's rights. To test Alda's hypothesis, we presented two groups of respondents with the following question. The questions presented to the two groups differed only in the statement appearing on either side of the slash within the brackets.

Problem 7 ($N = 149$)

As you know, the Equal Rights Amendment to the Constitution is currently being debated across the country. It says, "Equality of rights under law shall not be denied or abridged by the United States or by any state on account of sex." Supporters of the amendment say that it will [help eliminate discrimination against women/improve the rights of women] in job opportunities, salary, and social security benefits. Opponents of the amendment say that it will have a negative effect by denying women protection offered by special laws. Do you favor or oppose the Equal Rights Amendment? (check one)

Not surprisingly, a large majority of our sample of Stanford undergraduates indicated support for the ERA (74%). However, this support was greater when the problem was framed in terms of eliminating discrimination (78%) than in terms of improving women's rights (69%).

Just as the formulation of the issue may affect the attitude of the target audience, so might the prior attitude of the audience have an effect on the preferred formulation of the issue. Another group of respondents first indicated their opinion on the ERA, either pro or con. They then responded to the following question.

Problem 8 (N = 421)

The status and rights of women have been addressed in two different ways, which have different social and legal implications. Some people view it primarily as a problem of eliminating inequity and discrimination against women in jobs, salary, etc. Other people view it primarily as a problem of improving or strengthening the rights of women in different areas of modern society. How do you see the problem of women's rights? (check one only)

Of those who indicated support of the ERA, 72% chose to frame the issue in terms of eliminating inequity, whereas only 60% of those who opposed the ERA chose this frame. This finding is consistent with the common observation regarding the political significance of how issues are labeled. A familiar example involves abortion, whose opponents call themselves prolife, not antichoice.

Invariance, Framing, and the Ratio-Difference Principle

Perhaps the most fundamental principle of rational choice is the assumption of invariance. This assumption, which is rarely stated explicitly, requires that the preference order among prospects should not depend on how their outcomes and probabilities are described and thus that two alternative formulations of the same problem should yield the same choice. The responses to problems 7 and 8 above may be construed as a failure of invariance. In the present section, we present sharper tests of invariance in which the two versions of a given choice problem are unquestionably equivalent. Under these conditions, violations of invariance cannot be justified on normative grounds. To illustrate such failures of invariance and motivate the psychological analysis, consider the following pair of problems.

Problem 9 (N = 126)

Political decision making often involves a considerable number of trade-offs. A program that benefits one segment of the population may work to the disadvantage of another segment. Policies designed to lead to higher rates of employment frequently have an adverse effect on inflation. Imagine you were faced with the decision of adopting one of two economic policies.

If program *J* is adopted, 10% of the work force would be unemployed, while the rate of inflation would be 12%. If program *K* is adopted, 5% of the work force would be unemployed, while the rate of inflation would be 17%. The following table summarizes the alternative policies and their likely consequences:

Policy	Work force unemployed (%)	Rate of inflation (%)
Program *J*	10	12
Program *K*	5	17

Imagine you were faced with the decision of adopting program *J* or program *K*. Which would you select? [program *J*, 36%; program *K*, 64%]

A second group of respondents received the same cover story about trade-offs with the following description of the alternative policies:

Problem 10 (*N* = 133)

Policy	Work force employed (%)	Rate of inflation (%)
Program *J*	90	12
Program *K*	95	17

Imagine you were faced with the decision of adopting program *J* or program *K*. Which would you select? [program *J*, 54%; program *K*, 46%]

The modal response was program *K* in problem 9 and program *J* in problem 10. These choices constitute a violation of invariance in that each program produces the same outcomes in both problems. After all, to say that 10% or 5% of the work force will be unemployed is to say, respectively, that 90% or 95% of the work force will be employed. Yet respondents showed more sensitivity to the outcomes when these were described as rates of unemployment than as rates of employment. These results illustrate a "psychophysical" effect that we call the *ratio-difference principle*.

Psychophysics is the study of the functional relation between the physical and the psychological value of attributes such as size, brightness, or loudness. A utility function for money, therefore, can also be viewed as a psychophysical scale relating the objective to the subjective value of money. Recall that a concave value function for gains of the form depicted in figure 25.1 implies that a difference between $100 and $200 looms larger than the objectively equal difference between $200 and $300. More generally, the ratio-difference principle says that the impact of any fixed positive difference between two amounts increases with their ratio. Thus the difference between $200 and $100 yields a ratio of 2, whereas the difference between $300 and $200 yields a ratio of 1.5. The ratio-difference principle applies to many perceptual attributes. Increasing the illumination of a room by adding one candle has a much larger impact when the initial illumination is poor than when it is good. The same pattern is observed for many sensory attributes, and it appears that the same psychophysical principle is applicable to the perception of numerical differences as well.

Unlike perceptual dimensions, however, numerical scales can be framed in different ways. The labor statistics, for example, can be described in terms of employment or unemployment, yielding the same difference with very different ratios. If the ratio-difference principle applies to such scales, then the change from an unemployment rate of 10% to 5%, yielding a ratio of 2, should have more impact than the objectively equal change from an employment rate of 90% to 95%, yielding a ratio that is very close to unity. As a consequence, program K would be more popular in problem 9 and program J in problem 10. This reversal in preference was obtained, although the only difference between the two problems was the use of unemployment data in problem 9 and employment data in problem 10.

The ratio-difference principle has numerous applications to political behavior. For example, many political choices involve the allocation of limited funds to various sectors of the population. The following two problems demonstrate how the framing of official statistics can effect the perceived need for public assistance.

Problem 11 (N = 125)

The country of Delta is interested in reducing the crime rate among its immigrant groups. The Department of Justice has been allocated $100 million ($100M) for establishing a crime prevention program aimed at immigrant youths. The program would provide the youths with job opportunities and recreational facilities, inasmuch as criminal acts tend to be committed by unemployed youths who have little to do with their time. A decision must be made between two programs currently being considered. The programs differ from each other primarily in how the $100M would be distributed between Delta's two largest immigrant communities, the Alphans and the Betans. There are roughly the same number of Alphans and Betans in Delta. Statistics have shown that by the age of 25, 3.7% of all Alphans have a criminal record, whereas 1.2% of all Betans have a criminal record.

The following two programs are being considered. Program J would allocate to the Alphan community $55M and to the Betan community $45M. Program K would allocate $65M to the Alphan community and to the Betan community $35M. The following table summarizes these alternative programs:

Program	To Alphan community	To Betan community
Program *J*	$55M	$45M
Program *K*	$65M	$35M

Imagine you were faced with the decision between program *J* and program *K*. In light of the available crime statistics, which would you select? [program *J*, 41%; program *K*, 59%]

A second group of respondents received the same cover story and program description as in problem 11, with the criminal statistics framed as follows:

Problem 12 (*N* = 126)

Statistics have shown that by the age of 25, 96.3% of all Alphans have no criminal record whereas 98.8% of all Betans have no criminal record.... In light of the available crime statistics, which would you select? [program *J*, 71%; program *K*, 29%]

It should be apparent that the crime statistics on which respondents were to base their choice were the same across the two problems. Because of the ratio-difference principle, however, the Alphans are perceived as much more criminal than the Betans in problem 11—roughly three times as criminal—but they are seen as only slightly less noncriminal than the Betans in problem 12. As hypothesized, respondents selected that program in which differences in allocations between the groups matched as closely as possible differences in perceived criminality, resulting in a large reversal of preference ($p < .001$ by chi-square).

The preceding two problems illustrate an important social problem concerning the perception of crime rates among minority and nonminority segments of the population. It is generally believed that the members of minority groups, such as blacks, have much higher crime rates than do the members of nonminority groups, such as whites (Tursky et al. 1976). Indeed, according to the actual crime statistics compiled by the FBI in 1982, 2.76% of black citizens were arrested for a serious crime compared to .68% of white Americans. The between group difference does appear quite large. Problems 11 and 12 suggest, however, that judgments about the divergent crime rates in the two communities may be altered by how the data are framed. The apparently large difference between crime rates of 2.76% and .68% can be reframed as a relatively small difference between law-obedience rates of 97.24% and 99.32%.

Quattrone and Warren (1985) showed a sample of Stanford undergraduates the 1982 crime statistics, framed either in terms of the percentages of blacks and whites who were arrested for crime or the percentages who were not. Other respondents were not exposed to these data. As implied by the ratio-difference principle, the respondents who were exposed to the crime commission statistics considered the crime rate to be substantially higher in black communities than in white communities, whereas those exposed to the law-obedience statistics considered the communities to be more at par in crime. Furthermore, the subjects who were not shown the FBI crime data gave responses that were virtually indistinguishable from those given by subjects exposed to the crime commission statistics. This comparison suggests that people may generally formulate beliefs about the proportions of blacks and whites who commit crime, not the proportions who abide by the law.

In another question the subjects who had consulted the FBI statistics were asked to allocate $100M targeted for the prevention of crime between the two racial communities. It was observed that subjects exposed to the crime commission statistics allocated more money to the black community (mean = $58.4M) than did the subjects exposed to the law obedience statistics (mean = $47.2M). Hence, the basic results of this section were replicated for nonhypothetical groups. Moreover, a second study by Quattrone and Warren demonstrated that the same reversals due to framing are obtained when racial differences in crime must be inferred from a set of photographs rather than being explicitly pointed out in a neat statistical table. Taken as a whole, the results suggest that the decision of how to frame the data can have significant political consequences for individuals as well as for entire social groups. We suspect that the more successful practitioners of the art of persuasion commonly employ such framing effects to their personal advantage.

The Weighting of Chance Events

A cornerstone of the rational theory of choice is the expectation principle. In the expected utility model, the decision maker selects that option with the highest expected utility that equals the sum of the utilities of the outcomes, each weighted by its probability. The following example of Zeckhauser illustrates a violation of this rule. Consider a game of Russian roulette where you are allowed to purchase the removal of one bullet. Would you be willing to pay the same amount to reduce the number of bullets from four to three as you would to reduce the number from one to zero? Most people say that they would pay more to reduce the probability of death from one-sixth to zero, thereby eliminating the risk altogether, than to reduce the probability of death from four-sixths to three-sixths. This response, however, is incompatible with the expectation principle, according to which the former reduction from a possibility (one bullet) to a certainty (no bullets) cannot be more valuable than the latter reduction (from four to three bullets). To accommodate this and other

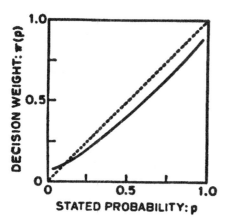

Figure 25.2
A hypothetical weighting function.

violations of the expectation principle, the value of each outcome in prospect theory is multiplied by decision weight that is a monotonic but nonlinear function of its probability.

Consider a simple prospect that yields outcome x with probability p, outcome y with probability q, and the status quo with probability $1 - p - q$. With the reference point set at the status quo, the outcomes are assigned values $v(x)$ and $v(y)$, and the probabilities are assigned *decision weights*, $\pi(p)$ and $\pi(q)$. The overall value of the prospect is

$$\pi(p)v(x) + \pi(q)v(y).$$

As shown in figure 25.2, π is a monotonic nonlinear function of p with the following properties:

1. Impossible events are discarded, that is, $\pi(0) = 0$, and the scale is normalized so that $\pi(1) = 1$. The function is not well behaved at the endpoints though, for people sometimes treat highly likely events as certain and highly unlikely events as impossible.

2. Low probabilities are overweighted, giving rise to some risk seeking in the domain of gains. For example, many people prefer one chance in a thousand to win $3,000 over $3 for sure. This implies

$$\pi(.001)v(\$3,000) > v(\$3),$$

hence

$\pi(.001) > v(\$3)/v(\$3,000) > .001,$

by the concavity of v for gains.

3. Although for low probabilities, $\pi(p) > p$, in general, $\pi(p) + \pi(1 - p) < 1$. Thus low probabilities are overweighted, moderate and high probabilities are underweighted, and the latter effect is more pronounced than the former.

4. For all $0 < p, q, r < 1$, $\pi(pq)/\pi(p) < \pi(pqr)/\pi(pr)$; that is, for any ratio of probabilities q, the ratio of decision weights is closer to unity when the probabilities are small than when they are large; for example, $\pi(.4)/\pi(.8) < \pi(.1)/\pi(.2)$. This property implies the common response to the Russian roulette problem because $\pi(1/6) - \pi(0) > \pi(4/6) - \pi(3/6)$.

Although the description of π has involved stated numerical probabilities, it can be extended to events whose probabilities are subjectively assessed or verbally implied. In these situations, however, the decision weights may also be affected by the vagueness or other details of the choice.

Certainty and Pseudocertainty
Many public policies involve the allocation of funds for projects whose outcomes cannot be known with certainty. The following problems illustrate how preferences among risky projects may be affected by the properties of π, and the results are contrasted with those predicted by the expected utility model.

Problem 13 (N = 88)

The state of Epsilon is interested in developing clean and safe alternative sources of energy. Its Department of Natural Resources is considering two programs for establishing solar energy within the state. If program X is adopted, then it is virtually certain that over the next four years the state will save $20 million ($20M) in energy expenditures. If program Y is adopted, then there is an 80% chance that the state will save $30M in energy expenditures over the next four years and a 20% chance that because of cost overruns, the program will produce no savings in energy expenditures at all. The following table summarizes the alternative policies and their probable consequences.

Policy	Savings in energy expenditures
Program X	$20M savings, with certainty
Program Y	80% chance of saving $30M, 20% chance of no savings

Imagine you were faced with the decision of adopting program X or program Y. Which would you select? [program X, 74%; program Y, 26%]

The same respondents who received problem 13 also received the following problem. Order of presenting the two problems was counterbalanced across booklets.

Problem 14 ($N = 88$)

The state of Gamma is also interested in developing clean and safe alternative sources of energy. Its Department of Natural Resources is considering two programs for establishing solar energy within the state. If program A is adopted, then there is a 25% chance that over the next four years the state will save $20 million ($20M) in energy expenditures and a 75% chance that because of cost overruns, the program will produce no savings in energy expenditures at all. If program B is adopted, there is a 20% chance that the state will save $30M in energy expenditures and an 80% chance that because of cost overruns, the program will produce no savings in energy expenditures at all. The following table summarizes the alternative policies and their probable consequences:

Policy	Savings in energy expenditures
Program A	25% chance of saving $20M, 75% chance of no savings
Program B	20% chance of saving $30M, 80% chance of no savings

Imagine you were faced with the decision of adopting program A or program B. Which would you select? [program A, 39%; program B, 61%]

Because the same respondents completed both problems 13 and 14, we can examine the number who selected each of the four possible pairs of programs: X and A, X and B, Y and A, Y and B. These data are shown below.

| | Problem 14 | |
Problem 13	Program A	Program B
Program X	27	38
Program Y	7	16

The pair most frequently selected is X and B, which corresponds to the modal choices of each problem considered individually. These modal choices pose a problem for the expected utility model. Setting $u(0) = 0$, the preference for X over Y in problem 13 implies that $u(\$20M) > (4/5)u(\$30M)$, or that $u(\$20M)/u(\$30M) > 4/5$. This inequality is inconsistent with that implied by problem 14, because the preference for A over B implies that $(1/4)u(\$20M) < (1/5)u(\$30M)$, or that $u(\$20M)/u(\$30M) < 4/5$. Note that programs A and B (in problem 14) can be obtained from programs X and Y (in problem 13), respectively, by multiplying the probability of nonnull outcomes by one-fourth. The substitution axiom of expected utility theory says that if X is preferred to Y, then a probability mixture that yields X with probability p and 0 otherwise should be preferred to a mixture that yields Y with probability p and 0 otherwise. If $p = 1/4$, this axiom implies that X is preferred to Y if and only if A is preferred to B. From the above table it is evident that more than half of our respondents (45 or 88) violated this axiom.

The modal choices, X and B, however, are consistent with prospect theory. Applying the equation of prospect theory to the modal choice of problem 13 yields $\pi(1)v(\$20\text{M}) > \pi(.8)v(\$30\text{M})$, hence $v(\$20\text{M})/v(\$30\text{M}) > \pi(.8)/\pi(1)$. Applied to problem 14, the equation yields $\pi(.2)/\pi(.25) > v(\$20\text{M})/v(\$30\text{M})$. Taken together, these inequalities imply the observed violation of the substitution axiom for those individuals for which $\pi(.8)/\pi(1) < v(\$20\text{M})/v(\$30\text{M}) < \pi(.2)/\pi(.25)$. Recall that for any ratio of probabilities $q < 1$, the ratio of decision weights is closer to unity when the probabilities are small than when they are large. In particular, $\pi(.8)/\pi(1) < \pi(.2)/\pi(.25)$. Indeed, 38 of the 45 pairs of choices that deviate from expected utility theory fit the above pattern, $p < .001$ by sign test.

It should be noted that prospect theory does not predict that all respondents will prefer X to Y and B to A. This pattern will be found only among those respondents for whom the value ratio, $v(\$20\text{M})/v(\$30\text{M})$, lies between the ratios of decision weights, $\pi(.8)/\pi(1)$ and $\pi(.2)/\pi(.25)$. The theory requires only that individuals who are indifferent between X and Y will prefer B to A and those who are indifferent between A and B will prefer X to Y. For group data, the theory does predict the observed shift in modal preferences. The only pair of choices *not* consistent with prospect theory is Y and A, for this pair implies that $\pi(.2)/\pi(.25) < \pi(.8)/\pi(1)$. This pair was in fact selected least often.

The modal preferences exhibited in the preceding two problems illustrate a phenomenon first reported by Allais (1953) that is referred to in prospect theory as the *certainty effect*: reducing the probability of an outcome by a constant factor has a greater impact when the outcome was initially certain than when it was merely possible. The Russian roulette game discussed earlier is a variant of the certainty effect.

Causal versus Diagnostic Contingencies

A classical problem in the analysis of political behavior concerns the rationality of voting and abstaining. According to Downs (1957), it may not be rational for an individual to register and vote in large elections because of the very low probability that the individual would cast a decisive vote coupled with the costs of registering and going to the polls. Objections to downs's view were raised by Riker and Ordes-hook (1968), who argued that an individual may derive from voting other benefits besides the possibility of casting a decisive ballot. These additional benefits are collectively referred to as *citizen's duty*, or *D*, and they include affirming one's allegiance to the democratic system, complying with a powerful ethic, participating in a common social ritual, as well as "standing up and being counted." To these rational consequences of voting, we suggest adding a somewhat less rational component.

Elsewhere (Quattrone and Tversky 1984) we have shown that people often fail to distinguish between causal contingencies (acts that produce an outcome) and diagnostic contingencies (acts that are merely correlated with an outcome). For example, there is a widespread belief that attitudes are correlated with actions. Therefore, some people may reason that if they decide to vote, that decision would imply that others with similar political attitudes would also decide to vote. Similarly, they may reason that if they decide to abstain, others who share their political attitudes will also abstain. Because the preferred candidates can defeat the opposition only if politically like-minded citizens vote in greater numbers than do politically unlike-minded citizens, the individual may infer that he or she had better vote; that is, each citizen may regard his or her single vote as diagnostic of *millions* of votes, which would substantially inflate the subjective probability of one's vote making a difference.

To test this hypothesis, which we call the *voter's illusion*, we had a sample of 315 Stanford undergraduates read about an imaginary country named Delta. Participants were to imagine that they supported party *A*, opposed party *B*, and that there were roughly four million supporters of each party in Delta as well as four million nonaligned voters. Subjects imagined that they were deliberating over whether to vote in the upcoming presidential election, having learned that voting in Delta can be costly in time and effort. To facilitate their decision, they were to consult one of two prevailing theories concerning the group of voters who would determine the electoral outcome.

Some subjects considered the *party supporter's theory*. According to this theory, the nonaligned voters would split their vote fairly equally across the two parties. The electoral outcome would be determined by whether the supporters of party *A* or party *B* became more involved in the election. The political experts were split as to whether the supporters of *A* or *B* would become more involved, but all agreed that the party whose members did become more involved would win by a margin of roughly 200 thousand to 400 thousand votes. Other subjects received the *nonaligned voter's theory*, which held that the supporters of each party would vote in equal numbers. The electoral outcome would in this account be determined by whether the nonaligned voters would swing their support primarily to party A or party B. The experts were split as to which party would capture the majority of the nonaligned voters, but all agreed that the fortunate party would win by a margin of at least 200 thousand votes.

Note that the consequences of voting included in the rational analysis are held constant across the two theories. In both, the "utility difference" between the two parties, the "probability" of casting a decisive vote, the costs of voting, and citizen's duty are the same. But according to the party supporter's theory, there is a correlation between political orientation and participation; that is, either the supporters of party A will vote in greater numbers than will the supporters of party B, or vice versa. In contrast, the nonaligned voter's theory holds that political orientation is independent of participation because party supporters will turn out in equal numbers. Therefore, only subjects presented with the former theory could infer that their decision to vote or to abstain would be diagnostic of what their politically like-minded peers would decide. If being able to make this inference is conducive to voting, then a larger "turnout" should be found among subjects presented with the party supporter's theory than among those presented with the nonaligned voter's theory. In fact, when asked, "Would you vote if the theory were true and voting in Delta were costly," significantly more subjects responded *no* under the party supporter's theory (16%) than under the nonaligned voter's theory (7%) ($p < .05$ by sign test).

An additional finding corroborated the analysis that this difference in turnout was attributable to the perceived diagnosticity of voting. Respondents were asked to indicate how likely it was that the supporters of party A would vote in greater numbers than the supporters of party B "given that you decided to vote" and "given that you decided to abstain." Responses to these two questions were made on nine-point scales with verbal labels ranging from "extremely likely" to "extremely unlikely." Subjects were informed that their decision to vote or abstain could not be communicated to others. Nonetheless, subjects exposed to the party supporter's theory thought that their individual choice would have a greater "effect" on what other decided to do than did subjects exposed to the nonaligned voter's theory, $F(1, 313) = 35.79$ ($p < .001$). Similar effects were observed in responses to a question probing how likely party A was to defeat party B "given that you decided to vote" and "given that you decided to abstain," $F(1, 313) = 40.18$ ($p < .001$). This latter difference was obtained despite subject's knowing that they could cast but one vote and that the likely margin of victory was about 200 thousand votes.

The observed differences between respondents exposed to the party supporter's and nonaligned voter's theory cannot be readily justified from a normative perspective (cf. Meehl 1977). The present analysis of causal versus diagnostic contingencies recalls the tragedy of the commons and it applies to other phenomena in which collective action dwarfs the causal significance of a single individual's contribution. The outcomes of most wars would not have changed had one fewer draftee been inducted, and the success or failure of most charity drives do not ordinarily depend on the dollars of an individual donor. These collective actions defy a routine rational analysis for the individual because if each citizen, draftee, or donor "rationally" refrains from making his or her paltry contribution, then the outcomes would be drastically affected. For this reason, exhortations to vote, to fight, and to help those less fortunate than oneself are usually framed, "If you don't vote/fight/contribute, think of what would happen if *everyone* felt the same way." This argument is compelling. Still, just how *does* an individual's private decision materially affect the decisions made by countless other persons?

Concluding Remarks

We contrasted the rational analysis of political decision making with a psychological account based on descriptive considerations. Although there is no universally accepted definition of rationality, most social scientists agree that rational choice should conform to a few elementary requirements. Foremost among these is the criterion of invariance (or extensionality [Arrow 1982]), which holds that the preference order among prospects should not depend on how they are described. Hence, no acceptable rational theory would allow reversals of preference to come about as a consequence of whether the choice is based on rates of employment or rates of unemployment, crime commission statistics or law obedience statistics. These alternate formulations of the problems convey the same information, and the problems differ from each other in no other way. We have seen, however, that these alternate frames led to predictable reversals in preference.

Whether our studies paint a humbling or flattering picture of human intellectual performance depends on the background from which they are viewed. The proponent of the rational theory of choice may find that we have focused on human limitations and have overlooked its many accomplishments. The motivational psychologist, accustomed to finding the root of all folly in deep-seated emotional needs, may find our approach much too rational and cognitive. Many readers are no doubt familiar with the versions of these opposing viewpoints found in political science. *The Authoritarian Personality* (Adorno et al. 1950), for example, well illustrates the use of motivational assumptions to explain the appeal of a particular ideology to certain elements of the population.

The descriptive failure of normative principles, such as invariance and coherence, does not mean that people are unintelligent or irrational. The failure merely indicates that judgment and choice—like perception and memory—are prone to distortion and error. The significance of the results stems from the observation that the errors are common and systematic, rather than idiosyncratic or random, hence they cannot be dismissed as noise. Accordingly, there is little hope for a theory of choice that is both normatively acceptable and descriptively adequate. A compelling analysis of the uses and abuses of rationality in theories of political behavior has been presented by Converse (1975) who has detailed the often arbitrary and inconsistent criteria by which rationality has been defined. Our intention was not to reopen the discussion about the meaning of rationality but rather to enrich the set of concepts and principles that could be used to analyze, explain, and predict the decisions made by individuals in their private lives, in the market place, and in the political arena.

Notes

The research reported in this article was funded by a grant awarded to Quattrone by the National Institute of Health 1 RO1 MH41382-01 and to Tversky by the Office of Naval Research ON00014-84-K-0615. We are indebted to Philip converse, Robyn Dawes, Alexander George, Robert Jervis, and Scott Plous for their helpful comments on an earlier draft.

References

Abelson, Robert, and Ariel Levi. 1985. Decision Making and Decision Theory. In *The Handbook of Social Psychology*, 3d ed., Gardner Lindzey and Elliot Aronson. Hillsdale, NJ: Lawrence Erlbaum.

Adorno, Theodor, Else Frenkel-Brunswik, Daniel Levinson, and R. Nevitt Sanford. 1950. *The Authoritarian Personality*. New York: Harper.

Allais, Maurice. 1953. Le comportement de l'homme rationnel devant le risque: Critique des postulates et axiomes de l'école americaine. *Econometrica* 21:503–46.

Arrow, Kenneth J. 1982. Risk Perception in Psychology and Economics. *Economic Inquiry* 20:1–9.

Bazerman, Max H. 1983. Negotiator Judgment. *American Behavioral Scientist* 27:211–28.

Bernoulli, Daniel. 1954. Exposition of a New Theory on the Measurement of Risk. *Econometrica* 22:23–36.

Converse, Philip. 1975. Public Opinion and Voting Behavior. In *Handbook of Political Science*, vol. 4, ed. Fred Greenstein and Nelson Polsby. Reading, MA: Addison-Wesley.

Dawes, Robyn. 1988. *Rational Choice in an Uncertain World*. New York: Harcourt, Brace, Jovanovich.

Downs, Anthony. 1957. *An Economic Theory of Democracy*. New York: Harper & Row.

Kahneman, Daniel, Paul Slovic, and Amos Tversky. 1982. *Judgment under Uncertainty: Heuristics and Biases*. New York: Cambridge University Press.

Kahneman, Daniel, and Amos Tversky. 1979. Prospect Theory: An Analysis of Decision under Risk. *Econometrica* 47:263–91.

Kahneman, Daniel, and Amos Tversky. 1984. Choices, Values, and Frames. *American Psychologist* 39:341–50.

Kiewiet, D. Roderick. 1982. The Rationality of Candidates Who Challenge Incumbents in congressional Elections. Social Science Working Paper no. 436, California Institute of Technology.

Kramer, Gerald H. 1971. Short-Term fluctuations in U.S. Voting Behavior, 1896–1964. *American Political Science Review* 65:131–43.

Lebow, Richard N., and Janice G. Stein. 1987. Beyond Deterrence. *Journal of Social Issues* 43:5–71.

Meehl, Paul. 1977. The Selfish Voter Paradox and the Thrown-away Vote Argument. *American Political Science Review* 71:11–30.

Quattrone, George A., and Amos Tversky. 1984. Causal versus Diagnostic Contingencies: On Self-Deception and one the Voter's Illusion. *Journal of Personality and Social Psychology* 46:237–48.

Quattrone, George A., and Diann Warren. 1985. The Ratio-Difference Principle and the Perception of Group Differences. Stanford University. Typescript.

Raiffa, Howard. 1968. *Decision Analysis: Introductory Lectures on Choices under Uncertainty*. Reading, MA: Addison-Wesley.

Riker, William, and Peter Ordeshook. 1968. A Theory of the Calculus of Voting. *American Political Science Review* 10:25–42.

Ross, Lee. 1986. Conflict Notes. Stanford University. Typescript.

Savage, Leonard. 1954. *The Foundations of Statistics*. New York: John Wiley & Sons.

Shepsle, Kenneth. 1972. The Strategy of Ambiguity: Uncertainty and Electoral Competition. *American Political Science Review* 66:555–68.

Simon, Herbert. 1955. A Behavioral Model of Rational Choice. *Quarterly Journal of Economics* 66:99–118.

Simon, Herbert. 1978. Rationality As Process and As Product of Thought. *American Economic Review (Papers and Proceedings)* 68:1–16.

Tursky, Bernard, Milton Lodge, Mary Ann Foley, Richard Reeder, and Hugh Foley. 1976. Evaluation of the Cognitive Component of Political Issues by Use of Classical Conditioning. *Journal of Personality and Social Psychology* 34:865–73.

Tversky, Amos, and Daniel Kahneman. 1986. Rational Choice and the Framing of Decisions. *The Journal of Business* 59:251–78.

Von Neumann, John, and Oskar Morgenstern. 1947. *Theory of Games and Economic Behavior*, 2d ed. Princeton: Princeton University Press.

26 Preference and Belief: Ambiguity and Competence in Choice under Uncertainty

Chip Heath and Amos Tversky

The uncertainty we encounter in the world is not readily quantified. We may feel that our favorite football team has a good chance to win the championship match, that the price of gold will probably go up, and that the incumbent mayor is unlikely to be reelected, but we are normally reluctant to assign numerical probabilities to these events. However, to facilitate communication and enhance the analysis of choice, it is often desirable to quantify uncertainty. The most common procedure for quantifying uncertainty involves expressing belief in the language of chance. When we say that the probability of an uncertain event is 30%, for example, we express the belief that this event is as probable as the drawing of a red ball from a box that contains 30 red and 70 green balls. An alternative procedure for measuring subjective probability seeks to infer the degree of belief from preference via expected utility theory. This approach, pioneered by Ramsey (1931) and further developed by Savage (1954) and by Anscombe and Aumann (1963), derives subjective probability from preferences between bets. Specifically, the subjective probability of an uncertain event E is said to be p if the decision maker is indifferent between the prospect of receiving \$x if E occurs (and nothing otherwise) and the prospect of receiving \$x if a red ball is drawn from a box that contains a proportion p of red balls.

The Ramsey scheme for measuring belief and the theory on which it is based were challenged by Daniel Ellsberg (1961; see also Fellner, 1961) who constructed a compelling demonstration of what has come to be called an ambiguity effect, although the term *vagueness* may be more appropriate. The simplest demonstration of this effect involves two boxes: one contains 50 red balls and 50 green balls, whereas the second contains 100 red and green balls in unknown proportion. You draw a ball blindly from a box and guess its color. If your guess is correct, you win \$20; otherwise you get nothing. On which box would you rather bet? Ellsberg argued that people prefer to bet on the 50/50 box rather than on the box with the unknown composition, even though they have no color preferences and so are indifferent between betting on red or on green in either box. This pattern of preferences, which was later confirmed in many experiments, violates the additivity of subjective probability because it implies that the sum of the probabilities of red and of green is higher in the 50/50 box than in the unknown box.

Ellsberg's work has generated a great deal of interest for two reasons. First, it provides an instructive counter example to (subjective) expected utility theory within the context of games of chance. Second, it suggests a general hypothesis that people prefer to bet on clear rather than on vague events, at least for moderate and high probability. For small probability, Ellsberg suggested, people may prefer vagueness to clarity. These observations present a serious problem for expected utility theory and other models of risky choice because, with the notable exception of games of chance, most decisions in the real world depend on uncertain events whose probabilities cannot be precisely assessed. If people's choices depend not only on the degree of uncertainty but also on the precision with which it can be assessed, then the applicability of the standard models of risky choice is severely limited. Indeed, several authors have extended the standard theory by invoking nonadditive measures of belief (e.g., Fishburn, 1988; Schmeidler, 1989) or second-order probability distributions (e.g., Gärdenfors and Sahlin, 1982; Skyrm, 1980) in order to account for the effect of ambiguity. The normative status of these models is a subject of lively debate. Several authors, notably Ellsberg (1963), maintain that aversion to ambiguity can be justified on normative grounds, although Raiffa (1961) has shown that it leads to incoherence.

Ellsberg's example, and most of the subsequent experimental research on the response to ambiguity or vagueness, were confined to chance processes, such as drawing a ball from a box, or problems in which the decision maker is provided with a probability estimate. The potential significance of ambiguity, however, stems from its relevance to the evaluation of evidence in the real world. Is ambiguity aversion limited to games of chance and stated probabilities, or does it also hold for judgmental probabilities? We found no answer to this question in the literature, but there is evidence that casts some doubt on the generality of ambiguity aversion.

For example, Budescu, Weinberg, and Wallsten (1988) compared the cash equivalents given by subjects for gambles whose probabilities were expressed numerically, graphically, or verbally. In the graphical display, probabilities were presented as the shaded area of a circle. In the verbal form, probabilities were described by expressions such as "very likely" or "highly improbable." Because the verbal and the graphical forms are more ambiguous than the numerical form, ambiguity aversion implies a preference for the numerical display. This prediction was not confirmed. Subjects priced the gambles roughly the same in all three displays. In a different experimental paradigm, Cohen and Hansel (1959) and Howell (1971) investigated subjects' choices between compound gambles involving both skill and chance components. For example, in the latter experiment the subject had to hit a target with a dart (where the subjects's hit rate equaled 75%) as well as spin a roulette wheel so that it would land on a marked section composing 40% of the area. Success involves a 75% skill component and 40% chance component with an overall probability of winning of $.75 \times .4 = .3$. Howell varied the skill and chance components of the gambles, holding the overall probability of winning constant. Because the chance level was known to the subject whereas the skill level was not, ambiguity aversion implies that subjects would shift as much uncertainty as possible to the chance component of the gamble. In contrast, 87% of the choices reflect a preference for skill over chance. Cohen and Hansel (1959) obtained essentially the same result.

The Competence Hypothesis

The preceding observations suggest that the aversion to ambiguity observed in a chance setup (involving aleatory uncertainty) does not readily extend to judgmental problems (involving espistemic uncertainty). In this article, we investigate an alternative account of uncertainty preferences, called the competence hypothesis, which applies to both chance and evidential problems. We submit that the willingness to bet on an uncertain event depends not only on the estimated likelihood of that event and the precision of that estimate; it also depends on one's general knowledge or understanding of the relevant context. More specifically, we propose that—holding judged probability constant—people prefer to bet in a context where they consider themselves knowledgeable or competent than in a context where they feel ignorant or uninformed. We assume that our feeling of competence[1] in a given context is determined by what we know relative to what can be known. Thus, it is enhanced by general knowledge, familiarity, and experience, and is diminished, for example, by calling attention to relevant information that is not available to the decision maker, especially if it is available to others.

There are both cognitive and motivational explanations for the competence hypothesis. People may have learned from lifelong experience that they generally do better in situations they understand than in situations where they have less knowledge. This expectation may carry over to situations where the chances of winning are no longer higher in the familiar than in the unfamiliar context. Perhaps the major reason for the competence hypothesis is motivational rather than cognitive. We propose that the consequences of each bet include, besides the monetary payoffs, the credit or blame associated with the outcome. Psychic payoffs of satisfaction or embarrassment can result from self-evaluation or from an evaluation by others. In either case, the credit and the blame associated with an outcome depend, we suggest, on the attributions for success and failure. In the domain of chance, both success and failure are attributed primarily to luck. The situation is different when a person bets on his or her judgment. If the decision maker has limited understanding of the problem at hand, failure will be attributed to ignorance, whereas success is likely to be attributed to chance. In contrast, if the decision maker is an "expert," success is attributable to knowledge, whereas failure can sometimes be attributed to chance.

We do not wish to deny that in situations where experts are supposed to know all the facts, they are probably more embarrassed by failure than are novices. However, in situations that call for an educated guess, experts are sometimes less vulnerable than novices because they can better justify their bets, even if they do not win. In betting on the winner of a football game, for example, people who consider themselves experts can claim credit for a correct prediction and treat an incorrect prediction as an upset. People who do not know much about football, on the other hand, cannot claim much credit for a correct prediction (because they are guessing), and they are exposed to blame for an incorrect prediction (because they are ignorant).

Competence or expertise, therefore, helps people take credit when they succeed and sometimes provides protection against blame when they fail. Ignorance or incompetence, on the other hand, prevents people from taking credit for success and exposes them to blame in case of failure. As a consequence, we propose, the balance of credit to blame is most favorable for bets in one's area of expertise, intermediate for chance events, and least favorable for bets in an area where one has only limited knowledge. This account provides an explanation of the competence hypothesis in terms of the asymmetry of credit and blame induced by knowledge or competence.

The preceding analysis readily applies to Ellsberg's example. People do not like to bet on the unknown box, we suggest, because there is information, namely the proportion of red and green balls in the box, that is knowable in principle but unknown to them. The presence of such data makes people feel less knowledgeable and less competent and reduces the attractiveness of the corresponding bet. A closely related interpretation of Ellsberg's example has been offered by Frisch and Baron (1988). The competence hypothesis is also consistent with the finding of Curley, Yates, and Abrams (1986) that the aversion to ambiguity is enhanced by anticipation that the contents of the unknown box will be shown to others.

Essentially the same analysis applies to the preference for betting on the future rather than on the past. Rothbart and Snyder (1970) asked subjects to roll a die and bet on the outcome either before the die was rolled or after the die was rolled but before the result was revealed. The subjects who predicted the outcome before the die was rolled expressed greater confidence in their guesses than the subjects who predicted the outcome after the die roll ("postdiction"). The former group also bet significantly more money than the latter group. The authors attributed this phenomenon to magical thinking or the illusion of control, namely the belief that one can exercise some control over the outcome before, but not after, the roll of the die.

However, the preference to bet on future rather than past events is observed even when the illusion of control does not provide a plausible explanation, as illustrated by the following problem in which subjects were presented with a choice between the two bets:

1. A stock is selected at random from the *Wall Street Journal*. You guess whether it will go up or down tomorrow. If you're right, you win $5.

2. A stock is selected at random from the *Wall Street Journal*. You guess whether it went up or down yesterday. You cannot check the paper. If you're right, you win $5.

Sixty-seven percent of the subjects ($N = 184$) preferred to bet on tomorrow's closing price. (Ten percent of the participants, selected at random, actually played their chosen bet.) Because the past, unlike the future, is knowable in principle, but not to them, subjects prefer the future bet where their relative ignorance is lower. Similarly, Brun and Teigen (1990) observed that subjects preferred to guess the result of a die roll, the sex of a child, or the outcome of a soccer game before the event rather than afterward. Most of the subjects found guessing before the event more "satisfactory if right" and less "uncomfortable if wrong." In prediction, only the future can prove you wrong; in postdiction, you could be wrong right now. The same argument applies to Ellsberg's problem. In the 50/50 box, a guess could turn out to be wrong only after drawing the ball. In the unknown box, on the other hand, the guess may turn out to be mistaken even before the drawing of the ball—if it turns out that the majority of balls in the box are of the opposite color. It is noteworthy that the preference to bet on future rather than on past events cannot be explained in terms of ambiguity because, in these problems, the future is as ambiguous as the past.

Simple chance events, such as drawing a ball from a box with a known composition involve no ambiguity; the chances of winning are known precisely. If betting preferences between equiprobable events are determined by ambiguity, people should prefer to bet on chance over their own vague judgments (at least for moderate and high probability). In contrast, the attributional analysis described above implies that people will prefer betting on their judgment over a matched chance event when they feel knowledgeable and competent, but not otherwise. This prediction is confirmed by the finding that people prefer betting on their skill rather than on chance. It is also consistent with the observation of March and Shapira (1987) that many top managers, who consistently bet on highly uncertain business propositions, resist the analogy between business decisions and games of chance.

We have argued that the present attributional analysis can account for the available evidence on uncertainty preferences, whether or not they involve ambiguity.

These include 1) the preference for betting on the known rather than on the unknown box in Ellsberg's problem, 2) the preference to bet on future rather than on past events, and 3) the preference for betting on skill rather than on chance. Furthermore, the competence hypothesis implies a *choice–judgment discrepancy*, namely a preference to bet on A rather than on B even though B is judged to be at least as probable as A. In the following series of experiments, we test the competence hypothesis and investigate the choice–judgment discrepancy. In experiment 1 we offer people the choice between betting on their judged probabilities for general knowledge items or on a matched chance lottery. Experiments 2 and 3 extend the test by studying real-world events and eliciting an independent assessment of knowledge. In experiment 4, we sort subjects according to their area of expertise and compare their willingness to bet on their expert category, a nonexpert category, and chance. Finally, in experiment 5, we test the competence hypothesis in a pricing task that does not involve probability judgment. The relations between belief and preference are discussed in the last section of the article.

Experiment 1: Betting on Knowledge
Subjects answered 30 knowledge questions in two different categories, such as history, geography, or sports. Four alternative answers were presented for each question, and the subject first selected a single answer and then rated his or her confidence in that answer on a scale from 25% (pure guessing) to 100% (absolute certainty). Participants were given detailed instructions about the use of the scale and the notion of calibration. Specifically, they were instructed to use the scale so that a confidence rating of 60%, say, would correspond to a hit rate of 60%. They were also told that these ratings would be the basis for a money-making game, and warned that both underconfidence and overconfidence would reduce their earnings.

After answering the questions and assessing confidence, subjects were given an opportunity to choose between betting on their answers or on a lottery in which the probability of winning was equal to their stated confidence. For a confidence rating of 75%, for example, the subject was given the choice between 1) betting that his or her answer was correct, or 2) betting on a 75% lottery, defined by drawing a numbered chip in the range 1–75 from a bag filled with 100 numbered poker chips. For half of the questions, lotteries were directly equated to confidence ratings. For the other half of the questions, subjects chose between the complement of their answer (betting that an answer other than the one they choose is correct) or the complement of their confidence rating. Thus, if a subject chose answer A with confidence of 65%, the subject could choose between betting that one of the remaining answers B, C, or D is correct, or betting on a $100\% - 65\% = 35\%$ lottery.

Two groups of subjects participated in the experiment. One group ($N = 29$) included psychology students who received course credit for participation. The second group ($N = 26$) was recruited from introductory economics classes and performed the experiment for cash earnings. To determine the subjects' payoffs, ten questions were selected at random, and the subjects played out the bets they had chosen. If subjects chose to gamble on their answer, they collected $1.50 if their answer was correct. If subjects chose to bet on the chance lottery, they drew a chip from the bag and collected $1.50 if the number on the chip fell in the proper range. Average earnings for the experiment were around $8.50.

Paid subjects took more time than unpaid subjects in selecting their answers and assessing confidence; they were slightly more accurate. Both groups exhibited overconfidence: the paid subjects answered correctly 47% of the questions and their average confidence was 60%. The unpaid subjects answered correctly 43% of the questions and their average confidence was 53%. We first describe the results of the simple lotteries; the complementary (disjunctive) lotteries are discussed later.

The results are summarized by plotting the percentage of choices (C) that favor the judgment bet over the lottery as a function of judged probability (P). Before discussing the actual data, it is instructive to examine several constrasting predictions, implied by five alternative hypotheses, which are displayed in figure 26.1.

The upper panel of figure 26.1 displays the predictions of three hypotheses in which C is independent of P. According to expected utility theory, decision makers will be indifferent between betting on their judgment or betting on a chance lottery; hence C should equal 50% throughout. Ambiguity aversion implies that people will prefer to bet on a chance event whose probability is well defined rather than on their judged probability, which is inevitably vague; hence C should fall below 50% everywhere. The opposite hypothesis, called chance aversion, predicts that people will prefer to bet on their judgment rather than on a matched chance lottery; hence C should exceed 50% for all P. In contrast to the flat predictions displayed in the upper panel, the two hypothesis in the lower panel imply that C depends on P. The regression hypothesis states that the decision weights, which control choice, will be regressive relative to stated probabilities. Thus, C will be relatively high for small probabilities and relatively low for high probabilities. This prediction also follows from the theory proposed by Einhorn and Hogarth (1985), who put forth a particular process model based on mental simulation, adjustment, and anchoring. The predictions of this model, however, coincide with the regression hypothesis.

Finally, the competence hypothesis implies that people will tend to bet on their judgment when they feel knowledgeable and on the chance lottery when they feel ignorant. Because higher stated probability generally entails higher knowledge, C

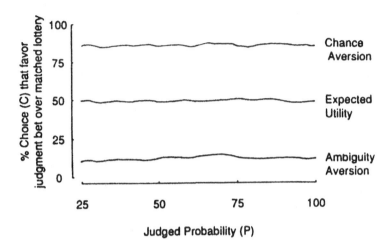

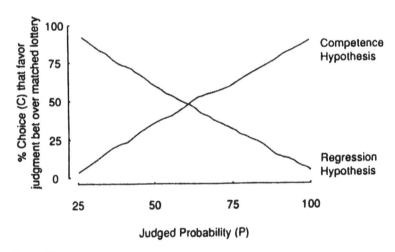

Figure 26.1
Five contrasting predictions of the results of an uncertainty preference experiment.

Table 26.1
Percentage of Paid and Nonpaid Subjects Who Preferred the Judgment Bet over the Lottery for Low, Medium, and High P (the Number of Observations Are Given in Parentheses)

	$25 \leq P \leq 50$	$50 < P < 75$	$75 \leq P \leq 100$
Paid	29	42	55
	(278)	(174)	(168)
Nonpaid	22	43	69
	(394)	(188)	(140)

will be an increasing function of P except at 100% where the chance lottery amounts to a sure thing.

The results of the experiment are summarized in table 26.1 and figure 26.2. Table 26.1 presents, for three different ranges of P, the percentage of paid and nonpaid subjects who bet on their answers rather than on the matched lottery. Recall that each question had four possible answers, so the lowest confidence level is 25%. Figure 26.2 displays the overall percentage of choices C that favored the judgment bet over the lottery as a function 2 of judged probability P. The graph shows that subjects chose the lottery when P was low or moderate (below 65%) and that they chose to bet on their answers when P was high. The pattern of results was the same for the paid and for the nonpaid subjects, but the effect was slightly stronger for the latter group. These results confirm the prediction of the competence hypothesis and reject the four alternative accounts, notably the ambiguity aversion hypothesis implied by second-order probability models (e.g., Gärdenfors and Sahlin, 1982), and the regression hypothesis implied by the model of Einhorn and Hogarth (1985).

To obtain a statistical test of the competence hypothesis, we computed, separately for each subject, the binary correlation coefficient (ϕ) between choice (judgment bet vs. lottery) and judged probability (above median vs. below median). The median judgment was .65. Seventy-two percent of the subjects yielded positive coefficients, and the average ϕ was .30, ($t(54) = 4.3$, $p < .01$). To investigate the robustness of the observed pattern, we replicated the experiment with one major change. Instead of constructing chance lotteries whose probabilities matched the values stated by the subjects, we constructed lotteries in which the probability of winning was either 6% higher or 6% lower than the subjects' judged probability. For high-knowledge questions ($P \geq 75\%$), the majority of responses (70%) favored the judgment bet over the lottery even when the lottery offered a (6%) higher probability of winning. Similarly, for low-confidence questions ($P \geq 50\%$) the majority of responses (52%) favored the lottery over the judgment bet even when the former offered a lower (6%) probability of winning.

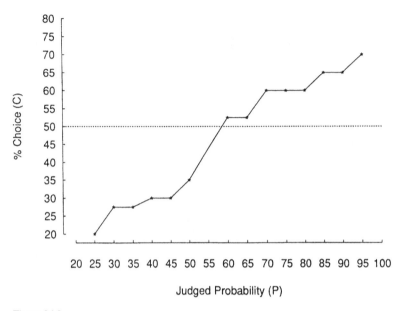

Figure 26.2
Percentage of choice (C) that favor a judgment bet over a matched lottery as a function of judged probability (P) in experiment 1.

Figure 26.3 presents the calibration curve for the data of experiment 1. The figure shows that, on the whole, people are reasonably well calibrated for low probability but exhibit substantial overconfidence for high probability. The preference for the judgment bet over the lottery for high probability, therefore, cannot be justified on an actuarial basis.

The analysis of the complementary bets, where subjects were asked in effect to bet that their chosen answer was incorrect, revealed a very different pattern. Across subjects, the judgment bet was favored 40.5% of the time, indicating a statistically significant preference for the chance lottery $(t(54) = 3.8\ p < .01)$. Furthermore, we found no systematic relation between C and P, in marked contrast to the monotonic relation displayed in figure 26.2. In accord with our attributional account, this result suggests that people prefer to bet on their beliefs rather than against them. These data, however, may also be explained by the hypothesis that people prefer to bet on simple rather than on disjunctive hypotheses.

Experiment 2: Football and Politics
Our next experiment differs from the previous one in three respects. First, it concerns the prediction of real-world future events rather than the assessment of general

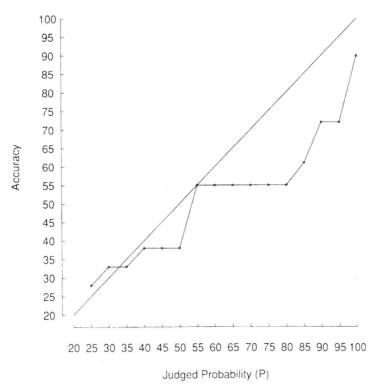

Figure 26.3
Calibration curve for experiment 1.

knowledge. Second, it deals with binary events so that the lowest level of confidence is .5 rather than .25 as in the previous experiment. Third, in addition to judgments of probability, subjects also rated their level of knowledge for each prediction.

A group of 20 students predicted the outcomes of 14 football games each week for five consecutive weeks. For each game, subjects selected the team that they thought would win the game and assessed the probability of their chosen team winning. The subjects also assessed, on a five-point scale, their knowledge about each game. Following the rating, subjects were asked whether they preferred to bet on the team they chose or on a matched chance lottery. The results summarized in figure 26.4 confirm the previous finding. For both high and low knowledge (defined by a median split on the knowledge rating scale), C was an increasing function of P. Moreover, C was greater for high knowledge than for low knowledge at any $P > .5$. Only 5% of the subjects produced negative correlations between C and P, and the average ϕ coefficient was .33, $(t(77) = 8.7, p < .01)$.

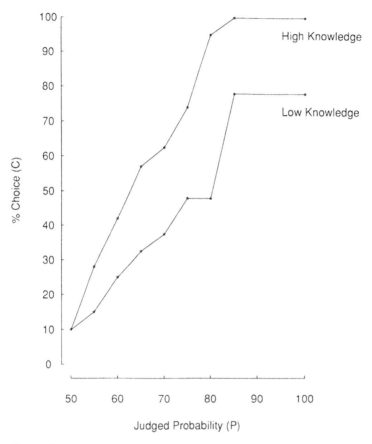

Figure 26.4
Percentage of choices (C) that favor a judgment bet over a matched lottery as a function of judged probability (P), for high- and low-knowledge items in the football prediction task (experiment 2).

We next took the competence hypothesis to the floor of the Republican National Convention in New Orleans during August of 1988. The participants were volunteer workers at the convention. They were given a one-page questionnaire that contained instructions and an answer sheet. Thirteen states were selected to represent a cross section of different geographical areas as well to include the most important states in terms of electoral votes. The participants $(N = 100)$ rates the probability of Bush carrying each of the 13 states in the November 1988 election on a scale from 0 (Bush is certain to lose) to 100 (Bush is certain to win). As in the football experiment, the participants rated their knowledge of each state on a five-point scale and indicated

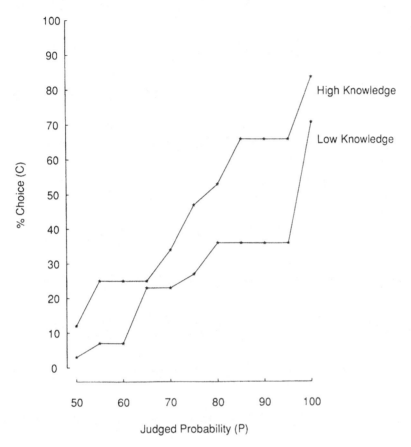

Figure 26.5
Percentage of choices (C) that favor a judgment bet over a matched lottery as a function of judged probability (P), for high- and low-knowledge items in experiment 2 (election data).

whether they would rather bet on their prediction or on a chance lottery. The results, summarized in figure 26.5, show that C increased with P for both levels of knowledge, and that C was greater for high knowledge than for low knowledge at all levels of P. When asked about their home state, 70% of the participants selected the judgment bet over the lottery. Only 5% of the subjects yielded negative correlations between C and P, and the average ϕ coefficient was .42, ($t(99) = 13.4$, $p < .01$).

The results displayed in figures 26.4 and 26.5 support the competence hypothesis in the prediction of real-world events: in both tasks C increases with P, as in experiment 1. In that study, however, probability and knowledge were perfectly correlated; hence the choice–judgment discrepancy could be attributed to a distortion of the probability scale in the judgement task. This explanation does not apply to the results of the present experiment, which exhibits an independent effect of rated knowledge. As seen in figures 26.4 and 26.5, the preference for the judgment bet over the chance lottery is greater for high-knowledge items than for low-knowledge items for all levels of judged probability. It is noteworthy that the strategy of betting on judgment was less successful than the strategy of betting on chance in both data sets. The former strategy yielded hit rates of 64% and 78% for football and election, respectively, whereas the latter strategy yielded hit rates of 73% and 80%. The observed tendency to select the judgment bet, therefore, does not yield better performance.

Experiment 3: Long Shots

The preceding experiments show that people often prefer to bet on their judgment than on a matched chance event, even though the former is more ambiguouis than the latter. This effect, summarized in figures 26.2, 26.4 and 26.5, was observed at the high end of the probability scale. These data could perhaps be explained by the simple hypothesis that people prefer the judgment bet when the probability of winning exceeds .5 and the chance lottery when the probability of winning is below .5. To test this hypothesis, we sought high-knowledge items in which the probability of winning is low, so the subject's best guess is unlikely to be true. In this case, the above hypothesis implies a preference for the chance lottery, whereas the competence hypothesis implies a preference for the judgment bet. These predictions are tested in the following experiment.

One hundred and eight students were presented with open-ended questions about 12 future events (e.g., what movie will win this year's Oscar for best picture? What football team will win the next Super Bowl? In what class next quarter will you have the highest grade?). They were asked to answer each question, to estimate the chances that their guess will turn out to be correct, and to indicate whether they have high or low knowledge of the relevant domain. The use of open-ended questions eliminates the lower bound of 50% imposed by the use of dichotomous predictions in the previous experiment. After the subjects completed these tasks, they were asked to consider, separately for each question, whether they would rather bet on their prediction or on a matched chance lottery.

On average, the subjects answered 10 out of 12 questions. Table 26.2 presents the percentage (C) of responses that favor the judgment bet over the chance lottery for high- and low-knowledge items, and for judged probabilities below or above .5. The number of responses in each cell is given in parentheses. The results show that, for high-knowledge items, the judgment bet was preferred over the chance lottery

Table 26.2
Percentage of Choices (C) That Favor a Judgment Bet over a Matched Lottery for High- and Low-rated
Knowledge and for Judged Probability below and above .5 (the Number of Responses Are Given in
Parentheses)

Rated knowledge	Judged probability	
	$P < .5$	$P \geq .5$
Low	36	58
	(593)	(128)
High	61	69
	(151)	(276)

regardless of whether P was above or below one half ($p < .01$ in both cases), as implied by the competence hypothesis. Indeed, the discrepancy between the low- and high-knowledge conditions was greater for $P < .5$ than for $P \geq .5$. Evidently, people prefer to bet on their high-knowledge predictions even when the predictions are unlikely to be correct.

Experiment 4: Expert Prediction

In the preceding experiments, we used the subjects' ratings of specific items to define high and know knowledge. In this experiment, we manipulate knowledge or competence by sorting subjects according to their expertise. To this end, we asked 110 students in an introductory psychology class to assess their knowledge of politics and of football on a nine-point scale. All subjects who rated their knowledge of the two areas on opposite sides of the midpoint were asked to take part in the experiment. Twenty-five subjects met this criterion, and all but two agreed to particpate. They included 12 political "experts" and 11 football "experts" defined by their strong area. To induce the subjects to give careful responses, we gave them detailed instructions including a discussion of calibration, and we employed the Brier scoring rule (see, e.g., Lichtenstein et al., 1982) designed to motivate subjects to give their best estimates. Subjects earned about $10, on average.

The experiment consisted of two sessions. In the first session, each subject made predictions for a set of 40 future events (20 political events and 20 football games). All the events were resolved within five weeks of the date of the initial session. The political events concerned the winner of the various states in the 1988 presidential election. The 20 football games included 10 professional and 10 college games. For each contest (politics or football), subjects chose a winner by circling the name of one of the contestants, and then assessed the probability that their prediction would come true (on a scale from 50% to 100%).

Table 26.3
Ranking Data for Expert Study

Type of bet	Rank			Mean rank
	1st	2nd	3rd	
High-knowledge	192	85	68	1.64
Chance	74	155	116	2.12
Low-knowledge	79	105	161	2.23

Using the results of the first session, 20 triples of bets were constructed for each participant. Each triple included three matched bets with the same probability of winning generated by 1) a chance device, 2) the subject's prediction in his or her strong category, 3) the subject's prediction in his or her weak category. Obviously, some events appeared in more than one triple. In the second session, subjects ranked each of the 20 triples of bets. The chance bets were defined as in experiment 1 with reference to a box containing 100 numbered chips. Subjects were told that they would actually play their choices in each of the triples. To encourage careful ranking, subjects were told that they would play 80% of their first choices and 20% of their second choices.

The data are summarized in table 26.3 and in figure 26.6, which plots the attractiveness of the three types of bets (mean rank order) against judged probability. The results show a clear preference for betting on the strong category. Across all triples, the mean ranks were 1.64 for the strong category, 2.12 for the chance lottery, and 2.23 for the weak category. The difference among the ranks is highly significant ($p < .001$) by the Wilcoxen rank sum test. In accord with the competence hypothesis, people prefer to bet on their judgment in their area of competence, but prefer to bet on chance in an area in which they are not well informed. As expected, the lottery became more popular than the high-knowledge bet only at 100%. This pattern of result is inconsistent with an account based on ambiguity or second-order probabilities because both the high-knowledge and the low-knowledge bets are based on vague judgmental probabilities whereas the chance lotteries have clear probabilities. Ambiguity aversion could explain why low-knowledge bets are less attractive than either the high-knowledge bet or the chance bet, but it cannot explain the major finding of this experiment that the vague high-knowledge bets are preferred to the clear chance bets.

A noteworthy feature of figure 26.6, which distinguishes it from the previous graphs, is that preferences are essentially independent of P. Evidently, the competence effect is fully captured in this case by the contrast between the categories; hence

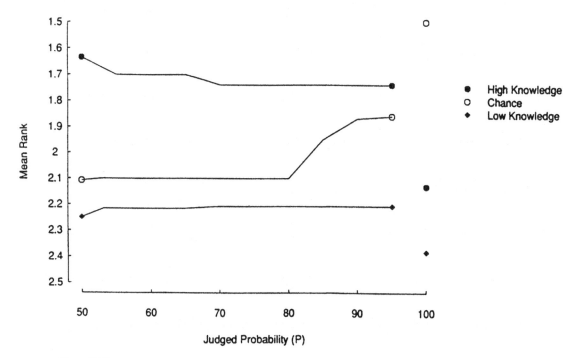

Figure 26.6
Ranking data for high-knowledge, low-knowledge, and chance bets as a function of P in experiment 4.

the added knowledge implied by the judged probability has little or no effect on the choice among the bets.

Figure 26.7 presents the average calibration curves for experiment 4, separately for the high- and low-knowledge categories. These graphs show that judgments were generally overconfident: subjects' confidence exceeded their hit rate. Furthermore, the overconfidence was more pronounced in the high-knowledge category than in the low-knowledge category. As a consequence, the ordering of bets did not mirror judgmental accuracy. Summing across all triples, betting on the chance lottery would win 69% of the time, betting on the novice category would win 64% of the time, and betting on the expert category would win only 60% of the time. By betting on the expert category therefore the subjects are losing, in effect, 15% of their expected earnings.

The preference for knowledge over chance is observed not only for judgments of probability for categorical events (win, loss), but also for probability distributions over numerical variables. Subjects ($N = 93$) were given an opportunity to set 80%

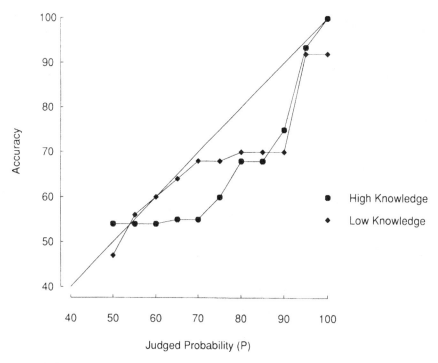

Figure 26.7
Calibration curves for high- and low-knowledge categories in experiment 4.

confidence intervals for a variety of quantities (e.g., average SAT score for entering freshmen at Stanford; driving distance from San Francisco to Los Angeles). After setting confidence intervals, subjects were given the opportunity to choose between 1) betting that their confidence interval contained the true value, or 2) an 80% lottery. Subjects preferred betting on the confidence interval in the majority of cases, although this strategy paid off only 69% of the time because the confidence intervals they set were generally too narrow. Again, subjects paid a premium of nearly 15% to bet on their judgment.

Experiment 5: Complementary Bets

The preceding experiments rely on judgments of probability to match the chance lottery and the judgment bet. To control for possible biases in the judgment process, out last test of the competence hypothesis is based on a pricing task that does not involve probability judgment. This experiment also provides an estimate of the premium that subjects are paying in order to bet on high-knowledge items.

Sixty-eight students were instructed to state their cash equivalent (reservation price) for each of 12 bets. They were told that one pair of bets would be chosen and a few students, selected at random, would play the bet for which they stated the higher cash equivalent. (For a discussion of this payoff scheme, see Tversky, Slovic, and Kahneman, 1990.) All bets in this experiment offered a prize of $15 if a given proposition were true, and nothing otherwise. Complementary propositions were presented to different subjects. For example, half the subjects were asked to price a bet that paid $15 if the air distance between New York and San Francisco is more 2500 miles, and nothing otherwise. The half of the subjects were asked to price the complementary bet that paid $15 if the air distance between New York and San Francisco is less than 2500 miles, and nothing otherwise.

To investigate uncertainty preferences, we paired high-knowledge and low-knowledge propositions. For example, we assumed that the subjects know more about the air distance between New York and San Francisco than about the air distance between Beijing and Bangkok. We also assumed that our respondents (Stanford students) know more about the percentage of undergraduate students who receive on-campus housing at Stanford than at the University of Nevada, Las Vegas. As before, we refer to these propositions as high-knowledge and low-knowledge items, respectively. Note that the selection of the stated value of the uncertain quantity (e.g., air distance, percentage of students) controls a subject's confidence in the validity of the proposition in question, independent of his or her general knowledge about the subject matter. Twelve pairs of complementary propositions were constructed, and each subject evaluated one of the four bets defined by each pair. In the air-distance problem, for example, the four propositions were $d(SF, NY) > 2500$, $d(SF, NY) < 2500$, $d(Be, Ba) > 3000$, $d(Be, Ba) < 3000$, where $d(SF, NY)$ and $d(Be, Ba)$ denote, respectively, the distances between San Francisco and New York and between Beijing and Bangkok.

Note that according to expected value, the average cash equivalent for each pair of complementary bets should be $7.50. Summing across all 12 pairs of complementary bets, subjects paid on average $7.12 for the high-knowledge bets and only $5.96 for the low-knowledge bets ($p < .01$). Thus, people were paying, in effect, a competence premium of nearly 20% in order to bet on the more familiar propositions. Furthermore, the average price for the (complementary) high-knowledge bets was greater than that for the low-knowledge bets in 11 out of 12 problems. For comparison, the average cash equivalent for a coin toss to win $15 was $7. In accord with out previous findings, the chance lottery is valued above the low-knowledge bets but not above the high-knowledge bets.

We next test the competence hypothesis against expected utility theory. Let H and $\overline{H}$ denote two complimentary high-knowledge propositions, and let L and $\overline{L}$ denote the corresponding low-knowledge propositions. Suppose a decision maker prefers betting on H over L and on $\bar{H}$ over $\bar{L}$. This pattern is inconsistent with expected utility theory because it implies that $P(H) > P(L)$ and $P(\bar{H}) > P(\bar{L})$, contrary to the additivity assumption $P(H) + P(\bar{H}) = P(L) + P(\bar{L}) = 1$. If, on the other hand, high-knowledge bets are preferred to low-knowledge bets, such a pattern is likely to arise. Because the four propositions $(H, \bar{H}, L, \bar{L})$ were evaluated by four different groups of subjects, we employ a between-subject test of additivity. Let $M(H_i)$ be the median price for the high-knowledge proposition H_i, etc. The responses in problem i violate additivity, in the direction implied by the competence hypothesis, whenever $M(H_i) > M(L_i)$ and $M(\bar{H}_i) \geq M(\bar{L}_i)$.

Five of the 12 pairs of problems exhibited this pattern indicating a preference for the high-knowledge bets, and none of the pairs exhibited the opposite pattern. For example, the median price for betting on the proposition "more than 85% of under-graduates at Stanford receive on-campus housing" was $7.50, and the median cash equivalent for betting on the complementary proposition was $10. In contrast, the median cash equivalent for betting on the proposition "more than 70% of under-graduates at UNLV receive on-campus housing" was $3, and the median value for the complementary bet was $7. The majority of respondents, therefore, were willing to pay more to bet on either side of a high-knowledge item than on either side of a low-knowledge item.

The preceding analysis, based on medians, can be extended as follows. For each pair of propositions (H_i, L_i), we computed the proportion of comparisons in which the cash equivalent of H_i exceeded the cash equivalent of L_i, denoted $P(H_i > L_i)$. We also computed $P(\bar{H}_i > \bar{L}_i)$ for the complementary propositions. All ties were excluded. Under expected utility theory,

$$P(H_i > L_i) + P(\bar{H}_i > \bar{L}_i) = P(L_i > H_i) + P(\bar{L}_i > \bar{H}_i) = 1,$$

because the additivity of probability implies that for every comparison that favors H_i over L_i, there should be another comparison that favors $\bar{L}_i$ over $\bar{H}_i$. On the other hand, if people prefer the high-knowledge bets, as implied by the competence hypothesis, we expect

$$P(H_i > L_i) + P(\bar{H}_i > \bar{L}_i) > P(L_i > H_i) + P(\bar{L}_i > \bar{H}_i).$$

Among the 12 pairs of complementary propositions, the above inequality was sat-isfied in 10 cases, the opposite inequality was satisfied in one case, and equality was observed in one case, indicating a significant violation of additivity in the direction implied by the competence hypothesis ($p < .01$ by sign test). These findings confirm the competence hypothesis in a test that does not rely on judgments of probability or on a comparison of a judgment bet to a matched lottery. Hence, the present results cannot be attributed to a bias in the judgment process or in the matching of high- and low-knowledge items.

Discussion

The experiments reported in this article establish a consistent and pervasive discrepancy between judgments of probability and choice between bets. Experiment 1 demonstrates that the preference for the knowledge bet over the chance lottery increases with judged confidence. Experiments 2 and 3 replicate this finding for future real-world events, and demonstrate a knowledge effect independent of judged probability. In experiment 4, we sort subjects into their strong and weak areas and show that people like betting on their strong category and dislike betting on their weak category; the chance bet is intermediate between the two. This pattern cannot be explained by ambiguity or by second-order probability because chance is unambiguous, whereas judgmental probability is vague. Finally, experiment 5 confirms the prediction of the competence hypothesis in a pricing task that does not rely on probability matchings, and shows that people are paying a premium of nearly 20% for betting on high-knowledge items.

These observations are consistent with our attributional account, which holds that knowledge induces an asymmetry in the internal balance of credit and blame. Competence, we suggest, allows people to claim credit when they are right, and its absence exposes people to blame when they are wrong. As a consequence, people prefer the high-knowledge bet over the matched lottery, and they prefer the matched lottery over the low-knowledge bet. This account explains other instances of uncertainty preferences reported in the literature, notably the preference for clear over vague probabilities in a chance setup (Ellsberg, 1961), the preference to bet on the future over the past (Rothbart and Snyder, 1970; Brun and Teigen, 1989), the preference for skill over chance (Cohen and Hansel,1959; Howell, 1971), and the enhancement of ambiguity aversion in the presence of knowledgeable others (Curley, Yates and Abrams, 1986). The robust finding that, in their area of competence, people prefer to bet on their (vague) beliefs over a matched chance event indicates that the impact of knowledge or competence outweighs the effect of vagueness.

In experiments 1–4 we used probability judgments to establish belief and choice data to establish preference. Furthermore, we have interpreted the choice–judgment discrepancy as a preference effect. In contrast, it could be argued that the choice–

judgment discrepancy is attributable to a judgmental bias, namely underestimation of the probabilities of high-knowledge items and an overestimation of the probabilities of low-knowledge items. This interpretation, however, is not supported by the available evidence. First, it implies less overconfidence for high-knowledge than for low-knowledge items contrary to fact (see figure 26.7). Second, judgments of probability cannot be dismissed as inconsequential because in the presence of a scoring rule, such as the one used in experiment 4, these judgments represent another form of betting. Finally, a judgmental bias cannot explain the results of experiment 5, which demonstrates preferences for betting on high-knowledge items in a pricing task that does not involve probability judgment.

The distinction between preference and belief lies at the heart of Bayesian decision theory. The standard interpretation of this theory assumes that 1) the expressed beliefs (i.e., probability judgments) of an individual are consistent with an additive probability measure, 2) the preferences of an individual are consistent with the expectation principle, and hence give rise to a (subjective) probability measure derived from choice, and 3) the two measures of subjective probability—obtained from judgment and from choice—are consistent. Note that points 1 and 2 are logically independent. Allais' counterexample, for instance, violates 2 but not 1. Indeed, many authors have introduced nonadditive decision weights, derived from preferences, to accommodate the observed violations of the expectation principle (see, e.g., Kahneman and Tversky, 1979). These decision weights, however, need not reflect the decision maker's beliefs. A person may believe that the probability of drawing the ace of spades from a well-shuffled deck is 1/52, yet in betting on this event he or she may give it a higher weight. Similarly, Ellsberg's example does not prove that people regard the clear event as more probable than the corresponding vague event; it only shows that people prefer to bet on the clear event. Unfortunately, the term *subjective probability* has been used in the literature to describe decision weights derived from preference as well as direct expressions of belief. Under the standard interpretation of the Bayesian theory, the two concepts coincide. As we go beyond this theory, however, it is essential to distinguish between the two.

Manipulations of Ambiguity

The distinction between belief and preference is particularly important for the interpretation of ambiguity effects. Several authors have concluded that, when the probability of winning is small or when the probability of losing is high, people prefer ambiguity to clarity (Curley and Yates, 1989; Einhorn and Hogarth, 1985; Hogarth and Kunreuther, 1989). However, this interpretation can be challenged because, as will be shown below, the data may reflect differences in belief rather than uncertainty preferences. In this section, we investigate the experimental procedures used to manipulate ambiguity and argue that they tend to confound ambiguity with perceived probability.

Perhaps the simplest procedure for manipulating ambiguity is to vary the decision maker's confidence in a given probability estimate. Hogarth and his collaborators have used two versions of this procedure. Einhorn and Hogarth (1985) presented the subject with a probability estimate, based on the "judgement of independent observers," and varied the degree of confidence attached to that estimate. Hogarth and Kunreuther (1989) "endowed" the subject with his or her "best estimate of the probability" of a given event, and manipulated ambiguity by varying the degree of confidence associated with this estimate. If we wish to interpret people's willingness to bet on these sorts of events as ambiguity seeking or ambiguity aversion, however, we must first verify that the manipulation of ambiguity did not affect the perceived probability of the events.

To investigate this question, we first replicated the manipulation of ambiguity used by Hogarth and Kunreuther (1989). One group of subjects ($N = 62$), called the high confidence group, received the following information:

Imagine that you head a department in a large insurance company. The owner of a small business comes to you seeking insurance against a $100,000 loss which could result from claims concerning a defective product. You have considered the manufacturing process, the reliabilities of the machines used, and evidence contained in the business records. After considering the evidence available to you, your best estimate of the probability of a defective product is .01. Given the circumstances, you feel confident about the precision of this estimate. Naturally you will update your estimate as you think more about the situation or receive additional information.

A second group of subjects ($N = 64$), called the low-confidence group, received the same information, except that the phrase "you feel confident about the precision of this estimate" was replaced by "you experience considerable uncertainty about the precision of this estimate." All subjects were then asked:

Do you expect that the new estimate will be (Check one):

Above .01   _____

Below .01   _____

Exactly .01   _____

The two groups were also asked to evaluate a second case in which the stated probability of a loss was .90. If the stated value (.01 or .90) is interpreted as the mean of the respective second-order probability distribution, then a subject's expectation for the updated estimate should coincide with the current "best estimate." Furthermore, if the manipulation of confidence affects ambiguity but not perceived probability,

Table 26.4
Subjective Assessments of Stated Probabilities of .01 and .90 under High-confidence and Low-confidence Instructions (the Entries are the Percentage of Subjects Who Chose Each of the Three Responses)

Stated value	Response	Your probability		Others' estimate	
		High confidence	Low confidence	High confidence	Low confidence
.01	Above .01	45	75	46	80
	Exactly .01	34	11	15	6
	Below .01	21	14	39	14
.90	Above .90	29	28	42	26
	Exactly .90	42	14	23	12
	Below .90	29	58	35	62

there should be no difference between the responses of the high-confidence and the low-confidence groups. The data presented in table 26.4, under the heading *Your probability*, clearly violate these assumptions. The distributions of responses in the low-confidence condition are considerably more skewed than the distributions in the high-confidence condition. Furthermore, the skewness is positive for .01 and negative for .90. Telling subjects that they "experience considerable uncertainty" about their best estimate produces a regressive shift: the expected probability of loss is above .01 in the first problem and below .90 in the second. The interaction between confidence (high–low) and direction (above–below) is statistically significant ($p < .01$).

We also replicated the procedure employed by Einhorn and Hogarth (1985) in which subjects were told that "independent observers have stated that the probability of a defective product is .01." Subjects ($N = 52$) in the high-confidence group were told that "you could feel confident about the estimate," whereas subjects ($N = 52$) in the low-confidence group were told that "you could experience considerable uncertainty about the estimate." Both groups were then asked whether their best guess of the probability of experiencing a loss is above .01, below .01, or exactly .01. The two groups also evaluated a second case in which the probability of loss was .90. The results presented in table 26.4, under the heading *Others' estimate*, reveal the pattern observed above. In the high-confidence condition, the distributions of responses are fairly symmetric, but in the low-confidence condition the distributions exhibit positive skewness at .01 and negative skewness at .90. Again, the interaction between confidence (high–low) and direction (above–below) is the statistically significant ($p < .01$).

These results indicate that the manipulations of confidence influenced not only the ambiguity of the event in question but also its perceived probability: they increased the perceived probability of the highly unlikely event and decreased the perceived probability of the likely event. A regressive shift of this type is not at all unreasonable and can even be rationalized by a suitable prior distribution. As a consequence of the shift in probability, the bet on the vaguer estimate should be more attractive when the probability of loss is high (.90) and less attractive when the probability of loss is low (.01). This is exactly the pattern of preferences observed by Einhorn and Hogarth (1985) and by Hogarth and Kunreuther (1989), but it does not entail either ambiguity seeking or ambiguity aversion because the events differ in perceived probability, not only in ambiguity.

The results of table 26.4 and the findings of Hogarth and his collaborators can be explained by the hypothesis that subjects interpret the stated probability value as the median (or the mode) of a second-order probability distribution. If the second-order distributions associated with extreme probabilities are skewed towards .5, the mean is less extreme than the median, and the difference between them is greater when ambiguity is high than when it is low. Consequently, the mean of the second-order probability distribution, which controls choice in the Bayesian model, will be more regressive (i.e., closer to .5) under low confidence than under high confidence.

The potential confounding of ambiguity and degree of belief arises even when ambiguity is manipulated by information regarding a chance process. Unlike Ellsberg's comparison of the 50/50 box with the unknown box, where symmetry precludes a bias in one direction or another, similar manipulations of ambiguity in asymmetric problems could produce a regressive shift, as demonstrated in an unpublished study by Parayre and Kahneman.[3]

These investigators compared a clear event, defined by the proportion of red balls in a box, with a vague event defined by the range of balls of the designated color. For a vague event [.8, 1], subjects were informed that the proportion of red balls could be anywhere between .8 and 1, compared with .9 for the clear event. Table 26.5 presents both choice and judgment data for three probability levels: low, medium, and high. In accord with previous work, the choice data show that subjects preferred to bet on the vague event when the probability of winning was low and when the probability of losing was high, and they preferred to bet on the clear event in all other cases. The novel feature of the Parayre and Kahneman experiment is the use of a perceptual rating scale based on a judgment of length, which provides a nonnumerical assessment of probability. Using this scale, the investigators showed that the judged probabilities were regressive. That is, the vague low-probability event [0, .10] was judged as more probable than the clear event, .05, and the vague high-probability event [.8, 1] was judged as less probable than the clear event, .9. For the medium probability, there was no significant difference in judgment between the vague event [0, 1]

Table 26.5
(Based on Parayre and Kahneman). Percentage of Subjects Who Favored the Clear Event and the Vague Event in Judgment and in Choice

	Probability (win/lose)	Judgment N = 72	Choice Win $100 N = 58	Lose $100 N = 58
Low	.05	28	12	66
	[0, .10]	47	74	22
Medium	.5	38	60	60
	[0, 1]	22	26	21
High	.9	50	50	22
	[.8, 1]	21	34	47

Note: The sum of the two values in each condition is less than 100%; the remaining responses expressed equivalence. In the choice task, the low probabilities were .075 and [0, .15]. N denotes sample size.

and the clear event, .5. These results, like the data of table 26.4, demonstrate that the preference for betting on the ambiguous event (observed at the low end for positive bets and at the high end for negative bets) could reflect a regressive shift in the perception of probability rather then a preference for ambiguity.

Concluding Remarks

The findings regarding the effect of competence and the relation between preferences and beliefs challenge the standard interpretation of choice models that assumes independence of preference and belief. The results are also at variance with post-Bayesian models that invoke second-order beliefs to explain the effects of ambiguity or partial knowledge. Moreover, our results call into question the basic idea of defining beliefs in terms of preferences. If willingness to bet on an uncertain event depends on more than the perceived likelihood of that event and the confidence in that estimate, it is exceedingly difficult—if not impossible—to derive underlying beliefs from preferences between bets.

Besides challenging existing models, the competence hypothesis might help explain some puzzling aspects of decisions under uncertainty. It could shed light on the observation that many decision makers do not regard a calculated risk in their area of competence as a gamble (see, e.g., March and Shapira, 1987). It might also help explain why investors are sometimes willing to forego the advantage of diversification and concentrate on a small number of companies (Blume, Crockett, and Friend, 1974) with which they are presumably familiar. The implications of the competence hypothesis to decision making at large are left to be explored.

Notes

This work was supported by Grant 89-0064 from The Air Force Office of Scientific Research to Stanford University. Funding for experiment 1 was provided by SES 8420240 to Ray Battalio. We have benefited from discussions with Max Bazerman, Daniel Ellsberg, Richard Gonzales, Robin Hogarth, Linda Ginzel, Daniel Kahneman, and Eldar Shafir.

1. We use the tern *competence* in a broad sense that includes skill, as well as knowledge or understanding.

2. In this and all subsequent figures, we plot the isotone regression of C on P—that is, the best-fitting monotone function in the least squares sense (see Barlow, Bartholomew, Bremner and Brunk, 1972).

3. We are grateful to Parayre and Kahneman for providing us with these data.

References

Anscombe, F. J., and R. J. Aumann. (1963). "A Definition of Subjective Probability," *Annals of Mathematical Statistics*, 34, 199–205.

Barlow, Richard E., et al. (1972). *Statistical Inference Under Order Restrictions: The Theory and Application of Isotonic Regression.* New York: J. Wiley.

Blume, Marshall E., Jean Crockett, and Irwin Friend. (1974). "Stock Ownership in the United States: Characteristics and Trends," *Survey of Current Business.*

Brun, Wibecke, and Karl Teigen. (1990). "Prediction and Postdiction Preferences in Guessing," *Journal of Behavioral Decision Making* 3, 17–28.

Budescu, David, Shalva Weinberg, and Thomas Wallsten. (1988). "Decisions Based on Numerically and Verbally Expressed Uncertainties," *Journal of Experimental Psychology: Human Perception and Performance* 14 (2), 281–294.

Cohen, John, and Mark Hansel. (1959). "Preferences for Different Combinations of Chance and Skill in Gambling," *Nature* 183, 841–843.

Curley, Shawn, and J. Frank Yates. (1989). "An Empirical Evaluation of Descriptive Models of Ambiguity Reactions in Choice Situations," *Journal of Mathematical Psychology* 33, 397–427.

Curley, Shawn, J. Frank Yates, and Richard Abrams. (1986). "Psychological Sources of Ambiguity Avoidance," *Organizational Behavior and Human Decision Processes* 38, 230–256.

Einhorn, Hillel, and Robin Hogarth. (1985). "Ambiguity and Uncertainty in Probabilistic Inference," *Psychological Review* 93, 433–461.

Ellsberg, Daniel. (1961). "Risk, Ambiguity, and the Savage Axioms," *Quarterly Journal of Economics* 75, 643–669.

Ellsberg, Daniel. (1963). "Risk, Ambiguity, and the Savage Axioms: Reply," *Quarterly Journal of Economics* 77, 336, 342.

Fellner, William. (1961). "Distortion of Subjective Probabilities as a Reaction to Uncertainty," *Quarterly Journal of Economics* 75, 670–689.

Fishburn, Peter. (1988). *Nonlinear Preference and Utility Theory.* Baltimore, MD: The Johns Hopkins University Press.

Frisch, Deborah, and Jonathan Baron. (1988). "Ambiguity and Rationality," *Journal of Behavioral Decision Making* 1, 149–157.

Gärdenfors, Peter, and Nils-Eric Sahlin. (1982). "Unreliable Probabilities, Risk Taking, and Decision Making," *Synthese* 53 (3), 361–386.

Hogarth, Robin, and Howard Kunreuther. (1988). *Pricing Insurance and Warranties: Ambiguity and Correlated Risks.* Unpublished manuscript, University of Chicago and University of Pennsylvania.

Hogarth, Robin, and Howard Kunreuther. (1989). "Risk, Ambiguity, and Insurance," *Journal of Risk and Uncertainty* 2, 5–35.

Howell, William. (1971). "Uncertainty from Internal and External Sources: A Clear Case of Overconfidence," *Journal of Experimental Psychology* 89 (2), 240–243.

Kahneman, Daniel, and Amos Tversky. (1979). "Prospect Theory: An Analysis of Decision under Risk," *Econometrica* 47, 263–291.

Lichtenstein, Sarah, Baruch Fischhoff, and Lawrence Phillips. (1982). "Calibration of Probabilities: The State of the Art to 1980." In D. Kahneman, P. Slovic and A. Tversky (eds.), *Judgment under Uncertainty: Heuristics and Biases*. New York: Cambridge University Press.

March, James, and Zur Shapira. (1987). "Managerial Perspectives on Risk and Risk Taking," *Management Science* 33 (11), 1404–1418.

Raiffa, Howard. (1961). "Risk, Ambiguity, and the Savage Axioms: Comment," *Quarterly Journal of Economics* 75, 690–694.

Ramsey, Frank. (1931). "Truth and Probability." In F. P. Ramsey, *The Foundations of Mathematics and Other Logical Essays*. New York: Harcourt, Brace and Co.

Rothbart, Myron, and Mark Snyder. (1970). "Confidence in the Prediction and Postdiction of an Uncertain Outcome," *Canadian Journal of Behavioral Science* 2 (1), 38–43.

Savage, Leonard. (1954). *The Foundations of Statistics*. New York: Wiley.

Schmeidler, David. (1989). "Subjective Probability and Expected Utility Without Additivity," *Econometrica* 57 (3), 571–587.

Skyrm, Brian. (1980). "Higher Order Degrees of Belief." In D. H. Mellor (ed.), *Prospects for Pragmatism. Essays in Memory of F. P. Ramsey*. Cambridge: Cambridge University Press, pp. 109–137.

Tversky, Amos, Paul Slovic, and Daniel Kahnemann. (1990). "The Causes of Preference Reversal," *American Economic Review* 80, 204–217.

27 Advances in Prospect Theory: Cumulative Representation of Uncertainty

Amos Tversky and Daniel Kahneman

Expected utility theory reigned for several decades as the dominant normative and descriptive model of decision making under uncertainty, but it has come under serious question in recent years. There is now general agreement that the theory does not provide an adequate description of individual choice: a substantial body of evidence shows that decision makers systematically violate its basic tenets. Many alternative models have been proposed in response to this empirical challenge (for reviews, see Camerer, 1989; Fishburn, 1988; Machina, 1987). Some time ago we presented a model of choice, called prospect theory, which explained the major violations of expected utility theory in choices between risky prospects with a small number of outcomes (Kahneman and Tversky, 1979; Tversky and Kahneman, 1986). The key elements of this theory are 1) a value function that is concave for gains, convex for losses, and steeper for losses than for gains, and 2) a nonlinear transformation of the probability scale, which overweights small probabilities and underweights moderate and high probabilities. In an important later development, several authors (Quiggin, 1982; Schmeidler, 1989; Yaari, 1987; Weymark, 1981) have advanced a new representation, called the rank-dependent or the cumulative functional, that transforms cumulative rather than individual probabilities. This chapter presents a new version of prospect theory that incorporates the cumulative functional and extends the theory to uncertain as well to risky prospects with any number of outcomes. The resulting model, called cumulative prospect theory, combines some of the attractive features of both developments (see also Luce and Fishburn, 1991). It gives rise to different evaluations of gains and losses, which are not distinguished in the standard cumulative model, and it provides a unified treatment of both risk and uncertainty.

To set the stage for the present development, we first list five major phenomena of choice, which violate the standard model and set a minimal challenge that must be met by any adequate descriptive theory of choice. All these findings have been confirmed in a number of experiments, with both real and hypothetical payoffs.

Framing effects The rational theory of choice assumes description invariance: equivalent formulations of a choice problem should give rise to the same preference order (Arrow, 1982). Contrary to this assumption, there is much evidence that variations in the framing of options (e.g., in terms of gains or losses) yield systematically different preferences (Tversky and Kahneman, 1986).

Nonlinear preferences According to the expectation principle, the utility of a risky prospect is linear in outcome probabilities. Allais's (1953) famous example challenged this principle by showing that the difference between probabilities of .99 and

1.00 has more impact on preferences than the difference between 0.10 and 0.11. More recent studies observed nonlinear preferences in choices that do not involve sure things (Camerer and Ho, 1991).

Source dependence   People's willingness to bet on an uncertain event depends not only on the degree of uncertainty but also on its source. Ellsberg (1961) observed that people prefer to bet on an urn containing equal numbers of red and green balls, rather than on an urn that contains red and green balls in unknown proportions. More recent evidence indicates that people often prefer a bet on an event in their area of competence over a bet on a matched chance event, although the former probability is vague and the latter is clear (Heath and Tversky, 1991).

Risk seeking   Risk aversion is generally assumed in economic analyses of decision under uncertainty. However, risk-seeking choices are consistently observed in two classes of decision problems. First, people often prefer a small probability of winning a large prize over the expected value of that prospect. Second, risk seeking is prevalent when people must choose between a sure loss and a substantial probability of a larger loss.

Loss aversion   One of the basic phenomena of choice under both risk and uncertainty is that losses loom larger than gains (Kahneman and Tversky, 1984; Tversky and Kahneman, 1991). The observed asymmetry between gains and losses is far too extreme to be explained by income effects or by decreasing risk aversion.

The present development explains loss aversion, risk seeking, and nonlinear preferences in terms of the value and the weighting functions. It incorporates a framing process, and it can accommodate source preferences. Additional phenomena that lie beyond the scope of the theory—and of its alternatives—are discussed later.

The present chapter is organized as follows. Section 1.1 introduces the (two-part) cumulative functional; section 1.2 discusses relations to previous work; and section 1.3 describes the qualitative properties of the value and the weighting functions. These properties are tested in an extensive study of individual choice, described in section 2, which also addresses the question of monetary incentives. Implications and limitations of the theory are discussed in section 3. An axiomatic analysis of cumulative prospect theory is presented in the appendix.

1   Theory

Prospect theory distinguishes two phases in the choice process: framing and valuation. In the framing phase, the decision maker constructs a representation of the acts, contingencies, and outcomes that are relevant to the decision. In the valuation phase, the decision maker assesses the value of each prospect and chooses accordingly. Although no formal theory of framing is available, we have learned a fair amount about the rules that govern the representation of acts, outcomes, and contingencies (Tversky and Kahneman, 1986). The valuation process discussed in subsequent sections is applied to framed prospects.

1.1 Cumulative Prospect Theory

In the classical theory, the utility of an uncertain prospect is the sum of the utilities of the outcomes, each weighted by its probability. The empirical evidence reviewed above suggests two major modifications of this theory: 1) the carriers of value are gains and losses, not final assets; and 2) the value of each outcome is multiplied by a decision weight, not by an additive probability. The weighting scheme used in the original version of prospect theory and in other models is a monotonic transformation of outcome probabilities. This scheme encounters two problems. First, it does not always satisfy stochastic dominance, an assumption that many theorists are reluctant to give up. Second, it is not readily extended to prospects with a large number of outcomes. These problems can be handled by assuming that transparently dominated prospects are eliminated in the editing phase, and by normalizing the weights so that they add to unity. Alternatively, both problems can be solved by the rank-dependent or cumulative functional, first proposed by Quiggin (1982) for decision under risk and by Schmeidler (1989) for decision under uncertainty. Instead of transforming each probability separately, this model transforms the entire cumulative distribution function. The present theory applies the cumulative functional separately to gains and to losses. This development extends prospect theory to uncertain as well as to risky prospects with any number of outcomes while preserving most of its essential features. The differences between the cumulative and the original versions of the theory are discussed in section 1.2.

Let S be a finite set of states of nature; subsets of S are called events. It is assumed that exactly one state obtains, which is unknown to the decision maker. Let X be a set of consequences, also called outcomes. For simplicity, we confine the present discussion to monetary outcomes. We assume that X includes a neutral outcome, denoted 0, and we interpret all other elements of X as gains or losses, denoted by positive or negative numbers, respectively.

An uncertain prospect f is a function from S into X that assigns to each state $s \in S$ a consequence $f(s) = x$ in X. To define the cumulative functional, we arrange the outcomes of each prospect in increasing order. A prospect f is then represented as a sequence of pairs (x_i, A_i), which yields x_i if A_i occurs, where $x_i > x_j$ iff $i > j$, and

(A_i) is a partition of S. We use positive subscripts to denote positive outcomes, negative subscripts to denote negative outcomes, and the zero subscript to index the neutral outcome. A prospect is called strictly positive or positive, respectively, if its outcomes are all positive or nonnegative. Strictly negative and negative prospects are defined similarly; all other prospects are called mixed. The positive part of f, denoted f^+, is obtained by letting $f^+(s) = f(s)$ if $f(s) > 0$, and $f^+(s) = 0$ if $f(s) \leq 0$. The negative part of f, denoted f^-, is defined similarly.

As in expected utility theory, we assign to each prospect f a number $V(f)$ such that f is preferred to or indifferent to g iff $V(f) \geq V(g)$. The following representation is defined in terms of the concept of *capacity* (Choquet, 1955), a nonadditive set function that generalizes the standard notion of probability. A capacity W is a function that assigns to each $A \subset S$ a number $W(A)$ satisfying $W(\phi) = 0$, $W(S) = 1$, and $W(A) \geq W(B)$ whenever $A \supset B$.

Cumulative prospect theory asserts that there exist a strictly increasing value function $v : X \to \mathrm{Re}$, satisfying $v(x_0) = v(0) = 0$, and capacities W^+ and W^-, such that for $f = (x_i, A_i)$, $-m \leq i \leq n$,

$$V(f) = V(f^+) + V(f^-),$$

$$V(f^+) = \sum_{i=0}^{n} \pi_i^+ v(x_i), \quad V(f^-) = \sum_{i=-m}^{0} \pi_i^- v(x_i), \tag{1}$$

where the decision weights $\pi^+(f^+) = (\pi_0^+, \ldots, \pi_n^+)$ and $\pi^-(f^-) = (\pi_{-m}^-, \ldots, \pi_0^-)$ are defined by:

$$\pi_n^+ = W^+(A_n), \quad \pi_{-m}^- = W^-(A_{-m}),$$

$$\pi_i^+ = W^+(A_i \cup \cdots \cup A_n) - W^+(A_{i+1} \cup \cdots \cup A_n), \quad 0 \leq i \leq n - 1,$$

$$\pi_i^- = W^-(A_{-m} \cup \cdots \cup A_i) - W^-(A_{-m} \cup \cdots \cup A_{i-1}), \quad 1 - m \leq i \leq 0.$$

Letting $\pi_i = \pi_i^+$ if $i \geq 0$ and $\pi_i = \pi_i^-$ if $i < 0$, equation (1) reduces to

$$V(f) = \sum_{i=-m}^{n} \pi_i v(x_i). \tag{2}$$

The decision weight π_i^+, associated with a positive outcome, is the difference between the capacities of the events "the outcome is at least as good as x_i" and "the outcome is strictly better than x_i." The decision weight π_i^-, associated with a negative outcome, is the difference between the capacities of the events "the outcome is at least as bad as x_i" and "the outcome is strictly worse than x_i." Thus, the decision weight associated with an outcome can be interpreted as the marginal contribution of the respective event,[1] defined in terms of the capacities W^+ and W^-. If each W is additive, and hence a probability measure, then π_i is simply the probability of A_i. It follows readily from the definitions of π and W that for both positive and negative prospects, the decision weights add to 1. For mixed prospects, however, the sum can be either smaller or greater than 1, because the decision weights for gains and for losses are defined by separate capacities.

If the prospect $f = (x_i, A_i)$ is given by a probability distribution $p(A_i) = p_i$, it can be viewed as a probabilistic or risky prospect (x_i, p_i). In this case, decision weights are defined by:

$$\pi_n^+ = w^+(p_n), \quad \pi_{-m}^- = w^-(p_{-m}),$$

$$\pi_i^+ = w^+(p_i + \cdots + p_n) - w^+(p_{i+1} + \cdots + p_n), \quad 0 \leq i \leq n-1,$$

$$\pi_i^- = w^-(p_{-m} + \cdots + p_i) - w^-(p_{-m} + \cdots + p_{i-1}), \quad 1 - m \leq i \leq 0.$$

where w^+ and w^- are strictly increasing functions from the unit interval into itself satisfying $w^+(0) = w^-(0) = 0$, and $w^+(1) = w^-(1) = 1$.

To illustrate the model, consider the following game of chance. You roll a die once and observe the result $x = 1, \ldots, 6$. If x is even, you receive $\$x$; if x is odd, you pay $\$x$. Viewed as a probabilistic prospect with equiprobable outcomes, f yields the consequences $(-5, -3, -1, 2, 4, 6)$, each with probability $1/6$. Thus, $f^+ = (0, 1/2; 2, 1/6; 4, 1/6; 6, 1/6)$, and $f^- = (-5, 1/6; -3, 1/6; -1, 1/6; 0, 1/2)$. By equation (1), therefore,

$$
\begin{aligned}
V(f) = V(f^+) + V(f^-) \\
&= v(2)[w^+(1/2) - w^+(1/3)] + v(4)[w^+(1/3) - w^+(1/6)] \\
&\quad + v(6)[w^+(1/6) - w^+(0)] \\
&\quad + v(-5)[w^-(1/6) - w^-(0)] + v(-3)[w^-(1/3) - w^-(1/6)] \\
&\quad + v(-1)[w^-(1/2) - w^-(1/3)].
\end{aligned}
$$

1.2 Relation to Previous Work

Luce and Fishburn (1991) derived essentially the same representation from a more elaborate theory involving an operation $\circ$ of joint receipt or multiple play. Thus, $f \circ g$ is the composite prospect obtained by playing both f and g, separately. The key feature of their theory is that the utility function U is additive with respect to $\circ$, that is, $U(f \circ g) = U(f) + U(g)$ provided one prospect is acceptable (i.e., preferred to the status quo) and the other is not. This condition seems too restrictive both normatively and descriptively. As noted by the authors, it implies that the utility of money is a linear function of money if for all sums of money x, y, $U(x \circ y) = U(x + y)$. This assumption appears to us inescapable because the joint receipt of x and y is tantamount to receiving their sum. Thus, we expect the decision maker to be indifferent between receiving a \$10 bill or receiving a \$20 bill and returning \$10 in change. The Luce–Fishburn theory, therefore, differs from ours in two essential respects. First, it extends to composite prospects that are not treated in the present theory. Second, it practically forces utility to be proportional to money.

The present representation encompasses several previous theories that employ the same decision weights for all outcomes. Starmer and Sugden (1989) considered a model in which $w^-(p) = w^+(p)$, as in the original version of prospect theory. In contrast, the rank-dependent models assume $w^-(p) = 1 - w^+(1 - p)$ or $W^-(A) = 1 - W^+(S - A)$. If we apply the latter condition to choice between uncertain assets, we obtain the choice model established by Schmeidler (1989), which is based on the Choquet integral.[2] Other axiomatizations of this model were developed by Gilboa (1987), Nakamura (1990), and Wakker (1989a, 1989b). For probabilistic (rather than uncertain) prospects, this model was first established by Quiggin (1982) and Yaari (1987), and was further analyzed by Chew (1989), Segal (1989), and Wakker (1990). An earlier axiomatization of this model in the context of income inequality was presented by Weymark (1981). Note that in the present theory, the overall value $V(f)$ of a mixed prospect is not a Choquet integral but rather a sum $V(f^+) + V(f^-)$ of two such integrals.

The present treatment extends the original version of prospect theory in several respects. First, it applies to any finite prospect and it can be extended to continuous distributions. Second, it applies to both probabilistic and uncertain prospects and can, therefore, accommodate some form of source dependence. Third, the present theory allows different decision weights for gains and losses, thereby generalizing the original version that assumes $w^+ = w^-$. Under this assumption, the present theory coincides with the original version for all two-outcome prospects and for all mixed three-outcome prospects. It is noteworthy that for prospects of the form $(x, p; y, 1 - p)$, where either $x > y > 0$ or $x < y < 0$, the original theory is in fact rank dependent. Although the two models yield similar predictions in general, the cumulative version—unlike the original one—satisfies stochastic dominance. Thus, it is no longer necessary to assume that transparently dominated prospects are eliminated in the editing phase—an assumption that was criticized by some authors. On the other hand, the present version can no longer explain violations of stochastic dominance in nontransparent contexts (e.g., Tversky and Kahneman, 1986). An axiomatic analysis of the present theory and its relation to cumulative utility theory and to expected utility theory are discussed in the appendix; a more comprehensive treatment is presented in Wakker and Tversky (1991).

1.3 Values and Weights

In expected utility theory, risk aversion and risk seeking are determined solely by the utility function. In the present theory, as in other cumulative models, risk aversion and risk seeking are determined jointly by the value function and by the capacities, which in the present context are called cumulative weighting functions, or weighting functions for short. As in the original version of prospect theory, we assume that v is concave above the reference point $(v''(x) \leq 0, x \geq 0)$ and convex below the reference point $(v''(x) \geq 0, x \leq 0)$. We also assume that v is steeper for losses than for gains $v'(x) < v'(-x)$ for $x \geq 0$. The first two conditions reflect the principle of diminishing sensitivity: the impact of a change diminishes with the distance from the reference point. The last condition is implied by the principle of loss aversion according to which losses loom larger than corresponding gains (Tversky and Kahneman, 1991).

The principle of diminishing sensitivity applies to the weighting functions as well. In the evaluation of outcomes, the reference point serves as a boundary that distinguishes gains from losses. In the evaluation of uncertainty, there are two natural boundaries—certainty and impossibility—that correspond to the endpoints of the certainty scale. Diminishing sensitivity entails that the impact of a given change in probability diminishes with its distance from the boundary. For example, an increase of .1 in the probability of winning a given prize has more impact when it changes the probability of winning from .9 to 1.0 or from 0 to .1, than when it changes the probability of winning from .3 to .4 or from .6 to .7. Diminishing sensitivity, therefore, gives rise to a weighting function that is concave near 0 and convex near 1. For uncertain prospects, this principle yields subadditivity for very unlikely events and superadditivity near certainty. However, the function is not well-behaved near the endpoints, and very small probabilities can be either greatly overweighted or neglected altogether.

Before we turn to the main experiment, we wish to relate the observed nonlinearity of preferences to the shape of the weighting function. For this purpose, we devised a new demonstration of the common consequence effect in decisions involving uncertainty rather than risk. Table 27.1 displays a pair of decision problems (I and II) presented in that order to a group of 156 money managers during a workshop. The participants chose between prospects whose outcomes were contingent on the difference d between the closing values of the Dow-Jones today and tomorrow. For

Table 27.1
A Test of Independence (Dow–Jones)

		A	B	C	
		if $d < 30$	if $30 \leq d \leq 35$	if $35 < d$	
Problem I	f	$25,000	$25,000	$25,000	[68]
	g	$25,000	0	$75,000	[32]
Problem II	f'	0	$25,000	$25,000	[23]
	g'	0	0	$75,000	[77]

Note: Outcomes are contingent on the difference d between the closing values of the Dow–Jones today and tomorrow. The percentage of respondents ($N = 156$) who selected each prospect is given in brackets.

Table 27.2
A Test of Independence (Stanford–Berkeley Football Game)

		A	B	C	
		if $d < 0$	if $0 \leq d \leq 10$	if $10 < d$	
Problem I	f	$10	$10	$10	[64]
	g	$10	$30	0	[36]
Problem II	f'	0	$10	$10	[34]
	g'	0	$30	0	[66]

Note: Outcomes are contingent on the point-spread d in a Stanford–Berkeley football game. The percentage of respondents ($N = 98$) who selected each prospect is given in brackets.

example, f' pays $25,000 if d exceeds 30 and nothing otherwise. The percentage of respondents who chose each prospect is given in brackets. The independence axiom of expected utility theory implies that f is preferred to g iff f' is preferred to g'. Table 27.1 shows that the modal choice was f in problem I and g' in problem II. This pattern, which violates independence, was chosen by 53% of the respondents.

Essentially the same pattern was observed in a second study following the same design. A group of 98 Stanford students chose between prospects whose outcomes were contingent on the point-spread d in the forthcoming Stanford–Berkeley football game. Table 27.2 presents the prospects in question. For example, g pays $10 if Stanford does not win, $30 if it wins by 10 points or less, and nothing if it wins by more than 10 points. Ten percent of the participants, selected at random, were actually paid according to one of their choices. The modal choice, selected by 46% of the subjects, was f and g', again in direct violation of the independence axiom.

To explore the constraints imposed by this pattern, let us apply the present theory to the modal choices in table 27.1, using $1,000 as a unit. Since f is preferred to g in problem I;

$$v(25) > v(75) W^+(C) + v(25)[W^+(A \cup C) - W^+(C)]$$

or

$$v(25)[1 - W^+(A \cup C) + W^+(C)] > v(75) W^+(C).$$

The preference for g' over f' in problem II, however, implies

$$v(75) W^+(C) > v(25) W^+(C \cup B);$$

hence,

$$W^+(S) - W^+(S - B) > W^+(C \cup B) - W^+(C). \tag{3}$$

Thus, "subtracting" B from certainty has more impact than "subtracting" B from $C \cup B$. Let $W_+(D) = 1 - W^+(S - D)$, and $w_+(p) = 1 - w^+(1 - p)$. It follows readily that equation (3) is equivalent to the subadditivity of W_+, that is, $W_+(B) + W_+(D) \geq W_+(B \cup D)$. For probabilistic prospects, equation (3) reduces to

$$1 - w^+(1 - q) > w^+(p + q) - w^+(p),$$

or

$$w_+(q) + w_+(r) \geq w_+(q + r), \quad q + r < 1.$$

Allais's example corresponds to the case where $p(C) = .10$, $p(B) = .89$, and $p(A) = .01$.

It is noteworthy that the violations of independence reported in tables 27.1 and 27.2 are also inconsistent with regret theory, advanced by Loomes and Sugden (1982, 1987), and with Fishburn's (1988) SSA model. Regret theory explains Allais's example by assuming that the decision maker evaluates the consequences as if the two prospects in each choice are statistically independent. When the prospects in question are defined by the same set of events, as in tables 27.1 and 27.2, regret theory (like Fishburn's SSA model) implies independence, since it is additive over states. The finding that the common consequence effect is very much in evidence in the present problems undermines the interpretation of Allais's example in terms of regret theory.

The common consequence effect implies the subadditivity of W_+ and of w_+. Other violations of expected utility theory imply the subadditivity of W^+ and of w^+ for small and moderate probabilities. For example, Prelec (1990) observed that most respondents prefer 2% to win \$20,000 over 1% to win \$30,000; they also prefer 1% to win \$30,000 and 32% to win \$20,000 over 34% to win \$20,000. In terms of the present theory, these data imply that $w^+(.02) - w^+(.01) \geq w^+(.34) - w^+(.33)$. More generally, we hypothesize

$$w^+(p+q) - w^+(q) \geq w^+(p+q+r) - w^+(q+r), \tag{4}$$

provided $p + q + r$ is sufficiently small. Equation (4) states that w^+ is concave near the origin; and the conjunction of the above inequalities implies that, in accord with diminishing sensitivity, w^+ has an inverted S-shape: it is steepest near the endpoints and shallower in the middle of the range. For other treatments of decision weights, see Hogarth and Einhorn (1990), Prelec (1989), Viscusi (1989), and Wakker (1990). Experimental evidence is presented in the next section.

2 Experiment

An experiment was carried out to obtain detailed information about the value and weighting functions. We made a special effort to obtain high-quality data. To this end, we recruited 25 graduate students from Berkeley and Stanford (12 men and 13 women) with no special training in decision theory. Each subject participated in three separate one-hour sessions that were several days apart. Each subject was paid $25 for participation.

2.1 Procedure
The experiment was conducted on a computer. On a typical trial, the computer displayed a prospect (e.g., 25% chance to win $150 and 75% chance to win $50) and its expected value. The display also included a descending series of seven sure outcomes (gains or losses) logarithmically spaced between the extreme outcomes of the prospect. The subject indicated a preference between each of the seven sure outcomes and the risky prospect. To obtain a more refined estimate of the certainty equivalent, a new set of seven sure outcomes was then shown, linearly spaced between a value 25% higher than the lowest amount accepted in the first set and a value 25% lower than the highest amount rejected. The certainty equivalent of a prospect was estimated by the midpoint between the lowest accepted value and the highest rejected value in the second set of choices. We wish to emphasize that although the analysis is based on certainty equivalents, the data consisted of a series of choices between a given prospect and several sure outcomes. Thus, the cash equivalent of a prospect was derived from observed choices, rather than assessed by the subject. The computer monitored the internal consistency of the responses to each prospect and rejected errors, such as the acceptance of a cash amount lower than one previously rejected. Errors caused the original statement of the problem to reappear on the screen.

The present analysis focuses on a set of two-outcome prospects with monetary outcomes and numerical probabilities. Other data involving more complicated pros-

Table 27.3
Median Cash Equivalents (in Dollars) for All Nonmixed Prospects

Outcomes	Probability								
	.01	.05	.10	.25	.50	.75	.90	.95	.99
(0, 50)			9		21		37		
(0, −50)			−8		−21		−39		
(0, 100)		14		25	36	52		78	
(0, −100)		−8		−23.5	−42	−63		−84	
(0, 200)	10		20		76		131		188
(0, −200)	−3		−23		−89		−155		−190
(0, 400)	12								377
(0, −400)	−14								−380
(50, 100)			59		71		83		
(−50, −100)			−59		−71		−85		
(50, 150)		64		72.5	86	102		128	
(−50, −150)		−60		−71	−92	−113		−132	
(100, 200)		118		130	141	162		178	
(−100, −200)		−112		−121	−142	−158		−179	

Note: The two outcomes of each prospect are given in the left-hand side of each row; the probability of the second (i.e., more extreme) outcome is given by the corresponding column. For example, the value of $9 in the upper left corner is the median cash equivalent of the prospect $(0, .9; \$50, .1)$.

pects, including prospects defined by uncertain events, will be reported elsewhere. There were 28 positive and 28 negative prospects. Six of the prospects (three non-negative and three nonpositive) were repeated on different sessions to obtain the estimate of the consistency of choice. Table 27.3 displays the prospects and the median cash equivalents of the 25 subjects.

A modified procedure was used in eight additional problems. In four of these problems, the subjects made choices regarding the acceptability of a set of mixed prospects (e.g., 50% chance to lose $100 and 50% chance to win x) in which x was systematically varied. In four other problems, the subjects compared a fixed prospect (e.g., 50% chance to lose $20 and 50% chance to win $50) to a set of prospects (e.g., 50% chance to lose $50 and 50% chance to win x) in which x was systematically varied. (These prospects are presented in table 27.6.)

2.2 Results

The most distinctive implication of prospect theory is the fourfold pattern of risk attitudes. For the nonmixed prospects used in the present study, the shapes of the value and the weighting functions imply risk-averse and risk-seeking preferences, respectively, for gains and for losses of moderate or high probability. Furthermore, the shape of the weighting functions favors risk seeking for small probabilities of gains and risk aversion for small probabilities of loss, provided the outcomes are not extreme. Note, however, that prospect theory does not imply perfect reflection in the sense that the preference between any two positive prospects is reversed when gains are replaced by losses. Table 27.4 presents, for each subject, the percentage of risk-seeking choices (where the certainty equivalent exceeded expected value) for gains and for losses with low $(p \leq .1)$ and with high $(p \geq .5)$ probabilities. Table 27.4 shows that for $p \geq .5$, all 25 subjects are predominantly risk averse for positive prospects and risk seeking for negative ones. Moreover, the entire fourfold pattern is observed for 22 of the 25 subjects, with some variability at the level of individual choices.

Although the overall pattern of preferences is clear, the individual data, of course, reveal both noise and individual differences. The correlations, across subjects, between the cash equivalents for the same prospects on successive sessions averaged .55 over six different prospects. Table 27.5 presents means (after transformation to Fisher's z) of the correlations between the different types of prospects. For example, there were 19 and 17 prospects, respectively, with high probability of gain and high probability of loss. The value of .06 in table 27.5 is the mean of the $17 \times 19 = 323$ correlations between the cash equivalents of these prospects.

The correlations between responses within each of the four types of prospects average $A1$, slightly lower than the correlations between separate responses to the same problems. The two negative values in table 27.5 indicate that those subjects who were more risk averse in one domain tended to be more risk seeking in the other. Although the individual correlations are fairly low, the trend is consistent: 78% of the 403 correlations in these two cells are negative. There is also a tendency for subjects who are more risk averse for high-probability gains to be less risk seeking for gains of low probability. This trend, which is absent in the negative domain, could reflect individual differences either in the elevation of the weighting function or in the curvature of the value function for gains. The very low correlations in the two remaining cells of table 27.5, averaging .05, indicate that there is no general trait of risk aversion or risk seeking. Because individual choices are quite noisy, aggregation of problems is necessary for the analysis of individual differences.

The fourfold pattern of risk attitudes emerges as a major empirical generalization about choice under risk. It has been observed in several experiments (see, e.g., Cohen, Jaffray, and Said, 1987), including a study of experienced oil executives involving significant, albeit hypothetical, gains and losses (Wehrung, 1989). It should be noted that prospect theory implies the pattern demonstrated in table 27.4 within the data of individual subjects, but it does not imply high correlations across subjects

Table 27.4
Percentage of Risk-seeking Choices

Subject	Gain		Loss	
	$p \leq .1$	$p \geq .5$	$p \leq .1$	$p \geq .5$
1	100	38	30	100
2	85	33	20	75
3	100	10	0	93
4	71	0	30	58
5	83	0	20	100
6	100	5	0	100
7	100	10	30	86
8	87	0	10	100
9	16	0	80	100
10	83	0	0	93
11	100	26	0	100
12	100	16	10	100
13	87	0	10	94
14	100	21	30	100
15	66	0	30	100
16	60	5	10	100
17	100	15	20	100
18	100	22	10	93
19	60	10	60	63
20	100	5	0	81
21	100	0	0	100
22	100	0	0	92
23	100	31	0	100
24	71	0	80	100
25	100	0	10	87
Risk seeking	78[a]	10	20	87[a]
Risk neutral	12	2	0	7
Risk averse	10	88[a]	80[a]	6

Note: The percentage of risk-seeking choices is given for low ($p \leq .1$) and high ($p \geq .5$) probabilities of gain and loss for each subject (risk-neutral choices were excluded). The overall percentage of risk-seeking, risk-neutral, and risk-averse choices for each type of prospect appear at the bottom of the table.
[a] Values that correspond to the fourfold pattern.

Table 27.5
Average Correlations between Certainty Equivalents in Four Types of Prospects

	L^+	H^+	L	H
L^+	.41	.17	.23	.05
H^+		.39	.05	.18
L			.40	.06
H				.44

Note: Low probability of gain = L^+; high probability of gain = H^+; low probability of loss = L; high probability of loss = H.

because the values of gains and of losses can vary independently. The failure to appreciate this point and the limited reliability of individual responses has led some previous authors (e.g., Hershey and Schoemaker, 1980) to underestimate the robustness of the fourfold pattern.

2.3   Scaling

Having established the fourfold pattern in ordinal and correlational analyses, we now turn to a quantitative description of the data. For each prospect of the form $(x, p; 0, 1 - p)$, let c/x be the ratio of the certainty equivalent of the prospect to the nonzero outcome x. Figures 27.1 and 27.2 plot the median value of c/x as a function of p, for positive and for negative prospects, respectively. We denote c/x by a circle if $|x| < 200$, and by a triangle if $|x| \geq 200$. The only exceptions are the two extreme probabilities (.01 and .99) where a circle is used for $|x| = 200$. To interpret figures 27.1 and 27.2, note that if subjects are risk neutral, the points will lie on the diagonal; if subjects are risk averse, all points will lie below the diagonal in figure 27.1 and above the diagonal in figure 27.2. Finally, the triangles and the circles will lie on top of each other if preferences are homogeneous, so that multiplying the outcomes of a prospect f by a constant $k > 0$ multiplies its cash equivalent $c(kf)$ by the same constant, that is, $c(kf) = kc(f)$. In expected utility theory, preference homogeneity gives rise to constant relative risk aversion. Under the present theory, assuming $X = \text{Re}$, preference homogeneity is both necessary and sufficient to represent v as a two-part power function of the form

$$v(x) = \begin{cases} x^\alpha & \text{if } x \geq 0 \\ -\lambda(-x)^\beta & \text{if } x < 0. \end{cases} \tag{5}$$

Figures 27.1 and 27.2 exhibit the characteristic pattern of risk aversion and risk seeking observed in table 27.4. They also indicate that preference homogeneity holds as a good approximation. The slight departures from homogeneity in figure 27.1

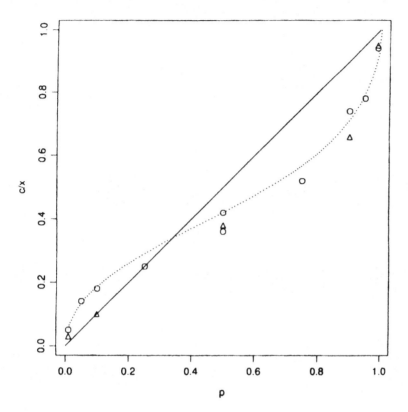

Figure 27.1
Median c/x for all positive prospects of the form $(x, p; 0, 1 - p)$. Triangles and circles, respectively, correspond to values of x that lie above or below 200.

suggest that the cash equivalents of positive prospects increase more slowly than the stakes (triangles tend to lie below the circles), but no such tendency is evident in figure 27.2. Overall, it appears that the present data can be approximated by a two-part power function. The smooth curves in figures 27.1 and 27.2 can be interpreted as weighting functions, assuming a linear value function. They were fitted using the following functional form:

$$w^+(p) = \frac{p^\gamma}{(p^\gamma + (1 - p)^\gamma)^{1/\gamma}}, \quad w^-(p) = \frac{p^\delta}{(p^\delta + (1 - p)^\delta)^{1/\delta}}. \tag{6}$$

This form has several useful features: it has only one parameter; it encompasses weighting functions with both concave and convex regions; it does not require

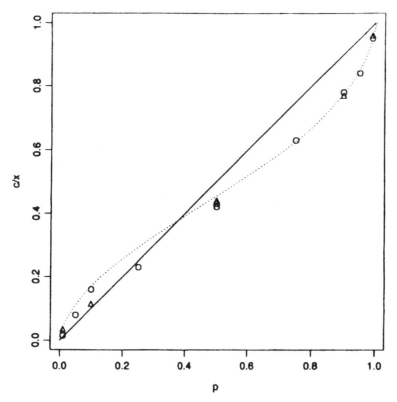

Figure 27.2
Median c/x for all negative prospects of the form $(x, p; 0, 1 - p)$. Triangles and circles, respectively, correspond to values of x that lie below or above -200.

$w(.5) = .5$; and most important, it provides a reasonably good approximation to both the aggregate and the individual data for probabilities in the range between .05 and .95.

Further information about the properties of the value function can be derived from the data presented in table 27.6. The adjustments of mixed prospects to acceptability (problems 1–4) indicate that, for even chances to win and lose, a prospect will only be acceptable if the gain is at least twice as large as the loss. This observation is compatible with a value function that changes slope abruptly at zero, with a loss-aversion coefficient of about 2 (Tversky and Kahneman, 1991). The median matches in problems 5 and 6 are also consistent with this estimate: when the possible loss is increased by k the compensating gain must be increased by about $2k$.

Table 27.6
A Test of Loss Aversion

Problem	a	b	c	x	θ
1	0	0	−25	61	2.44
2	0	0	−50	101	2.02
3	0	0	−100	202	2.02
4	0	0	−150	280	1.87
5	−20	50	−50	112	2.07
6	−50	150	−125	301	2.01
7	50	120	20	149	0.97
8	100	300	25	401	1.35

Note: In each problem, subjects determined the value of x that makes the prospect $(\$a, \frac{1}{2}; \$b, \frac{1}{2})$ as attractive as $(\$c, \frac{1}{2}; \$x, \frac{1}{2})$. The median values of x are presented for all problems along with the fixed values a, b, c. The statistic $\theta = (x - b)/(c - a)$ is the ratio of the "slopes" at a higher and a lower region of the value function.

Problems 7 and 8 are obtained from problems 5 and 6, respectively, by positive translations that turn mixed prospects into strictly positive ones. In contrast to the large values of θ observed in problems 1–6, the responses in problems 7 and 8 indicate that the curvature of the value function for gains is slight. A decrease in the smallest gain of a strictly positive prospect is fully compensated by a slightly larger increase in the largest gain. The standard rank-dependent model, which lacks the notion of a reference point, cannot account for the dramatic effects of small translations of prospects illustrated in table 27.6.

The estimation of a complex choice model, such as cumulative prospect theory, is problematic. If the functions associated with the theory are not constrained, the number of estimated parameters for each subject is too large. To reduce this number, it is common to assume a parametric form (e.g., a power utility function), but this approach confounds the general test of the theory with that of the specific parametric form. For this reason, we focused here on the qualitative properties of the data rather than on parameter estimates and measures of fit. However, in order to obtain a parsimonious description of the present data, we used a nonlinear regression procedure to estimate the parameters of equations (5) and (6), separately for each subject. The median exponent of the value function was 0.88 for both gains and losses, in accord with diminishing sensitivity. The median λ was 2.25, indicating pronounced loss aversion, and the median values of γ and δ, respectively, were 0.61 and 0.69, in agreement with equations (3) and (4) above.[3] The parameters estimated from the median data were essentially the same. Figure 27.3 plots w^+ and w^- using the median estimates of γ and δ.

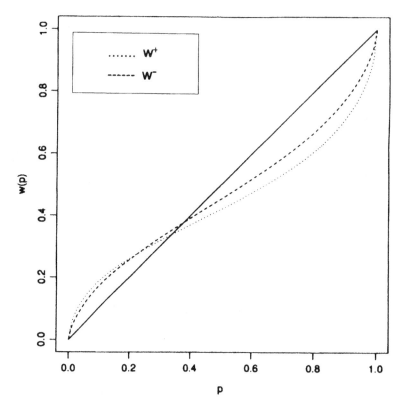

Figure 27.3
Weighting functions for gains (w^+) and for losses (w^-) based on median estimates of γ and δ in equation
(12).

Figure 27.3 shows that, for both positive and negative prospects, people overweight low probabilities and underweight moderate and high probabilities. As a
consequence, people are relatively insensitive to probability difference in the middle
of the range. Figure 27.3 also shows that the weighting functions for gains and for
losses are quite close, although the former is slightly more curved than the latter (i.e.,
$\gamma < \delta$). Accordingly, risk aversion for gains is more pronounced than risk seeking for
losses, for moderate and high probabilities (see table 27.3). It is noteworthy that
the condition $w^+(p) = w^-(p)$, assumed in the original version of prospect theory,
accounts for the present data better than the assumption $w^+(p) = 1 - w^-(1 - p)$,
implied by the standard rank-dependent or cumulative functional. For example, our
estimates of w^+ and w^- show that all 25 subjects satisfied the conditions $w^+(.5) < .5$

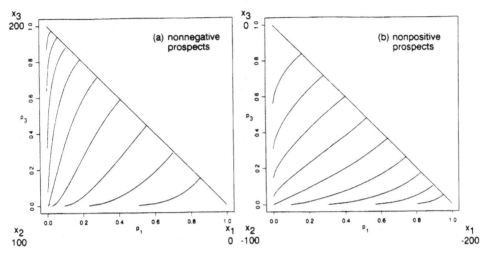

Figure 27.4
Indifference curves of cumulative prospect theory (a) for nonnegative prospects $(x_1 = 0,\ x_2 = 100,\ x_3 = 200)$, and (b) for nonpositive prospects $(x_1 = -200,\ x_2 = -100,\ x_3 = 0)$. The curves are based on the respective weighting functions of figure 3, $(\gamma = .61,\ \delta = .69)$ and on the median estimates of the exponents of the value function $(\alpha = \beta = .88)$. The broken line through the origin represents the prospects whose expected value is x_2.

and $w^-(.5) < .5$, implied by the former model, and no one satisfied the condition $w^+(.5) < .5$ iff $w^-(.5) > .5$, implied by the latter model.

Much research on choice between risky prospects has utilized the triangle diagram (Marschak, 1950; Machina, 1987) that represents the set of all prospects of the form $(x_1, p_1; x_2, p_2; x_3, p_3)$, with fixed outcomes $x_1 < x_2 < x_3$. Each point in the triangle represents a prospect that yields the lowest outcome (x_1) with probability p_1, the highest outcome (x_3) with probability p_3, and the intermediate outcome (x_2) with probability $p_2 = 1 - p_1 - p_3$. An indifference curve is a set of prospects (i.e., points) that the decision maker finds equally attractive. Alternative choice theories are characterized by the shapes of their indifference curves. In particular, the indifference curves of expected utility theory are parallel straight lines. Figures 27.4a and 27.4b illustrate the indifference curves of cumulative prospect theory for nonnegative and nonpositive prospects, respectively. The shapes of the curves are determined by the weighting functions of figure 27.3; the values of the outcomes (x_1, x_2, x_3) merely control the slope.

Figures 27.4a and 27.4b are in general agreement with the main empirical generalizations that have emerged from the studies of the triangle diagram; see Camerer

(1992), and Camerer and Ho (1991) for reviews. First, departures from linearity, which violate expected utility theory, are most pronounced near the edges of the triangle. Second, the indifference curves exhibit both fanning in and fanning out. Third, the curves are concave in the upper part of the triangle and convex in the lower right. Finally, the indifference curves for nonpositive prospects resemble the curves for nonnegative prospects reflected around the 45° line, which represents risk neutrality. For example, a sure gain of $100 is equally as attractive as a 71% chance to win $200 or nothing (see figure 27.4a), and a sure loss of $100 is equally as aversive as a 64% chance to lose $200 or nothing (see figure 27.4b). The approximate reflection of the curves is of special interest because it distinguishes the present theory from the standard rank-dependent model in which the two sets of curves are essentially the same.

2.4   Incentives

We conclude this section with a brief discussion of the role of monetary incentives. In the present study we did not pay subjects on the basis of their choices because in our experience with choice between prospects of the type used in the present study, we did not find much difference between subjects who were paid a flat fee and subjects whose payoffs were contingent on their decisions. The same conclusion was obtained by Camerer (1989), who investigated the effects of incentives using several hundred subjects. He found that subjects who actually played the gamble gave essentially the same responses as subjects who did not play; he also found no differences in reliability and roughly the same decision time. Although some studies found differences between paid and unpaid subjects in choice between simple prospects, these differences were not large enough to change any significant qualitative conclusions. Indeed, all major violations of expected utility theory (e.g. the common consequence effect, the common ratio effect, source dependence, loss aversion, and preference reversals) were obtained both with and without monetary incentives.

As noted by several authors, however, the financial incentives provided in choice experiments are generally small relative to people's incomes. What happens when the stakes correspond to three- or four-digit rather than one- or two-digit figures? To answer this question, Kachelmeier and Shehata (1991) conducted a series of experiments using Masters students at Beijing University, most of whom had taken at least one course in economics or business. Due to the economic conditions in China, the investigators were able to offer subjects very large rewards. In the high payoff condition, subjects earned about three times their normal monthly income in the course of one experimental session! On each trial, subjects were presented with a simple bet that offered a specified probability to win a given prize, and nothing otherwise. Subjects were instructed to state their cash equivalent for each bet. An incentive compatible procedure (the BDM scheme) was used to determine, on each trial, whether the subject would play the bet or receive the "official" selling price. If departures from the standard theory are due to the mental cost associated with decision making and the absence of proper incentives, as suggested by Smith and Walker (1992), then the highly paid Chinese subjects should not exhibit the characteristic nonlinearity observed in hypothetical choices, or in choices with small payoffs.

However, the main finding of Kachelmeier and Shehata (1991) is massive risk seeking for small probabilities. Risk seeking was slightly more pronounced for lower payoffs, but even in the highest payoff condition, the cash equivalent for a 5% bet (their lowest probability level) was, on average, three times larger than its expected value. Note that in the present study the median cash equivalent of a 5% chance to win $100 (see table 27.3) was $14, almost three times the expected value of the bet. In general, the cash equivalents obtained by Kachelmeier and Shehata were higher than those observed in the present study. This is consistent with the finding that minimal selling prices are generally higher than certainty equivalents derived from choice (see, e.g., Tversky, Slovic, and Kahneman, 1990). As a consequence, they found little risk aversion for moderate and high probability of winning. This was true for the Chinese subjects, at both high and low payoffs, as well as for Canadian subjects, who either played for low stakes or did not receive any payoff. The most striking result in all groups was the marked overweighting of small probabilities, in accord with the present analysis.

Evidently, high incentives do not always dominate noneconomic considerations, and the observed departures from expected utility theory cannot be rationalized in terms of the cost of thinking. We agree with Smith and Walker (1992) that monetary incentives could improve performance under certain conditions by eliminating careless errors. However, we maintain that monetary incentives are neither necessary nor sufficient to ensure subjects' cooperativeness, thoughtfulness, or truthfulness. The similarity between the results obtained with and without monetary incentives in choice between simple prospects provides no special reason for skepticism about experiments without contingent payment.

3   Discussion

Theories of choice under uncertainty commonly specify 1) the objects of choice, 2) a valuation rule, and 3) the characteristics of the functions that map uncertain events and possible outcomes into their subjective counterparts. In standard applications of expected utility theory, the objects of choice are probability distributions over wealth, the valuation rule is expected utility, and utility is a concave function of wealth. The empirical evidence reported here and elsewhere requires major revisions of all three elements. We have proposed an alternative descriptive theory in which 1) the objects of choice are prospects framed in terms of gains and losses, 2) the valuation rule is a two-part cumulative functional, and 3) the value function is S-shaped and the weighting functions are inverse S-shaped. The experimental findings confirmed the qualitative properties of these scales, which can be approximated by a (two-part) power value function and by identical weighting functions for gains and losses.

The curvature of the weighting function explains the characteristic reflection pattern of attitudes to risky prospects. Overweighting of small probabilities contributes to the popularity of both lotteries and insurance. Underweighting of high probabilities contributes both to the prevalence of risk aversion in choices between probable gains and sure things, and to the prevalence of risk seeking in choices between probable and sure losses. Risk aversion for gains and risk seeking for losses are further enhanced by the curvature of the value function in the two domains. The pronounced asymmetry of the value function, which we have labeled loss aversion, explains the extreme reluctance to accept mixed prospects. The shape of the weighting function explains the certainty effect and violations of quasi-convexity. It also explains why these phenomena are most readily observed at the two ends of the probability scale, where the curvature of the weighting function is most pronounced (Camerer, 1992).

The new demonstrations of the common consequence effect, described in tables 27.1 and 27.2, show that choice under uncertainty exhibits some of the main characteristics observed in choice under risk. On the other hand, there are indications that the decision weights associated with uncertain and with risky prospects differ in important ways. First, there is abundant evidence that subjective judgments of probability do not conform to the rules of probability theory (Kahneman, Slovic and Tversky, 1982). Second, Ellsberg's example and more recent studies of choice under uncertainty indicate that people prefer some sources of uncertainty over others. For example, Heath and Tversky (1991) found that individuals consistently preferred bets on uncertain events in their area of expertise over matched bets on chance devices, although the former are ambiguous and the latter are not. The presence of systematic preferences for some sources of uncertainty calls for different weighting functions for different domains, and suggests that some of these functions lie entirely above others. The investigation of decision weights for uncertain events emerges as a promising domain for future research.

The present theory retains the major features of the original version of prospect theory and introduces a (two-part) cumulative functional, which provides a convenient mathematical representation of decision weights. It also relaxes some descriptively inappropriate constraints of expected utility theory. Despite its greater generality, the cumulative functional is unlikely to be accurate in detail. We suspect that decision weights may be sensitive to the formulation of the prospects, as well as to the number, the spacing and the level of outcomes. In particular, there is some evidence to suggest that the curvature of the weighting function is more pronounced when the outcomes are widely spaced (Camerer, 1992). The present theory can be generalized to accommodate such effects, but it is questionable whether the gain in descriptive validity, achieved by giving up the separability of values and weights, would justify the loss of predictive power and the cost of increased complexity.

Theories of choice are at best approximate and incomplete. One reason for this pessimistic assessment is that choice is a constructive and contingent process. When faced with a complex problem, people employ a variety of heuristic procedures in order to simplify the representation and the evaluation of prospects. These procedures include computational shortcuts and editing operations, such as eliminating common components and discarding nonessential differences (Tversky, 1969). The heuristics of choice do not readily lend themselves to formal analysis because their application depends on the formulation of the problem, the method of elicitation, and the context of choice.

Prospect theory departs from the tradition that assumes the rationality of economic agents; it is proposed as a descriptive, not a normative, theory. The idealized assumption of rationality in economic theory is commonly justified on two grounds: the conviction that only rational behavior can survive in a competitive environment, and the fear that any treatment that abandons rationality will be chaotic and intractable. Both arguments are questionable. First, the evidence indicates that people can spend a lifetime in a competitive environment without acquiring a general ability to avoid framing effects or to apply linear decision weights. Second, and perhaps more important, the evidence indicates that human choices are orderly, although not always rational in the traditional sense of this word.

Appendix: Axiomatic Analysis

Let $F = \{f : S \to X\}$ be the set of all prospects under study, and let F^+ and F^- denote the positive and the negative prospects, respectively. Let $\gtrsim$ be a binary preference relation on F, and let $\approx$ and $>$ denote its symmetric and asymmetric parts, respectively. We assume that $\gtrsim$ is complete, transitive, and strictly monotonic, that is, if $f \neq g$ and $f(s) \geq g(s)$ for all $s \in S$, then $f > g$.

For any $f, g \in F$ and $A \subset S$, define $h = fAg$ by: $h(s) = f(s)$ if $s \in A$, and $h(s) = g(s)$ if $s \in S - A$. Thus, fAg coincides with f on A and with g on $S - A$. A preference relation $\gtrsim$ on F satisfies *independence* if for all $f, g, f', g' \in F$ and $A \subset S$, $fAg \gtrsim fAg'$ iff $f'Ag \gtrsim f'Ag'$. This axiom, also called the sure thing principle (Savage, 1954), is one of the basic qualitative properties underlying expected utility theory, and it is violated by Allais's common consequence effect. Indeed, the attempt to accommodate Allais's example has motivated the development of numerous models, including cumulative utility theory. The key concept in the axiomatic analysis of that theory is the relation of comonotonicity, due to Schmeidler (1989). A pair of prospects $f, g \in F$ are *comonotonic* if there are no $s, t \in S$ such that $f(s) > f(t)$ and $g(t) > g(s)$. Note that a constant prospect that yields the same outcome in every state is comonotonic with all prospects. Obviously, comonotonicity is symmetric but not transitive.

Cumulative utility theory does not satisfy independence in general, but it implies independence whenever the prospects fAg, fAg', $f'Ag$, and $f'Ag'$ above are pairwise comonotonic. This property is called *comonotonic independence*.[4] It also holds in cumulative prospect theory, and it plays an important role in the characterization of this theory, as will be shown below. Cumulative prospect theory satisfies an additional property, called *double matching:* for all $f, g \in F$, if $f^+ \approx g^+$ and $f^- \approx g^-$, then $f \approx g$.

To characterize the present theory, we assume the following structural conditions: S is finite and includes at least three states; $X = \text{Re}$; and the preference order is continuous in the product topology on Re^k, that is, $\{f \in F : f \gtrsim g\}$ and $\{f \in F : g \gtrsim f\}$ are closed for any $g \in F$. The latter assumptions can be replaced by restricted solvability and a comonotonic Archimedean axiom (Wakker, 1991).

THEOREM 1.   Suppose $(F^+, \gtrsim)$ and $(F^-, \gtrsim)$ can each be represented by a cumulative functional. Then $(F, \gtrsim)$ satisfies cumulative prospect theory iff it satisfies double matching and comonotonic independence.

The proof of the theorem is given at the end of the appendix. It is based on a theorem of Wakker (1992) regarding the additive representation of lower-diagonal structures. Theorem 1 provides a generic procedure for characterizing cumulative prospect theory. Take any axiom system that is sufficient to establish an essentially unique cumulative (i.e., rank-dependent) representation. Apply it separately to the preferences between positive prospects and to the preferences between negative prospects, and construct the value function and the decision weights separately for F^+ and for F^-. Theorem 1 shows that comonotonic independence and double matching ensure that, under the proper rescaling, the sum $V(f^+) + V(f^-)$ preserves the preference order between mixed prospects. In order to distinguish more sharply between the conditions that give rise to a one-part or a two-part representation, we need to focus on a particular axiomatization of the Choquet functional. We chose Wakker's (1989a, 1989b) because of its generality and compactness.

For $x \in X$, $f \in F$, and $r \in S$, let $x\{r\}f$ be the prospect that yields x in state r and coincides with f in all other states. Following Wakker (1989a), we say that a preference relation satisfies *tradeoff consistency*[5] (TC) if for all $x, x', y, y' \in X, f, f', g, g' \in F$, and $s, t \in S$.

$$x\{s\}f \precsim y\{s\}g, \ x'\{s\}f \succsim y'\{s\}g \ \text{ and } \ x\{t\}f' \succsim y\{t\}g' \ \text{ imply } \ x'\{t\}f' \succsim y'\{t\}g'.$$

To appreciate the import of this condition, suppose its premises hold but the conclusion is reversed, that is, $y'\{t\}g' > x'\{t\}f'$. It is easy to verify that under expected utility theory, the first two inequalities, involving $\{s\}$, imply $u(y) - u(y') \geq u(x) - u(x')$, whereas the other two inequalities, involving $\{t\}$, imply the opposite conclusion. Tradeoff consistency, therefore, is needed to ensure that "utility intervals" can be consistently ordered. Essentially the same condition was used by Tversky, Sattath, and Slovic (1988) in the analysis of preference reversal, and by Tversky and Kahneman (1991) in the characterization of constant loss aversion.

A preference relation satisfies *comonotonic tradeoff consistency* (CTC) if TC holds whenever the prospects $x\{s\}f$, $y\{s\}g$, $x'\{s\}f$, and $y'\{s\}g$ are pairwise comonotonic, as are the prospects $x\{t\}f'$, $y\{t\}g'$, $x'\{t\}f'$, and $y'\{t\}g'$ (Wakker, 1989a). Finally, a preference relation satisfies *sign-comonotonic tradeoff consistency* (SCTC) if CTC holds whenever the consequences x, x', y, y' are either all nonnegative or all nonpositive. Clearly, TC is stronger than CTC, which is stronger than SCTC. Indeed, it is not difficult to show that 1) expected utility theory implies TC, 2) cumulative utility theory implies CTC but not TC, and 3) cumulative prospect theory implies SCTC but not CTC. The following theorem shows that, given our other assumptions, these properties are not only necessary but also sufficient to characterize the respective theories.

THEOREM 2.   Assume the structural conditions described above.

a. (Wakker, 1989a) Expected utility theory holds iff $\succsim$ satisfies TC.

b. (Wakker, 1989b) Cumulative utility theory holds iff $\succsim$ satisfies CTC.

c. Cumulative prospect theory holds iff $\succsim$ satisfies double matching and SCTC.

A proof of part c of the theorem is given at the end of this section. It shows that, in the presence of our structural assumptions and double matching, the restriction of tradeoff consistency to sign-comonotonic prospects yields a representation with a reference-dependent value function and different decision weights for gains and for losses.

Proof of Theorem 1. The necessity of comonotonic independence and double matching is straightforward. To establish sufficiency, recall that, by assumption, there exist functions π^+, π^-, v^+, v^-, such that $V^+ = \sum \pi^+ v^+$ and $V^- = \sum \pi^- v^-$ preserve $\gtrsim$ on F^+ and on F^-, respectively. Furthermore, by the structural assumptions, π^+ and π^- are unique, whereas v^+ and v^- are continuous ratio scales. Hence, we can set $v^+(1) = 1$ and $v^-(-1) = \theta < 0$, independently of each other.

Let Q be the set of prospects such that for any $q \in Q$, $q(s) \neq q(t)$ for any distinct $s, t \in S$. Let F_g denote the set of all prospects in F that are comonotonic with G. By comonotonic independence and our structural conditions, it follows readily from a theorem of Wakker (1992) on additive representations for lower-triangular subsets of Re^k that, given any $q \in Q$, there exist intervals scales $\{U_{qi}\}$, with a common unit, such that $U_q = \sum_i U_{qi}$ preserves $\gtrsim$ on F_q. With no loss of generality we can set $U_{qi}(0) = 0$ for all i and $U_q(1) = 1$. Since V^+ and V^- above are additive representations of $\gtrsim$ on F_q^+ and F_q^-, respectively, it follows by uniqueness that there exist $a_q, b_q > 0$ such that for all i, U_{qi} equals $a_q \pi_i^+ v^+$ on Re^+, and U_{qi} equals $b_q \pi_i^- v^-$ on Re^-.

So far the representations were required to preserve the order only within each F_q. Thus, we can choose scales so that $b_q = 1$ for all q. To relate the different representations, select a prospect $h \neq q$. Since V^+ should preserve the order on F^+, and U_q should preserve the order within each F_q, we can multiply V^+ by a_h, and replace each a_q by a_q/a_h. In other words, we may set $a_h = 1$. For any $q \in Q$, select $f \in F_q$, $g \in F_h$ such that $f^+ \approx g^+ > 0$, $f^- \approx g^- > 0$, and $g \approx 0$. By double matching, then, $f \approx g \approx 0$. Thus, $a_q V^+(f^+) + V^-(f^-) = 0$, since this form preserves the order on F_q. But $V^+(f^+) = V^+(g^+)$ and $V^-(f^-) = V^-(g^-)$, so $V^+(g^+) + V^-(g^-) = 0$ implies $V^+(f^+) + V^-(f^-) = 0$. Hence, $a_q = 1$, and $V(f) = V^+(f^+) + V^-(f^-)$ preserves the order within each F_q.

To show that V preserves the order on the entire set, consider any $f, g \in F$ and suppose $f \gtrsim g$. By transitivity, $c(f) \geq c(g)$ where $c(f)$ is the certainty equivalent of f. Because $c(f)$ and $c(g)$ are comonotonic, $V(f) = V(c(f)) \geq V(c(g)) = V(g)$. Analogously, $f > g$ implies $V(f) > V(g)$, which complete the proof of theorem 1.

Proof of Theorem 2 (part c). To establish the necessity of SCTC, apply cumulative prospect theory to the hypotheses of SCTC to obtain the following inequalities:

$$V(x\{s\}f) = \pi_s v(x) + \sum_{r \in S-s} \pi_r v(f(r))$$

$$\leq \pi'_s v(y) + \sum_{r \in S-s} \pi'_r v(g(r)) = V(y\{s\}g)$$

$$V(x'\{s\}f) = \pi_s v(x') + \sum_{r \in S-s} \pi_r v(f(r))$$

$$\geq \pi'_s v(y') + \sum_{r \in S-s} \pi'_r v(g(r)) = V(y'\{s\}g).$$

The decision weights above are derived, assuming SCTC, in accord with equations (1) and (2). We use primes to distinguish the decision weights associated with g from those associated with f. However, all the above prospects belong to the same comonotonic set. Hence, two outcomes that have the same sign and are associated with the same state have the same decision weight. In particular, the weights associated with $x\{s\}f$ and $x'\{s\}f$ are identical, as are the weights associated with $y\{s\}g$ and with $y'\{s\}g$. These assumptions are implicit in the present notation. It follows that

$$\pi_s v(x) - \pi'_s v(y) \leq \pi_s v(x') - \pi'_s v(y').$$

Because x, y, x', y' have the same sign, all the decision weights associated with state s are identical, that is, $\pi_s = \pi'_s$. Cancelling this common factor and rearranging terms yields $v(v) - v(y') \geq v(x) - v(x')$.

Suppose SCTC is not valid, that is, $x\{t\}f \succsim y\{t\}g'$ but $x'\{t\}f' < y'\{t\}g'$. Applying cumulative prospect theory, we obtain

$$V(x\{t\}f') = \pi_t v(x) + \sum_{r \in S-t} \pi_r v(f'(r))$$

$$\geq \pi_t v(y) + \sum_{r \in S-t} \pi_r v(g'(r)) = V(y\{t\}g')$$

$$V(x'\{t\}f') = \pi_t v(x') + \sum_{r \in S-t} \pi_r v(f'(r))$$

$$< \pi_t v(y') + \sum_{r \in S-t} \pi_r v(g'(r)) = V(y'\{t\}g').$$

Adding these inequalities yields $v(x) - v(x') > v(y) - v(y')$ contrary to the previous conclusion, which establishes the necessity of SCTC. The necessity of double matching is immediate.

To prove sufficiency, note that SCTC implies comonotonic independence. Letting $x = y$, $x' = y'$, and $f = g$ in TC yields $x\{t\}f' \gtrsim x\{t\}g'$ implies $x'\{t\}f' \gtrsim x'\{t\}g'$, provided all the above prospects are pairwise comonotonic. This condition readily entails comonotonic independence (see Wakker, 1989b).

To complete the proof, note that SCTC coincides with CTC on $(F^+, \gtrsim)$ and on $(F^-, \gtrsim)$. By part b of this theorem, the cumulative functional holds, separately, in the nonnegative and in the nonpositive domains. Hence, by double matching and comonotonic independence, cumulative prospect theory follows from theorem 1.

Notes

An earlier version of this article was entitled "Cumulative Prospect Theory: An Analysis of Decision under Uncertainty."

This article has benefited from discussions with Colin Camerer, Chew Soo-Hong, David Freedman, and David H. Krantz. We are especially grateful to Peter P. Wakker for his invaluable input and contribution to the axiomatic analysis. We are indebted to Richard Gonzalez and Amy Hayes for running the experiment and analyzing the data. This work was supported by Grants 89-0064 and 88-0206 from the Air Force Office of Scientific Research, by Grant SES-9109535 from the National Science Foundation, and by the Sloan Foundation.

1. In keeping with the spirit of prospect theory, we use the decumulative form for gains and the cumulative form for losses. This notation is vindicated by the experimental findings described in section 2.

2. This model appears under different names. We use *cumulative utility theory* to describe the application of a Choquet integral to a standard utility function, and *cumulative prospect theory* to describe the application of two separate Choquet integrals to the value of gains and losses.

3. Camerer and Ho (1991) applied equation (6) to several studies of risky choice and estimated γ from aggregate choice probabilities using a logistic distribution function. Their mean estimate (.56) was quite close to ours.

4. Wakker (1989b) called this axiom *comonotonic coordinate independence*. Schmeidler (1989) used *comonotonic independence* for the mixture space version of this axiom: $f \gtrsim g$ iff $\alpha f + (1 - \alpha)h \gtrsim \alpha g + (1 - \alpha)h$.

5. Wakker (1989a, 1989b) called this property *cardinal coordinate independence*. He also introduced an equivalent condition, called the absence of *contradictory tradeoffs*.

References

Allais, Maurice. (1953). "Le comportement de l'homme rationel devant le risque, critique des postulates et axiomes de l'ecole americaine," *Econometrica* 21, 503–546.

Arrow, Kenneth J. (1982). "Risk Perception in Psychology and Economics," *Economic Inquiry* 20, 1–9.

Camerer, Colin F. (1989). "An Experimental Test of Several Generalized Utility Theories," *Journal of Risk and Uncertainty* 2, 61–104.

Camerer, Colin F. (1992). "Recent Tests of Generalizations of Expected Utility Theory." In W. Edwards (ed.), *Utility: Theories, Measurement and Applications*, Boston, MA: Kluwer Academic Publishers.

Camerer, Colin F. and Teck-Hua Ho. (1991). "Nonlinear Weighting of Probabilities and Violations of the Betweenness Axiom." Unpublished manuscript, The Wharton School, University of Pennsylvania.

Chew, Soo-Hong. (1989). "An Axiomatic Generalization of the Quasilinear Mean and the Gini Mean with Application to Decision Theory," Unpublished manuscript, Department of Economics, University of California at Irvine.

Choquet, Gustave. (1955). "Theory of Capacities," *Annales de L'Institut Fourier* 5, 131–295.

Cohen, Michele, Jean-Yves Jaffray, and Tanios Said. (1987). "Experimental Comparison of Individual Behavior Under Risk and Under Uncertainty for Gains and for Losses," *Organizational Behavior and Human Decision Processes* 39, 1–22.

Ellsberg, Daniel. (1961). "Risk, Ambiguity, and the Savage Axioms," *Quarterly Journal of Economics* 75, 643–669.

Fishburn, Peter C. (1988). *Nonlinear Preference and Utility Theory*. Baltimore, MD: The Johns Hopkins University Press.

Gilboa, Itzhak. (1987). "Expected Utility with Purely Subjective Non-additive Probabilities," *Journal of Mathematical Economics* 16, 65–88.

Heath, Chip and Amos Tversky. (1991). "Preference and Belief: Ambiguity and Competence in Choice Under Uncertainty," *Journal of Risk and Uncertainty* 4, 5–28.

Hershey, John C. and Paul J. H. Schoemaker. (1980). "Prospect Theory's Reflection Hypothesis: A Critical Examination," *Organizational Behavior and Human Performance* 25, 395–418.

Hogarth, Robin and Hillel Einhorn. (1990). "Venture Theory: A Model of Decision Weights," *Management Science* 36, 780–803.

Kachelmeier, Steven J. and Mohamed Shehata. (1991). "Examining Risk Preferences Under High Monetary Incentives: Experimental Evidence from The People's Republic of China," *American Economic Review*, forthcoming.

Kahneman, Daniel, Paul Slovic, and Amos Tversky (eds.). (1982). *Judgment Under Uncertainty: Heuristics and Biases*. New York: Cambridge University Press.

Kahneman, Daniel and Amos Tversky. (1979). "Prospect Theory: An Analysis of Decision Under Risk," *Econometrica* 47, 263–291.

Kahneman, Daniel and Amos Tversky. (1984). "Choices, Values and Frames," *American Psychologist* 39, 341–350.

Loomes, Graham and Robert Sugden. (1987). "Regret Theory: An Alternative Theory of Rational Choice Under Uncertainty," *The Economic Journal* 92, 805–824.

Loomes, Graham and Robert Sugden. (1987). "Some Implications of a More General Form of Regret Theory," *Journal of Economic Theory* 41, 270–287.

Luce, E. Duncan and Peter C. Fishburn. (1991). "Rank- and Sign-dependent Linear Utility Models for Finite First-order Gambles," *Journal of Risk and Uncertainty* 4, 29–59.

Machina, Mark J. (1987). "Choice Under Uncertainty: Problems Solved and Unsolved," *Economic Perspectives* 1(1), 121–154.

Marschak, Jacob. (1950). "Rational Behavior, Uncertain Prospects, and Measurable Utility," *Econometrica* 18, 111–114.

Nakamura, Yutaka. (1990). "Subjective Expected Utility with Non-additive Probabilities on Finite State Space," *Journal of Economic Theory* 51, 346–366.

Prelec, Drazen. (1989). "On the Shape of the Decision Weight Function." Unpublished manuscript, Harvard Graduate School of Business Administration.

Prelec, Drazen. (1990). "A 'Pseudo-endowment' Effect, and its Implications for Some Recent Nonexpected Utility Models," *Journal of Risk and Uncertainty* 3, 247–259.

Quiggin, John. (1982). "A Theory of Anticipated Utility," *Journal of Economic Behavior and Organization* 3, 323–343.

Savage, Leonard J. (1954). *The Foundations of Statistics*. New York: Wiley.

Schmeidler, David. (1989). "Subjective Probability and Expected Utility without Additivity," *Econometrica* 57, 571–587.

Segal, Uzi. (1989). "Axiomatic Representation of Expected Utility with Rank-dependent Probabilities," *Annals of Operations Research* 19, 359–373.

Smith, Vernon L. and James M. Walker. (1992). "Monetary Rewards and Decision Cost in Experimental Economics," Unpublished manuscript, Economic Science Lab. University of Arizona.

Starmer, Chris and Robert Sugden. (1989). "Violations of the Independence Axiom in Common Ratio Problems: An Experimental Test of Some Competing Hypotheses," *Annals of Operations Research* 19, 79–102.

Tversky, Amos. (1969). "The Intransitivity of Preferences," *Psychology Review* 76, 31–48.

Tversky, Amos and Daniel Kahneman. (1986). "Rational Choice and the Framing of Decisions," *The Journal of Business* 59(4), part 2, S251–S278.

Tversky, Amos and Daniel Kahneman. (1991). "Loss Aversion in Riskless Choice: A Reference Dependent Model," *Quarterly Journal of Economics* 107(4), 1039–1061.

Tversky, Amos, Shmuel Sattath, and Paul Slovic. (1988). "Contingent Weighting in Judgment and Choice," *Psychological Review* 95(3), 371–384.

Tversky, Amos, Paul Slovic, and Daniel Kahneman. (1990). "The Causes of Preference Reversal," *The American Economic Review* 80(1), 204–217.

Viscusi, Kip W. (1989). "Prospective Reference Theory: Toward an Explanation of the Paradoxes," *Journal of Risk and Uncertainty* 2, 235–264.

Wakker, Peter P. (1989a). *Additive Representations of Preferences: A New Foundation in Decision Analysis.* Dordrecht, The Netherlands: Kluwer Academic Publishers.

Wakker, Peter P. (1989b). "Continuous Subjective Expected Utility with Nonadditive Probabilities," *Journal of Mathematical Economics* 18, 1–27.

Wakker, Peter P. (1990). "Separating Marginal Utility and Risk Aversion." Unpublished manuscript, University of Nijmegen, The Netherlands.

Wakker, Peter P. (1991). "Additive Representations of Preferences, a New Foundation of Decision Analysis; the Algebraic Approach." In J. D. Doignon and J. C. Falmagne (eds.), *Mathematical Psychology: Current Developments.* Berlin: Springer, pp. 71–87.

Wakker, Peter P. (1992). "Additive Representations on Rank-ordered Sets; Part II: The Topological Approach," *Journal of Mathematical Economics*, forthcoming.

Wakker, Peter P. and Amos Tversky. (1991). "An Axiomatization of Cumulative Prospect Theory." Unpublished manuscript, University of Nijmegan, the Netherlands.

Wehrung, Donald A. (1989). "Risk Taking over Gains and Losses: A Study of Oil Executives," *Annals of Operations Research* 19, 115–139.

Weymark, J. A. (1981). "Generalized Gini Inequality Indices," *Mathematical Social Sciences* 1, 409–430.

Yaari, Menahem E. (1987). "The Dual Theory of Choice Under Risk," *Econometrica* 55, 95–115.

28 Thinking through Uncertainty: Nonconsequential Reasoning and Choice

Eldar Shafir and Amos Tversky

Much of everyday thinking and decision making involves uncertainty about the objective state of the world and about our subjective moods and desires. We may be uncertain about the future state of the economy, our mood following an upcoming examination, or whether we will want to vacation in Hawaii during the holidays. Different states of the world, of course, often lead to different decisions. If we do well on the exam, we may feel that we deserve a break and want to go to Hawaii; if we do poorly, we may prefer to stay at home. When making decisions under uncertainty we need to consider the possible states of the world and their potential implications for our desires and actions. Uncertain situations may be thought of as disjunctions of possible states: either one state will obtain, or another. A student who is uncertain about her performance on an exam, for instance, faces a disjunction of outcomes: passing the exam or failing the exam. In deciding whether or not to plan a vacation in Hawaii, the student needs to consider whether she would want to go to Hawaii if she were to pass the exam, and whether she would want to go if she were to fail, as diagrammed in figure 28.1. (As is customary, decision nodes are denoted by squares; chance nodes are denoted by circles.)

Most conceptions of decision making under uncertainty—both normative and descriptive—are *consequentialist* in the sense that decisions are determined by an assessment of the potential consequences and their perceived likelihood. According to this view, the student's decision to buy the Hawaiian vacation will depend on her subjective value of staying and going in the event that she passes the exam and in the event that she fails, and on her subjective probability of passing and failing.[1] Choices based on a consequentialist evaluation of anticipated outcomes are expected to satisfy a basic axiom of decision under uncertainty known as Savage's sure-thing principle (Savage, 1954, p. 21). The sure-thing principle (henceforth STP) says that if we prefer x to y given any possible state of the world, then we should prefer x to y even when the exact state of the world is not known. In the context of figure 28.1, it implies that if the student prefers going to staying both if she passes and if she fails the exam, then she should prefer going to staying even when the exam's outcome is not known. STP is an important implication of the consequentialist view. It captures a fundamental intuition of what it means for a decision to be determined by the anticipated consequences. It is a cornerstone of Expected Utility Theory, and it holds in other models which impose less stringent criteria of rationality.

If, however, people do not always choose in a consequentialist manner, then STP may sometimes be violated. For example, we have shown elsewhere that many peo-

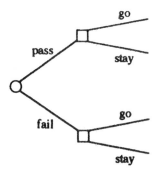

Figure 28.1
A tree diagram for the Hawaiian vacation problem.

ple who chose to purchase a vacation to Hawaii if they were to pass an exam *and* if they were to fail, decided to postpone buying the vacation in the disjunctive case, when the exam's outcome was not known (Tversky & Shafir, 1992). Having passed the exam, the vacation is presumably seen as a time of celebration following a successful semester; having failed the exam, the vacation becomes a consolation and time of recovery. Not knowing the outcome of the exam, we suggest, the decision maker lacks a clear reason for going and, as a result, may prefer to wait and learn the outcome before deciding to go, contrary to STP.

For another example of nonconsequential reasoning, imagine that you have agreed to bet on a toss of a coin in which you had equal chances to win $200 or lose $100. Suppose that the coin has been tossed, but that you do not know whether you have won or lost. Would you now want to play this gamble a second time? Alternatively, how would you feel about accepting the second gamble if you knew that you lost $100 on the first gamble? And finally, would you play the second gamble having discovered that you won $200 on the first gamble? We have shown that, contrary to STP, a majority of respondents accepted the second gamble both after having won as well as after having lost the first, but a majority rejected the second gamble when the outcome of the first was not known (Tversky & Shafir, 1992). This pattern—accept when win, accept when lose, but reject when do not know—was the single most frequent pattern of preferences exhibited by our subjects. We have suggested that people have a good reason for accepting the second gamble following a gain (namely, "I am up and no matter what happens I cannot lose"), and that they have a compelling albeit different reason for accepting the second gamble following a loss (namely, "I am down and this is my chance to get out of the red"). But when the outcome of the first gamble is unknown, people do not know whether they are ahead and cannot lose or whether they are behind and need to recover their losses. In this condition, we have argued, they may have no clear reason for accepting the additional gamble which, on its own, is not particularly attractive. We call the above pattern of preferences a *disjunction effect*. A disjunction effect occurs when people prefer *x* over *y* when they know that event *A* obtains, and they also prefer *x* over *y* when they know that event *A* does not obtain, but they prefer *y* over *x* when it is unknown whether or not *A* obtains. The disjunction effect amounts to a violation of STP, and hence of consequentialism.

In the present chapter we explore nonconsequential behavior in several reasoning and decision making tasks. We suggest that various reasons and considerations are weighted differently in the presence of uncertainty than in its absence, giving rise to violations of STP. Our previous studies explored situations in which the reasons for a particular option (like going to Hawaii, or taking the gamble) were more compelling once the uncertainty was resolved than when the outcome was uncertain. The present studies focus on scenarios in which arguments that seem appealing while the outcome is uncertain lose much of their force once the uncertainty is resolved. It is proposed that the shift in perspective induced by the resolution of uncertainty may shed light on several puzzling manifestations of nonconsequential behavior. In the first part of the chapter we explore one-shot Prisoner's Dilemmas, and a version of Newcomb's Problem played against a computer program. We then extend the analysis from decision making to reasoning. We suggest that nonconsequential reasoning plays an important role in Wason's selection task, and then describe a scenario in which the U.S. financial markets seem to exhibit nonconsequential behavior. Finally, we explore the implications of the present findings to the analysis of thinking in the face of uncertainty, and consider their relevance to the comparison between natural and artificial intelligence.

Games and Decisions

Prisoner's Dilemma

The theory of games provides an analysis of the interaction among players who act according to specific rules. One particular two-person game which has received enormous attention is the Prisoner's Dilemma, or PD for short. (For extensive discussion, see Rapoport & Chammah, 1965; Rapoport, 1988). A typical PD is presented in figure 28.2. The cell entries indicate the payoffs (e.g., the number of points) received by each player. Thus, if both you and your opponent cooperate, each receives 75 points. On the other hand, if the other cooperates and you compete, you

OTHER

	cooperates	competes
cooperate	You: 75 Other: 75	You: 25 Other: 85
compete	You: 85 Other: 25	You: 30 Other: 30

YOU

Figure 28.2
A typical Prisoner's Dilemma. The cell entries indicate the number of points that you and the other player receive contingent on your choices.

receive 85 points while the other receives 25, etc. What characterizes the PD is that regardless of the opponent's choice, each player fares better by competing than by cooperating; yet, if they both compete they do less well than if they had both cooperated. While many interesting strategies arise in the context of repeated games (see, e.g., Axelrod, 1984; Kreps & Wilson, 1982; Luce & Raiffa, 1957), the present discussion is confined to PD's that are played only once.

This is the simplest and sharpest form of a dilemma. Because the opponent is encountered only once, there is no opportunity for conveying strategic messages, inducing reciprocity, developing a reputation, or otherwise influencing the other player's choice of strategy. Because regardless of what the other does on this single encounter you will receive more points if you compete than if you cooperate, the dominant strategy is to compete. Nevertheless, some—presumably on ethical grounds—choose to cooperate. When Douglas Hofstadter (1983) presented a problem of this kind to a group of experts, roughly a third chose cooperation. Similar rates of cooperation were observed in a number of experimental studies (see, e.g., Rapoport, Guyer, & Gordon, 1976; Rapoport, 1988). The philosopher Dan Dennett captured the guiding ethical motivation when he remarked: "I'd rather be the person who bought the Brooklyn Bridge than the person who sold it. Similarly, I'd feel better spending $3 gained by cooperating than $10 gained by defecting." Evidently, some people are willing to forego some gains in order to make the cooperative, ethical decision.

Our previous discussion of nonconsequential reasoning suggests an alternative interpretation of the cooperation observed in one-shot PD games. Once the player knows that the other has chosen either to compete or to cooperate, it is clear that competition will be more advantageous to him than cooperation. But as long as the other has not made his decision, mutual cooperation looms as an attractive solution for both players. Although each player cannot affect the other's decision, he may be tempted to do his best (in this case, cooperate) to bring about the mutually desired state. This reasoning, of course, no longer applies once the outcome has occurred. Voting behavior is a case in point. We know that our individual vote is unlikely to affect the outcome of elections. Nevertheless, many of us who would not bother to vote once the outcome has been determined, are inclined to vote when the outcome of the elections is still pending. If this interpretation of cooperation in the PD game is correct, we expect a greater rate of cooperation in the disjunctive condition, when the other player's strategy is not known, than when the other player has chosen to compete or when the other has chosen to cooperate. This hypothesis is tested in the following study.

Method   Eighty Princeton undergraduates were presented with PD games displayed on a computer screen one at a time, in the format given in figure 28.2. On each trial, they chose whether to compete or cooperate by pressing the appropriate button. Subjects responded at their own pace, and once they chose their strategy, the screen cleared and the next game was presented. Each subject was presented with 40 games, of which only six were PD's. Other two-person games (with different payoff structures) were interspersed among the PD's in order to force subjects to consider each game anew, rather than adopt a "standard" strategy. Subjects were told that these games were being played with other students currently on the computer system, and that the outcomes would be determined by their choice and that of a new participant in each game. Their choices would not be made available to anyone playing with them. Thus, subjects were playing a series of one-shot games, each against a different opponent. In addition, subjects were told that they had been randomly assigned to a bonus group: this meant that, occasionally, they would be given information about the other player's already-chosen strategy before they had to choose their own. This information appeared on the screen along with the game, so that subjects could use it in making their decision. Subjects were to be paid according to the number of points that they accumulated throughout the session. They were paid $6.00 on average, and the entire session lasted approximately 40 min. The complete instructions appear in the appendix.

We focus now on the six PD games that the subjects played. Each of these appeared three times throughout the session: once in the standard version where the other player's strategy was not known, a second time with the information that the

Table 28.1
Prisoner's Dilemma

		Other player competes		
		S competes	*S* cooperates	
A. Other's strategy known[a]				
Other player cooperates	*S* competes	364	7	371 (84%)
	S cooperates	66	7	73 (16%)
		430	14	444
		(97%)	(3%)	
B. Other's strategy not known[b]				
Other player cooperates	*S* competes	113 cooperate	3 cooperate	
		251 compete	4 compete	
	S cooperates	43 cooperate	5 cooperate	
		23 compete	2 compete	

[a] Joint distribution of subjects' (*S*) strategies when the other player competes and when the other player cooperates.
[b] Distribution of subjects' strategies when the other player's strategy is not known, broken down—as in A—according to subjects' choice of strategy when the other player competes and cooperates.

other had competed, and a third time with the information that the other had cooperated. The standard version of each PD game appeared first, and the order of the other two was counterbalanced across subjects. The three versions of each game were separated by a number of other games in between. We refer to the three versions of each PD game as a PD "triad." The first 18 subjects were presented with four PD triads, and the remaining subjects played six PD triads each, yielding a total of 444 triads.

Results and Discussion Subjects' responses to the PD triads are presented in table 28.1. Table 28.1A summarizes subjects' chosen strategies, over all 444 games, when the other player competes and when the other player cooperates. Table 28.1B shows these same subjects' chosen strategy in the disjunctive case, when the other player's strategy is not known. When informed that the other has chosen to compete, the great majority of subjects reciprocate by competing. To cooperate would mean to turn the other cheek and forfeit points. Of the 444 games in which subjects were informed that the other had chosen to compete (table 28.1A), only 3% resulted in cooperation. When informed that the other has chosen to cooperate, a larger percentage of subjects choose cooperation. This confirms the widespread sentiment that there is an ethical inclination to reciprocate when the other cooperates. Of the 444 games in which subjects were told that the other player had cooperated, 16% resulted

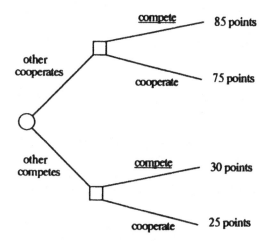

Figure 28.3
A tree diagram illustrating the Prisoner's Dilemma presented in figure 28.2. Decision nodes and chance nodes are denoted by squares and circles, respectively. Modal choices are underlined.

in cooperation. Now what should subjects do when the other's strategy is not known? Since 3% cooperate when the other competes and 16% cooperate when the other cooperates, we would expect an intermediate rate of cooperation when the other's strategy is not known. Instead, of the 444 games in which the other's strategy was unknown (table 28.1B), a full 37% resulted in cooperation (the cooperation rates in the three versions are all significantly different, $p < .001$ in all cases). The increased tendency to cooperate when uncertain about the other's chosen strategy cannot be attributed to a moral imperative of the type articulated by Dennett. Any account based on ethical considerations implies that the rate of cooperation should be highest when the other player is known to have cooperated, contrary to table 28.1.

As expected, competition was the most popular strategy in all conditions. Consequently, the single most frequent choice pattern was to compete in all three versions. The next most frequent pattern, however, representing 25% of all response triads (113 out of 444 triads in table 28.1B), was of the form: compete when the other competes, compete when the other cooperates, but cooperate when the other's strategy is not known. Sixty-five percent of the subjects exhibited such a disjunction effect on at least one of the six PD triads that they played. Of all triads yielding cooperation when the other player's strategy was unknown, 69% resulted in competition both when the other competed and when the other cooperated. This pattern is illustrated using the tree diagram of figure 28.3. The majority of subjects choose to compete at the upper branch (when the other cooperates) as well as at the lower branch (when the other competes). Contrary to STP, however, many cooperate when they do not know on which branch they are.

A behavioral pattern that violates a simple normative rule calls for both a positive analysis, which explains the specific factors that produce the observed response, and a negative analysis, which explains why the correct response is not made (Kahneman & Tversky, 1982). The conjunction fallacy (Tversky & Kahneman, 1983) is a case in point. The positive analysis of this phenomenon has invoked judgmental heuristics, such as availability and representativeness, whereas the negative analysis attributes conjunction errors to people's failure to detect the fact that one event is included in the other, or to their failure to appreciate the implication of this inclusion. Analogously, a negative analysis of the disjunction effect suggests that people do not evaluate appropriately all the relevant outcomes. This may occur because people sometimes fail to consider all the branches of the relevant decision tree, especially when the number of outcomes is large. Alternatively, people may consider all the relevant outcomes but, due to the presence of uncertainty, may not see their own preferences very clearly. Consider the Hawaii scenario described earlier. A person who has just taken the exam but does not know the outcome may feel, without specifically considering the implications of success and failure, that this is not the time to choose to go to Hawaii. Alternatively, the person might contemplate the outcomes, but—uncertain about which outcome will occur—may feel unsure about her own preferences. For example, she may feel confident about wanting to go to Hawaii if she passes the exam, but unsure about whether she would want to go in case she failed. Only when she focuses exclusively on the possibility of failing the exam, does her preference for going to Hawaii become clear. A similar analysis applies to the present PD game. Not knowing the opponent's strategy, a player may realize that he wishes to compete if the other competes, but he may not be sure about his preference if the other were to cooperate. Having focused exclusively on the latter possibility, the player now sees more clearly that he wishes to compete in this case as well. The presence of uncertainty, we suggest, makes it difficult to focus sharply on any single branch; broadening the focus of attention results in a loss of acuity. The failure to appreciate the force of STP, therefore, is attributed to people's reluctance to consider all the outcomes, or to their reluctance to formulate a clear preference in the presence of uncertainty about those outcomes. This interpretation is consistent with the finding that, once people are made aware of their preferences given each possible outcome, STP is no longer violated (Tversky & Shafir, 1992).

Several factors may contribute to a positive analysis of the disjunction effect in the PD game. The game is characterized by the fact that an individually rational decision by each player results in an outcome that is not optimal collectively. Our subjects seem to exhibit a change of perspective that may be described as a shift from individual to collective rationality. Once the other's strategy is known, a player is "on her own." Only one column of the PD table is relevant (that which corresponds to the strategy chosen by the other), and the outcome of the game depends on her and her alone. The individually rational strategy, of course, is to compete. In the disjunctive condition, on the other hand, all four cells of the table are in play. The outcome of the game depends on the collective decision of both players, and the collectively optimal decision is for both to cooperate. Thus, the pattern of behavior observed in the PD may be explained, in part at least, by the greater tendency to adopt the collective perspective in the disjunctive version of the game.[2] Note, incidentally, that collective—albeit uncoordinated—action is quite viable. To the extent that our nonconsequentialist subjects play against one another, they stand to receive more points (for reaching the cooperate–cooperate cell) than would be awarded to consequentialist subjects (for their compete–compete cell). The potential benefits of cooperation in social dilemmas are discussed by Dawes and Orbell (1992).

A consequentialist subject who chooses to compete both when the other competes and when the other cooperates, should also compete when the other's decision—as is usually the case—is not known. Instead, uncertainty promotes a tendency to cooperate, which disappears once the other player's decision has been determined. It appears that many subjects did not appropriately evaluate each possible outcome and its implications. Rather, when the opponent's response was not known, many subjects preferred to cooperate, perhaps as a way of "inducing" cooperation from the other. Because subjects naturally assume that the other player—a fellow student—will approach the game in much the same way they do, whatever they decide to do, it seems, the other is likely to do the same. Along these lines, Messe and Sivacek (1979) have argued that people overestimate the likelihood that others will act the way they do in mixed-motive games. Such an attitude may lead subjects to cooperate in the hope of achieving joint cooperation and thereby obtaining the largest mutual benefit, rather than compete and risk joint competition. If they were able to coordinate a binding agreement, subjects would certainly agree on mutual cooperation. Being unable to secure a binding agreement in the PD game, subjects are nevertheless tempted to act in accord with the agreement that both players would have endorsed. Although they cannot actually affect the other's decision, subjects choose to "do their share" to bring about the mutually preferred state. This interpretation is consistent with the finding of Quattrone and Tversky (1984) that people often select actions that are diagnostic of favorable outcomes even though they do not cause those outcomes. A discussion of the relation between causal and diagnostic reasoning is resumed in the next section.

We have interpreted violations of STP in the above PD games as an indication that people do not evaluate the outcomes in a consequentialist manner. We now consider two alternative interpretations of the above findings. First, subjects might have cooperated in the disjunctive version of the game because they were afraid that their choices will be relayed to the other player before she had made her decision. This concern, of course, would not arise once the other's decision has already been made. Recall that subjects were specifically told that their choices would not be communicated to anyone playing with them. Nevertheless, they could have been suspicious. Post-experimental interviews, however, revealed that while a few subjects were suspicious about the actual, simultaneous presence of other players on the system, none were concerned that their choices would be surreptitiously divulged. It is unlikely that suspicion could account for subjects' strategies in the present experiment.

Second, it could be argued that the present results can be explained by the hypothesis that the tendency to compete increases as the experiment progresses. In order to observe subjects' untainted strategies in the standard prisoner's dilemmas, we presented these games before the known-outcome games. Hence, an increase in the tendency to compete as the experiment progressed could contribute to the observed pattern because the disjunctive problems—where cooperation was highest —generally occurred earlier in the experiment. However, no such temporal change was observed. The rate of cooperation in the first disjunction encountered (the sixth game played), the fourth disjunction (game number 15), and the last disjunction (game number 19), were 33%, 30%, and 40%, respectively. Similarly, the rate of cooperation when subjects were told that the other had cooperated averaged 13% for the first three occurrences and 21% for the last three. In effect, cooperation tended to increase as the experiment progressed, which would diminish the observed frequency of disjunction effects.

Recall that, like Hofstadter's experts, nearly 40% of our subjects chose to cooperate in a single-shot Prisoner's Dilemma. Once they discovered the other's strategy, however, nearly 70% of these cooperators chose to compete both when the other competed and when the other cooperated. These players followed a variant of Kant's Categorical Imperative: act in the way you wish others to act. They felt less compelled, however, to act in ways others have already acted. This pattern suggests that some of the cooperation observed in one-shot PD games may stem not from a moral imperative of the kind described by Dennett but, rather, from a combination of wishful thinking and nonconsequential evaluation. A similar analysis may apply to a related decision problem to which we turn next.

Newcomb's Problem

First published by Nozick (1969), Newcomb's Problem has since generated a lively philosophical debate that touches upon the nature of rational decision. The standard version of the problem proceeds roughly as follows.

Suppose that you have two options: to take the contents of a closed box in front of you, or to take the contents of the closed box *plus* another, open box that you can see contains $1000 in cash. The closed box contains either one million dollars ($M) or nothing, depending on whether a certain being with miraculous powers of foresight, called the Predictor, has or has not placed $M there prior to the time at which you are to make your decision. You know that the Predictor will have placed the $M in the closed box if he has predicted that you will choose the closed box alone; he will have left the closed box empty if he has predicted that you will choose both boxes. You also know that almost everyone who has chosen both boxes found the closed box empty and received just $1000, while almost everyone who has chosen just the closed box has found $M in it. What is your choice?

A number of authors (e.g., Brams, 1975; Lewis, 1979; Sobel, 1991) have commented on the logical affinity of Newcomb's Problem with the Prisoner's Dilemma. In both cases, the outcome depends on the choice that you make and on that made by another being—the other player in the Prisoner's Dilemma, and the Predictor in Newcomb's Problem. In both cases, one option (competing or taking both boxes) dominates the other, yet the other option (cooperating or taking just one box) seems preferable if the being—the Predictor or the other player—knows what you will do, or will act like you.

The conflicting intuitions generated by Newcomb's problem proceed roughly as follows (see Nozick, 1969, for a more complete treatment).

ARGUMENT 1 (FOR ONE BOX). If I choose both boxes, the Predictor, almost certainly, will have predicted this and will not have put the $M in the closed box, and so I will get only $1000. If I take only the closed box, the Predictor, almost certainly, will have predicted this and will have put the $M in that box, and so I will get $M. Thus, if I take both boxes I, almost certainly, will get $1000, and if I take just the closed box I, almost certainly, will get $M. Therefore, I should choose just the closed box.

ARGUMENT 2 (FOR TWO BOXES). The Predictor has already made his prediction and has already either put the $M in the closed box or has not. If the Predictor has already put the $M in the closed box, and I take both boxes I get $M + $1000, whereas if I take only the closed box, I get only $M. If the Predictor has not put the $M in the closed box, and I take both boxes I get $1000, whereas if I take only the closed box I get no money. Therefore, whether the $M is there or not, I get $1000 more by taking both boxes rather than only the closed box. So I should take both boxes.

When Martin Gardner (1973, 1974) published Newcomb's Problem in *Scientific American* and invited readers to send in their responses, roughly 70% of the readers who indicated a preference found Argument 1 more compelling and chose to take just the closed box, while 30% were driven by Argument 2 to take both boxes.

Argument 2 relies on consequential reasoning reminiscent of STP, namely, whatever the state of the boxes, I will do better choosing both boxes than one only. Argument 1, on the other hand, is more problematic. While couched in terms of expected utility, it seems to suppose that what the Predictor will have predicted—although he has done so already—depends somehow on what I decide to do now. Excluding trickery, there are two interpretations of the Predictor's unusual powers. According to the first interpretation, the Predictor is simply an excellent judge of human character. Using some database (including, e.g., gender, background, and appearance), a predictor might be able to predict the decision maker's response with remarkable success. If this interpretation is correct, then you have no reason to take just one box: however insightful the Predictor's forecast, you will do better if you take both boxes rather than one box only. The second interpretation is that the Predictor has truly supernatural powers of insight. If you are unwilling to dismiss this possibility, then you may be justified in deferring to the mysterious powers of the Predictor and taking just one box (cf., Bar-Hillel & Margalit, 1972). This puzzle has captured the imagination of many people. An interesting collection of articles on Newcomb's Problem and its relation to the Prisoner's Dilemma is provided in Campbell & Sowden (1985).

Like Gardner's readers, many people presented with Newcomb's problem opt for one box only, contrary to the consequential logic of Argument 2. The choice of the single box may result from a belief in the Predictor's supernatural abilities. Alternatively, it may reflect a nonconsequential evaluation of the options in question. To distinguish between these interpretations, we created a credible version of Newcomb's problem that involves no supernatural elements. The role of the predictor is played by a fictitious computer program, whose predictions of subjects' choices are based on a previously established database. The experiment proceeded as follows. Upon completing the PD study described in the previous section, subjects ($N = 40$) were presented with the following scenario, displayed on the computer screen:

You now have one more chance to collect additional points. A program developed recently at MIT was applied during this entire session to analyze the pattern of your preferences. Based on that analysis, the program has predicted your preference in this final problem.

20 points	?
Box A	Box B

Consider the two boxes above. Box A contains 20 points for sure. Box B may or may not contain 250 points. Your options are to:

(1) Choose both boxes (and collect the points that are in both).

(2) Choose Box B only (and collect only the points that are in Box B).

If the program predicted, based on observation of your previous preferences, that you will take both boxes, then it left Box B empty. On the other hand, if it predicted that you will take only Box B, then it put 250 points in that box. (So far, the program has been remarkably successful: 92% of the participants who chose only Box B found 250 points in it, as opposed to 17% of those who chose both boxes.)

To insure that the program does not alter its guess after you have indicated your preference, please indicate to the person in charge whether you prefer both boxes or Box B only. After you indicate your preference, press any key to discover the allocation of points.

This scenario provides a believable version of Newcomb's Problem. While the computer program is quite successful, it is by no means infallible.[3] Also, any suspicion of backward causality has been removed: assuming the experimenter does not cheat in some sophisticated fashion (and our post-experimental interviews indicated that no subject thought he would), it is clear that the program's prediction has been made, and can be observed at any point, without further feedback about the subject's decision. This problem has a clear "common cause" structure (see Eells, 1982): the subject's strategic tendencies in games of this kind, as observed in the preceding PD games, are supposedly predictive of both his preferred strategy in the next game and of the prediction made by the program. While the choice of a single box is diagnostic of the presence of 250 points in it, there can be no relevant causal influence between the two events. Under these conditions, there seems to be no defensible rationale for taking just one box. As Nozick (1969) points out, "if the actions or decisions ... do not affect, help bring about, influence, and so on *which* state obtains, then whatever the conditional probabilities ..., one should perform the dominant action," namely, take both boxes. In this situation, it would appear, people should choose both boxes since both boxes are better than one no matter what.

The results were as follows: 35% (14 of the 40 subjects) chose both boxes, while 65% preferred to take Box B only. The present scenario, which removed all supernatural elements from the original formulation of Newcomb's problem, yielded roughly the same proportions of choices for one and for both boxes as those obtained by Gardner from the readers of *Scientific American*. What can be said about the majority of subjects who preferred to take just one box? Had they known for certain that the 250 points were in that box (and could see that 20 were in the other), they surely would have taken both rather than just one. And certainly, if they knew that the 250 points were not in that box, they would have taken both rather than just the one that is empty. These subjects, in other words, would have taken both boxes had they known that Box B is full, and they also would have taken both boxes had they known that Box B is empty. Consequentialist subjects should then choose both boxes even when it is not known whether Box B is full or empty. The majority, however, chose Box B alone when its contents were not known. Note that the hypothesis, discussed earlier, that attributes the disjunction effect to subjects' failure to predict their own preferences, cannot account for the present finding. No subject would have had any difficulty predicting his preference for more rather than fewer points, had he considered the possible states of the unknown box. Evidently, many subjects do not consider separately the consequences of the program's predictions, and as a result succumb to the temptation to choose the single box, which happens to be correlated with the higher prize.

Quasi-magical Thinking   Magical thinking refers to the erroneous belief that one can influence an outcome (e.g., the role of a die) by some symbolic or other indirect act (e.g., imagining a particular number) even though the act has no causal link to the outcome. We introduce the term quasi-magical thinking to describe cases in which people act as if they erroneously believe that their action influences the outcome, even though they do not really hold that belief. As in the Prisoner's Dilemma, the pattern of preferences observed in Newcomb's problem, may be described as quasi-magical thinking. When the program's prediction is known, the outcome depends entirely on the subject's decision and the obvious choice is to take both boxes. But as long as the program's prediction is not known and the eventual outcome depends on the behavior of both subject and program, there is a temptation to act as if one's decision could affect the program's prediction. As Gibbard and Harper (1978) suggest in an attempt to explain people's choice of a single box, "a person may ... want to bring about an indication of a desired state of the world, even if it is known that the act that brings about the indication in no way brings about the desired state itself." Most people, of course, do not actually believe that they are able to alter the decision made by the program or the other player. Nevertheless, they feel compelled to "do their bit" in order to bring about the desired outcome. Another demonstration of such quasi-magical thinking was provided by Quattrone and Tversky (1984), whose subjects in effect "cheated" on a medical exam by selecting actions (e.g., holding their hand in very cold water for an extended period of time) that they believed were diagnostic of favorable outcomes (e.g., a strong heart) even though they must have known that their actions could not possibly produce the desired outcomes.

Quasi-magical thinking, we believe, underlies several phenomena related to self-deception and the illusion of control. Quattrone and Tversky (1984), for example, noted that Calvinists act as if their behavior will determine whether they will go to heaven or to hell, despite their belief in divine pre-determination, which entails that their fate has been determined prior to their birth. Several authors, notably Langer

(1975), showed that people often behave as if they can exert control over chance events and, as a result, exhibit different attitudes and place larger bets when betting before rather than after a coin has been tossed (Rothbart & Snyder, 1970; Strickland, Lewicki, & Katz, 1966).[4] Most people, however, do not really believe that they can control the toss of a coin, nor that the choice of a single box in the Newcomb experiment can influence the program's already-made prediction. In these and other cases, people probably know that they cannot affect the outcome, but they act as if they could. It is told of Niels Bohr that, when asked by a journalist about a horse-shoe (purported to bring good luck) hanging over his door, he explained that he of course does not believe in such nonsense, but heard that it helped even if one did not believe.

It is exceedingly difficult, of course, to ascertain what people really believe. The preceding discussion suggests that we cannot always infer belief from action. People may behave as if they could influence uncontrollable events even though they do not actually believe in being able to do so. For example, dice players who throw softly for low numbers and hard for high numbers (Henslin, 1967) may not necessarily believe that the nature of the throw influences the outcome. People who exhibit superstitious behaviors, such as wearing a good luck charm or avoiding crossing a black cat's path, may not actually believe that their actions can affect the future. There is a sense in which quasi-magical thinking appears more rational than magical thinking because it does not commit one to patently absurd beliefs. On the other hand, quasi-magical thinking appears even more puzzling because it undermines the link between belief and action. Whereas magical thinking involves indefensible beliefs, quasi-magical thinking yields inexplicable actions. The presence of uncertainty, we suggest, is a major contributor to quasi-magical thinking; few people act as if they can undo an already certain event by performing an action that is diagnostic of an alternative event. In this vein, subjects in Quattrone and Tversky's (1984) experiment would have been less willing to keep their hands in painfully cold water if they knew that they had strong or weak hearts than when their "diagnosis" was uncertain. And Calvinists would perhaps do fewer good deeds if they knew that they had already been assigned to heaven, or to hell, than while their fate remains a mystery.

General Discussion

As demonstrated in the previous section, people often fail to consider the possible outcomes and consequences of uncertain events. The difficulties of thinking through uncertainty manifest themselves in a variety of situations: they encompass reasoning as well as decision making tasks, and they are observed both inside and outside the laboratory. In the present section, we extend the analysis of nonconsequential evaluation to deductive reasoning and economic forecast.

Wason's Selection Task

One of the best known tasks in research on human reasoning is the selection task, devised by Wason (1966). In a typical version of the task, subjects are presented with four cards, each of which has a letter on one side and a number on the other. Only one side of each card is displayed. For example:

$\boxed{\text{E}}$ $\boxed{\text{D}}$ $\boxed{\text{4}}$ $\boxed{\text{7}}$

Subjects' task is to indicate which cards must be turned over to test the rule: "If there is a vowel on one side of the card, then there is an even number on the other side of the card." The simplicity of the problem is deceptive—the great majority of subjects fail to solve it.[5] Most select only the *E*, or the *E* and the *4* cards, whereas the correct choices are the *E* and the *7* cards. The difficulty of the selection task is puzzling, especially because people generally have no trouble evaluating the relevance of the items that may be hidden on the other side of each card. Wason and Johnson-Laird (1970; see also Wason, 1969) have commented on the discrepancy between subjects' ability to evaluate the relevance of potential outcomes (i.e., to understand the truth conditions of the rule), and their inappropriate selection of the relevant cards. Subjects, for example, understand that neither a vowel nor a consonant on the other side of the *4* card contributes to the possible falsification of the rule, but they choose to turn the *4* card when its other side is not known. Similarly, subjects understand that a consonant on the other side of the *7* card would not falsify the rule and that a vowel *would* falsify it, yet they neglect to turn the *7* card. The above pattern, which resembles a disjunction effect, arises when subjects who are easily able to evaluate the relevance of a specific outcome, fail to apply this knowledge when facing a disjunction of outcomes. As Evans (1984, 458) notes, "this strongly confirms the view that card selections are not based upon any analysis of the consequences of turning the cards." Like the people who postpone the trip to Hawaii when the exam's outcome is not known, and those who cooperate in the disjunctive version of the Prisoner's Dilemma, subjects performing the selection task fail to consider the consequences of each of the events. Instead of considering the consequences of each particular kind of symbol on the other side of the card, they appear to remain behind a veil of uncertainty when the card's other side is not known.

Numerous studies have explored the elusive thought process that underlies subjects' performance on the selection task. Indeed, a complex pattern of content effects has emerged from a number of variations on the original task (see, e.g., Johnson-Laird, Legrenzi, & Legrenzi, 1972; Griggs & Cox, 1982; Wason, 1983; Evans, 1989, for a review; although see also Manktelow & Evans, 1979, for conflicting reports). To explain these findings, researchers have suggested verification biases (Johnson-Laird & Wason, 1970), matching biases (Evans & Lynch, 1973; Evans, 1984), memories of domain-specific experiences (Griggs & Cox, 1982; Manktelow & Evans, 1979), pragmatic reasoning schemas (Cheng & Holyoak, 1985, 1989), and an innate propensity to look out for cheaters (Cosmides, 1989). What these explanations have in common is an account of performance on the selection task that fails to refer to formal reasoning. Instead, people are assumed to focus on items that have been explicitly mentioned, to apply pre-stored knowledge structures, or to remember relevant past experiences. "The inferential processes that occur in these cases," concludes Wason (1983, p. 69), "are not ... instances of 'logical' reasoning." Thus, people find it relatively easy to reason logically about each isolated outcome, but a disjunction of outcomes leads them to suspend logical reasoning. This is reminiscent of the eight-year-olds studied by Osherson and Markman (1974–75) who when asked about a concealed, single-color poker chip, whether it is true that "Either the chip in my hand is yellow or it is not yellow?", responded "I don't know" because they could not see it. While most adults find the poker chip disjunction trivial, subtler disjunctions can lead to a temporary suspension of judgment.

The Disjunction Effect in Financial Markets   One result of nonconsequential decision making is that people will sometimes seek information that has no impact on their decision. In the Hawaii problem described earlier, for example, subjects were willing to effect to pay for information that was not going to change their choice but—as we have interpreted it—was merely going to clarify their reasons for choosing. In a variation on the earlier PD experiment, we presented a new group of subjects with the same PD games, but this time, instead of being told the other's decision, subjects were offered, for a very small fee, the opportunity to learn the other's decision before making their own choice. The great majority of subjects chose to compete regardless of whether the opponent had decided to compete or to cooperate, but on 81% of the trials subjects first chose to pay to discover the opponent's decision. Although this behavior can be attributed to curiosity, we conjecture that people's willingness to pay for the information would have diminished had they realized that it would not affect their decision. Searching for information that has no impact on decision may be quite frequent in situations of uncertainty. For example, we may call to find out whether a beach hotel has a pool before making a reservation, despite the fact we will end up going whether it has a pool or not. One intriguing case of a nonconsequential evaluation of information is provided by the following account regarding the U.S. financial markets.

In the weeks preceding the 1988 U.S. Presidential election, the financial markets in the U.S. remained relatively inactive and stable "because of caution before the Presidential election" (*The New York Times*, Nov. 5, 1988). "Investors were reluctant to make major moves early in a week full of economic uncertainty and 7 days away from the Presidential election" (*The Wall Street Journal*, Nov. 2). The market, reported the *Wall Street Journal*, was "killing time." "There is literally nothing going on, and there probably won't be at least until Wednesday" observed the head of a trading desk at Shearson Lehman Hutton, referring to the day following the election (*WSJ*, Nov. 8). "Once the uncertainty of the election is removed, investors could begin to develop a better feeling about the outlook for the economy, inflation and interest rates," remarked the president of an investment firm (*NYT*, Nov. 2). "The outcome of the election had cast a decided cloud over the market in recent days. Its ture direction is likely to surface rapidly in coming days," explained a portfolio strategist (*NYT*, Nov. 9). And, in fact, immediately following the election, a clear direction surfaced. The dollar plunged sharply to its lowest level in 10 months, and stock and bond prices declined. During the week following Bush's victory the DOW Jones industrial average fell a total of 78 points.[6] "The post-election reality is setting in," explained the co-chairman of an investment committee at Goldman, Sachs & Co. (*WSJ*, Nov. 21). The dollar's decline, explained the analysts, "reflected continued worry about the U.S. trade and budget deficits," "the excitement of the election is over, the honeymoon is over, and economic reality has set back in" (*WSJ*, Nov. 10). The financial markets, said the front page of the *NYT* on November 12, "had generally favored the election of Mr. Bush and had expected his victory, but in the three days since the election they have registered their concern about where he goes from here." Of course, the financial markets would likely have registered at least as much concern had Mr. Dukakis been elected. Most traders agree, wrote the *WSJ* on election day, "the stock market would drop significantly if Democratic candidate Michael Dukakis stages a come-from-behind victory." In fact, the market reacted to Bush's victory just as it would have reacted to Dukakis's. "When I walked in and looked at the screen," explained one trader after the election, "I thought Dukakis had won" (*NYT*, Nov. 10).

After long days of inactivity preceding the election, the market declined immediately following Bush's victory, and certainly would have declined at least as much had Dukakis been the victor. Of course, a thorough analysis of the financial markets' behavior is likely to reveal numerous complications. There is, for example, the possibility that an unexpected margin of victory, a surprising last-minute outcome, could have contributed to the paradoxical effect. As it happens, however, "newspapers and television networks came about as close as polling specialists believe is possible to forecasting the results of [the] election" (*NYT*, Nov. 10, 1988). In the week preceding the election, while some thought a Dukakis "surge" still possible, polls conducted by Gallup, ABC News/*Washington Post*, NBC/*Wall Street Journal*, and *New York Times*/CBS News predicted a Bush victory by an average margin of 9 percentage points, 1 point off the eventual 8-point margin. Similarly, the Democrats were expected to retain control of both the Congress (where they were predicted to pick up one or two seats) and the House of Representatives, which is precisely what occurred. The election results do not appear to have been a surprise. At least on the surface, this incident has all the makings of a disjunction effect: the markets were going to decline if Bush was elected, they were going to decline if Dukakis was elected, but they resisted any change until they knew which of the two had been elected. Being at the node of such a momentous disjunction seems to have stopped Wall Street from seriously addressing the consequences of the election. While either elected official would have led the financial markets to "register their concern about where he goes from here," the interim situation of uncertainty highlighted the need for "caution before the election." After all, how can we worry about "where he goes from here" before we know who is doing the going?

Concluding Comments

Patterns of decision and reasoning that violate STP were observed in simple contexts involving uncertainty. These patterns, we suggest, reflect a failure on the part of people to detect and apply this principle rather than a lack of appreciation for its normative appeal. When we first asked subjects to indicate their preferred course of action under each outcome and only then to make a decision in the disjunctive condition, the majority of subjects who opted for the same option under every outcome chose that option also when the precise outcome was not known (Tversky & Shafir, 1992). The frequency of disjunction effects, in other words, substantially diminishes when the logic of STP is made salient. Like other normative principles of decision making, STP is generally satisfied when its application is transparent, but is sometimes violated when it is not (Tversky & Kahneman, 1986).

A number of factors may contribute to the reluctance to think consequentially. Thinking through an event tree requires people to assume momentarily as true something that may in fact be false. People may be reluctant to make this assumption, especially when another plausible alternative (another branch of the tree) is readily available. It is apparently difficult to devote full attention to each of several branches of an event tree (see also Slovic & Fischhoff, 1977). As a result, people may be reluctant to entertain the various hypothetical branches. Furthermore, they may lack the motivation to traverse the tree simply because they presume, as is often the case, that the problem will not be resolved by separately evaluating the branches. We usually tend to formulate problems in ways that have sifted through the irrelevant disjunctions: those that are left are normally assumed to involve genuine conflict.

The disjunctive scenarios investigated in this chapter were relatively simple, involving just two possible outcomes. Disjunctions of multiple outcomes are more difficult to think through and, as a result, are more likely to give rise to nonconsequential reasoning. This is particularly true for economic, social, or political decisions, where the gravity and complexity of situations may conceal the fact that all possible outcomes are eventually—perhaps for different reasons—likely to lead to a similar decision. Critics of U.S. nuclear first-strike strategies, for example, have maintained that while every plausible array of Russian missiles argues against the viability of an American first-strike, American strategists have insisted on retaining that option while the exact array of Russian arsenals is not known. Of course, the strategies involved in such scenarios are exceedingly complex, but it is conceivable that a first-strike option appears attractive partly *because* the adversary's precise arsenals are not known.

Shortcomings in reasoning have typically been attributed to quantitative limitations of human beings as processors of information. "Hard problems" are typically characterized by reference to the "amount of knowledge required," the "memory load," or the "size of the search space" (cf. Kotovsky, Hayes, & Simon, 1985; Kotovsky & Simon, 1990). These limitations play a critical role in many problems. They explain why we cannot remember all the cards that have previously come up in a poker game, or why we are severely limited in the number of steps that we can plan ahead in a game of chess. Such limitations, however, are not sufficient to account for all that is difficult about thinking. In contrast to many complicated tasks that people perform with relative ease, the problems investigated in this paper are computationally very simple, involving a single disjunction of two well-defined states. The present studies highlight the discrepancy between logical complexity on the one hand and psychological difficulty on the other. In contrast with the "frame problem" (McCarthy & Hayes, 1969; Hayes, 1973), for example, which is trivial for people but exceedingly difficult for AI, the task of thinking through disjunctions is trivial for AI (which routinely implements "tree search" and "path finding" algorithms) but very difficult for people. The failure to reason consequentially may constitute a fundamental difference between natural and artificial intelligence.

Appendix
Instructions Given to Subjects in Prisoner's Dilemma Game

Welcome to the Intercollegiate Computer Game. The game will be conducted on an IBM PC. In this game you will be presented with situations involving you and one other player. Each situation will require that you make a strategic decision: to cooperate or to compete with the other player. The other player will have to make a similar decision.

Each situation will present a payoff-matrix that will determine how many points each of you earns depending on whether you compete or cooperate. One such matrix looks like the following.

	Other cooperates	Other competes
You cooperate	You: 20	You: 5
	Other: 20	Other: 25
You compete	You: 25	You: 10
	Other: 5	Other: 10

According to this matrix, if you both cooperate you will both earn a considerable number of points (20 points each). If you cooperate and the other competes, the other will earn 25 points and you will earn only 5 points. Similarly, if you compete and the other cooperates, you will earn 25 points and the other will earn only 5 points. Finally, if you both choose to compete, you will earn only 10 points each.

You will be presented with numerous matrices of the kind shown above. In each case, you will be asked to indicate whether you choose to compete or to cooperate. As in the matrix above, you will frequently do rather well if you both cooperate, you will do worse if you both compete, and one will often do better than the other if one competes and the other cooperates.

You will be playing with other students who are currently on the computer system. For each new matrix you will be matched with a different person. Thus, you will never play against the same person more than once.

You have been arbitrarily assigned to the bonus group. A random bonus program will occasionally inform you of the strategy that the other player has already chosen.

Thus, for example, upon being presented with a new matrix, you may be told that the other player has chosen to compete. You are free to use the bonus information to help you choose your own strategy. (Your strategy will not be revealed to anyone who is playing with you.)

At the end of the game, the points that you accumulate will be converted (via a pre-determined algorithm) to actual money that will be paid to you. The more points you accumulate, the more money you will earn.

Of course, there are no "correct" choices. People typically find certain situations more conductive to cooperation and others to competition. The matrices differ significantly, and their outcomes depend both on your choice and on that of a different player at each turn. Please observe each matrix carefully and decide separately on your preferred strategy in each particular case. Also, be sure to note those cases where the bonus program informs you of the other player's choice. If you have any questions, please ask the person in charge. Otherwise, turn to the terminal and begin.

Notes

This research was supported by US Public Health Service Grant 1-R29-MH46885 from the National Institute of Mental Health to the first author, by Grant 89-0064 from the Air Force Office of Scientific Research to the second author, and by a grant from the Hewlett Foundation to the Stanford Center on Conflict and Negotiation.

1. The notion of consequentialism appears in the philosophical and decision theoretic literature in a number of different senses. See, e.g., Hammond (1988), Levi (1991), and Bacharach and Hurley (1991) for technical discussion.

2. A "collective action" interpretation of cooperative behavior in one-shot PD games is proposed by Hurley (1989, 1991). She interprets such behavior as "quite rational" since, according to her, it is motivated by "a concern to be part of, do one's part in, participate in . . . a valuable form of collective agency" (1989, p. 150). As with the ethical arguments mentioned earlier, however, this interpretation entails that subjects should certainly be inclined to cooperate when the other has cooperated, contrary to the present findings.

3. In retrospect, the remarkably simple program, "Put 250 points in Box B if the subject has produced at least two disjunction effects in the PD experiment; otherwise, leave Box B empty," would have rewarded 70% of the one-boxers and only 29% of the two-boxers with 250 points in Box B. More sophisticated rules cold probably come closer to the alleged performance of the MIT program.

4. One may distinguish between uncertainty about the outcome of a future event and uncertainty about the outcome of an event that has already occurred. While the present study does not systematically differentiate between the two, Greene and Yolles (1990) present data which give reason to expect more non-consequential reasoning in the former than the latter.

5. The success rate of initial choices in dozens of studies employing the basic form of the selection task (with "abstract" materials) typically ranges between 0 and somewhat over 20%. See Evans (1989) and Gilhooly (1988) for reviews.

6. Some believed that the central banks were actually involved in preventing the dollar from plummeting just before the U.S. presidential election (see, e.g., *WSJ*, 11/2–4).

References

Axelrod, R. (1984). *The evolution of cooperation*. New York: Basic Books.

Bacharach, M., & Hurley, S. (1991). Issues and advances in the foundations of decision theory. In M. Bacharach & S. Hurley (Eds.), *Foundations of decision theory: Issues and advances* (pp. 1–38). Oxford: Basil Blackwell.

Bar-Hillel, M., & Margalit, A. (1972). Newcomb's paradox revisited. *British Journal for the Philosophy of Science*, 23, 295–304.

Brams, S. J. (1975). Newcomb's Problem and Prisoner's Dilemma. *Journal of Conflict Resolution*, 19(4), 596–612.

Campbell, R., & Sowden, L. (Eds.). (1985). *Paradoxes of rationality and cooperation: Prisoner's Dilemma and Newcomb's Problem*. Vancouver: The University of British Columbia Press.

Cheng, P. W., & Holyoak, K. J. (1985). Pragmatic reasoning schemas. *Cognitive Pyschology*, 17, 391–416.

Cheng, P. W., & Holyoak, K. J. (1989). On the natural selection of reasoning theories. *Cognition*, 33, 285–313.

Cosmides, L. (1989). The logic of social exchange: has natural selection shaped how humans reason? *Cognition*, 31, 187–276.

Dawes, R. M., & Orbell, J. M. (1992). The potential benefit of optional play in a one-shot prisoner's dilemma game. To appear in K. Arrow et al. (Eds.), *Barriers to conflict resolution*, New York: Norton.

Eells, E. (1982). *Rational decision and causality*. Cambridge: Cambridge University Press.

Evans, J. St B. T. (1984). Heuristic and analytic processes in reasoning. *British Journal of Psychology*, 75, 451–468.

Evans, J. St B. T. (1989). *Bias in human reasoning: Causes and consequences*. Hillsdale, NJ: Lawrence Erlbaum Associates.

Evans, J. St B. T., & Lynch, J. S. (1973). Matching bias in the selection task. *British Journal of Psychology*, 64, 391–397.

Gardner, M. (1973, July). Free will revisited, with a mind-bending prediction paradox by William Newcomb. *Scientific American*, Vol. 229, No. 1, pp. 104–108.

Gardner, M. (1974, March). Reflections on Newcomb's problem: a prediction and free-will dilemma. *Scientific American*, Vol. 230, No. 3, pp. 102–109.

Gibbard, A., & Harper, W. L. (1978). Counterfactuals and two kinds of expected utility. In C. A. Hooker, J. J. Leach, & E. F. McClennen, (Eds.), *Foundations and applications of decision theory* (Vol. 1, pp. 125–162). Dordrecht: Reidel.

Gilhooly, K. J. (1988). *Thinking: Directed, undirected, and creative* (2nd ed). San Diego, CA: Academic Press.

Greene, S. B., & Yolles, D. J. (1990). *Perceived determinacy of unknown outcomes*. Unpublished manuscript, Princeton University.

Griggs, R. A., & Cox, J. R. (1982). The elusive thematic-materials effect in Wason's selection task. *British Journal of Psychology*, 73, 407–420.

Hammond, P. (1988). Consequentialist foundations for expected utility. *Theory and Decision*, 25, 25–78.

Hayes, P. (1973). The frame problem and related problems in artificial intelligence. In A. Elithorn & D. Jones (Eds.), *Artificial and human thinking*. San Francisco: Jossey-Bass.

Henslin, J. M. (1967). Craps and magic. *American Journal of Sociology*, 73, 316–330.

Hofstadter, D. R. (1983, June). Dilemmas for superrational thinkers, leading up to a luring lottery. *Scientific American*. Reprinted in Hofstadter, D. R. (1985). *Metamagical themas: Questing for the essence of mind and pattern*. New York: Basic Books.

Hurley, S. L. (1989). *Natural reasons: Personality and Polity*. New York: Oxford University Press.

Hurley, S. L. (1991). Newcomb's Problem, Prisoner's Dilemma, and collective action. *Synthese*, 86, 173–196.

Johnson-Laird, P. N., Legrenzi, P., & Legrenzi, S. M. (1972). Reasoning and a sense of reality. *British Journal of Psychology*, 63, 395–400.

Johnson-Laird, P. N., & Wason, P. C. (1970). A theoretical analysis of insight into a reasoning task. *Cognitive Psychology*, 1, 134–148.

Kahneman, D., & Tversky, A. (1982). On the study of statistical intuitions. *Cognition*, 11, 123–141.

Kotovsky, K., Hayes, J. R., & Simon, H. A. (1985). Why are some problems hard?: Evidence from Tower of Hanoi. *Cognitive Psychology*, 17, 284–294.

Kotovsky, K., & Simon, H. A. (1990). What makes some problems really hard: Explorations in the problem space of difficulty. *Cognitive Psychology*, 22, 143–183.

Kreps, D., & Wilson, R. (1982). Reputations and imperfect information. *Journal of Economic Theory*, 27, 253–279.

Langer, E. J. (1975). The illusion of control. *Journal of Personality and Social Psychology*, 32, 311–328.

Levi, I. (1991). Consequentialism and sequential choice. In M. Bacharach & S. Hurley (Eds.), *Foundations of decision theory: Issues and advances* (pp. 92–122). Oxford: Basil Blackwell.

Lewis, D. (1979). Prisoner's Dilemma is a Newcomb Problem. *Philosophy and Public Affairs*, 8, 235–240.

Luce, R. D., & Raiffa, H. (1957). *Games and decisions*. New York: Wiley.

Manktelow, K. I., & Evans, J. St B. T. (1979). Facilitation of reasoning by realism: Effect or non-effect? *British Journal of Psychology*, 70, 477–488.

McCarthy, J., & Hayes, P. (1969). Some philosophical problems from the standpoint of Artificial Intelligence. In B. Meltzer & D. Michie (Eds.), *Machine intelligence*. New York: American Elsevier.

Messe, L. A., & Sivacek, J. M. (1979). Predictions of others' responses in a mixed-motive game: Self-justification or false consensus? *Journal of Personality and Social Psychology*, 37(4), 602–607.

Nozick, R. (1969). Newcomb's problem and two principles of choice. In Nicholas Rescher (Ed.), *Essays in honor of Carl G. Hempel*. Dordrecht: Reidel.

Osherson, D. N., & Markman, E. (1974–75). Language and the ability to evaluate contradictions and tautologies. *Cognition*, 3(3), 213–226.

Quattrone, G. A., & Tversky, A. (1984). Causal versus diagnostic contingencies: On self-deception and on the voter's illusion. *Journal of Personality and Social Psychology*, 46(2), 237–248.

Rapoport, A. (1988). Experiments with n-person social traps I: Prisoner's Dilemma, weak Prisoner's Dilemma, Volunteer's Dilemma, and Largest Number. *Journal of Conflict Resolution*, 32(3), 457–472.

Rapoport, A., & Chammah, A. (1965). *Prisoner's Dilemma*. Ann Arbor: University of Michigan Press.

Rapoport, A., Guyer, M. J., & Gordon, D. G. (1976). *The 2 × 2 game*. Ann Arbor: University of Michigan Press.

Rothbart, M., & Snyder, M. (1970). Confidence in the prediction and postdiction of an uncertain event. *Canadian Journal of Behavioral Science*, 2, 38–43.

Savage, L. J. (1954). *The foundations of statistics*. New York: Wiley & Sons.

Slovic, P., & Fischhoff, B. (1977). On the psychology of experimental surprises. *Journal of Experimental Psychology: Human Perception and Performance*, 3, 544–551.

Sobel, J. H. (1991). Some versions of Newcomb's Problem are Prisoner's Dilemmas. *Synthese*, 86, 197–208.

Strickland, L. H., Lewicki, R. J., & Katz, A. M. (1966). Temporal orientation and perceived control as determinants of risk-taking. *Journal of Experimental Social Psychology*, 2, 143–151.

Tversky, A., & Kahneman, D. (1983). Extensional versus intuitive reasoning: The conjunction fallacy in probability judgment. *Psychological Review*, 90, 293–315.

Tversky, A., & Kahneman, D. (1986). Rational choice and the framing of decisions. *Journal of Business*, 59(4, 2), 251–278.

Tversky, A., & Shafir, E. (1992). The disjunction effect in choice under uncertainty. *Psychological Science*, in press.

Wason, P. C. (1966). Reasoning. In B. M. Foss (Ed.), *New horizons in psychology* (Vol. 1). Harmandsworth: Penguin.

Wason, P. C. (1969). Structural simplicity and psychological complexity: Some thoughts on a novel problem. *Bulletin of the British Psychological Society*, 22, 281–284.

Wason, P. C. (1983). Realism and rationality in the selection task. In J. St B. T. Evans (Ed.), *Thinking and reasoning: Psychological approaches*. London: Routledge & Kegan Paul.

Wason, P. C., & Johnson-Laird, P. N. (1970). A conflict between selecting and evaluating information in an inferential task. *British Journal of Psychology*, 61, 509–515.

29 Conflict Resolution: A Cognitive Perspective

Daniel Kahneman and Amos Tversky

Many different disciplines deal with the resolution of conflict. Even within the single discipline of psychology, conflict can be approached from different perspectives. For example, there is an emotional aspect to interpersonal conflict, and a comprehensive psychological treatment of conflict should address the role of resentment, anger, and revenge. In addition, conflict resolution and negotiation are processes that generally extend over time, and no treatment that ignores their dynamics can be complete. In this chapter we do not attempt to develop, or even sketch, a comprehensive psychological analysis of conflict resolution. Instead, we explore some implications for conflict resolution of a particular cognitive analysis of individual decision making. We focus on three relevant phenomena: optimistic overconfidence, the certainty effect, and loss aversion. Optimistic overconfidence refers to the common tendency of people to overestimate their ability to predict and control future outcomes; the certainty effect refers to the common tendency to overweight outcomes that are certain relative to outcomes that are merely probable; and loss aversion refers to the asymmetry in the evaluation of positive and negative outcomes, in which losses loom larger than the corresponding gains. We shall illustrate these phenomena, which were observed in studies of individual judgment and choice, and discuss how these biases could hinder successful negotiation. The present discussion complements the treatment offered by Neale and Bazerman (1991).

Some preliminary remarks are in order. First, the three phenomena described above represent departures from the rational theory of judgment and decision making. The barriers to conflict resolution discussed in this chapter, therefore, would be reduced or eliminated if people were to behave in accord with the standard rational model. It would be inappropriate to conclude, however, that departures from rationality always inhibit the resolution of conflict. There are many situations in which less-than-rational agents may reach agreement while perfectly rational agents do not. The prisoner's dilemma is a classic example in which rationality may not be conducive for achieving the most desirable social solution. The present chapter focuses on the obstacles imposed by the presence of optimistic overconfidence, the certainty effect, and loss aversion. We do not wish to imply, however, that these phenomena are necessarily detrimental to conflict resolution.

Optimistic Overconfidence

In this section we discuss two phenomena of judgment that have each attracted a considerable amount of research attention in recent years: overconfidence and optimism. Overconfidence in human judgment is indicated by a cluster of robust findings: uncalibrated assignments of probability that are more extreme than the judge's knowledge can justify (Lichtenstein, Fischhoff, and Phillips 1982), confidence intervals that are two narrow (Alpert and Raiffa 1982), and nonregressive predictions (Kahneman and Tversky 1973). Overconfidence is prevalent but not universal, and there are different views of the main psychological processes that produce it. One source of overconfidence is the common tendency to undervalue those aspects of the situation of which the judge is relatively ignorant. A recent study by Brenner, Koehler, and Tversky (1992) illustrates this effect, which is likely to be common in situations of conflict.

Participants were presented with factual information about several court cases. In each case, the information was divided into three parts: background data, the plaintiff's argument, and the defendant's argument. Four groups of subjects participated in this study. One group received only the background data. Two other groups received the background data and the arguments for one of the two sides, selected at random. The arguments for the plaintiff or the defendant contained no new evidence; they merely elaborated the facts included in the background data. A fourth group was given all the information presented to the jury. The subjects were all asked to predict the percentage of people in the jury who would vote for the plaintiff. The responses of the people who received one-sided evidence were strongly biased in the direction of the information they had received. Although the participants knew that their evidence was one-sided, they were not able to make the proper adjustment. In most cases, those who received all the evidence were more accurate in predicting the jury vote than those who received only one side. However, the subjects in the one-sided condition were generally more confident in their prediction than those who received both sides. Thus, subjects predicted the jury's decision with greater confidence when they had only one-half, rather than all, of the evidence presented to it.

Conflicts and disputes are characterized by the presence of asymmetric information. In general, each side knows a great deal about the evidence and the arguments that support its position and much less about those that support the position of the other side. The difficulty of making proper allowance for missing information, demonstrated in the preceding experiment, entails a bias that is likely to hinder successful negotiation. Each side will tend to overestimate its chances of success, as well as its ability to impose a solution on the other side and to prevent such an attempt by an opponent. Many years ago, we suggested that participants in a conflict are susceptible to a fallacy of initiative—a tendency to attribute less initiative and less imagination to the opponent than to oneself (Tversky and Kahneman 1973). The difficulty of adopting the opponent's view of the chessboard or of the battlefield may help explain why people often discover many new moves when they switch sides in a game. A related phenomenon has been observed in the response to mock trials that are sometimes conducted when a party to a dispute considers the possibility of litigation. Observers of mock trials have noted (Hans Zeisel, personal communication) that the would-be litigators are often surprised and dismayed by the strength of the position put forth by their mock opponent. In the absence of such a vivid demonstration of their bias, disputants are likely to hold an overly optimistic assessment of their chances in court. More generally, a tendency to underestimate the strength of the opponent's position could make negotiators less likely to make concessions and thereby reduce the chances of a negotiated settlement. Neale and Bazerman (1983) illustrated this effect in the context of a final arbitration procedure, in which the parties submit final offers, one of which is selected by the arbitrator. Negotiators overestimated (by more than 15 percent, on the average) the chance that their offer would be chosen. In this situation, a more realistic appraisal would probably result in more concilatory final offers.

Another cognitive mechanism that may contribute to overconfident optimism is the tendency to base forecasts and estimates mostly on the particular features of the case at hand, including extrapolations of current achievements and assessments of the strength of relevant causal factors. This preferred "inside approach" to prediction is contrasted with an "outside approach," which draws the prediction of an outcome from the statistics of similar cases in the past, with no attempt to divine the history of the events that will yield that outcome (Kahneman and Lovallo 1993; Kahneman and Tversky 1979a). The neglect of relevant statistical information in the inside approach to forecasting is one of many manifestations of a general tendency to represent any situation in terms of a concrete (and preferably causal) model, rather than in more abstract, statistical terms. This tendency can produce an inconsistency between people's general beliefs and their beliefs about particular cases. One example of such an inconsistency applies to the overconfidence effect: respondents who are on the average much too confident in their opinions about a series of questions are likely to be less optimistic, or even slightly pessimistic, in their guess about the total number of questions that they have answered correctly (Gigerenzer, Hoffrage, and Kleinbolting 1991; Griffin and Tversky 1992). The effect is not restricted to laboratory studies. Cooper, Woo, and Dunkelberg (1988) interviewed entrepreneurs about their chances of success, and about the base rate of success for enterprises of the same kind. Over 80 percent of the respondents perceived their chances of success as 70 percent or better, and fully 33 percent of them described their success as certain. The average chance of success that these entrepreneurs attributed to a business like theirs was only 59 percent, an estimate that is also too optimistic: the five-year survival rate for new firms is around 33 percent (Dun and Bradstreet 1967). In general, of course, the individuals who freely choose to engage in an economic activity tend to be among those who have the most favorable expectations for that activity in general, and for their own prospects in particular. This is a version of a statistical selection effect that is known in other contexts as the "winner's curse." It is possible in principle for an agent to anticipate this bias and to correct for it, but the data suggest that the entrepreneurs studied by Cooper et al. did not do so.

The inside approach to forecasts is not by itself sufficient to yield an optimistic bias. However, in the special case of a decision maker considering a course of action, the preference for the inside view makes it likely that the forecast will be anchored on plans and intentions and that relevant statistical considerations will be underweighted or ignored. If we plan to complete a project in a couple of months, it is natural to take this date as a starting point for the assessment of completion time, maybe adding an additional month for unforeseen factors. This mode of thinking leads us to neglect the many ways in which a plan might fail. Because plans tend to be best-case estimates, such anchoring leads to optimism. Indeed, the optimism of forecasts made in the planning context is a well-documented effect (Arnold 1986; Merrow, Phillips, and Myers 1981; Davis 1985). In the context of conflict, unwarranted optimism can be a serious obstacle, especially when it is bolstered by professional authority. Optimistic overconfidence is not a desirable trait for generals recommending a war or for attorneys urging a lawsuit, even if their expressions of confidence and optimism are pleasantly reassuring to their followers or clients at the time.

There are other sources and other manifestations of optimism than those mentioned so far (Taylor and Brown 1988). For example, there is evidence that most normal people expect others to rate them more favorably than they actually do, whereas mildly depressed people tend to be more realistic (Lewinsohn, Mischel, Chaplin, and Barton 1980). Similarly, people rate themselves above the mean on most desirable qualities, from effectiveness to sense of humor (Taylor and Brown 1988). People also exaggerate their ability to control their environment (Langer 1975; Crocker 1981) and accordingly prefer to bet on their skills rather than on a matched chance event (Howell 1971; Heath and Tversky 1991).

The claim that optimistic delusions are often adaptive has recently attracted much attention (Taylor and Brown 1988; Seligman 1991). To put this claim in perspective, it is useful to consider separately the effects of optimistic overconfidence on the two main phases of any undertaking: the setting of goals and plans, and the execution of a plan. When goals are chosen and plans are set, unrealistic optimism favors excessive risk-taking. Indeed, there are indications of large biases of optimistic planning in the domain of business decisions (Davis 1985), and the daily newspaper offers many examples in the political domain. However, decision makers are also very risk averse in most situations. The conjunction of overconfident optimism and risk aversion brings about a situation in which decision makers often accept risks because they deny them (Kahneman and Lovallo 1993; March and Shapira 1987). Thus, the benefit of unrealistic optimism in the decision phase may be to prevent paralysis by countering excessive aversion to risk, but this is hardly an unequivocal blessing— especially in situations of conflict.

The main advantages of optimism may be found in increasing persistence and commitment during the phase of action toward a chosen goal, and in improving the ability to tolerate uncontrollable suffering. Taylor (1989) has reviewed the role of irrational hope in promoting the adjustment of some cancer patients, and Seligman (1991) has claimed that an optimistic explanatory style, in which one takes credit for successes but views failures as aberrations, promotes persistence in the face of diffi- culties in diverse activities, ranging from the sale of insurance to competitive sports. The role of optimism in sports is of particular interest for a treatment of conflict. On the one hand, optimistic overconfidence will sometimes encourage athletes to take on competitors that are too strong for them. On the other hand, confidence, short of complacency, is surely an asset once the contest begins. The hope of victory increases effort, commitment, and persistence in the face of difficulty or threat of failure, and thereby raises the chances of success. A characteristic of competitive sports is that the option of abandoning the contest is not normally available to a competitor, even if defeat is certain. Under those circumstances, stubborn perseverance against the odds can only be beneficial. The situation is more complex when leaving the field is a via- ble option, and continuing the struggle is costly. Under these conditions, it is rarely easy to distinguish justified perseverance from irrational escalation of commitment.

In other situations of conflict, as in sports, optimism and confidence are likely to increase effort, commitment, and persistence in the conduct of the struggle. This is particularly true in conflicts that involve severe attrition. When maximal effort is exerted by both contestants, then it would appear that optimism offers a competitive advantage. In some competitive situations, the advantages of optimism and over- confidence may stem not from the deception of self, but from the deception of the opponent. This is how intimidation works—and successful intimidation accom- plishes all that could be obtained by an actual victory, usually at a much lower cost. An animal that is capable of intimidating competitors away from a desirable mate, prey, or territory would have little need for techniques of conflict resolution. It is also recognized in analyses of conflict, from the game of chicken to treatments of pariah [or "outlaw"] states, that the appearance of complete confidence often pays off. Because complete confidence may be hard to fake, a tendency to sincere overconfidence could have adaptive advantages (see Frank 1988).

Certainty and Pseudocertainty

A significant aspect of conflict resolution is the presence of uncertainty not only about the nature of an agreement but also about its actual outcomes. The outcomes of agreement can be classified into three types: (1) assured or certain outcomes—exchanges that are executed immediately, or promises for future actions that are unambiguous, unconditional, and enforceable; (2) contingently certain outcomes—enforceable undertakings that are conditional on objectively observed external events; and (3) uncertain outcomes—consequences (e.g., goodwill) that are more likely in the presence of agreement than in its absence. Uncertain outcomes are often stated as intentions of the parties in the "cheap talk" that precedes or accompanies the agreement.

Sure things and definite contingencies are the stuff of explicit agreements, contracts, and treaties; but the uncertain consequences of agreements are sometimes no less important. For example, a mutually satisfactory agreement between a supplier and a customer on a particular transaction can increase the probability of long-term association between them. A peace treaty between Israel and Syria might reduce the probability that Syria would seek to build or acquire nuclear weapons, but this significant consequence is not guaranteed. As these examples illustrate, an increase in the other side's goodwill is sometimes an important outcome of agreement, albeit an uncertain one. Future goodwill differs from many other consequences in that it is not necessarily in limited supply; negotiations in which goodwill is (implicitly or explicitly) a significant factor present a sharp contrast to zero-sum games. However, the characteristics of the way people think about uncertain outcomes favor a systematic underweighting of such consequences of agreement, compared to certain and to contingently certain benefits that are assured in the formal contract. This tendency reduces, in effect, the perceived value of an agreement for both parties in a dispute.

Research on individual decision making has identified a major bias in the weights that are assigned to probabilistic advantages and to sure things, which we have called the *certainty effect* (Kahneman and Tversky, 1979b, 1984). The classic demonstration of this effect is the Allais paradox, named after the French Nobel laureate in economics who in 1952 demonstrated to an audience of famous economists (several of them future Nobel laureates) that their preferences were inconsistent with expected utility theory. More specifically, these preferences imply that the difference between probabilities of 0.99 and 1.00 looms larger than the difference between 0.10 and 0.11. The intuition that the two differences are not equally significant is compelling. Indeed, it comes as a surprise to the uninitiated that the standard analysis of rational choice (expected utility theory) requires that a probability difference of, say 1 percent, be given equal weight, regardless of whether the difference lies in the middle of the range (0.30 to 0.31) or whether it involves the transition from impossibility to possibility (zero to 0.01) or from near-certainty to certainty (0.99 to 1). Intuitively, however, the qualitative distinctions between impossibility and possibility and between probability and certainty have special significance. As a consequence, many people consider it prudent to pay more to increase the probability of a desirable outcome from .99 to 1 than from .80 to .85. Similarly, people may well pay more to reduce the probability of harm from .0005 to zero than to reduce the same risk from .0015 to .0005 (Viscusi, Magat, and Huber 1987). The certainty effect has been confirmed when the probabilities are associated with well-defined chance processes and are expressed numerically. Most decisions under uncertainty, however, involve vague contingencies and ambiguous probabilities. The evidence suggests that the certainty effect is further enhanced by vagueness and ambiguity (Hogarth and Einhorn 1990; Tversky and Kahneman 1991). Thus, there is good reason to believe that uncertain outcomes, such as goodwill, are underweighted when people evaluate alternative agreements.

The principle that uncertain benefits are underweighted does not apply to *contingently certain outcomes*. The payment of insurance in the event of a specified property loss or in the event of a medical need is a prime example of a contingently certain outcome. The evidence indicates that people are willing to pay disproportionately more for insurance that will certainly be provided if the relevant contingencies arise than for insurance that is merely probabilistic. There is also strong evidence for a closely related phenomenon, which has been labeled the *pseudocertainty effect* (Kahneman and Tversky 1984; Tversky and Kahneman 1986), and is illustrated using the following pair of decision problems.

Problem 1.   Consider the following two-stage game. In the first stage there is a 75 percent chance to end the game without winning anything and a 25 percent chance to move into the second stage. If you reach the second stage you have a choice between

A. a sure win of $30

B. an 80 percent chance to win $45

Your choice must be made before the game starts, i.e., before the outcome of the first stage is known. Please indicate the option you prefer.

Problem 2.   Which of the following options do you prefer?

C. 25 percent chance to win $30

D. 20 percent chance to win $45

Because there is one chance in four to move into the second stage of problem 1, prospect A offers a .25 probability to win $30 and prospect B offers a $.25 \times .80 = .20$ probability to win $45. Problems 1 and 2 are therefore identical in terms of probabilities and outcomes. However, the two problems elicit different preferences, which we have observed with both real and hypothetical payoffs. A clear majority of respondents preferred A over B in problem 1, whereas the majority preferred D over C in problem 2 (Tversky and Kahneman 1986). We have attributed this phenomenon to the combination of the certainty effect and the tendency to focus on the outcomes that are directly relevant to the decision at hand. Because the failure to reach the second stage of the game yields the same outcome (i.e., no gain) regardless of whether the decision maker chooses A or B, people compare these prospects as if they had reached the second stage. In this case, they face a choice between a sure gain of $30 and a .80 chance to win $45. The tendency to overweight sure things relative to uncertain outcomes (the certainty effect) favors the former option in the sequential version. Because an uncertain event (reaching the second stage of the game) is weighted as if it were certain, we called the phenomenon the pseudo-certainty effect.

A study by Viscusi, Magat, and Huber (1987) provides compelling examples of both the certainty and the pseudocertainty effects. Participants in that study were exposed to a container of insecticide that was allegedly available for a stated price. After reading the warning label, they were asked to state their willingness to pay more for a product that would be safer in various ways. Two risks were mentioned (inhalation and child poisoning), each with a .0015 probability. The average willingness to pay to reduce both risks from .0015 to .0005 was $2.38 (in families with children), but the respondents were willing to pay an additional $5.71 to eliminate the last .0005 chance of harm. This large difference illustrates the certainty effect. The same respondents were also willing to pay $2.69 or $4.29, respectively, to eliminate the risk of inhalation or of child poisoning, without reducing the other risk. However, they were only willing to pay $1.84 to reduce both risks to .0005. This is an instance of a pseudocertainty effect. The respondents were willing to pay for the comfort of completely eliminating an identified risk, but the certainty they wished to purchase was illusory: the pesticide they would buy would still be associated with some danger, and in any event the amount paid to eliminate the risk of toxic inhalation or child poisoning would only reduce the overall risk of such harms, which can also occur in many other ways.

Contingently certain outcomes are important in many negotiations, in at least two ways. First, there are penalties and insurance provisions that are intended to protect one party against a failure of the other to comply with the agreement. The present analysis suggests that these provisions will loom large in the parties' view—but of course only to the extent that they are fully enforceable, and therefore contingently certain. Second, contingent certainty is involved in a less obvious way in negotiations about assets that will be significant if conflict breaks out between the parties. The negotiations between Israel and its neighbors provide many examples. Strategic assets, such as the Mitla Pass in the Sinai, or the Golan Heights near the Syrian border, provide contingently certain benefits to Israel in case of war. However, the retention of such assets raises tensions and surely increases the probability of armed conflict. An Israeli leader intent on minimizing the probability of catastrophic defeat should consider the probability that war will occur, multiplied by the probability of defeat given a war—separately for the case of withdrawal and nonwithdrawal. We do not presume to assess these probabilities; we merely suggest that the side that argues for retaining the strategic asset is likely to have the upper hand in a political debate—because of the superiority of contingent certainty over mere probability. Thus, the definite advantage of a strategic asset in case of war is likely to offset the uncertain reduction in the probability of war that might be brought about by a strategic or territorial concession.

The tendency to undervalue uncertain benefits sometimes leads to what might be described as the *pseudodominance effect*. If it is advantageous to hold strategic assets both in war and in peace, territorial concession appears to be dominated by the strategy of holding on to key strategic positions. The fallacy in this argument is that it does not take into account the possibility that an agreement based on territorial concessions can decrease the chances of war. Even if holding to the strategic positions in question is in a country's best interest both in war and in peace, it could still make sense to give them up if this act could greatly reduce the probability of war. Since this outcome is uncertain, and its probability is in some sense unknowable, both politicians and citizens are likely to undervalue or neglect its contribution. The present discussion, of course, does not imply that strategic concessions should always be made. It only points out that the perception of dominance in such cases is often illusory.

Loss Aversion

Loss aversion refers to the observation that losses generally loom larger than the corresponding gains. This notion may be captured by a value function that is steeper in the negative than in the positive domain. In decisions under risk, loss aversion entails a reluctance to accept even-chance gambles, unless the payoffs are very favorable. For example, many people will accept such a gamble only if the gain is at least twice as large as the loss. In decisions under certainty, loss aversion entails a systematic discrepancy in the assessments of advantages and disadvantages (Tversky and Kahneman 1991; Kahneman, Knetsch, and Thaler 1991). The general principle is quite simple: When an option is compared to the reference point, the comparison is coded in terms of the advantages and disadvantages of that option. A particularly important case of loss aversion arises when the reference point is the status quo, and when the retention of the status quo is an option. Because the disadvantages of any alternative to the status quo are weighted more heavily than its advantages, a strong bias in favor of the status quo is observed (Samuelson and Zeckhauser 1988). The argument has been extended to the context of international conflict and negotiation. Jervis (1992) notes: "If loss aversion is widespread, states defending the status quo should have a big bargaining advantage. That is, a state will be willing to pay a higher price and run higher risks if it is facing losses than if it is seeking to make gains" (p. 162).

The location of the reference point also affects the evaluation of *differences* between other pairs of options. Differences between disadvantages will generally have greater weight than corresponding differences between advantages, because disadvantages are evaluated on a steeper limb of the value function. For example, the difference between salary offers of $40,000 and $45,000 will be viewed as a difference between two gains by someone whose current income is now $35,000, and as a difference between two losses if current income is $50,000. The psychological differences between the alternatives is likely to be greater in the latter case, reflecting the steeper slope of the value function in the domain of losses. Acceptance of the lower salary will be experienced as an increased loss if the reference point is high and as a forgone gain if it is low. It will be more painful in the former case.

The following classroom demonstration illustrates the principle of loss aversion (Kahneman, Knetsch, and Thaler 1990; see also Knetsch and Sinden 1984). An attractive object (e.g., a decorated mug) is distributed to one-third of the students. The students who have been given mugs are *sellers*—perhaps better described as owners. They are informed that there will be an opportunity to exchange the mug for a predetermined amount of money. The subjects state what their choice will be for

different amounts, and thereby indicate the minimal amount for which they are willing to give up their mug. Another one-third of the students are *choosers*. They are
told that they will have a choice between a mug like the one in the hands of their
neighbor and an amount of cash; they indicate their choices for different amounts.
The remaining students are *buyers:* they indicate whether they would pay each of the
different amounts to acquire a mug. In a representative experiment, the median price
set by sellers was $7.12, the median cash equivalent set by the choosers was $3.12,
and the median buyer was willing to pay $2.88 for the mug.

The difference between the valuations of owners and choosers occurs in spite of
the fact that both groups face the same choice: go home with a mug or with a pre-
specified sum of money. Subjectively, however, the choosers and owners are in different states: the former evaluate the mug as a gain, the latter as something to be
given up. Because of loss aversion, more cash is required to persuade the owners to
give up the mug than to match the attractiveness of the mug to the choosers. In the
same vein, Thaler (1980) tells of a wine lover who will neither sell a bottle that has
gained value in his cellar nor buy another bottle at the current price. The experimental studies of the discrepant valuation of owners, choosers, and buyers demonstrate that loss aversion can be induced instantaneously; it does not depend on a
progressive attachment to objects in one's possession. Unlike the differences between
buyers and sellers observed in some bargaining experiments (Neale, Huber, and
Northcraft 1987), the above effect does not depend on the labels attached to the
roles.

The market experiments conducted by Kahneman, Knetsch, and Thaler (1990)
demonstrated a significant consequence of the discrepancy between the valuations of
owners and buyers: far fewer transactions take place than economic theory would
predict. Consider an experiment in which half the subjects are given mugs, and a
market is set up where these subjects can sell their mugs to potential buyers. Economic theory predicts that when all market changes are completed, the mugs will be
in the hands of the subjects who value them most. Because the initial allocation was
random, half the mugs initially allocated should change hands. In an extended series
of experiments, however, the observed volume of trade was about one-fourth, that is,
only half the number predicted. The same result was obtained when owners and
potential buyers had an opportunity to bargain directly over a possible price.

Concession Aversion
Loss aversion, we argue, could have a significant impact on conflict resolution.
Imagine two countries negotiating the number of missiles that they will keep and aim
at each other. Each country derives security from its own missiles and is threatened

by those of the other side. Thus, missiles eliminated by the other side are evaluated as gains, and missiles one must give up are evaluated as losses, relative to the status quo. If losses have twice the impact of gains, then each side will require that its opponent will eliminate twice as many missiles as it eliminates—not a promising start for the achievement of an agreement. The symmetry of the positions might help negotiators reframe the problem to trade missiles at par, but in most negotiations the sacrifices made by the two sides are not easily compared. In labor negotiations, for example, a union may be asked to give up a third pilot in the cockpit, and might be offered improved benefits or a more generous retirement plan in return. These are the circumstances under which we expect to find *concession aversion*, a systematically different evaluation of concessions made and of concessions received.

Concession aversion appears similar to the phenomenon of *reactive devaluation*, a negotiator's tendency to value a possible concession less if it is made by the opponent than by one's own side, as discussed in the previous chapter. However, the processes are quite different: reactive devaluation reflects a change in the evaluation of a proposal in response to an offer by an opponent, while concession aversion reflects the asymmetric valuation of gains and losses. Both processes could operate together to make agreement difficult.

Loss aversion does not affect all transactions: it applies to goods held for use, not goods held for exchange. Three categories of exchange goods are money held for spending, goods held specifically for sale, and "bargaining chips," goods that are valued only because they can be traded. The significance of missiles, for example, is substantially reduced when they are treated not as strategic assets but as bargaining chips. Concession aversion, we suggest, will only inhibit agreement in the latter case. Loss aversion plays little role in routine economic transactions, in which a seller and a buyer exchange a good and money, both of which were held for that purpose. In contrast, many of the objects of bargaining in labor negotiations (e.g., job security, benefits, grievance procedures) are "use goods" rather than exchange goods. Labor negotiations in which both sides seek to modify an existing contract to their advantage therefore provide the paradigm case of concession aversion.

The analysis of concession aversion has an immediate prescriptive implication. It suggests that the most effective concessions you can make are those that reduce or eliminate your opponent's losses; the least effective concessions are those that improve an attribute in which the other side is already "in the gains." Reductions of losses are evaluated on the steep lower limb of the value function—and the eliminations of losses are evaluated at its steepest region. In contrast, increments to already large gains are expected to add relatively little value.

The suggestion that it is more efficient to reduce the opponent's losses than to offset them by gains is compatible with a negotiating strategy discussed by Pruitt (1983). The *cost-cutting strategy* requires a side that seeks a concession to find ways to reduce the costs of that concession to the other side—in other words, to avoid imposing losses. The cost-cutting strategy is implicitly preferred to a strategy of offering concessions that the other side will evaluate as gains. In the terms of the present analysis, the losses that the cost-cutting strategy eliminates are evaluated in the steep region of the value function, whereas the marginal value of offsetting gains is relatively slight.

Gains, Losses, and Fairness

"I only want what is fair" is a common cry in negotiations, although adversaries who make this claim are not necessarily close to agreement. In addition to their effect on the valuation of outcomes, reference points also affect negotiations by influencing judgments of what is fair or unfair. Such judgments have impact on the outcome of bargaining—perhaps because offers that are perceived as unfair as well as disadvantageous are especially likely to evoke anger and resistance. It is generally accepted, of course, that fairness does not always govern behavior, that the rules of fairness are often ambiguous, and that disputants' interpretation of these ambiguities are likely to be self-serving (Messick and Sentis 1983; Thompson and Loewenstein 1992).

The role of reference points in judgments of fairness has been studied in the context of business practices. Judgments of fairness were obtained in a series of telephone surveys, in which the respondents assessed vignettes describing actions of price or wage setting by merchants, landlords, and employers (Kahneman, Knetsch, and Thaler 1986). The judgments appeared to be governed by a small number of rules of fairness, which treated gains and losses asymmetrically. The most prominent rule of fairness is that a firm should not impose a loss on its transactors (customers, employees, or tenants) merely in order to increase its own gain. For example, people consider it extremely unfair for a hardware store to raise the price of snow shovels after a blizzard, and they also think it unacceptable for a firm to cut the wages of employees merely because they could be replaced by cheaper labor. On the other hand, the standards of fairness allow a firm to protect itself from losses by raising the price it charges its customers or by reducing the pay of its employees. Thus, a firm can fairly use its market power to protect its reference profit, but not to increase it. In a further indication of the asymmetric treatment of gains and losses, the rules of fairness do not obligate a firm to share increases in its profits with its customers or employees. We summarized these rules by a *principle of dual entitlement:* the firm is entitled to its reference profit; customers, employees, and tenants are entitled to a reference price, wage, or rent; and in case of conflict between these entitlements the firm is allowed to protect itself from a threatened loss by transferring it to its transactors. Note that the principle defends the *rights* of both parties to a reference state, without imposing a more general egalitarian norm of sharing both pain and gain.

What determines the reference transaction? The precedent of previous transactions between the firm and the same individual transactor can be important. Thus, it is unfair to reduce the wage of an employee during a period of high unemployment, although an employee who quits can be replaced at a lower wage. The previous history of transactions between the firm and its employee defines an entitlement, which does not extend to the replacement. Note also that the wage that the new employee was paid elsewhere is entirely irrelevant. Thus, it is not the task of the firm to protect new employees from a loss relative to their previous earnings, because these are not part of the relevant reference transaction. The prevailing wage is the standard reference transaction for a new contract, especially if the new employee's job is not directly comparable to that of anyone currently in the organization.

Similar principles find expression in legal practice. Cohen and Knetsch (1992) have compiled an illuminating review of the judicial impact of the distinction between losses and forgone gains. They cite a legal expert to the effect that "To deprive somebody of something which he merely expected to receive is a less serious wrong, deserving of less protection, than to deprive somebody of the expectation of continuing to hold something which he already possesses." The familiar expression that possession is nine points of the law is another manifestation of the importance of the reference point.

The asymmetric treatment of losses and gains has generally conservative implications, for judgments of economic fairness as well as for individual choice. We saw earlier that loss aversion induces a bias toward the retention of the status quo; the rules of fairness exhibit a similar bias favoring the retention of the reference transaction. There are other similarities between the two domains. For example, losses are given greater weight than forgone gains in individual choice, in judicial decisions (Cohen and Knetsch 1992), and also in lay rules of fairness. A firm is (barely) allowed to deny its transactors any share of its gains, but is definitely prohibited from imposing losses on them. No one would seriously suggest that these principles extend to all human interactions. There are domains in which fairness demands that gains be shared, and competitive contexts in which the imposition of losses on others is sanctioned. It appears, however, that one common principle may apply across contexts: Actions that impose losses relative to an acceptable reference standard are viewed much more severely than actions (or omissions) that merely fail to provide a gain.

The notion of rights or entitlements is associated with a more extreme form of loss aversion, called *enhanced loss aversion*. Losses that are compounded by outrage are much less acceptable than losses that are caused by misfortune or by legitimate actions of others. An example is the difference between two customers who face a steep increase in price, which one of the customers regards as unfair and the other as legitimate. According to the present analysis both customers face the same loss, but whether they perceive that a right has been violated depends on their coding of the supplier's choice. Suppose, for example, that the supplier follows others in raising the price. If the prevailing price is accepted as a legitimate reference, the option of maintaining the old price would be coded as a loss to the supplier, which the rules of fairness do not require. If the price charged by other merchants is considered irrelevant, maintaining the old price merely forgoes an illegitimate gain.

As this example illustrates, the rules of fairness are often ambiguous, and the ambiguity typically involves the selection of the specific reference standard, rather than a more general principle. Customer and supplier could agree on the general principles that prices should be fair and that arbitrary increases beyond a proper reference price are unfair, but disagree on the proper reference price for the case at hand. Another important possibility is that the reference point by which an action is evaluated may not be unique. "Seeing the other person's point of view" might make a difference even when one does not fully accept it. There is at least a possibility that a discussion of fairness may have some persuasive effect even when it does not achieve a complete conversion.

Concluding Remarks

In this chapter we have discussed three major phenomena (optimistic overconfidence, the certainty effect, and loss aversion) which have emerged from the cognitive analysis of individual judgment and decision making. These phenomena represent systematic departures from the standard rational theory in which individuals are assumed to have realistic expectations, to weight outcomes by their probabilities, and to evaluate consequences as asset positions, not as gains and losses. We have argued that these biases in the assessment of evidence and the evaluation of consequences can hinder the successful resolution of conflict. In particular, optimistic overconfidence is likely to make opponents believe that they can prevail and hence they do not have to make concessions. The certainty effect leads disputants to undervalue some outcomes, such as goodwill, because they are not certain. Finally, loss aversion is likely to reduce the range of acceptable agreements because one's own concessions are evaluated as losses and the opponent's concessions are evaluated as gains. Although these phenomena do not exhaust the psychological barriers to the successful resolution of interpersonal conflict, they represent serious obstacles that often stand in the way of successful negotiation.

An understanding of the cognitive obstacles to conflict resolution could provide insight on two levels. On the first level, a negotiator may recognize that her opponent may not behave according to the standard rules of rational behavior, that he is likely to be overconfident, to undervalue uncertain concessions, and to be loss averse. In the spirit of Raiffa's prescriptive analysis (see Bell, Raiffa, and Tversky 1988), a rational negotiator may wish to take into account the fact that her opponent may not be entirely rational. On a higher level of insight, a negotiator may realize that she, too, does not always behave in accord with the maxims of rationality, and that she also exhibits overconfidence, the certainty effect, and loss aversion. The literature on judgment and choice (see Bazerman 1994; Dawes 1988; Kahneman, Slovic, and Tversky 1982) indicates that biases and cognitive illusions are not readily eliminated by knowledge or warning. Nevertheless, knowing the opponent's biases, as well as our own, may help us understand the barriers to conflict resolution and could even suggest methods to overcome them.

Note

Parts of this chapter are borrowed from an article by the first author entitled Reference points, anchors, norms, and mixed feelings, that appeared in a special issue of *Organizational Behaviour and Human Decision Processes*.

References

Alpert, M., and Raiffa, H. (1982). A progress report on the training of probability assessors. In D. Kahneman, P. Slovic, and A. Tversky, eds., *Judgment under uncertainty: Heuristics and biases*. Cambridge, England: Cambridge University Press.

Arnold, III, J. (1986). Assessing capital risk: You can't be too conservative. *Harvard Business Review* 64(5): 113–121.

Bazerman, M. H. (1994). *Judgment in managerial decision making*, 3rd ed. New York: John Wiley.

Bell, D. E., Raiffa, H., and Tversky, A. (1988). Descriptive, normative, and prescriptive interactions in decision making. In D. E. Bell, H. Raiffa, and A. Tversky, eds., *Decision making: Descriptive, normative, and prescriptive interactions*. 9–30. New York: Cambridge University Press.

Brenner, L., Koehler, D., and Tversky, A. (1992). *On the evaluation of one-sided evidence*. Working Paper. Stanford: Stanford University Press.

Cohen, D., and Knetsch, J. L. (1992). Judicial choice and disparities between measures of economic value. *Osgoode Hall Law Review, 30*, 737–770.

Cooper, A. C., Woo, C. Y., and Dunkelberg, W. C. (1988). Entrepreneurs' perceived chances for success. *Journal of Business Venturing* 3(2): 97–108.

Crocker, J. (1981). Judgment of covariation by social perceivers. *Psychology Bulletin* 90: 272–92.

Davis, D. (1985). New projects: Beware of false economies. *Harvard Business Review* 63(2): 95–101.

Dawes, R. M. (1988a). *Rational choice in an uncertain world.* San Diego: Harcourt, Brace, Jovanovich.

Dun and Bradstreet (1967). *Patterns of success in managing a business.* New York: Dun and Bradstreet.

Frank, R. H. (1988). *Passions within reason: The strategic role of the emotions.* New York: W. W. Norton.

Gigerenzer, G., Hoffrage, U., and Kleinbolting, H. (1991). Probabilistic mental models: A Brunswikian theory of confidence. *Psychological Review* 98(4): 506–28.

Griffin, D., and Tversky, A. (1992). The weighing of evidence and the determinants of confidence. *Cognitive Psychology* 24(3): 411–35.

Heath, F., and Tversky, A. (1991). Preference and belief: Ambiguity and competence in choice under uncertainty. *Journal of Risk and Uncertainty* 4: 4–28.

Hogarth, R. M., and Einhorn, H. J. (1990). Venture theory: A model of decision weights. *Management Science* 36(7): 780–803.

Howell, W. (1971). Uncertainty from internal and external sources: A clear case of overconfidence. *Journal of Experimental Psychology* 89(2): 240–43.

Jervis, R. (1992). Political implications of loss aversion. Unpublished manuscript. New York: Columbia University.

Kahneman, D. (1992). Reference points, anchors, herms, and mixed feelings. *Organizational Behavior and Human Decision Processes* 51: 296–312.

Kahneman, D., Knetsch, J. L., and Thaler, R. H. (1986). Fairness as a constraint on profit seeking: Entitlements in the market. *The American Economic Review* 76(4): 728–41.

——— (1990). Experimental tests of the endowment effect and the Coase theorem. *Journal of Political Economy* 98(6): 1325–48.

——— (1991). The endowment effect, loss aversion, and the status quo bias. *Journal of Economic Perspectives* 5: 193–206.

Kahneman, D., and Lovallo, D. (1993). Timid choices and bold forecasts: A cognitive perspective on risk taking. *Management Science* 39: 17–31.

Kahneman, D., Slovic, P., and Tversky, A. (1982). *Judgment under uncertainty: Heuristics and biases.* Cambridge, England: Cambridge University Press.

Kahneman, D., and Tversky, A. (1973). On the psychology of prediction. *Psychological Review* 80: 237–51.

——— (1979a). Intuitive prediction: Biases and corrective procedures. *TIMS Studies in Management Science* 12: 313–27.

——— (1979b). Prospect theory: An analysis of decision under risk. *Econometrica* 47(2): 263–91.

——— (1984). Choices, values and frames. *American Psychologist* 39: 341–50.

Knetsch, J. L., and Sinden, J. A. (1984). Willingness to pay and compensation demanded: Experimental evidence of an unexpected disparity in measures of value. *Quarterly Journal of Economics* 99(3): 507–21.

Langer, E. J. (1975). The illusion of control. *Journal of Personality and Social Psychology* 32: 311–28.

Lewinsohn, P. M., Mischel, W., Chaplin, W., and Barton, R. (1980). Social competence and depression: The role of illusory self-perceptions. *Journal of Abnormal Psychology* 89: 203–12.

Lichtenstein, S., Fischhoff, B., and Phillips, L. (1982). Calibration of probabilities: The state of the art to 1980. In D. Kahneman, et al., eds., *Judgment under uncertainty: Heuristics and biases*. Cambridge, England: Cambridge University Press.

March, J., and Shapira, Z. (1987). Managerial perspectives on risk and risk taking. *Management Science* 33(11): 1404–18.

Merrow, E., Phillips, K., and Myers, C. (1981). *Understanding cost growth and performance shortfalls in pioneer process plants*. Santa Barbara, Calif.: Rand Corporation.

Messick, D. M., and Sentis, K. (1983). Fairness, preference, and fairness bias. In D. M. Messick and K. S. Cook, eds., *Equity theory: Psychological and sociological perspectives*, 61–94. New York: Praeger.

Neale, M. A., and Bazerman, M. H. (1983). The effects of perspective-taking ability under alternate forms of arbitration on the negotiation process. *Industrial and Labor Relations Review* 36: 378–88.

——— (1991). *Cognition and rationality in negotiation*. New York: The Free Press.

Neale, M. A., Huber, V. L., and Northcraft, G. B. (1987). The framing of negotiations: Context versus task frames. *Organizational Behavior and Human Decision Processes* 39(2): 228–41.

Pruitt, D. G. (1983). Achieving integrative agreements. In M. H. Bazerman, and R. J. Lewicki, eds., *Negotiating in organizations*. Beverly Hills, Calif.: Sage Publications.

Samuelson, W., and Zeckhauser, R. (1988). Status quo bias in decision making. *Journal of Risk and Uncertainty* 1: 7–59.

Seligman, M. E. P. (1991). *Learned optimism*. New York: A. A. Knopf.

Taylor, S. E. (1989). *Positive illusions: Creative self-deception and the healthy mind*. New York: Basic Books.

Taylor, S. E., and Brown, J. D. (1988). Illusion and well-being: A social psychological perspective on mental health. *Psychological Bulletin* 103(2): 193–210.

Thaler, R. (1980). Toward a positive theory of consumer choice. *Journal of Economic Behavior and Organization* 1(1): 39–60.

Thompson, L., and Loewenstein, G. F. (1992). Egocentric interpretations of fairness and interpersonal conflict. *Organizational Behavior and Human Decision Processes* 51(2): 176–97.

Tversky, A., and Fox, C. (1995). Weighing risk and uncertainty. *Psychological Review*, in press.

Tversky, A., and Kahneman, D. (1973). Availability: A heuristic for judging frequency and probability. *Cognitive Psychology* 5: 207–32.

——— (1986). Rational choice and the framing of decisions. Part 2. *The Journal of Business* 59(4): S251–S78.

——— (1991). Loss aversion in riskless choice: A reference-dependent model. *Quarterly Journal of Economics* 106(4): 1039–61.

Viscusi, W. K., Magat, W. A., and Huber, J. C. (1987). An investigation of the rationality of consumer valuations of multiple health risks. *Rand Journal of Economics* 18(4): 465–79.

30 Weighing Risk and Uncertainty

Amos Tversky and Craig R. Fox

Decisions are generally made without definite knowledge of their consequences. The decisions to invest in the stock market, to undergo a medical operation, or to go to court are generally made without knowing in advance whether the market will go up, the operation will be successful, or the court will decide in one's favor. Decision under uncertainty, therefore, calls for an evaluation of two attributes: the desirability of possible outcomes and their likelihood of occurrence. Indeed, much of the study of decision making is concerned with the assessment of these values and the manner in which they are—or should be—combined.

In the classical theory of decision under risk, the utility of each outcome is weighted by its probability of occurrence. Consider a simple prospect of the form (x, p) that offers a probability p to win \$$x$ and a probability $1 - p$ to win nothing. The expected utility of this prospect is given by $pu(x) + (1 - p)u(0)$, where u is the utility function for money. Expected utility theory has been developed to explain attitudes toward risk, namely, risk aversion and risk seeking. Risk aversion is defined as a preference for a sure outcome over a prospect with an equal or greater expected value. Thus, choosing a sure \$100 over an even chance to win \$200 or nothing is an expression of risk aversion. Risk seeking is exhibited if a prospect is preferred to a sure outcome with equal or greater expected value. It is commonly assumed that people are risk averse, which is explained in expected utility theory by a concave utility function.

The experimental study of decision under risk has shown that people often violate both the expected utility model and the principle of risk aversion that underlie much economic analysis. Table 30.1 illustrates a common pattern of risk seeking and risk aversion observed in choice between simple prospects (adapted from Tversky & Kahneman, 1992), where $C(x, p)$ is the median certainty equivalent of the prospect (x, p). Thus, the upper left-hand entry in the table shows that the median participant is indifferent between receiving \$14 for sure and a 5% chance of receiving \$100. Because the expected value of this prospect is only \$5, this observation reflects risk seeking.

Table 30.1 illustrates a fourfold pattern of risk attitudes: risk seeking for gains and risk aversion for losses of low probability, coupled with risk aversion for gains and risk seeking for losses of high probability. Choices consistent with this pattern have been observed in several studies, with and without monetary incentives[1] (Cohen, Jaffray, & Said, 1987; Fishburn & Kochenberger, 1979; Hershey & Schoemaker, 1980; Kahneman & Tversky, 1979; Payne, Laughhunn, & Crum, 1981; Wehrung,

Table 30.1
The Fourfold Pattern of Risk Attitudes

Probability	Gain	Loss
Low	$C(\$100, .05) = \$14$ (risk seeking)	$C(-\$100, .05) = -\$8$ (risk aversion)
High	$C(\$100, .95) = \$78$ (risk aversion)	$C(-\$100, .95) = -\$84$ (risk seeking)

Note: C is the median certainty equivalent of the prospect in question.

1989). Risk seeking for low-probability gains may contribute to the popularity of gambling, whereas risk seeking for high-probability losses is consistent with the tendency to undertake risk in order to avoid a sure loss.

Because the fourfold pattern is observed for a wide range of payoffs, it cannot be explained by the shape of the utility function as proposed earlier by Friedman and Savage (1948) and by Markowitz (1952). Instead, it suggests a nonlinear transformation of the probability scale, first proposed by Preston and Baratta (1948) and further discussed by Edwards (1962) and others. This notion is one of the cornerstones of prospect theory (Kahneman & Tversky, 1979; Tversky & Kahneman, 1992), which provides the theoretical framework used in the present chapter. According to this theory, the value of a simple prospect that offers a probability p to win \$$x$ (and probability $1 - p$ to win nothing) is given by $w(p)v(x)$, where v measures the subjective value of the outcome x, and w measures the impact of p on the desirability of the prospect. The values of w are called decision weights; they are normalized so that $w(0) = 0$, and $w(1) = 1$. It is important to note that w should not be interpreted as a measure of degree of belief. A decision maker may believe that the probability of heads on a toss of a coin is one-half but give this event a lower weight in the evaluation of a prospect.

According to prospect theory, the value function v and the weighting function w exhibit diminishing sensitivity: marginal impact diminishes with distance from a reference point. For monetary outcomes, the status quo generally serves as the reference point that distinguishes gains from losses. Thus, diminishing sensitivity gives rise to an S-shaped value function, with $v(0) = 0$, that is concave for gains and convex for losses. For probability, there are two natural reference points—certainty and impossibility—that correspond to the endpoints of the scale. Therefore, diminishing sensitivity implies that increasing the probability of winning a prize by .1 has more impact when it changes the probability of winning from .9 to 1.0 or from 0 to .1 than when it changes the probability from, say, .3 to .4 or from .6 to .7. This gives rise to a weighting function that is concave near zero and convex near one. Figure 30.1

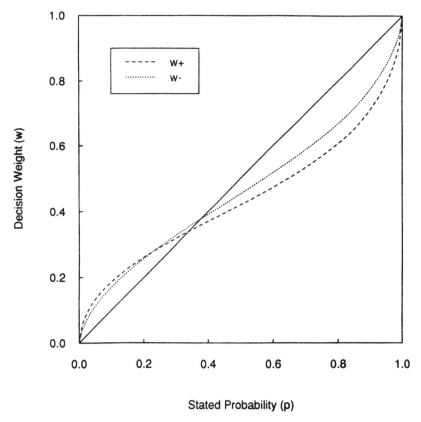

Figure 30.1
Weighting functions for gains (w^+) and losses (w^-).

depicts the weighting functions for gains and for losses, estimated from the median data of Tversky and Kahneman (1992).[2] Such a function overweights small probabilities and underweights moderate and high probabilities, which explains the four-fold pattern of risk attitudes illustrated in table 30.1. It also accounts for the well-known certainty effect discovered by Allais (1953). For example, whereas most people prefer a sure $30 to an 80% chance of winning $45, most people also prefer a 20% chance of winning $45 to a 25% chance of winning $30, contrary to the substitution axiom of expected utility theory (Tversky & Kahneman, 1986). This observation is consistent with an S-shaped weighting function satisfying $w(.20)/w(.25) \geq w(.80)/w(1.0)$. Such a function appears to provide a unified account of a wide range of empirical findings (see Camerer & Ho, 1994).

A choice model that is based on a nonlinear transformation of the probability scale assumes that the decision maker knows the probabilities associated with the possible outcomes. With the notable exception of games of chance, however, these probabilities are unknown, or at least not specified in advance. People generally do not know the probabilities associated with events such as the guilt of a defendant, the outcome of a football game, or the future price of oil. Following Knight (1921), decision theorists distinguish between risky (or chance) prospects where the probabilities associated with outcomes are assumed to be known, and uncertain prospects where these probabilities are not assumed to be known. To describe individual choice between uncertain prospects, we need to generalize the weighting function from risk to uncertainty. When the probabilities are unknown, however, we cannot describe decision weights as a simple transformation of the probability scale. Thus, we cannot plot the weighting function as we did in figure 30.1, nor can we speak about the overweighting of low probabilities and underweighting of high probabilities.

This article extends the preceding analysis from risk to uncertainty. To accomplish this, we first generalize the weighting function and introduce the principle of bounded subadditivity. We next describe a series of studies that demonstrates this principle for both risk and uncertainty, and we show that it is more pronounced for uncertainty than for risk. Finally, we discuss the relationship between decision weights and judged probabilities, and the role of ambiguity in choice under uncertainty. An axiomatic treatment of these concepts is presented in Tversky and Wakker (in press).

Theory

Let S be a set whose elements are interpreted as states of the world. Subsets of S are called *events*. Thus, S corresponds to the certain event, and ϕ is the null event. A weighting function W (on S) is a mapping that assigns to each event is S a number between 0 and 1 such that $W(\phi) = 0$, $W(S) = 1$, and $W(A) \geq W(B)$ if $A \supset B$. Such a function is also called a *capacity*, or a nonadditive probability.

As in the case of risk, we focus on simple prospects of the form (x, A), which offer x if an uncertain event A occurs and nothing if A does not occur. According to prospect theory, the value of such a prospect is $W(A)v(x)$, where W is the decision weight associated with the uncertain event A. (We use W for uncertainty and w for risk.) Because the present treatment is confined to simple prospects with a single positive outcome, it is consistent with both the original and the cumulative versions of prospect theory (Tversky & Kahneman, 1992). It is consistent with expected utility theory if and only if W is additive, that is, $W(A \cup B) = W(A) + W(B)$ whenever $A \cap B = \phi$.[3]

Prospect theory assumes that W satisfies two conditions.

(i) Lower subadditivity: $W(A) \geq W(A \cup B) - W(B)$, provided A and B are disjoint and $W(A \cup B)$ is bounded away from one.[4] This inequality captures the possibility effect: The impact of an event A is greater when it is added to the null event than when it is added to some nonnull event B.

(ii) Upper subadditivity: $W(S) - W(S - A) \geq W(A \cup B) - W(B)$, provided A and B are disjoint and $W(B)$ is bounded away from zero.[5] This inequality captures the certainty effect: The impact of an event A is greater when it is subtracted from the certain event S than when it is subtracted from some uncertain event $A \cup B$.

A weighting function W satisfies bounded subadditivity, or subadditivity (SA) for short, if it satisfies both (i) and (ii) above. According to such a weighting function, an event has greater impact when it turns impossibility into possibility or possibility into certainty than when it merely makes a possibility more or less likely. To illustrate, consider the possible outcome of a football game. Let H denote the event that the home team wins the game, V denote the event that the visiting team wins, and T denote a tie. Hence, $S = H \cup V \cup T$. Lower SA implies that $W(T)$ exceeds $W(H \cup T) - W(H)$, whereas upper SA implies that $W(H \cup V \cup T) - W(H \cup V)$ exceeds $W(H \cup T) - W(H)$. Thus, adding the event T (a tie) to ϕ has more impact than adding T to H, and subtracting T from S has more impact than subtracting T from $H \cup T$. These conditions extend to uncertainty the principle that increasing the probability of winning a prize from 0 to p has more impact than increasing the probability of winning from q to $q + p$, and decreasing the probability of winning from 1 to $1 - p$ has more impact than decreasing the probability of winning from $q + p$ to q. To investigate these properties empirically, consider four simple prospects, each of which offers a fixed prize if a particular event (H, T, $H \cup V$, or $H \cup T$) occurs and nothing if it does not. By asking people to price these prospects, we can estimate the decision weights associated with the respective events and test both lower and upper SA, provided the value function is scaled independently.

Several comments concerning this analysis are in order. First, risk can be viewed as a special case of uncertainty where probability is defined through a standard chance device so that the probabilities of outcomes are known. Under this interpretation, the S-shaped weighting function of figure 30.1 satisfies both lower and upper SA. Second, we have defined these properties in terms of the weighting function W that is not directly observable but can be derived from preferences (see Wakker &

Table 30.2
A Demonstration of Subadditivity in Betting on the Outcome of a Stanford–Berkeley Football Game

Problem	Option	Events A	B	C	D	Preference (%)
1	f_1	$25	0	0	0	61
	g_1	0	0	$10	$10	39
2	f_2	0	0	0	$25	66
	g_2	$10	$10	0	0	34
3	f_3	$25	0	0	$25	29
	g_3	$10	$10	$10	$10	71

Note: A = Stanford wins by 7 or more points; B = Stanford wins by less than 7 points; C = Berkeley ties or wins by less than 7 points; D = Berkeley wins by 7 or more points. Preference = percentage of respondents ($N = 112$) that chose each option.

Tversky, 1993). Necessary and sufficient conditions for bounded SA in terms of the observed preference order are presented by Tversky and Wakker (in press) in the context of cumulative prospect theory. Third, the concept of bounded SA is more general than the property of diminishing sensitivity, which gives rise to a weighting function that is concave for relatively unlikely events and convex for relatively likely events. Finally, there is evidence to suggest that the decision weights for complementary events typically sum to less than one, that is, $W(A) + W(S - A) \leq 1$ or equivalently, $W(A) \leq W(S) - W(S - A)$. This property, called *subcertainty* (Kahneman & Tversky, 1979), can also be interpreted as evidence that upper SA has more impact than lower SA; in other words, the certainty effect is more pronounced than the possibility effect. Some data consistent with this property are presented below.

An Illustration
We next present an illustration of SA that yields a new violation of expected utility theory. We asked 112 Stanford students to choose between prospects defined by the outcome of an upcoming football game between Stanford and the University of California at Berkeley. Each participant was presented with three pairs of prospects, displayed in table 30.2. The percentage of respondents who chose each prospect appears on the right. Half of the participants received the problems in the order presented in the table; the other half received the problems in the opposite order. Because we found no significant order effects, the data were pooled. Participants were promised that 10% of all respondents, selected at random, would be paid according to one of their choices.

Table 30.2 shows that, overall, f_1 was chosen over g_1, f_2 over g_2, and g_3 over f_3. Furthermore, the triple (f_1, f_2, g_3) was the single most common pattern, selected by 36% of the respondents. This pattern violates expected utility theory, which implies that a person who chooses f_1 over g_1 and f_2 over g_2 should also choose f_3 over g_3. However, 64% of the 55 participants who chose f_1 and f_2 in problems 1 and 2 chose g_3 in problem 3, contrary to expected utility theory. This pattern, however, is consistent with the present account. To demonstrate, we apply prospect theory to the modal choices in table 30.2. The choice of f_1 over g_1 in problem 1 implies that

$$v(25) W(A) > v(10) W(C \cup D).$$

Similarly, the choice of f_2 over g_2 in problem 2 implies that

$$v(25) W(D) > v(10) W(A \cup B).$$

Adding the two inequalities and rearranging terms yields

$$\frac{W(A) + W(D)}{W(A \cup B) + W(C \cup D)} > \frac{v(10)}{v(25)}.$$

On the other hand, the choice of g_3 over f_3 in problem 3 implies that

$$v(10) W(A \cup B \cup C \cup D) > v(25) W(A \cup D), \quad \text{or}$$

$$\frac{v(10)}{v(25)} > \frac{W(A \cup D)}{W(A \cup B \cup C \cup D)}.$$

Consequently, the modal choices imply

$$\frac{W(A) + W(D)}{W(A \cup B) + W(C \cup D)} > \frac{W(A \cup D)}{W(A \cup B \cup C \cup D)}.$$

It can be shown that this inequality is consistent with a subadditive weighting function. Moreover, the inequality follows from such a weighting function, provided that subcertainty holds. To demonstrate, note that according to lower SA, $W(A) + W(D) \geq W(A \cup D)$. Furthermore, it follows from subcertainty that

$$W(A \cup B) + W(C \cup D) \leq W(A \cup B \cup C \cup D) = 1.$$

Thus, the left-hand ratio exceeds the right-hand ratio, in accord with the modal choices. Note that under expected utility theory W is an additive probability measure, hence the left-hand ratio and the right-hand ratio must be equal.

Relative Sensitivity

As noted earlier, prospect theory assumes SA for both risk and uncertainty. We next propose that this effect is stronger for uncertainty than for risk. In other words, both lower and upper SA are amplified when outcome probabilities are not specified.

To test this hypothesis, we need a method for comparing different domains or sources of uncertainty (e.g., the outcome of a football game or the spin of a roulette wheel). Consider two sources, **A** and **B**, and suppose that the decision weights for both sources satisfy bounded subadditivity. We say that the decision maker is less sensitive to **B** than to **A** if the following two conditions hold for all disjoint events A_1, A_2 in **A**, and B_1, B_2 in **B**, provided all values of W are bounded away from 0 and 1.

If $W(B_1) = W(A_1)$ and $W(B_2) = W(A_2)$

then $W(B_1 \cup B_2) \leq W(A_1 \cup A_2)$. $\qquad (1)$

If $W(S - B_1) = W(S - A_1)$ and $W(S - B_2) = W(S - A_2)$,

then $W(S - [B_1 \cup B_2]) \geq W(S - [A_1 \cup A_2])$. $\qquad (2)$

The first condition says that the union of disjoint events from **B** "loses" more than the union of matched events from **A**. The second condition imposes the analogous requirement on the dual function. Thus, a person is less sensitive[6] to **B** than to **A** if **B** produces more lower SA and more upper SA than does **A**.

This definition can be readily stated in terms of preferences. To illustrate, consider a comparison between uncertainty and chance.[7] Suppose B_1 and B_2 are disjoint uncertain events (e.g., the home team wins or the home team ties a particular football game). Let A_1 and A_2 denote disjoint chance events (e.g., a roulette wheel landing red or landing green). The hypothesis that people are less sensitive to the uncertain source **B** than to the chance source **A** implies the following preference condition. If one is indifferent between receiving \$50 if the home team wins the game or if a roulette wheel lands red ($p = 18/38$), and if one is also indifferent between receiving \$50 if the home team ties the game or if a roulette wheel lands green (i.e., zero or double zero, $p = 2/38$), then one should prefer receiving \$50 if a roulette wheel lands either green or red ($p = 20/38$) to receiving \$50 if the home team either wins or ties the game.

The following studies test the two hypotheses discussed above. First, decision makers exhibit bounded subadditivity under both risk and uncertainty. Second, decision makers are generally less sensitive to uncertainty than to risk.

Table 30.3
Outline of Studies

	Study 1	Study 2	Study 3
Participants	NBA fans	NFL fans	Psychology students
	($N = 27$)	($N = 40$)	($N = 45$)
Sources	Chance	Chance	Chance
	NBA playoffs	Super Bowl	San Francisco temperature
	San Francisco temperature	Dow–Jones	Beijing temperature

Note: NBA = National Basketball Association; NFL = National Football League.

Experimental Tests

We conducted three studies using a common experimental paradigm. On each trial, participants chose between an uncertain (or risky) prospect and various cash amounts. These data were used to estimate the certainty equivalents of each prospect (i.e., the sure amount that the participant considers as attractive as the prospect) and to derive decision weights. The basic features of the studies are outlined in table 30.3.

Method

Participants.   The participants in the first study were 27 male Stanford students (median age $= 21$) who responded to advertisements calling for basketball fans to take part in a study of decision making. Participants received $15 for participating in two 1-hour sessions, spaced a few days apart. The participants in the second study were 40 male football fans (median age $= 21$), recruited in a similar manner. They were promised that in addition to receiving $15 for their participation in two 1-hour sessions, some of them would be selected at random to play one of their choices for real money. The participants in the third study were 45 Stanford students enrolled in an introductory psychology course (28 men, 17 women, median age $= 20$) who took part in a 1-hour session for course credit. The responses of a few additional participants (one from study 1, four from study 2, and three from study 3) were excluded from the analysis because they exhibited a great deal of internal inconsistency. We also excluded a very small number of responses that were completely out of line with an individual's other responses.

Procedure.   The experiment was run using a computer. Each trial involved a series of choices between a prospect that offered a prize contingent on chance or an uncertain event (e.g., a 25% chance to win a prize of $150) and a descending series of sure payments (e.g., receive $40 for sure). In study 1, the prize was always $75 for half the respondents and $150 for the other half; in studies 2 and 3, the prize for all respondents was $150. Certainty equivalents were inferred from two rounds of such choices. The first round consisted of six choices between the prospect and sure payments, spaced roughly evenly between $0 and the prize amount. After completing the first round of choices, a new set of seven sure payments was presented, spanning the narrower range between the lowest payment that the respondent had accepted and highest payment that the respondent had rejected. The program enforced internal consistency. For example, no respondent was allowed to prefer $30 for sure over a prospect and also prefer the same prospect over a sure $40. The program allowed respondents to backtrack if they felt they had made a mistake in the previous round of choices.

The certainty equivalent of each prospect was determined by a linear interpolation between the lowest value accepted and the highest value rejected in the second round of choices. This interpolation yielded a margin of error of $\pm\$2.50$ for the $150 prospects and $\pm\$1.25$ for the $75 prospects. We wish to emphasize that although our analysis is based on certainty equivalents, the data consisted of a series of choices between a given prospect and sure outcomes. Thus, respondents were not asked to generate certainty equivalents; instead, these values were inferred from choices.

Each session began with detailed instructions and practice. In study 1, the first session consisted of chance prospects followed by basketball prospects; the second session replicated the chance prospects followed by prospects defined by a future temperature in San Francisco. In study 2, the first session consisted of chance prospects followed by Super Bowl prospects; the second session replicated the chance prospects followed by prospects defined by a future value of the Dow–Jones index. Study 3 consisted of a single session in which the chance prospects were followed by prospects defined by a future temperature in San Francisco and Beijing; the order of the latter two sources was counterbalanced. The order of the prospects within each source was randomized.

Sources of Uncertainty. Chance prospects were described in terms of a random draw of a single poker chip from an urn containing 100 chips numbered consecutively from 1 to 100. Nineteen prospects of the form (x, p) were constructed where p varied from .05 to .95 in multiples of .05. For example, a typical chance prospect would pay $150 if the number of the poker chip is between 1 and 25, and nothing otherwise. This design yields 90 tests of lower SA and 90 tests of upper SA for each participant.

Basketball prospects were defined by the result of the first game of the 1991 National Basketball Association (NBA) quarter final series between the Portland

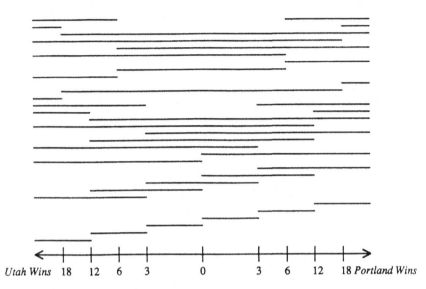

Figure 30.2
Event space for prospects defined by the result of the Utah–Portland basketball game. The horizontal axis refers to the point spread in that game. Each row denotes a target event that defines a prospect used in study 1. Segments that extend up to the arrowhead represent unbounded intervals. Each interval includes the more extreme endpoint relative to 0, but not the less extreme endpoint.

Trailblazers and the Utah Jazz. For example, a typical prospect would pay $150 if Portland beats Utah by more than 6 points. The event space is depicted in figure 30.2. Each of the 32 rows in the figure represents a target event A that defines an uncertain prospect (x, A). For example, the top row in figure 30.2, which consists of two segments, represents the event "the margin of victory exceeds 6 points." This design yields 28 tests of lower SA and 12 tests of upper SA. For example, one test of lower SA is obtained by comparing the decision weight for the event "Utah wins" to the sum of the decision weights for the two events "Utah wins by up to 12 points" and "Utah wins by more than 12 points."

Super Bowl prospects were defined by the result of the 1992 Super Bowl game between the Buffalo Bills and the Washington Redskins. The event space is depicted in figure 30.3. It includes 28 target events yielding 30 tests of lower SA and 17 tests of upper SA.

Dow–Jones prospects were defined by the change in the Dow–Jones Industrial Average over the subsequent week. For example, a typical prospect would pay $150 if the Dow–Jones goes up by more than 50 points over the next seven days. The event space has the same structure as that of the Super Bowl (figure 30.3).

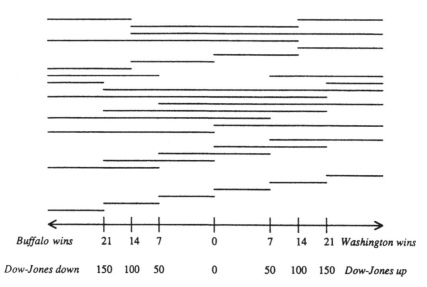

Figure 30.3
Event space for prospects defined by the result of the Super Bowl game between Washington and Buffalo (and for the Dow–Jones prospects). The horizontal axis refers to the point spread in the Super Bowl (and the change in the Dow–Jones in the next week). Each row denotes a target event that defines a prospect used in study 2. Segments that extend up to the arrowhead represent unbounded intervals. Each interval includes the more extreme endpoint relative to 0, but not the less extreme endpoint.

San Francisco temperature prospects were defined by the daytime high temperature in San Francisco on a given future date. The 20 target events used in studies 1 and 3 are depicted in figure 30.4. This design yields 30 tests of lower SA and 10 tests of upper SA. For example, a typical prospect would pay $75 if the daytime high temperature in downtown San Francisco on April 1, 1992, is between 65° and 80°. Similarly, Beijing temperature prospects were defined by the daytime high temperature in Beijing on a given future day. The event space is identical to the San Francisco temperature in study 3, as depicted in figure 30.4.

Results

To test lower and upper SA, the decision weights for each respondent were derived as follows. Using the choice data, we first estimated the certainty equivalent C of each prospect by linear interpolation, as described earlier. According to prospect theory, if $C(x, A) = y$, then $v(y) = W(A)v(x)$ and $W(A) = v(y)/v(x)$. The decision weight associated with an uncertain event A, therefore, can be computed if the value function v for gains is known. Previous studies (e.g., Tversky, 1967) have indicated that

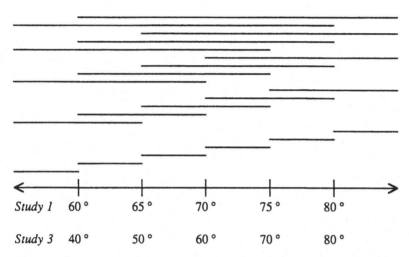

Figure 30.4
Event space for prospects defined by future temperatures in San Francisco and Beijing. The horizontal axis refers to the daytime high temperature on a given date. Each row denotes a target event that defines a prospect used in studies 1 and 3. Segments that extend up to the arrowhead represent unbounded intervals. Each interval includes the left endpoint but not the right endpoint.

the value function for gains can be approximated by a power function of the form $v(x) = x^\alpha$, $0 \le \alpha \le 1$. This form is characterized by the assumption that multiplying the prize of a prospect by a positive constant multiplies its certainty equivalent by the same constant.[8] This prediction was tested using the data from study 1 in which each event was paired both with a prize of $75 and with a prize of $150. Consistent with a power value function, we found no significant difference between $C(150, A)$ and $2C(75, A)$ for any of the sources.

Although the present data are consistent with a power function, the value of the exponent cannot be estimated from simple prospects because the exponent α can be absorbed into W. To estimate the exponent for gains, we need prospects with two positive outcomes. Such prospects were investigated by Tversky and Kahneman (1992), using the same experimental procedure and a similar subject population. They found that estimates of the exponent did not vary markedly across respondents and the median estimate of the exponent was .88. In the analysis that follows, we first assume a power value function with an exponent of .88 and test lower and upper SA using this function. We then show that the test of SA is robust with respect to substantial variations in the exponent. Further analyses are based on an ordinal method that makes no assumption about the functional form of v.

Table 30.4
Proportion of Tests that Strictly Satisfy Lower and Upper Subadditivity (SA)

	Study 1		Study 2		Study 3	
Source	Lower SA	Upper SA	Lower SA	Upper SA	Lower SA	Upper SA
Chance	.80	.81	.77	.83	.81	.79
Basketball	.88	.83				
Super Bowl			.86	.87		
Dow–Jones			.77	.87		
S.F. temp.	.83	.89			.85	.89
Beijing temp.					.89	.91

Note: S.F. = San Francisco; temp. = temperature.

Using the estimated W for each source of uncertainty, we define measures of the degree of lower and upper SA as follows. Recall that lower SA requires that $W(A) \geq W(A \cup B) - W(B)$, for $A \cap B = \phi$. Hence, the difference between the two sides of the inequality,

$$D(A, B) \equiv W(A) + W(B) - W(A \cup B),$$

provides a measure of the degree of lower SA. Similarly, recall that upper SA requires that $1 - W(S - A) \geq W(A \cup B) - W(B)$, for $A \cap B = \phi$. Hence, the difference between the two sides of the inequality,

$$D'(A, B) \equiv 1 - W(S - A) - W(A \cup B) + W(B),$$

provides a measure of the degree of upper SA.

Table 30.4 presents the overall proportion of tests, across participants, that strictly satisfy lower and upper SA (i.e., $D > 0$, $D' > 0$) for each source of uncertainty. Note that if W were additive (as implied by expected utility theory), then both D and D' are expected to be zero; hence, all entries in table 30.4 should be close to one-half. However, each entry in table 30.4 is significantly greater than one-half ($p < .01$, by a binomial test), as implied by SA.

To obtain global measures of lower and upper SA, let d and d', respectively, be the mean values of D and D' for a given respondent. Besides serving as summary statistics, these indexes have a simple geometric interpretation if the risky weighting function is roughly linear except near the endpoints. It is easy to verify that within the linear portion of the graph, D and D' do not depend on A and B, and the summary measures d and d' correspond to the "lower" and "upper" intercepts of the weighting function (see figure 30.5). Its slope, $s = 1 - d - d'$, can then be interpreted as a measure of sensitivity to probability changes. For uncertainty, we cannot plot d and

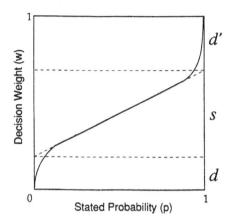

Figure 30.5
A weighting function that is linear except near the endpoints (d = "lower" intercept of the weighting function; d' = "upper" intercept of the weighting function; s = slope).

d' as in figure 30.5. However, d and d' have an analogous interpretation as a "possibility gap" and "certainty gap," respectively, if W is roughly linear except near the endpoints.[9] Note that under expected utility theory, $d = d' = 0$ and $s = 1$, whereas prospect theory implies $d \geq 0$, $d' \geq 0$, and $s \leq 1$. Thus, prospect theory implies less sensitivity to changes in uncertainty than is required by expected utility theory. To test these predictions, we computed the values of d, d', and s, separately for each respondent. Table 30.5 presents the median values of these indexes, across respondent for each source of uncertainty.

In accord with SA, each value of d and d' in table 30.5 is significantly greater than zero ($p < .05$). Furthermore, both indexes are larger for uncertainty than for chance: The mean values of d and of d' for the uncertain sources are significantly greater than each of the corresponding indexes for chance ($p < .01$, separately for each study). Finally, consistent with subcertainty, d' tends to exceed d, though this difference is statistically significant only in studies 2 and 3 ($p < .05$).

Recall that all participants evaluated the same set of risky prospects, and that respondents in each of the three studies evaluated two different types of uncertain prospects (see table 30.3). Figure 30.6 plots, for each respondent, the average sensitivity measure s for the two uncertain sources against s for the risky source. (One respondent who produced a negative s was excluded from this analysis.) These data may be summarized as follows. First, all values of s for the uncertain prospects and all but two values of s for the risky prospects were less than or equal to one as implied by SA. Second, the values of s are considerably higher for risk (mean $s = .74$)

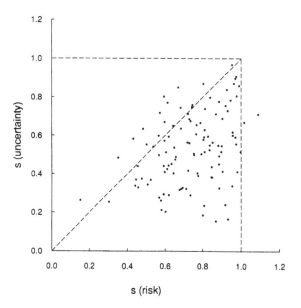

Figure 30.6
Joint distribution for all respondents of the sensitivity measure *s* for risk and uncertainty.

than for uncertainty (mean $s = .53$), as demonstrated by the fact that 94 out of 111 points lie below the identity line ($p < .01$ by a sign test). Third, the data reveal a significant correlation between the sensitivity measures for risk and for uncertainty ($r = .37$, $p < .01$). The average correlation between the uncertain sources is .40. If we restrict the analysis to studies 1 and 2 that yielded more stable data (in part because the risky prospects were replicated), the correlation between sensitivity for risk and for uncertainty increases to .51, and the mean correlation between the uncertain sources increases to .54. These correlations indicate the presence of consistent individual differences in SA and suggest that sensitivity to uncertainty is an important attribute that distinguishes among decision makers. An axiomatic analysis of the conditions under which one individual is consistently more SA than another is presented in Tversky and Wakker (in press).

Robustness. The preceding analysis summarized in table 30.5 assumes a power value function with an exponent $\alpha = .88$. To investigate whether the above conclusions depend on the particular choice of the exponent, we reanalyzed the data using different values of α varying from one-half to one. To appreciate the impact of this difference, consider the prospect that offers a one-third chance to win $100. [We

Table 30.5
Median Values of d, d', and s, across Respondents, Measuring the Degree of Lower and Upper Sub-additivity (SA) and Global Sensitivity, Respectively

Source	Study 1			Study 2			Study 3		
	d	d'	s	d	d'	s	d	d'	s
Chance	.06	.10	.81	.05	.19	.75	.11	.14	.72
Basketball	.21	.19	.61						
Super Bowl				.15	.23	.57			
Dow–Jones				.12	.22	.67			
S.F. temp.	.20	.26	.51				.27	.23	.50
Beijing temp.							.28	.32	.42

Note: S.F. = San Francisco; temp. = temperature.

choose one-third because, according to figure 30.1, $w(1/3)$ is approximately one-third.] The certainty equivalent of this prospect is \$33.33 if $\alpha = 1$, but it is only \$11.11 if $\alpha = .5$. Table 30.6 shows that as α decreases (indicating greater curvature), d increases and d' decreases. More important, however, both d and d' are positive throughout the range for all sources, and the values of s are significantly smaller than one ($p < .01$) in all cases. SA, therefore, holds for a fairly wide range of variation in the curvature of the value function.

Ordinal Analysis. The preceding analysis confirmed our hypothesis that people are less sensitive to uncertainty than to chance using the sensitivity measure s. We next turn to an ordinal test of this hypothesis that makes no assumptions about the value function. Let B_1, B_2 denote disjoint uncertain events, and let A_1, A_2 denote disjoint chance events. We searched among the responses of each participant for patterns satisfying

$$C(x, B_1) \geq C(x, A_1) \quad \text{and} \quad C(x, B_2) \geq C(x, A_2) \quad \text{but}$$
$$C(x, B_1 \cup B_2) < C(x, A_1 \cup A_2), \tag{3}$$

or

$$C(x, S - B_1) \leq C(x, S - A_1) \quad \text{and}$$
$$C(x, S - B_2) \leq C(x, S - A_2) \quad \text{but} \tag{4}$$
$$C(x, S - [B_1 \cup B_2]) > C(x, S - [A_1 \cup A_2]).$$

A response pattern that satisfies either condition 3 or 4 provides support for the hypothesis that the respondent is less sensitive to uncertainty (**B**) than to chance (**A**).

Table 30.6
Median Values of d, d', and s across Respondents, Measuring the Degree of Lower Subadditivity, Upper Subadditivity, and Global Sensitivity, Respectively, for Several Values of α Between .5 and 1

Source and index	α				
	0.500	0.625	0.750	0.875	1.00
Chance (Study 1)					
d	.29	.19	.12	.06	.01
d'	.02	.05	.07	.10	.12
s	.66	.73	.77	.81	.83
Chance (Study 2)					
d	.28	.18	.11	.05	.003
d'	.09	.12	.15	.19	.23
s	.66	.70	.74	.75	.75
Chance (Study 3)					
d	.33	.24	.17	.11	.06
d'	.05	.08	.11	.14	.17
s	.59	.65	.69	.72	.75
Basketball					
d	.40	.33	.26	.21	.16
d'	.10	.14	.17	.19	.22
s	.50	.56	.58	.61	.63
Super Bowl					
d	.36	.28	.20	.15	.11
d'	.15	.18	.20	.23	.25
s	.49	.54	.55	.57	.60
Dow–Jones					
d	.34	.25	.17	.11	.07
d'	.12	.15	.19	.22	.25
s	.54	.61	.64	.67	.70
SF temp (Study 1)					
d	.40	.32	.26	.20	.15
d'	.15	.18	.22	.26	.30
s	.42	.48	.49	.51	.52
SF temp (Study 3)					
d	.47	.39	.33	.27	.22
d'	.15	.18	.20	.23	.26
s	.39	.43	.48	.50	.52
Beijing temp					
d	.48	.40	.34	.28	.23
d'	.21	.25	.29	.32	.35
s	.33	.38	.42	.42	.43

Note: SF = San Francisco; temp = temperature.

Table 30.7
Ordinal Analysis of Differential Sensitivity

Source comparison	Study 1		Study 2		Study 3	
	m	m'	m	m'	m	m'
Basketball vs. chance	.85	.64				
Super Bowl vs. chance			.91	.89		
Dow–Jones vs. chance			.79	.76		
S.F. temp. vs. chance	.76	.93			.87	.87
Beijing temp. vs. chance					.83	.94

Note: Each entry corresponds to the median value, across respondents, of m and m' measuring the degree to which respondents are less sensitive to uncertainty than to chance. S.F. = San Francisco; temp. = temperature.

Several comments regarding this test are in order. First, note that if we replace the weak inequalities in conditions 3 and 4 with equalities, then these conditions reduce to the definition of relative sensitivity (see equations 1 and 2). The above conditions are better suited for the present experimental design because participants were not asked to "match" intervals from different sources. Second, the present analysis is confined to contiguous intervals; conditions 3 and 4 may not hold when comparing contiguous to noncontiguous intervals (see Tversky & Koehler, 1994). Third, because of measurement error, the above conditions are not expected to hold for all comparisons; however, the conditions indicating less sensitivity to uncertainty than to chance are expected to be satisfied more frequently than the opposite conditions.

Let $M(\mathbf{B}, \mathbf{A})$ be the number of response patterns that satisfy condition 3 above (i.e., less sensitivity to uncertainty than to chance). Let $M(\mathbf{A}, \mathbf{B})$ be the number of response patterns that satisfy 3 with the As and Bs interchanged (i.e., less sensitivity to chance than to uncertainty). The ratio $m(\mathbf{B}, \mathbf{A}) = M(\mathbf{B}, \mathbf{A})/(M(\mathbf{B}, \mathbf{A}) + M(\mathbf{A}, \mathbf{B}))$ provides a measure of the degree to which a respondent is less sensitive to uncertainty than to chance, in the sense of condition 3. We define $M'(\mathbf{B}, \mathbf{A})$, $M'(\mathbf{A}, \mathbf{B})$, and $m'(\mathbf{B}, \mathbf{A})$ similarly for preference patterns that satisfy condition 4. If the respondent is invariably less sensitive to $\mathbf{B}$ than to $\mathbf{A}$, then the ratios $m(\mathbf{B}, \mathbf{A})$ and $m'(\mathbf{B}, \mathbf{A})$ should be close to one. On the other hand, if the respondent is not more sensitive to one source than to another, these ratios should be close to one-half. Table 30.7 presents the median ratios, across respondent, comparing each of the five uncertain sources to chance. As predicted, all entries in the table are significantly greater than one-half ($p < .05$, by t tests), indicating that people are generally less sensitive to uncertainty than to chance.

We conclude this section with a brief methodological discussion. We have attributed the findings of bounded subadditivity and lower sensitivity for uncertainty than for risk to basic psychological attitudes toward risk and uncertainty captured by the weighting function. Alternatively, one might be tempted to account for these findings by a statistical model that assumes that the assessment of certainty equivalents, and hence the estimation of decision weights, is subject to random error that is bounded by the endpoints of the outcome scale, because $C(x, A)$ must lie between 0 and x. Although bounded error could contribute to SA, this model cannot adequately account for the observed pattern of results. First, it cannot explain the subadditivity observed in simple choice experiments that do not involve (direct or indirect) assessment of certainty equivalents, such as the Stanford–Berkeley problem presented in table 30.2. More extensive evidence for both lower and upper SA in simple choices between risky prospects is reported by Wu and Gonzalez (1994), who also found some support for the stronger hypothesis that w is concave for low probabilities and convex for moderate and high probabilities. Second, a statistical model cannot readily account for the result of the ordinal analysis reported above that respondents were less sensitive to uncertainty than to chance. Third, because a random error model implies a bias toward one-half, it cannot explain the observation that the decision weight of an event that is as likely as not to occur is generally less than one-half (see figures 30.7, 30.8, and 30.9 below). Finally, it should be noted that subadditivity and differential sensitivity play an important role in the pricing of risky and uncertain prospects, regardless of whether these phenomena are driven primarily by psychological or by statistical factors.

Discussion

The final section of this article addresses three topics. First, we explore the relationship between decision weights and judged probabilities. Second, we investigate the presence of preferences for betting on particular sources of uncertainty. Finally, we discuss descriptive and normative implications of the present results.

Preference and Belief

The present account distinguishes between decision weights derived from preferences and degree of belief expressed by probability judgments. What is the relation between the judged probability, $P(A)$, of an uncertain event, A, and its associated decision weight $W(A)$? To investigate this problem, we asked respondents, after they completed the choice task, to assess the probabilities of all target events. Following

Table 30.8
Median Values of d, d', and s, across Respondents, That Measure the Degree of Lower and Upper Sub-additivity, SA, and Global Sensitivity, Respectively, for Judged Probability

	Study 1			Study 2			Study 3		
Source	d	d'	s	d	d'	s	d	d'	s
Basketball	.08	.11	.74						
Super Bowl				.11	.08	.81			
Dow–Jones				.07	.08	.84			
S.F. temp.	.13	.16	.70				.29	.21	.51
Beijing temp.							.24	.25	.53

Note: SA = Subadditivity; S.F. = San Francisco; temp. = temperature; s = degree of global sensitivity.

the analysis of decision weights, we define measures of the degree of lower and upper SA in probability judgments as follows:

$$D(A, B) \equiv P(A) + P(B) - P(A \cup B),$$

$$D'(A, B) \equiv 1 - P(S - A) + P(B) - P(A \cup B),$$

provided $A \cap B = \phi$. Clearly, P is additive if and only if $D = D' = 0$ for all disjoint A, B in S. As before, let d and d' be the mean values of D and D', respectively, and let $s = 1 - d - d'$. Table 30.8, which is the analog of table 30.5, presents the median values of d, d', and s, across respondents, for each of the five uncertain sources.

All values of d and d' in table 30.8 are significantly greater than zero ($p < .05$), demonstrating both lower and upper SA for probability judgments. Comparing table 30.8 and table 30.5 reveals that the values of s for judged probabilities (overall mean .70) are greater than the corresponding uncertain decision weights (overall mean .55). Thus, probability judgments exhibit less SA than do uncertain decision weights. This finding is consistent with a two-stage process in which the decision maker first assesses the probability P of an uncertain event A, then transforms this value by the risky weighting function w. Thus, $W(A)$ may be approximated by $w[P(A)]$.

We illustrate this model using the median risky and uncertain decision weights derived from study 2 (assuming $\alpha = .88$). In figure 30.7 we plot decision weights for chance prospects as a function of stated (objective) probabilities. In figures 30.8 and 30.9, respectively, we plot decision weights for Super Bowl prospects and for Dow–Jones prospects as functions of (median) judged probabilities. The comparison of these figures reveals that the data in figures 30.8 and 30.9 are less orderly than those in figure 30.7. This is not surprising because judged probability (unlike stated probability) is measured with error, and because the uncertain decision weights exhibit

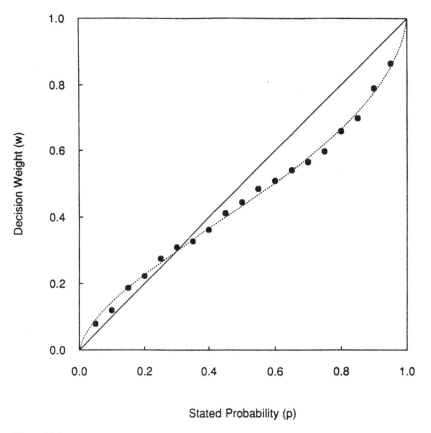

Figure 30.7
Median decision weights for chance prospects, from study 2, plotted as a function of stated (objective) probabilities.

greater variability (both within and between subjects) than risky decision weights. However, the underlying relation between probability and decision weights is nearly identical in the three figures.[10] This is exactly what we would expect if the uncertain weighting function W is obtained by applying the risky weighting function w to judged probabilities.

The subadditivity of probability judgments reported in table 30.8 is consistent with support theory[11] (Tversky & Koehler, 1994), according to which $P(A) + P(B) \geq P(A \cup B)$. The combination of the two-stage model (which is based on prospect theory) with an analysis of probability judgments (which is based on support theory) can therefore explain our main finding that decision weights are more subadditive for

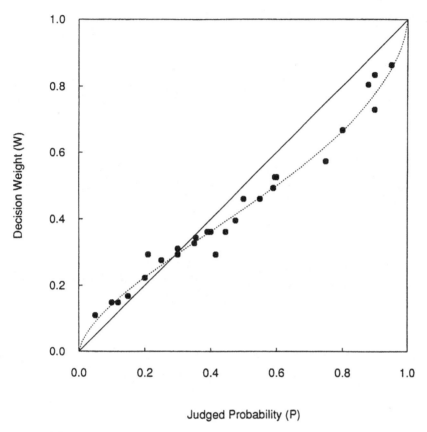

Figure 30.8
Median decision weights for Super Bowl prospects, from study 2, plotted as a function of median judged probabilities.

uncertainty than for chance. This model also implies that the decision weight associated with an uncertain event (e.g., an airplane accident) increases when its description is unpacked into its constituents (e.g., an airplane accident caused by mechanical failure, terrorism, human error, or acts of God; see Johnson, Hershey, Meszaros, & Kunreuther, 1993). Furthermore, this model predicts greater subadditivity, ceteris paribus, when $A \cup B$ is a contiguous interval (e.g., future temperature between 60° and 80°) than when $A \cup B$ is not a contiguous interval (e.g., future temperature less than 60° or more than 80°). A more detailed treatment of this model will be presented elsewhere.

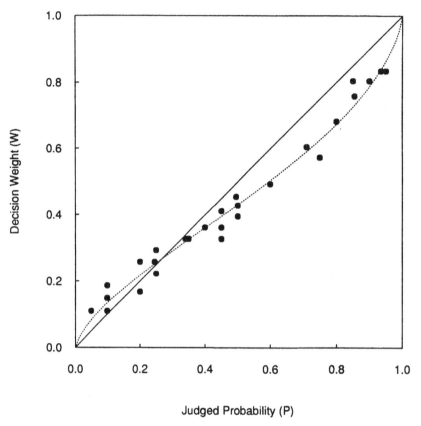

Figure 30.9
Median decision weights for Dow–Jones prospects, from study 2, plotted as a function of median judged probability.

Source Preference

The finding that people are less sensitive to uncertainty than to risk should be distinguished from the observation of ambiguity aversion: People often prefer to bet on known rather than unknown probabilities (Ellsberg, 1961). For example, people generally prefer to bet on either side of a fair coin than on either side of a coin with an unknown bias. These preferences violate expected utility theory because they imply that the sum of the subjective probabilities of heads and of tails is higher for the unbiased coin than for the coin with the unknown bias.

Recent research has documented some significant exceptions to ambiguity aversion. Heath and Tversky (1991) showed that people who were knowledgeable about sports but not about politics preferred to bet on sports events rather than on chance events that these people had judged equally probable. However, the same people preferred to bet on chance events rather than on political events that they had judged equally probable. Likewise, people who were knowledgeable about politics but not about sports exhibited the reverse pattern. These data support what Heath and Tversky call the competence hypothesis: People prefer to bet on their beliefs in situations where they feel competent or knowledgeable, and they prefer to bet on chance when they feel incompetent or ignorant. This account is consistent with the preference to bet on the fair rather than the biased coin, but it predicts additional preferences that are at odds with ambiguity aversion.

The preceding studies allow us to test the competence hypothesis against ambiguity aversion. Recall that the participants in studies 1 and 2 were recruited for their knowledge of basketball and football, respectively. Ambiguity aversion implies a preference for chance over uncertainty because the probabilities associated with the sports events (e.g., Utah beating Portland) are necessarily vague or imprecise. In contrast, the competence hypothesis predicts that the sports fans will prefer to bet on the game than on chance.

To establish source preference, let $\mathbf{A}$ and $\mathbf{B}$ be two different sources of uncertainty. A decision maker is said to prefer source $\mathbf{A}$ to source $\mathbf{B}$ if for any events A in $\mathbf{A}$ and B in $\mathbf{B}$. $W(A) = W(B)$ implies $W(S - A) > W(S - B)$, or equivalently, $C(x, A) = C(x, B)$ implies $C(x, S - A) > C(x, S - B)$, $x > 0$. To test for source preference we searched among the responses of each participants for patterns that satisfy $C(x, A) \geq C(x, B)$ and $C(x, S - A) > C(x, S - B)$. Thus, a decision maker who prefers to bet on event A than to bet on event B, and also prefers to bet against A than to bet against B exhibits a preference for source $\mathbf{A}$ over source $\mathbf{B}$. The preference to bet on either side of a fair coin rather than on either side of a coin with an unknown bias illustrates such a preference for chance over uncertainty.

Let $K(\mathbf{A}, \mathbf{B})$ be the number of response patterns indicating a preference for source $\mathbf{A}$ over source $\mathbf{B}$, as defined above, and let $K(\mathbf{B}, \mathbf{A})$ be the number of response patterns indicating the opposite preference. For each pair of sources, we computed the ratio $k(\mathbf{A}, \mathbf{B}) = K(\mathbf{A}, \mathbf{B})/(K(\mathbf{A}, \mathbf{B}) + K(\mathbf{B}, \mathbf{A}))$, separately for each respondent. This ratio provides a comparative index of source preference; it should equal one-half if neither source is preferred to the other, and it should be substantially greater than one-half if source $\mathbf{A}$ is generally preferred to source $\mathbf{B}$.

The present data reveal significant source preferences that are consistent with the competence hypothesis but not with ambiguity aversion. In all three studies, participants preferred to bet on their uncertain beliefs in their area of competence rather than on known chance events. The basketball fans in study 1 preferred betting on basketball than on chance (median $k = .76$, $p < .05$ by t test); the football fans in study 2 preferred betting on the Super Bowl than on chance (median $k = .59$, though this effect is not statistically significant); and the students in study 3 (who live near San Francisco) preferred betting on San Francisco temperature than on chance (median $k = .76$, $p < .01$). Two other comparisons consistent with the competence hypothesis are the preference for basketball over San Francisco temperature in study 1 (median $k = .76$, $p < .05$), and the preference for San Francisco temperature over Beijing temperature in study 3 (median $k = .86$, $p < .01$). For further discussions of ambiguity aversion and source preference, see Camerer and Weber (1992), Fox and Tversky (in press), and Frisch and Baron (1988).

Concluding Comments

Several authors (e.g., Ellsberg, 1961; Fellner, 1961; Keynes, 1921; Knight, 1921), critical of expected utility theory, distinguished among uncertain prospects according to the degree to which the uncertainty can be quantified. At one extreme, uncertainty is characterized by a known probability distribution; this is the domain of decision under risk. At the other extreme, decision makers are unable to quantify their uncertainty; this is the domain of decision under ignorance. Most decisions under uncertainty lie somewhere between these two extremes: People typically do not know the exact probabilities associated with the relevant outcomes, but they have some vague notion about their likelihood. The role of vagueness or ambiguity in decision under uncertainty has been the subject of much experimental and theoretical research.

In the present chapter we have investigated this issue using the conceptual framework of prospect theory. According to this theory, uncertainty is represented by a weighting function that satisfies bounded subadditivity. Thus, an event has more impact when it turns impossibility into possibility, or possibility into certainty, than when it merely makes a possibility more likely. This principle explains Allais's examples (i.e., the certainty effect) as well as the fourfold pattern of risk attitudes illustrated in table 30.1. The experiments reported in this article demonstrate SA for both risk and uncertainty. They also show that this effect is more pronounced for uncertainty than for risk. The latter finding suggests the more general hypothesis that SA, and hence the departure from expected utility theory, is amplified by vagueness or ambiguity. Consequently, studies of decision under risk are likely to underestimate the degree of SA that characterizes decisions involving real-world uncertainty.[12] Subadditivity, therefore, emerges as a unifying principle of choice that is manifested to varying degrees in decisions under risk, uncertainty, and ignorance.

The psychological basis of bounded subadditivity includes both judgmental and preferential elements. As noted earlier, SA holds for judgments of probability (see table 30.8), but it is more pronounced for decision weights (see table 30.5). This amplification may reflect people's affective responses to positive and negative outcomes. Imagine owning a lottery ticket that offers some hope of winning a great fortune. Receiving a second ticket to the same lottery, we suggest, will increase one's hope of becoming rich but will not quite double it. The same pattern appears to hold for negative outcomes. Imagine waiting for the results of a biopsy. Receiving a preliminary indication that reduces the probability of malignancy by one-half, we suggest, will reduce fear by less than one-half. Thus, hope and fear seem to be subadditive in outcome probability. To the extent that the experience of hope and fear is treated as a consequence of an action, subadditivity may have some normative basis. If lottery tickets are purchased primarily for entertaining a fantasy, and protective action is undertaken largely to achieve peace of mind, then it is not unreasonable to value the first lottery ticket more than the second, and to value the elimination of a hazard more than a comparable reduction in its likelihood.

Notes

This research was supported by National Science Foundation Grants SES-9109535 and SBR-9408684. The article benefitted from discussions with Daniel Kahneman and Peter Wakker.

1. Risk seeking for long shots was reported by Kachelmeier and Shehata (1992) in an experiment conducted in China with real payoffs that were considerably higher than the normal monthly incomes of the participants.

2. Figure 30.1 corrects a minor error in the original drawing.

3. For other discussions of decision weights for uncertain events, see Hogarth and Einhorn (1990), Viscusi (1989), and Wakker (1994).

4. The boundary conditions are needed to ensure that we always compare an interval that includes an endpoint to an interval that is bounded away from the other endpoint (see Tversky & Wakker, in press, for a more rigorous formulation).

5. The upper subadditivity of W is equivalent to the lower subadditivity of the dual function $W'(A) = 1 - W(S - A)$.

6. Relative sensitivity is closely related to the concept of relative curvature for subjective dimensions introduced by Krantz and Tversky (1975).

7. Although probabilities could be generated by various chance devices, we do not distinguish between them here, and treat risk or chance as a single source of uncertainty.

8. This follows from the fact that for $t > 0$, the value of the prospect (tx, A) is $W(A)(tx)^\alpha$; hence, $C(tx, A) = W(A)^{1/\alpha} tx$, which equals $tC(x, A)$.

9. More formally, this holds when $W(A \cup B) - W(A)$ does not depend on A, for all $A \cap B = \phi$, provided $W(A)$ is not too close to zero and $W(A \cup B)$ is not too close to 1.

10. The smooth curves in figures 30.5 and 30.6 were obtained by fitting the parametric form $w(p) = \delta p^\gamma / (\delta p^\gamma + [1 - p]^\gamma)$, used by Lattimore, Baker, and Witte (1992). It assumes that the relation between w

and p is linear in a log odds metric. The estimated values of the parameters in figures 30.7, 30.8, and 30.9, respectively, are .69, .69, and .72 for γ, and .77, .76, and .76 for δ.

11. In this theory, $P(A) + P(S - A) = 1$; hence, the equations for lower and upper SA coincide.

12. Evidence for substantial SA in the decisions of professional options traders is reported by Fox, Rogers, and Tversky (1995).

References

Allais, A. M. (1953). Le comportement de l'homme rationel devant le risque, critique des postulates et axiomes de l'ecole americaine. *Econometrica, 21*, 503–546.

Camerer, C. F., & Ho, T.-H. (1994). Violations of the betweenness axiom and nonlinearity in probability. *Journal of Risk and Uncertainty, 8*, 167–196.

Camerer, C. F., & Weber, M. (1992). Recent developments in modeling preferences: Uncertainty and ambiguity. *Journal of Risk and Uncertainty, 5*, 325–370.

Cohen, M., Jaffray, J. Y., & Said, T. (1987). Experimental comparisons of individual behavior under risk and under uncertainty for gains and for losses. *Organizational Behavior and Human Decision Processes, 39*, 1–22.

Edwards, W. (1962). Subjective probabilities inferred from decisions. *Psychological Review, 69*, 109–135.

Ellsberg, D. (1961). Risk, ambiguity, and the Savage axioms. *Quarterly Journal of Economics, 75*, 643–669.

Fellner, W. (1961). Distortion of subjective probabilities as a reaction to uncertainty. *Quarterly Journal of Economics, 75*, 670–689.

Fishburn, P. C., & Kochenberger, G. A. (1979). Two-piece von Neumann–Morganstern utility functions. *Decision Sciences, 10*, 503–518.

Fox, C. R., Rogers, B., & Tversky, A. (1995). *Options traders reveal subadditive decision weights.* Unpublished manuscript, Stanford University.

Fox, C. R., & Tversky, A. (in press). Ambiguity aversion and comparative ignorance. *Quarterly Journal of Economics.*

Friedman, M., & Savage, L. J. (1948). The utility analysis of choices involving risk. *Journal of Political Economy, 56*, 279–306.

Frisch, D., & Baron, J. (1988). Ambiguity and rationality. *Journal of Behavioral Decision Making, 1*, 149–157.

Heath, F., & Tversky, A. (1991). Preference and belief: Ambiguity and competence in choice under uncertainty. *Journal of Risk and Uncertainty, 4*, 4–28.

Hershey, J. C., & Schoemaker, P. H. J. (1980). Prospect theory's reflection hypothesis: A critical examination. *Organizational Behavior and Human Performance, 25*, 395–418.

Hogarth, R., & Einhorn, H. (1990). Venture theory: A model of decision weights. *Management Science, 36*, 780–803.

Johnson, E. J., Hershey, J., Meszaros, J., & Kunreuther, H. (1993). Framing, probability distortions, and insurance decisions. *Journal of Risk and Uncertainty, 7*, 35–51.

Kachelmeier, S. J., & Shehata, M. (1992). Examining risk preferences under high monetary incentives: Experimental evidence from the People's Republic of China. *American Economic Review, 82*, 1120–1141.

Kahneman, D., & Tversky, A. (1979). Prospect theory: An analysis of decision under risk. *Econometrica, 4*, 263–291.

Keynes, J. M. (1921). *A treatise on probability*. London: Macmillan.

Knight, F. H. (1921). *Risk, uncertainty, and profit.* New York: Houghton Mifflin.

Krantz, D. H., & Tversky, A. (1975). Similarity of rectangles: An analysis of subjective dimensions. *Journal of Mathematical Psychology, 12,* 4–34.

Lattimore, P. M., Baker, J. R., & Witte, A. D. (1992). The influence of probability on risky choice. *Journal of Economic Behavior and Organization, 17,* 377–400.

Markowitz, H. (1952). The utility of wealth. *Journal of Political Economy, 60,* 151–158.

Payne, J. W., Laughhunn, D. J., & Crum, R. (1981). Aspiration level effects in risky behavior. *Management Science, 27,* 953–958.

Preston, M. G., & Baratta, P. (1948). An experimental study of the auction value of an uncertain outcome. *American Journal of Psychology, 61,* 183–193.

Tversky, A. (1967). Utility theory and additivity analysis of risky choices. *Journal of Experimental Psychology, 75,* 27–36.

Tversky, A., & Kahneman, D. (1986). Rational choice and the framing of decisions. *Journal of Business, 59*(4, Part 2), 251–278.

Tversky, A., & Kahneman, D. (1992). Advances in prospect theory: Cumulative representation of uncertainty. *Journal of Risk and Uncertainty, 5,* 297–323.

Tversky, A., & Koehler, D. K. (1994). Support theory: A nonextensional representation of subjective probability. *Psychological Review, 101,* 547–567.

Tversky, A., & Wakker, P. P. (in press). Risk attitudes and decision weights. *Econometrica.*

Viscusi, W. K. (1989). Prospective reference theory: Toward an explanation of the paradoxes. *Journal of Risk and Uncertainty, 2,* 235–264.

Wakker, P. P. (1994). Separating marginal utility and probabilistic risk aversion. *Theory and Decision, 30,* 1–44.

Wakker, P. P., & Tversky, A. (1993). An axiomatization of cumulative prospect theory. *Journal of Risk and Uncertainty, 7,* 147–176.

Wehrung, D. A. (1989). Risk taking over gains and losses: A study of oil executives. *Annals of Operations Research, 19,* 115–139.

Wu, G., & Gonzalez, R. (1994). Curvature of the probability weighting function. Unpublished manuscript, Harvard Business School.

31 Ambiguity Aversion and Comparative Ignorance

Craig R. Fox and Amos Tversky

Introduction

One of the fundamental problems of modern decision theory is the analysis of decisions under ignorance or ambiguity, where the probabilities of potential outcomes are neither specified in advance nor readily assessed on the basis of the available evidence. This issue was addressed by Knight [1921], who distinguished between *measurable uncertainty* or *risk*, which can be represented by precise probabilities, and *unmeasurable uncertainty*, which cannot. Furthermore, he suggested that entrepreneurs are compensated for bearing unmeasurable uncertainty as opposed to risk. Contemporaneously, Keynes [1921] distinguished between *probability*, representing the balance of evidence in favor of a particular proposition and the *weight of evidence*, representing the quantity of evidence supporting that balance. He then asked, "If two probabilities are equal in degree, ought we, in choosing our course of action, to prefer that one which is based on a greater body of knowledge?" [p. 313]. The distinction between clear and vague probabilities has been rejected by proponents of the subjectivist school. Although Savage [1954] acknowledged that subjective probabilities are commonly vague, he argued that vagueness has no role in a rational theory of choice.

Interest in the problem of decision under ignorance was revived by a series of papers and commentaries published in the early sixties in this *Journal*. The most influential of these papers, written by Ellsberg [1961], presented compelling examples in which people prefer to bet on known rather than on unknown probabilities (see also Fellner [1961]). Ellsberg's simplest example, known as the "two-color" problem, involves two urns each containing red and black balls. Urn 1 contains 50 red and 50 black balls, whereas urn 2 contains 100 red and black balls in an unknown proportion. Suppose that a ball is drawn at random from an urn and one receives $100 or nothing depending on the outcome. Most people seem indifferent between betting on red or on black for either urn, yet they prefer to bet on the 50-50 urn rather than on the urn with the unknown composition. This pattern of preferences is inconsistent with expected utility theory because it implies that the subjective probabilities of black and of red are greater in the 50-50 urn than in the unknown urn, and therefore cannot sum to one for both urns.

Essentially the same problem was discussed by Keynes some 40 years earlier: "In the first case we know that the urn contains black and white balls in equal proportions; in the second case the proportion of each color is unknown, and each ball is as likely to be black as white. It is evident that in either case the probability of drawing a white ball is $\frac{1}{2}$, but that the weight of the argument in favor of this conclusion is greater in the first case" [1921, p. 75]. In the spirit of Knight and Keynes, Ellsberg [1961] argued that people's willingness to act in the presence of uncertainty depends not only on the perceived probability of the event in question, but also on its vagueness or ambiguity. Ellsberg characterized ambiguity as "a quality depending on the amount, type, and 'unanimity' of information, and giving rise to one's degree of 'confidence' in an estimate of relative likelihoods" [p. 657].

The preference for the clear over the vague bet has been demonstrated in many experiments using several variations of Ellsberg's original problems (for a comprehensive review of the literature, see Camerer and Weber [1992]). As noted above, these observations provide evidence against the descriptive validity of expected utility theory. Furthermore, many authors have attempted to justify the preference for risk over ambiguity on normative grounds, although Raiffa [1961] has argued that ambiguity can be reduced to risk by tossing a coin to decide whether to guess red or black.

Ambiguity aversion has attracted much attention because, with the notable exception of games of chance, decision makers usually do not know the precise probabilities of potential outcomes. The decisions to undertake a business venture, to go to court, or to undergo medical treatment are commonly made in the absence of a clear idea of the chances that these actions will be successful. The question arises, then, whether the ambiguity aversion demonstrated using the Ellsberg urn applies to such decisions. In other words, is the preference for clear over vague probabilities confined to the domain of chance, or does it extend to uncertain beliefs based on world knowledge?

To answer this question, Heath and Tversky [1991] conducted a series of experiments comparing people's willingness to bet on their uncertain beliefs with their willingness to bet on clear chance events. Contrary to ambiguity aversion, they found that people prefer to bet on their vague beliefs in situations where they feel especially competent or knowledgeable, although they prefer to bet on chance when they do not. In one study, subjects were asked to choose among bets based on three sources of uncertainty: the results in various states of the 1988 presidential election, the results of various professional football games, and the results of random draws from an urn with a known composition. Subjects who were preselected for their knowledge of politics and lack of knowledge of football preferred betting on political events rather than on chance events that they considered equally probable. However, these subjects preferred betting on chance events rather than on sports events that they considered equally probable. Analogously, subjects who were preselected for their knowledge of football and lack of knowledge of politics exhibited the opposite pattern, preferring football to chance and chance to politics. Another finding that is consistent with Heath and Tversky's competence hypothesis but not with ambiguity aversion is people's preference to bet on their physical skills (e.g., throwing darts) rather than on matched chance events despite the fact that the perceived probability of success is vague for skill and clear for chance [Cohen and Hansel 1959; Howell 1971].

If ambiguity aversion is driven by the feeling of incompetence, as suggested by the preceding discussion, the question arises as to what conditions produce this state of mind. We propose that people's confidence is undermined when they contrast their limited knowledge about an event with their superior knowledge about another event, or when they compare themselves with more knowledgeable individuals. Moreover, we argue that this contrast between states of knowledge is the predominant source of ambiguity aversion. When evaluating an uncertain event in isolation, people attempt to assess its likelihood—as a good Bayesian would—paying relatively little attention to second-order characteristics such as vagueness or weight of evidence. However, when people compare two events about which they have different levels of knowledge, the contrast makes the less familiar bet less attractive or the more familiar bet more attractive. The main implication of this account, called the *comparative ignorance hypothesis*, is that ambiguity aversion will be present when subjects evaluate clear and vague prospects jointly, but it will greatly diminish or disappear when they evaluate each prospect in isolation.

A review of the experimental literature reveals a remarkable fact: virtually every test of ambiguity aversion to date has employed a within-subjects design in which respondents compared clear and vague bets, rather than a between-subjects design in which different respondents evaluated each bet. This literature, therefore, does not answer the question of whether ambiguity aversion exists in the absence of a contrast between clear and vague bets. In the following series of studies we test the hypothesis that ambiguity aversion holds in a comparative context (or a within-subjects design) but that it is reduced or eliminated in a noncomparative context (or a between-subjects design).

Experiments

Study 1
The following hypothetical problem was presented to 141 undergraduates at Stanford University. It was included in a questionnaire consisting of several unrelated items that subjects completed for class credit.

Table 31.1
Results of Study 1

	Clear bet		Vague bet	
Comparative	$24.34		$14.85	
	(2.21)	$N = 67$	(1.80)	$N = 67$
Noncomparative	$17.94		$18.42	
	(2.50)	$N = 35$	(2.87)	$N = 39$

Imagine that there is a bag on the table (*Bag A*) filled with exactly 50 red poker chips and 50 black poker chips, and a second bag (*Bag B*) filled with 100 poker chips that are red and black, but you do not know their relative proportion. Suppose that you are offered a ticket to a game that is to be played as follows: First, you are to guess a color (red or black). Next, without looking, you are to draw a poker chip out of one of the bags. If the color that you draw is the same as the one you predicted, then you will win $100; otherwise you win nothing. What is the most that you would pay for a ticket to play such a game for each of the bags? ($0–$100)

Bag A	*Bag B*
50 red chips	? red chips
50 black chips	? black chips
100 total chips	100 total chips

The most that I would be willing to pay for a ticket to *Bag A* (50 red; 50 black) is: __
The most that I would be willing to pay for a ticket to *Bag B* (? red; ? black) is: __

Approximately half the subjects performed the comparative task described above; the order in which the two bets were presented was counterbalanced. The remaining subjects performed a noncomparative task: approximately half evaluated the clear bet alone, and the remaining subjects evaluated the vague bet alone.

Mean willingness to pay for each bet is presented in table 31.1. As in all subsequent tables, standard errors (in parentheses) and sample sizes (N) are listed below the means. The data support our hypothesis. In the comparative condition, there is strong evidence of ambiguity aversion: subjects were willing to pay on average $9.51 more for the clear bet than for the vague bet, $t(66) = 6.00$, $p < 0.001$. However, in the noncomparative condition, there is no trace of ambiguity aversion as subjects paid slightly less for the clear bet than for the vague bet, $t(72) = -.12$, n.s. This interaction is significant ($z = 2.42$, $p < 0.01$).

Study 2

Our next study tested the comparative ignorance hypothesis with real money at stake. Subjects were recruited via signs posted in the psychology building at Stanford

Table 31.2
Results of Study 2

	Clear bet	Vague bet
Comparative	$9.74	$8.53
	(0.49) $N = 52$	(0.58) $N = 52$
Noncomparative	$7.58	$8.04
	(0.62) $N = 26$	(0.43) $N = 26$

University, promising a chance to win up to $20 for participation in a brief study. We recruited 110 students, faculty, and staff; six subjects were excluded because of inconsistent responses.

Subjects were run individually. Participants in the comparative condition priced both the clear bet and the vague bet. Half the subjects in the noncomparative condition priced the clear bet alone; the other half priced the vague bet alone. The clear bet involved a draw from a bag containing one red ping-pong ball and one green ping-pong ball. The vague bet involved a draw from a bag containing two ping-pong balls, each of which could be either red or green. Subjects were first asked to guess the color of the ball to be drawn. Next, they were asked to make a series of choices between receiving $20 if their guess is correct (and nothing otherwise) or receiving $X for sure. Subjects marked their choices on a response sheet that listed the various sure amounts ($X) in descending order from $19.50 to $0.50 in steps of 50 cents. They were informed that some participants would be selected at random to play for real money. For these subjects, one choice would be selected at random, and the subjects would either receive $X or play the bet, depending on the preference they had indicated. This procedure is incentive-compatible because subjects can only make themselves worse off by misrepresenting their preferences.

Cash equivalents were estimated by the midpoint between the lowest amount of money that was preferred to the uncertain bet, and the highest amount of money for which the bet was preferred. Mean cash equivalents are listed in table 31.2. The procedural variations introduced in this study (real bets, monetary incentive, individual administration) did not affect the pattern of results. In the comparative condition, subjects priced the clear bet $1.21 higher on average than the vague bet, $t(51) = 2.70$, $p < 0.01$. However, in the noncomparative condition, subjects priced the vague bet slightly above the clear bet, $t(50) = -.61$, n.s. Again, the interaction is significant ($z = 1.90$, $p < 0.05$).

Two comments regarding the interpretation of studies 1 and 2 are in order. First, subjects in both the comparative and noncomparative conditions were clearly aware of the fact that they did not know the composition of the vague urn. Only in the

Table 31.3
Ellsberg's Three-Color Problem

		10 balls	20 balls	
	Bet	white	red	blue
Decision 1	f_1	$50	0	0
	g_1	0	$50	0
Decision 2	f_2	$50	0	$50
	g_2	0	$50	$50

comparative task, however, did this fact influence their prices. Hence, ambiguity aversion seems to require a direct comparison between the clear and the vague bet; an awareness of missing information is not sufficient (cf. Frisch and Baron [1988]). Second, it is noteworthy that in both studies 1 and 2, the comparative context enhanced the attractiveness of the clear bet somewhat more than it diminished the attractiveness of the vague bet. The comparative ignorance hypothesis, however, makes no prediction about the relative magnitude of these effects.

Study 3

In addition to the two-color problem described above, Ellsberg [1961] introduced a three-color problem, depicted in table 31.3. Consider an urn that contains ten white balls, and twenty balls that are red and blue in unknown proportion. In decision 1 subjects are asked to choose between f_1, winning on white $\left(p = \frac{1}{3}\right)$; or g_1, winning on red $\left(0 \leq p \leq \frac{2}{3}\right)$. In decision 2 subjects are asked to choose between f_2, winning on either white or blue $\left(\frac{1}{3} \leq p \leq 1\right)$, or g_2, winning on either red or blue $\left(p = \frac{2}{3}\right)$. As suggested by Ellsberg, people typically favor f_1 over g_1 in decision 1, and g_2 over f_2 in decision 2, contrary to the independence axiom of expected utility theory.

From the standpoint of the comparative ignorance hypothesis, this problem differs from the two-color problem because here the description of the bets (especially f_2) involves both clear and vague probabilities. Consequently, we expect some ambiguity aversion even in a noncomparative context in which each subject evaluates only one bet. However, we expect a stronger effect in a comparative context in which each subject evaluates both the clear and vague bets. The present study tests these predictions.

Subjects were 162 first-year law students at Willamette University who completed a short questionnaire in a classroom setting. Three subjects who violated dominance were excluded from the analysis. Subjects were informed that some people would be selected at random to be paid on the basis of their choices. The instructions included

Table 31.4
Results of Study 3

	Clear bet	Vague bet
Comparative	$55.60	$44.92
	(2.66) $N = 53$	(3.27) $N = 53$
Noncomparative	$51.69	$47.85
	(2.94) $N = 54$	(3.65) $N = 52$

a brief description of an incentive-compatible payoff scheme (based on Becker, DeGroot, and Marschak [1964]). Subjects were asked to state their minimum selling price for the bets displayed in table 31.3. In the comparative condition, subjects priced all four bets. In the noncomparative condition, approximately half the subjects priced the two complementary clear bets (f_1 and g_2), and the remaining subjects priced the two complementary vague bets (f_2 and g_1). The order of the bets was counterbalanced.

Let $c(f)$ be the stated price of bet f. As expected, most subjects in the comparative condition priced the clear bets above the vague bets. In particular, we observed $c(f_1) > c(g_1)$ for 28 subjects, $c(f_1) = c(g_1)$ for 17 subjects, and $c(f_1) < c(g_1)$ for 8 subjects, $p < 0.01$. Similarly, we observed $c(g_2) > c(f_2)$ for 36 subjects, $c(g_2) = c(f_2)$ for 12 subjects, and $c(g_2) < c(f_2)$ for 5 subjects, $p < 0.001$. Moreover, the pattern implied by ambiguity aversion (i.e., $c(f_1) \geq c(g_1)$ and $c(f_2) \leq c(g_2)$, where at least one inequality is strict) was exhibited by 62 percent of the subjects.

In order to contrast the comparative and the noncomparative conditions, we have added for each subject the selling prices of the two complementary clear bets (i.e., $c(f_1) + c(g_2)$) and the selling prices of the two complementary vague bets (i.e., $c(g_1) + c(f_2)$). Obviously, for subjects in the noncomparative condition, we can compute only one such sum. These sums measure the attractiveness of betting on either side of the clear and of the vague bets. The means of these sums are presented in table 31.4. The results conform to expectation. In the comparative condition, subjects priced clear bets $10.68 higher on average than vague bets, $t(52) = 6.23$, $p < 0.001$. However, in the noncomparative condition, the difference was only $3.85, $t(104) = 0.82$, n.s. This interaction is marginally significant ($z = 1.37$, $p < 0.10$).

Inspection of the individual bets reveals that for the more probable bets, f_2 and g_2, there was a strong preference for the clear over the vague in the comparative condition ($c(g_2) = \$33.75$, $c(f_2) = \$24.66$, $t(52) = 5.85$, $p < 0.001$) and a moderate preference for the clear over the vague in the noncomparative condition ($c(g_2) = \$31.67$, $c(f_2) = \$26.71$, $t(104) = 2.05$, $p < 0.05$). However, for the less probable bets, f_1 and g_1, we found no significant differences between selling prices for clear and vague bets in either the comparative condition $(c(g_1) = \$20.26, \; c(f_1) = \$21.85, \; t(52) = 1.05$, n.s.) or the noncomparative condition $(c(g_1) = \$21.13, \; c(f_1) = \$20.02, \; t(104) = 0.43$, n.s.). The aggregate pattern displayed in table 31.4, therefore, is driven primarily by the more probable bets.

Study 4

In the preceding three studies, uncertainty was generated using a chance device (i.e., drawing a ball from an urn with a known or an unknown composition). Our next study tests the comparative ignorance hypothesis using natural events. Specifically, we asked subjects to price hypothetical bets contingent on future temperature in a familiar city (San Francisco) and an unfamiliar city with a similar climate (Istanbul). Ambiguity aversion suggests that our subjects (who were living near San Francisco) should prefer betting on San Francisco temperature, with which they were highly familiar, to betting on Istanbul temperature, with which they were not.

Subjects were asked how much they would be willing to pay to bet on each side of a proposition that offered a fixed prize if the temperature in a given city is above or below a specified value. The exact wording was as follows.

Imagine that you have been offered a ticket that will pay you $100 if the afternoon high temperature in [San Francisco/Istanbul] is *at least* 60 degrees Fahrenheit one week from today. What is the most you would be willing to pay for such a ticket?

The most I would be willing to pay is $___

Imagine that you have been offered a ticket that will pay you $100 if the afternoon high temperature in [San Francisco/Istanbul] is *less than* 60 degrees Fahrenheit one week from today. What is the most you would be willing to pay for such a ticket?

The most I would be willing to pay is $___

In the noncomparative condition one group of subjects priced the above two bets for San Francisco, and a second group of subjects priced the same two bets for Istanbul. In the comparative condition, subjects performed both tasks, pricing all four bets. The order of the events (less than 60 degrees/at least 60 degrees) and of the cities was counterbalanced. To minimize order effects, all subjects were asked before answering the questions to consider their best guess of the afternoon high temperature in the city or cities on which they were asked to bet.

Subjects were 189 pedestrians on the University of California at Berkeley campus who completed a five-minute survey (that included a few unrelated items) in exchange for a California lottery ticket. Ten subjects who violated dominance were excluded from the analysis. There were no significant order effects. Let $c(SF \geq 60)$ denote willingness to pay for the prospect "Win $100 if the high temperature in San

Table 31.5
Results of Study 4

	San Francisco bets	Istanbul bets
Comparative	$40.53	$24.69
	(4.27) $N = 90$	(3.09) $N = 90$
Noncomparative	$39.89	$38.37
	(5.06) $N = 44$	(6.10) $N = 45$

Francisco one week from today is at least 60 degrees," etc. As in Study 3 we added for each subject his or her willingness to pay for both sides of complementary bets. In particular, we computed $c(SF \geq 60) + c(SF < 60)$ for the San Francisco bets and $c(Ist \geq 60) + c(Ist < 60)$ for the Istanbul bets. Table 31.5 presents the means of these sums. The results again support our hypothesis. In the comparative condition subjects were willing to pay on average $15.84 more to bet on familiar San Francisco temperature than on unfamiliar Istanbul temperature, $t(89) = 5.05$, $p < 0.001$. However, in the noncomparative condition subjects were willing to pay on average a scant $1.52 more to bet on San Francisco than on Istanbul, $t(87) = 0.19$, n.s. This interaction is significant ($z = 1.68$, $p < 0.05$).

The same pattern holds for the individual bets. In the comparative condition, $c(SF \geq 60) = \$22.74$, and $c(Ist \geq 60) = \$15.21$, $t(89) = 3.13$, $p < 0.01$. Similarly, $c(SF < 60) = \$17.79$ and $c(Ist < 60) = \$9.49$, $t(89) = 4.25$, $p < 0.001$ In the non-comparative condition, however, $c(SF \geq 60) = \$21.95$, and $c(Ist \geq 60) = \$21.07$, $t(87) = 0.17$, n.s. Similarly, $c(SF < 60) = \$17.94$, and $c(Ist < 60) = \$17.29$, $t(87) = 0.13$, n.s. Thus, subjects in the comparative condition were willing to pay significantly more for either side of the San Francisco proposition than they were willing to pay for the corresponding sides of the Istanbul proposition. However, no such pattern is evident in the noncomparative condition. Note that unlike the effect observed in studies 1 and 2, the present effect is produced by the reduction in the attractiveness of the less familiar bet.

Study 5

We have interpreted the results of the preceding studies in terms of comparative ignorance. Alternatively, it might be argued that these results can be explained at least in part by the more general hypothesis that the difference between cash equivalents of prospects evaluated in isolation will be enhanced by a direct comparison between them. Such enhancement would apply whether or not the prospects in question involve different sources of uncertainty that vary with respect to familiarity or ambiguity.

Table 31.6
Results of Study 5

	Bet A			Bet B		
Comparative	$25.77			$6.42		
	(3.68)	N = 47		(1.84)	N = 47	
Noncomparative	$23.07			$5.32		
	(3.42)	N = 42		(1.27)	N = 40	

To test this hypothesis, we recruited 129 Stanford undergraduates to answer a one-page questionnaire. Subjects were asked to state their maximum willingness to pay for hypothetical bets that offered $100 if the daytime high temperature in Palo Alto (where Stanford is located) on a particular day falls in a specified range. The two bets were described as follows:

[A] Imagine that you have been offered a ticket that will pay you $100 if the afternoon high temperature *two weeks* from today in Palo Alto is *more than* 70 degrees Fahrenheit. What is the most you would be willing to pay for such a ticket?

The most I would be willing to pay is $___

[B] Imagine that you have been offered a ticket that will pay you $100 if the afternoon high temperature *three weeks* from today in Palo Alto is *less than* 65 degrees Fahrenheit. What is the most you would be willing to pay for such a ticket?

The most I would be willing to pay is $___

Subjects in the comparative condition evaluated both [A] and [B] (the order was counterbalanced). Approximately half the subjects in the noncomparative condition evaluated [A] alone, and the remaining subjects evaluated [B] alone.

Because Palo Alto temperature in the springtime (when the study was conducted) is more likely to be above 70 degrees than below 65 degrees, we expected bet [A] to be generally more attractive than bet [B]. The enhancement hypothesis, therefore, implies that the difference between $c(A)$ and $c(B)$ will be greater in the comparative than in the noncomparative condition. The mean values of $c(A)$ and $c(B)$ are presented in table 31.6. The results do not support the enhancement hypothesis. In this study, $c(A)$ was greater than $c(B)$. However, the difference $c(A) - c(B)$ was roughly the same in the two conditions (interaction $z = 0.32$, n.s). In fact, there were no significant differences between the comparative and noncomparative conditions in the cash equivalents of either prospect ($t(87) = 0.53$ for A; n.s.; $t(85) = 0.48$ for B, n.s.). This pattern contrasts sharply with the results of the preceding studies (see especially table 31.5), that reveal substantially larger differences between stated prices in the comparative than in the noncomparative conditions. We conclude that the comparative ignorance effect observed in studies 1–4 cannot be explained by the more general enhancement hypothesis.

Study 6

The comparative ignorance hypothesis attributes ambiguity aversion to the contrast between states of knowledge. In the first four studies we provided subjects with a comparison between more and less familiar events. In our final study we provided subjects with a comparison between themselves and more knowledgeable individuals.

Subjects were undergraduates at San Jose State University. The following hypothetical problem was included in a questionnaire containing several unrelated items that subjects completed for class credit.

Kaufman Broad Homes (KBH) is one of the largest home sellers in America. Their stock is traded on the New York Stock Exchange.

[1] Do you think that KBH stock will close higher or lower Monday than it did yesterday? (Circle one)

· KBH will close higher.

· KBH will close the same or lower.

[2] Which would you prefer? (Circle one)

· receive $50 for sure

· receive $150 if my prediction about KBH is correct.

Subjects in the noncomparative condition ($N = 31$) answered the above questions. Subjects in the comparative condition ($N = 32$) answered the same questions with the following additional item inserted between questions 1 and 2.

We are presenting this survey to undergraduates at San Jose State University, graduate students in economics at Stanford University, and to professional stock analysts.

Subjects were then asked to rate their knowledge of the item on a scale from 0 to 10.

The present account implies that the suggested comparison to more knowledgeable individuals (i.e., graduate students in economics and professional stock analysts) will undermine the subjects' sense of competence and consequently decrease their willingness to bet on their own judgment. The results support this prediction. The uncertain prospect of winning $150 was preferred to the sure payment of $50 by 68 percent of subjects in the noncomparative condition and by only 41 percent of subjects in the comparative condition, $\chi^2(1) = 4.66$, $p < 0.05$.

We replicated this effect using a different subject population (undergraduates at Stanford University enrolled in an introductory psychology course) and a different uncertain event. The following hypothetical problem was included in a questionnaire that contained several unrelated items that was completed for class credit.

[1] Do you think that the inflation rate in Holland over the past 12 months is greater than or less than 3.0 percent? (Circle one)

- *less than* 3.0 percent
- *at least* 3.0 percent

  [2] Which of the following do your prefer? (Circle one)

- receive $50 for sure
- receive $150 if I am right about the inflation rate.

As before, subjects in the noncomparative condition ($N = 39$) evaluated the items above, and subjects in the comparative condition ($N = 37$) answered the same questions with the following additional item inserted between questions [1] and [2].

We are presenting this survey to undergraduates in Psych 1, graduate students in economics, and to professional business forecasters.

Subjects were then asked to rate their knowledge of the item on a scale from 0 to 10.

The uncertain prospect was preferred to the sure payment by 38 percent of subjects in the noncomparative condition and by only 11 percent of subjects in the comparative condition, $\chi^2(1) = 7.74$, $p < 0.01$. Thus, the tendency to bet on a vague event is reduced by a suggested comparison to more knowledgeable individuals. Note that the results of this study, obtained by the mere mention of a more expert population, should be distinguished from the finding of Curley, Yates, and Abrams [1986] that ambiguity aversion is enhanced when people anticipate that their decision will be evaluated by their peers.

Market Experiments
Before we turn to the implications of the present findings, the question arises whether the effects of ambiguity and comparative ignorance persist when decision-makers are given an opportunity to make multiple decisions in a market setting that provides incentives and immediate feedback. A positive answer to this question has been provided by Sarin and Weber [1993], who compared subjects' bids for clear and for vague bets in several experimental markets using sealed bid and double oral auctions. In one series of studies involving graduate students of business administration from Cologne University, the clear bet paid 100 Deutsche Marks (DM) if a yellow ball was drawn from an opaque urn containing ten yellow and ten white tennis balls, and nothing otherwise. The vague bet was defined similarly except that the subject did

not know the proportion of yellow and white balls, which was sampled from a uniform distribution. In some studies, subjects traded both clear and vague bets in each market. In other studies, subjects traded clear bets in some markets and vague bets in other markets. Thus, all subjects evaluated both clear and vague bets. The comparative ignorance hypothesis predicts that (1) the clear bet will be generally priced above the vague bet, and (2) the discrepancy between the prices will be more pronounced when clear and vague bets are traded jointly than when they are traded separately. The data support both predictions. The difference between the average market price of the clear and the vague bets across both auction types (for the last trading period in experiments 11 through 14) was more than DM 20 in the joint markets and less than DM 5 in the separate markets. This effect was especially pronounced in the double oral auctions where there was no difference between the market price of the clear and the vague bets in the separate markets, and a substantial difference (DM 18.5) in the joint markets. Evidently, market setting is not sufficient to eliminate the effects of ambiguity and comparative ignorance.

Discussion

The preceding studies provide support for the comparative ignorance hypothesis, according to which ambiguity aversion is driven primarily by a comparison between events or between individuals, and it is greatly reduced or eliminated in the absence of such a comparison. We hasten to add that the distinction between comparative and noncomparative assessment refers to the state of mind of the decision-maker, which we have attempted to control through the experimental context. Of course, there is no guarantee that subjects in the comparative conditions actually performed the suggested comparison, or that subjects in the noncomparative conditions did not independently generate a comparison. In Ellsberg's two-color problem, for example, people who are presented with the vague urn alone may spontaneously invoke a comparison to a 50-50 urn, especially if they have previously encountered such a problem. However, the consistent results observed in the preceding studies suggest that the experimental manipulation was successful in inducing subjects to make a comparison in one condition but not in the other.

The comparative ignorance hypothesis suggests that when people price an uncertain prospect in isolation (e.g., receive $100 if Istanbul temperature one week from today exceeds 60 degrees), they pay little or no attention to the quality or precision of their assessment of the likelihood of the event in question. However, when people are asked to price this prospect in the context of another prospect (e.g., receive $100 if

San Francisco temperature one week from today exceeds 60 degrees), they become
sensitive to the contrast in their knowledge regarding the two events, and as a result
price the less familiar or vaguer prospect lower than the more familiar or clearer
prospect (see, e.g., Heath and Tversky [1991] and Keppe and Weber [forthcoming]).
Similarly, an uncertain prospect becomes less attractive when people are made aware
that the same prospect will also be evaluated by more knowledgeable individuals.
Thus, ambiguity aversion represents a reluctance to act on inferior knowledge, and
this inferiority is brought to mind only through a comparison with superior knowledge about other domains or of other people.

Theoretical Implications

The comparative ignorance effect violates the principle of procedure invariance,
according to which strategically equivalent elicitation procedures should produce the
same preference order (cf. Tversky, Sattath, and Slovic [1988]). In the preceding
studies, the vague and clear bets were equally valued when priced in isolation, yet the
latter was strictly preferred to the former when the two bets were priced jointly. Like
other instances of preference reversal (see, e.g., Tversky and Thaler [1990]), a particular attribute (in this case knowledge of probabilities) looms larger in comparative
than in noncomparative evaluation. However, the most noteworthy finding is not the
illustration of a new variety of preference reversal, but rather the conclusion that the
Ellsberg phenomenon is an inherently comparative effect.

This discrepancy between comparative and noncomparative evaluation raises the
question of which preference should be considered more rational. On the one hand, it
could be argued that the comparative judgment reflects people's "true" preferences
and in the absence of comparison, people fail to properly discount for their ignorance. On the other hand, it might the argued that the noncomparative judgments
are more rational, and that subjects are merely intimidated by a comparison with
superior knowledge. As we see it, there is no compelling argument to favor one interpretation over the other. The rational theory of choice (or more specifically, the
principle of procedure invariance) requires that the comparative and noncomparative
evaluations will coincide, but the theory does not provide a method for reconciling
inconsistent preferences.

What are the implications of the present findings for the analysis of individual
decision-making? To answer this question, it is important to distinguish two phenomena that have emerged from the descriptive study of decision under uncertainty:
source preference and source sensitivity [Tversky and Fox 1995; Tversky and Wakker forthcoming]. Source preference refers to the observation that choices between
prospects depend not only on the degree of uncertainty but also on the source of

uncertainty (e.g., San Francisco temperature versus Istanbul temperature). Source preference is demonstrated by showing that a person prefers to bet on a proposition drawn from one source than on a proposition drawn from another source, and also prefers to bet against the first proposition than against the second (e.g., $c(SF \geq 60) > c(Ist \geq 60)$, and $c(SF < 60) > c(Ist < 60)$; see Study 4 above). We have interpreted ambiguity aversion as a special case of source preference, in which risk is preferred to uncertainty, as in Ellsberg's examples.[1]

Source sensitivity refers to nonadditivity of decision weights. In particular, the descriptive analysis of decision under risk indicates that the impact of a given event on the value of a prospect is greater when it turns an impossibility into a possibility or a possibility into a certainty than when it merely makes an uncertain event more or less probable [Kahneman and Tversky 1979]. For example, increasing the probability of winning a fixed prize from 0 to 0.1 or 0.9 to 1.0 has a greater impact than increasing the probability from, say, 0.3 to 0.4 Tversky and Fox [1995] have further shown that this pattern, called bounded subadditivity, is more pronounced for uncertainty than for chance (i.e., for vague than for clear probabilities). In other words, people are less sensitive to uncertainty to chance, regardless of whether or not they prefer uncertainty than to chance. Thus, source preference and source sensitivity are logically independent.

The present experiments show that source preference, unlike source sensitivity, is an inherently comparative phenomenon, and it does not arise in an independent evaluation of uncertain prospects. This suggests that models based on decision weights or nonadditive probabilities (e.g., Quiggin [1982]; Gilboa [1987]; Schmeidler [1989]; Tversky and Wakker [forthcoming]) can accommodate source sensitivity, but they do not provide a satisfactory account of source preference because they do not distinguish between comparative and noncomparative evaluation. One might attempt to model the comparative ignorance effect using a contingent weighting approach [Tversky, Sattath, and Slovic 1988] in which the weight associated with an event depends on whether it is evaluated in a comparative or noncomparative context. The major difficulties with this, or any other attempt to model the comparative ignorance effect, is that it requires prior specification of the decision-maker's sense of his or her competence regarding the event in question and the salience of alternative states of knowledge. Although these variables can be experimentally manipulated, as we did in the preceding studies, they cannot easily be measured and incorporated into a formal model.

Despite the difficulties in modeling comparative ignorance, it could have significant economic implications. For example, an individual who is knowledgeable about the computer industry but not about the energy industry may exhibit ambiguity aversion in choosing whether to invest in a high-tech startup or an oil exploration, but not when each investment is evaluated independently. Furthermore, the present account suggests that the order in which the two investments are considered could affect their valuation. In particular, the less familiar investment might be valued more when it is considered before rather than after the more familiar investment.[2] In light of the present analysis, recent attempts to model ambiguity aversion in financial markets (e.g., Dow, and Werlang [1991] and Epstein and Wang [1994]) may be incomplete because they do not distinguish between comparative and noncomparative evaluation. In particular, such models are likely to overestimate the degree of ambiguity aversion in settings in which uncertain prospects are evaluated in isolation (cf. Sarin and Weber [1993]). The role of comparative ignorance in economic transactions awaits further empirical investigation.

Notes

This work was supported by grants SES-9109535 and SBR-9408684 from the National Science Foundation. It has benefited from discussion with Martin Weber.

1. Some authors have interpreted as ambiguity aversion the finding that people prefer to bet on a more reliable rather than on a less reliable estimate of a given probability p (e.g., Einhorn and Hogarth [1985]). This demonstration, however, does not establish source preference because it does not also consider the complements of the events in question. Hence, the above finding can be attributed to the fact that the subjective probability associated with the less reliable estimate of p is less extreme (i.e., closer to 0.5) than that associated with the more reliable estimate of p (see Heath and Tversky [1991, Table 4]). More generally, the oft-cited conclusion that people are ambiguity-averse for high probabilities and ambiguity-seeking for small probabilities is questionable because the demonstrations on which it is based do not properly control for variations in subjective probability.

2. Unpublished data, collected by Fox and Weber, showed that an unfamiliar prospect was priced lower when evaluated after a familiar prospect than when evaluated before that prospect.

References

Becker, Gordon, Morris DeGroot, and Jacob Marschak, "Measuring Utility by a Single-Response Sequential Method," *Behavioral Science*, IX (1964), 226–232.

Camerer, Colin, and Martin Weber, "Recent Developments in Modeling Preferences: Uncertainty and Ambiguity," *Journal of Risk and Uncertainty*, V (1992), 325–370.

Cohen, John, and Mark Hansel, "Preferences for Different Combinations of Chance and Skill in Gambling," *Nature*, CLXXXIII (1959), 841–843.

Curley, Shawn P., J. Frank Yates, and Richard A. Abrams, "Psychological Sources of Ambiguity Avoidance," *Organizational Behavior and Human Decision Processes*, XXXVIII (1986), 230–256.

Dow, James, and Sergio Ribeiro da Costa Werlang, "Uncertainty Aversion, Risk Aversion, and the Optimal Choice of Portfolio," *Econometrica*, LX (1991), 197–204.

Einhorn, Hillel J., and Robyn M. Hogarth, "Ambiguity and Uncertainty in Probabilistic Inference," *Psychological Review*, XCIII (1985), 433–461.

Ellsberg, Daniel, "Risk, Ambiguity and the Savage Axioms," *Quarterly Journal of Economics*, LXXV (1961), 643–669.

Epstein, Larry G., and Tan Wang, "Intertemporal Asset Pricing under Knightian Uncertainty," *Econometrica*, LXII (1994), 283–322.

Fellner, William, "Distortion of Subjective Probabilities as a Reaction to Uncertainty," *Quarterly Journal of Economics*, LXXV (1961), 670–689.

Frisch, Deborah, and Jonathan Baron, "Ambiguity and Rationality," *Journal of Behavioral Decision Making*, I (1988), 149–157.

Gilboa, Itzhak, "Expected Utility with Purely Subjective Non-additive Probabilities," *Journal of Mathematical Economics*, XVI (1987), 65–88.

Heath, Chip, and Amos Tversky, "Preference and Belief: Ambiguity and Competence in Choice under Uncertainty," *Journal of Risk and Uncertainty*, IV (1991), 5–28.

Howell, William, "Uncertainty from Internal and External Sources: A Clear Case of Overconfidence," *Journal of Experimental Psychology*, LXXXI (1971), 240–243.

Kahneman, Daniel, and Amos Tversky, "Prospect Theory: An Analysis of Decision under Risk," *Econometrica*, XLVII (1979), 263–291.

Keppe, Hans-Jürgen, and Martin Weber, "Judged Knowledge and Ambiguity Aversion," *Theory and Decision*, forthcoming.

Keynes, John Maynard, *A Treatise on Probability* (London: Macmillan, 1921).

Knight, Frank H., *Risk, Uncertainty, and Profit* (Boston: Houghton Mifflin, 1921).

Quiggin, John, "A Theory of Anticipated Utility," *Journal of Economic Behavior and Organization*, III (1982), 323–343.

Raiffa, Howard, "Risk Ambiguity and the Savage Axioms: Comment." *Quarterly Journal of Economics*, LXXV (1961), 690–694.

Sarin, Rakesh K., and Martin Weber, "Effects of Ambiguity in Market Experiments," *Theory and Decision*, XXXIX (1993), 602–615.

Savage, Leonard J., *The Foundation of Statistics* (New York: John Wiley & Sons, 1954).

Schmeidler, David, "Subjective Probability and Expected Utility without Additivity," *Econometrica*, LVII (1989), 571–587.

Tversky, Amos and Craig R. Fox, "Weighing Risk and Uncertainty," *Psychological Review*, CXLIX (1995), 269–283.

Tversky, Amos, Shmuel Sattath, and Paul Slovic, "Contingent Weighting in Judgment and Choice," *Psychological Review*, XCV (1988), 371–384.

Tversky, Amos, and Richard Thaler, "Preference Reversals," *Journal of Economic Perspectives*, IV (1990), 201–211.

Tversky, Amos, and Peter Wakker, "Risk Attitudes and Decision Weights," *Econometrica*, forthcoming.

32 A Belief-Based Account of Decision under Uncertainty

Craig R. Fox and Amos Tversky

Introduction

It seems obvious that the decisions to invest in the stock market, undergo a medical treatment, or settle out of court depend on the strength of people's beliefs that the market will go up, that the treatment will be successful, or that the court will decide in their favor. It is less obvious how to elicit and measure such beliefs. The classical theory of decision under uncertainty derives beliefs about the likelihood of uncertain events from people's choices between prospects whose consequences are contingent on these events. This approach, first advanced by Ramsey (1931),[1] gives rise to an elegant axiomatic theory that yields simultaneous measurement of utility and subjective probability, thereby bypassing the thorny problem of how to interpret direct expressions of belief.

From a psychological (descriptive) perspective, the classical theory can be questioned on several counts. First, it does not correspond to the common intuition that belief precedes preference. People typically choose to bet $50 on team A rather than team B because they believe that A is more likely to win; they do not infer this belief from the observation that the former bet is more attractive than the latter. Second and perhaps more important, the classical theory does not consider probability judgments that could be useful in explaining and predicting decisions under uncertainty. Third, and most important, the empirical evidence indicates that the major assumptions of the classical theory that underlie the derivation of belief from preference are not descriptively valid.

This chapter develops a belief-based account in which probability judgments are used to predict decisions under uncertainty. We first review recent work on probability judgment and on the weighting function of prospect theory that serves as the basis for the present development. We next formulate a two-stage model of decision under uncertainty, and explore its testable implications. This model is tested against the classical theory in two experiments. Finally, we address some empirical, methodological, theoretical, and practical issues raised by the present development.

Theoretical Background

There is an extensive body of research indicating that people's choices between risky prospects depart systematically from expected utility theory (for a review, see Camerer 1995). Many of these violations can be explained by a nonlinear weighting

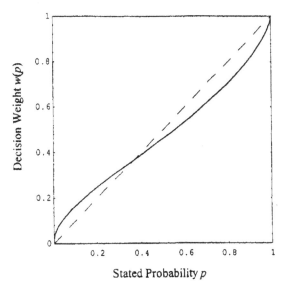

Figure 32.1
Weighting function for decision under risk, $w(p) = \exp(-\beta(-\ln p)^{\alpha})$, with $\alpha = 0.7$, $\beta = 1$ (Prelec 1998).

function (see figure 32.1) that overweights low probabilities and underweights moderate to high probabilities (Kahneman and Tversky 1979, Tversky and Kahneman 1992, Prelec 1998). Such a function accounts for violations of the independence axiom (the common consequence effect) and the substitution axiom (the common ratio effect), first demonstrated by Allais (1953). It also accommodates the commonly observed fourfold pattern of risk attitudes: risk seeking for gains and risk aversion for losses of low probability, together with risk aversion for gains and risk seeking for losses of high probability (Tversky and Kahneman 1992). Finally, it is consistent with the observed pattern of fanning in and fanning out in the probability triangle (Camerer and Ho 1994, Wu and Gonzalez 1998a).

Although most empirical studies have employed risky prospects, where probabilities are assumed to be known, virtually all real-world decisions (with the notable exception of games of chance) involve uncertain prospects (e.g., investments, litigation, insurance) where this assumption does not hold. In order to model such decisions we need to extend the key features of the risky weighting function to the domain of uncertainty. Tversky and Wakker (1995) established such a generalization, within the framework of cumulative prospect theory, by assuming that an event has more impact on choice when it turns an impossibility into a possibility or a possibility into a certainty than when it merely makes a possibility more or less likely.

Formally, let W denote the weighting function defined on subsets of a sample space S, where $W(\phi) = 0$ and $W(S) = 1$. W satisfies *bounded subadditivity* if:

(i) $W(A) \geq W(A \cup B) - W(B)$, and

(ii) $W(S) - W(S - A) \geq W(A \cup B) - W(B)$,

provided A and B are disjoint and $W(B)$ and $W(A \cup B)$ are bounded away from 0 and 1, respectively.[2] Condition (i) generalizes the notion that increasing the probability of winning a prize from 0 to p has more impact than increasing the probability of winning from q to $q + p$, provided $q + p < 1$. This condition reflects the *possibility effect*. Condition (ii) generalizes the notion that decreasing the probability of winning from 1 to $1 - p$ has more impact than decreasing the probability of winning from $q + p$ to q, provided $q > 0$. This condition reflects the *certainty effect*. Note that risk can be viewed as a special case of uncertainty where probability is defined via a standard chance device so that the probabilities of outcomes are known.

Tversky and Fox (1995) tested bounded subadditivity in a series of studies using both risky prospects and uncertain prospects whose outcomes were contingent on upcoming sporting events, future temperature in various cities, and changes in the Dow Jones index. The data satisfied bounded subadditivity for both risk and uncertainty. Furthermore, this effect was more pronounced for uncertainty than for risk, indicating greater departures from expected utility theory when probabilities are not known. The results of these experiments are consistent with a two-stage model in which the decision maker first assesses the probability P of an uncertain event A, then transforms this value using the risky weighting function,[3] w.

In the present chapter we elaborate this two-stage model and investigate its consequences. To simplify matters, we confine the present treatment to simple prospects of the form (x, A) that pay \$$x$ if the target event A obtains, and nothing otherwise.[4] We assume that the overall value V of such prospects is given by

$$V(x, A) = v(x)W(A) = v(x)w[P(A)], \tag{1}$$

where v is the value function for monetary gains, w is the risky weighting function, and $P(A)$ is the judged probability of A. The key feature of this model, which distinguishes it from other theories of decision under uncertainty, is the inclusion of probability judgments. Note that if $W(A)$ can be expressed as $w[P(A)]$, as implied by equation (1), we can predict decisions under uncertainty from decisions under risk and judgments of probability. We further assume that risky choices satisfy prospect theory[5] (Kahneman and Tversky 1979, Tversky and Kahneman 1992) and that judged probabilities satisfy support theory (Tversky and Koehler 1994, Rottenstreich and Tversky 1997), a psychological model of degree of belief to which we now turn.

There is ample evidence that people's intuitive probability judgments are often inconsistent with the laws of chance. In particular, different descriptions of the same event often give rise to systematically different responses (e.g., Fischhoff et al. 1978), and the judged probability of the union of disjoint events is generally smaller than the sum of judged probabilities of these events (e.g., Teigen 1974). To accommodate such findings, support theory assumes that (subjective) probability is not attached to events, as in other models, but rather to descriptions of events, called *hypotheses*; hence, two descriptions of the same event may be assigned different probabilities. Support theory assumes that each hypothesis A has a nonnegative support value $s(A)$ corresponding to the strength of the evidence for this hypothesis. The judged probability $P(A, B)$, that hypothesis A rather than B holds, assuming that one and only one of them obtains, is given by:

$$P(A, B) = \frac{s(A)}{s(A) + s(B)},$$

(2)

where

$$s(A) \leq s(A_1 \vee A_2) \leq s(A_1) + s(A_2),$$

(3)

provided (A_1, A_2) is recognized as a partition of A.

In this theory, judged probability is interpreted as the support of the focal hypothesis A relative to the alternative hypothesis B (equation 2). The theory further assumes that (i) unpacking a description of an event A (e.g., homicide) into disjoint components $A_1 \vee A_2$ (e.g., homicide by an acquaintance, A_1, or homicide by a stranger, A_2) generally increases its support, and (ii) the sum of the support of the component hypotheses is at least as large as the support of their disjunction (equation (3)). The rationale for these assumptions is that (i) unpacking may remind people of possibilities that they have overlooked, and (ii) the separate evaluation of hypotheses tends to increase their salience and enhance their support.

Equation (2) implies *binary complementarity*: $P(A, B) + P(B, A) = 1$. For finer partitions, however, equations (2) and (3) imply *subadditivity*: the judged probability of A is less than or equal to the sum of judged probabilities of its disjoint components. These predictions have been confirmed in several studies reviewed by Tversky and Koehler (1994). For example, experienced physicians were provided with medical data regarding the condition of a particular patient who was admitted to the emergency ward, and asked to evaluate the probabilities of four mutually exclusive and exhaustive prognoses. The judged probability of a prognosis (e.g., that the patient will survive the hospitalization) against its complement, evaluated by different groups of physicians, summed to one, in accord with binary complementarity. However, the sum of the judged probabilities for the four prognoses was substantially greater than one, in accord with subadditivity (Redelmeier et al. 1995).

Implications

Perhaps the most striking contrast between the two-stage model and the classical theory (i.e., expected utility theory with risk aversion) concerns the effect of partitioning. Suppose $(A_1, \ldots, A_n)$ is a partition of A, and $C(x, A)$ is the certainty equivalent of the prospect that pays $\$x$ if A occurs, and nothing otherwise. The classical theory implies the following *partition inequality*:

$$C(x, A_1) + \cdots + C(x, A_n) \leq C(x, A), \tag{4}$$

for all real x and $A \subset S$. That is, the certainty equivalent of an uncertain prospect exceeds the sum of certainty equivalents of the subprospects (evaluated independently) obtained by partitioning the target event. In the context of expected utility theory, the partition inequality is implied by risk aversion.[6] However, if people follow the two-stage model, defined in equation (1), and if the judged probabilities are subadditive, as implied by support theory, then the partition inequality is not expected to hold. Such failures are especially likely when the curvature of the value function (between 0 and $\$x$) is not very pronounced and the target event (A) is partitioned into many components. Thus, the partition inequality provides a simple method for testing the classical theory and contrasting it to the two-stage model.

To test the two-stage model, we predict the certainty equivalent of an uncertain prospect, $C(x, A)$, from two independent responses: the judged probability of the target event, $P(A)$, and the certainty equivalent of the risky prospect, $C(x, P(A))$. It follows readily from equation (1) that

$$\text{if } P(A) = p, \quad \text{then } C(x, A) = C(x, p). \tag{5}$$

This condition provides a method for testing the two-stage model that does not require an estimation of the value function. The following two studies test the partition inequality and compare the predictions derived from equation (5) to those of the classical theory.

Experiments

Study 1: Basketball Playoffs

Method

PARTICIPANTS. The participants in this study were 50 students at Northwestern University (46 men, 4 women; median age = 20) who responded to fliers calling for fans of professional basketball to take part in a study of decision making. Subjects indicated that they had watched several games of the National Basketball Association (NBA) during the regular season (median = 25). They received $10 for completing a one-hour session and were told that some participants would be selected at random to play one of their choices for real money and that they could win up to $160.

PROCEDURE. The experiment was run using a computer. All subjects were run on the same day, during the beginning of the NBA quarterfinals. Subjects were given detailed instructions and an opportunity for supervised practice. The study consisted of four tasks.

The first task was designed to estimate subjects' certainty equivalents (abbreviated C) for risky prospects. These prospects were described in terms of a random draw of a single poker chip from an urn containing 100 chips numbered consecutively from 1 to 100. Nineteen prospects of the form ($160, p$) were constructed where p varied from 0.05 to 0.95 in multiples of .05. For example, the ($160, .25$) prospect would pay $160 if the number of the poker chip is between 1 and 25, and nothing otherwise.

Each trial involved a series of choices between a prospect and an ascending series of sure payments (e.g., receive $40 for sure). The order of the 19 risky prospects was randomized separately for each subject. Certainty equivalents were inferred from two rounds of such choices. The first round consisted of nine choices between the prospect and sure payments that were spaced evenly from $0 to $160. After completing the first round of choices, a new set of nine sure payments was presented, spanning the narrower range between the lowest payment that the subject had accepted and the highest payment that the subject had rejected (excluding the endpoints). The program enforced dominance and internal consistency within a given trial. For example, the program did not allow a respondent to prefer $30 over a prospect and also prefer the same prospect over $40. The program allowed subjects to backtrack if they felt they had made a mistake in the previous round of choices.

For each risky prospect, C was determined by linear interpolation between the lowest value accepted and the highest value rejected in the second round of choices,

Table 32.1
Values of a, b, and c Used in the Spinner Games of Study 1 and Median Value of Subjects' Responses (x)

Probability outcome	Fixed prospect			Variable prospect		
	0.25 $a	0.25 $b	0.50 $0	0.25 $c	0.25 $x (Median)	0.50 $0
1)	50	100		25	131	
2)	30	60		10	86.5	
3)	20	90		40	70	
4)	10	110		35	82	
5)	85	55		120	31	
6)	50	45		75	29	
7)	95	25		70	42	
8)	115	15		80	43	

yielding a margin of error of $\pm\$1.00$. Note that although our analysis is based on C, the data consisted of a series of choices between a given prospect and sure outcomes. Thus, respondents were not asked to generate C; it was inferred from their choices.

The second task was designed to estimate certainty equivalents for uncertain prospects. Each prospect offered to pay $160 if a particular team, division, or conference would win the 1995 NBA championship. At the time of the study, eight teams remained (Chicago, Indiana, Orlando, New York, Los Angeles, Phoenix, San Antonio, Houston) representing four divisions (Central, Atlantic, Pacific, Midwestern) and two conferences (Eastern, Western). Fourteen prospects of the form ($160, A$) were constructed that offered to pay $160 if a particular team, division, or conference were to win the 1995 NBA championship. For example, a typical prospect would pay $160 if the Chicago Bulls win the championship. The elicitation method was identical to that of the first task.

The third task was designed to provide an independent test of risk aversion that makes no assumptions regarding the additivity of subjective probabilities or decision weights. Subjects were presented with a "fixed" prospect of the form ($a, 0.25; \$b, 0.25; \$0, 0.50$) and a "variable" prospect of the form ($c, 0.25; \$x, 0.25; \$0, 0.50$). These prospects were displayed as "spinner games" that would pay the designated amount depending on the particular region on which the spinner would land. In each trial, the values of a, b, and c were fixed, while the value of x varied. The initial value of x was set equal to b. Eight such pairs of prospects were constructed (see table 32.1), presented in an order that was randomized separately for each subject. On each trial, participants were asked to indicate their preference between the prospects. When a subject preferred the fixed prospect, the value of x increased by $16;

when a subject preferred the variable prospect, the value of x decreased by \$16. When a subject's preference switched from the fixed prospect to the variable prospect or from variable to fixed, the change in x reversed direction and the increment was cut in half (i.e., from \$16 to \$8, from \$8 to \$4, and so forth) until the increment was \$1. This process was repeated until the subject indicated that the two prospects were equally attractive. The program did not allow subjects to violate dominance.

The fourth task required participants to estimate the probability of each target event (i.e., that a particular team, division, or conference would win the NBA play-offs). The fourteen events were presented in an order that was randomized separately for each subject. On each trial, subjects could respond by either typing a number between 0 and 100, or by clicking and dragging a "slider" on a visual scale.

Subjects performed two additional tasks. They judged the probability that one team rather than another would win the NBA championship assuming that two particular teams reach the finals, and they rated the "strength" of each team. These data are discussed in Fox (1998).

Results

JUDGED PROBABILITY.   The median judged probability for each target event is listed in figure 32.2. The figure shows that the sum of these probabilities is close to one for the two conferences, nearly one and a half for the four divisions, and more than two for the eight teams. This pattern is consistent with the predictions of support theory that

$$\sum_{\text{teams}} P \geq \sum_{\text{divisions}} P \geq \sum_{\text{conferences}} P \ , \tag{6}$$

and the sum over the two conferences equals one. Moreover, in every case the sum of the probabilities for the individual teams is greater than the probability of the respective division, and the sum of the probabilities for the divisions is greater than the probability of the respective conference, consistent with support theory.[7]

The same pattern holds in the analysis of individual subjects. The median sum of probabilities for the eight teams was 2.40, the median sum for the four divisions was 1.44, and the median sum of probabilities for the two conferences was 1.00. More-over, 41 of 50 respondents satisfied equation (6) with strict inequalities, and 49 of 50 respondents reported probabilities for the eight teams that summed to more than one ($p < 0.001$ by sign test in both cases).

CERTAINTY EQUIVALENTS.   Figure 32.3 presents the median normalized C for each prospect; that is, the median certainty equivalent divided by \$160. The choice data in

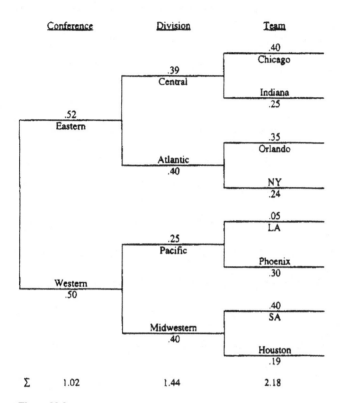

Figure 32.2
Median judged probabilities for all target events in study 1.

figure 32.3 echo the judgment data in figure 32.2. In every case, the sum of Cs for the individual teams is greater than C for the respective division, and the sum of Cs for the divisions is greater than C for the respective conference.[8] Furthermore, the sum of Cs for the 8 teams exceeds \$160; that is, the sum of the normalized Cs is greater than one.

Again, the same pattern holds in the analysis of individual subjects. The median sum of normalized Cs for the 8 teams was 2.08, the median sum for the 4 divisions was 1.38, and the median sum for the 2 conferences was 0.93. Moreover, the pattern implied by the partition inequality (equation (4)):

$$\sum_{\text{teams}} C \le \sum_{\text{divisions}} C \le \sum_{\text{conferences}} C ,$$

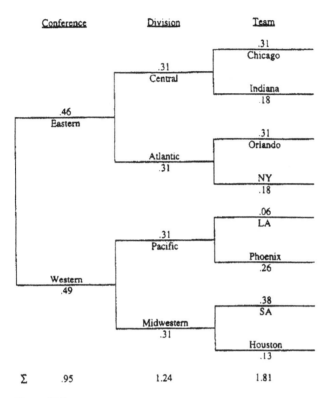

Figure 32.3
Median normalized certainty equivalents for all prospects in study 1.

was satisfied by only one respondent, whereas 41 of the 50 respondents satisfied the reverse pattern that is consistent with the two-stage model ($p < 0.001$):

$$\sum_{\text{teams}} C > \sum_{\text{divisions}} C > \sum_{\text{conferences}} C \ .$$

Furthermore, only 5 subjects produced Cs for the 8 teams that summed to less than \$160, whereas 44 subjects produced Cs that summed to more than \$160 ($p < 0.001$). This pattern violates the partition inequality, with $A = S$.

COMPARING MODELS.   We next compare the fit of the classical theory to that of the two-stage model. For each event A, we observed the median judged probability $P(A)$, then searched for the median C of the risky prospect (x, p) where $p = P(A)$. For example, the median judged probability that the San Antonio Spurs (SAS) would win the NBA championship was 0.40, and the median value of $C(\$160, .40)$, was \$59. According to equation (5), therefore, $C(\$160, \mathrm{SAS})$ should equal \$59; the actual value was \$60. In cases where the $P(A)$ is not a multiple of 5 percent, we determined the certainty equivalent by linear interpolation.

To fit the classical theory, let C_A be the certainty equivalent of the prospect $(\$160, A)$. Setting $u(0) = 0$, the classical theory yields $u(C_A) = u(160)\mathscr{P}(A)$, where u is concave and $\mathscr{P}(A)$ is an additive (subjective) probability measure. Hence, $\mathscr{P}(A) = u(C_A)/u(160)$. Previous studies (e.g., Tversky 1967, Tversky and Kahneman 1992) have indicated that the value function for small to moderate gains can be approximated by a power function of the form $u(x) = x^\alpha$, $\alpha > 0$. To estimate the exponent, we used data from the "spinner games" described above. If a subject is indifferent between the fixed prospect $(\$a, 0.25; \$b, 0.25; \$0, 0.5)$ and the variable prospect $(\$c, 0.25; \$x, 0.25; \$0, 0.5)$ then assuming a power utility function, $a^\alpha + b^\alpha = c^\alpha + x^\alpha$. Because a, b, and c are given and the value of x is determined by the subject, one can solve for $\alpha > 0$. The exponent for each subject was estimated using the median value of α over the eight problems listed in table 32.1. This analysis showed that participants were generally risk-averse: 32 subjects exhibited $\alpha < 1.00$ (risk aversion); 14 exhibited $\alpha = 1.00$ (risk neutrality); and 4 exhibited $\alpha > 1.00$ (risk seeking) ($p < 0.001$ by sign test). The median response to each of the eight trials yielded $\alpha = 0.80$. The finding that the majority of subjects exhibited risk aversion in this task shows that the violations of the partition inequality described earlier cannot be explained by a convex utility function.

Subjective probabilities were estimated as follows. For each elementary target event A, we computed $(C_A/160)^\alpha$ and divided these values by their sum to ensure additivity. Figure 32.4 displays the median C for each of the eight teams along with the predictions of the two-stage model and the standard theory (assuming $\alpha = 0.80$, based on the median response to each item). It is evident from the figure that the two-stage model fits the data (mean absolute error = \$5.83) substantially better than does the standard theory (mean absolute error = \$23.71).[9] The same pattern is evident in the responses of individual subjects. The two-stage model fits the data better than does the classical theory for 45 of the 50 subjects ($p < 0.001$).

Note that the predictions of the two-stage model were derived from two independent tasks; no parameters were estimated from the fitted data. In contrast, the predictions of the classical theory were derived by estimating a parameter for each of the fitted data points; these estimates were constrained only by the requirement that the subjective probabilities sum to unity. In light of the substantial advantage conferred to the classical theory in this comparison, its inferior fit provides compelling evidence against the additivity of subjective probabilities that are inferred from choice.

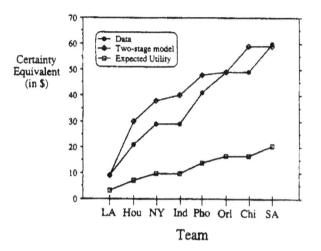

Figure 32.4
Median certainty equivalents of bets for all eight teams, and predictions of two-stage model and classical
theory (with $\alpha = 0.80$).

STUDIES OF UNPACKING.   We have attributed the failure of the partition inequality
to the subadditivity of judged probability that is implied by support theory. A
more radical departure from the classical theory is suggested by the *unpacking
principle* of support theory, according to which unpacking the description of an
event into an explicit disjunction of constituent events generally increases its judged
probability. Under the two-stage model, therefore, unpacking the description of an
event is also expected to increase the attractiveness of a prospect whose outcome
depends on this event. Furthermore, if this effect is sufficiently pronounced, it can
give rise to violations of monotonicity where $C(x, A) < C(x, A_1 \vee \cdots \vee A_n)$ even
when $A_1 \vee \cdots \vee A_n$ is a proper subset of A.

To explore this possibility, we presented a brief questionnaire to 58 business students at Northwestern University shortly before the beginning of the 1996 NBA
playoffs. The survey was administered in a classroom setting. Prior to the survey,
respondents were presented with the records of all NBA teams listed by their division
and conference. Subjects were randomly assigned to one of two groups. Subjects in
the first group ($N = 28$) stated their certainty equivalent for two prospects: a prospect that offered \$75 if the winner of the 1996 playoffs belongs to the Eastern con-
ference, and a prospect that offered \$75 if one of the four leading Western conference
teams (Seattle, Utah, San Antonio, or Los Angeles) would win the 1996 playoffs.
Subjects in the second group ($N = 30$) stated their certainty equivalent for the two

Table 32.2
Median Judged Probability and Certainty Equivalent for the Two Conferences and Respective Leading Teams for the 1996 NBA Playoffs

	Judged probability	Certainty equivalents
Eastern Conference	0.78	$50
Chi ∨ Orl ∨ Ind ∨ NY	0.90	$60
Western Conference	0.18	$15
Seattle ∨ Utah ∨ Sa ∨ LA	0.20	$15

parallel prospects: a prospect that offered $75 if the winner of the 1996 playoffs belongs to the Western conference, and a prospect that offered $75 if one of the four leading Eastern conference teams (Chicago, Orlando, Indiana, or New York) would win the 1996 playoffs.[10] Each group also assessed the probability of the two target events that defined the prospects evaluated by the other group. For example, the group that evaluated the prospect that would pay if an Eastern team will win assessed the probability that a Western team will win, and vice versa.

Table 32.2 presents the median judged probability and certainty equivalent for the two conferences, and the four leading teams in each conference. Although these teams had the best record in their respective conferences, some strong teams (e.g., the defending champion Houston Rockets) were not included in the list. Monotonicity requires, therefore, that the judged probability and certainty equivalent assigned to each conference should exceed those assigned to their leading teams. The unpacking principle, on the other hand, suggests that a nontransparent comparison (e.g., a between-subjects test) may produce violations of monotonicity. Indeed, the data of table 32.2 do not satisfy the monotonicity requirement. There is essentially no difference in either judged probability or the certainty equivalent between the Western conference and its four leading teams, whereas the judged probability and the certainty equivalent assigned to the Eastern conference are significantly smaller than those assigned to its four leading teams ($p < 0.05$, by a t-test in each case).[11]

Violations of monotonicity (or dominance) induced by unpacking have been observed by several investigators. Johnson et al. (1993), for example, reported that subjects were willing to pay more for a health insurance policy that covers hospitalization for all diseases and accidents than for a policy that covers hospitalization for any reason. Wu and Gonzalez (1998b) found similar effects in the evaluation of prospects contingent on diverse events such as the winner of the World Series, the outcomes of the 1996 elections, and future temperature in Boston. Although the effects observed in the above studies are not very pronounced, they indicate that unpacking can give rise to nonmonotonicity in judgments of probability as well as the pricing of uncertain prospects.

Study 2: Economic Indicators

The above study, like previous tests of bounded subadditivity, relied on subjects' beliefs regarding the occurrence of various real-world events. In the following study, subjects were given an opportunity to learn the probability of target events by observing changes in inflation and interest rates in a simulated economy. This design allows us to test both the classical theory and the two-stage model in a controlled environment in which all subjects are exposed to identical information. It also allows us to compare subjects' judged probabilities to the actual probabilities of the target events.

Method

PARTICIPANTS.   Subjects were students ($N = 92$) enrolled in an introductory class in judgment and decision making at Stanford University. Students were asked to download a computer program from a world wide web page, run the program, and e-mail their output to a class account. At the time of the study, the students had been exposed to discussions of probability theory and judgmental biases, but they were unfamiliar with decision theory. We received 86 complete responses. Four subjects were dropped because they apparently did not understand the instructions. The 82 remaining subjects included 49 men and 33 women (median age = 21.5). Most of them completed the study in less than an hour (median = 47 minutes).

PROCEDURE.   Subjects were first given an opportunity to learn the movement of two indicators (inflation and interest rates) in a simulated economy. Each indicator could move either up or down relative to the previous quarter. In this economy both indicators went up 60 percent of the time, inflation went up and interest went down 25 percent of the time, inflation went down and interest went up 10 percent of the time, and both indicators went down 5 percent of the time. The order of these events was randomized over 60 quarters of learning, separately for each subject. Participants were informed that the probabilities of the target events were the same for each quarter.

The learning procedure was divided into two parts. During the first 20 quarters, subjects merely clicked the mouse to advance to the next quarter and observed what happened. During the remaining 40 quarters, subjects also played a game in which they predicted the direction that each indicator would move in the subsequent quarter, and they made (hypothetical) bets on their predictions. After each prediction, subjects were given feedback and the computer adjusted their "bank balance" according to whether they had predicted correctly.

The second task was designed to estimate C for risky prospects. We constructed eleven prospects of the form ($1600, p$) that offered to pay $1600 with probability $(0.01, 0.05, 0.10, 0.15, 0.25, 0.50, 0.75, 0.85, 0.90, 0.95, 0.99)$. The elicitation procedure was identical to that used in the basketball study, except that all dollar amounts were multiplied by 10. Using this method we could estimate C for $1600 prospects within $\pm$10.

The third task was designed to estimate C for uncertain prospects. Subjects were first given an opportunity to review up to three times a 35-second "film" that very briefly displayed changes in the two indicators over each of the 60 quarters that subjects had previously observed. They were then presented with prospects that offered $1600 contingent on the movement of the indicators in the next (i.e., 61st) quarter. The first four trials involved movement of a single indicator (e.g., win $1600 if inflation up). The next four trials involved movement of both indicators (e.g., win $1600 if inflation up and interest down). The final four trials involved negations of the previous four events (e.g., win $1600 *unless* inflation up and interest down). The order of prospects within each set of trials was randomized separately for each subject. C was elicited through a series of choices between uncertain prospects and sure payments, as in the previous task.

The fourth task was designed to obtain an independent test of risk aversion. The procedure was essentially identical to the third task of the basketball study, except that the dollar amounts were multiplied by 10, and the initial value of x for the variable prospect was set so that the expected value of the two spinner games was equal (see table 32.7).

In the fifth task, subjects judged the probability of each target event. Subjects were first given an opportunity to review again up to three times a "film" of the 60 quarters they had previously observed. The first eight trials involved the movement of a single economic indicator (e.g., what is the probability that the following happens: inflation up) or combination of indicators (e.g., inflation up and interest down). The last four trials involved complementary events (e.g., what is the probability that the following does *not* happen: inflation up and interest down). The order of these events within each set was randomized separately for each subject, and responses were elicited as in the basketball study.

Subjects performed one additional task involving the acceptability of mixed prospects. The results of this task will not be discussed here.

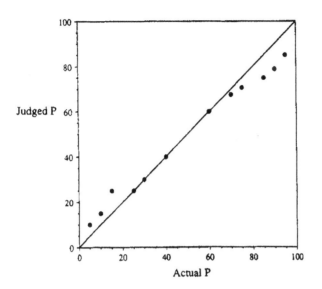

Figure 32.5
Median judged probability as a function of actual probabilities for all target events in study 2.

Results

JUDGED PROBABILITIES.   Figure 32.5 plots for each target event the median judged probability against the actual probability. The figure shows that participants had learned the probabilities of the target events with impressive accuracy ($r = 0.995$). The mean absolute difference (MAD) between median judged probability and actual probability was 0.048. The median correlation for individual subjects was 0.89 (median MAD $= 0.14$). Subjects also exhibited a tendency to overestimate low probabilities and underestimate high probabilities. Of the 82 subjects, 60 both over-estimated, on average, events with true probabilities less than 50 percent, and underestimated, on average, events with true probabilities greater than 50 percent ($p < 0.001$ by sign test).

The median judged probability for each target event is listed in table 32.3. Each cell displays the probability that the two indicators move as specified. The median judged probabilities of the complementary events are given in brackets. For example, the median judged probability that both indicators go up is 0.60, the probability that it is not the case that both indicators go down is 0.85, and the probability that inflation goes up is 0.75.

Table 32.3
Median Judged Probability of All Target Events in Study 2 (Data for Complementary Events Are Given in Brackets)

Inflation	Interest		
	Up	Down	
Up	0.60	0.25	
	[0.40]	[0.71]	0.75
Down	0.15	0.10	0.25
	[0.79]	[0.85]	
	0.68	0.30	

Table 32.4a
Tests of Binary Complementarity for Median Judged Probabilities in Study 2

Partition	$\sum P_i$	$\Delta = \sum P_i - 1$
$U\bullet$, $D\bullet$	1.00	0.00
$\bullet U$, $\bullet D$	0.98	−0.02
UU, $\overline{UU}$	1.00	0.00
UD, $\overline{UD}$	0.96	−0.04
DU, $\overline{DU}$	0.94	−0.06
DD, $\overline{DD}$	0.95	−0.05
Mean	0.97	−0.03

Note: The first column presents binary partitions of S, the second column $(\sum P_i)$ presents the sum of median judged probabilities for this partition, and the third column (Δ) presents the difference between this sum and one.

Recall that support theory predicts that the judged probability of an event and its complement will sum to unity (binary complementarity), but in all other cases the sum of the judged probabilities of disjoint events will be greater than or equal to the judged probability of their union (subadditivity). Table 32.4a presents six tests of binary complementarity, based on the median response to each item. Each row presents a binary partition of the sample space, along with the sum of median judged probabilities for this partition. The column labeled Δ lists the difference between this sum and one. For each event, the first letter corresponds to inflation (U for up, D for down) and the second to interest. For example, UD is the event "inflation up and interest down," $U\bullet$ is the event "inflation up," and $\bullet D$ is the event "interest down." Complements are denoted by a bar. For example, $\overline{UU}$ is the event "it is not the case that interest up and inflation up." As expected, the sum of median judged probabilities for complementary events is close to unity (mean = 0.97). However, these values were systematically smaller than one: the median value of the mean of these

Table 32.4b
Tests of Subadditivity for Median Judged Probabilities in Study 2

Event	Partition	$\sum P_i$	P	$\Delta = \sum P_i - P$
$U\bullet$	UU, UD	0.85	0.75	0.10
$D\bullet$	DU, DD	0.25	0.25	0.00
$\bullet U$	UU, DU	0.75	0.68	0.07
$\bullet D$	UD, DD	0.35	0.30	0.05
$\overline{UU}$	UD, DU, DD	0.50	0.40	0.10
$\overline{UD}$	UU, DU, DD	0.85	0.71	0.14
$\overline{DU}$	UU, UD, DD	0.95	0.79	0.16
$\overline{DD}$	UU, UD, DU	1.00	0.85	0.15
Mean		0.69	0.59	0.10

Note: The first column presents a target event, the second column presents a partition of that event, the third column ($\sum P_i$) presents the sum of median judged probabilities over the partition, the fourth column (P) presents the median judged probability of the target event, and the fifth column (Δ) presents the difference between these two values.

tests for each subject is 0.98; 48 subjects exhibited a mean less than 1.00, 10 exhibited a mean equal to 1.00, and 24 exhibited a mean greater than 1.00 ($p < 0.01$).

Table 32.4b presents eight tests of subadditivity based on median judged probabilities. Each row presents the sum of judged probabilities of disjoint events, the judged probability of their union, and the difference between them (Δ). For example, the first row shows that $P(inflation\ Up\ and\ interest\ Up) + P(inflation\ Up\ and\ interest\ Down) = 0.85$, and $P(inflation\ Up) = 0.75$, so that $\Delta = 0.10$. As expected, table 32.4b shows that in every case the sum of judged probabilities of disjoint events is greater than or equal to the judged probability of their union,[12] and the mean difference between them is 0.10. Furthermore, 60 of 82 subjects exhibited this pattern (i.e., mean $\Delta > 0$) on average ($p < 0.001$ by sign test).

CERTAINTY EQUIVALENTS.   The median normalized C_A for each target event A is presented in table 32.5. The corresponding medians for the complementary events are given in brackets. For example, the median normalized C for the event that both indicators go up is 0.43 and the median for the complementary event is 0.29. It can be shown that whenever $w(p) + w(1 - p) \leq 1$ and the value function is concave, the two-stage model implies the partition inequality for binary partitions of the sample space[13] (i.e., $C(x, A) + C(x, S - A) \leq C(x, S) = x$), but it does not imply the partition inequality for finer partitions of S or for binary partitions of other events.

Table 32.6a presents six tests of the partition inequality for binary partitions of the sample space. Analogous to table 32.4a, each row presents a binary partition of S along with the sum of median normalized Cs for this partition and the difference (Δ)

Table 32.5
Median Normalized Certainty Equivalents of All Target Events in Study 2 (Data for Complementary Events Are Given in Brackets)

	Interest		
Inflation	Up	Down	
Up	0.43	0.22	
	[0.29]	[0.48]	0.62
Down	0.13	0.10	0.18
	[0.59]	[0.76]	
	0.49	0.28	

Table 32.6a
Tests of the Partition Inequality for Binary Partitions of S in Study 2

Partition	$\sum C_i$	$\Delta = \sum C_i - 1$
$U\bullet, D\bullet$	0.79	−0.21
$\bullet U, \bullet D$	0.78	−0.22
$UU, \overline{UU}$	0.73	−0.27
$UD, \overline{UD}$	0.70	−0.30
$DU, \overline{DU}$	0.72	−0.28
$DD, \overline{DD}$	0.86	−0.14
Mean	0.76	−0.24

Note: The first column presents a partition of S, the second column ($\sum C_i$) presents the sum of median normalized certainty equivalents for this partition, and the third column (Δ) presents the difference between this sum and one.

Table 32.6b
Tests of the Partition Inequality in Study 2 for Proper Subsets of S

Event	Partition	$\sum C_i$	C	$\Delta = \sum C_i - C$
$U\bullet$	UU, UD	0.65	0.62	0.03
$D\bullet$	DU, DD	0.23	0.18	0.05
$\bullet U$	UU, DU	0.56	0.49	0.07
$\bullet D$	UD, DD	0.32	0.28	0.04
$\overline{UU}$	UD, DU, DD	0.45	0.29	0.16
$\overline{UD}$	UU, DU, DD	0.66	0.48	0.18
$\overline{DU}$	UU, UD, DD	0.75	0.59	0.16
$\overline{DD}$	UU, UD, DU	0.78	0.76	0.02
Mean		0.55	0.46	0.09

Note: The first column presents a target event, the second column presents a partition of that event, the third column ($\sum C_i$) presents the sum of median normalized certainty equivalents over the partition, the fourth column (C) presents the median normalized certainty equivalent of the target event, and the fifth column (Δ) presents the difference between these two values.

Table 32.7
Values of a, b, and c Used in Spinner Games of Study 2, and Median Value of Subjects' Responses (x)

Probability outcome	Fixed prospect			Variable prospect		
	0.25 a	0.25 b	0.50 $0	0.25 c	0.25 x (median)	0.50 $0
1)	500	1000		250	1330	
2)	500	700		250	990	
3)	200	1200		400	985	
4)	200	800		400	600	
5)	650	550		800	400	
6)	650	350		800	210	
7)	1100	100		750	360	
8)	1100	250		750	520	

between this sum and one. As predicted by both the classical theory and the present account, the partition inequality holds for all comparisons listed in table 32.6a (mean $\Delta = -0.24$). It also holds on average for 68 of 82 subjects ($p < 0.001$).

Table 32.6b presents eight additional tests of the partition inequality based on proper subsets of S. Analogous to table 32.4b, each entry presents the sum of median normalized Cs of disjoint events, the normalized C of their union, and the difference between them. Table 32.6b shows that the partition inequality fails in all cases (mean $\Delta = 0.09$).[14] Furthermore, 51 of 82 subjects exhibited this pattern on average (i.e., $\Delta > 0$, $p < 0.05$ by sign test).

The preceding results can be summarized as follows. For binary partitions of the sample space S, judged probabilities (nearly) satisfy binary complementarity (table 32.4a), and certainty equivalents satisfy the partition inequality (table 32.6a). This pattern is consistent with both the classical theory and the present account. For finer partitions, however, the data yield subadditivity for judged probabilities (table 32.4b) and reversal of the partition inequality for certainty equivalents (table 32.6b). This pattern is consistent with the two-stage model but not with the classical theory.

COMPARING MODELS. We next compare the fit of the classical theory to that of the two-stage model using the same method as in the previous study. To fit the classical theory, the exponent α of the utility function was estimated from the spinner games and the exponent for each subject was estimated using the median value of α derived from that subject's responses to the eight problems listed in table 32.7. Subjects were generally risk-averse: 48 subjects exhibited $\alpha < 1.00$ (risk aversion); 32 exhibited $\alpha = 1.00$ (risk neutrality); and 2 exhibited $\alpha > 1.00$ (risk seeking) ($p < 0.001$). Applying the same analysis to the median response to each of the eight trials yields $\alpha = 0.80$.

According to the classical theory with a power utility function, $C_A^\alpha = 1600^\alpha \mathscr{P}(A)$. Recall that in this study subjects learned probabilities by observing the frequencies of the four elementary events (e.g., inflation up and interest up). For each elementary target event A, we computed $(C_A/1600)^\alpha$, and divided these values by their sum to ensure additivity. The subjective probabilities of all other events were derived from these estimates, assuming additivity.

The two-stage model was estimated using equation (5) as in the previous study. The data show that this model fits the median certainty equivalents (mean absolute error = \$69) better than the classical theory (mean absolute error = \$128).[15] The same holds within the data of individual subjects. Using individual estimates of the parameters, the two-stage model fits the data better than the standard theory for 50 of the 82 participants ($p < 0.05$).

Discussion

The two preceding studies indicate that to a reasonable first approximation, the certainty equivalents of uncertain prospects can be predicted from independent judgments of probability and certainty equivalents for risky prospects, without estimating any parameters from the fitted data. Moreover, this model can account for the observed violations of the partition inequality. We conclude this chapter with a review of related studies, a comment regarding response bias, a discussion of the problem of source preference, and some closing thoughts concerning practical implications of the two-stage model.

Previous Studies

In the basketball study reported above, the event space has a hierarchical structure (conferences, divisions, teams). In the economic indicators study, the event space has a product structure (inflation up/down × interest up/down). Previous tests of bounded subadditivity employed a dimensional structure in which a numerical variable (e.g., the closing price per share of Microsoft stock two weeks in the future) was partitioned into intervals (e.g., less than \$88, \$88 to \$94, more than \$94). Subjects priced prospects contingent on these events and assessed their probabilities.

The results of these studies, summarized in table 32.8, are consistent with the present account. First, consider probability judgments. The column labeled (A, $S - A$) presents the median sum of judged probabilities for binary partitions of S,

Table 32.8
Summary of Previous Studies

Study/Population	N^*	Sources of uncertainty	Judged probabilities		Certainty equivalents	
			$(A, S - A)$	$(A_1, \ldots, A_n)$	$\sum C$	$\%V$
a. NBA fans	27	Playoff game	0.99	1.40	1.40	93
		SF temperature	0.98	1.47	1.27	77
b. NFL fans	40	Super Bowl	1.01	1.48	1.31	78
		Dow-Jones	0.99	1.25	1.16	65
c. Stanford students	45	SF temperature	1.03	2.16	1.98	88
		Beijing temperature	1.01	1.88	1.75	82
d. Options traders (San Francisco)	32	Microsoft	1.00	1.40	1.53	89
		General Electric	0.96	1.43	1.50	89
e. Options traders (Chicago)	28	IBM	1.00	1.27	1.47	82
		Gannett Co.	0.99	1.20	1.13	64
		Median	1.00	1.42	1.44	82

Note: The first three columns identify the subject population, sample sizes, and sources of uncertainty. Studies *a*, *b*, and *c* are reported in Tversky and Fox (1995) and are based on a sixfold partition. Studies *d*, and *e* are reported in Fox et al. (1996), and are based on a fourfold partition. The next two columns present the median sum of judged probabilities for a binary partition $(A, S - A)$ and for *n*-fold partitions $(A_1, \ldots, A_n)$ of *S*. The next column, labeled $\sum C$, presents the median sum of normalized certainty equivalents over an *n*-fold partition of *S*. The final column, labelled $\%V$, presents the percentage of subjects who violated the partition inequality. A few table entries are based on smaller samples than indicated because of missing data.

and the column labeled $(A_1, \ldots, A_n)$ presents the median sum of judged probabilities for finer partitions of *S*. The results conform to support theory: sums for binary partitions of *S* are close to one, whereas sums for *n*-fold partitions are consistently greater than one. Next, consider certainty equivalents. The column labeled $\sum C$ presents the median sum of normalized certainty equivalents for the finest partition of *S* in each study, and the column labeled $\%V$ presents the corresponding percentage of subjects who violated the partition inequality. In accord with the present findings, the majority of subjects in every study violated the partition inequality, and the sum of certainty equivalents was often substantially greater than the prize. This pattern holds for a wide range of sources, with and without monetary incentives, and for both naive and expert subjects. Taken together, these findings suggest that subadditivity of judged probability is a major cause of violations of the partition inequality.

The studies of Fox et al. (1996) are particularly interesting in this respect. Participants were professional options traders who priced prospects contingent on the closing price of various stocks. Unlike typical subjects, the options traders priced risky prospects by their expected value, yielding $v(x) = x$ and $w(p) = p$. Like most other subjects, however, their judged probabilities were subadditive (i.e., $P(A_1) + \cdots + P(A_n) > P(A)$). Under these circumstances, the two-stage model predicts

$$C(x, A_1) + \cdots + C(x, A_n) = P(A_1)x + \cdots + P(A_n)x > P(A)x = C(x, A),$$

whereas the classical theory requires equality throughout. The data for the options traders, summarized in table 32.8, confirms the prediction of the two-stage model.

Response Bias

We have attributed the subadditivity of judged probabilities and of decision weights to basic psychological principles advanced in support theory and prospect theory. Alternatively, one might be tempted to account for these findings by a bias toward the midpoint of the response scale. This bias could be induced by anchoring on the midpoint of the scale, or by a symmetric error component that is bounded by the endpoints of the response scale. Although such response bias may contribute to subadditivity in some studies, it cannot provide a satisfactory account of this phenomenon. First, there is compelling evidence for bounded subadditivity in simple choices between uncertain prospects (see e.g., Tversky and Kahneman 1992, tables 32.1 and 32.2; Wu and Gonzalez 1996) that cannot be explained as a response bias.[16] Second, response bias cannot account for the observation that unpacking the description of a target event can increase the attractiveness of the corresponding prospect, nor can it account for the resulting nonmonotonicities described above. Third, a symmetric bias toward the midpoint of the response scale cannot explain the observation that both cash equivalents and decision weights for complementary prospects generally sum to less than one. Finally, it should be noted that the significance of subadditivity to the prediction of judgment and choice is not affected by whether it is interpreted as a feature of the evaluation process, as a response bias, or as a combination of the two.

Source Preference

There is evidence that people's willingness to bet on an uncertain event depends not only on the degree of uncertainty but also on its source. We next review this phenomenon and discuss its relation to the belief-based account.

A person exhibits source preference if he or she prefers to bet on a proposition drawn from one source rather than on a proposition drawn from another source, and also prefers to bet against the first proposition rather than against the second. Source preference was first illustrated by Ellsberg (1961) using the following example. Consider an urn containing 50 red and 50 black balls, and a second urn containing 100 red and black balls in an unknown proportion. Suppose you are offered a cash prize if you correctly guess the color of a ball drawn blindly from one of the urns. Ellsberg argued that most people would rather bet on a red ball from the first urn than on a red ball from the second, and they also would rather bet on a black ball from the first urn than on a black ball from the second. This pattern has been observed in several studies (see Camerer and Weber 1992 for a review). The preference to bet on clear or known probabilities rather than vague or unknown probabilities has been called *ambiguity aversion*.

More recent research has shown that although people exhibit ambiguity aversion in situations of complete ignorance (e.g., Ellsberg's urn), they often prefer betting on their vague beliefs than on matched chance events. Indeed, the evidence is consistent with a more general account, called the *competence hypothesis*: people prefer to bet on their vague beliefs in situations in which they feel particularly competent or knowledgeable, and they prefer to bet on chance when they do not (Heath and Tversky 1991). For example, subjects who were knowledgeable about football but not about politics preferred to bet on the outcome of professional football games than on matched chance events, but they preferred to bet on chance than on the results of a national election. Analogously, subjects who were knowledgeable about politics but not about football preferred to bet on the results of an election than on matched chance events, but they preferred to bet on chance than on football.[17]

The present studies provide some evidence for source preference that is consistent with the competence hypothesis. Recall that subjects in study 1 were recruited for their interest in professional basketball. Indeed, these subjects preferred betting on basketball to betting on matched chance events: the median certainty equivalent for the Eastern Conference ($79) and the Western Conference ($74) were both greater than the median certainty equivalent for the 50-percent chance prospect ($69). In contrast, subjects in study 2 did not have special expertise regarding the simulated economy. Indeed, these subjects generally preferred betting on chance to betting on the economic indicators. For example, the median certainty equivalent for both inflation and interest going up ($690) was the same as the median certainty equivalent for the 50-percent chance prospect, but the median certainty equivalent for the complementary event ($470) was considerably lower.

It is evident that source preference cannot be explained by the present model, though it can be accommodated by a more general belief-based account. For example, we can generalize equation (1) by letting $W(A) = F[P(A)]$ so that the transformation F of judged probability depends on the source of uncertainty. One convenient parameterization may be defined by $W(A) = (w[P(A)])^{\theta}$, where $\theta > 0$ is inversely related to the attractiveness of the source.[18] These generalizations no longer satisfy equation (5), but they maintain the decomposition of W into two components: P, which reflects a person's belief in the likelihood of the target event; and F (or w^{θ}), which reflects a person's preference to bet on that belief.

Practical Implications

The two-stage model may have important implications for the management sciences and related fields. First, the unpacking principle implies that the particular descriptions of events on which outcomes depend may affect a person's willingness to act. Hence, the attractiveness of an opportunity such an investment might be increased by unpacking the ways in which the investment could be profitable; willingness to take protective action such as the purchase of insurance might be increased by unpacking the ways in which a relevant mishap might occur.

Second, violations of the partition inequality suggest that people are willing to pay more for a prospect when components are evaluated separately; thus, they are willing to pay a premium, on average, for specificity. When such decisions are aggregated over time or across individuals within an organization, this pattern can lead to certain losses. To illustrate, the first author ran a classroom exercise in which MBA students were divided into six "firms" of eight students each, and each student was asked to decide their firm's maximum willingness to pay for an "investment" that would yield $100,000 depending on future movement of indicators in the U.S economy. The state space was partitioned into eight events (one for each student) so that each firm's portfolio of investments resulted in a certain return of exactly $100,000. Nevertheless, the six firms reported willingness-to-pay for the eight investments that summed to between $107,000 and $210,000.

Concluding Remarks

We have provided evidence that decision weights under uncertainty can be predicted from judged probabilities of events and risky decision weights. To the extent that the two-stage model reflects the psychological process underlying decision under uncertainty, this model suggests two independent sources of departure from the classical theory: a belief-based source (subadditivity of judged probability) and a preference-based source (nonlinear weighting of chance events). While the development of effective prescriptions for correcting such bias awaits future investigation, this decomposition of the weighting function offers a new approach to the modeling of decision under uncertainty that integrates probability judgment into the analysis of choice.[19]

Notes

1. The notion that beliefs can be measured based on preferences was anticipated by Borel (1924).

2. The boundary conditions are needed to ensure that we always compare an interval that includes an endpoint to an interval that is bounded away from the other endpoint (see Tversky and Wakker 1995 for a more rigorous formulation).

3. We use the lower case w to denote the weighting function for risk and the upper case W to denote the weighting function for uncertainty.

4. The two-stage model has not yet been extensively tested for multiple nonzero outcomes; however, see Wu and Gonzalez (1998c) for a preliminary investigation.

5. For the simple prospects considered here, the separable and cumulative versions of the theory are identical.

6. To demonstrate, set $u(0) = 0$. Hence, $C(x, A_1) + \cdots + C(x, A_n) = u^{-1}(u(x)\mathscr{P}(A_1)) + \cdots + u^{-1}(u(x)\mathscr{P}(A_n)) \leq u^{-1}(u(x)\mathscr{P}(A)) = C(x, A)$ if u is concave. We use $\mathscr{P}$ to denote an additive probability measure, to be distinguished from P, that denotes judged probability.

7. In every case this also holds for a significant majority of subjects ($p < 0.01$ by sign tests).

8. In every case this also holds for a significant majority of subjects ($p < 0.01$).

9. A more conservative test of the standard theory assuming $\alpha = 1.00$ yields a mean absolute error of $13.29.

10. Eight teams qualified for the playoffs from each conference.

11. Violations of monotonicity are also evident in the certainty equivalent data for study 1 reported in figure 32.3. Note that the median certainty equivalent for San Antonio is higher than the median certainty equivalent for the Midwestern Division; Chicago and Orlando are priced as high as their respective divisions. While these results are consistent with the present account, none of these differences is statistically significant.

12. In every case $\Delta > 0$ for a significant majority of subjects ($p < 0.05$).

13. The condition $w(p) + w(1 - p) \leq 1$, called *subcertainty*, is generally supported by empirical data (see e.g., Tversky and Kahneman 1992). It says that the certainty effect is more pronounced than the possibility effect, and it implies the common finding that $w(0.5) < 0.5$ (see figure 32.1).

14. In every case $\Delta > 0$ for a majority of subjects; this majority is statistically significant ($p < 0.05$ by sign test) for all tests but the first and fourth listed in the table.

15. A least-square procedure for estimating all subjective probabilities simultaneously subject to the additivity constraint did not improve the fit of the classical theory.

16. The studies of Wu and Gonzalez (1996) provide evidence of concavity for low probabilities and convexity for moderate to high probabilities, which are stronger than lower and upper subadditivity, respectively.

17. To complicate matters further, Fox and Tversky (1995) have shown that ambiguity aversion, which has been commonly observed when people evaluate both clear and vague propositions jointly, seems to diminish or disappear when people evaluate only one of these propositions in isolation.

18. Alternatively, one might accommodate source preference by varying a parameter of the risky weighting function that increases or decreases weights throughout the unit interval. For example, one can vary β of Prelec's (1998) two-parameter risky weighting function, $w(p) = \exp(-\beta(-\ln p)^{\alpha})$, where $\beta > 0$ is inversely related to the attractiveness of the source. This has the advantage of manipulating the "elevation" of

the function somewhat independently of its degree of "curvature." For more on elevation and curvature of the weighting function, see Gonzalez and Wu (1998).

19. This research was conducted while the first author was visiting at Northwestern University. It was supported in part by grant SBR-9408684 from the National Science Foundation to the second author. The authors thank George Wu and Peter Wakker for helpful discussions and suggestions.

References

Allais, M., "Le Comportement de l'Homme Rationel Devant le Risque, Critique des Postulates et Axiomes de l'Ecole Americaine," *Econometrica*, 21 (1953), 503–546.

Borel. É., "Apropos of a Treatise on Probability," in H. Kyburg and H. Smokler (eds.), *Studies in Subjective Probability* (lst Edition), John Wiley & Sons, New York, 1924.

Camerer, C. F., "Individual Decision Making," Chapter 8 in J. H. Kagel and A. E. Roth (eds.), *Handbook of Experimental Economics*, Princeton University Press, Princeton, NJ, 1995.

———— and T.-H. Ho, "Violations of the Betweenness Axiom and Nonlinearity in Probability," *J. Risk and Uncertainty*, 8 (1994), 167–196.

———— and M. Weber, "Recent Developments in Modeling Preferences: Uncertainty and Ambiguity," *J. Risk and Uncertainty*, 5 (1992), 325–370.

Ellsberg, D., "Risk, Ambiguity, and the Savage Axioms," *Quarterly J. Economics*, 75 (1961), 643–669.

Fischhoff, B., P. Slovic, and S. Lichtenstein, "Fault Trees: Sensitivity of Estimated Failure Probabilities to Problem Representation," *J. Experimental Psychology*: *Human Perception and Performance*, 4 (1978), 330–344.

Fox, C. R., "Subadditivity in Judgment and Choice: A Test of the Major Axioms and Implications of Support Theory," Unpublished Manuscript, Duke University Fuqua School of Business, Durham, NC, 1998.

————, B. A. Rogers, and A. Tversky, "Options Traders Exhibit Subadditive Decision Weights," *J. Risk and Uncertainty*, 13 (1996), 5–17.

———— and A. Tversky, "Ambiguity Aversion and Comparative Ignorance," *Quarterly J. Economics*, 110 (1995), 585–603.

Gonzalez, R. and G. Wu, "On the Form of the Probability Weighting Function," Unpublished Manuscript, Department of Psychology, University of Michigan, Ann Arbor, MI, 1998.

Heath, C. and A. Tversky, "Preference and Belief: Ambiguity and Competence in Choice under Uncertainty," *J. Risk and Uncertainty*, 4 (1991), 4–28.

Johnson, E. J., J. Hershey, J. Meszaros, and H. Kunreuther, "Framing, Probability Distortions, and Insurance Decisions," *J. Risk and Uncertainty*, 7 (1993), 35–51.

Kahneman, D. and A. Tversky, "Prospect Theory: An Analysis of Decision under Risk," *Econometrica*, 4 (1979), 263–291.

Prelec, D., "The Probability Weighting Function," *Econometrica*, 60 (1998), 497–528.

Ramsey, F. P., "Truth and Probability," in R. B. Braithwaite (ed.), *The Foundations of Mathematics and Other Logical Essays by FP Ramsey*, Harcourt, Brace and Co., NY, 1931.

Redelmeier, D. A., D. J. Koehler, V. Liberman, and A. Tversky, "Probability Judgment in Medicine: Discounting Unspecified Possibilities," *Medical Decision Making*, 15 (1995), 227–230.

Rottenstreich, Y. and A. Tversky, "Unpacking, Repacking, and Anchoring: Advances in Support Theory," *Psychological Review*, 2 (1997), 406–415.

Teigen, K. H., "Subjective Sampling Distributions and the Additivity of Estimates," *Scandinavian J. Psychology*, 24 (1974), 97–105.

Tversky, A., "Utility Theory and Additivity Analysis of Risky Choices," *J. Experimental Psychology*, 75 (1967), 27–36.

Tversky, A. and C. R. Fox, "Weighing Risk and Uncertainty," *Psychological Rev.*, 102 (1995), 269–283.

———— and D. Kahneman, "Advances in Prospect Theory: Cumulative Representation of Uncertainty," *J. Risk and Uncertainty*, 5 (1992), 297–323.

Tversky, A. and D. J. Koehler, "Support Theory: A Nonextensional Representation of Subjective Probability," *Psychological Review*, 101 (1994), 547–567.

———— and P. P. Wakker, "Risk Attitudes and Decision Weights," *Econometrica*, 63 (1995), 1255–1280.

Wu, G. and R. Gonzalez, "Common Consequence Effects in Decision Making under Risk," *Risk and Uncertainty*, 16 (1998a), 113–135.

———— and ————, "Dominance Violations and Event Splitting," Unpublished Manuscript, University of Chicago Graduate School of Business, Chicago, IL, 1998b.

———— and ————, "Nonlinearity of Decision Weights in Decision Making under Uncertainty," Unpublished Manuscript, University of Chicago Graduate School of Business, Chicago, IL, 1998c.

———— and ————, "Curvature of the Probability Weighting Function," *Management Sci.*, 42 (1996), 1676–1690.

Contingent Preferences

33 Self-Deception and the Voter's Illusion

George A. Quattrone and Amos Tversky

A major problem in the analysis of choice concerns the relationship between actions and outcomes. A common assumption is that actions have a causal effect on outcomes. Some actions, however, may be primarily diagnostic of outcomes in that actions and outcomes may both be consequences of a common antecedent cause. When actions are merely diagnostic of outcomes, rather than causal, the analysis of choice becomes more problematic. The extensive literature on Newcomb's paradox is a case in point. In this chapter, we first discuss the normative problem of causal versus diagnostic contingencies. We then turn from the logical to the psychological analysis, where we argue that decision-makers sometimes fail to distinguish between causal and diagnostic contingencies. We further relate our psychological analysis to the theory of cognitive dissonance and to the concept of self-deception. Next, we describe an experiment in which subjects selected actions that were diagnostic of the outcomes, "good health and longevity," although it was clear to subjects that the actions would have no causal effect on their state of health. A second experiment is presented to demonstrate that an individual may view his own choices as diagnostic of the choices likely to be made by his like-minded peers. The results of the experiment, which are indicative of what we call the "voter's illusion", may help explain why some people vote in large elections despite the low probability of casting a decisive ballot. Finally, we discuss further implications and extensions of these ideas.

The Logic of Decision

Because the outcome of a decision often depends on past or future states of nature that cannot be known with certainty, it is reasonable for the decision-maker to weigh the possible outcomes of an action by the probability of the states on which they depend. In many situations, the relevant states of nature are independent of one's choice. Despite numerous anecdotes to the contrary, the probability of rain does not depend on whether one has decided to wash one's car. We shall use the conventional notation for conditional probabilities, $P(S/A)$, to refer to the probability of a state, S, given act, A. Thus, the state "rain" is independent of the act "car wash" in the sense that $P(S/A) = P(S/\text{not } A) = P(S)$, the marginal (i.e., pre-decisional) probability of rain.

It is not always true that the relevant states of nature are independent of one's choice. In deliberating over whether to stop smoking, for example, the decision-maker must weigh the pleasures of tobacco and the pain of withdrawal against the possibility of premature death. Clearly, the risk of contracting lung cancer (S) is not independent of whether one abstains (A) from smoking in that $P(S/A) < P(S/\text{not } A)$. Because states may not be independent of one's choice, the value of each outcome associated with a particular act should be weighted by the probability of the outcome conditional on selecting the act (Jeffrey 1965).

This conception becomes problematic when it is recognized that acts may be *causal* or *diagnostic* of outcomes with which they are correlated. Consider the historical controversy over how to interpret the correlation between smoking and cancer. It is now widely acknowledged that smoking has a direct causal effect on the etiology of lung cancer. But it has not always been so clear. As late as 1959, R. A. Fisher, the great statistician, argued that the correlation could be attributable to a genetic trait that predisposed the individual towards both smoking and cancer. To Fisher, smoking was diagnostic of lung cancer, not causal, in that smoking was merely a sign that the individual had been born with the pre-cancerous gene. Despite the fact that smoking may have a lower expected desirability than abstaining if the value of the outcomes are weighted by the respective conditional probabilities, Fisher cited his genetic thesis as reason enough for lighting up.

One may certainly object to Fisher's theory about the linkage between smoking and cancer. But if the theory were true, Fisher's decision to continue smoking is defensible. According to this theory one either has or does not have the pre-cancerous gene, and hence one's decision to smoke or not does not facilitate or inhibit the emergence of cancerous cells. True, smokers are more likely to die of cancer than non-smokers. But the correlation is channelled through the presence or absence of a genetic trait beyond the individual's control.

One way to conceptualize the problem is to imagine that the hypothetical pre-cancerous gene exerts its influence on smoking by first producing a yen or an urge to smoke (Jeffrey 1981). The knowledge that one does not have the urge (A^*) or that one does, effectively "screens off" the correlation between the act of smoking (not-A) and cancer (S), in the sense that $P(S/A \ \& \ A^*) = P(S/\text{not } A \ \& \ A^*) < P(S/A \ \& \ \text{not } A^*) = P(S/\text{not } A \ \& \ \text{not } A^*)$. The inequality indicates that among people without the urge and among people with the urge, smoking is independent of cancer. The overall correlation between smoking and cancer is merely a consequence of there being more smokers and pre-cancerous persons among people with the gene-induced urge than among people without the urge. Hence, upon recognizing that one has the urge to smoke, one who subscribes to Fisher's theory ought to light up because, given the urge, cancer is independent of smoking. Most philosophical analyses of the problem (Nozick 1969; Gibbard and Harper 1978; Skyrms 1980; Jeffrey 1981) defend smoking under the above assumptions, but question whether it is always possible to screen off the correlation between action and outcome.

The Psychology of Choice

We now turn from the logical to the psychological analysis, which is complicated by the fact that causal and diagnostic contingencies are usually confounded in the real world. Suppose undergraduates know that students who attend a review session for the final examination get better grades than students who do not attend. Does the correlation between attendance and grade mean that the review session really helps? Or does it mean that reviews are attended primarily by conscientious students who would do well, session or no? Insofar as there is uncertainty about the causal or diagnostic significance of the action (attendance) with respect to the outcome (grade), it is reasonable for students to entertain the causal hypothesis, play it safe and attend the session. We hypothesize, however, that people would select an action correlated with an auspicious outcome even if they believed that the action is only diagnostic of the outcome and in no way causal. Thus even if students were presented with compelling evidence that review sessions have no causal influence on their examination performance, and they accept the evidence, they might nonetheless be tempted to attend, so long as better grades are associated with attendance than with non-attendance.

This problem is reminiscent of the well-known dilemma faced by Calvinists, who subscribe to divine pre-determination. As drawn in the left-hand side of figure 33.1, Calvinists believe that there are two kinds of people, the chosen and the not-chosen. Whether one is chosen or not has already been decided by the deity prior to one's birth. There are at least two consequences of the deity's decision. First, the chosen will enter paradise after death, whereas the not-chosen will suffer eternal damnation in hell. Second, the chosen will lead a life of virtue, whereas the not-chosen will lead a life of sin. Calvinists do not know who among them are the chosen. But they know that avarice, lust and sloth are sinful acts correlated with eternal damnation. Conversely, they know that charity, purity and hard work are virtuous acts correlated

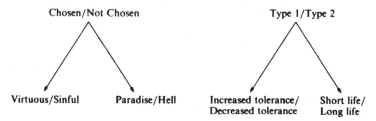

Figure 33.1
Illustrated causal structures.

with eternal post-mortal bliss. Although the acts are not believed to influence one's posthumous fate, most Calvinists conclude that they had better live by the *Book* in that the immediate gratifications of the flesh seem hardly worth an eternity in hell. That Calvinists may confuse diagnostic and causal contingencies is illustrated by the following letter circulated by Baptists in 1770: "Every soul that comes to Christ to be saved ... is to be encouraged ... The coming soul need not fear that he is not elected, for none but such would be willing to come."

What about the "urge" or the temptation to sin? Do Calvinists not recognize that temptation itself should screen off the correlation between the virtuousness of one's act and the location of one's life after death? After all, only the not-chosen would even contemplate a dissolute deed. The normative analysis of Fisher's smoking theory would suggest that Calvinists ought to transgress upon experiencing the desire to do so, *ceteris paribus*, for heaven and hell are independent of action conditional on the urge to sin. Contrary to this analysis, we believe that many Calvinists would nonetheless resist the temptation and choose instead the virtuous acts correlated with paradise.

The notion that people may confuse causal and diagnostic contingencies is familiar to social psychologists (see Abelson et al. 1968). The theory of cognitive dissonance (Festinger 1957) is an illustrative case. According to this theory, an individual who holds two or more cognitions (i.e., attitudes and beliefs) that are psychologically inconsistent will experience an uncomfortable state of tension, called dissonance. The individual will then be "driven" to reduce dissonance by changing one or more of the cognitions so that they are no longer inconsistent. For example, suppose a college freshman suffers embarrassment and exerts considerable physical effort as part of an initiation procedure to join a fraternity. Having become a member, he discovers that the organization falls far short of his previous expectations: the food is tasteless, and the parties are dull. The cognition, "this is a lousy fraternity," can be regarded as psychologically inconsistent with the cognition, "I incurred costs to enter the fraternity," in the sense that people do not ordinarily expend great effort to attain an undesirable goal. The resulting dissonance can be reduced by re-evaluating the fraternity: "the food is not really all that bad, and the parties are as good as any on campus." This hypothesized process can be analysed in terms of the confusion between causal and diagnostic contingencies. It is commonly thought that there is a relationship between the costs one bears to join a group and the overall desirability of the group. The causal impact usually flows from "desirability" to "costs." That is, one is willing to bear costs to enter a group because it is desirable; the group does not become desirable because one bore costs to enter it. Dissonance theory predicts, however, that people may reverse the causal and diagnostic relationships. Thus an individual who, in the absence of bearing costs, would rate two groups as equally desirable would subsequently rate as more desirable the group for which he bore more costs to enter. Hence, the cost one bears comes to influence one's evaluation of the group rather than being merely diagnostic of one's evaluation of the group. The example also illustrates how causal and diagnostic contingencies are confounded in the real world. If we knew only that an individual evaluates highly a group he exerted much effort to join, it is difficult to discern whether he was willing to exert the effort because he had already evaluated the group highly, or whether he evaluated the group highly because of the effort he expended. Finally, dissonance theory does not claim that people must engage in actions that are diagnostic of an inference *in order to* accept the inference. The freshman does not have to act as though the fraternity were desirable to accept the belief that it is. The re-evaluation may be achieved solely through cognitive means. Once the belief is accepted, however, the individual may, according to dissonance theory, act in line with the belief; for example, he may praise the fraternity in public. In contrast, we suspect that these actions may not simply "follow from" the newly accepted belief. The actions may in part be motivated by the individual's attempt to convince himself that the belief is valid.

Dissonance theory is not inconsistent with the notion that people may select *actions* enabling them to make favourable inferences. The theory allows dissonance to be reduced either through cognitive or behavioural means. What has not been investigated in the social psychological literature are the conditions under which people would be "taken in" by their own actions. How could actors reasonably make a favourable diagnosis from their behaviour when the behaviour was enacted in order to make the diagnosis? What comfort could a Calvinist derive from a virtuous act if performed while one is tempted to sin? One possibility is that people do not quite recognize that for diagnostic contingencies the urge to act (e.g., to smoke or to sin) screens off the correlation between action and outcome. People may adopt a quasi-behaviouristic doctrine in which actions speak louder than urges and related inner states. This account is consistent with Bem's (1972) theory of self-perception in that inferences about the self are assumed to be based solely on the observation of one's own behaviour and on the external circumstances in which one behaves. It is also possible, however, that a certain degree of self-deception may contribute to the acceptance of the diagnosis implied by one's behaviour. That is, actors may have to avoid admitting to themselves that the behaviour was produced more by the motive to infer an auspicious antecedent cause than by the auspicious antecedent cause itself. Calvinists may deny their temptation to sin and convince themselves that the virtuous act was not selected merely to defend against the inference of not being chosen.

Gur and Sackheim (1979) have characterized self-deception by the following criteria: (a) the individual simultaneously holds two contradictory beliefs, (b) the individual is not aware of holding one of the beliefs and (c) the lack of awareness is motivated. We are arguing that when people select actions to infer an auspicious antecedent cause, then, to accept the inference as valid, they often render themselves unaware of the fact that they selected the action just in order to infer the cause. Unless they deny to themselves that their action was purposefully chosen to make a favourable diagnosis, they may not attribute the action to the target antecedent cause but rather to the motive to infer that cause. This view is compatible with the criteria put forth by Gur and Sackheim. The beliefs, "I purposefully engaged in the behaviour to make a favourable diagnosis," and "I did not purposefully engage in the behaviour to make a favourable diagnosis," are clearly contradictory (a), and one's lack of awareness (b) regarding the former belief is motivated by the individual's desire to accept the diagnosis implied by behaviour (c). When people select an action to make a favourable diagnosis, but fail to realize that they purposefully selected the action in order to make the diagnosis, we classify the action and the denial collectively as a form of *deceptive diagnosis*.

Deceptive Diagnosis

We now describe an experiment that tested our basic thesis that people select actions diagnostic of favourable outcomes, even if it is clear that the action does not facilitate the outcome. Self-report measures were also included to test the notion that, even if people do engage in the diagnostic behaviour, the favourable diagnosis would be made primarily by subjects who deny that the action was purposefully selected. We chose to investigate these issues in a medical context. Medical examinations consist of tests that are diagnostic or indicative of one's underlying state of health. How one does on the examination does not, in general, affect one's state of health. Rather, it is one's state of health that determines how one does on the examination. If people were given an opportunity, we predict that they would "cheat" on a medical examination in a direction correlated with desirable outcomes, such as good health and longevity. To test this hypothesis, we constructed an analogue of the Calvinist dilemma in the medical realm. Subjects learned that there were two kinds of hearts, namely, type 1 and type 2. Heart type allegedly had two sets of consequences. First, people with type 1 heart are frequently ill, are prone to heart disease, and have a shorter-than-average life expectancy. People with type 2 heart enjoy good health, have a low risk of heart disease, and show a longer-than-average life expectancy. Second, heart type was said to determine how exercise would change an individual's tolerance to cold water. Half of our subjects were informed that a type 1 heart would increase tolerance to cold water after exercise whereas a type 2 heart would decrease tolerance. The remaining subjects learned that a type 1 heart would decrease tolerance to cold water after exercise, whereas a type 2 heart would increase tolerance. We shall refer to these treatments as the decrease and increase conditions, respectively, to indicate the change in tolerance associated with good health and longevity. The righthand side of figure 33.1 illustrates the correlational structure received by subjects in the decrease condition. All three variables (i.e., heart type, life expectancy and shifts in tolerance) were treated as continuous. For example, subjects in the increase condition were led to believe that the closer they are to having a type 2 heart, the more would exercise increase their tolerance and the longer would their life expectancy be.

Subjects first underwent a baseline trial of the cold-pressor pain task (Hilgard et al. 1974), which requires them to submerge their forearms into a chest of circulating cold water until they can no longer tolerate it. Subjects then pedalled an exercycle for one minute, which was followed by the information about heart types, life expectancy, and tolerance shifts. Subjects then repeated the cold-pressor task to their tolerance threshold in the presence of a second "blind" experimenter. Finally, subjects indicated on a questionnaire whether they believed they were type 1 or type 2 and whether they had purposefully tried to alter the amount of time they kept their arm in the water on the post-exercise trial. We tested the following three hypotheses:

1. On the post-exercise or "experimental" trial, subjects would shift their tolerance threshold in the direction correlated with health and longevity: that is, a downward shift in the decrease condition and an upward shift in the increase condition. The prediction for the increase condition is especially noteworthy because it implies that people will incur painful consequences of their action so long as the action were diagnostic of an outcome more important than transient pain.

2. By and large, subjects will deny that they purposefully tried to shift their tolerance on the post-exercise trial.

3. Those subjects who do admit that they had purposefully tried to shift their tolerance would be less likely to infer that they had the preferred type 2 heart than would subjects who deny the attempt to shift.

Procedure

The subjects were 38 undergraduates at Stanford University. They arrived for an experiment on the "psychological and medical aspects of athletics." The experimental room was on the physiological floor of the psychology building where animals, chemicals and electronic equipment are readily visible. The location was selected to establish credibility for our alleged interest in cardiovascular matters. A female experimenter, wearing a white lab coat, told subjects that the purpose of the study was to examine the effects of rapid changes in temperature on heart rate after exercise. The research question was allegedly inspired by wondering what were the coronary implications of athletes' jumping into a cold shower after working out on a hot day. Subjects were given an overview of the entire experimental procedure. The cold-pressor task was said to provide the necessary "change in temperature," pulse-readings to provide the measures of "heart rate," and pedalling an exercycle to provide the "exercise." Subjects understood that they would undergo two trials of the cold-pressor task, each followed by a pulse-reading, and separated from each other by a minute of exercycling. Thus the first trial would provide a baseline measure of heart rate in response to temperature change, which could then be compared to heart rate in response to temperature change following exercise. After subjects understood the procedure and were forewarned of the discomfort associated with the cold-pressor task, they were asked to express their informed consent. All subjects consented.

The baseline trial of the cold-pressor was administered after subjects had given their consent. The apparatus consisted of a picnic chest, partitioned in the middle and filled with water. Ice cubes were placed in one side of the partition, and a motor circulated the water to maintain its temperature at about 35 °F. Subjects immersed their bare hands and forearms into the water. After every five seconds they reported a number from one to ten to express their discomfort. The number ten was taken to mean that point at which subjects would rather not tolerate the cold any longer. When subjects reached ten, they were asked to remove their arm from the chest. Subjects reported their numbers in response to a letter called out by the experimenter. Subjects heard "A" after five seconds, "B" after ten seconds, "C" after fifteen seconds and so on. This procedure was used to help subjects to recall how long they tolerated the water on the baseline trial thus providing them with a target for the experimental trial. Subjects then had their pulse taken and pedalled an exercycle vigorously for one minute.

A brief "rest period" was inserted between the exercycling and the experimental cold-pressor trial. This interval gave the experimenter the opportunity to present the correlational structure discussed previously. To prevent subjects from discovering the true purpose of the study, the crucial information was embedded in a mini-lecture on psychophysics. Subjects learned that the cold-pressor was used to study the psychophysics of pain. Psychophysics was defined as the attempt to relate mathematically the perception of a stimulus to the physical properties of a stimulus. Subjects were shown a curve on a blackboard that related time of immersion in cold water to subjective discomfort (i.e., numbers from one to ten). The curve depicted the typical relationship and it was said to be based on data averaged over many people. Individual differences were said to exist, illustrated by showing two curves that reached ten at different rates. Skin type was said to be one factor that distinguished between people with high or low tolerance to cold water. Heart type was said to be another factor. Subjects learned that people could be characterized as having either one of two cardiovascular complexes, referred to as type 1 and type 2 hearts. Subjects viewed a histogram, on a glossy photograph, which showed that longer life expectancies were associated with increasing degrees of type 2 hearts and that shorter life expectancies were associated with increasing degrees of type 1 hearts. Allegedly, some investigators had suggested that type 1 subjects do not differ from type 2 subjects in tolerance on the pre-exercise trial. However, exercise supposedly may create a difference between the two types. Subjects were then randomly assigned to either the decrease or increase described earlier. The information was conveyed verbally and displayed in a histogram.

A second female experimenter administered the experimental cold-pressor trial. To guard against experimenter bias, she was blind to subjects' condition and performance on the baseline trial. We also tried to reduce the likelihood that subjects would show self-presentational shifts in tolerance to impress the experimenter that they were healthy. First, it was made clear to subjects that there was a lot of variability within types 1 and 2 on both trials. Thus, the second experimenter could not infer from the length of the second trial subjects' likely type. Only shifts between trials would be telling. Second, subjects were assured that the first experimenter would be kept ignorant of their performance on the second trial and that the second experimenter would be kept ignorant of their performance on the baseline trial. Thus, neither experimenter would have the data required to infer subjects' likely type. Finally, the experimenter who administered the post-experimental trial was presented as a secretary, wearing ordinary clothing, employed here simply to administer the trial. Thus her appearance and behaviour were designed to make it seem as though she knew nothing of the study's hypotheses, description or rationale. After the second cold-pressor trial, subjects completed a brief questionnaire. They were asked to infer whether they were type 1 or 2, and they checked either "Yes" or "No" to the question, "Did you purposefully try to alter the amount of time you kept your hand in the water after exercise?" Finally, subjects were thoroughly debriefed of all deception and sworn to secrecy. Prior to the debriefing, no subject could articulate the hypotheses when probed.

Table 33.1
Mean Time of Immersion in Seconds

Condition	Trial		Change
	Baseline	Experimental	
Decrease	44.74	37.11	−7.63
Increase	34.21	46.05	+11.84

Table 33.2
Mean Time in Tolerance

Condition	Subjects' self-reported group	
	Non-Deniers	Deniers
Decrease	−5.00	−8.13
Increase	+19.11	+8.08
Difference	24.17	16.21
$F(1, 34)$	11.54	18.61
p	.005	.001

Results

The number of seconds during which subjects kept their arms in the cold water was recorded after each of the two trials. The cell means are shown in table 33.1. In line with our first hypothesis, subjects in the decrease condition showed significantly less tolerance on the experimental trial than on the baseline trial, $F(1, 36) = 9.41$, $p < .005$, whereas subjects in the increase condition showed significantly more tolerance, $F(1, 36) = 23.25$, $p < .001$.

Of the 38 subjects tested, 27 showed the predicted shift (13 of 19 in the decrease condition and 14 of 19 in the increase condition), and 11 did not, $p < .01$ by the sign test. Five subjects in each condition showed no shift, whereas one subject in the decrease condition, a "suicidal type," showed a shift opposite from prediction.

Only 9 of our 38 subjects indicated on the anonymous questionnaire that they had purposefully tried to change the amount of time they held their hand in the water after exercise. In line with our second hypothesis, this number was smaller than the number (i.e., 29) who indicated no attempt to shift, $p < .005$ by sign test. The tendency to deny or to admit an attempt to shift could not be attributed to actual differences in behaviour. That is, the percentage of subjects who did shift as predicted was no greater among subjects who indicated that they tried to shift (67%) than it was among subjects who indicated that they did not try to shift (72%). Table 33.2 shows the mean changes in tolerance in the decrease and increase conditions both for the group of subjects who indicated that they did try to shift ("non-deniers") and for the group who indicated that they did not try to shift ("deniers"). The predicted difference between conditions was significant within each group of subjects, and no interaction between condition and subjects' group was observed, $F(1, 34) < 1$.

We have shown that a majority of subjects show the hypothesized shift and that a majority deny that they attempted to shift. Moreover, the deniers did not differ from the non-deniers in the degree to which their behaviour was diagnostic of having a type 2 heart. In line with our third hypothesis, however, the two groups of subjects *did* differ in their acceptance of the diagnosis implied by their behaviour. Only two of the nine non-deniers (or 22%) inferred having a type 2 heart, whereas 20 of the 29 deniers (or 69%) inferred a type 2 heart, $p < .05$.

To summarize, the preceding experiment employed a procedure that resembles a medical examination. Subjects believed that a directional change in tolerance to cold water correlated with their state of health and expected lifespan. It should have been clear to subjects that shifts in tolerance would have no *causal* impact on their life expectancy. Shifts would be merely *diagnostic* of their life expectancy in that both shifts and life expectancy were affected by an individual's heart type. As predicted, subjects "cheated" on this medical examination in a direction that correlated with having a robust heart and long expected life. Subjects who believed that longevity was associated with an exercise-induced decrease in tolerance removed their arm from near-freezing water sooner after exercise than before exercise. Subjects who believed that longevity was associated with an exercise-induced increase in tolerance removed their arm from the water later after exercise than before exercise. The latter result indicated that people are willing to bear painful behavioural consequences so long as the behaviour is a sign, though not a cause, of good health and long life.

As hypothesized, a majority of subjects indicated that they had not purposefully tried to alter the amount of time they kept their hand in the cold. Moreover, the few subjects who indicated that they did try to shift were no more likely to show the predicted shift than were the many subjects who indicated no attempt to shift. In the post-experimental interview, the first experimenter asked subjects who shifted why they had done so. Subjects in the decrease condition would typically say something like, "The water felt a lot colder," whereas subjects in the increase condition would say something like, "The water just didn't feel so cold anymore." By themselves, these data may signify only that subjects were reluctant to admit to the experimenter that they had "falsified" their scores. The self-presentational account appears less plausible, however, when we consider these data in conjunction with subjects' private inferences as to whether they were type 1 or type 2. A majority of the subjects who indicated on the anonymous questionnaire that they tried to shift inferred that they were type 1, fated to a life of illness. But the majority of subjects who indicated no attempt to shift inferred that they were type 2. These inferential differences were obtained despite there being no behavioural differences between the deniers and non-deniers. The data therefore suggest that a majority of subjects may have been reluctant to admit to *themselves* that they acted with a target inference in mind. Subjects probably sensed the dubious legitimacy of an inference based on behaviour that was motivated by the desire to make the inference. Denying the ulterior motive makes it easier for subjects to make the comforting diagnosis. Conversely, the difficulty of denying one's intentions may help explain the limited success of behavioural therapies. Clients are trained to act assertively, but they do not feel like assertive people because they know that the behaviour is a deliberate attempt to create an assertive image and is thus an invalid indicator.[1] To be sure, self-deception and denial are not matters of all-or-none. Deceptive diagnosis may come in finer gradations than would be apparent from dichotomous reports. Even subjects who indicated no attempt to shift may have harboured a lingering doubt to the contrary.

The Voter's Illusion

The idea that people may select an action to make a favourable self-diagnosis is not new. The first experiment went beyond earlier treatments of the problem by demonstrating that self-deception may contribute to accepting the diagnosis implied by behaviour. The second experiment extends our analysis of the problem further by testing the hypothesis that people would select actions correlated with auspicious outcomes, even if the actions do not directly involve inferences about oneself. For example, an individual may regard his or her own decisions as diagnostic of the decisions likely to be made by other "like-minded" persons. If the individual recognizes that beneficial outcomes would ensue if very many like-minded persons select a particular alternative, then the individual may select that alternative, even if the choice is costly, not witnessed by others and not likely by itself to affect the final outcome. In these circumstances, the choice is made to "induce" others who think and act like oneself to do the same, rather than to make comforting diagnoses about one's own attributes. The following analysis of voting is a case in point.

  Political scientists have long noted the paradoxical nature of an individual's voting in large national elections. A single vote is highly unlikely to be decisive, and the time and effort required to register and vote can be considerable. To understand voting in terms of rational choice, political scientists have maintained that an individual may derive from voting other benefits than just the prospect of casting the decisive ballot (cp. Riker and Ordeshook 1968). These additional benefits may include fulfilling one's duty as a citizen, participating in a common social ritual and signalling to others that voting is essential for the survival of democracy. To these rational *causal* consequences of voting, we suggest adding a less rational *diagnostic* aspect. People may reason that, within the electorate, there are citizens whose political orientation is similar to theirs (i.e., like-minded persons) as well as citizens whose political orientation is dissimilar (i.e., unlike-minded persons). The political dichotomy may be based on a single important issue, like abortion, or on an entire ideology, like liberalism/ conservatism. Two sets of consequences may follow from political orientation. First, like-minded persons would prefer one line of candidates, whereas unlike-minded persons would prefer the opposing line. Second, political orientation may also affect the likelihood of voting. There are three relevant possibilities to consider: like-minded persons may vote in larger numbers than do unlike-minded persons; unlike-minded persons may vote in larger numbers than do like-minded persons; or there may be no relationship between political orientation and likelihood of voting. One may not know which of these three states of the world will be in effect in the upcoming election. But one may reason that if one votes, then one's politically like-minded peers, who think and act like oneself, will also vote. Conversely, if one abstains, then one's like-minded peers will also abstain. Because the preferred candidates could defeat the opposition only if like-minded citizens vote in larger numbers than do unlike-minded citizens, the individual may conclude that he or she had better vote. That is, an individual may regard his or her *single* vote as diagnostic of *millions* of votes, and hence as a sign that the preferred candidates will emerge victorious. This analysis of voting can be likened to a Prisoner's Dilemma game played by identical twins, which is a variant of the well-known Newcomb's paradox (Nozick 1969). The twins reason that each will eventually select the same option. Therefore, each twin should select the dominated cooperative response to "induce" the other to do the same.

To explore the plausibility of "diagnostic voting," we created a political scenario about an imaginary country named Delta, whose electorate consisted of 4 million supporters of Party *A*, 4 million supporters of Party *B* and 4 million non-aligned voters. Subjects were asked to imagine that they support Party *A*, and that they wonder whether it is worthwhile to vote in the upcoming election. They were presented with one of two theories about who would determine the margin of victory in the election. Both theories maintained that the victorious party would win by a margin of 200,000 to 400,000 votes. But according to the "Non-Aligned Voters Theory," party supporters will vote in roughly equal numbers; hence the margin of victory will be determined by the non-aligned voters, who will either swing disproportionately for Party *A* or for Party *B* depending on which group of political

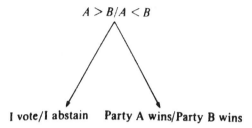

$A > B / A < B$

I vote/I abstain   Party A wins/Party B wins

Figure 33.2
Voting decisions faced by subjects in the party supporters' condition.

experts one consulted. In contrast, the Party Supporters Theory held that non-aligned voters will split their vote equally between the two parties. The margin of victory would therefore depend on which of the two parties voted in greater numbers. That is, supporters of one party will be more likely to vote than supporters of the other party, although the political experts did not agree as to which party it would be.

Note that the Party Supporters Theory holds that there will be a correlation between political orientation and vote turnout. That is, either the supporters of Party A will vote in greater numbers than the supporters of Party B (i.e., $A > B$) or vice-versa (i.e., $A < B$). In contrast, the Non-aligned Voters Theory holds that there will be no correlation ($A = B$). The correlational structure expected to be generated by subjects in the Party Supporters condition is shown in figure 33.2. Thus although the causal consequences of voting were held constant across the two theories, only subjects who receive the Party Supporters Theory could regard their decision to vote or to abstain as diagnostic of the decision reached by the other supporters of Party A. Because one's decision to vote would be diagnostic of a favourable electoral outcome only for subjects exposed to the Party Supporters Theory, these subjects should show a greater willingness to vote than should subjects who receive the Non-aligned Voters Theory. To test these hypotheses, we asked subjects a number of questions after they had read the respective theory, four of which assessed conditional probabilities. Assuming the theory were true, the subjects were asked how likely is it that the supporters of Party A will vote in greater numbers than the supporters of Party B (i.e., $A > B$) given that the subject votes (i.e., V) and given that the subject abstains. The next two questions were similar in that the subject now estimated the probability of Party A's defeating Party B conditional on the subject's voting or abstaining. Finally, subjects were asked whether they would vote, assuming the theory were true and voting were costly. We made the following predictions:

1. The differences in inferred probabilities conditional on voting and abstaining will be greater among subjects who receive the Party Supporters Theory than among those who receive the Non-aligned Voters Theory. That is $P(A > B/V) - P(A > B/\text{not } V)$ will be greater in the former condition than in the latter condition, and this difference will hold for "$A > B$" as well as for "Party A defeats Party B".

2. Subjects who receive the Party Supporters Theory will indicate a greater willingness to vote than will subjects who receive the Non-aligned Voters Theory.

3. The greater the difference in inferred probabilities conditional on voting and abstaining, the greater the willingness to vote. That is, the more a subject believes that his or her voting is diagnostic of what other supporters of Party A would do, the more willing is the subject to vote.

Procedure

The subjects were 315 Stanford undergraduate volunteers. The diagnostic voting problem was included in a questionnaire that subjects completed in their dormitories. It presented the information given in the introduction to this experiment in greater detail. Subjects were asked to imagine themselves citizens of the nation, Delta, which was said to have two major opposing parties. Party A favours peace and prosperity. Party B favours offensive warfare. Subjects imagined they were supporters of Party A, which consists of politically like-minded persons. Delta was about to hold an election with the presidency and other important offices being contested. A recent poll showed that 4 million eligible voters supported Party A, 4 million supported Party B and 4 million were not aligned with either party. Subjects imagined that they were deciding whether to vote, for registering to vote in Delta is costly in time and effort. They could not ask others if they would vote, because it is considered impolite in Delta to inquire into the voting intentions of others. To facilitate the decision, they were to consult the prevailing theory about the sort of voters that determine the margin of victory for the winning party. The proponents of the theory were said to be expert political analysts.

Subjects who received the Party Supporters Theory learned that the non-aligned voters would split their votes equally between the two parties. The outcome of the election would be due to the fact that the supporters of Party A will differ from the supporters of Party B in how involved they become in the election. Half of the experts believed that Party A supporters would become more involved than Party B supporters and half believed that Party B supporters would become more involved than Party A supporters. All experts agreed that the party whose supporters became more involved would win by a margin of 200,000 to 400,000 votes. The Non-aligned

Voters Theory informed the remaining subjects that Party *A* and Party *B* supporters will vote in equal numbers. But the majority of the non-aligned voters will side with one unspecified party (the experts were split as to which party it would be), and that party will win by a margin of 200,000 to 400,000 votes.

Having read the theory, subjects responded to six questions. The first four questions assessed the conditional probabilities hypothesized in part to motivate the vote: (1) if you vote, how likely is it that the other supporters of Party *A* will vote in larger numbers than the supporters of Party *B*? (2) If you abstain, how likely is it that the other supporters of Party *A* will vote in larger numbers than the supporters of Party *B*? (3) If you vote, how likely is it that Party *A* will defeat Party *B*? And (4), if you abstain, how likely is it that Party *A* will defeat Party *B*? Responses were made on 9-point scales labelled in the middle and at the endpoints. On a similar scale, subjects were asked, "How likely are you to vote if the theory were true and voting in Delta were costly?" and, finally, subjects checked "yes" or "no" to the question, "Would you vote if the theory were true and voting in Delta were costly?"

Results

Each subject was asked to estimate the likelihood that Party *A* would vote in larger numbers than Party *B* if the subject voted and if the subject abstained. The subject was also asked the likelihood that Party *A* would defeat Party *B* conditional on the subjects' voting and abstaining. The cell means are shown in table 33.3, and data relevant to the predictions are found in the row labelled "difference." As expected, the differences in inferred likelihoods conditional on voting and abstaining were significantly greater among subjects in the Party Supporters condition than among

Table 33.3
The Inferred Likelihood of States Given Subject's Decision

Condition	Subject's decision	States	
		Party *A* votes in greater numbers than Party *B*	Party *A* defeats Party *B*
Party supporters theory	Vote	5.81	6.06
	Abstain	4.13	4.09
	Difference	1.68	1.97
Non-aligned voters theory	Vote	4.20	5.12
	Abstain	3.87	4.60
	Difference	0.33	0.52

subjects in the Non-aligned Voters condition, both for the question concerning whether Party *A* would vote in greater numbers than Party *B*, $F(1, 313) = 35.79$, $p < .001$, and for the question concerning whether Party *A* would defeat Party *B*, $F(1, 313) = 40.18$, $p < .001$.

The difference between conditions in the assumed diagnostic significance of voting translated into differences between conditions in assumed voting intentions. Subjects in the Non-aligned Voters condition assumed that they would be less willing to vote (M = 6.43) than did subjects in the Party Supporters condition (M = 7.17), $F(1, 313) = 7.85$, $p < .05$. In a like manner, a greater percentage of subjects in the former condition (16%) than in the latter (7%) indicated that they would not vote, $p < .05$. Evidence for the hypothesized linkage between the inferred diagnostic significance of voting and willingness to vote was most directly demonstrated through correlational measures. In the Party Supporters condition, subjects were more willing to vote the more they believed that their decision to vote or to abstain was diagnostic of (a) whether Party *A* would vote in greater numbers than Party *B* (i.e., $P(A > B/V) - P(A > B/\text{not } V)$), $r = .27$, $p < .001$ and (b) whether Party *A* would defeat Party *B* (i.e., $P(A \text{ defeats } B/V) - P(A \text{ defeats } B/\text{not } V)$), $r = .32$, $p < .001$. In the Non-aligned Voters condition, the correlations were non-significantly smaller, $r = .07$, n.s. and $r = .17$, $p < .01$, respectively, perhaps because of the smaller variance in the conditional probability differences.

Discussion

From the perspective of the individual citizen, voting is both causal and diagnostic with respect to a desired electoral outcome. Causally, a single vote may create or break a tie, and the citizen may communicate with like-minded peers, persuading them also to vote. Diagnostically, one's decision to vote or to abstain is an indicator that others who think and act like oneself are likely to make the same decision. The Party Supporters and Non-aligned Voters theories were equivalent in the causal significance of voting. But subjects perceived the Party Supporters Theory as having more diagnostic significance than the Non-aligned Voters Theory. As a consequence, they indicated a greater willingness to vote given the validity of the former theory than given the validity of the latter. These results obtained despite the margin of victory's being kept at from 200,000 to 400,000 votes for both theories.

One could identify additional circumstances, analogous to voting, in which collective action dwarfs the causal significance of a single individual's decision. The outcomes of most wars would not have changed had one fewer draftee been inducted, and the success or failure of many telethons do not hinge on the contributions of a single viewer. The paradox is that if each citizen, draftee or viewer abstains from making his or her paltry contribution upon acknowledging its relative insignificance, then the outcomes would be dramatically affected. Indeed, the moral imperatives to vote, to fight and to help the disabled draws its strength from the argument, "If you believe that your vote/fighting/contribution doesn't help, then consider what would happen if *everyone* felt that way." The argument is compelling. Nonetheless, just how *does* an individual's private decision materially affect the decision reached by countless other people?

To summarize, actions may be causal or diagnostic of outcomes with which they are correlated. The normative analysis of choice maintains that, in the evaluation of alternative actions, an outcome ought to be weighted by its probability conditional on selecting the actions only if the actions have a causal effect on the outcome. We have hypothesized, however, that people may weigh an outcome by its subjective conditional probability, even though the alternative actions may be merely diagnostic of the outcome. That is, if both action and outcome are believed to be consequences of a common antecedent cause, people may reason that by selecting the action they have increased the probability of the desirable outcome. Thus, in the first experiment, subjects selected actions that correlated with longevity despite their recognition that the actions would not affect their state of health. The actions, which were directional changes in tolerance to cold water, were mere signs that one possessed the sort of heart that would endure for longer than the normal span of years. The experiment further showed that the comforting diagnosis was accepted primarily by subjects who denied that they had purposefully tried to alter their tolerance to the cold. A certain degree of self-deception was probably involved, for otherwise the action may not have been attributed to the auspicious antecedent cause but rather to the motive to infer that cause. The second experiment demonstrated that people may make decisions diagnostic not only of their own attributes but of the decisions likely to be made by their like-minded peers. The experiment may shed light on why some people may vote in spite of the low probability of casting a decisive ballot.

We suspect that the assumed physiological mechanism of pain and heart responses may have facilitated self-deception in the first experiment. Most people believe that such responses are not under an individual's voluntary control. This widespread belief makes it very easy to deny to oneself that the action was deliberately enacted to make a cheerful diagnosis, for how does one intentionally "pull the strings." That self-deception may occur more often and be more successful for actions (incorrectly) believed to be uncontrollable than controllable is an interesting question for further research. The possibility of a "motivational placebo effect," in which the desire to have one's tolerance shifted produces actual changes in physiological tolerance thresholds, seems worth exploring.

We have argued that people often select *actions* to make favourable diagnoses. But favourable diagnoses may be reached also by varying the *circumstances* under which an action is performed. Suppose subjects in the first experiment were required to keep their arm in the cold as long on the second trial as on the first, but they were allowed to adjust the temperature of the water on the second trial. Then subjects who learned that longevity was associated with an exercise-induced increase or decrease in tolerance may have, respectively, lowered or raised the water's temperature on the second trial. That is, by making the water temperature either colder or hotter, they could still infer an increase or a decrease in tolerance without altering the time of immersion. This point is reminiscent of the self-handicapping strategies discussed by Jones and Berglas (1978). These authors have argued that people may alter the circumstances of diagnostic performance to protect the belief that they are basically competent. For example, by drinking or taking drugs, any level of intellectual performance would not destroy the belief that one is basically bright, for even failure could be attributed to the debilitating effects of alcohol.

Finally, subsequent research should explicitly manipulate whether people believe an action to be causal or diagnostic of a favourable outcome. Intuitively, it appears as though the action would be chosen more often by subjects with a causal theory than by subjects with a diagnostic theory. But ironically, the intuition may not always be valid.[2] Compare the Catholic to the Calvinist. Both believe that one's conduct on earth (virtuous or sinful) is correlated with one's post-mortal fate (paradise or hell). But the Catholic subscribes to a causal theory in which the location of one's soul after death is a direct consequence of how one led one's life on earth. In contrast, the Calvinist champions a diagnostic theory in which earthly conduct and post-mortal fate are both consequences of the deity's prior decision. Although Catholics believe they can influence the location of their life after death, whereas Calvinists believe they cannot, Calvinists may be even more motivated than Catholics to select the virtuous acts correlated with paradise. To the Calvinist, even a single sinful deed is evidence enough that he or she is not among the chosen. To the Catholic, it is more a matter of one's total good and bad deeds that determines heaven or hell. And besides, there is always confession.

Notes

This research was supported in part by ONR Grant N00014-79-C-0077. The authors would like to acknowledge the assistance of Jane Boreta, Doug Passaro, and Nellie Yoshida in serving as experimenters.

This chapter is adapted from an article that appeared in the *Journal of Personality and Social Psychology*, 40.

1. We are indebted to an anonymous reviewer for bringing this point to our attention.

2. We wish to thank Lee Ross for this idea.

References

Abelson, R. P., Aronson, E., McGuire, W. J., Newcomb, T. M., Rosenberg, M. J., and Tannenbaum, P. H. (eds.) (1968) *Theories of Cognitive Consistency: A Source-book*, Chicago: Rand McNally.

Bem, D. J. (1972) "Self-perception theory," in L. Berkowitz (ed.), *Advances in Experimental Social Psychology*, vol. 6, New York: Academic Press.

Festinger, L. (1957) *A Theory of Cognitive Dissonance*, Evanston, Ill.: Row, Peterson.

Fisher, R. A. (1959) *Smoking*, London: Oliver and Boyd.

Gibbard, A., and Harper, W. L. (1978) "Counterfactuals and two kinds of expected utility," in C. A. Hooker, J. J. Leach, and E. F. McClennan (eds.), *Foundations and Applications of Decision Theory*, vol. 1, Dordrecht, Holland: D. Reidel Publishing Co.

Gur, R. C., and Sackheim, H. A. (1979) "Self-deception: A concept in search of a phenomenon," *Journal of Personality and Social Psychology* 37, 147–169.

Hilgard, E. R., Ruch, J. C., Lange, A. F., Lenox, J. R., Morgan, A. H., and Sachs, L. B. (1974) "The psychophysics of cold pressor pain and its modification through hypnotic suggestion," *American Journal of Psychology* 87, 17–31.

Jeffrey, R. (1965) *The Logic of Decision*, New York: McGraw-Hill.

Jeffrey, R. (1981) "The logic of decision defended," *Synthese* 48, 473–492.

Jones, E. E., and Berglas, S. C. (1978) "Control of attributions about the self through self-handicapping strategies: the appeal of alcohol and the role of underachievement," *Personality and Social Psychology Bulletin* 4, 200–206.

Nozick, R. (1969) "Newcomb's problem and two principles of choice," in N. Racher (ed.), *Essays in Honor of Carl G. Hempel*. Dordrecht, Holland: D. Reidel Publishing Co.

Riker, W. H., and Ordeshook, P. C. (1968) "A theory of the calculus of voting," *American Political Science Review* 62, 25–42.

Skyrms, B. (1980) "*Causal Necessity*," New Haven, Conn: Yale University Press.

34 Contingent Weighting in Judgment and Choice

Amos Tversky, Shmuel Sattath, and Paul Slovic

The relation of preference between acts or options is the key element of decision theory that provides the basis for the measurement of utility or value. In axiomatic treatments of decision theory, the concept of preference appears as an abstract relation that is given an empirical interpretation through specific methods of elicitation, such as choice and matching. In choice the decision maker selects an option from an offered set of two or more alternatives. In matching the decision maker is required to set the value of some variable in order to achieve an equivalence between options (e.g., what chance to win $750 is as attractive as 1 chance in 10 to win $2,500?).

The standard analysis of choice assumes procedure invariance: Normatively equivalent procedures for assessing preferences should give rise to the same preference order. Indeed, theories of measurement generally require the ordering of objects to be independent of the particular method of assessment. In classical physical measurement, it is commonly assumed that each object possesses a well-defined quantity of the attribute in question (e.g., length, mass) and that different measurement procedures elicit the same ordering of objects with respect to this attribute. Analogously, the classical theory of preference assumes that each individual has a well-defined preference order (or a utility function) and that different methods of elicitation produce the same ordering of options. To determine the heavier of two objects, for example, we can place them on the two sides of a pan balance and observe which side goes down. Alternatively, we can place each object separately on a sliding scale and observe the position at which the sliding scale is balanced. Similarly, to determine the preference order between options we can use either choice or matching. Note that the pan balance is analogous to binary choice, whereas the sliding scale resembles matching.

The assumption of procedure invariance is likely to hold when people have well-articulated preferences and beliefs, as is commonly assumed in the classical theory. If one likes opera but not ballet, for example, this preference is likely to emerge regardless of whether one compares the two directly or evaluates them independently. Procedure invariance may hold even in the absence of precomputed preferences, if people use a consistent algorithm. We do not immediately know the value of $7(8 + 9)$, but we have an algorithm for computing it that yields the same answer regardless of whether the addition is performed before or after the multiplication. Similarly, procedure invariance is likely to be satisfied if the value of each option is computed by a well-defined criterion, such as expected utility.

Studies of decision and judgment, however, indicate that the foregoing conditions for procedure invariance are not generally true and that people often do not have well-defined values and beliefs (e.g., Fischhoff, Slovic & Lichtenstein, 1980; March, 1978; Shafer & Tversky, 1985). In these situations, observed preferences are not simply read off from some master list; they are actually constructed in the elicitation process. Furthermore, choice is contingent or context sensitive: It depends on the framing of the problem and on the method of elicitation (Payne, 1982; Slovic & Lichtenstein, 1983; Tversky & Kahneman, 1986). Different elicitation procedures highlight different aspects of options and suggest alternative heuristics, which may give rise to inconsistent responses. An adequate account of choice, therefore, requires a psychological analysis of the elicitation process and its effect on the observed response.

What are the differences between choice and matching, and how do they affect people's responses? Because our understanding of the mental processes involved is limited, the analysis is necessarily sketchy and incomplete. Nevertheless, there is reason to expect that choice and matching may differ in a predictable manner. Consider the following example. Suppose Joan faces a choice between two job offers that vary in interest and salary. As a natural first step, Joan examines whether one option dominates the other (i.e., is superior in all respects). If not, she may try to reframe the problem (e.g., by representing the options in terms of higher order attributes) to produce a dominant alternative (Montgomery, 1983). If no dominance emerges, she may examine next whether one option enjoys a decisive advantage: that is, whether the advantage of one option far outweighs the advantage of the other. If neither option has a decisive advantage, the decision maker seeks a procedure for resolving the conflict. Because it is often unclear how to trade one attribute against another, a common procedure for resolving conflict in such situations is to select the option that is superior on the more important attribute. This procedure, which is essentially lexicographic, has two attractive features. First, it does not require the decision maker to assess the trade-off between the attributes, thereby reducing mental effort and cognitive strain. Second, it provides a compelling argument for choice that can be used to justify the decision to oneself as well as to others.

Consider next the matching version of the problem. Suppose Joan has to determine the salary at which the less interesting job would be as attractive as the more interesting one. The qualitative procedure described earlier cannot be used to solve the matching problem, which requires a quantitative assessment or a matching of intervals. To perform this task adequately, the decision maker should take into account both the size of the intervals (defined relative to the natural range of variation of the attributes in question) and the relative weights of these attributes. One method of matching first equates the size of the two intervals, and then adjusts the constructed interval according to the relative weight of the attribute. This approach is particularly compelling when the attributes are expressed in the same units (e.g., money, percent, test scores), but it may also be applied in other situations where it is easier to compare ranges than to establish a rate of exchange. Because adjustments are generally insufficient (Tversky & Kahneman, 1974) this procedure is likely to induce a relatively flat or uniform weighting of attributes.

The preceding discussion is not meant to provide a comprehensive account of choice or of matching. It merely suggests different heuristics or computational schemes that are likely to be used in the two tasks. If people tend to choose according to the more important dimension, or if they match options by adjusting unweighed intervals, then the two procedures are likely to yield different results. In particular, choice is expected to be more lexicographic than matching: That is, the more prominent attribute will weigh more heavily in choice than in matching. This is the *prominence hypothesis* investigated in the following section.

The discrepancy between choice and matching was first observed in a study by Slovic (1975) that was motivated by the ancient philosophical puzzle of how to choose between equally attractive alternatives. In this study the respondents first matched different pairs of (two-dimensional) options and, in a later session, chose between the matched options. Slovic found that the subjects did not choose randomly but rather tended to select the option that was superior on the more important dimension. This observation supports the prominence hypothesis, but the evidence is not conclusive for two reasons. First, the participants always matched the options prior to the choice hence the data could be explained by the hypothesis that the more important dimension looms larger in the later trial. Second, and more important, each participant chose between matched options hence the results could reflect a common tie-breaking procedure rather than a genuine reversal of preferences. After all, rationality does not entail a random breaking of ties. A rational person may be indifferent between a cash amount and a gamble but always pick the cash when forced to take one of the two.

To overcome these difficulties we develop in the next section a method for testing the prominence hypothesis that is based entirely on interpersonal (between-subjects) comparisons, and we apply this method to a variety of choice problems. In the following two sections we present a conceptual and mathematical analysis of the elicitation process and apply it to several phenomena of judgment and choice. The theoretical and practical implications of the work are discussed in the final section.

Tests of the Prominence Hypothesis

Interpersonal Tests

We illustrate the experimental procedure and the logic of the test of the prominence hypothesis in a problem involving a choice between job candidates. The participants in the first set of studies were young men and women (ages 20–30 years) who were taking a series of aptitude tests at a vocational testing institute in Tel Aviv, Israel. The problems were presented in writing, and the participants were tested in small groups. They all agreed to take part in the study, knowing it had no bearing on their test scores. Some of the results were replicated with Stanford undergraduates.

Problem 1 (Production Engineer)

Imagine that, as an executive of a company, you have to select between two candidates for a position of a Production Engineer. The candidates were interviewed by a committee who scored them on two attributes (technical knowledge and human relations) on a scale from 100 (superb) to 40 (very weak). Both attributes are important for the position in question, but technical knowledge is more important than human relations. On the basis of the following scores, which of the two candidates would you choose?

	Technical knowledge	Human relations	$[N = 63]$
Candidate X	86	76	[65%]
Candidate Y	78	91	[35%]

The number of respondents (N) and the percentage who chose each option are given in brackets on the right side of the table. In this problem, about two thirds of the respondents selected the candidate who has a higher score on the more important attribute (technical knowledge).

Another group of respondents received the same data except that one of the four scores was missing. They were asked "to complete the missing score so that the two candidates would be equally suitable for the job." Suppose, for example, that the lower left value (78) were missing from the table. The respondent's task would then be to generate a score for Candidate Y in technical knowledge so as to match the two candidates. The participants were reminded that "Y has a higher score than X in human relations, hence, to match the two candidates Y must have a lower score than X in technical knowledge."

Assuming that higher scores are preferable to lower ones, it is possible to infer the response to the choice task from the response to the matching task. Suppose, for example, that one produces a value of 80 in the matching task (when the missing value is 78). This means that X's score profile (86, 76) is judged equivalent to the profile $(80, 91)$, which in turn dominates Y's profile $(78, 91)$. Thus, a matching value of 80 indicates that X is preferable to Y. More generally, a matching response above 78 implies a preference for X; a matching response below 78 implies a preference for Y; and a matching response of 78 implies indifference between X and Y.

Formally, let (X_1, X_2) and (Y_1, Y_2) denote the values of options X and Y on Attributes 1 and 2, respectively. Let V be the value of Y_1 for which the options are matched. We show that, under the standard assumptions, X is preferred to Y if and only if $V > Y_1$. Suppose $V > Y_1$, then (X_1, X_2) is equivalent to (V, Y_2) by matching, (V, Y_2) is preferred to (Y_1, Y_2) by dominance, hence, X is preferred to Y by transitivity. The other cases are similar.

We use the subscript 1 to denote the primary, or the more important dimension, and the subscript 2 to denote the secondary, or the less important dimension—whenever they are defined. If neither option dominates the other, X denotes the option that is superior on the primary dimension and Y denotes the option that is superior on the secondary dimension. Thus, X_1 is better than Y_1 and Y_2 is better than X_2.

Let C denote the percentage of respondents who chose X over Y, and let M denote the percentage of people whose matching response favored X over Y. Thus, C and M measure the tendency to decide according to the more important dimension in the choice and in the matching tasks, respectively. Assuming random allocation of subjects, procedure invariance implies $C = M$, whereas the prominence hypothesis implies $C > M$. As was shown earlier, the two contrasting predictions can be tested by using aggregate between-subjects data.

To estimate M, we presented four different groups of about 60 respondents each with the data of problem 1, each with a different missing value, and we asked them to match the two candidates. The following table presents the values of M derived from the matching data for each of the four missing values, which are given in parentheses.

	1. Technical Knowledge	2. Human Relations
Candidate X	32% (86)	33% (76)
Candidate Y	44% (78)	26% (91)

There were no significant differences among the four matching groups, although M was greater when the missing value was low rather than high ($M_L = 39 > 29 = M_H$) and when the missing value referred to the primary rather than to the secondary attribute ($M_1 = 38 > 30 = M_2$). Overall, the matching data yielded $M = 34\%$ as compared with $C = 65\%$ obtained from choice ($p < .01$). This result supports the hypothesis that the more important attribute (e.g., technical knowledge) looms larger in choice than in matching.

In problem 1, it is reasonable to assume—as stated—that for a production engineer, technical knowledge is more important than human relations. Problem 2 had the same structure as problem 1, except that the primary and secondary attributes were manipulated. Problem 2 dealt with the choice between candidates for the position of an advertising agent. The candidates were characterized by their scores on two dimensions: creativity and competence. One half of the participants were told that "for the position in question, creativity is more important than competence," whereas the other half of the participants were told the opposite. As in problem 1, most participants (65%, $N = 60$) chose according to the more important attribute (whether it was creativity or competence) but only 38% ($N = 276$) of the matching responses favored X over Y. Again, M was higher for the primary than for the secondary attribute, but all four values of M were smaller than C. The next two problems involve policy choices concerning safety and the environment.

Problem 3 (Traffic Accidents)

About 600 people are killed each year in Israel in traffic accidents. The ministry of transportation investigates various programs to reduce the number of casualties. Consider the following two programs, described in terms of yearly costs (in millions of dollars) and the number of casualties per year that is expected following the implementation of each program.

	Expected number of casualties	Cost	[$N = 96$]
Program X	500	$55M	[67%]
Program Y	570	$12M	[33%]

Which program do you favor?

The data on the right side of the table indicate that two thirds of the respondents chose Program X, which saves more lives at a higher cost per life saved. Two other groups matched the cost of either Program X or Program Y so as to make the two programs equally attractive. The overwhelming majority of matching responses in both groups (96%, $N = 146$) favored the more economical Program Y that saves fewer lives. Problem 3 yields a dramatic violation of invariance: $C = 68\%$ but $M = 4\%$. This pattern follows from the prominence hypothesis, assuming the number of casualties is more important than cost. There was no difference between the groups that matched the high ($55M) or the low ($12M) values.

A similar pattern of responses was observed in problem 4, which involves an environmental issue. The participants were asked to compare two programs for the control of a polluted beach:

Program X: A comprehensive program for a complete clean-up of the beach at a yearly cost of $750,000 to the taxpayers.

Program Y: A limited program for a partial clean-up of the beach (that will not make it suitable for swimming) at a yearly cost of $250,000 to the taxpayers.

Assuming the control of pollution is the primary dimension and the cost is secondary, we expect that the comprehensive program will be more popular in choice than in matching. This prediction was confirmed: $C = 48\%$ $(N = 104)$ and $M = 12\%$ $(N = 170)$. The matching data were obtained from two groups of respondents who assessed the cost of each program so as to match the other. As in problem 3, these groups gave rise to practically identical values of M.

Because the choice and the matching procedures are strategically equivalent, the rational theory of choice implies $C = M$. The two procedures, however, are not informationally equivalent because the missing value in the matching task is available in the choice task. To create an informationally equivalent task we modified the matching task by asking respondents, prior to the assessment of the missing value, (a) to consider the value used in the choice problem and indicate first whether it is too high or too low, and (b) to write down the value that they consider appropriate. In problem 3, for example, the modified procedure read as follows:

	Expected number of casualties	Cost
Program X	500	?
Program Y	570	$12M

You are asked to determine the cost of Program X that would make it equivalent to Program Y. (a) Is the value of $55M too high or too low? (b)What is the value you consider appropriate?

The modified matching procedure is equivalent to choice not only strategically but also informationally. Let C^* be the proportion of responses to question (a) that lead to the choice of X (e.g., "too low" in the preceding example). Let M^* be the proportion of (matching) responses to question (b) that favor option X (e.g., a value that exceeds $55M in the preceding example). Thus, we may view C^* as choice in a matching context and M^* as matching in a choice context. The values of C^* and M^* for problems 1–4 are presented in table 34.1, which yields the ordering $C > C^* > M^* > M$. The finding $C > C^*$ shows that merely framing the question in a matching context reduces the relative weight of the primary dimension. Conversely, $M^* > M$ indicates that placing the matching task after a choice-like task increases the relative weight of the primary dimension. Finally, $C^* > M^*$ implies a within-subject and within-problem violation of invariance in which the response to Question

Table 34.1
Percentages of Responses Favoring the Primary Dimension under Different Elicitation Procedures

Problem	Dimensions		Choice (C)	Information control		Matching (M)	θ
	Primary	Secondary		C^*	M^*		
1. Engineer	Technical	Human	65	57	47	34	.82
N	knowledge	relations	63	156	151	267	
2. Agent	Competence	Creativity	65	52	41	38	.72
N			60	155	152	276	
3. Accidents	Casualities	Cost	68	50	18	4	.19
N			105	96	82	146	
4. Pollution	Health	Cost	48	32	12	12	.45
N			104	103	94	170	
5. Benefits	1 year	4 years	59			46	.86
N			56			46	
6. Coupons	Books	Travel	66			11	.57
N			58			193	
Unweighted mean			62	48	30	24	

Note: C = percentage of respondents who chose X over Y; M = percentage of respondents whose matching responses favored X over Y; C^* = percentage of responses to Question a that lead to the choice of X; M^* = percentage of matching responses to Question b that favor option X.

a favors X and the response to Question b favors Y. This pattern of responses indicates a failure, on the part of some subjects, to appreciate the logical connection between Questions a and b. It is noteworthy, however, that 86% of these inconsistencies follow the pattern implied by the prominence hypothesis.

In the previous problems, the primary and the secondary attributes were controlled by the instructions, as in problems 1 and 2, or by the intrinsic value of the attributes, as in problems 3 and 4. (People generally agree that saving lives and eliminating pollution are more important goals than cutting public expenditures.) The next two problems involved benefit plans in which the primary and the secondary dimensions were determined by economic considerations.

Problem 5 (Benefit Plans)

Imagine that, as a part of a profit-sharing program, your employer offers you a choice between the following plans. Each plan offers two payments, in one year and in four years.

	Payment in 1 year	Payment in 4 years	
			[N = 36]
Plan X	$2,000	$2,000	[59%]
Plan Y	$1,000	$4,000	[41%]

Which plan do you prefer?

Table 34.2

Percentages of Respondents ($N = 101$) Who Chose Between-Matched Alternatives ($M = 50\%$) According to the Primary Dimension (after Slovic, 1975)

	Dimensions			
Alternatives	Primary	Secondary	Choice criterion	C
1. Baseball players	Batting average	Home runs	Value to team	62
2. College applicants	Motivation	English	Potential success	69
3. Gifts	Cash	Coupons	Attractiveness	85
4. Typists	Accuracy	Speed	Typing ability	84
5. Athletes	Chin-ups	Push-ups	Fitness	68
6. Routes to work	Time	Distance	Attractiveness	75
7. Auto tires	Quality	Price	Attractiveness	67
8. TV commercials	Number	Time	Annoyance	83
9. Readers	Comprehension	Speed	Reading ability	79
10. Baseball teams	% of games won against first place team	% of games won against last place team	Standing	86
Unweighted mean				76

Note: C = percentage of respondents who chose X over Y.

Because people surely prefer to receive a payment sooner rather than later, we assume that the earlier payment (in 1 year) acts as the primary attribute, and the later payment (in 4 years) acts as the secondary attribute. The results support the hypothesis: $C = 59\%$ ($N = 56$) whereas $M = 46\%$ ($N = 46$).

Problem 6 resembled problem 5 except that the employee was offered a choice between two bonus plans consisting of a different combination of coupons for books and for travel. Because the former could be used in a large chain of bookstores, whereas the latter were limited to organized tours with a particular travel agency, we assumed that the book coupons would serve as the primary dimension. Under this interpretation, the prominence effect emerged again: $C = 66\%$ ($N = 58$) and $M = 11\%$ ($N = 193$). As in previous problems, M was greater when the missing value was low rather than high ($M_L = 17 > 3 = M_H$) and when the missing value referred to the primary rather than the secondary attribute ($M_1 = 19 > 4 = M_2$). All values of M, however, were substantially smaller than C.

Intrapersonal Tests

Slovic's (1975) original demonstration of the choice-matching discrepancy was based entirely on an intrapersonal analysis. In his design, the participants first matched the relevant option and then selected between the matched options at a later date. They were also asked afterward to indicate the more important attribute in each case. The main results are summarized in table 34.2, which presents for each choice problem the options, the primary and the secondary attributes, and the resulting values of C. In every case, the value of M is 50% by construction.

The results indicate that, in all problems, the majority of participants broke the tie between the matched options in the direction of the more important dimension as implied by the prominence hypothesis. This conclusion held regardless of whether the estimated missing value belonged to the primary or the secondary dimension, or whether it was the high value or the low value on the dimension. Note that the results of table 34.2 alone could be explained by a shift in weight following the matching procedure (because the matching always preceded the choice) or by the application of a common tie-breaking procedure (because for each participant the two options were matched). These explanations, however, do not apply to the interpersonal data of table 34.1.

On the other hand, table 34.2 demonstrates the prominence effect within the data of each subject. The value of C was only slightly higher (unweighted mean: 78) when computed relative to each subject's ordering of the importance of the dimensions (as was done in the original analysis), presumably because of the general agreement among the respondents about which dimension was primary.

Theoretical Analysis

The data described in the previous section show that the primary dimension looms larger in choice than in matching. This effect gives rise to a marked discrepancy between choice and matching, which violates the principle of procedure invariance assumed in the rational theory of choice. The prominence effect raises three general questions. First, what are the psychological mechanisms that underlie the choice-matching discrepancy and other failures of procedure invariance? Second, what changes in the traditional theory are required in order to accommodate these effects? Third, what are the implications of the present results to the analysis of choice in general, and the elicitation of preference in particular? The remainder of this article is devoted to these questions.

The Compatibility Principle

One possible explanation of the prominence effect, introduced earlier in this article, is the tendency to select the option that is superior on the primary dimension, in situations where the other option does not have a decisive advantage on the secondary dimension. This procedure is easy to apply and justify because it resolves conflict on the basis of qualitative arguments (i.e., the prominence ordering of the dimensions) without establishing a rate of exchange. The matching task, on the other hand, cannot be resolved in the same manner. The decision maker must resort to quantitative comparisons to determine what interval on one dimension matches a given interval on the second dimension. This requires the setting of a common metric in which the attributes are likely to be weighted more equally, particularly when it is natural to match their ranges or to compute cost per unit (e.g., the amount of money spent to save a single life).

It is instructive to distinguish between qualitative and quantitative arguments for choice. Qualitative, or ordinal, arguments are based on the ordering of the levels within each dimension, or on the prominence ordering of the dimensions. Quantitative, or cardinal, arguments are based on the comparison of value differences along the primary and the secondary dimensions. Thus, dominance and a lexicographic ordering are purely qualitative decision rules, whereas most other models of multiattribute choice make essential use of quantitative considerations. The prominence effect indicates that qualitative considerations loom larger in the ordinal procedure of choice than in the cardinal procedure of matching, or equivalently, that quantitative considerations loom larger in matching than in choice. The prominence hypothesis, therefore, may be construed as an example of a more general principle of compatibility.

The choice-matching discrepancy, like other violations of procedure invariance, indicates that the weighting of the attributes is influenced by the method of elicitation. Alternative procedures appear to highlight different aspects of the options and thereby induce different weights. To interpret and predict such effects, we seek explanatory principles that relate task characteristics to the weighting of attributes and the evaluation of options. One such explanation is the compatibility principle. According to this principle, the weight of any input component is enhanced by its compatibility with the output. The rationale for this principle is that the characteristics of the task and the response scale prime the most compatible features of the stimulus. For example, the pricing of gambles is likely to emphasize payoffs more than probability because both the response and the payoffs are expressed in dollars. Furthermore, noncompatibility (in content, scale, or display) between the input and the output requires additional mental transformations, which increase effort and error, and reduce confidence and impact (Fitts & Seeger, 1953; Wickens, 1984). We shall next illustrate the compatibility principle in studies of prediction and similarity and then develop a formal theory that encompasses a variety of compatibility effects, including the choice-matching discrepancy and the preference reversal phenomenon.

A simple demonstration of scale compatibility was obtained in a study by Slovic, Griffin, and Tversky (1988). The subjects ($N = 234$) were asked to predict the judgments of an admission committee of a small, selective college. For each of 10 applicants the subjects received two items of information: a rank on the verbal section of the Scholastic Aptitude Test (SAT) and the presence or absence of strong extracurricular activities. The subjects were told that the admission committee ranks all 500 applicants and accepts about the top fourth. Half of the subjects predicted the rank assigned to each applicant, whereas the other half predicted whether each applicant was accepted or rejected.

The compatibility principle implies that the numerical data (i.e., SAT rank) will loom larger in the numerical prediction task, whereas the categorical data (i.e., the presence or absence of extracurricular activities) will loom larger in the categotical prediction of acceptance or rejection. The results confirmed the hypothesis. For each pair of applicants, in which neither one dominates the other, the percentage of responses that favored the applicant with the higher SAT was recorded. Summing across all pairs, this value was 61.4% in the numerical prediction task and 44.6% in the categorical prediction task. The difference between the groups is highly significant. Evidently, the numerical data had more impact in the numerical task, whereas the categorical data had more impact in the categorical task. This result demonstrates the compatibility principle and reinforces the proposed interpretation of the choice-matching discrepancy in which the relative weight of qualitative arguments is larger in the qualitative method of choice than in the quantitative matching procedure.

In the previous example, compatibility was induced by the formal correspondence between the scales of the dependent and the independent variables. Compatibility effects can also be induced by semantic correspondence, as illustrated in the following example, taken from the study of similarity. In general, the similarity of objects (e.g., faces, people, letters) increases with the salience of the features they share and decreases with the salience of the features that distinguish between them. More specifically, the contrast model (Tversky, 1977) represents the similarity of objects as a linear combination of the measures of their common and their distinctive features. Thus, the similarity of a and b is monotonically related to

$$\theta f(A \cap B) - g(A \Delta B),$$

where $A \cap B$ is the set of features shared by a and b, and $A \Delta B = (A - B) \cup (B - A)$ is the set of features that belongs to one object and not to the other. The scales f and g are the measures of the respective feature sets.

The compatibility hypothesis suggests that common features loom larger in judgments of similarity than in judgments of dissimilarity, whereas distinctive features loom larger in judgments of dissimilarity than in judgments of similarity. As a consequence, the two judgments are not mirror images. A pair of objects with many common and many distinctive features could be judged as more similar, as well as more dissimilar, than another pair of objects with fewer common and fewer distinctive features. Tversky and Gati (1978) observed this pattern in the comparison of pairs of well-known countries with pairs of countries that were less well-known to the respondents. For example, most subjects in the similarity condition selected East Germany and West Germany as more similar to each other than Sri Lanka and Nepal, whereas most subjects in the dissimilarity condition selected East Germany and West Germany as more different from each other than Sri Lanka and Nepal. These observations were explained by the contrast model with the added assumption that the relative weight of the common features is greater in similarity than in dissimilarity judgments (Tversky, 1977).

Contingent Trade-Off Models

To accommodate the compatibility effects observed in studies of preference, prediction and judgment, we need models in which the trade-offs among inputs depend on the nature of the output. In the present section we develop a hierarchy of models of this type, called contingent trade-off models. For simplicity, we investigate the two-dimensional case and follow the choice-matching terminology. Extensions and applications are discussed later. It is convenient to use $A = \{a, b, c, \ldots\}$ and $Z = \{z, y, x, \ldots\}$ to denote the primary and the secondary attributes, respectively, whenever they are properly defined. The object set S is given by the product set $A \times Z$, with typical elements az, by, and so on. Let $\geq_c$ be the preference relation obtained by choice, and let $\geq_m$ be the preference relation derived from matching.

As in the standard analysis of indifference curves (e.g., Varian, 1984, chap. 3), we assume that each $\geq_i$, $i = c, m$, is a weak order, that is, reflexive, connected, and transitive. We also assume that the levels of each attribute are consistently ordered, independent of the (fixed) level of the other attribute. That is,

$$az \geq_i bz \quad \text{iff} \quad ay \geq_i by \quad \text{and} \quad az \geq_i ay \quad \text{iff} \quad bz \geq_i by, \quad i = c, m.$$

Under these assumptions, in conjunction with the appropriate structural conditions (see, e.g., Krantz, Luce, Suppes, & Tversky, 1971, chap. 7), there exist functions F_i, G_i, and U_i, defined on A, Z, and $Re \times Re$, respectively, such that

$$az \geq_i by \quad \text{iff} \quad U_i[F_i(a), G_i(z)] \geq U_i[F_i(b), G_i(y)], \tag{1}$$

where U_i, $i = c, m$ is monotonically increasing in each of its arguments.

Equation 1 imposes no constraints on the relation between choice and matching. Although our data show that the two orders do not generally coincide, it seems reason-

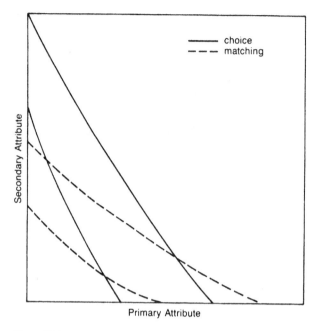

Figure 34.1
A dual indifference map induced by the general model (equations 1 and 2).

able to suppose that they do coincide in unidimensional comparisons. Thus, we assume

$$az \geq_c bz \quad \text{iff} \quad az \geq_m bz \quad \text{and} \quad az \geq_c ay \quad \text{iff} \quad az \geq_m ay.$$

It is easy to see that this condition is both necessary and sufficient for the monotonicity of the respective scales. That is,

$$F_c(b) \geq F_c(a) \quad \text{iff} \quad F_m(b) \geq F_m(a) \quad \text{and}$$

$$G_c(z) \geq G_c(y) \quad \text{iff} \quad G_m(z) \geq G_m(y). \tag{2}$$

Equations 1 and 2 define the general contingent trade-off model that is assumed throughout. The other models discussed in this section are obtained by imposing further restrictions on the relation between choice and matching. The general model corresponds to a dual indifference map, that is, two families of indifference curves, one induced by choice and one induced by matching. A graphical illustration of a dual map is presented in figure 34.1.

We next consider a more restrictive model that constrains the relation between the rates of substitution of the two attributes obtained by the two elicitation procedures.

Suppose the indifference curves are differentiable, and let RS_i denote the rate of substitution between the two attributes (A and Z) according to procedure $i = c, m$. Thus, $RS_i = F'_i / G'_i$, where F'_i and G'_i, respectively, are the partial derivatives of U_i with respect to F_i and G_i. Hence, $RS_i(az)$ is the negative of the slope of the indifference curve at the point az. Note that RS_i is a meaningful quantity even though F_i, G_i and U_i are only ordinal scales.

A contingent trade-off model is proportional if the ratio of RS_c to RS_m is the same at each point. That is,

$$RS_c(az) / RS_m(az) = \text{constant.} \tag{3}$$

Recall that in the standard economic model, the foregoing ratio equals 1. The proportional model assumes that this ratio is a constant, but not necessarily one. The indifference maps induced by choice and by matching, therefore, can be mapped into each other by multiplying the RS value at every point by the same constant.

Both the general and the proportional model impose few constraints on the utility functions U_i. In many situations, preferences between multiattribute options can be represented additively. That is, there exist functions F_i and G_i defined on A and Z, respectively, such that

$$az \geq_i by \quad \text{iff} \quad F_i(a) + G_i(z) \geq F_i(b) + G_i(y), \quad i = c, m, \tag{4}$$

where F_i and G_i are interval scales with a common unit. The existence of such an additive representation is tantamount to the existence of a monotone transformation of the axes that maps all indifference curves into parallel straight lines.

Assuming the contingent trade-off model, with the appropriate structural conditions, the following cancellation condition is both necessary and sufficient for additivity (equation 4), see Krantz et al. (1971, chap. 6):

$$ay \geq_i bx \quad \text{and} \quad bz \geq_i cy \quad \text{imply} \quad az \geq_i cx, \quad i = c, m.$$

If both proportionality and additivity are assumed, we obtain a particularly simple form, called the contingent weighting model, in which the utility scales F_c, F_m and G_c, G_m are linearly related. In other words, there is a monotone transformation of the axes that simultaneously linearizes both sets of indifference curves. Thus, if both equations 3 and 4 hold, there exist functions F and G defined on A and Z, respectively, and constants $\alpha_i \beta_i$, $i = c, m$, such that

$$
\begin{aligned}
az \geq_i by \quad &\text{iff} \quad \alpha_i F(a) + \beta_i G(z) \geq \alpha_i F(b) + \beta_i G(y) \\
&\text{iff} \quad F(a) + \theta_i G(z) \geq F(b) + \theta_i G(y),
\end{aligned} \tag{5}
$$

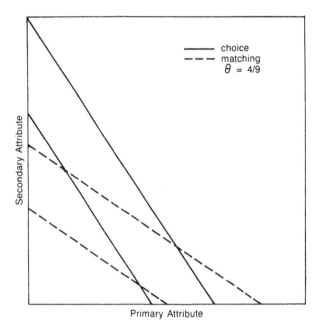

Figure 34.2
A dual indifference map induced by the additive model (equation 4).

where $\theta_i = \beta_i/\alpha_i$. In this model, therefore, the indifference maps induced by choice and by matching are represented as two sets of parallel straight lines that differ only in slope $-\theta_i$, $i = c, m$ (see figure 34.2). We are primarily interested in the ratio $\theta = \theta_c/\theta_m$ of these slopes.

Because the rate of substitution in the additive model is constant, it is possible to test proportionality (equation 3) without assessing local RS_i. In particular, the contingent weighting model (equation 5) implies the following interlocking condition;

$$ax \geq_c bw, \quad dw \geq_c cx, \quad \text{and} \quad by \geq_m az \quad \text{imply} \quad dy \geq_m cz,$$

and the same holds when the attributes (A and Z) and the orders ($\geq_c$ and $\geq_m$) are interchanged. Figure 34.3 presents a graphic illustration of this condition. The interlocking condition is closely related to triple cancellation, or the Reidemeister condition (see Krantz et al., 1971, 6.2.1), tested by Coombs, Bezembinder, and Goode (1967). The major difference between the assumptions is that the present interlocking condition involves two orders rather than one. This condition says, in effect, that the intradimensional ordering of A-intervals or Z-intervals is independent of the method

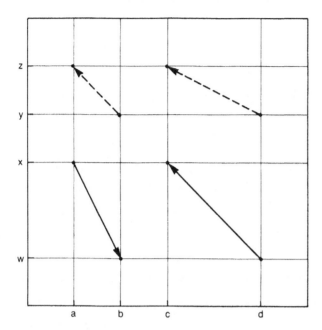

Figure 34.3
A graphic illustration of the interlocking condition where arrows denote preferences.

of elicitation. This can be seen most clearly by deriving the interlocking condition from the contingent weighting model. From the hypotheses of the condition, in conjunction with the model, we obtain

$$F(a) + \theta_c G(x) \geq F(b) + \theta_c G(w) \quad \text{or} \quad \theta_c[G(x) - G(w)] \geq F(b) - F(a)$$

$$F(d) + \theta_c G(w) \geq F(c) + \theta_c G(x) \quad \text{or} \quad F(d) - F(c) \geq \theta_c[G(x) - G(w)]$$

$$F(b) + \theta_m G(y) \geq F(a) + \theta_m G(z) \quad \text{or} \quad F(b) - F(a) \geq \theta_m[G(z) - G(y)].$$

The right-hand inequalities yield

$$F(d) - F(c) \geq \theta_m[G(z) - G(y)] \quad \text{or} \quad F(d) + \theta_m G(y) \geq F(c) + \theta_m G(z),$$

hence $dy \geq_m cz$ as required.

The interlocking condition is not only necessary but also sufficient, because it implies that the inequalities

$$F_i(d) - F_i(c) \geq F_i(b) - F_i(a) \quad \text{and} \quad G_i(z) - G_i(y) \geq G_i(x) - G_i(w)$$

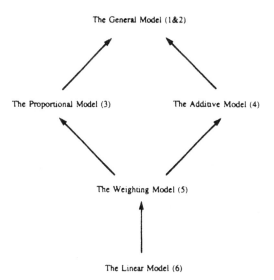

Figure 34.4
A hierarchy of contingent preference models. (Implications are denoted by arrows.)

are independent of $i = c, m$, that is, the two procedures yield the same ordering of intradimensional intervals. But because F_c and F_m (as well as G_c and G_m) are interval scales, they must be linearly related. Thus, there exist functions F and G and constants α_i, β_i such that

$$az \geq_i by \quad \text{iff} \quad \alpha_i F(a) + \beta_i G(z) \geq \alpha_i F(b) + \beta_i G(y).$$

Thus, we have established the following result.

THEOREM: Assuming additivity (equation 4), the contingent weighting model (equation 5) holds iff the interlocking condition is satisfied.

Perhaps the simplest, and most restrictive, instance of equation 5 is the case where A and Z are sets of real numbers and both F and G are linear. In this case, the model reduces to

$$
\begin{aligned}
az \geq_i by \quad &\text{iff} \quad \alpha_i a + \beta_i z \geq \alpha_i b + \beta_i y \\
&\text{iff} \quad a + \theta_i z \geq b + \theta_i y, \quad \theta_i = \beta_i/\alpha_i, \quad i = c, m.
\end{aligned}
\tag{6}
$$

The hierarchy of contingent trade-off models is presented in figure 34.4, where implications are denoted by arrows.

In the following section we apply the contingent weighting model to several sets of data and estimate the relative weights of the two attributes under different elicitation procedures. Naturally, all the models of figure 34.4 are consistent with the compatibility hypothesis. We use the linear model (equation 6) because it is highly parsimonious and reduces the estimation to a single parameter $\theta = \theta_c/\theta_m$. If linearity of scales or additivity of attributes is seriously violated in the data, higher models in the hierarchy should be used. The contingent weighting model can be readily extended to deal with more than two attributes and methods of elicitation.

The same formal model can be applied when the different preference orders $\geq_i$ are generated by different individuals rather than by different procedures. Indeed, the interlocking condition is both necessary and sufficient for representing the (additive) preference orders of different individuals as variations in the weighting of attributes. (This notion underlies the INDSCAL approach to multidimensional scaling, Carroll, 1972). The two representations can be naturally combined to accommodate both individual differences and procedural variations. The following analyses focus on the latter problem.

Applications

The Choice-Matching Discrepancy

We first compute $\theta = \theta_c/\theta_m$ from the choice and matching data, summarized in table 34.1. Let $C(az, by)$ be the percentage of respondents who chose az over by, and let $M(az, by)$ be the percentage of respondents whose matching response favored az over by. Consider the respondents who matched the options by adjusting the second component of the second option. Because different respondents produced different values of the missing component (y), we can view $M(az, b.)$ as a (decreasing) function of the missing component. Let $\bar{y}$ be the value of the second attribute for which $M(ax, b\bar{y}) = C(az, by)$.

If the choice and the matching agree, $\bar{y}$ should be equal to y, whereas the prominence hypothesis implies that $\bar{y}$ lies between y and z (i.e., $|z - y| > |z - \bar{y}|$). To estimate θ from these data, we introduce an additional assumption, in the spirit of probabilistic conjoint measurement (Falmagne, 1985, chap. 11), which relates the linear model (6) to the observed percentage of responses.

$$M(az, b\bar{y}) = C(az, by) \quad \text{iff} \quad (a + \theta_m z) - (b + \theta_m \bar{y}) = (a + \theta_c z) - (b + \theta_c y)$$

$$\text{iff} \quad \theta_m(z - \bar{y}) = \theta_c(z - y). \tag{7}$$

Under this assumption we can compute

$$\theta = \theta_{\mathrm{c}}/\theta_{\mathrm{m}} = (z - \bar{y})/(z - y),$$

and the same analysis applies to the other three components (i.e., $\bar{a}$, $\bar{b}$, and $\bar{z}$).

We applied this method to the aggregate data from problems 1 to 6. The average values of θ, across subjects and components, are displayed in table 34.1 for each of the six problems. The values of $\theta = \theta_{\mathrm{c}}/\theta_{\mathrm{m}}$ are all less than unity, as implied by the prominence hypothesis. Note that θ provides an alternative index of the choice-matching discrepancy that is based on equations 6 and 7—unlike the difference between C and M that does not presuppose any measurement structure.

Prediction of Performance

We next use the contingent weighting model to analyze the effect of scale compatibility observed in a study of the prediction of students' performance, conducted by Slovic et al. (1988). The subjects ($N = 234$) in this study were asked to predict the performance of 10 students in a course (e.g., History) on the basis of their performance in two other courses (e.g., Philosophy and English). For each of the 10 students, the subjects received a grade in one course (from A to D), and a class rank (from 1 to 100) in the other course. One half of the respondents were asked to predict a grade, and the other half were asked to predict class rank. The courses were counterbalanced across respondents. The compatibility principle implies that a given predictor (e.g., grade in Philosophy) will be given more weight when the predicted variable is expressed on the same scale (e.g., grade in History) than when it is expressed on a different scale (e.g., class rank in History). The relative weight of grades to ranks, therefore, will be higher in the group that predicts grades than in the group that predicts ranks.

Let $(r_{\mathrm{i}}, g_{\mathrm{j}})$ be a student profile with rank i in the first course and grade j in the second. Let r_{ij} and g_{ij} denote, respectively, the predicted rank and grade of that student. The ranks range from 1 to 100, and the grades were scored as A+ = 10, A = 9, ..., D = 1. Under the linear model (Equation 6), we have

$$r_{\mathrm{ij}} = \alpha_{\mathrm{r}} r_{\mathrm{i}} + \beta_{\mathrm{r}} g_{\mathrm{j}} \quad \text{and} \quad g_{\mathrm{ij}} = \alpha_{\mathrm{g}} r_{\mathrm{i}} + \beta_{\mathrm{g}} g_{\mathrm{j}}$$

By regressing the 10 predictions of each respondent against the predictors, r_{i} and g_{j}, we obtained for each subject in the rank condition an estimate of $\theta_{\mathrm{r}} = \beta_{\mathrm{r}}/\alpha_{\mathrm{r}}$, and for each subject in the grade condition an estimate of $\theta_{\mathrm{g}} = \beta_{\mathrm{g}}/\alpha_{\mathrm{g}}$. These values reflect the relative weight of grades to ranks in the two prediction tasks. As implied by the compatibility hypothesis, the values of θ_{g} were significantly higher than the values of θ_{r}, $p < .001$ by a Mann-Whitney test.

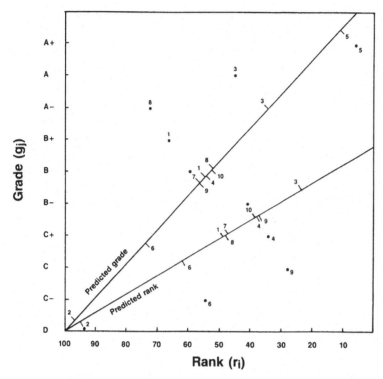

Figure 34.5
Contingent weighting representation of predicted ranks and grades. (The dots characterize the input information for each of the 10 students. The slopes of the two lines correspond to the relative weight of grades to ranks in the two prediction tasks.)

Figure 34.5 represents each of the 10 students as a point in the rank $\times$ grade plane. The slopes of the two lines, θ_r and θ_g, correspond to the relative weights of grade to rank estimated from the average predictions of ranks and grades, respectively. The multiple correlation between the inputs (r_i, g_j) and the average predicted scores was .99 for ranks and .98 for grades, indicating that the linear model provides a good description of the aggregate data. Recall that in the contingent weighting model, the predicted scores are given by the perpendicular projections of the points onto the respective lines, indicated by notches. The two lines, then, are orthogonal to the equal-value sets defined by the two tasks. The figure shows that grades and ranks were roughly equally weighted in the prediction of grades ($\theta_g = 1.06$), but grades were given much less weight than ranks in the prediction of ranks ($\theta_r = .58$). As a consequence, the two groups generated different ordering of the students. For example, the predicted rank of Student 9 was higher than that of Student 8, but the order of the predicted grades was reversed. Note that the numbered points in figure 34.5 represent the design, not the data. The discrepancy between the two orderings is determined jointly by the angle between the lines that is estimated from subjects' predictions, and by the correlation between the two dimensions that is determined by the design.

These data suggest a more detailed account based on a process of anchoring and adjustment (Slovic & Lichtenstein, 1971; Tversky & Kahneman, 1974). According to this heuristic, the subject uses the score on the compatible attribute (either rank or grade) as an anchor, and adjusts it upward or downward on the basis of the other score. Because adjustments are generally insufficient, the compatible attribute is overweighted. Although the use of anchoring and adjustment probably contribute to the phenomenon in question, Slovic et al. (1988) found a significant compatibility effect even when the subject only predicted which of the two students would obtain a higher grade (or rank), without making any numerical prediction that calls for anchoring and adjustment.

Preference Reversals

The contingent weighting model (equation 5) and the compatibility principle can also be used to explain the well-known preference reversals discovered by Lichtenstein and Slovic (1971; see also Slovic and Lichtenstein, 1968, 1983). These investigators compared two types of bets with comparable expected values—an H bet that offers a high probability of winning a relatively small amount of money (e.g., 32/36 chance to win \$4) and an L bet that offers a low probability of winning a moderate amount of money (e.g., 9/36 chance to win \$40). The results show that people generally choose the H bet over the L bet (i.e., $H >_c L$) but assign a higher cash equivalent to the L bet than to the H bet (i.e., $C_L > C_H$, where C_L and C_H are the amounts of money that are as desirable as L and H respectively). This pattern of preferences, which is inconsistent with the theory of rational choice, has been observed in numerous experiments, including a study conducted on the floor of a Las Vegas casino (Lichtenstein & Slovic, 1973), and it persists even in the presence of monetary incentives designed to promote consistent responses (Grether & Plott, 1979).

Although the basic phenomenon has been replicated in many studies, the determinants of preference reversals and their causes have remained elusive heretofore. It is easy to show that the reversal of preferences implies either intransitive choices or a choice-pricing discrepancy (i.e., a failure of invariance), or both. In order to understand this phenomenon, it is necessary to assess the relative contribution of these factors because they imply different explanations. To accomplish this goal, however, one must extend the traditional design and include, in addition to the bets H and L, a cash amount X that is compared with both. If procedure invariance holds and preference reversals are due to intransitive choices, then we should obtain the cycle $L >_c X >_c H >_c L$. If, on the other hand, transitivity holds and preference reversals are due to an inconsistency between choice and pricing, then we should obtain either $X >_c L$ and $C_L > X$, or $H >_c X$ and $X > C_H$. The first pattern indicates that L is *overpriced* relative to choice, and the second pattern indicates that H is *underpriced* relative to choice. Recall that $H >_c X$ refers to the choice between the bet H and the sure thing X, while $X > C_H$ refers to the ordering of cash amounts.

Following this analysis, Tversky, Slovic, and Kahneman (1988) conducted an extensive study of preference reversals, using 18 triples (H, L, X) that cover a wide range of probabilities and payoffs. A detailed analysis of response patterns showed that, by far, the most important determinant of preference reversals is the overpricing of L. Intransitive choices and the underpricing of H play a relatively minor role, each accounting for less than 10% of the total number of reversals. Evidently, preference reversals represent a choice-pricing discrepancy induced by the compatibility principle: Because pricing is expressed in monetary units, the payoffs loom larger in pricing than in choice.

We next apply the contingent weighting model to a study reported by Tversky et al. (1988) in which 179 participants (a) chose between 6 pairs consisting of an H bet and an L bet, (b) rated the attractiveness of all 12 bets, and (c) determined the cash equivalent of each bet. In order to provide monetary incentives and assure the strategic equivalence of the three methods, the participants were informed that a pair of bets would be selected at random, and that they would play the member of the pair that they had chosen, or the bet that they had priced or rated higher. The present discussion focuses on the relation between pricing and rating, which can be readily analyzed using multiple regression. In general, rating resembles choice in favoring the H bets, in contrast to pricing that favors the L bets. Note that in rating and pricing each gamble is evaluated separately, whereas choice (and matching) involve a comparison between gambles. Because the discrepancy between rating and pricing is even more pronounced than that between choice and pricing, the reversal of preferences cannot be explained by the fact that choice is comparative whereas pricing is singular. For further discussions of the relation between rating, choice, and pricing, see Goldstein and Einhom (1987), and Schkade and Johnson (1987).

We assume that the value of a simple prospect (q, y) is approximated by a multiplicative function of the probability q and the payoff y. Thus, the logarithms of the pricing and the rating can be expressed by

$$\theta_i \log y + \log q, \quad i = r, p, \tag{8}$$

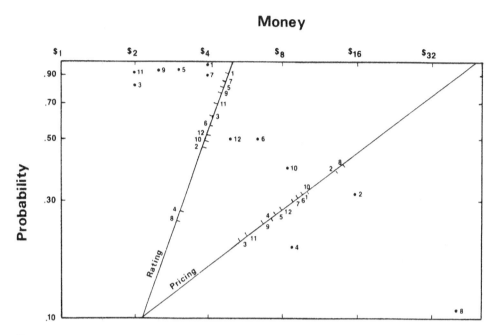

Figure 34.6
Contingent weighting representation of rating and pricing. (The dots characterize the six H bets and six L bets denoted by odd and even numbers, respectively, in logarithmic coordinates. The slopes of the two lines correspond to the weight of money relative to probability in rating and pricing.)

where θ_r and θ_p denote the relative weight of the payoff in the rating and in the pricing tasks, respectively. Note that this model implies a power utility function with an exponent θ_i. The average transformed rating and pricing responses for each of the 12 bets were regressed, separately, against log q and log y. The multiple correlations were .96 and .98 for the ratings and the pricing, respectively, indicating that the relation between rating and pricing can be captured, at least in the aggregate data, by a very simple model with a single parameter.

Figure 34.6 represents each of the 12 bets as a (numbered) point in the plane whose coordinates are probability and money, plotted on a logarithmic scale. The rating and pricing lines in the figure are perpendicular to the respective sets of linear indifference curves (see figure 34.2). Hence, the projections of each bet on the two lines (denoted by notches) correspond to their values derived from rating and pricing, respectively. The angle between these lines equals the (smaller) angle between the intersecting families of indifference curves. Figure 34.6 reveals a dramatic difference between the slopes: $\theta_r = 2.7$, $\theta_p = .75$, hence $\theta = \theta_p/\theta_r = .28$. Indeed, these data give rise to a negative correlation ($r = -.30$) between the rating and the pricing, yielding numerous reversals of the ordering of the projections on the two lines. For example, the most extreme L bet (No. 8) has the lowest rating and the highest cash equivalent in the set.

The preceding analysis shows that the compatibility principle, incorporated into the contingent weighting model, provides a simple account of the well-known preference reversals. It also yields new predictions, which have been confirmed in a recent study. Note that if preference reversals are caused primarily by the overweighting of payoffs in the pricing task, then the effect should be much smaller for nonmonetary payoffs. Indeed, Slovic et al. (1988) found that the use of nonmonetary payoffs (e.g., a dinner for two at a very good restaurant or a free weekend at a coastal resort) greatly reduced the incidents of preference reversals. Furthermore, according to the present analysis, preference reversals are not limited to risky prospects. Tversky et al. (1988) constructed riskless options of the form ($\$x, t$) that offers a payment of $\$x$ at some future time, t (e.g., 3 years from now). Subjects chose between such options, and evaluated their cash equivalents. The cash equivalent (or the price) of the option ($\$x, t$) is the amount of cash, paid immediately, that is as attractive as receiving $\$x$ at time t. Because both the price and the payment are expressed in dollars, compatibility implies that the payment will loom larger in pricing than in choice. This prediction was confirmed. Subjects generally chose the option that paid sooner, and assigned a higher price to the option that offered the larger payment. For example, 85% of the subjects ($N = 169$) preferred $2,500 in 5 years over $3,550 in 10 years, but 71% assigned a higher price to the second option. Thus, the replacement of risk by time gives rise to a new type of reversals. Evidently, preference reversals are determined primarily by the compatibility between the price and the payoff, regardless of the presence or absence of risk.

We conclude this section with a brief discussion of alternative accounts of preference reversals proposed in the literature. One class of comparative theories, developed by Fishburn (1984, 1985) and Loomes and Sugden (1982, 1983), treat preference reversals as intransitive choices. As was noted earlier, however, the intransitivity of choice accounts for only a small part of the phenomenon in question, hence these theories do not provide a fully satisfactory explanation of preference reversals. A different model, called expression theory, has been developed by Goldstein and Einhorn (1987). This model is a special case of the contingent model defined by Equation 1. It differs from the present treatment in that it focuses on the expression of preferences rather than on the evaluation of prospects. Thus, it attributes preference reversals to the mapping of subjective value onto the appropriate response scale, not to the compatibility between the input and the output. As a consequence, this model does not imply many of the compatibility effects described in this article, such as the contingent weighting of grades and ranks in the prediction of students' performance, the marked reduction in preference reversals with non-monetary payoffs, and the differential weighting of common and of distinctive features in judgments of similarity and dissimilarity.

A highly pertinent analysis of preference reversals based on attention and anchoring data was proposed by Schkade and Johnson (1987). Using a computer-controlled experiment in which the subject can see only one component of each bet at a time, these investigators measured the amount of time spent by each subject looking at probabilities and at payoffs. The results showed that in the pricing task, the percentage of time spent on the payoffs was significantly greater than that spent on probabilities, whereas in the rating task, the pattern was reversed. This observation supports the hypothesis, suggested by the compatibility principle, that subjects attended to payoffs more in the pricing task than in the rating task.

The relation between preference reversals and the choice-matching discrepancy was explored in a study by Slovic et al. (1988). Subjects matched twelve pairs of H and L bets by completing the missing probability or payoff. The overall percentage of responses that favored H over L was 73% for probability matches and 49% for payoff matches. (For comparison, 76% preferred H over L in a direct choice.) This result follows from scale compatibility: The adjusted attribute, either probability or money, looms larger than the nonadjusted attribute. However, the pattern differs from the prominence effect described earlier, which produced relatively small differences between the matches on the primary and the secondary attributes and large differences between choice and matching (see, e.g., problem 1). This contrasts with the present finding of large differences between probability and payoff matches, and no difference between probability matches and choice. Evidently, preference reversals are induced primarily by scale compatibility, not by the differential prominence of attributes that underlies the choice-matching discrepancy. Indeed, there is no obvious reason to suppose that probability is more prominent than money or vice versa. For further examples and discussions of elicitation biases in risky choice, see Fischer, Damodaran, Laskey, and Lincoln (1987), and Hershey and Schoemaker (1985).

Discussion

The extensive use of rational theories of choice (e.g., the expected utility model or the theory of revealed preference) as descriptive models (e.g., in economics, management, and political science) has stimulated the experimental investigation of the descriptive validity of the assumptions that underlie these models. Perhaps the most basic assumption of the rational theory of choice is the principle of invariance (Kahneman and Tversky, 1984) or extensionality (Arrow, 1982), which states that the relation of preference should not depend on the description of the options (description invariance) or on the method of elicitation (procedure in variance). Empirical tests of description invariance have shown that alternative framing of the same options can lead to different choices (Tversky and Kahneman, 1986). The present studies provide evidence against the assumption of procedure invariance by demonstrating a systematic discrepancy between choice and matching, as well as between rating and pricing. In this section we discuss the main findings and explore their theoretical and practical implications.

In the first part of the article we showed that the more important dimension of a decision problem looms larger in choice than in matching. We addressed this phenomenon at three levels of analysis. First, we presented a heuristic account of choice and matching that led to the prominence hypothesis; second, we related this account to the general notion of input-output compatibility; and third, we developed the formal theory of contingent weighting that represents the prominence effect as well as other elicitation phenomena, such as preference reversals. The informal analysis, based on compatibility, provides a psychological explanation for the differential weighting induced by the various procedures.

Although the prominence effect was observed in a variety of settings using both intrapersonal and interpersonal comparisons, its boundaries are left to be explored. How does it extend to options that vary on a larger number of attributes? The present analysis implies that the relative weights of any pair of attributes will be less extreme (i.e., closer to unity) in matching than in choice. With three or more attributes, however, additional considerations may come into play. For example, people may select the option that is superior on most attributes (Tversky, 1969, experiment 2). In this case, the prominence hypothesis does not always result in a lexicographic bias. Another question is whether the choice-matching discrepancy applies to other judgmental or perceptual tasks. The data on the prediction of students' performance indicate that the prominence effect is not limited to preferential choice, but it is not clear whether it applies to psychophysics. Perceived loudness, for example, depends primarily on intensity and to a lesser degree on frequency. It could be interesting to test the prominence hypothesis in such a context.

The finding that the qualitative information about the ordering of the dimensions looms larger in the ordinal method of choice than in the cardinal method of matching has been construed as an instance of the compatibility principle. This principle states that stimulus components that are compatible with the response are weighted more heavily than those that are not presumably because (a) the former are accentuated, and (b) the latter require additional mental transformations that produce error and reduce the diagnosticity of the information. This effect may be induced by the nature of the information (e.g., ordinal vs. cardinal), by the response scale (e.g., grades vs. ranks), or by the affinity between inputs and outputs (e.g., common features loom larger in similarity than in dissimilarity judgments). Compatibility, therefore, appears to provide a common explanation to many phenomena of judgment and choice.

The preceding discussion raises the intriguing normative question as to which method, choice or matching, better reflects people's "true" preferences. Put differently, do people overweigh the primary dimension in choice or do they underweigh it in matching? Without knowing the "correct" weighting, it is unclear how to answer this question, but the following study provides some relevant data. The participants in a decision-making seminar performed both choice and matching in the traffic-accident problem described earlier (problem 3). The two critical (choice and matching) questions were embedded in a questionnaire that included similar questions with different numerical values. The majority of the respondents (21 out of 32) gave inconsistent responses that conformed to the prominence hypothesis. After the session, each participant was interviewed and confronted with his or her answers. The subjects were surprised to discover that their responses were inconsistent and they offered a variety of explanations, some of which resemble the prominence hypothesis. One participant said, "When I have to choose between programs I go for the one that saves more lives because there is no price for human life. But when I match the programs I have to pay attention to money." When asked to reconsider their answers, all respondents modified the matching in the direction of the choice, and a few reversed the original choice in the direction of the matching. This observation suggests that choice and matching are both biased in opposite directions, but it may reflect a routine compromise rather than the result of a critical reassessment.

Real-world decisions can sometimes be framed either as a direct choice (e.g., should I buy the used car at this price?) or as a pricing decision (e.g., what is the most I should pay for that used car?). Our findings suggest that the answers to the two questions are likely to diverge. Consider, for example, a medical decision problem where the primary dimension is the probability of survival and the secondary dimension is the cost associated with treatment or diagnosis. According to the present analysis, people are likely to choose the option that offers the higher probability of survival with relatively little concern for cost. When asked to price a marginal increase in the probability of survival, however, people are expected to appear less generous. The choice-matching discrepancy may also arise in resource allocation and budgeting decisions. The prominence hypothesis suggests that the most important item in the budget (e.g., health) will tend to dominate a less important item (e.g., culture) in a direct choice between two allocations, but the less important item is expected to fare better in a matching procedure.

The lability of preferences implied by the demonstrations of framing and elicitation effects raises difficult questions concerning the assessment of preferences and values. In the classical analysis, the relation of preference is inferred from observed responses (e.g., choice, matching) and is assumed to reflect the decision maker's underlying utility or value. But if different elicitation procedures produce different ordeaings of options, how can preferences and values be defined? And in what sense do they exist? To be sure, people make choices, set prices, rate options and even explain their decisions to others. Preferences, therefore, exist as observed data. However, if these data do not satisfy the elementary requirements of invariance, it is unclear how to define a relation of preference that can serve as a basis for the measurement of value. In the absence of well-defined preferences, the foundations of choice theory and decision analysis are called into question.

Notes

This work was supported by Contract N00014-84-K-0615 from the Office of Naval Research to Stanford University and by National Science Foundation Grant 5ES-8712-145 to Decision Research.

The article has benefited from discussions with Greg Fischer, Dale Griffin, Eric Johnson, Daniel Kahneman, and Lennart Sjöberg.

References

Arrow, K. J. (1982). Risk perception in psychology and economics. *Economic Inquiry, 20*, 1–9.

Carroll, J. D. (1972). Individual differences and multidimensional scaling. In R. N. Shepard, A. K. Romney, & S. Neriove (Eds.), *Multidimensional scaling: Theory and applications in the behavioral sciences: Vol. 1. Theory* (pp. 105–155). New York: Seminar Press.

Coombs, C. H., Bezembinder, T. C. G., & Goode, F. M. (1967). Testing expectation theories of decision making without measuring utility and subjective probability. *Journal of Mathematical Psychology, 4*, 72–103.

Falmagne, J.-C. (1985). Elements of psychophysical theory. New York: Oxford University Press.

Fischer, G. W., Damodaran, N., Laskey, K. B., & Lincoln, D. (1987). Preferences for proxy attributes. *Management Science, 33*, 198–214.

Fischhoff, B., Slovic, P., & Lichtenstein, S. (1980). Knowing what you want: Measuring labile values. In T. Wallstein (Ed.), *Cognitive processes in choice and decision behavior* (pp. 117–141). Hillsdale, NJ: Erlbaum.

Fishburn, P. C. (1984). SSB utility theory: An economic perspective. *Mathematical Social Sciences, 8*, 63–94.

Fishburn, P. C. (1985). Nontransitive preference theory and the preference reversal phenomenon. *Rivista Internazionale di Scienze Economiche e Commerciali, 32*, 39–50.

Fitts, P. M., & Seeger, C. M. (1953). S-R compatibility: Spatial characteristics of stimulus and response codes. *Journal of Experimental Psychology, 46*, 199–210.

Goldstein, W. M., & Einhom, H. J. (1987). Expression theory and the preference reversal phenomena. *Psychological Review, 94*, 236–254.

Grether, D. M., & Plott, C. R. (1979). Economic theory of choice and the preference reversal phenomenon. *American Economic Review, 69*, 623–638.

Hershey, J., & Schoemaker, P. J. (1985). Probability vs. certainty equivalence methods in utility measurement: Are they equivalent? *Management Science, 31,* 1213–1231.

Kahneman, D., and Tversky, A. (1984). Choices, values and frames. *American Psychologist, 39,* 341–350.

Krantz, D. H., Luce, R. D., Suppes, P., & Tversky, A. (1971). *Foundations of measurement* (vol. 1). New York: Academic Press.

Lichtenstein, S., & Slovic, P. (1971). Reversals of preference between bids and choices in gambling decisions. *Journal of Experimental Psychology, 89,* 46–55.

Lichtenstein, S., & Slovic, P. (1973). Response-induced reversals of preference in gambling: An extended replication in Las Vegas. *Journal of Experimental Psychology, 101,* 16–20.

Loomes, G., & Sugden, R. (1982). Regret theory: An alternative theory of rational choice under uncertainty. *Economic Journal, 92,* 805–824.

Loomes, G., & Sugden, R. (1983). A rationale for preference reversal. *American Economic Review, 73,* 428–432.

March, J. G. (1978). Bounded rationality, ambiguity, and the engineering of choice. *The Bell Journal of Economics, 9,* 587–608.

Montgomery, H. (1983). Decision rules and the search for a dominance structure: Towards a process model of decision making. In P. C. Humphreys, O. Svenson, & A. Vari (Eds.), *Analyzing and aiding decision processes* (pp. 343–369). Amsterdam/Budapest: North-Holland and Hungarian Academic Press.

Payne, J. W. (1982). Contingent decision behavior. *Psychological Bulletin, 92,* 382–401.

Schkade, D. A., & Johnson, E. J. (1988). *Cognitive processes in preference reversals.* Working paper, Department of Management, University of Texas.

Shafer, G., & Tversky, A. (1985). Languages and designs for probability judgment. *Cognitive Science, 9,* 309–339.

Slovic, P. (1975). Choice between equally valued alternatives. *Journal of Experimental Psychology: Human Perception and Performance, 1,* 280–287.

Slovic, P., Griffin, D. P., & Tversky, A. (1988). *Compatibility effects in judgment and choice.* Unpublished manuscript, Stanford University, Stanford, CA.

Slovic, P., & Lichtenstein, S. (1968). The relative importance of probabilities and payoffs in risk-taking. *Journal of Experimental Psychology Monograph Supplement, 78*(3, pt. 2).

Slovic, P., & Lichtenstein, S. (1971). Comparison of Bayesian and regression approaches to the study of information processing in judgment. *Organizational Behavioral and Human Performance, 6,* 649–744.

Slovic, P., & Lichtenstein, S. (1983). Preference reversals: A broader perspective. *American Economic Review, 73,* 596–605.

Tversky, A. (1969). The intransitivity of preferences. *Psychological Review, 76,* 31–48.

Tversky, A. (1977). Features of similarity. *Psychological Review, 84,* 327–352.

Tversky, A., & Gati, L. (1978). Studies of similarity. In E. Rosch & B. Lloyd (Eds.), *Cognition and categorization* (pp. 79–98). Hillsdale, NJ: Erlbaum.

Tversky, A., & Kahneman, D. (1974). Judgment under uncertainty: Heuristics and biases. *Science, 185,* 1124–1131.

Tversky, A., & Kahneman, D. (1986). Rational choice and the framing of decisions. *The Journal of Business, 59*(4), pt. 2, 251–278.

Tversky, A., Slovic, P., & Kahneman, D. (1988). *The determinants of preference reversals.* Unpublished manuscript, Stanford University, Stanford, CA.

Varian, H. R. (1984). *Macroeconomic analysis.* New York: Norton & Co.

Wickens, C. D. (1984). *Engineering psychology and human performance.* Columbus, OH: Merrill.

35 Anomalies: Preference Reversals

Amos Tversky and Richard H. Thaler

Introduction

Imagine, if you will, that you have been asked to advise the Minister of Transportation for a small Middle Eastern country regarding the choice of a highway safety program. At the current time, about 600 people per year are killed in traffic accidents in that country. Two programs designed to reduce the number of casualties are under consideration. Program A is expected to reduce the yearly number of casualities to 570; its annual cost is estimated at $12 million. Program B is expected to reduce the yearly number of casualities to 500; its annual cost is estimated at $55 million. The Minister tells you to find out which program would make the electorate happier.

You hire two polling organizations. The first firm asks a group of citizens which program they like better. It finds that about two-thirds of the respondents prefer Program B which saves more lives, though at a higher cost per life saved. The other firm uses a "matching" procedure. It presents respondents with the same information about the two programs except that the cost of Program B is not specified. These citizens are asked to state the cost that would make the two programs equally attractive. The polling firm reasons that respondents' preferences for the two programs can be inferred from their responses to this question. That is, a respondent who is indifferent between the two programs at a cost of less than $55 million should prefer A to B. On the other hand, someone who would be willing to spend over $55 million should prefer Program B. This survey finds, however, that more than 90 percent of the respondents provided values smaller than $55 million indicating, in effect, that they prefer Program A over Program B.

This pattern is definitely puzzling. When people are asked to choose between a pair of options, a clear majority favors B over A. When asked to price these options, however, the overwhelming majority give values implying a preference for A over B. Indeed, the implicit value of human life derived from the simple choice presented by the first firm is more than twice that derived from the matching procedure used by the other firm.

What are you going to tell the Minister? You decide to call a staff meeting where various explanations for the results are offered. Perhaps one of the pollsters has made a mistake. Perhaps people cannot think straight about problems involving the value of a human life, especially in the Middle East. However, one staff member points out that there is a good reason to trust both surveys, since recent research by some psychologists[1] has produced exactly the same pattern using a wide range of problems such as selecting job applicants, consumer products, and saving plans. The psychologists conclude that the notion of preference that underlies modern decision theory is more problematic than economists normally assume because different methods of elicitation often give rise to systematically different orderings. Well? The Minister is waiting.

For almost two decades, economists and psychologists have been intrigued by a similar inconsistency involving risky prospects. Subjects are first asked to choose between two gambles with nearly the same expected values. One gamble, called the H bet (for high chance of winning) has a high chance of winning a relatively small prize (say, 8/9 chance to win $4), while the other gamble, the L bet, offers a lower chance to win a larger prize (say, a 1/9 chance to win $40). Most subjects choose the H bet. Subjects are then asked to price each of the gambles. Specifically, they are asked to state the lowest price at which they would be willing to sell each gamble if they owned it. Surprisingly, most subjects put a higher price on the L bet. (In a recent study that used this particular pair of bets, for example, 71 percent of the subjects chose the H bet, while 67 percent priced L above H.) This pattern is called a *preference reversal*. Sarah Lichtenstein and Paul Slovic (1971, 1973) first demonstrated such reversals in a series of studies, one of which was conducted for real money with gamblers on the floor of the Four Queens Casino in Las Vegas.

Lichtenstein and Slovic did not come upon this result by chance. In an earlier study (Slovic and Lichtenstein, 1968), they observed that both buying and selling prices of gambles were more highly correlated with payoffs than with chances of winning, whereas choices between gambles (and ratings of their attractiveness) were more highly correlated with the probabilities of winning and losing than with the payoffs. The authors reasoned that if the method used to elicit preferences affected the weighting of the gamble's components, it should be possible to construct pairs of gambles such that the same individual would choose one member of the pair but set a higher price for the other. Experimental tests supported this conjecture.

The preference reversal phenomenon raises an issue rarely discussed in economics: How is the notion of preference to be operationalized? We say that option A is preferred to option B if A is selected when B is available *or* if A has a higher reservation price than B. The standard analysis of choice assumes that these procedures give rise to the same ordering. This requirement—called procedure invariance—seldom appears as an explicit axiom, but it is needed to ensure that the preference relation is well defined. The assumption of procedure invariance is not unique to the study of preference. When measuring mass, for example, we can use either a pan balance or a spring to determine which of the objects is heavier, and we expect the two measurement procedures to yield the same ordering. Unlike the measurement of physical attributes such as mass or length, however, different methods of eliciting preference often give rise to systematically different orderings. This column summarizes the evidence regarding this puzzling result, and discusses its implications for economics.

Economists were introduced to the preference reversal phenomenon by David Grether and Charles Plott (1979) who designed a series of experiments "to discredit the psychologists' work as applied to economics" (p. 623). These authors began by generating a list of 13 objections and potential artifacts that would render the preference reversal phenomenon irrelevant to economic theory. Their list included poor motivation, income effects, strategic responding, and the fact that the experimenters were psychologists (thereby creating suspicions leading to peculiar behavior). Grether and Plott attempted to eliminate preference reversals by various means (like offering a special incentive system), but to no avail. Indeed, preference reversals were somewhat more common among subjects responding under financial incentives than in a control group facing purely hypothetical questions. Subsequent studies by both psychologists and economists, using a wide range of procedural variations, led to similar conclusions. (See Slovic and Lichtenstein (1983) for a review of the early literature and Tversky, Slovic and Kahneman (1990) for later references.)

Although these experimental studies have established the validity and the robustness of the preference reversal phenomenon, its interpretation and explanation has remained unclear. To formulate the problem, we must introduce some notation. Let C_H and C_L denote the cash equivalents (or minimum selling price) of H and L (the gambles with high and low chances of winning, respectively). Let $\succ$ and $\approx$ denote strict preference and indifference, respectively. Recall that a preference reversal occurs when H is preferred to L but L is priced higher than H; that is, $H \succ L$ and $C_L > C_H$. Note that $\succ$ refers to preference between options, whereas $>$ refers to the ordering of cash amounts.[2] It is not difficult to see that a preference reversal implies either the intransitivity of the preference relation, $\succ$, or a failure of procedure invariance, or both. Now, recall that if procedure invariance holds, a decision maker will be indifferent when choosing between a bet B and some cash amount X, if and only if the cash equivalent for B is equal to X, that is $C_B = X$. So, if procedure invariance holds, then a preference reversal implies the following intransitive pattern of preferences:

$$C_H \approx H \succ L \approx C_L \succ C_H$$

where the two inequalities are implied by the assumed preference reversal and the two equivalences follow from procedure invariance.

Because procedure invariance is commonly taken for granted, many authors have interpreted preference reversals as intransitivities, and some have proposed nontransitive choice models to account for this phenomenon (Loomes and Sugden, 1983; Fishburn, 1985). A preference reversal, however, does not imply cyclic choice; it can be consistent with transitivity if procedure invariance does not hold. Two types of discrepancies between choice and pricing could produce the standard pattern of preference reversal,[3] that is, preferring H but assigning a higher value to L: either overpricing of L or underpricing of H. Overpricing of L is evident if the decision maker prefers her reservation price for the bet over the bet itself when offered a choice between them on another occasion (i.e., $C_L \succ L$). Underpricing of H is evident if the decision maker prefers the bet over its price in a direct choice on another occasion (i.e., $H \succ C_H$). (The terms overpricing and underpricing merely identify the sign of the discrepancy between pricing and choice; the labels are not meant to imply that the choice represents one's "true" preference and the bias resides in pricing.)

The third possible explanation of the preference reversal implicates the payoff scheme used to elicit cash equivalence. To encourage subjects to produce careful and truthful responses, several investigators have employed the following payoff scheme called the BDM procedure after its originators Becker, DeGroot, and Marschak (1964). After the subject states a selling price for a gamble, an offer is generated by some random process. The subject receives the offer if it exceeds the stated selling price, and plays the gamble if the stated price exceeds the offer. The price stated by the subject, therefore, serves only to determine whether the subject will play the bet or receive the cash, but it does not determine the actual amount. As long as the subject is an expected utility maximizer, this procedure is incentive compatible: the decision maker has no incentive to state a selling price that departs from his or her actual cash equivalent. However, as noted by Holt (1986), Karni, and Safra (1987), and Segal (1988), if the decision maker does not obey the independence (or reduction) axiom of expected utility theory, the BDM procedure no longer ensures that the stated price will correspond to the cash equivalent of the gamble. Indeed, Karni, and Safra have shown that preference reversals observed under the BDM scheme are consistent with a generalized version of expected utility theory with nonlinear probabilities.

So we now have three alternative interpretations of preference reversals. They can arise from violations of transitivity, procedure invariance, or the independence axiom. To determine which interpretation is correct we need to solve two problems. First, we need an experimental procedure that can distinguish between failures of transitivity and failures of procedure invariance. Second, we need an incentive-compatible payoff scheme that does not rely on the expectation principle. Both requirements have been met in a recent study by Tversky, Slovic, and Kahneman (1990).

To discriminate between the intransitivity and procedure invariance explanations, these investigators extended the original design to include, in addition to the standard H and L bets, a cash amount X that was compared to both of them. That is, subjects indicated their preferences between each of the pairs in the triple $\{H, L, X\}$. Subjects also produced cash equivalents, C_L and C_H, (using a method described below) for both of the bets. By focusing on standard preference reversal patterns in which the pre-specified cash amount X happened to lie between the values of C_L and C_H generated by this subject (that is, $H \succ L$ and $C_L > X > C_H$), it is possible to diagnose each preference reversal pattern according to whether it was produced by an intransitivity, by an overpricing of L, by an underpricing of H, or by both. For example, if subjects indicated that $L \succ X$, and that $X \succ H$, then their preferences are intransitive since we are confining our attention to those cases in which $H \succ L$. Alternatively, if subjects overprice the L bet, then their pattern of responses will be $X \succ L$ and $X \succ H$. (The subjects produce a price for L that is greater than X, but when offered a choice between X and L, they choose X.) This pattern is transitive, though it is a preference reversal.

The results of this study were very clear. Using 18 triples of the form $\{H, L, X\}$ that cover a wide range of payoffs, the experiment yielded the usual rate of preference reversal (between 40 and 50 percent), but only 10 percent of preference reversal patterns were intransitive, and the remaining 90 percent violated procedure invariance. By far, the major source of preference reversal was the overpricing of the L bet, which accounted for nearly two-thirds of the observed patterns. (Note that if subjects were choosing at random, the expected rate of the standard preference reversal is 25 percent.)

Having eliminated intransitivity as the major cause of preference reversal, let us turn now to the effect of the payoff scheme. Karni and Safra (1987) have shown that it is exceedingly difficult, if not impossible, to devise an incentive compatible payoff scheme for the elicitation of cash equivalence that does not rely on expected utility theory. Fortunately, to demonstrate preference reversal, it is not necessary to elicit the actual selling prices; it is sufficient to establish their order—which can be obtained under much weaker conditions. Suppose the subject is presented with two tasks: pricing each bet separately and choosing between pairs of bets. The subjects are told that one of these pairs will be selected at random at the end of the session, and that they will play one of these bets. To determine which bet they will play, first a random device will be used to select either choices or pricing as the criteria for selection. If the choice data are used, then the subject plays the bet chosen. If the pricing data are used, then the subject will play whichever gamble was priced higher.

In this latter procedure, called the *ordinal payoff scheme*, the prices offered by the subjects are only used to order the bets within each pair. Consistency, therefore, requires that the price orderings and choice orderings should agree, whether or not the subjects are expected utility maximizers. Thus, if the previously observed reversals were caused by a failure of expected utility theory, then they should not occur under the ordinal payoff scheme. This prediction was clearly refuted. The incidence of reversals was roughly the same (40 percent to 50 percent) whether the experiment employed the BDM scheme, the above ordinal scheme, or even no payoff scheme at all. This finding shows that preference reversal is not caused by the BDM procedure, hence it cannot be explained as a violation of the independence or reduction axioms of expected utility theory.

The conclusions of the Tversky, Slovic, and Kahneman study may be summarized as follows. First, intransitivity alone accounts for only a small portion of preference reversal patterns. Second, preference reversal is hardly affected by the payoff scheme, hence, it is not attributable to the failure of expected utility theory. Third, the major cause of preference reversal is the failure of procedure invariance and, more specifically, the overpricing of the L bets. That is, the minimum selling prices associated with L bets (but not with H bets) are too high in comparison to the choices between the bets and cash amounts. These conclusions are further supported by a recent study of Bostic, Herrnstein and Luce (1990) using a somewhat different design.

This analysis raises a new question: Why do people overprice the low-probability high-payoff bets? Why do people who prefer, say, $10 for sure over a 1/3 chance to win $40, assign to this bet a cash equivalent that exceeds $10? Research suggests that this counterintuitive finding is a consequence of a general principle of compatibility that appears to play an important role in human judgment and choice.

The Compatibility Hypothesis

The concept of stimulus-response compatibility has been introduced by students of human factors who studied perceptual and motor performance. For example, a square array of four burners on a stove is easier to control with a matching square array of knobs than with a linear array. Slovic, Griffin, and Tversky (1990) have extended this concept and proposed that the weight of a stimulus attribute in judgment or in choice is enhanced by its compatibility with the response scale. The rationale for this scale compatibility hypothesis is two-fold. First, if the stimulus and the response do not match, additional mental operations are needed to map one into the other. This increases effort and error and may reduce the impact of the stimulus.

Second, a response mode tends to focus attention on the compatible features of the stimulus. Because there is neither a formal definition of compatibility nor an independent measurement procedure, the analysis is both informal and incomplete. Nevertheless, in many contexts the compatibility order is sufficiently clear so that it can be investigated experimentally.

A simple study by Slovic, Griffin, and Tversky illustrates a case in which the compatibility hypothesis makes a clear prediction. Subjects were given two pieces of information about each of 12 large companies taken from *Business Week*'s Top 100: the company's 1986 market value (in billions of dollars), and the company's rank (among the Top 100) with respect to 1987 profits. Half of the subjects were then asked to predict the 1987 market value in billions of dollars, whereas the other half were asked to predict the company's rank with respect to its 1987 market value. Thus each subject has one predictor measured on the same scale (that is, money or rank) as the dependent variable, and one predictor measured on a different scale. As implied by compatibility, each predictor was given more weight when the predicted variable was expressed on the same scale. As a consequence, the relative weight of the 1986 market value was twice as high for those who predicted in dollars than for those who predicted the corresponding rank. This effect produced many reversals in which one company was ranked above another but the order of their predicted values was reversed.

Because the cash equivalence of a bet is expressed in dollars, compatibility implies that the payoffs, which are expressed in the same units, will be weighted more heavily in pricing bets than in chosing between bets. Furthermore, since the payoffs of L bets are much larger than the payoffs of H bets, the major consequence of a compatibility bias is the overpricing of the L bet. The compatibility hypothesis, therefore, explains the major source of preference reversal, namely the overpricing of the low-probability high-payoff bets. This account has been supported by several additional findings. Slovic, Griffin, and Tversky presented subjects with H and L bets involving nonmonetary outcomes, such as a one-week pass for all movie theaters in town, or a dinner for two at a good restaurant. If preference reversals are due primarily to the compatibility of prices and payoffs, which are both expressed in dollars, their incidence should be substantially reduced by the use of nonmonetary outcomes. This is precisely what happened. The prevalence of preference reversals was reduced by nearly 50 percent. Schkade and Johnson (1989) found additional support for the role of compatibility in preference reversals in a computer-controlled experiment which allowed subjects to see only one component of each bet at a time. The percentage of time spent looking at the payoff was significantly greater in a pricing task than in a choice task. This pattern was pronounced when the subject produced a preference reversal, but not when the subject produced consistent responses. The finding that subjects attend to the payoffs more in pricing than in choice supports the hypothesis that people focus their attention on the stimulus components that are most compatible with the response mode.

Although the compatibility hypothesis can explain preference reversals between pairs of bets, the explanation does not depend on the presence of risk. Indeed, this hypothesis implies a similar discrepancy between choice and pricing for riskless options with a monetary component, such as delayed payments. Let (X, T) be a prospect that offers a payment of $\$X$, T years from now. Consider a lone-term prospect L ($2500, 5 years from now) and a short-term prospect S ($1600, $1\frac{1}{2}$ years from now). Suppose that subjects (i) choose between L and S, and (ii) price both prospects by stating the smallest immediate cash payment for which they would be willing to exchange the delayed payment. According to the compatibility hypothesis, the monetary component X would loom larger in pricing than in choice. As a consequence, subjects should produce preference reversals in which the short-term option is preferred over the long-term option in a direct choice, but the latter is priced higher than the former (that is, $S \succ L$ and $C_L > C_S$). This was precisely the pattern observed by Tversky, Slovic and Kahneman (1990). These investigators presented a large group of subjects with pairs of S and L options with comparable present values. The subjects chose between pairs of options, and also priced each option separately. Subjects exhibited the predicted pattern of preference. Overall, subjects chose the short-term option 74 percent of the time but priced the long-term option above the short-term option 75 percent of the time, and the rate of reversals exceeded 50 percent. The incidence of the non-predicted reversals was less than 10 percent. Further analysis revealed that—as in the risky case—the major source of preference reversal was the overpricing of the long-term option, as entailed by compatibility. These findings indicate that the preference reversal phenomenon is an example of a general pattern, rather than a peculiar characteristic of choice between bets.

Indeed, the preference reversal phenomenon is not the only example of a failure of procedure invariance. As illustrated by the life-saving example discussed in the introduction to this article, Tversky, Sattath, and Slovic (1988) have demonstrated a related discrepancy between choice and matching. These investigators observed that the more prominent dimension looms larger in choice than in matching. In the highway safety problem, for example, human lives are valued much higher in a direct choice than in the price matching procedure. Recall that in this study subjects selected the program that saved more lives when making a direct choice, but their stated prices favored the less expensive program. As a consequence, choice is more lexicographic than matching—the most important dimension is weighted more heavily in choice. Other violations of procedure invariance in the context of risky choice have been documented by Hershey and Schoemaker (1985). They first ask subjects to provide a certainty equivalent for some gamble, such as a 50 percent chance to win $100. Suppose the subject says $40. Later the subject is asked to indicate what probability of winning $100 would make the gamble just as attractive as a sure $40. If procedural invariance holds, then subjects should respond with .5. However, subjects do not reproduce the probability they started with, and their departures are systematic rather than random. Other violations of procedure invariance involving choice and ratings of gambles are presented by Goldstein and Einhorn (1987).

Commentary

Taken at face value the data [showing preference reversals] are simply inconsistent with preference theory and have broad implications about research priorities within economics. The inconsistency is deeper than the mere lack of transitivity or even stochastic transitivity. It suggests that no optimization principles of any sort lie behind the simplest of human choices and that the uniformities in human choice behavior which lie behind market behavior may result from principles which are of a completely different sort from those generally accepted (Grether and Plott, 1979, p. 623).

The preference reversal phenomenon has been established in numerous studies during the last two decades, but its causes have only recently been uncovered. It appears that preference reversals cannot be attributed to an intransitivity or to a violation of the independence axiom of expected utility theory. Rather, they seem to be driven primarily by the discrepancy between choice and pricing, which in turn is induced by scale compatibility. This account is supported by several new experiments, and it gives rise to a new type of reversal in the domain of time preference. What are the implications of preference reversals to economics and decision theory? This phenomenon, or cluster of phenomena, challenges the traditional assumption that the decision maker has a fixed preference order that is captured accurately by any reliable elicitation procedure. If option A is priced higher than option B, we cannot always assume that A is preferred to B in a direct comparison. The evidence shows that different methods of elicitation could change the relative weighting of the attributes and give rise to different orderings.

The findings are in contrast to the standard economic formulation of choice which assumes that, in the presence of complete information, people act as if they could look up their preferences in a book, and respond to situations accordingly: choose the item most preferred; pay up to the value of an item to obtain it; sell an item if offered more than its value; and so on. The principle of procedure invariance is likely to hold under two conditions. First, people could have preestablished preferences. If you prefer football to opera, then this preference will emerge whether you are choosing between activities or bidding for tickets. However, procedure invariance could also hold even if people do not have preestablished preferences. We do not immediately know the value of $7(8 + 9)$, but we have an algorithm for computing it that yields the same answer whether we do the addition before or after the multiplication. The results of the experiments reported here indicate that neither condition holds. First, people do not possess a set of pre-defined preferences for every contingency. Rather, preferences are constructed in the process of making a choice or judgment. Second, the context and procedures involved in making choices or judgments influence the preferences that are implied by the elicited responses. In practical terms, this implies that behavior is likely to vary across situations that economists consider identical. For example, alternative auction mechanisms which are equivalent in theory might produce different outcomes if the auction procedures themselves influence bidding behavior.

The discussion of the meaning of preference and the status of value may be illuminated by the well-known exchange among three baseball umpires. "I call them as I see them," said the first. "I call them as they are," claimed the second. The third disagreed, "They ain't nothing till I call them." Analogously, we can describe three different views regarding the nature of values. First, values exist—like body temperature—and people perceive and report them as best they can, possibly with bias (I call them as I see them). Second, people know their values and preferences directly—as they know the multiplication table (I call them as they are). Third, values or preferences are commonly constructed in the process of elicitation (they ain't nothing till I call them). The research reviewed in this article is most compatible with the third view of preference as a constructive, context-dependent process.

Notes

Amos Tversky's research is supported, in part, by Grant 89-0064 from the Air Force Office of Scientific Research. Richard H. Thaler's research is supported, in part, by Concord Capital Management and the Russell Sage Foundation. The authors thank Barach Fischhoff and Paul Slovic for helpful comments.

1. See Tversky, Sattath, and Slovic (1988). The data regarding the two highway safety programs are taken from this paper.

2. We assume that for sure outcomes measured in dollars $X > Y$ implies $X \succ Y$; that is, more money is preferred to less.

3. This is the standard preference reversal pattern. The other possible preference reversal, choosing L but assigning a higher value to H is rarely observed. We use the term "preference reversal" to refer to this standard pattern.

References

Becker, Gordon M., Morris H. DeGroot, and Jacob Marschak, "Measuring Utility by a Single-Response Sequential Method," *Behavioral Science*, July 1964, *9*, 226–232.

Bostic, Raphael, Richard J. Herrnstein, and R. Duncan Luce, "The Effect on the Preference-Reversal Phenomenon of Using Choice Indifferences," *Journal of Economic Behavior and Organization*, 1990, in press.

Fishburn, Peter C. "Nontransitive Preference Theory and the Preference Reversal Phenomenon," *Rivista Internazionale di Scienze Economiche e Commerciali*, January 1985, *32*, 39–50.

Goldstein, William M., and Hillel J. Einhorn, "Expression Theory and the Preference Reversal Phenomena," *Psychological Review*, April 1987, *94*, 236–254.

Grether, David M., and Charles R. Plott, "Economic Theory of Choice and the Preference Reversal Phenomenon," *American Economic Review*, September 1979, *69*, 623–638.

Hershey, John C., and Paul J. H. Schoemaker, "Probability Versus Certainty Equivalence Methods in Utility Measurement: Are they Equivalent?" *Management Science*, October 1985, *31*, 1213–1231.

Holt, Charles A., "Preference Reversals and the Independence Axiom," *The American Economic Review*, June 1986, *76*, 508–515.

Karni, Edi, and Zvi Safra, " 'Preference Reversal' and the Observability of Preferences by Experimental Methods," *Econometrica*, May 1987, *55*, 675–685.

Lichtenstein, Sarah, and Paul Slovic, "Reversals of Preference Between Bids and Choices in Gambling Decisions," *Journal of Experimental Psychology*, January 1971, *89*, 46–55.

Lichtenstein, Sarah, and Paul Slovic, "Response-induced Reversals of Preference in Gambling: An Extended Replication in Las Vegas," *Journal of Experimental Psychology*, November 1973, *101*, 16–20.

Loomes, Graham, and Robert Sugden, "A Rationale for Preference Reversal," *American Economic Review*, June 1983, *73*, 428–432.

Schkade, David A., and Eric J. Johnson, "Cognitive Processes in Preference Reversals," *Organization Behavior and Human Performance*, June 1989, *44*, 203–231.

Segal, Uzi, "Does the Preference Reversal Phenomenon Necessarily Contradict the Independence Axiom?" *The American Economic Review*, March 1988, *78*, 233–236.

Slovic, Paul, Dale Griffin, and Amos Tversky, "Compatibility Effects in Judgment and Choice." In Hogarth, Robin M., ed., *Insights in Decision Making: Theory and Applications*. Chicago: The University of Chicago Press, 1990.

Slovic, Paul, and Sarah Lichtenstein, "The Relative Importance of Probabilities and Payoffs in Risk-Taking," *Journal of Experimental Psychology Monograph Supplement*, November 1968, Part 2, *78*, 1–18.

Slovic, Paul, and Sarah Lichtenstein, "Preference Reversals: A Broader Perspective," *American Economic Review*, September 1983, *73*, 596–605.

Tversky, Amos, Shmuel Sattath, and Paul Slovic, "Contingent Weighting in Judgment and Choice," *Psychological Review*, July 1988, *95*, 371–384.

Tversky, Amos, Paul Slovic, and Daniel Kahneman, "The Causes of Preference Reversal," *American Economic Review*, March 1990, *80*, in press.

36 Discrepancy between Medical Decisions for Individual Patients and for Groups

Donald A. Redelmeier and Amos Tversky

Tension between health policy and medical practice exists in many situations. For example, regional variations in practice patterns persist despite extensive shared information,[1-3] there are substantial deviations from accepted guidelines daily in the care of patients,[4-7] and disproportionate amounts of care are given to selected individuals.[8-10] These observations indicate that decisions in the clinical arena, which focus on the individual patient, may be at variance with general medical policies, which are based on wider considerations. Our study investigated this discrepancy.

Imagine a patient presenting to a physician with a specific problem. Normally the physician treats each patient as a unique case and selects the treatment that seems best for that person. Over time, however, the physician may encounter many similar patients. Does the physician make a different judgment when a case is viewed as unique rather than as one of a group of comparable cases? There is evidence that people make different choices between financial gambles when they face single rather than repeated situations.[11-13] Furthermore, studies of both economic and medical decisions show that looking at a problem from different perspectives can change the relative weight given to its attributes and lead to different choices.[14-16]

We hypothesized that physicians give more weight to a patient's personal concerns when they consider the patient as an individual and more weight to general criteria of effectiveness when they consider the patient as part of a group. More specifically, we suggested that in viewing a patient as an individual rather than as a member of a group, physicians are more likely to do the following: recommend an additional test with a low cost and a possible benefit, examine a patient directly rather than follow progress by telephone, avoid troubling problems such as discussing organ donation, and recommend a therapy with a high probability of success but the chance of an adverse outcome. In this study we explored these issues to address the question: Do physicians make different judgments in evaluating an individual patient as compared with considering a group of similar patients? Our data suggest that they do, that the discrepancy is recognized by physicians trained in health-services research, and that lay people also make this distinction.

Methods

In our first experiment we invited practicing physicians to participate in a study of medical decision making. The questionnaire we used contained clinical scenarios describing problems in patient management about which reasonable physicians could disagree. Each physician was asked to select the most appropriate treatment.

We presented the problems in two versions, each from a different perspective. The individual version concerned the treatment of one patient. The aggregate version concerned the treatment of a group of comparable patients. In all other respects, the two versions contained the same information. For example, the individual version of one scenario was as follows.

The literature provides little information on the use of the telephone as an instrument of medical care. For example, H.B. is a young woman well known to her family physician and free from any serious illnesses. She contacts her family physician by phone because of 5 days of fever without any localizing symptoms. A tentative diagnosis of viral infection is made, symptomatic measures are prescribed, and she is told to stay "in touch." After about 36 hours she phones back reporting feeling about the same: no better, no worse, no new symptoms. The choice must be made between continuing to follow her a little longer by telephone or else telling her to come in now to be examined. Which management would you select for H.B.?

The aggregate version of this scenario was similar, except that we replaced all references to the individual patient with terms denoting a group of patients.

The literature provides little information on the use of the telephone as an instrument of medical care. For example, consider young women who are well known to their family physicians and free from any serious illnesses. They might contact their respective family physicians by phone because of 5 days of fever without any localizing symptoms. Frequently a tentative diagnosis of viral infection is made, symptomatic measures are prescribed, and they are told to stay "in touch." Suppose that after about 36 hours they phone back reporting feeling about the same: no better, no worse, no new symptoms. The choice must be made between continuing to follow them a little longer by telephone or else telling them to come in now to be examined. Which management strategy would you recommend?

Four groups of doctors participated in this part of the study: house staff in the Department of Medicine at Stanford University Hospital, physicians who were practicing full time in a regional health maintenance organization (HMO), academic physicians affiliated with Stanford's Department of Internal Medicine, and full-time physicians associated with a county medical center. Within each group we randomly assigned physicians to receive either the individual or the aggregate version of the questionnaire. We then compared their responses to the two versions using the Mann–Whitney test.[17]

In our second experiment we presented scenarios analogous to those in experiment 1 and asked participants to compare the two perspectives directly. For this questionnaire we surveyed a group of internists, psychiatrists, and pediatricians who had advanced training in both clinical medicine and health-services research. For each scenario the participants indicated whether they thought that physicians were more likely to recommend a particular action from the individual-patient perspective or the general-policy perspective. We presented, for example, the following scenario: "A 25-year-old man who rides a motorcycle is being seen for routine medical reasons. From which perspective do you think the option of discussing organ donation is more likely to be recommended?"

In our third experiment, we asked undergraduate students at Stanford to consider a hypothetical medical case that could be understood without technical knowledge. As in the first experiment, half the students were presented with the individual version, and half the aggregate version. Participants in all three experiments received the questionnaires, completed them at their leisure, and then returned them anonymously.

Results

Experiment 1
In the first experiment, 59 house officers returned completed questionnaires, as did 94 university-affiliated physicians, 75 HMO physicians, and 128 physicians associated with the county hospital. The overall rate of response was 78 percent. As expected, the two groups that had received the different versions of the questionnaire were similar in age, sex, experience, and rate of response. The four issues we have raised are discussed below.

Blood Test   To explore the first issue, we asked the physicians to consider the scenario of a college student presenting with fatigue, insomnia, and difficulty in concentrating. In addition to the usual evaluation we described an extra blood test that might detect a rare, treatable condition but that entailed a $20 cost, which the student would have to pay out of pocket. The physicians chose to perform the test more frequently when given the individual version, which referred to one patient, than when given the aggregate version, which referred to a group of patients (30 vs. 17 percent; $P < 0.005$). The difference was evident among the house staff (26 vs. 4 percent; $P < 0.05$), the HMO physicians (28 vs. 7 percent; $P < 0.10$), the academic physicians (40 vs. 19 percent; $P < 0.01$), and doctors at the county hospital (43 vs. 22 percent; $P < 0.05$).

Telephone Medicine   To explore the second, we asked the physicians to consider the scenario of an otherwise healthy young woman who calls her family doctor because of a persistent mild fever. The physicians recommended following by telephone, rather than asking the patient to come in for an examination, more frequently in the aggregate version than in the individual version (13 vs. 9 percent; $P < 0.005$). The difference was evident among the academic physicians (15 vs. 6 percent; P < 0.01) and the doctors at the county hospital (12 vs. 2 percent; P < 0.05), but not among the HMO physicians (14 vs. 24 percent; P not significant). The house staff were not presented with this scenario.

Experiment 2

In contrast with the physicians in experiment 1, who each evaluated only one version of a problem, the physicians in experiment 2 compared the aggregate and the individual perspectives directly. A total of 89 completed questionnaires were returned, representing a rate of response of 77 percent. The results confirmed the findings of our first experiment. In the case of the college student with fatigue, 81 percent of the respondents (P < 0.005) thought that the additional test would be recommended more frequently if considered from the individual rather than the aggregate perspective. In the case of the young woman with a fever, 87 percent of the respondents (P < 0.005) thought that the option of following by telephone would be selected more frequently from the group perspective.

Organ Donation   To explore the third issue, we also presented the health-service researchers with the scenario of a healthy motorcycle rider who was being seen for a minor medical problem. When asked about discussing organ donation, 93 percent of the respondents (P < 0.005) thought that it would be recommended more frequently from the aggregate perspective.

Adverse Outcomes   To explore the fourth issue, we presented the health-service researchers with a scenario of a woman with a blood condition. We described a medication, which could be added to her therapy, that sometimes improves longevity but sometimes makes things worse. The medication offered an 85 percent chance of adding two years to her life and a 15 percent chance of shortening it by two years. In this case, 59 percent of the respondents (P < 0.10) thought that the medication would be recommended more frequently from the individual perspective.

Experiment 3

This experiment tested whether the difference between the perspectives was also evident in the judgments of lay people. A total of 327 students were presented with the adverse-outcomes scenario, selected because it involved no technical knowledge of medicine. As in the first experiment, each student received either the individual or the aggregate version. In accordance with our previous finding, the medication was recommended more frequently by those given the individual version than by those given the aggregate version (62 vs. 42 percent; P < 0.005).

Discussion

Our results indicate that physicians make different decisions when evaluating an individual patient than when considering a group of comparable patients (experiment 1). This discrepancy is recognized as a professional norm (experiment 2) and is also found in the judgments of lay people (experiment 3). We explored four issues that highlight the discrepancy. From the individual as compared with the aggregate perspective, physicians are more likely to order an additional test, expend time directly assessing a patient, avoid raising some troubling issues, and recommend a therapy with a high probability of success but the chance of an adverse outcome.

The discrepancy between the aggregate and individual perspectives demonstrated in these experiments cannot be attributed to differences in either medical information or economic incentives; hence it is difficult to explain on normative grounds.[18,19] Our results are consistent with the notion that physicians give more weight to the personal concerns of patients when considering them as individuals and more weight to general criteria of effectiveness when considering them as a group. For example, the responses to our adverse-outcomes scenario suggest that small probabilities are taken less seriously when deciding about just one case. Such differences in giving weight to various aspects of a problem may help to explain why general principles, which reflect a group perspective, are not always followed in clinical practice, which proceeds on a case-by-case basis. As a consequence, the discrepancy between the aggregate and individual perspectives may create tension between health policy makers and medical practitioners even when the pertinent facts are accepted by both.

Several characteristics of medical decision making may amplify the discrepancy between perspectives. Schelling has discussed the distinction between statistical lives and identified lives, emphasizing the higher value society places on the life of an identified person.[20] Fuchs has suggested a "technologic imperative" in doctor–patient relationships that reflects physicians' desires to do everything they have been trained to do in treating individual patients.[21] Evans has addressed the physician's conflict between being a perfect agent for the patient and being the protector of society.[22] Financial incentives, of course, may also contribute to the tension between policy and practice.[23,24]

Although the discrepancy between the aggregate and individual perspectives calls for resolution, we do not suggest discarding either perspective. The individual perspective emphasizes the particular concerns of the patient and is more in accord with the personal nature of the doctor–patient relationship. The aggregate perspective acknowledges the fact that over time doctors will treat many similar patients. Physicians and policy makers may wish to examine problems from both perspectives to ensure that treatment decisions are appropriate whether applied to one or to many patients. An awareness of the two perspectives may enhance clinical judgment and enrich health policy.

Note

We are indebted to Tammy Tengs, Joan Esplin, Marcus Krupp, Edward Harris, Eliott Wolfe, and Patrick Kearns for assistance with the questionnaires; to Halsted Holman, Dianna Dutton, Alan Garber, Robert Wachter, and Mitchel Wilson for help in preparing the manuscript; and to our respondents for their thoughtful effort.

References

1. Chassin MR, Brook RH, Park RE, et al. Variations in the use of medical and surgical services by the Medicare population. N Engl J Med 1986; 314:285–290.

2. Wennberg J. Which rate is right? N Engl J Med 1986; 314:310–311.

3. Iglehart JK, ed. Variations in medical practice. Health Aff (Millwood) 1984; 3(2):6–148.

4. Woo B, Woo B, Cook EF, Weisberg M, Goldman L. Screening procedures in the asymptomatic adult: comparison of physicians' recommendations, patients' desires, published guidelines, and actual practice. JAMA 1985; 254:1480–1484.

5. Kosecoff J, Kanouse DE, Rogers WH, McCloskey L, Winslow CM, Brook RH. Effects of the National Institutes of Health Consensus Development Program on physician practice. JAMA 1987; 258:2708–2713.

6. Eddy DM. Clinical policies and the quality of clinical practice. N Engl J Med 1982; 307:343–347.

7. Lomas J, Anderson GM, Domnick-Pierre K, Vayda E, Enkin MW, Hannah WJ. Do practice guidelines guide practice? The effect of a consensus statement on the practice of physicians. N Engl J Med 1989; 321:1306–1311.

8. Woolley FR. Ethical issues in the implantation of the total artificial heart. N Engl J Med 1984; 310:292–296.

9. Bunker JP. When the medical interests of society are in conflict with those of the individual, who wins? Pharos 1976; 39(1):64–66.

10. Levinsky NG. The doctor's master. N Engl J Med 1984; 311:1573–1575.

11. Samuelson PA. Risk and uncertainty: a fallacy of large numbers. Scientia 1963; 98:108–113.

12. Keren G, Wagenaar WA. Violation of expected utility theory in unique and repeated gambles. J Exp Psychol [Learn Mem Cogn] 1987; 13:382–391.

13. Montgomery H, Adelbratt T. Gambling decisions and information about expected value. Organ Behav Hum Performance 1982; 29:39–57.

14. McNeil BJ, Pauker SG, Sox HC Jr, Tversky A. On the elicitation of preferences for alternative therapies. N Engl J Med 1982; 306:1259–1262.

15. Eraker SA, Sox HC Jr. Assessment of patients' preferences for therapeutic outcomes. Med Decis Making 1981; 1:29–39.

16. Tversky A, Kahneman D. Rational choice and the framing of decisions. J Bus 1986; 59:S251–S278.

17. Moses LE. Think and explain with statistics. Reading, Mass.: Addison-Wesley, 1986.

18. Sox HC Jr, Blatt MA, Higgins MC, Marton KI. Medical decision making. Boston: Butterworths, 1988.

19. Raiffa H. Decision analysis. Reading, Mass.: Addison–Wesley, 1968.

20. Schelling TC. The life you save may be your own. In: Chase SB Jr, ed. Problems in public expenditure analysis. Washington, D.C.: Brookings Institution, 1968.

21. Fuchs VR. Who shall live? Health, economics, and social choice. New York: Basic Books, 1974.

22. Evans RW. Health care technology and the inevitability of resource allocation and rationing decisions. JAMA 1983; 249:2208–2219.

23. Bock RS. The pressure to keep prices high at a walk-in clinic: a personal experience. N Engl J Med 1988; 319:785–787.

24. Scovern H. Hired help: a physician's experiences in a for-profit staff-model HMO. N Engl J Med 1988; 319:787–790.

37 Loss Aversion in Riskless Choice: A Reference-Dependent Model

Amos Tversky and Daniel Kahneman

The standard models of decision making assume that preferences do not depend on current assets. This assumption greatly simplifies the analysis of individual choice and the prediction of trades: indifference curves are drawn without reference to current holdings, and the Coase theorem asserts that, except for transaction costs, initial entitlements do not affect final allocations. The facts of the matter are more complex. There is substantial evidence that initial entitlements do matter and that the rate of exchange between goods can be quite different depending on which is acquired and which is given up, even in the absence of transaction costs or income effects. In accord with a psychological analysis of value, reference levels play a large role in determining preferences. In the present paper we review the evidence for this proposition and offer a theory that generalizes the standard model by introducing a reference state.

The present analysis of riskless choice extends our treatment of choice under uncertainty [Kahneman and Tversky, 1979, 1984; Tversky and Kahneman, 1991], in which the outcomes of risky prospects are evaluated by a value function that has three essential characteristics. *Reference dependence:* the carriers of value are gains and losses defined relative to a reference point. *Loss aversion:* the function is steeper in the negative than in the positive domain; losses loom larger than corresponding gains. *Diminishing sensitivity:* the marginal value of both gains and losses decreases with their size. These properties give rise to an asymmetric S-shaped value function, concave above the reference point and convex below it, as illustrated in figure 37.1.

In this article we apply reference dependence, loss aversion, and diminishing sensitivity to the analysis of riskless choice. To motivate this analysis, we begin with a review of selected experimental demonstrations.

Empirical Evidence

The examples discussed in this section are analyzed by reference to figure 37.2. In every case we consider two options x and y that differ on two valued dimensions and show how the choice between them is affected by the reference point from which they are evaluated. The common reason for these reversals of preference is that the relative weight of the differences between x and y on dimensions 1 and 2 varies with the location of the reference value on these attributes. Loss aversion implies that the impact of a difference on a dimension is generally greater when that difference is evaluated as a loss than when the same difference is evaluated as a gain. Diminishing

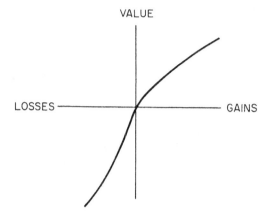

Figure 37.1
An illustration of a value function.

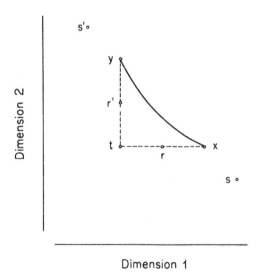

Figure 37.2
Multiple reference points for the choice between x and y.

sensitivity implies that the impact of a difference is attenuated when both options are remote from the reference point for the relevant dimension. This simple scheme serves to organize a large set of observations. Although isolated findings may be subject to alternative interpretations, the entire body of evidence provides strong support for the phenomenon of loss aversion.

a. Instant Endowment.   An immediate consequence of loss aversion is that the loss of utility associated with giving up a valued good is greater than the utility gain associated with receiving it. Thaler [1980] labeled this discrepancy the endowment effect, because value appears to change when a good is incorporated into one's endowment. Kahneman, Knetsch, and Thaler [1990] tested the endowment effect in a series of experiments, conducted in a classroom setting. In one of these experiments a decorated mug (retail value of about $5) was placed in front of one third of the seats after students had chosen their places. All participants received a questionnaire. The form given to the recipients of a mug (the "sellers") indicated that "You now own the object in your possession. You have the option of selling it if a price, which will be determined later, is acceptable to you. For each of the possible prices below indicate whether you wish to (x) Sell your object and receive this price; (y) Keep your object and take it home with you. . . ." The subjects indicated their decision for prices ranging from $0.50 to $9.50 in steps of 50 cents. Some of the students who had not received a mug (the "choosers") were given a similar questionnaire, informing them that they would have the option of receiving either a mug or a sum of money to be determined later. They indicated their preferences between a mug and sums of money ranging from $0.50 to $9.50.

The choosers and the sellers face precisely the same decision problem, but their reference states differ. As shown in figure 37.2, the choosers' reference state is t, and they face a positive choice between two options that dominate t; receiving a mug or receiving a sum in cash. The sellers evaluate the same options from y; they must choose between retaining the status quo (the mug) or giving up the mug in exchange for money. Thus, the mug is evaluated as a gain by the choosers, and as a loss by the sellers. Loss aversion entails that the rate of exchange of the mug against money will be different in the two cases. Indeed, the median value of the mug was $7.12 for the sellers and $3.12 for the choosers in one experiment, $7.00 and $3.50 in another. The difference between these values reflects an endowment effect which is produced, apparently instantaneously, by giving an individual property rights over a consumption good.

The interpretation of the endowment effect may be illuminated by the following thought experiment.

Imagine that as a chooser you prefer \$4 over a mug. You learn that most sellers prefer the mug to \$6, and you believe that if you had the mug you would do the same. In light of this knowledge, would you now prefer the mug over \$5?

If you do, it is presumably because you have changed your assessment of the pleasure associated with owning the mug. If you still prefer \$4 over the mug—which we regard as a more likely response—this indicates that you interpret the effect of endowment as an aversion to giving up your mug rather than as an unanticipated increase in the pleasure of owning it.

b. Status Quo Bias.   The retention of the status quo is an option in many decision problems. As illustrated by the analysis of the sellers' problem in the example of the mugs, loss aversion induces a bias that favors the retention of the status quo over other options. In figure 37.2, a decision maker who is indifferent between x and y from t will prefer x over y from x, and y over x from y. Samuelson and Zeckhauser [1988] introduced the term "status quo bias" for this effect of reference position.

Knetsch and Sinden [1984] and Knetsch [1989] have offered compelling experimental demonstrations of the status quo bias. In the latter study two undergraduate classes were required to answer a brief questionnaire. Students in one of the classes were immediately given a decorated mug as compensation; students in another class received a large bar of Swiss chocolate. At the end of the session students in both classes were shown the alternative gift and were allowed the option of trading the gift they had received for the other, by raising a card with the word "Trade" written on it. Although the transaction cost associated with the change was surely slight, approximately 90 percent of the participants retained the gift they had received.

Samuelson and Zeckhauser [1988] documented the status quo bias in a wide range of decisions, including hypothetical choices about jobs, automobile color, financial investments, and policy issues. Alternative versions of each problem were presented to different subjects: each option was designated as the status quo in one of these versions; one (neutral) version did not single out any option. The number of options presented for each problem was systematically varied. The results were analyzed by regressing the proportions of subjects choosing an option designated as status quo $P(SQ)$, or an alternative to the status quo $P(ASQ)$, on the choice proportions for the same options in the neutral version $P(N)$. The results were well described by the equations,

$$P(SQ) = 0.17 + 0.83P(N) \quad \text{and} \quad P(ASQ) = 0.83P(N).$$

The difference (0.17) between $P(SQ)$ and $P(ASQ)$ is a measure of the status quo bias in this experiment.

Samuelson and Zeckhauser [1988] also obtained evidence of status quo bias in a field study of the choice of medical plans by Harvard employees. They found that a new medical plan is generally more likely to be chosen by new employees than by employees hired before that plan became available—in spite of the yearly opportunity to review the decision and the minimal cost of changing it. Furthermore, small changes from the status quo were favored over larger changes: enrollees who did transfer from the originally most popular Blue Cross/Blue Shield plan tended to favor a new variant of that plan over other new alternatives. Samuelson and Zeckhauser also observed that the allocations of pension reserves to TIAA and CREF tend to be very stable from year to year, in spite of large variations in rate of return. They invoked the status quo bias as an explanation of brand loyalty and pioneer firm advantage, and noted that rational models that ignore status quo effects "will present excessively radical conclusions, exaggerating individuals' responses to changing economic variables and predicting greater instability than is observed in the world" [p. 47].

Loss aversion implies the status quo bias. As noted by Samuelson and Zeckhauser [1988], however, there are several factors, such as costs of thinking, transaction costs, and psychological commitment to prior choices that can induce a status quo bias even in the absence of loss aversion.

c. Improvements versus Tradeoffs.   Consider the evaluation of the options x and y in figure 37.2 from the reference points r and r'. When evaluated from r, option x is simply a gain (improvement) on dimension 1, whereas y combines a gain in dimension 2 with a loss in dimension 1. These relations are reversed when the same options are evaluated from r'. Considerations of loss aversion suggest that x is more likely to be preferred from r than from r'.

Ninety undergraduates took part in a study designed to test this hypothesis. They received written instructions indicating that some participants, selected at random, would receive a gift package. For half the participants (the dinner group) the gift consisted of "one free dinner at MacArthur Park Restaurant and a monthly Stanford calendar." For the other half (the photo group) the gift was "one 8 × 10 professional photo portrait and a monthly Stanford calendar." All subjects were informed that some of the winners, again selected at random, would be given an opportunity to exchange the original gift for one of the following options:

x: two free dinners at MacArthur Park Restaurant

y: one 8 × 10 professional photo portrait plus two 5 × 7 and three wallet size prints.

The subjects were asked to indicate whether they preferred to (i) keep the original gift, (ii) exchange it for x, or (iii) exchange it for y. If people are averse to giving up the reference gift, as implied by loss aversion, then the preference for a dinner-for-two (x) over multiple photos (y) should be more common among the subjects whose reference gift was a dinner-for-one (r) than among subjects whose reference gift was the single photo (r'). The results confirmed this prediction. Only ten participants chose to keep the original gift. Among the remaining subjects, option x was selected by 81 percent of the dinner group and by 52 percent of the photo group ($p < 0.01$).

d. Advantages and Disadvantages. In our next demonstration a combination of a small gain and a small loss is compared with a combination of a larger gain and a larger loss. Loss aversion implies that the same difference between two options will be given greater weight if it is viewed as a difference between two disadvantages (relative to a reference state) than if it is viewed as a difference between two advantages. In the representation of figure 37.2, x is more likely to be preferred over y from s than from s', because the difference between x and y in dimension 1 involves disadvantages relative to s and advantages relative to s'. A similar argument applies to dimension 2. In a test of this prediction subjects answered one of two versions of the following question:

Imagine that as part of your professional training you were assigned to a part-time job. The training is now ending, and you must look for employment. You consider two possibilities. They are like your training job in most respects except for the amount of social contact and the convenience of commuting to and from work. To compare the two jobs to each other and to the present one, you have made up the following table:

	Social contact	Daily travel time
Present job	isolated for long stretches	10 min.
Job x	limited contact with others	20 min.
Job y	moderately sociable	60 min.

The second version of this problem included the same options x and y, but a different reference job (s'), described by the following attributes: "much pleasant social interaction and 80 minutes of daily commuting time."

In the first version both options are superior to the current reference job on the dimension of social contact and both are inferior in commuting time. The different amounts of social contact in jobs x and y are evaluated as advantages (gains), whereas the commuting times are evaluated as disadvantages (losses). These relations are reversed in the second version. Loss aversion implies that a given difference between two options will generally have greater impact when it is evaluated as a difference between two losses (disadvantages) than when it is viewed as a difference between two gains (or advantages). This prediction was confirmed: Job x was chosen by 70 percent of the participants in version 1 and by only 33 percent of the participants in version 2 ($N = 106$, $p < 0.01$).

Reference Dependence

In order to interpret the reversals of preference that are induced by shifts of reference, we introduce, as a primitive concept, a preference relation indexed to a given reference state. As in the standard theory, we begin with a choice set $X = \{x, y, z, \ldots\}$ and assume, for simplicity, that it is isomorphic to the positive quadrant of the real plane, including its boundaries. Each option, $x = (x_1, x_2)$ in X, $x_1, x_2 \geq 0$, is interpreted as a bundle that offers x_1 units of good 1 and x_2 units of good 2, or as an activity characterized by its levels on two dimensions of value. The extension to more than two dimensions is straightforward.

A *reference structure* is a family of indexed preference relations, where $x \geq_r y$ is interpreted as x is weakly preferred to y from reference state r. The relations $>_r$ and $=_r$ correspond to strict preference and indifference, respectively. Throughout this article we assume that each $\geq_r$, $r \in X$, satisfies the standard assumptions of the classical theory. Specifically, we assume that $\geq_r$ is complete, transitive, and continuous; that is, $\{x: x \geq_r y\}$ and $\{x: y \geq_r x\}$ are closed for any y. Furthermore, each preference order is strictly monotonic in the sense that $x \geq_r y$ and $x \neq y$ imply that $x >_r y$. Under these assumptions each $\geq_r$ can be represented by a strictly increasing continuous utility function U_r (see, e.g., Varian [1984], ch. 3).

Because the standard theory does not recognize the special role of the reference state, it implicitly assumes *reference independence*; that is, $x \geq_r y$ iff $x \geq_s y$ for all $x, y, r, s \in X$. This property, however, was consistently violated in the preceding experiments. To accommodate these observations, we describe individual choice not by a single preference order but by a family or a book of indexed preference orders $\{\geq_r: r \in X\}$. For convenience, we use the letters r, s to denote reference states and x, y to denote options, although they are all elements of X.

A treatment of reference-dependent choice raises two questions: what is the reference state, and how does it affect preferences? The present analysis focuses on the second question. We assume that the decision maker has a definite reference state in X, and we investigate its impact on the choice between options. The question of the origin and the determinants of the reference state lies beyond the scope of the present article. Although the reference state usually corresponds to the decision maker's current position, it can also be influenced by aspirations, expectations, norms, and social comparisons [Easterlin, 1974; van Praag, 1971; van de Stadt, Kapteyn, and van de Geer, 1985].

In the present section we first define loss aversion and diminishing sensitivity in terms of the preference orders $\geq_r$, $r \in X$. Next we introduce the notion of a decomposable reference function and characterize the concept of constant loss aversion. Finally, we discuss some empirical estimates of the coefficient of loss aversion.

Loss Aversion

The basic intuition concerning loss aversion is that losses (outcomes below the reference state) loom larger than corresponding gains (outcomes above the reference state). Because a shift of reference can turn gains into losses and vice versa, it can give rise to reversals of preference, as implied by the following definition.

A reference structure satisfies *loss aversion* (LA) if the following condition holds for all x, y, r, s in X. Suppose that $x_1 \geq r_1 > s_1 = y_1$, $y_2 > x_2$ and $r_2 = s_2$; see figure 37.3. Then $x =_s y$ implies that $x >_r y$; the same holds if the subscripts 1 and 2 are interchanged throughout. (Note that the relations $>$ and $=$ refer to the numerical components of the options; whereas $>_r$ and $=_r$ refer to the preference between options in reference state r.) Loss aversion implies that the slope of the indifference curve through y is steeper when y is evaluated from r than when it is evaluated from s. In other words, $U_r^*(y) > U_s^*(y)$, where $U_r^*(y)$ is the marginal rate of substitution of U_r at y.

To motivate the definition of loss aversion, it is instructive to restate it in terms of advantages and disadvantages, relative to a reference point r. An ordered pair $[x_i, r_i]$, $i = 1, 2$, is called an advantage or a disadvantage, respectively, if $x_i > r_i$, or $x_i < r_i$. We use brackets to distinguish between the pair $[x_i, r_i]$ and the two-dimensional option (x_1, x_2). Suppose that there exist real-valued functions v_1, v_2 such that $U_r(x)$ can be expressed as $U(v_1[x_1, r_1], v_2[x_2, r_2])$. To simplify matters, suppose that $x_1 = r_1$ and $x_2 > r_2$, as in figure 37.3. Hence, $x =_s y$ implies that the combination of the two advantages, $[x_1, s_1]$ and $[x_2, s_2]$, relative to the reference state s, has the same impact as the combination of the advantage $[y_2, s_2]$ and the null interval $[y_1, y_1]$. Similarly, $x >_r y$ implies that the combination of the advantage $[x_2, r_2]$ and the null interval $[x_1, x_1]$ has greater impact than the combination of the advantage $[y_2, r_2]$ and the disadvantage $[y_1, r_1]$. As the reference state shifts from s to r, therefore, the disadvantage $[y_1, r_1] = [s_1, r_1]$, enters into the evaluation of y, and the advantage $[x_1, s_1] = [r_1, s_1]$ is deleted from the evaluation of x. But since $[s_1, r_1]$ and $[r_1, s_1]$ differ by sign only, loss aversion implies that the introduction of a disadvantage has a

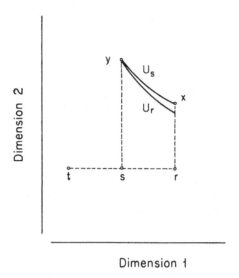

Figure 37.3
A graphic illustration of loss aversion.

bigger effect than the deletion of the corresponding advantage. A similar argument applies to the case where $x_1 > r_1 > s_1$.

The present notion of loss aversion accounts for the endowment effect and the status quo bias described in the preceding section. Consider the effect of different reference points on the preference between x and y, as illustrated in figure 37.2. Loss aversion entails that a decision maker who is indifferent between x and y from t will prefer x over y from x, and y over x from y. That is, $x =_t y$ implies that $x >_x y$ and $y >_y x$. This explains the different valuations of a good by sellers and choosers and other manifestations of the status quo bias.

Diminishing Sensitivity
Recall that, according to the value function of figure 37.1, marginal value decreases with the distance from the reference point. For example, the difference between a yearly salary of \$60,000 and a yearly salary of \$70,000 has a bigger impact when current salary is \$50,000 than when it is \$40,000. A reference structure satisfies *diminishing sensitivity* (DS) if the following condition holds for all x, y, s, t in X. Suppose that $x_1 > y_1$, $y_2 > x_2$, $s_2 = t_2$, and either $y_1 \geq s_1 \geq t_1$ or $t_1 \geq s_1 \geq x_1$; see figure 37.3. Then $y =_s x$ implies that $y \geq_t x$; the same holds if the subscripts 1 and 2 are interchanged throughout. *Constant sensitivity* is satisfied if the same hypotheses

imply that $y =_t x$. DS states that the sensitivity to a given difference on a dimension is smaller when the reference point is distant than when it is near. It follows from DS that the slope of the indifference curve through x is steeper when evaluated from s than from t, or $U_s^*(x) > U_t^*(x)$. It is important to distinguish between the present notion of diminishing sensitivity, which pertains to the effect of the reference state, and the standard assumption of diminishing marginal utility. Although the two hypotheses are conceptually similar, they are logically independent. In particular, diminishing sensitivity does not imply that the indifference curves are concave below the reference point.

Each reference state r partitions X into four quadrants defined by treating r as the origin. A pair of options, x and y, belong to the same quadrant with respect to r whenever $x_i \geq r_i$ iff $y_i \geq r_i$, $i = 1, 2$. A reference structure satisfies *sign dependence* if for all x, y, r, s in X $x \geq_r y$ iff $x \geq_s y$ whenever (i) x and y belong to the same quadrant with respect to r and with respect to s, and (ii) r and s belong to the same quadrant with respect to x and with respect to y. This condition implies that reference independence can be violated only when a change in reference turns a gain into a loss or vice versa. It is easy to verify that sign dependence is equivalent to constant sensitivity. Although sign dependence may not hold in general, it serves as a useful approximation whenever the curvature induced by the reference state is not very pronounced.

The assumption of diminishing (or constant) sensitivity allows us to extend the implications of loss aversion to reference states that do not coincide with x or y on either dimension. Consider the choice between x and y in figure 37.4. Note that r is dominated by x but not by y, whereas s is dominated by y but not by x. Let t be the meet of r and s; that is, $t_i = \min(r_i, s_i)$, $i = 1, 2$. It follows from loss aversion and diminishing sensitivity that if $x =_t y$, then $x >_r y$ and $y >_s x$. Thus, x is more likely to be chosen over y when evaluated from r than when evaluated form s. This proposition is illustrated by our earlier observation that a gift was more attractive when evaluated as a moderate improvement on one attribute than when evaluated as a combination of a large improvement and a loss (see example c above).

Consider two exchangeable individuals (i.e., hedonic twins), each of whom holds position t, with low status and low pay; see figure 37.4. Suppose that both are indifferent between position x (very high status, moderate pay) and position y (very high pay, moderate status). Imagine now that both individuals move to new positions, which become their respective reference points; one individual moves to r (high status, low pay), and the other moves to s (high pay, low status). LA and DS imply that the person who moved to r now prefers x, whereas the person who moved to s now prefers y, because they are reluctant to give up either salary or status.

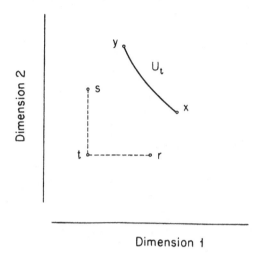

Figure 37.4
An illustration of reference-dependent preferences.

Constant Loss Aversion

The present section introduces additional assumptions that constrain the relation among preference orders evaluated from different reference points. A reference structure $(X, \geq_r)$, $r \in X$, is *decomposable* if there exists a real-valued function U, increasing in each argument, such that for each $r \in X$, there exist increasing functions $R_i : X_i \to$ Reals, $i = 1, 2$ satisfying

$$U_r(x_1, x_2) = U(R_1(x_1), R_2(x_2)).$$

The functions R_i are called the reference functions associated with reference state r. In this model the effect of the reference point is captured by separate monotonic transformations of the two axes. Decomposability has testable implications. For example, suppose that U_r is additive; that is, $U_r(x_1, x_2) = R_1(x_1) + R_2(x_2)$. It follows then that, for any $s \in X$, U_s is also additive although the respective scales may not be linearly related.

In this section we focus on a special case of decomposability in which the reference functions assume an especially simple form. A reference structure $(X, \geq_r)$ satisfies *constant loss aversion* if there exist functions $u_i : X_i \to$ Reals, constants $\lambda_i > 0$, $i = 1, 2$, and a function U such that $U_r(x_1, x_2) = U(R_1(x_1), R_2(x_2))$, where

$$R_i(x_i) = \begin{cases} u_i(x_i) - u_i(r_i) & \text{if } x_i \geq r_i \\ (u_i(x_i) - u_i(r_i))/\lambda_i & \text{if } x_i < r_i. \end{cases}$$

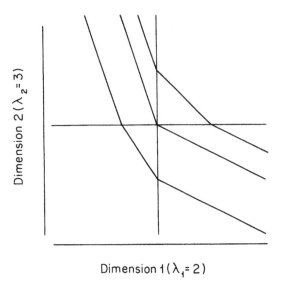

Figure 37.5
A set of indifference curves illustrating constant loss aversion.

Thus, the change in the preference order induced by a shift of reference is described in terms of two constants, λ_1 and λ_2, which can be interpreted as the coefficients of loss aversion for dimensions 1 and 2, respectively. Figure 37.5 illustrates constant loss aversion, with $\lambda_1 = 2$ and $\lambda_2 = 3$. For simplicity, we selected a linear utility function, but this is not essential.

Although we do not have an axiomatic characterization of constant loss aversion in general, we characterize below the special case where U is additive, called additive constant loss aversion. This case is important because additivity serves as a good approximation in many contexts. Indeed, some of the commonly used utility functions (e.g., Cobb-Douglas, or CES) are additive. Recall that a family of indifference curves is additive if the axes can be monotonically transformed so that the indifference curves become parallel straight lines. The following cancellation condition, also called the Thomsen condition, is both necessary and sufficient for additivity in the present context [Debreu, 1960; Krantz, Luce, Suppes, and Tversky, 1971].

For all $x_1, y_1, z_1 \in X_1$, $x_2, y_2, z_2 \in X_2$, and $r \in X$,

    if $(x_1, z_2) \geq_r (z_1, y_2)$ and $(z_1, x_2) \geq_r (y_1, z_2)$, then $(x_1, x_2) \geq_r (y_1, y_2)$.

Assuming cancellation for each $\geq_r$, we obtain an additive representation for each reference state. In order to relate the separate additive representations to each other,

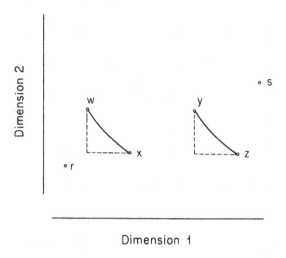

Figure 37.6
A graphic illustration of reference interlocking.

we introduce the following axiom. Consider $w, w', x, x', y, y', z, z'$ in X that (i) belong to the same quadrant with respect to r as well as with respect to s, and (ii) satisfy $w_1 = w_1'$, $x_1 = x_1'$, $y_1 = y_1'$, $z_1 = z_1'$ and $x_2 = z_2$, $w_2 = y_2$, $x_2' = z_2'$, $w_2' = y_2'$; see figure 37.6. A reference structure $(X, \geq_r)$, $r \in X$, satisfies *reference interlocking* if, assuming (i) and (ii) above, $w =_r x$, $y =_r z$ and $w' =_s x'$ imply that $y' =_s z'$. Essentially the same condition was invoked by Tversky, Sattah, and Slovic [1988] in the treatment of preference reversals, and by Wakker [1988] and Tversky and Kahneman [1991] in the analysis of decision under uncertainty.

To appreciate the content of reference interlocking, note that, in the presence of additivity, indifference can be interpreted as a matching of an interval on one dimension to an interval on the second dimension. For example, the observation $w =_r x$ indicates that the interval $[x_1, w_1]$ on the first dimension matches the interval $[w_2, x_2]$ on the second dimension. Similarly, $y =_r z$ indicates that $[z_1, y_1]$ matches $[y_2, z_2]$. But since $[w_2, x_2]$ and $[y_2, z_2]$ are identical by construction (see figure 37.6), we conclude that $[x_1, w_1]$ matches $[z_1, y_1]$. In this manner we can match two intervals on the *same* dimension by matching each of them to an interval on the *other* dimension. Reference interlocking states that if two intradimensional intervals are matched as gains, they are also matched as losses. It is easy to verify that reference interlocking follows from additive constant loss aversion. Furthermore, the following theorem shows that in the presence of cancellation and sign-dependence, reference interlocking is not only necessary but it is also sufficient for additive constant loss aversion.

THEOREM.   A reference structure $(X, \geq_r)$, $r \in X$, satisfies additive constant loss aversion iff it satisfies cancellation, sign-dependence, and reference interlocking.

The proof of the theorem is presented in the appendix. An estimate of the coefficients of loss aversion can be derived from an experiment described earlier, in which two groups of subjects assigned a monetary value to the same consumption good: sellers who were given the good and the option of selling it, and choosers who were given the option of receiving the good or a sum of money [Kahneman, Knetsch, and Thaler, 1990]. The median value of the mug for sellers was $7.12 and $7.00 in two separate replications of the experiments; choosers valued the same object at $3.12 and $3.50. According to the present analysis, the sellers and the choosers differ only in that the former evaluate the mug as a loss, the latter as a gain. If the value of money is linear in that range, the coefficient of loss aversion for the mug in these experiments was slightly greater than two.

There is an intriguing convergence between this estimate of the coefficient of loss aversion and estimates derived from decisions under risk. Such estimates can be obtained by observing the ratio G/L that makes an even chance to gain G or lose L just acceptable. We have observed a ratio of just over 2:1 in several experiments. In one gambling experiment with real payoffs, for example, a 50-50 bet to win $25 or lose $10 was barely acceptable, yielding a ratio of 2.5:1. Similar values were obtained from hypothetical choices regarding the acceptability of larger gambles, over a range of several hundred dollars [Tversky and Kahneman, 1990]. Although the convergence of estimates should be interpreted with caution, these findings suggest that a loss aversion coefficient of about two may explain both risky and riskless choices involving monetary outcomes and consumption goods.

Recall that the coefficient of loss aversion could vary across dimensions, as illustrated in figure 37.5. We surmise that the coefficient of loss aversion associated with different dimensions reflects the importance or prominence of these dimensions [Tversky, Sattath, and Slovic, 1988]. For example, loss aversion appears to be more pronounced for safety than for money [Viscusi, Magat, and Huber, 1987], and more pronounced for income than for leisure.

Implications of Loss Aversion

Loss aversion is an important component of a phenomenon that has been much discussed in recent years: the large disparity often observed between the minimal amount that people are willing to accept (WTA) to give up a good they own and the maximal amount they would be willing to pay (WTP) to acquire it. Other potential sources of this discrepancy include income effect, strategic behavior, and the legitimacy of transactions. The buying-selling discrepancy was initially observed in hypothetical questions involving public goods (see Cummings, Brookshire, and Schulze [1986], for a review), but it has also been confirmed in real exchanges [Heberlein and Bishop, 1985; Kahneman, Knetsch, and Thaler, 1990; Loewenstein, 1988]. It also survived, albeit reduced, in experiments that attempted to eliminate it by the discipline of market experience [Brookshire and Coursey, 1987; Coursey, Hovis, and Schulze, 1987]; see also Knetsch and Sinden [1984, 1987]. Kahneman, Knetsch, and Thaler [1990] showed that the disparate valuations of consumption goods by owners and by potential buyers inhibits trade. They endowed half the participants with a consumption good (e.g., a mug) and set up a market for that good. Because the mugs were allocated at random, standard theory predicts that half the sellers should trade their mugs to buyers who value them more. The actual volume of trade was consistently observed to be about half the predicted amount. Control experiments in which subjects traded tokens redeemable for cash produced nearly perfect efficiency and no disparity between the values assigned by buyers and sellers.

A trade involves two dimensions, and loss aversion may operate on one or both. Thus, the present analysis suggests two ways in which loss aversion could contribute to the disparity between WTA and WTP. The individual who states WTA for a good considers giving it up; the individual who states WTP for that good considers acquiring it. If there is loss aversion for the good, the owner will be reluctant to sell. If the buyer views the money spent on the purchase as a loss, there will be reluctance to buy. The relative magnitude of the two effects can be estimated by comparing sellers and buyers to choosers, who are given a choice between the good and cash, and are therefore not susceptible to loss aversion. Results of several comparisons indicated that the reluctance to sell is much greater than the reluctance to buy [Kahneman, Knetsch, and Thaler, 1990]. The buyers in these markets do not appear to value the money they give up in a transaction as a loss. These observations are consistent with the standard theory of consumer choice, in which the decision of whether or not to purchase a good is treated as a choice between it and other goods that could be purchased instead.

Loss aversion is certainly not involved in the exchange of a $5 bill for $5, because the transaction is evaluated by its net outcome. Similarly, reluctance to sell is surely absent in routine commercial transactions, in which goods held for sale have the status of tokens for money. However, the present analysis implies that asymmetric evaluations of gains and losses will affect the responses of both buyers and sellers to changes of price of profit, relative to the reference levels established in prior transactions [Kahneman, Knetsch, and Thaler, 1986; Winer, 1986]. The response to changes is expected to be more intense when the changes are unfavorable (losses) than when they are for the better. Putler [1988] developed an analysis of demand that incorporates an asymmetric effect of price increases and decreases. He tested the model by estimating separate demand elasticities for increases and for decreases in the retail price of shell eggs, relative to a reference price estimated from the series of earlier prices. The estimated elasticities were −1.10 for price increases and −0.45 for price decreases, indicating that price increases have a significantly greater impact on consumer decisions. (This analysis assumes that the availability of substitutes eliminates loss aversion in the response to the reduced consumption of eggs.) A similar result was observed in scanner-panel data in the coffee market [Kalwani, Yim, Rinne, and Sugita, 1990]. The reluctance to accept losses may also affect sellers: a study of the stock market indicated that the volume of trade tends to be higher when prices are rising than when prices are falling [Shefrin and Statman, 1985].

Loss aversion can complicate negotiations. Experimental evidence indicates that negotiators are less likely to achieve agreement when the attributes over which they bargain are framed as losses than when they are framed as gains [Bazerman and Carroll, 1987]. This result is expected if people are more sensitive to marginal changes in the negative domain. Furthermore, there is a natural asymmetry between the evaluations of the concessions that one makes and the concessions offered by the other party; the latter are normally evaluated as gains, whereas the former are evaluated as losses. The discrepant evaluations of concessions significantly reduces the region of agreement in multi-issue bargaining.

A marked asymmetry in the responses to favorable or unfavorable changes of prices or profits was noted in a study of the rules that govern judgments of the fairness of actions that set prices or wages [Kahneman, Knetsch, and Thaler, 1986]. In particular, most people reject as highly unfair price increases that are not justified by increased costs and cuts in wages that are not justified by a threat of bankruptcy. On the other hand, the customary norms of economic fairness do not absolutely require the firm to share the benefits of reduced costs or increased profits with its customers or its employees. In contrast to economic analysis, which does not distinguish losses from forgone gains, the standards of fairness draw a sharp distinction between actions that impose losses on others and actions (or failures to act) that do not share benefits. A study of court decisions documented a similar distinction in the treatment of losses and forgone gains; in cases of negligence, for example, compensation is more likely to be awarded for out-of-pocket costs than for unrealized profits [Cohen and Knetsch, 1990].

Because actions that are perceived as unfair are often resisted and punished, considerations of fairness have been invoked as one of the explanations of wage stickiness and of other cases in which markets clear only sluggishly [Kahneman, Knetsch, and Thaler, 1986; Okun, 1981; Olmstead and Rhode, 1985]. For example, the difference in the evaluation of losses and of forgone gains implies a corresponding difference in the reactions to a wage cut and to a failure to increase wages when such an increase would be feasible. The terms of previous contracts define the reference levels for collective as well as for individual bargaining; in the bargaining context the aversion to losses takes the form of an aversion to concessions. The rigidity induced by loss aversion may result in inefficient labor contracts that fail to respond adequately to changing economic circumstances and technological developments. As a consequence, new firms that bargain with their workers without the burden of previous agreements may gain a competitive advantage.

Is loss aversion irrational? This question raises a number of difficult normative issues. Questioning the values that decision makers assign to outcomes requires a criterion for the evaluation of preferences. The actual experience of consequences provides such a criterion: the value assigned to a consequence in a decision context can be justified as a prediction of the quality of the experience of that consequence [Kahneman and Snell, 1990]. Adopting this predictive stance, the value function of figure 37.1, which was initially drawn to account for the pattern of risky choices, can be interpreted as a prediction of the psychophysics of hedonic experience. The value function appropriately reflects three basic facts: organisms habituate to steady states, the marginal response to changes is diminishing, and pain is more urgent than pleasure. The asymmetry of pain and pleasure is the ultimate justification of loss aversion in choice. Because of this asymmetry a decision maker who seeks to maximize the experienced utility of outcomes is well advised to assign greater weight to negative than to positive consequences.

The demonstrations discussed in the first part of this paper compared choices between the same two objective states, evaluated from different reference points. The effects of reference levels on decisions can only be justified by corresponding effects of these reference levels on the experience of consequences. For example, a bias in favor of the status quo can be justified if the disadvantages of any change will be experienced more keenly than its advantages. However, some reference levels that are naturally adopted in the context of decision are irrelevant to the subsequent experience of outcomes, and the impact of such reference levels on decisions is normatively dubious. In evaluating a decision that has long-term consequences, for example, the initial response to these consequences may be relatively unimportant, if adaptation eventually induces a shift of reference. Another case involves principal-agent relations: the principal may not wish the agent's decisions to reflect the agent's aversion to losses, because the agent's reference level has no bearing on the principal's experience of outcomes. We conclude that there is no general answer to the question about the normative status of loss aversion or of other reference effects, but there is a principled way of examining the normative status of these effects in particular cases.

Appendix

THEOREM. A reference structure $(X, \geq_r)$, $r \in X$, satisfies additive constant loss aversion iff it satisfies cancellation, sign dependence, and reference interlocking.

Proof. Necessity is straightforward. To establish sufficiency, note that, under the present assumptions, cancellation implies additivity [Debreu, 1960; Krantz et al., 1971]. Hence, for any $r \in X$ there exist continuous functions $R_i : X_i \rightarrow$ Reals, unique up to a positive linear transformation, such that $R(x) = R_1(x_1) + R_2(x_2)$ represents $\geq_r$. That is, for any $x, y \in X$, $x \geq_r y$ iff $R(x) \geq R(y)$. We next establish the following two lemmas.

LEMMA 1. Let A be a set of options that belong to the same quadrant with respect to r and with respect to s. Then there exist $\lambda_i > 0$ such that for all x, y in A,

$$R_i(y_i) - R_i(x_i) = (S_i(y_i) - S_i(x_i))/\lambda_i, \quad i = 1, 2.$$

Proof. We wish to show that for all $r, s, w, x, y, z \in X$,

$$R_i(z_i) - R_i(y_i) = R_i(x_i) - R_i(w_i) \quad \text{implies that}$$

$$S_i(z_i) - S_i(y_i) = S_i(x_i) - S_i(w_i), \quad i = 1, 2.$$

This proposition follows from continuity, additivity, and reference interlocking whenever the i-intervals in question can be matched by intervals on the other dimension. If such matching is not possible, we use continuity to divide these i-intervals into sufficiently small subintervals that could be matched by intervals on the other dimension. Because equality of R_i differences implies equality of S_i differences, Lemma 1 follows from continuity and additivity.

LEMMA 2. Suppose that $r, s \in X$, with $s_1 < r_1$ and $s_2 = r_2$. Let S be a representation of $\geq_s$ satisfying $S_1(s_1) = 0$. If sign-dependence and reference interlocking hold, then there exist $\lambda_1 > 0$, $\lambda_2 = 1$, such that $R^*(x) = R_1^*(x_1) + R_2^*(x_2)$ represents $\geq_r$, where

$$R_1^*(x_1) = \begin{cases} S_1(x_1) - S_1(r_1) & \text{if } x_1 \geq r_1 \\ (S_1(x_1) - S_1(r_1))/\lambda_1 & \text{if } s_1 \leq x_1 \leq r_1 \\ S_1(x_1) - S_1(r_1)/\lambda_1 & \text{if } x_1 \leq s_1 \end{cases}$$

and $R_2^*(x_2) = S_2(x_2) - S_2(r_2)/\lambda_2$. The same holds if the indices 1 and 2 are interchanged throughout.

Proof. By sign-dependence $\geq_r$ and $\geq_s$ coincide for all pairs of elements of $\{x \in X : x_1 \geq r_1, x_2 \geq r_2\}$ and of $\{x \in X : x_1 \geq r_1, x_2 \leq r_2\}$. To prove that $\geq_r$ and $\geq_s$ also coincide on their union, suppose that y belongs to the former set and z belongs to the latter. It suffices to show that $y =_r z$ implies that $y =_s z$. By monotonicity and continuity there exists w such that $y =_r w =_r z$ and $w_2 = r_2 = s_2$. Since w belongs to the intersection of the two sets, $y =_r w$ implies that $y =_s w$ and $z =_r w$ implies that $z =_s w$ hence $y =_s z$.

Therefore, we can select the scales so that $R_i = S_i$, $i = 1, 2$, on $\{x \in X : x_1 \geq r_1\}$. Next we show that $R^*(x) + S(r) = R(x)$. We consider each dimension separately. For $i = 2$, $R_2^*(x_2) + S_2(r_2) = S_2(x_2)$. We show that $S_2(x_2) = R_2(x_2)$. Select an $x_1 \geq r_1$. By construction, $S(x) = R(x)$—hence $S_2(x_2) = R_2(x_2)$.

For $i = 1$, if $x_1 \geq r_1$, we get $R_1^*(x_1) + S_1(r_1) = S_1(x_1)$ and $R_1(x_1) = S_1(x_1)$, by construction. Hence

$$R_1^*(x_1) + S_1(r_1) = S_1(x_1) = R_1(x_1).$$

For $s_1 < x_1 < r_1$, we want to show that there exists λ_1 such that

$$R_1(x_1) = S_1(r_1) + (S_1(x_1) - S_1(r_1))/\lambda_1, \quad \text{or}$$

$$R_1(x_1) - R_1(r_1) = (S_1(x_1) - S_1(r_1))/\lambda_1,$$

which follows from Lemma 1.

For $x_1 \leq s_1$, $\geq_r$ and $\geq_s$ coincide, by sign-dependence—hence $R_1 = \alpha S_1 + \beta$, $\alpha > 0$. Because $R_2 = S_2$, $\alpha = 1$, and because $S_1(s_1) = 0$, $\beta = R_1(s_1)$—hence $R_1(x_1) = S_1(x_1) + R_1(s_1)$. Consequently,

$$R_1(x_1) - R_1^*(x_1) = S_1(x_1) + R_1(s_1) - (S_1(x_1) - S_1(r_1)/\lambda_1)$$

$$= R_1(s_1) + S_1(r_1)/\lambda_1.$$

It suffices to show that this expression equals $S_1(r_1)$. Consider the case $s_1 < x_1 < r_1$, by continuity at s_1,

$$R_1(s_1) - R_1(r_1) = (S_1(s_1) - S_1(r_1))/\lambda_1, \quad \text{hence}$$

$$R_1(s_1) + S_1(r_1)/\lambda_1 = R_1(r_1)$$

$$= S_1(r_1), \quad \text{by construction,}$$

which completes the proof of Lemma 2.

Next we show that λ_i, $i = 1, 2$, is independent of r. Select $r, s, t \in X$ such that $r_2 = s_2 = t_2$ and $s_1 < r_1 < t_1$. By the previous lemma there exist R^* and T^*, defined in terms of S, with constants $\lambda^{(r)}$ and $\lambda^{(t)}$, respectively. Because $\geq_r$ and $\geq_t$ coincide on $\{x \in X : x_1 \leq r_1\}$, by sign-dependence, $\lambda^{(r)} = \lambda^{(t)}$. The same argument applies when indices 1 and 2 are interchanged, and when $r_1 < s_1$.

To establish sufficiency for the general case, consider $r, s \in X$, with $r_1 > s_1$, $r_2 \leq s_2$ and $t = (r_1, s_2)$. By applying the previous (one-dimensional) construction twice, once for (s, t) and then for (t, r), we obtain the desired result.

Notes

This paper has benefited from the comments of Kenneth Arrow, Peter Diamond, David Krantz, Matthew Rabin, and Richard Zeckhauser. We are especially grateful to Shmuel Sattath and Peter Wakker for their helpful suggestions.

This work was supported by Grants No. 89-0064 and 88-0206 from the Air Force Office of Scientific Research, and by the Sloan Foundation.

References

Bazerman, Max, and John S. Carroll, "Negotiator Cognition," in B. Staw and L. L. Cummings, eds., *Research in Organizational Behavior*, vol. VIIII (Greenwich, CT: JAI Press, 1987), pp. 247–288.

Brookshire, David S., and Don L. Coursey, "Measuring the Value of a Public Good: An Empirical of Elicitation Procedures," *American Economic Review*, LXXVII (1987), 554–566.

Cohen, David, and Jack L. Knetsch, "Judicial Choice and Disparities Between Measures of Economic Values," Simon Fraser University Working Paper, 1990.

Coursey, Don L., John L. Hovis, and William D. Schulze, "The Disparity between Willingness to Accept and Willingness to Pay Measures of Value," *Quarterly Journal of Economics*, CII (1987), 679–690.

Cummings, Ronald G., David S. Brookshire, and William D. Schulze, eds., *Valuing Environmental Goods* (Totowa, NJ: Rowman and Allanheld, 1986).

Debreu, Gerald, "Topological Methods in Cardinal Utility Theory," in Kenneth J. Arrow, Sam Karlin, and Patrick Suppes, eds., *Mathematical Methods in the Social Sciences* (Stanford, CA: Stanford University Press, 1960), pp. 16–26.

Easterlin, Richard A., "Does Economic Growth Improve the Human Lot? Some Empirical Evidence," in P. A. David and M. W. Reder, eds., *Nations and Households in Economic Growth* (New York, NY: Academic Press, 1974), pp. 89–125.

Heberlein, Thomas A., and Richard C. Bishop, "Assessing the Validity of Contingent Valuation: Three Field Experiments," Paper presented at the International Conference on Man's Role in Changing the Global Environment, Italy, 1985.

Kahneman, Daniel, Jack L. Knetsch, and Richard Thaler, "Fairness as a Constraint on Profit Seeking: Entitlements in the Market," *American Economic Review*, LXXVI (1986), 728–741.

——, ——, and ——, "Experimental Tests of the Endowment Effect and the Coase Theorem," *Journal of Political Economy*, XCVIII (1990), 1325–1348.

Kahneman, Daniel, and Jackie Snell, "Predicting Utility," in Robin Hogarth, ed., *Insights in Decision Making* (Chicago, IL: University of Chicago Press, 1990).

Kahneman, Daniel, and Amos Tversky, "Prospect Theory: An Analysis of Decision Under Risk," *Econometrica*, XLVII (1979), 263–291.

——, and ——, "Choices, Values and Frames," *American Psychologist*, XXXIX (1984), 341–350.

Kalwani, Manohar U., Chi Kin Yim, Heikki J. Rinne, and Yoshi Sugita, "A Price Expectations Model of Customer Brand Choice," *Journal of Marketing Research*, XXVII (1990), 251–262.

Knetsch, Jack L., "The Endowment Effect and Evidence of Nonreversible Indifference Curves," *American Economic Review*, LXXIX (1989), 1277–1284.

——, and J. A. Sinden, "Willingness to Pay and Compensation Demanded: Experimental Evidence of an Unexpected Disparity in Measures of Value," *Quarterly Journal of Economics*, XCIX (1984), 507–521.

——, and ——, "The Persistence of Evaluation Disparities," *Quarterly Journal of Economics*, CII (1987), 691–695.

Krantz, David H., R. Duncan Luce, Patrick Suppes, and Amos Tversky, *Foundations of Measurement*, vol. I (New York, NY: Academic Press, 1971).

Loewenstein, George, "Frames of Mind in Intertemporal Choice," *Management Science*, XXXIV (1988), 200–214.

Okun, Arthur, *Prices and Quantities: A Macroeconomic Analysis* (Washington, DC: The Brookings Institution, 1981).

Olmstead, Alan L., and Paul Rhode, "Rationing Without Government: The West Coast Gas Famine of 1920," *American Economic Review*, LXXV (1985), 1044–1055.

Putler, Daniel S., "Reference Price Effects and Consumer Behavior," unpublished, Economic Research Service, U. S. Department of Agriculture, Washington, DC, 1988.

Samuelson, William, and Richard Zeckhauser, "Status Quo Bias in Decision Making," *Journal of Risk and Uncertainty*, I (1988), 7–59.

Shefrin, Hersh, and Meir Statman, "The Disposition to Sell Winners Too Early and Ride Losers Too Long: Theory and Evidence," *Journal of Finance*, XL (1985), 777–790.

Thaler, Richard, "Toward a Positive Theory of Consumer Choice," *Journal of Economic Behavior and Organization*, I (1980), 39–60.

Tversky, Amos, Shmuel Sattath, and Paul Slovic, "Contingent Weighting in Judgment and Choice," *Psychological Review*, XCV (1988), 371–384.

Tversky, Amos, and Daniel Kahneman, "Advances in Prospect Theory: Cumulative Representation of Uncertainty," unpublished, Stanford University, 1991.

van de Stadt, Huib, Arie Kapteyn, and Sara van der Geer, "The Relativity of Utility: Evidence from Panel Data," *Review of Economics and Statistics*, LXVII (1985), 179–187.

van Praag, Bernard M. S., "The Individual Welfare Function of Income in Belgium: An Empirical Investigation," *European Economic Review*, XX (1971), 337–369.

Varian, Hal R., *Microeconomic Analysis* (New York, NY: Norton, 1984).

Viscusi, W. Kip, Wesley A. Magat, and Joel Huber, "An Investigation of the Rationality of Consumer Valuations of Multiple Health Risks," *Rand Journal of Economics*, XVIII (1987), 465–479.

Wakker, Peter P., *Additive Representations of Preferences: A New Foundation of Decision Analysis* (Dordrecht, The Netherlands: Kluwer Academic Publishers, 1989).

Winer, Russell S., "A Reference Price Model of Brand Choice for Frequently Purchased Products," *Journal of Consumer Research*, XIII (1986), 250–256.

38 Endowment and Contrast in Judgments of Well-Being

Amos Tversky and Dale Griffin

Introduction

In a recent educational television programme, an amnesic patient was asked about his childhood and high-school experiences. Verbally fluent, he was able to converse about daily events, but could not remember any details about his past. Finally, the interviewer asked him how happy he was. The patient pondered this question for a few seconds before answering, "I don't know."

Clearly, memory plays a crucial role in the assessment of well-being. The present evidently does not provide enough information to define happiness without reference to the past. Yet memories have a complex effect on our current sense of well-being. They represent a direct source of happiness or unhappiness, and they also affect the criteria by which current events are evaluated. In other words, a salient hedonic event (positive or negative) influences later evaluations of well-being in two ways: through an *endowment* effect and a *contrast* effect. The endowment effect of an event represents its direct contribution to one's happiness or satisfaction. Good news and positive experiences enrich our lives and make us happier; bad news and hard times diminish our well-being. Events also exercise an indirect contrast effect on the evaluation of subsequent events. A positive experience makes us happy, but it also renders similar experiences less exciting. A negative experience makes us unhappy, but it also helps us appreciate subsequent experiences that are less bad. The hedonic impact of an event, we suggest, reflects a balance of its endowment[1] and contrast effects. The present chapter explores some descriptive and prescriptive implications of this notion.

A few examples illustrate the point. Consider a professor from a small midwestern town who attends a conference in New York and enjoys having dinner at an outstanding French restaurant. This memorable event contributes to her endowment— she is happier for having had that experience—but it also gives rise to a contrast effect. A later meal in the local French restaurant becomes somewhat less satisfying by comparison with the great meal she had in New York. Similarly, exposure to great theatre is enriching, but makes it harder to enjoy the local repertory company. The same principle applies to accomplishments. A successful first novel contributes a great deal to the author's endowment and self-esteem, but it also reduces the satisfaction derived from future novels if they are less good.

The effects of endowment and contrast also apply to negative events. Some people, dominated by a negative endowment, become depressed and unable to enjoy life in the aftermath of a bad experience; others are elated by the contrast between the present and the bleak past. People may vary in the degree to which their reactions are dominated by endowment or by contrast. Note that the endowment-contrast dimension of individual differences is orthogonal to the more familiar dimension of optimism-pessimism. Both endowment and contrast, of course, are memory based. The stronger the memory of the past, the greater its impact on present well-being. With no memory, there can be no endowment and no contrast, just immediate pleasures and pains.

There is little novelty in suggesting that well-being depends both on the nature of the experience that is being evaluated and on the standard of evaluation. Furthermore, many authors have observed that satisfaction is directly related to the quality of the experience, or its endowment, and inversely related to the evaluation standard, which serves as a contrast. What is perhaps less obvious is the observation that the same (past) event makes a dual contribution to well-being—a direct contribution as endowment and an inverse contribution as contrast. Although these effects have been discussed in the well-being literature (under various names), we know of no explicit attempt to integrate them.

The distinction between endowment and contrast has nothing to do with the character of the event itself; any hedonic experience affects our well-being both through the endowment it generates and through the contrast to which it gives rise. The endowment depends primarily on the quality and the intensity of the event, whereas the contrast depends primarily on its similarity or relevance to subsequent events. A great meal at a French restaurant in New York will probably not reduce your ability to enjoy a Chinese meal back home; similarly, while a great theatre performance may spoil your taste for the local repertory company, you will probably continue to take pleasure in concerts or even high-school plays.

Because the contrast effect depends on similarity or perceived relevance, it is susceptible to framing and other cognitive manipulations. The same sequence of events can produce varying degrees of satisfaction depending on whether an early event is viewed as similar or relevant to the evaluation of later events. Thus, happiness should be maximized by treating positive experiences as endowments and negative experiences as contrasts. To achieve this goal, one should find ways to treat the positive experiences of the past as different from the present (to avoid comparisons with the glorious past). By the same token, one should compare present conditions to worse situations in the past (to enjoy the benefits of a positive contrast). This prescription raises some intriguing questions that lie beyond the scope of this chapter. Are people who emphasize the endowment of positive events and the contrast of negative events generally happier than those who do not? And how much freedom do people have in the framing of hedonic events?

The present chapter reports some preliminary explorations based on experimental manipulations of endowment and contrast. In the next section we vary the quality and the relevance of past events and investigate their effects on judgments of well-being. We develop a simple method for assessing the relative contributions of endowment and contrast in these studies, and we apply this analysis to some experiments of Schwarz, Strack and their colleagues, and to the study of expectation effects. In the last section of the chapter, we discuss the use of choice and of judgment for the assessment of well-being, illustrate the discrepancy between the two procedures, and relate it to the relative contribution of endowment and contrast.

Studies of Endowment and Contrast

The following two experiments employ the same design to study the impact of a past event on present judgments of happiness. In the first study, we use fictitious scripts to investigate the role of endowment and contrast in judgments regarding the well-being of another person. In the second study, subjects rated their own satisfaction following an actual experience.

In our first study, subjects were given a "story"—a description of two events, allegedly taken from an interview with a student—and were asked to rate the happiness of that student. In each case, the earlier event was either positive or negative, and the later event was neutral. Four types of events were used in the study: a date, a term paper, a party, and a movie. The two events presented to the subject could be of the same type (e.g. two term papers or two parties) or of different types (e.g. a date followed by a party or vice versa). This arrangement gives rise to a 2×2 (between subjects) design in which a neutral event is preceded by either a positive or a negative event that could be of the same type or of a different type.

Because the second event is always neutral, we can focus on the endowment and the contrast effects produced by the first event. For events of different types, we expect an endowment effect, with little or no contrast. Judged happiness, therefore, should be high when the first event is positive and low when the first event is negative. For events of the same type, however, both contrast and endowment effects are expected. As a consequence, a related positive event should produce less happiness than an unrelated positive event, whereas a related negative event should produce greater happiness than an unrelated negative event. For example, an excellent paper followed by an average paper should produce less satisfaction than an excellent paper followed by an average party because the original paper makes a subsequent paper (but not a subsequent party) somewhat disappointing by contrast. On the

other hand, a bad paper followed by an average paper should produce more satisfaction than a bad paper followed by an average party.

Sixty-four students participated in our first experiment, which was administered in
a class setting in four groups of approximately sixteen students each. All subjects
received the following instructions:

On the next few pages you will find several descriptions of life events experienced by high-
school students. These are everyday sorts of events that you or your friends have probably
experienced some time in your high-school career.

Your task will be to read these stories carefully and try to understand how the person felt
during these episodes. Each individual narrator will present two vignettes from his or her own
high-school experience. The vignettes were all gathered during the narrator's junior year in
high school. After each pair of stories, you will be asked to rate the feelings of the narrator.

Each storyteller was asked to recount two experiences. First, they were asked to describe an
experience from the week before, and then they were asked to describe something that had
happened that very day. These narratives were given orally, so the grammar and prose are not
perfect.

Each story is very short, so please take your time and try to imagine what the scene looked like
and felt like to the narrator. Especially try to imagine how the narrator was feeling as he or she
recounted the story.

The stories refer to four domains: a date with a young woman, performance in
a course, the planning of a party, and the reaction to an Australian movie. Three
events were constructed for each domain: positive, neutral, and negative. Recall
that for each pair of events, the present event was always neutral and it was
preceded either by a positive or a negative event that was either related or unrelated.
Each respondent evaluated four stories, one in each quality/relation condition (i.e.
positive/related, positive/unrelated, negative/related, and negative/unrelated). The
following story describes a negative event regarding class performance followed by a
related neutral event; an unrelated neutral event is also given for comparison.

Tim's Story
(Past, Negative)
What happened last week? Last week, let's see. I had a bad day. A really, really bad day. In the
morning, I had a quiz in French. I was so tired and I just couldn't keep my mind on the
problems. And then with about 10 minutes to go in the period, I sort of woke up and realized
that I was in bad trouble. I had sort of puttered on the first page of a three-page quiz and there
was no way I was going to finish. I almost broke out in a cold sweat; the quiz wasn't very
important or anything, but it was like a dream where I was racing against time and my heart
was pounding and there was no way I was going to get finished. So I felt bad about that all
morning, not to mention embarrassed at blowing the quiz, and then in the afternoon I got a
test back in Chemistry. I had almost failed it; it was a pretty hard test and everything, but it

just made me want to give up. I was just stunned, not to mention tired. Good grades in Chemistry are important to me because I want to take sciences in college. So I skipped track practice that day and just went home. I didn't want to deal with anything else bad that could happen to me.

(Present, Related)

What happened today? I had three classes this morning, but since one of them is Civics, it wasn't too bad. In Civics, we discussed political issues that have been in the news. That was o.k., mostly a break from taking notes in other classes. First period I had Geometry, and we had a substitute teacher so we just did our homework in class. Before lunch I had French, which I am taking instead of Spanish this year. We practiced our conversations, which we have to present next week. That's pretty much it, I think.

Story 2 (Present, Unrelated)

What happened today? Well, I had another lunch with Susan. We had a pretty good time. We talked most of the time, about classes and some people we both know. Mostly we talked about the English class, though, and the way that exams were given. We argued some about whether the professor was fair, but we both agreed that the exams were aimed more at trivial detail than were the lectures. We ate pretty slowly, but both made it to our one o'clock classes. It was hard to get a feeling for what was going on, but I think she liked me well enough.

The dependent variable was a rating of happiness on a scale ranging from one (very unhappy) to ten (very happy). Subjects were asked "On the day that Tim answered these questions: how happy do you think he was with his life overall?" Because there were no significant differences between the responses to the stories, the results were pooled. Figure 38.1 displays the average rating of happiness in each of the four conditions, averaged across subjects and stories. The results confirmed our predictions. There was a significant interaction between the quality of the past event (positive or negative) and its relation (related, unrelated) to the present event, $F(1, 60) = 6.71$, $p < .02$. As expected, we observed a significant endowment effect: in both the related and unrelated conditions, judged satisfaction was higher for the positive than for the negative prior event. Furthermore, there was a significant contrast effect: for the positive event, satisfaction was higher in the unrelated ($M = 7.1$) than in the related condition ($M = 6.8$), whereas for the negative event, the pattern was reversed ($M = 4.9$ for the unrelated condition, and $M = 5.5$ for the related condition). For example, the memory of a good date last week diminished the satisfaction with a neutral date this week, but it enhanced the satisfaction with a neutral movie this week. The memory of a painful date, on the other hand, enhanced the satisfaction with a neutral date this week, while it diminished the satisfaction with a neutral movie this week.

To aid in the interpretation of experimental data, we find it useful to express judgments of satisfaction as an additive combination of endowment and contrast

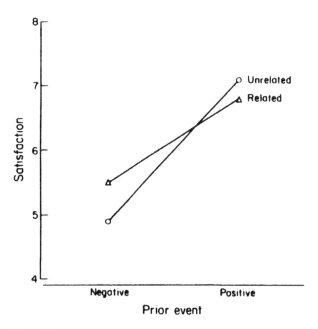

Figure 38.1
The effect of prior events.

effects. We assume that the endowment effect E_{12} is given by the sum of the endowments of the first and second events denoted E_1 and E_2, respectively, and that the contrast effect C_{12} is expressible as the signed hedonic discrepancy between the two events d_{12}, weighted by their degree of relatedness r_{12}. Thus, we obtain the form

$$\text{Satisfaction} = \text{Endowment} + \text{Contrast}$$
$$= E_{12} + C_{12}$$
$$= E_1 + E_2 + r_{12}d_{12}.$$

To apply this scheme to the results of our first study, let S denote the rating of satisfaction. For simplicity, we suppose that the grand mean has been substracted from all observations, so S is expressed as a deviation score. Let S^+ and S^- be respectively the responses in a condition where the first event was positive or negative, and let S_r and S_u denote the responses in a condition where the two events were related or unrelated. Let E^+ and E denote the endowment associated with a positive or negative event, and let C^+ and C^- denote the contrast associated with a positive or negative event, respectively. Because the second event in this study was always neutral we can neglect its endowment, and set $E_2 = 0$. Naturally, the contrast associated with a prior positive event is negative, $C^+ < 0$, and the contrast associated with a prior negative event is positive, $C^- > 0$. We also assume that, for unrelated events, $r_{12} = 0$, hence the contrast term vanishes in that case. Judgments of satisfaction in the present design can be represented as:

	Negative	Positive
Unrelated	$S_u^- = E^-$	$S_u^+ = E^+$
Related	$S_r^- = E^- + C^-$	$S_r^+ = E^+ + C^+$

We use this model to estimate the effect of contrast and endowment. The total endowment effect is:

$$E = E^+ - E^- = S_u^+ - S_u^- = 7.1 - 4.9 = 2.2$$

As we assume the unrelated events involve no contrast, the overall endowment effect is simply the difference between mean satisfaction in the cells representing positive versus negative unrelated events. The contrast associated with the positive first event is:

$$C^+ = S_r^+ - S_u^+ = 6.8 - 7.1 = -.3.$$

Similarly, the contrast associated with the negative first event is:

$$C^- = S_r^- - S_u^- = 5.5 - 4.9 = .6.$$

Thus, the total contrast effect in this experiment is $C^- - C^+ = .9$, which is considerably smaller than the endowment effect, as can be seen in figure 38.1.

In our second study, subjects rated their own satisfaction with actual experiences. Seventy-two subjects took part in a computer-controlled stock-market game played for real money. Subjects were given information about different stocks and were instructed to construct a portfolio from these stocks. They were told that the computer would simulate the market and that their actual payoffs would depend on the performance of their portfolios. Each session included an initial game (with a payoff of $2 or $6) and a later game (with a payoff of $4) separated by a filler task involving no gains or losses. As in the first study, we manipulated two variables: (a) the payoff in the first game and (b) the similarity or relatedness between the first and the second games. In the related condition, subjects played essentially the same game with different stocks. In the unrelated condition, the games involved different markets (stocks versus commodities) and used different procedures for portfolio construction.

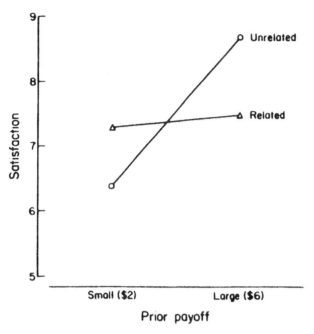

Figure 38.2
The effect of prior payoffs.

After subjects played both games, they were asked to rate their overall satisfaction with the experience, using a 10-point scale.

This design allows us to test the following hypotheses regarding judged satisfaction. First, the difference between the low ($2) and the high ($6) payoffs will be greater in the unrelated than in the related condition. This prediction follows from the assumption that for the unrelated games, the difference reflects a pure endowment effect. In the related games, however, the positive endowment will be reduced by the negative contrast, whereas the negative endowment will be reduced by the positive contrast. Second, the negative contrast effect following the high payoff (when $d_{12} > 0$) will be larger than the positive contrast effect following the low payoff (when $d_{12} < 0$), as suggested by the notion of loss aversion in prospect theory (Kahneman and Tversky, 1979).

The pattern of results displayed in figure 38.2 supported the endowment-contrast analysis. In the unrelated condition, where there is pure endowment and no contrast, those who received the larger payoff in the first game were generally more satisfied ($M = 8.7$) than those who received the smaller payoff in the first game ($M = 6.4$),

$t(33) = 1.95$, $p < .05$, one-tailed. However, in the related condition, where contrast and endowment worked in the opposite directions, there was essentially no difference between the satisfaction of those who received the larger reward in the first game ($M = 7.5$) and those who received the smaller reward in the first game ($M = 7.3$).

The decomposition scheme introduced in the first study is applicable to the results of the present study. In this study too, E_2 is a constant, and hence can be ignored in the analysis. To simplify matters, we also assume that the difference between the satisfaction derived from the high prior payoff and the low prior payoff in the unrelated games yields an estimate of the total endowment effect:

$$E = S_u^+ - S_u^- = 8.7 - 6.4 = 2.3.$$

The positive contrast (the increase in satisfaction caused by a low expectation) was:

$$C^- = S_r^- - S_u^- = 7.3 - 6.4 = .9;$$

and the negative contrast (the decrease in satisfaction caused by a large expectation) was:

$$C^+ = S_r^+ - S_u^+ = 7.5 - 8.7 = -1.2.$$

Note that the overall endowment effect was about the same in the two experiments, but the overall contrast effect, $C = C^- - C^+ = 2.1$ was doubled in the present study. As implied by loss aversion, people's disappointment with a "loss" of $2 was greater than their satisfaction with a "gain" of $2.

Applications of the Endowment-Contrast Scheme

Our conceptual scheme for the integration of endowment and contrast effects, described above, can be applied to two studies conducted by Schwarz, Strack and their colleagues. In one experiment, Strack, Schwarz, and Gschneidinger (1985) instructed subjects in one group to recall and write down a very negative event in their lives; subjects in another group were instructed to recall and write down a very positive event in their lives. Within each group, half of the subjects were asked to recall a present event, and half were asked to recall a past event. Subjects were then asked to rate their well-being on a 10-point scale. This procedure yields a 2×2 (between-subjects) design in which the recalled event was either positive or negative, in the present or in the past. For the events in the present, the results were hardly surprising. Recalling a positive present event made people feel good, whereas thinking about a negative present event made people feel less happy. The results for past

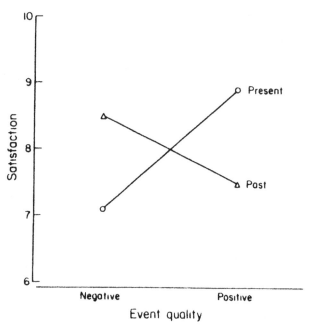

Figure 38.3
The effect of past versus present events.

events were more surprising: ratings of well-being were higher for those who recalled a past negative event than for those who recalled a past positive event (see figure 38.3). We have replicated this result at Stanford.

The endowment-contrast scheme provides a natural account of these findings. For the events in the present, there is no room for contrast, hence we get a positive endowment effect for the positive event and a negative endowment effect for the negative event. The recall of past events, however, introduces a contrast with the present, which is positive for negative events and negative for positive ones. Because present events are more salient than past events, the endowment effect is greater for present than past events. Thus, for past events, the contrast component offsets the endowment component and produces the observed reversal.

Again, let S^+ and S^- refer to judged satisfaction when a positive or negative event, respectively, has been brought to mind. (As before, we first subtract the grand mean from each observation and operate on deviation scores). Let S_c and S_p refer to the judgments associated with a current and a past event, respectively. We can represent the average judgment in each cell as follows:

	Negative	Positive
Current	$S_c^- = E^-$	$S_c^+ = E^+$
Past	$S_p^- = E^- + C^-$	$S_p^+ = E^+ + C^+$

The total endowment effect is:

$$E = E^+ - E^- = S_c^+ - S_c^- = 8.9 - 7.1 = 1.8.$$

The contrast associated with the positive first event is:

$$C^+ = S_p^+ - S_c^+ = 7.5 - 8.9 = -1.4.$$

The contrast associated with the negative first event is:

$$C^- = S_p^- - S_c^- = 8.5 - 7.1 = 1.4.$$

The total contrast effect in this experiment is thus $C = C^- - C^+ = 2.8$. In this study, therefore, the contrast effect is considerably greater than the endowment effect.

More generally, thinking about positive events in the past (e.g. a tour of the Greek islands, or a happy time at summer camp) calls attention to the less exciting present. This is the stuff of which nostalgia is made. On the other hand, recalling some bad times in the past (e.g. failing a test or being lonely) reminds us that the present, although imperfect, could be a great deal worse. While Strack et al., (1985) see mood as the carrier of endowment, we do not regard mood as a necessary condition for an endowment effect. We shall address this difference in emphasis at the conclusion of this section.

In another study, Schwarz, Strack, Kommer, and Wagner (1987) required subjects to spend an hour either in an extremely pleasant room (spacious, nicely furnished and decorated with posters and flowers) or in an extremely unpleasant room (small, dirty, smelly, noisy and overheated). After the session, subjects were asked to assess general satisfaction as well as satisfaction with regard to their current housing situation. The room influenced the rating of overall satisfaction; subjects who were placed in the pleasant room reported higher overall life satisfaction than those in the unpleasant room. However, subjects' rating of their normal living conditions exhibited the opposite pattern (see figure 38.4). Those placed in the unpleasant room reported higher satisfaction with their housing than those who had been in the pleasant room. This pattern is naturally interpreted as a contrast effect. One's own room appears less attractive when compared with the pleasant room than when compared with the unpleasant room. Because contrast depends on the relevance or the similarity of the standard to the target, the contrast effect of the experimental room was confined to the evaluation of housing, and did not extend to the rating of

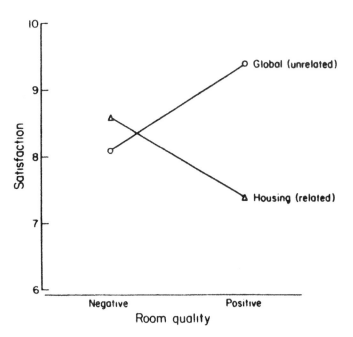

Figure 38.4
The effect of room quality.

life satisfaction. A specific event, therefore, is likely to have a significant contrast effect in the domain to which it belongs, and little or no contrast effect in others.

Using the notation introduced earlier, let S^+ and S^- denote, respectively, judgments of satisfaction for the pleasant and unpleasant rooms, and let S_r and S_u denote, respectively, judgments of satisfaction for the related (housing) and unrelated (life satisfaction) domains. The analysis of these results is then identical to the analysis of study 1. In particular, the total endowment effect is:

$$E = S_u^+ - S_u^- = E^+ - E^- = 9.4 - 8.1 = 1.3.$$

The contrast effect associated with the positive first event is:

$$C^+ = S_r^+ - S_u^+ = 7.4 - 9.4 = -2.0.$$

The contrast effect associated with the negative first event is:

$$C^- = S_r^- - S_u^- = 8.6 - 8.1 = .5.$$

As one might expect, the contrast effect produced by the room is considerably larger ($C = C^- - C^+ = 2.5$) than its endowment effect.

Although different in focus, our analysis is generally compatible with that offered by Schwarz and Strack. They assume the operation of contrast effects and focus on the role of emotion or mood in generating endowment. Our account assumes the existence of endowment effects, produced through either mood or other processes, and focuses on the factors that control the relative strength of endowment and contrast.

Expectations as Contrast and Endowment

Much psychological research on the assessment of well-being has focused on the role of expectations. It has been shown in many contexts that the same event can be perceived as more or less satisfying, depending on whether a positive or negative expectation has been induced (Feather, 1966; Shrauger, 1975). Whether a given test score is pleasing or disappointing will depend on whether the student was led to expect a low or a high score (Schul, 1989). Expectation effects are generally interpreted as contrast. Indeed, people are commonly advised to lower their expectations in order to avoid disappointment. In line with our previous analysis, we propose that expectations produce endowment as well as contrast. We are relieved when a dreaded event does not happen, but the memory of anxiety and fear still haunts us long afterward. Imagine that you have been living two weeks with the possibility that your child has leukemia. Further tests now prove your worries unfounded. Despite your elation at this news, we suspect that you are worse off for the experience. In such circumstances, the endowment effect of a negative expectation has a strong impact on your well-being long after the specific worry has been relieved.

Much as unrealized fears can generate negative endowment, unrealized hopes can give rise to positive endowment. Consider the experience of someone who owns a lottery ticket. Because the probability of winning is very small, the failure to win does not cause much disappointment. However, the dream of becoming an overnight millionaire could produce enough pleasure to offset the mild disappointment of not winning the lottery. Indeed, it appears that many people enjoy playing the lottery even when they do not win. Probability plays here a critical role. As the probability of winning increases, the costs of disappointment seem to increase faster than the benefits of hope. Holding expected value constant, therefore, playing hong odds should be more pleasurable than playing short odds. Losers on long odds had sweeter dreams than losers on short odds; and their disappointment was also less bitter. This analysis suggests another reason for the attractiveness of long shots, in addition to the overweighting of small probabilities (Kahneman and Tversky, 1979).

The present treatment adopts a symbolic rather than a consummatory conception of well-being. We derive pleasure and pain not merely from the positive and the negative events we experience, but also from the memory of past events and the anticipation of future events (Schelling, 1984). Like the memories of past events, expectations of future events, we suggest, serve both as endowment and as contrast. Expectations not only control the evaluation of future events, they have a hedonic impact of their own—whether or not the event they refer to actually comes to pass. Our hedonic portfolio encompasses memories and expectations; successes and failures of the past, hopes and fears of the future.

The Assessment of Well-Being: Choice versus Judgment

The preceding studies were concerned, like most of the empirical work discussed in this volume, with judgments of satisfaction or happiness, which have served as a major source of data for students of well-being (Argyle, 1987; Diener, 1984). Another paradigm for the study of welfare, dominant in economics, focuses on choice rather than on judgment. In this paradigm, a person is said to be better off in State A than in State B if he or she chooses State A over State B. Indeed, the concept of utility has been used in economics and decision theory in two different senses: (a) experience value, the degree of pleasure or pain associated with the actual experience of an outcome, and (b) decision value, the contribution of an anticipated outcome to the overall attractiveness of an option (Kahneman and Tversky, 1984). Experience values are generally measured by judgmental methods (e.g. self-reports or judgments by observers), although physiological measures (e.g. blood pressure or heart rate) are occasionally used. Decision values are inferred from choices using an appropriate model such as expected utility theory or the theory of revealed preference. The distinction between experience and decision values is rarely made explicit because, with a few notable exceptions (e.g. March, 1978; Schelling, 1984; Sen, 1982), it is commonly assumed that judgment and choice yield the same ordering. In many situations, however, experience values, as expressed in self-ratings, appear to diverge from decision values, as inferred from choice.

First, choice and judgment may yield different results because of moral considerations and problems of self-control. We commonly avoid certain pleasurable experiences because they are immoral, illegal, or fattening. On the other hand, there are times we cannot resist experiences that will ultimately make us unhappy, because of a lack of self-control. Choice, therefore, could conceal rather than reveal one's "true preferences." Second, a choice-judgment discrepancy is likely to arise if the decision maker's prediction of the consequences of choice is inaccurate or biased. A common bias in the prediction of utility is a tendency to overweight one's present state or mood. Some perceptive consumers have learned to avoid doing their weekly grocery shopping either when they are very hungry (because they would buy too much) or after a very large meal (because they would not buy enough). A related source of error is the failure to anticipate our remarkable ability to adapt to new states. People tend to overestimate the long-term impact of both positive events, such as winning a lottery or receiving tenure, and negative events, such as injury or personal loss (Brickman, Coates, and Janoff-Bulman, 1978). The ability to predict future well-being depends largely on the nature of the experience. People generally have a reasonable idea of what it is like to lose money or to have a bad cold, but they probably do not have a clear notion of what it means to go bankrupt, or to lose a limb. For illuminating discussions of the role of adaptation and the problems of predicting one's own future satisfaction, see Kahneman and Snell (in press), and Kahneman and Varey (in press).

But even if the judgment, like the choice, precedes the experience of the consequence, the two tasks can give rise to different answers because they highlight different aspects of the problem. When people are asked to assess the hedonic value of some future states (e.g. job offers) they try to imagine what it would feel like to experience those states. But when asked to choose among these states, they tend to search for reasons or arguments to justify their choice. Consequently, the two procedures could lead to different results. For example, Tversky, Sattath, and Slovic (1988) have shown that the most important attribute of a multi-dimensional decision problem is weighted more heavily in choice than in judgment, presumably because it provides a convenient rationale for choice. Recall the stock-market study, presented in the first section of this chapter. Given a choice, subjects would surely elect to participate in the negative contrast condition, where they earn $10, rather than in the positive contrast condition, where they earn $6. Yet subjects who had a lower total endowment ($6) and a positive contrast were just as satisfied as subjects who had a higher total endowment ($10) and a negative contrast. It appears that the choice depends primarily on the payoffs whereas judgments of satisfaction are more sensitive to the contrast.

To explore the choice-judgment discrepancy, we presented the following information to some sixty-six undergraduate students.

Imagine that you have just completed a graduate degree in Communications and you are considering one-year jobs at two different magazines.

(A) At Magazine A, you are offered a job paying $35,000. However, the other workers who have the same training and experience as you do are making $38,000.

(B) At Magazine B, you are offered a job paying $33,000. However, the other workers who have the same training and experience as you do are making $30,000.

Approximately half the subjects were asked "Which job would you choose to take?" while the other half were asked "At which job would you be happier?" The results confirmed our prediction that the comparison with others would loom larger in judgment, and that the salary would dominate the choice. Eighty-four per cent of the subjects (twenty-seven out of thirty-two) preferred the job with the higher absolute salary and lower relative position, while sixty-two per cent (twenty-one out of thirty-four) of the subjects anticipated higher satisfaction in the job with the lower absolute salary and higher relative position ($\chi^2(1) = 14.70$, $p < .01$).

We further explored the relation between choice and judgment in the assessment of an actual experience using a within-subjects design. Thirty-eight undergraduate students participated in a study of "verbal creativity" involving two different tasks. One was described as a test of "cognitive production": the ability to come up with many words that fit a sentence. The other task was described as a test of "grammatical production": the ability to produce many words of a particular grammatical type. Subjects were told that their payoffs would depend on their performance in these tasks.

All subjects performed both tasks, each of which consisted of a practice trial followed by a payoff trial. In one task, subjects were told that their performance was below average on the practice trial, and about average on the payoff trial. In the other task, subjects were told that they performed above average on the practice trial, and about average on the payoff trial. Thus, the performance of each subject "improved" on one task and "declined" on the other task. The order and type of task were counterbalanced. The payoff in the declining condition ($3) was higher than the payoff in the improving condition ($1). Thus, one task paired a larger payoff with an unfavourable comparison. The other task paired a smaller payoff with a favourable comparison. After each task, subjects were asked to rate their satisfaction with their performance on a 10-point scale. Following the completion of both tasks, subjects were asked "If you could do just one task, which would you choose to do?"

As predicted, the payoffs loomed larger in choice than in judgment, or (equivalently) the contrast was weighted more heavily in judgment than in choice. Of the twenty-eight subjects whose ratings were not identical on the two tasks, 75 per cent chose the high-payoff task while 54 per cent expressed greater satisfaction with the low-payoff task. This reversal pattern is significant ($p < .05$ by a McNemar test of symmetry).

These studies show that judgments of satisfaction and choice can yield systematically different orderings. Furthermore, it appears that choice is determined primarily by the payoffs, which reflect the endowment effect, whereas the judgment is more sensitive to comparison or contrast. The salary or payoff one receives provides a more compelling reason for choice than the contrast between one's own salary and the salary of others. This contrast, however, is a very salient feature of the anticipated experience, as reflected in the judgment task. Note that the present use of *contrast* is consistent with, but considerably broader than, the concept invoked in the first part of the chapter. There the term refers to the indirect contribution of a past event to current well-being, whereas here it refers to the standard of reference by which the relevant outcomes are evaluated, which may be determined by prior experience or by other factors, such as the salary of colleagues.

The choice-judgment discrepancy raises an intriguing question: which is the correct or more appropriate measure of well-being? This question cannot be readily answered, and perhaps it cannot be answered at all, because we lack a gold standard for the measurement of happiness. We believe that both choice and judgment provide relevant data for the assessment of well-being, although neither one is entirely satisfactory. Since, as we argue below, the two methods seem to be biased in opposite directions, a compromise between them may have some merit.

Perhaps the most basic principle of welfare economics is Pareto optimality: an allocation of resources is acceptable if it improves everybody's lot. Viewed as a choice criterion, this principle is irresistible. It is hard to object to a policy that improves your lot just because it improves the lot of someone else even more. This is a pure endowment argument that neglects contrast altogether. Policies that ignore contrast effects can create widespread unhappiness. Consider, for example, a policy that doubles the salary of a few people in an organization and increases all other salaries by 5 per cent. Even though all salaries rise, it is doubtful that this change will make most people happier. There is a great deal of evidence (e.g. Brickman, 1975; Brickman and Campbell, 1971; Crosby, 1976) that people's reported satisfaction depends largely on their relative position, not only on their objective situation.

Both experimental and survey research on happiness have shown that judgments of well-being are highly sensitive to comparison or contrast and relatively insensitive to endowment effects. Perhaps the most dramatic illustration of this phenomenon concerns the effect of windfall gains and tragedies. Judged by their ratings, lottery winners are no happier than normal controls, and quadriplegics are only slightly less happy than healthy people and no less happy than paraplegics (Brickman et al., 1978). Surveys indicate that wealther people are slightly happier than people with less money, but substantial increases in everyone's income and standard of living do not raise the reported level of happiness (Easterlin, 1974).

Do these data reflect rapid adaptation that negates the immediate impact of any endowment—as implied by the treadmill theory of happiness (Brickman & Campbell, 1971)? Or do they reflect a normalization of the response scale that makes the ratings of ordinary people and paraplegics essentially incomparable? (As if the paraplegic answers the question: how do I feel relative to other paraplegics?) There are no simple answers to these questions. Obviously, everyone would choose to be healthy rather than paraplegic, and rich rather than poor. But it is not obvious how to demonstrate that the rich are actually happier than the poor if both groups report the same level of well-being. At the same time, it is clear that an adequate measure of well-being must distinguish between rich and poor, and between paraplegic and quadriplegic.

It seems that judgments of well-being are insufficiently sensitive to endowment, whereas choice is insufficiently sensitive to contrast. The exclusive reliance on either method can lead to unreasonable conclusions and unsound recommendations. Welfare policy derived from Pareto optimality could result in allocations that make most people less happy because it ignores the effect of social comparison. On the other hand, a preoccupation with judgment has led some psychologists to the view that "persons with a few ecstatic moments in their lives may be doomed to unhappiness" (Diener, 1984, p. 568), hence, "if the best can come only rarely, it is better not to include it in the range of experiences at all" (Parducci, 1968, p. 90). These conclusions are justified only if endowment effects are essentially ignored. A few glorious moments could sustain a lifetime of happy memories for those who can cherish the past without discounting the present.

Notes

This work was supported by a grant from the Alfred P. Sloan Foundation. It has benefited from discussions with Daniel Kahneman and Lee Ross.

1. Our use of this term to denote a component of hedonic experience should be distinguished from the endowment effect demonstrated by Thaler (1980), which refers to the impact of acquiring material goods on subsequent choices.

References

Argyle, M. *The psychology of happiness.* London: Methuen, 1987.

Brickman, P. Adaptation level determinants of satisfaction with equal and unequal outcome distributions in skill and chance situations. *Journal of Personality and Social Psychology*, 1975; 32, 191–198.

Brickman, P., and Campbell, D. T. Hedonic relativism and planning the good society. In M. H. Appley (ed.), *Adaptation level theory: A symposium* (pp. 287–302). New York; Academic Press, 1971.

Brickman, P., Coates, D., and Janoff-Bulman, R. Lottery winners and accident victims: Is happiness relative? *Journal of Personality and Social Psychology*, 1978; 36, 917–927.

Crosby, F. A model of egoistical relative deprivation. *Psychological Review*, 1976; 83, 85–113.

Diener, E. Subjective well-being. *Psychological Bulletin*, 1984; 95(3), 542–575.

Easterlin, R. A. Does economic growth improve the human lot? Some empirical evidence. In P. A. David and M. W. Reder (eds.), *Nations and households in economic growth* (pp. 89–125). New York; Academic Press, 1974.

Feather, N. T. Effects of prior success and failure on expectations of success and failure. *Journal of Personality and Social Psychology*, 1966; 3, 287–298.

Kahneman, D., and Snell, J. Predicting utility. In R. Hogarth (ed.), *Insights in decision making*. Chicago, IL: University of Chicago Press, in press.

Kahneman, D., and Tversky, A. Prospect theory: An analysis of decision under risk. *Econometrica*, 1979; 47, 263–291.

Kahneman, D., and Tversky, A. Choices, values and frames. *American Psychologist*, 1984; 39, 341–350.

Kahneman, D., and Varey, C. Notes on the psychology of utility. In J. Roemer, & J. Elster (eds.), *Interpersonal comparisons of well-being*. Chicago, IL: University of Chicago Press, in press.

March, J. G. Bounded rationality, ambiguity, and the engineering of choice. *The Bell Journal of Economics*, 1978; 9(2), 587–608.

Parducci, A. The relativism of absolute judgments. *Scientific American*, 1968; 219, 84–90.

Schelling, T. A. *Choice and consequence*. Cambridge, MA: Harvard University Press, 1984.

Schul, Y. *Expectations, performance, and satisfaction*. Unpublished manuscript, The Hebrew University of Jerusalem, 1989.

Schwarz, N., Strack, F., Kommer, D., and Wagner, D. Soccer, rooms, and the quality of your life: Mood effects on judgments of satisfaction with life in general and with specific domains. *European Journal of Social Psychology*, 1987; 17, 69–79.

Sen, A. *Choice, welfare and measurement*. Cambridge, MA: MIT Press, 1982.

Shrauger, J. S. Responses to evaluation as a function of initial self-perception. *Psychological Bulletin*, 1975; 82, 581–596.

Strack, F., Schwarz, N., and Gschneidinger, E. Happiness and reminiscing: The role of time perspective, affect, and mode of thinking. *Journal of Personality and Social Psychology*, 1985; 49(6), 1460–1469.

Thaler, R. Toward a positive theory of consumer choice. *Journal of Economic Behavior and Organization*, 1980; 1, 39–60.

Tversky, A., Sattath, S., and Slovic, P. Contingent weighting in judgment and choice. *Psychological Review*, 1988; 95(3), 371–384.

39 Reason-Based Choice

Eldar Shafir, Itamar Simonson, and Amos Tversky

The result is that peculiar feeling of inward unrest known as indecision. *Fortunately it is too familiar to need description, for to describe it would be impossible. As long as it lasts, with the various objects before the attention, we are said to* deliberate; *and when finally the original suggestion either prevails and makes the movement take place, or gets definitively quenched by its antagonists, we are said to* decide ... *in favor of one or the other course. The reinforcing and inhibiting ideas meanwhile are termed the* reasons *or* motives *by which the decision is brought about.*
—William James (1890/1981)

My way is to divide half a sheet of paper by a line into two columns; writing over the one Pro, *and over the other* Con. *Then, during three or four days' consideration, I put down under the different heads short hints of the different motives, that at different times occur to me for or against the measure. When I have thus got them all together in one view, I endeavor to estimate the respective weights ... find at length where the balance lies ... And, though the weight of reasons cannot be taken with the precision of algebraic quantities, yet, when each is thus considered, separately and comparatively, and the whole matter lies before me. I think I can judge better, and am less liable to make a rash step; and in fact I have found great advantage for this kind of equation, in what may be called* moral *or* prudential algebra.
—Benjamin Franklin, 1772 (cited in Bigelow, 1887)

Introduction

The making of decisions, both big and small, is often difficult because of uncertainty and conflict. We are usually uncertain about the exact consequences of our actions, which may depend on the weather or the state of the economy, and we often experience conflict about how much of one attribute (e.g., savings) to trade off in favor of another (e.g., leisure). In order to explain how people resolve such conflict, students of decision making have traditionally employed either formal models or reason-based analyses. The formal modeling approach, which is commonly used in economics, management science, and decision research, typically associates a numerical value with each alternative, and characterizes choice as the maximization of value. Such value-based accounts include normative models, like expected utility theory (von Neumann & Morgenstern, 1947), as well as descriptive models, such as prospect theory (Kahneman & Tversky, 1979). An alternative tradition in the study of decision making, characteristic of scholarship in history and the law, and typical of political and business discourse, employs an informal, reason-based analysis. This approach identifies various reasons and arguments that are purported to enter into and influence decision, and explains choice in terms of the balance of reasons for and against the various alternatives. Examples of reason-based analyses can be found in studies of historic presidential decisions, such as those taken during the Cuban missile crisis (e.g., Allison, 1971), the Camp David accords (Telhami, 1990), or the Vietnam war (e.g., Berman, 1982; Betts & Gelb, 1979). Furthermore, reason-based analyses are commonly used to interpret "case studies" in business and law schools. Although the reasons invoked by researchers may not always correspond to those that motivated the actual decision makers, it is generally agreed that an analysis in terms of reasons may help explain decisions, especially in contexts where value-based models can be difficult to apply.

Little contact has been made between the two traditions, which have typically been applied to different domains. Reason-based analyses have been used primarily to explain non-experimental data, particularly unique historic, legal and political decisions. In contrast, value-based approaches have played a central role in experimental studies of preference and in standard economic analyses. The two approaches, of course, are not incompatible: reason-based accounts may often be translated into formal models, and formal analyses can generally be paraphrased as reason-based accounts. In the absence of a comprehensive theory of choice, both formal models and reason-based analyses may contribute to the understanding of decision making.

Both approaches have obvious strengths and limitations. The formal, value-based models have the advantage of rigor, which facilitates the derivation of testable implications. However, value-based models are difficult to apply to complex, real world decisions, and they often fail to capture significant aspects of people's deliberations. An explanation of choice based on reasons, on the other hand, is essentially qualitative in nature and typically vague. Furthermore, almost anything can be counted as a "reason," so that every decision may be rationalized after the fact. To overcome this difficulty, one could ask people to report their reasons for decision. Unfortunately, the actual reasons that guide decision may or may not correspond to those reported by the subjects. As has been amply documented (e.g., Nisbett & Wilson, 1977), subjects are sometimes unaware of the precise factors that determine their choices, and generate spurious explanations when asked to account for their decisions. Indeed, doubts about the validity of introspective reports have led many students of decision making to focus exclusively on observed choices. Although verbal reports and introspective accounts can provide valuable information, we use "reasons" in the present article to describe factors or motives that affect decision, whether or not they can be articulated or recognized by the decision maker.

Despite its limitations, a reason-based conception of choice has several attractive features. First, a focus on reasons seems closer to the way we normally think and talk about choices. When facing a difficult choice (e.g., between schools, or jobs) we try to come up with reasons for and against each option—we do not normally attempt to estimate their overall values. Second, thinking of choice as guided by reasons provides a natural way to understand the conflict that characterizes the making of decisions. From the perspective of reason-based choice, conflict arises when the decision maker has good reasons for and against each option, or conflicting reasons for competing options. Unlike numerical values, which are easy to compare, conflicting reasons may be hard to reconcile. An analysis based on reasons can also accommodate framing effects (Tversky & Kahneman, 1986) and elicitation effects (Tversky, Sattath, & Slovic, 1988), which show that preferences are sensitive to the ways in which options are described (e.g., in terms of gains or losses), and to the methods through which preferences are elicited (e.g., pricing versus choice). These findings, which are puzzling from the perspective of value maximization, are easier to interpret if we assume that different frames and elicitation procedures highlight different aspects of the options and thus bring forth different reasons to guide decision. Finally, a conception of choice based on reasons may incorporate comparative considerations (such as relative advantages, or anticipated regret) that typically remain outside the purview of value maximization.

In this chapter, we explore the logic of reason-based choice, and test some specific hypotheses concerning the role of reasons in decision making. The chapter proceeds as follows. Section 1 considers the role of reasons in choice between equally attractive options. Section 2 explores differential reliance on reasons for and against the selection of options. Section 3 investigates the interaction between high and low conflict and people's tendency to seek other alternatives, whereas section 4 considers the relation between conflict and the addition of alternatives to the choice set. Section 5 contrasts the impact of a specific reason for choice with that of a disjunction of reasons. Section 6 explores the role that irrelevant reasons can play in the making of decisions. Concluding remarks are presented in section 7.

1. Choice between Equally Attractive Options

How do decision makers resolve the conflict when faced with a choice between two equally attractive options? To investigate this question, Slovic (1975) first had subjects equate pairs of alternatives, and later asked them to make choices between the equally valued alternatives in each pair. One pair, for example, were gift packages consisting of a combination of cash and coupons. For each pair, one component of one alternative was missing, as shown below, and subjects were asked to determine the value of the missing component that would render the two alternatives equally attractive. (In the following example, the value volunteered by the subject may be, say, $10).

	Gift package A	Gift package B
Cash	—	$20
Coupon book worth	$32	$18

A week later, subjects were asked to choose between the two equated alternatives. They were also asked, independently, which dimension—cash or coupons—they considered more important. Value-based theories imply that the two alternatives— explicitly equated for value—are equally likely to be selected. In contrast, in the choice between gift packages above, 88% of the subjects who had equated these alternatives for value then proceeded to choose the alternative that was higher on the dimension that the subject considered more important.

As Slovic (1975, 1990) suggests, people seem to be following a choice mechanism that is easy to explain and justify: choosing according to the more important dimension provides a better reason for choice than, say, random selection, or selection of the right-hand option. Slovic (1975) replicated the above pattern in numerous domains, including choices between college applicants, auto tires, baseball players, and routes to work. (For additional data and a discussion of elicitation procedures, see Tversky et al., 1988.) All the results were consistent with the hypothesis that people do not choose between the equated alternatives at random. Instead, they resolve the conflict by selecting the alternative that is superior on the more important dimension, which seems to provide a compelling reason for choice.

2. Reasons Pro and Con

Consider having to choose one of two options or, alternatively, having to reject one of two options. Under the standard analysis of choice, the two tasks are interchangeable. In a binary choice situation it should not matter whether people are asked which option they prefer, or which they would reject. Because it is the options themselves that are assumed to matter, not the way in which they are described, if people prefer the first they will reject the second, and vice versa.

As suggested by Franklin's opening quote, our decision will depend partially on the weights we assign to the options' pros and cons. We propose that the positive features of options (their pros) will loom larger when choosing, whereas the negative features of options (their cons) will be weighted more heavily when rejecting. It is natural to select an option because of its positive features, and to reject an option because of its negative features. To the extent that people base their decisions on reasons for and against the options under consideration, they are likely to focus on reasons for choosing an option when deciding which to choose, and to focus on reasons for rejecting an option when deciding which to reject. This hypothesis leads to a straightforward prediction: consider two options, an *enriched* option, with more positive and more negative features, and an *impoverished* option, with fewer positive and fewer negative features. If positive features are weighted more heavily when choosing than when rejecting and negative features are weighted relatively more when rejecting than when choosing, then an enriched option could be both chosen and rejected when compared to an impoverished option. Let P_c and P_r denote, respectively, the percentage of subjects who choose and who reject a particular option. If choosing and rejecting are complementary, then the sum $P_c + P_r$ should equal 100. On the other hand, according to the above hypothesis, $P_c + P_r$ should be greater than 100 for the enriched option and less than 100 for the impoverished option. This pattern was observed by Shafir (1993). Consider, for example, the following problem which was presented to subjects in two versions that differed only in the bracketed questions. One half of the subjects received one version, the other half received the other. The enriched option appears last, although the order presented to subjects was counterbalanced.

Problem 1 ($n = 170$):
Imagine that you serve on the jury of an only-child sole-custody case following a relatively messy divorce. The facts of the case are complicated by ambiguous economic, social, and emotional considerations, and you decide to base your decision entirely on the following few observations. [To which parent would you award sole custody of the child?/Which parent would you deny sole custody of the child?]

		Award	Deny
Parent A:	average income average health average working hours reasonable rapport with the child relatively stable social life	36%	45%
Parent B:	above-average income very close relationship with the child extremely active social life lots of work-related travel minor health problems	64%	55%

Parent A, the impoverished option, is quite plain—with no striking positive or negative features. There are no particularly compelling reasons to award or deny this parent custody of the child. Parent B, the enriched option, on the other hand, has good reasons to be awarded custody (a very close relationship with the child and a good income), but also good reasons to be denied sole custody (health problems and extensive absences due to travel). To the right of the options are the percentages of subjects who chose to award and to deny custody to each of the parents. Parent B is the majority choice both for being awarded custody of the child and for being denied it. As predicted, $P_c + P_r$ for parent B $(64 + 55 = 119)$ is significantly greater than 100, the value expected if choosing and rejecting were complementary $(z = 2.48, p < .02)$. This pattern is explained by the observation that the enriched parent (parent B) provides more compelling reasons to be awarded as well as denied child custody.

The above pattern has been replicated in hypothetical choices between monetary gambles, college courses, and political candidates (Shafir, 1993). For another example, consider the following problem, presented to half the subjects in the "prefer" and to the other half in the "cancel" version.

Problem 2 ($n = 172$):

Prefer:
Imagine that you are planning a week vacation in a warm spot over spring break. You currently have two options that are reasonably priced. The travel brochure gives only a limited amount of information about the two options. Given the information available, which vacation spot would you prefer?

Cancel:
Imagine that you are planning a week vacation in a warm spot over spring break. You currently have two options that are reasonably priced, but you can no longer retain your reservation in both. The travel brochure gives only a limited amount of information about the two options. Given the information available, which reservation do you decide to cancel?

		Prefer	Cancel
Spot A:	average weather average beaches medium-quality hotel medium-temperature water average nightlife	33%	52%
Spot B:	lots of sunshine gorgeous beaches and coral reefs ultra-modern hotel very cold water very strong winds no nightlife	67%	48%

The information about the two spots is typical of the kind of information we have available when deciding where to take our next vacation. Because it is difficult to estimate the overall value of each spot, we are likely to seek reasons on which to base our decision. Spot A, the impoverished option, seems unremarkable yet unobjectionable on all counts. On the other hand, there are obvious reasons—gorgeous beaches, an abundance of sunshine, and an ultra-modern hotel—for choosing spot B. Of course, there are also compelling reasons—cold water, winds, and a lack of nightlife—why spot B should be rejected. We suggest that the gorgeous beaches are likely to provide a more compelling reason when we choose than when we reject, and the lack of nightlife is likely to play a more central role when we reject than when we choose. Indeed, spot B's share of being preferred and rejected exceeds that of spot A ($P_c + P_r = 67 + 48 = 115$, $p < .05$). These results demonstrate that options are not simply ordered according to value, with the more attractive selected and the less attractive rejected. Instead, it appears that the relative importance of options' strengths and weaknesses varies with the nature of the task. As a result, we are significantly more likely to end up in spot B when we ask ourselves which we prefer than when we contemplate which to cancel (67% vs. 52%, $z = 2.83$, $p < .001$).

One of the most basic assumptions of the rational theory of choice is the principle of procedure invariance, which requires strategically equivalent methods of elication to yield identical preferences (see Tversky et al., 1988, for discussion). The choose–reject discrepancy represents a predictable failure of procedure invariance. This phenomenon is at variance with value maximization, but is easily understood from the point of view of reason-based choice: reasons for choosing are more compelling when we choose than when we reject, and reasons for rejecting matter more when we reject than when we choose.

3. Choice under Conflict: Seeking Options

The need to choose often creates conflict: we are not sure how to trade off one attribute relative to another or, for that matter, which attributes matter to us most. It is a commonplace that we often attempt to resolve such conflict by seeking reasons for choosing one option over another. At times, the conflict between available alternatives is hard to resolve, which may lead us to seek additional options, or to maintain the status quo. Other times, the context is such that a comparison between alternatives generates compelling reasons to choose one option over another. Using reasons to resolve conflict has some non-obvious implications, which are addressed below. The present section focuses on people's decision to seek other alternatives; the next section explores some effects of adding options to the set under consideration.

In many contexts, we need to decide whether to opt for an available option or search for additional alternatives. Thus, a person who wishes to buy a used car may settle for a car that is currently available or continue searching for additional models. Seeking new alternatives usually requires additional time and effort, and may involve the risk of losing the previously available options. Conflict plays no role in the classical theory of choice. In this theory, each option x has a value $v(x)$ such that, for any offered set, the decision maker selects the option with the highest value. In particular, a person is expected to search for additional alternatives only if the expected value of searching exceeds that of the best option currently available. A reliance on reasons, on the other hand, entails that we should be more likely to opt for an available option when we have a convincing reason for its selection, and that we should be more likely to search further when a compelling reason for choice is not readily available.

To investigate this hypothesis, Tversky and Shafir (1992b) presented subjects with pairs of options, such as bets varying in probability and payoff, or student apartments varying in monthly rent and distance from campus, and had subjects choose one of the two options or, instead, request an additional option, at some cost. Subjects first reviewed the entire set of 12 options (gambles or apartments) to familiarize themselves with the available alternatives. In the study of choice between bets some subjects then received the following problem.

Conflict:
Imagine that you are offered a choice between the following two gambles:

(x) 65% chance to win $15

(y) 30% chance to win $35

You can either select one of these gambles or you can pay $1 to add one more gamble to the choice set. The added gamble will be selected at random from the list you reviewed.

Other subjects received a similar problem except that option y was replaced by option x', to yield a choice between the following.

Dominance:

(x) 65% chance to win $15

(x') 65% chance to win $14

Subjects were asked to indicate whether they wanted to add another gamble or select between the available alternatives. They then chose their preferred gamble from the resulting set (with or without the added option). Subjects were instructed that the gambles they chose would be played out and that their payoff would be proportional to the amount of money they earned minus the fee they paid for the added gambles.

A parallel design presented choices between hypothetical student apartments. Some subjects received the following problem.

Conflict:

Imagine that you face a choice between two apartments with the following characteristics:

(x) $290 a month, 25 minutes from campus

(y) $350 a month, 7 minutes from campus

Both have one bedroom and a kitchenette. You can choose now between the two apartments or you can continue to search for apartments (to be selected at random from the list you reviewed). In that case, there is some risk of losing one or both of the apartments you have found.

Other subjects received a similar problem except that option y was replaced by option x', to yield a choice between the following.

Dominance:

(x) $290 a month, 25 minutes from campus

(x') $330 a month, 25 minutes from campus

Note that in both pairs of problems the choice between x and y—the *conflict* condition—is non-trivial because the xs are better on one dimension and the ys are better on the other. In contrast, the choice between x and x'—the *dominance* condition—involves no conflict because the former strictly dominates the latter. Thus, while there is no obvious reason to choose one option over the other in the conflict condition, there is a decisive argument for preferring one of the two alternatives in the dominance condition.

On average, subjects requested an additional alternative 64% of the time in the conflict condition, and only 40% of the time in the dominance condition ($p < .05$). Subjects' tendency to search for additional options, in other words, was greater when the choice among alternatives was harder to rationalize, than when there was a compelling reason and the decision was easy.

These data are inconsistent with the principle of value maximization. According to value maximization, a subject should search for additional alternatives if and only if the expected (subjective) value of searching exceeds that of the best alternative currently available. Because the best alternative offered in the dominance condition is also available in the conflict condition, value maximization implies that the percentage of subjects who seek an additional alternative cannot be greater in the conflict than in the dominance condition, contrary to the observed data.

It appears that the search for additional alternatives depends not only on the value of the best available option, as implied by value maximization, but also on the difficulty of choosing among the options under consideration. In situations of dominance, for example, there are clear and indisputable reasons for choosing one option over another (e.g., "This apartment is equally distant and I save $40!"). Having a compelling argument for choosing one of the options over the rest reduces the temptation to look for additional alternatives. When the choice involves conflict, on the other hand, reasons for choosing any one of the options are less immediately available and the decision is more difficult to justify (e.g., "Should I save $60 a month, or reside 18 minutes closer to campus?"). In the absence of compelling reasons for choice, there is a greater tendency to search for other alternatives.

4. Choice under Conflict: Adding Options

An analysis in terms of reasons can help explain observed violations of the principle of independence of irrelevant alternatives, according to which the preference ordering between two options should not be altered by the introduction of additional alternatives. This principle follows from the standard assumption of value maximization, and has been routinely assumed in the analysis of consumer choice. Despite its intuitive appeal, there is a growing body of evidence that people's preferences depend on the context of choice, defined by the set of options under consideration. In particular, the addition and removal of options from the offered set can influence people's preferences among options that were available all along. Whereas in the previous section we considered people's tendency to seek alternatives in the context of a given set of options, in this section we illustrate phenomena that arise through the addition of options, and interpret them in terms of reasons for choice.

A major testable implication of value maximization is that a non-preferred option cannot become preferred when new options are added to the offered set. In particular, a decision maker who prefers y over the option to defer the choice should not prefer to defer the choice when both y and x are available. That the "market share" of an option cannot be increased by enlarging the offered set is known as the *regularity condition* (see Tversky & Simonson, in press). Contrary to regularity, numerous experimental results indicate that the tendency to defer choice can increase with the addition of alternatives. Consider, for instance, the degree of conflict that arises when a person is presented with one attractive option (which he or she prefers to deferring the choice), compared to two competing alternatives. Choosing one out of two competing alternatives can be difficult: the mere fact that an alternative is attractive may not in itself provide a compelling reason for its selection, because the other option may be equally attractive. The addition of an alternative may thus make the decision harder to justify, and increase the tendency to defer the decision.

A related phenomenon was aptly described by Thomas Schelling, who tells of an occasion in which he had decided to buy an encyclopedia for his children. At the bookstore, he was presented with two attractive encyclopedias and, finding it difficult to choose between the two, ended up buying neither—this, despite the fact that had only one encyclopedia been available he would have happily bought it. More generally, there are situations in which people prefer each of the available alternatives over the status quo but do not have a compelling reason for choosing among the alternatives and, as a result, defer the decision, perhaps indefinitely.

The phenomenon described by Schelling was demonstrated by Tversky and Shafir (1992b) in the following pair of problems, which were presented to two groups of students ($n = 124$ and 121, respectively).

High conflict:
Suppose you are considering buying a compact disk (CD) player, and have not yet decided what model to buy. You pass by a store that is having a 1-day clearance sale. They offer a popular SONY player for just $99, and a top-of-the-line AIWA player for just $169, both well below the list price. Do you?:

(*x*) buy the AIWA player.	27%
(*y*) buy the SONY player.	27%
(*z*) wait until you learn more about the various models.	46%

Low conflict:
Suppose you are considering buying a CD player, and have not yet decided what model to buy. You pass by a store that is having a 1-day clearance sale. They offer a popular SONY player for just $99, well below the list price. Do you?:

(*y*) buy the SONY player.	66%
(*z*) wait until you learn more about the various models.	34%

The results indicate that people are more likely to buy a CD player in the latter, *low-conflict*, condition than in the former, *high-conflict*, situation ($p < .05$). Both models—the AIWA and the SONY—seem attractive, both are well priced, and both are on sale. The decision maker needs to determine whether she is better off with a cheaper, popular model, or with a more expensive and sophisticated one. This conflict is apparently not easy to resolve, and compels many subjects to put off the purchase until they learn more about the various options. On the other hand, when the SONY alone is available, there are compelling arguments for its purchase: it is a popular player, it is very well priced, and it is on sale for 1 day only. In this situation, having good reasons to choose the offered option, a greater majority of subjects decide to opt for the CD player rather than delay the purchase.

The addition of a competing alternative in the preceding example increased the tendency to delay decision. Clearly, the level of conflict and its ease of resolution depend not only on the number of options available, but on how the options compare. Consider, for example, the following problem, in which the original AIWA player was replaced by an inferior model ($n = 62$).

Dominance:
Suppose you are considering buying a CD player, and have not yet decided what model to buy. You pass by a store that is having a 1-day clearance sale. They offer a popular SONY player for just $99, well below the list price, and an inferior AIWA player for the regular list price of $105. Do you?:

(x')	buy the AIWA player.	3%
(y)	buy the SONY player.	73%
(z)	wait until you learn more about the various models.	24%

In this version, contrary to the previous *high-conflict* version, the AIWA player is dominated by the SONY: it is inferior in quality and costs more. Thus, the presence of the AIWA does not detract from the reasons for buying the SONY, it actually supplements them: the SONY is well priced, it is on sale for 1 day only, *and* it is clearly better than its competitor. As a result, the SONY is chosen more often than before the inferior AIWA was added. The ability of an asymmetrically dominated or relatively inferior alternative, when added to a set, to increase the attractiveness and choice probability of the dominating option is known as the asymmetric dominance effect (Huber, Payne, & Puto, 1982). Note that in both the *high-conflict* and the *dominance* problems subjects were presented with two CD players and an option to delay choice. Subjects' tendency to delay, however, is much greater when they lack clear reasons for buying either player, than when they have compelling reasons to buy one player and not the other ($p < .005$).

The above patterns violate the regularity condition, which is assumed to hold so long as the added alternatives do not provide new and relevant information. In the above scenario, one could argue that the added options (the superior player in one case and the inferior player in the other) conveyed information about the consumer's chances of finding a better deal. Recall that information considerations could not explain the search experiments of the previous section because there subjects reviewed all the potentially available options. Nevertheless, to test this interpretation further, Tversky and Shafir (1992b) devised a similar problem, involving real payoffs, in which the option to defer is not available. Students ($n = 80$) agreed to fill out a brief questionnaire for $1.50. Following the questionnaire, one half of the subjects were offered the opportunity to exchange the $1.50 (the default) for one of two prizes: a metal Zebra pen (henceforth, Zebra), or a pair of plastic Pilot pens (henceforth, Pilot). The other half of the subjects were only offered the opportunity to exchange the $1.50 for the Zebra. The prizes were shown to the subjects, who were also informed that each prize regularly costs a little over $2.00. Upon indicating their preference, subjects received their chosen option. The results were as follows. Seventy-five per cent of the subjects chose the Zebra over the payment when the Zebra was the only alternative, but only 47% chose the Zebra *or* the Pilot when both were available ($p < .05$). Faced with a tempting alternative, subjects had a compelling reason to forego the payment: the majority took advantage of the opportunity to obtain an attractive prize of greater value. The availability of competing alternatives of comparable value, on the other hand, did not present an immediate reason for choosing either alternative over the other, thus increasing the tendency to retain the default option. Similar effects in hypothetical medical decisions made by expert physicians are documented in Redelmeier and Shafir (1993).

In the above study the addition of a competing alternative was shown to increase the popularity of the default option. Recall that the popularity of an option may also be enhanced by the addition of an inferior alternative. Thus, in accord with the asymmetric dominance effect, the tendency to prefer *x* over *y* can be increased by adding a third alternative *z* that is clearly inferior to *x* but not to *y* (see figure 39.1). The phenomenon of asymmetric dominance was first demonstrated, by Huber, Payne, and Puto (1982), in choices between hypothetical options. Wedell (1991) reports similar findings using monetary gambles. The following example involving real choices is taken from Simonson and Tversky (1992). One group ($n = 106$) was offered a choice between $6 and an elegant Cross pen. The pen was selected by 36% of the subjects, and the remaining 64% chose the cash. A second group ($n = 115$) was given a choice among three options: $6 in cash, the same Cross pen, and a sec-

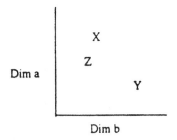

Figure 39.1
A schematic representation of asymmetric dominance. The tendency to prefer *x* over *y* can be increased by adding an alternative, *z*, that is clearly inferior to *x* but not to *y*.

ond pen that was distinctly less attractive. Only 2% of the subjects chose the less attractive pen, but its presence increased the percentage of subjects who chose the Cross pen from 36% to 46% ($p < .10$). This pattern again violates the regularity condition discussed earlier. Similar violations of regularity were observed in choices among other consumer goods. In one study, subjects received descriptions and pictures of microwave ovens taken from a "Best" catalogue. One group ($n = 60$) was then asked to choose between an Emerson priced at $110, and a Panasonic priced at $180. Both items were on sale, one third off the regular price. Here, 57% chose the Emerson and 43% chose the Panasonic. A second group ($n = 60$) was presented with these options along with a $200 Panasonic at a 10% discount. Only 13% of the subjects chose the more expensive Panasonic, but its presence increased the percentage of subjects who chose the less expensive Panasonic from 43% to 60% ($p < .05$).[1]

Simonson and Tversky (1992) have interpreted these observations in terms of "tradeoff contrast." They proposed that the tendency to prefer an alternative is enhanced or hindered depending on whether the tradeoffs within the set under consideration are favorable or unfavorable to that alternative. A second cluster of context effects, called *extremeness aversion*, which refers to the finding that, within an offered set, options with extreme values are relatively less attractive than options with intermediate values (Simonson, 1989). For example, consider two-dimensional options x, y, and z, such that y lies between x and z (see figure 39.2). Considerations of value maximization imply that the middle alternative, y, should be relatively less popular in the trinary choice than in either one of the binary comparisons (y compared to x, or y compared to z). Extremeness aversion, on the other hand, yields the opposite prediction because y has small advantages and disadvantages with respect to x and to z, whereas both x and z have more extreme advantages and disadvantages with respect to each other. This pattern was observed in several experiments. For example, subjects were shown five 35 mm cameras varying in quality and price.

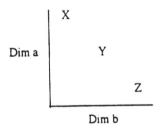

Figure 39.2
A schematic representation of extremeness aversion. Option y is relatively more popular in the trinary choice, when both x and z are available, than in either one of the binary comparisons, when either x or z are removed.

One group ($n = 106$) was then given a choice between two cameras: a Minolta X-370 priced at \$170 and a Minolta 3000i priced at \$240. A second group ($n = 115$) was given an additional option, the Minolta 7000i priced at \$470. Subjects in the first group were split evenly between the two options, yet 57% of the subjects in the second group chose the middle option (Minolta 3000i), with the remaining divided about equally between the two extreme options. Thus, the introduction of an extreme option reduced the "market share" of the other extreme option, but not of the middle option. Note that this effect cannot be attributed to information conveyed by the offered set because respondents had reviewed the relevant options prior to making their choice.

We suggest that both tradeoff contrast and extremeness aversion can be understood in terms of reasons. Suppose a decision maker faces a choice between two alternatives, x and y, and suppose x is of higher quality whereas y is better priced. This produces conflict if the decision maker finds it difficult to determine whether the quality difference outweighs the price difference. Suppose now that the choice set also includes a third alternative, z, that is clearly inferior to y but not to x. The presence of z, we suggest, provides an argument for choosing y over x. To the extent that the initial choice between x and y is difficult, the presence of z may help the decision maker break the tie. In the pen study, for example, the addition of the relatively unattractive pen, whose monetary value is unclear but whose inferiority to the elegant Cross pen is apparent, provides a reason for choosing the Cross pen over the cash. Similarly, in the presence of options with extreme values on the relevant dimensions, the middle option can be seen as a compromise choice that is easier to defend than either extremes. Indeed, verbal protocols show that the accounts generated by subjects while making these choices involve considerations of asymmetric advantage and compromise; furthermore, asymmetric dominance is enhanced when subjects anticipate having to justify their decisions to others (Simonson, 1989). It is noteworthy that the arguments leading to tradeoff contrast and extremeness aversion are comparative in nature; they are based on the positions of the options in the choice set, hence they cannot be readily translated into the values associated with single alternatives.

Tversky and Simonson (in press) have proposed a formal model that explains the above findings in terms of a tournament-like process in which each option is compared against other available options in terms of their relative advantages and disadvantages. This model can be viewed as a formal analog of the preceding qualitative account based on reasons for choice. Which analysis—the formal or the qualitative—proves more useful is likely to depend, among other things, on the nature of the problem and on the purpose of the investigation.

5. Definite versus Disjunctive Reasons

People sometimes encounter situations of uncertainty in which they eventually opt for the same course of action, but for very different reasons, depending on how the uncertainty is resolved. Thus, a student who has taken an exam may decide to take a vacation, either to reward herself in case she passes or to console herself in case she fails. However, as illustrated below, the student may be reluctant to commit to a vacation while the outcome of the exam is pending. The following problem was presented by Tversky and Shafir (1992a) to 66 undergraduate students.

Disjunctive version:
Imagine that you have just taken a tough qualifying examination. It is the end of the fall quarter, you feel tired and run-down, and you are not sure that you passed the exam. In case you failed you have to take the exam again in a couple of months—after the Christmas holidays. You now have an opportunity to buy a very attractive 5-day Christmas vacation package in Hawaii at an exceptionally low price. The special offer expires tomorrow, while the exam grade will not be available until the following day. Would you?:

(a) buy the vacation package.   32%

(b) not buy the vacation package.   7%

(c) pay a $5 non-refundable fee in order to retain the rights to   61%
     buy the vacation package at the same exceptional price the
     day after tomorrow—after you find out whether or not you
     passed the exam.

The percentage of subjects who chose each option appears on the right. Two additional versions, called *pass* and *fail*, were presented to two different groups of 67 students each. These two versions differed only in the expression in brackets.

Pass/fail versions:
Imagine that you have just taken a tough qualifying examination. It is the end of the fall quarter, you feel tired and run-down, and you find out that you [passed the exam./failed the exam. You will have to take it again in a couple of months—after the Christmas holidays.] You now have an opportunity to buy a very attractive 5-day Christmas vacation package in Hawaii at an exceptionally low price. The special offer expires tomorrow. Would you?:

	Pass	*Fail*
(a) buy the vacation package.	54%	57%
(b) not buy the vacation package.	16%	12%
(c) pay a $5 non-refundable fee in order to retain the rights to buy the vacation package at the same exceptional price the day after tomorrow.	30%	31%

The data show that more than half of the students chose the vacation package when they knew that they passed the exam and an even larger percentage chose the vacation when they knew that they failed. However, when they did not know whether they had passed or failed, less than one third of the students chose the vacation and 61% were willing to pay $5 to postpone the decision until the following day, when the results of the exam would be known.[2] Once the outcome of the exam is known, the student has good—albeit different—reasons for taking the trip: having passed the exam, the vacation is presumably seen as a reward following a hard but successful semester; having failed the exam, the vacation becomes a consolation and time to recuperate before a re-examination. Not knowing the outcome of the exam, however, the student lacks a definite reason for going to Hawaii. Notice that the outcome of the exam will be known long before the vacation begins. Thus, the uncertainty characterizes the actual moment of decision, not the eventual vacation.

The indeterminacy of reasons for going to Hawaii discourages many students from buying the vacation, even when both outcomes—passing or failing the exam— ultimately favor this course of action. Tversky and Shafir (1992a) call the above pattern of decisions a *disjunction effect*. Evidently, a disjunction of different reasons (reward in case of success or consolation in case of failure) is often less compelling than either definite reason alone. A significant proportion of the students above were willing to pay, in effect, for information that was ultimately not going to affect their decision—they would choose to go to Hawaii in either case—but that promised to leave them with a more definite reason for making that choice. The willingness to pay for non-instrumental information is at variance with the classical model, in which the worth of information is determined only by its potential to influence decision.

People's preference for definite as opposed to disjunctive reasons has significant implications in cases where the option to defer decision is not available. Consider the following series of problems presented by Tversky and Shafir (1992a) to 98 students.

Win/lose version:
Imagine that you have just played a game of chance that gave you a 50% chance to win $200 and a 50% chance to lose $100. The coin was tossed and you have [won $200/lost $100]. You are now offered a second identical gamble: 50% chance to win $200 and 50% chance to lose $100. Would you?:

	Won	*Lost*
(a) accept the second gamble.	69%	59%
(b) reject the second gamble.	31%	41%

The students were presented with the *win* version of the problem above, followed a week later by the *lose* version, and 10 days after that by the following version that is a disjunction of the previous two. The problems were embedded among other, similar problems so that the relation between the various versions was not transparent. Subjects were instructed to treat each decision separately.

Disjunctive version:
Imagine that you have just played a game of chance that gave you a 50% chance to win $200 and a 50% chance to lose $100. Imagine that the coin has already been tossed, but that you will not know whether you have won $200 or lost $100 until you make your decision concerning a second, identical gamble: 50% chance to win $200 and 50% chance to lose $100. Would you?:

(a) accept the second gamble.   36%
(b) reject the second gamble.   64%

The data show that a majority of subjects accepted the second gamble after having won the first gamble and a majority also accepted the second gamble after having lost the first gamble. However, the majority of subjects rejected the second gamble when the outcome of the first was not known. An examination of individual choices reveals that approximately 40% of the subjects accepted the second gamble both after a gain in the first and after a loss. Among these, however, 65% rejected the second gamble in the disjunctive condition, when the outcome of the first gamble was not known. Indeed, this response pattern (accepting in both conditions but rejecting in the disjunction) was the single most frequent pattern, exhibited by 27% of all subjects. This pattern, which violates Savage's (1954) sure-thing principle, cannot be attributed to unreliability (Tversky & Shafir, 1992a).

The students above were offered a gamble with a positive expected value, and an even chance of a non-trivial loss. Different reasons were likely to arise for accepting the second gamble depending on the outcome of the first. In the *win* condition, the decision maker is already up $200, so even a loss on the second gamble leaves him or her ahead overall, which makes this option quite attractive. In the *lose* condition, on the other hand, the decision maker is down $100. Playing the second gamble offers a chance to "get out of the red", which for many is more attractive than accepting a sure $100 loss. In the *disjunctive* condition, however, the decision maker does not know whether she is up $200 or down $100; she does not know, in other words, whether her reason for playing the second gamble is that it is a no-loss proposition or, instead, that it provides a chance to escape a sure loss. In the absence of a definite reason, fewer subjects accept the second gamble.

This interpretation is further supported by the following modification of the above problem, in which both outcomes of the first gamble were increased by $400 so that the decision maker could not lose in either case.

Imagine that you have just played a game of chance that gave you a 50% chance to win $600 and a 50% chance to win $300. Imagine that the coin has already been tossed, but that you will not know whether you have won $600 or $300 until you make your decision concerning a second gamble: 50% chance to win $200 and 50% chance to lose $100.

A total of 171 subjects were presented with this problem, equally divided into three groups. One group was told that they had won $300 on the first gamble, a second group was told that they had won $600 on the first gamble, and the third group was told that the outcome of the first gamble—$300 or $600—was not known (the disjunctive version). In all cases, subjects had to decide whether to accept or to reject the second gamble which, as in the previous problem, consisted of an even chance to win $200 or lose $100. The percentage of subjects who accepted the second gamble in the $300, $600, and disjunctive versions, were 69%, 75%, and 73%, respectively. (Recall that the corresponding figures for the original problem were 59%, 69%, and 36%; essentially identical figures were obtained in a between-subjects replication of that problem.) In contrast to the original problem, the second gamble in this modified problem was equally popular in the disjunctive as in the non-disjunctive versions. Whereas in the original scenario the second gamble amounted to either a no-loss proposition or a chance to avoid a sure loss, in the modified scenario the second gamble amounts to a no-loss proposition regardless of the outcome of the first gamble. The increased popularity of the second gamble in the modified problem shows that it is not the disjunctive situation itself that discourages people from playing. Rather, it is the lack of a specific reason that seems to drive the effect: when the same reason applies regardless of outcome, the disjunction no longer reduces the tendency to accept the gamble.

As illustrated above, changes in the context of decision are likely to alter the reasons that subjects bring to mind and, consequently, their choices. Elsewhere (Shafir & Tversky, 1992) we describe a disjunction effect in the context of a one-shot prisoner's dilemma game, played on a computer for real payoffs. Subjects ($n = 80$) played a series of prisoner's dilemma games, without feedback, each against a different unknown player. In this setup, the rate of cooperation was 3% when subjects knew that the other player had defected, and 16% when they knew that the other had cooperated. However, when subjects did not know whether the other player had cooperated or defected (the standard version of the prisoner's dilemma game) the rate of cooperation rose to 37%. Thus, many subjects defected when they knew the other's choice—be it cooperation or defection—but cooperated when the other player's choice was not known. Shafir and Tversky (1992) attribute this pattern to the different perspectives that underlie subjects' behavior under uncertainty as opposed to when the uncertainty is resolved. In particular, we suggest that the reasons for competing are more compelling when the other player's decision is known and the payoff depends on the subject alone, than when the other's chosen strategy is uncertain, and the outcome of the game depends on the choices of both players.

The above "disjunctive" manipulation—which has no direct bearing from the point of view of value maximization—appears to influence the reasons for decision that people bring to mind. Another kind of manipulation that seems to alter people's reasons without bearing directly on options' values is described in what follows.

6. Non-Valued Features

Reasons for choice or rejection often refer to specific features of the options under consideration. The positive features of an option typically provide reasons for choosing that option and its negative features typically provide reasons for rejection. What happens when we add features that are neither attractive nor aversive? Can choice be influenced by features that have little or no value?

Simonson and his colleagues have conducted a number of studies on the effects of non-valued features, and tested the hypothesis that people are reluctant to choose alternatives that are supported by reasons that they do not find appealing. In one study, for example, Simonson, Nowlis, and Simonson (in press) predicted that people would be less likely to choose an alternative that was chosen by another person for a reason that does not apply to them. UC Berkeley business students ($n = 113$) were told that, because of budget cuts and in order to save paper and duplicating costs, a questionnaire that they will receive was designed for use by two respondents. Thus, when subjects had to enter a choice, they could see the choice made by the previous "respondent" and the reason given for it. The choices and reasons of the previous respondents were systematically manipulated. One problem, for example, offered a choice between attending the MBA programs at Northwestern and UCLA. In one version of the questionnaire, the previous respondent had selected Northwestern, and provided the (handwritten) reason, "I have many relatives in the Chicago area." Because this reason does not apply to most subjects, it was expected to reduce their likelihood of choosing Northwestern. In a second version, no reason was given for the choice of Northwestern. As expected, those exposed to an irrelevant reason were less likely to choose Northwestern than subjects who saw the other respondent's choice but not his or her reason (23% vs. 43%, $p < .05$). It should be noted that both Northwestern and UCLA are well known to most subjects (Northwestern currently has the highest ranked MBA program; the UCLA program is ranked high and belongs to the same UC system as Berkeley). Thus, it is unlikely that subjects made inferences about the quality of Northwestern based on the fact that another respondent chose it because he or she had relatives in Chicago.

In a related study, Simonson, Carmon, and O'Curry (in press) showed that endowing an option with a feature that was intended to be positive but, in fact, has no value for the decision maker can reduce the tendency to choose that option, even when subjects realize that they are not paying for the added feature. For example, an offer to purchase a collector's plate—that most did not want—if one buys a particular brand of cake mix was shown to lower the tendency to buy that particular brand relative to a second, comparable cake mix brand (from 31% to 14%, $p < .05$). Choosing brands that offer worthless bonuses was judged (in a related study) as more difficult to justify and as more susceptible to criticism. An analysis of verbal protocols showed that a majority of those who failed to select the endowed option explicitly mentioned not needing the added feature. It should be noted that sale promotions, such as the one involving the collector's plate offer above, are currently employed by a wide range of companies and there is no evidence that they lead to any inferences about the quality of the promoted product (e.g., Blattberg & Neslin, 1990).

The above manipulations all added "positive," albeit weak or irrelevant, features, which should not diminish an option's value; yet, they apparently provide a reason against choosing the option, especially when other options are otherwise equally attractive. Evidently, the addition of a potentially attractive feature that proves useless can provide a reason to reject the option in favor of a competing alternative that has no "wasted" features.

7. Concluding Remarks

People's choices may occasionally stem from affective judgments that preclude a thorough evaluation of the options (cf. Zajonc, 1980). In such cases, an analysis of the reasons for choice may prove unwarranted and, when attempted by the decision maker, may actually result in a different, and possibly inferior, decision (Wilson & Schooler, 1991). Other choices, furthermore, may follow standard operating procedures that involve minimal reflective effort. Many decisions, nonetheless, result from a careful evaluation of options, in which people attempt to arrive at what they believe is the best choice. Having discarded the less attractive options and faced with a choice that is hard to resolve, people often search for a compelling rationale for choosing one alternative over another. In this chapter, we presented an analysis of the role of reasons in decision making, and considered ways in which an analysis based on reasons may contribute to the standard quantitative approach based on the maximization of value. A number of hypotheses that derive from this perspective were investigated in experimental settings.

The reasons that enter into the making of decisions are likely to be intricate and diverse. In the preceding sections we have attempted to identify a few general principles that govern the role of reasons in decision making, and thus some of the fundamental ways in which thinking about reasons is likely to contribute to our understanding of the making of decisions. A reliance on the more important dimensions—those likely to provide more compelling reasons for choice—was shown in section 1 to predict preferences between previously equated options. The notions of compatibility and salience were summoned in section 2 to account for the differential weighting of reasons in a choice versus rejection task. Reasons, it appears, lend themselves to certain framing manipulations that are harder to explain from the perspective of value maximization. In section 3, manipulating the precise relationships between competing alternatives was shown to enhance or reduce conflict, yielding decisions that were easier or more difficult to rationalize and justify. Providing a context that presents compelling reasons for choosing an option apparently increases people's tendency to opt for that option, whereas comparing alternatives that render the aforementioned reasons less compelling tends to increase people's tendency to maintain the status quo or search for other alternatives. The ability of the context of decision to generate reasons that affect choice was further discussed in section 4, where the addition and removal of competing alternatives was interpreted as generating arguments for choice based on comparative considerations of relative advantages and compromise. The relative weakness of disjunctive reasons was discussed in section 5. There, a number of studies contrasted people's willingness to reach a decision based on a definite reason for choice, with their reluctance to arrive at a decision in the presence of uncertainty about which reason is actually relevant to the case at hand. Section 6 briefly reviewed choice situations in which the addition of purported reasons for choosing an option, which subjects did not find compelling, was seen to diminish their tendency to opt for that option, even though its value had not diminished.

The nature of the reasons that guide decision, and the ways in which they interact, await further investigation. There is evidence to suggest that a wide variety of arguments play a role in decision making. We often search for a convincing rationale for the decisions that we make, whether for inter-personal purposes, so that we can explain to others the reasons for our decision, or for intra-personal motives, so that we may feel confident of having made the "right" choice. Attitudes toward risk and loss can sometimes be rationalized on the basis of common myths or clichés, and choices are sometimes made on the basis of moral or prudential principles that are used to override specific cost–benefit calculations (cf. Prelec & Herrnstein, 1991). Formal decision rules, moreover, may sometimes act as arguments in people's deliberations. Thus, when choosing between options x and z, we may realize that, sometime earlier, we had preferred x over y and y over z and that, therefore, by transitivity, we should now choose x over z. Montgomery (1983) has argued that people look for dominance structures in decision problems because they provide a compelling reason for choice. Similarly, Tversky, and Shafir (1992a) have shown that detecting the applicability of the sure-thing principle to a decision situation leads people to act in accord with this principle's compelling rationale. Indeed, it has been repeatedly observed that the axioms of rational choice which are often violated in non-transparent situations are generally satisfied when their application is transparent (e.g., Tversky & Kahneman, 1986). These results suggest that the axioms of rational choice act as compelling arguments, or reasons, for making a particular decision when their applicability has been detected, not as universal laws that constrain people's choices.

In contrast to the classical theory that assumes stable values and preferences, it appears that people often do not have well-established values, and that preferences are actually constructed—not merely revealed—during their elicitation (cf. Payne, Bettman, & Johnson, 1992). A reason-based approach lends itself well to such a constructive interpretation. Decisions, according to this analysis, are often reached by focusing on reasons that justify the selection of one option over another. Different frames, contexts, and elicitation procedures highlight different aspects of the options and bring forth different reasons and considerations that influence decision.

The reliance on reasons to explain experimental findings has been the hallmark of social psychological analyses. Accounts of dissonance (Wicklund & Brehm, 1976) and self-perception (Bem, 1972), for example, focus on the reasons that people muster in an attempt to explain their counter-attitudinal behaviors. Similarly, attribution theory (Heider, 1980) centers around the reasons that people attribute to others' behavior. These studies, however, have primarily focused on postdecisional rationalization rather than predecisional conflict. Although the two processes are closely related, there are nevertheless some important differences. Much of the work in social psychology has investigated how people's decisions affect the way they think. The present paper, in contrast, has considered how the reasons that enter into people's thinking about a problem influence their decision. A number of researchers have recently begun to explore related issues. Billig (1987), for example, has adopted a rhetorical approach to understanding social psychological issues, according to which "our inner deliberations are silent arguments conducted within a single self" (p. 5). Related "explanation-based" models of decision making have been applied by Pennington and Hastie (1988, 1992) to account for judicial decisions, and the importance of social accountability in choice has been addressed by Tetlock (1992). From a philosophical perspective, a recent essay by Schick (1991) analyzes various decisions from the point of view of practical reason. An influential earlier work is Toulmin's (1950) study of the role of arguments in ethical reasoning.

In this chapter, we have attempted to explore some of the ways in which reasons and arguments enter into people's decisions. A reason-based analysis may come closer to capturing part of the psychology that underlies decision and thus may help shed light on a number of phenomena that remain counterintuitive from the perspective of the classical theory. It is instructive to note that many of the experimental studies described in this chapter were motivated by intuitions stemming from a qualitative analysis based on reasons, not from a value-based perspective, even if they can later be interpreted in that fashion. We do not propose that accounts based on reasons replace value-based models of choice. Rather, we suggest that an analysis of reasons may illuminate some aspects of reflective choice, and generate new hypotheses for further study.

Notes

This research was supported by US Public Health Service Grant No. 1-R29-MH46885 from the National Institute of Mental Health, by Grant No. 89-0064 from the Air Force Office of Scientific Research and by Grant No. SES-9109535 from the National Science Foundation. The chapter was partially prepared while the first author participated in a Summer Institute on Negotiation and Dispute Resolution at the Center for Advanced Study in the Behavioral Sciences, and while the second author was at the University of California, Berkeley. Funds for support of the Summer Institute were provided by the Andrew W. Mellon Foundation. We thank Robyn Dawes for helpful comments on an earlier draft.

1. These effects of context on choice can naturally be used in sales tactics. For example, Williams-Sonoma, a mail-order business located in San Francisco, used to offer a bread-baking appliance priced at $279. They later added a second bread-baking appliance, similar to the first but somewhat larger, and priced at $429—more than 50% higher than the original appliance. Not surprisingly, Williams-Sonoma did not sell many units of the new item. However, the sales of the less expensive appliance almost doubled. (To the best of our knowledge, Williams-Sonoma did not anticipate this effect.)

2. An additional group of subjects ($n = 123$) were presented with both the fail and the pass versions, and asked whether or not they would buy the vacation package in each case. Two thirds of the subjects made the same choice in the two conditions, indicating that the data for the disjunctive version cannot be explained by the hypothesis that those who like the vacation in case they pass the exam do not like it in

case they fail, and vice versa. Note that while only one third of the subjects made different decisions depending on the outcome of the exam, more than 60% of the subjects chose to wait when the outcome was not known.

References

Allison, G. T. (1971). *Essence of decision: explaining the Cuban missile crisis*. Boston: Little Brown.

Bem, D. J. (1972). Self-perception theory. In L. Berkowitz (Ed.), *Advances in experimental social psychology* (vol. 6). New York: Academic Press.

Berman, L. (1982). *Planning a tragedy*. New York: Norton.

Betts, R., & Gelb, L. (1979). *The irony of Vietnam: the system worked*. Washington, DC: Brookings Institution.

Bigelow, J. (Ed.) (1887). *The complete works of Benjamin Franklin* (vol. 4). New York: Putnam.

Billig, M. (1987). *Arguing and thinking: a rhetorical approach to social psychology*. New York: Cambridge University Press.

Blattberg, R. C., & Neslin, S. A. (1990). *Sales promotion: concepts, methods, and strategies*. Englewood Cliffs, NJ: Prentice-Hall.

Heider, F. (1980). *The psychology of interpersonal relations*. New York: Wiley.

Huber, J., Payne, J. W., and Puto, C. (1982). Adding asymmetrically dominated alternatives: violations of regularity and the similarity hypothesis. *Journal of Consumer Research, 9*, 90–98.

James, W. (1981). *The principles of psychology* (vol. 2). Cambridge, MA: Harvard University Press.

Kahneman, D., & Tversky, A. (1979). Prospect theory: an analysis of decision under risk. *Econometrica, 47*, 263–291.

Montgomery, H. (1983). Decision rules and the search for a dominance structure: towards a process model of decision making. In P. Humphreys, O. Svenson, & A. Vari (Eds.), *Analyzing and aiding decision processes*. Amsterdam: North-Holland.

Nisbett, R. E., & Wilson, T. D. (1977). Telling more than we can know: verbal reports on mental processes. *Psychological Review, 84*, 231–259.

Payne, J. W., Bettman, J. R., & Johnson, E. J. (1992). Behavioral decision research: a constructive process perspective. *Annual Review of Psychology, 43*, 87–131.

Pennington, N., & Hastie, R. (1988). Explanation-based decision making: effects of memory structure on judgment. *Journal of Experimental Psychology: Learning, Memory, and Cognition, 14*, 521–533.

Pennington, N., & Hastie, R. (1992). Explaining the evidence: tests of the story model for juror decision making. *Journal of Personality and Social Psychology, 62*, 189–206.

Prelec, D., & Herrnstein, R. J. (1991). Preferences or principles: alternative guidelines for choice. In R. J. Zeckhauser (Ed.), *Strategy and choice*. Cambridge, MA: MIT Press.

Redelmeter, D., & Shafir, E. (1993). Medical decisions over multiple alternatives. Working paper, University of Toronto.

Savage, L. J. (1954). *The foundations of statistics*. New York: Wiley.

Schick, F. (1991). *Understanding action: an essay on reasons*. New York: Cambridge University Press.

Shater, G. (1986). Savage revisited. *Statistical Science, 1*, 463–485.

Shafir, E. (1993). Choosing versus rejecting: why some options are both better and worse than others. *Memory & Cognition, 21*, 546–556.

Shafir, E., & Tversky, A. (1992). Thinking through uncertainty: nonconsequential reasoning and choice. *Cognitive Psychology, 24*, 449–474.

Simonson, I. (1989). Choice based on reasons: the case of attraction and compromise effects. *Journal of Consumer Research, 16,* 158–174.

Simonson, I., Carmon, Z., & O'Curry, S. (in press). Experimental evidence on the negative effect of unique product features and sales promotions on brand choice. *Marketing Science.*

Simonson, I., Nowlis, S., & Simonson, Y. (in press). The effect of irrelevant preference arguments on consumer choice. *Journal of Consumer Psychology.*

Simonson, I., & Tversky, A. (1992). Choice in context: tradeoff contrast and extremeness aversion. *Journal of Marketing Research, 29,* 281–295.

Slovic, P. (1975). Choice between equally valued alternatives. *Journal of Experimental Psychology: Human Perception and Performance, 1,* 280–287.

Slovic, P. (1990). Choice. In D. Osherson & E. Smith (Eds.), *An invitation to cognitive science* (vol. 3). Cambridge, MA: MIT Press.

Telhami, S. (1990). *Power and leadership in international bargaining: the path to the Camp David accords.* New York: Columbia University Press.

Tetlock, P. E. (1992). The impact of accountability on judgment and choice: toward a social contingency model. In M. P. Zanna (Ed.), *Advances in experimental social psychology* (vol. 25). New York: Academic Press.

Toulmin, S. (1950). *The place of reason in ethics.* New York: Cambridge University Press.

Tversky, A., & Kahneman, D. (1986). Rational choice and the framing of decisions. *Journal of Business, 59,* 251–278.

Tversky, A., Sattath, S., & Slovic, P. (1988). Contingent weighting in judgment and choice. *Psychological Review, 95,* 371–384.

Tversky, A., & Shafir, E. (1992a). The disjunction effect in choice under uncertainty. *Psychological Science, 3,* 305–309.

Tversky, A., & Shafir, E. (1992b). Choice under conflict: the dynamics of deferred decision. *Psychological Science, 3,* 358–361.

Tversky, A., & Simonson, I. (in press). Context-dependent preferences. *Management Science.*

von Neumann, J., & Morgenstern, O. (1947). *Theory of games and economic behavior.* Princeton, NJ: Princeton University Press.

Wedell, D. H. (1991). Distinguishing among models of contextually induced preference reversals. *Journal of Experimental Psychology: Learning, Memory, and Cognition, 17,* 767–778.

Wicklund, R. A., & Brehm, J. W. (1976). *Perspectives on cognitive dissonance.* Hillsdale, NJ: Erlbaum.

Wilson, T. D., & Schooler, J. W. (1991). Thinking too much: introspection can reduce the quality of preferences and decisions. *Journal of Personality and Social Psychology, 60,* 181–192.

Zajonc, B. (1980). Preferences without inferences. *American Psychologist, 35,* 151–175.

40 Context-Dependence in Legal Decision Making

Mark Kelman, Yuval Rottenstreich, and Amos Tversky

Introduction

Normative analyses of choice commonly assume *value maximization:* a numerical value or utility is associated with each option such that, given a set of options, the decision maker chooses the one with the highest value. An immediate consequence of value maximization, called *context-independence*, is that the relative ranking of any two options should not vary with the addition or deletion of other options.[1] A person who prefers chicken over pasta should not change this preference on learning that fish is also available.[2] Despite its intuitive appeal, there is evidence[3] that decision makers do not always satisfy this condition. In this article, we test the descriptive validity of context-independence in legal settings and discuss its prescriptive implications.

Two types of violations of context-independence—*compromise effects* and *contrast effects*—have recently been demonstrated. "Compromise effect" refers to the finding that the same option is evaluated more favorably when it is seen as intermediate in the set of options under consideration than when it is extreme. Consequently, compromise implies that the relative ranking of two options depends on the presence or absence of other options. Salespeople sometimes exploit this tendency by showing both bare bones and fancy products in order to induce customers to buy an intermediate product. Several experiments have demonstrated compromise effects. In one experiment subjects first reviewed several available Minolta cameras in a catalog. One group chose between a mid-level Minolta camera and a low-end camera; 50 percent chose each camera. Another group could also choose a third, high-end camera. In this group, of those choosing either the mid-level or low-end camera, 72 percent chose the mid-level camera.[4]

"Trade-off contrast," or simply "contrast," refers to the observation that the same option is evaluated more favorably in the presence of similar options clearly inferior to it than in the absence of such options. Contrast effects, more generally, are ubiquitous in perception and judgment. The same circle appears larger when surrounded by small circles and smaller when surrounded by large ones. Similarly, the same product may appear attractive on the background of less attractive alternatives and unattractive on the background of more attractive ones.[5] Real estate agents interested in selling a particular home sometimes show customers a similar home that is clearly less attractive. Experimental studies also demonstrate contrast effects. Given the choice between $6 and a Cross pen, only 36 percent of subjects chose the Cross pen. However, when given the choice between $6, the Cross pen, and a less attractive pen, the percentage choosing the Cross pen rose to 46 percent (only 2 percent of subjects chose the other pen, confirming its inferiority).[6]

Our goal was to test compromise and contrast in two types of legal decisions. First, we investigated the degree to which decision makers made contested *legal judgments* (grading or sentencing decisions in the criminal law) independently of the set of available judgments. Second, we investigated the degree to which consumers of *heavily legalized products* (plaintiffs or their lawyers facing distinct settlement offers) chose between such consumption bundles independently of the set of options available.

We report five experiments. Two tested for compromise and one for contrast in legal judgments, two for contrast in choices between heavily legalized products. The experimental methodology was as follows. Subjects read case summaries and made decisions. Each subject read one or two cases. The case summaries (reprinted in the appendix) contained (1) a presentation of established facts, (2) a list of possible options (verdicts for experimental jurors, sentences for experimental judges, settlement offers for experimental lawyers acting as client advisors), and (3) legal definitions where relevant (for example, definitions of offenses for jurors selecting an appropriate verdict). Subjects read individually, spent about 10 minutes on each case, and did not discuss the cases with others. Subjects reading the first two cases were students in "Introductory Psychology" at Stanford University and San Jose State University, as well as random persons recruited in two public places (White Plaza at Stanford and downtown Palo Alto) to participate in exchange for a lottery ticket. Cases 3 and 5 were read only by students in Stanford's "Introductory Psychology" class. Case 4 was read only by students enrolled in a "Psychology of Gender" class at Stanford. Subjects in the classroom settings participated for course credit and were recruited by methods normally used at the two schools. Since the responses in the distinct settings were extremely similar, we report aggregated data. The experimental results were inconsistent with the context-independence condition implied by value maximization. We present the experiments, detail limitations of the data, and discuss implications of the results.

Experimental Tests of Compromise

Case 1
Subjects first read the following summary of facts:[7]

On January 1, 1993, at 9:00 A.M., the Defendant gave her second husband a cup of coffee into which she poured twenty crushed sleeping pills. He died within hours of drinking it. You should take it as given that he suffered a great deal of physical pain in the last several hours of his life. The Defendant concedes that after she gave him the coffee, she typed a suicide note on his computer screen in the basement and that she did so hoping that the police would believe she had nothing to do with his death. She concedes, too, that she gave him the coffee and ground up pills hoping that he would die. The prosecution concedes that at 8:05 A.M. the Defendant had overheard her seventeen year old daughter from her first marriage sobbing on the phone. The daughter was telling her best friend that her stepfather (the deceased) had "once again" attempted to molest her sexually the previous evening. At the same time, the prosecutor argues, and the Defendant concedes, that she stood to inherit a large amount of money from the deceased, and that she had been involved with another man for more than six months prior to her husband's death.

One group of subjects was told the incident occurred in the District of Columbia; members of this group were told to choose either murder or manslaughter as the verdict since there is no category of special circumstances murder in the jurisdiction. A second group of subjects was told the incident occurred in California; members of this group were given the additional option of choosing the verdict of special circumstances murder and told that potentially relevant special circumstances were (*a*) that the defendant killed for financial gain; (*b*) that she killed in an exceptionally heinous fashion, manifesting exceptional depravity (and that that finding was appropriate if the crime were conscienceless or pitiless and was unnecessarily torturous to the victim); and (*c*) that the defendant killed by the administration of poison.[8]

Jurors should choose the manslaughter verdict if they believe the defendant was acting under the influence of extreme emotional disturbance for which there is a reasonable explanation and an available murder verdict otherwise. The choice between manslaughter and the other verdicts should not be sensitive to whether, if the defendant were acting deliberately, she killed for financial gain, or in a heinous fashion, or using something that would be considered poison. Thus, context-independence requires a juror who prefers manslaughter over murder in the two-option condition to prefer manslaughter over both murder and special circumstances murder in the three-option condition;[9] implying, in the aggregate, that manslaughter will be chosen by as many jurors facing a two-option choice set as jurors facing a three-option choice set. Compromise, however, predicts that a smaller proportion of jurors will select manslaughter in the three-option choice set than in the two-option choice set. The logic follows directly from the definition of compromise. If each person is more likely to choose murder than manslaughter when a third option, involving still more serious penalties than murder, is present, that tendency should be revealed in the aggregate.

The data show that 47 percent of 167 subjects chose manslaughter when given only murder and manslaughter as options; when special circumstances murder

Table 40.1
Choices of Subjects Reading Case 1

	% choosing manslaughter	% choosing murder	% choosing murder with special circumstances	N
Group 1 (D.C.)	47	53	...	167
Group 2 (California)	19	39	42	183
Group 3	52	48	...	151

Note: See text for explanation.

was also present, only 19 percent of 183 subjects chose manslaughter ($\chi^2 = 32.96$, $p < .0001$).[10]

It is possible that the presence of the special circumstances option communicated relevant information about the appropriateness of choosing murder rather than manslaughter. A fact finder forced to focus (by the presence of the special circumstances instruction) on the fact that the defendant used particular means to kill (poison) and may have had a particular motive (greed) may be more likely to adopt the view that the murder was premeditated and planned, rather than committed "in the heat of passion." To respond to this concern, a third group of subjects read about special circumstances murder, so that they received the information potentially describing the defendant's form of killing but were told that special circumstances murder was not an available option in their jurisdiction. The hypothesis that the above finding is attributable to relevant information available to one, but not both, experimental groups was not borne out by the data; 52 percent of the 151 subjects in the third group chose manslaughter, a rate comparable to that of the two-option group and substantially higher than that of the initial three-option group ($\chi^2 = 40.61$, $p < .0001$). See table 40.1.

Case 2

Subjects were told to take the following as proven:

Donald Dewey, the defendant, who is an African-American, is walking in the inner courtyard of a shopping mall well after all the shops have closed. However, the mall is still open. Fifteen minutes earlier, one of the jewelry shops in the mall was burglarized, but not by Dewey. Nonetheless, a security guard, an off-duty policeman hired by the owners of the mall, approaches Dewey and asks whether he would mind if he patted him down, telling him that there had been a burglary. The guard intended to check both for burglar's tools and for some of the cash and the missing jewelry. The guard realized he had no probable cause to detain Dewey. Nonetheless, when Dewey refused, the guard reached out to grab him, and felt a bulge, which proved to be a gun, in his coat pocket. Dewey tried to spin away from the guard's hold, screaming, "You've got no business stopping me!" The guard then shouted a racist epithet. Dewey was able to break the guard's grip, and knock him over. While the guard was lying on the ground, he shot him with his gun, killing him. All sides concede that Dewey purposely killed the victim.

Subjects were informed that special circumstances murder, murder, voluntary manslaughter, and involuntary manslaughter were possible verdicts; that involuntary manslaughter would be appropriate only if the defendant subjectively, but unreasonably, believed he was entitled to defend himself;[11] and that the distinction between murder and special circumstances murder depended solely on whether the off-duty policeman acting as a guard should be treated as an officer acting in the line of duty since the murder of officers was sufficient grounds for the finding of special circumstances. Note that the question of whether Dewey committed murder or voluntary manslaughter depends only on whether the defendant was, in the minds of the fact finder, adequately provoked (to use common-law language) or "acting under the influence of severe emotional disturbance for which there is a reasonable explanation" (to use the portions of the Model Penal Code language that subjects were in fact given). The distinction between special circumstances murder and murder is irrelevant to this question. The possibility of involuntary manslaughter is likewise orthogonal.[12]

One group was told the judge had ruled, as a matter of law, that off-duty police employed as private security guards are not "police officers in the performance of their duties" so that they could not grade the homicide as special circumstances murder. A second group was told the judge had ruled, as a matter of law, that Dewey was not entitled to use deadly force and that there was no evidence that he subjectively believed, even unreasonably, that he was defending himself; thus they could not grade the homicide as involuntary manslaughter. Since every subject was initially informed about all four possible verdicts, differences across groups do not involve information about the existence of possible alternatives.[13]

The proportion of subjects choosing voluntary manslaughter rose from 31 percent among those choosing from the "upper set" of special circumstances murder, murder, and manslaughter to 55 percent among those choosing from the "lower set" of involuntary manslaughter, manslaughter, and murder. The proportion choosing murder fell from 57 percent in the upper set to 39 percent in the lower set (χ^2 for murder vs. all other verdicts was 7.66, $p < .01$). This pattern indicates a strong compromise effect.

It seems reasonable to assume in this case that the options are naturally ordered in terms of "severity." (Special circumstances murder is more severe than murder, which is more severe than voluntary manslaughter, which is more severe than involuntary manslaughter.) Consider any subset consisting of three of the options. Preferences satisfy *betweenness* if someone who prefers one of the extreme options in the subset over the intermediate option in the subset is more likely to prefer the intermediate option over the other extreme option than someone who does not. In the Dewey case, betweenness is natural: someone preferring special circumstances murder to murder would almost surely prefer murder to voluntary manslaughter.[14] Someone preferring murder to voluntary manslaughter would almost surely prefer voluntary manslaughter to involuntary manslaughter.

Given betweenness, context-independence requires that the ratio of murder verdicts to voluntary manslaughter verdicts be lower in the upper group than in the lower group. To see why, take choices in the upper group as given and consider how these choices should be translated into the lower group. Anyone choosing special circumstances murder should select murder. Any movement to involuntary manslaughter should come from voluntary manslaughter. Thus, as we move from the upper to the lower group, the number of murder verdicts should rise, and the number of manslaughter verdicts should decline.

Compromise predicts the opposite pattern. In the set of available options, murder is intermediate option for the upper group, voluntary manslaughter is intermediate option for the lower group. Thus, compromise predicts that murder will be seen more favorably in the upper group and manslaughter will be seen more favorably in the lower group. If this holds for each individual, it will be reflected in the aggregate. Consequently, the ratio of murder to manslaughter verdicts will be higher in the upper rather than in the lower group.

The data support the compromise prediction. Of 103 upper-group subjects choosing either murder or manslaughter, 65 percent chose murder. Of 100 lower-group subjects choosing either murder or voluntary manslaughter, only 41 percent chose murder ($\chi^2 = 11.79$, $p < .001$). Thus, an option does better by being intermediate in the choice set presented, in violation of the requirement that preference between two options be independent of the presence or absence of other options. See table 40.2.

Experimental Tests of Contrast

Case 3

Subjects read the following established facts:

The defendant has been convicted of violating a section of the state's criminal code. Any licensed real estate broker who knowingly conceals a substantial and material defect from a purchaser of residential property shall be adjudged in violation of the Code. The Code pro-

Table 40.2
Choices of Subjects Reading Case 2

Choices	Upper group ($N = 118$)	Lower group ($N = 107$)
Murder with special circumstances (%)	13	...
Murder (%)	57	38
Voluntary manslaughter (%)	30	55
Involuntary manslaughter (%)	...	7
Proportion of manslaughter/murder*	35	59

Note: See text for explanation.
* The proportion of manslaughter to murder is voluntary manslaughter divided by voluntary manslaughter plus murder.

vides that brokers need not necessarily make efforts to ascertain the condition of the dwelling units they offer. However, brokers must inform buyers of all substantial and material defects of which they have been apprised. Additionally, in those cases in which the brokers make no efforts to learn about the dwelling unit's condition, they must inform buyers that they have made no such efforts. In this particular case the broker had in his possession at the time of sale a four month old engineer's report indicating that the house he was representing had sustained substantial dry rot damage to the foundation. The report indicated that the damage would cost close to $100,000 to repair. The broker did not inform the would-be buyers of this fact, and they purchased the house for $200,000, which was estimated by appraisers to be within $10,000 of the fair market value of the home without dry rot. At trial, the broker claimed that he believed the report was dated. He testified that he surmised that the foundation had probably been repaired during the six weeks time between the time the engineer's report was prepared and the time the house was first listed by his real estate agency. The jury apparently did not believe this claim for they convicted the defendant of knowingly withholding material information.

Subjects were instructed to act as the judge in the case and to sentence the defendant. One group was asked to choose either the prosecutor's recommendation of a $2,500 fine and 1 month in jail or the probation department's recommendation of a $2,500 fine plus 6 months' probation during which the defendant would perform 50 hours of community service. A second group was given these choices plus the additional alternative of selecting a distinct probation recommended by the probation department as an additional option for the judge's consideration: a $2,500 fine plus 6 months' probation during which the defendant would undergo "50 hours of counseling sessions ... [focusing] on the importance of ethical business practices and the connection between dishonesty and impaired self-esteem." We tested the hypothesis that the community service probation recommendation would be seen more favorably when contrasted with the counseling probation. We believed most subjects would be skeptical of the utility of counseling for an offender seemingly motivated by

Table 40.3
Decisions of Those Subjects Choosing Either Community Service Probation or Jail in Case 3

	% choosing community service probation	% choosing jail	N
Two-option group	74	26	73
Three-option group	88	12	85

Note: An inferior probation option was also available to subjects in the three-option group. See text for further explanation.

greed. Thus we suggest that the community service probation option dominated the similar counseling probation option.

Assuming context-independence, the ratio of community service probation choices to jail choices should be higher in the two-option group than in the three-option group. To see why, take choices in the three-option set as given and consider how they should be translated into the two-option set. Anyone choosing either community service probation or jail from the three-option set should do so from the two-option set as well. Those choosing counseling probation from the three-option set hold one of two rank orders of the three options.[15] We expect few people to hold the rank order: counseling probation, jail, community service probation. The alternative rank order—counseling probation, community service probation, jail—is far more likely. Those choosing counseling probation from the three-option set are more likely than not to choose community service probation from the two-option set. As a result, under context-independence, the ratio of community service probation choices to jail choices should be higher in the two-option group than in the three option group.

Contrast predicts the opposite pattern. If community service probation is evaluated more favorably when contrasted with the inferior counseling probation, that effect should be reflected in a higher ratio of community service probation choices to jail choices in the three-option set than in the two-option set. The data support the contrast prediction. Seventy-four percent of the 73 subjects chose the community service probation over jail in the two-option set; in the three-option set 88 percent of the 85 subjects choosing either community service probation or jail chose community service probation ($\chi^2 = 4.55$, $p < .05$). See table 40.3.

Case 4

Subjects were asked to act as lawyers evaluating a series of settlement offers proffered by the defendant and to recommend one of the offers to their clients. Subjects read the following background facts:

The Economics Department of a major university voted, two years ago, to recommend that your client, then an Associate Professor at the University, not be promoted to a tenured position. She claims that she was discriminated against on account of her gender. She notes, first, that male colleagues with parallel publication records had been promoted though none had, like her, received undergraduate teaching awards. She notes, second, that the Department had neither hired nor promoted a number of qualified women it had considered over the past two decades.

Your client is interested in (1) being compensated for wrongs done to her and in (2) having the University publicly admit guilt in her case. At the same time, your client is very interested in the progress of women generally and wants (3) to do her part to push for affirmative action plans that would help women in Economics. Your client is not sure how to weigh and compare these three interests. The University counsel's office has contacted you and asked you to communicate settlement offers to your client.

One group of subjects faced three settlement offers. One bound the university to an affirmative action plan for the economics department without admitting guilt or paying damages. A second consisted of a public admission of guilt and $45,000 in damages. A third consisted of a public admission of guilt, plus a donation of $35,000 in the client's name to her favorite charity. We predicted that few subjects would select the third proposal; it appears inferior to the proposal in which the university pays $45,000 in damages. The professor could always accept the $45,000, give $35,000 to charity and keep $10,000 for herself.[16] However, the third proposal is not clearly inferior to the affirmative action proposal. A second group of subjects faced only the first two options. Additionally, all subjects were given information about the client's underlying preferences, her financial condition, her charitable giving plans, and her estimates of the possibility that the affirmative action plan would be adopted with or without her intervention.

Contrast predicts that subjects are more likely to prefer, and hence recommend, the $45,000 proposal over the affirmative action proposal when the third inferior proposal is offered than when it is not. Context-independence implies that an option can never be "more popular" in a three-option offered set than in a corresponding two-option offered set.[17] Thus, if the percentage of people choosing the $45,000 proposal is actually larger when three options are available, it is clear that violations of context-independence, attributable to contrast effects, are prevalent.

The data indicate a strong contrast effect. Only 50 percent of 36 subjects chose the $45,000 proposal from the two-option set, while 76 percent of 31 subjects chose it when the option clearly inferior to it was also available ($\chi^2 = 4.54$, $p < .05$). The presence of an inferior option leads to a markedly more favorable evaluation of a similar but superior option.[18] See table 40.4.

Table 40.4
Choices of Subjects Reading Case 4

	% choosing $45,000	% choosing $35,000 for charity	% choosing admission of guilt	N
Two-option group	50	. . .	50	36
Three-option group	74	6	20	31

Note: See text for explanation.

Case 5

Once more, subjects are asked to advise a client selecting among settlement offers. The client, Mr. Wells, is the sole neighbor of a nightclub. The nightclub was excessively noisy on weekends, and the owner concedes that were Wells to file a nuisance suit, he would and should prevail in court. The club owner thus communicates a number of settlement offers.

One group received two offers: (1) the club would not lower the noise level but would pay for Wells to stay in a fancy hotel each weekend and give him $120 a week, or (2) the nightclub would reduce the noise level. Another group received an additional proposal (3) the nightclub would pay for Wells to stay in a fancy hotel and give him $40 in cash plus $85 of vouchers per week redeemable at several nightclubs. The third proposal is clearly inferior to the hotel/unrestricted cash proposal but is not clearly inferior to the noise reduction proposal. That $85 in "restricted" money plus $40 in cash is inferior to $120 in cash was highlighted by noting that Wells attended nightclubs only three times a year and spent only $50 per visit when alone and $90 when accompanied by a date. We hypothesized that the presence of the hotel/vouchers proposal creates a contrast in which the hotel/money proposal looks more favorable than it does when standing alone.

As in case 4, the presence of contrast and a belief that few people will choose the hotel/vouchers option, gives rise to a prediction that the overall popularity of the hotel/money option will rise with the addition of the latter option. Recall that context-independence implies that no option can become more popular with the introduction of additional options.

The results show a marked increase in overall popularity of the hotel/money option. This option was chosen by 47 percent of the 32 subjects in the two-option condition and by 74 percent of the 31 subjects in the three-option condition ($\chi^2 = 4.91$, $p < .05$). The presence of an inferior option again leads to a more favorable evaluation of the similar superior option. See table 40.5.

Table 40.5
Choices of Subjects Reading Case 5

	% choosing weekend lodging	% choosing inferior weekend lodging	% choosing sound decrease	N
Two-option group	47	. . .	53	32
Three-option group	74	0	26	31

Note: See text for explanation.

Interpreting the Data

There are two distinct interpretive issues. The first issue concerns the validity of our findings. Do the experiments demonstrate the presence of genuine compromise or contrast effects that undermine our faith that decision makers will make context-independent decisions? This question turns both on whether the experimental subjects actually made context-dependent decisions (an internal validity question) and whether the experimental setting permits us to make reasonable inferences about decision makers in ostensibly parallel real world settings (an external validity question).

The second issue concerns the response to the presence of context-dependent decision making. The present findings, we suggest, provide at least prima facie evidence that the decisions of judges or juries may be prone to compromise and contrast effects. It could be argued that this conclusion is of limited practical significance either because the observed biases are not particularly troubling from a normative standpoint or because there is little that can be done to reduce or eliminate them. We shall discuss these issues in turn.

Have We Demonstrated Genuine Context-Dependence in Legal Decision Making?
Preferences are said to be context-dependent only if the choice between two options is affected by the presence of a third option that does not provide new information about the relative merits of the remaining options. It is important to consider whether preferences we labeled "context-dependent" can be explained on the basis that the additional options conveyed "added relevant information" that could reasonably cause preferences to change. We have addressed this issue in discussing the experiments in turn, but we thought it important to systematize prior discussions.

The results of our experiments closely parallel results of experiments in consumer choice where no meaningful information was conveyed about the options present.

For instance, the presence of an unattractive pen does not convey additional information about the attractiveness of a Cross pen. Similarly, we argue that no additional relevant information was provided by the added options in the second, fourth, and fifth experiments. This might be true for formal or procedural reasons—as in the second (Dewey) experiment, where all subjects read all four possible verdicts and were simply told to rule out one of the extreme ones. This might also be true for substantive reasons—that is, because focusing on the additional option does not lead one to reconsider any features of the other options that are salient in reaching a decision. In the Dewey case, for instance, the choice between murder and manslaughter, given the prevailing definitions of the two offenses in the experiment, turns only on the presence or absence of "extreme emotional disturbance for which there is a reasonable explanation." Directions either to attend to (or ignore) whether a security guard is a police officer acting in the line of duty or whether the defendant was acting in imperfect self-defense are irrelevant to that question.[19] In case 4, one does not learn more about the value of $45,000 in untied money by being presented with the option of $35,000 in tied money. Similarly, in case 5, one would not learn more about the value of $120 a week by being presented with the option of receiving $40 plus $85 in vouchers.[20]

In the first and third studies, it is plausible that subjects substantively "learned" about the core options by being offered additional ones. One could argue that in the first experiment (in which the wife kills her husband), the presence of the special circumstances murder instruction alerts readers to three features of the case that are more consistent with the claim that the defendant was a premeditated murderer than one who acted in something resembling the "heat of passion": first, that she had a long-term motive (financial gain); second, that she killed by administering poison; and, third, that she arguably killed in a torturous manner, all of which seem less consistent with the standard model of manslaughter in which the defendant simply lashes out. (The argument that the experiment involving group 3 [in table 40.1] does not cure this defect, by exposing all subjects to this account of the crime, is that they have not been asked to apply this account to the particular facts if they are in the experimental group that chooses only between murder and manslaughter. Subjects may, thus, pay less attention to this account of the killing. In a sense they have been told that "authorities"—experimenters in our cases, judges in a courtroom—do not credit such an account of the case.) Similarly, in the third experiment (in which a judge is asked to choose between incarceration and probation for the real estate agent) one could argue that subjects given the "inferior" probation option (counseling) in addition to the superior one (community service) choose some probation more often because the presence of the counseling option suggests that the real estate agent acted not out of the maliciousness some might think necessary to justify imprisonment but out of psychological pathology.

In summary, the second, fourth, and fifth experiments most strongly suggest that subjects' preferences are context-dependent, while the first and third experiments are consistent with this conclusion, although they are more open to alternative accounts.

Finally, it might be argued that the behavior of jurors and judges in real trials is quite different than the behavior of students in experimental situations. The question, however, is not whether our experimental task captures the essential features of legal decision making but whether compromise and contrast effects observed in our studies are likely to disappear in a real world setting. Although this possibility cannot be ruled out, it is not supported by available data.[21] There is evidence to suggest that the qualitative patterns observed in hypothetical studies are generally replicated in more realistic conditions involving real payoffs and significant consequences.[22] Thus, we believe the present findings provide at least prima facie evidence that context effects are likely to influence jurors and judges.

How Should We Respond to Context-Dependent Decision Making?

There are two separate questions policy makers might pose if they believed context-dependent decisions were commonplace. First, they must ascertain whether such decisions are problematic, harming some cognizable interests of some party. Second, they must determine whether the decisions they deem harmful can be avoided by reducing the decision makers' authority, "educating" them about their tendencies, or designing procedures to reduce context-dependence.

Do Context-Dependent Decisions Cause Harm? Violations of context-independence may be more troubling in legal decision making than in consumer choice. Unlike consumer choice, where the decision maker does not have clearly defined ends, legal processes have been designed with specific purposes in mind. Legal rule makers (legislatures, administrative agencies) typically state, rather explicitly, a set of goals to be met by legal judgment in particular cases. It is, therefore, easier to argue that the failure to meet those goals efficaciously is troublesome. Once we declare, for instance, that the purpose of differentiating murder from manslaughter is (for instance) to show a certain level of mercy to those acting in atypically stressful circumstances, then we have failed to meet that stated goal if we differentiate defendants on some other basis (for example, the presence of an option in which we condemn murderers of policemen more than ordinary murderers). Whether a violator deserves "reasonable" probation or imprisonment should similarly turn on some explicit set of policy judgments: if the decision is likely to be different when we learn facts unrelated to those policy judgments (that is, that we could choose between rea-sonable and "silly" probation), it is far less likely that we are attending to the set of policy judgments we have declared relevant.[23]

Because consumers do not have explicit "policies" or goals, it is less clear in what sense differential evaluation of options on the basis of context hinders con-sumers' interests. The notion that the consumer harms herself by breaches of context-independence is grounded in two observations. First, we suspect that the consumer herself would be prone to reevaluate (if not alter) her decision if she became aware of the fact that she made it on the basis of nonprobative facts. In this sense, a pragmatic test of the problematic nature of context-dependent choices is simply that such choices are prone to be ones the decision maker would prefer to reconsider or revisit.[24] Second, to the extent that people do not have a stable, context-independent preference order, their choices can be manipnulated by the composition of the set of options under consideration. As we have noted, such manipulations are common in the marketplace. They suggest that harm befalls context-dependent consumers since someone manipulated into choosing the option favored by another party, with her own set of interests, is less likely to maximize his own well-being.[25]

Going beyond the question of possible harm, it is perfectly possible to read the experiments as (a) describing a regular pattern in human behavior, and (b) giving lawyers (like marketers of consumer goods) information about how better to manip-ulate those they deal with (or defend themselves from manipulation). A lawyer pre-fers that the party suing her accept one of two realistic settlement offers: knowledge of contrast effects permits her to increase the probability that her adversary will accept her preferred offer.

We have little doubt that some lawyers already implicitly incorporate informal intuitions about context dependence, even if unaware of the formal category. "Compromise" effects are well known to both district attorneys and defenders: as a tactical matter, one side and/or the other might choose not to request that judges instruct jurors to consider lesser included charges,[26] hoping to force the jury to elect between acquittal and conviction of a serious charge, believing that the jury will otherwise be unduly prone to pick the compromise judgment, even if that judgment would attract little support in a two-option set (against acquittal alone, or against conviction of the serious offense alone, assuming one could decide to convict and then, sequentially, grade). The fact that clients are rarely able to challenge the com-petence of lawyers who fail to ask for instructions on lesser included offenses, even when conviction of those offenses would have been legally tenable, reflects not only generally high burdens in challenging lawyer competency,[27] but the recognition that the decision to offer a compromise verdict diminishes the probability of acquittal and is, as a result, a tactical judgment[28] that the client must make in consultation with his attorney.[29]

Can We Reduce Context-Dependence and Improve Legal Decision Making? The experiments do not tell whether an experimental group alerted to the existence of contrast or compromise effects avoids them any better than an experimental group not so alerted. Thus it is not clear whether we can "educate" people to avoid context-dependent decisions, even one effect at a time, let alone whether more general education would lead to context-independence more globally.

We can, of course, eliminate irrelevant options when we have a substantive theory of irrelevance and, more interestingly, weigh the value of including a relevant option against the costs that will be borne because inclusion shifts preferences among other options for irrelevant reasons. However, if we believe, for instance, that it is impossible to eliminate compromise biases because people might still implicitly consider an unstated option more extreme than one or the other pole in the option set, then the goal of eliminating irrelevant options may not be achievable. It would appear, though, that we should retain at least presumptive faith that eliminating explicit irrelevant options will reduce context-dependent decisions.

The question appears most salient and obvious in relation to the issue of "lesser included offenses," offenses in which the underlying act might be consistent with a variety of criminal charges but in which culpability is differentiated for some reason (mental state, motivation, deliberativeness, victim status, and so on). Presumably, the legislative decision to subdivide a potentially unified offense and the judicial decision to instruct a jury to consider all subdivided offenses are based on policy decisions about each additional subdivided offense. In the absence of context-dependent decision making, the legislature should subdivide an offense when it believes that distinctions in defendant conduct within a historically unified (or conceptually unifiable) category reasonably differentiate offenders (along dimensions like blameworthiness, deterrability, signaling dangerousness, and so forth). Similarly, the judge should instruct the fact finder to consider convictions for an additional category that the legislature has created so long as she believes a reasonable jury could find beyond a reasonable doubt that the defendant committed the (contested) suboffense, rather than some other suboffense (even if the judge herself believes the other suboffense a more plausible conviction pigeonhole).[30]

Given context-dependent decision making, though, it appears that neither of these decision rules is adequately complete. A legislature that adds capital murder to the list of crimes and attempts to distinguish it from "ordinary" murder (and manslaughter) must understand that it is not only creating a new substantive

category—based on the substantive belief that certain killings are morally more rep-
rehensible, or harder to deter in the absence of aggravated punishments, or socially
more harmful—but it must also understand that it is altering the balance of convictions between murder and manslaughter (though the legislature might not intend
to alter the substantive grounds for distinguishing, say, provoked, partly mitigated
homicides from unprovoked murders). This will be true, at least arguably, both
because murder will more frequently become a compromise verdict between capital
murder and manslaughter and because it may frequently be the case that murder
clearly dominates capital murder (or vice versa) and that the "murders" thus benefit
(as a result of contrast effects) relative to manslaughter. To put the point more generally, a legislature must recognize that, in establishing what one might concede,
at least for argument's sake, is a substantively distinguishable new category, it may
alter substantive judgments among other categories even when the substantive lines
between those categories have formally remained constant.[31]

Similarly, when a judge decides that a reasonable jury might convict a defendant
of a particular option—even though the judge believes that rather unlikely—she
must recognize that she has altered the probability of convicting the defendant of
yet another option (that would have been offered the jurors in any case, uncon-
troversially). A judge's decision, say, to refuse to instruct on special circumstances
murder might not appear reasonable if we focus solely on the question of whether
special circumstances murder is a plausible charge, but it may appear more reasonable if we understand the judge must weigh what we will accept as one form of loss in
decision-making capacity (the refusal to let the jury hear an option that it might in
fact accept) against what might be perceived as a larger gain (preventing the jury
from making the choice between options it is more likely to consider seriously on
grounds that are irrelevant to the distinction between these options).[32]

Conclusion

Past research has demonstrated context-dependence in consumer choice. We
extended this work to legal decision making and showed that violations of context-
independence are prevalent in this domain. We have argued that, from a normative
standpoint, context-dependence is more problematic in legal decision making than
in consumer choice because legal decision makers, unlike consumers, are guided by
explicit principles declaring certain factors to be relevant and others to be irrelevant.
Moreover, legal decision makers make choices that invariably affect others, while
consumers routinely make only self-regarding decisions. Given the fact that context-

dependent decision making is problematic when actors make legal judgments, it would appear that both legislatures and judges (instructing jurors) must carefully consider the option sets available to decision makers. They must account for the fact that, whether it is their intention to do so or not, additional alternatives will not only introduce what may seem a substantively plausible decision option but will alter the choice patterns among other options.

Appendix
Experimental Materials

Below are the full experimental materials from all five cases. In each of the five cases, all subjects read the same background, introductory materials. Materials read by only certain experimental groups are clearly marked.

Case 1

Below is a description of a homicide case. Please read the summary of the facts and the potential verdicts. Then, please indicate which verdict you think is the correct one.

You should take the following facts as proven:

On January 1, 1993, at 9:00 A.M., the Defendant gave her second husband a cup of coffee into which she had poured twenty crushed sleeping pills. He died within hours of drinking it. You should take it as a given that he suffered a great deal of physical pain in the last several hours of his life. The Defendant concedes that after she gave him the coffee, she typed a suicide note on his computer screen in the basement, and that she did so hoping that the police would believe she had nothing to do with his death. She concedes, too, that she gave him the coffee and ground up pills hoping that he would die. The prosecution concedes that at 8:05 A.M. the Defendant had overheard her seventeen year old daughter from her first marriage sobbing on the phone. The daughter was telling her best friend that her stepfather (the deceased) had once again attempted to molest her sexually the previous evening. At the same time, the prosecutor argues, and the Defendant concedes, that she stood to inherit a large amount of money from the deceased, and that she had been involved with another man for more than six months prior to her husband's death.

Your Task All the other jurors believe that the defendant is guilty of homicide, the unlawful killing of another human being. You believe your task, at this point, is simply to grade the unlawful homicide, to determine the level of culpability.

Group 1 Subjects Were Given the Following Materials This trial is being held in the District of Columbia. In the District of Columbia there are two grades of homicide that are relevant to this case:

A. Murder

B. Manslaughter

One the next page you will find a summary of the legal code relevant to deciding upon a grade for the homicide in question. We then ask you to indicate which verdict you would choose.

RELEVANT LAW   District of Columbia law provides in part:

A. Murder. (1) Murder is the unlawful killing of a human being when there is manifested malice, a deliberate intention unlawfully to take away the life of a fellow creature. A defendant found guilty of murder shall receive a penalty of confinement in prison for a term of from 25 years to life with the possibility of parole.

B. Manslaughter. (2) Criminal homicide constitutes manslaughter when a homicide which would otherwise be murder is committed under the influence of extreme mental or emotional disturbance for which there is reasonable explanation or excuse. The reasonableness of such explanation or excuse shall be determined from the viewpoint of a person in the actor's situation under the circumstances as he believes them to be. A defendant who has had an adequate period to cool off following a severe disturbance will be presumed not to act under the influence of such disturbance. Manslaughter shall be punished by a term in prison of eight years.

Group 2 Subjects Were Given the Following Materials   This trial is being held in the State of California. In the State of California there are three grades of homicide that are relevant to this case:

A. Special Circumstances Murder

B. Murder

C. Manslaughter

On the next page you will find a summary of the legal code relevant to deciding upon a grade for the homicide in question. We then ask you to indicate which verdict you would choose.

RELEVANT LAW   California law provides in part: (1) Murder is the unlawful killing of a human being when there is manifested malice, a deliberate intention unlawfully to take away the life of a fellow creature.

A. Special Circumstances Murder. (2) The penalty for a defendant found guilty of murder shall be either death or confinement in prison for a term of life without the possibility of parole in any case in which one or more special circumstances are found.

(3) The potentially relevant special circumstances are: (*a*) The murder was intentional and carried out for financial gain. (*b*) The murder was exceptionally heinous, atrocious, or cruel, manifesting exceptional depravity. You should find this to be the case if the crime is conscienceless or pitiless and is unnecessarily torturous to the victim. (*c*) The defendant intentionally killed the victim by the administration of poison.

(4) If you, as juror, find that the defendant has committed murder with special circumstances, there shall be a separate hearing to determine whether the defendant is sentenced to death or simply to life imprisonment without possibility of parole. You do not have to attend to the bases for that decision.

B. Murder. (5) A defendant found guilty of murder and not of murder with special circumstances shall receive a penalty of confinement in prison for a term of from 25 years to life with the possibility of parole.

C. Manslaughter. (6) Criminal homicide constitutes manslaughter when a homicide which would otherwise be murder is committed under the influence of extreme mental or emotional disturbance for which there is reasonable explanation or excuse. (*a*) The reasonableness of such explanation or excuse shall be determined from the viewpoint of a person in the actor's situation under the circumstances as he believes them to be. A defendant who has had an adequate period to "cool off" following a severe disturbance will be presumed not to act under the influence of such disturbance. (*b*) Manslaughter shall be punished by a term in prison of eight years.

Group 3 Subjects Were Given the Following Materials

OTHER JURISDICTIONS   In some jurisdictions, special circumstances murder is a possible verdict. Here is a summary of legal code pertaining to special circumstances murder:

(*a*) Murder is the unlawful killing of a human being when there is manifested malice, a deliberate intention unlawfully to take away the life of a fellow creature. (*b*) The penalty for a defendant found guilty of murder shall be either death or confinement in prison for a term of life without parole when one or more special circumstances are found: (*c*) The potentially relevant special circumstances are:

(i) The murder was intentional and carried out for financial gain.

(ii) The murder was exceptionally heinous, atrocious, or cruel, manifesting exceptional depravity. You should find this to be the case if the crime is conscienceless or pitiless and is unnecessarily torturous to the victim.

(iii) The defendant intentionally killed the victim by the administration of poison. (*d*) If it is found the defendant has committed murder with special circumstances, there shall be a separate hearing to determine whether the defendant is sentenced to death or simply to life imprisonment without parole.

THIS JURISDICTION   This trial is being held in the District of Columbia where special circumstances murder is not part of the law. Thus, the only possible grades for the homicide in question are:

A. Murder

B. Manslaughter

On the next page you will find a summary of legal code defining murder and manslaughter. Please indicate which of these two verdicts is the appropriate one for this case.

RELEVANT LAW

A. Murder. (1) Murder is the unlawful killing of a human being when there is manifested malice, a deliberate intention unlawfully to take away the life of a fellow creature. A defendant found guilty of murder shall receive a penalty of confinement in prison for 25 years to life with the possibility of parole.

B. Manslaughter. (2) Criminal homicide constitutes manslaughter when a homicide which would otherwise be murder is committed under the influence of extreme mental or emotional disturbance for which there is reasonable explanation or excuse. The reasonableness of such explanation or excuse shall be determined from the viewpoint of a person in the actor's situation under the circumstances as he believes them to be. A defendant who has had an adequate period to cool off following a severe disturbance will be presumed not to act under the influence of such disturbance. Manslaughter shall be punished by a term in prison of eight years.

Case 2

Below is a description of a legal case. Please read the summary of the facts and the potential verdicts. Then, please indicate which verdict you think is the correct one.

The defense and prosecution agree that the following is an accurate depiction of the event in question:

Donald Dewey, the defendant, who is an African-American, is walking in the inner courtyard of a shopping mall well after all the shops have closed. However, the mall is still open. Fifteen minutes earlier, one of the jewelry shops in the mall was burglarized, but not by

Dewey. Nonetheless, a security guard, an off-duty policeman hired by the owners of the mall, approaches Dewey and asks whether he would mind if he patted him down, telling him that there had been a burglary. The guard intended to check both for burglar's tools and for some of the cash and missing jewelry. The guard realized he had no probable cause to detain Dewey. Nonetheless, when Dewey refused, the security guard reached out to grab him, and felt a bulge, which proved to be a gun, in his coat pocket. Dewey tried to spin away from the guard's hold, screaming, "You've got no business stopping me!" The guard then shouted a racist epithet. Dewey was able to break the guard's grip, and knock him over. While the guard was lying on the ground, he shot him with his gun, killing him.

All sides concede that Dewey purposely killed the victim.

Your Task   Homicide is defined generally as the unlawful killing of another human being. There are four grades of homicide in this jurisdiction:

A. Special Circumstances Murder

B. Murder

C. Voluntary Manslaughter

D. Involuntary Manslaughter

Given the facts of the case, your task as a juror at this trial is simply to grade the unlawful homicide. That is, you must decide of which of the different grades of homicide Donald Dewey is guilty.

Grades of Homicide—Definitions and Relevance to This Case

UPPER GROUP SUBJECTS

A. Special Circumstances Murder. A person is guilty of Special Circumstances Murder if he purposely or knowingly kills another human being and if the victim of the killing is a police officer who is in the course of performing his official duties. The penalty for Special Circumstances Murder is either life imprisonment without the possibility of parole or death (exactly which is determined later in a separate hearing). The District Attorney [DA] argues for Special Circumstances Murder in this case on the basis that the guard was acting with the authority he would have had as a police officer and thus should be deemed a police officer acting in his official capacity. Although he was not formally on duty at the time, police officers always have the rights of officials to make arrests.

B. Murder. A person is guilty of Murder if he purposely kills another human being. The penalty for Murder is imprisonment for a term of 25 years to life with the possibility of parole.

C. Voluntary Manslaughter. A homicide is to be graded as Voluntary Manslaughter when it would otherwise be considered Murder but is committed under the influence of extreme mental or emotional disturbance for which there is a reasonable explanation. The penalty for manslaughter is imprisonment for a term of up to eight years. The DA maintains that Dewey was not sufficiently provoked to warrant a decision of Voluntary Manslaughter. That is, the DA maintains that Dewey was not under the influence of extreme mental or emotional disturbance. Dewey's lawyer argues that his defendant was provoked to kill by both the illegal, unwarranted arrest, and by the guard's use of a racist epithet. That is, Dewey's lawyer maintains that the unwarranted arrest plus racist epithet constitute sufficient cause for extreme mental or emotional disturbance.

D. Involuntary Manslaughter. If a person kills another human being when he subjectively but unreasonably believes he is entitled to use deadly force to defend himself, a judgment of Involuntary Manslaughter is appropriate. However, the judge has ruled that as a matter of law, Dewey is not entitled to use deadly force against an unwarranted arrest, and finds that there is no credible evidence to back a claim that Dewey believed that he was legally entitled to use deadly force to defend himself. Thus, this homicide cannot be graded as an Involuntary Manslaughter.

LOWER GROUP SUBJECTS

A. Special Circumstances Murder. A person is guilty of Special Circumstances Murder if he purposely or knowingly kills another human being and if the victim of the killing is a police officer who is in the course of performing his official duties. The penalty for Special Circumstances Murder is either life imprisonment without the possibility of parole or death (exactly which is determined later in a separate hearing). However, the judge has ruled that as a matter of law, off-duty police employed as private security guards are not police officers in the performance of their official duties. Thus, the homicide in question cannot be graded as a Special Circumstances Murder.

B. Murder. A person is guilty of Murder if he purposely kills another human being. The penalty for Murder is imprisonment for a term of 25 years to life with the possibility of parole.

C. Voluntary Manslaughter. A homicide is to be graded as Voluntary Manslaughter when it would otherwise be considered Murder but is committed under the influence of extreme mental or emotional disturbance for which there is a reasonable explanation. The penalty for manslaughter is imprisonment for a term of up to eight years. The District Attorney maintains that Dewey was not sufficiently provoked to warrant a decision of Voluntary Manslaughter. That is, the DA maintains that Dewey was not under the influence of extreme mental or emotional disturbance. Dewey's lawyer argues that his defendant was provoked to kill by both the illegal, unwarranted arrest, and by the guard's use of a racist epithet. That is, Dewey's lawyer maintains that the unwarranted arrest plus racist epithet constitute sufficient cause for extreme mental or emotional disturbance.

D. Involuntary Manslaughter. If a person kills another human being when he subjectively but unreasonably believes he is entitled to use deadly force to defend himself, a judgment of Involuntary Manslaughter is appropriate. The judge has ruled that as a matter of law, Dewey is not entitled to use deadly force against an unwarranted arrest. However, if you judge that Dewey mistakenly believed that he was entitled to use deadly force to defend himself, you should then grade the homicide as Involuntary Manslaughter. Dewey's lawyer argues just such a position. He states that Dewey believed he was entitled to use deadly force to resist an illegal arrest and that, in addition, Dewey feared the guard would seriously injure or kill him.

Case 3

The Situation   Take the following as given:

The defendant has been convicted of violating a section of the state's criminal code. Any licensed real estate broker who knowingly conceals a substantial and material defect in a dwelling unit from a purchaser of residential property shall be adjudged in violation of the Code. The Code provides that brokers need not necessarily make efforts to ascertain the condition of the dwelling units they offer. However, brokers must inform buyers of all substantial and material defects of which they have been apprised. Additionally, in those cases in which brokers make no efforts to learn about the dwelling unit's condition, they must inform buyers that they have made no such efforts.

In this particular case, the broker had in his possession at the time of sale a four month old engineer's report indicating that the house he was representing had sustained substantial dry rot damage to the foundation. The report indicated that the damage would cost close to $100,000 to repair. The broker did not inform the would-be buyers of this fact, and they purchased the home for $200,000, which was estimated by appraisers to be within $10,000 of the fair market value of the home without dry rot. At trial, the broker claimed that he believed the report was dated. He testified that he surmised that the foundation had probably been repaired during the six weeks between the time the engineer's report was prepared and the time the house was first listed by his real estate agency. The jury apparently did not believe this claim for they convicted the defendant of knowingly withholding material information.

Your Task   You are the judge. You must decide upon a sentence for the offender in this case. On the next page is a short summary of recommended sentences.

Your Options   Below are sentences recommended by the prosecutor's office and the county probation department:

TWO-OPTION GROUP

A. Prosecutor's Recommendation. The prosecutor has recommended that the defendant be imprisoned for one month and fined $2,500.

B. Probation Department's Recommendation. The probation department recommends that the defendant be fined $2,500 and placed on probation for six months. During his probation the defendant would perform 50 hours of community service, largely working to find new dwelling places for persons displaced by redevelopment in the city in which he lives.

THE ADDITIONAL OPTION AVAILABLE TO THE THREE-OPTION GROUP

C. Probation Department's Recommendation. Alternatively, the probation department recommends that the defendant the fined $2,500 and placed on probation for six months, during which time he would be asked to report for 50 hours of counseling sessions. The counseling sessions would focus on the importance of ethical business practices and the connection between dishonesty and impaired self-esteem.

Case 4

Imagine that you are an attorney working for the plaintiff in the legal case described below. Please indicate which course of action you would take.

Background   The Economics Department of a major university voted, two years ago, to recommend that your client, then an Associate Professor at the University, not be promoted to a tenured position. She claims that she was discriminated against on account of her gender. She notes, first, that male colleagues with parallel publication records had been promoted though none had, like her, received undergraduate teaching awards. She notes, second, that the Department had neither hired nor promoted a number of qualified women it had considered over the past two decades.

Your client is interested in (1) being compensated for the wrongs done her and in (2) having the University publicly admit guilt in her case.

At the same time, your client is very interested in the progress of women generally and wants (3) to do her part in helping to push for affirmative action plans that would help women in Economics.

Your client is not sure how to weigh and compare these three interests.

The University counsel's office has contacted you and asked you to communicate three distinct settlement proposals to your client.

The Situation   Your client asks you to recommend one of the settlement proposals. The proposals appear on the back.

TWO-OPTION GROUP: THE PROPOSALS   Offer including admission of guilt by the University:

Proposal 1. (*a*) The University would pay your client $45,000 in damages. (*b*) The University would publicly admit guilt in your client's case.

Note. Your client now has a job at another university making $70,000 per year. She would find the $45,000 helpful but not utterly life changing.

Offer including a plan to increase female representation in Economics:

Proposal 2. (*a*) The University would agree to what your client would feel is an acceptable affirmative action plan to increase female representation in the Department. (*b*) The University, though, would not admit guilt in your client's case.

Note. It is conceivable that the University might enact an affirmative action plan whether or not your client agrees to this settlement proposal.

THE ADDITIONAL OPTION AVAILABLE TO THE THREE-OPTION GROUP

Proposal 3. (*a*) The University would contribute $35,000 in your client's name to her favorite charity. (*b*) The University would publicly admit guilt in you client's case.

Note. Your client would probably not wish to contribute such a large amount of money. Also, your client could always contribute a portion of the money she receives from Proposal 1.

Case 5

Imagine that you are a lawyer. Which choice would you make in the case below?

Background   Your client, Wells, is the sole neighbor of a dance club that stays open until 3 A.M. The club owner acknowledges that the noise levels from midnight to three exceed levels that Wells should have to tolerate; he concedes that the activity would be judged a "nuisance" if Wells sued him in court.

The club owner would prefer not to be forced to diminish the noise too radically, especially on Friday and Saturday nights, and he communicates three offers to your client.

Your client asks you to advise him. Which settlement offer would you recommend that he take?

TWO-OPTION GROUP

Sound Decrease Alternative: Proposal X. The club owner would (*a*) lower the sound system by ten decibels and (*b*) plant a hedge outside the club that would muffle away more of the sound. Wells would usually no longer be bothered by the noise. Every now and then he would still hear the loud music from the club and find it aggravating.

Weekend Lodgings Alternative: Proposal Y. The club owner would (*a*) put Wells up at a nearby plush hotel every Friday and Saturday night, and (*b*) pay Wells $120 per week in cash. Wells would enjoy staying at the hotel although he may get tired of it after a while. If some time he didn't want to go to the hotel, he could stay home. Wells makes $25,000 per year and the $120 would be helpful.

THE ADDITIONAL OPTION AVAILABLE TO THE THREE-OPTION GROUP

Proposal Z. The club owner would (*a*) put Wells up at a nearby plush hotel every Friday and Saturday, and (*b*) pay Wells $40 in cash per week and give Wells $85 per week in credit for use at this or three other dance clubs. Wells would enjoy staying at the hotel although he may get tired of it. Wells attends the clubs where he would have credit about three times a year, spending $50 if alone and $90 if on a date. He probably would not go to these clubs every weekend.

Notes

This work was supported by grant no. SBR-9408684 from the National Science Foundation and grant no. MH-53046 from the National Institute of Health to Tversky; and by the Stanford Legal Research Fund, made possible by a bequest from Ira S. Lillick and by gifts from other friends of Stanford Law School to Kelman.

1. This condition is often called *independence of irrelevant alternatives.*

2. We exclude the case where availability of the third option may convey relevant information about the relative merits of the other two. For instance, the availability of veal parmesan might suggest that the restaurant specializes in Italian dishes.

3. See, for example, Joel Huber, John W. Payne, & Christopher Puto, Adding Asymmetrically Dominated Alternatives: Violations of Regularity and the Similarity Hypothesis, 9 J. Consumer Res. 90 (1982); Joel Huber & Christopher Puto, Market Boundaries and Product Choice: Illustrating Attraction and Substitution Effects, 10 J. Consumer Res. 31 (1983); Itamar Simonson & Amos Tversky, Choice in Context: Tradeoff Contrast and Extremeness Aversion, 29 J. Marketing Res. 281, 282 (1992); and D. A. Redelmeir & E. Shafir, Medical Decision Making in Situations That Offer Multiple Alternatives, 273 J. Am. Med. Ass'n 302 (1995). Discussions and attempts to model the phenomena appear in Amos Tversky & Itamar Simonson, Context-Dependent Preferences, 39 Mgmt. Sci. 1179 (1993); and Eldar Shafir, Itamar Simonson, & Amos Tversky, Reason-Based Choice, 49 Cognition 11 (1993).

4. Simonson & Tversky, *supra* note 3, at 290.

5. If one considers the choice between options that vary along two dimensions and assumes that neither option dominates the other, the comparison between them involves an evaluation of differences along the

two attributes. Consider a consumer evaluating two personal computers: x has 960K memory and costs $1,200, while y has 640K memory and costs $1,000. The choice between the two depends on whether the consumer is willing to pay $200 more for an additional 320K of memory. The contrast hypothesis implies that the tendency to prefer x over y will be enhanced if the decision maker encounters other choices in which the exchange rate between price and quality is higher than that implied by x and y. *Id.*

6. *Id.*

7. The full text of the experiments is in the appendix.

8. The precise legal definitions subjects saw are reprinted in the appendix.

9. The "two-option" set is indeed a two-option set, not a three-option set in which acquittal is an option (and manslaughter intermediate between acquittal and murder) since the subjects are told that all the jurors believe the defendant is guilty of homicide and that their only task is to grade the unlawful homicide.

10. More specifically, the data support the prediction that manslaughter will be chosen less frequently when it is an "extreme" choice than when there are simply no extreme choices because there are only two options. The proportion of people choosing murder in the two-option study was 53 percent, and it in fact fell to 39 percent in the three-option set because 42 percent of the people chose special circumstances murder. We suggest that people become more predisposed to find murder than manslaughter when murder is seen as a compromise choice, rather than an extreme one, and they are less predisposed to find manslaughter when it is an extreme choice than when there simply *are* no extreme choices. *Then*, subjects decide between murder and special circumstances murder. In this case, it strikes us that finding murder at all, rather than special circumstances murder, *once one has found murder rather than manslaughter*, is explicable *only* as a compromise verdict: the defendant almost certainly killed the victim by administering poison. (While it is plausible to find that other special circumstances existed—to determine that the killing was done in a heinous fashion or was done for financial gain—these findings are not so uncontroversial that one would expect anyone who finds murder rather than manslaughter to accept them unquestioningly.)

11. The actual instructions on involuntary manslaughter appear from a lawyer's vantage point to blur together "mistake of law" and "mistake of fact" issues that would almost surely be differentiated in an actual case. (If one looks at the experimental jury instructions, it appears that Dewey would be guilty of involuntary manslaughter whether he unreasonably believed the guard physically threatened him or if he unreasonably believed it to be permissible to use deadly force to resist illegal detention.) In most American jurisdictions, though, a mistake about the scope of justification norms would be considered a mistake about the governing norm; no mistakes about the content of governing norms are deemed exculpatory (unless the legislature intends such a "mistake of law" defense or unless due process constitutional norms preclude convicting a defendant ignorant of a particular norm). It may well be the case that one could construct an argument that the defendant in such a case simply makes a (potentially exculpatory) mistake about some legal circumstance attendant to the definition of the offense, but such an argument would, for a wide variety of reasons, appear to be unavailing. Unfortunately, the initial instructions (in the pretest experiment), which paid heed to these subtle distinctions, were too difficult for experimental subjects to cope with in the short time frame of these experiments.

12. In a real case, jurors might conceivably have been instructed to find the defendant guilty of voluntary manslaughter if he had either acted under extreme emotional disturbance or if he recklessly believed that he was entitled to use force to defend himself against the deceased. (One should recognize that, even in a jurisdiction in which such a reckless belief in the need to use deadly force would result in a manslaughter conviction, many judges would, in this case, refuse to give such an instruction.) What is critical, however, is that the "experimental judge's" refusal to allow one experimental group to consider involuntary manslaughter should not affect a juror's choice between murder or manslaughter. The judge's refusal to credit the possibility that Dewey subjectively believed he was defending himself is irrelevant to the form of voluntary manslaughter the decision makers are asked to consider. If voluntary manslaughter could be predicated on a form of imperfect self-defense (one in which the defendant took a conscious risk that he was not entitled to defend himself), then one possible criticism might hold that voluntary manslaughter is less plausible once it has been concluded that the defendant did not subjectively though unreasonably believe there was a substantial risk that he might not be entitled to defend himself. The criticism does not hold

here, however, since, for our subjects, grading the killing as voluntary manslaughter is appropriate only when the defendant acted under the influence of explicable emotional disturbance.

13. It is remotely plausible, though not necessary to consider in reviewing our results, that more, not fewer, subjects should choose manslaughter when told by the judge, in effect, that the off-duty policeman is not clearly a person acting without official state penal authority (for these purposes, that is the relevant message of allowing the jury to consider special circumstances murder). One would think that jurors would find it (very marginally) more reasonable and explicable for a person to "act under the influence of extreme emotional disturbance" when confronted by official, rather than private, racism and unreasonableness in making decisions to detain so that the judge's instruction to consider special circumstances murder might serve as a (weak) informational reminder of the official status of the victim.

14. To the limited extent that some subjects reacted as we discussed in note 13 *supra*, focusing on the official status of the victim so that they felt the relevant choice was between those categories in which official status was arguably salient (special circumstances murder or manslaughter) vs. those in which it was not (murder), then we should not expect all experimental subjects who are "deprived" of the chance to choose special circumstances murder to choose murder, rather than manslaughter. Still, the "betweenness" hypothesis we detail in the text appears overwhelmingly more plausible.

15. For convenience, we exclude the possibility of ranking two options as tied.

16. It is conceivable that some people would prefer to direct a lower sum of money to charity rather than receive a larger sum, which they could personally donate to charity, in order to demonstrate to the defendant university that some people (including the plaintiff herself) make decisions without any regard to selfish concerns. Our ex ante prediction, borne out in fact, was that the number of people who either want to demonstrate such selflessness, and believed one would better demonstrate it if one never controlled the funds at all, would be very small.

17. We again exclude the possibility that the presence of the third option communicates information relevant to the assessment of the others.

18. We doubt that the results here reflect a combination of contrast and compromise effects. It is difficult to see the second option as "intermediate" along salient dimensions. It is possible that the options could be aligned in terms of how costly they are for the university to implement. However, it cannot be clear to subjects whether the affirmative action plan is more or less expensive than the $45,000 settlement, although the $45,000 settlement is clearly more expensive for the defendant than the $35,000 donation. Likewise, if the options are to be "aligned" in accord with the degree to which the defendant gains from the settlement, they appear incommensurable in significant ways.

19. See note 13 *supra* for a qualification, but one which implies that the "informational" role of the added option is to make manslaughter seem more attractive to those exposed to the special circumstances murder charge.

20. The substantive barriers appear more meaningful to us than the formal ones in assessing the probative value of the experiments. One could argue, reasonably plausibly, that reading the full option set is not the sole way subjects gather information about options so that "formal" or "procedural" techniques to insure that no information is gained by altering option sets are, in the final analysis, never quite adequate: it may well be the case that subjects reasonably "tilt" in a particular direction when certain options are "on the table." The fact that an option is "on the table" may signal that the perspective embodied in the option is a serious one, and the substantive positions that underlie it should be embodied, at least to some extent, in any final judgment.

21. One might reasonably argue that internal and external validity issues are related in the following sense: if experimental jurors or experimental consumers are not like real jurors or real consumers, they may not be seeking the same goal as their real counterparts. Experimental subjects may always seek, for instance, simply to give the "answer" they anticipate the experimenter wants to hear, or the answer that is "correct" or smart in some sense. If that is the case, the consumer is not trying to express her authentic preferences. However, it is not the least bit clear what answer is the "correct" answer (or the one experimenters expect). It might be that what we see as compromise and contrast effects are efforts to pick up on clues about the experimenters' wishes. Naturally, it is also possible that the real counterparts face quite parallel complex

agendas (real jurors may be trying to guess what the judge wants; real consumers may be trying not to look foolish in front of the salesman); if this were the case, though, one would say that the experiments are externally valid (real actors behave like experimental actors) but that we have not demonstrated context-dependence so much as the possibility that people's goals are less straightforward than they might appear.

22. See, in particular, Colin Camerer, Behavioral Decision Theory, in The Handbook of Experimental Economics (John H. Kagel & Alvin E. Roth eds. 1995).

23. In a similar vein, social choice theorists have discussed the distinction between relevant and irrelevant grounds for social choice: it is deemed worrisome that agenda setting (whether deliberate or inadvertent) determines political outcomes. See Kenneth Arrow, Social Choice and Individual Values (2d ed. 1963). For further discussions, see, for example, Frank Easterbrook, Ways of Criticizing the Court, 95 Harv. L. Rev. 802, 823 (1982). What we have noted is that even for individual decision makers, inadvertent or manipulative agenda setting (presentation of distinct option sets) may alter substantive outcomes.

24. The proposed pragmatic test suggests that one is more likely to express a "true" preference when irrelevant options are eliminated, that is, from two-option choice sets. However, even if contrast effects are monumentally fleeting—so that the consumer's preferences may change each time we expose her to new option sets—it is not clear that *any* of these short-lived choices is inferior to a preference revealed in some initial two-option set, precisely because we lack a theory of what inferiority would mean here.

25. One possible account would hold that forming preferences is itself a costly activity so that rules of thumb reducing that cost could be globally optimal, even if such rules mandated inclusion of informationally valueless clues on particular occasions. Thus, it might be that we have learned that we are most typically satisfied if we pick the compromise good from a range of alternatives or that we make decisions with least stress if we rely on contrast.

Two aspects of such an account should be stressed. First, it is important to recognize that the notion of costly preference formation represents a major departure from the standard model. In the traditional picture, preferences are the starting point of analysis: the decision maker is assumed to know her preferences. Second, it is far from clear that any theory holding that departures from the normative standard are the result of "thinking costs" can account for the remarkable lability of preferences, which are not only context-dependent but also sensitive to the way a choice problem is described or "framed" and to the mode of response used to express preference (see Paul Slovic, The Construction of Preference, 50 Am. Psychologist 364 (1995), for an excellent, though brief, review).

26. Lesser included offenses are offenses composed of elements already contained in the charged offense or that must be committed during the perpetration of the charged offenses. Only North Carolina, Tennessee, and Oklahoma require that lesser included offense instructions be raised sua sponte: in other jurisdictions, one of the parties must request the instruction before it can be given. The judge must then grant the request by either party for the lesser included offense instruction so long as there is some evidence that would justify conviction of the lesser offense and the proof of the element or elements differentiating the two crimes is sufficiently in dispute that the jury may consistently find the defendant innocent of the greater, but guilty of the lesser included offense. Initially, the lesser included offense doctrine was developed as a way for the prosecution to obtain a conviction in cases where it had overcharged or was unable to prove some element of the crime (for example, premeditation in the homicide context) while proving others (for example, causing death intentionally in that same homicide context). Defendants, though, began to request the instructions, hoping that it might allow jurors to temper convictions when they were sympathetic to the defendants but still felt them culpable to some extent. For basic discussions of lesser included offense law, see Beck v. Alabama, 447 U.S. 625, 700 S.Ct. 2382, 65 L.Ed. 2d 392 (U.S. Ala. 1980); Note, Improving Jury Deliberations: A Reconsideration of Lesser Included Offense Instructions, 16 U. Mich. J. L. Ref. 561 (1983) (Michael Craig); Tracy L. Hamrick, Looking at Lesser Included Offenses on an "All or Nothing" Basis: State v. Bullard and the Sporting Approach to Criminal Justice, 69 N.C. L. Rev. 1470 (1991); Janis L. Ettinger, In Search of a Reasoned Approach to the Lesser Included Offense, 50 Brook. L. Rev. 191 (1984); Edward G. Mascolo, Procedural Due Process and the Lesser Included Offense Doctrine, 50 Alb. L. Rev. 263 (1986); or Comment, Jury Deliberations and the Lesser Included Offense Rule: Getting the Courts Back in Step, 23 U.C. Davis L. Rev. 375 (1990) (David F. Abele).

27. See Strickland v. Washington, 466 U.S. 668 (1984).

28. Van Alstine v. State, 263 Ga. 1, 426 S.E. 2d 360 (1993); Wisconsin v. Hollsten, 170 Wis. 2d 734, 492 N.W. 2d 191 (1992). The lawyers' refusal to request a lesser included offense instruction may be successfully challenged only in situations in which the court has a reason to doubt that it was tactically motivated, most obviously in situations in which the lawyer is paid contingent on acquittal, either as a result of a formal contingency fee contract or some factual equivalent. See, for instance, United States v. Murphy, 349 F. Supp. 818 (E.D. Pa. 1972) (lawyer's fees to be paid out of insurance proceeds that were payable only if defendant acquitted; lawyer's decision not to inform client that prosecutor had offered to cap charges at second-degree murder if client plead guilty before trial or to seek lesser included charge instructions at trial constituted incompetent assistance).

29. See ABA Standards for Criminal Justice, Rule 4-5.2 (comment at 4) (client must ultimately make the decision whether to seek a lesser included offense instruction).

30. See, for example, Sansone v. United States, 380 U.S. 343, 351 (1965); Beck v. Alabama, 447 U.S. 625, 636 n. 12 (1980) (citing state and federal cases supporting the proposition that a defendant is entitled "to a requested lesser included offense instruction if the evidence warrants it"); United States v. Thompson, 492 F.2d 359, 362 (8th Cir. 1974) (lesser included offense charge must be given when there is some evidence that would justify conviction of the lesser included offense and the proof on the element or elements differentiating the two offenses is sufficiently in dispute so that the jury may consistently find the defendant innocent of the greater and guilty of the lesser included offense).

31. While the model applies most readily to subdivided criminal offenses, it applies in rather obvious fashions to any situation in which the legislature increases the option set of decision makers entitled to respond to a particular set of behaviors or to situations in which the judge must choose whether to allow fact finders to choose from the full menu of options a lawmaker has provided. Thus, decisions about whether to increase the range of remedies available in a class of civil cases may be analyzed "traditionally" (that is, the legislature should increase the remedy range if additional remedies seem apt for a subclass of cases and the court should instruct the jury to consider any remedy that a reasonable juror could find fits the legislatively established criteria to apply that remedy) and/or in light of context-dependence (the legislature and judge must consider the effect of additional options on choices among the options that might more frequently be chosen as well).

32. Currently, when judges instruct jurors to consider lesser included offenses, they indeed make some efforts to "separate" decisions, to try to insure that jurors do not look at their actual menu of choices as an option set. Thus, typically, judges instruct that the jury must acquit the defendant, unanimously, of the most serious offense he is charged with committing before considering the lesser included offense. See, for example, Nell v. State, 642 P.2d 1361, 1367 (Alaska App. 1982); Stone v. Superior Court of San Diego County, 31 Cal. 3d 503, 646 P.2d 809, 183 Cal. Rptr. 647 (1982) ("The jury must be cautioned, of course, that it should first decide whether the defendant is guilty of the greater offense before considering the lesser offense, and that if it finds the defendant guilty of the greater offense, or if it is unable to agree on that offense, it should not return a verdict on the lesser offense." 646 P.2d at 820). Still other states attempt to separate decisions on the distinct charges by submitting each charge to the jury in guilty/not guilty form. See, for example, State v. Dippre, 121 Ariz. 596, 592 P.2d 1252 (1979). Finally, in some states, jurors are informed that they should not consider lesser included offense charges unless they have reasonable doubts about whether the defendant is guilty of the higher charge, but there appears to be no requirement in such states that the jury as a whole unanimously vote to acquit (that is, unanimously shares such reasonable doubts) before considering the lesser included offenses. See, for example, People v. McGregor, 635 P.2d 912 (Colo. App. 1981); State v. Santiago, 516 P.2d 1256 (Haw. 1973). While it is possible that the first and third procedure produce distinct jury dynamics—a juror or jurors committed to convicting the defendant of the higher charge would seem to have more leverage under the first procedure—the fact remains that jurors informed, as they are in the third class of states, that "[i]f you are not satisfied beyond a reasonable doubt that the defendant is guilty of an offense charged, or you entertain a reasonable doubt of the defendant's guilt, you may consider whether he is guilty of a lesser offense ..." (McGregor, 635 P.2d at 914) may interpret the charge to do no more or less than remind them that juries are supposed to acquit of offense (whether "higher" charges or the only charge) when they are not satisfied beyond a reasonable doubt that the charges have been proven. Thus, in some jurisdictions, the courts explicitly disclaim the idea that the first and third instructions are significantly distinct. See, for example, People v. Padilla, 638 P.2d

15 (Colo. 1981). The jury instructions read: "If you are not satisfied beyond a reasonable doubt that the defendant is guilty of the offense charged, he may, however, be found guilty of any lesser offense" (*id.* at 17). The court notes that it is unclear whether the jury would have first had to acquit the defendant of the higher charge before considering the lesser offense (*id.*) but notes that, even if the instruction does require a finding of acquittal, it withstands the defendant's challenge (*id.*). See also State v. McNeal, 288 N.W.2d 874 (Wis. App. 1980) (while instructions seem to require that the jury acquit the defendant first of the greater charge before considering the lesser included offense, the court *describes* the instructions as allowing the jury to consider the lesser included offense if it fails to find the defendant guilty).

In any case, it is by no means clear that any effort to make the jurors consider each charge in isolation from context will succeed. Each juror who favors the compromise position (the lesser included offense) that he knows is available once the lesser included offense instruction has been given will be more prone to vote to acquit on the more serious charge.

We should note, though, that a judge-imposed rule of the sort we suggest in the text is quite invasive of the jury's traditional fact-finding role. To protect the jury from making a context-dependent decision, the judge, in essence, refuses to give instructions about the requisite elements of a crime although it is a concededly plausible option to convict of that crime. Obviously, distrust of juror capacity drives a good deal of restrictiveness in admitting evidence (one can think of the suggestion that judges be more circumspect in giving lesser included offense instructions as a variant on the traditional idea that certain information is likely to be more prejudicial than probative). One would be hard-pressed, though, to find a situation in which the jury is not told of a legal option that the jury formally possesses for fear that they would misuse the information, but jurors are indeed sometimes left unaware of salient features of the legal system for fear that they will perform their fact-finding function less capably if they are more informed. For instance, in capital trials, jurors may not hear that each executive will have the power to commute what are formally labeled "life sentences" without possibility of parole (or, for that matter, that the executive at the time of scheduled execution could commute a death sentence), presumably on the supposition that they will make the choice between life imprisonment and the death penalty on the basis of an inadequately policy-salient fact: the risk of the sentence not being carried out.

Amos Tversky's Complete Bibliography
(in chronological order)

Books

1. Edwards, W., and Tversky, A. (Eds.). (1967). *Decision Making: Selected Readings*. Middlesex, England: Penguin Books, Ltd.

2. Coombs, C. H., Dawes, R. M., and Tversky, A. (1970). *Mathematical Psychology: An Elementary Introduction*. Englewood Cliffs, N.J.: Prentice-Hall.

3. Krantz, D. H., Luce, R. D., Suppes, P., and Tversky, A. (1971). *Foundations of Measurement (vol. 1)*. New York: Academic Press.

4. Kahneman, D., Slovic, P., and Tversky, A. (Eds.). (1982). *Judgment under Uncertainty: Heuristics and Biases*. New York: Cambridge University Press.

5. Bell, D. E., Raiffa, H., and Tversky, A. (Eds.). (1988). *Decision Making: Descriptive, Normative, and Prescriptive Interactions*. New York: Cambridge University Press.

6. Suppes, P., Krantz, D. H., Luce, R. D., and Tversky, A. (1989). *Foundations of Measurement (vol. 2)*. New York: Academic Press.

7. Luce, R. D., Krantz, D. H., Suppes, P., and Tversky, A. (1990). *Foundations of Measurement (vol. 3)*. New York: Academic Press.

8. Arrow, K., Mnookin, R., Ross, L., Tversky, A., and Wilson, R. (Eds.). (1995). *Barriers to Conflict Resolution*. New York: Norton.

9. Liberman, V., and Tversky, A. (forthcoming). *Critical Thinking: Statistical Reasoning and Intuitive Judgment* (in Hebrew). Tel Aviv, Israel: Open University Press.

10. Kahneman, D., and Tversky, A. (Eds.). (2000). *Choices, Values, and Frames*. New York: Cambridge University Press and the Russell Sage Foundation.

Articles and Book Chapters

1. Tversky, A. (1964). On the optimal number of alternatives at a choice point. *Journal of Mathematical Psychology*, 2, 386–391.

2. Rapoport, A., and Tversky, A. (1966). Cost and accessibility of offers as determinants of optimal stopping in a sequential decision task. *Psychonomic Science*, 4, 145–146.

3. Tversky, A., and Edwards, W. (1966). Information versus reward in binary choices. *Journal of Experimental Psychology*, 71, 680–683.

4. Tversky, A. (1967). Additivity analysis of risky choices. *Journal of Experimental Psychology*, 75, 27–36.

5. Tversky, A. (1967). Additivity, utility, and subjective probability. *Journal of Mathematical Psychology*, 4, 175–202.

6. Tversky, A. (1967). A general theory of polynomial conjoint measurement. *Journal of Mathematical Psychology*, 4, 1–20.

7. Beals, R., Krantz, D. H., and Tversky, A. (1968). The foundations of multidimensional scaling. *Psychological Review*, 75, 127–142.

8. Tversky, A. (1969). The intransitivity of preferences. *Psychological Review*, 76, 31–48.

9. Tversky, A., and Krantz, D. H. (1969). Similarity of schematic faces: A test of interdimensional additivity. *Perception & Psychophysics*, 5, 125–128.

10. Tversky, A., and Russo, E. J. (1969). Substitutability and similarity in binary choices. *Journal of Mathematical Psychology*, 6, 1–12.

11. Pollatsek, A., and Tversky, A. (1970). A theory of risk. *Journal of Mathematical Psychology*, 7, 540–553.

12. Rapoport, A., and Tversky, A. (1970). Choice behavior in an optimal stopping task. *Organizational Behavior and Human Performance*, 5, 105–120.

13. Tversky, A., and Krantz, D. H. (1970). The dimensional representation and the metric structure of similarity data. *Journal of Mathematical Psychology*, 7, 572–597.

14. Krantz, D. H., and Tversky, A. (1971). Conjoint-measurement analysis of composition rules in psychology. *Psychological Review*, 78, 151–169.

15. Kubovy, M., Rapoport, A., and Tversky, A. (1971). Deterministic versus probabilistic strategies in detection. *Perception & Psychophysics*, 9, 427–429.

16. Tversky, A., and Kahneman, D. (1971). Belief in the law of small numbers. *Psychological Bulletin*, 76, 105–110.

17. Kahneman, D., and Tversky, A. (1972). Subjective probability: A judgment of representativeness. *Cognitive Psychology*, 3, 430–454.

18. Tversky, A. (1972). Choice by elimination. *Journal of Mathematical Psychology*, 9, 341–367.

19. Tversky, A. (1972). Elimination by aspects: A theory of choice. *Psychological Review*, 79, 281–299.

20. Kahneman, D., and Tversky, A. (1973). On the psychology of prediction. *Psychological Review*, 80, 237–251.

21. Tversky, A., and Kahneman, D. (1973). Availability: A heuristic for judging frequency and probability. *Cognitive Psychology*, 5, 207–232.

22. Slovic, P., and Tversky, A. (1974). Who accepts Savage's axiom? *Behavioral Science*, 19, 368–373.

23. Tversky, A. (1974). Assessing uncertainty. *Journal of the Royal Statistical Society*, Series B, 36, 148–159.

24. Tversky, A., and Kahneman, D. (1974). Judgment under uncertainty: Heuristics and biases. *Science*, 185, 1124–1131.

25. Krantz, D. H., and Tversky, A. (1975). Similarity of rectangles: An analysis of subjective dimensions. *Journal of Mathematical Psychology*, 12, 4–34.

26. Tversky, A. (1975). A critique of expected utility theory: Descriptive and normative consideration. *Erkenntnis*, 9, 163–173.

27. Sattath, S., and Tversky, A. (1976). Unite and conquer: A multiplicative inequality for choice probabilities. *Econometrica*, 44, 79–89.

28. Sattath, S., and Tversky, A. (1977). Additive similarity trees. *Psychometrika*, 42, 319–345.

29. Tversky, A. (1977). Features of similarity. *Psychological Review*, 84, 327–352.

30. Tversky, A. (1977). On the elicitation of preferences: Descriptive and prescriptive considerations. In D. Bell, R. L. Kenney, and H. Raiffa (Eds.), *Conflicting Objectives in Decisions*. International Series on Applied Systems Analysis. New York: Wiley.

31. Tversky, A., and Gati, I. (1978). Studies of similarity. In E. Rosch and B. Lloyd (Eds.), *Cognition and Categorization*. Hillsdale, N.J.: Erlbaum.

32. Kahneman, D., and Tversky, A. (1979). Intuitive prediction: Biases and corrective procedures. *TIMS Studies in Management Science*, 12, 313–327.

33. Kahneman, D., and Tversky, A. (1979). Prospect theory: An analysis of decision under risk. *Econometrica*, 47, 263–291.

34. Lindley, D. V., Tversky, A., and Brown, R. V. (1979). On the reconciliation of probability assessments. *Journal of the Royal Statistical Society*, 142, 146–180.

35. Tversky, A., and Sattath, S. (1979). Preference trees. *Psychological Review*, 86, 542–573.

36. Schwarz, G., and Tversky, A. (1980). On the reciprocity of proximity relations. *Journal of Mathematical Psychology*, 22, 157–175.

37. Tversky, A., and Kahneman, D. (1980). Causal schemas in judgments under uncertainty. In M. Fishbein (Ed.), *Progress in Social Psychology*. Hillsdale, N.J.: Erlbaum.

38. Tversky, A., and Kahneman, D. (1981). The framing of decisions and the psychology of choice. *Science*, 211, 453–458.

39. Gati, I., and Tversky, A. (1982). Representations of qualitative and quantitative dimensions. *Journal of Experimental Psychology: Human Perception and Performance*, 8, 325–340.

40. Kahneman, D., and Tversky, A. (1982). On the study of statistical intuitions. *Cognition*, 11, 123–141.

41. Kahneman, D., and Tversky, A. (1982). The psychology of preferences. *Scientific American*, 246, 160–173.

42. Kahneman, D., and Tversky, A. (1982). The simulation heuristic. In D. Kahneman, P. Slovic, and A. Tversky (Eds.), *Judgment under Uncertainty: Heuristics and Biases*. New York: Cambridge University Press.

43. Kahneman, D., and Tversky, A. (1982). Variants of uncertainty. *Cognition*, 11, 143–157.

44. McNeil, B., Pauker, S., Sox, H. Jr., and Tversky, A. (1982). On the elicitation of preferences for alternative therapies. *New England Journal of Medicine*, 306, 1259–1262.

45. Pruzansky, S., Tversky, A., and Carroll, J. D. (1982). Spatial versus tree representation of proximity data. *Psychometrika*, 47, 3–24.

46. Tversky, A., and Gati, I. (1982). Similarity, separability, and the triangle inequality. *Psychological Review*, 89, 123–154.

47. Tversky, A., and Kahneman, D. (1982). Evidential impact of base rates. In D. Kahneman, P. Slovic, and A. Tversky (Eds.), *Judgment under Uncertainty: Heuristics and Biases*. New York: Cambridge University Press.

48. Tversky, A., and Kahneman, D. (1982). Judgments of and by representativeness. In D. Kahneman, P. Slovic, and A. Tversky (Eds.), *Judgment under Uncertainty: Heuristics and Biases*. New York: Cambridge University Press.

49. Johnson, E. J., and Tversky, A. (1983). Affect, generalization and the perception of risk. *Journal of Personality and Social Psychology*, 45, 20–31.

50. Newman, C. M., Rinott, Y., and Tversky, A. (1983). Nearest neighbors and Voronoi regions in certain point processes. *Advances in Applied Probability*, 15, 726–751.

51. Tversky, A., and Bar-Hillel, M. (1983). Risk: The long and the short. *Journal of Experimental Psychology: Learning, Memory, and Cognition*, 9, 713–717.

52. Tversky, A., and Kahneman, D. (1983). Extensional vs. intuitive reasoning: The conjunction fallacy in probability judgment. *Psychological Review*, 91, 293–315.

53. Tversky, A., Rinott, Y., and Newman, C. M. (1983). Nearest neighbor analysis of point processes: Applications to multidimensional scaling. *Journal of Mathematical Psychology*, 27, 235–250.

54. Gati, I., and Tversky, A. (1984). Weighting common and distinctive features in perceptual and conceptual judgments, *Cognitive Psychology*, 16, 341–370.

55. Johnson, E., and Tversky, A. (1984). Representations of perceptions of risk. *Journal of Experimental Psychology: General*, 113, 55–70.

56. Kahneman, D., and Tversky, A. (1984). Choices, values, and frames. *American Psychologist*, 39, 341–350.

57. Quattrone, G. A., and Tversky, A. (1984). Causal versus diagnostic contingencies: On self-deception and on the voter's illusion. *Journal of Personality and Social Psychology*, 46, 237–248.

58. Gilovich, T., Vallone, B., and Tversky, A. (1985). The hot hand in basketball: On the misconception of random sequences. *Cognitive Psychology*, 17, 295–314.

59. Shafer, G., and Tversky, A. (1985). Languages and designs for probability judgment. *Cognitive Science*, 9, 309–339.

60. Corter, J., and Tversky, A. (1986). Extended similarity trees. *Psychometrika*, 51, 429–451.

61. Quattrone, G. A., and Tversky, A. (1986). Self-deception and the voter's illusion. In Jon Elster (Ed.), *The Multiple Self*. New York: Cambridge University Press.

62. Tversky, A. (1986). Cognitive illusions in judgment and choice. In E. Ullmann-Margalit (Ed.), *The Kaleidoscope of Science* (75–87). Dordrecht, Holland: D. Reidel Publishing Co.

63. Tversky, A., and Hutchinson, J. W. (1986). Nearest neighbor analysis of psychological spaces. *Psychological Review*, 93, 3–22.

64. Tversky, A., and Kahneman, D. (1986). Rational choice and the framing of decisions. *The Journal of Business*, 59, Part 2, S251–S278.

65. Gati, J., and Tversky, A. (1987). Recall of common and distinctive features of verbal and pictorial stimuli. *Memory and Cognition*, 15, 97–100.

66. Sattath, S., and Tversky, A. (1987). On the relation between common and distinctive feature models. *Psychological Review*, 94, 16–22.

67. Bell, D. E., Raiffa, H., and Tversky, A. (1988). Descriptive, normative, and prescriptive interactions in decision making. In D. E. Bell, H. Raiffa, and A. Tversky (Eds.), *Decision Making: Descriptive, Normative, and Prescriptive Interactions*. New York: Cambridge University Press.

68. McNeil, B. J., Pauker, S. G., and Tversky, A. (1988). One the framing of medical decisions. In D. E. Bell, H. Raiffa, and A. Tversky (Eds.), *Decision Making: Descriptive, Normative, and Prescriptive Interactions*. New York: Cambridge University Press.

69. Quattrone, G. A., and Tversky, A. (1988). Contrasting rational and psychological analyses of political choice. *American Political Science Review*, 82 (3), 719–736.

70. Tversky, A., Sattath, S., and Slovic, P. (1988). Contingent weighting in judgment and choice. *Psychological Review*, 95 (3), 371–384.

71. Dawes, R. M., and Tversky, A. (1989). Clyde Hamilton Coombs (1912–1988). *American Psychologist*, 44 (11), 1415–1416.

72. Tversky, A., and Gilovich, T. (1989). The cold facts about the "hot hand" in basketball. *Chance*, 2 (1), 16–21.

73. Tversky, A., and Gilovich, T. (1989). The hot hand: Statistical reality or cognitive illusion? *Chance*, 2 (4), 31–34.

74. Redelmeier, D. A., and Tversky, A. (1990). Discrepancy between medical decisions for individual patients and for groups. *New England Journal of Medicine*, 322, 1162–1164.

75. Ritov, I., Gati, I., and Tversky, A. (1990). Differential weighting of common and distinctive components. *Journal of Experimental Psychology: General*, 119 (1), 30–41.

76. Ritov, I., Gati, I., and Tversky, A. (1990). Reply to Keren. *Journal of Experimental Psychology: General*, 119 (1), 44.

77. Slovic, P., Griffin, D., and Tversky, A. (1990). Compatibility effects in judgment and choice. In R. M. Hogarth (Ed.), *Insights in Decision Making: Theory and Applications*. Chicago: University of Chicago Press.

78. Tversky, A., Slovic, P., and Kahneman, D. (1990). The causes of preference reversal. *The American Economic Review*, 80 (1), 204–217.

79. Tversky, A., and Thaler, R. (1990). Anomalies: Preference reversals. *Journal of Economic Perspectives*, 4 (2), 201–211.

80. Gonzalez, R., and Tversky, A. (1990). The impact of others' choice on investment decisions. In K. Borcherding, O. I. Larichev, and D. Messick (Eds.), *Contemporary Issues in Decision Making* (367–373). North-Holland: Elsevier Science Publishers B.V.

81. Gerrig, R. J., Maloney, L. T., and Tversky, A. (1991). Validating the dimensional structure of psychological spaces: Applications to personality and emotions. In D. R. Brown and J. E. K. Smith (Eds.),

Frontiers of Mathematical Psychology: Essays in Honor of Clyde Coombs (138–165). New York: Springer-Verlag.

82. Heath, F., and Tversky, A. (1991). Preference and belief: Ambiguity and competence in choice under uncertainty. *Journal of Risk and Uncertainty*, 4 (1), 5–28.

83. Tversky, A., and Griffin, D. (1991). Endowment and contrast in judgments of well-being. In F. Strack, M. Argyle, and N. Schwartz (Eds.), *Subjective Well-Being: An Interdisciplinary Perspective* (101–118). Elmsford, NY: Pergamon Press.

84. Tversky, A., and Kahneman, D. (1991). Loss aversion in riskless choice: A reference dependent model. *Quarterly Journal of Economics*, 107 (4), 1039–1061.

85. Simonson, I., and Tversky, A. (1992). Choice in context: Tradeoff contrast and extremeness aversion. *Journal of Marketing Research*, 29, 281–295.

86. Griffin, D., and Tversky, A. (1992). The weighing of evidence and the determinants of confidence. *Cognitive Psychology*, 24, 411–435.

87. Redelmeier, D. A., and Tversky, A. (1992). On the framing of multiple prospects. *Psychological Science*, 3 (3), 191–193.

88. Tversky, A., and Shafir, E. (1992). The disjunction effect in choice under uncertainty. *Psychological Science*, 3 (5), 305–309.

89. Shafir, E., and Tversky, A. (1992). Thinking through uncertainty: Nonconsequential reasoning and choice. *Cognitive Psychology*, 24 (4), 449–474.

90. Tversky, A. (1992). Clyde Hamilton Coombs 1912–1988. In *Biographical Memoirs,* vol. 61 (59–77). Washington, DC: The National Academy Press.

91. Tversky, A., and Kahneman, D. (1992). Advances in prospect theory: Cumulative representation of uncertainty. *Journal of Risk and Uncertainty*, 5, 297–323.

92. Tversky, A., and Shafir, E. (1992). Choice under conflict: The dynamics of deferred decision. *Psychological Science*, 3 (6), 358–361.

93. Liberman, V., and Tversky, A. (1993). On the evaluation of probability judgments: Calibration, resolution, and monotonicity. *Psychological Bulletin*, 114, 162–173.

94. Gidron, D., Koehler, D., and Tversky, A. (1993). Implicit quantification of personality traits. *Personality and Social Psychology Bulletin*, 19, 594–604.

95. Wakker, P., and Tversky, A. (1993). An axiomatization of cumulative prospect theory. *Journal of Risk and Uncertainty*, 7, 147–176.

96. Tversky, A., and Simonson, I. (1993). Context-dependent preferences. *Management Science*, 39, 1178–1189.

97. Shafir, E., Simonson, I., and Tversky, A. (1993). Reason-based choice. *Cognition*, 49, 11–36.

98. Tversky, A. (1994). Contingent preferences: Loss Aversion and tradeoff contrast in decision making. *Japanese Psychological Research*, 36, 3–9.

99. Tversky, A., and Koehler, D. J. (1994). Support theory: A nonextensional representation of subjective probability. *Psychological Review*, 101, 547–567.

100. Shafir, E., and Tversky, A. (1995). Decision making. In D. N. Osherson and E. E. Smith (Eds.), *Invitation to Cognitive Science, volume 3: Thinking* (77–100). Cambridge, Mass.: MIT Press.

101. Tversky, A., and Fox, C. R. (1995). Weighing risk and uncertainty. *Psychological Review*, 102 (2), 269–283.

102. Redelmeier, D. A., Koehler, D. J., Liberman, V., and Tversky, A. (1995). Probability judgment in medicine: Discounting unspecified possibilities. *Medical Decision Making*, 15, 227–230.

103. Fox, C. R., and Tversky, A. (1995). Ambiguity aversion and comparative ignorance. *Quarterly Journal of Economics*, 110, 585–603.

104. Kahneman, D., and Tversky, A. (1995). Conflict resolution: A cognitive perspective. In K. Arrow, R. Mnookin, L. Ross, A. Tversky, and R. Wilson (Eds.), *Barriers to the Negotiated Resolution of Conflict* (49–67). New York: Norton.

105. Tversky, A., and Wakker, P. (1995). Risk attitudes and decision weights. *Econometrica*, 63 (6), 1255–1280.

106. Tversky, A. (1995). Rational theory and constructive choice. In K. J. Arrow et al. (Eds.), *The Rational Foundations of Economics Behavior*. United Kingdom: Macmillan.

107. Kahneman, D., and Tversky, A. (1996). On the reality of cognitive illusion: A reply to Gigerenzer's critique. *Psychological Review*, 103, 582–591.

108. Kelman, M., Rottenstreich, Y., and Tversky, A. (1996). Context-dependence in legal decision making. *The Journal of Legal Studies*, 25, 287–318.

109. Tversky, A. (1996). Contrasting rational and psychological principles of choice. In R. J. Zeckhauser, R. K. Keeney, and J. K. Sebenius (Eds.), *Wise Choices: Games, Decisions, and Negotiations* (5–21). Boston: Harvard Business School Press.

110. Redelmeier, D. A., and Tversky, A. (1996). On the belief that arthritis pain is related to the weather. *Procedings of the National Academy of Sciences*, 93, 2895–2896.

111. Brenner, L. A., Koehler, D. J., and Tversky, A. (1996). On the evaluation of one-sided evidence. *Journal of Behavioral Decision Making*, 9, 1–12.

112. Koehler, D. J., Brenner, L. A., Liberman, V., and Tversky, A. (1996). Confidence and accuracy in trait inference: Judgment by similarity. *Acta Psychologica*, 475, 1–24.

113. Brenner, L. A., Koehler, D. J., Liberman, V., and Tversky, A. (1996). Overconfidence in probability and frequency judgments: A critical examination. *Organizational Behavior and Human Decision Processes*, 65, 212–219.

114. Fox, C. F., Rogers, B. A., and Tversky, A. (1996). Option traders exhibit subadditive decision weights. *Journal of Risk and Uncertainty*, 13, 5–17.

115. Rubinstien, A., Tversky, A., and Heller, D. (1996). Naive strategies in Zero-sum games. In W. Guth et al. (Eds.), *Understanding Strategic Interaction: Essays in Honor of Reinhard Selten*. Springer-Verlag, 394–402.

116. Wakker, P., Thaler, R., and Tversky, A. (1997). Probabilistic Insurance. *Journal of Risk and Uncertainty*, 15, 7–28.

117. Shafir, E., Diamond, P., and Tversky, A. (1997). On money illusion. *The Quarterly Journal of Economics*, CXII, 2, 341–374.

118. Rottenstreich, Y., and Tversky, A. (1997). Unpacking, repacking, and anchoring: Advances in support theory. *Psychological Review*, 104, 2, 406–415.

119. Thaler, R. H., Tversky, A., Kahneman, D., and Schwarz, A. (1997). The effect of myopia and loss aversion on risk taking: An experimental test. *Quarterly Journal of Economics*, 112, 647–661.

120. Koehler, D. J., Brenner, L. A., and Tversky, A. (1997). The enhancement effect in probability judgment. *Journal of Behavioral Decision Making*, 10, 293–313.

121. Fox, C. R., and Tversky, A. (1998). A belief-based account of decision under uncertainty. *Management Science*, 44, 7, 879–895.

122. Drolet, A., Simonson, I., and Tversky, A. (2000). Indifference curves that travel with the choice set. *Marketing Letters*, 11 (3), 199–209.

Index

CPSIA information can be obtained
at www.ICGtesting.com
Printed in the USA
BVOW04s1018090217
475531BV00016B/5/P